Since I moved here last year, my landlord next door has taken a real liking to me. His wife even cooks for me. The food's great and I'm thankful, but I feel bad because I've never told them that I can't eat onions.

Tite Kubo

久保帯人

Recent photo of author

BLEACH is author Tite Kubo's second title. Kubo made his debut with **ZOMBIE POWDER**, a four-volume series for **WEEKLY SHONEN JUMP**. To date, **BLEACH** has been translated into numerous languages and has also inspired an animated TV series that began airing in Japan in 2004. Beginning its serialization in 2001, **BLEACH** is still a mainstay in the pages of **WEEKLY SHONEN JUMP**.

W9-DEV-640

BLEACH
3-in-1 Edition

SHONEN JUMP Manga Omnibus Edition Volume 3
A compilation of the graphic novel volumes 7–9

STORY AND ART BY
TITE KUBO

English Adaptation/Lance Caselman
Translation/Joe Yamazaki
Touch-up Art & Lettering/Dave Lanphear, Andy Ristaino
Design - Manga Edition/Sean Lee
Design - Omnibus Edition/Fawn Lau
Editor - Manga Edition/Kit Fox
Editor - Omnibus Edition/Alexis Kirsch

Printed in the U.S.A.

Published by VIZ Media, LLC
P.O. Box 77010
San Francisco, CA 94107

10 9 8 7
Omnibus edition first printing, October 2011
Seventh printing, November 2017

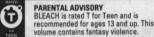

PARENTAL ADVISORY
BLEACH is rated T for Teen and is
recommended for ages 13 and up. This
volume contains fantasy violence.
ratings.viz.com

www.viz.com

We should not shed tears
That is a surrender of the body to the heart
It is only proof
That we are beings that do not know
What to do with our hearts

BLEACH 7 | THE BROKEN CODA

Shonen Jump Manga

STARS AND

柘木ルキア
Rukia Kuchiki

Orihime Inoue

Ichigo Kurosaki

井上織姫

黒崎一護

plot

Fifteen-year-old Ichigo "Strawberry" Kurosaki can see ghosts. Otherwise, he was a typical (?) high school student until the day a Hollow—a malevolent lost soul—came to eat him, and the Soul Reaper Rukia Kuchiki stepped into his life. To defeat the Hollow and save his family, Ichigo let Rukia transfer some of her Soul Reaper powers to him. But when Rukia was left powerless, she recruited Ichigo for her war against the murderous, soul-gobbling Hollows.

In mid-duel, Ichigo and Uryû Ishida, the Quincy, team up to fight the gigantic Menos Grande. In the process, Ichigo discovers latent power he was not aware of! In the aftermath of the battle, Rukia decides she has lingered in this world long enough. But things take a disturbing turn when she finds herself face to face with two hunters from the Soul Society!!

BLEACH ALL

朽木白哉
Byakuya Kuchiki

浦原喜助
Kisuke Urahara

Renji Abarai

阿散井恋次

STORIES

BLEACH 7

THE BROKEN CODA

Contents

53. Nice to meet you. (I will beat you.)

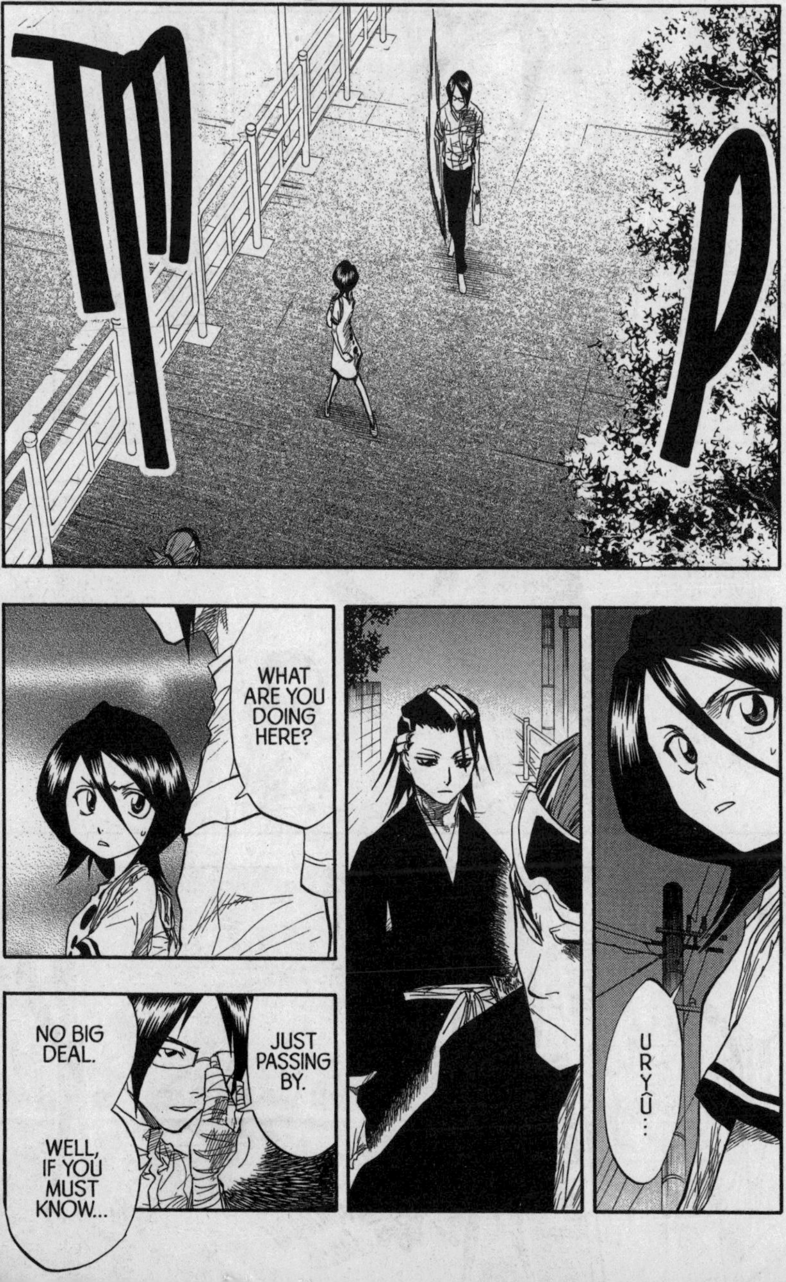
URYÛ...
WHAT ARE YOU DOING HERE?
NO BIG DEAL.
JUST PASSING BY.
WELL, IF YOU MUST KNOW...

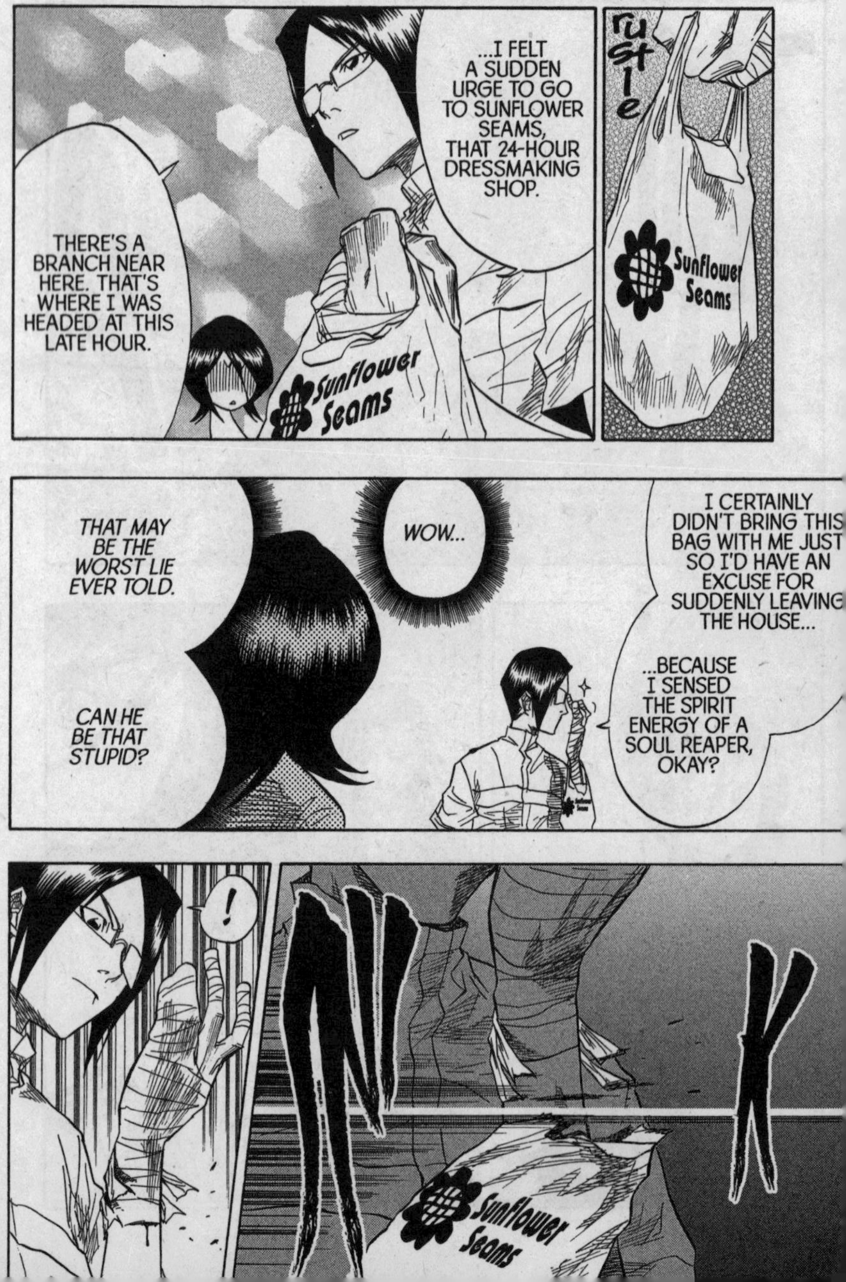
rustle
Sunflower Seams
...I FELT A SUDDEN URGE TO GO TO SUNFLOWER SEAMS, THAT 24-HOUR DRESSMAKING SHOP.
THERE'S A BRANCH NEAR HERE. THAT'S WHERE I WAS HEADED AT THIS LATE HOUR.
Sunflower Seams
I CERTAINLY DIDN'T BRING THIS BAG WITH ME JUST SO I'D HAVE AN EXCUSE FOR SUDDENLY LEAVING THE HOUSE...
...BECAUSE I SENSED THE SPIRIT ENERGY OF A SOUL REAPER, OKAY?
WOW...
THAT MAY BE THE WORST LIE EVER TOLD.
CAN HE BE THAT STUPID?
!
Sunflower Seams

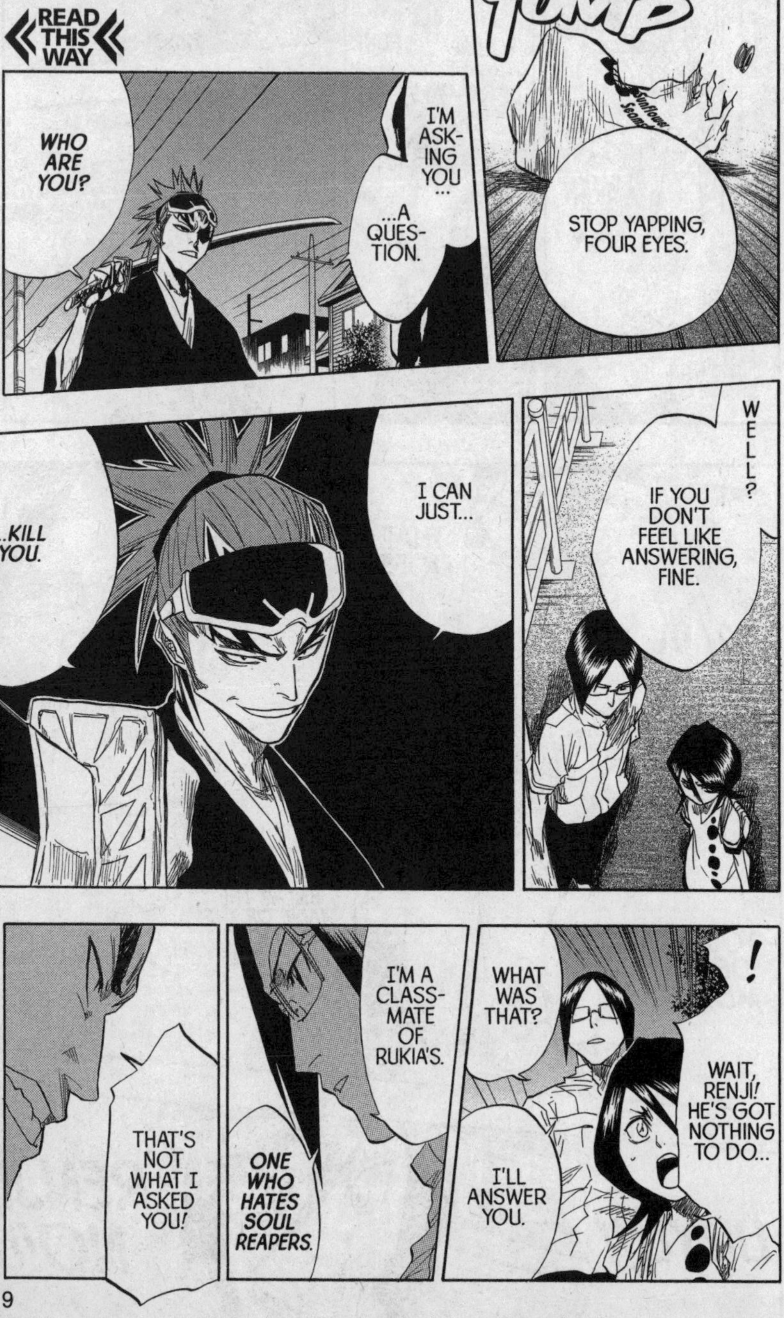
READ THIS WAY
TUMP
STOP YAPPING, FOUR EYES.
I'M ASKING YOU...
...A QUESTION.
WHO ARE YOU?
WELL?
IF YOU DON'T FEEL LIKE ANSWERING, FINE.
I CAN JUST...
...KILL YOU.
!
WAIT, RENJI! HE'S GOT NOTHING TO DO...
WHAT WAS THAT?
I'LL ANSWER YOU.
I'M A CLASSMATE OF RUKIA'S.
ONE WHO HATES SOUL REAPERS.
THAT'S NOT WHAT I ASKED YOU!

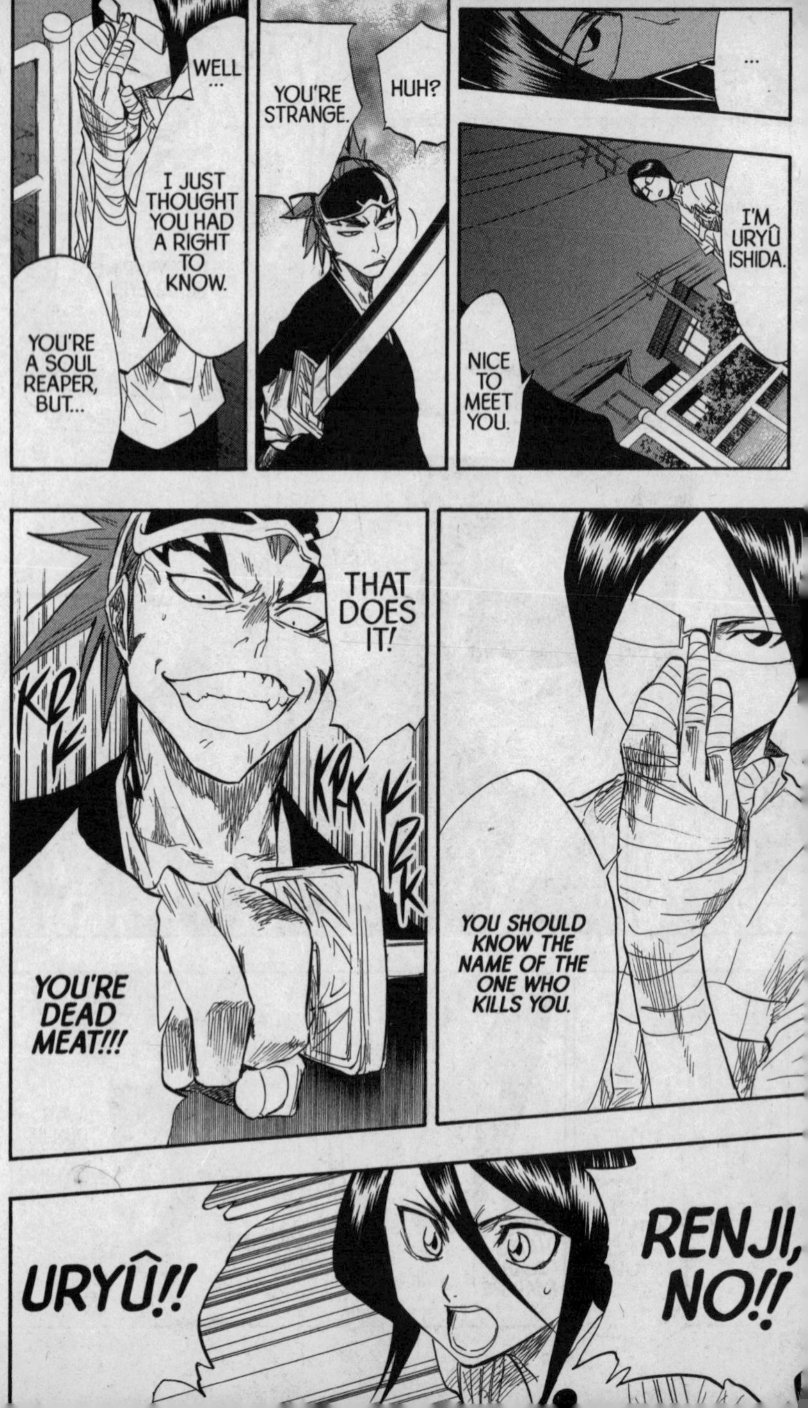

...
I'M URYÛ ISHIDA.
NICE TO MEET YOU.
HUH?
YOU'RE STRANGE.
WELL ...
I JUST THOUGHT YOU HAD A RIGHT TO KNOW.
YOU'RE A SOUL REAPER, BUT...
YOU SHOULD KNOW THE NAME OF THE ONE WHO KILLS YOU.
THAT DOES IT!
KRK
KRK
KRK
YOU'RE DEAD MEAT!!!
RENJI, NO!!
URYÛ!!

beat you.)

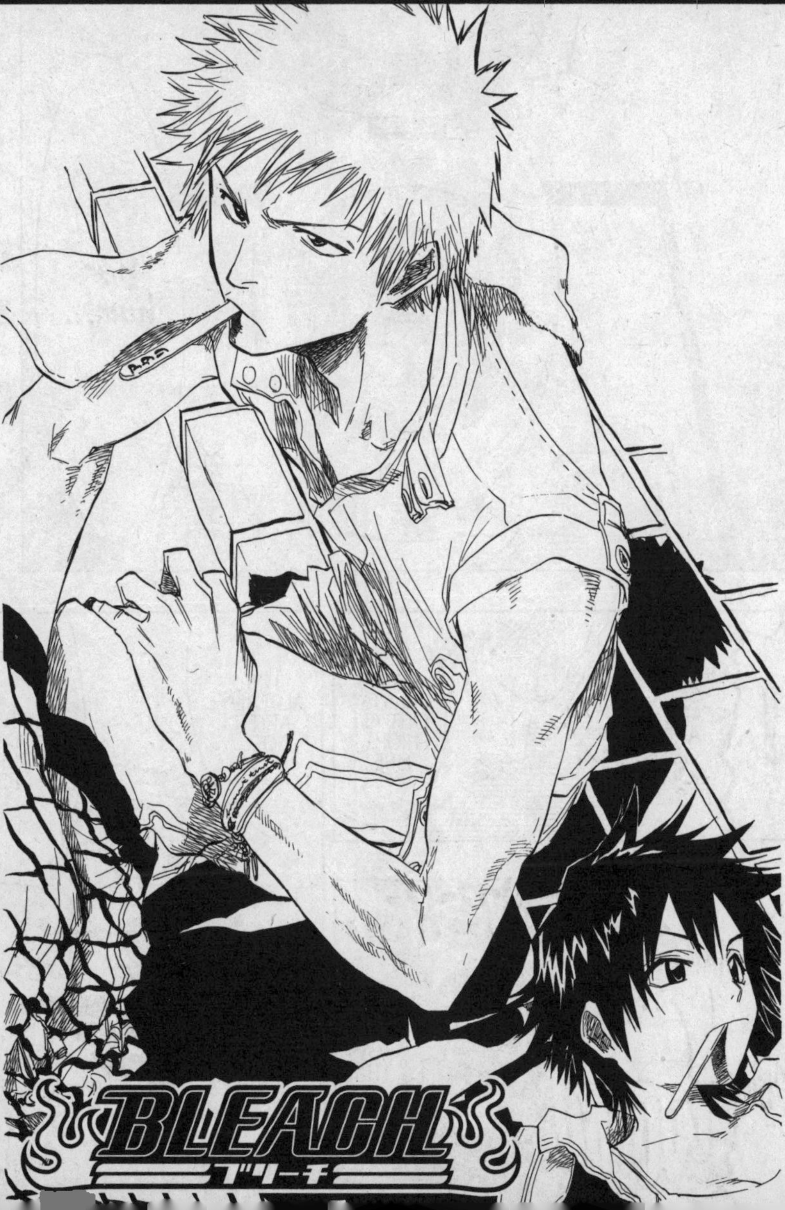
BLEACH
ブリーチ

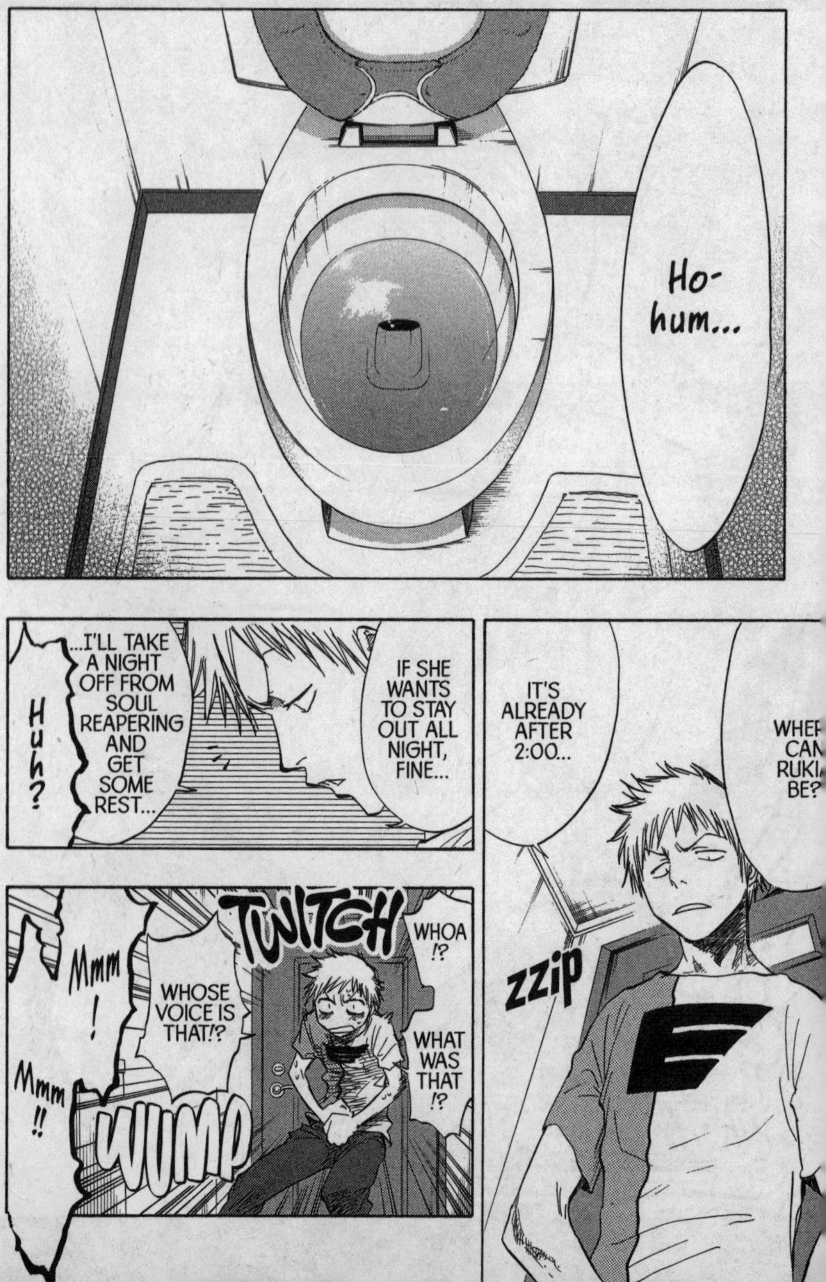
Ho-hum...
WHER CAN RUKI BE?
IT'S ALREADY AFTER 2:00...
ZZIP
IF SHE WANTS TO STAY OUT ALL NIGHT, FINE...
...I'LL TAKE A NIGHT OFF FROM SOUL REAPERING AND GET SOME REST...
Huh?
TWITCH
WHOA!?
WHAT WAS THAT!?
WHOSE VOICE IS THAT!?
Mmm!
Mmm!!
WUMP

READ THIS WAY

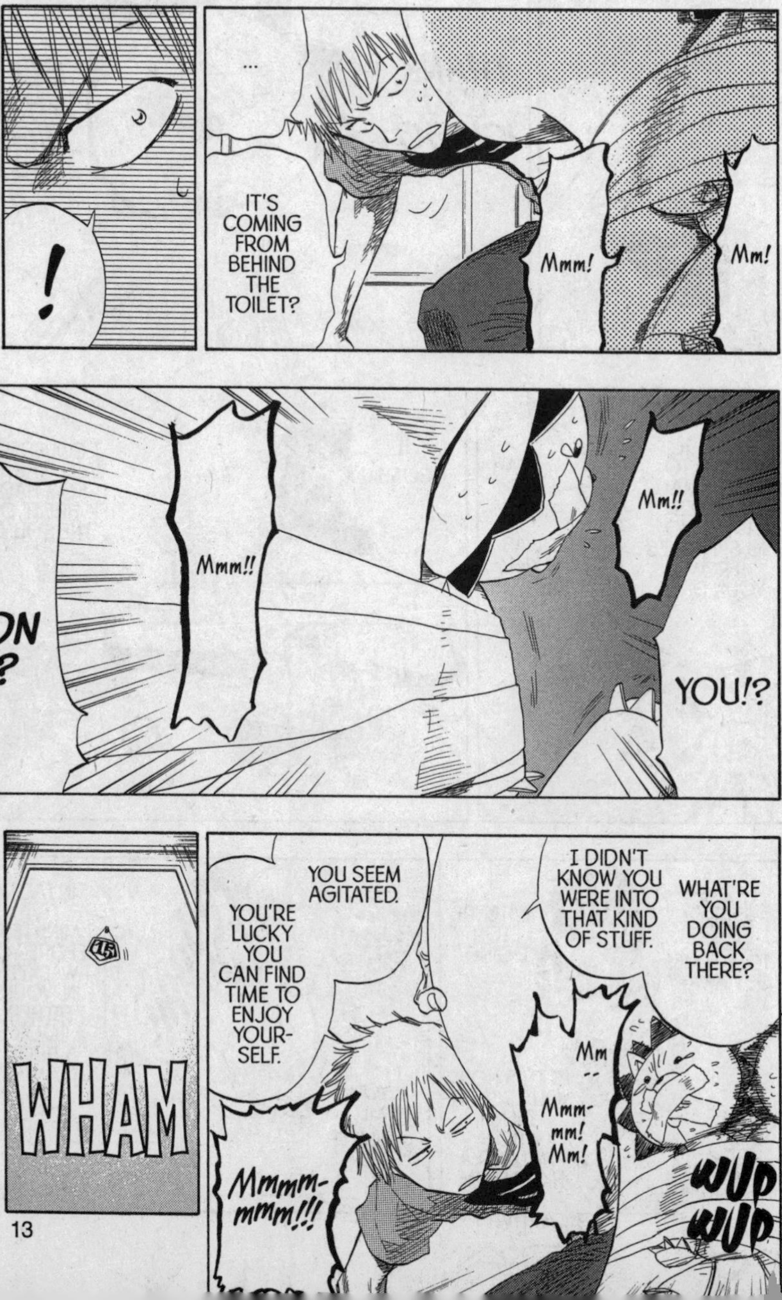
Mm!
Mmm!
...
IT'S COMING FROM BEHIND THE TOILET?
!
YOU!?
Mm!!
Mmm!!
KON !?
WHAT'RE YOU DOING BACK THERE?
I DIDN'T KNOW YOU WERE INTO THAT KIND OF STUFF.
YOU SEEM AGITATED.
YOU'RE LUCKY YOU CAN FIND TIME TO ENJOY YOURSELF.
Mm--
Mmm-mm! Mm!
WUP WUP
Mmmm-mmm!!!
15
WHAM

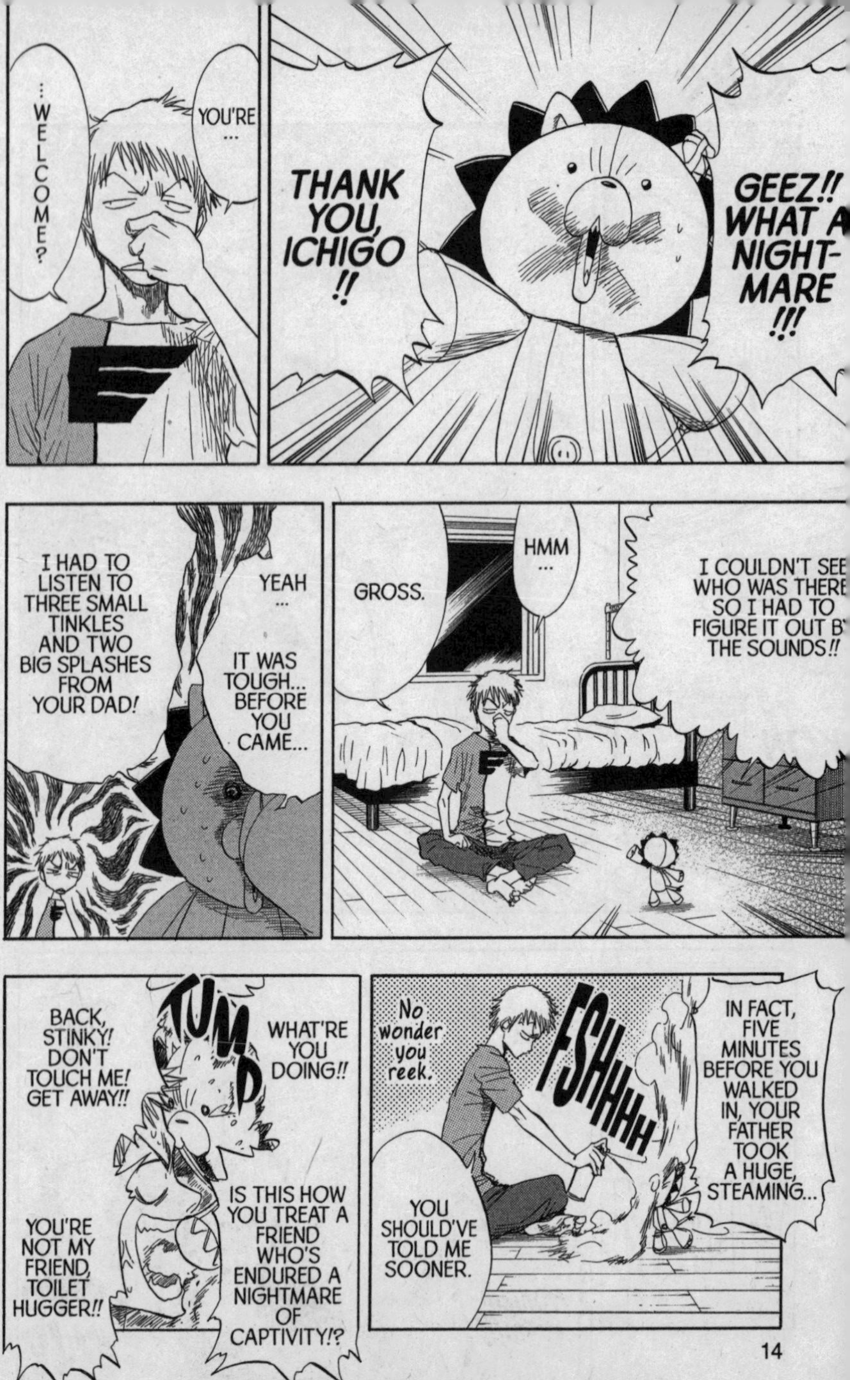
GEEZ!! WHAT A NIGHTMARE!!!
THANK YOU, ICHIGO!!
YOU'RE...
...WELCOME?
I COULDN'T SEE WHO WAS THERE SO I HAD TO FIGURE IT OUT BY THE SOUNDS!!
HMM...
GROSS.
YEAH...
IT WAS TOUGH... BEFORE YOU CAME...
I HAD TO LISTEN TO THREE SMALL TINKLES AND TWO BIG SPLASHES FROM YOUR DAD!
IN FACT, FIVE MINUTES BEFORE YOU WALKED IN, YOUR FATHER TOOK A HUGE, STEAMING...
FSHHHH
No wonder you reek.
YOU SHOULD'VE TOLD ME SOONER.
WHAT'RE YOU DOING!!
TUMP
BACK, STINKY! DON'T TOUCH ME! GET AWAY!!
IS THIS HOW YOU TREAT A FRIEND WHO'S ENDURED A NIGHTMARE OF CAPTIVITY!?
YOU'RE NOT MY FRIEND, TOILET HUGGER!!

READ THIS WAY

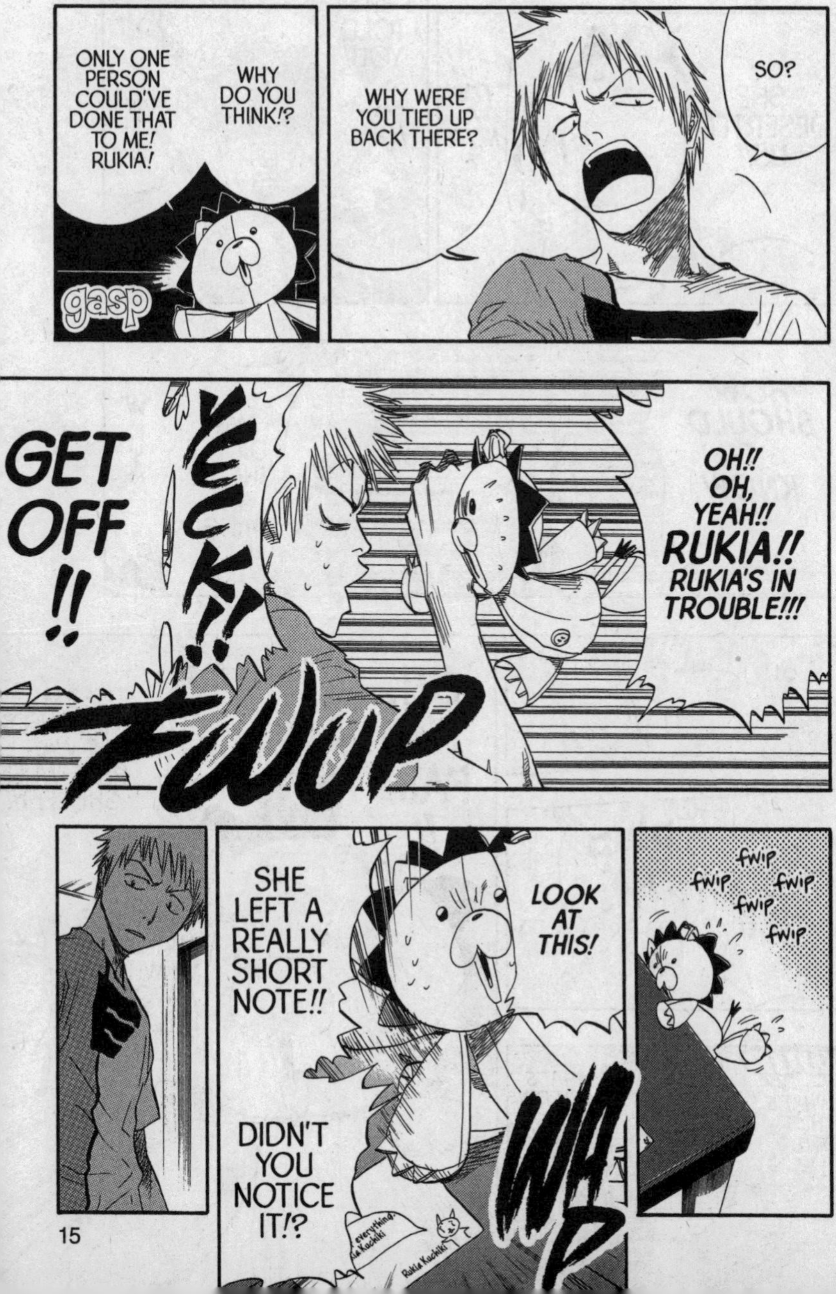

SO?
WHY WERE YOU TIED UP BACK THERE?
WHY DO YOU THINK!?
ONLY ONE PERSON COULD'VE DONE THAT TO ME! RUKIA!
gasp
OH!! OH, YEAH!! RUKIA!! RUKIA'S IN TROUBLE!!!
GET OFF!!
YECK!!
FWUP
fwip fwip fwip fwip fwip
LOOK AT THIS!
SHE LEFT A REALLY SHORT NOTE!!
DIDN'T YOU NOTICE IT!?
Rukia Kuchiki
WAP

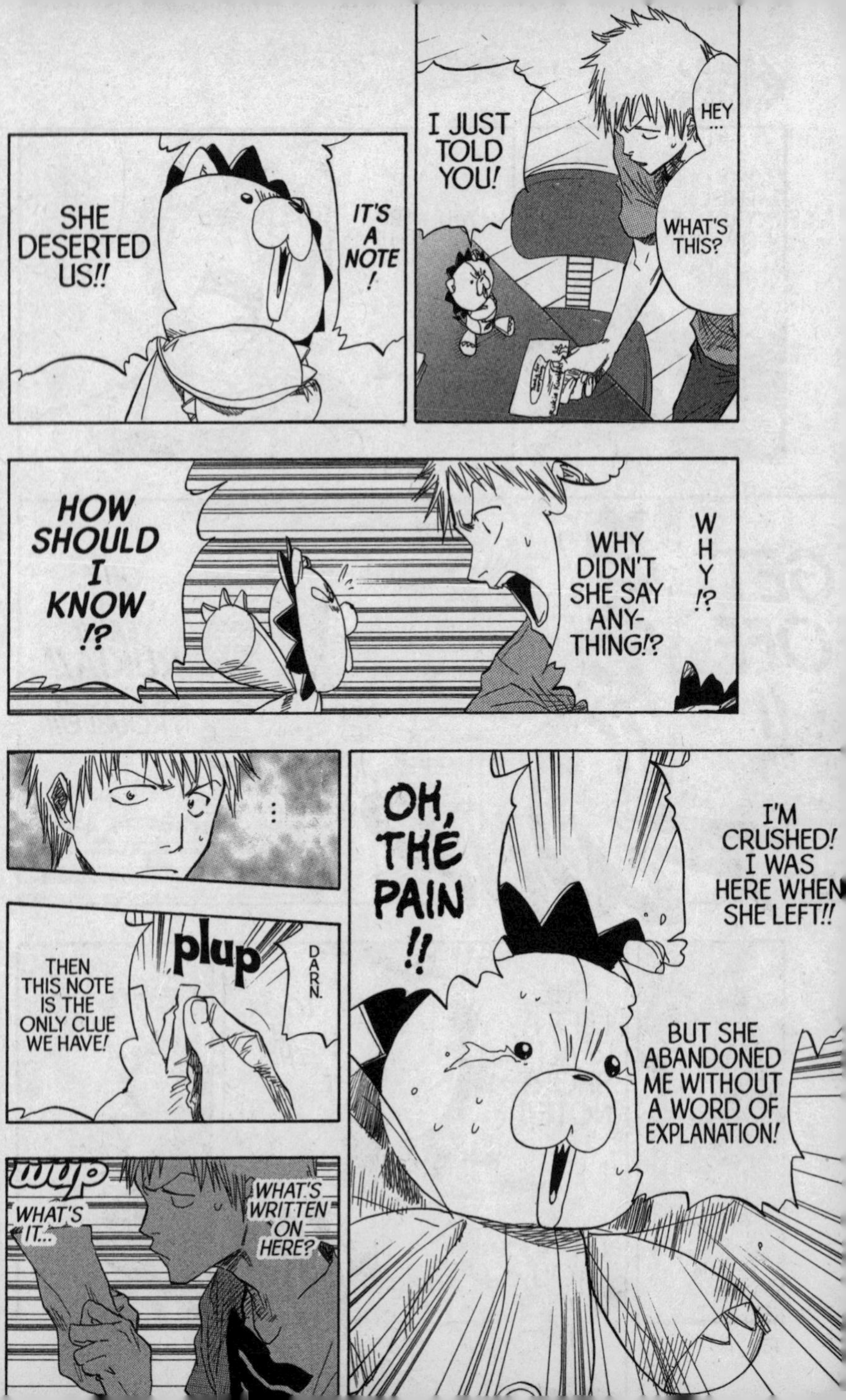

HEY...
WHAT'S THIS?
I JUST TOLD YOU!
IT'S A NOTE!
SHE DESERTED US!!
WHY DIDN'T SHE SAY ANYTHING!?
WHY!?
HOW SHOULD I KNOW!?
I'M CRUSHED! I WAS HERE WHEN SHE LEFT!!
BUT SHE ABANDONED ME WITHOUT A WORD OF EXPLANATION!
OH, THE PAIN!!
...
DARN.
plup
THEN THIS NOTE IS THE ONLY CLUE WE HAVE!
wup
WHAT'S WRITTEN ON HERE?
WHAT'S IT...

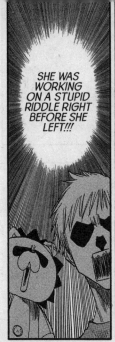

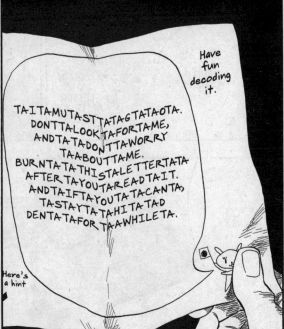

Have fun decoding it.
TAITAMUTASTTATAGTATAOTA. DONTTALOOKTAFORTAME, ANDTATADONTTAWORRY TAABOUTTAME. BURNTATATHISTALETTERTATA AFTERTAYOUTAREADTAIT. ANDTAIFTAYOUTATACANTA, TASTAYTATAHITATAD DENTATAFORTAAWHILETA.
Here's a hint
SHE WAS WORKING ON A STUPID RIDDLE RIGHT BEFORE SHE LEFT!!!
Here's a hint
WHAT'S THIS!?
WHY A TANUKI?!! OH, I GET IT, "TA-NUKI"! "NUKI" MEANS "WITHOUT"!
SO I'LL READ IT WITHOUT THE TA'S!!
UM...
"I... MUST... GO."

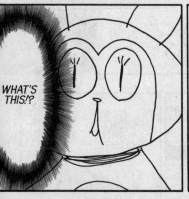

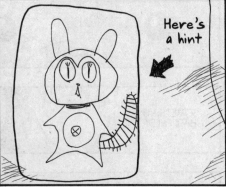

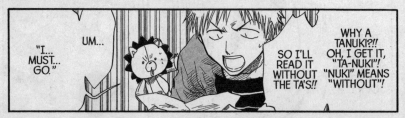

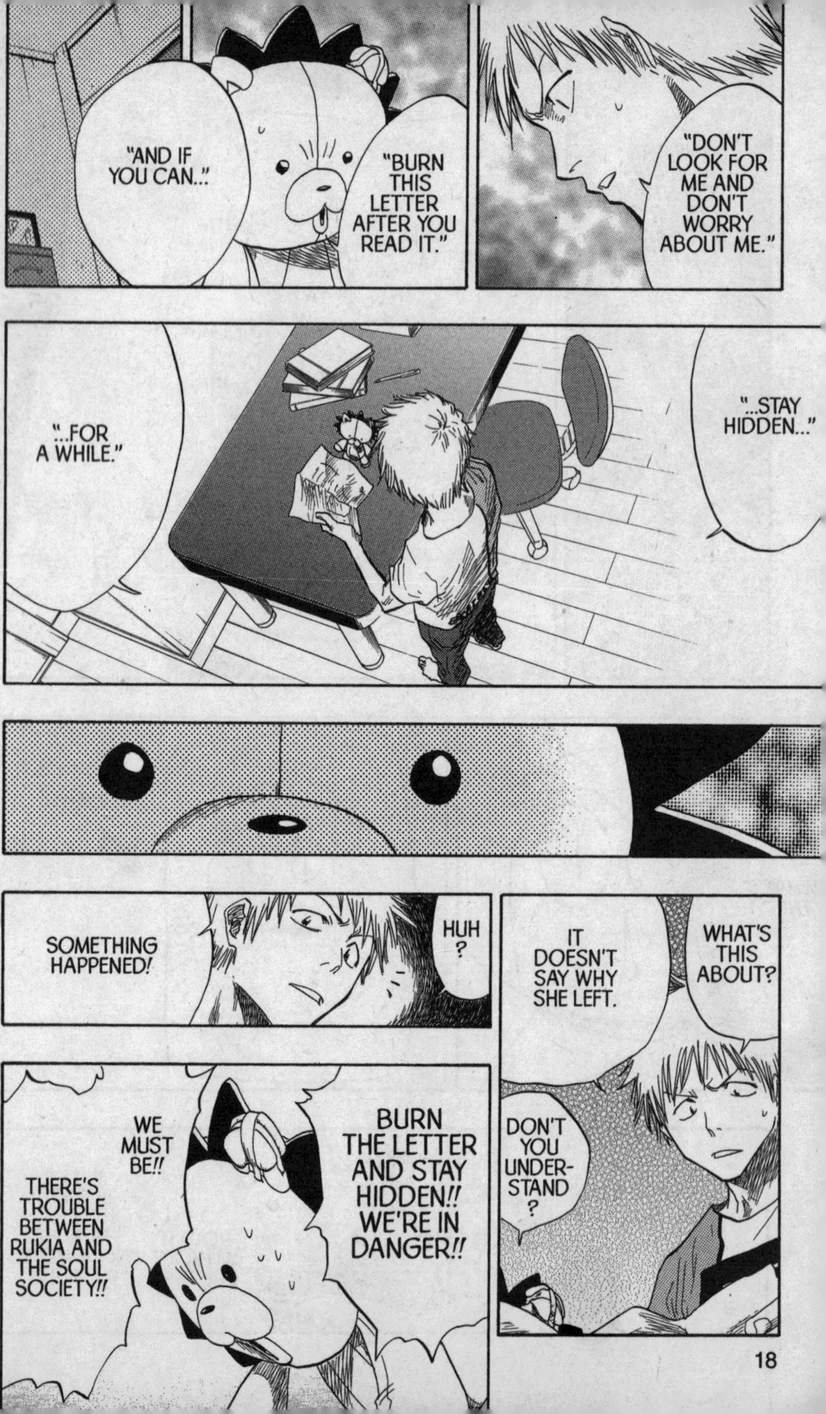
"DON'T LOOK FOR ME AND DON'T WORRY ABOUT ME."
"BURN THIS LETTER AFTER YOU READ IT."
"AND IF YOU CAN..."
"...STAY HIDDEN..."
"...FOR A WHILE."
WHAT'S THIS ABOUT?
IT DOESN'T SAY WHY SHE LEFT.
HUH?
SOMETHING HAPPENED!
DON'T YOU UNDER-STAND?
BURN THE LETTER AND STAY HIDDEN!! WE'RE IN DANGER!!
WE MUST BE!!
THERE'S TROUBLE BETWEEN RUKIA AND THE SOUL SOCIETY!!

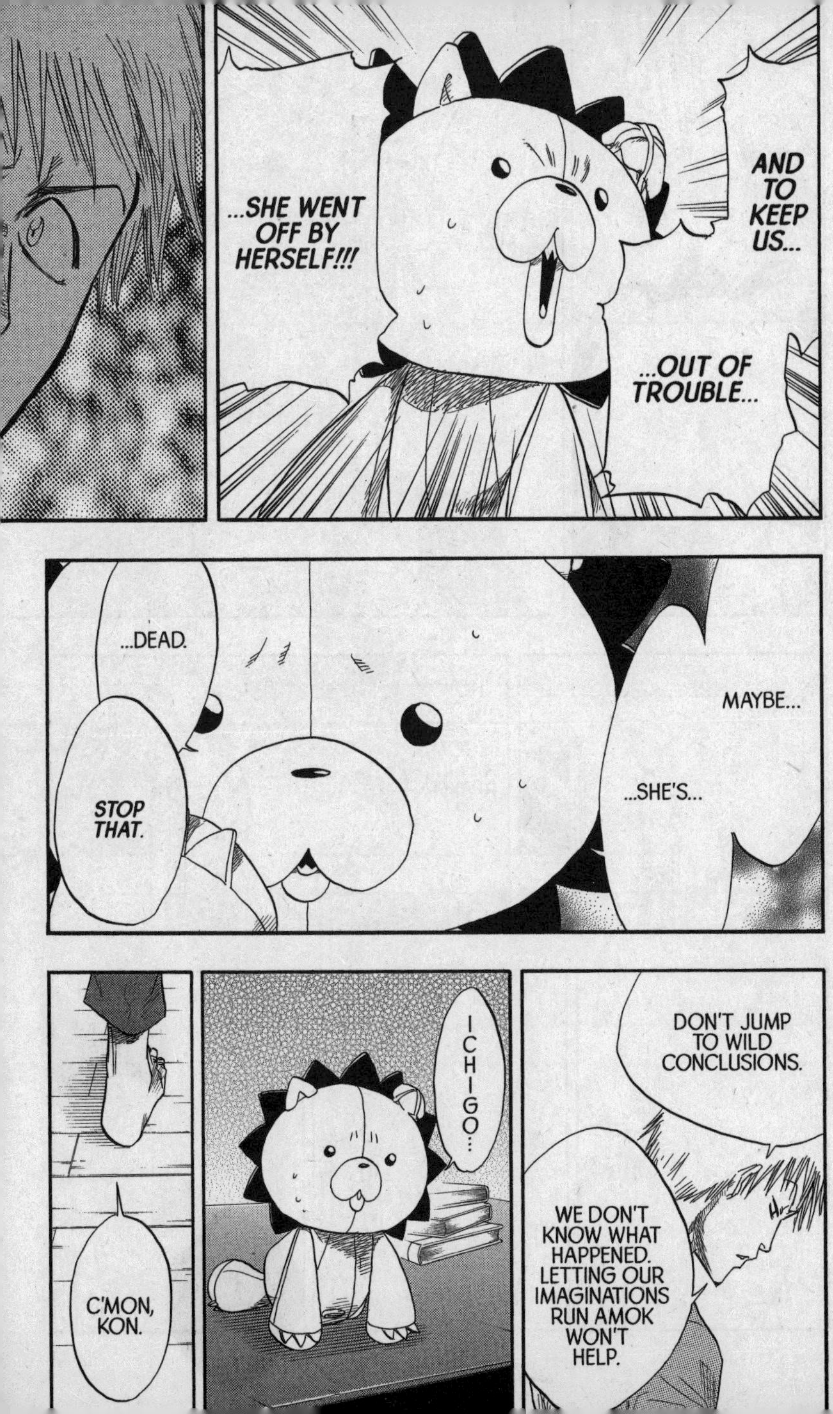

AND TO KEEP US...
...OUT OF TROUBLE...
...SHE WENT OFF BY HERSELF!!!
MAYBE...
...SHE'S...
...DEAD.
STOP THAT.
DON'T JUMP TO WILD CONCLUSIONS.
WE DON'T KNOW WHAT HAPPENED. LETTING OUR IMAGINATIONS RUN AMOK WON'T HELP.
ICHIGO...
C'MON, KON.

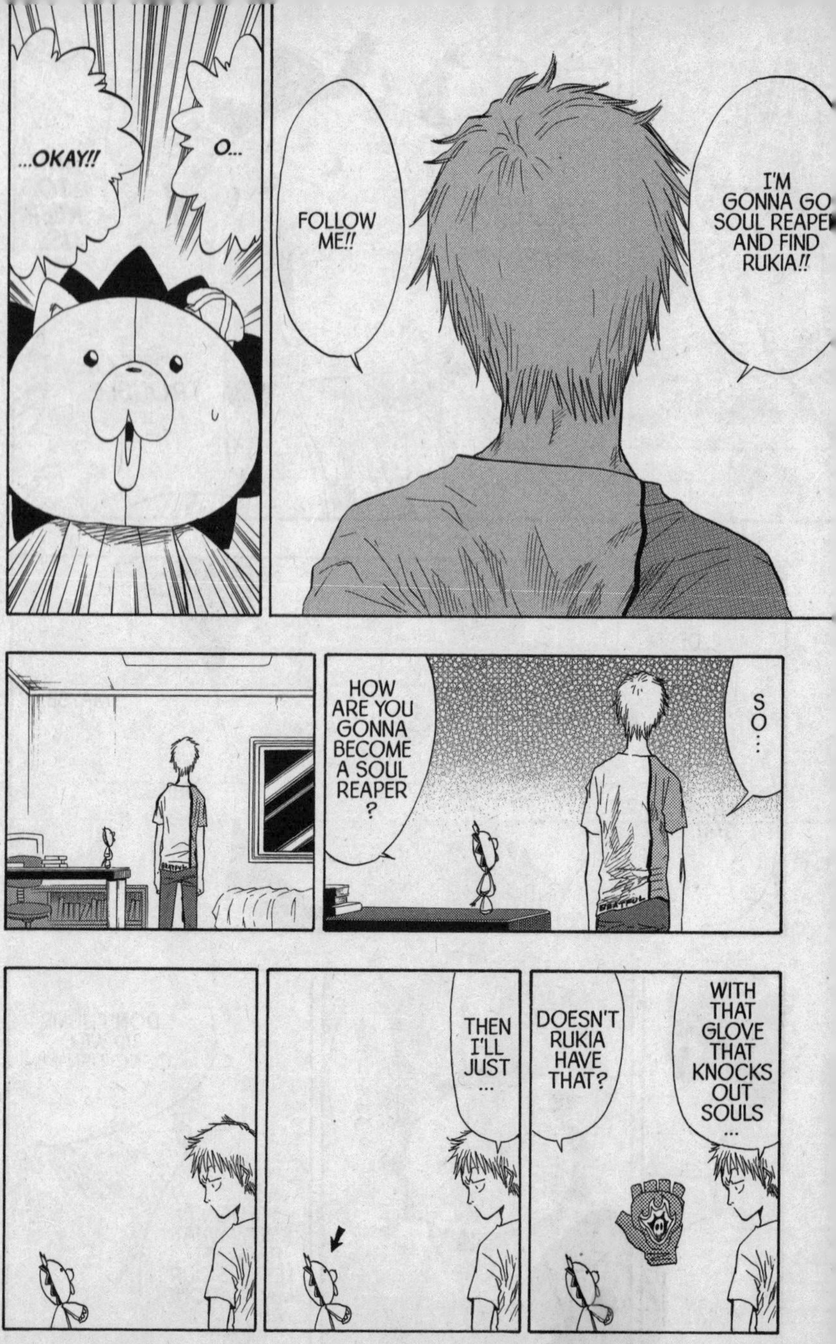
I'M GONNA GO SOUL REAPE AND FIND RUKIA!!
FOLLOW ME!!
O...
...OKAY!!
SO...
HOW ARE YOU GONNA BECOME A SOUL REAPER?
WITH THAT GLOVE THAT KNOCKS OUT SOULS...
DOESN'T RUKIA HAVE THAT?
THEN I'LL JUST...

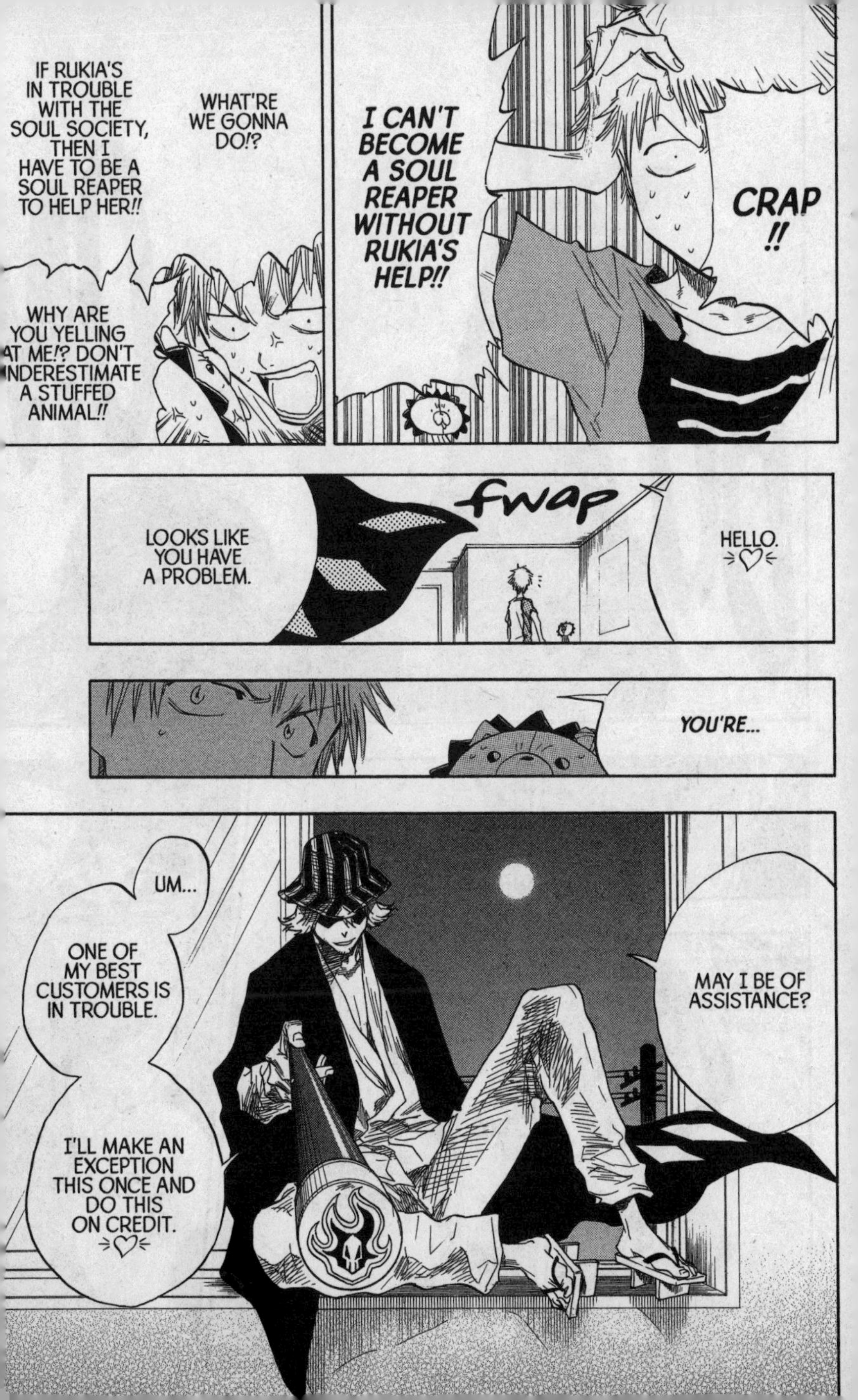
CRAP!!
I CAN'T BECOME A SOUL REAPER WITHOUT RUKIA'S HELP!!
WHAT'RE WE GONNA DO!?
IF RUKIA'S IN TROUBLE WITH THE SOUL SOCIETY, THEN I HAVE TO BE A SOUL REAPER TO HELP HER!!
WHY ARE YOU YELLING AT ME!? DON'T NDERESTIMATE A STUFFED ANIMAL!!
HELLO. ♡
fwap
LOOKS LIKE YOU HAVE A PROBLEM.
YOU'RE...
MAY I BE OF ASSISTANCE?
UM...
ONE OF MY BEST CUSTOMERS IS IN TROUBLE.
I'LL MAKE AN EXCEPTION THIS ONCE AND DO THIS ON CREDIT. ♡

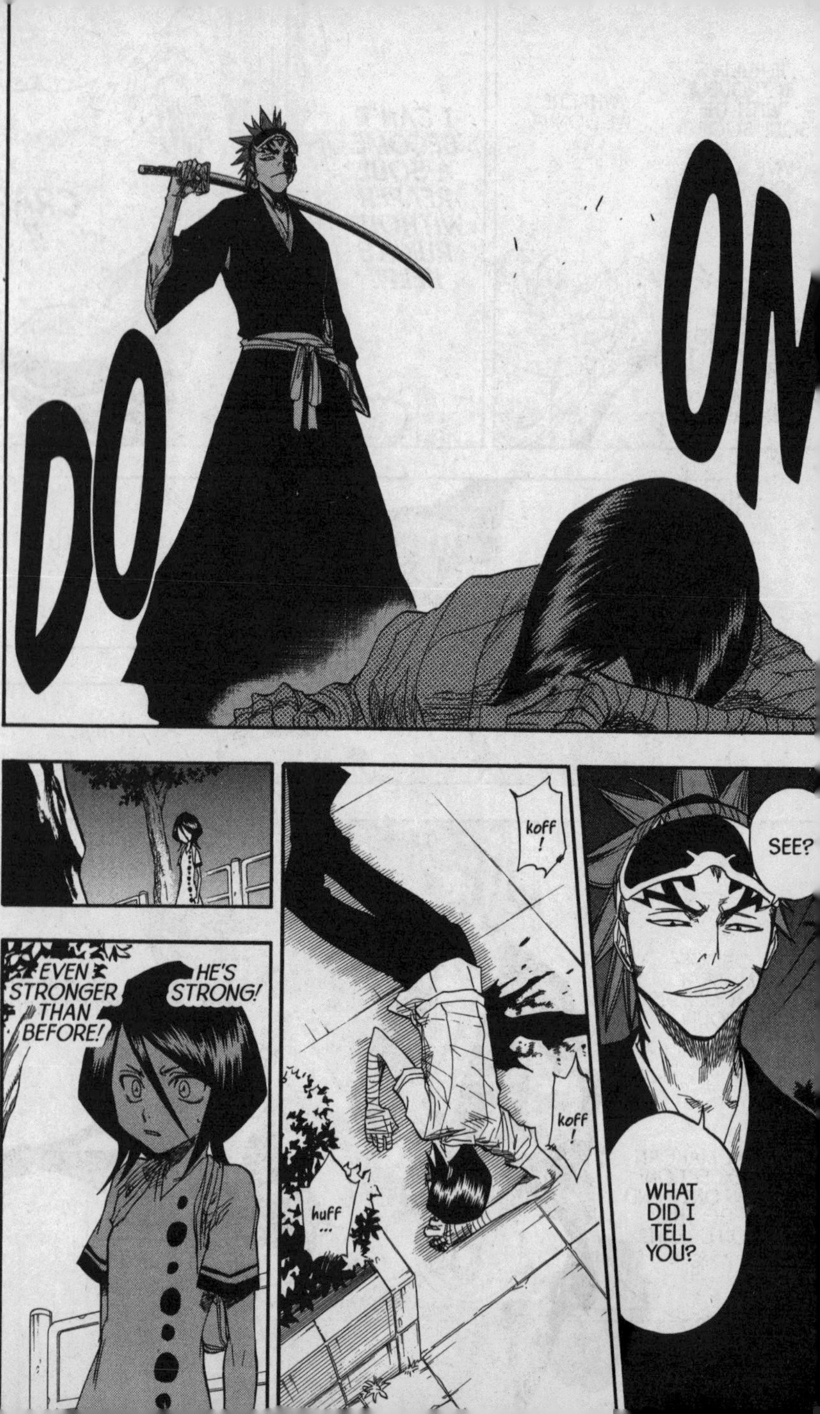
DO
ON
SEE?
WHAT DID I TELL YOU?
koff!
koff!
huff...
HE'S STRONG!
EVEN STRONGER THAN BEFORE!

READ THIS WAY

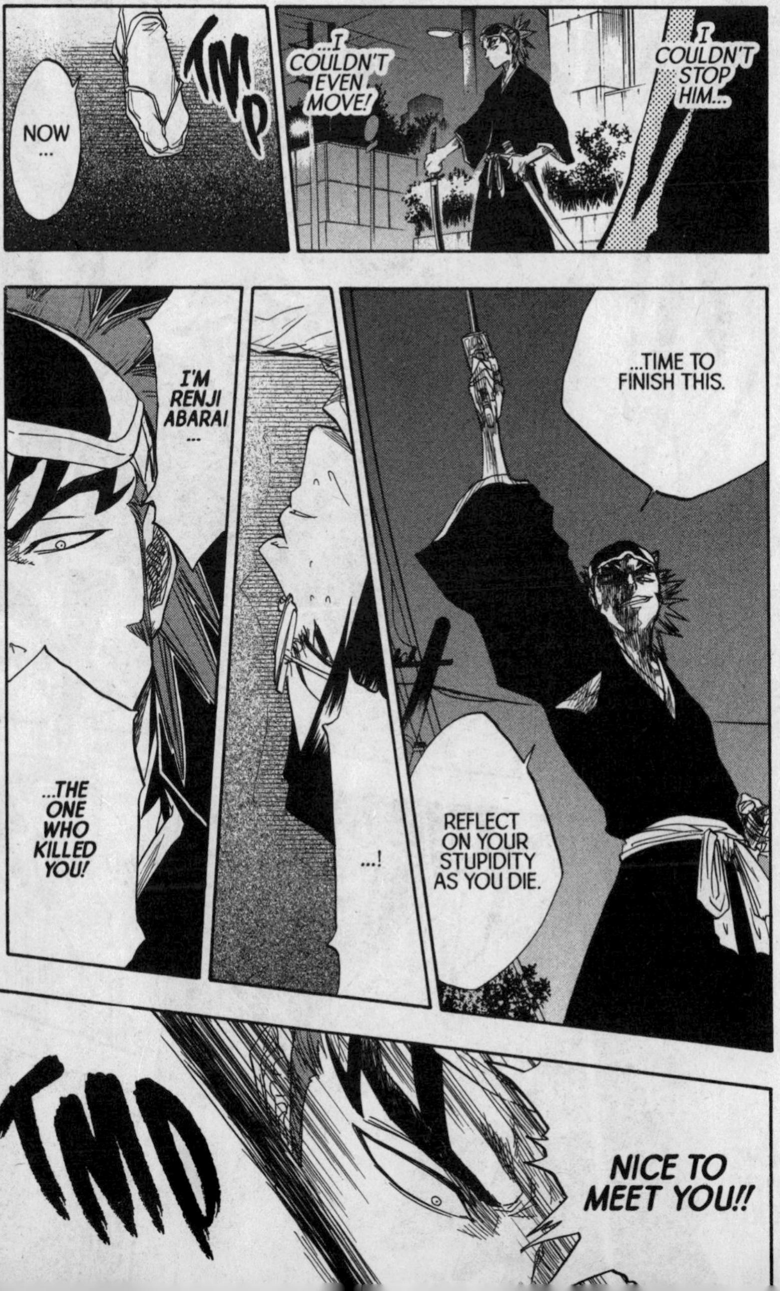

I COULDN'T STOP HIM...
...I COULDN'T EVEN MOVE!
TMP
NOW...
...TIME TO FINISH THIS.
REFLECT ON YOUR STUPIDITY AS YOU DIE.
...!
I'M RENJI ABARAI...
...THE ONE WHO KILLED YOU!
NICE TO MEET YOU!!
TMP

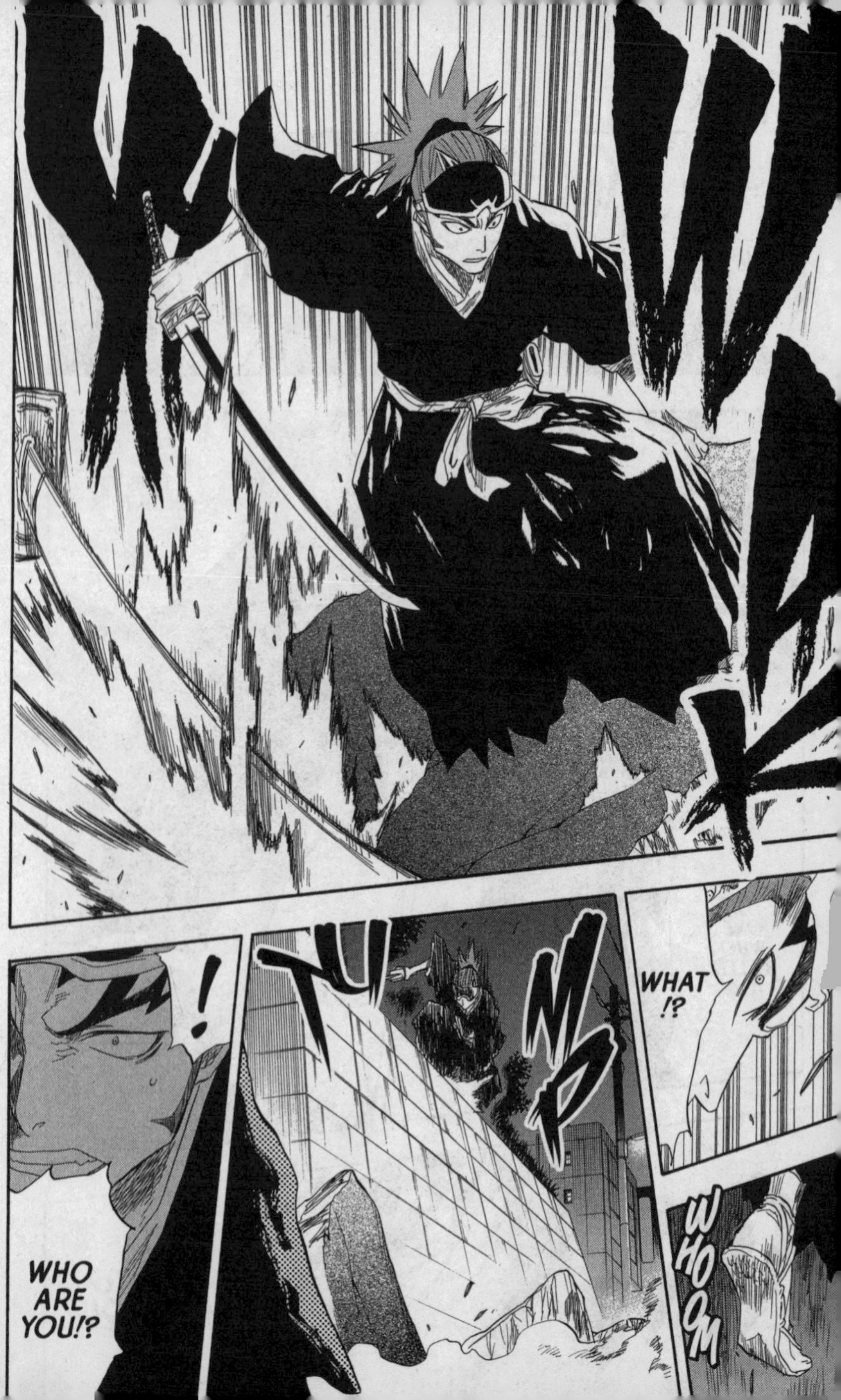
WHAT !?
WHOOM
!
WHO ARE YOU!?

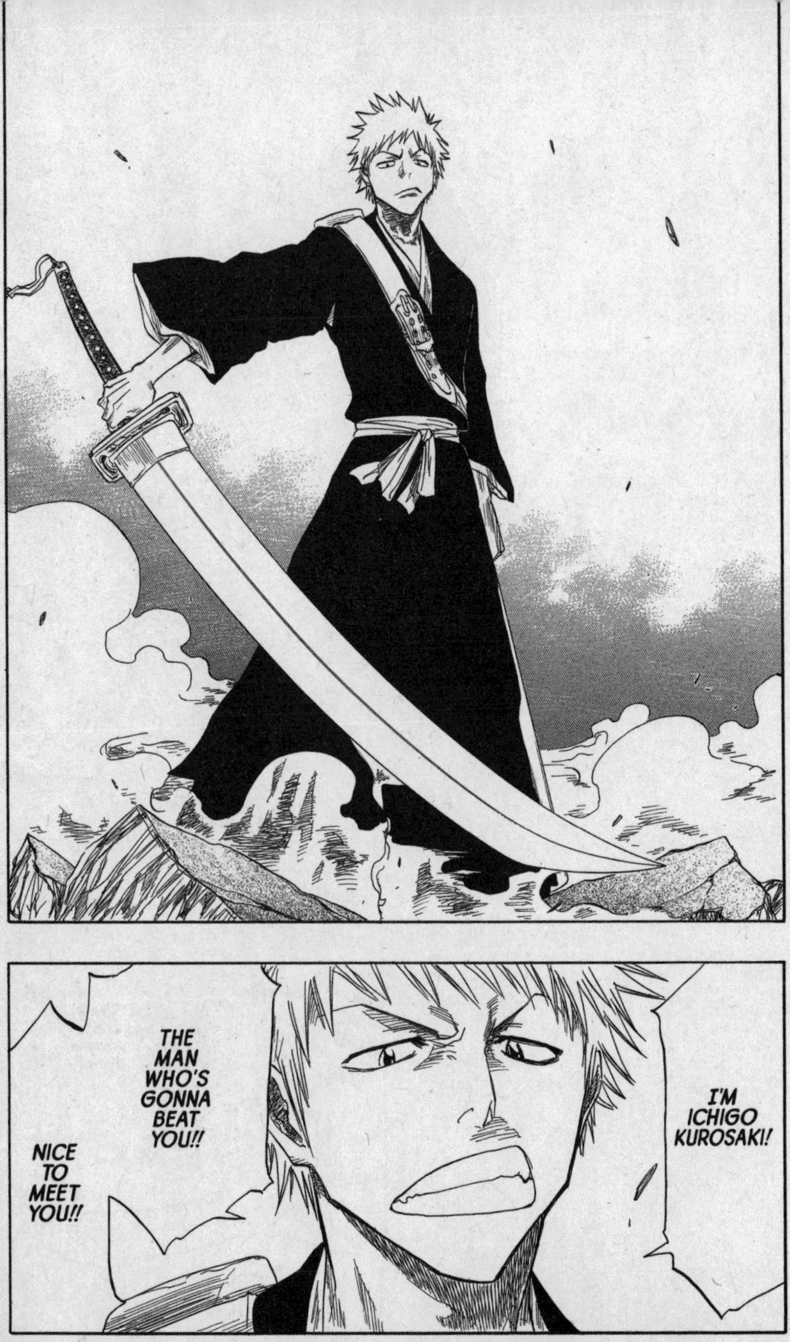
I'M ICHIGO KUROSAKI!
THE MAN WHO'S GONNA BEAT YOU!!
NICE TO MEET YOU!!

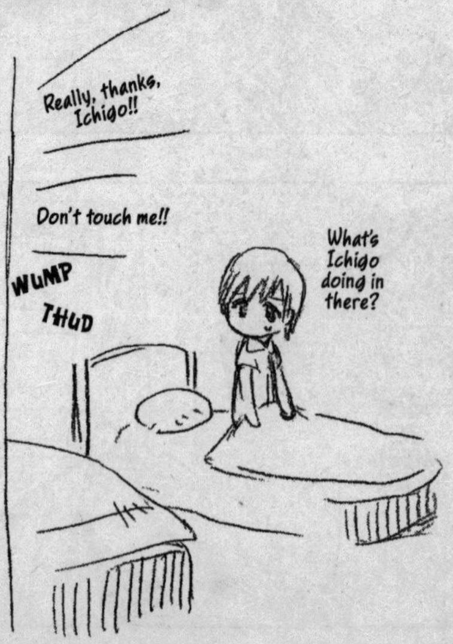
Really, thanks, Ichigo!!
Don't touch me!!
WUMP
THUD
What's Ichigo doing in there?

54. The Nameless Boy

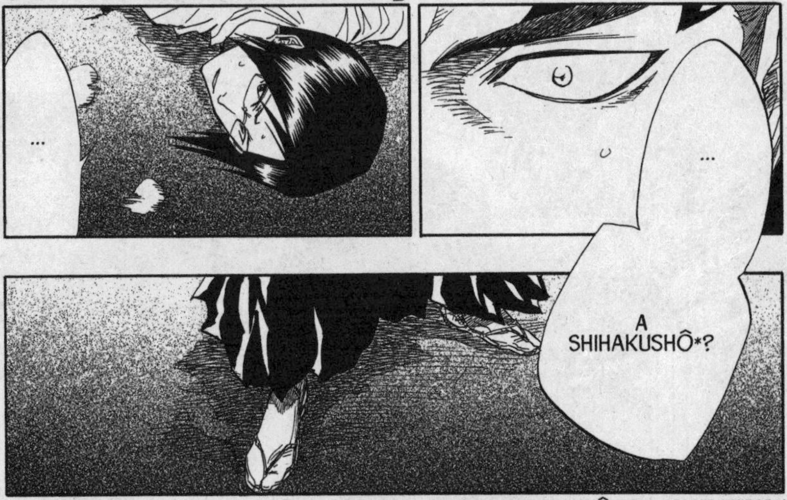
...
...
A SHIHAKUSHÔ*?

*SHIHAKUSHÔ: SOUL REAPER UNIFORM

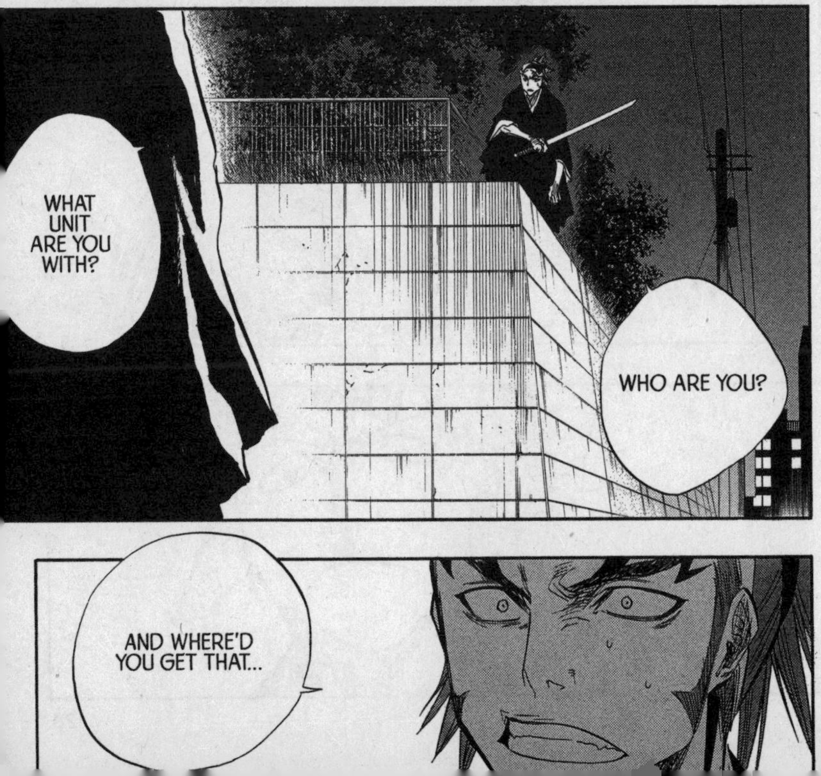
WHO ARE YOU?
WHAT UNIT ARE YOU WITH?
AND WHERE'D YOU GET THAT...

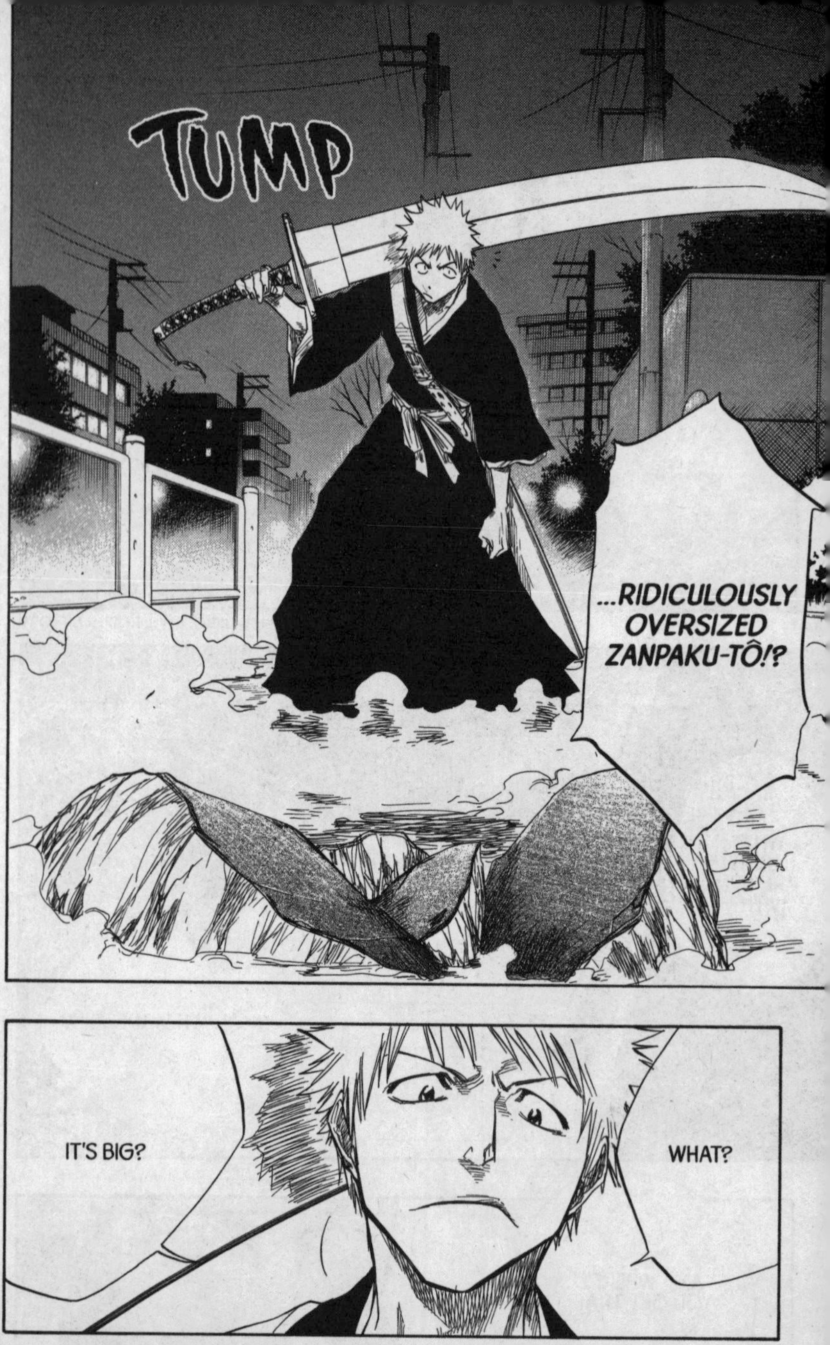
TUMP
...RIDICULOUSLY OVERSIZED ZANPAKU-TÔ!?
WHAT?
IT'S BIG?

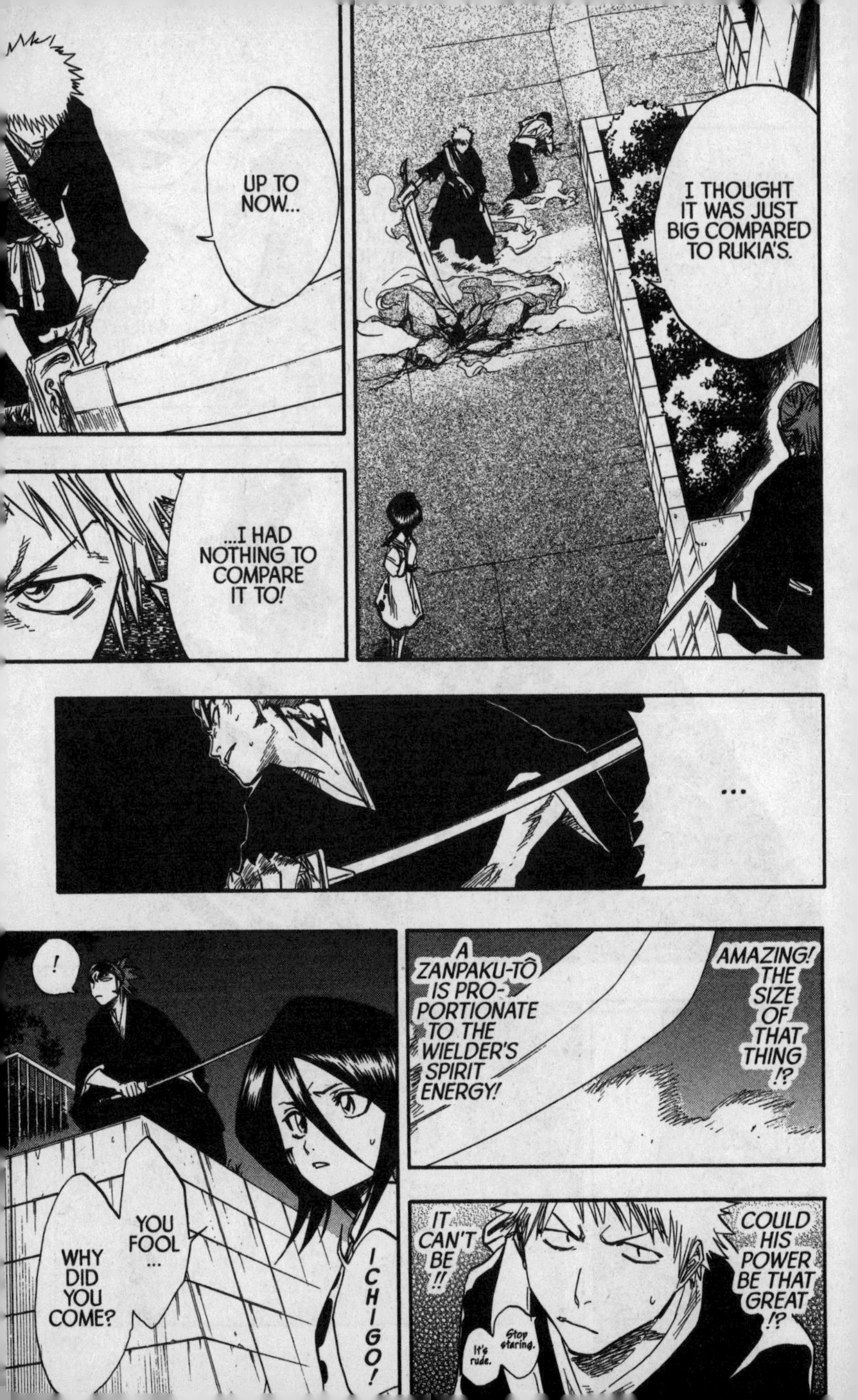
I THOUGHT IT WAS JUST BIG COMPARED TO RUKIA'S.
UP TO NOW...
...I HAD NOTHING TO COMPARE IT TO!
...
AMAZING! THE SIZE OF THAT THING !?
A ZANPAKU-TÔ IS PRO-PORTIONATE TO THE WIELDER'S SPIRIT ENERGY!
!
COULD HIS POWER BE THAT GREAT !?
IT CAN'T BE !!
Stop staring.
It's rude.
ICHIGO!
YOU FOOL ...
WHY DID YOU COME?

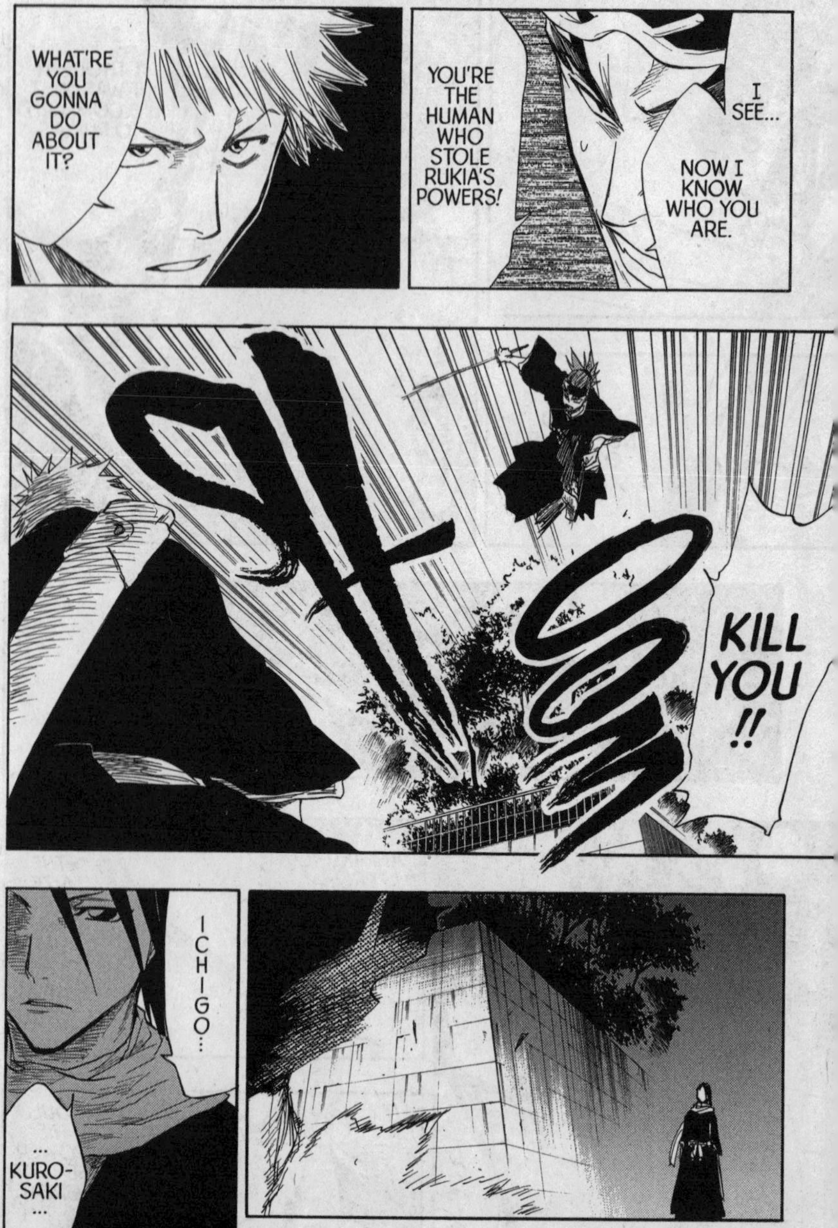
I SEE...
NOW I KNOW WHO YOU ARE.
YOU'RE THE HUMAN WHO STOLE RUKIA'S POWERS!
WHAT'RE YOU GONNA DO ABOUT IT?
KILL YOU!!
ICHIGO...
...KUROSAKI...

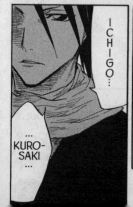

54. The Nameless Boy

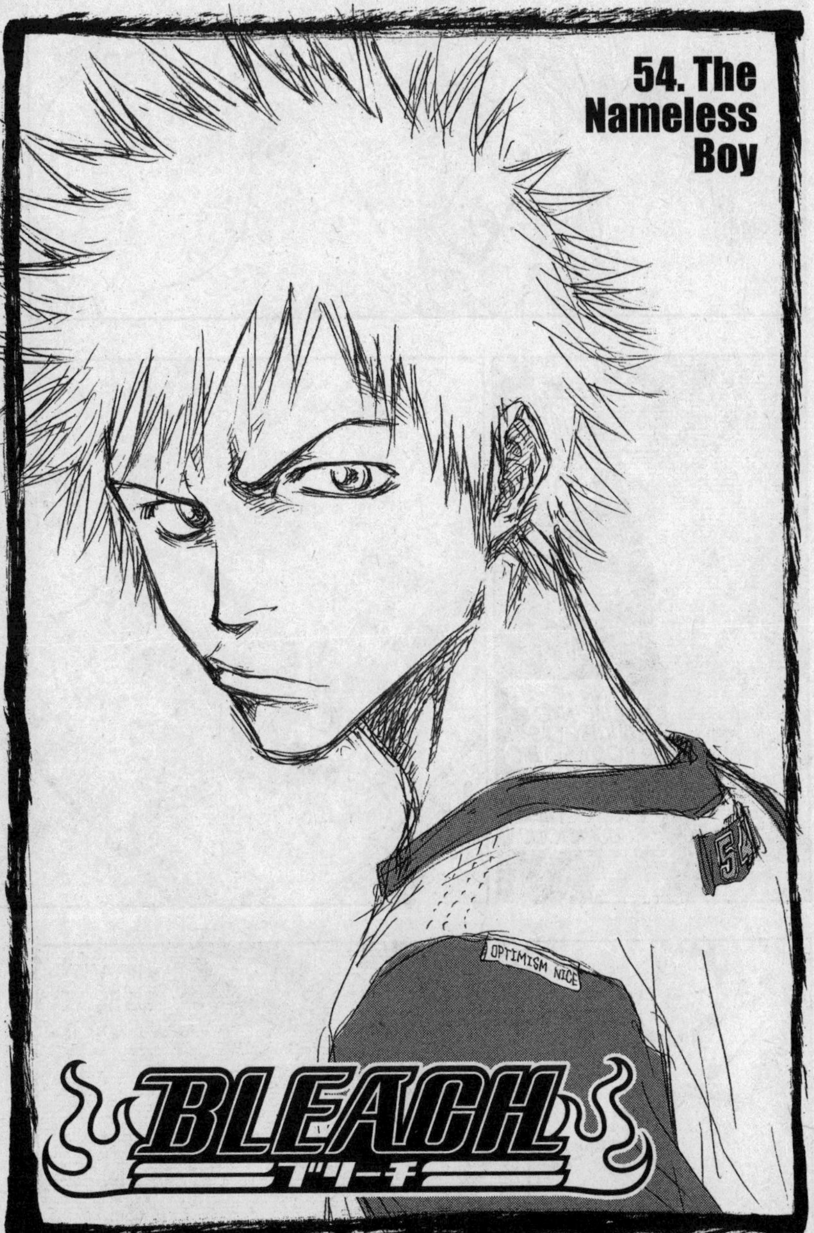
OPTIMISM NICE
54
BLEACH
ブリーチ

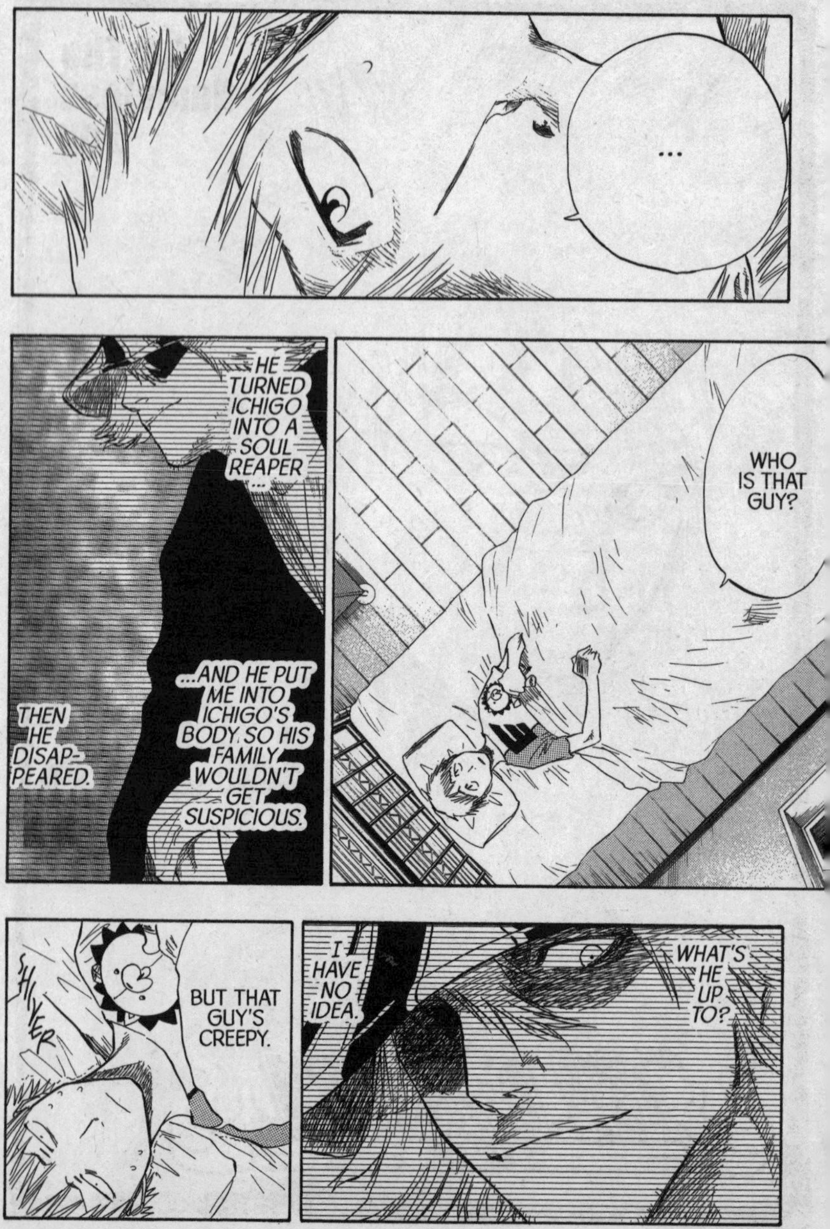
...
WHO IS THAT GUY?
HE TURNED ICHIGO INTO A SOUL REAPER...
...AND HE PUT ME INTO ICHIGO'S BODY SO HIS FAMILY WOULDN'T GET SUSPICIOUS.
THEN HE DISAPPEARED.
WHAT'S HE UP TO?
I HAVE NO IDEA.
BUT THAT GUY'S CREEPY.
SHIVER

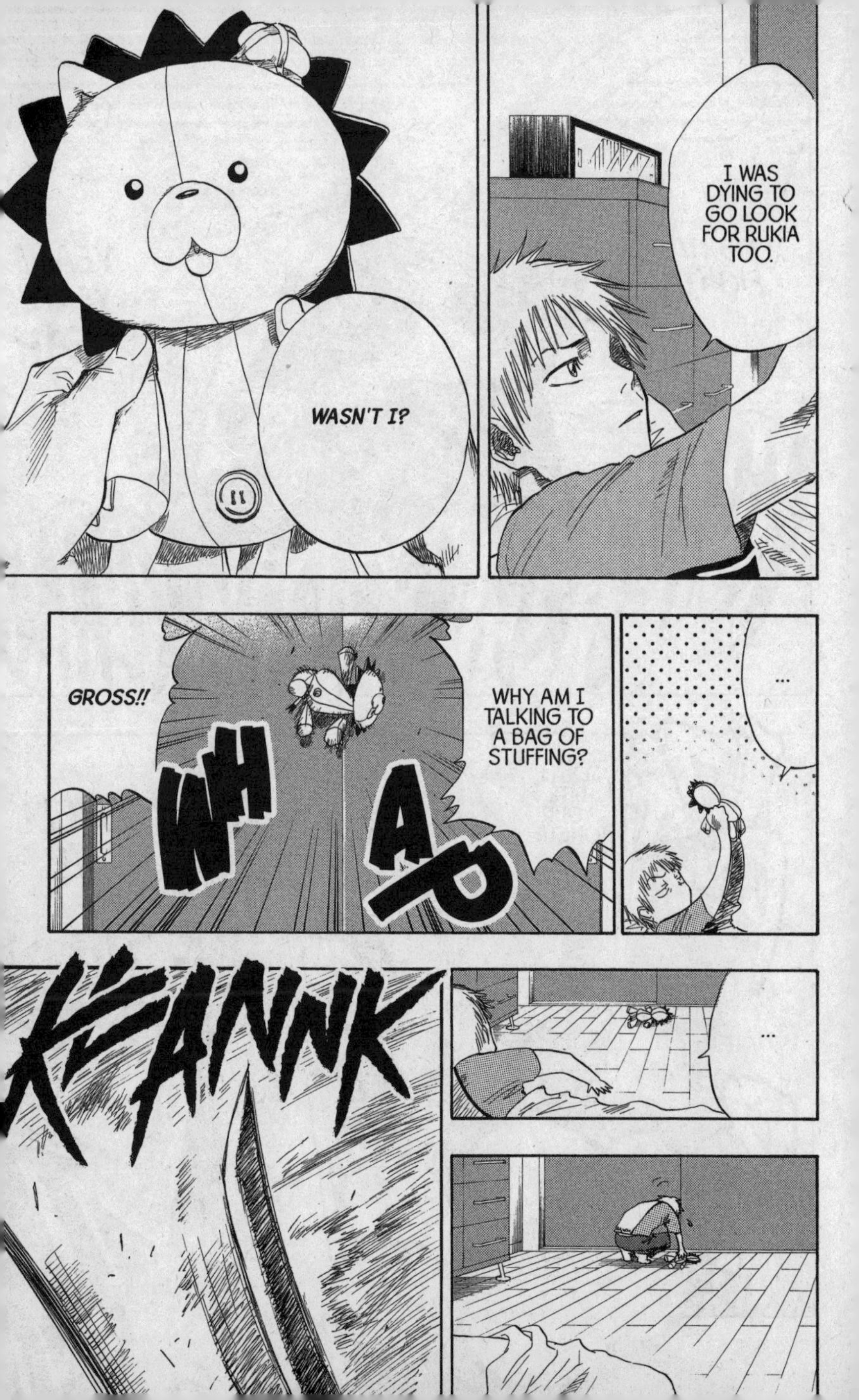
I WAS DYING TO GO LOOK FOR RUKIA TOO.
WASN'T I?
...
WHY AM I TALKING TO A BAG OF STUFFING?
GROSS!!
WHAP
...

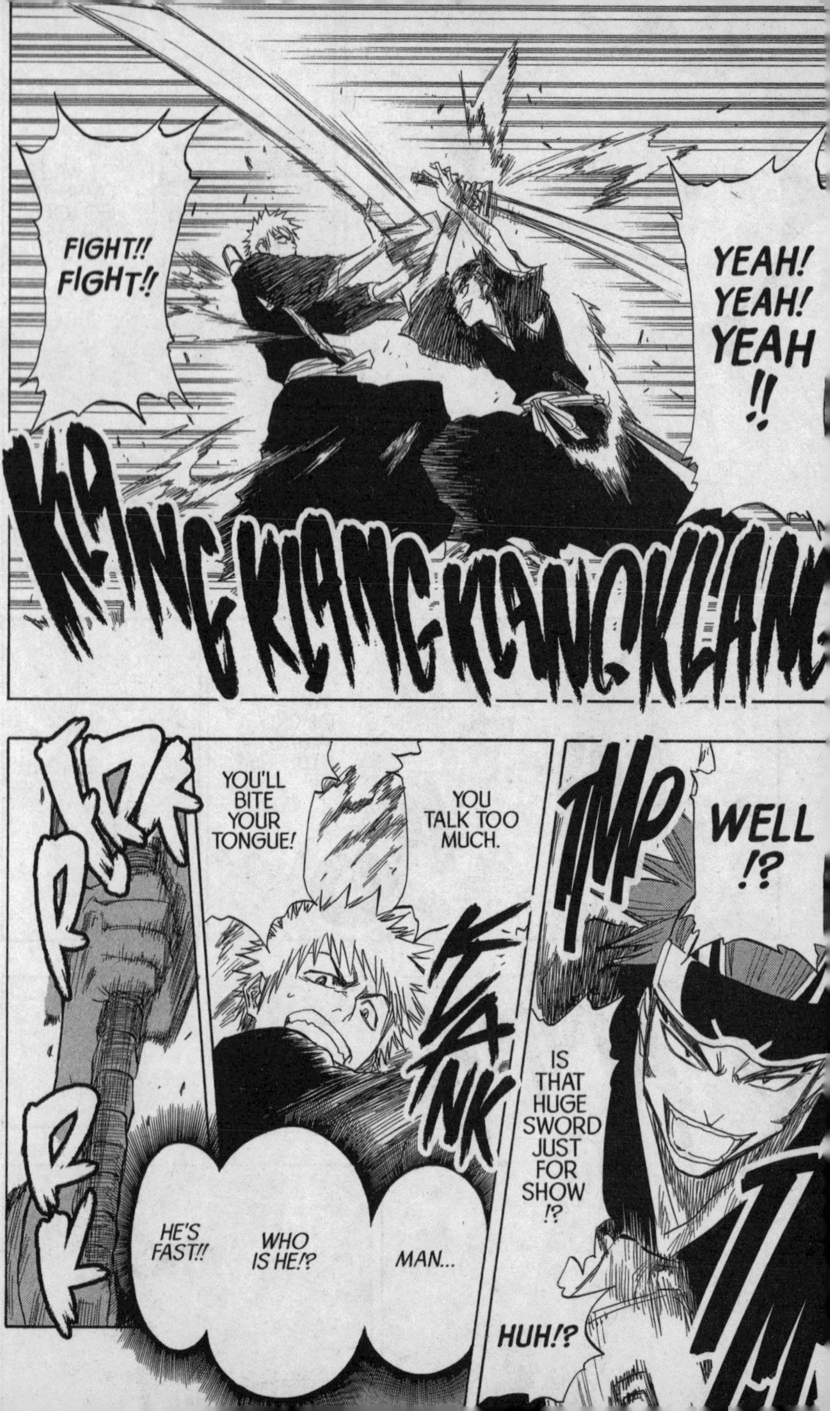
YEAH! YEAH! YEAH!!
FIGHT!! FIGHT!!
WELL!?
YOU TALK TOO MUCH.
YOU'LL BITE YOUR TONGUE!
IS THAT HUGE SWORD JUST FOR SHOW!?
HUH!?
MAN...
WHO IS HE!?
HE'S FAST!!

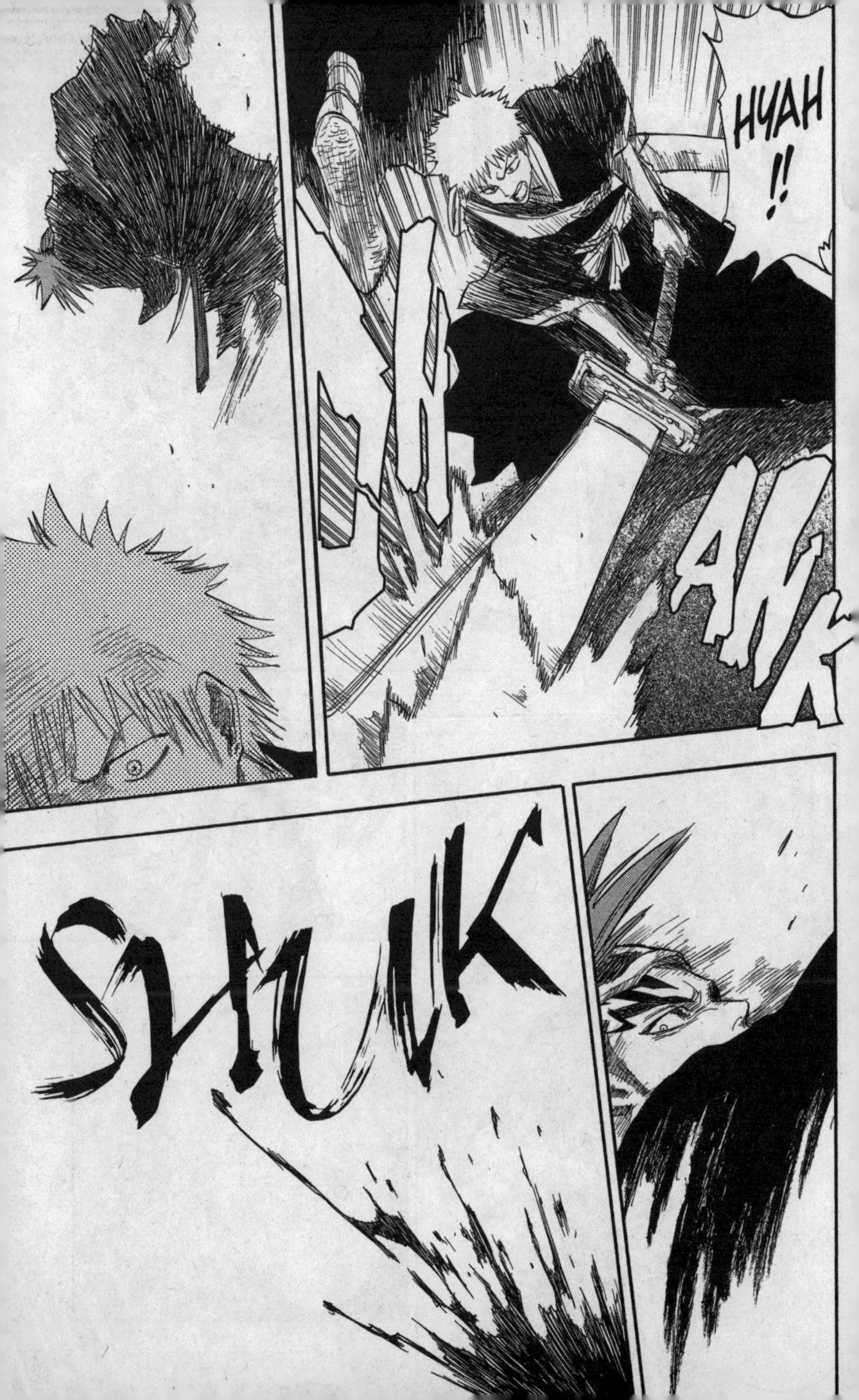
HYAH !!
SHUK

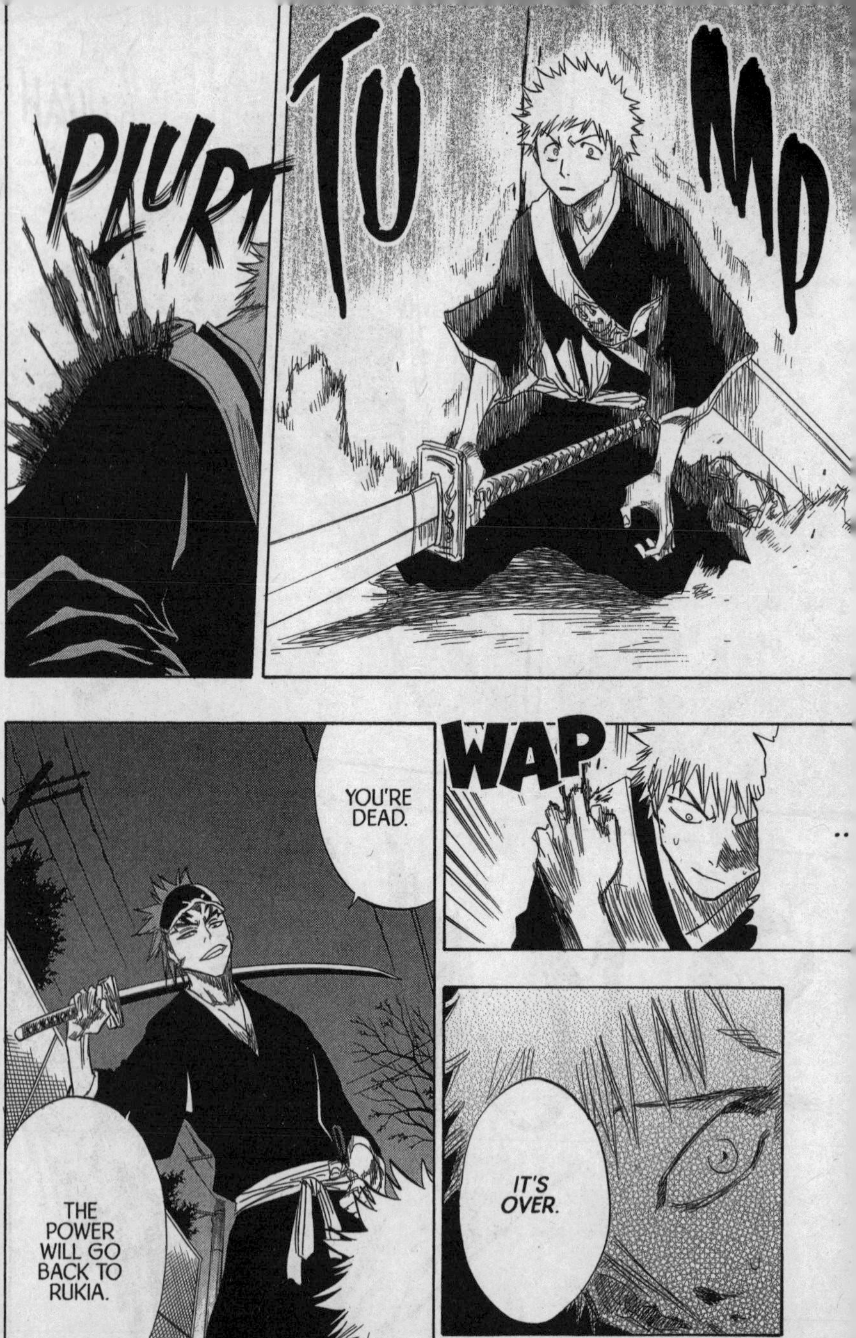
TUMP
PLURT
WAP
..
IT'S OVER.
YOU'RE DEAD.
THE POWER WILL GO BACK TO RUKIA.

READ THIS WAY

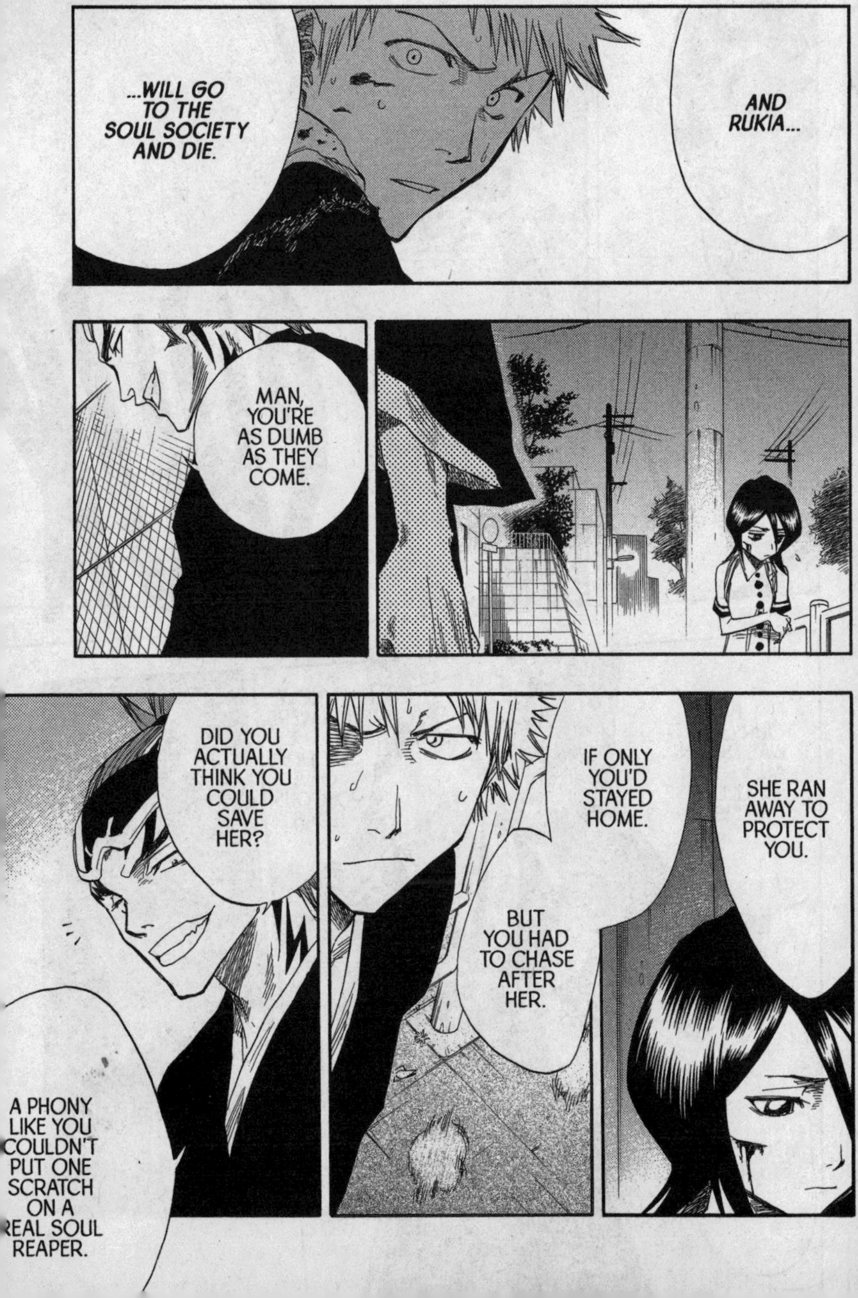
AND RUKIA...
...WILL GO TO THE SOUL SOCIETY AND DIE.
MAN, YOU'RE AS DUMB AS THEY COME.
SHE RAN AWAY TO PROTECT YOU.
IF ONLY YOU'D STAYED HOME.
BUT YOU HAD TO CHASE AFTER HER.
DID YOU ACTUALLY THINK YOU COULD SAVE HER?
A PHONY LIKE YOU COULDN'T PUT ONE SCRATCH ON A REAL SOUL REAPER.

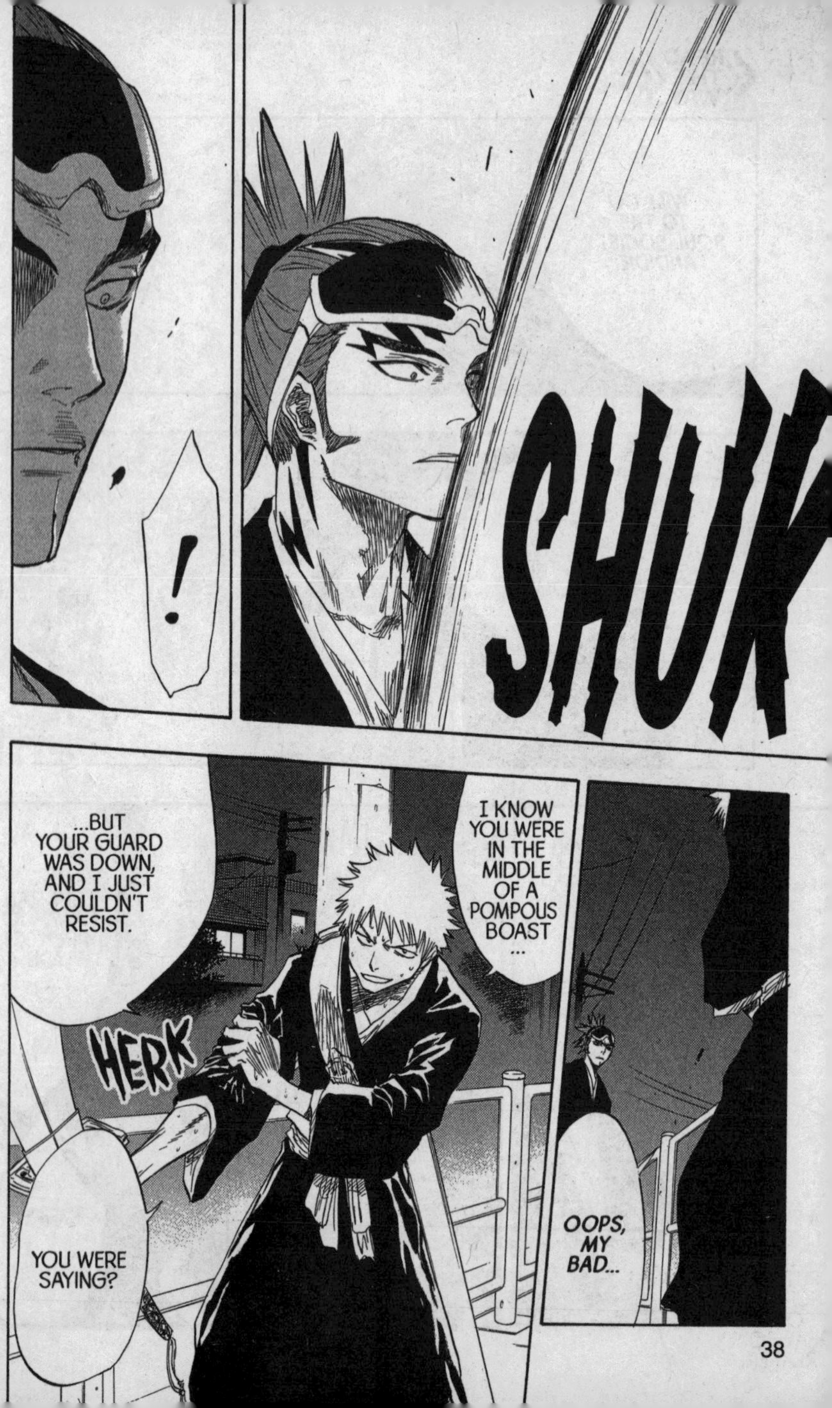
SHUK
!
OOPS, MY BAD...
I KNOW YOU WERE IN THE MIDDLE OF A POMPOUS BOAST ...
...BUT YOUR GUARD WAS DOWN, AND I JUST COULDN'T RESIST.
HERK
YOU WERE SAYING?

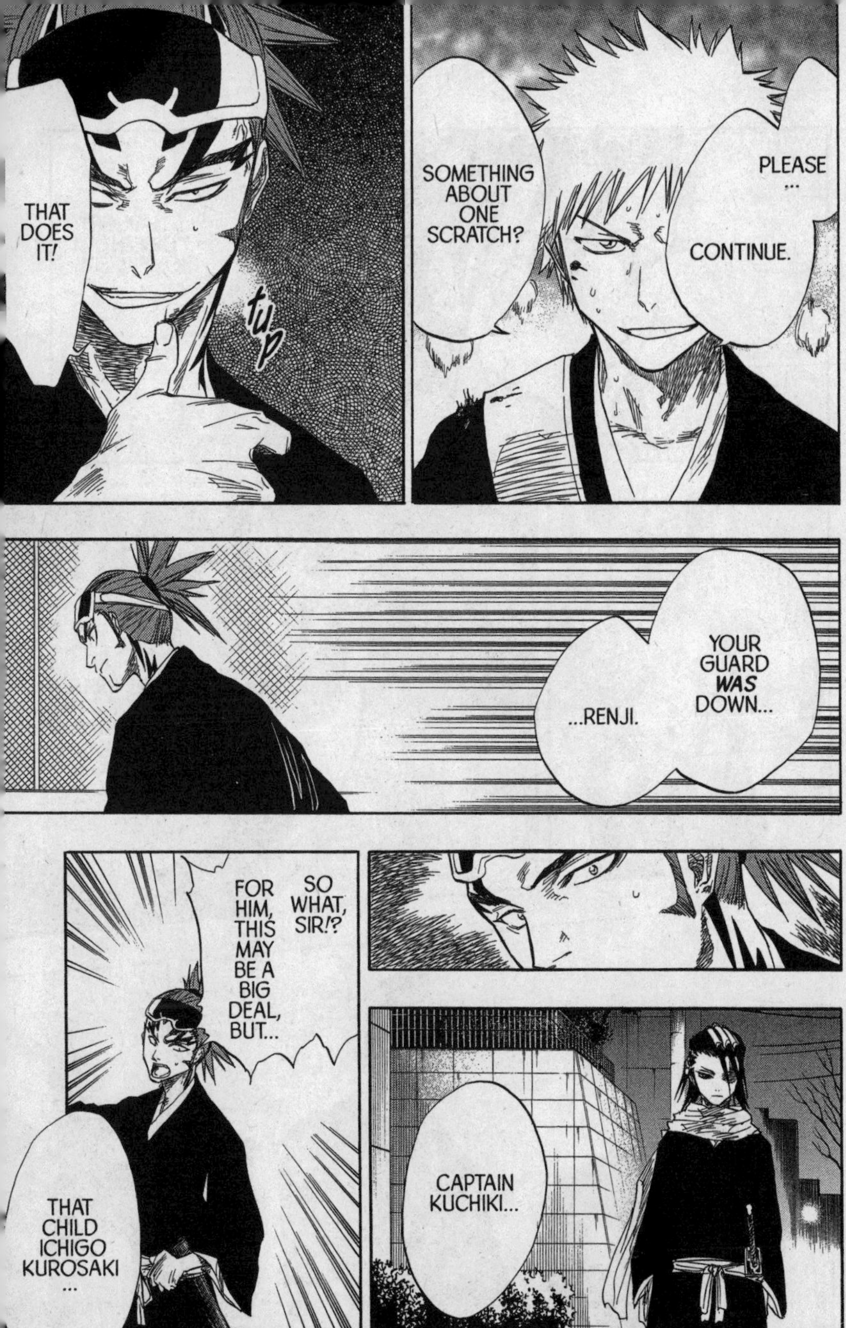
PLEASE ... CONTINUE.
SOMETHING ABOUT ONE SCRATCH?
THAT DOES IT!
tup
YOUR GUARD WAS DOWN...
...RENJI.
CAPTAIN KUCHIKI...
SO WHAT, SIR!?
FOR HIM, THIS MAY BE A BIG DEAL, BUT...
THAT CHILD ICHIGO KUROSAKI ...

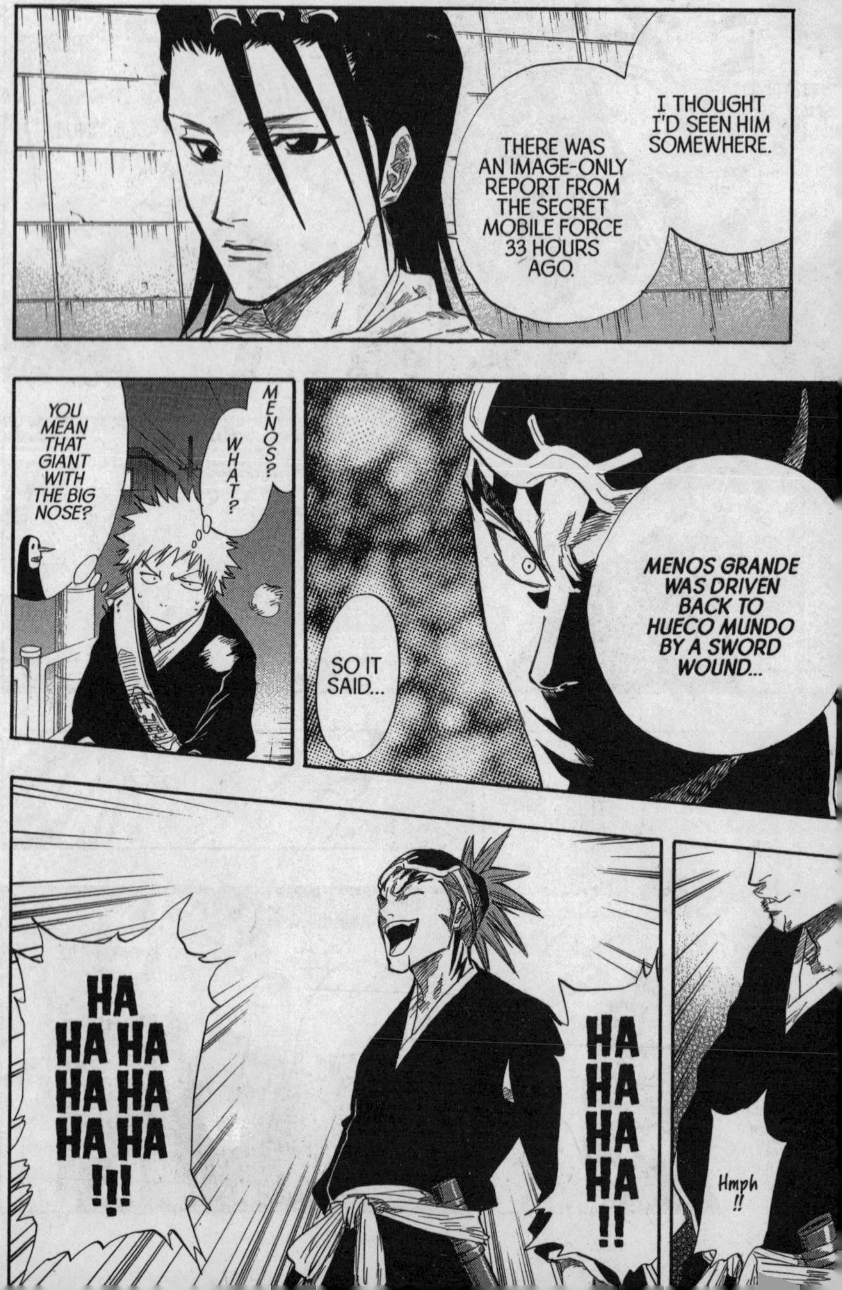
I THOUGHT I'D SEEN HIM SOMEWHERE.
THERE WAS AN IMAGE-ONLY REPORT FROM THE SECRET MOBILE FORCE 33 HOURS AGO.
MENOS GRANDE WAS DRIVEN BACK TO HUECO MUNDO BY A SWORD WOUND...
SO IT SAID...
MENOS? WHAT?
YOU MEAN THAT GIANT WITH THE BIG NOSE?
Hmph!!
HA HA HA HA HA!!
HA HA HA HA HA HA HA!!!

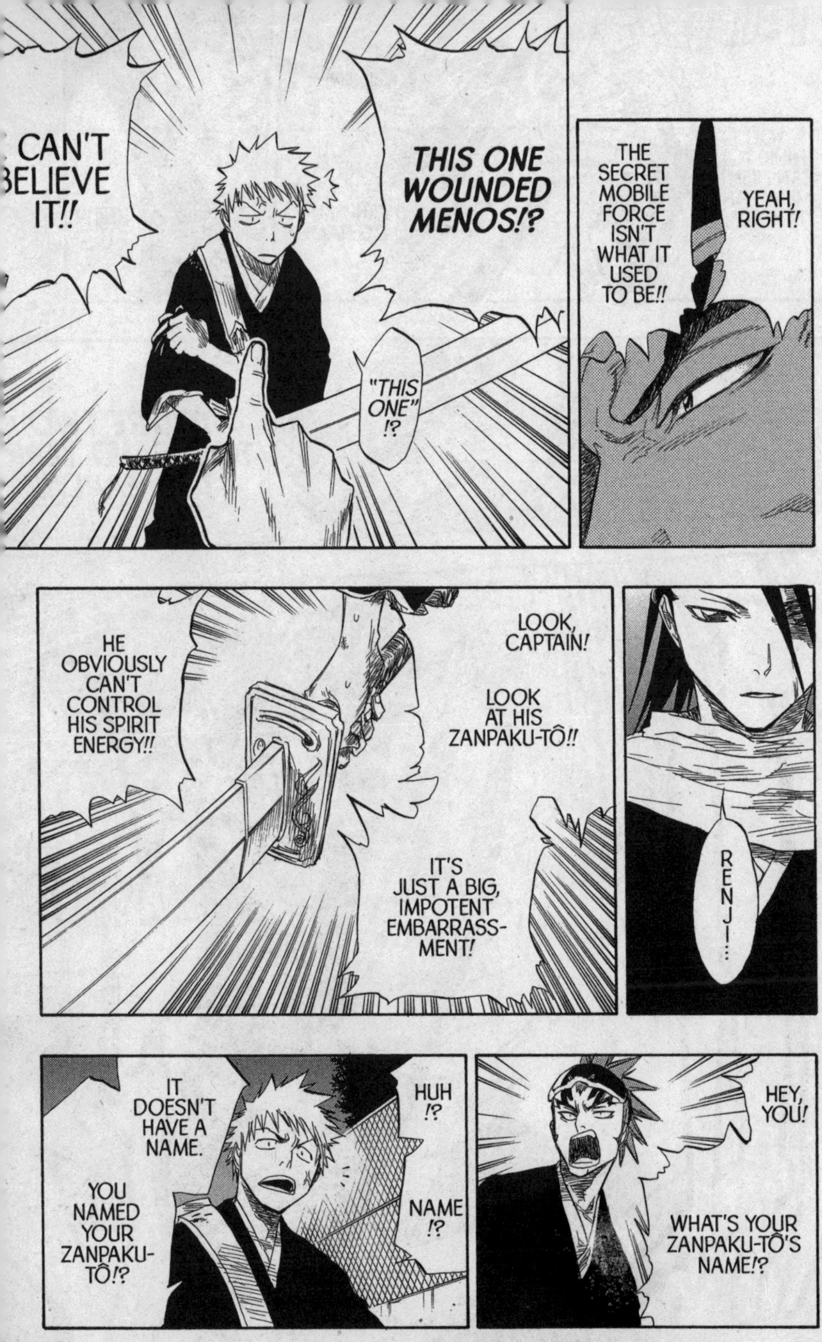
THIS ONE WOUNDED MENOS!?
CAN'T BELIEVE IT!!
"THIS ONE" !?
YEAH, RIGHT!
THE SECRET MOBILE FORCE ISN'T WHAT IT USED TO BE!!
RENJI...
LOOK, CAPTAIN!
LOOK AT HIS ZANPAKU-TÔ!!
HE OBVIOUSLY CAN'T CONTROL HIS SPIRIT ENERGY!!
IT'S JUST A BIG, IMPOTENT EMBARRASS-MENT!
HEY, YOU!
WHAT'S YOUR ZANPAKU-TÔ'S NAME!?
HUH !?
NAME !?
IT DOESN'T HAVE A NAME.
YOU NAMED YOUR ZANPAKU-TÔ!?

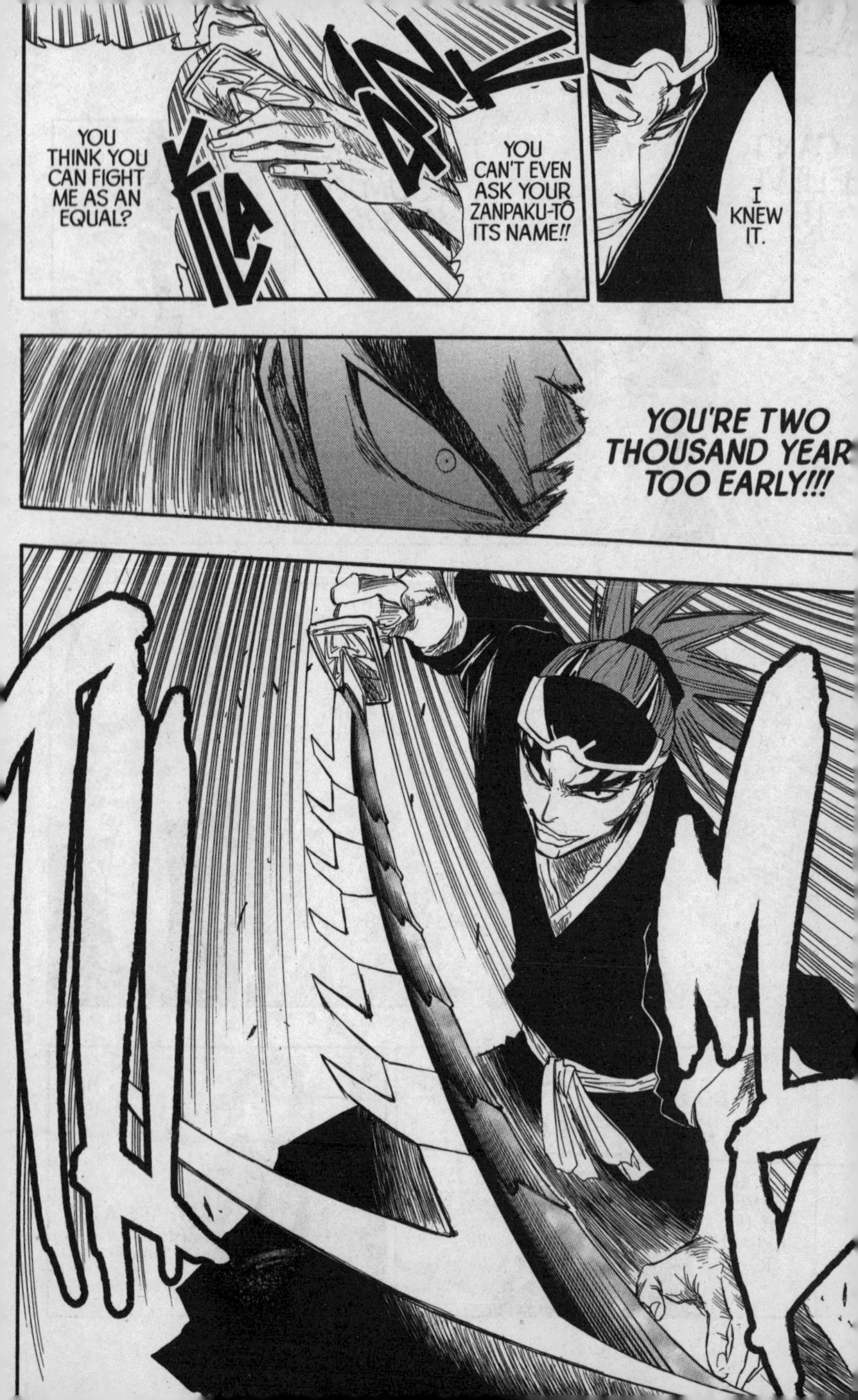
I KNEW IT.
YOU CAN'T EVEN ASK YOUR ZANPAKU-TÔ ITS NAME!!
KLANK
YOU THINK YOU CAN FIGHT ME AS AN EQUAL?
YOU'RE TWO THOUSAND YEAR TOO EARLY!!!

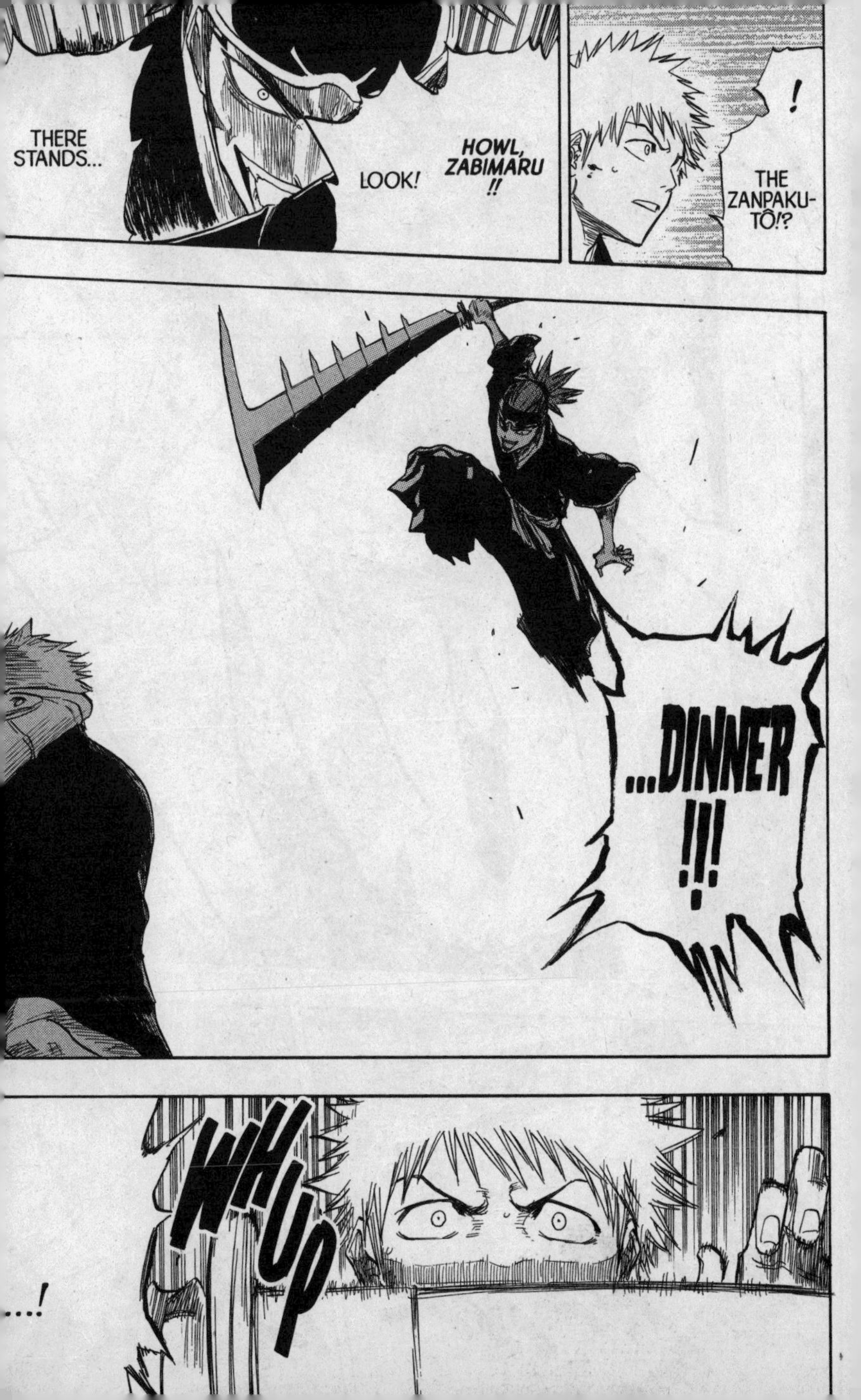

!
THE ZANPAKU-TÔ!?
THERE STANDS...
LOOK!
HOWL, ZABIMARU !!
...DINNER !!!
WHUP
...!

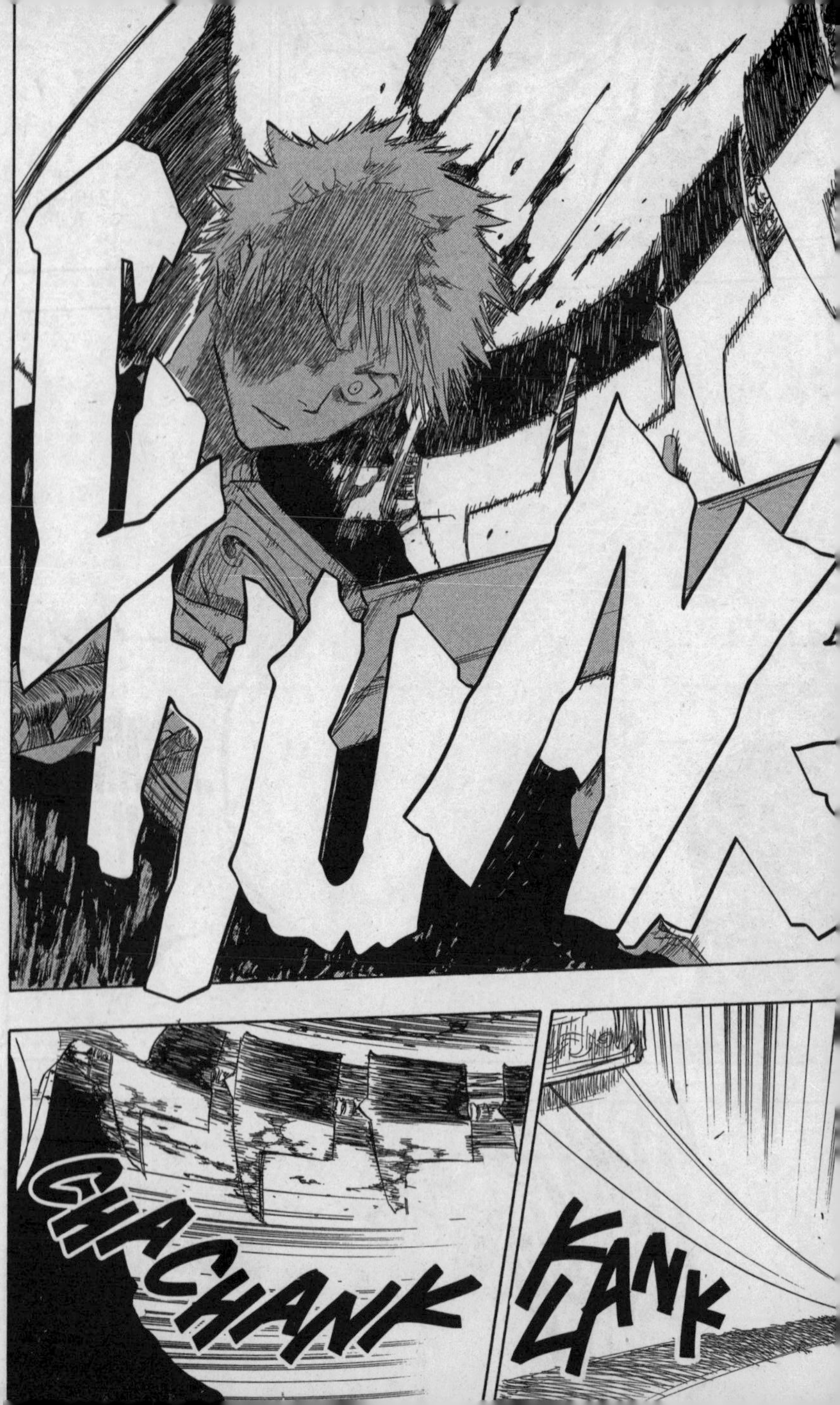
CHUNK
KANK
LANK
CHACHANK

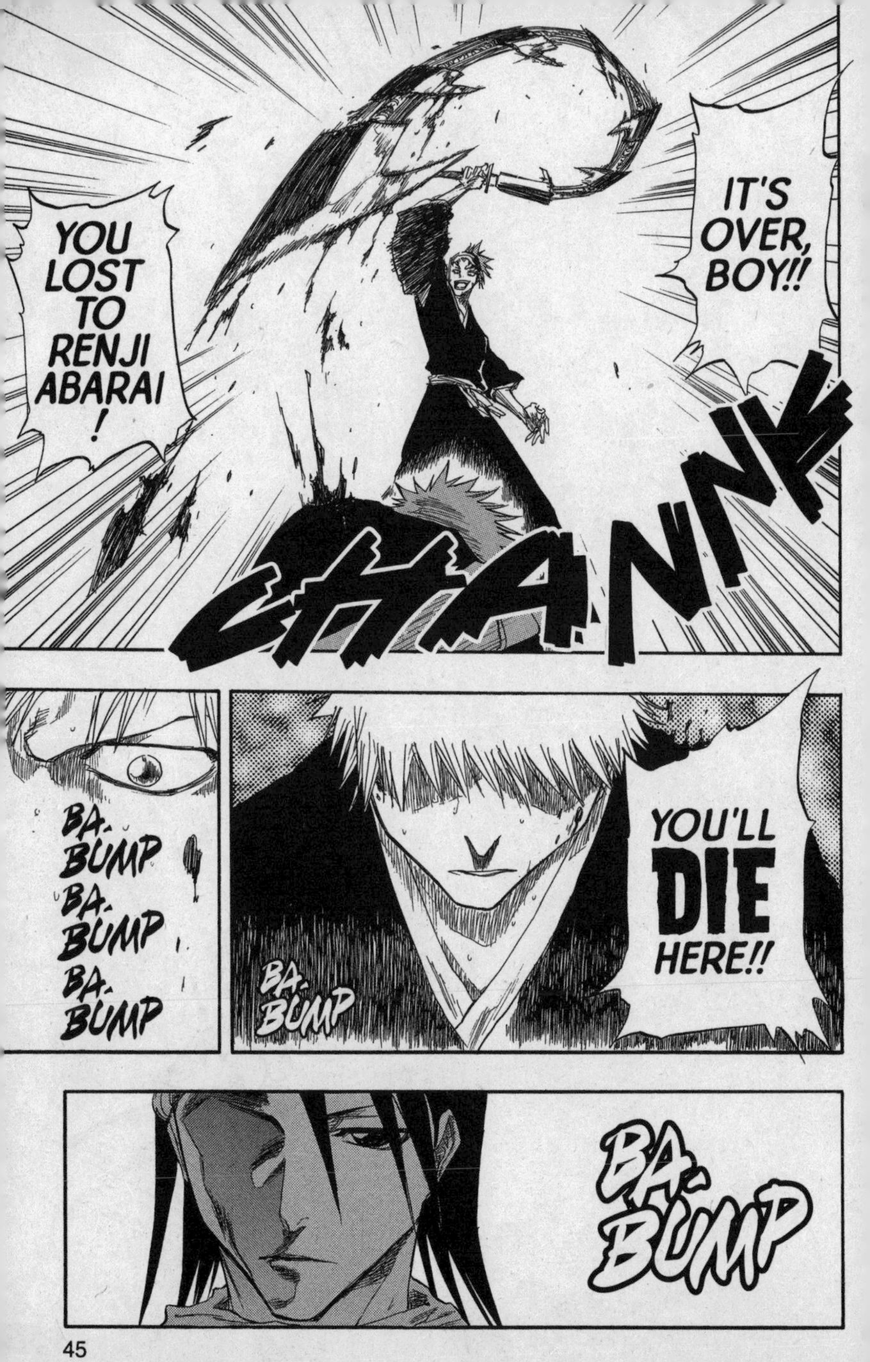
IT'S OVER, BOY!!
YOU LOST TO RENJI ABARAI!
CHANNK
YOU'LL DIE HERE!!
BA-BUMP
BA-BUMP BA-BUMP BA-BUMP
BA-BUMP

55. SHUT

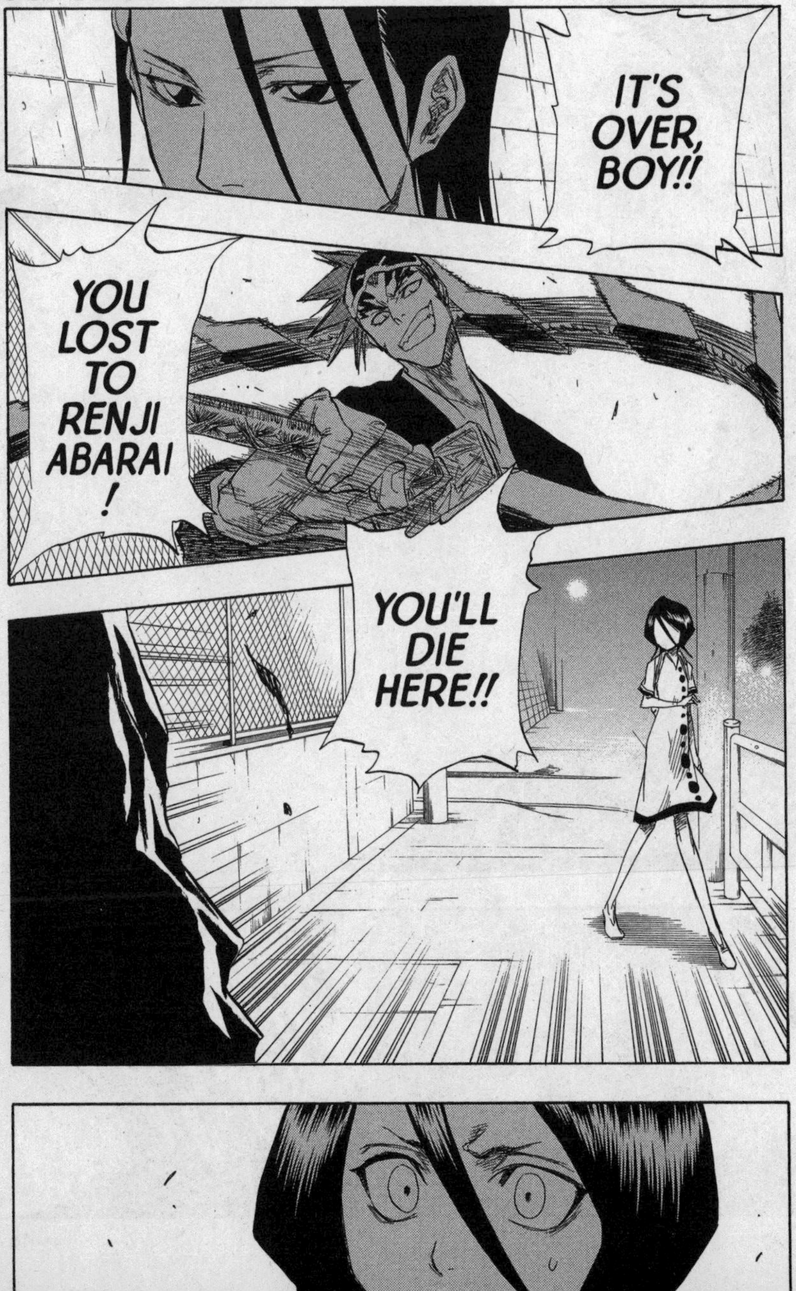
IT'S OVER, BOY!!
YOU LOST TO RENJI ABARAI!
YOU'LL DIE HERE!!

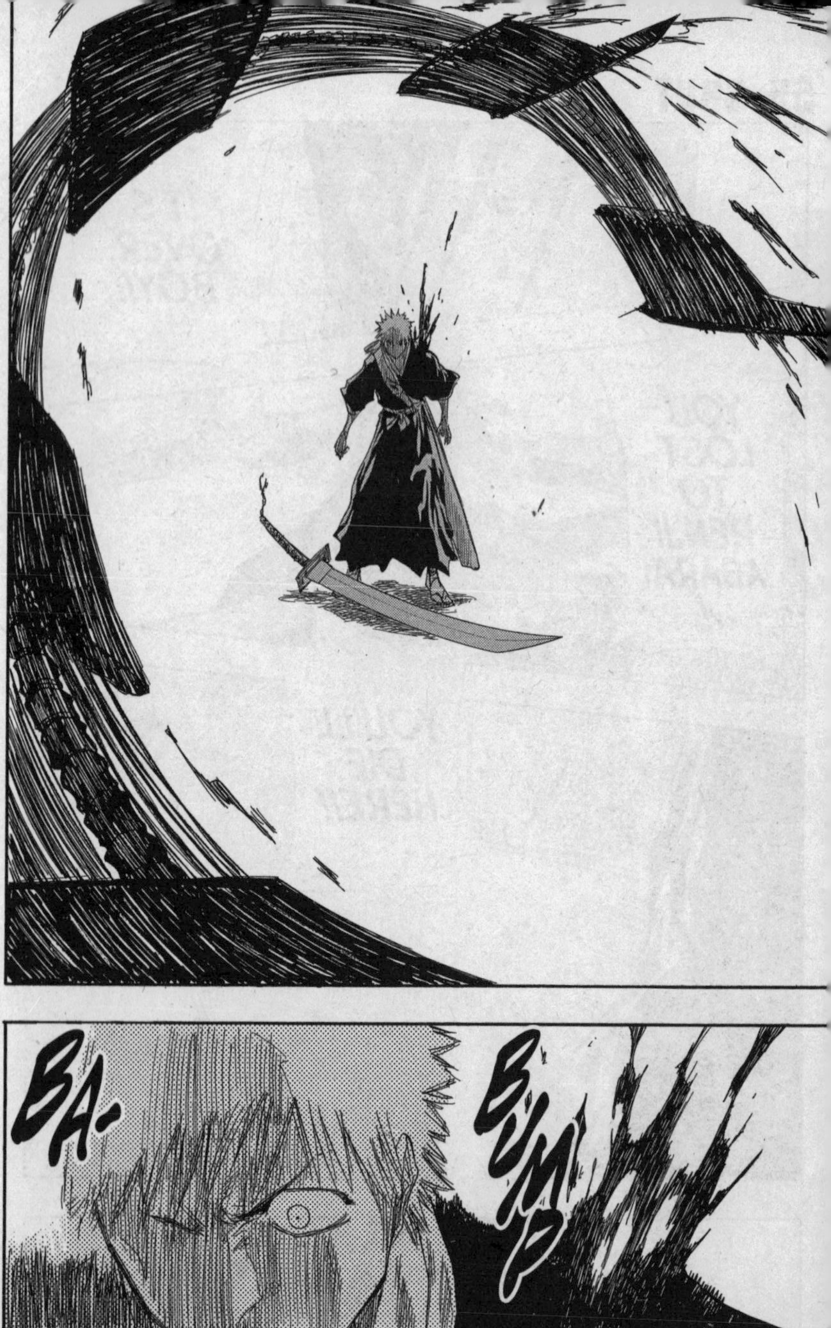
BA-
BUMP

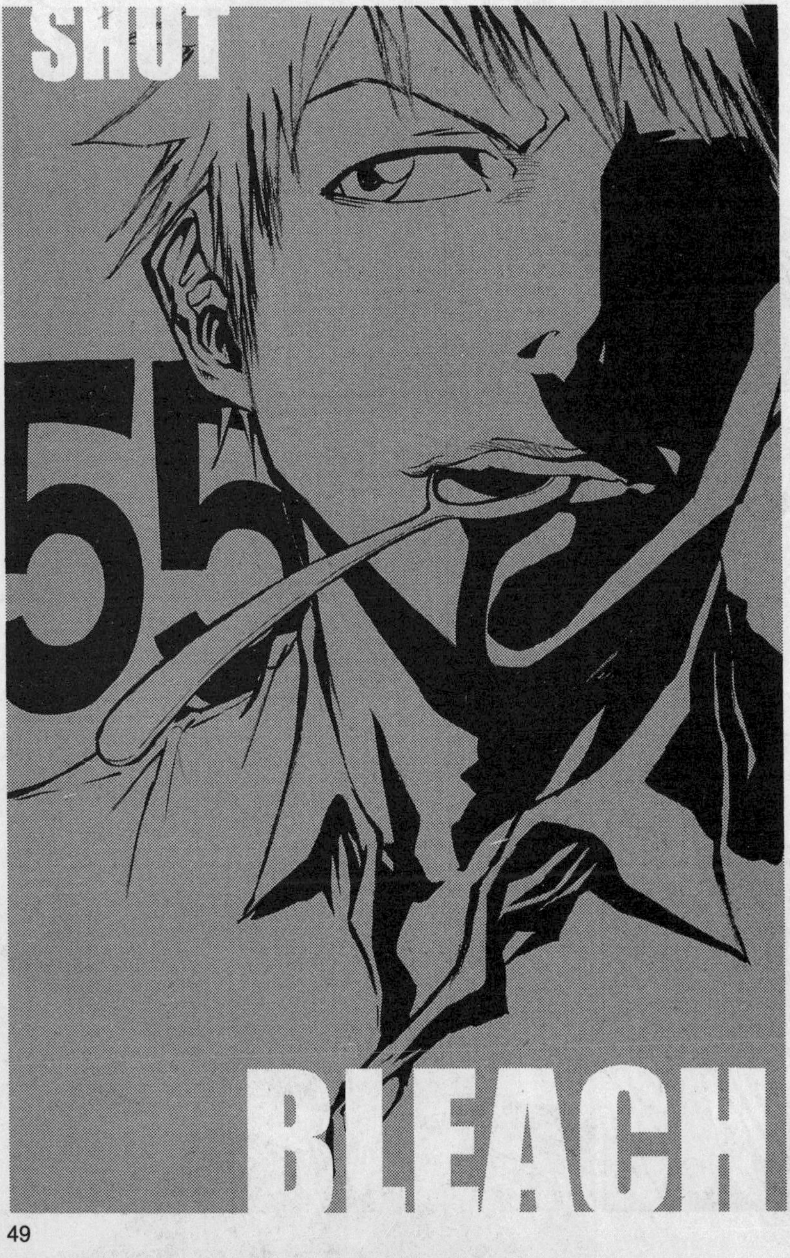
SHOT
55
BLEACH

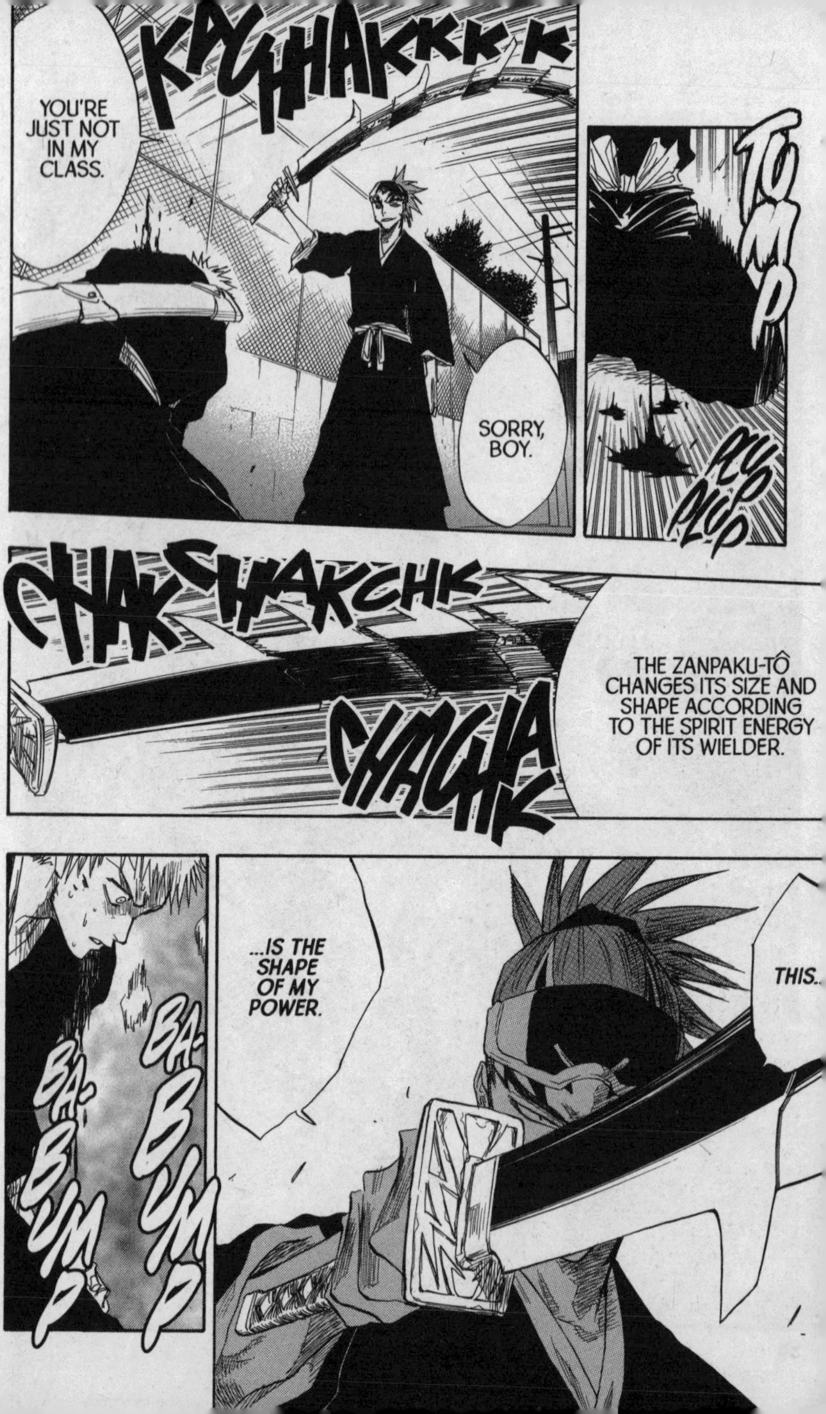

TOMP
PLIP PLOP
KACHHAKKKK
SORRY, BOY.
YOU'RE JUST NOT IN MY CLASS.
THE ZANPAKU-TÔ CHANGES ITS SIZE AND SHAPE ACCORDING TO THE SPIRIT ENERGY OF ITS WIELDER.
CHAKSHAKCHK
CHAGHAK
THIS...
...IS THE SHAPE OF MY POWER.
BA-BUMP
BA-BUMP

READ THIS WAY

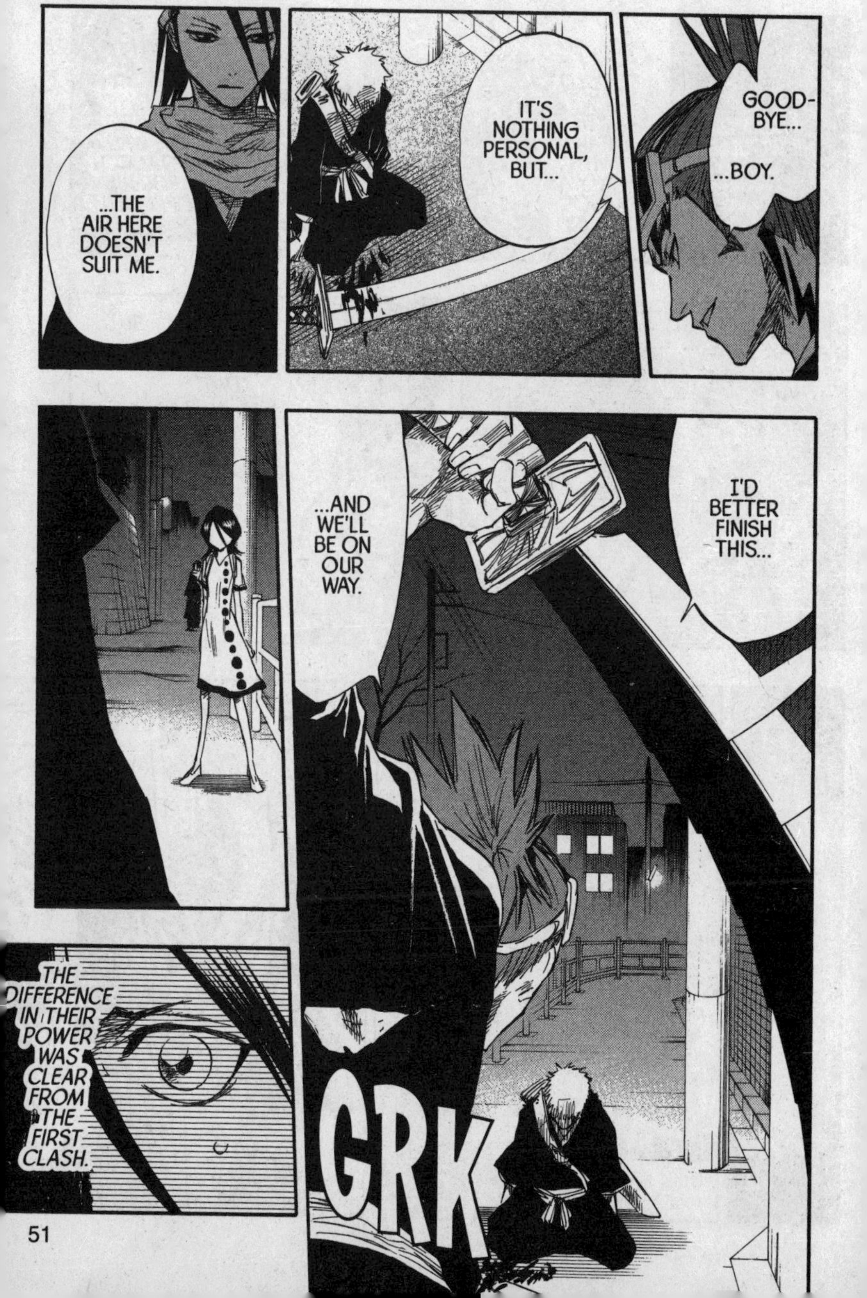
GOOD-BYE...
...BOY.
IT'S NOTHING PERSONAL, BUT...
...THE AIR HERE DOESN'T SUIT ME.
I'D BETTER FINISH THIS...
...AND WE'LL BE ON OUR WAY.
GRK
THE DIFFERENCE IN THEIR POWER WAS CLEAR FROM THE FIRST CLASH.

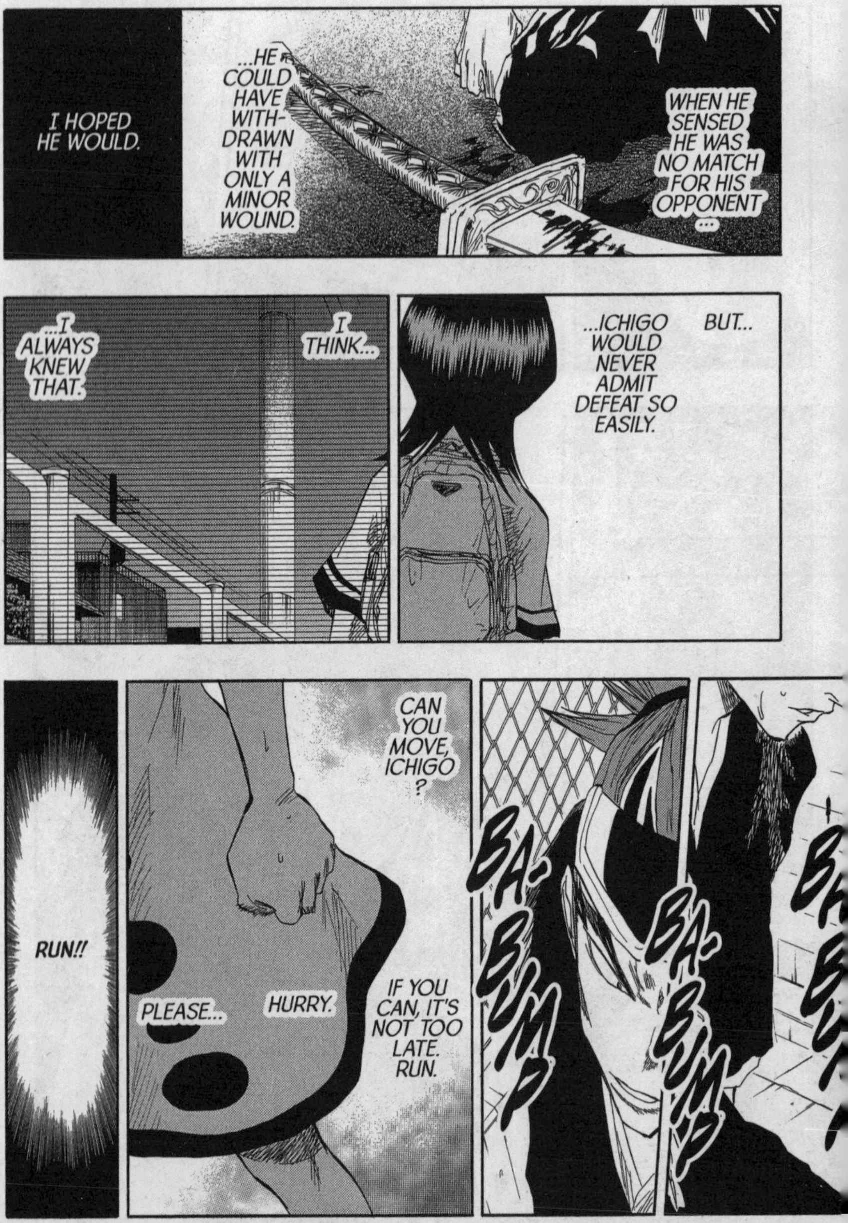
WHEN HE SENSED HE WAS NO MATCH FOR HIS OPPONENT...
...HE COULD HAVE WITHDRAWN WITH ONLY A MINOR WOUND.
I HOPED HE WOULD.
BUT...
...ICHIGO WOULD NEVER ADMIT DEFEAT SO EASILY.
I THINK...
...I ALWAYS KNEW THAT.
BA-BUMP
BA-BUMP
CAN YOU MOVE, ICHIGO?
IF YOU CAN, IT'S NOT TOO LATE. RUN.
HURRY.
PLEASE...
RUN!!

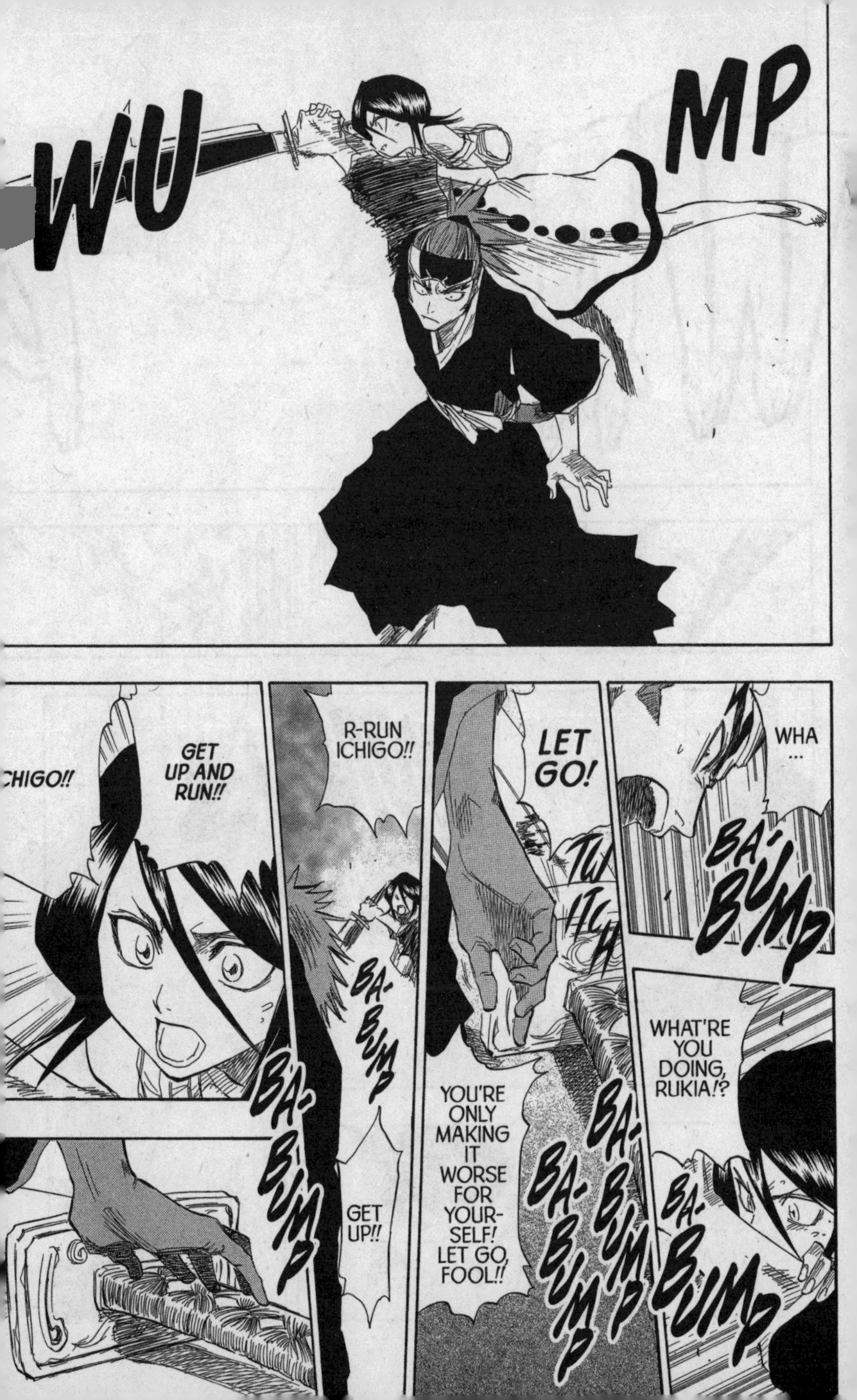
WU
MP
WHA
...
BA-BUMP
WHAT'RE YOU DOING, RUKIA!?
BA-BUMP
LET GO!
TWITCH
YOU'RE ONLY MAKING IT WORSE FOR YOUR-SELF! LET GO, FOOL!!
BA-BUMP
BA-BUMP
R-RUN ICHIGO!!
BA-BUMP
GET UP!!
GET UP AND RUN!!
CHIGO!!
BA-BUMP

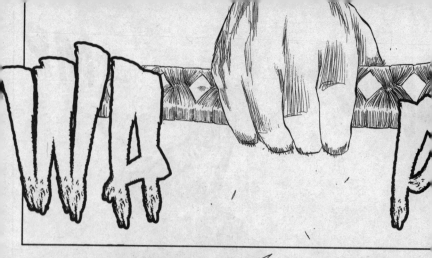

!!

WUMP

WHAT?

YOU CAN STILL MOVE?

EXCELLENT.

IT'S NO FUN BUTCHERING A CRIPPLED PIG, ANYWAY.

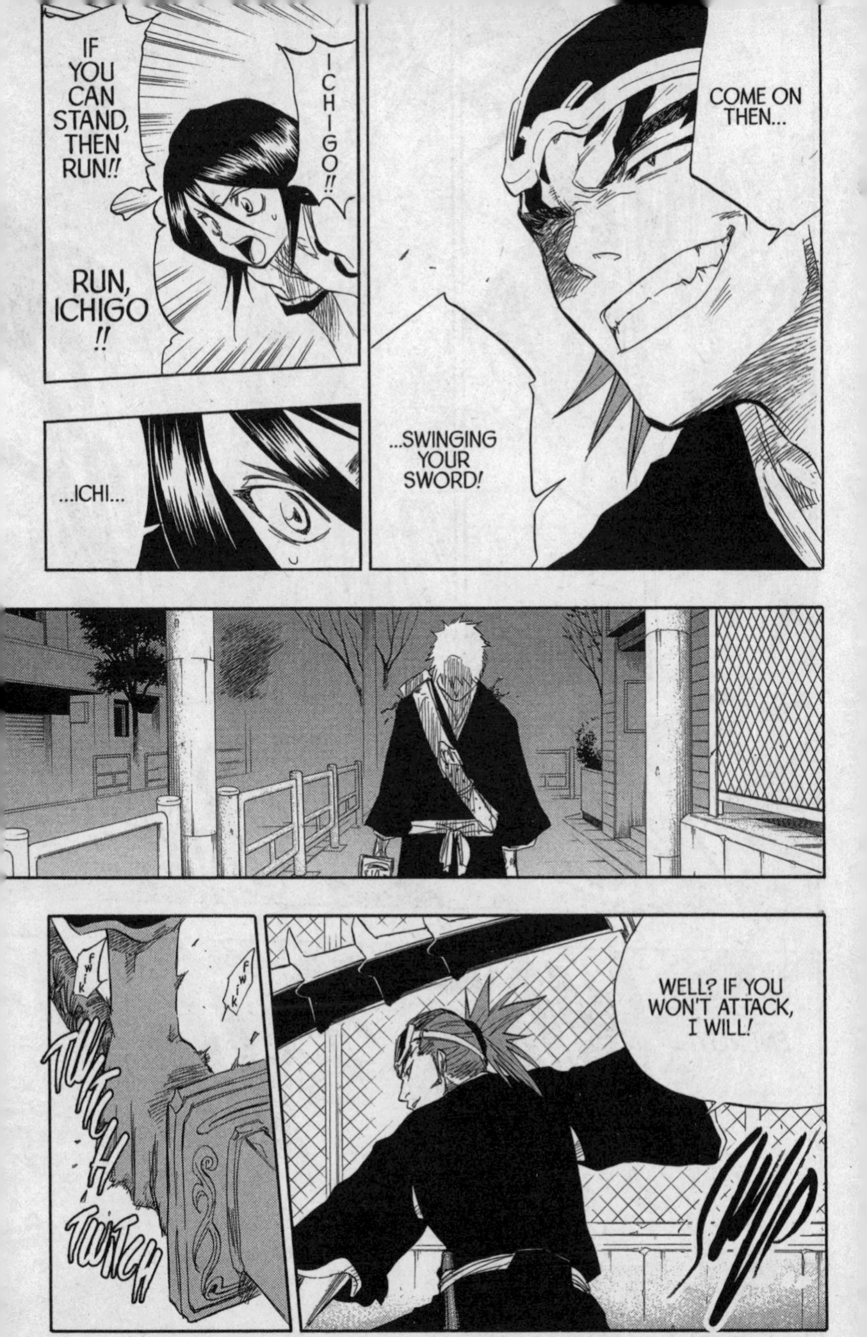
COME ON THEN...
...SWINGING YOUR SWORD!
ICHIGO!!
IF YOU CAN STAND, THEN RUN!!
RUN, ICHIGO!!
...ICHI...
WELL? IF YOU WON'T ATTACK, I WILL!
SWIP
TWITCH
TWITCH
fwik
fwik

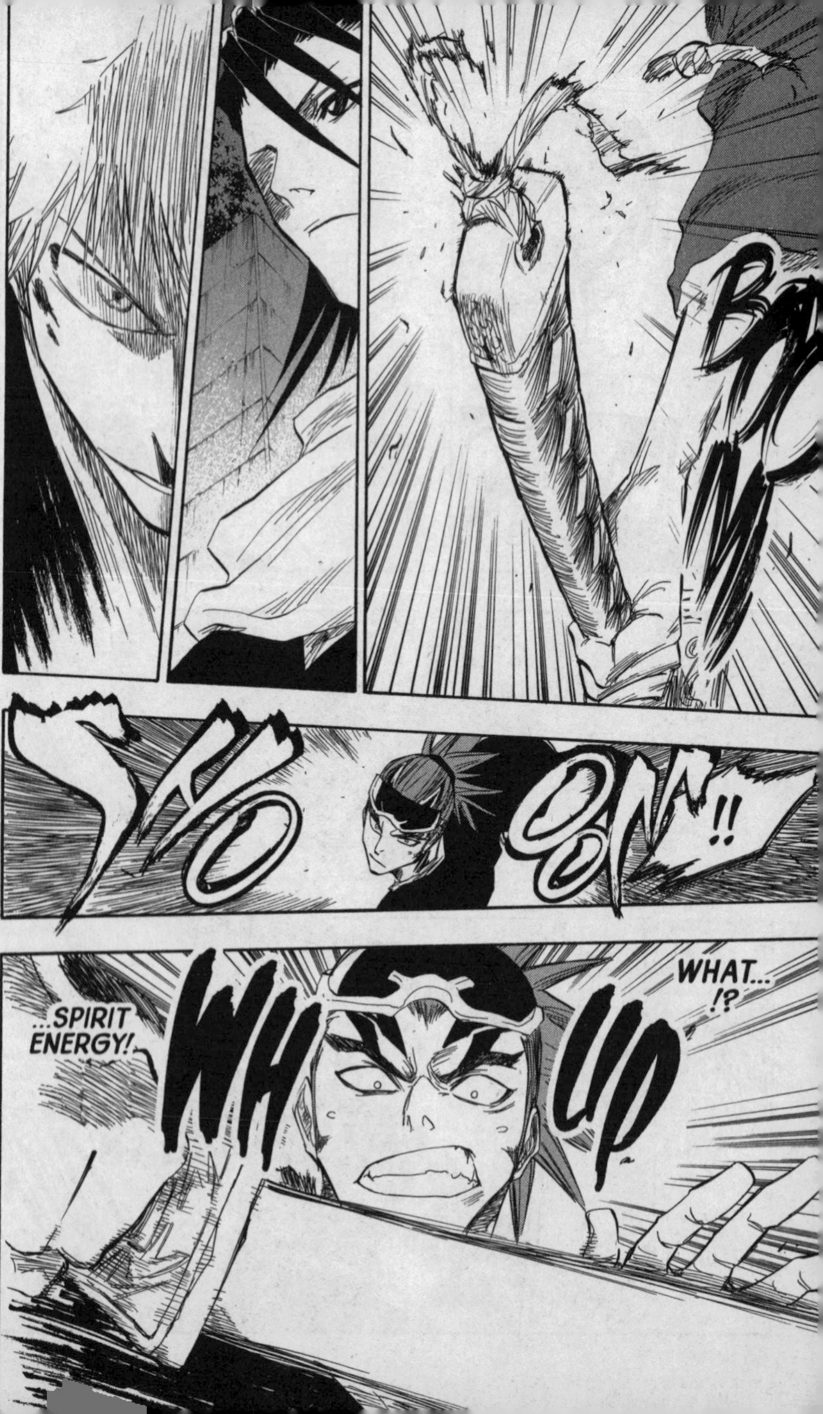
WHAT... !?
WHUP
...SPIRIT ENERGY!

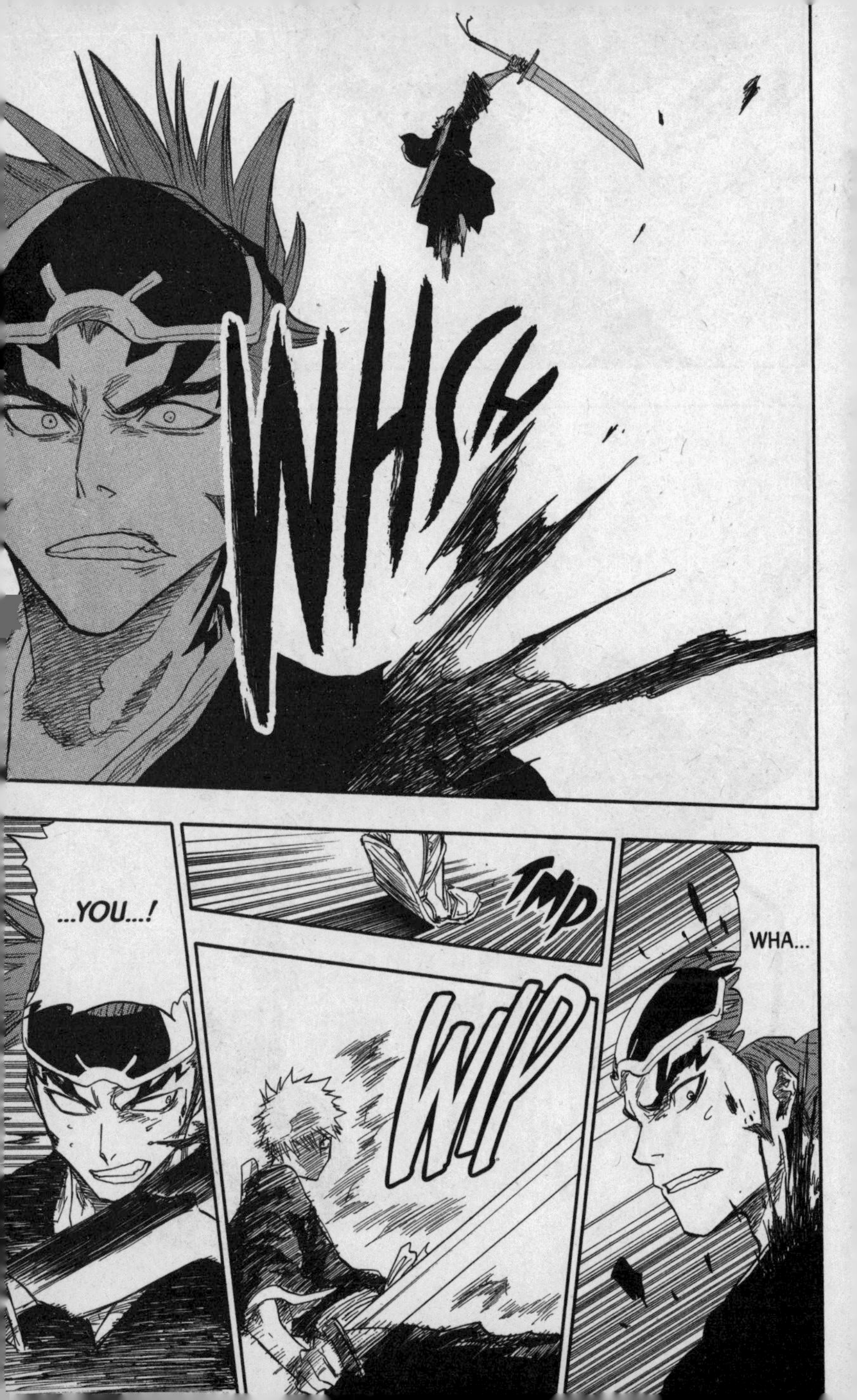
WHSH
WHA...
TMP
WHP
...YOU...!

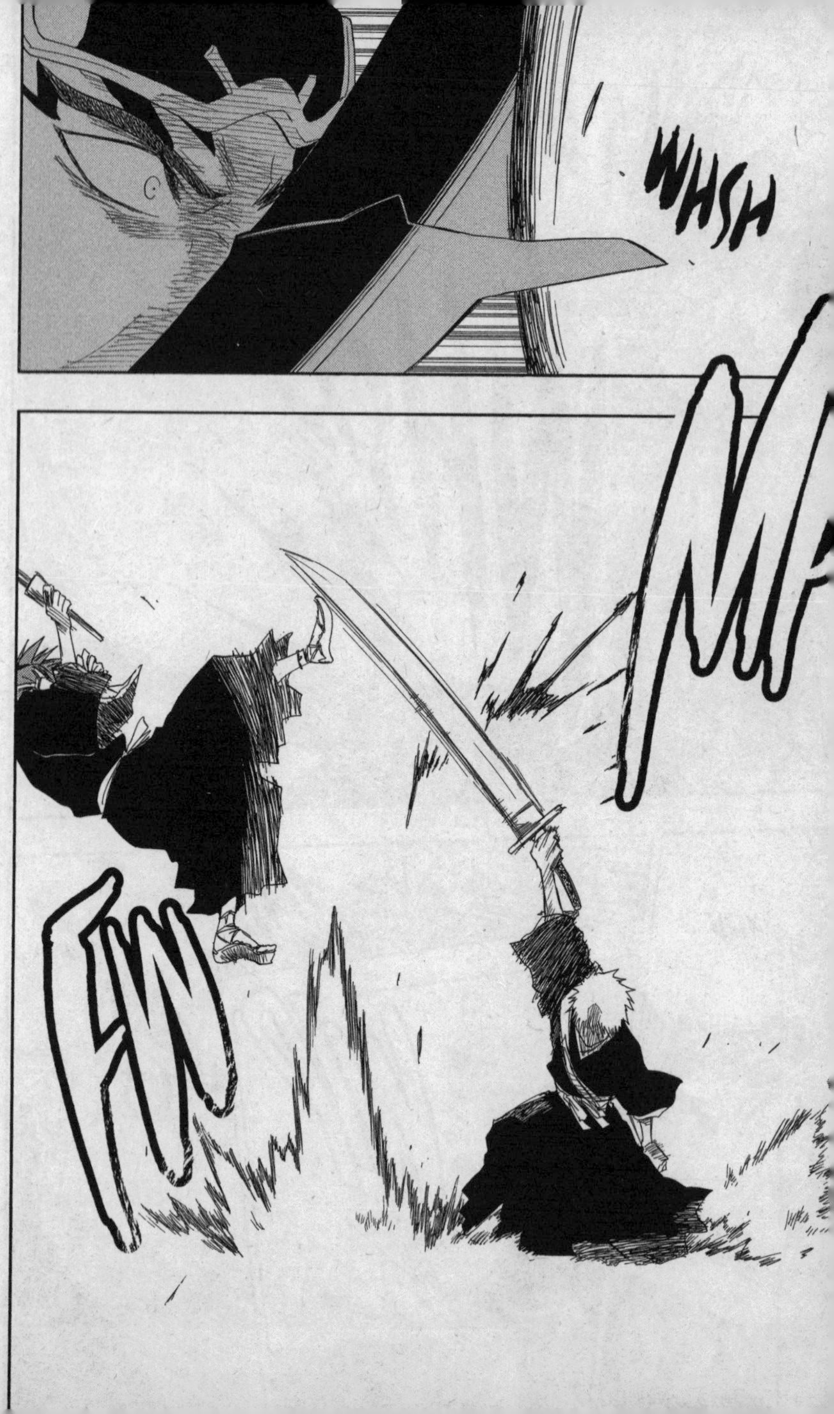
WHSH

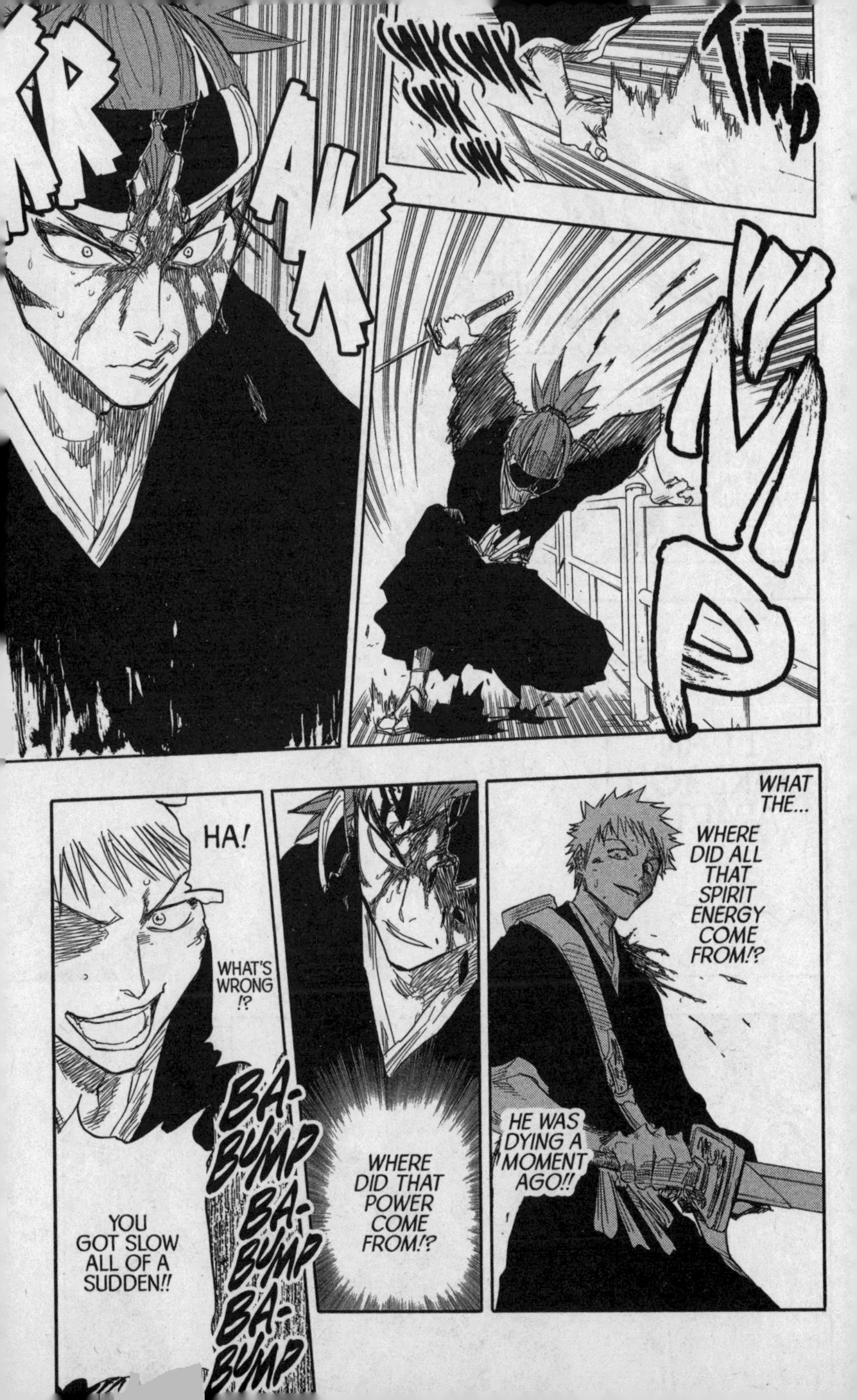
TMP
WHAT THE...
WHERE DID ALL THAT SPIRIT ENERGY COME FROM!?
HE WAS DYING A MOMENT AGO!!
WHERE DID THAT POWER COME FROM!?
HA!
WHAT'S WRONG!?
YOU GOT SLOW ALL OF A SUDDEN!!
BA-BUMP BA-BUMP BA-BUMP

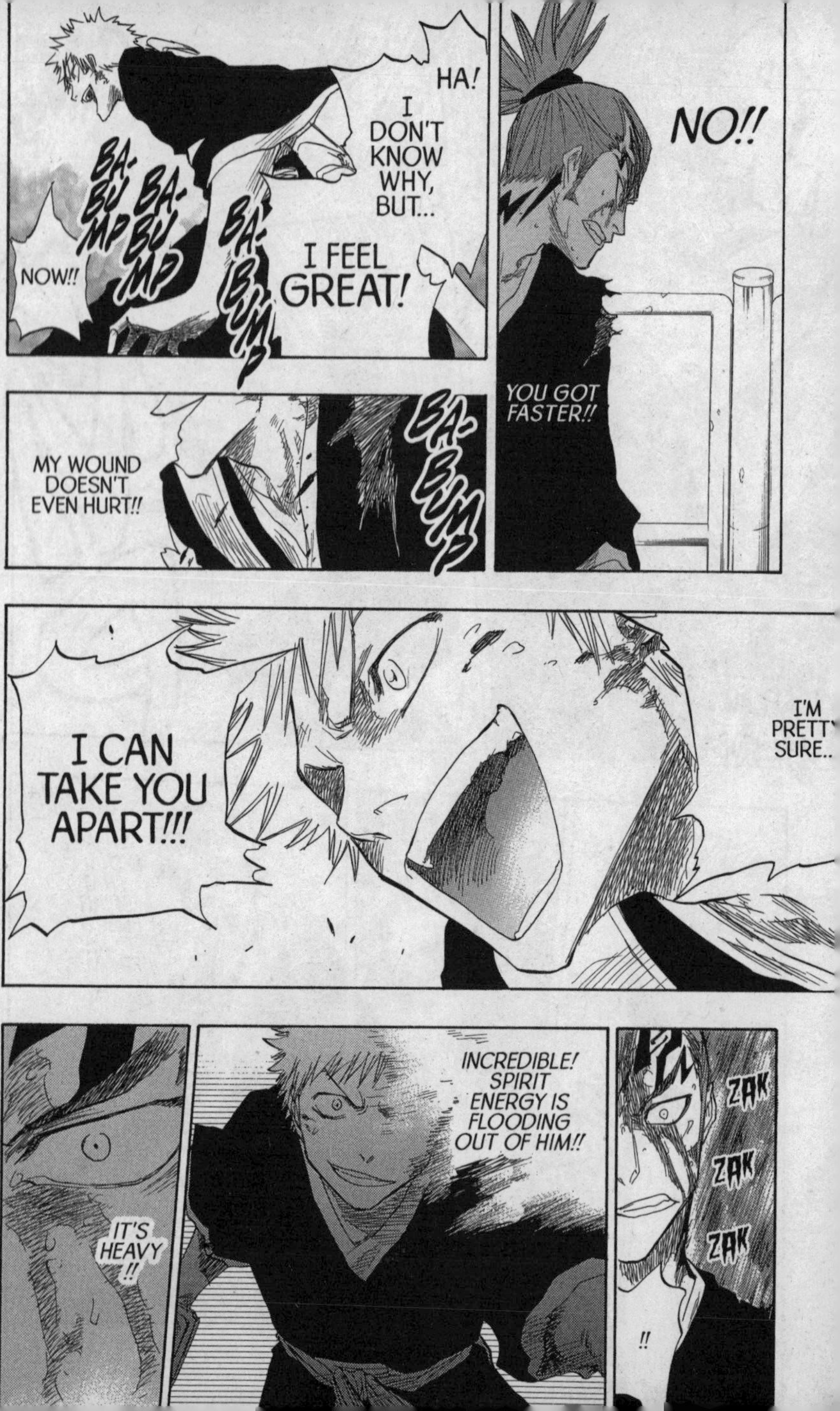
NO!!
YOU GOT FASTER!!
HA!
I DON'T KNOW WHY, BUT...
I FEEL GREAT!
NOW!!
BA-BUMP BA-BUMP BA-BUMP
MY WOUND DOESN'T EVEN HURT!!
BA-BUMP
I'M PRETTY SURE...
I CAN TAKE YOU APART!!!
ZAK ZAK ZAK
!!
INCREDIBLE! SPIRIT ENERGY IS FLOODING OUT OF HIM!!
IT'S HEAVY!!

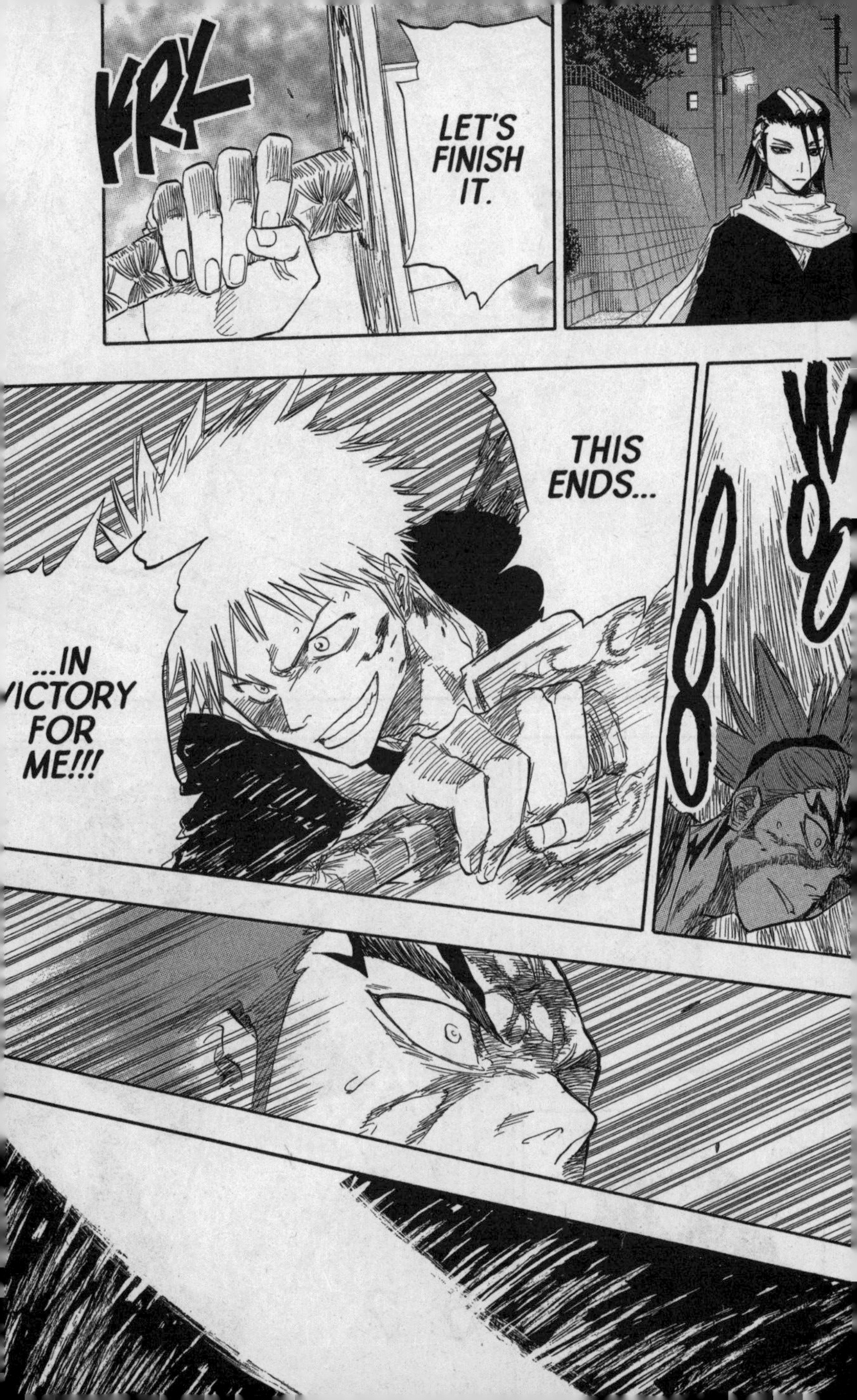
KRK
LET'S FINISH IT.
THIS ENDS...
...IN VICTORY FOR ME!!!

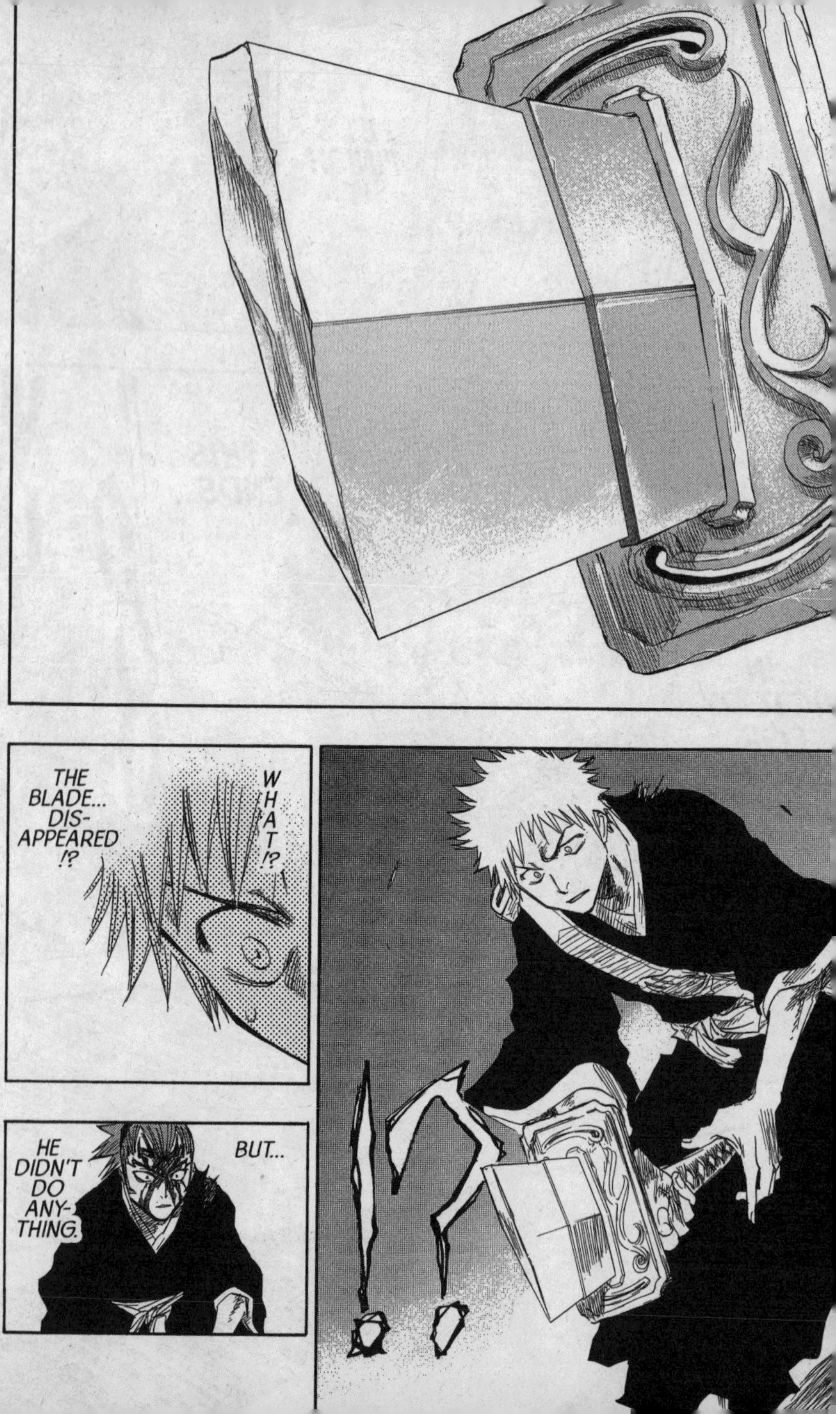
WHAT!?
THE BLADE... DIS-APPEARED!?
BUT...
HE DIDN'T DO ANY-THING.
!?

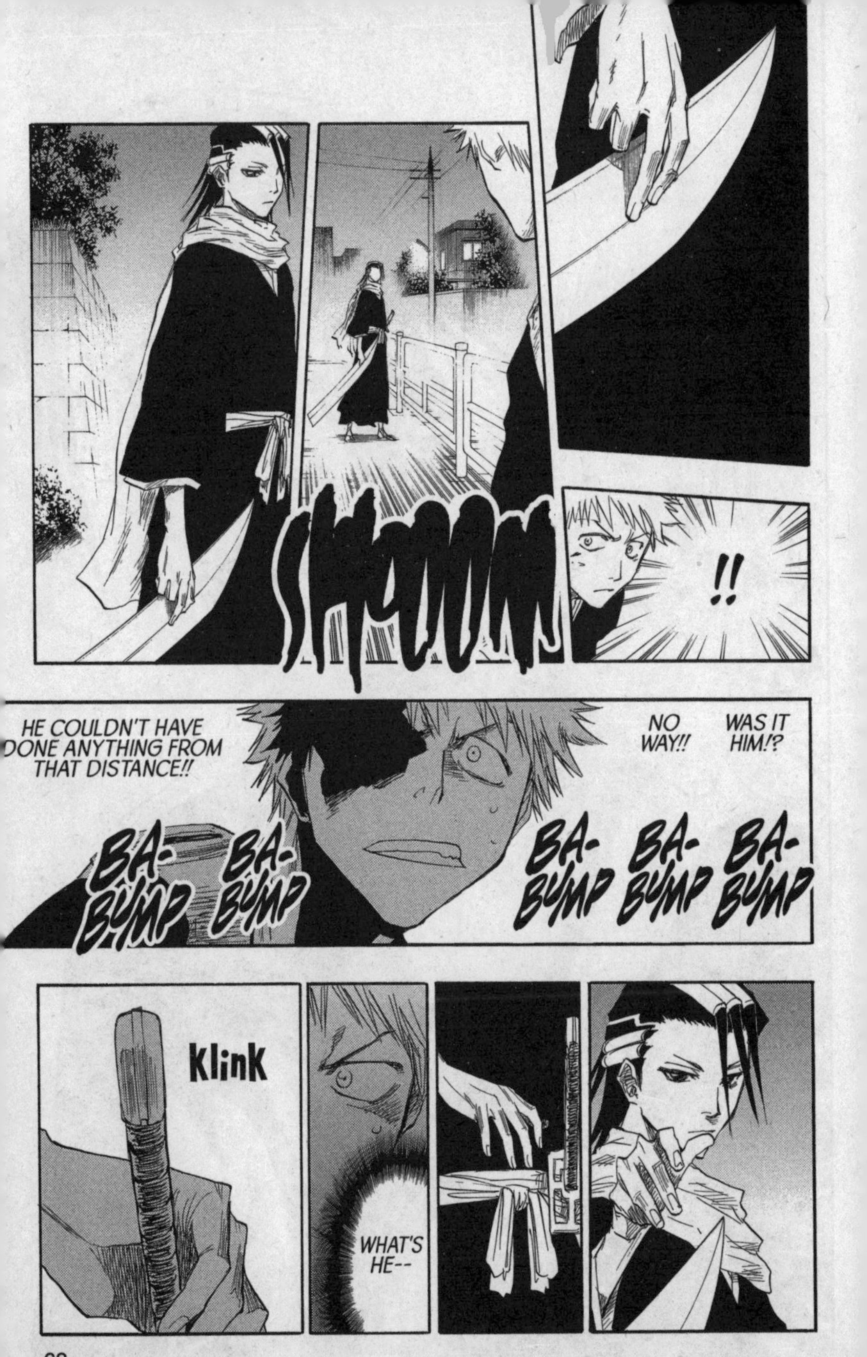
!!
WAS IT HIM!?
NO WAY!!
HE COULDN'T HAVE DONE ANYTHING FROM THAT DISTANCE!!
BA-BUMP
BA-BUMP
BA-BUMP
BA-BUMP
BA-BUMP
WHAT'S HE--
Klink

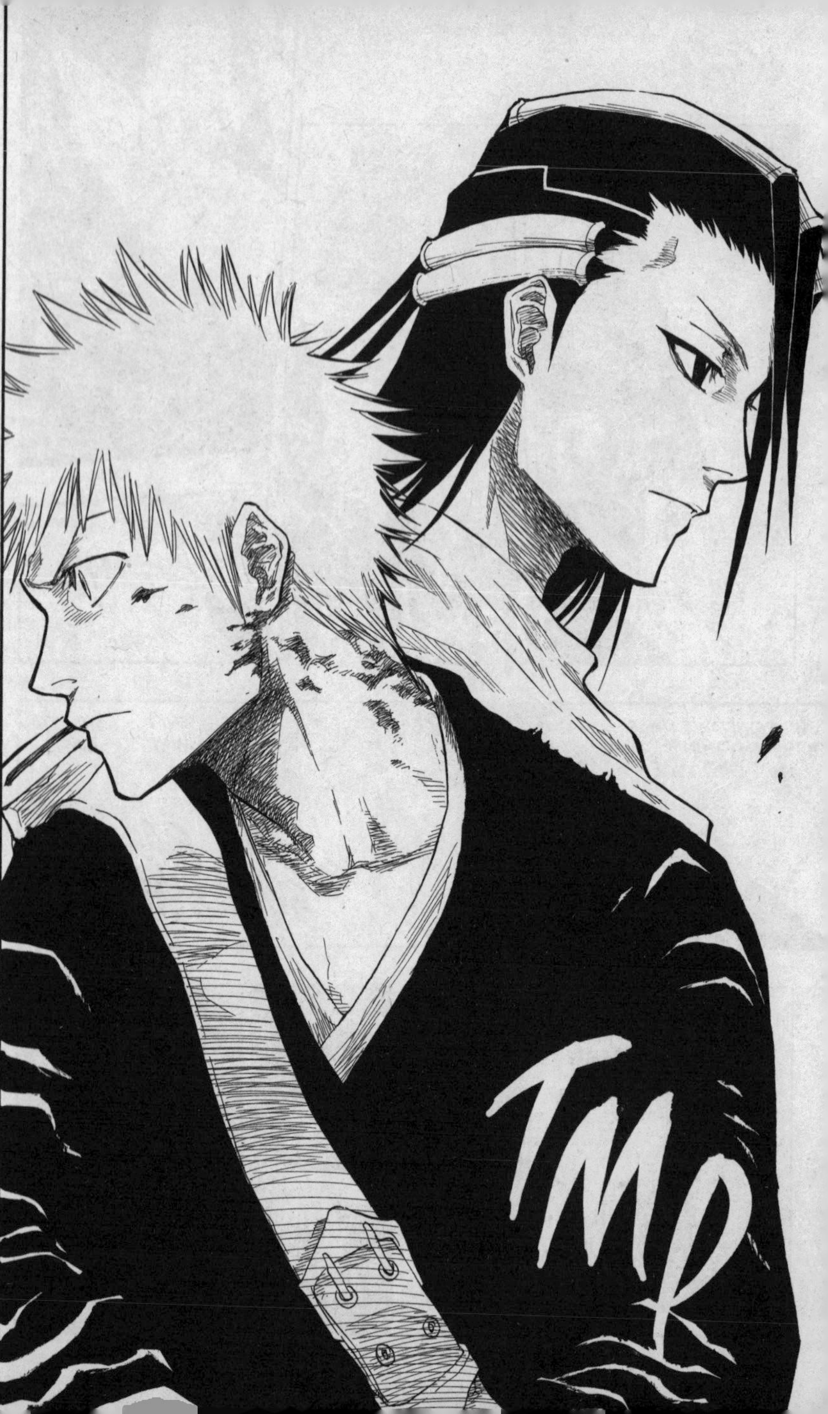
TMP

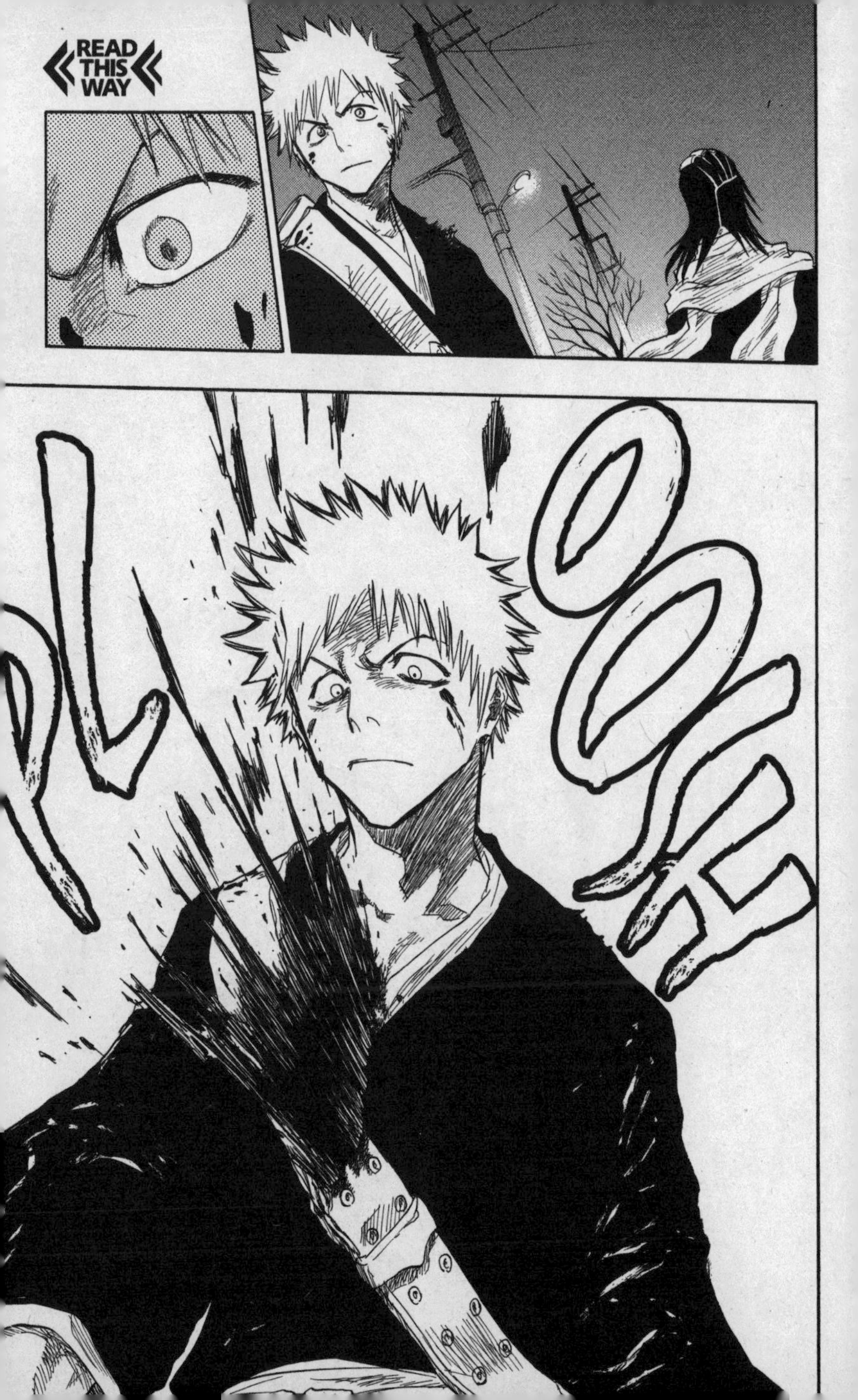
READ THIS WAY

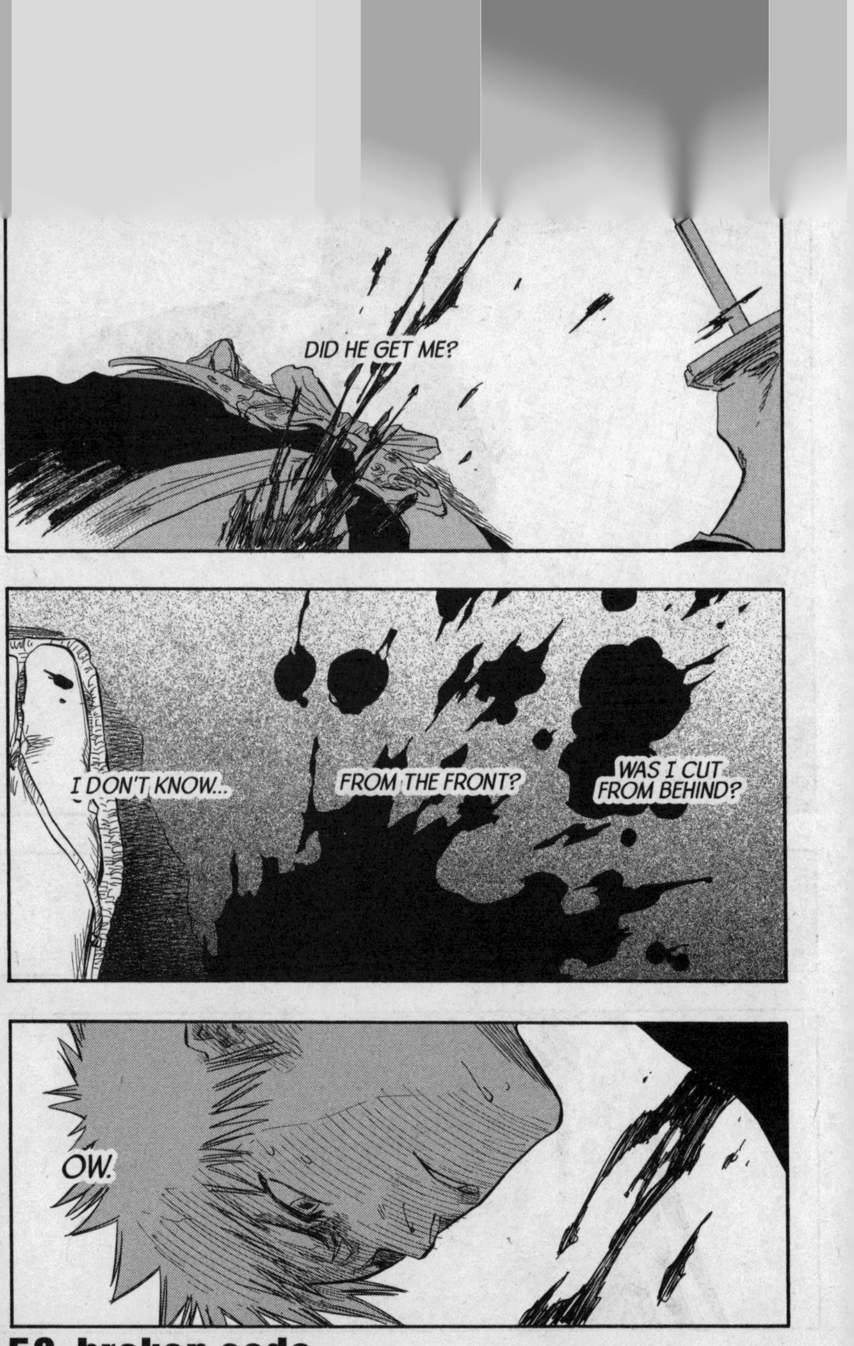
DID HE GET ME?
WAS I CUT FROM BEHIND?
FROM THE FRONT?
I DON'T KNOW...
OW.

56. broken coda

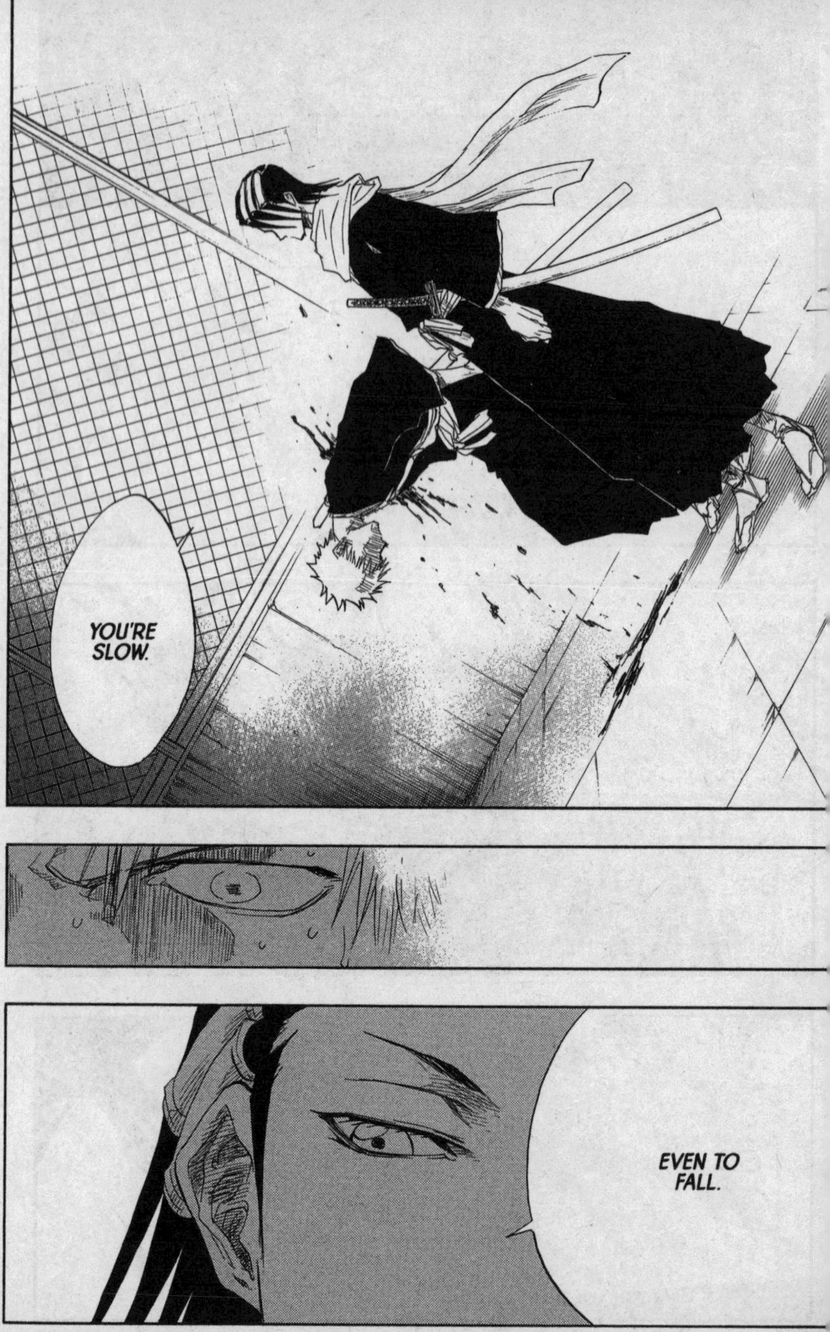
YOU'RE SLOW.
EVEN TO FALL.

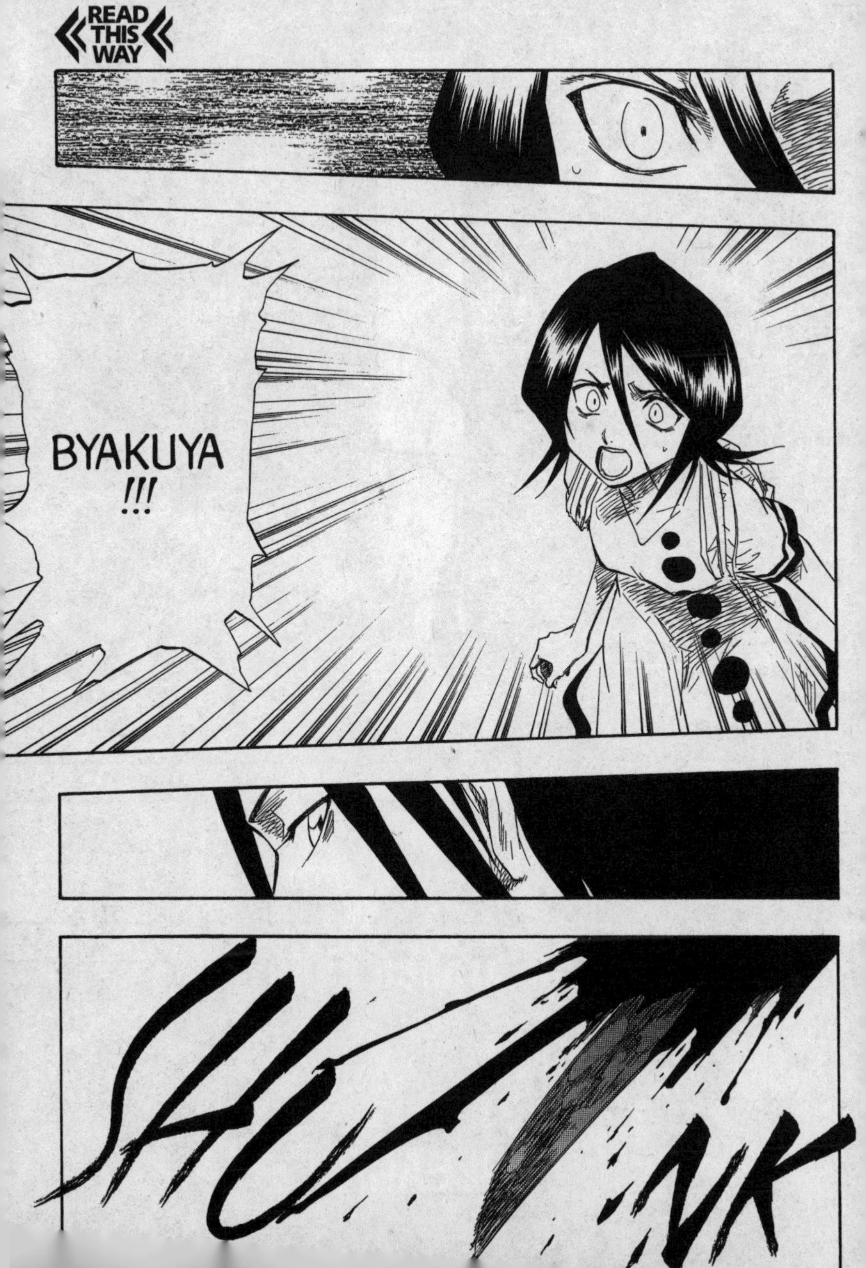
READ THIS WAY
BYAKUYA !!!
SHUNK

56. broken coda

BLEACH

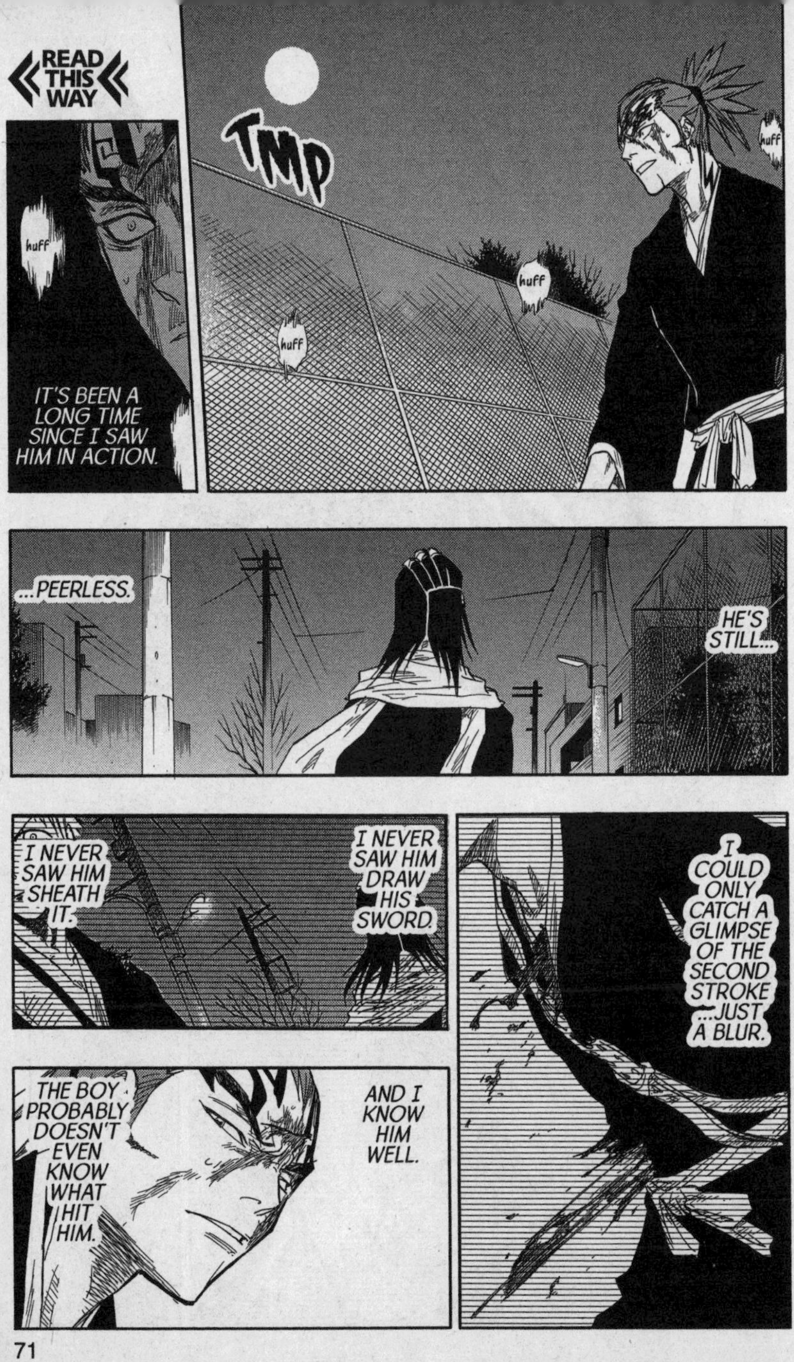
READ THIS WAY
TMP
huff
huff
huff
huff
IT'S BEEN A LONG TIME SINCE I SAW HIM IN ACTION.
HE'S STILL...
...PEERLESS.
I NEVER SAW HIM DRAW HIS SWORD.
I NEVER SAW HIM SHEATH IT.
I COULD ONLY CATCH A GLIMPSE OF THE SECOND STROKE ...JUST A BLUR.
AND I KNOW HIM WELL.
THE BOY PROBABLY DOESN'T EVEN KNOW WHAT HIT HIM.

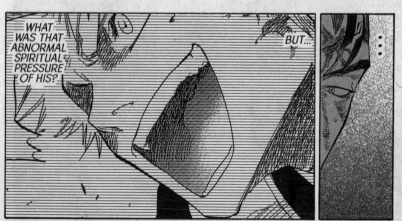

WHAT WAS THAT ABNORMAL SPIRITUAL PRESSURE OF HIS?

BUT...

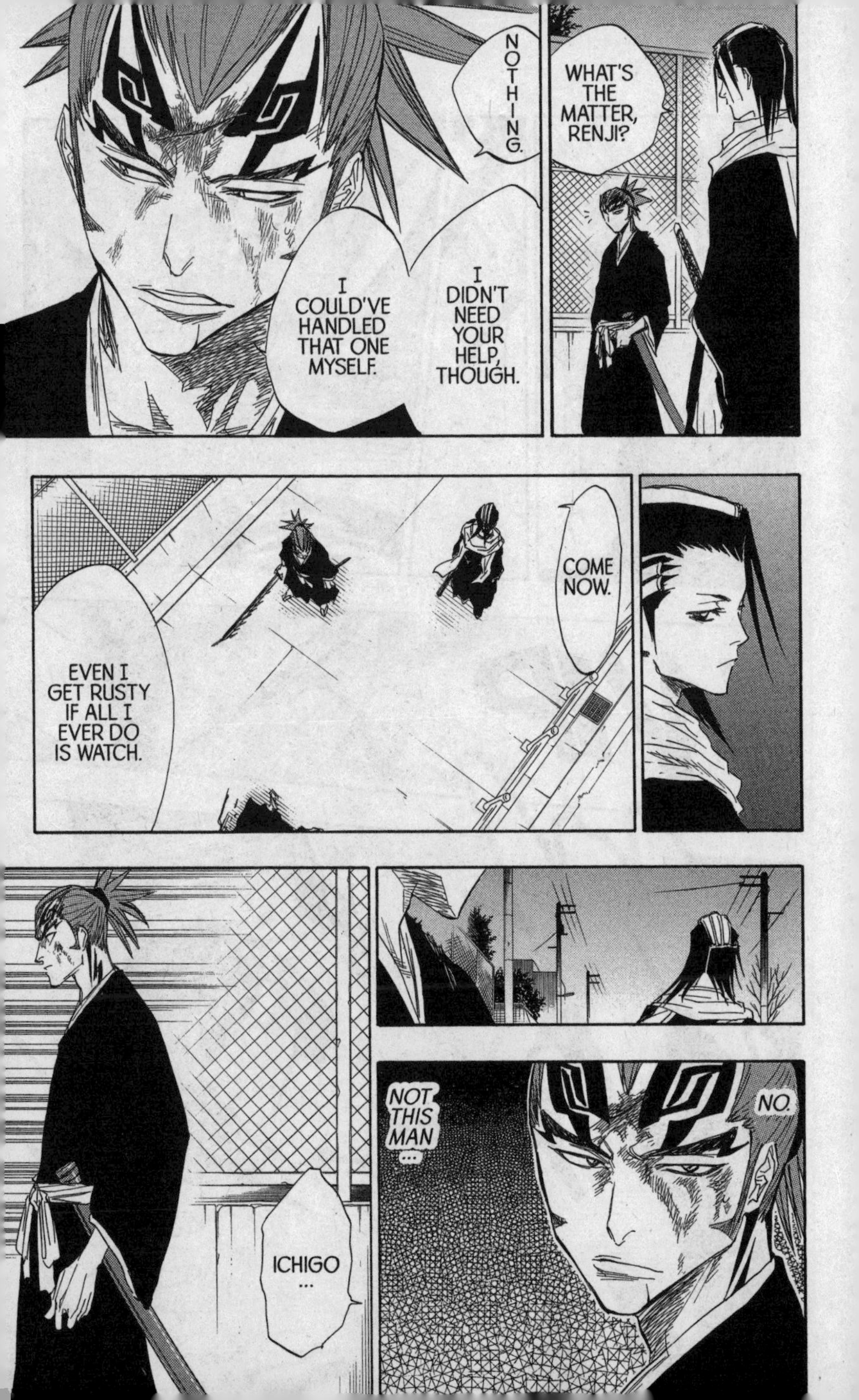
WHAT'S THE MATTER, RENJI?
NOTHING.
I DIDN'T NEED YOUR HELP, THOUGH.
I COULD'VE HANDLED THAT ONE MYSELF.
COME NOW.
EVEN I GET RUSTY IF ALL I EVER DO IS WATCH.
NO.
NOT THIS MAN...
ICHIGO...

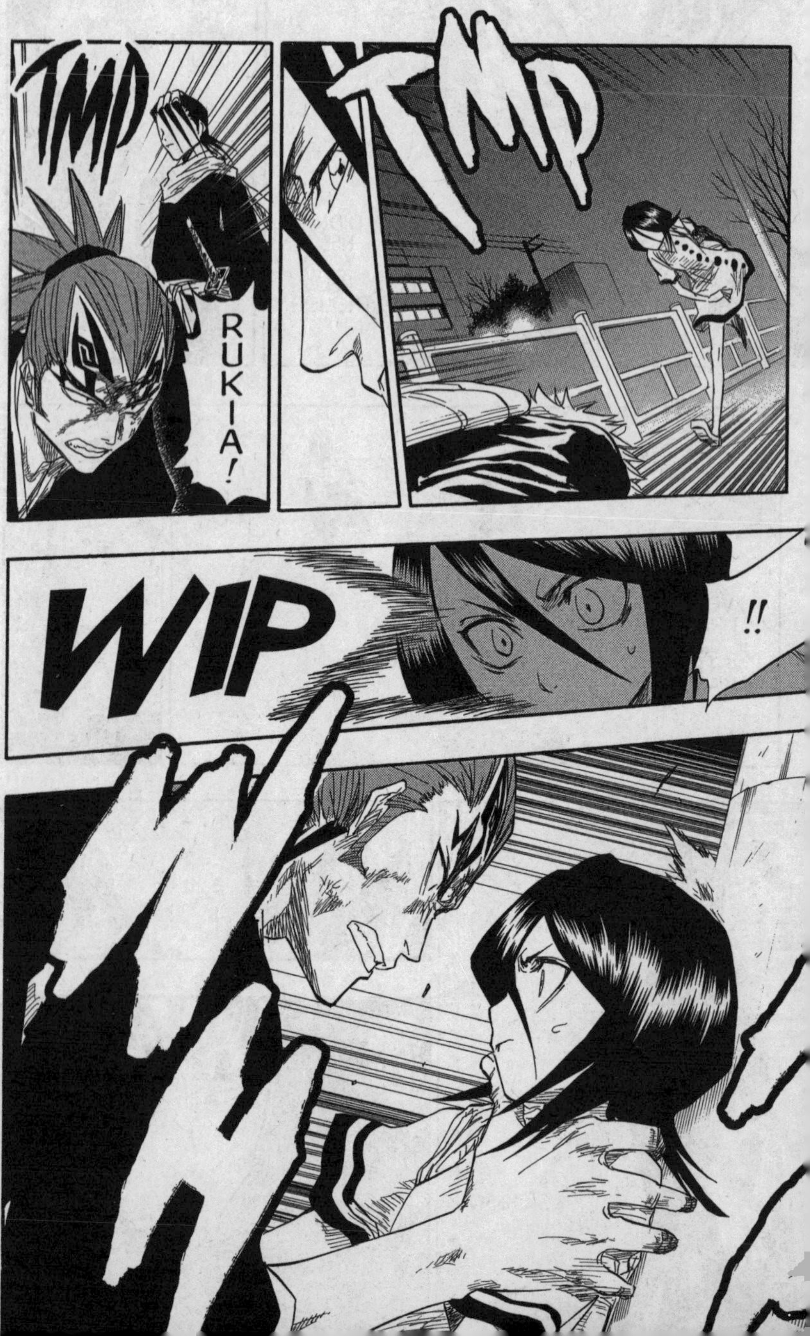
TMP
TMP
RUKIA!
!!
WIP

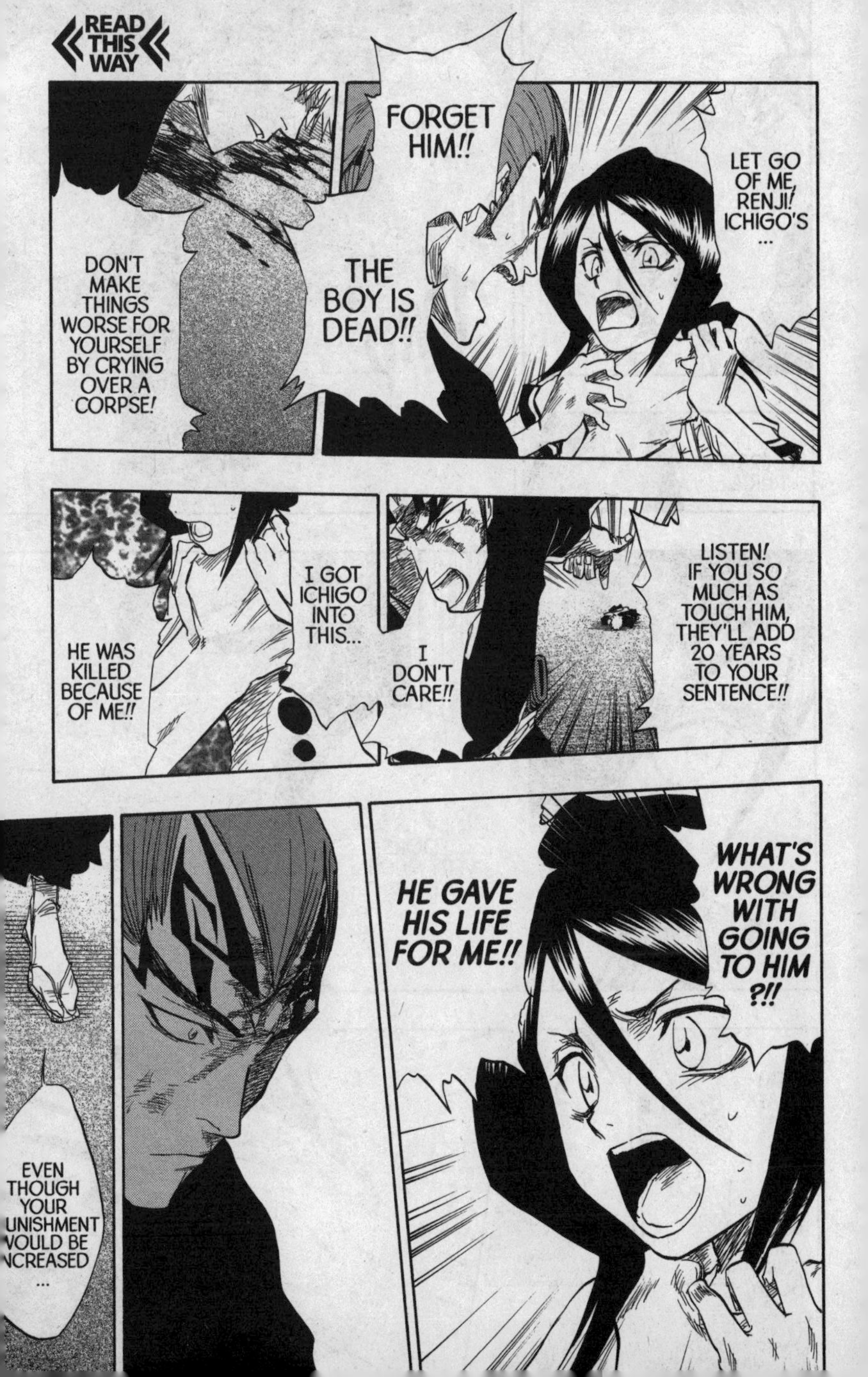
READ THIS WAY
LET GO OF ME, RENJI! ICHIGO'S ...
FORGET HIM!!
THE BOY IS DEAD!!
DON'T MAKE THINGS WORSE FOR YOURSELF BY CRYING OVER A CORPSE!
LISTEN! IF YOU SO MUCH AS TOUCH HIM, THEY'LL ADD 20 YEARS TO YOUR SENTENCE!!
I DON'T CARE!!
I GOT ICHIGO INTO THIS...
HE WAS KILLED BECAUSE OF ME!!
WHAT'S WRONG WITH GOING TO HIM ?!!
HE GAVE HIS LIFE FOR ME!!
EVEN THOUGH YOUR UNISHMENT VOULD BE NCREASED ...

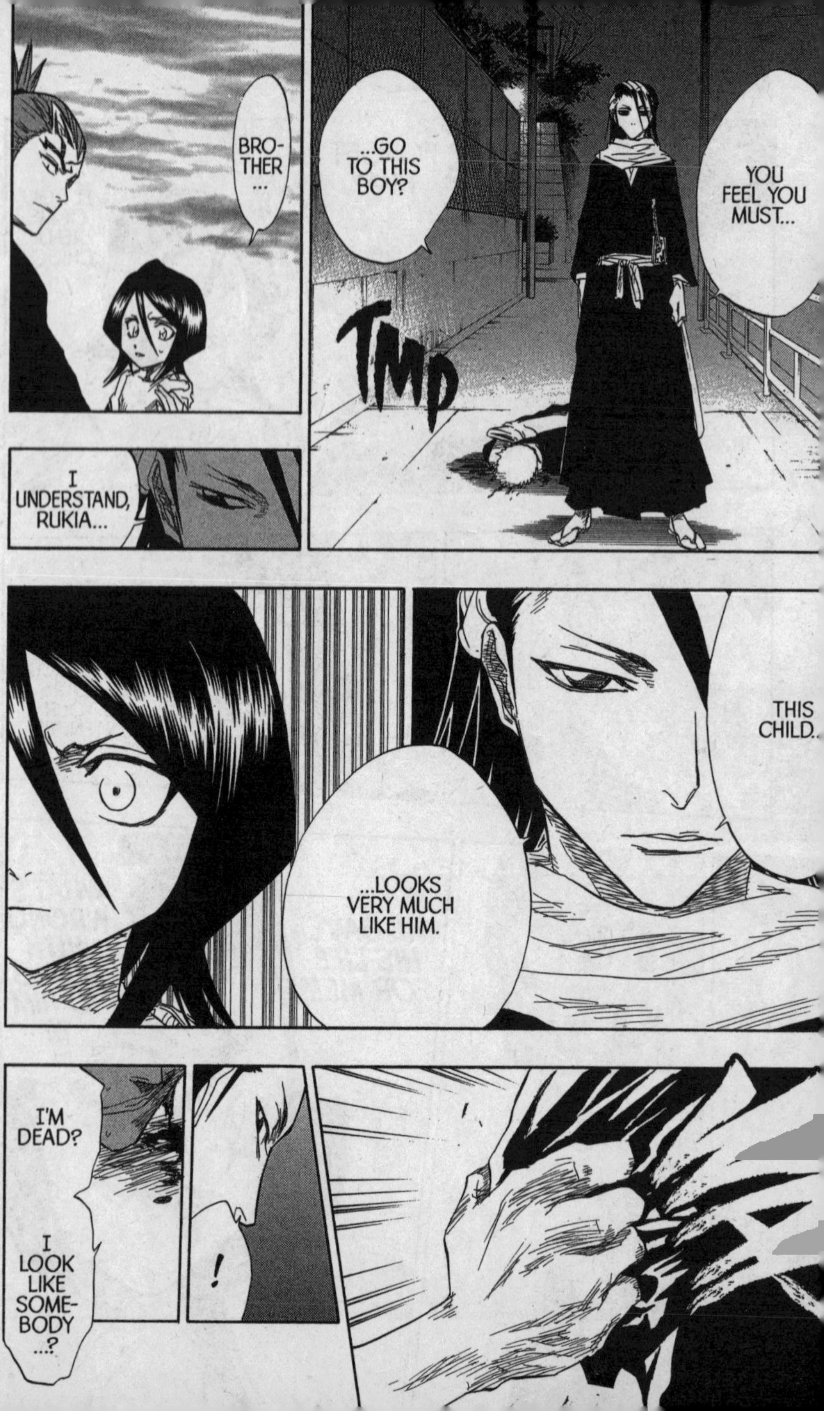
YOU FEEL YOU MUST...
...GO TO THIS BOY?
TMP
BROTHER...
I UNDERSTAND, RUKIA...
THIS CHILD...
...LOOKS VERY MUCH LIKE HIM.
!
I'M DEAD?
I LOOK LIKE SOMEBODY...?

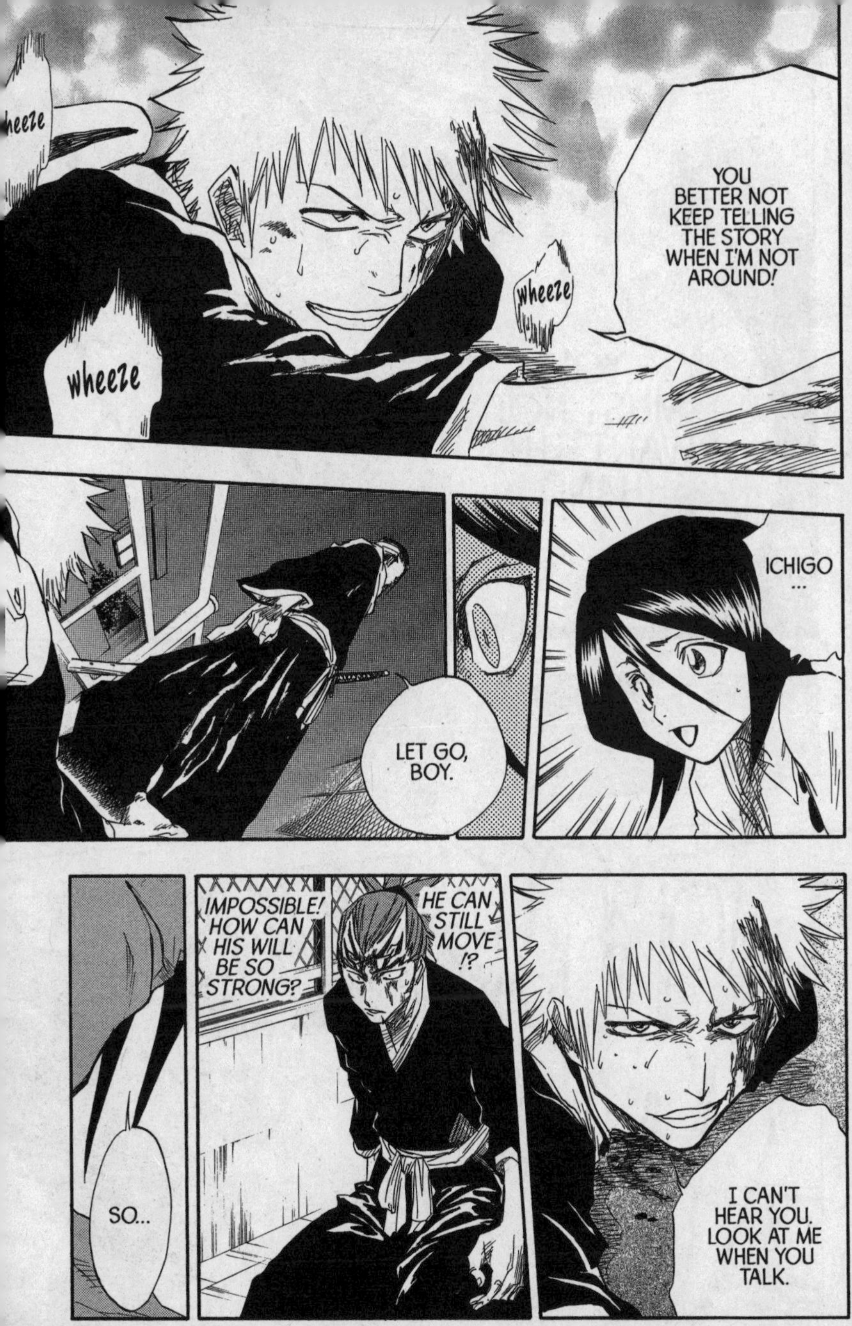
YOU BETTER NOT KEEP TELLING THE STORY WHEN I'M NOT AROUND!
wheeze
heeze
wheeze
ICHIGO ...
LET GO, BOY.
I CAN'T HEAR YOU. LOOK AT ME WHEN YOU TALK.
HE CAN STILL MOVE !?
IMPOSSIBLE! HOW CAN HIS WILL BE SO STRONG?
SO...

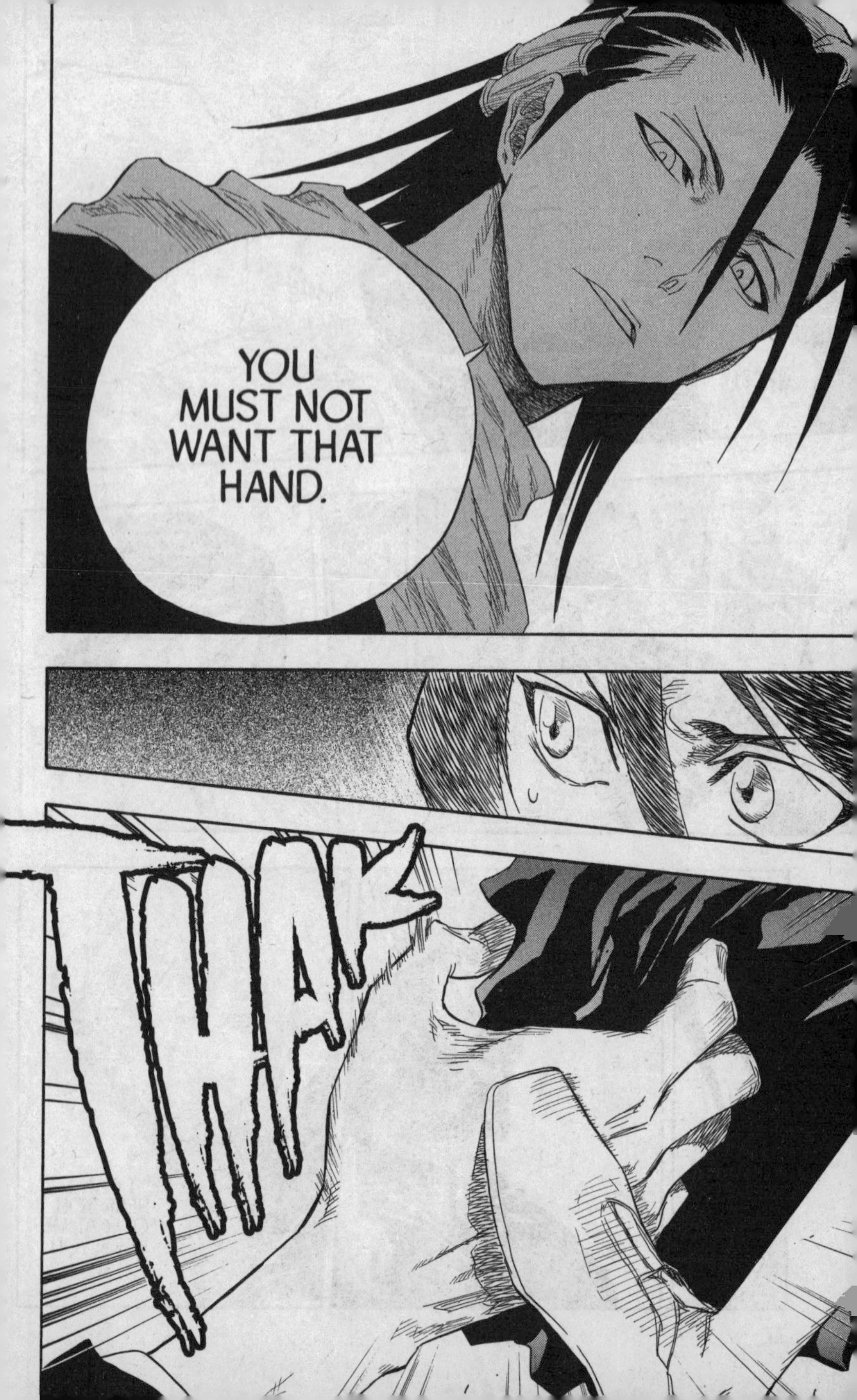
YOU MUST NOT WANT THAT HAND.
THAP

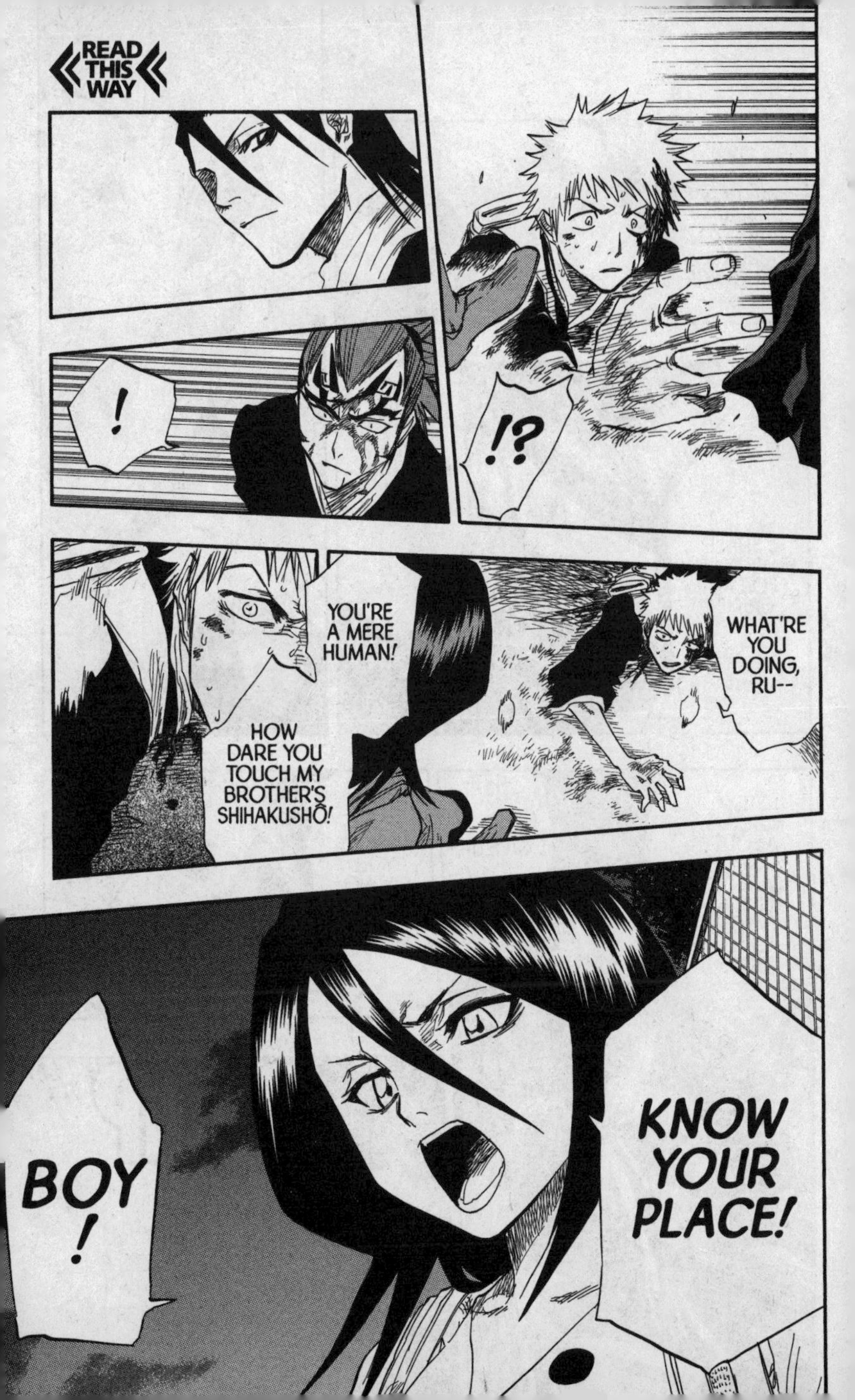
READ THIS WAY
!?
!
WHAT'RE YOU DOING, RU--
YOU'RE A MERE HUMAN!
HOW DARE YOU TOUCH MY BROTHER'S SHIHAKUSHŌ!
KNOW YOUR PLACE!
BOY!

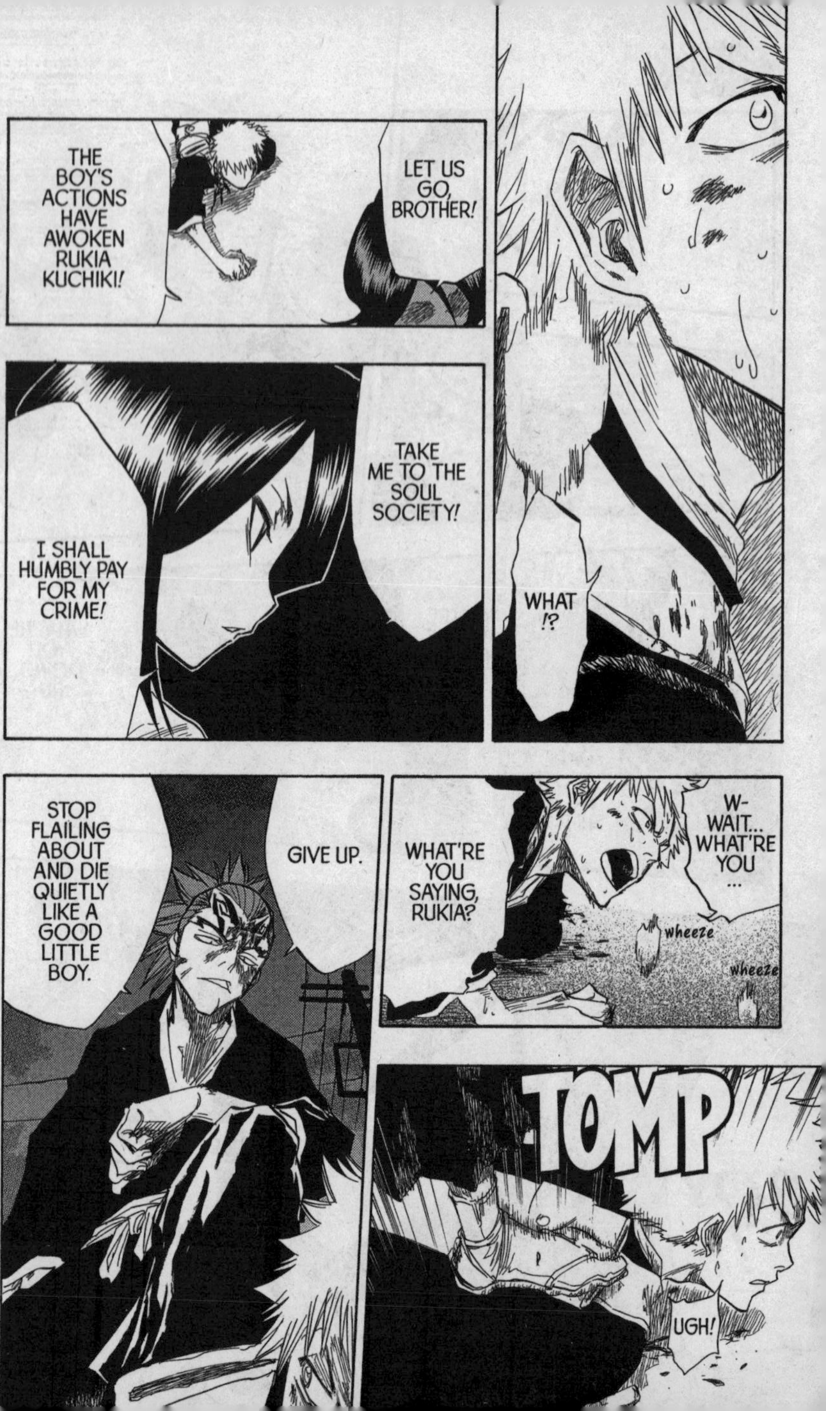
LET US GO, BROTHER!
THE BOY'S ACTIONS HAVE AWOKEN RUKIA KUCHIKI!
TAKE ME TO THE SOUL SOCIETY!
I SHALL HUMBLY PAY FOR MY CRIME!
WHAT !?
W-WAIT... WHAT'RE YOU ...
WHAT'RE YOU SAYING, RUKIA?
wheeze
wheeze
GIVE UP.
STOP FLAILING ABOUT AND DIE QUIETLY LIKE A GOOD LITTLE BOY.
TOMP
UGH!

READ THIS WAY

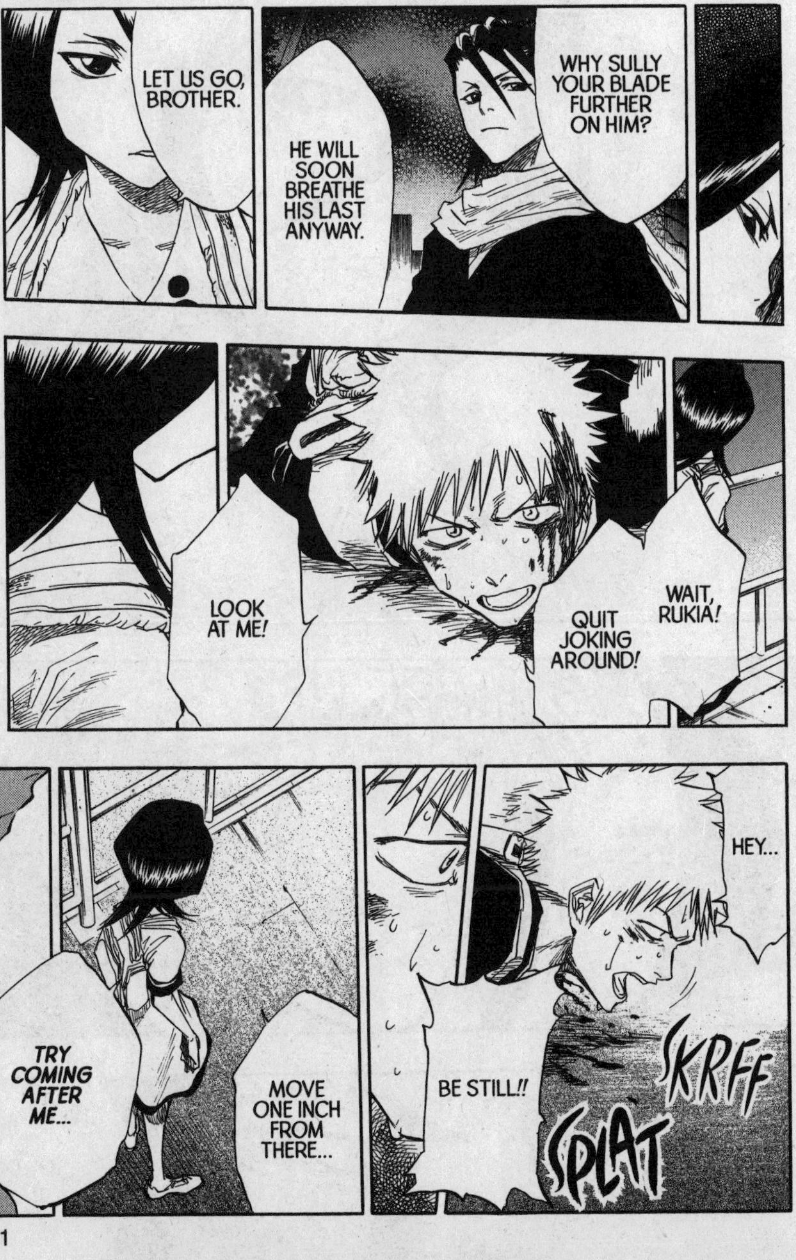

WHY SULLY YOUR BLADE FURTHER ON HIM?
HE WILL SOON BREATHE HIS LAST ANYWAY.
LET US GO, BROTHER.
WAIT, RUKIA!
QUIT JOKING AROUND!
LOOK AT ME!
HEY...
SKRFF
SPLAT
BE STILL!!
MOVE ONE INCH FROM THERE...
TRY COMING AFTER ME...

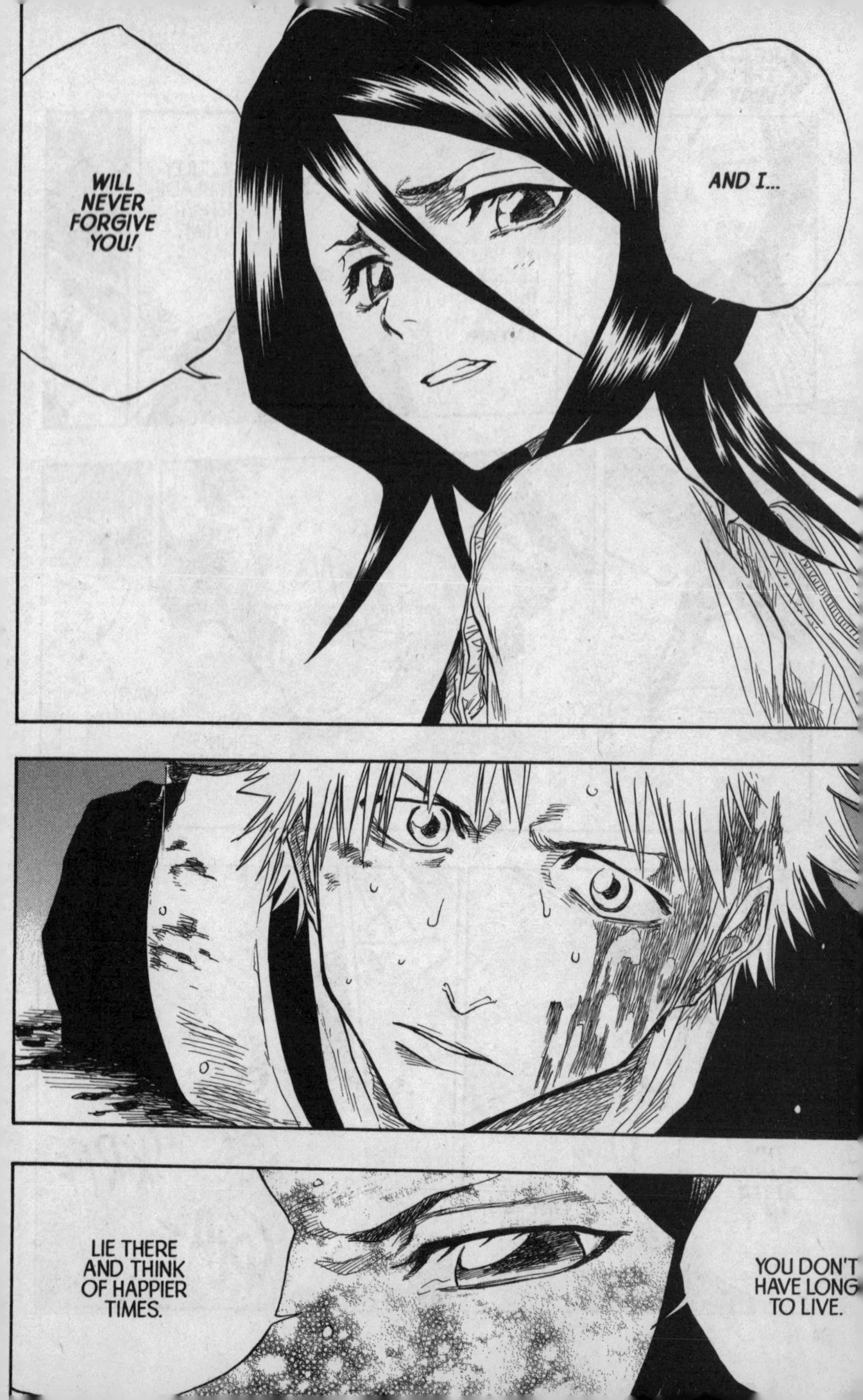
AND I...
WILL NEVER FORGIVE YOU!
YOU DON'T HAVE LONG TO LIVE.
LIE THERE AND THINK OF HAPPIER TIMES.

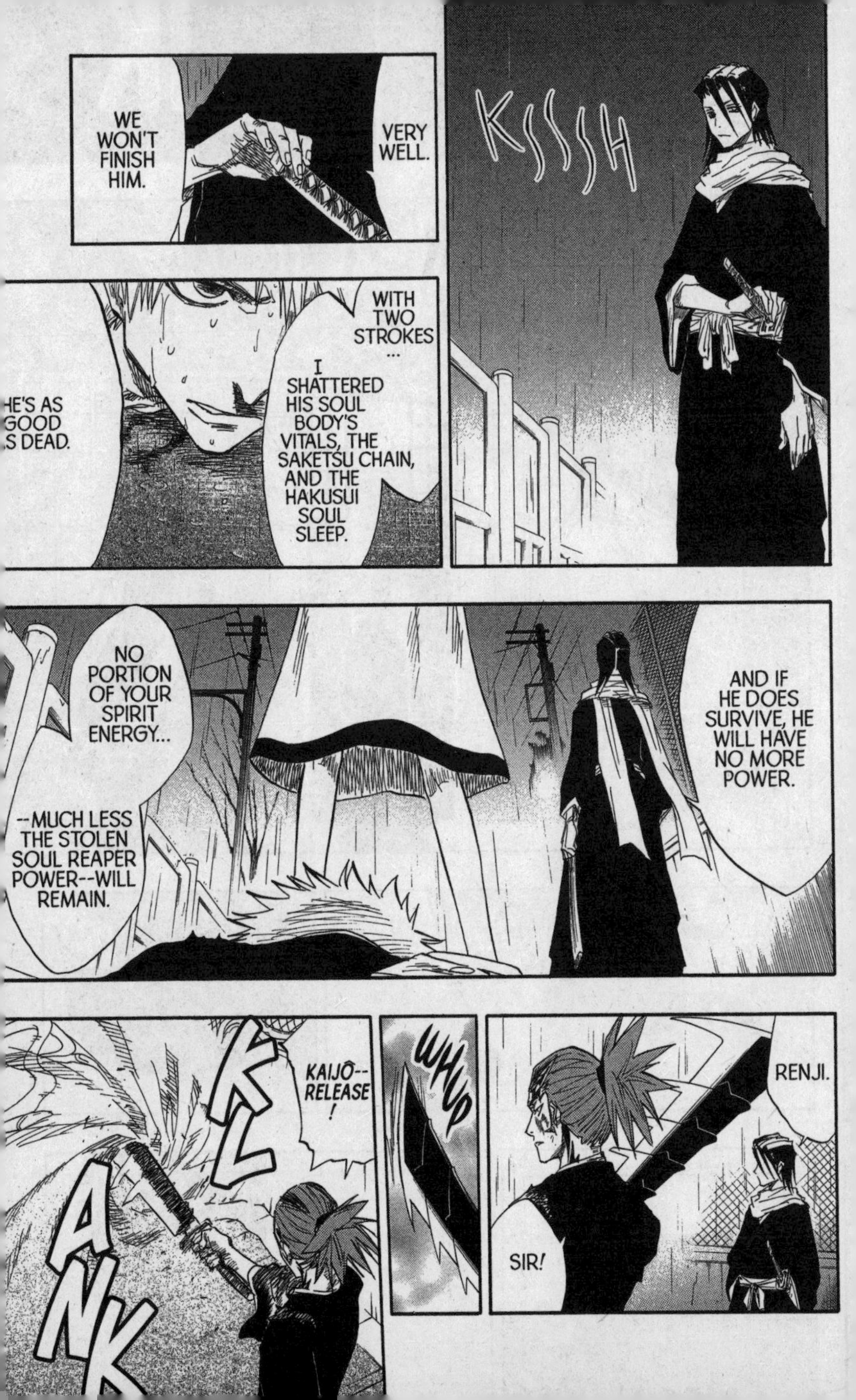
KSSSH
VERY WELL.
WE WON'T FINISH HIM.
WITH TWO STROKES...
I SHATTERED HIS SOUL BODY'S VITALS, THE SAKETSU CHAIN, AND THE HAKUSUI SOUL SLEEP.
HE'S AS GOOD S DEAD.
AND IF HE DOES SURVIVE, HE WILL HAVE NO MORE POWER.
NO PORTION OF YOUR SPIRIT ENERGY...
--MUCH LESS THE STOLEN SOUL REAPER POWER--WILL REMAIN.
RENJI.
SIR!
WHUP
KAIJÔ--RELEASE!
KLANK

SHSSISK

I CAN'T MOVE...

I CAN'T TALK...

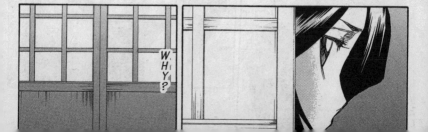

WHY?

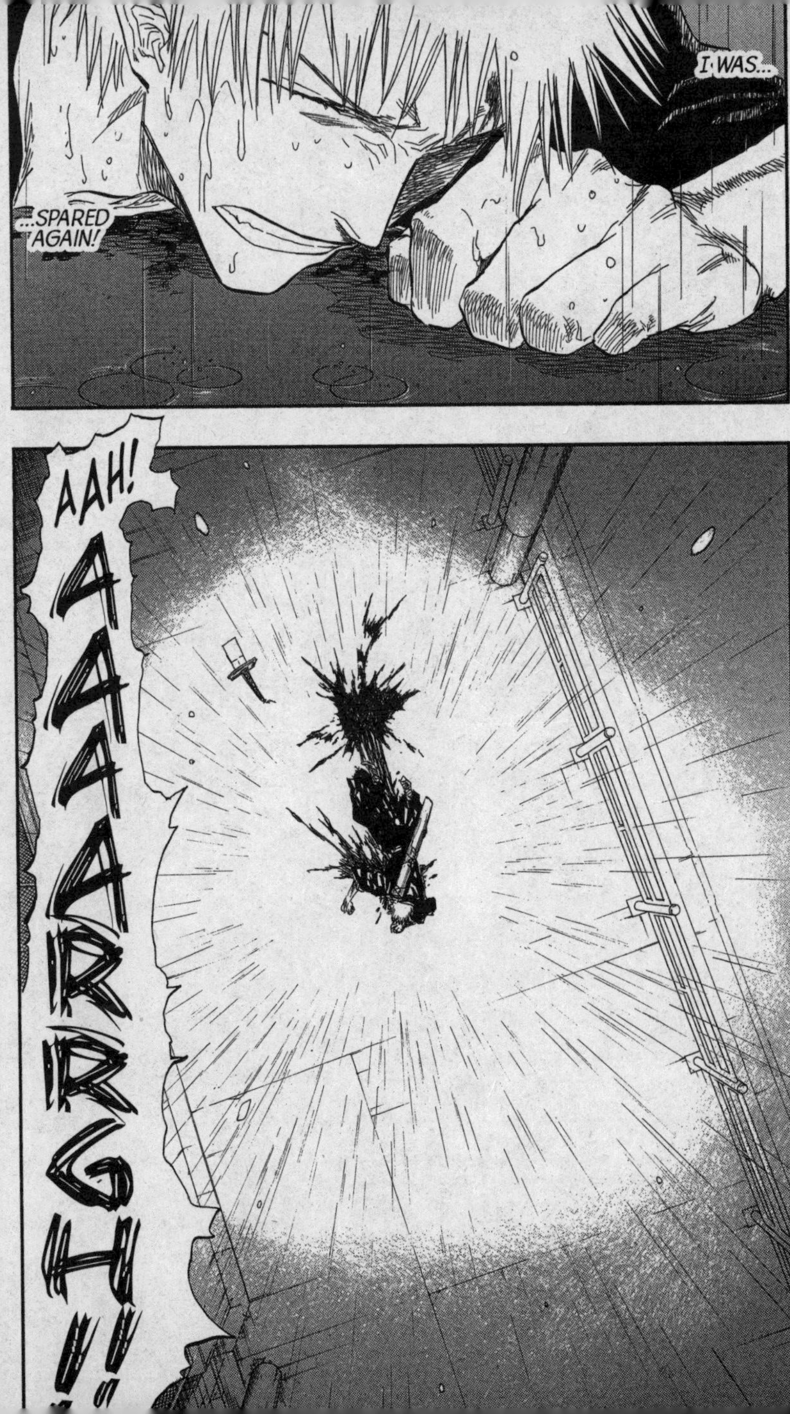
I WAS...
...SPARED AGAIN!
AAH!
AAAARRGH!!

57. July Rain, Interrupted

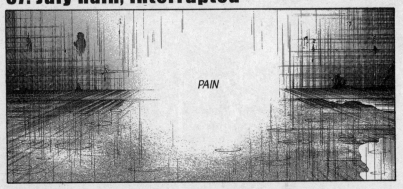

PAIN

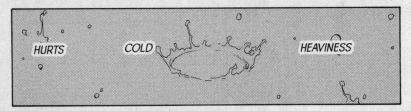

HURTS   COLD   HEAVINESS

WON'T
STOP

BLEEDING

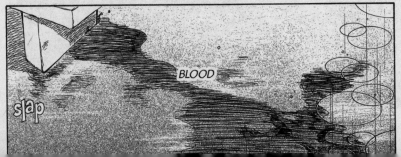

BLOOD

slap

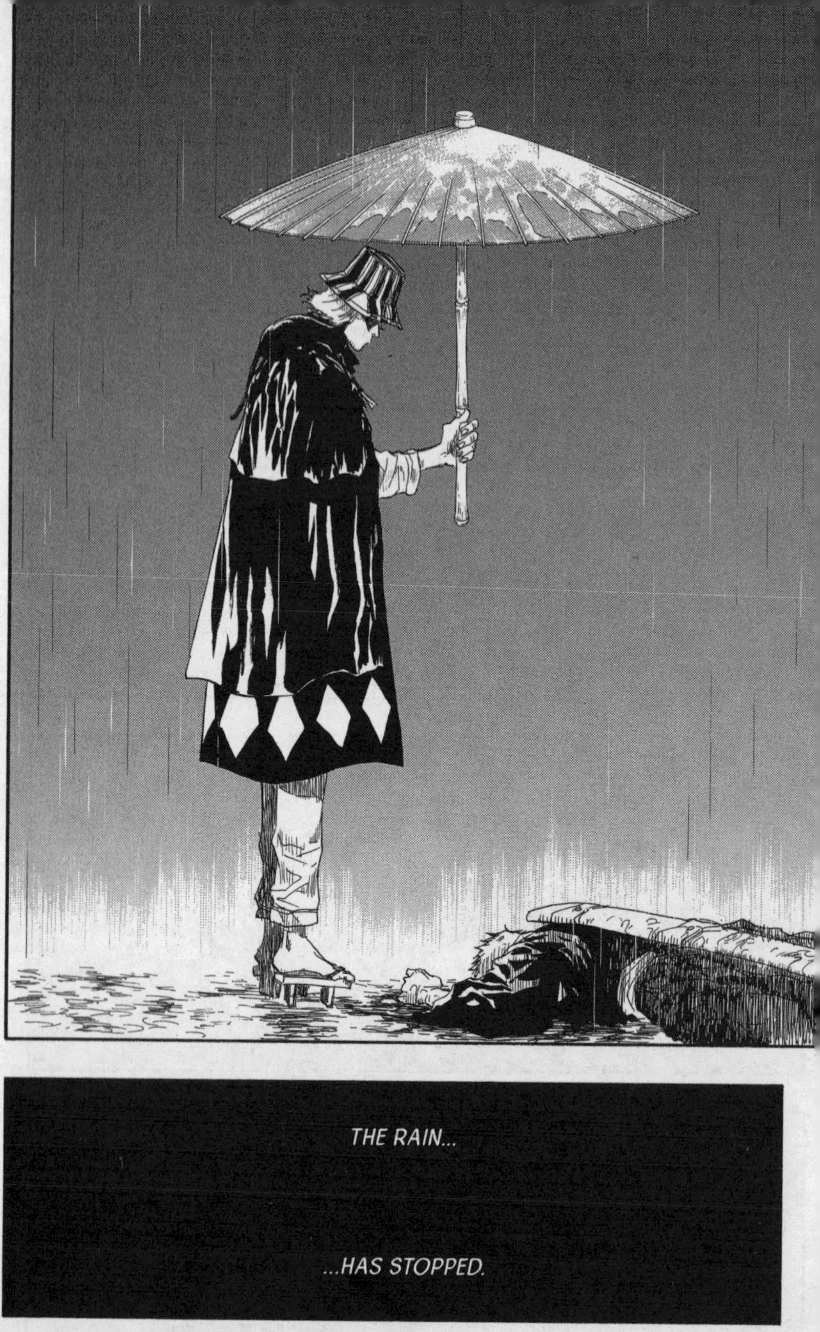
THE RAIN...
...HAS STOPPED.

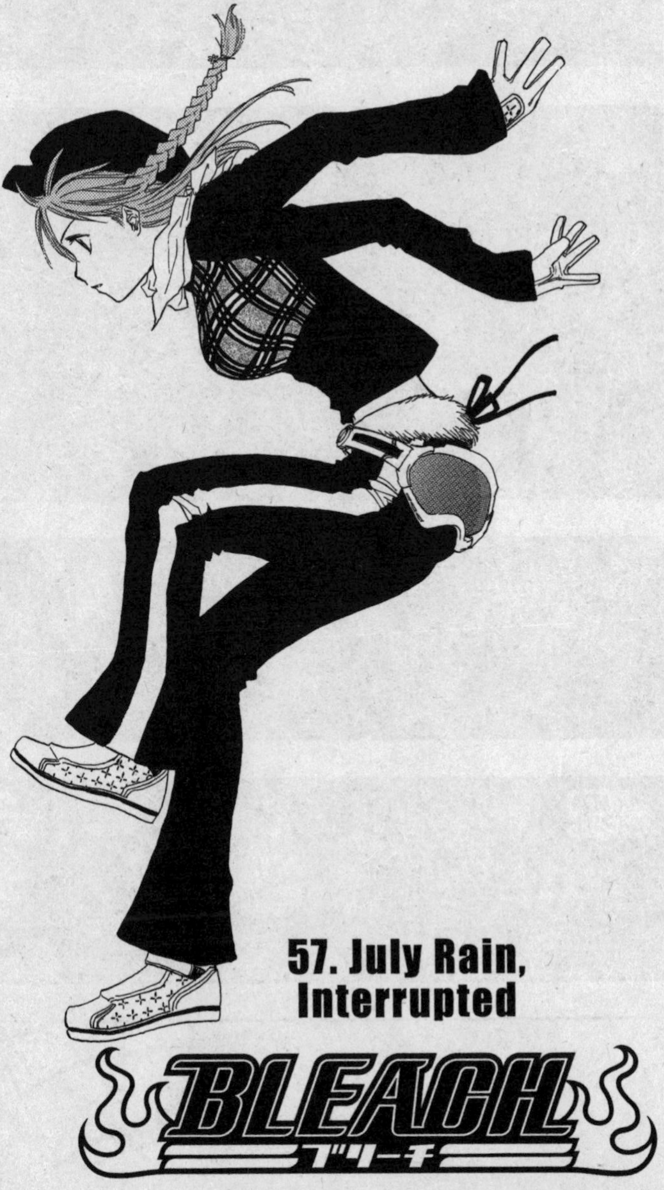

57. July Rain, Interrupted

BLEACH

ブリーチ

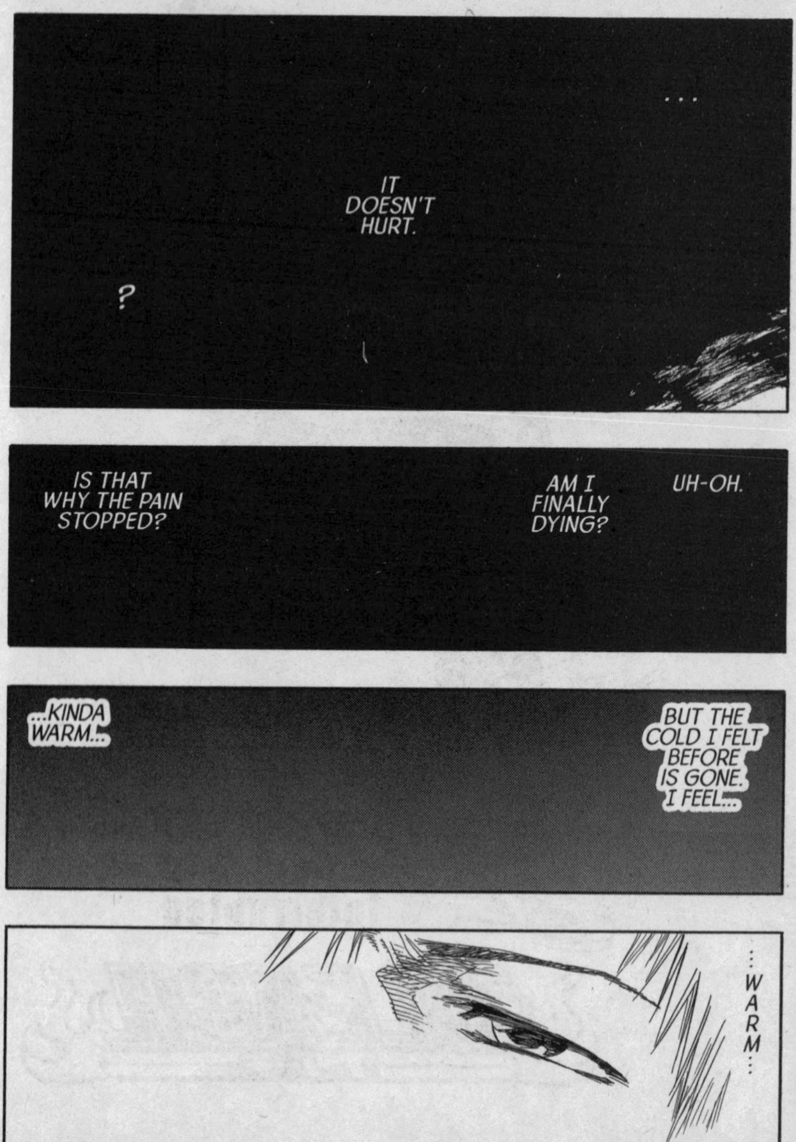
...
IT DOESN'T HURT.
?
UH-OH.
AM I FINALLY DYING?
IS THAT WHY THE PAIN STOPPED?
BUT THE COLD I FELT BEFORE IS GONE. I FEEL...
...KINDA WARM...
...WARM...

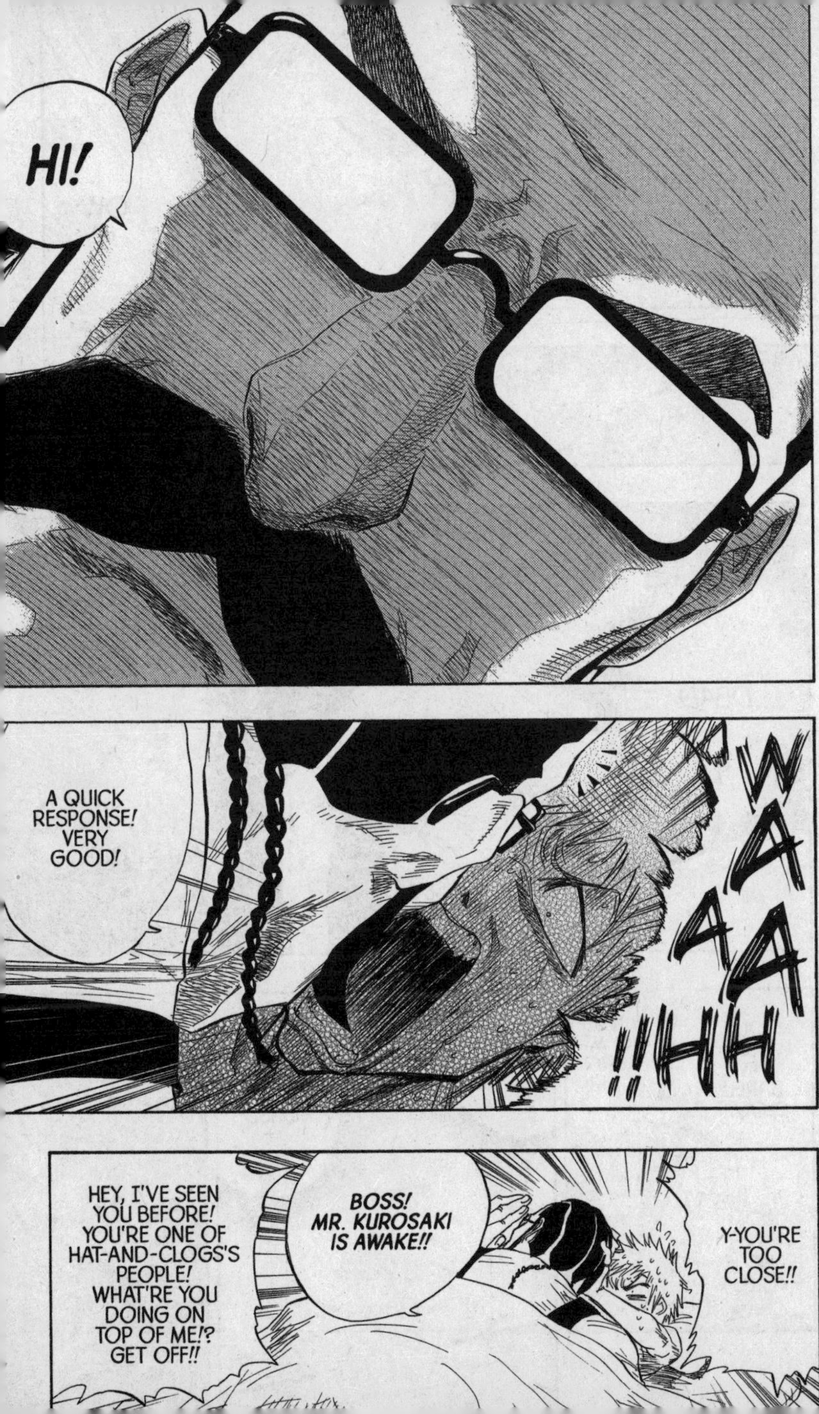
HI!
WAAAHH!!
A QUICK RESPONSE! VERY GOOD!
Y-YOU'RE TOO CLOSE!!
BOSS! MR. KUROSAKI IS AWAKE!!
HEY, I'VE SEEN YOU BEFORE! YOU'RE ONE OF HAT-AND-CLOGS'S PEOPLE! WHAT'RE YOU DOING ON TOP OF ME!? GET OFF!!

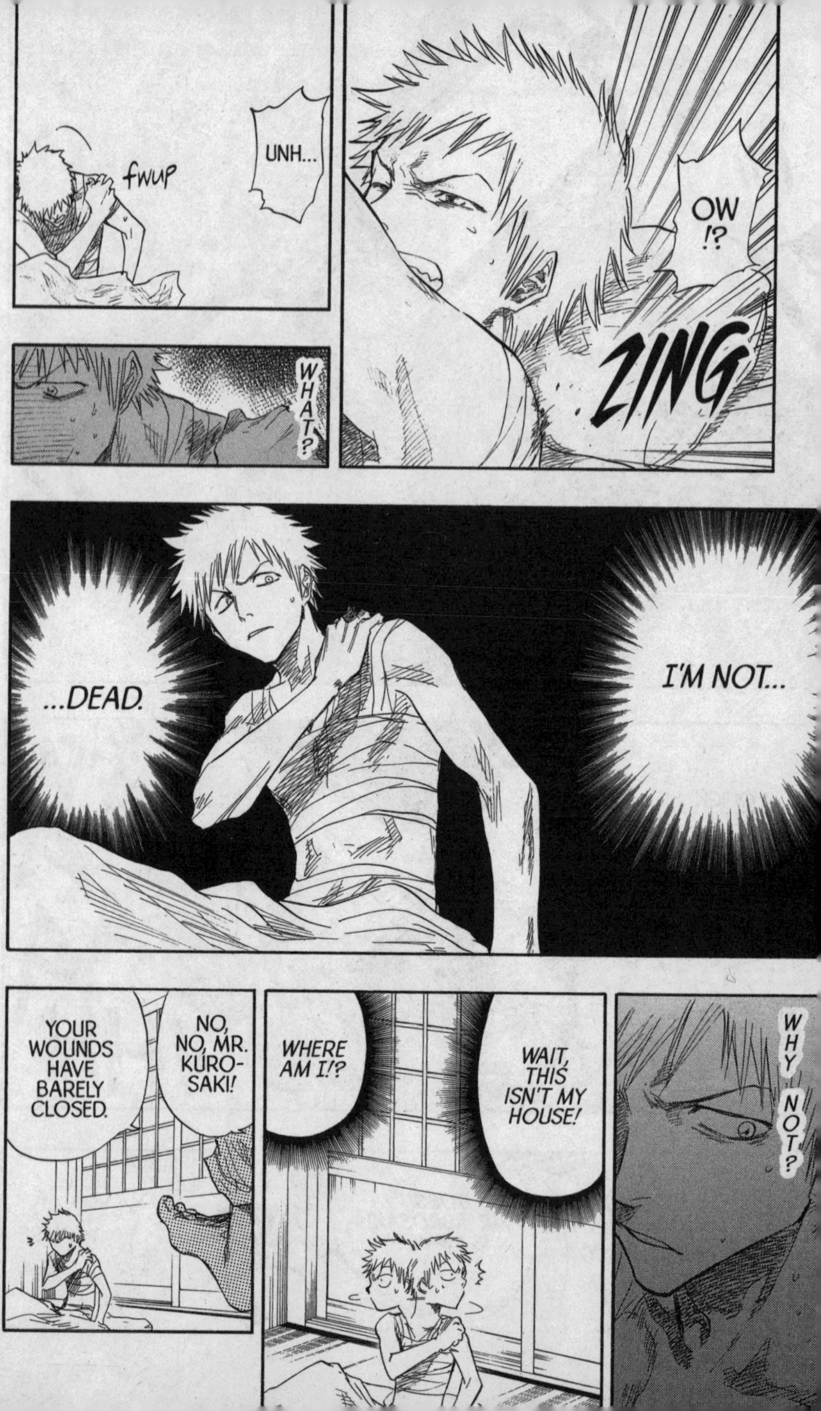
OW!?
ZING
UNH...
fwup
WHAT?
I'M NOT...
...DEAD.
WHY NOT?
WAIT, THIS ISN'T MY HOUSE!
WHERE AM I!?
NO, NO, MR. KUROSAKI!
YOUR WOUNDS HAVE BARELY CLOSED.

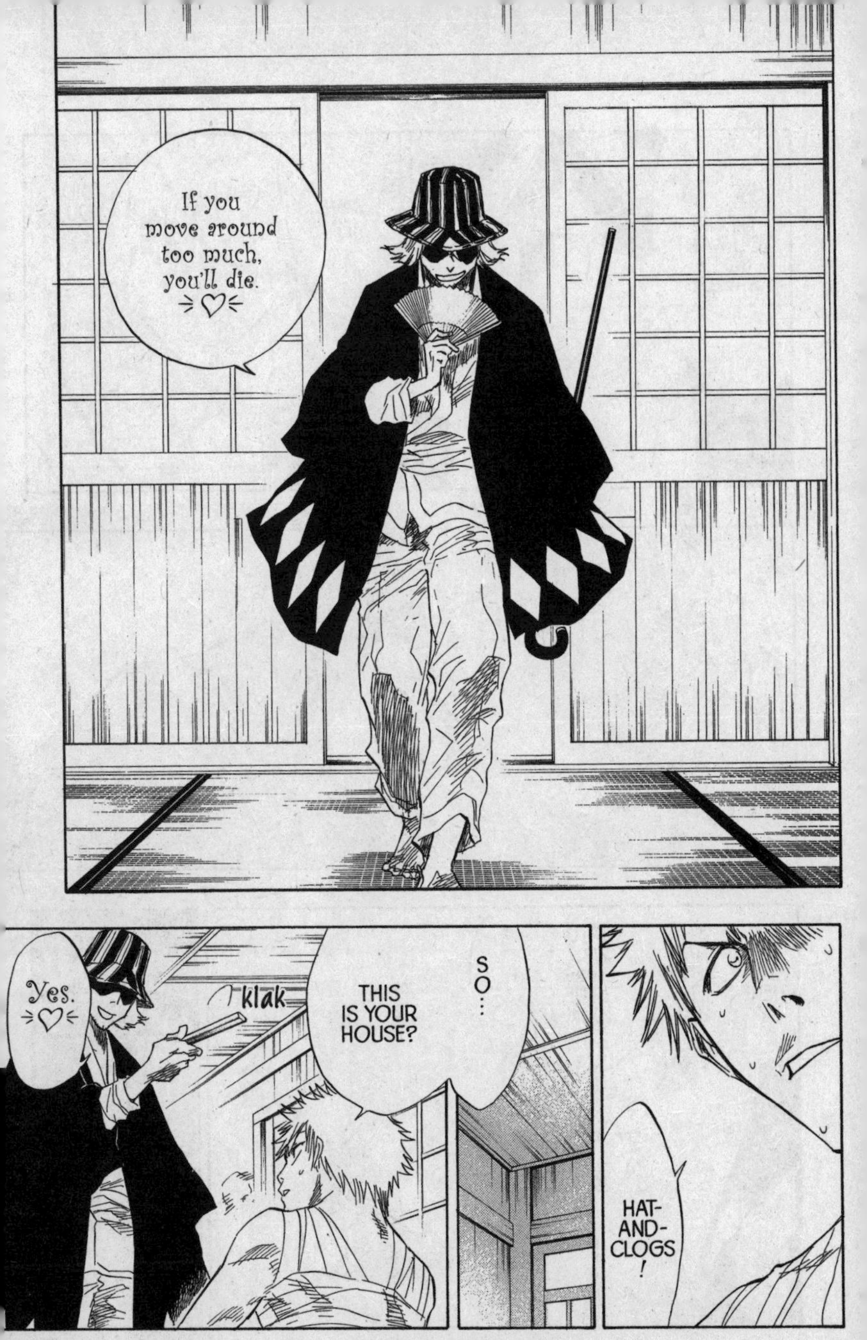
If you move around too much, you'll die. ♡
HAT-AND-CLOGS!
SO... THIS IS YOUR HOUSE?
Yes. ♡
klak

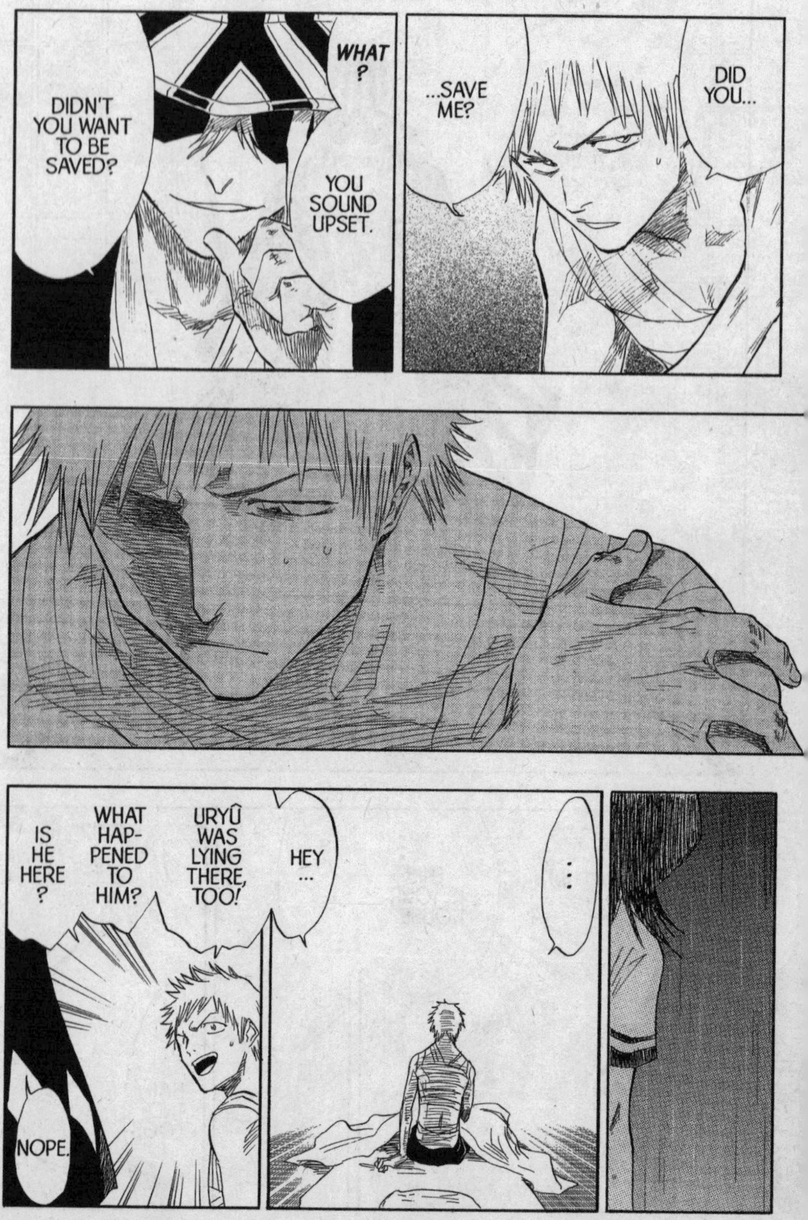
DID YOU...
...SAVE ME?
WHAT ?
YOU SOUND UPSET.
DIDN'T YOU WANT TO BE SAVED?
...
HEY ...
URYÛ WAS LYING THERE, TOO!
WHAT HAP-PENED TO HIM?
IS HE HERE ?
NOPE.

READ THIS WAY

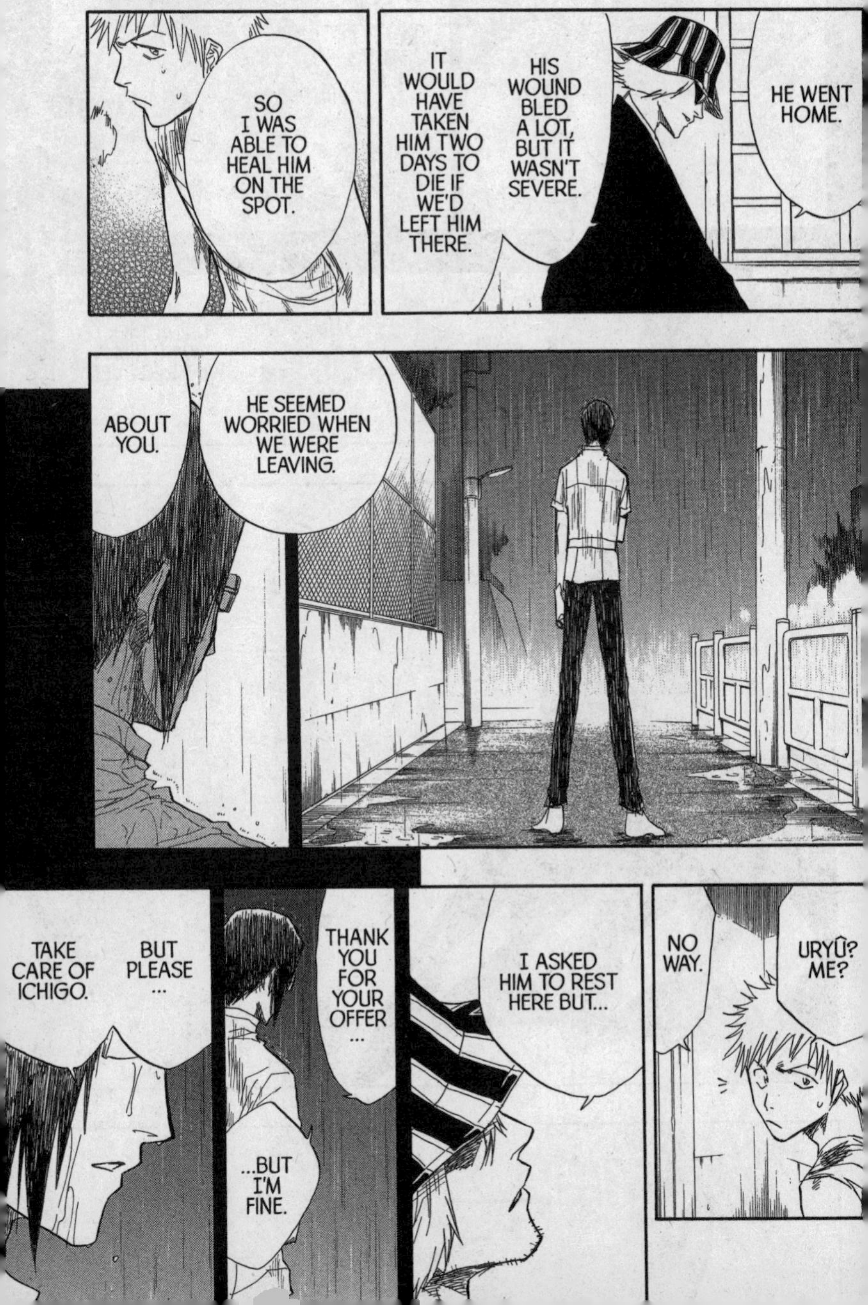

HE WENT HOME.
HIS WOUND BLED A LOT, BUT IT WASN'T SEVERE.
IT WOULD HAVE TAKEN HIM TWO DAYS TO DIE IF WE'D LEFT HIM THERE.
SO I WAS ABLE TO HEAL HIM ON THE SPOT.
HE SEEMED WORRIED WHEN WE WERE LEAVING.
ABOUT YOU.
URYÛ? ME?
NO WAY.
I ASKED HIM TO REST HERE BUT...
THANK YOU FOR YOUR OFFER ...
...BUT I'M FINE.
BUT PLEASE ...
TAKE CARE OF ICHIGO.

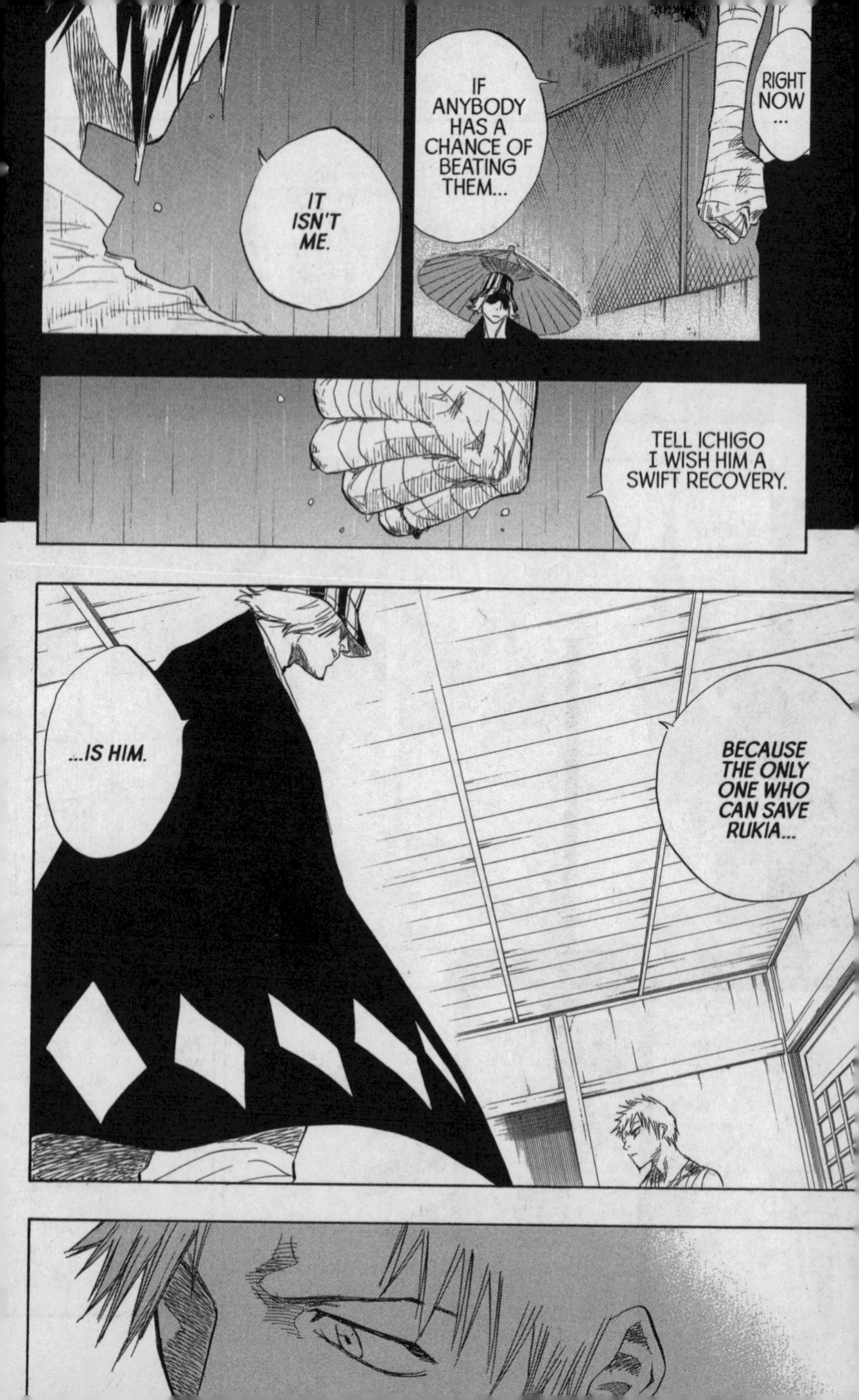
RIGHT NOW...
IF ANYBODY HAS A CHANCE OF BEATING THEM...
IT ISN'T ME.
TELL ICHIGO I WISH HIM A SWIFT RECOVERY.
BECAUSE THE ONLY ONE WHO CAN SAVE RUKIA...
...IS HIM.

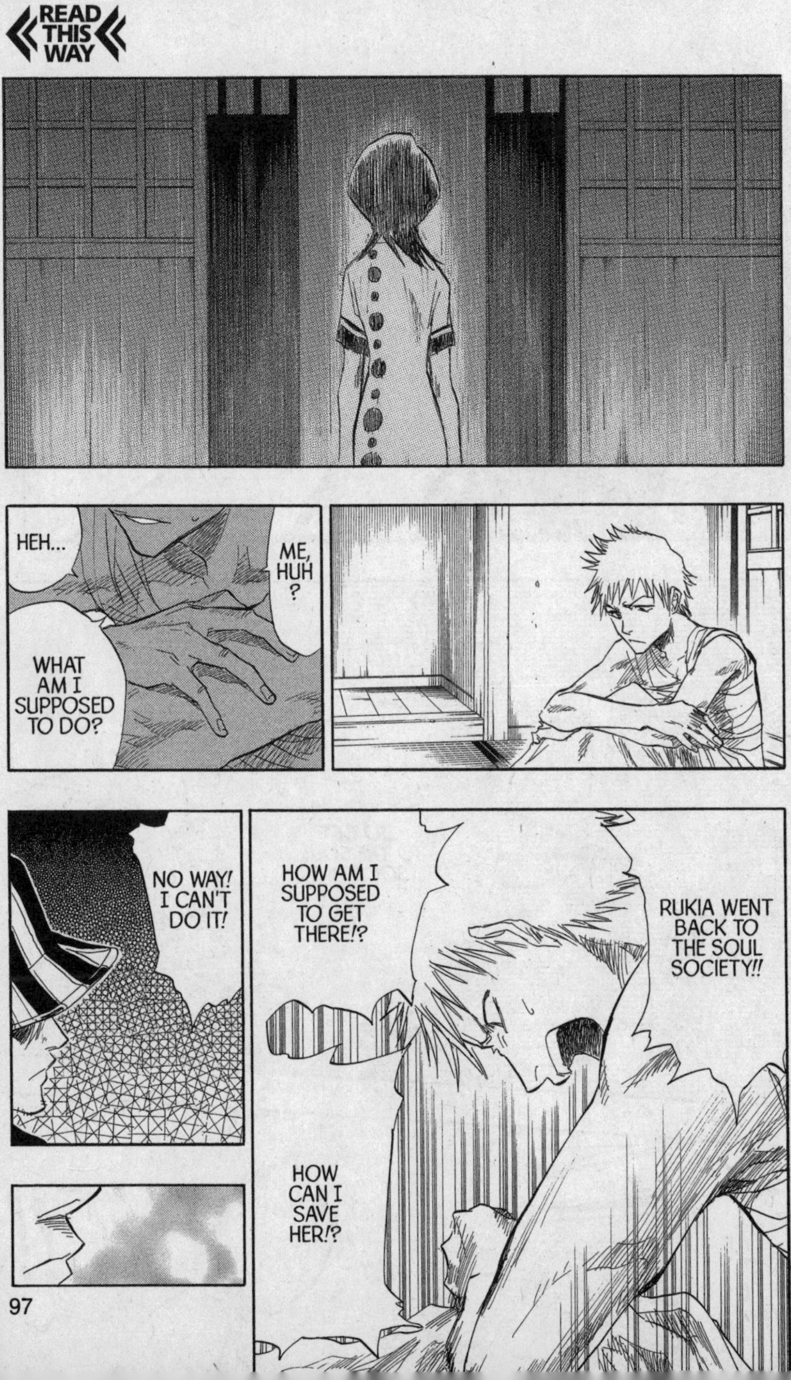
READ THIS WAY
ME, HUH?
HEH...
WHAT AM I SUPPOSED TO DO?
RUKIA WENT BACK TO THE SOUL SOCIETY!!
HOW AM I SUPPOSED TO GET THERE!?
HOW CAN I SAVE HER!?
NO WAY! I CAN'T DO IT!

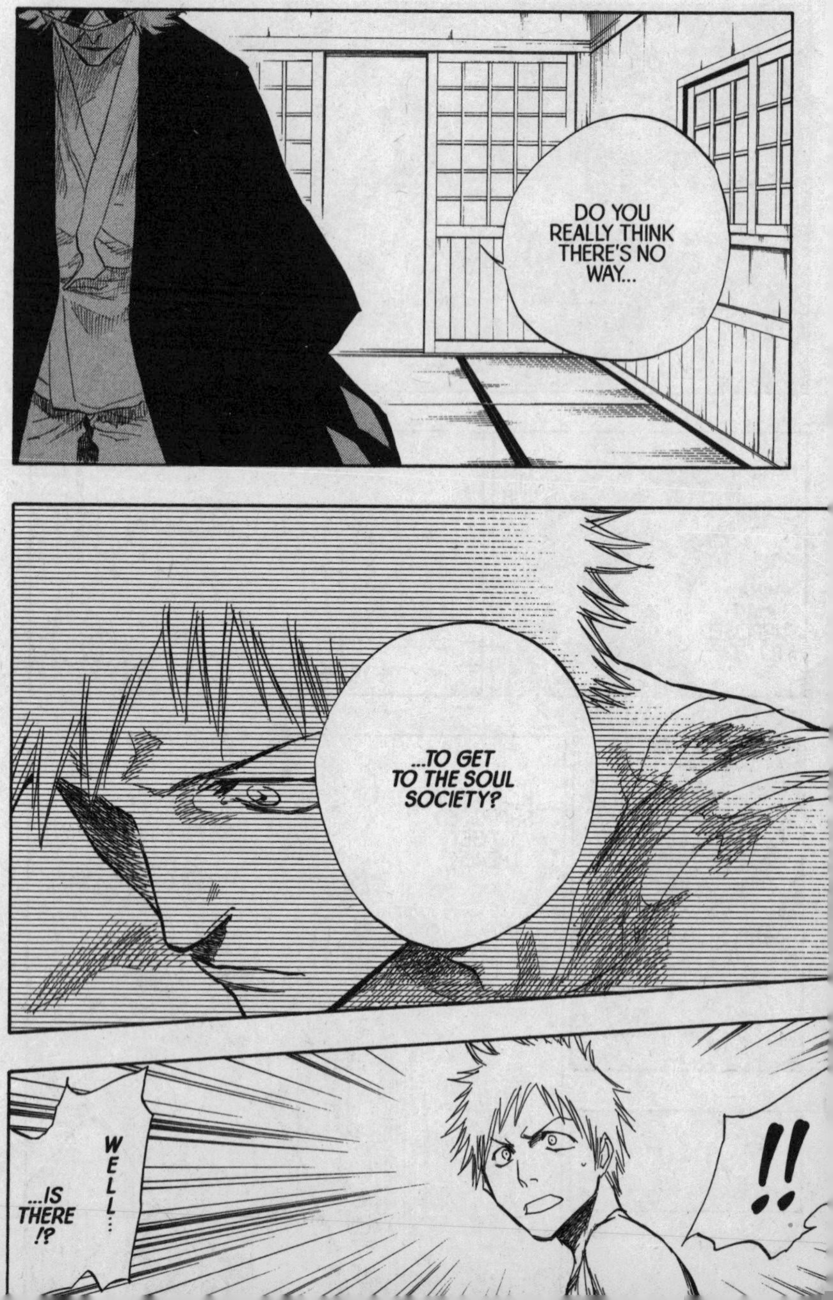
DO YOU REALLY THINK THERE'S NO WAY...
...TO GET TO THE SOUL SOCIETY?
!!
WELL...
...IS THERE !?

READ THIS WAY

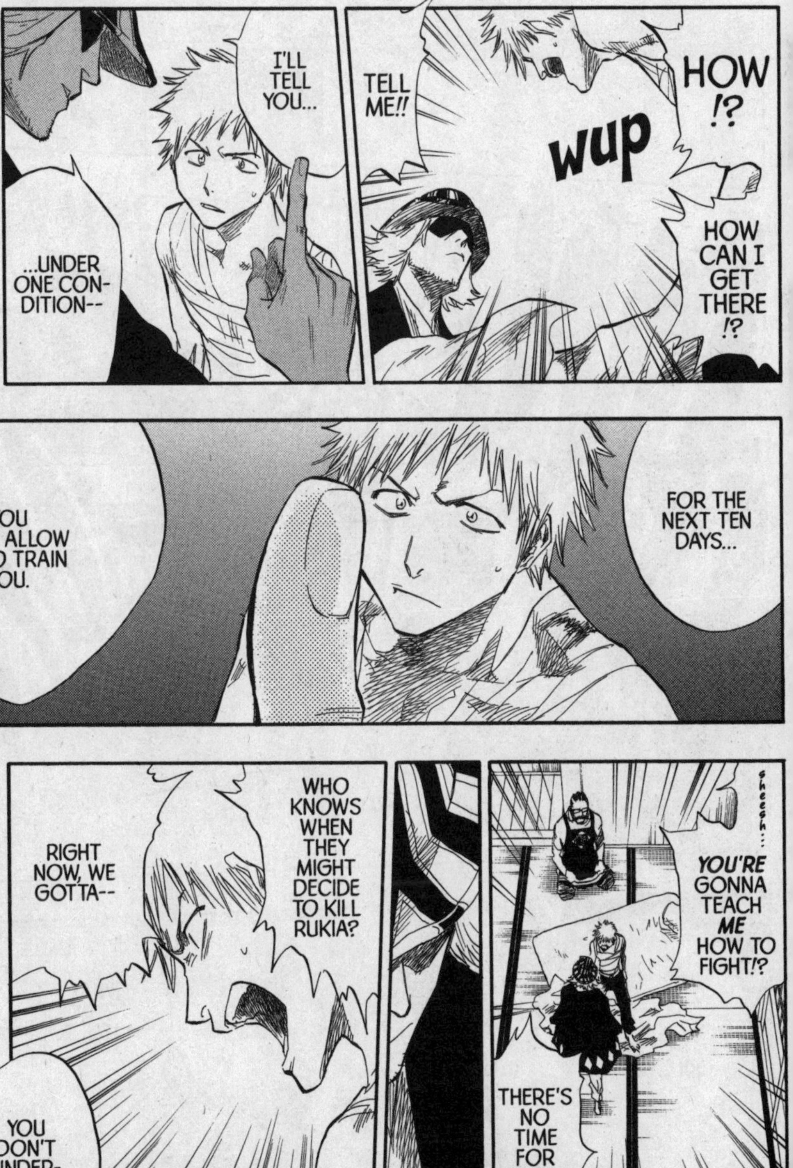
HOW !?
wup
HOW CAN I GET THERE !?
TELL ME!!
I'LL TELL YOU...
...UNDER ONE CON-DITION--
FOR THE NEXT TEN DAYS...
YOU MUST ALLOW ME TO TRAIN YOU.
sheesh...
YOU'RE GONNA TEACH *ME* HOW TO FIGHT!?
THERE'S NO TIME FOR THAT!
WHO KNOWS WHEN THEY MIGHT DECIDE TO KILL RUKIA?
RIGHT NOW, WE GOTTA--
YOU DON'T UNDER-STAND.

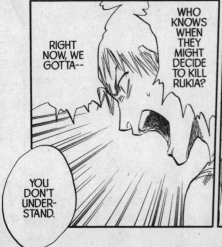

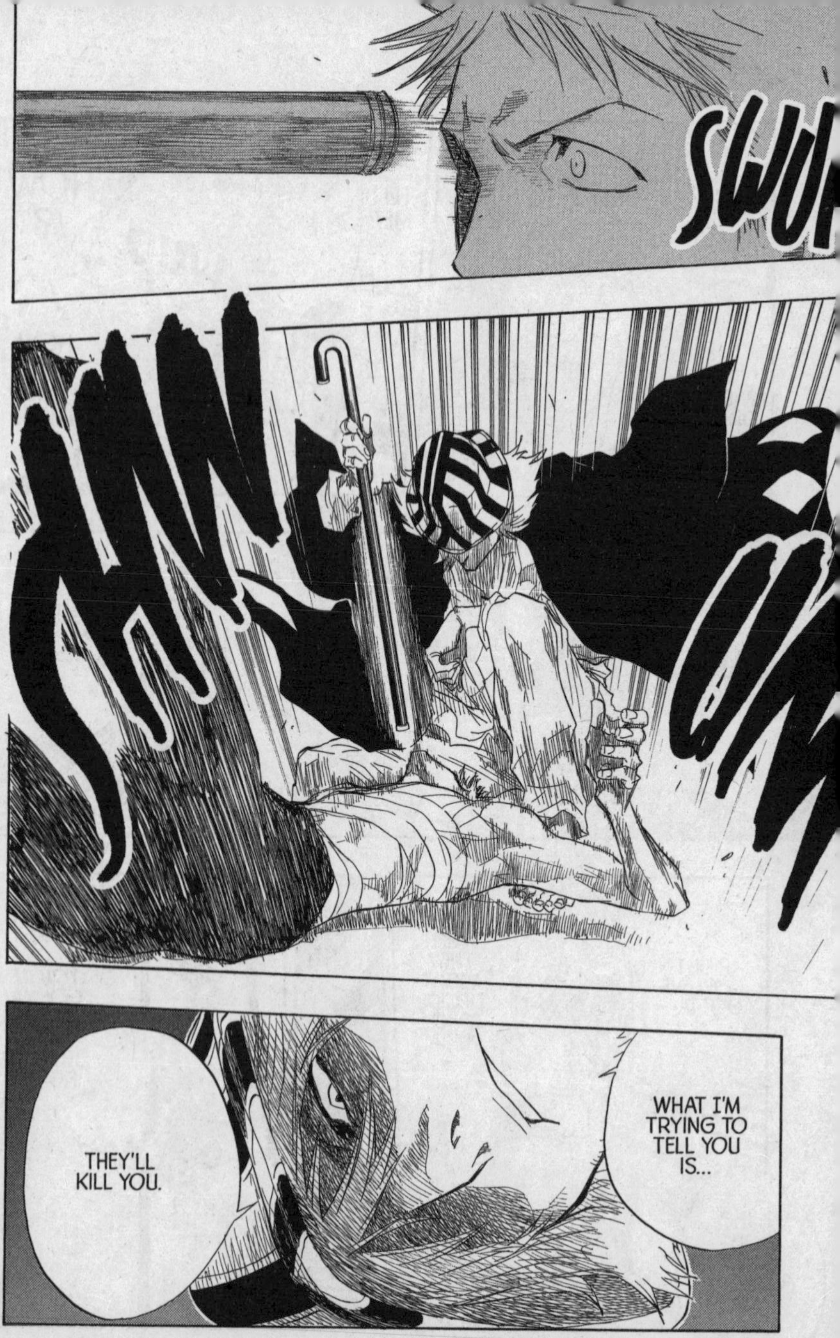
WHAT I'M TRYING TO TELL YOU IS...
THEY'LL KILL YOU.

READ THIS WAY

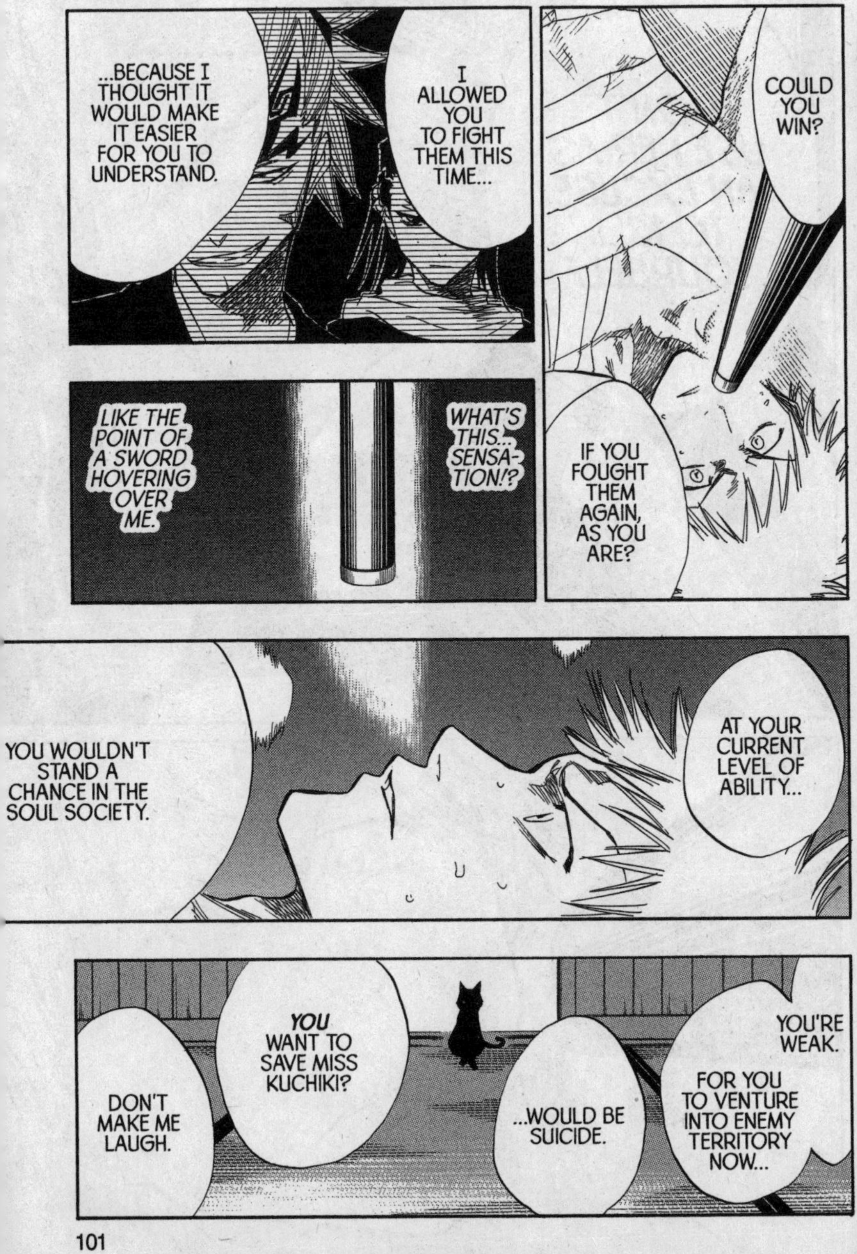

COULD YOU WIN?
IF YOU FOUGHT THEM AGAIN, AS YOU ARE?
I ALLOWED YOU TO FIGHT THEM THIS TIME...
...BECAUSE I THOUGHT IT WOULD MAKE IT EASIER FOR YOU TO UNDERSTAND.
WHAT'S THIS... SENSA-TION!?
LIKE THE POINT OF A SWORD HOVERING OVER ME.
AT YOUR CURRENT LEVEL OF ABILITY...
YOU WOULDN'T STAND A CHANCE IN THE SOUL SOCIETY.
YOU'RE WEAK.
FOR YOU TO VENTURE INTO ENEMY TERRITORY NOW...
...WOULD BE SUICIDE.
YOU WANT TO SAVE MISS KUCHIKI?
DON'T MAKE ME LAUGH.

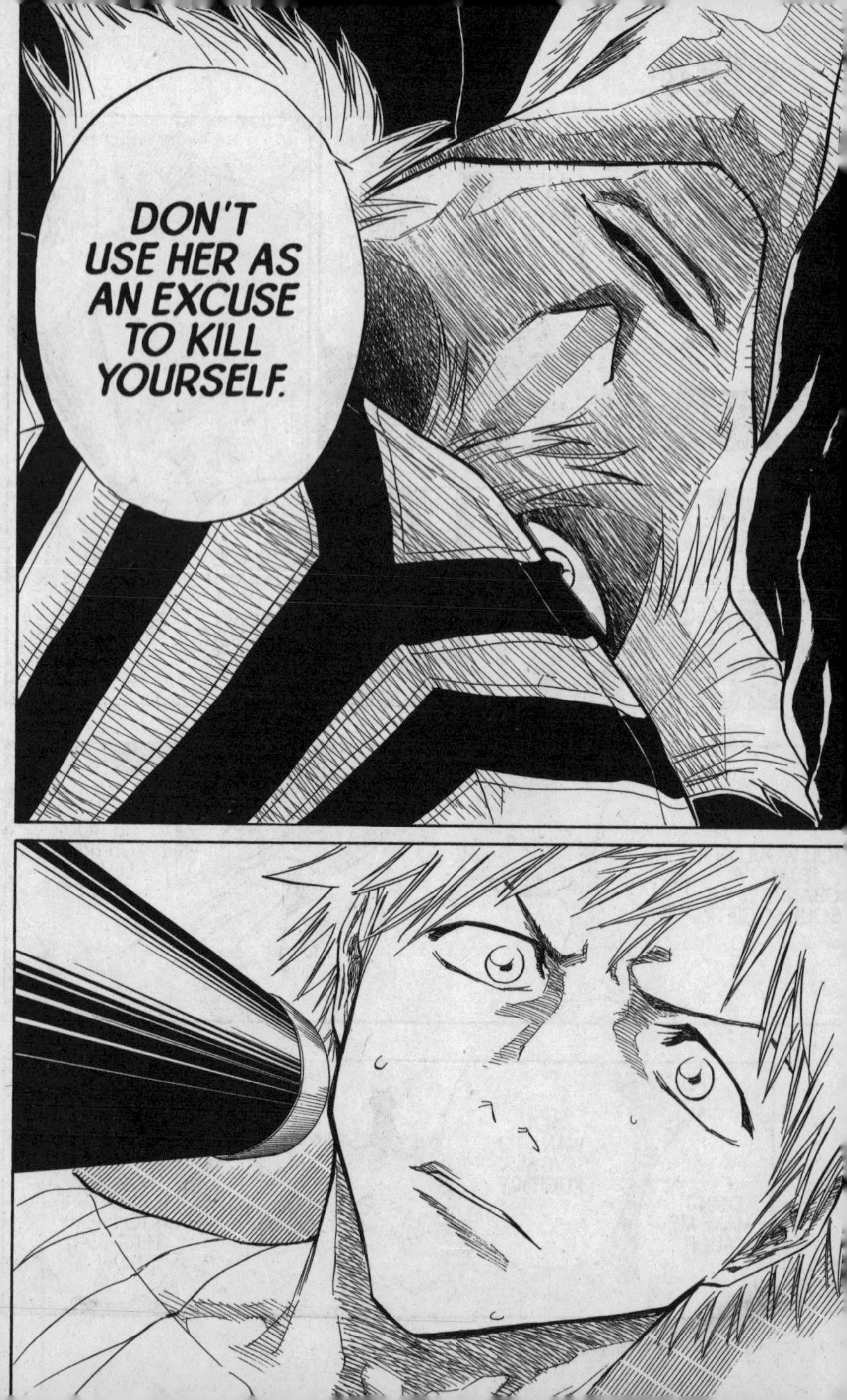
DON'T USE HER AS AN EXCUSE TO KILL YOURSELF.

READ THIS WAY

*KYOKUSHÛ: A CAPITAL OFFENDER.

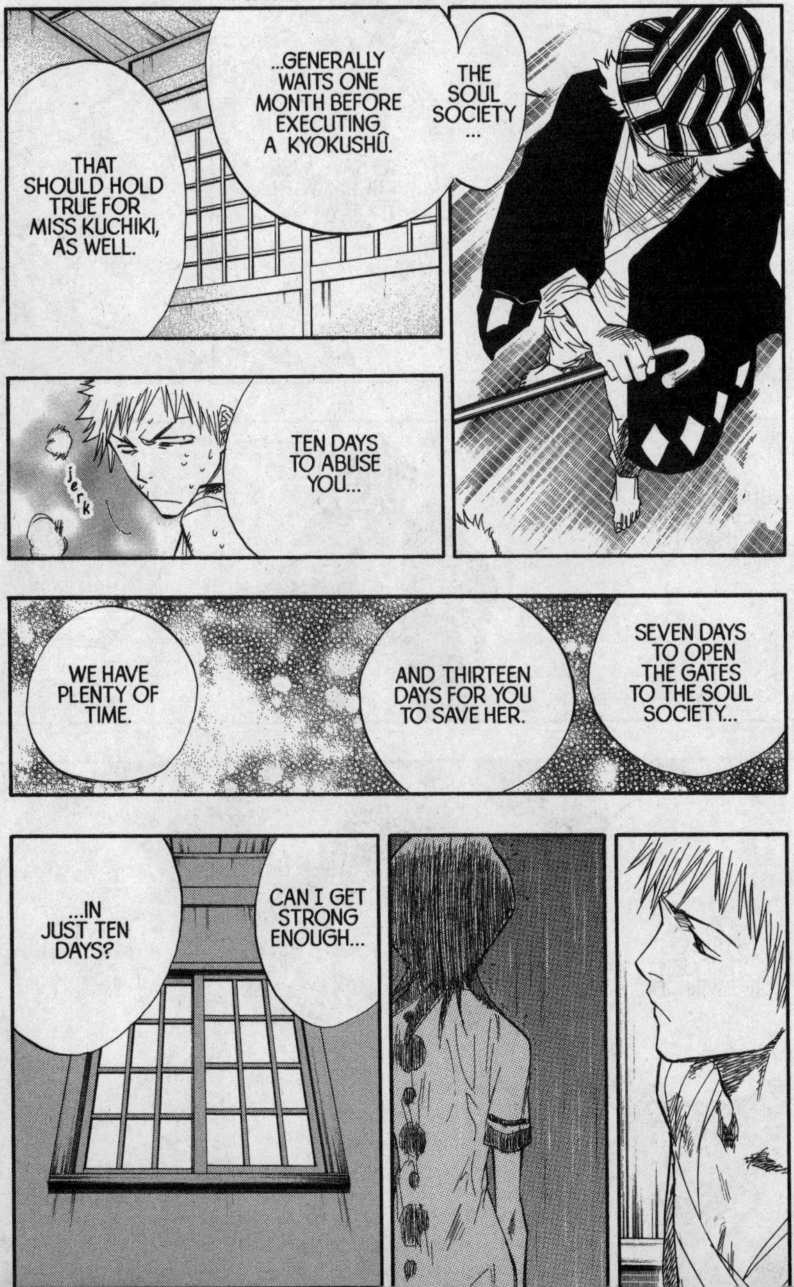
THE SOUL SOCIETY ...
...GENERALLY WAITS ONE MONTH BEFORE EXECUTING A KYOKUSHÛ.
THAT SHOULD HOLD TRUE FOR MISS KUCHIKI, AS WELL.
TEN DAYS TO ABUSE YOU...
jerk
SEVEN DAYS TO OPEN THE GATES TO THE SOUL SOCIETY...
AND THIRTEEN DAYS FOR YOU TO SAVE HER.
WE HAVE PLENTY OF TIME.
CAN I GET STRONG ENOUGH...
...IN JUST TEN DAYS?

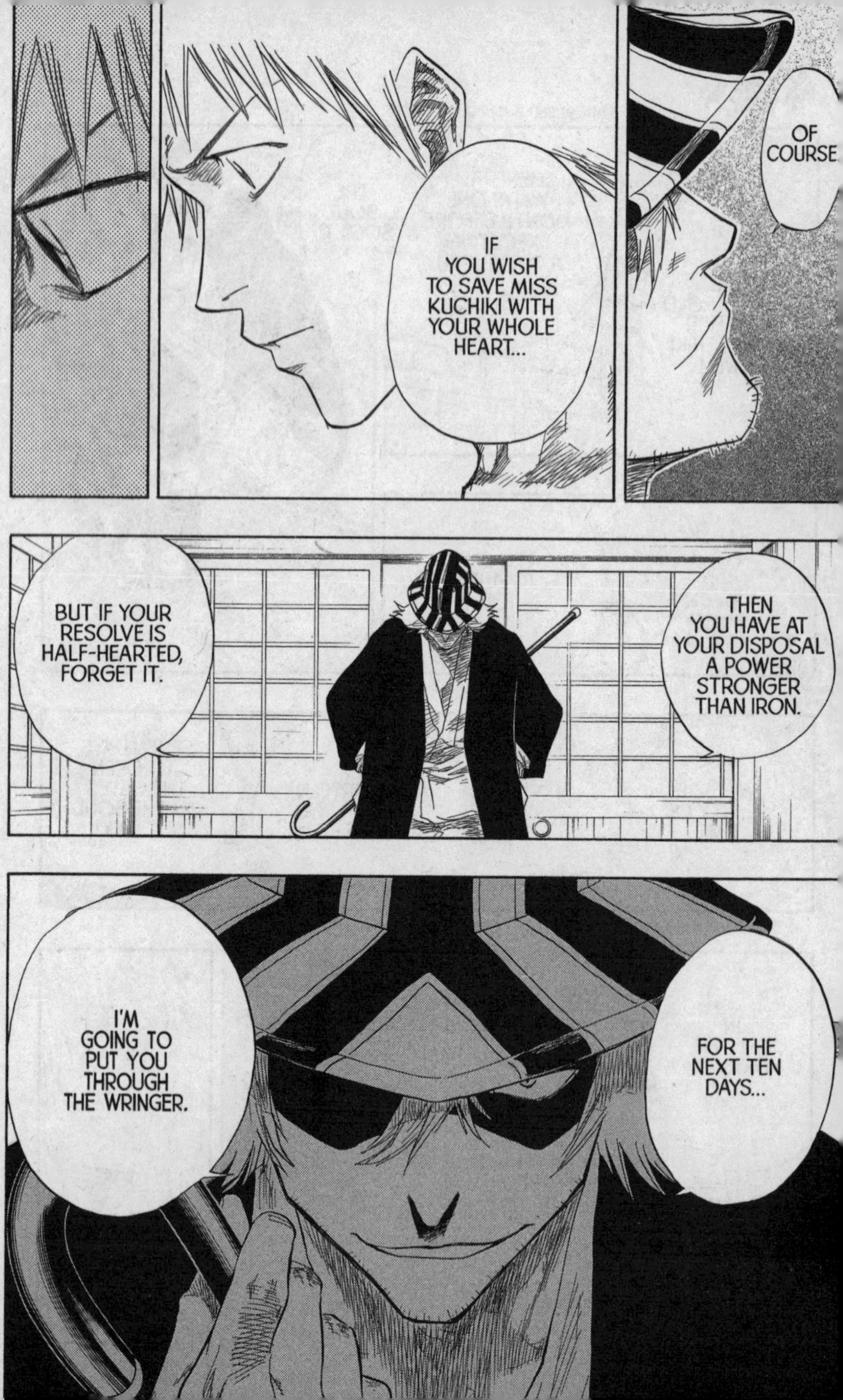

OF COURSE.
IF YOU WISH TO SAVE MISS KUCHIKI WITH YOUR WHOLE HEART...
THEN YOU HAVE AT YOUR DISPOSAL A POWER STRONGER THAN IRON.
BUT IF YOUR RESOLVE IS HALF-HEARTED, FORGET IT.
FOR THE NEXT TEN DAYS...
I'M GOING TO PUT YOU THROUGH THE WRINGER.

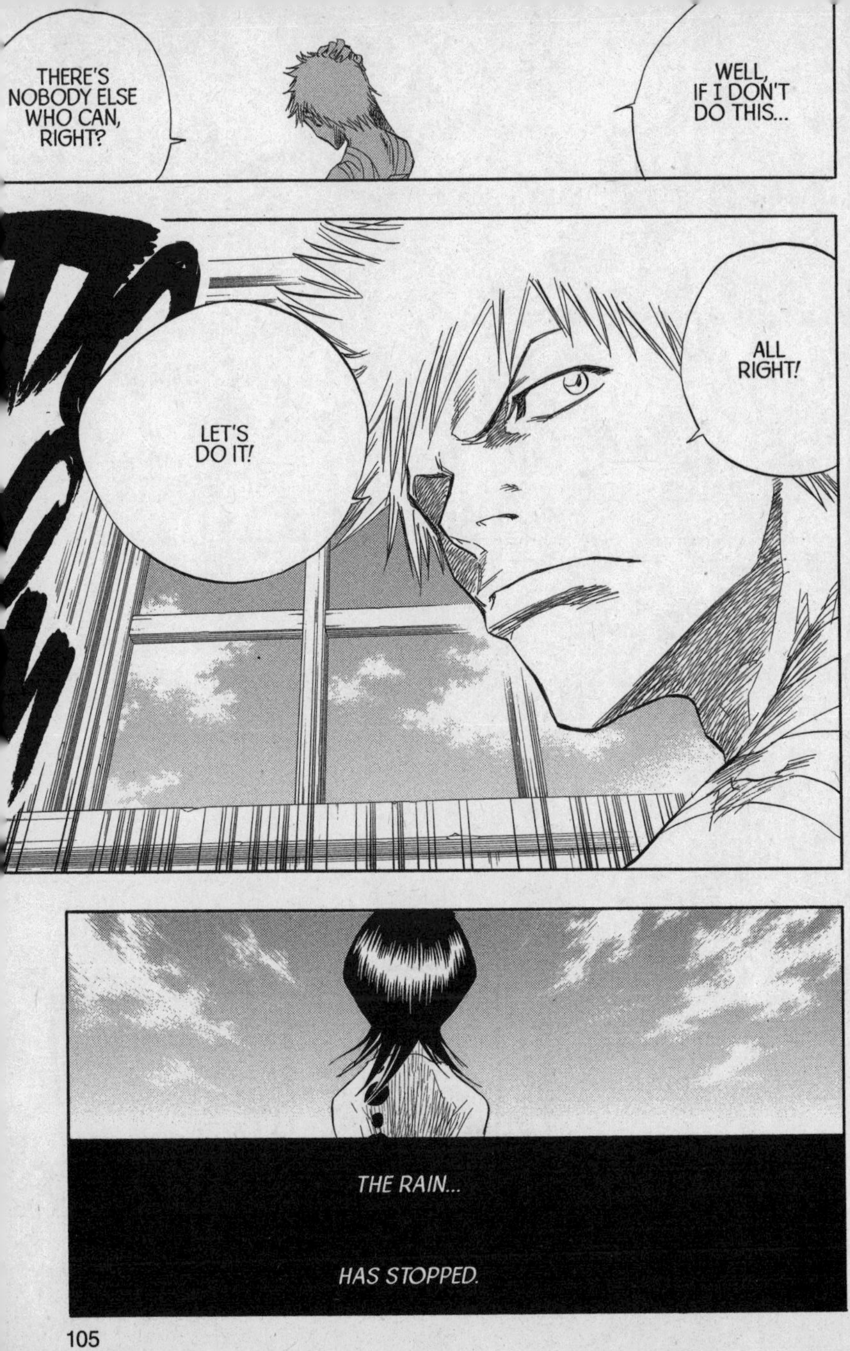
WELL, IF I DON'T DO THIS...
THERE'S NOBODY ELSE WHO CAN, RIGHT?
ALL RIGHT!
LET'S DO IT!
THE RAIN...
HAS STOPPED.

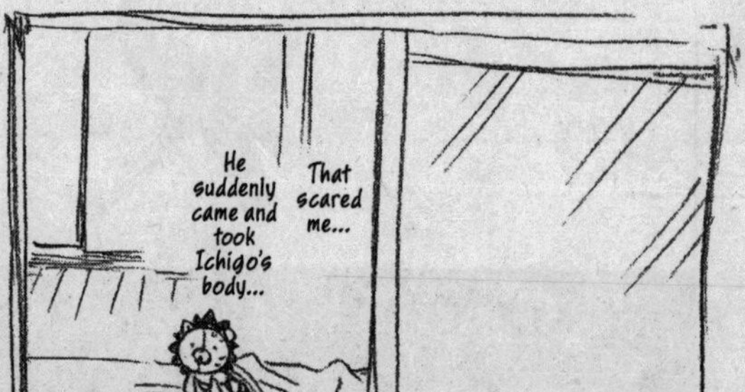
He suddenly came and took Ichigo's body...
That scared me...

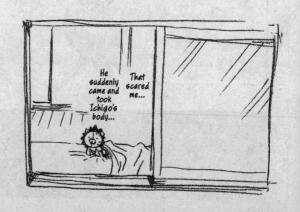

58. blank

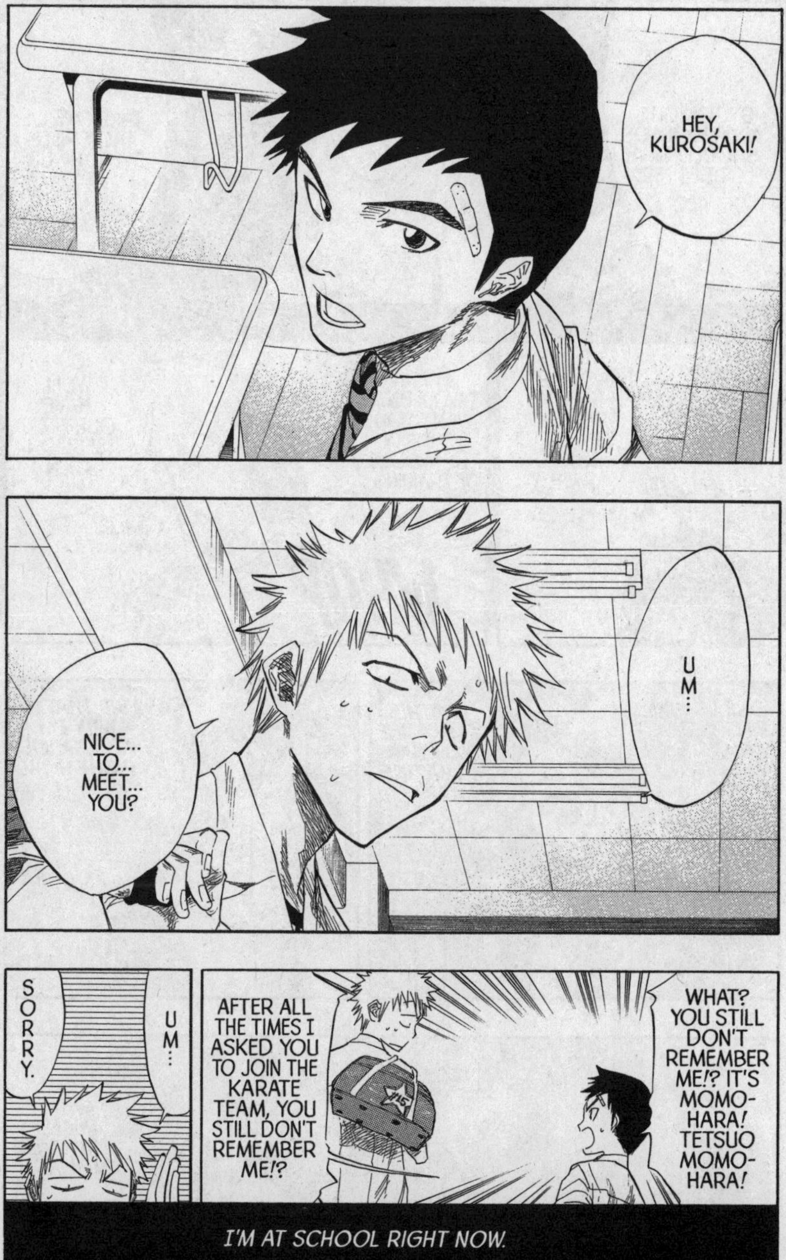
HEY, KUROSAKI!
UM...
NICE... TO... MEET... YOU?
WHAT? YOU STILL DON'T REMEMBER ME!? IT'S MOMO-HARA! TETSUO MOMO-HARA!
AFTER ALL THE TIMES I ASKED YOU TO JOIN THE KARATE TEAM, YOU STILL DON'T REMEMBER ME!?
UM...
SORRY.
I'M AT SCHOOL RIGHT NOW.

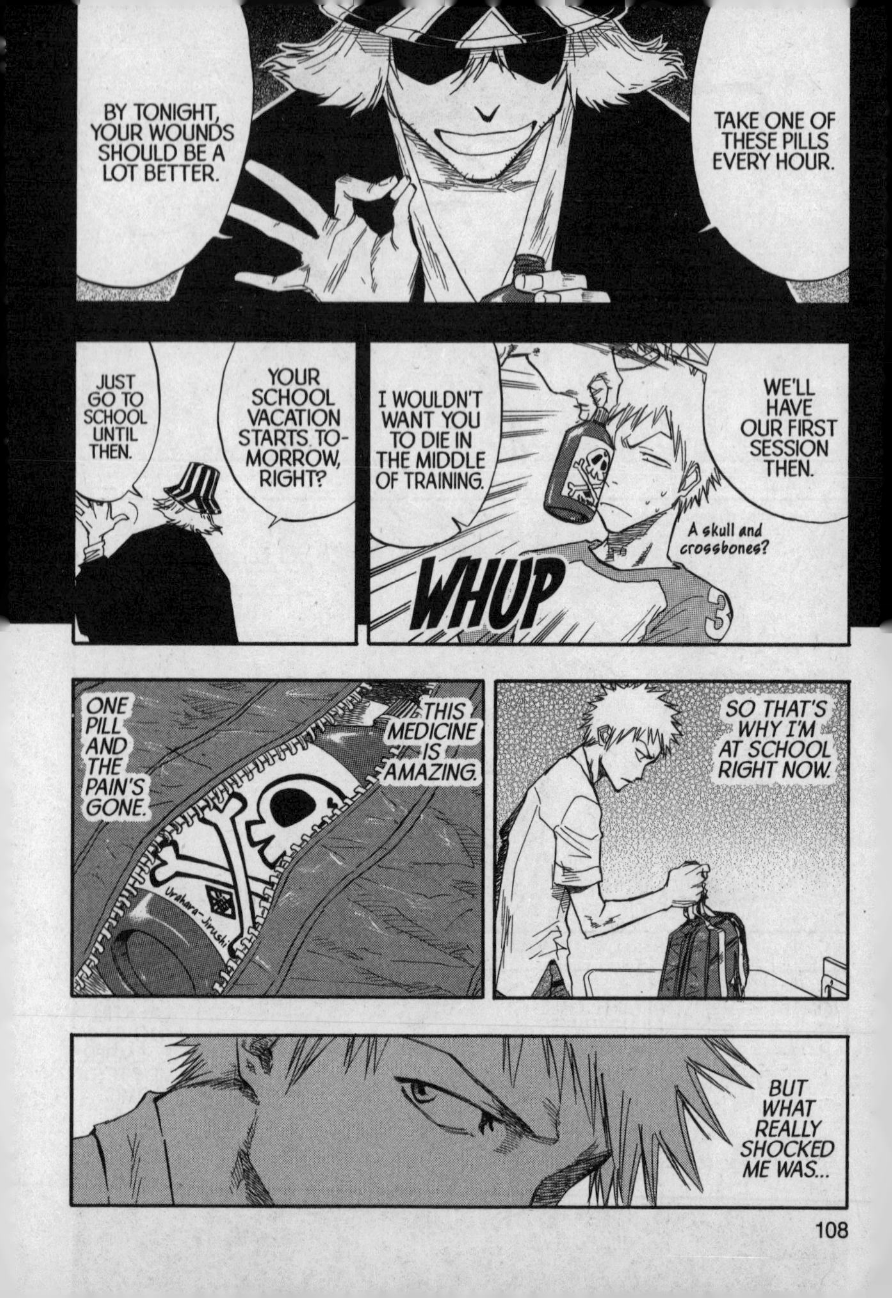

TAKE ONE OF THESE PILLS EVERY HOUR.
BY TONIGHT, YOUR WOUNDS SHOULD BE A LOT BETTER.
WE'LL HAVE OUR FIRST SESSION THEN.
A skull and crossbones?
WHUP
I WOULDN'T WANT YOU TO DIE IN THE MIDDLE OF TRAINING.
YOUR SCHOOL VACATION STARTS TO-MORROW, RIGHT?
JUST GO TO SCHOOL UNTIL THEN.
SO THAT'S WHY I'M AT SCHOOL RIGHT NOW.
THIS MEDICINE IS AMAZING.
ONE PILL AND THE PAIN'S GONE.
Urahara-Jirushi
BUT WHAT REALLY SHOCKED ME WAS...

READ THIS WAY

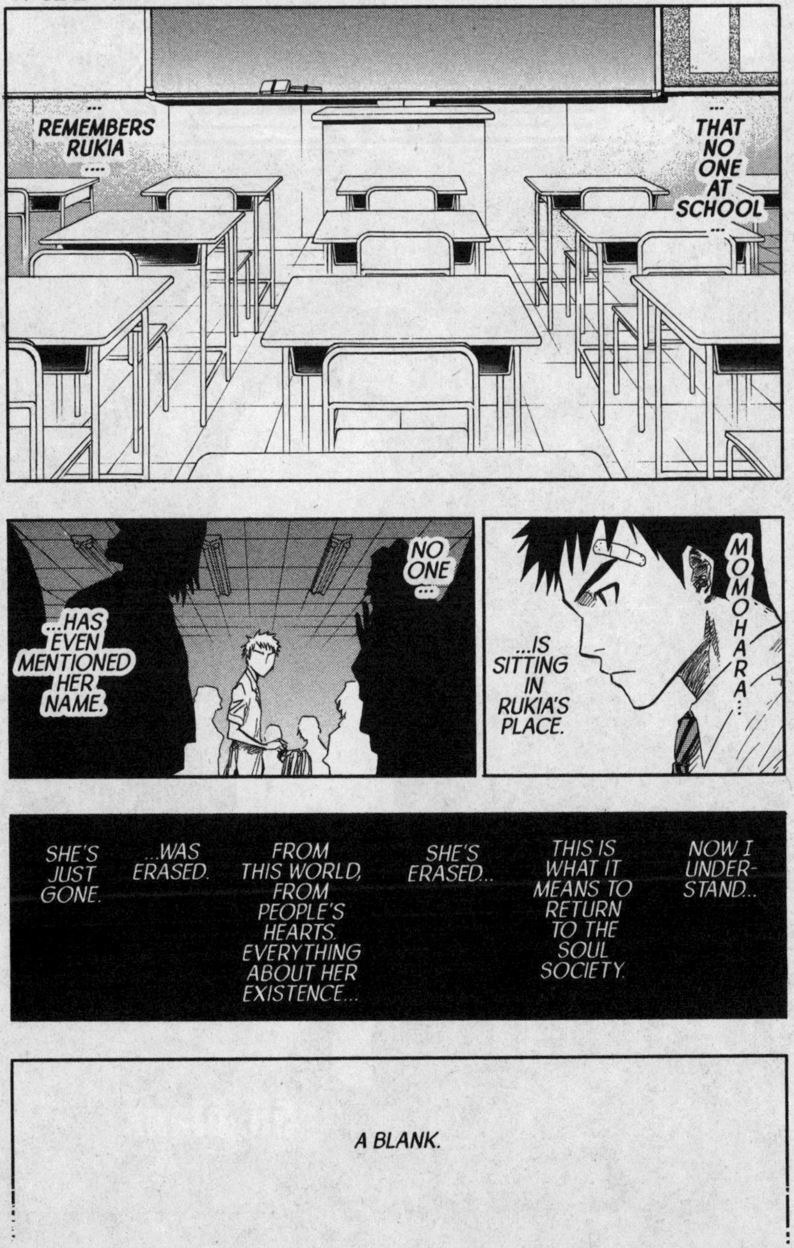
...THAT NO ONE AT SCHOOL...
...REMEMBERS RUKIA....
MOMOHARA...
...IS SITTING IN RUKIA'S PLACE.
NO ONE...
...HAS EVEN MENTIONED HER NAME.
NOW I UNDERSTAND...
THIS IS WHAT IT MEANS TO RETURN TO THE SOUL SOCIETY.
SHE'S ERASED...
FROM THIS WORLD, FROM PEOPLE'S HEARTS. EVERYTHING ABOUT HER EXISTENCE...
...WAS ERASED.
SHE'S JUST GONE.
A BLANK.

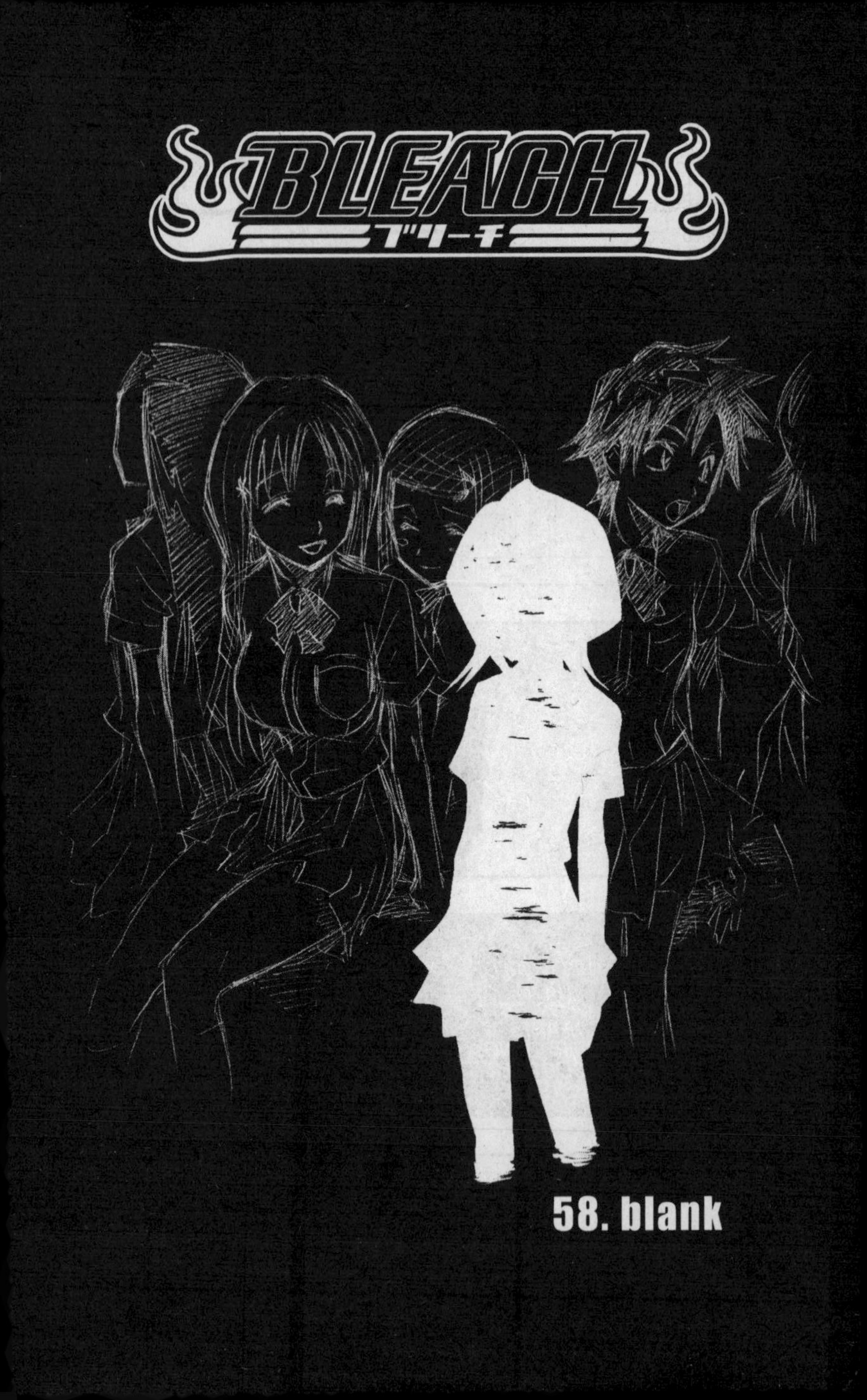
BLEACH
ブリーチ
58. blank

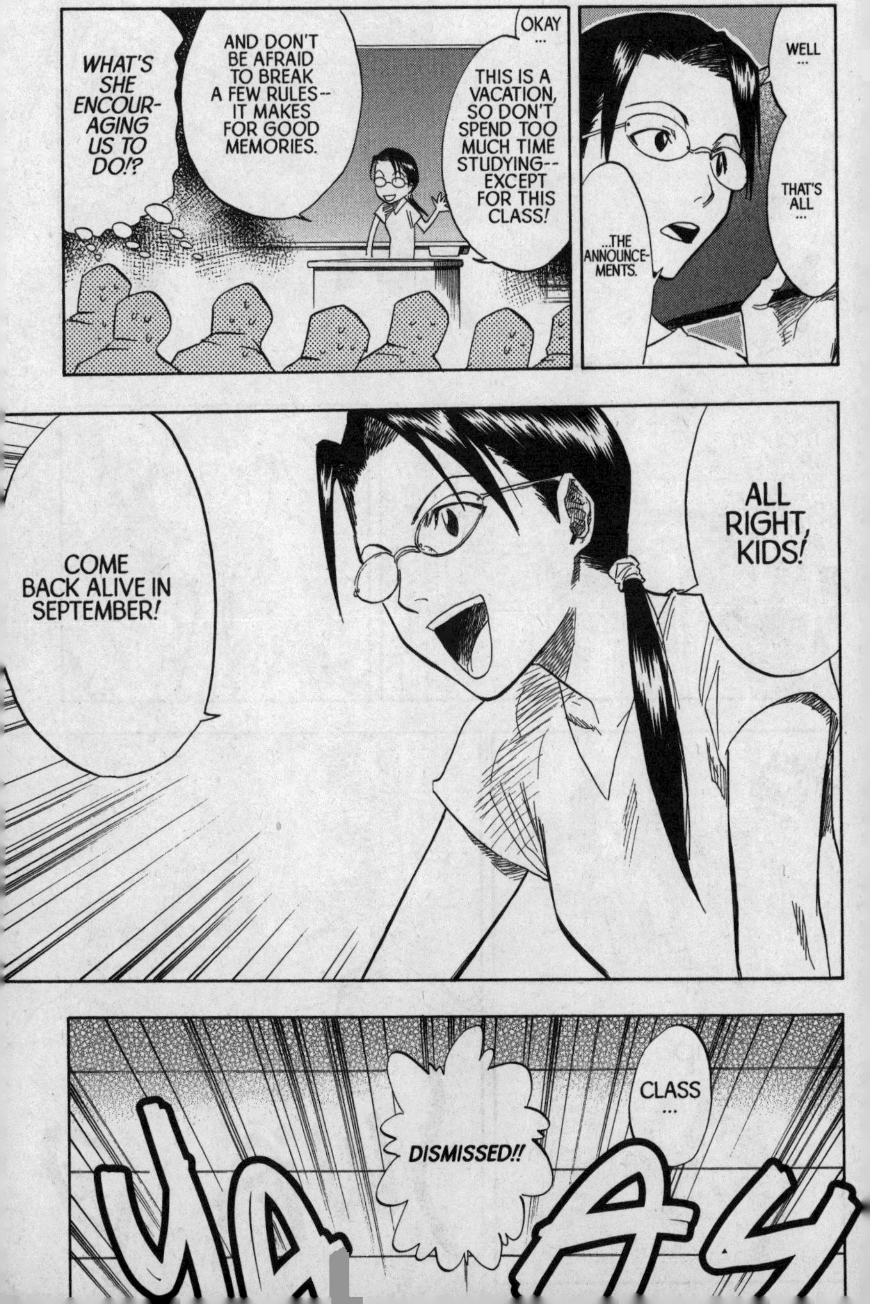
WELL ...
THAT'S ALL ...
...THE ANNOUNCEMENTS.
OKAY ...
THIS IS A VACATION, SO DON'T SPEND TOO MUCH TIME STUDYING-- EXCEPT FOR THIS CLASS!
AND DON'T BE AFRAID TO BREAK A FEW RULES-- IT MAKES FOR GOOD MEMORIES.
WHAT'S SHE ENCOURAGING US TO DO!?
ALL RIGHT, KIDS!
COME BACK ALIVE IN SEPTEMBER!
CLASS ...
DISMISSED!!

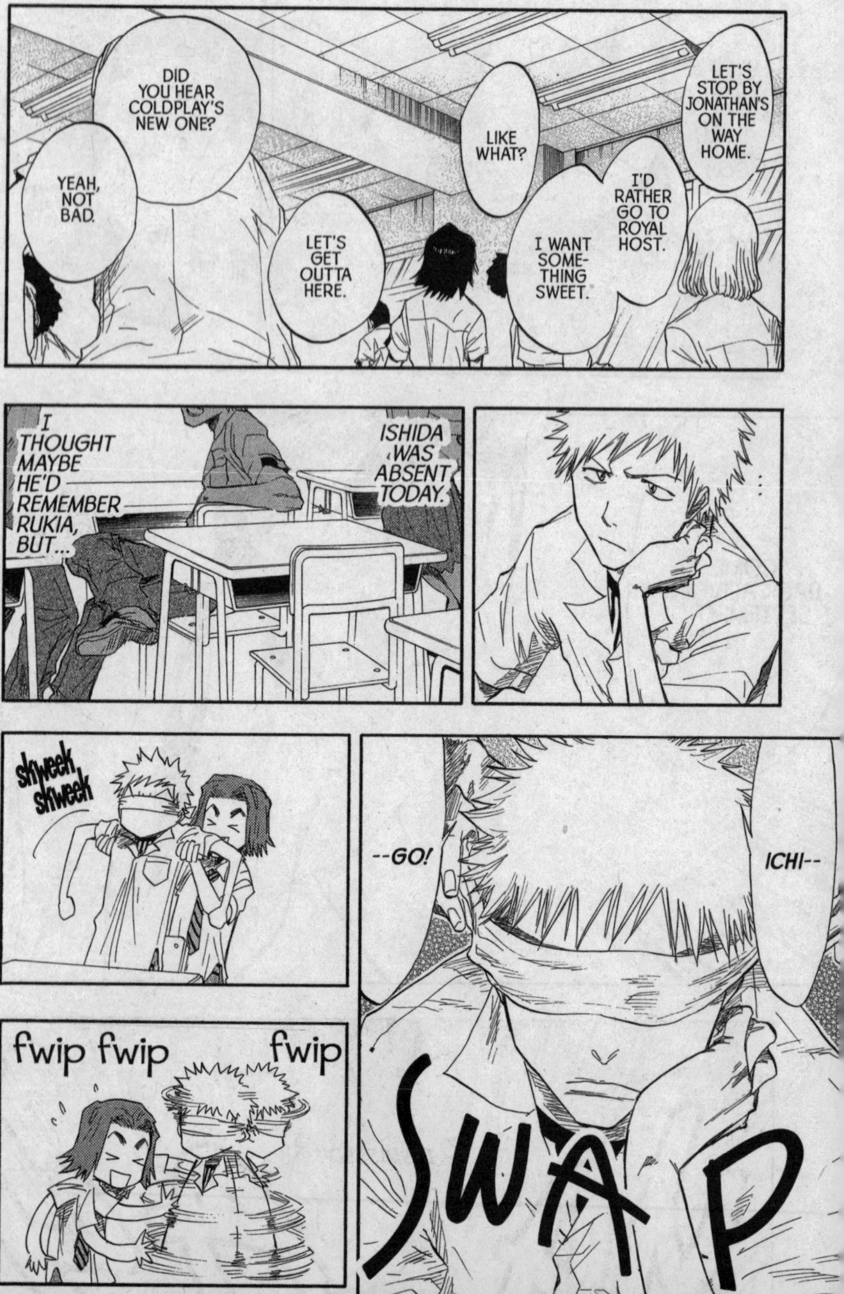

LET'S STOP BY JONATHAN'S ON THE WAY HOME.
I'D RATHER GO TO ROYAL HOST.
LIKE WHAT?
I WANT SOME-THING SWEET.
DID YOU HEAR COLDPLAY'S NEW ONE?
LET'S GET OUTTA HERE.
YEAH, NOT BAD.
...
ISHIDA WAS ABSENT TODAY.
I THOUGHT MAYBE HE'D REMEMBER RUKIA, BUT...
ICHI--
--GO!
SWAP
skweek skweek
fwip fwip fwip

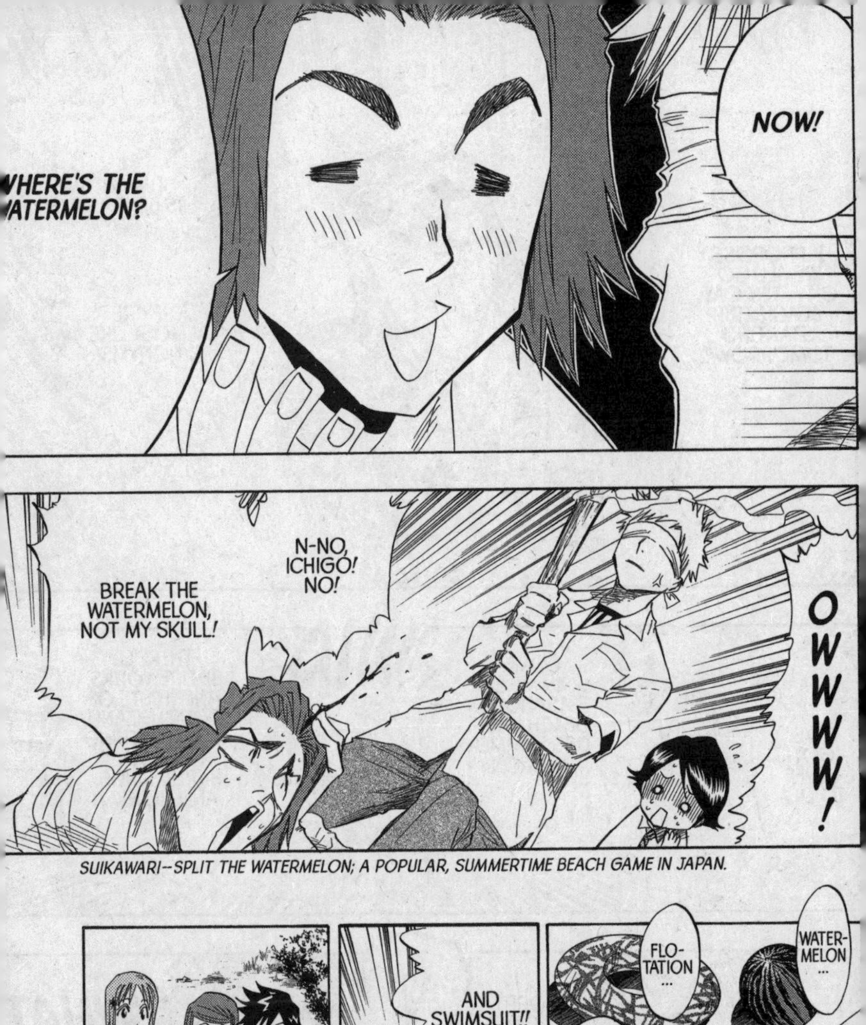
NOW!
WHERE'S THE WATERMELON?
OWWWWW!
N-NO, ICHIGO! NO!
BREAK THE WATERMELON, NOT MY SKULL!

SUIKAWARI--SPLIT THE WATERMELON; A POPULAR, SUMMERTIME BEACH GAME IN JAPAN.

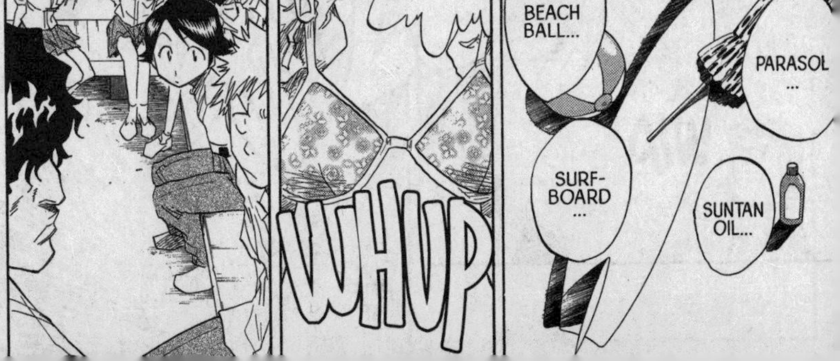
WATER-MELON...
FLO-TATION...
BEACH BALL...
PARASOL...
SURF-BOARD...
SUNTAN OIL...
AND SWIMSUIT!!
WHUP

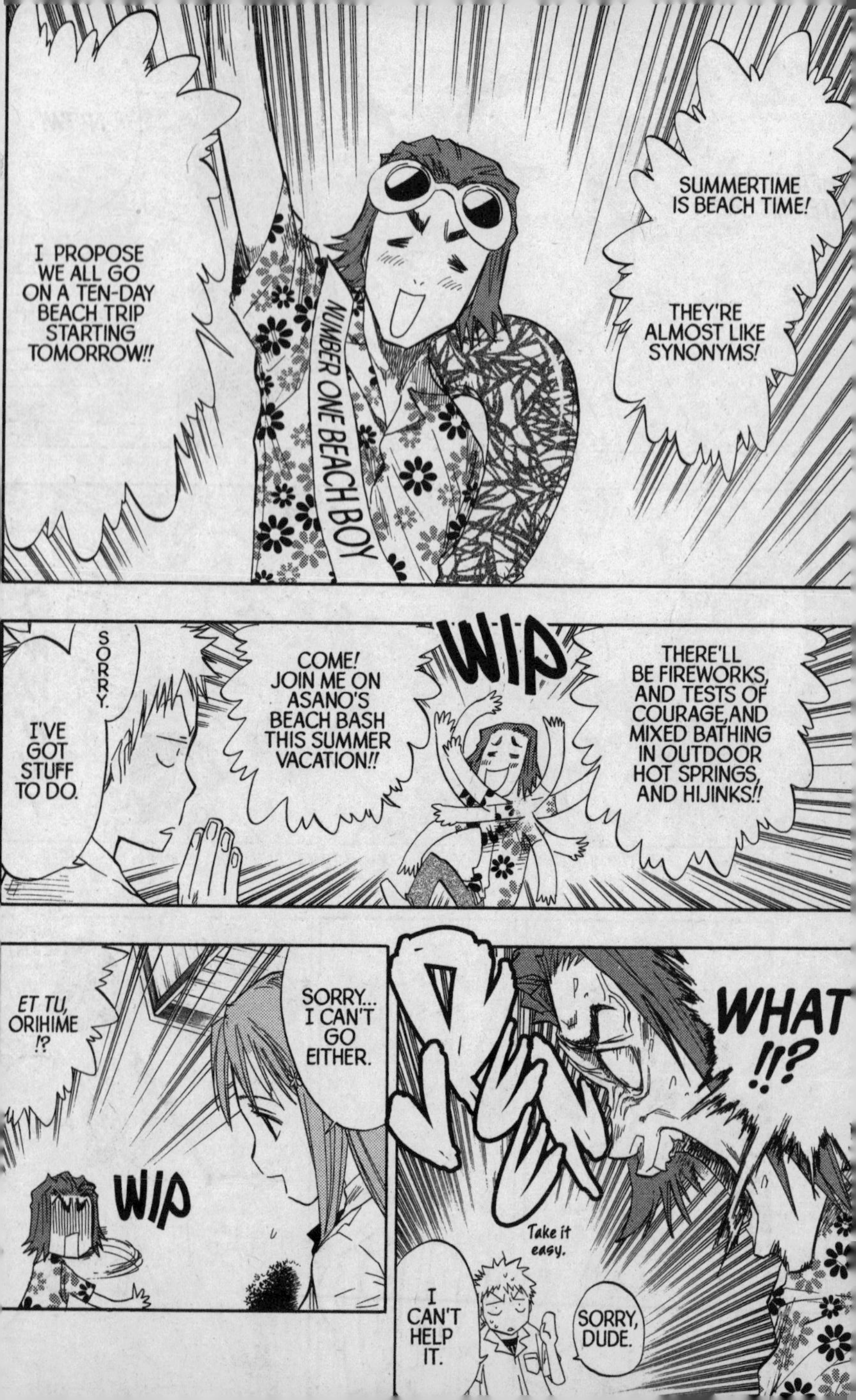
SUMMERTIME IS BEACH TIME!
THEY'RE ALMOST LIKE SYNONYMS!
NUMBER ONE BEACH BOY
I PROPOSE WE ALL GO ON A TEN-DAY BEACH TRIP STARTING TOMORROW!!
THERE'LL BE FIREWORKS, AND TESTS OF COURAGE, AND MIXED BATHING IN OUTDOOR HOT SPRINGS, AND HIJINKS!!
WIP
COME! JOIN ME ON ASANO'S BEACH BASH THIS SUMMER VACATION!!
SORRY.
I'VE GOT STUFF TO DO.
WHAT!!?
Take it easy.
SORRY, DUDE.
I CAN'T HELP IT.
SORRY... I CAN'T GO EITHER.
ET TU, ORIHIME!?
WIP

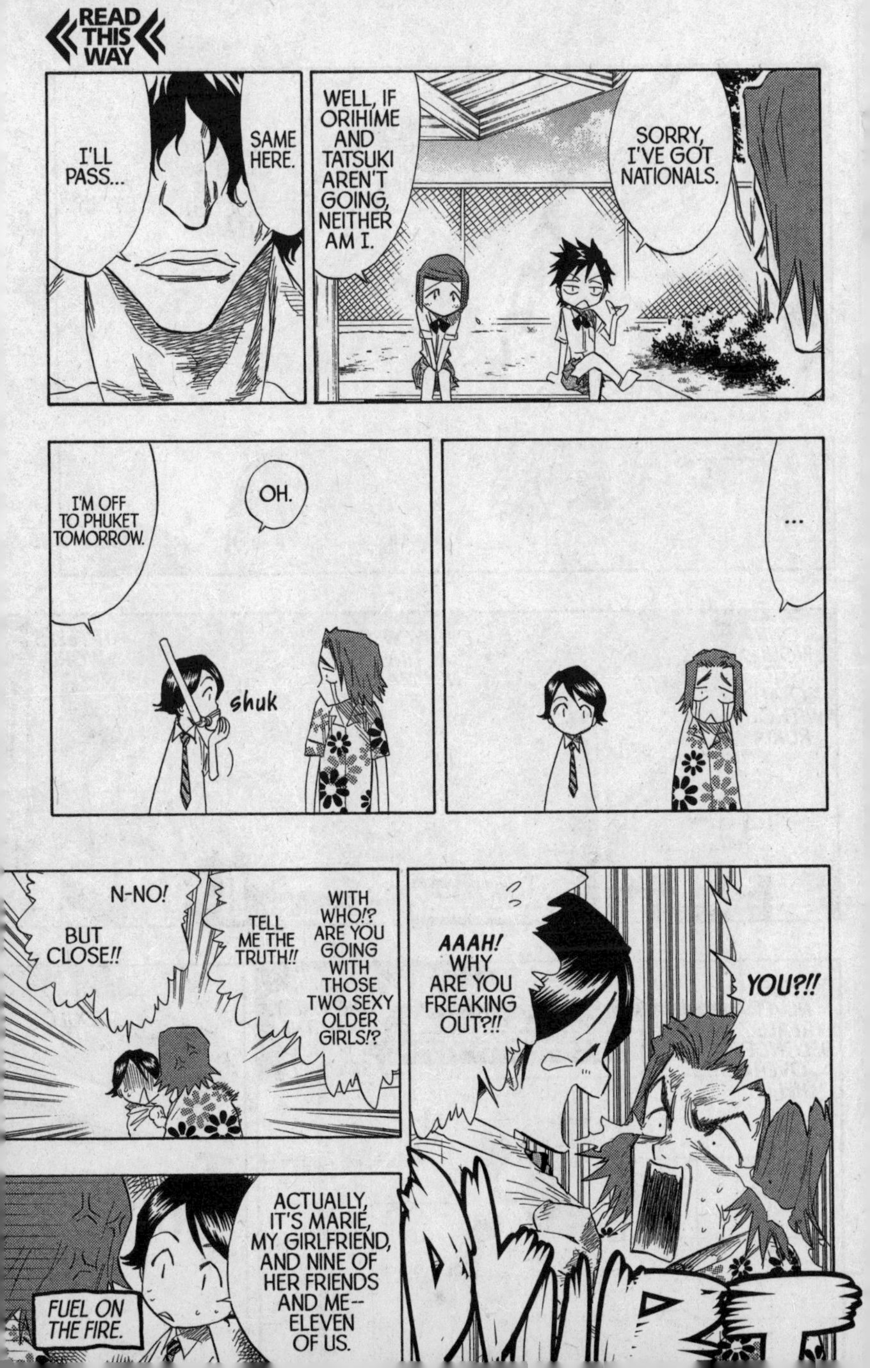
READ THIS WAY
SORRY, I'VE GOT NATIONALS.
WELL, IF ORIHIME AND TATSUKI AREN'T GOING, NEITHER AM I.
SAME HERE.
I'LL PASS...
...
OH.
I'M OFF TO PHUKET TOMORROW.
shuk
YOU?!!
AAAH! WHY ARE YOU FREAKING OUT?!!
WITH WHO!? ARE YOU GOING WITH THOSE TWO SEXY OLDER GIRLS!?
TELL ME THE TRUTH!!
N-NO! BUT CLOSE!!
ACTUALLY, IT'S MARIE, MY GIRLFRIEND, AND NINE OF HER FRIENDS AND ME-- ELEVEN OF US.
FUEL ON THE FIRE.

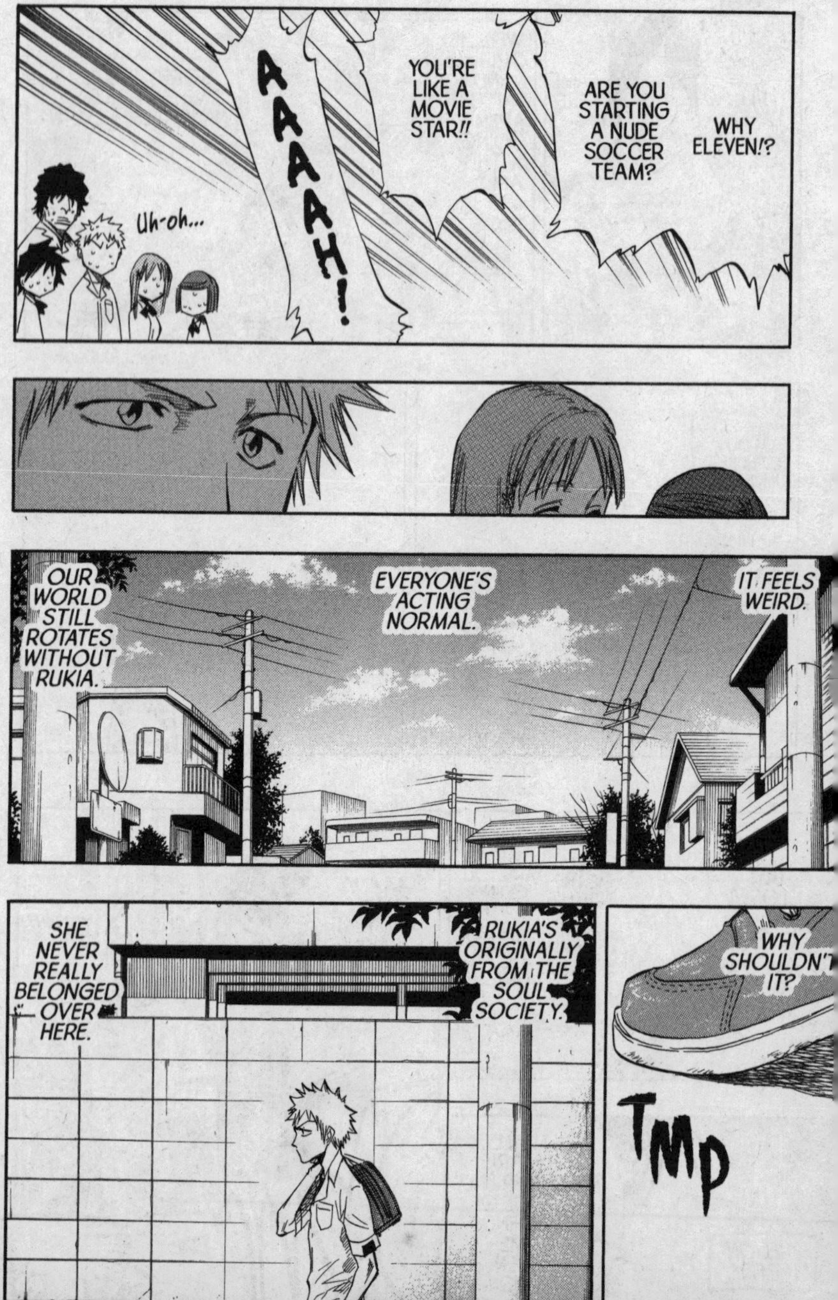

WHY ELEVEN!?
ARE YOU STARTING A NUDE SOCCER TEAM?
YOU'RE LIKE A MOVIE STAR!!
AAAAH!!
Uh-oh...
IT FEELS WEIRD.
EVERYONE'S ACTING NORMAL.
OUR WORLD STILL ROTATES WITHOUT RUKIA.
WHY SHOULDN'T IT?
TMP
RUKIA'S ORIGINALLY FROM THE SOUL SOCIETY.
SHE NEVER REALLY BELONGED OVER HERE.

READ THIS WAY

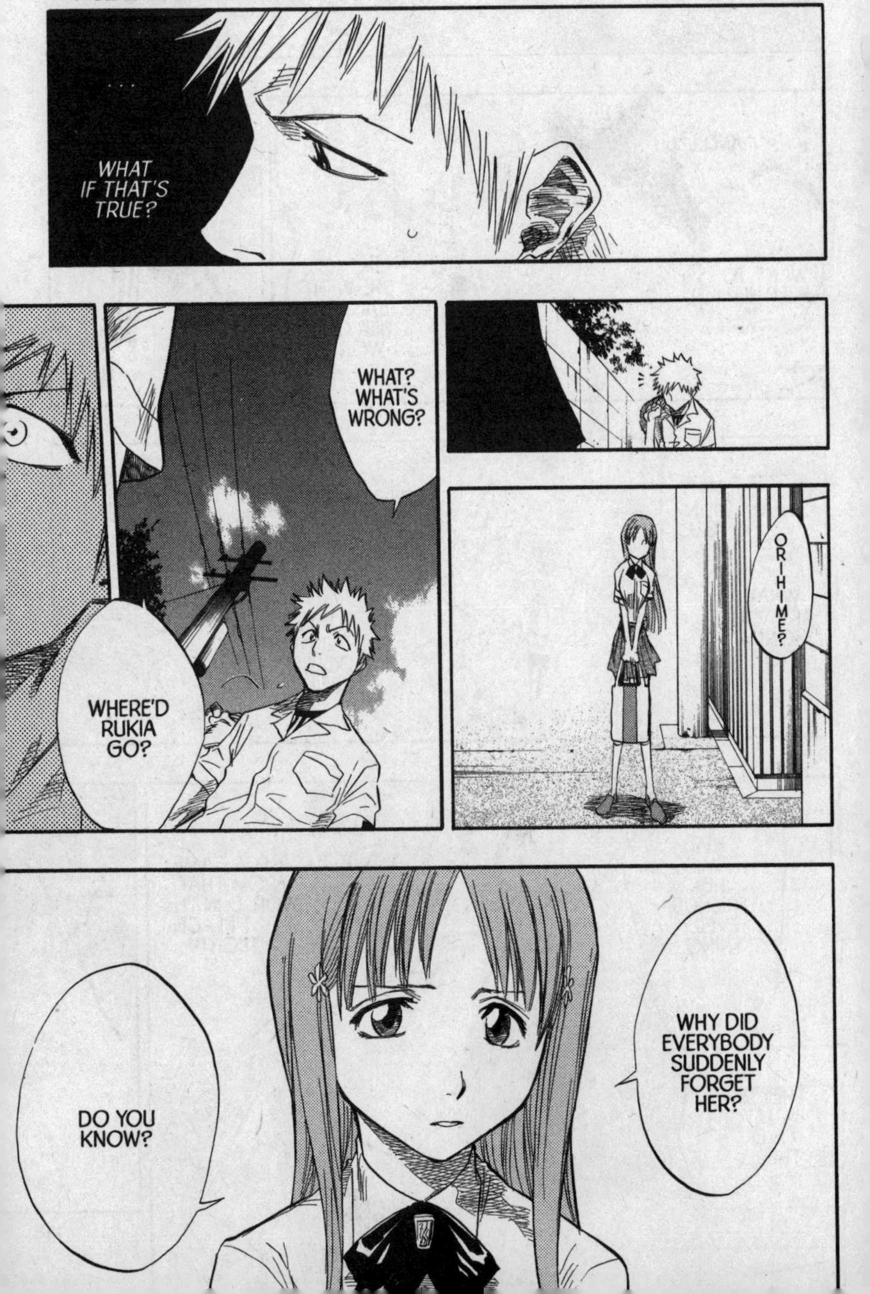
...
WHAT IF THAT'S TRUE?
ORIHIME?
WHAT? WHAT'S WRONG?
WHERE'D RUKIA GO?
WHY DID EVERYBODY SUDDENLY FORGET HER?
DO YOU KNOW?

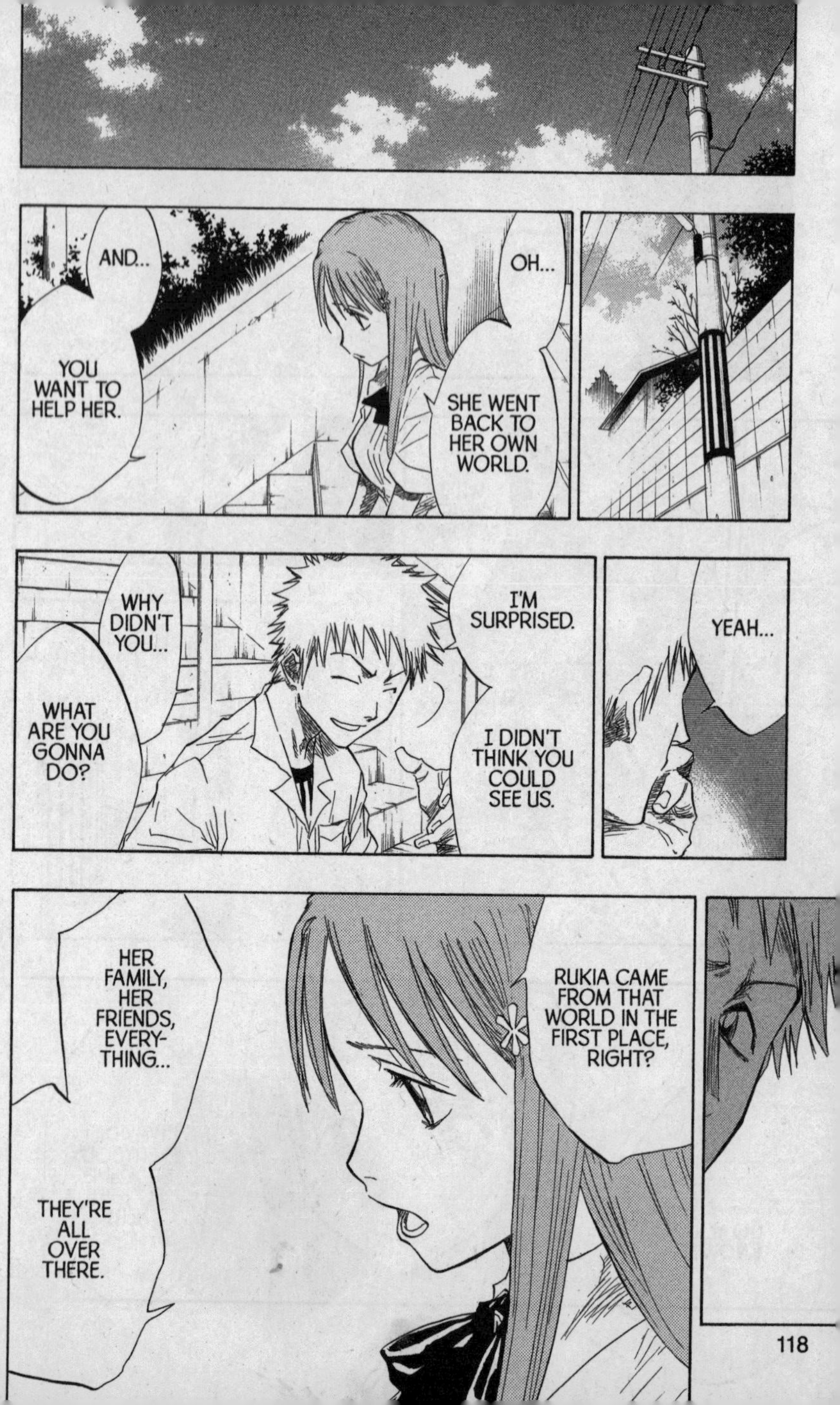
OH...
SHE WENT BACK TO HER OWN WORLD.
AND...
YOU WANT TO HELP HER.
YEAH...
I'M SURPRISED.
I DIDN'T THINK YOU COULD SEE US.
WHY DIDN'T YOU...
WHAT ARE YOU GONNA DO?
RUKIA CAME FROM THAT WORLD IN THE FIRST PLACE, RIGHT?
HER FAMILY, HER FRIENDS, EVERY-THING...
THEY'RE ALL OVER THERE.

READ THIS WAY

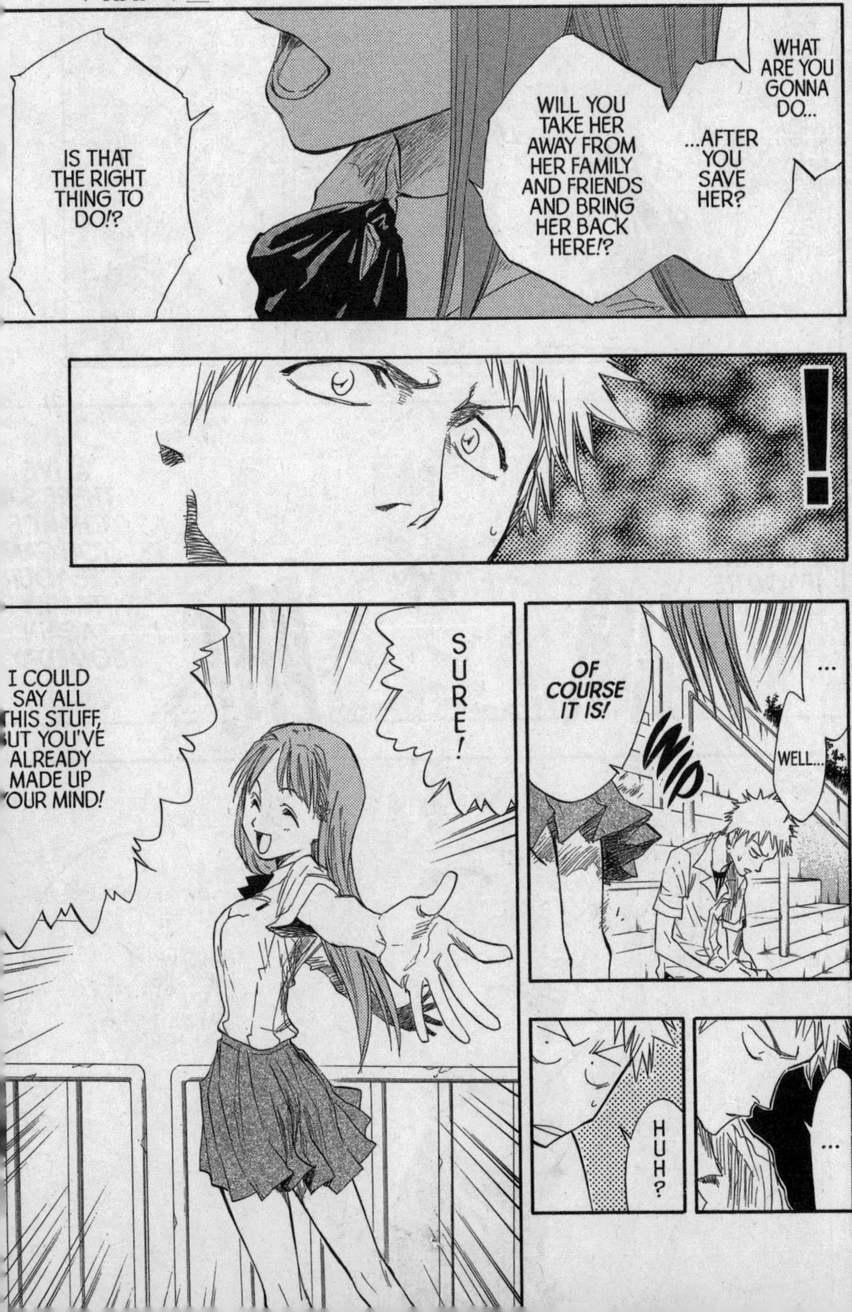
WHAT ARE YOU GONNA DO...
...AFTER YOU SAVE HER?
WILL YOU TAKE HER AWAY FROM HER FAMILY AND FRIENDS AND BRING HER BACK HERE!?
IS THAT THE RIGHT THING TO DO!?
!
...
WELL...
OF COURSE IT IS!
WIP
SURE!
I COULD SAY ALL THIS STUFF, UT YOU'VE ALREADY MADE UP OUR MIND!
...
HUH?

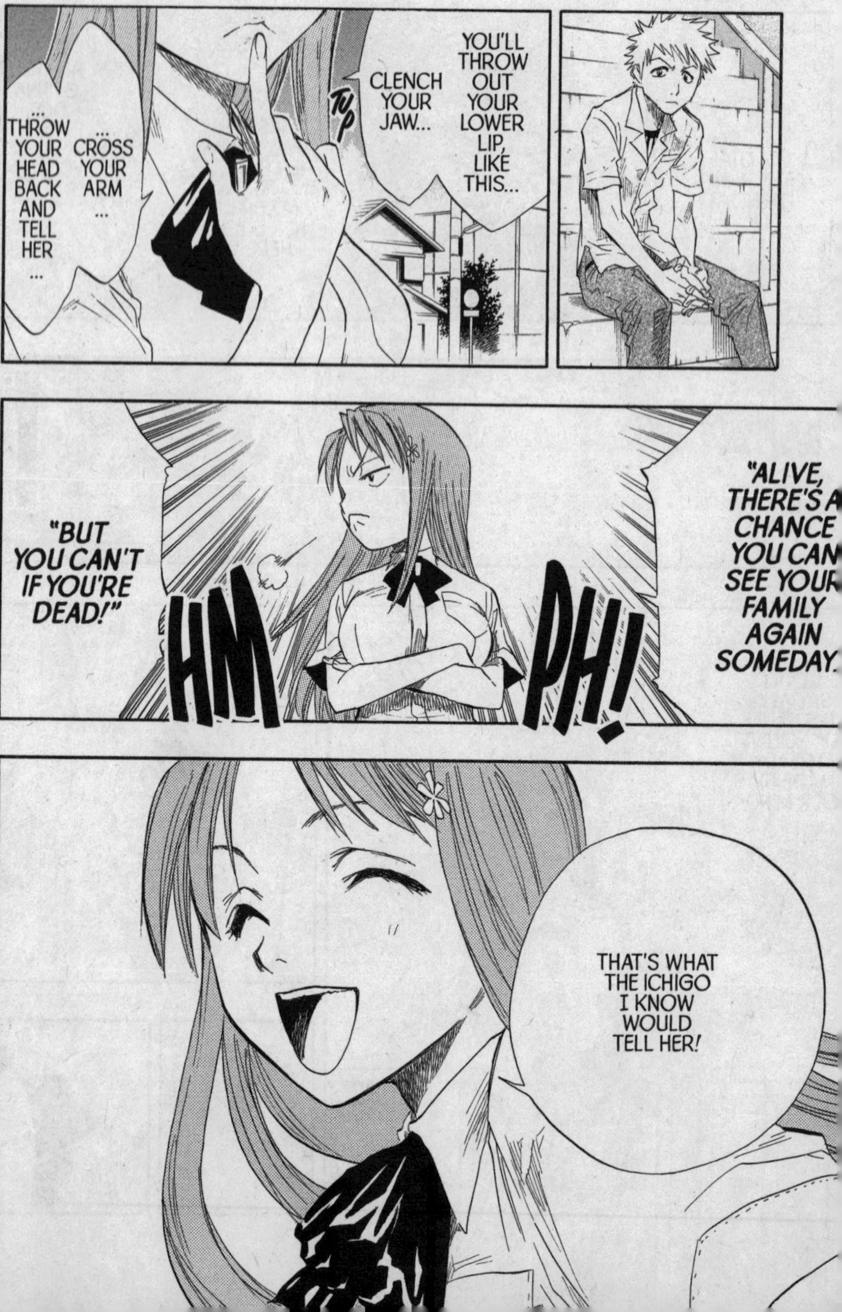
YOU'LL THROW OUT YOUR LOWER LIP, LIKE THIS...
CLENCH YOUR JAW...
TYP
...CROSS YOUR ARM...
...THROW YOUR HEAD BACK AND TELL HER...
"ALIVE, THERE'S A CHANCE YOU CAN SEE YOUR FAMILY AGAIN SOMEDAY.
HMPH!
"BUT YOU CAN'T IF YOU'RE DEAD!"
THAT'S WHAT THE ICHIGO I KNOW WOULD TELL HER!

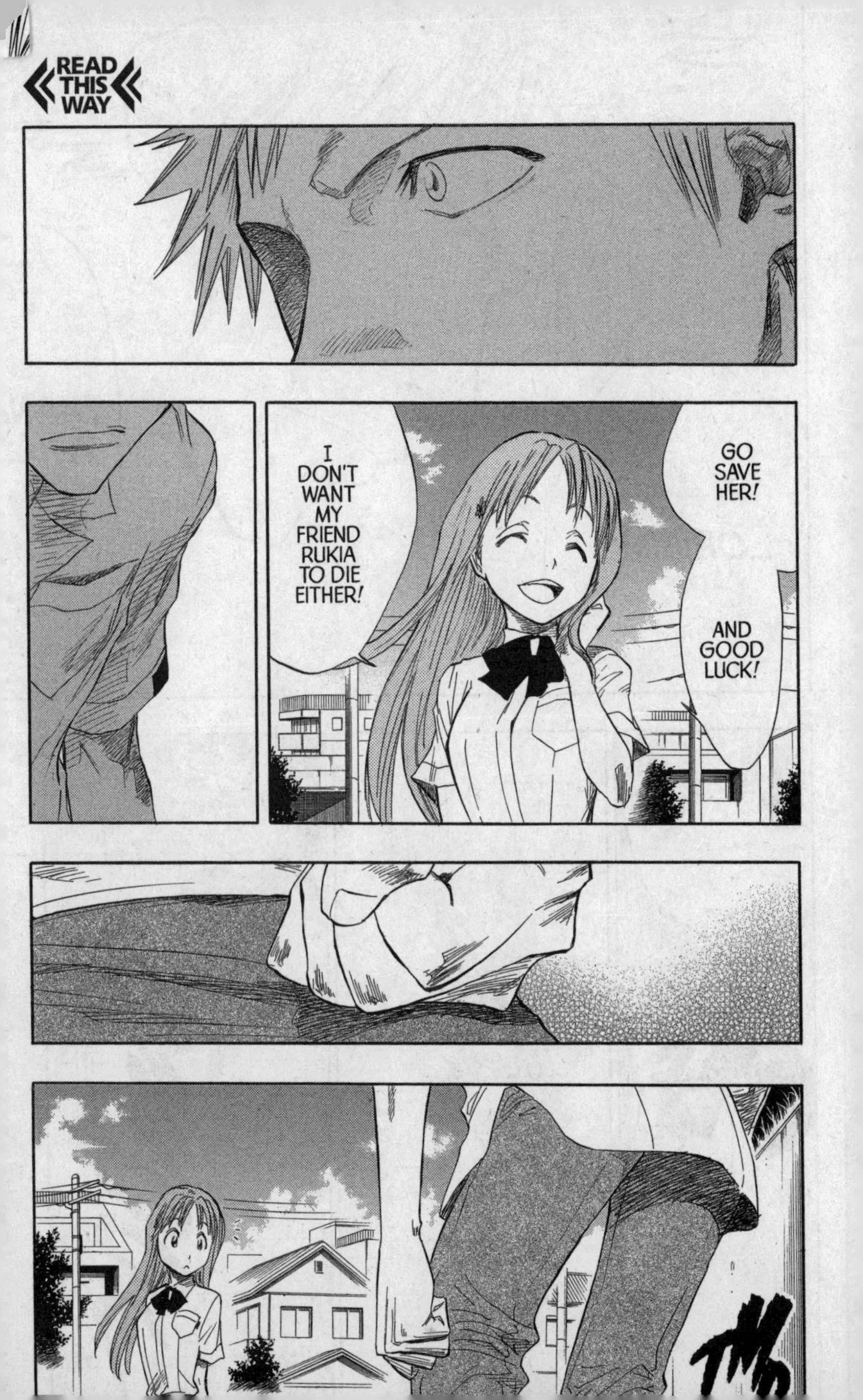
READ THIS WAY
GO SAVE HER!
AND GOOD LUCK!
I DON'T WANT MY FRIEND RUKIA TO DIE EITHER!

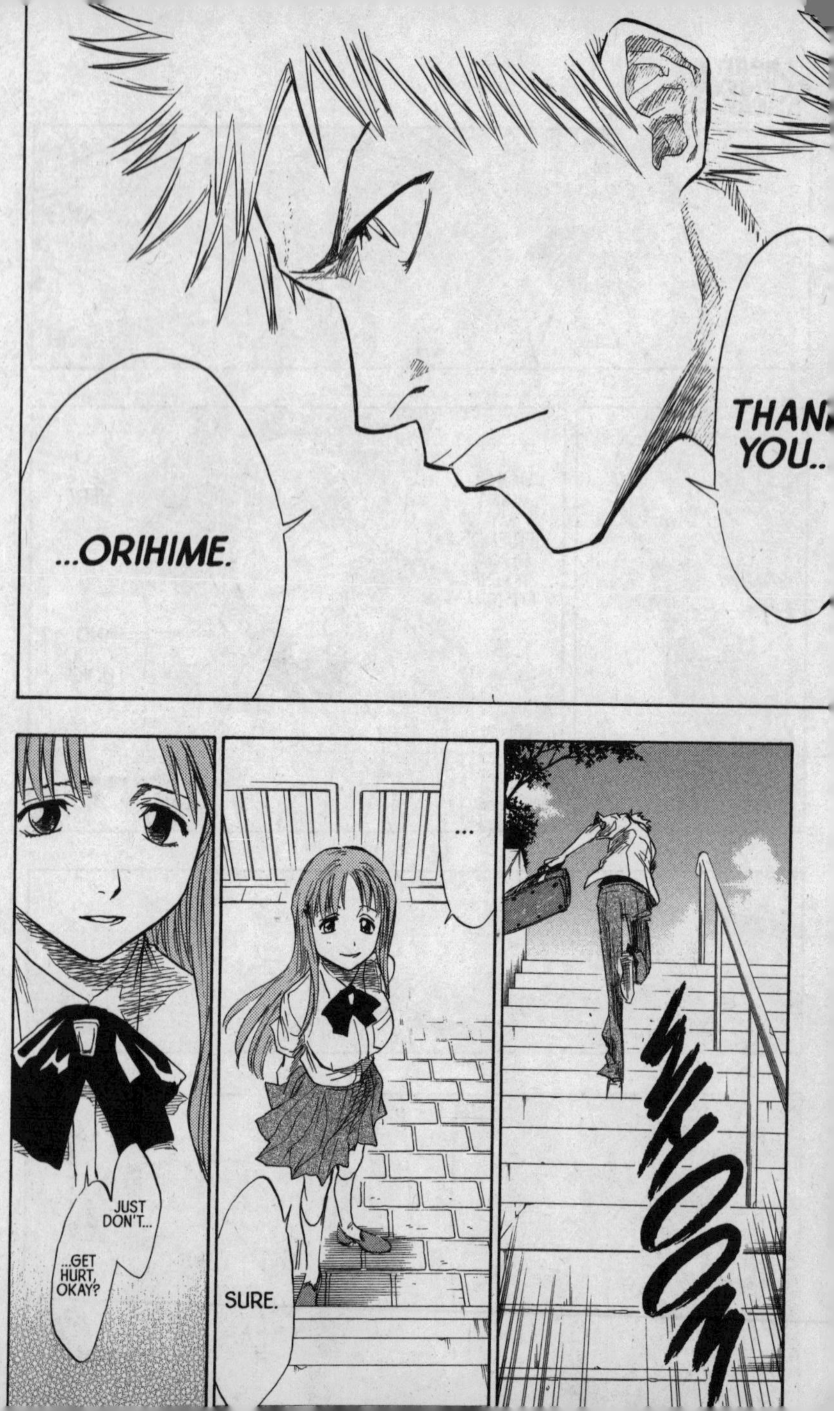
THAN
YOU..
...ORIHIME.
WHOOM
...
SURE.
JUST DON'T...
...GET HURT, OKAY?

I WON'T LET HIM.

NO.

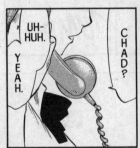

UH-HUH.

YEAH.

CHAD?

UH-HUH.

I'VE MADE UP MY MIND.

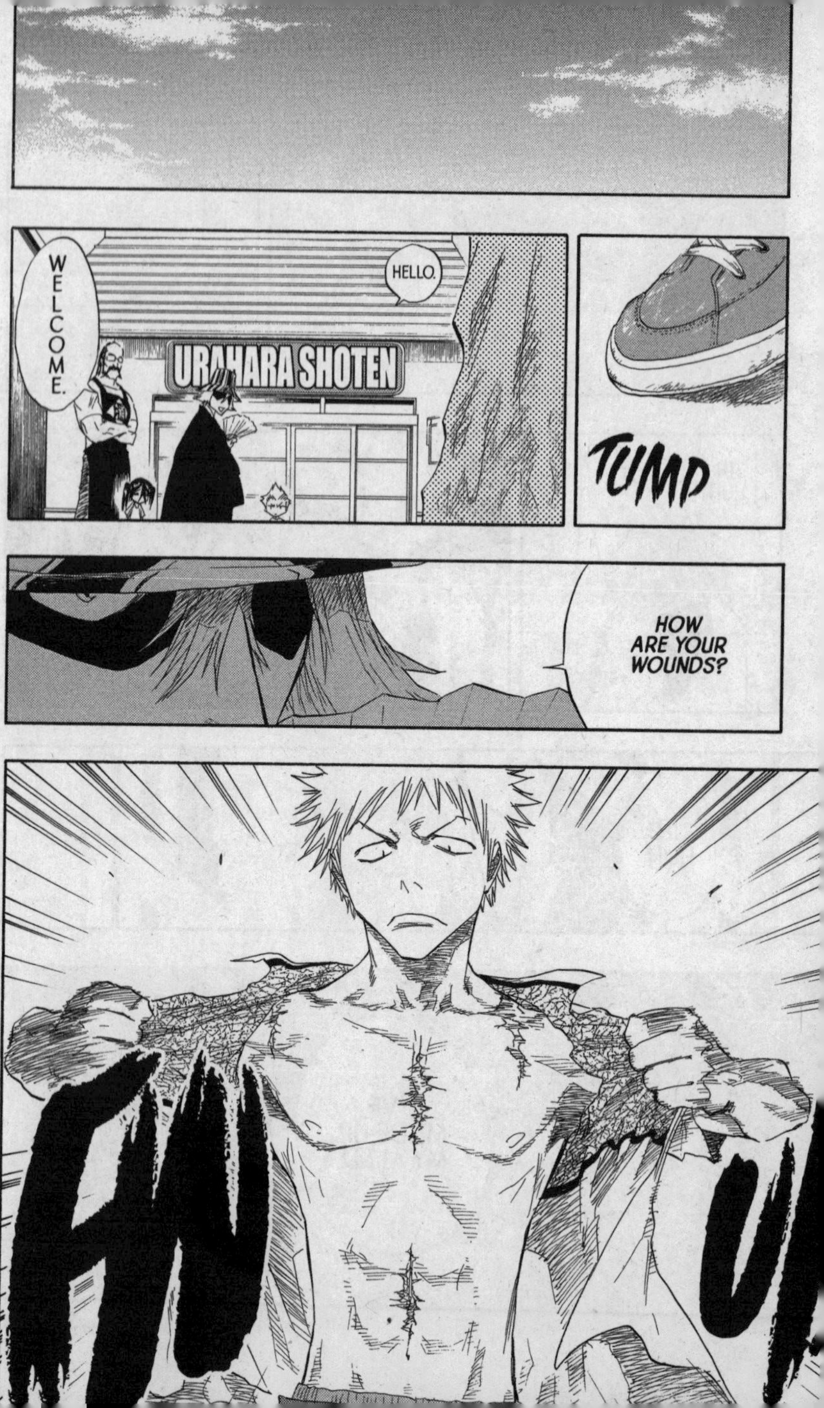
TUMP
HELLO.
WELCOME.
URAHARA SHOTEN
HOW ARE YOUR WOUNDS?

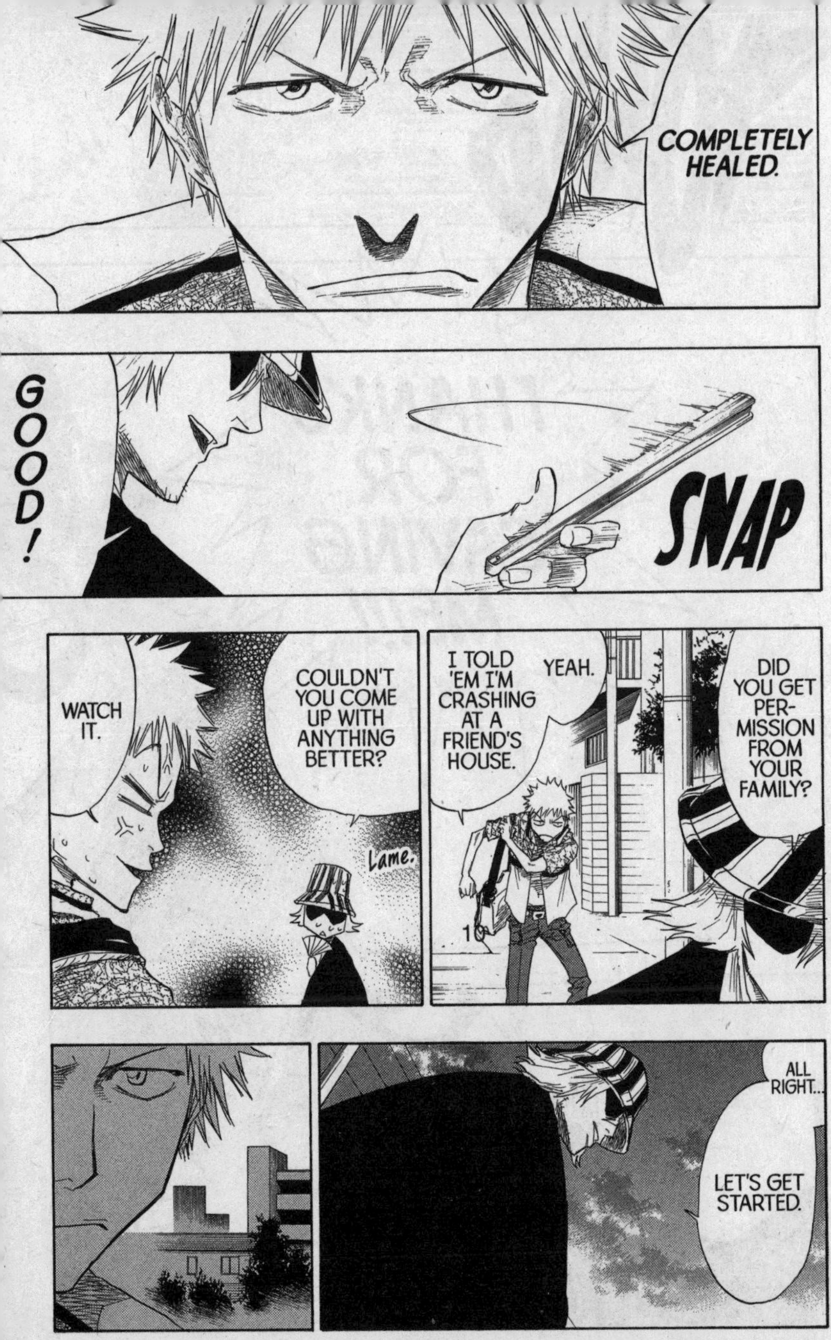
COMPLETELY HEALED.
GOOD!
SNAP
DID YOU GET PER-MISSION FROM YOUR FAMILY?
YEAH.
I TOLD 'EM I'M CRASHING AT A FRIEND'S HOUSE.
COULDN'T YOU COME UP WITH ANYTHING BETTER?
Lame.
WATCH IT.
ALL RIGHT...
LET'S GET STARTED.

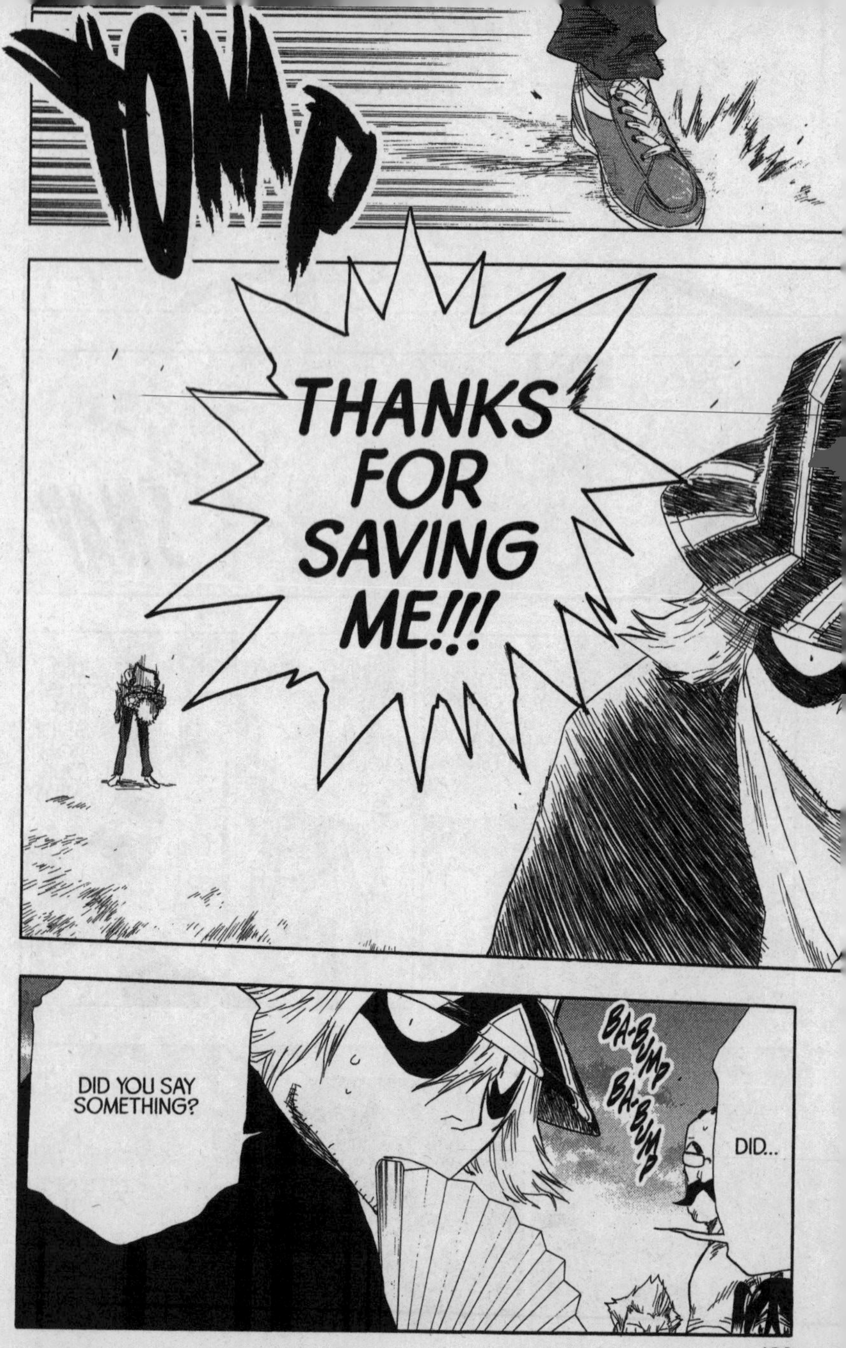

TOMP
THANKS FOR SAVING ME!!!
DID...
BA-BUMP BA-BUMP
DID YOU SAY SOMETHING?

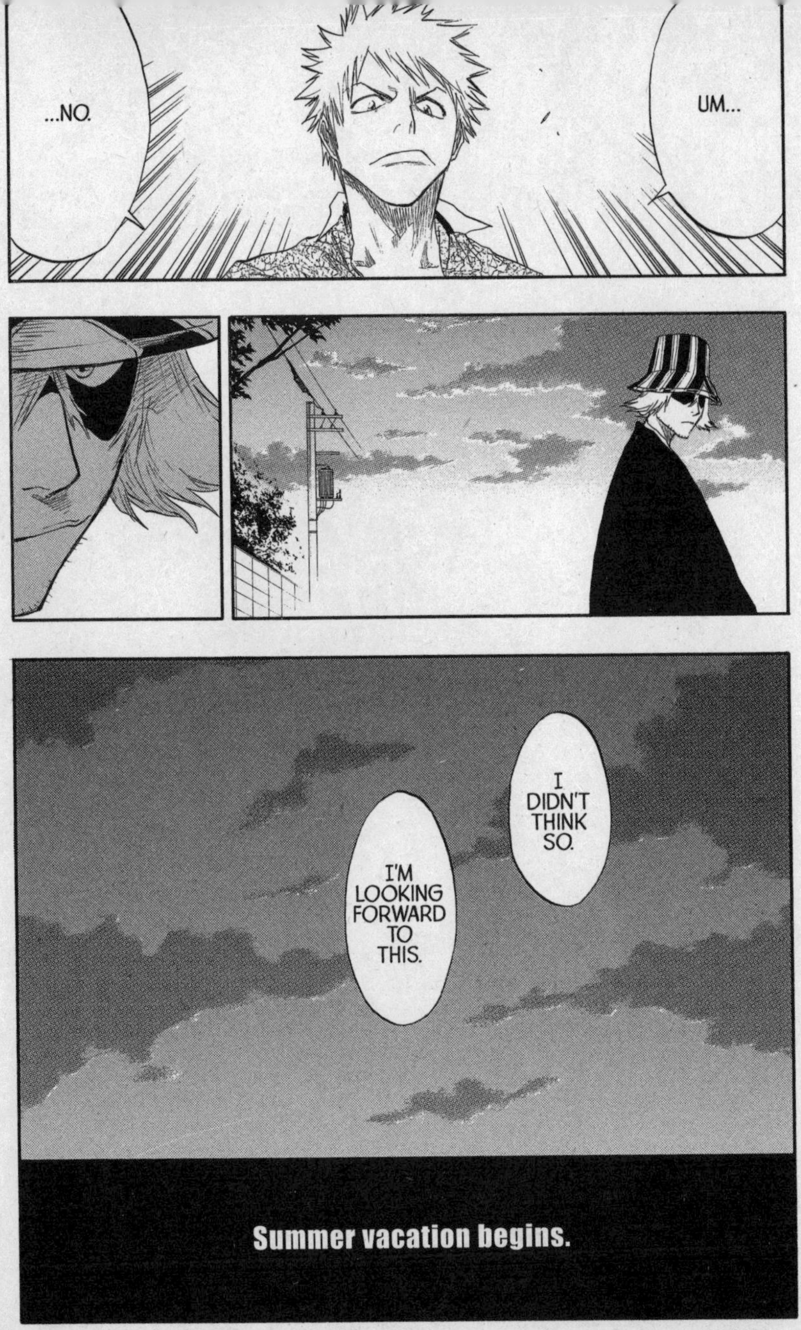
UM...
...NO.
I DIDN'T THINK SO.
I'M LOOKING FORWARD TO THIS.
Summer vacation begins.

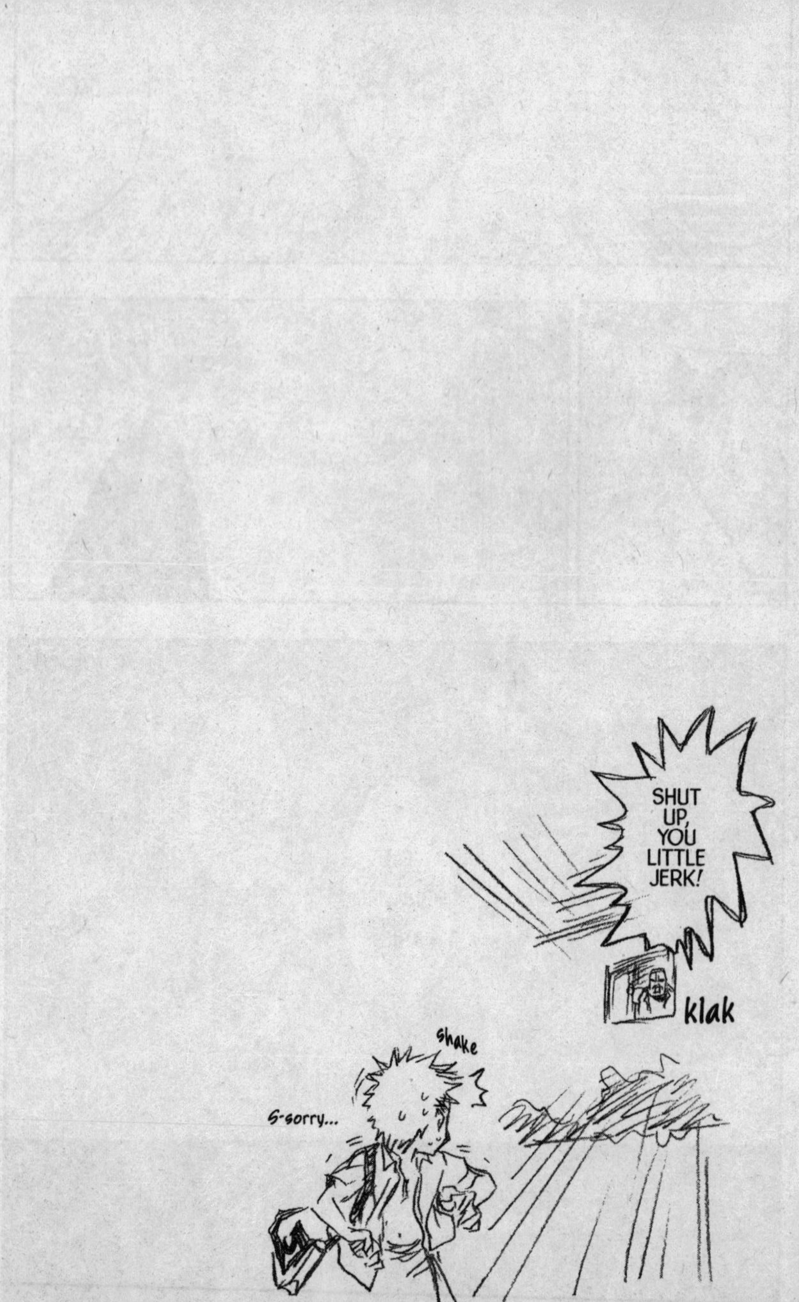
SHUT UP, YOU LITTLE JERK!
klak
shake
S-sorry...

59. Lesson 1: One Strike! + Jailed at Home

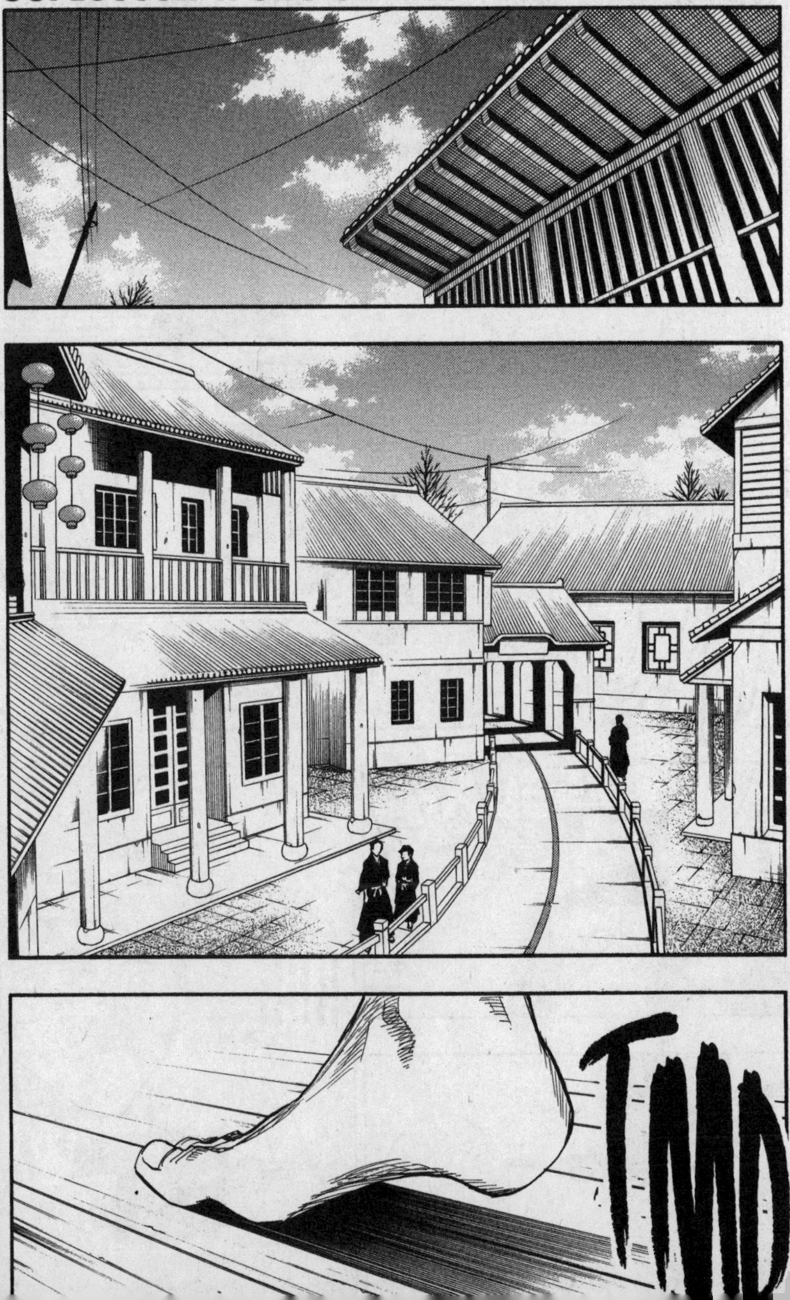
TMD

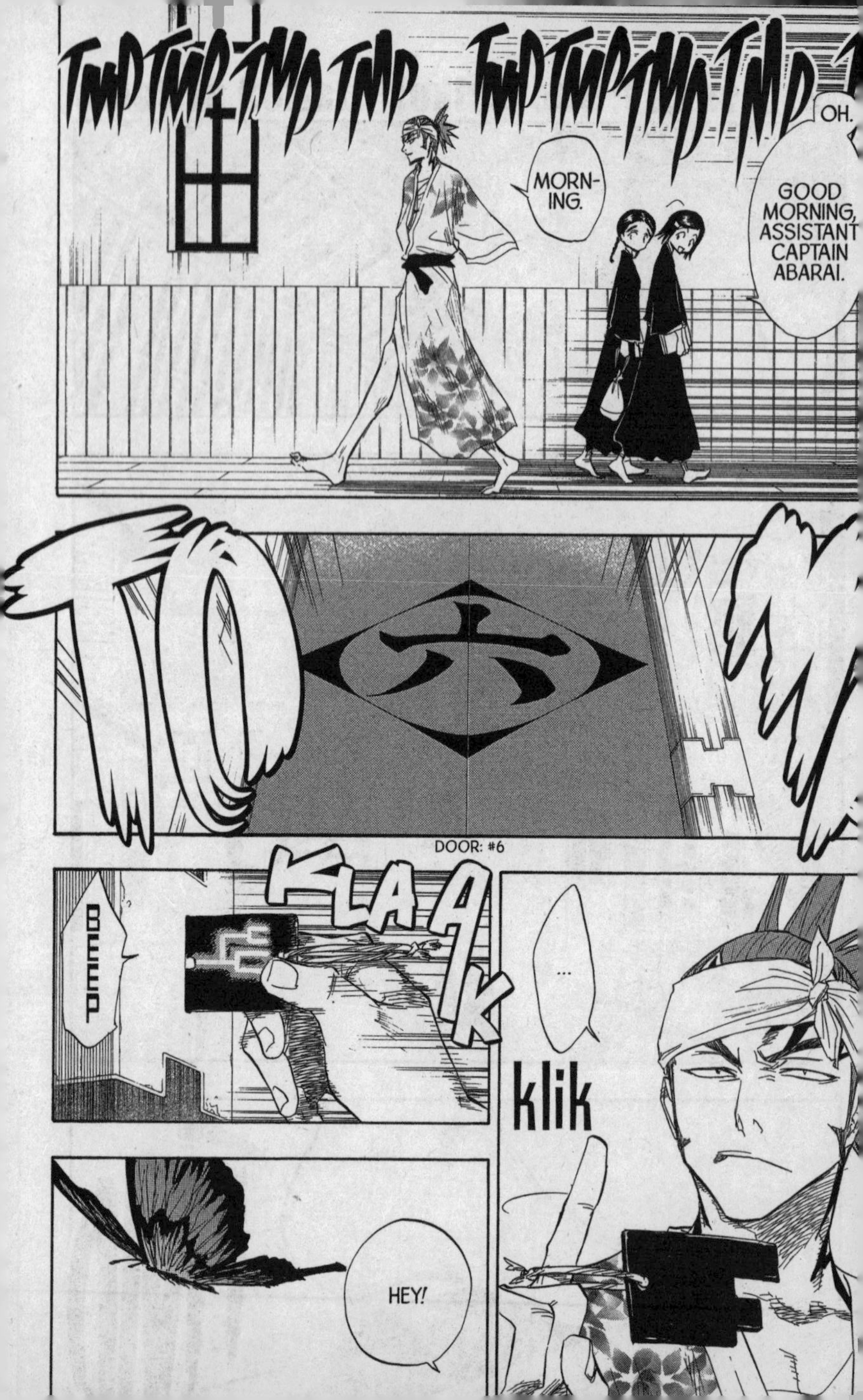
TMP TMP TMP TMP
TMP TMP TMP TMP TMP
OH.
GOOD MORNING, ASSISTANT CAPTAIN ABARAI.
MORN-ING.
DOOR: #6
...
klik
KLAAK
BEEEP
HEY!

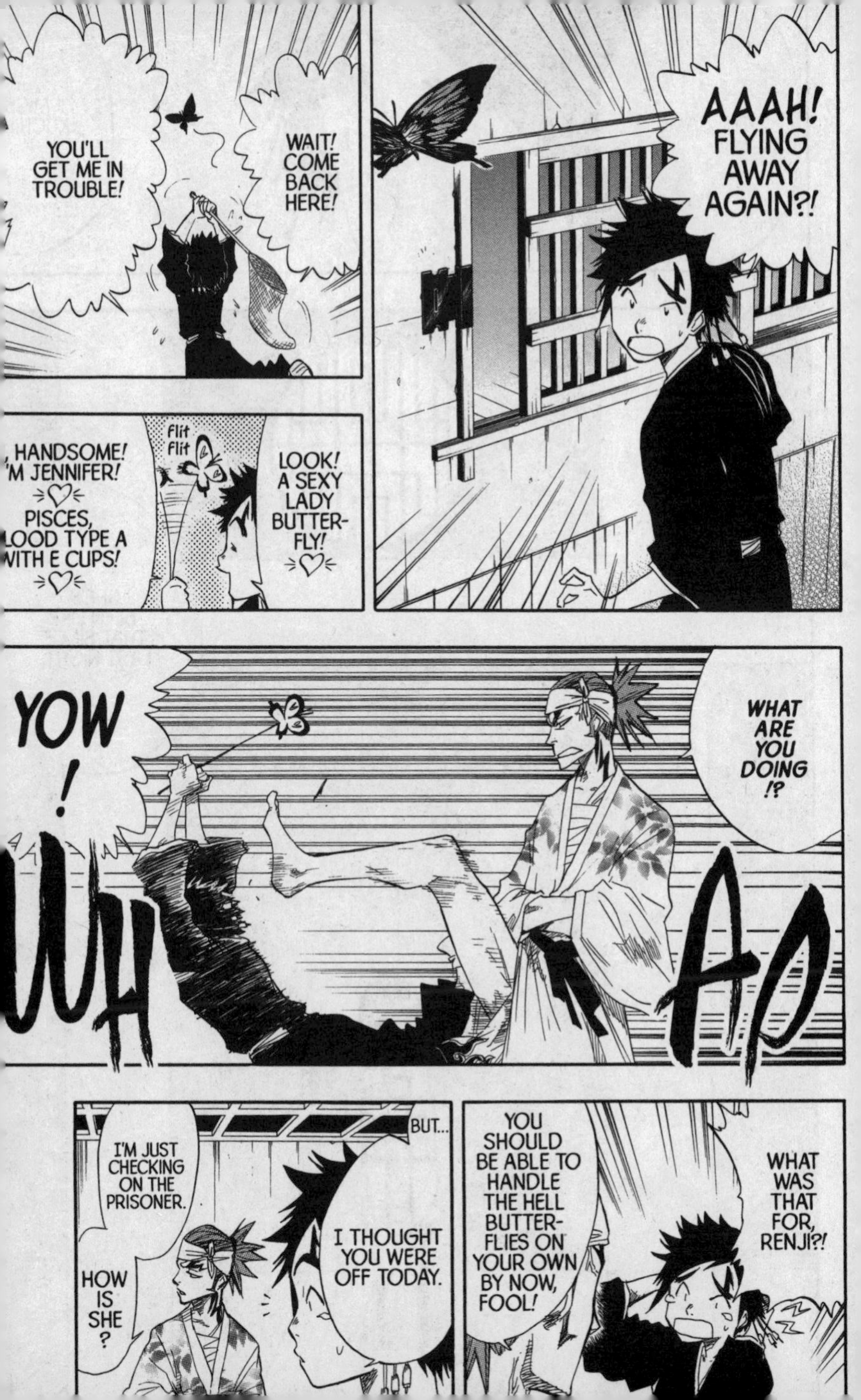
AAAH! FLYING AWAY AGAIN?!
WAIT! COME BACK HERE!
YOU'LL GET ME IN TROUBLE!
LOOK! A SEXY LADY BUTTERFLY!
Flit Flit
, HANDSOME! 'M JENNIFER! PISCES, LOOD TYPE A WITH E CUPS!
WHAT ARE YOU DOING !?
YOW !
WHAP
WHAT WAS THAT FOR, RENJI?!
YOU SHOULD BE ABLE TO HANDLE THE HELL BUTTERFLIES ON YOUR OWN BY NOW, FOOL!
BUT...
I THOUGHT YOU WERE OFF TODAY.
I'M JUST CHECKING ON THE PRISONER.
HOW IS SHE ?

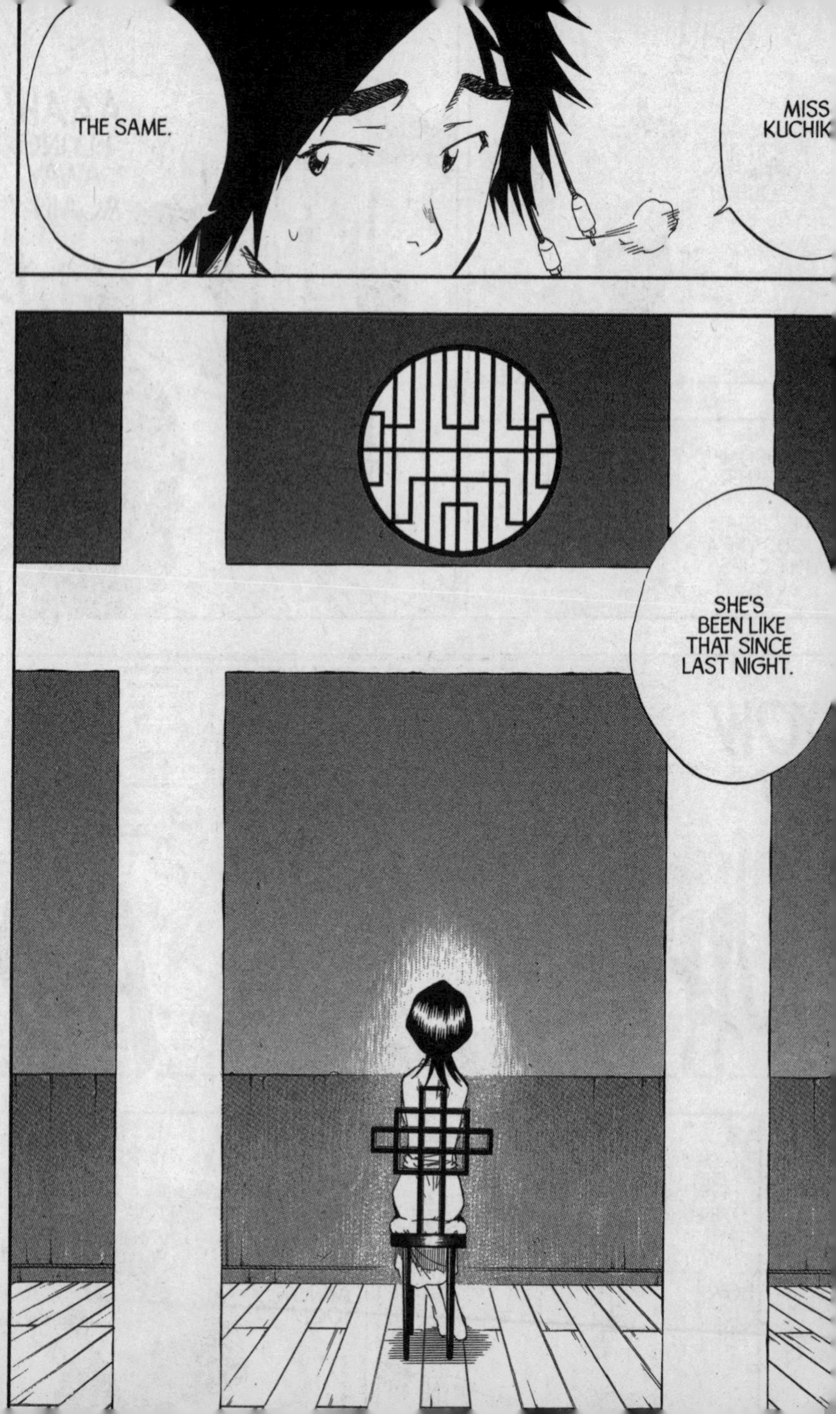
MISS KUCHIK
THE SAME.
SHE'S BEEN LIKE THAT SINCE LAST NIGHT.

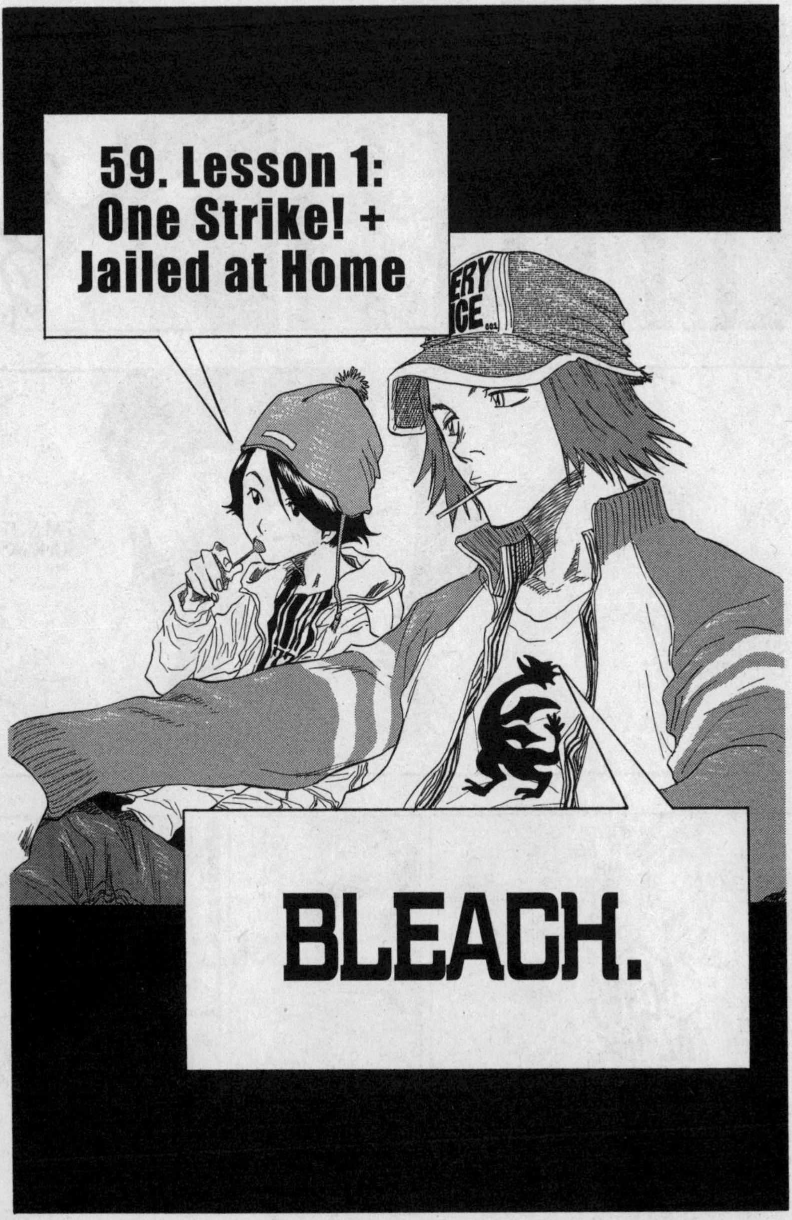
59. Lesson 1: One Strike! + Jailed at Home
BLEACH.

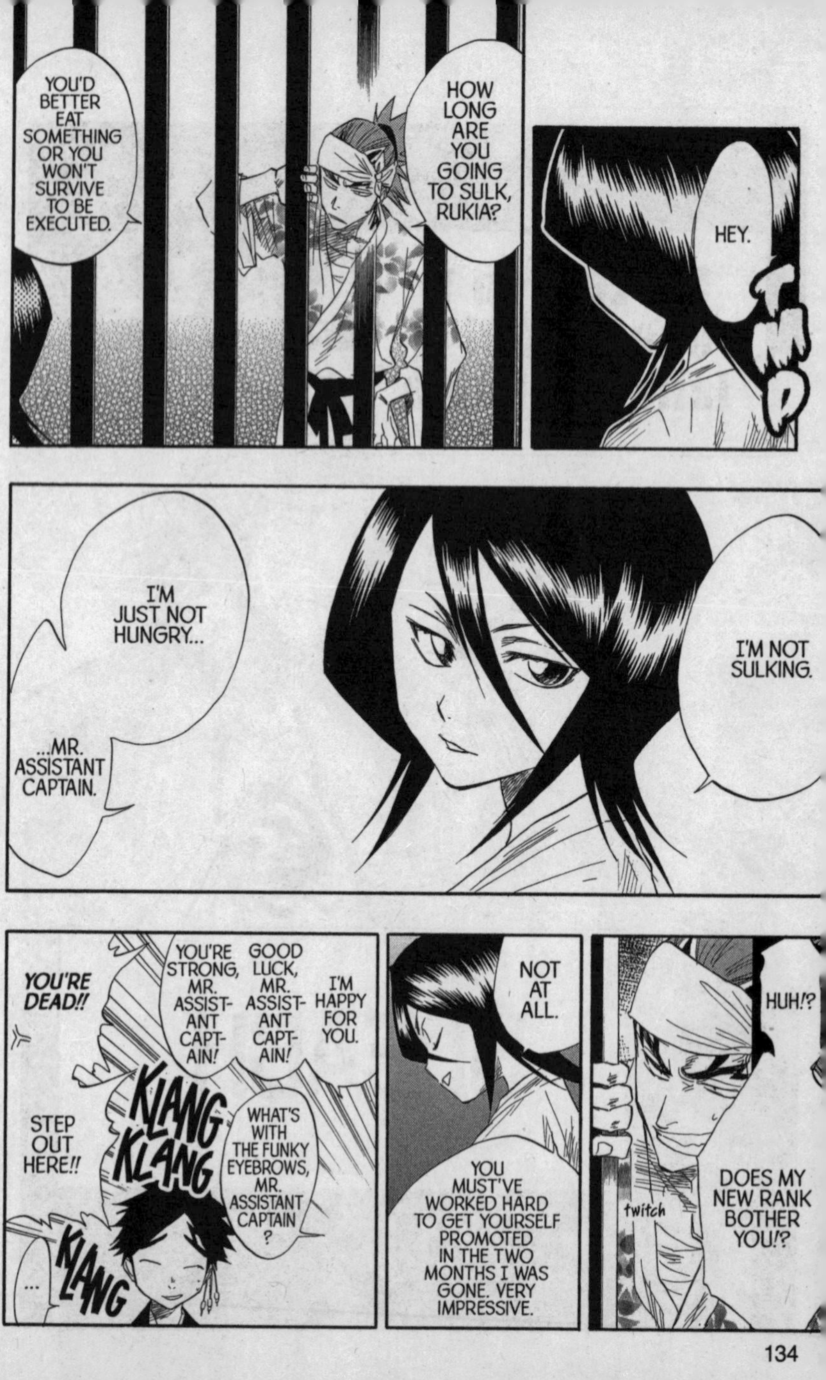
HEY.
TMP
HOW LONG ARE YOU GOING TO SULK, RUKIA?
YOU'D BETTER EAT SOMETHING OR YOU WON'T SURVIVE TO BE EXECUTED.
I'M NOT SULKING.
I'M JUST NOT HUNGRY...
...MR. ASSISTANT CAPTAIN.
HUH!?
DOES MY NEW RANK BOTHER YOU!?
twitch
NOT AT ALL.
YOU MUST'VE WORKED HARD TO GET YOURSELF PROMOTED IN THE TWO MONTHS I WAS GONE. VERY IMPRESSIVE.
I'M HAPPY FOR YOU.
GOOD LUCK, MR. ASSIST-ANT CAPT-AIN!
YOU'RE STRONG, MR. ASSIST-ANT CAPT-AIN!
WHAT'S WITH THE FUNKY EYEBROWS, MR. ASSISTANT CAPTAIN?
YOU'RE DEAD!!
STEP OUT HERE!!
KLANG KLANG
KLANG
...

READ THIS WAY

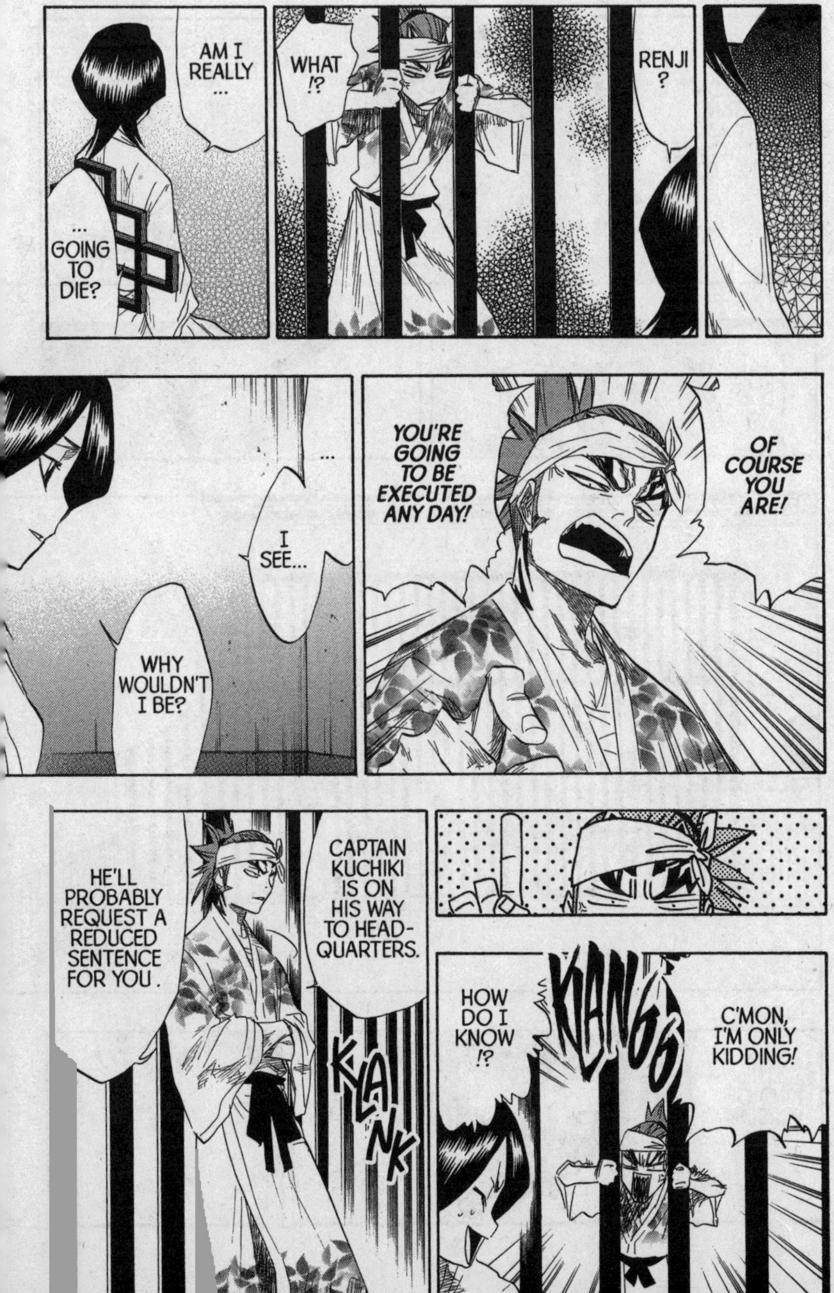
RENJI?
WHAT!?
AM I REALLY ...
... GOING TO DIE?
OF COURSE YOU ARE!
YOU'RE GOING TO BE EXECUTED ANY DAY!
...
I SEE...
WHY WOULDN'T I BE?
C'MON, I'M ONLY KIDDING!
KLANG
HOW DO I KNOW!?
CAPTAIN KUCHIKI IS ON HIS WAY TO HEAD-QUARTERS.
HE'LL PROBABLY REQUEST A REDUCED SENTENCE FOR YOU.
KLANK

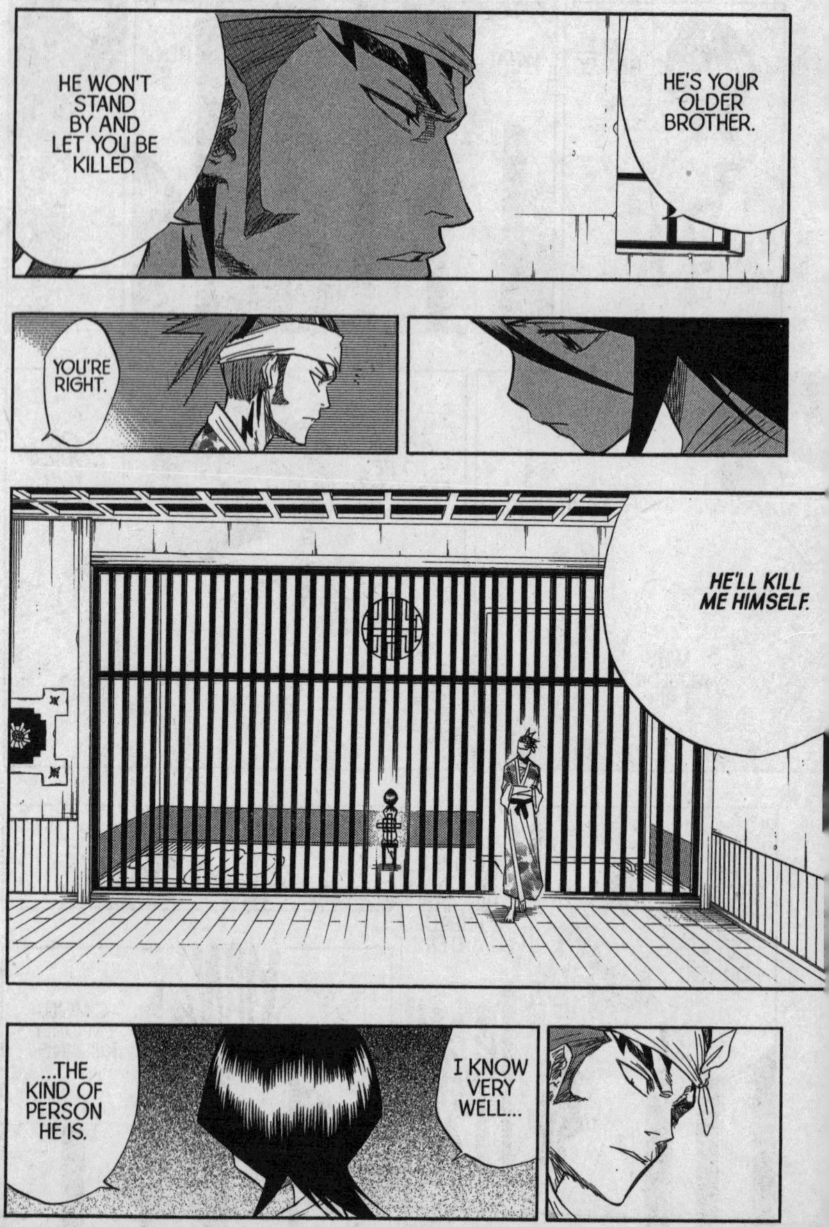
HE'S YOUR OLDER BROTHER.
HE WON'T STAND BY AND LET YOU BE KILLED.
YOU'RE RIGHT.
HE'LL KILL ME HIMSELF.
I KNOW VERY WELL...
...THE KIND OF PERSON HE IS.

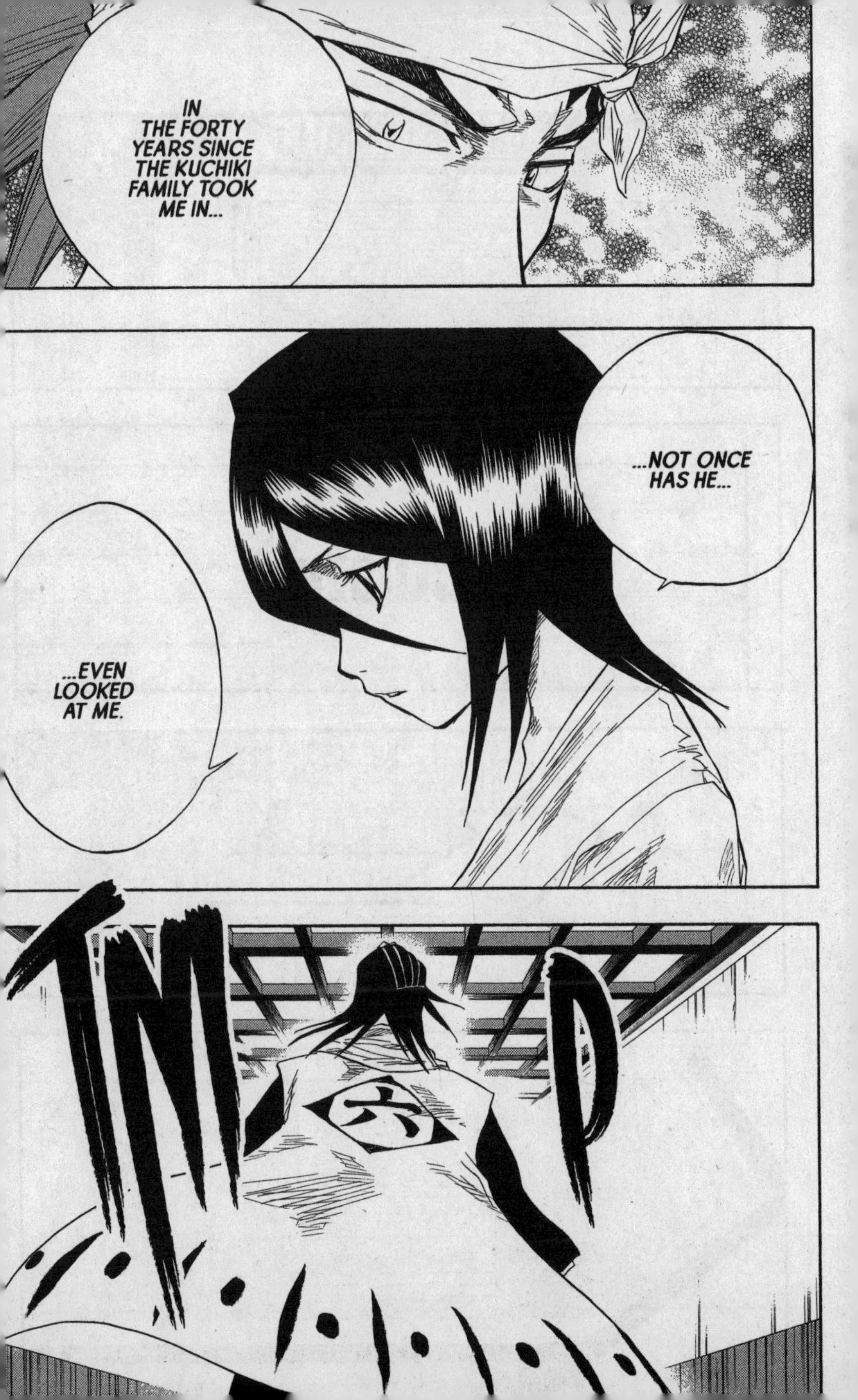
IN THE FORTY YEARS SINCE THE KUCHIKI FAMILY TOOK ME IN...
...NOT ONCE HAS HE...
...EVEN LOOKED AT ME.
TMP

URAHARA SHOTEN
CLOSED
CLOSED

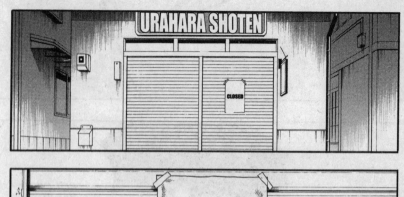

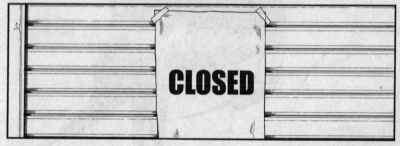

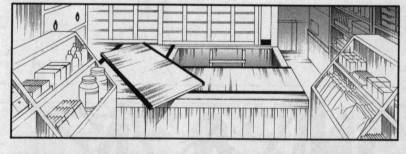

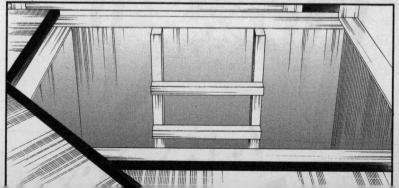

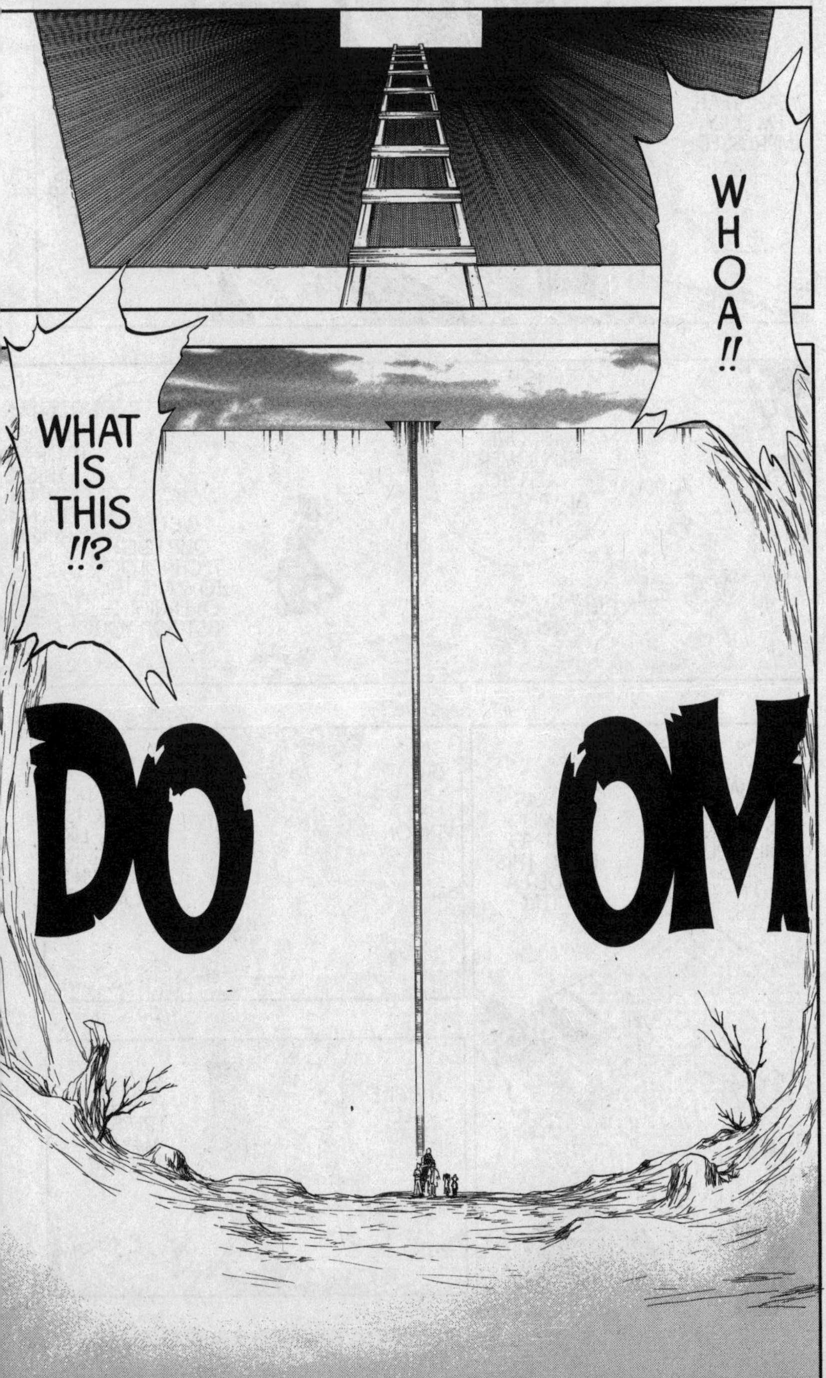
WHOA!!
WHAT IS THIS!!?
DOOM

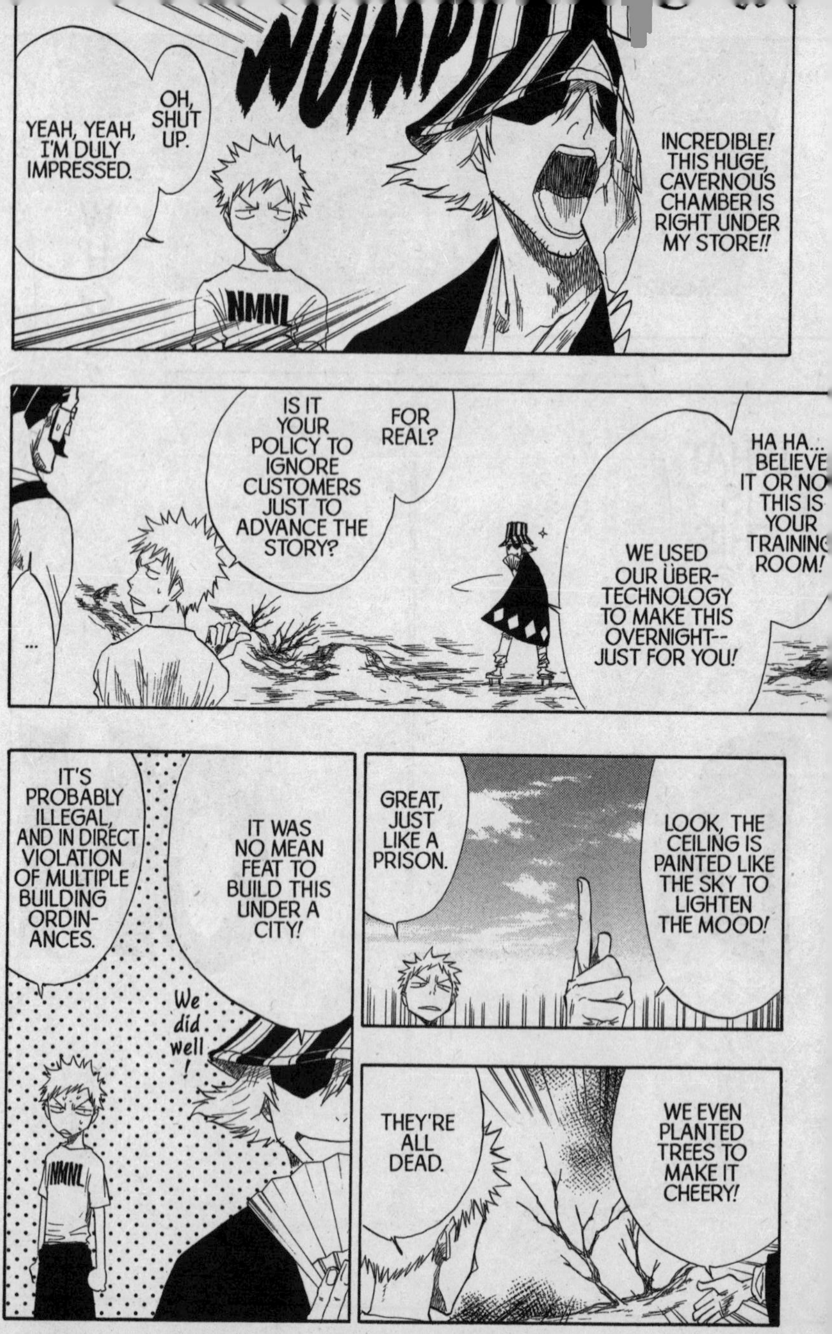
WUMP
INCREDIBLE! THIS HUGE, CAVERNOUS CHAMBER IS RIGHT UNDER MY STORE!!
OH, SHUT UP.
YEAH, YEAH, I'M DULY IMPRESSED.
NMNL
HA HA... BELIEVE IT OR NO THIS IS YOUR TRAININ ROOM!
WE USED OUR ÜBER-TECHNOLOGY TO MAKE THIS OVERNIGHT-- JUST FOR YOU!
FOR REAL?
IS IT YOUR POLICY TO IGNORE CUSTOMERS JUST TO ADVANCE THE STORY?
...
LOOK, THE CEILING IS PAINTED LIKE THE SKY TO LIGHTEN THE MOOD!
GREAT, JUST LIKE A PRISON.
WE EVEN PLANTED TREES TO MAKE IT CHEERY!
THEY'RE ALL DEAD.
IT WAS NO MEAN FEAT TO BUILD THIS UNDER A CITY!
We did well!
IT'S PROBABLY ILLEGAL, AND IN DIRECT VIOLATION OF MULTIPLE BUILDING ORDINANCES.
NMNL

READ THIS WAY

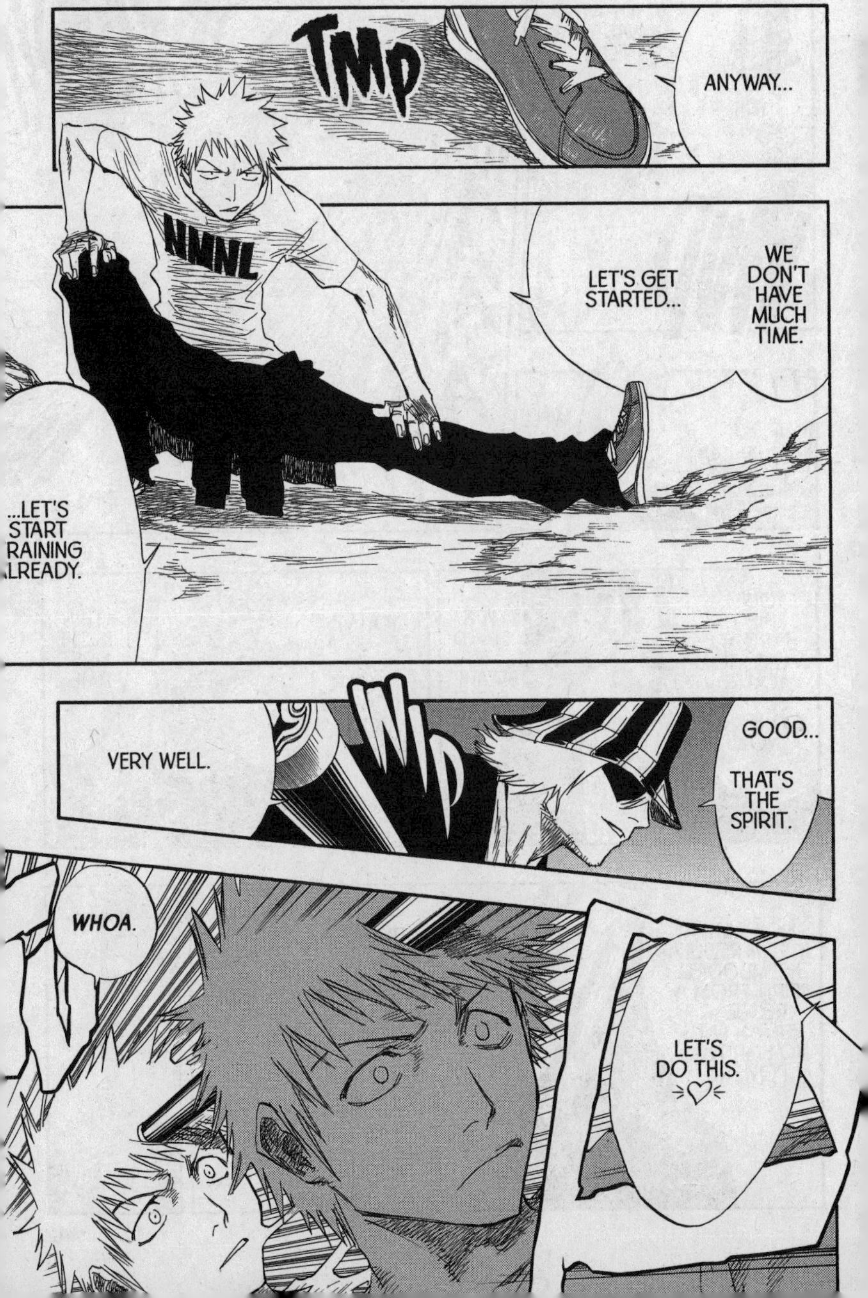
TMP
ANYWAY...
WE DON'T HAVE MUCH TIME.
LET'S GET STARTED...
...LET'S START RAINING LREADY.
GOOD... THAT'S THE SPIRIT.
VERY WELL.
LET'S DO THIS. ♡
WHOA.

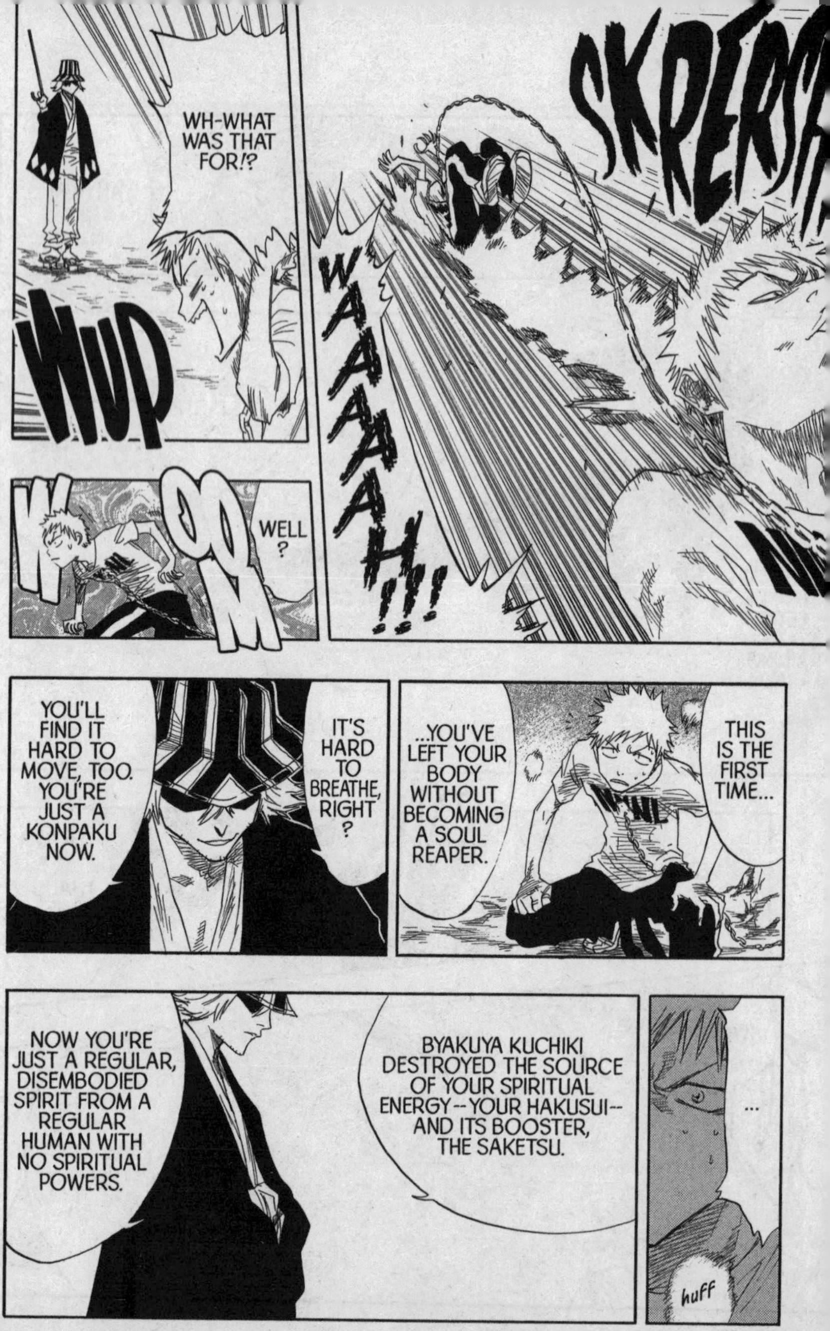
WAAAAAH!!!
WH-WHAT WAS THAT FOR!?
WHUP
WELL?
WOOM
THIS IS THE FIRST TIME...
...YOU'VE LEFT YOUR BODY WITHOUT BECOMING A SOUL REAPER.
IT'S HARD TO BREATHE, RIGHT?
YOU'LL FIND IT HARD TO MOVE, TOO. YOU'RE JUST A KONPAKU NOW.
...
huff
BYAKUYA KUCHIKI DESTROYED THE SOURCE OF YOUR SPIRITUAL ENERGY--YOUR HAKUSUI--AND ITS BOOSTER, THE SAKETSU.
NOW YOU'RE JUST A REGULAR, DISEMBODIED SPIRIT FROM A REGULAR HUMAN WITH NO SPIRITUAL POWERS.

READ THIS WAY

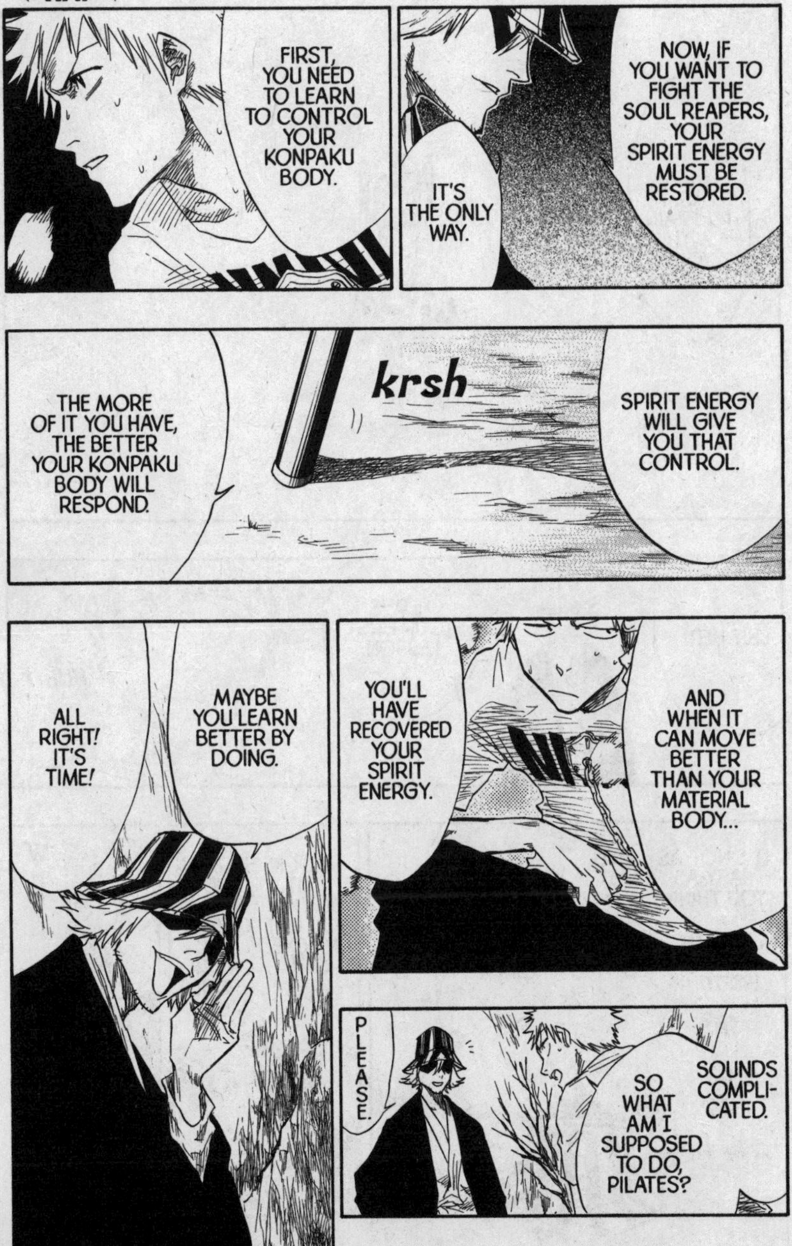

NOW, IF YOU WANT TO FIGHT THE SOUL REAPERS, YOUR SPIRIT ENERGY MUST BE RESTORED.
IT'S THE ONLY WAY.
FIRST, YOU NEED TO LEARN TO CONTROL YOUR KONPAKU BODY.
SPIRIT ENERGY WILL GIVE YOU THAT CONTROL.
krsh
THE MORE OF IT YOU HAVE, THE BETTER YOUR KONPAKU BODY WILL RESPOND.
AND WHEN IT CAN MOVE BETTER THAN YOUR MATERIAL BODY...
YOU'LL HAVE RECOVERED YOUR SPIRIT ENERGY.
SOUNDS COMPLI-CATED.
SO WHAT AM I SUPPOSED TO DO, PILATES?
PLEASE.
MAYBE YOU LEARN BETTER BY DOING.
ALL RIGHT! IT'S TIME!

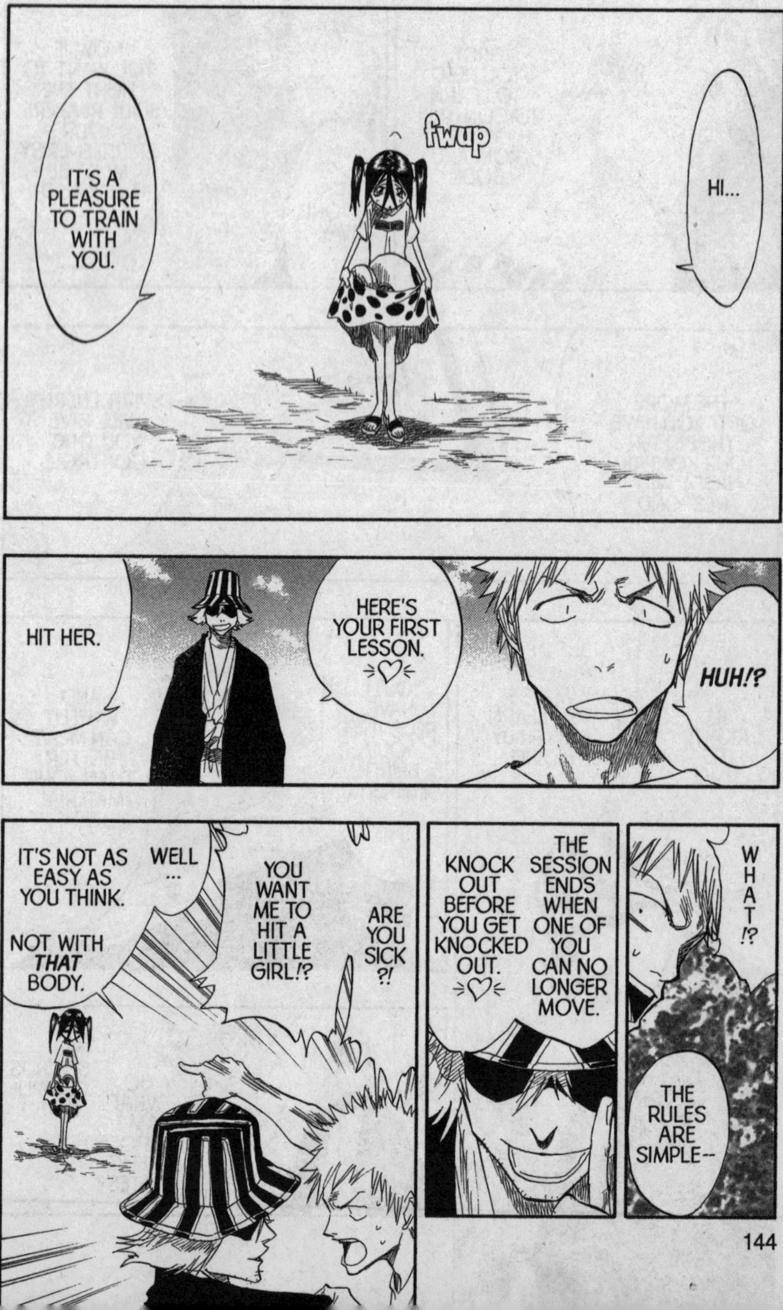
HI...
fwup
IT'S A PLEASURE TO TRAIN WITH YOU.
HUH!?
HERE'S YOUR FIRST LESSON. ♡
HIT HER.
WHAT!?
THE RULES ARE SIMPLE--
THE SESSION ENDS WHEN ONE OF YOU CAN NO LONGER MOVE.
KNOCK OUT BEFORE YOU GET KNOCKED OUT. ♡
ARE YOU SICK?!
YOU WANT ME TO HIT A LITTLE GIRL!?
WELL ...
IT'S NOT AS EASY AS YOU THINK.
NOT WITH *THAT* BODY.

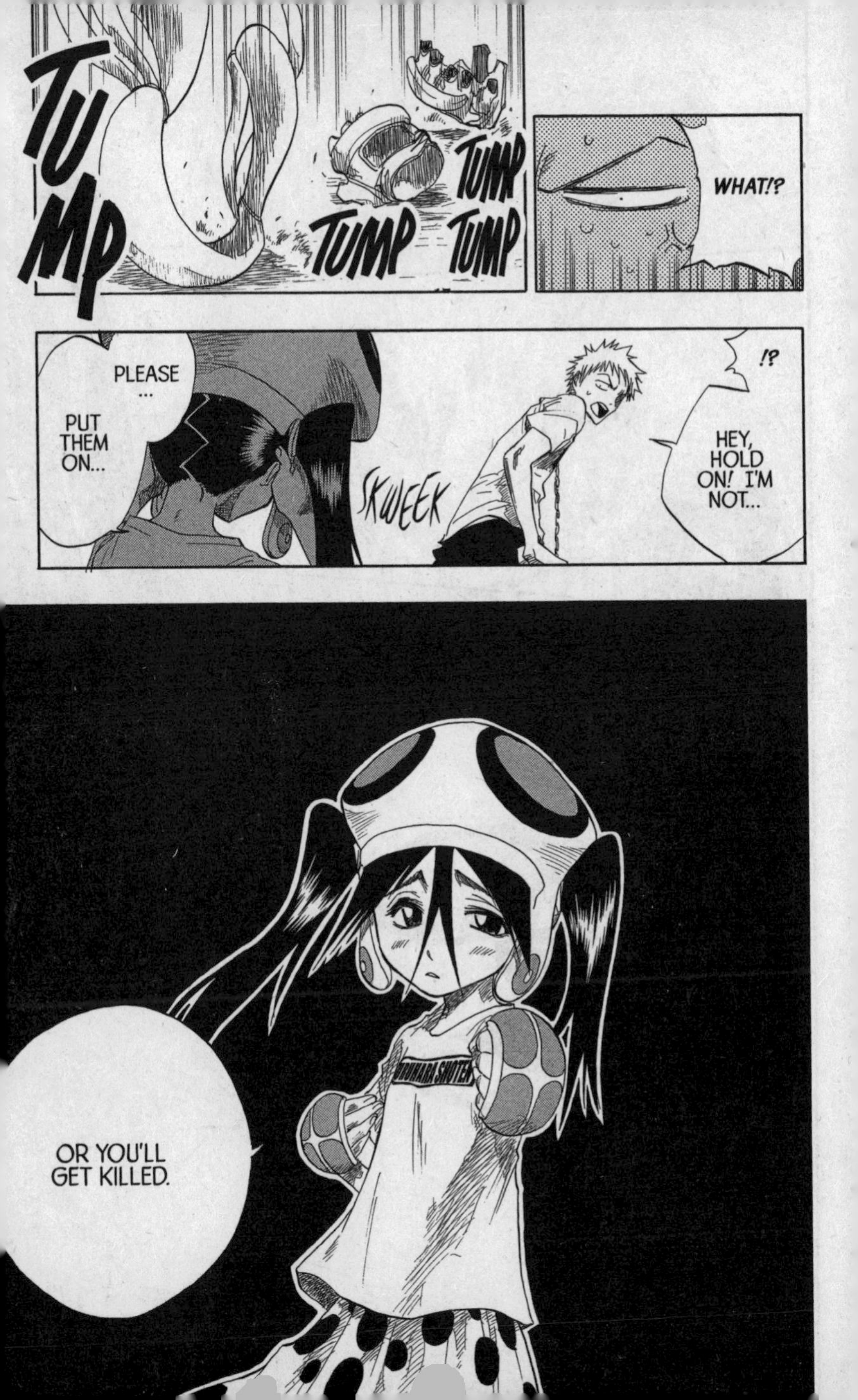
TUMP
TUMP
TUMP
TUMP
TUMP
WHAT!?
!?
HEY, HOLD ON! I'M NOT...
SKWEEK
PLEASE ... PUT THEM ON...
OR YOU'LL GET KILLED.

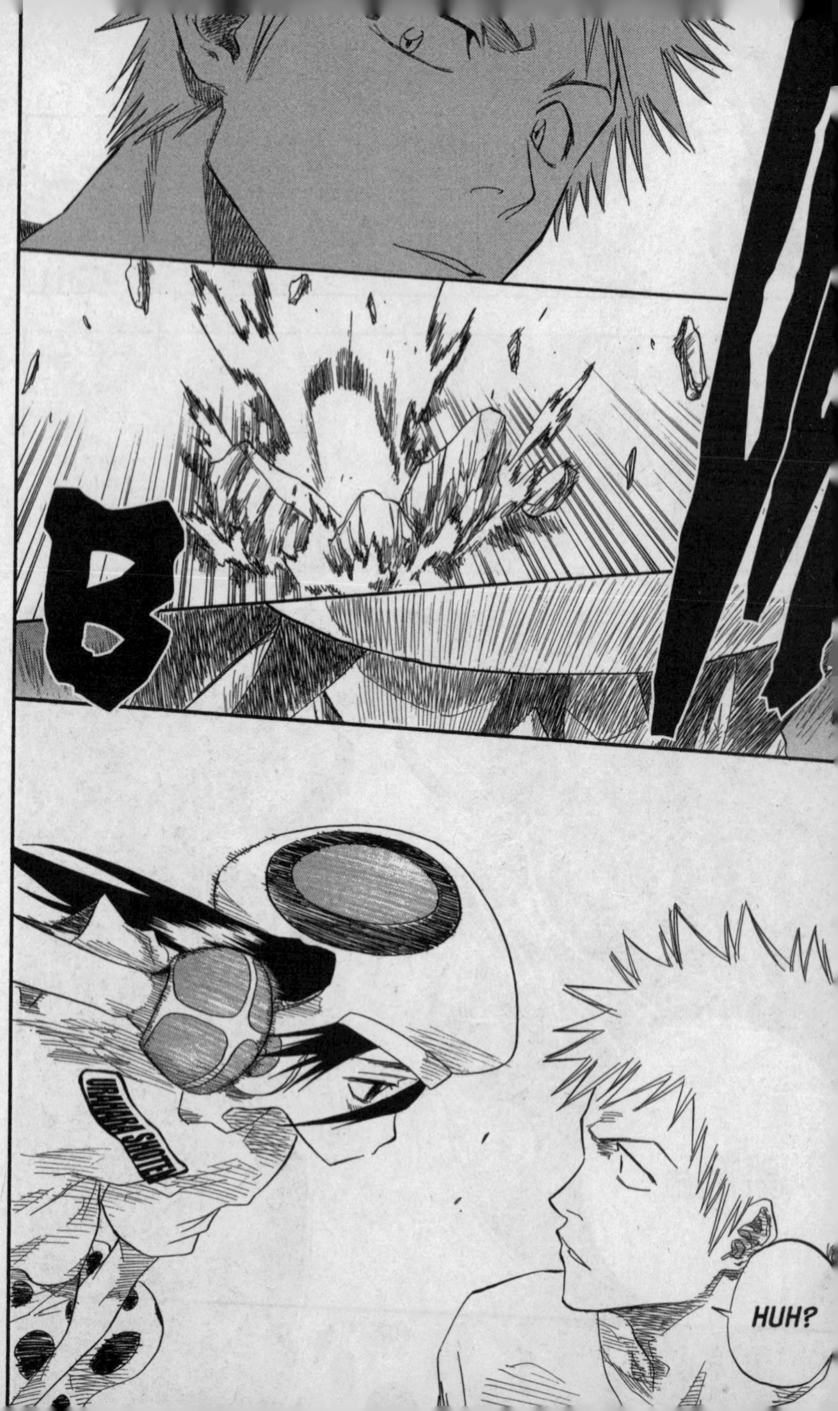
B
HUH?
URAHARA SHOTEN

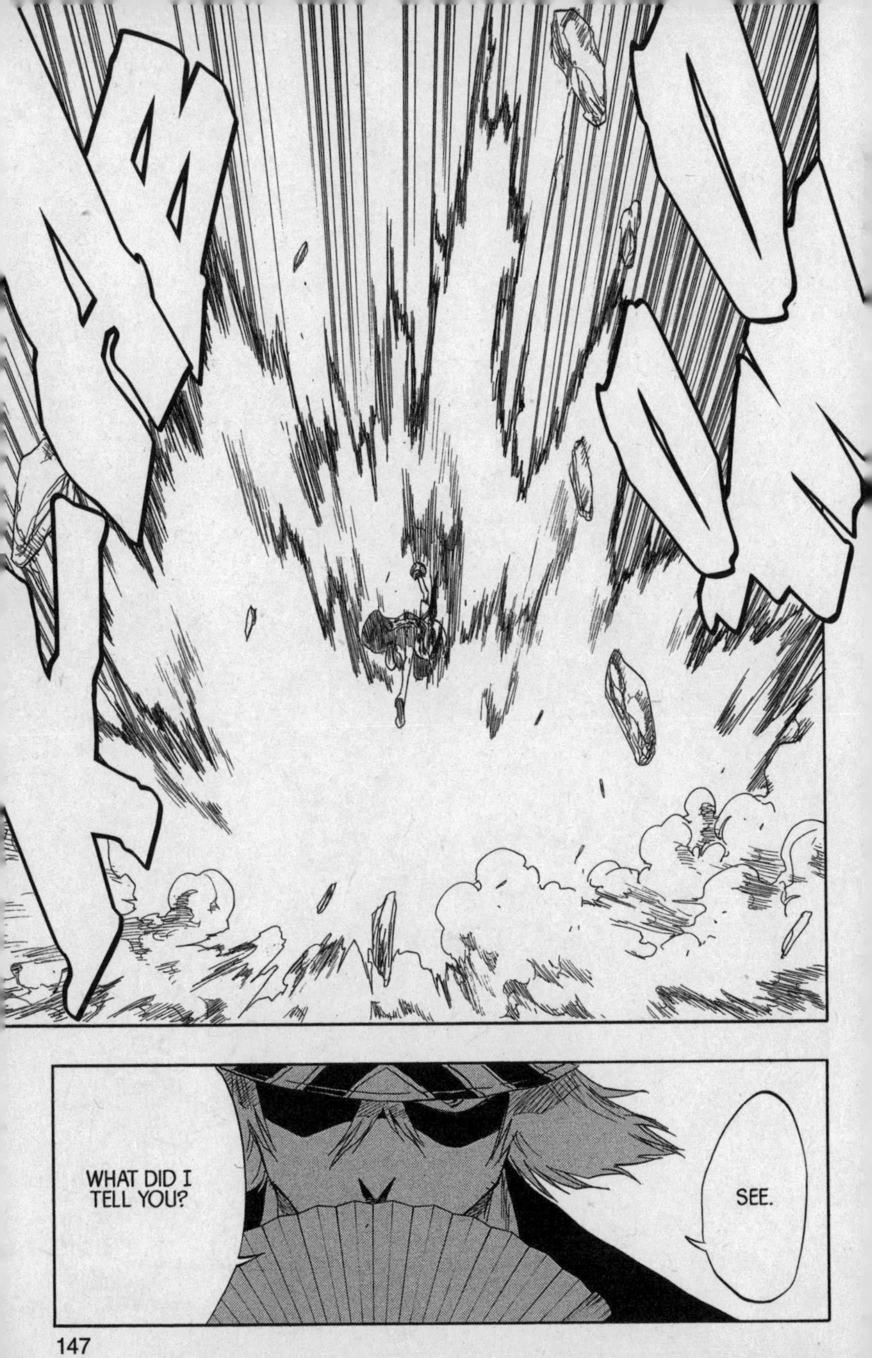
SEE.
WHAT DID I TELL YOU?

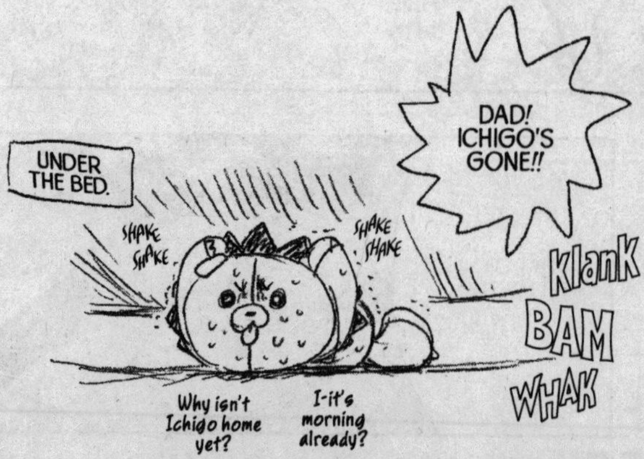
DAD! ICHIGO'S GONE!!
Klank
BAM
WHAK
UNDER THE BED.
SHAKE SHAKE
SHAKE SHAKE
I-it's morning already?
Why isn't Ichigo home yet?

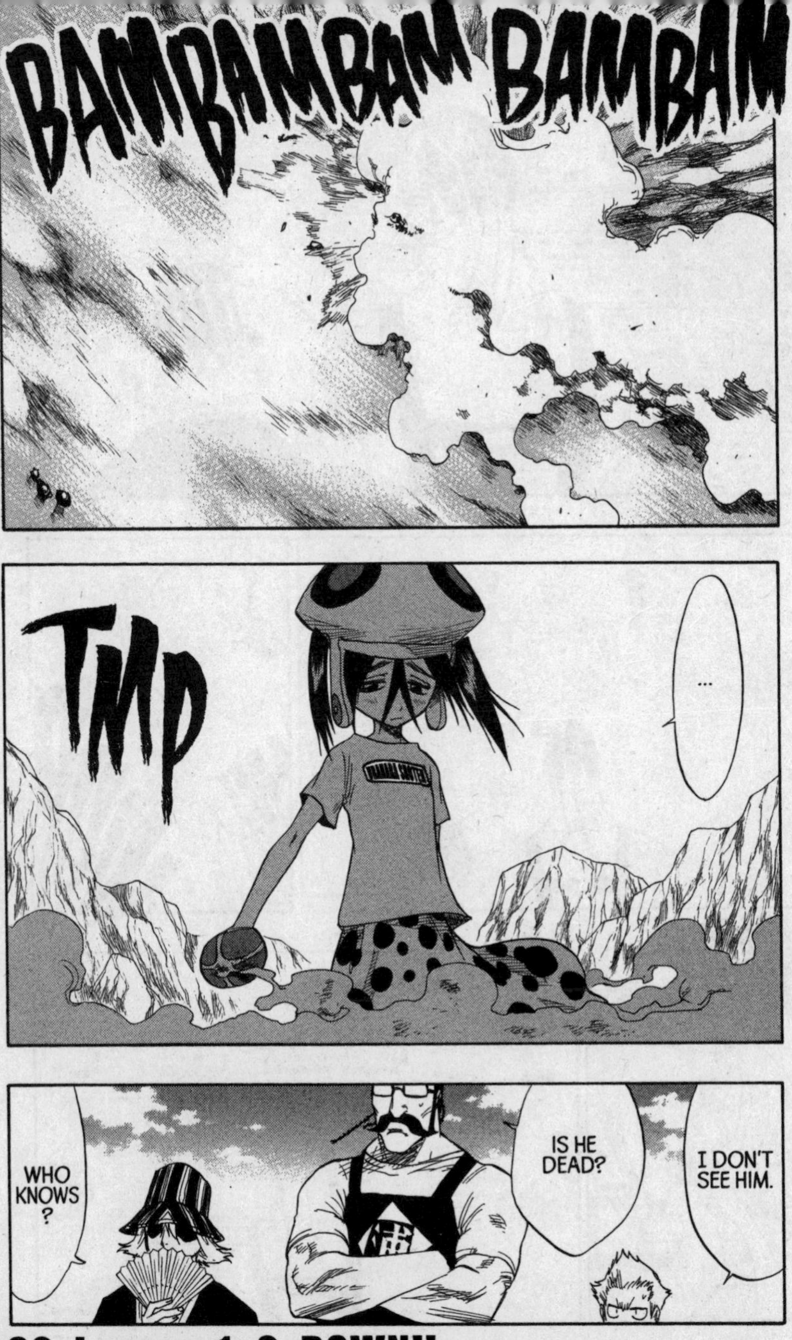
BAMBAMBAM BAMBAM
TMP
...
I DON'T SEE HIM.
IS HE DEAD?
WHO KNOWS?

60. Lesson 1–2: DOWN!!

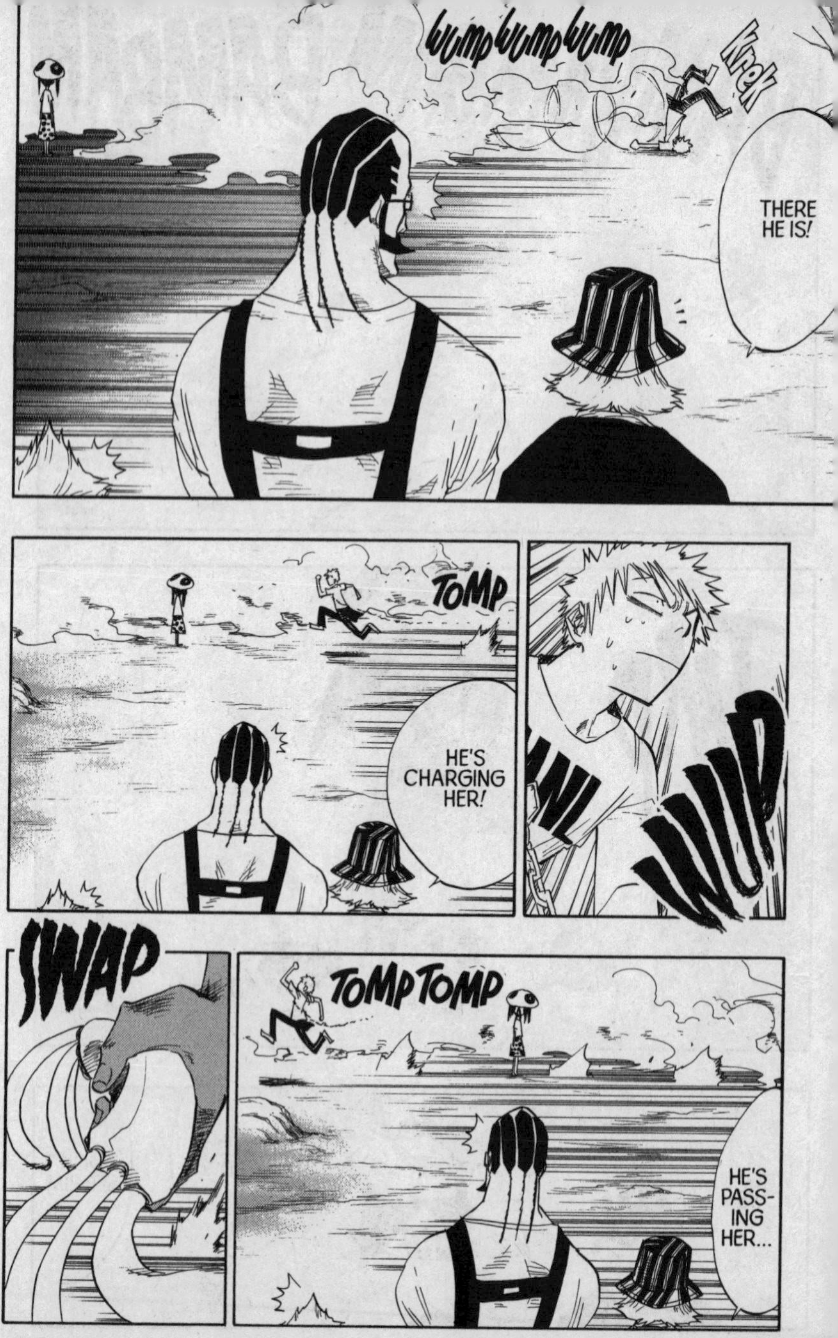
bump bump bump
Krek
THERE HE IS!
WUP
TOMP
HE'S CHARGING HER!
TOMP TOMP
HE'S PASSING HER...
SWAP

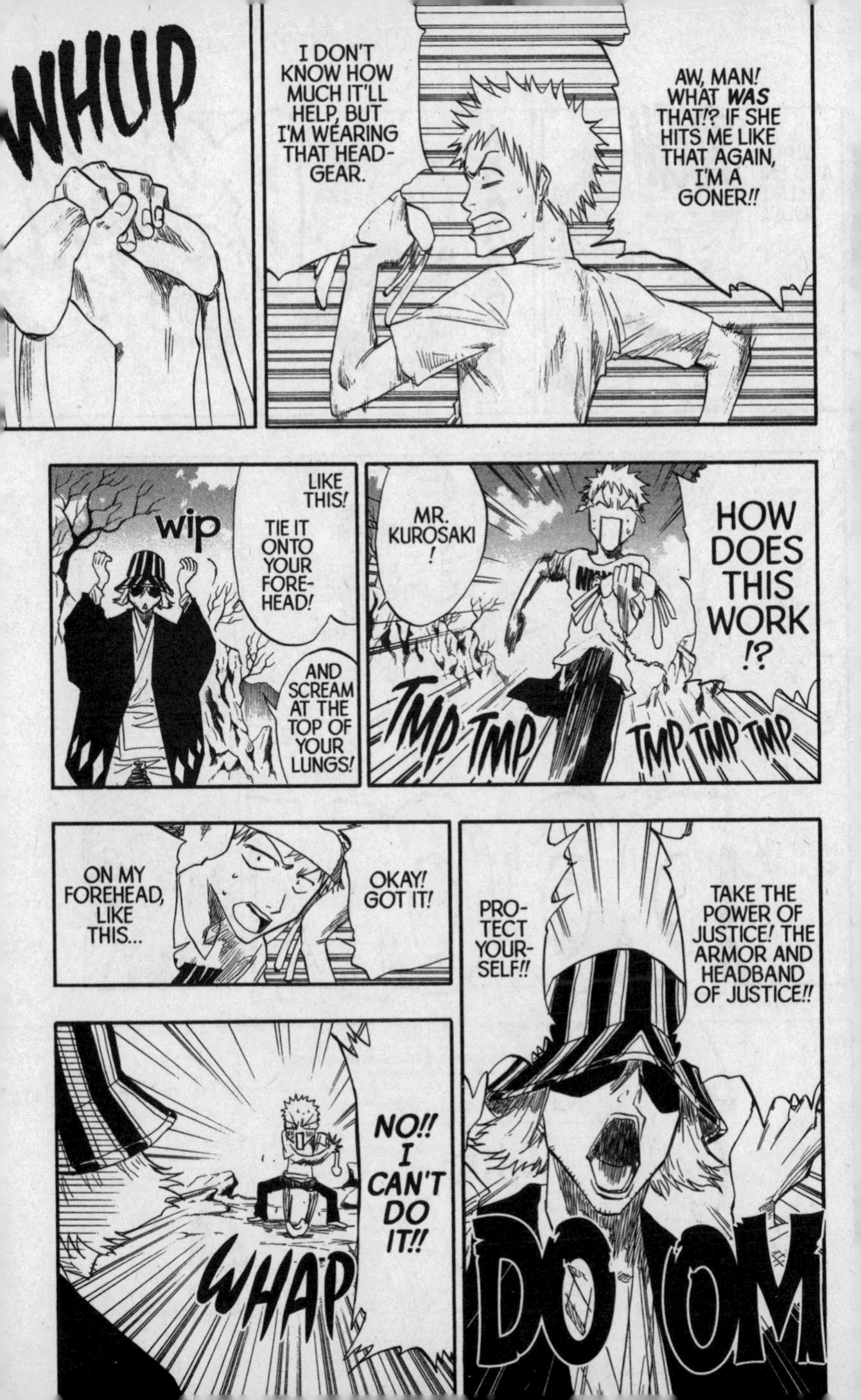
AW, MAN! WHAT WAS THAT!? IF SHE HITS ME LIKE THAT AGAIN, I'M A GONER!!
I DON'T KNOW HOW MUCH IT'LL HELP, BUT I'M WEARING THAT HEAD-GEAR.
WHUP
HOW DOES THIS WORK!?
MR. KUROSAKI!
TMP TMP
TMP TMP TMP
LIKE THIS!
TIE IT ONTO YOUR FORE-HEAD!
AND SCREAM AT THE TOP OF YOUR LUNGS!
wip
TAKE THE POWER OF JUSTICE! THE ARMOR AND HEADBAND OF JUSTICE!!
PRO-TECT YOUR-SELF!!
DOOM
OKAY! GOT IT!
ON MY FOREHEAD, LIKE THIS...
NO!! I CAN'T DO IT!!
WHAP

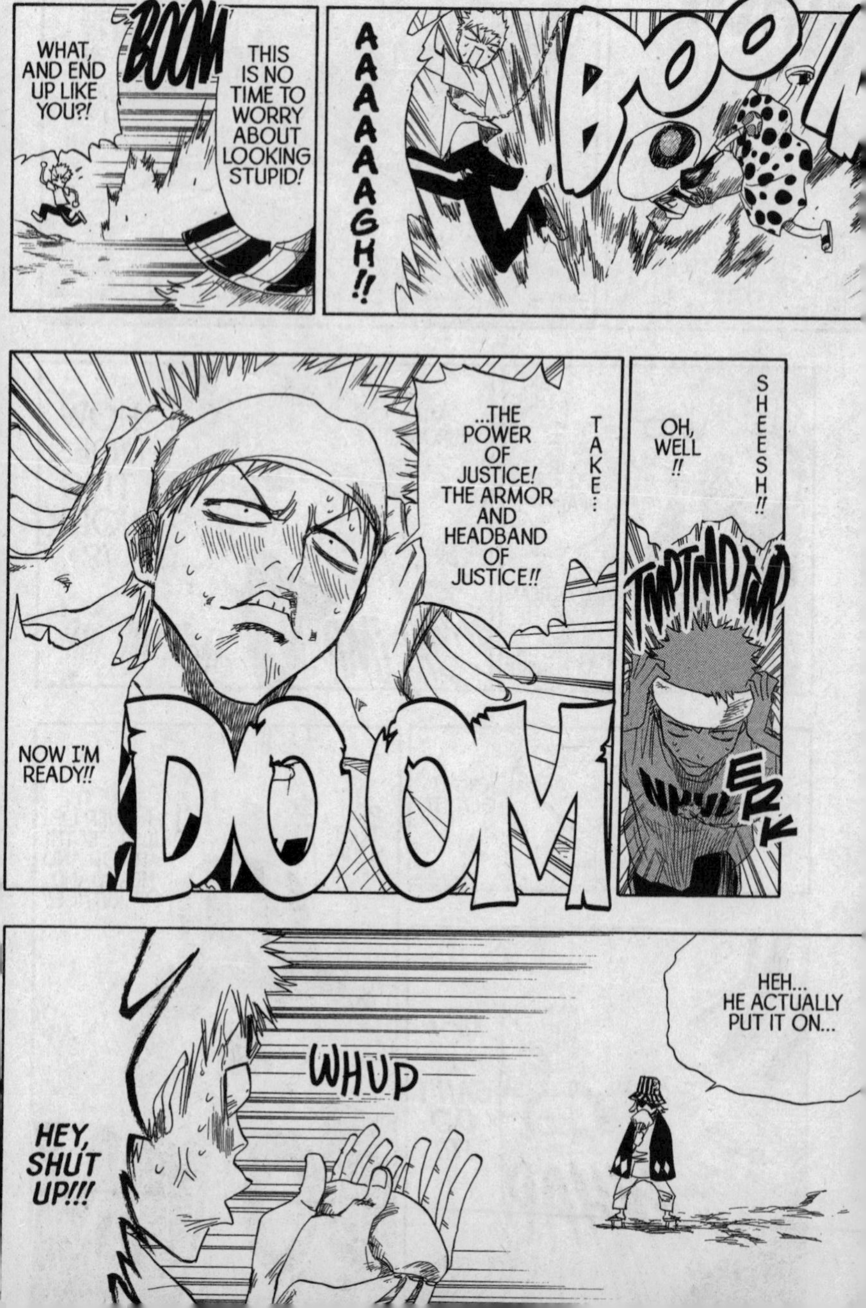
BOOM
AAAAAAAAGH!!
THIS IS NO TIME TO WORRY ABOUT LOOKING STUPID!
BOOM
WHAT, AND END UP LIKE YOU?!
SHEESH!!
OH, WELL!!
TMPTMPTMP
ERK
TAKE...
...THE POWER OF JUSTICE! THE ARMOR AND HEADBAND OF JUSTICE!!
DOOM
NOW I'M READY!!
HEH... HE ACTUALLY PUT IT ON...
WHUP
HEY, SHUT UP!!!

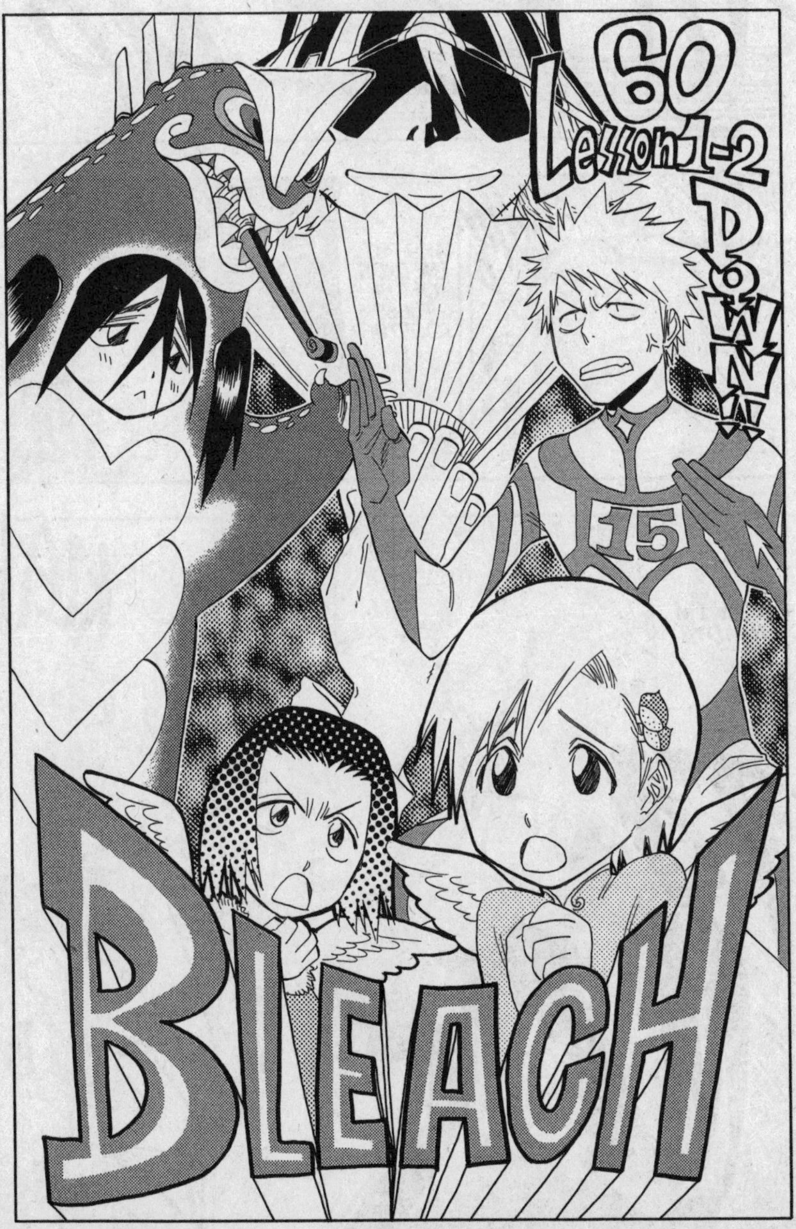

60
Lesson1-2
DOWN!!
15
BLEACH

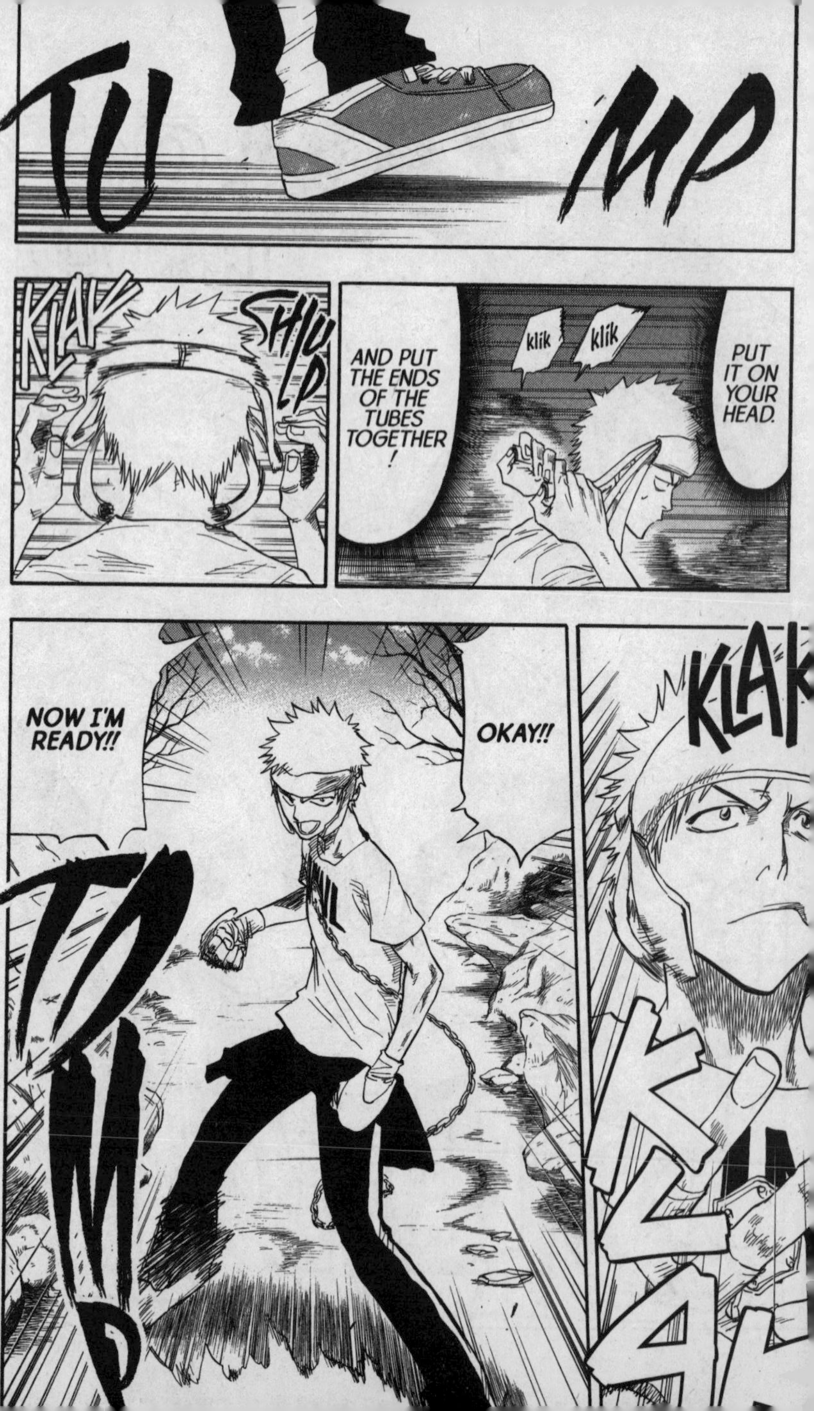
TUMP
PUT IT ON YOUR HEAD.
klik
klik
AND PUT THE ENDS OF THE TUBES TOGETHER!
SHULP
KLAK
KLAK
OKAY!!
NOW I'M READY!!

READ THIS WAY

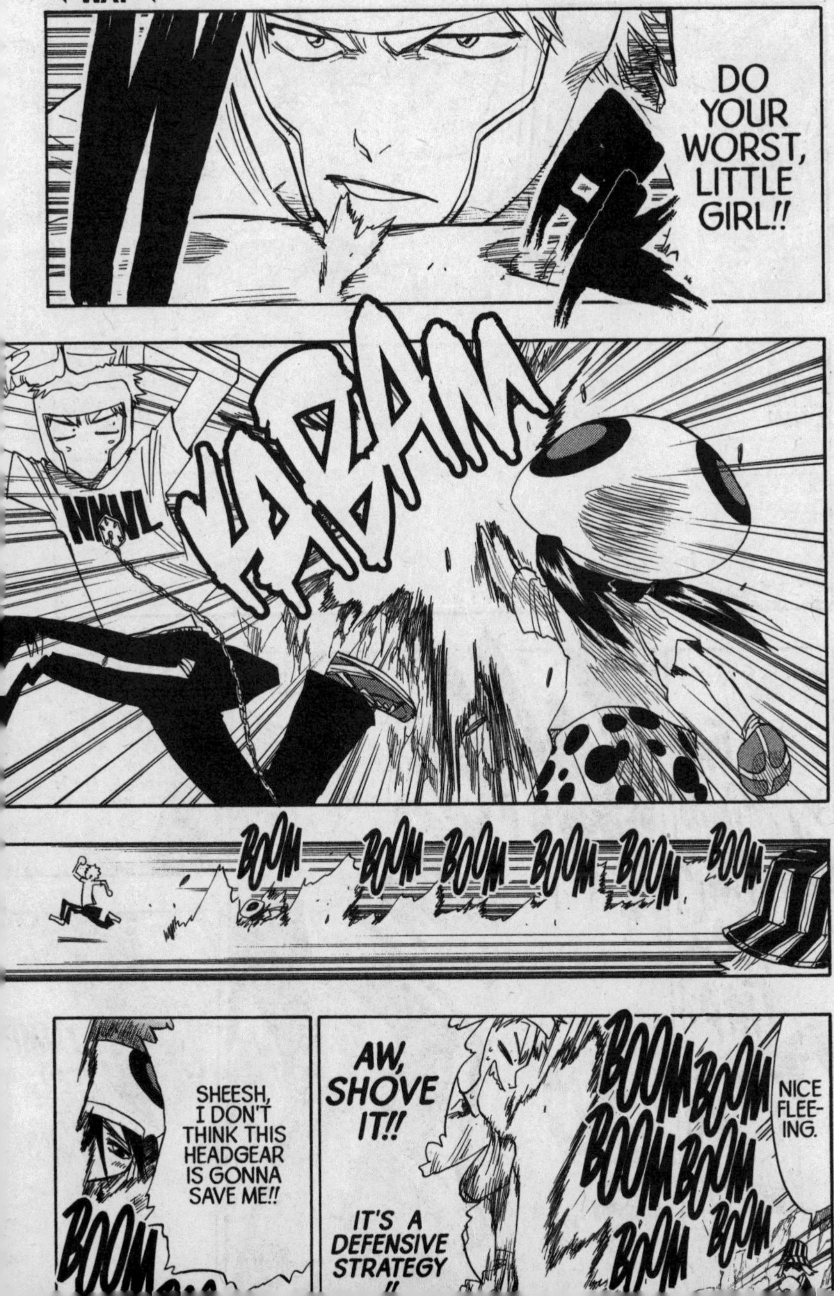
DO YOUR WORST, LITTLE GIRL!!
KABAM
BOOM BOOM BOOM BOOM BOOM BOOM
NICE FLEEING.
AW, SHOVE IT!!
IT'S A DEFENSIVE STRATEGY!!
BOOM BOOM BOOM BOOM BOOM BOOM BOOM BOOM
SHEESH, I DON'T THINK THIS HEADGEAR IS GONNA SAVE ME!!
BOOM

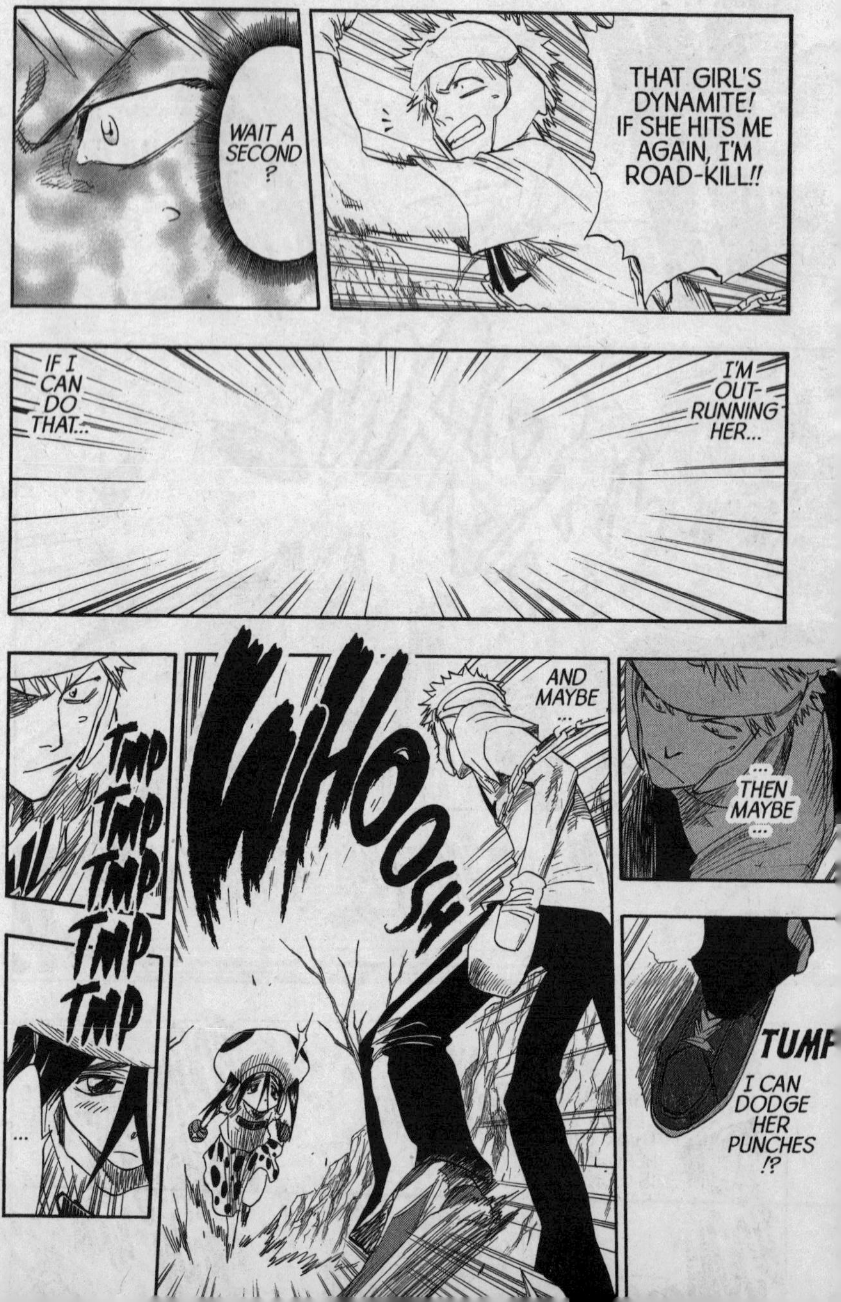
THAT GIRL'S DYNAMITE! IF SHE HITS ME AGAIN, I'M ROAD-KILL!!
WAIT A SECOND ?
I'M OUT-RUNNING HER...
IF I CAN DO THAT...
...THEN MAYBE...
TUMF
I CAN DODGE HER PUNCHES !?
AND MAYBE ...
WHOOSH
TMP TMP TMP TMP TMP TMP
...

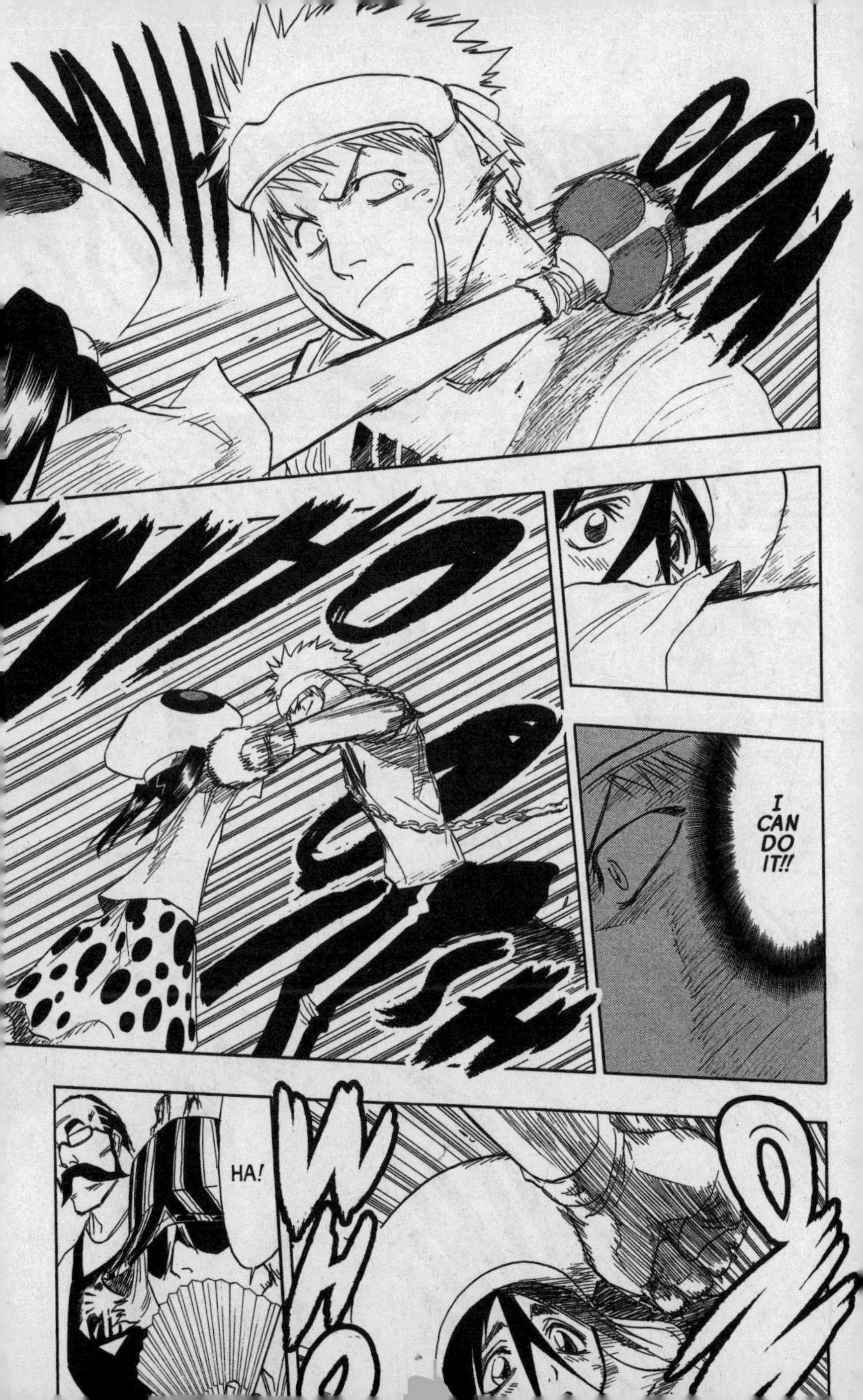

I CAN DO IT!!
WHOOSH
HA!

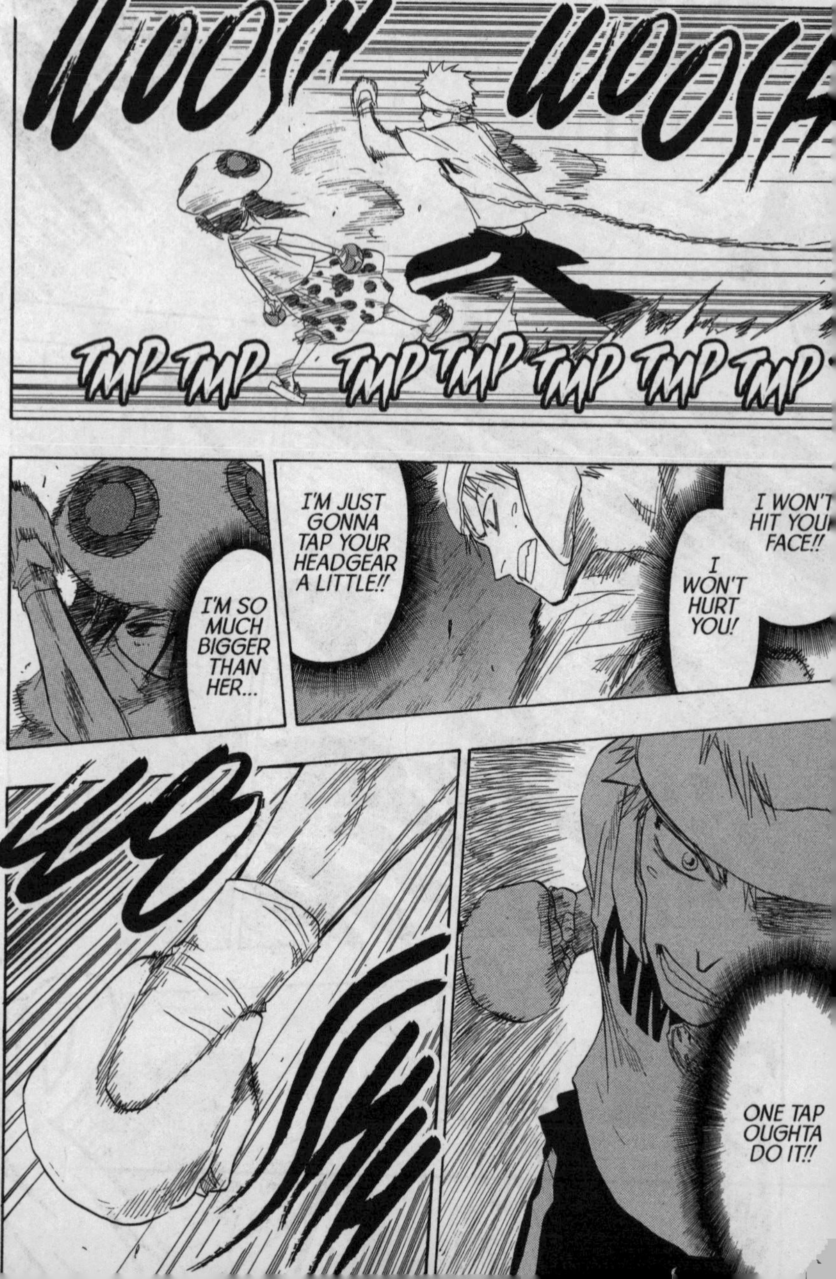
WOOSH WOOSH
TMP TMP TMP TMP TMP TMP TMP TMP TMP
I WON'T HIT YOU FACE!!
I WON'T HURT YOU!
I'M JUST GONNA TAP YOUR HEADGEAR A LITTLE!!
I'M SO MUCH BIGGER THAN HER...
ONE TAP OUGHTA DO IT!!
WOOSH

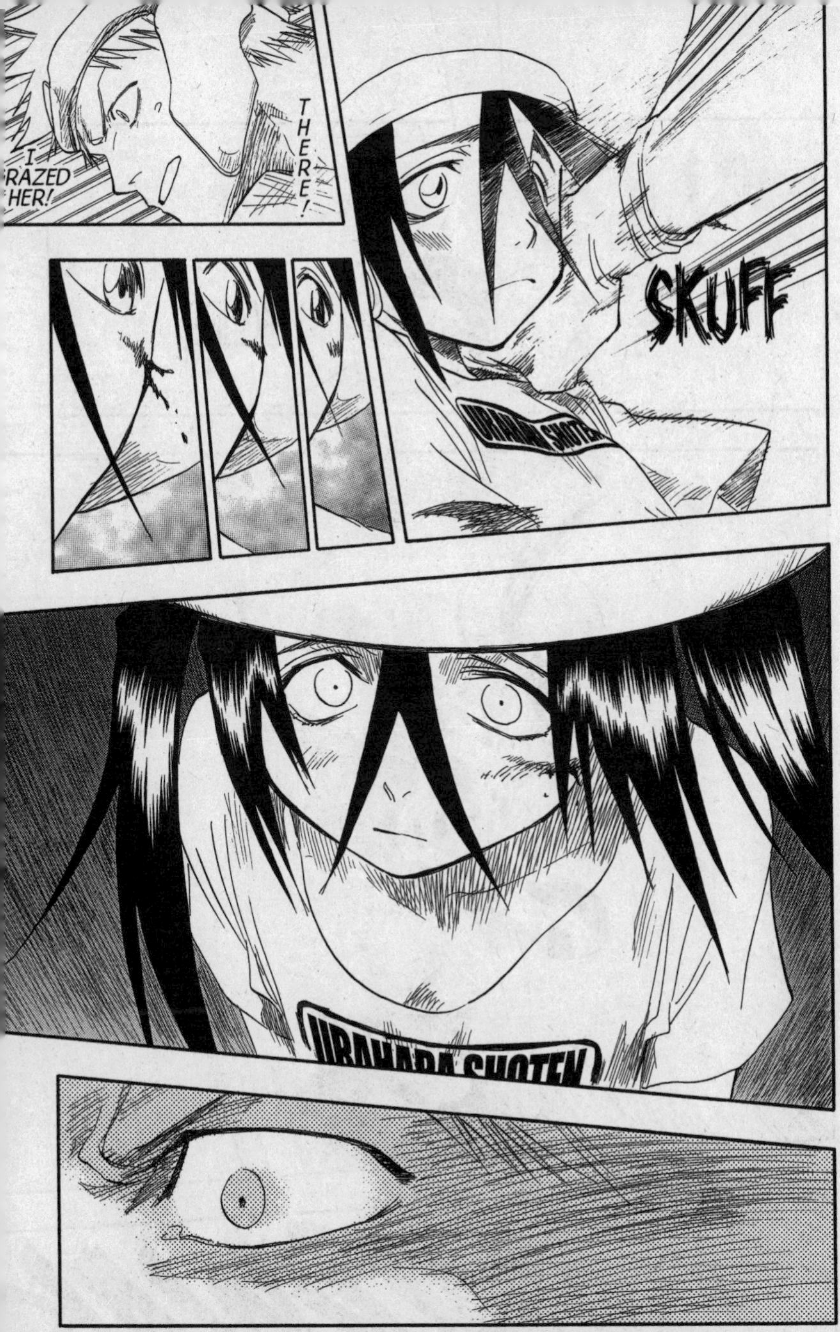
THERE!
I
RAZED
HER!
SKUFF

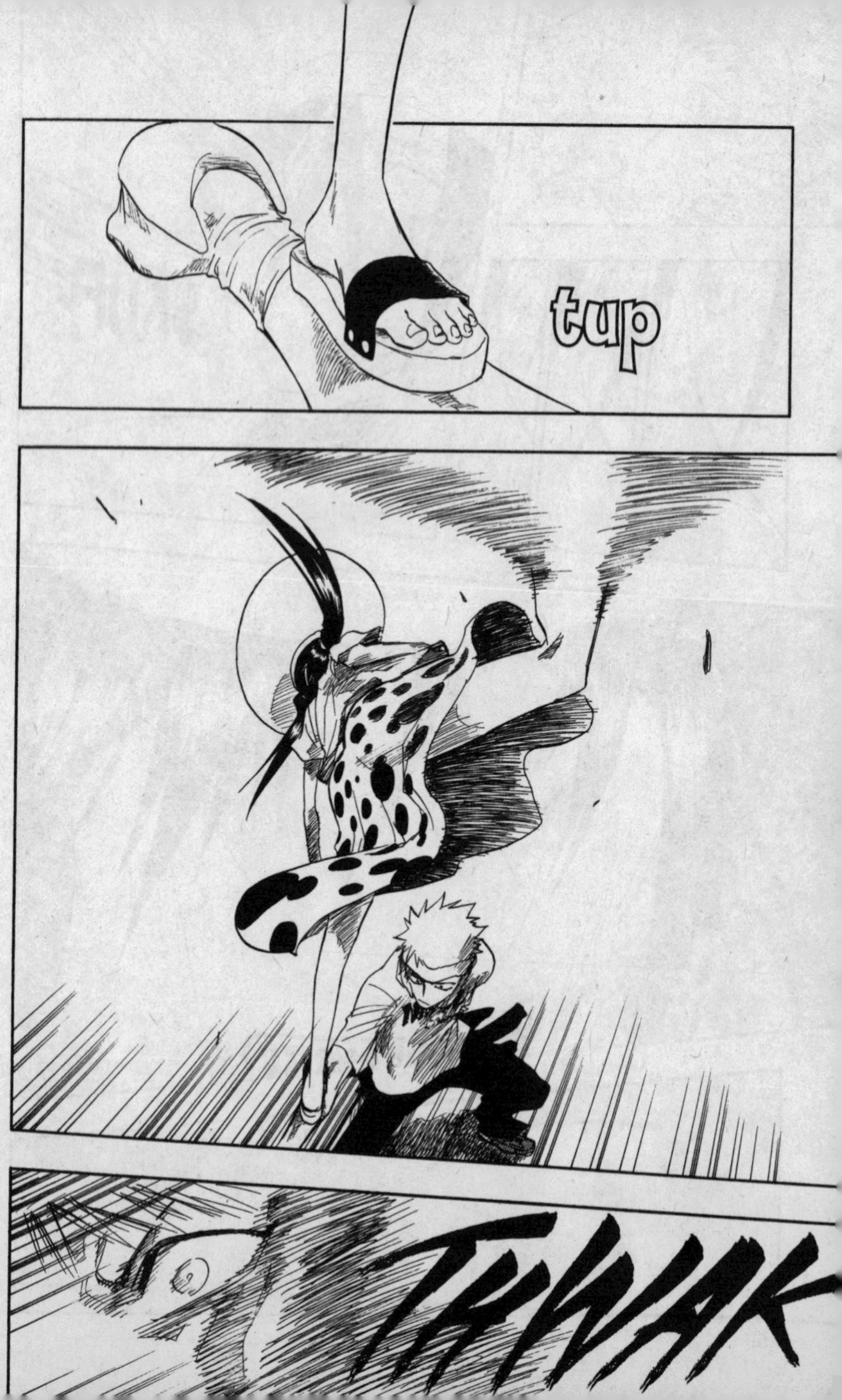
tup
THWAK

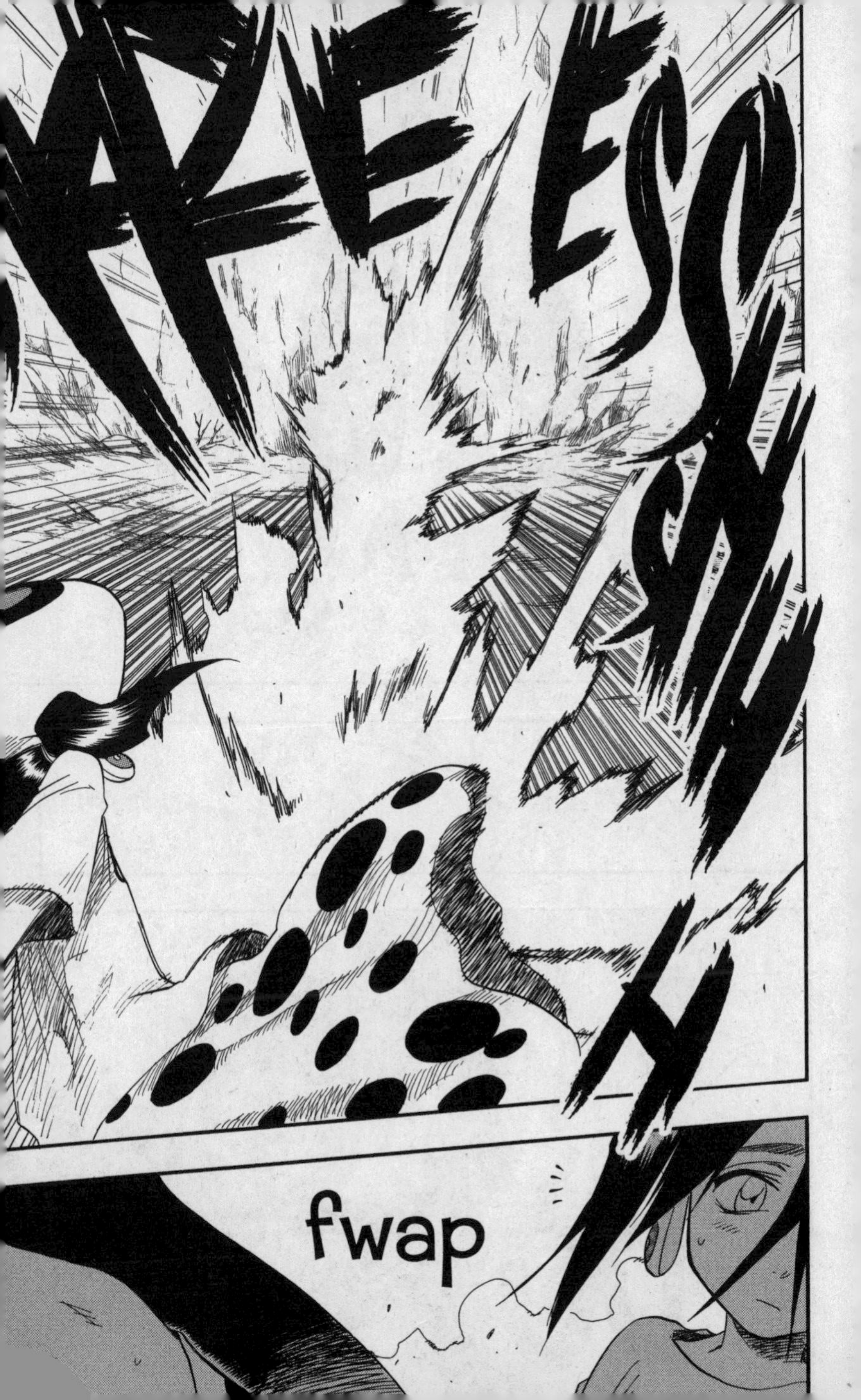
fwap

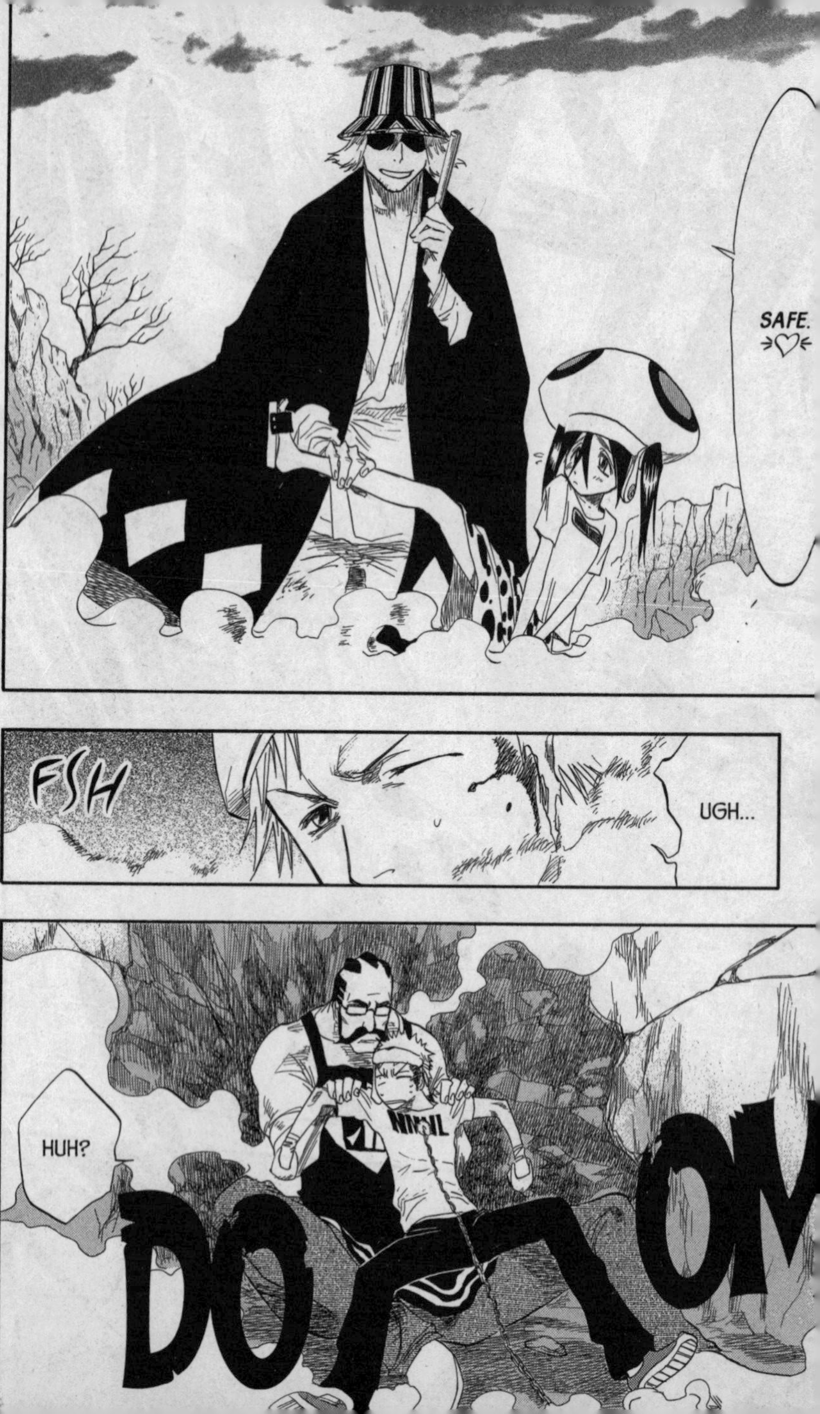
SAFE. ♡
FSH
UGH...
HUH?
DOOM

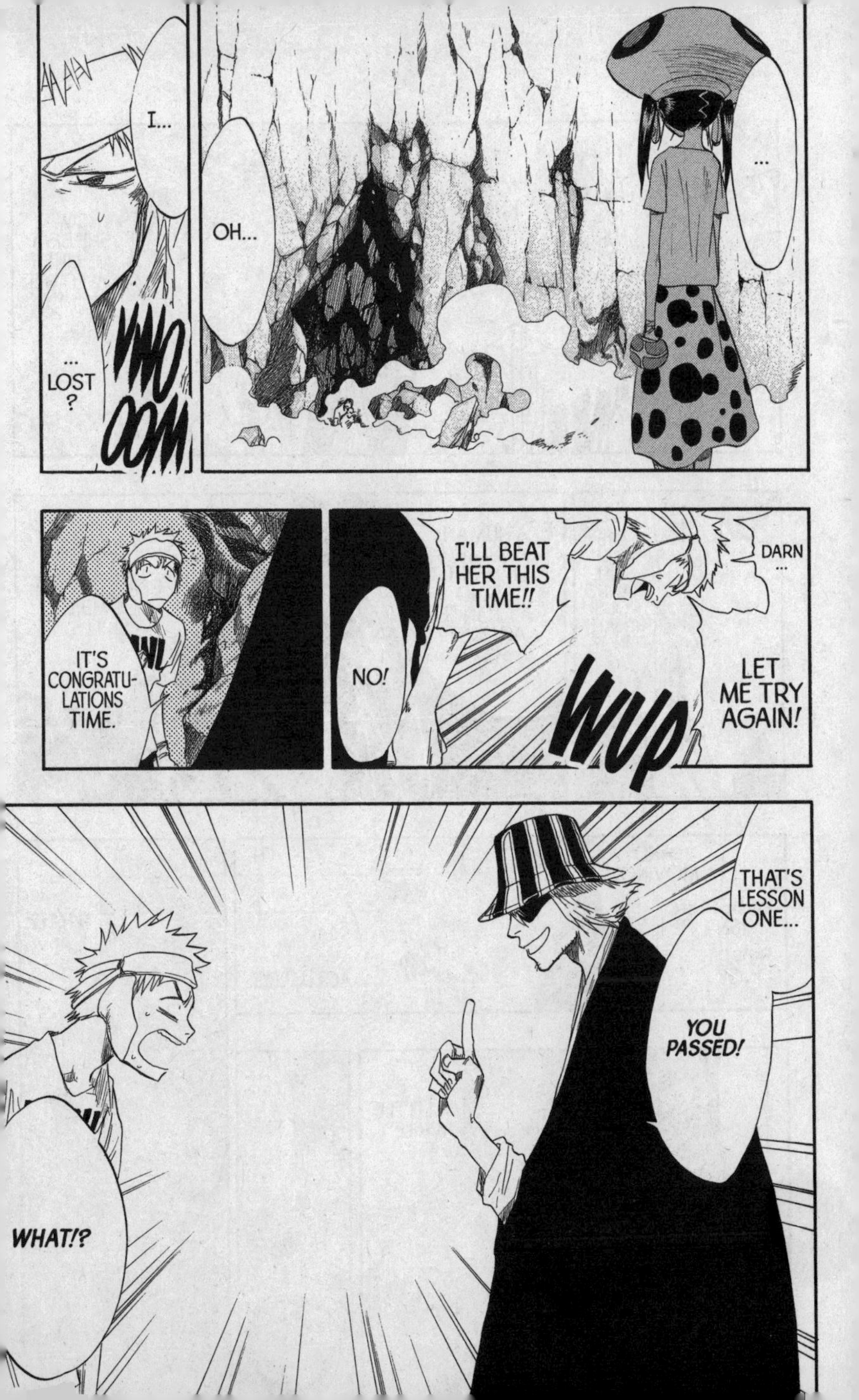
...
OH...
I...
... LOST ?
VWOOOM
DARN ...
LET ME TRY AGAIN!
I'LL BEAT HER THIS TIME!!
WUP
NO!
IT'S CONGRATU-LATIONS TIME.
THAT'S LESSON ONE...
YOU PASSED!
WHAT!?

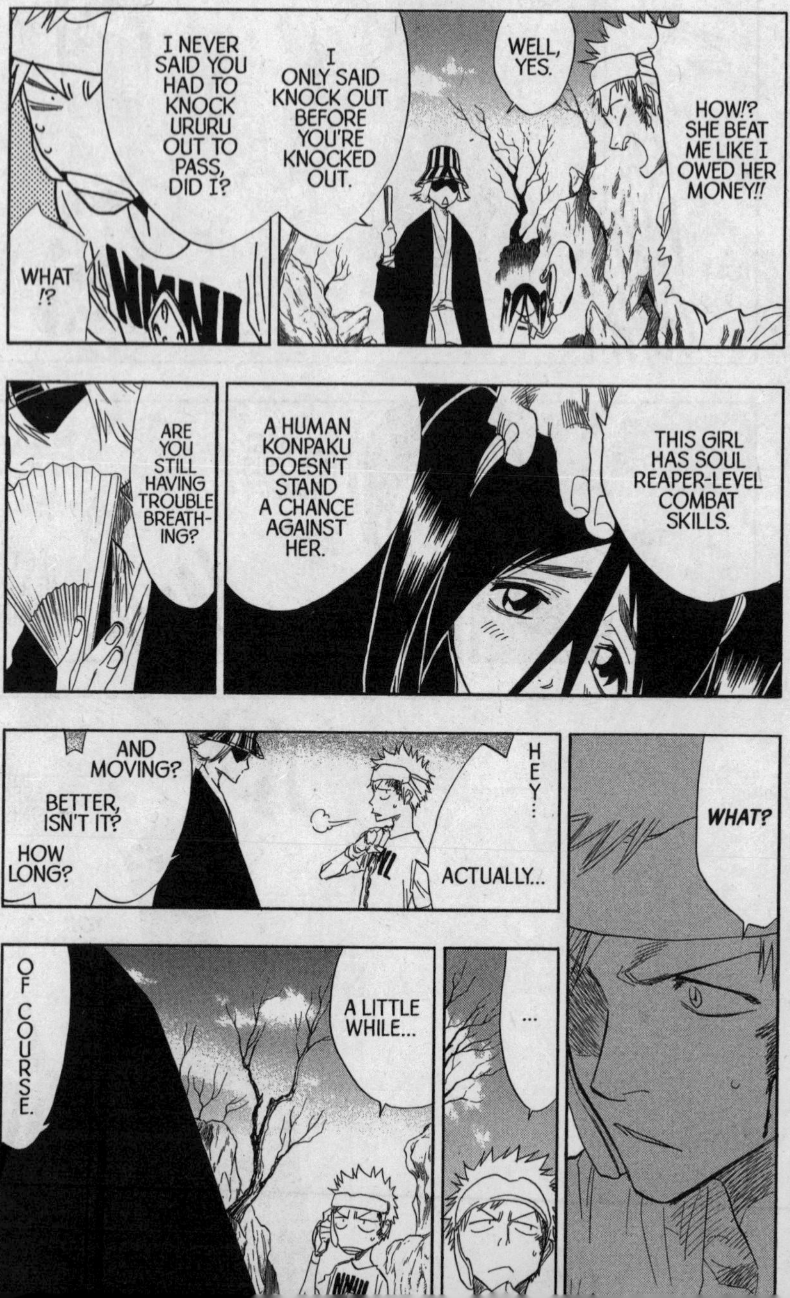
HOW!? SHE BEAT ME LIKE I OWED HER MONEY!!
WELL, YES.
I ONLY SAID KNOCK OUT BEFORE YOU'RE KNOCKED OUT.
I NEVER SAID YOU HAD TO KNOCK URURU OUT TO PASS, DID I?
WHAT!?
THIS GIRL HAS SOUL REAPER-LEVEL COMBAT SKILLS.
A HUMAN KONPAKU DOESN'T STAND A CHANCE AGAINST HER.
ARE YOU STILL HAVING TROUBLE BREATHING?
HEY...
ACTUALLY...
AND MOVING?
BETTER, ISN'T IT?
HOW LONG?
WHAT?
...
A LITTLE WHILE...
OF COURSE.

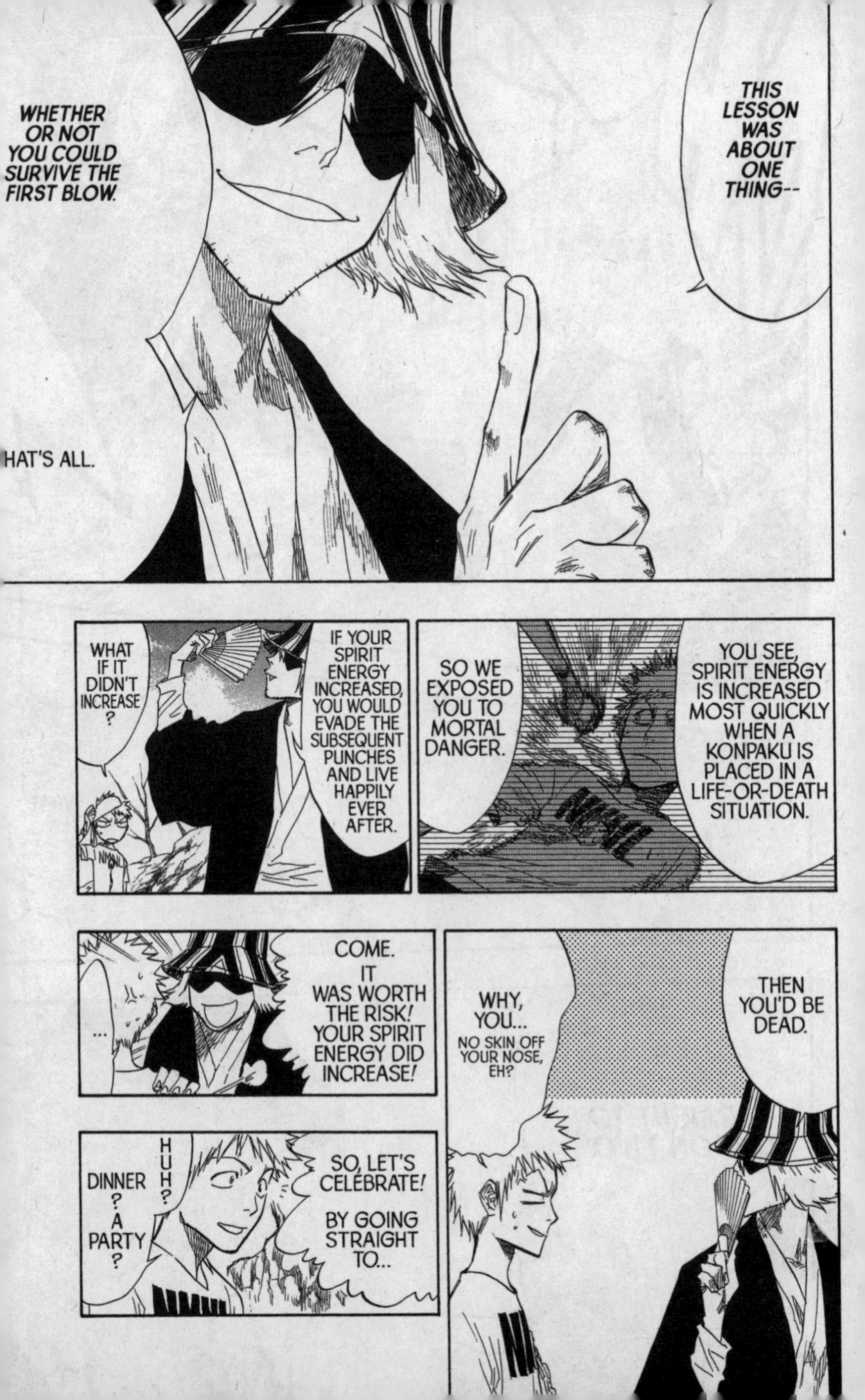
THIS LESSON WAS ABOUT ONE THING--
WHETHER OR NOT YOU COULD SURVIVE THE FIRST BLOW.
HAT'S ALL.
YOU SEE, SPIRIT ENERGY IS INCREASED MOST QUICKLY WHEN A KONPAKU IS PLACED IN A LIFE-OR-DEATH SITUATION.
SO WE EXPOSED YOU TO MORTAL DANGER.
IF YOUR SPIRIT ENERGY INCREASED, YOU WOULD EVADE THE SUBSEQUENT PUNCHES AND LIVE HAPPILY EVER AFTER.
WHAT IF IT DIDN'T INCREASE?
THEN YOU'D BE DEAD.
WHY, YOU... NO SKIN OFF YOUR NOSE, EH?
COME. IT WAS WORTH THE RISK! YOUR SPIRIT ENERGY DID INCREASE!
...
SO, LET'S CELEBRATE! BY GOING STRAIGHT TO...
HUH?
DINNER? A PARTY?

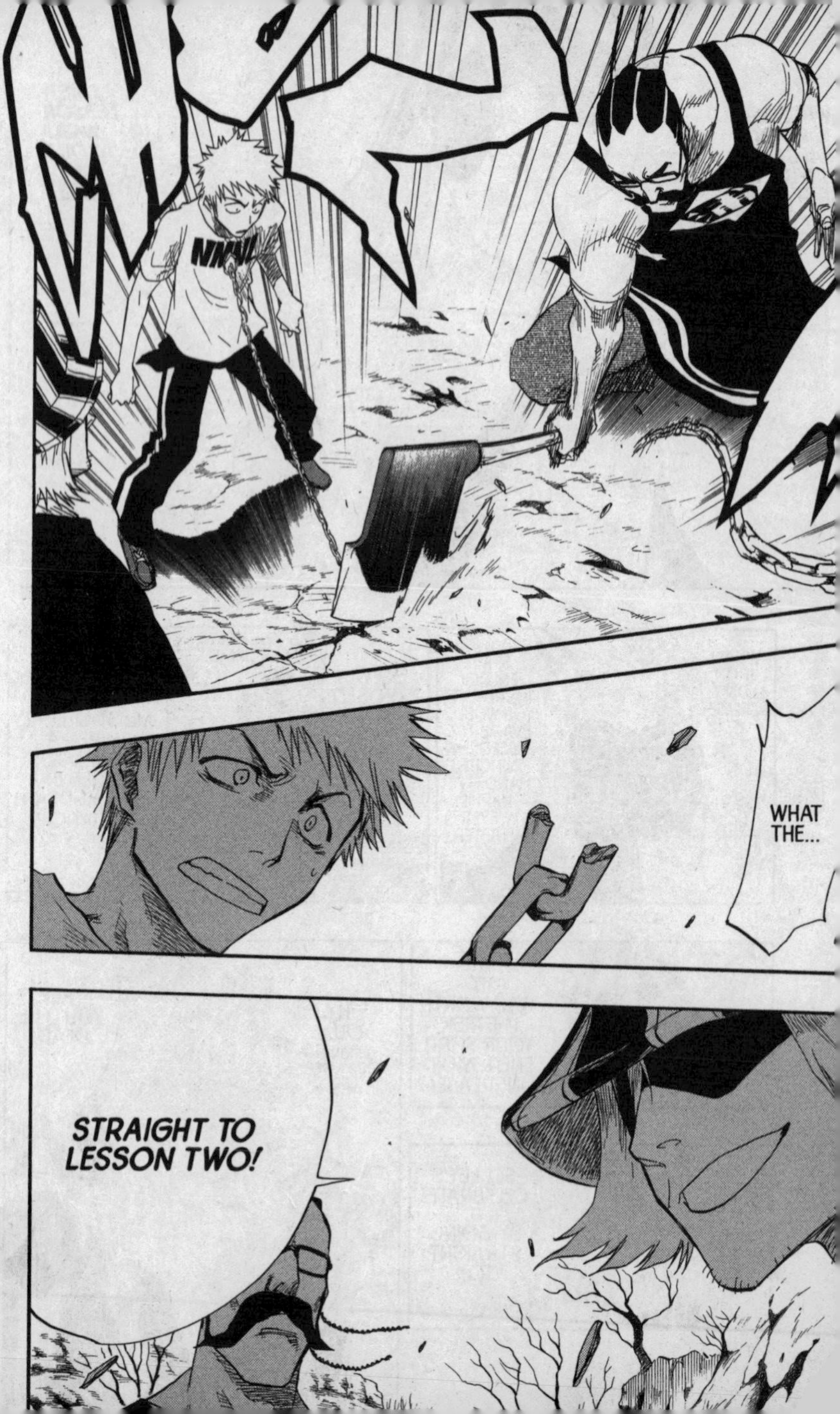
WHAT THE...
STRAIGHT TO LESSON TWO!

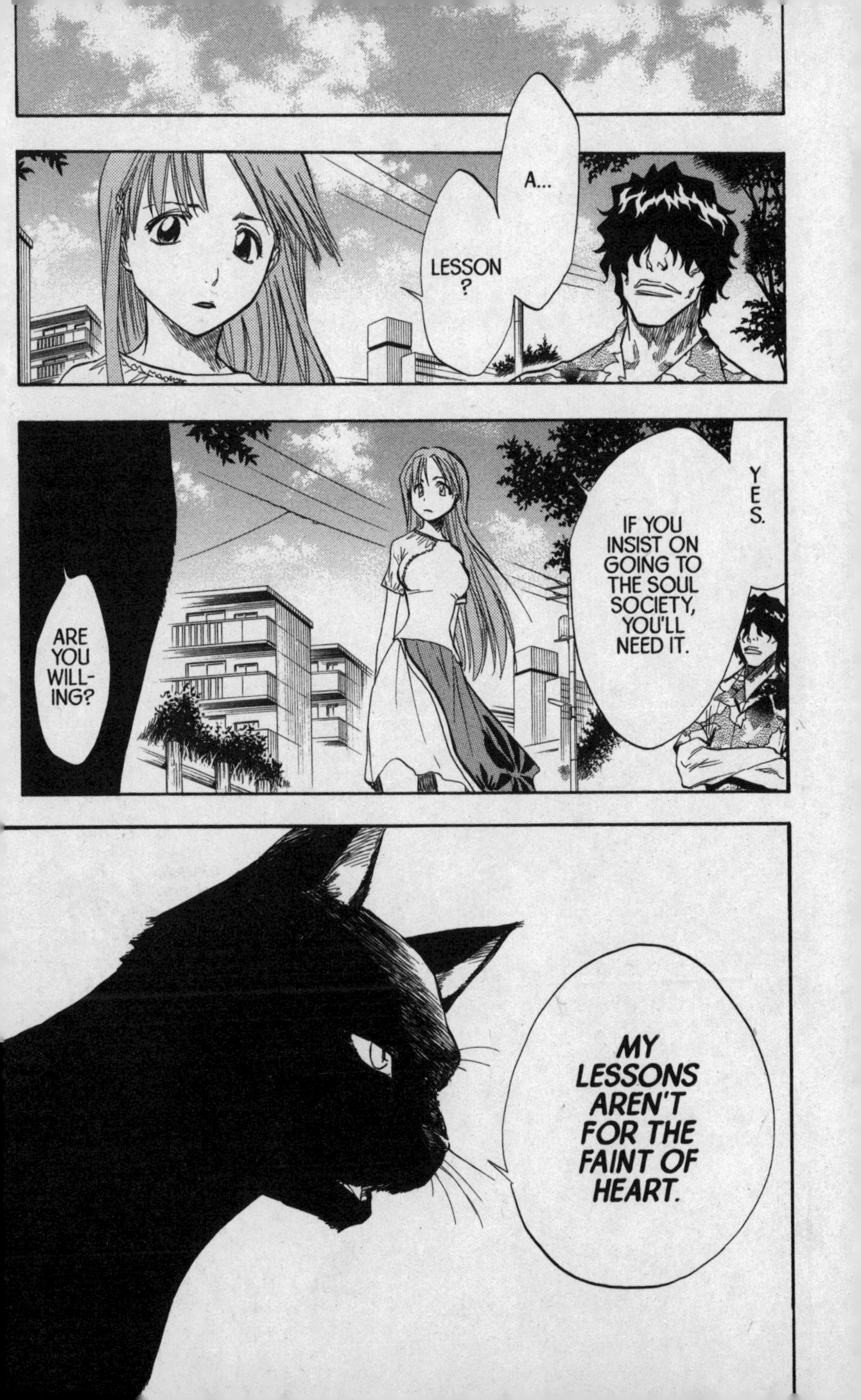
A...
LESSON?
YES.
IF YOU INSIST ON GOING TO THE SOUL SOCIETY, YOU'LL NEED IT.
ARE YOU WILL-ING?
MY LESSONS AREN'T FOR THE FAINT OF HEART.

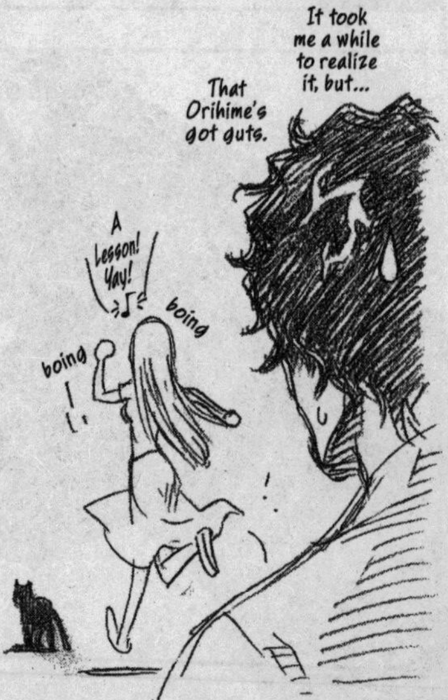
It took me a while to realize it, but...
That Orihime's got guts.
A Lesson! Yay!
boing
boing

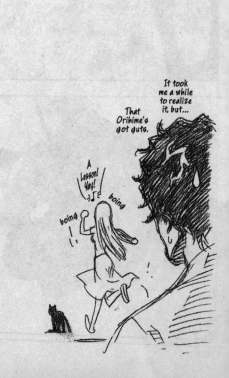

61. Lesson 2: Shattered Shaft

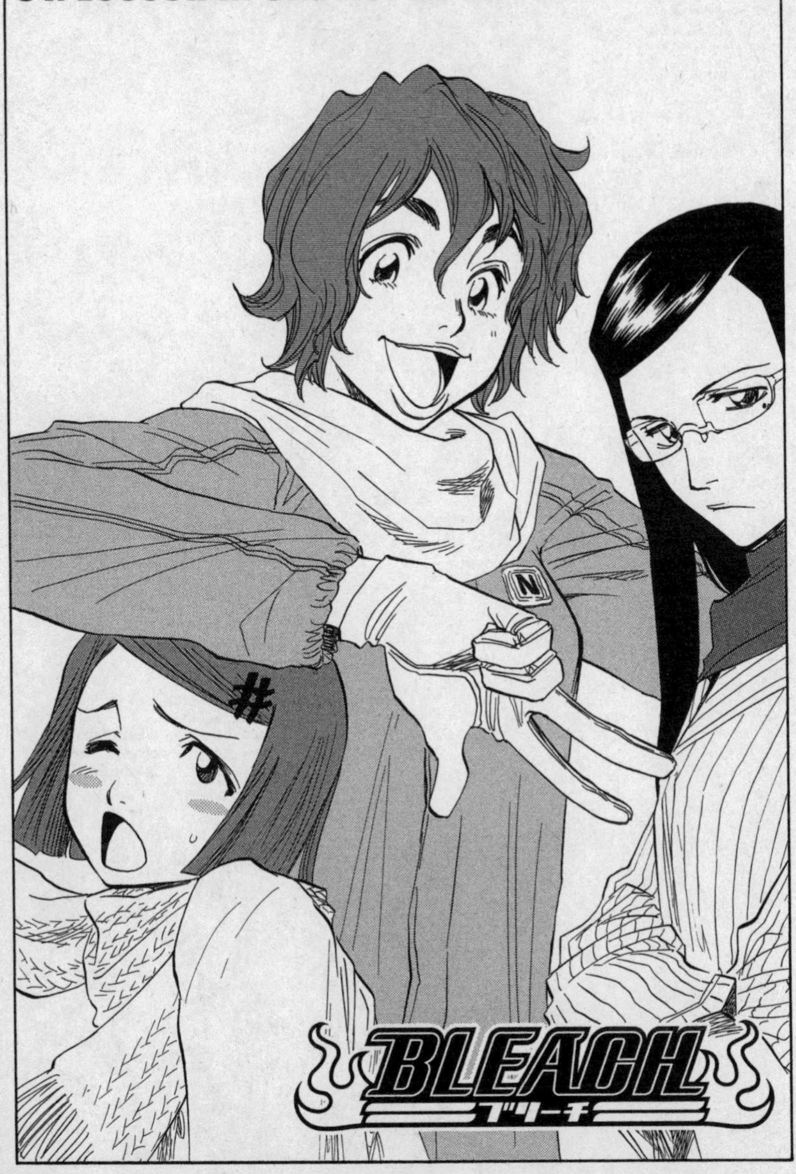
BLEACH
ブリーチ

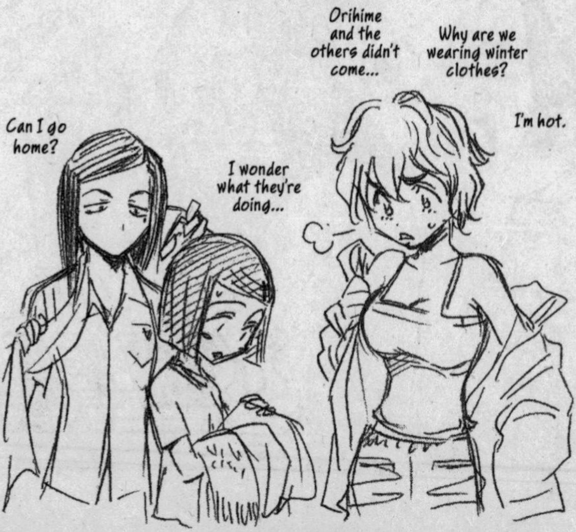
I'm hot.
Why are we wearing winter clothes?
Orihime and the others didn't come...
I wonder what they're doing...
Can I go home?

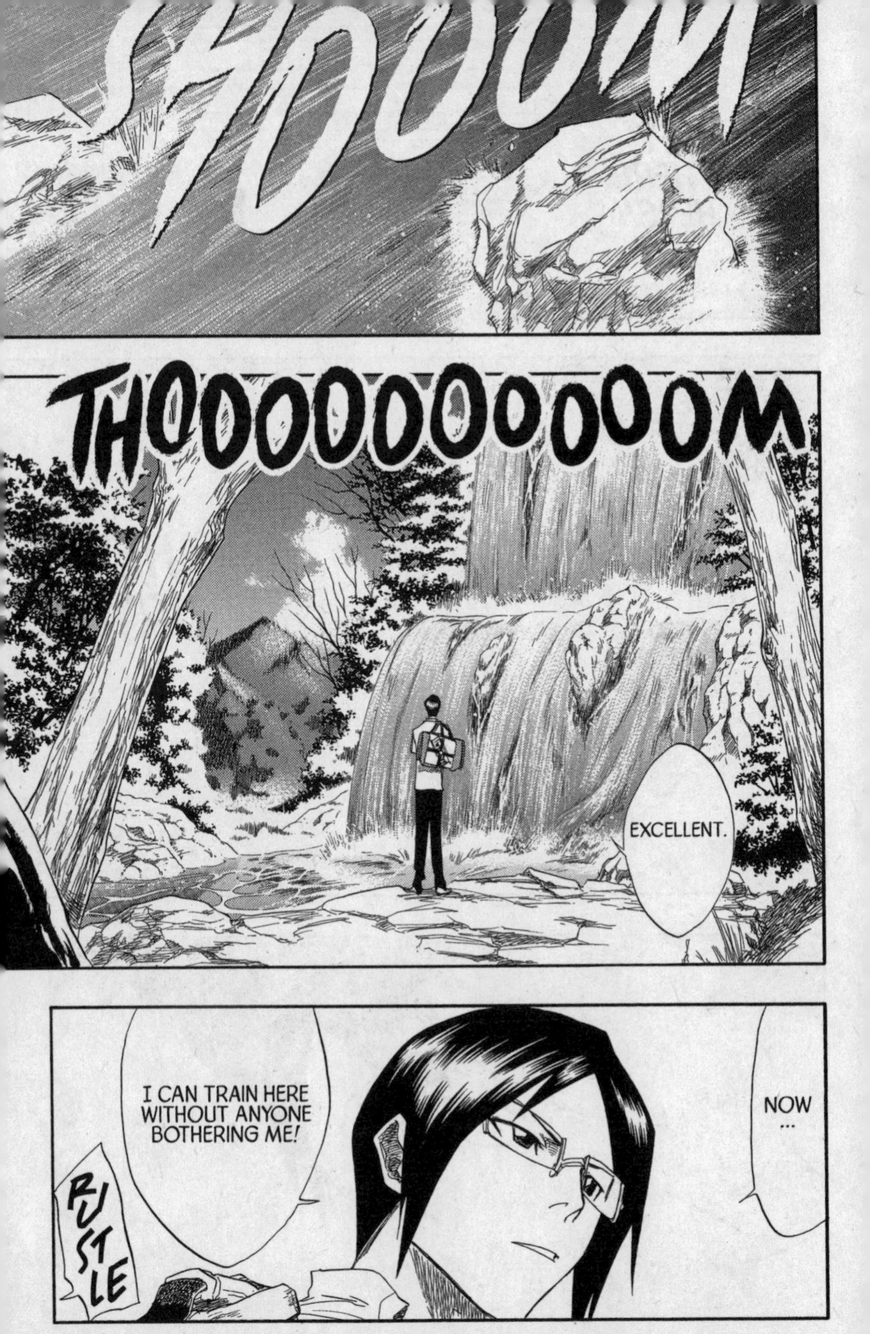
SHOOOM
THOOOOOOOOOM
EXCELLENT.
NOW ...
I CAN TRAIN HERE WITHOUT ANYONE BOTHERING ME!
RUSTLE

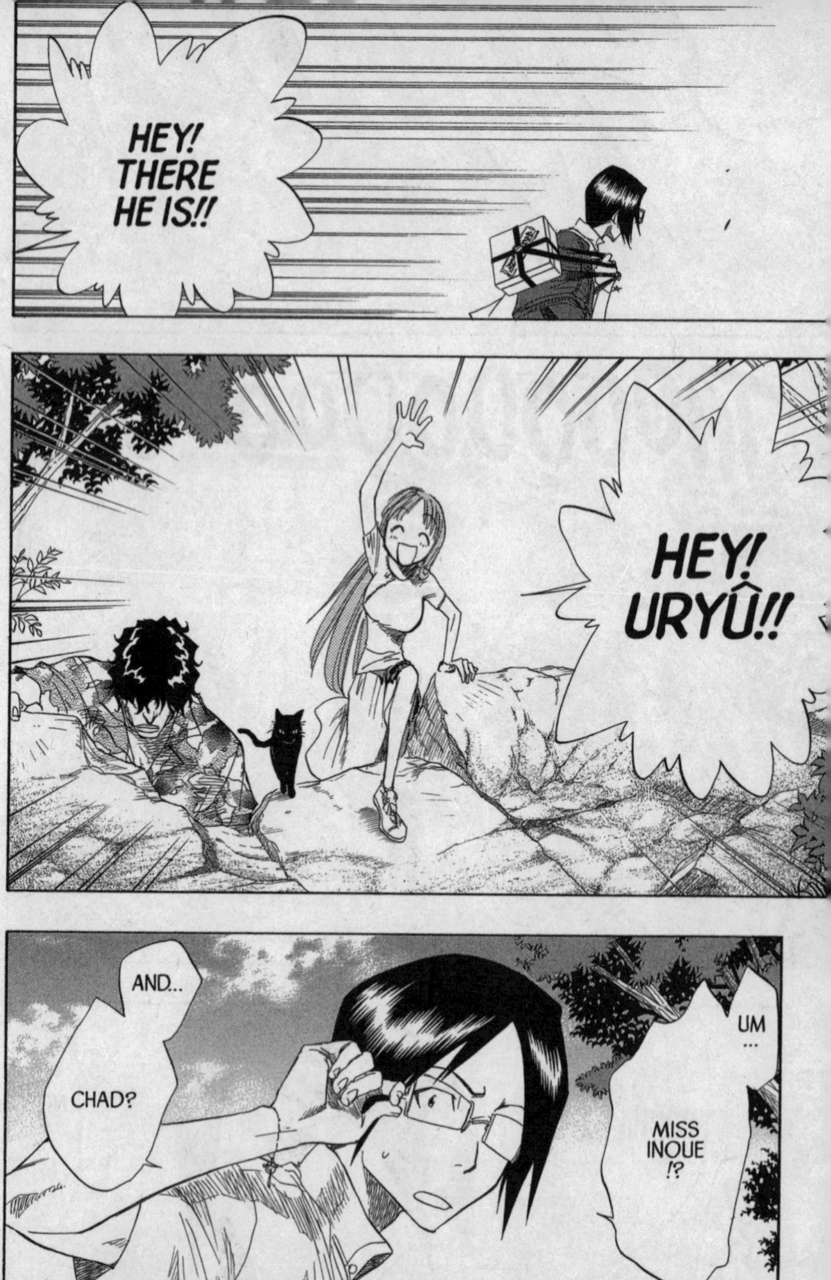
HEY! THERE HE IS!!
HEY! URYÛ!!
UM ... MISS INOUE !?
AND... CHAD?

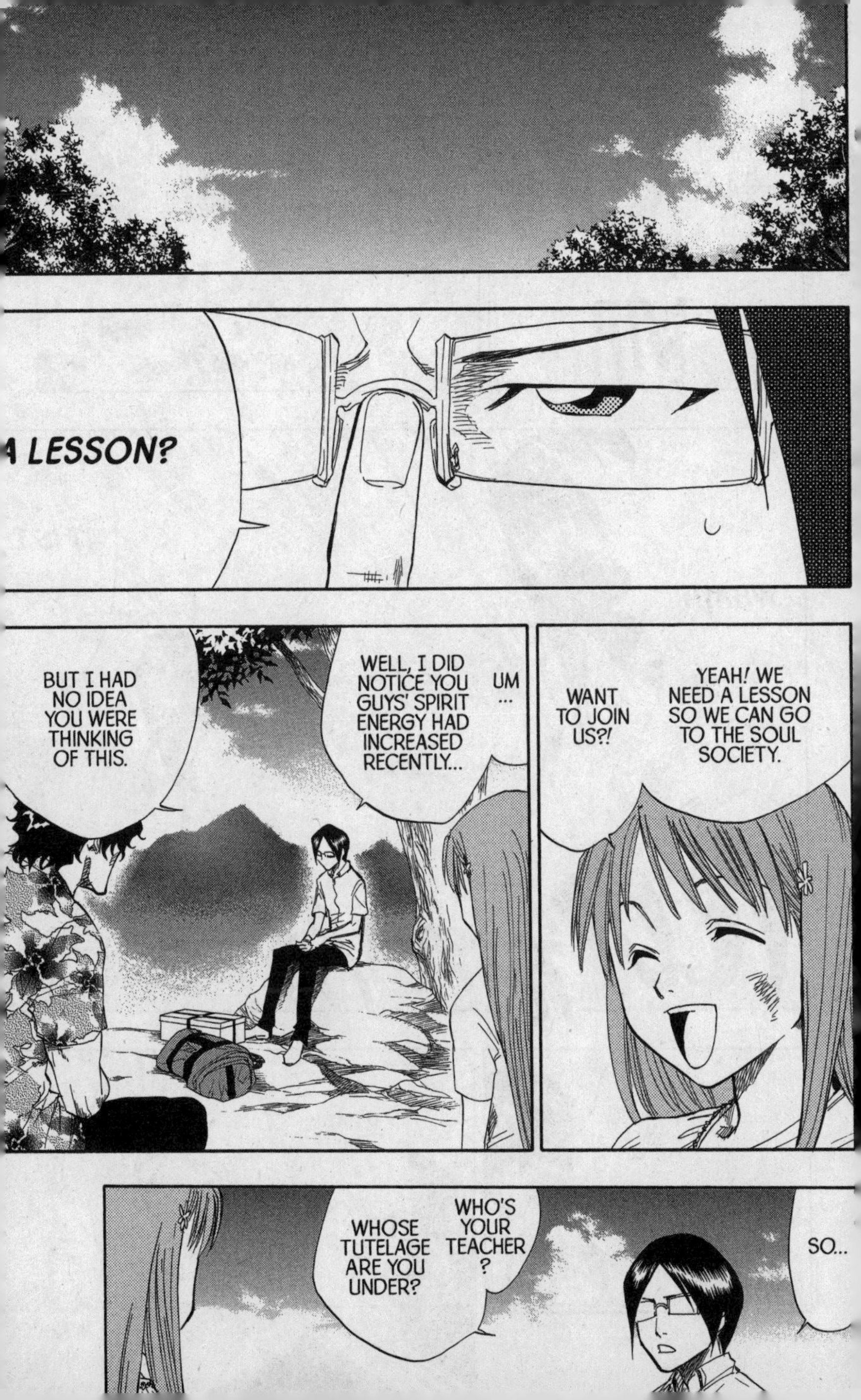
A LESSON?
YEAH! WE NEED A LESSON SO WE CAN GO TO THE SOUL SOCIETY.
WANT TO JOIN US?!
UM ...
WELL, I DID NOTICE YOU GUYS' SPIRIT ENERGY HAD INCREASED RECENTLY...
BUT I HAD NO IDEA YOU WERE THINKING OF THIS.
SO...
WHO'S YOUR TEACHER ?
WHOSE TUTELAGE ARE YOU UNDER?

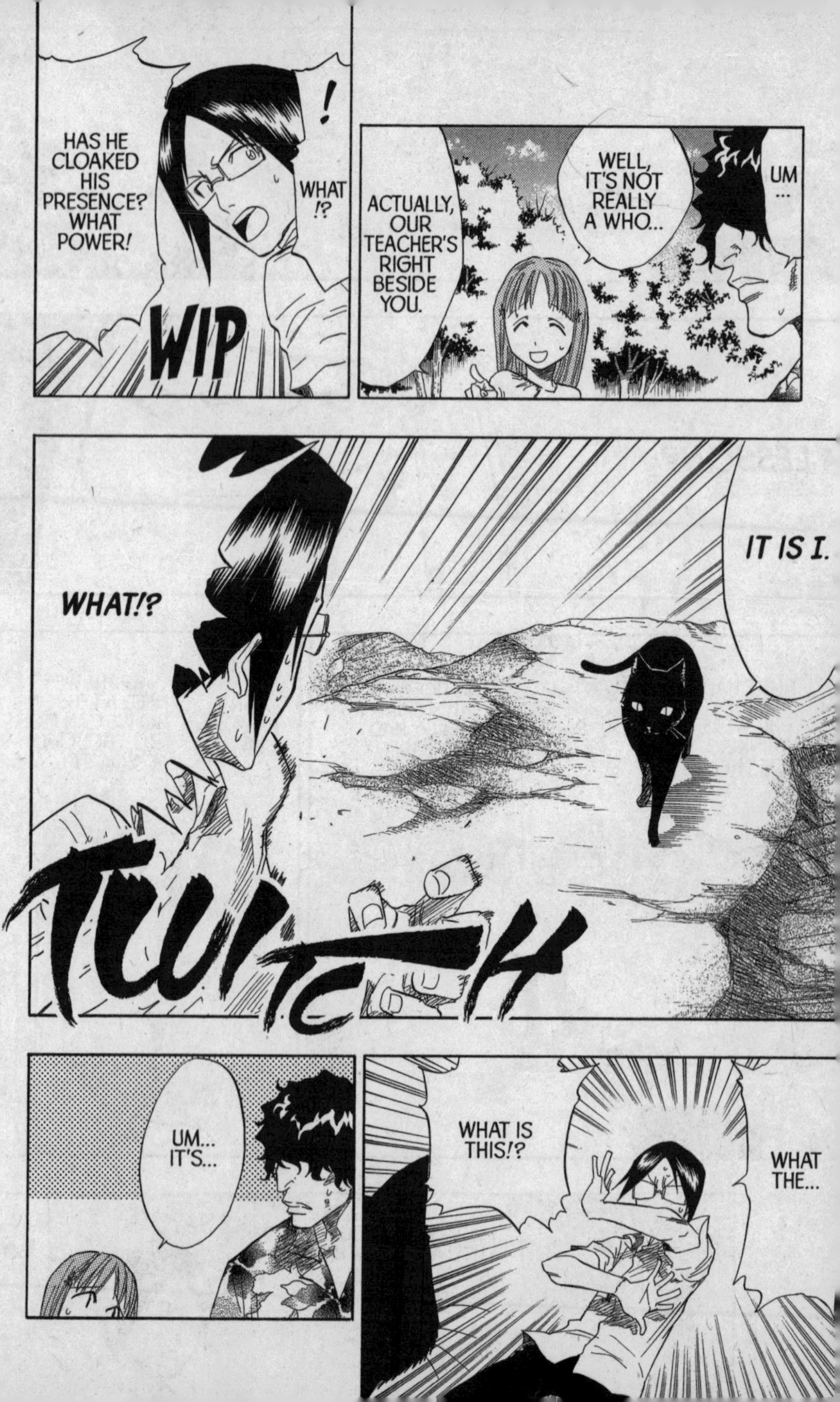
UM ...
WELL, IT'S NOT REALLY A WHO...
ACTUALLY, OUR TEACHER'S RIGHT BESIDE YOU.
!
WHAT!?
HAS HE CLOAKED HIS PRESENCE? WHAT POWER!
WIP
IT IS I.
WHAT!?
TWITCH
WHAT THE...
WHAT IS THIS!?
UM... IT'S...

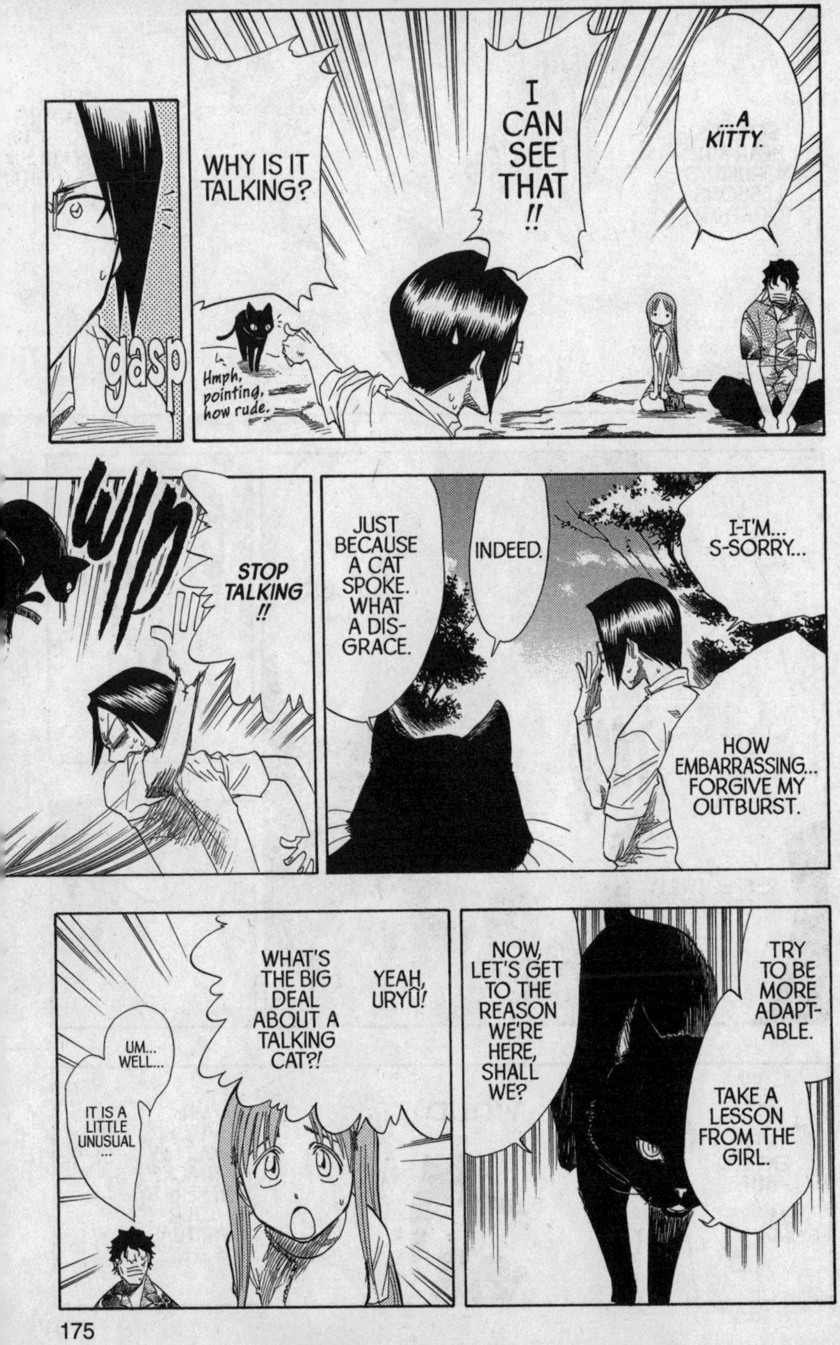

...A KITTY.
I CAN SEE THAT!!
WHY IS IT TALKING?
Hmph, pointing, how rude.
gasp
I-I'M... S-SORRY...
HOW EMBARRASSING... FORGIVE MY OUTBURST.
INDEED.
JUST BECAUSE A CAT SPOKE. WHAT A DISGRACE.
STOP TALKING!!
TRY TO BE MORE ADAPTABLE.
TAKE A LESSON FROM THE GIRL.
NOW, LET'S GET TO THE REASON WE'RE HERE, SHALL WE?
YEAH, URYÛ!
WHAT'S THE BIG DEAL ABOUT A TALKING CAT?!
UM... WELL...
IT IS A LITTLE UNUSUAL...

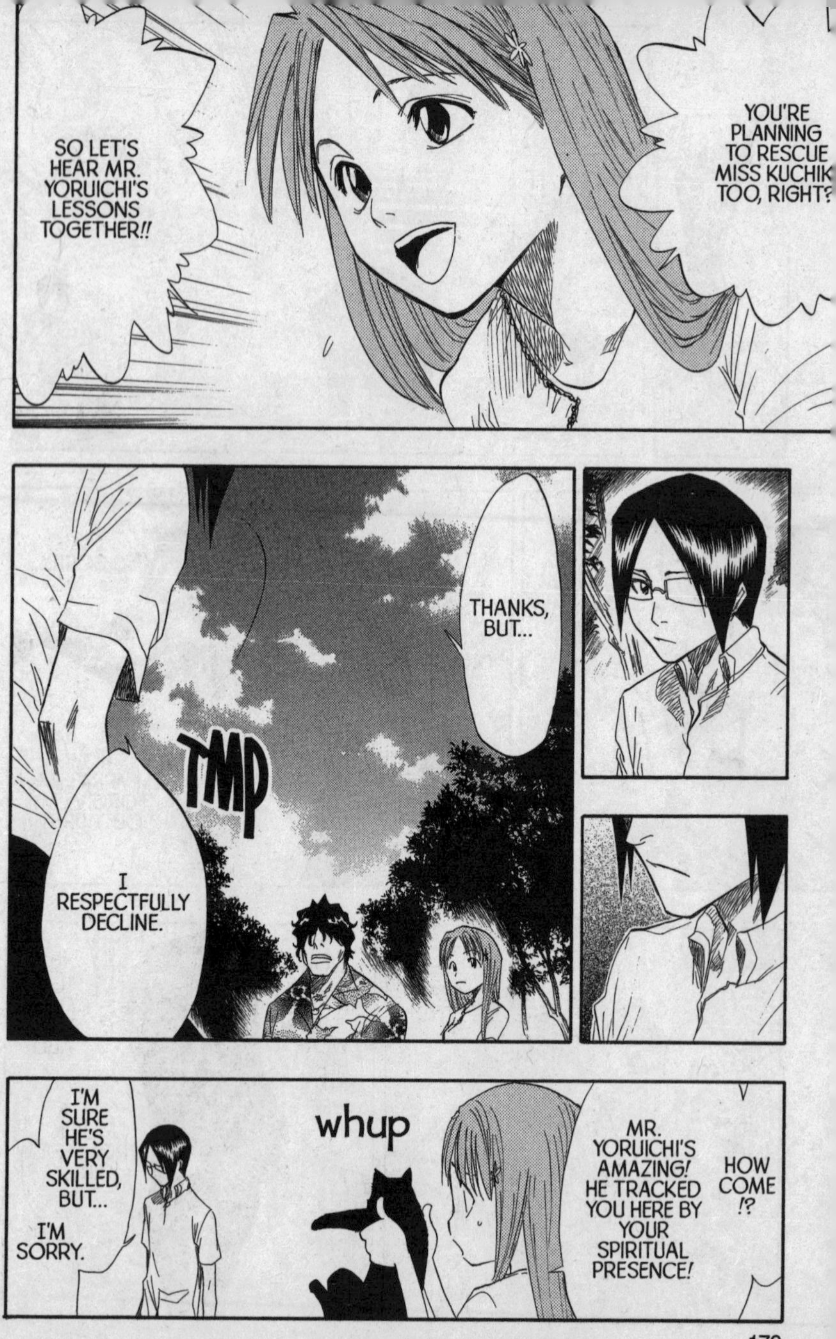
YOU'RE PLANNING TO RESCUE MISS KUCHIK TOO, RIGHT?
SO LET'S HEAR MR. YORUICHI'S LESSONS TOGETHER!!
THANKS, BUT...
TMP
I RESPECTFULLY DECLINE.
HOW COME !?
MR. YORUICHI'S AMAZING! HE TRACKED YOU HERE BY YOUR SPIRITUAL PRESENCE!
whup
I'M SURE HE'S VERY SKILLED, BUT...
I'M SORRY.

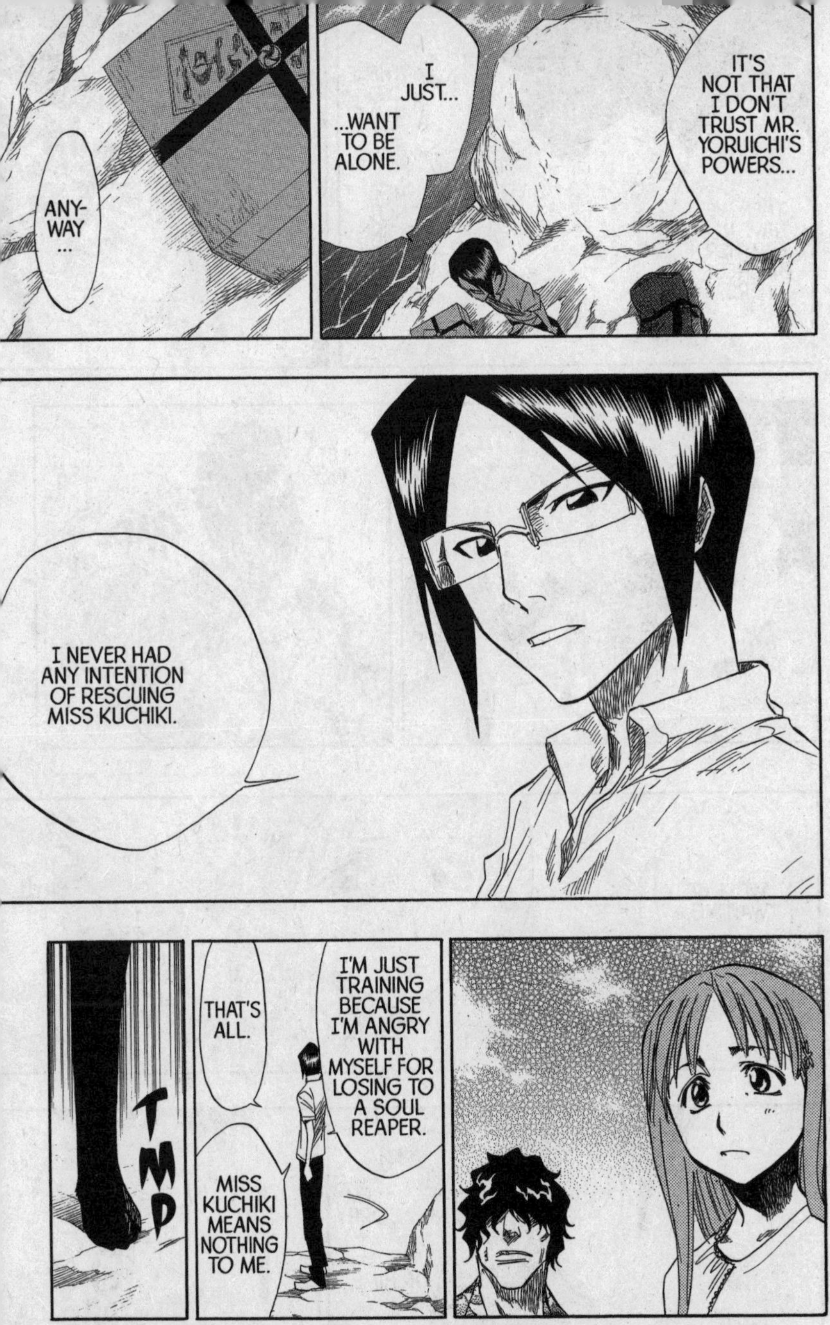
IT'S NOT THAT I DON'T TRUST MR. YORUICHI'S POWERS...
I JUST...
...WANT TO BE ALONE.
ANY-WAY ...
I NEVER HAD ANY INTENTION OF RESCUING MISS KUCHIKI.
I'M JUST TRAINING BECAUSE I'M ANGRY WITH MYSELF FOR LOSING TO A SOUL REAPER.
THAT'S ALL.
MISS KUCHIKI MEANS NOTHING TO ME.
TMP

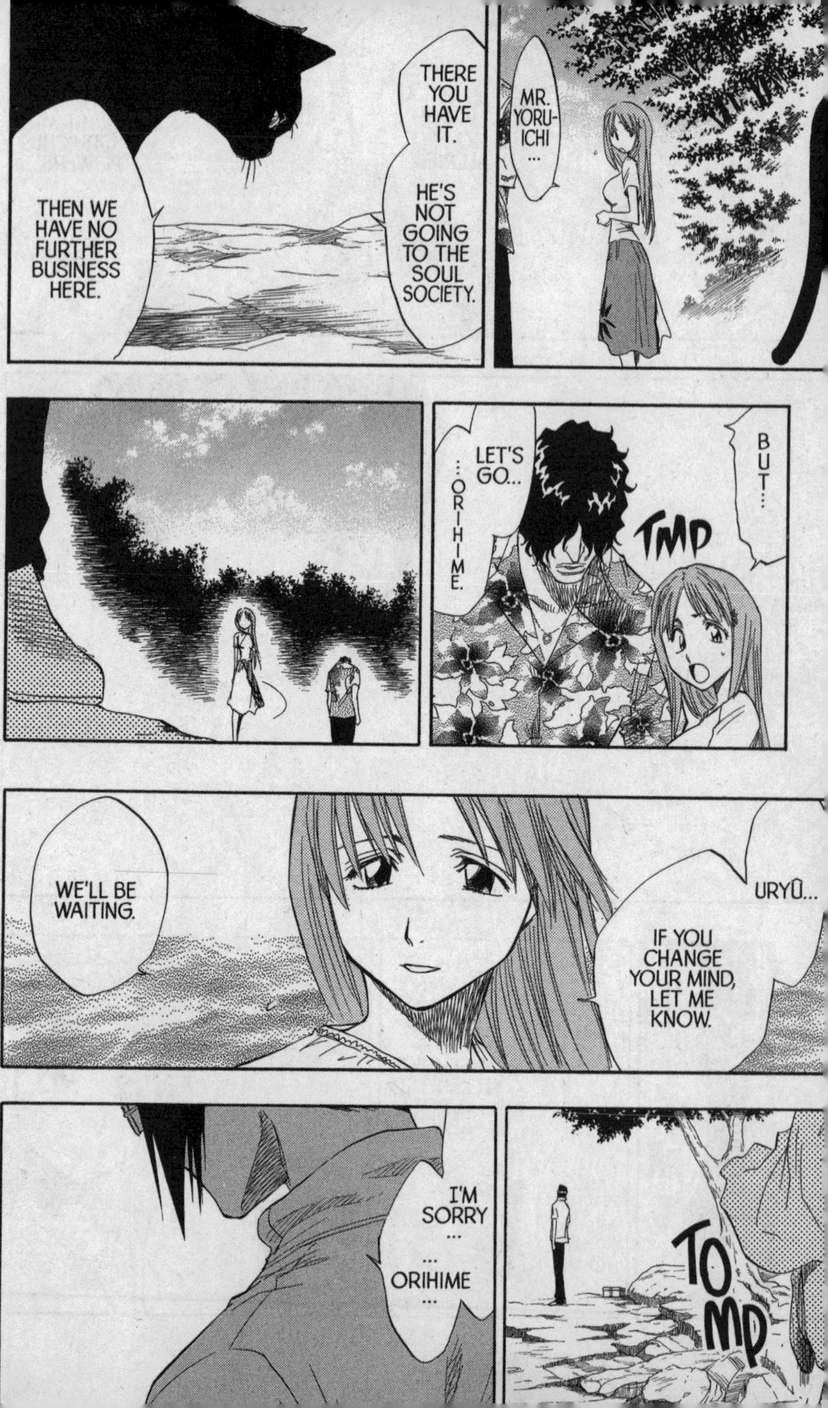
MR. YORUICHI...
THERE YOU HAVE IT.
HE'S NOT GOING TO THE SOUL SOCIETY.
THEN WE HAVE NO FURTHER BUSINESS HERE.
BUT...
TMP
LET'S GO...
...ORIHIME.
URYŪ...
IF YOU CHANGE YOUR MIND, LET ME KNOW.
WE'LL BE WAITING.
TOMP
I'M SORRY...
...ORIHIME...

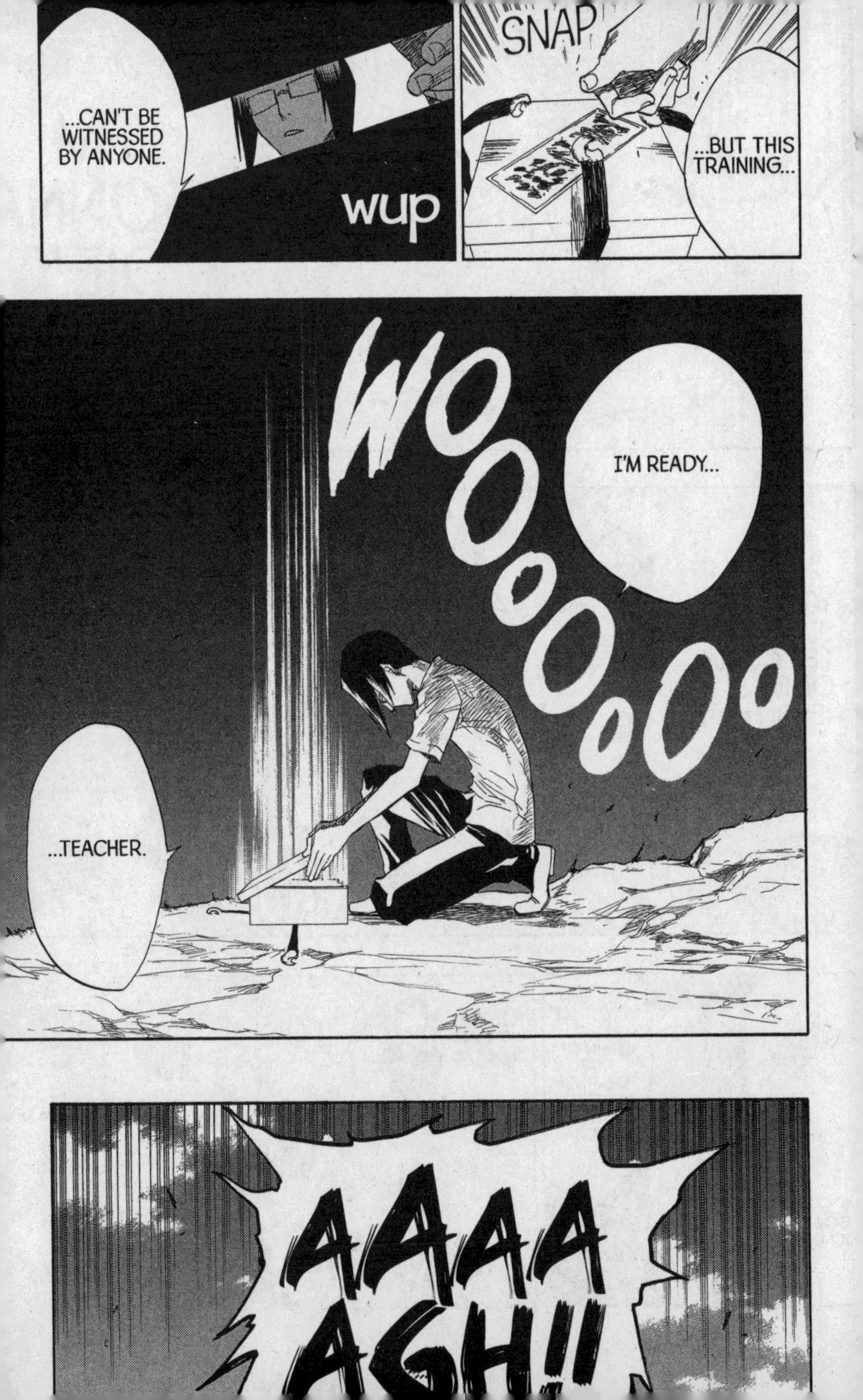
SNAP
...BUT THIS TRAINING...
...CAN'T BE WITNESSED BY ANYONE.
wup
WOOOOOOOO
I'M READY...
...TEACHER.
AAAA AGH!!

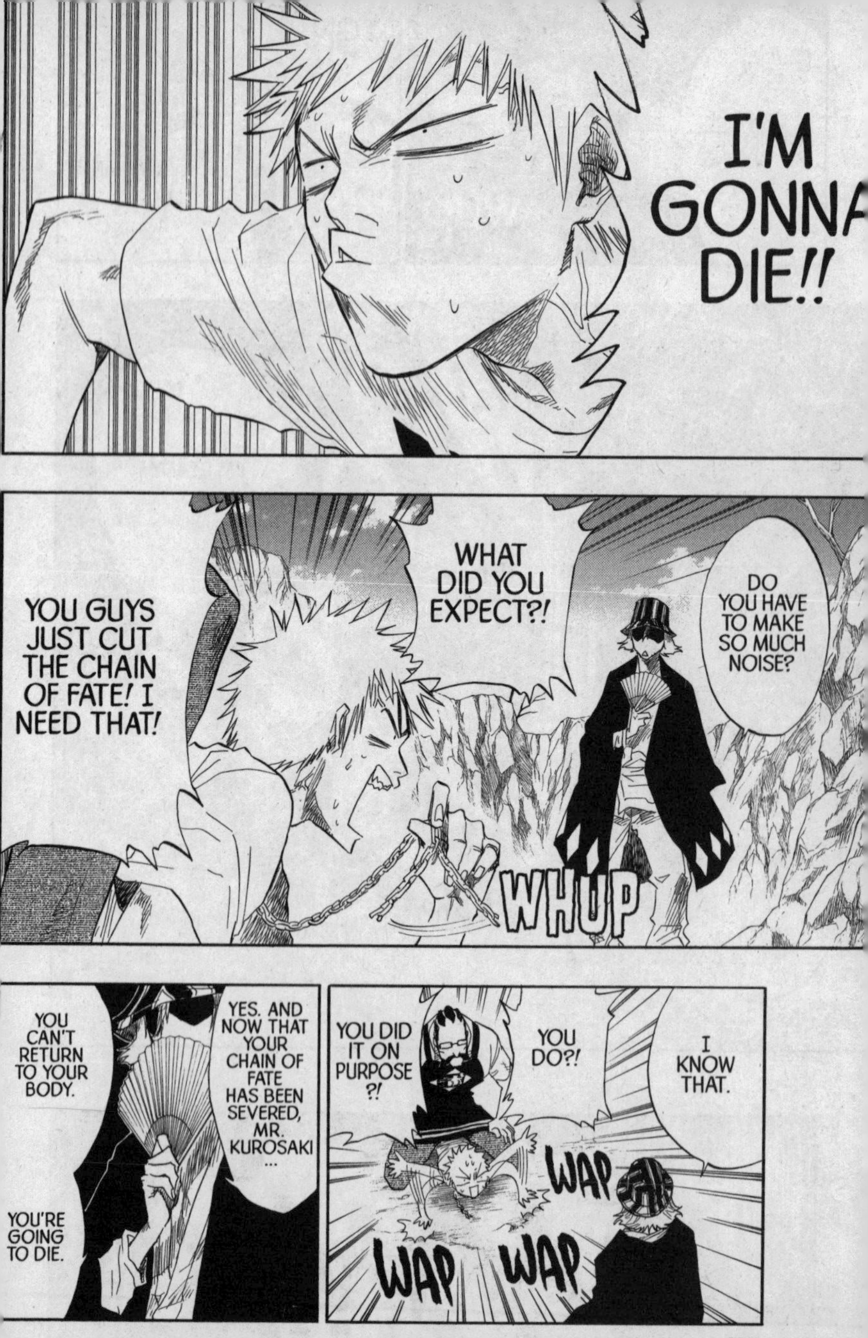
I'M GONNA DIE!!
DO YOU HAVE TO MAKE SO MUCH NOISE?
WHAT DID YOU EXPECT?!
YOU GUYS JUST CUT THE CHAIN OF FATE! I NEED THAT!
WHUP
I KNOW THAT.
YOU DO?!
YOU DID IT ON PURPOSE ?!
WAP
WAP
WAP
YES. AND NOW THAT YOUR CHAIN OF FATE HAS BEEN SEVERED, MR. KUROSAKI ...
YOU CAN'T RETURN TO YOUR BODY.
YOU'RE GOING TO DIE.

READ THIS WAY

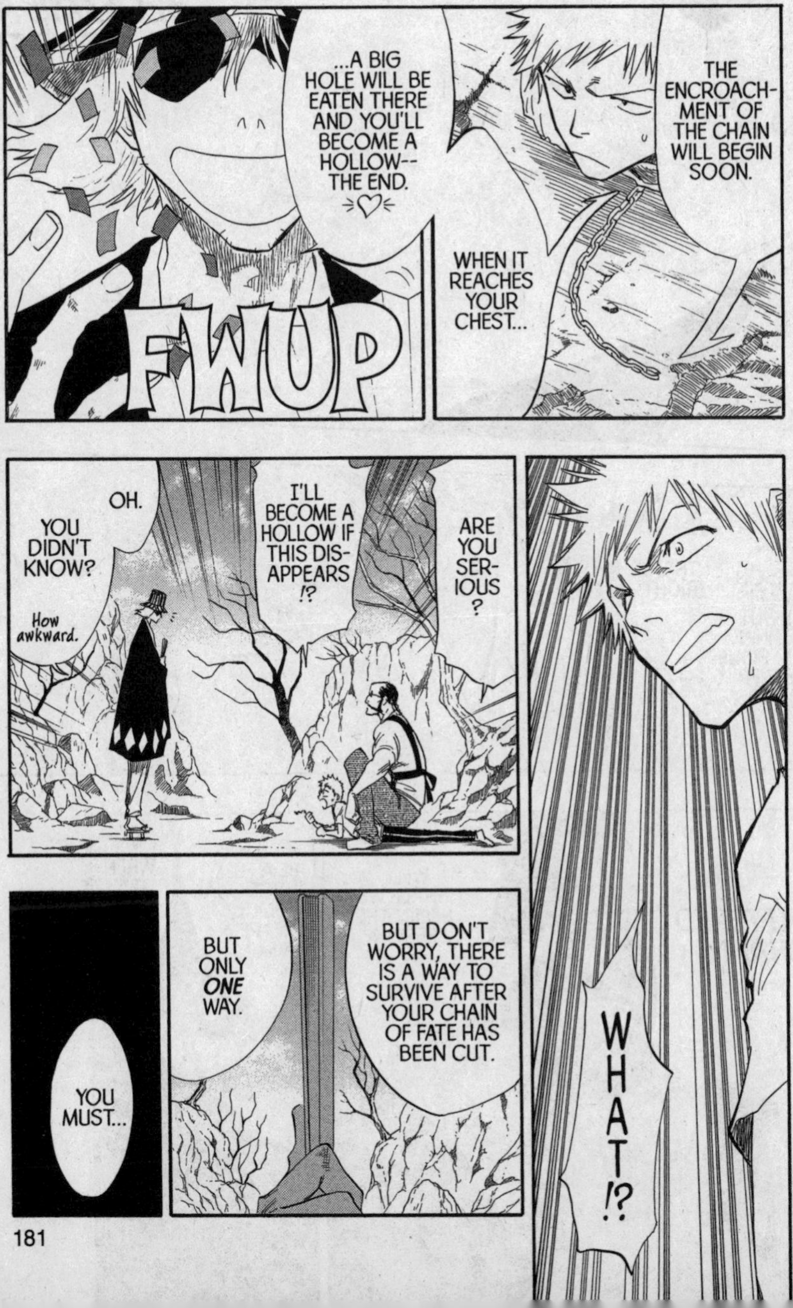
THE ENCROACHMENT OF THE CHAIN WILL BEGIN SOON.
WHEN IT REACHES YOUR CHEST...
...A BIG HOLE WILL BE EATEN THERE AND YOU'LL BECOME A HOLLOW-- THE END. ♡
FWUP
WHAT!?
ARE YOU SERIOUS?
I'LL BECOME A HOLLOW IF THIS DISAPPEARS!?
OH.
YOU DIDN'T KNOW?
How awkward.
BUT DON'T WORRY, THERE IS A WAY TO SURVIVE AFTER YOUR CHAIN OF FATE HAS BEEN CUT.
BUT ONLY ONE WAY.
YOU MUST...

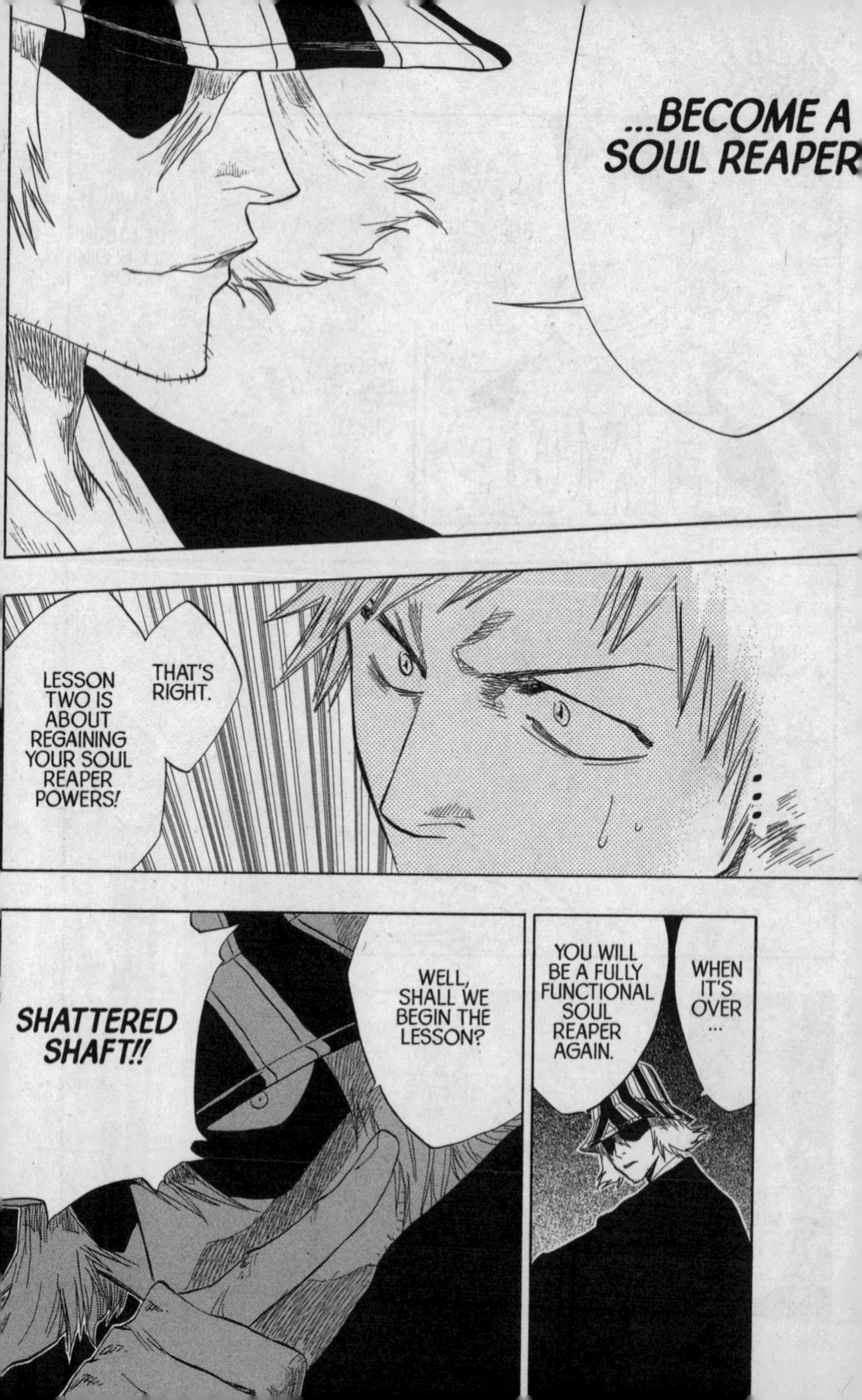
...BECOME A SOUL REAPER
THAT'S RIGHT.
LESSON TWO IS ABOUT REGAINING YOUR SOUL REAPER POWERS!
...
WHEN IT'S OVER ...
YOU WILL BE A FULLY FUNCTIONAL SOUL REAPER AGAIN.
WELL, SHALL WE BEGIN THE LESSON?
SHATTERED SHAFT!!

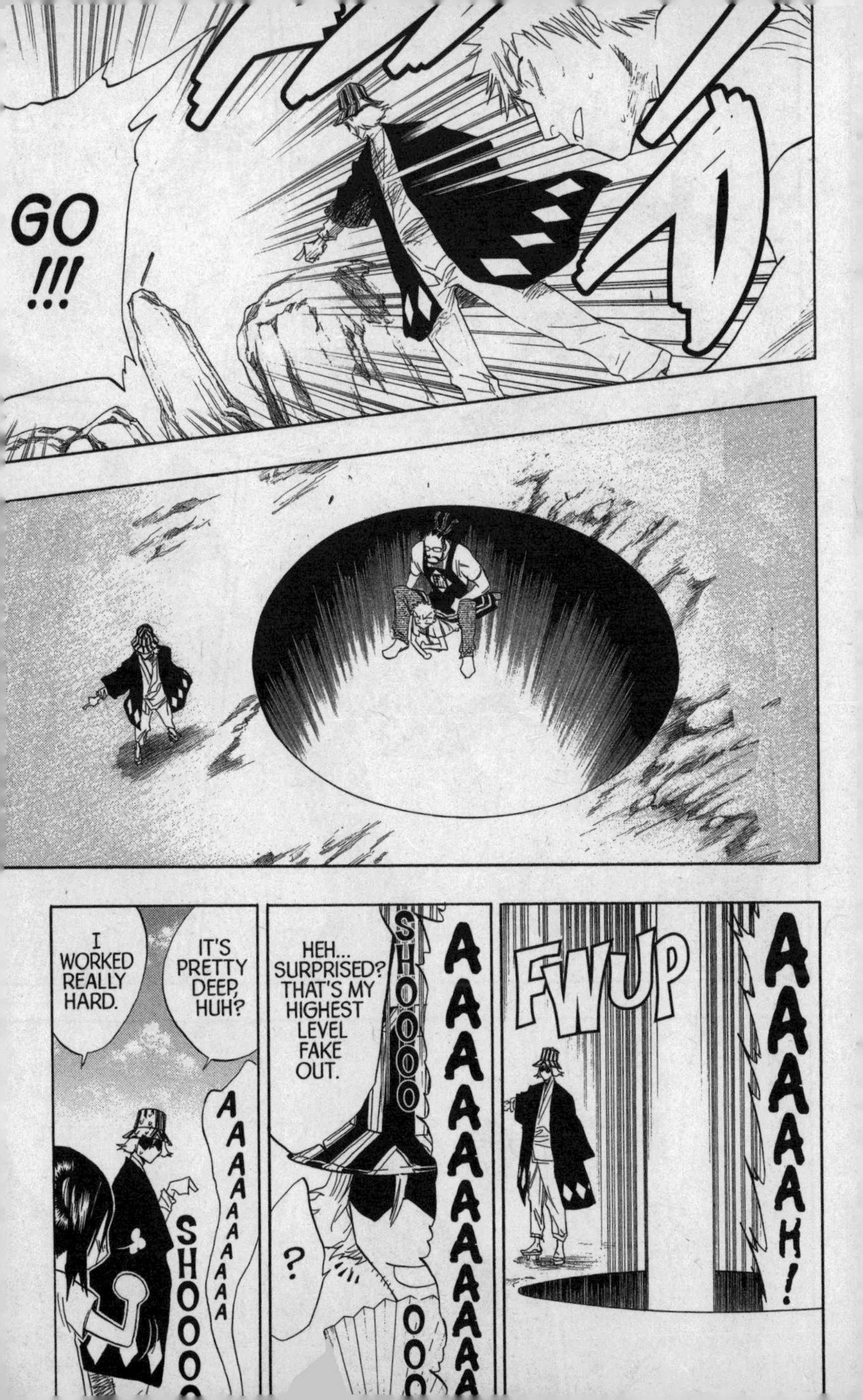
GO !!!
FWUP
AAAAAAAH!
SHOOOO
AAAAAAAAAAA
HEH... SURPRISED? THAT'S MY HIGHEST LEVEL FAKE OUT.
?
IT'S PRETTY DEEP, HUH?
I WORKED REALLY HARD.
AAAAAAAAAAA
SHOOOO

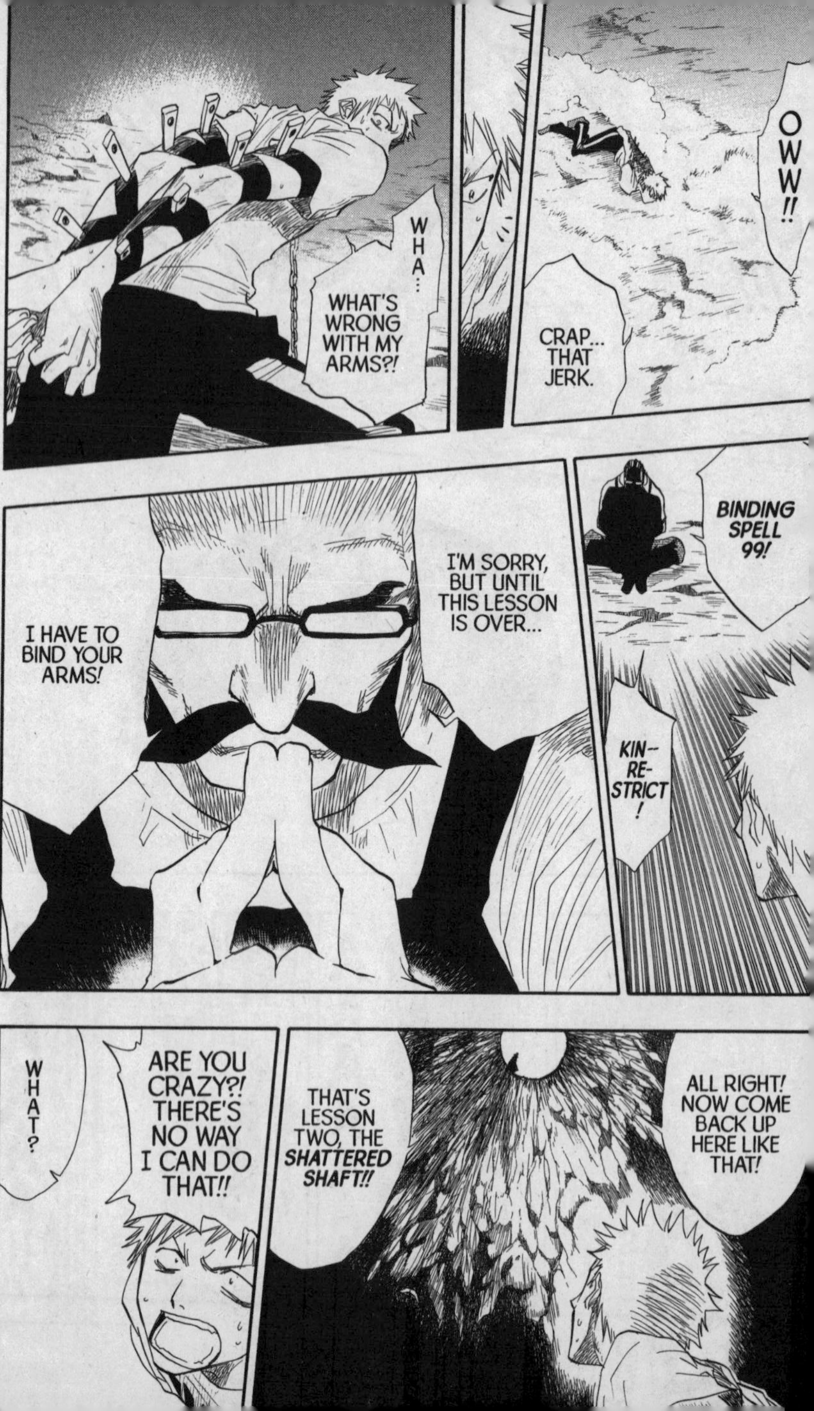
OWW!!
CRAP... THAT JERK.
WHA...
WHAT'S WRONG WITH MY ARMS?!
BINDING SPELL 99!
KIN-- RE- STRICT!
I'M SORRY, BUT UNTIL THIS LESSON IS OVER...
I HAVE TO BIND YOUR ARMS!
ALL RIGHT! NOW COME BACK UP HERE LIKE THAT!
THAT'S LESSON TWO, THE *SHATTERED SHAFT!!*
ARE YOU CRAZY?! THERE'S NO WAY I CAN DO THAT!!
WHAT?

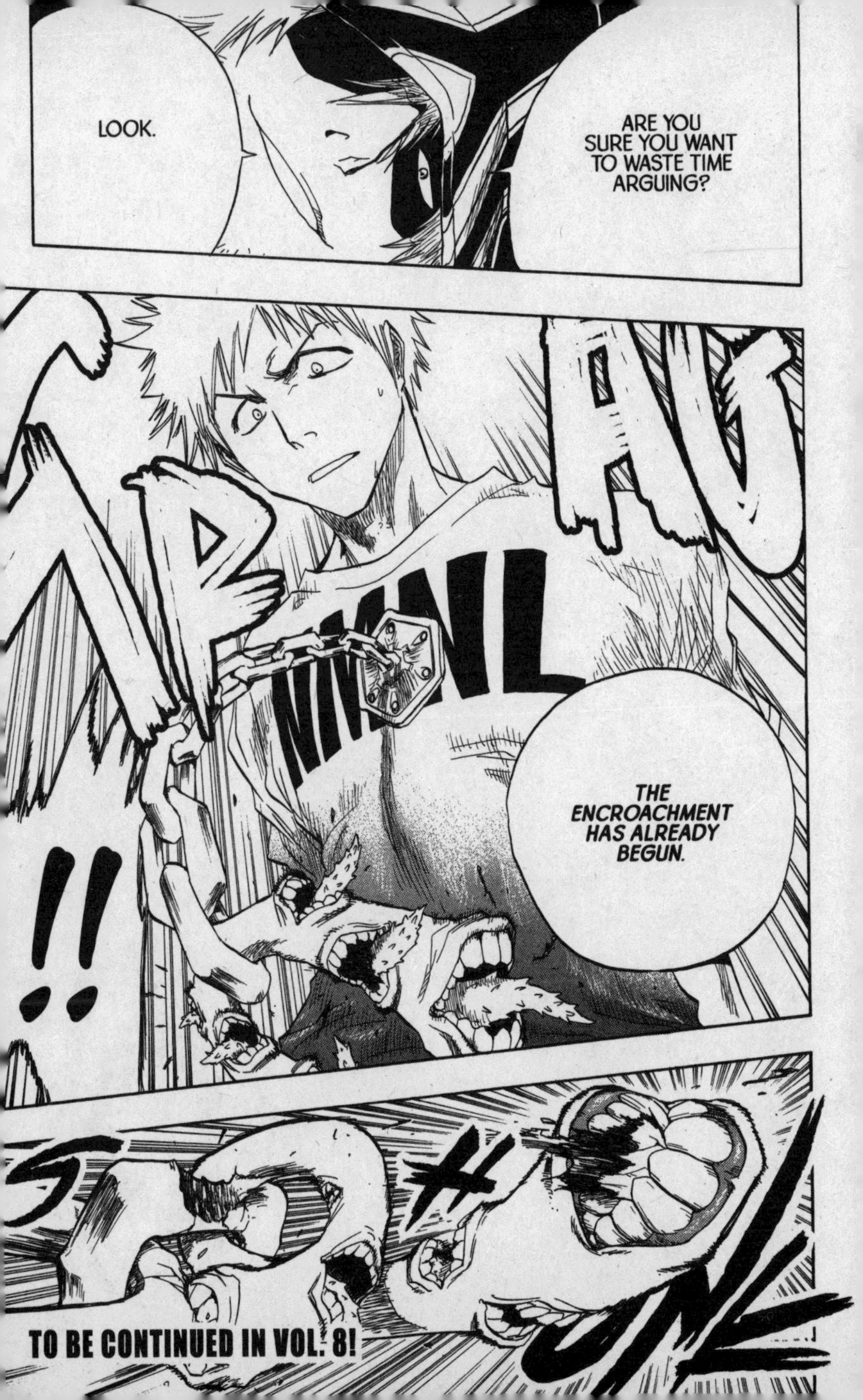
ARE YOU SURE YOU WANT TO WASTE TIME ARGUING?
LOOK.
THE ENCROACHMENT HAS ALREADY BEGUN.
TO BE CONTINUED IN VOL. 8!

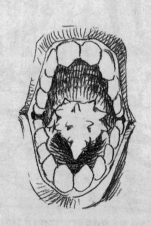

BLEACH EXTRA!!!
RADIO-KON

BLEACH EXTRA!!!
RADIO-KON2

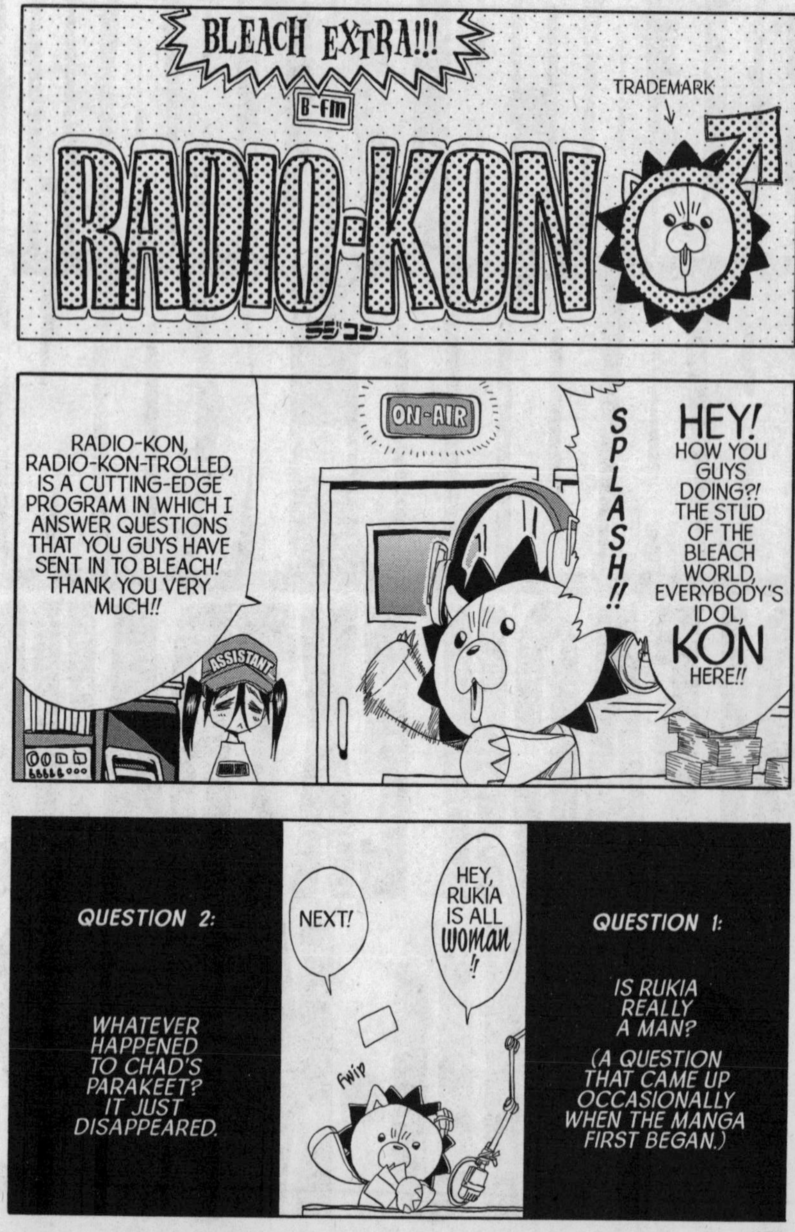
BLEACH EXTRA!!!
B-FM
TRADEMARK
RADIO-KON
ラジコン
HEY! HOW YOU GUYS DOING?! THE STUD OF THE BLEACH WORLD, EVERYBODY'S IDOL, KON HERE!!
SPLASH!!
ON-AIR
RADIO-KON, RADIO-KON-TROLLED, IS A CUTTING-EDGE PROGRAM IN WHICH I ANSWER QUESTIONS THAT YOU GUYS HAVE SENT IN TO BLEACH! THANK YOU VERY MUCH!!
ASSISTANT
QUESTION 1:
IS RUKIA REALLY A MAN?
(A QUESTION THAT CAME UP OCCASIONALLY WHEN THE MANGA FIRST BEGAN.)
HEY, RUKIA IS ALL WOMAN!!
NEXT!
FWIP
QUESTION 2:
WHATEVER HAPPENED TO CHAD'S PARAKEET? IT JUST DISAPPEARED.

READ THIS WAY

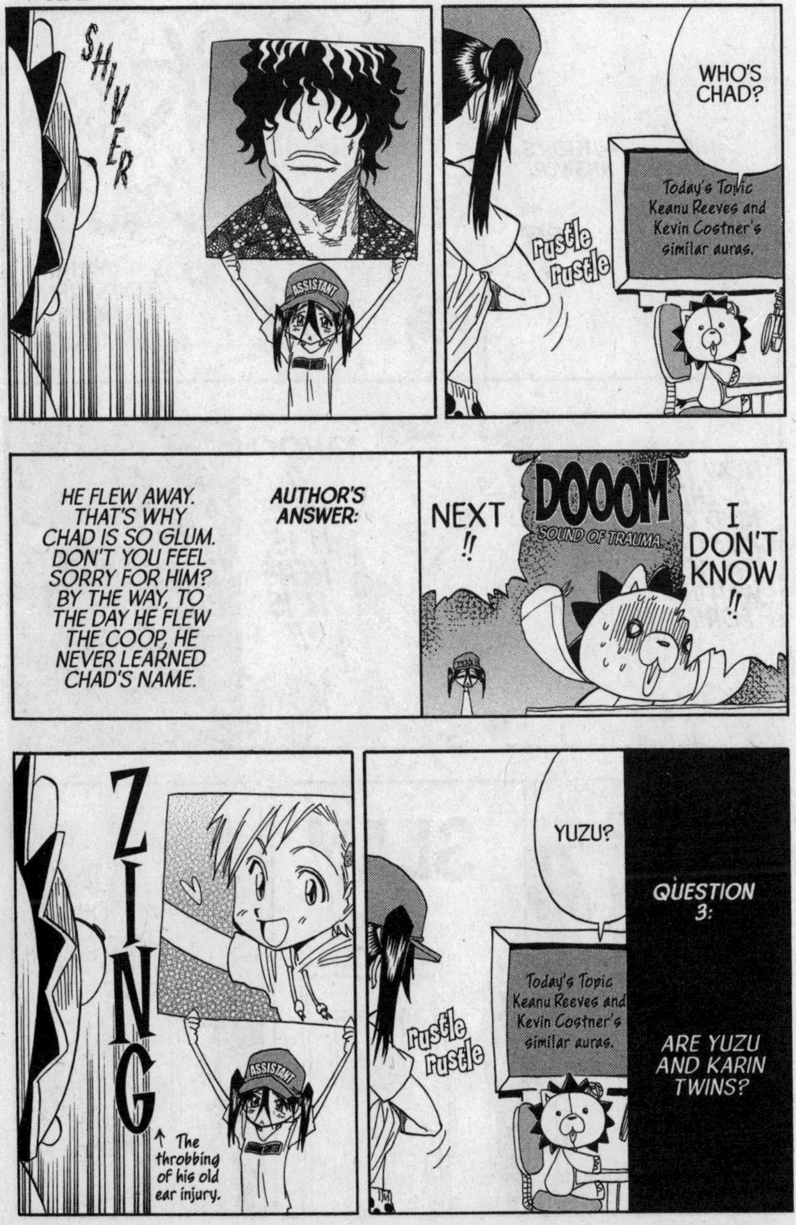
WHO'S CHAD?
Today's Topic Keanu Reeves and Kevin Costner's similar auras.
rustle rustle
SHIVER
ASSISTANT
I DON'T KNOW!!
DOOOM
SOUND OF TRAUMA
NEXT!!
AUTHOR'S ANSWER:
HE FLEW AWAY. THAT'S WHY CHAD IS SO GLUM. DON'T YOU FEEL SORRY FOR HIM? BY THE WAY, TO THE DAY HE FLEW THE COOP, HE NEVER LEARNED CHAD'S NAME.
QUESTION 3:
ARE YUZU AND KARIN TWINS?
YUZU?
Today's Topic Keanu Reeves and Kevin Costner's similar auras.
rustle rustle
ZING
ASSISTANT
↑ The throbbing of his old ear injury.

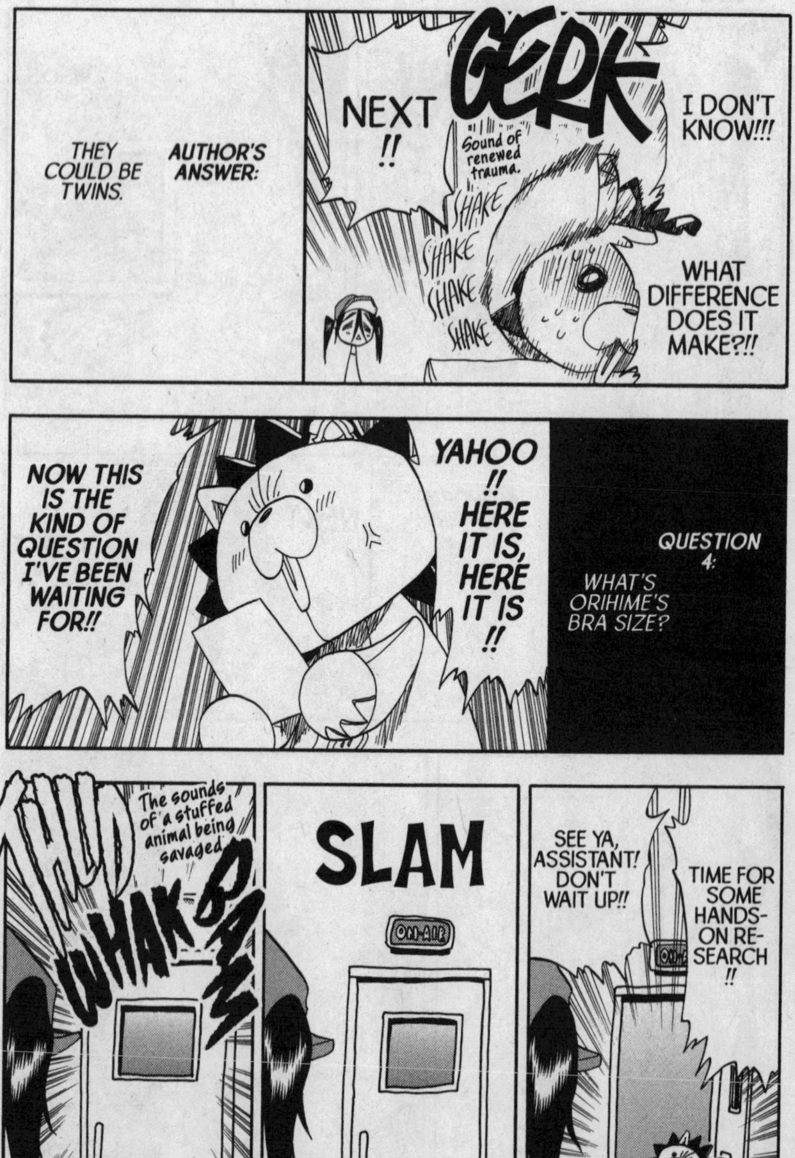

I DON'T KNOW!!!
WHAT DIFFERENCE DOES IT MAKE?!!
GERK
Sound of renewed trauma.
SHAKE SHAKE SHAKE SHAKE
NEXT!!
AUTHOR'S ANSWER:
THEY COULD BE TWINS.
QUESTION 4:
WHAT'S ORIHIME'S BRA SIZE?
YAHOO!! HERE IT IS, HERE IT IS!!
NOW THIS IS THE KIND OF QUESTION I'VE BEEN WAITING FOR!!
TIME FOR SOME HANDS-ON RE-SEARCH!!
SEE YA, ASSISTANT! DON'T WAIT UP!!
SLAM
ON-AIR
THUD WHAK BAM
The sounds of a stuffed animal being savaged

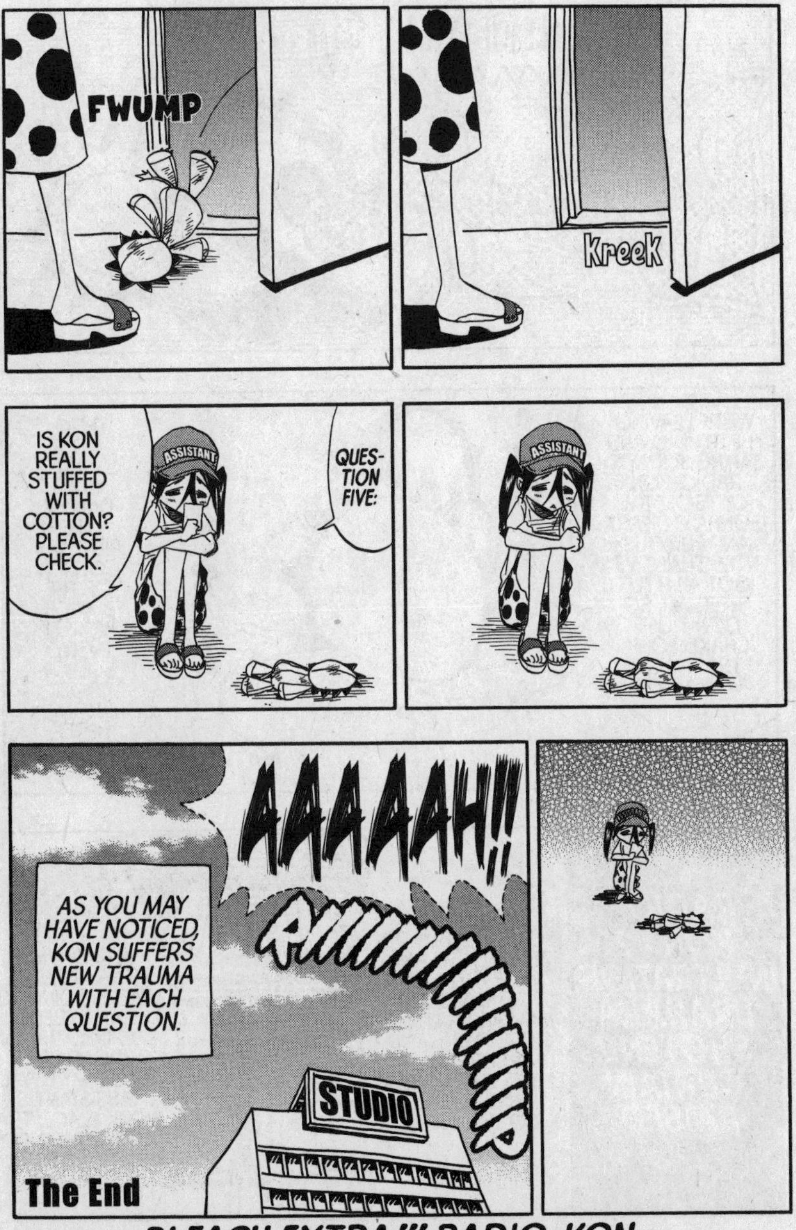
Kreek
FWUMP
QUES-TION FIVE:
IS KON REALLY STUFFED WITH COTTON? PLEASE CHECK.
AAAAAH!!
RIIIIIIIIIIIIP
STUDIO
AS YOU MAY HAVE NOTICED, KON SUFFERS NEW TRAUMA WITH EACH QUESTION.
The End

BLEACH EXTRA!!! RADIO-KON

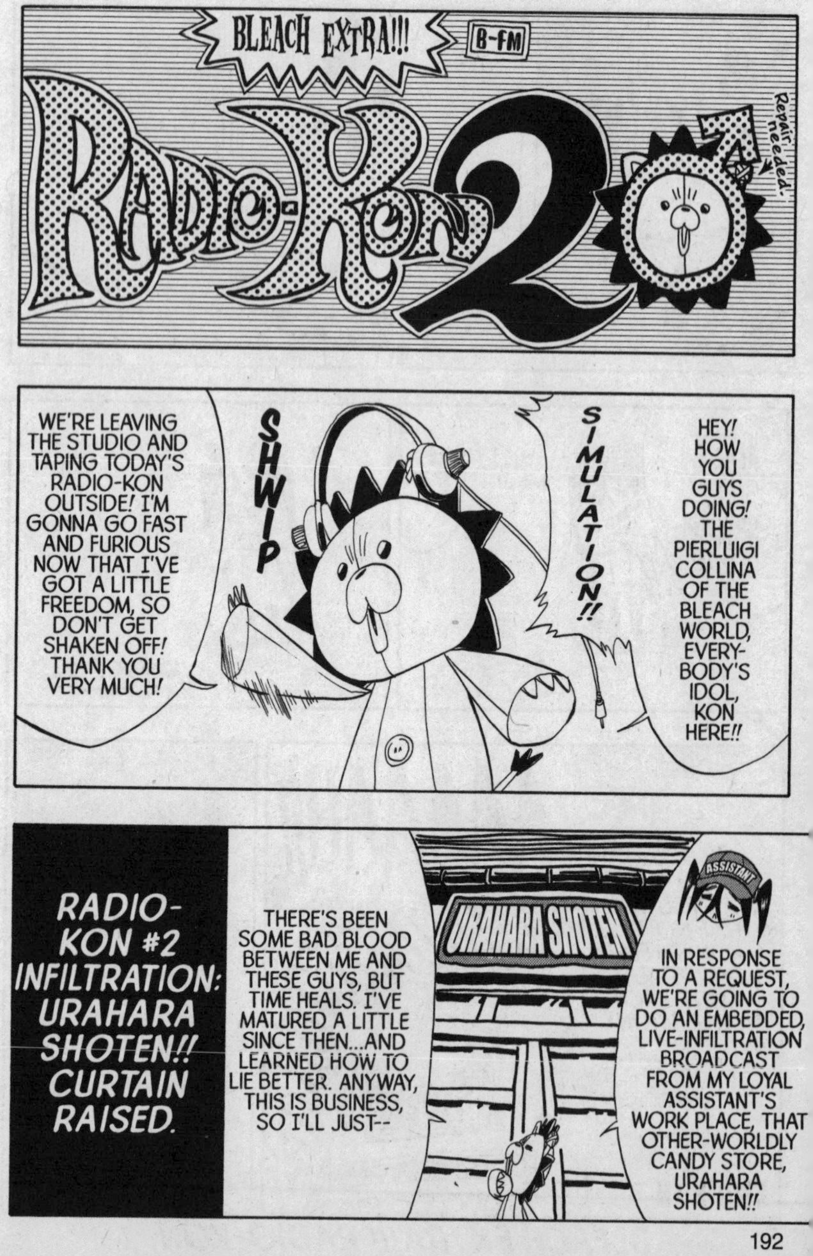

BLEACH EXTRA!!!
B-FM
RADIO-KON 2
Repair needed.
HEY! HOW YOU GUYS DOING! THE PIERLUIGI COLLINA OF THE BLEACH WORLD, EVERYBODY'S IDOL, KON HERE!!
SIMULATION!!
SHWIP
WE'RE LEAVING THE STUDIO AND TAPING TODAY'S RADIO-KON OUTSIDE! I'M GONNA GO FAST AND FURIOUS NOW THAT I'VE GOT A LITTLE FREEDOM, SO DON'T GET SHAKEN OFF! THANK YOU VERY MUCH!
ASSISTANT
IN RESPONSE TO A REQUEST, WE'RE GOING TO DO AN EMBEDDED, LIVE-INFILTRATION BROADCAST FROM MY LOYAL ASSISTANT'S WORK PLACE, THAT OTHER-WORLDLY CANDY STORE, URAHARA SHOTEN!!
URAHARA SHOTEN
THERE'S BEEN SOME BAD BLOOD BETWEEN ME AND THESE GUYS, BUT TIME HEALS. I'VE MATURED A LITTLE SINCE THEN...AND LEARNED HOW TO LIE BETTER. ANYWAY, THIS IS BUSINESS, SO I'LL JUST--
RADIO-KON #2 INFILTRATION: URAHARA SHOTEN!! CURTAIN RAISED.

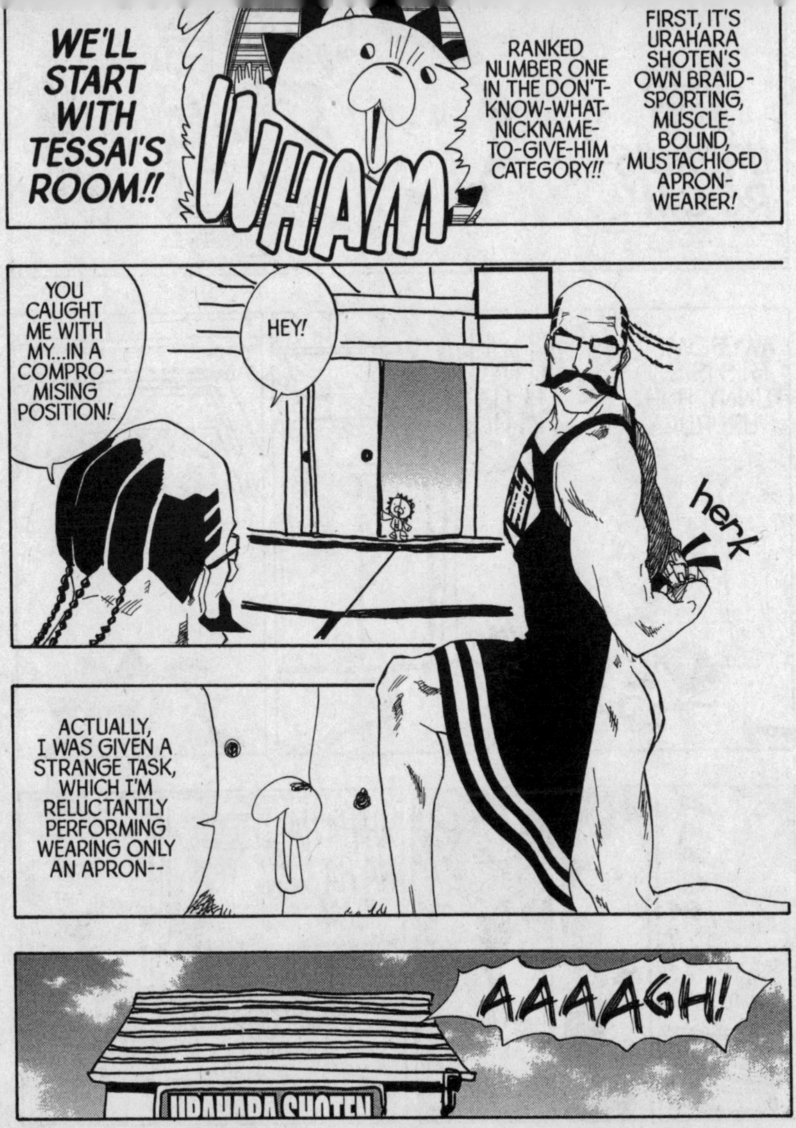
FIRST, IT'S URAHARA SHOTEN'S OWN BRAID-SPORTING, MUSCLE-BOUND, MUSTACHIOED APRON-WEARER!
RANKED NUMBER ONE IN THE DON'T-KNOW-WHAT-NICKNAME-TO-GIVE-HIM CATEGORY!!
WHAM
WE'LL START WITH TESSAI'S ROOM!!
HEY!
YOU CAUGHT ME WITH MY...IN A COMPROMISING POSITION!
herk
ACTUALLY, I WAS GIVEN A STRANGE TASK, WHICH I'M RELUCTANTLY PERFORMING WEARING ONLY AN APRON--
AAAAGH!

Part 2: Jinta and Ururu's Room

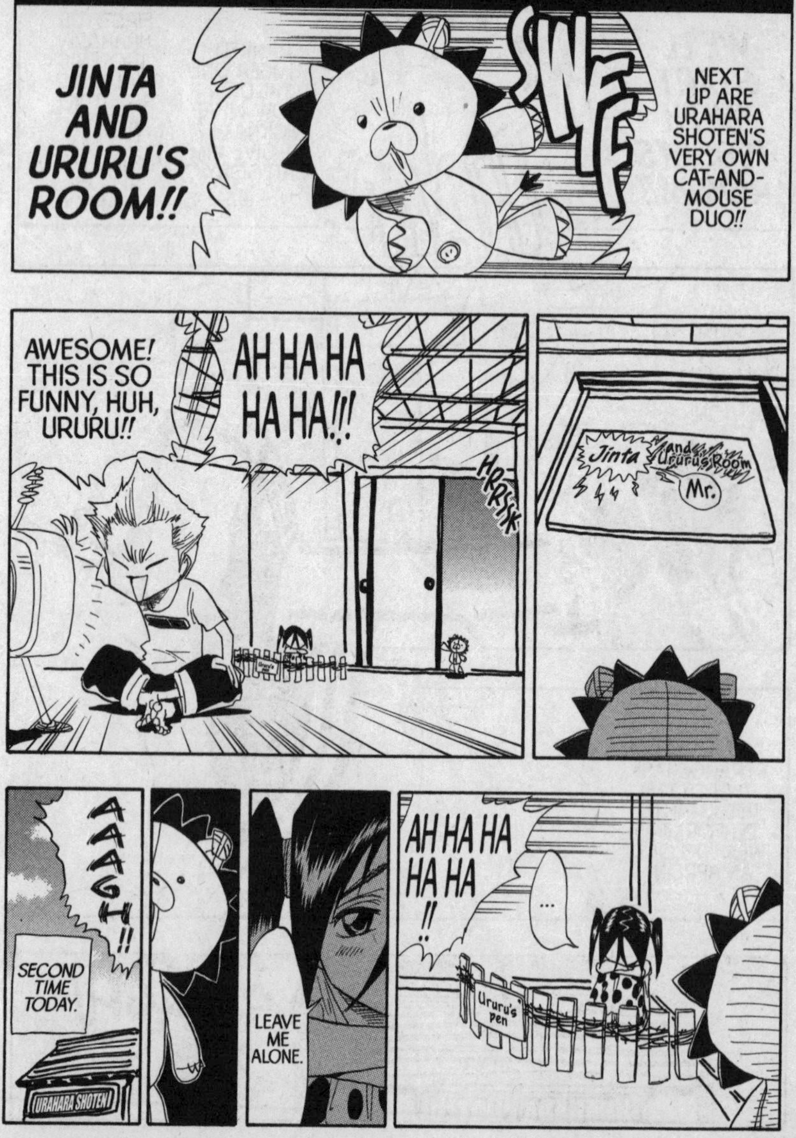

NEXT UP ARE URAHARA SHOTEN'S VERY OWN CAT-AND-MOUSE DUO!!
SNIFF
JINTA AND URURU'S ROOM!!
Jinta and Ururu's Room
Mr.
AH HA HA HA HA!!!
AWESOME! THIS IS SO FUNNY, HUH, URURU!!
HRRSSK
AH HA HA HA HA !!
...
Ururu's pen
LEAVE ME ALONE.
AAAAGH!!
SECOND TIME TODAY.
URAHARA SHOTEN

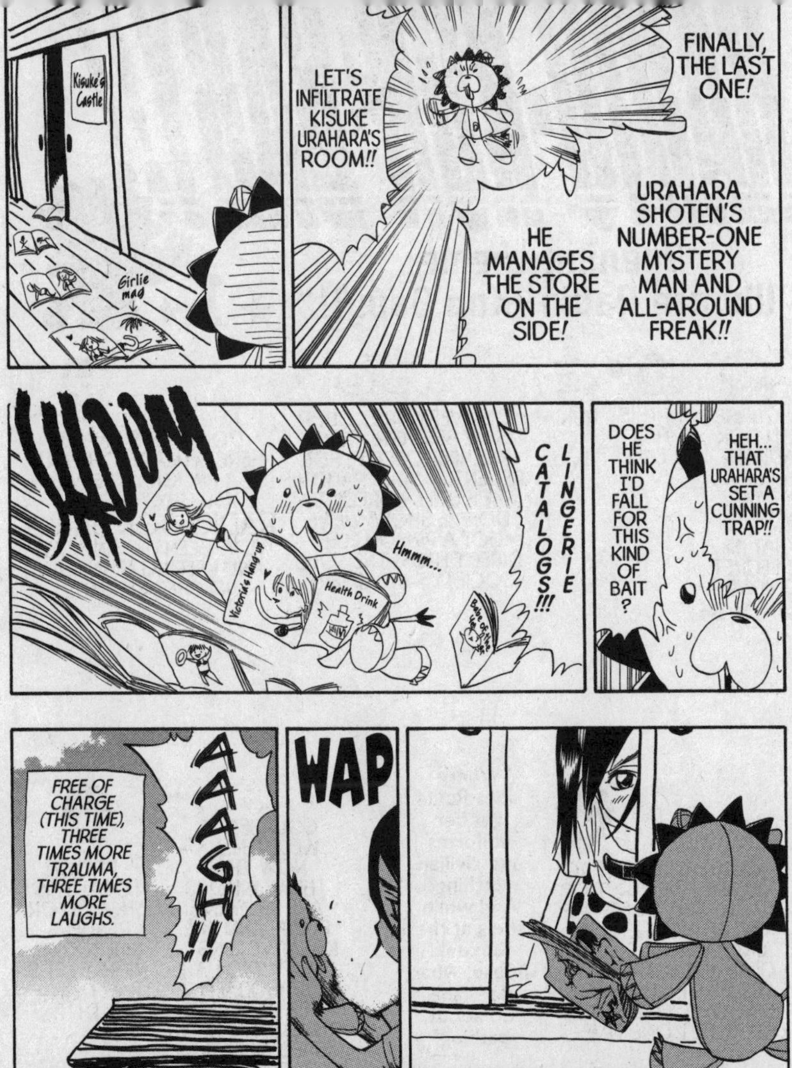
FINALLY, THE LAST ONE!
URAHARA SHOTEN'S NUMBER-ONE MYSTERY MAN AND ALL-AROUND FREAK!!
HE MANAGES THE STORE ON THE SIDE!
LET'S INFILTRATE KISUKE URAHARA'S ROOM!!
Kisuke's Castle
Girlie mag
HEH... THAT URAHARA'S SET A CUNNING TRAP!!
DOES HE THINK I'D FALL FOR THIS KIND OF BAIT?
LINGERIE CATALOGS!!!
Hmmm...
Victoria's Hang-up
Health Drink
WAP
AAAGH!!
FREE OF CHARGE (THIS TIME), THREE TIMES MORE TRAUMA, THREE TIMES MORE LAUGHS.
URAHARA SHOTEN
...THE END

← BLEACH EXTRA!!! RADIO-KON 2

ラジコンベイビー

RADIO-KON★BABY!!

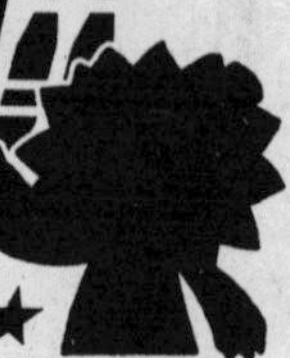

Opening theme: "We are Radio-Kon Baby!!" ★7★

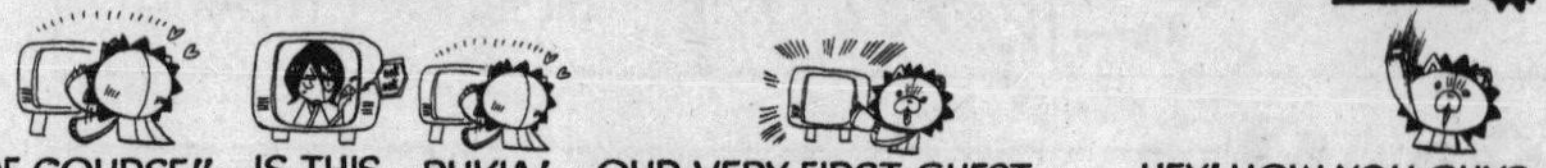

HEY! HOW YOU GUYS DOING? IT'S FINALLY HERE, A HEART-TO-HEART Q&A PROGRAM BETWEEN YOU GUYS AND ME! **RADIO-KON BABY!!** WE'VE BEEN DIGGING DEEP AND KEEPING IT UNREAL, SO CHECK IT OUT!!

OUR VERY FIRST GUEST IS MY BEST GIRL RUKIA KUCHIKI!! DESPITE HER RECENT INCARCERATION, SHE'S STILL AGREED TO DO THE SHOW! WE'VE GOT A PRISON FEED DIRECT FROM THE SOUL SOCIETY'S SLAMMER!!

RUKIA! ♡ ♡

IS THIS FOR REAL?

OF COURSE!! YOU LOOK RADIANT, AS ALWAYS, MY DEAR! ♡ WHAT IS THE SECRET TO YOUR BEAUTY!?

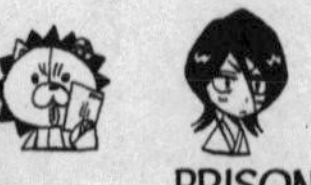

PRISON FOOD. THIS SHOW'S FOR READERS' QUESTIONS, RIGHT? LET'S GET ON WITH IT.

OF COURSE!! WELL THEN, NOW THAT THE MONITORS ARE SHOWING RUKIA, AND THE NEGATIVE IONS IN THE STUDIO HAVE DRASTICALLY INCREASED, LET ME READ THE MOST ASKED QUESTION OUT OF THE TONS OF LETTERS WE'VE RECEIVED!

Where does Rukia get her uniforms and civilian clothing? And while she's at the Kurosaki house, what does she do about bathing?

Naomi Kishino--Ishikawa, Japan

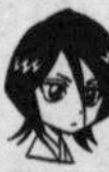

YOU REALLY WANT TO KNOW? FINE. FIRST OF ALL, THE UNIFORMS WERE ALL PROVIDED BY URAHARA. AS FOR MY CIVILIAN CLOTHING, AT FIRST I WAS BORROWING ICHIGO'S LITTLE SISTER YUZU'S, BUT ONE TIME...

...SHE CAUGHT ICHIGO GOING THROUGH HER DRESSER, AND...IT WAS AWKWARD. SINCE THEN, I'VE BEEN BORROWING OR BUYING FROM URAHARA ON CREDIT. AS FOR BATHS, AT FIRST I'D SNEAK ONE LATE AT NIGHT WHILE ICHIGO KEPT A LOOKOUT, BUT IT WAS TOO RISKY, SO AFTER ABOUT TWO WEEKS I STARTED GOING TO URAHARA'S TO BATHE.

THAT SEEMS EVEN RISKIER, TO ME, BUT...

Mr. Kubo, if you weren't a manga artist, what do you think you would be?

Ayaka Yokoyama-- Chiba, Japan

WHO CARES?!!

HEY, THIS IS A QUESTION FOR TITE. WE CAN'T ANSWER IT. IF YOU HAVE A QUESTION FOR HIM, I'M SURE HE'LL BE INVITED AS A GUEST EVENTUALLY. SAVE IT UNTIL THEN.

NO WAY! I DON'T LIKE THAT GUY!! IF HE SHOWS UP, I'M OUTTA HERE! HE CAN DO THE SHOW BY HIMSELF!!

YOU'D BETTER WATCH IT. YOUR APPEARANCES MIGHT DECREASE IF YOU KEEP SAYING STUFF LIKE THAT...

Is Kon more of a Kyoko Fukada or Haruka Igawa fan?

Gunma-- Everyday is Special

HARUKA IGAWA!!! BECAUSE HER SERVINGS ARE BIGGER!!

WHO? WHO ARE THESE PEOPLE?

I have a problem. I like someone, but we're in different classes so I just end up teasing her whenever I see her. What can I do so I won't tease her? Mr. Kon, please help me.

Hyogo-- Baseball Player

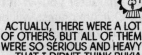

HMMM... HERE IT IS. I THOUGHT NOBODY WOULD SEND A SERIOUS LOVE QUESTION TO A MANGA, BUT WE'VE GOT ONE.

ACTUALLY, THERE WERE A LOT OF OTHERS, BUT ALL OF THEM WERE SO SERIOUS AND HEAVY THAT I DIDN'T THINK RUKIA OR I COULD HANDLE THEM. IF ONLY I HAD A GUEST WHO WAS GOOD AT THIS KIND OF THING. OH, WELL. RUKIA! WHAT DO YOU THINK ABOUT THIS?

WELL, THERE WERE GUYS LIKE THAT WHEN I WAS IN SCHOOL, BOYS WHO'D PINCH ME OR SAY MEAN THINGS TO ME EVERY TIME I PASSED THEM IN THE HALL.

WHAT?! THE NERVE OF THOSE GUYS, TO TEASE MY RUKIA!!

KREEK

UNFORTUNATELY, HE'S GOT TO DECIDE WHETHER HE'D RATHER SUFFER A LITTLE EMBARRASSMENT OR BE HATED.

BUT IT'S HARD FOR HIM TO ACT NORMAL AROUND HER.

LOOKING BACK NOW, I REALIZE THEY JUST WANTED ATTENTION, BUT AT THE TIME I THOUGHT THEY WERE JERKS. OF COURSE, IT DEPENDS ON WHAT KIND OF RELATIONSHIP YOU HAVE WITH THEM AND THE KIND OF TEASING IT IS, BUT GENERALLY THE CHANCE OF A GIRL LIKING A BOY WHO TEASES HER IS LESS THAN ONE IN A MILLION. EVEN IF YOU'RE EMBARRASSED, THE FIRST STEP IS TO SMILE CONFIDENTLY AND SAY HELLO. WHEN SOMEONE WHO USUALLY TEASES YOU APPROACHES YOU IN A NORMAL WAY, THE EFFECT CAN BE DRAMATIC.

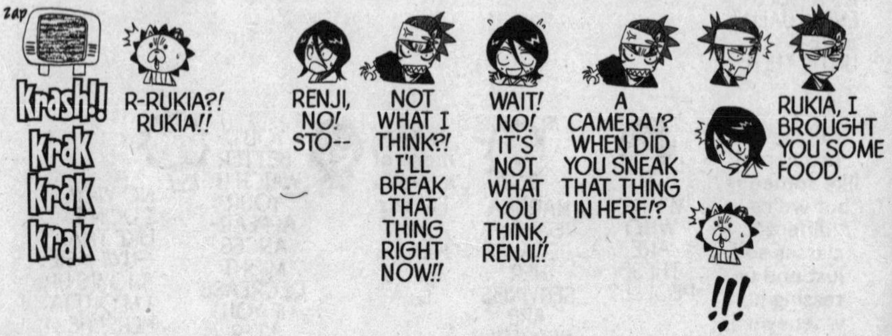
zap
Krash!! krak krak krak
R-RUKIA?! RUKIA!!
RENJI, NO! STO--
NOT WHAT I THINK?! I'LL BREAK THAT THING RIGHT NOW!!
WAIT! NO! IT'S NOT WHAT YOU THINK, RENJI!!
A CAMERA!? WHEN DID YOU SNEAK THAT THING IN HERE!?
RUKIA, I BROUGHT YOU SOME FOOD.
!!!

Accepting letters!! Any question is okay!!

We're accepting letters now!! And tell us which character you want the letters to be read by!! Our next guest will be Tatsuki Arisawa!! Include your question, name, address, age, and telephone number and send it all to the address below!

SHONEN JUMP c/o VIZ, LLC
P.O. Box 77010, San Francisco, CA 94107
ATTN: "Bleach" Radio-Kon Baby!!

Single: "Good night! Radio-Kon Baby!"

Ending theme music: SMAP "Lion Heart"

--Fade out...

The other day I received a letter from a reader who said they named their son Ichigo. The realization that my work had influenced someone I didn't even know was both exciting and terrifying. So I've decided to shape up. I hope this human Ichigo can be proud to be named after my Ichigo when he grows up.

-Tite Kubo

BLEACH

BLEACH
ブリーチ

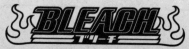

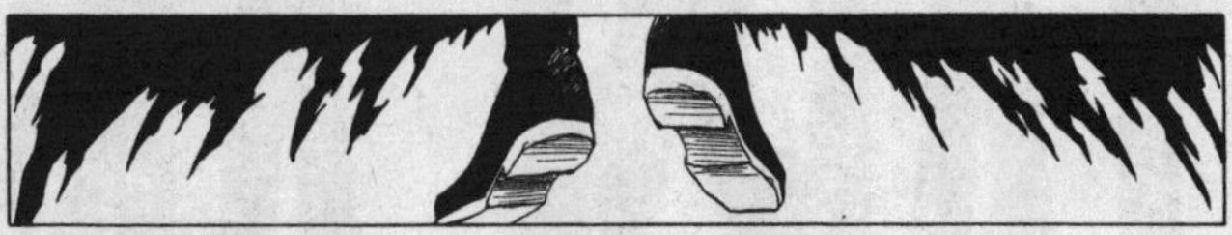

If it rusts, it can never be trusted
If its owner fails to control it, it will cut him
Yes, pride is
Like a blade

BLEACH 8
THE BLADE AND ME

Shonen Jump Manga

STARS AND

Kisuke Urahara

Tessai Tsukabishi

Ichigo Kurosaki

plot

In a series of strange events, Ichigo Kurosaki encountered Rukia Kuchiki and came to possess her Soul Reaper powers. Now his job is to cleanse fallen souls called Hollows and guide them to the Soul Society. Eventually Ichigo's powers grow strong, enabling him to defeat the colossal Menos Grande.

Now Rukia languishes in a Soul Society jail with a death sentence hanging over her. In order to regain his lost powers and rescue Rukia, Ichigo allows Kisuke Urahara to train him. But Lesson 2, the Shattered Shaft, will either restore Ichigo's powers, or destroy his very soul....

BLEACH ALL

夜一
Yoruichi

花刈ジン太
Jinta Hanakari

Ururu Tsumugiya
紬屋雨

STORIES

BLEACH 8

THE BLADE AND ME

Contents

62. Lesson 2-2: Bad Ending in the Shaft

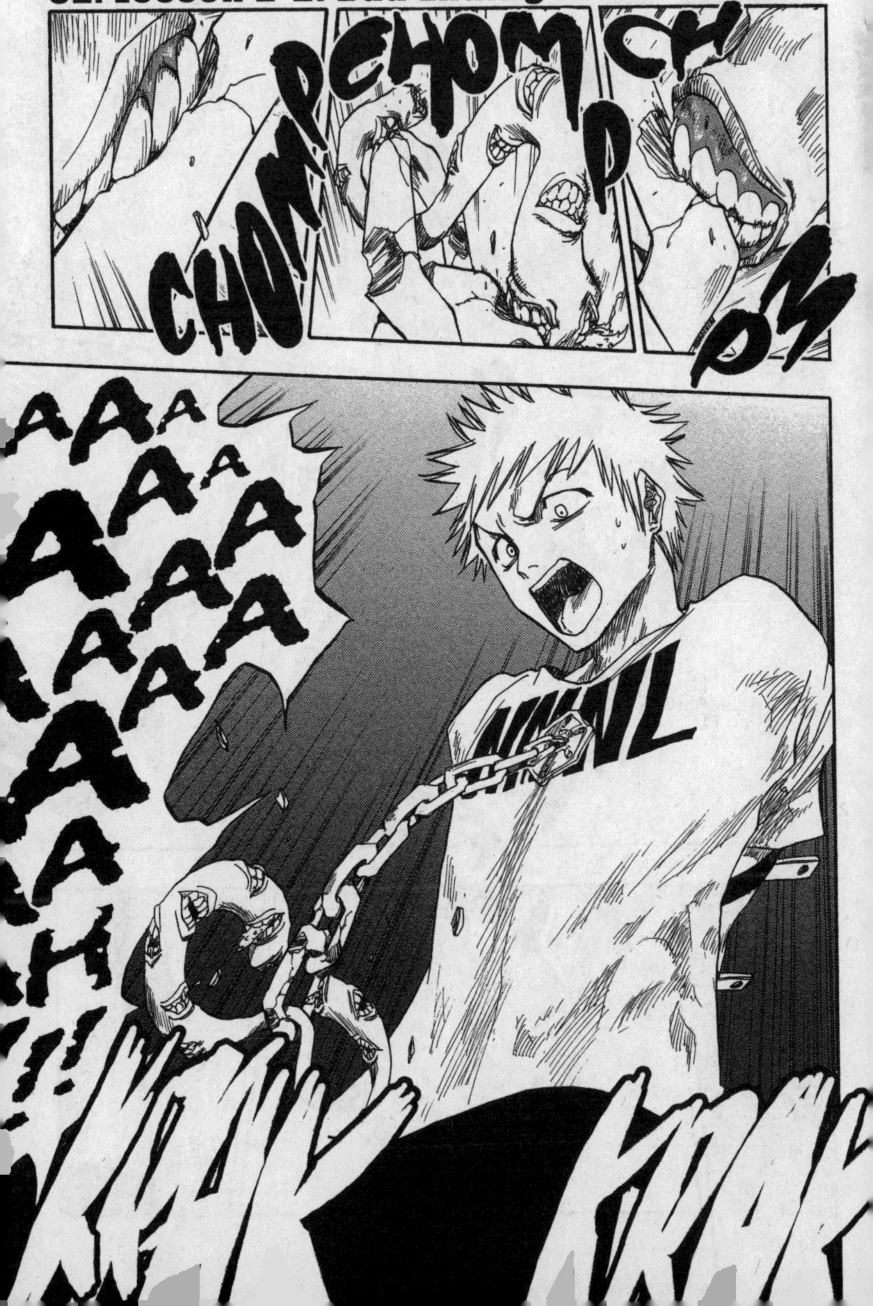
CHOMP
CHOMP
CHOMP
AAAAAAAAAAAAAAH!!

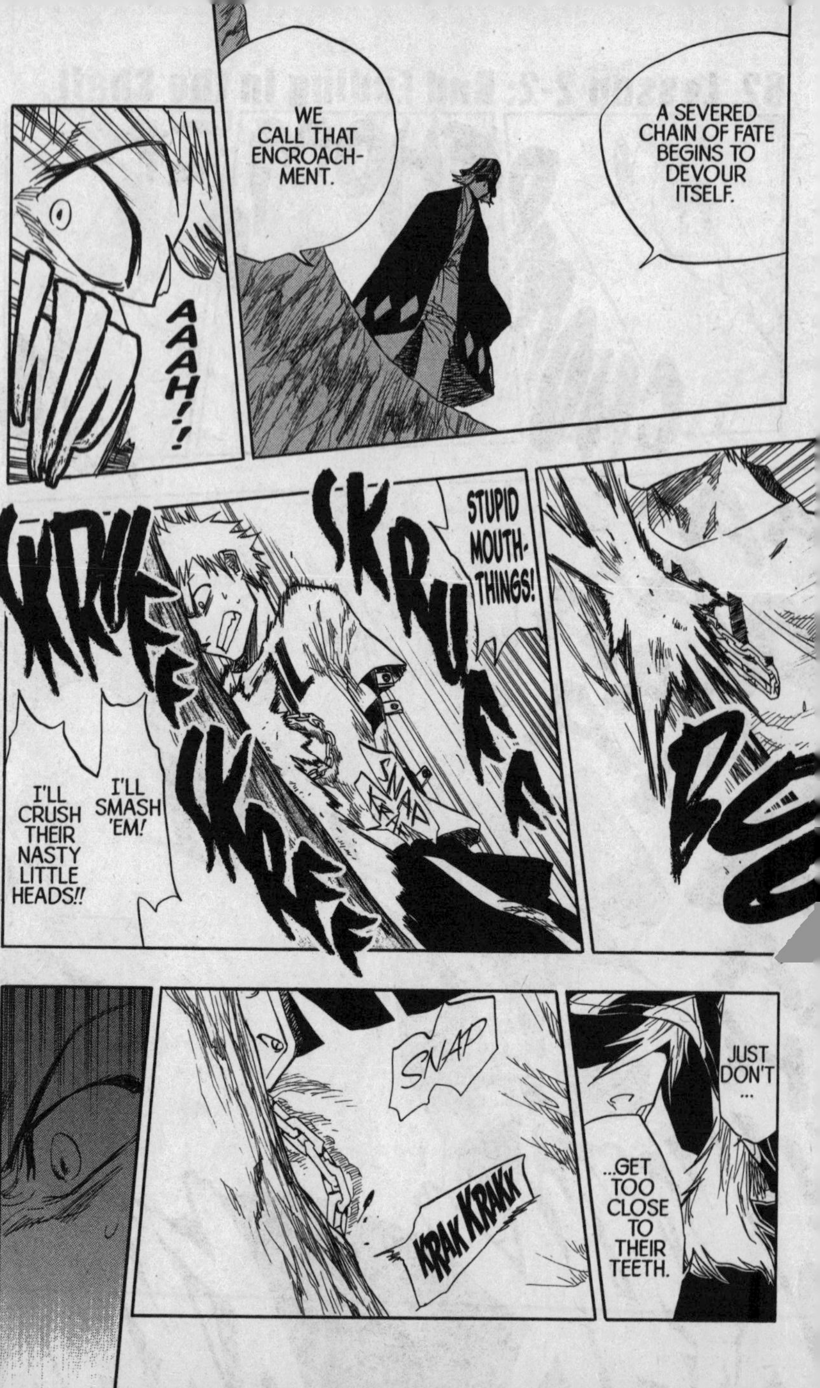
A SEVERED CHAIN OF FATE BEGINS TO DEVOUR ITSELF.
WE CALL THAT ENCROACH-MENT.
AAAAH!!
STUPID MOUTH-THINGS!
SNAP KRAK
I'LL SMASH 'EM!
I'LL CRUSH THEIR NASTY LITTLE HEADS!!
JUST DON'T ...
...GET TOO CLOSE TO THEIR TEETH.
SNAP
KRAK KRAKK

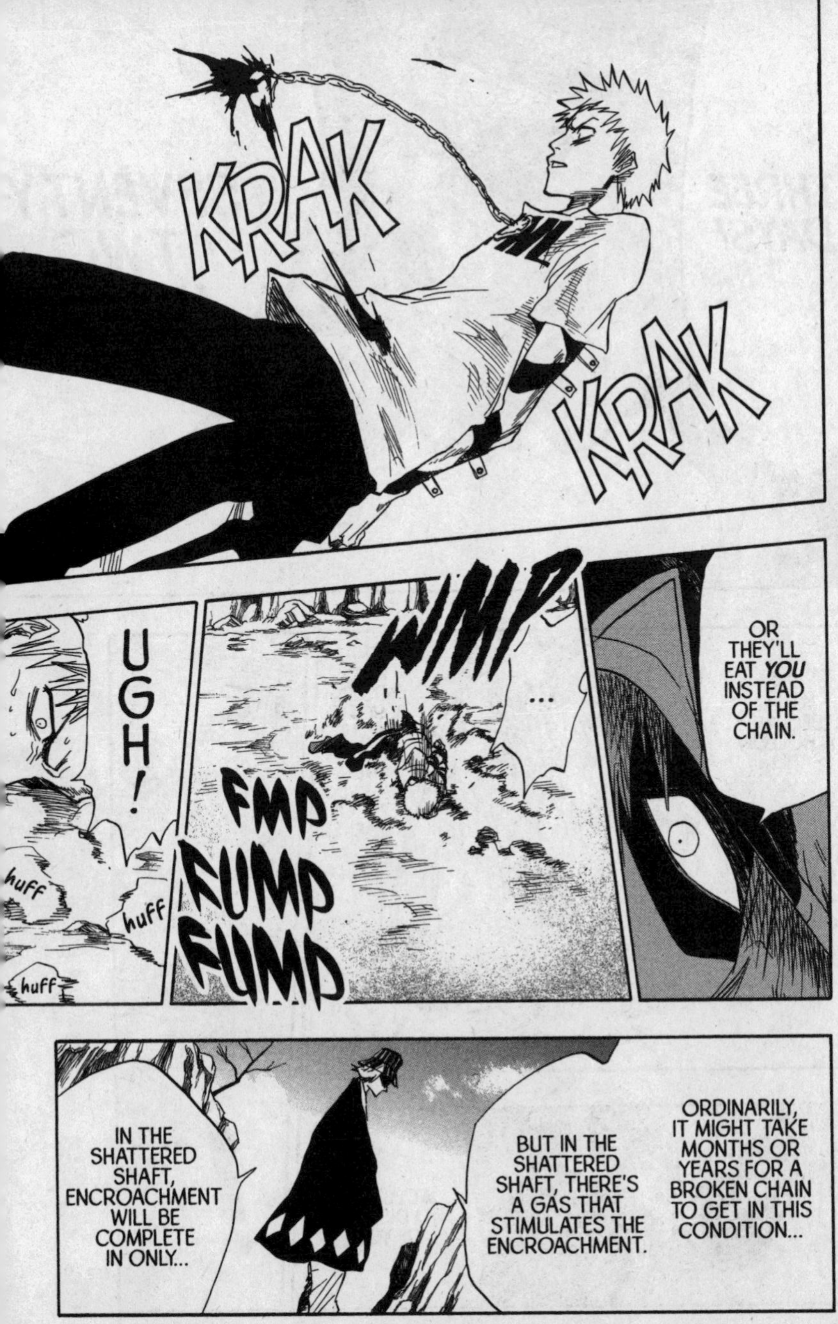
KRAK
KRAK
OR THEY'LL EAT *YOU* INSTEAD OF THE CHAIN.
WMP
...
FMP
FUMP
FUMP
UGH!
huff
huff
huff
ORDINARILY, IT MIGHT TAKE MONTHS OR YEARS FOR A BROKEN CHAIN TO GET IN THIS CONDITION...
BUT IN THE SHATTERED SHAFT, THERE'S A GAS THAT STIMULATES THE ENCROACHMENT.
IN THE SHATTERED SHAFT, ENCROACHMENT WILL BE COMPLETE IN ONLY...

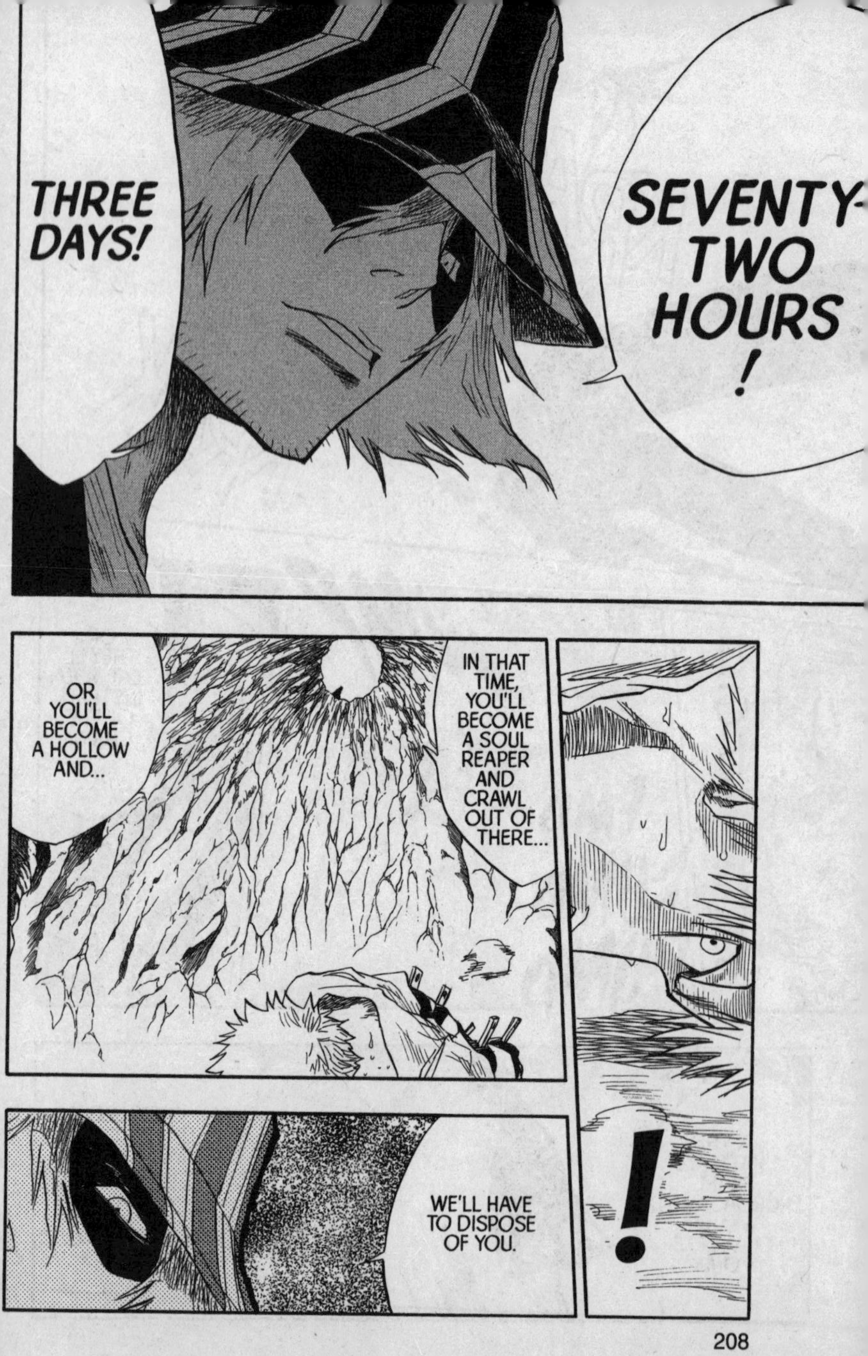
SEVENTY-TWO HOURS!
THREE DAYS!
IN THAT TIME, YOU'LL BECOME A SOUL REAPER AND CRAWL OUT OF THERE...
OR YOU'LL BECOME A HOLLOW AND...
!
WE'LL HAVE TO DISPOSE OF YOU.

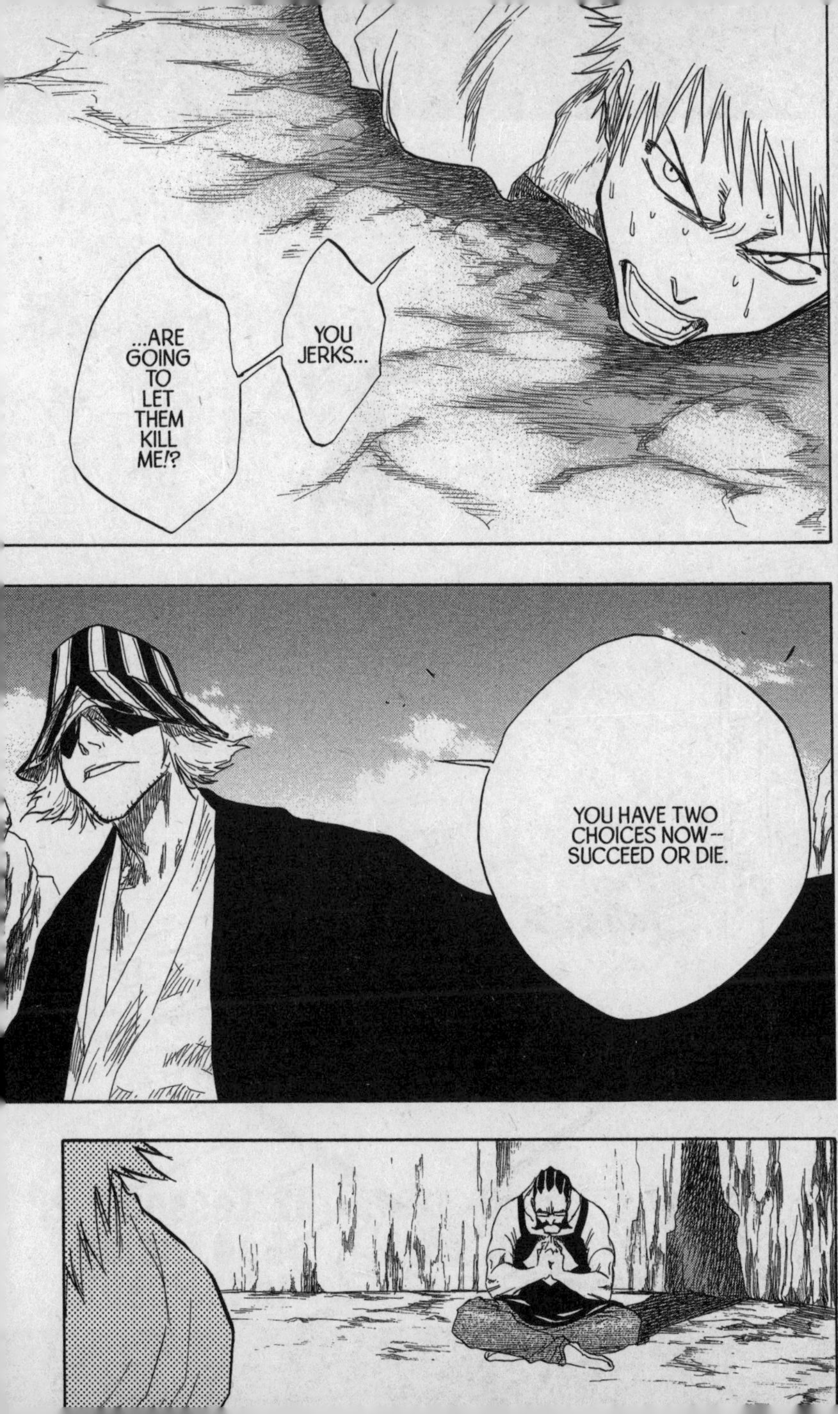
YOU JERKS...
...ARE GOING TO LET THEM KILL ME!?
YOU HAVE TWO CHOICES NOW-- SUCCEED OR DIE.

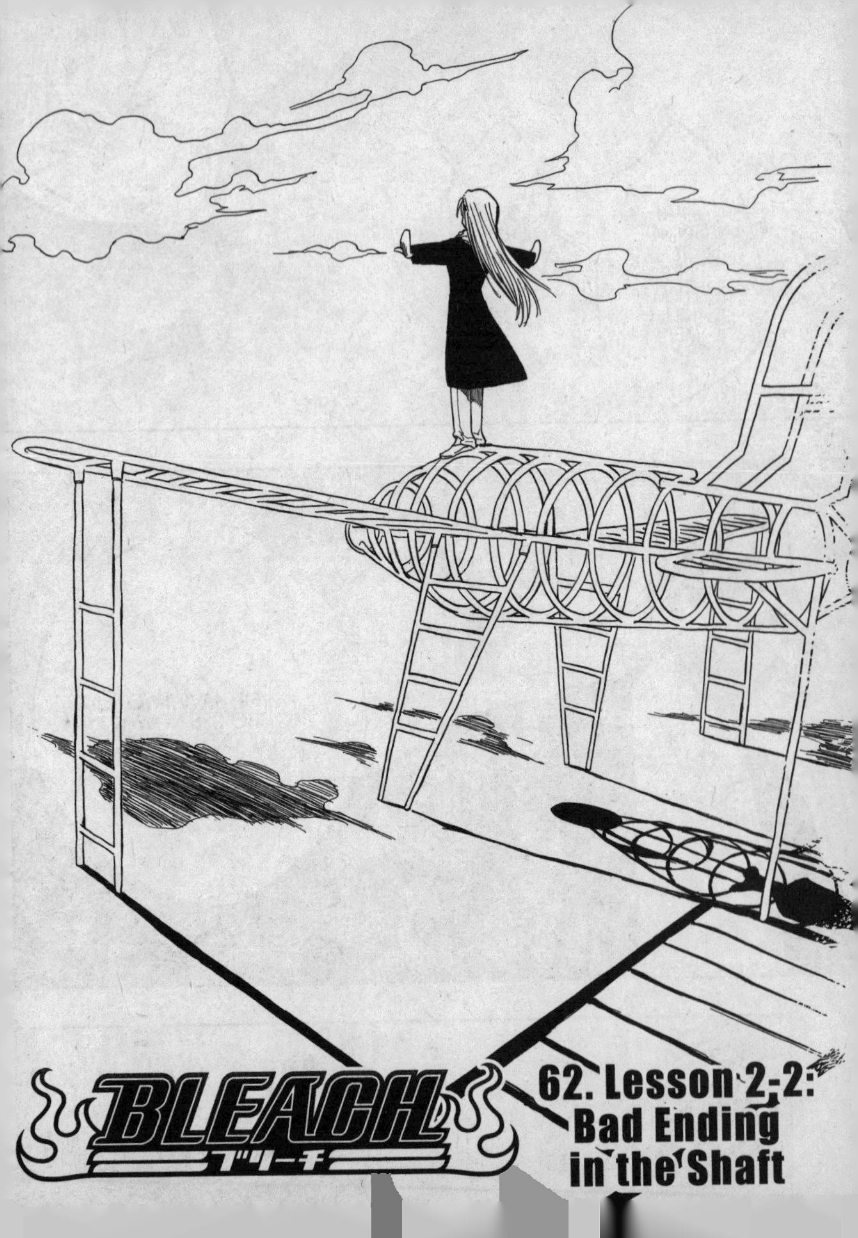
BLEACH
ブリーチ
62. Lesson 2-2:
Bad Ending
in the Shaft

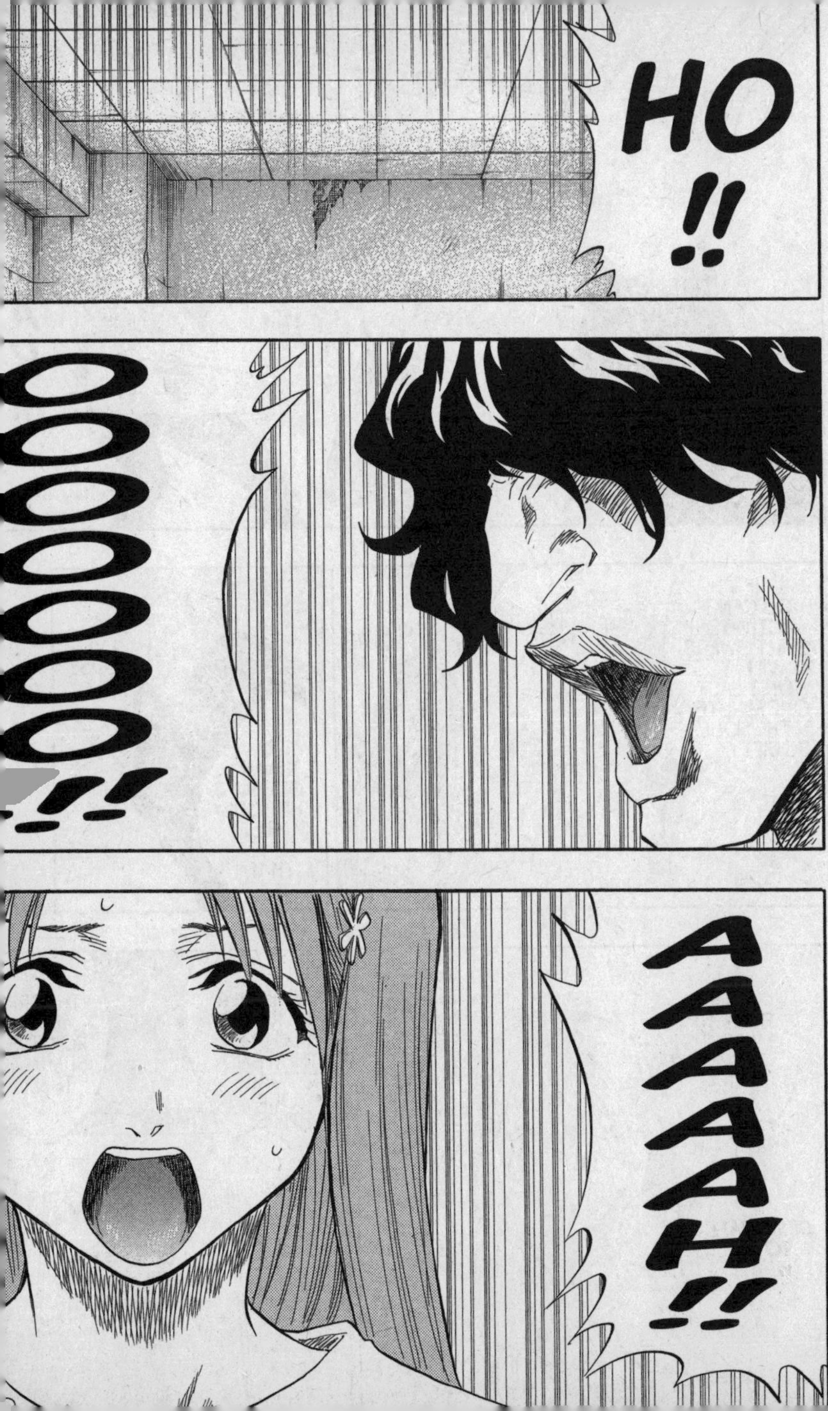
HO!!
OOOOOOO!!
AAAAH!!

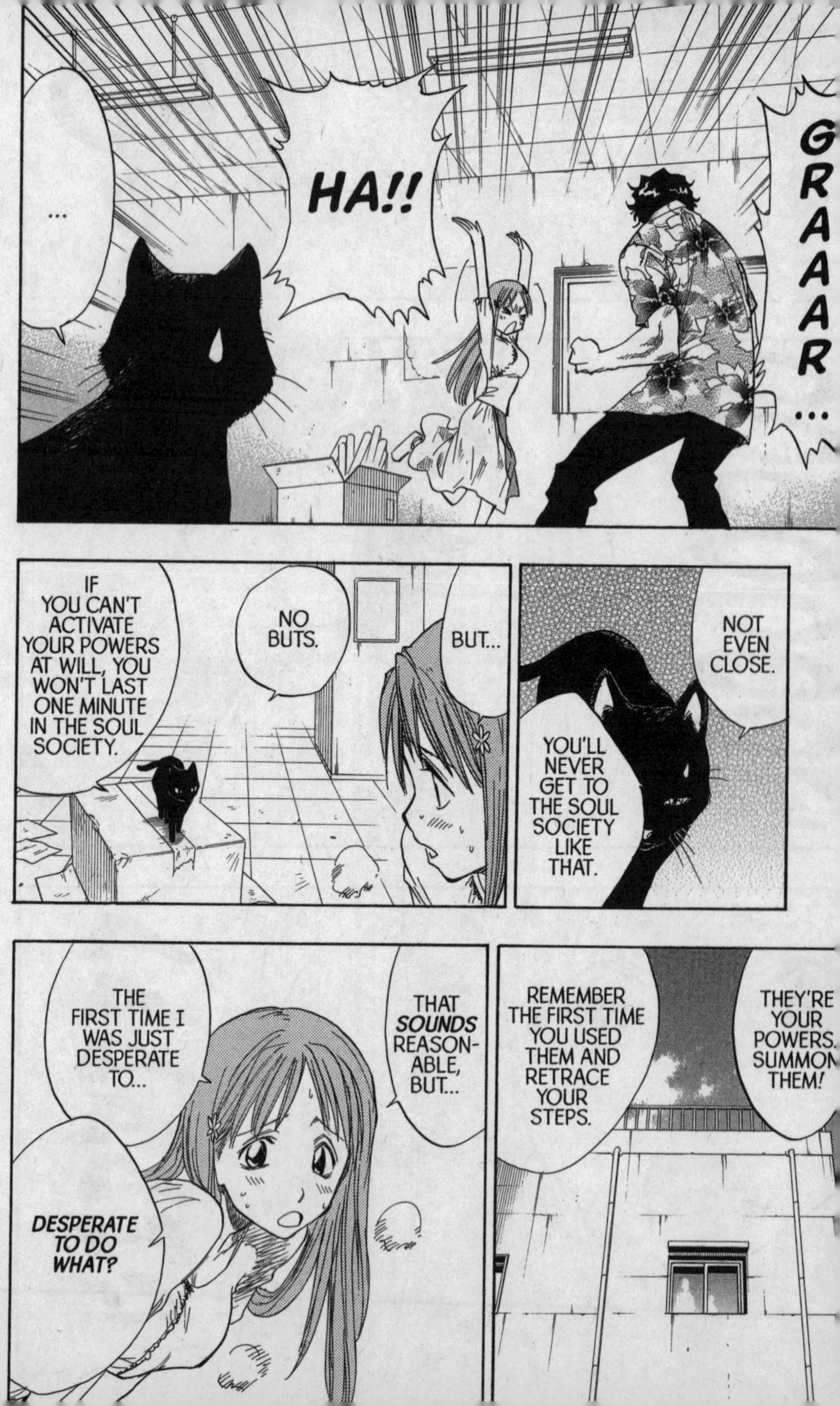
GRAAAR...
HA!!
...
NOT EVEN CLOSE.
YOU'LL NEVER GET TO THE SOUL SOCIETY LIKE THAT.
BUT...
NO BUTS.
IF YOU CAN'T ACTIVATE YOUR POWERS AT WILL, YOU WON'T LAST ONE MINUTE IN THE SOUL SOCIETY.
THEY'RE YOUR POWERS. SUMMON THEM!
REMEMBER THE FIRST TIME YOU USED THEM AND RETRACE YOUR STEPS.
THAT *SOUNDS* REASONABLE, BUT...
THE FIRST TIME I WAS JUST DESPERATE TO...
DESPERATE TO DO WHAT?

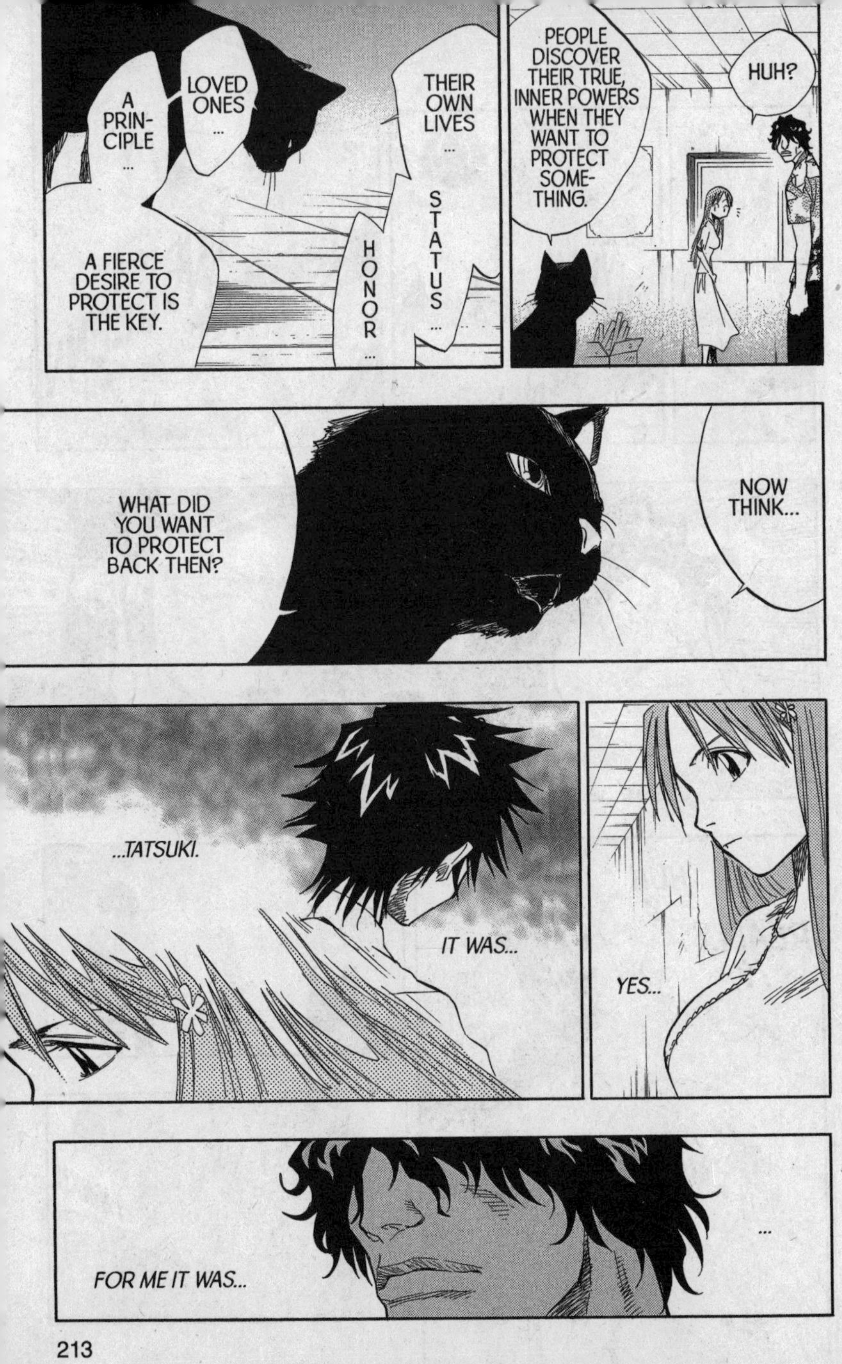

PEOPLE DISCOVER THEIR TRUE, INNER POWERS WHEN THEY WANT TO PROTECT SOMETHING.
HUH?
THEIR OWN LIVES...
STATUS...
HONOR...
LOVED ONES...
A PRINCIPLE...
A FIERCE DESIRE TO PROTECT IS THE KEY.
NOW THINK...
WHAT DID YOU WANT TO PROTECT BACK THEN?
YES...
IT WAS...
...TATSUKI.
...
FOR ME IT WAS...

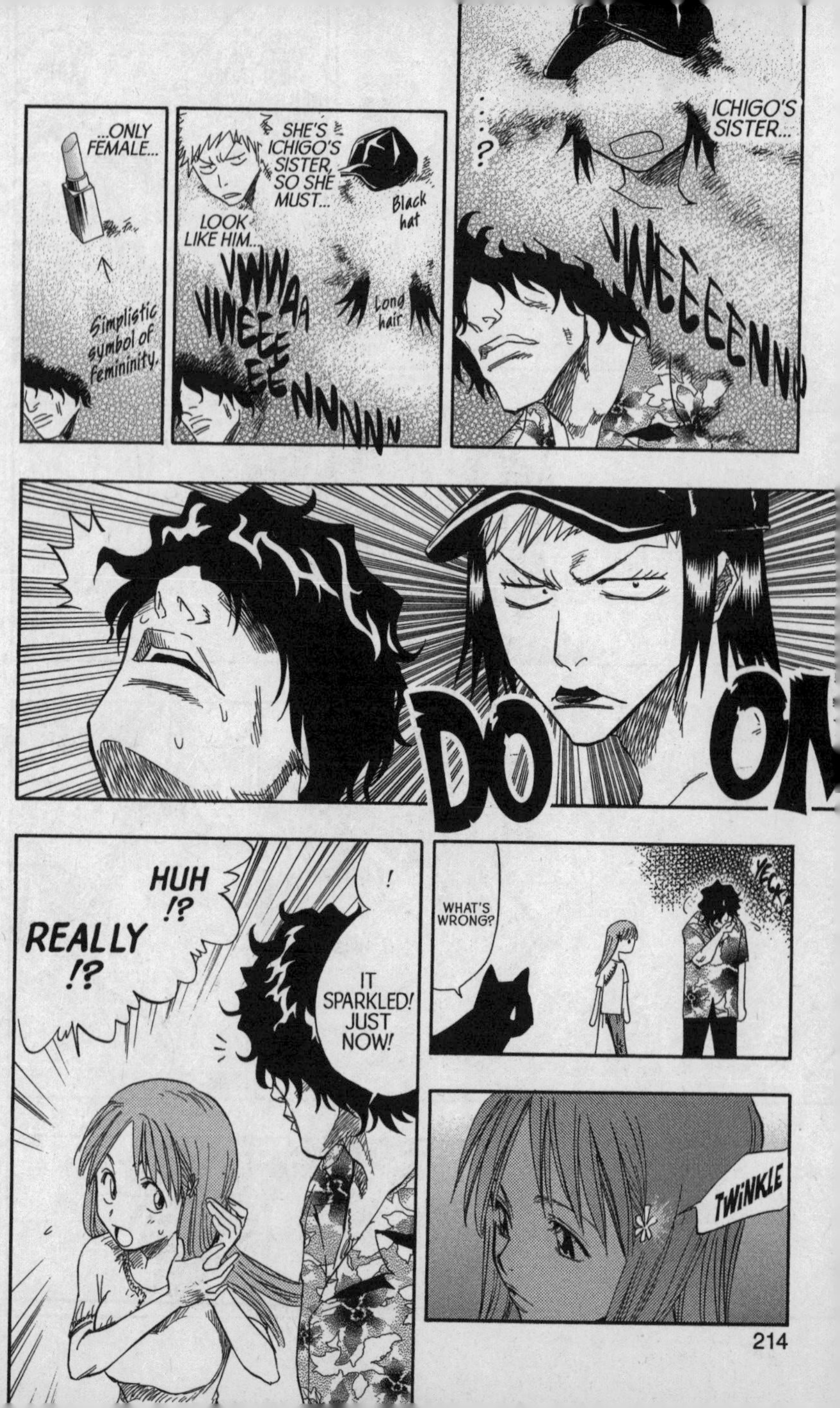
ICHIGO'S SISTER...
...?
SHE'S ICHIGO'S SISTER, SO SHE MUST...
LOOK LIKE HIM...
Black hat
Long hair
VWWAA VWEEEEENNNNN
...ONLY FEMALE...
Simplistic symbol of femininity.
VWEEEENNN
DO ON
WHAT'S WRONG?
IT SPARKLED! JUST NOW!
HUH !?
REALLY !?
TWINKLE

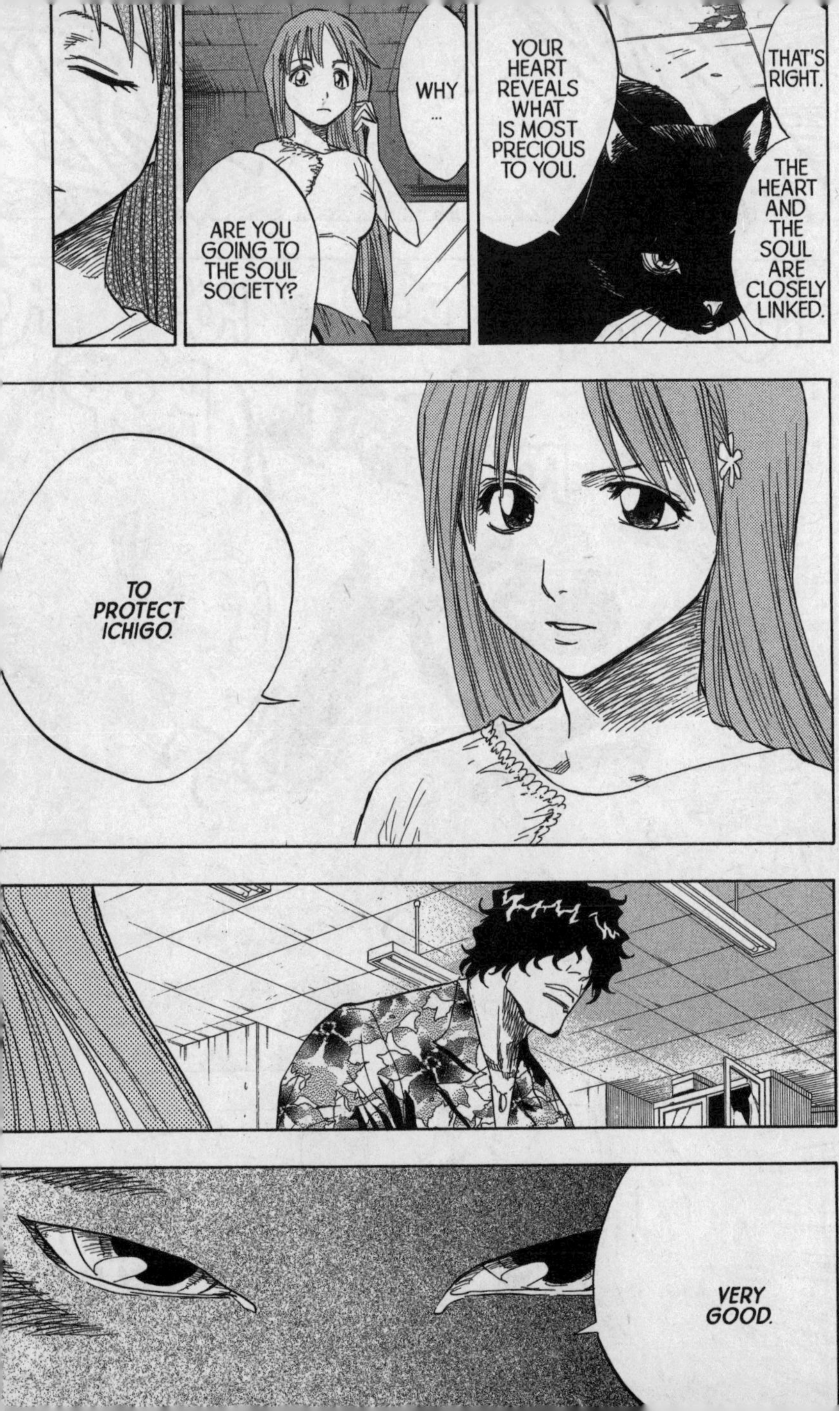
THAT'S RIGHT.
THE HEART AND THE SOUL ARE CLOSELY LINKED.
YOUR HEART REVEALS WHAT IS MOST PRECIOUS TO YOU.
WHY ...
ARE YOU GOING TO THE SOUL SOCIETY?
TO PROTECT ICHIGO.
VERY GOOD.

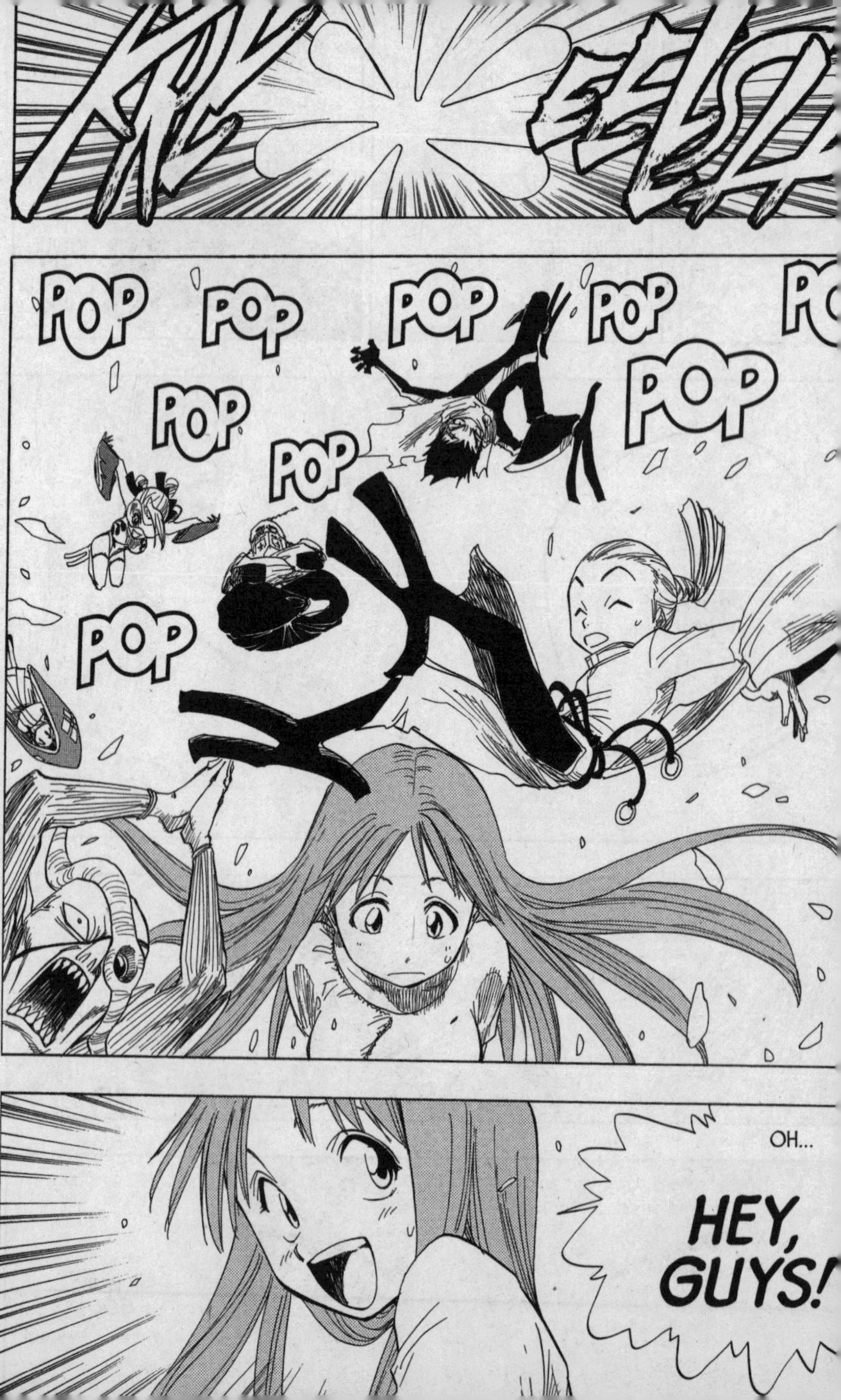
POP
POP
POP
POP
POP
POP
POP
POP
OH...
HEY, GUYS!

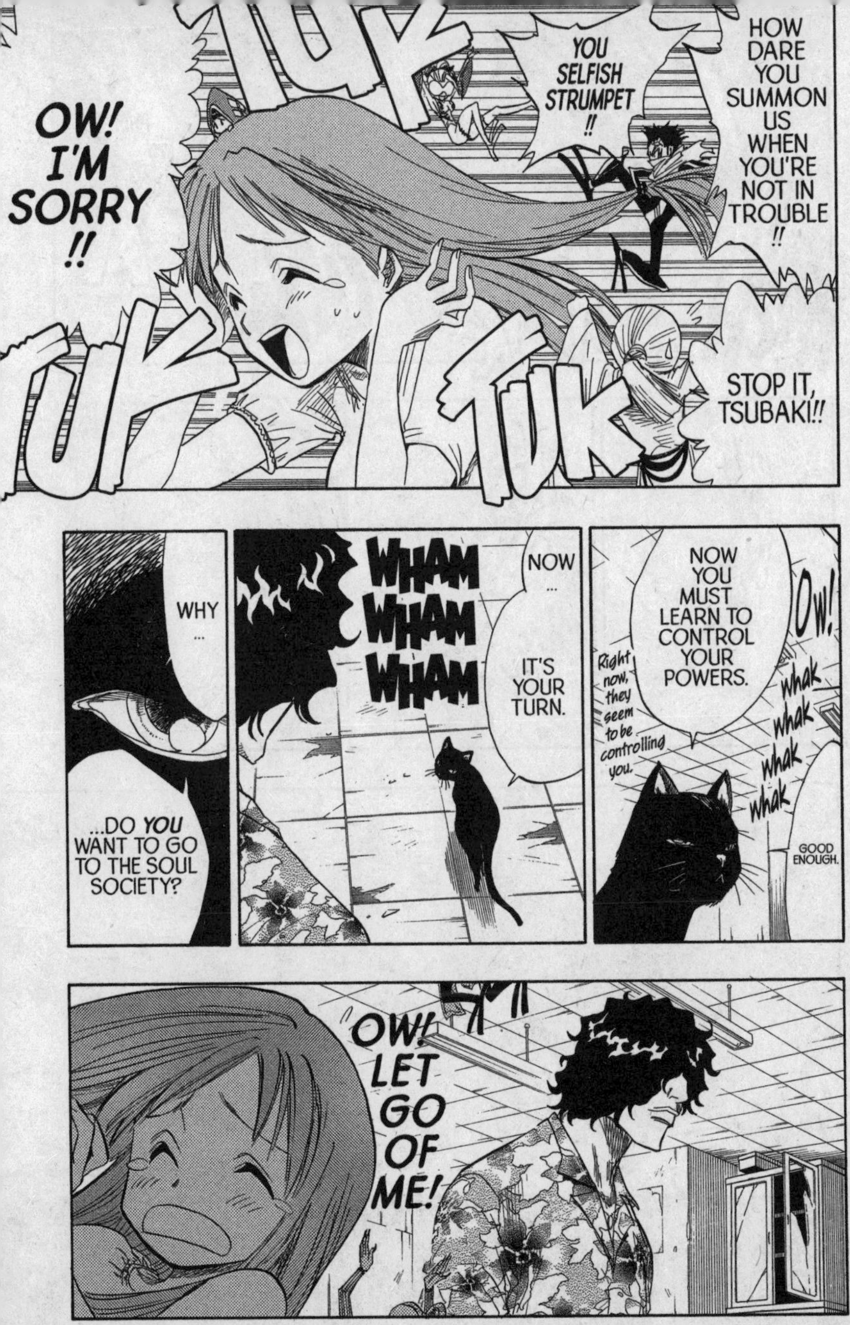
HOW DARE YOU SUMMON US WHEN YOU'RE NOT IN TROUBLE!!
YOU SELFISH STRUMPET!!
OW! I'M SORRY!!
TUK
TUK
TUK
STOP IT, TSUBAKI!!
NOW YOU MUST LEARN TO CONTROL YOUR POWERS.
Right now, they seem to be controlling you.
OW!
whak whak whak whak
GOOD ENOUGH.
NOW...
IT'S YOUR TURN.
WHAM WHAM WHAM
WHY...
...DO YOU WANT TO GO TO THE SOUL SOCIETY?
OW! LET GO OF ME!

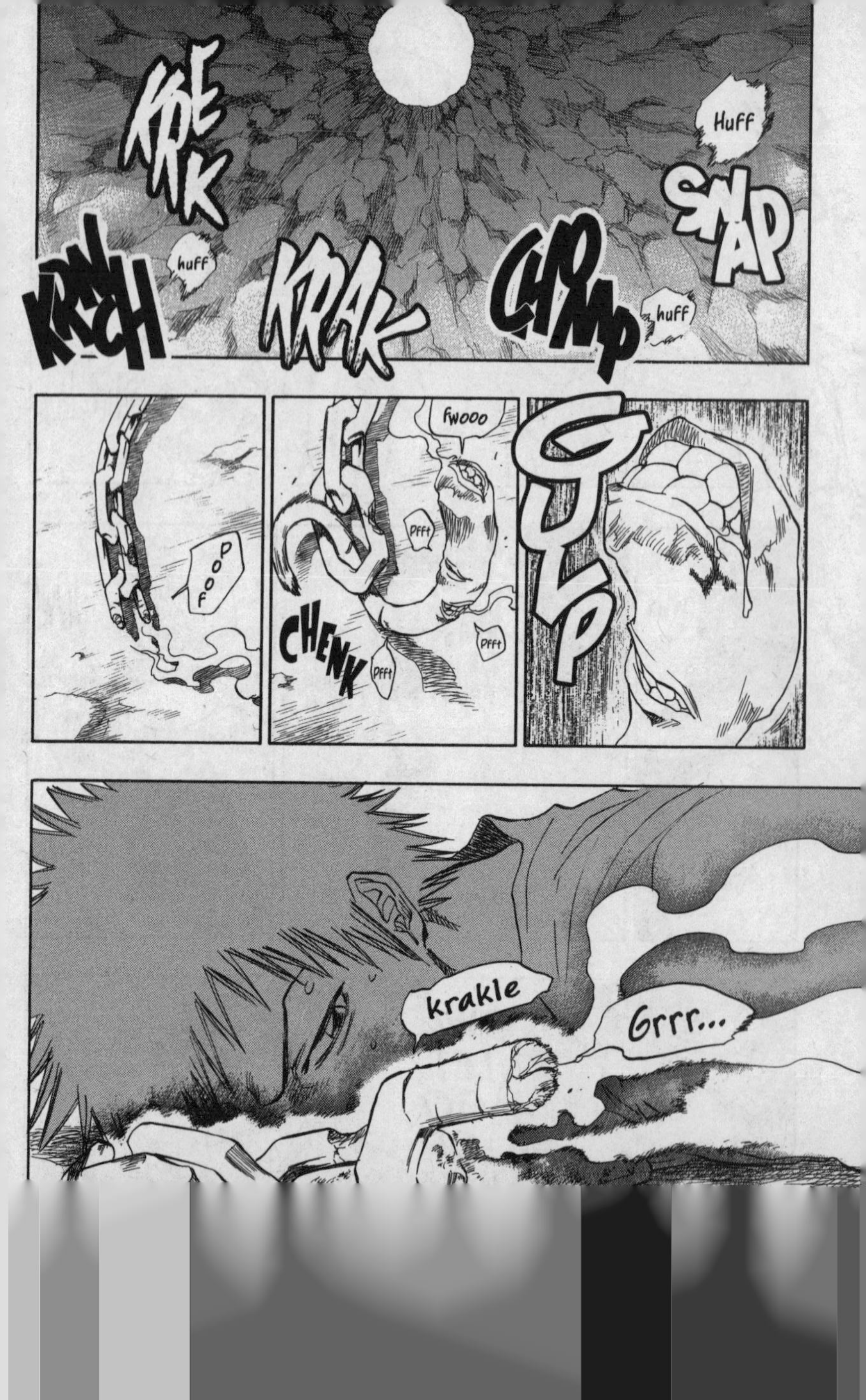
Huff
SNAP
huff
CHOMP
KRAK
huff
GULP
fwooo
Pfft
Pfft
Pfft
CHENK
Poof
Grrr...
krakle

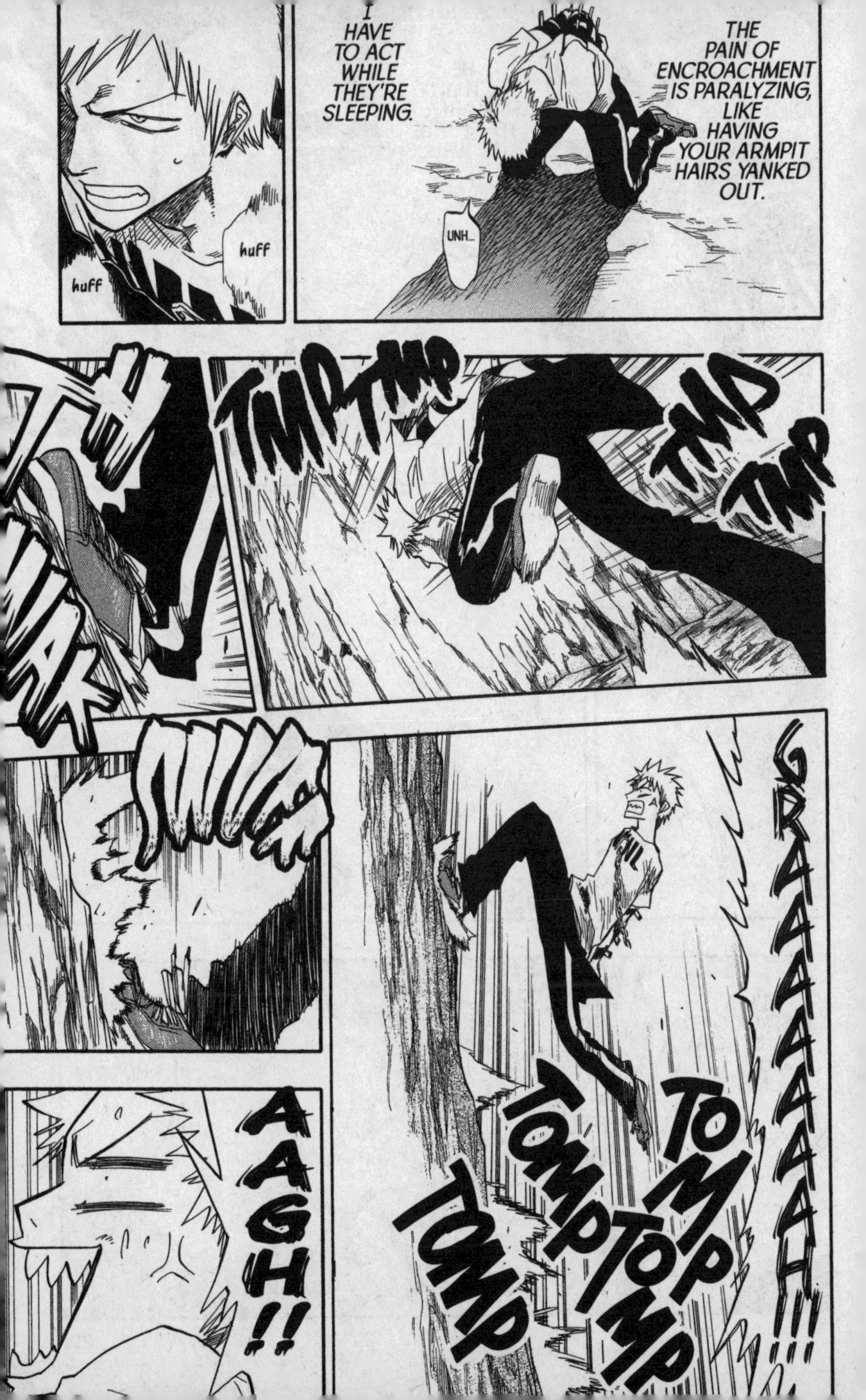
THE PAIN OF ENCROACHMENT IS PARALYZING, LIKE HAVING YOUR ARMPIT HAIRS YANKED OUT.
I HAVE TO ACT WHILE THEY'RE SLEEPING.
UNH...
huff
huff
TMP TMP
TMP TMP
THWAK
GRAAAAAAAAAH!!
TOMTOMP
TOMPTOMP
TOMP
AAGH!!

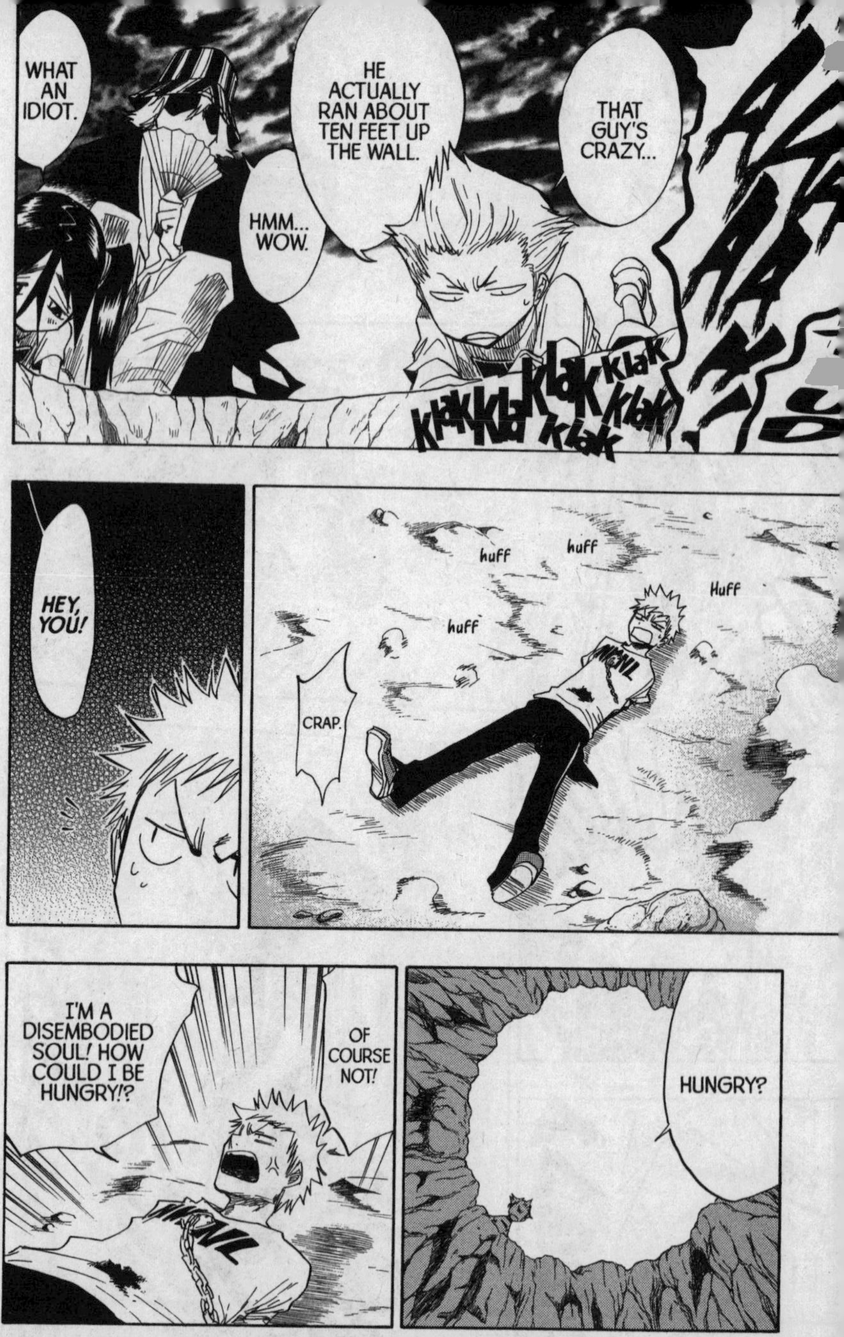
THAT GUY'S CRAZY...
HE ACTUALLY RAN ABOUT TEN FEET UP THE WALL.
HMM... WOW.
WHAT AN IDIOT.
KLAK KLAK KLAK KLAK KLAK KLAK
huff huff Huff huff
CRAP.
HEY, YOU!
HUNGRY?
OF COURSE NOT!
I'M A DISEMBODIED SOUL! HOW COULD I BE HUNGRY!?

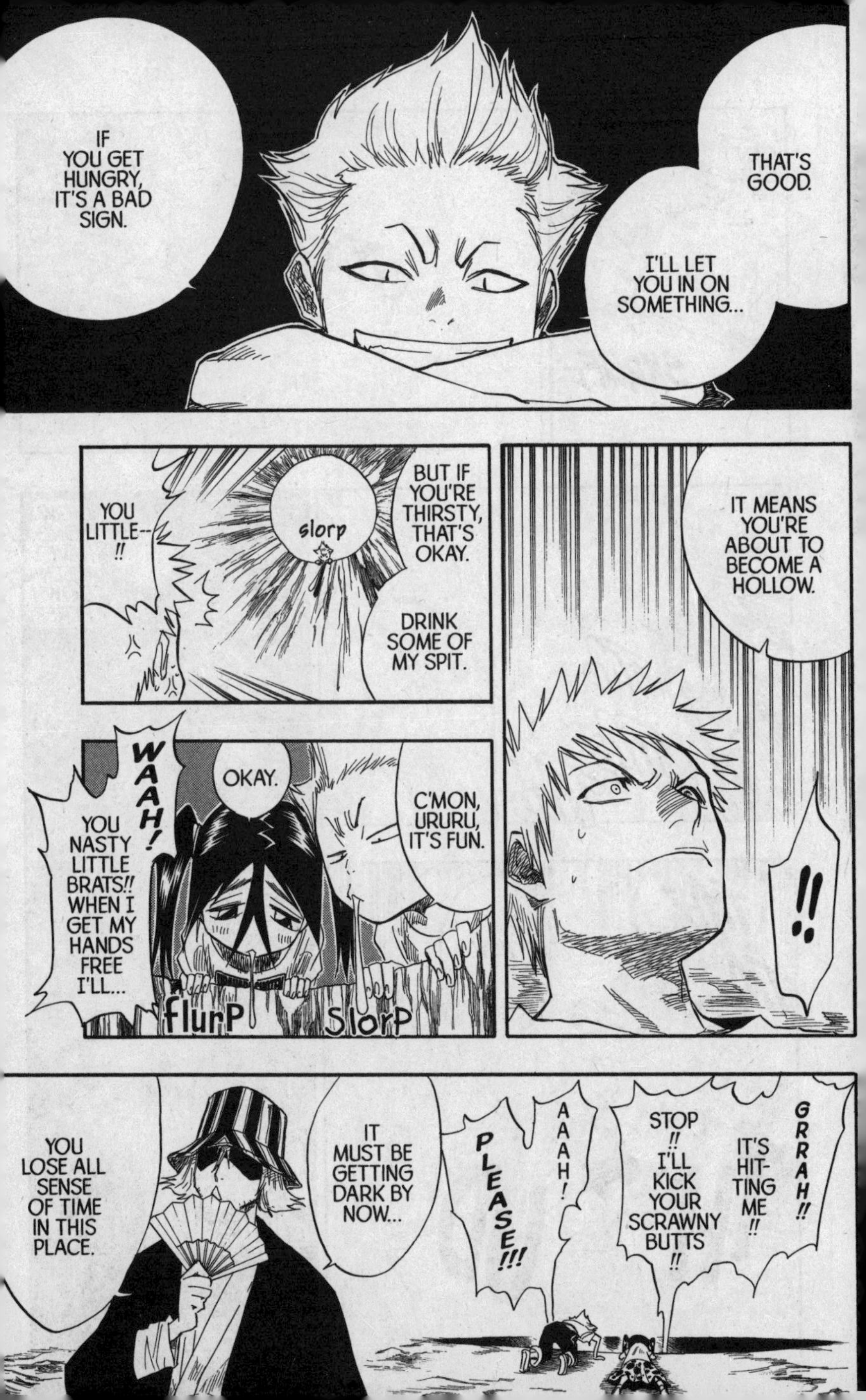
THAT'S GOOD.
I'LL LET YOU IN ON SOMETHING...
IF YOU GET HUNGRY, IT'S A BAD SIGN.
IT MEANS YOU'RE ABOUT TO BECOME A HOLLOW.
!!
BUT IF YOU'RE THIRSTY, THAT'S OKAY.
DRINK SOME OF MY SPIT.
slorp
YOU LITTLE-- !!
C'MON, URURU, IT'S FUN.
OKAY.
WAAAH!
YOU NASTY LITTLE BRATS!! WHEN I GET MY HANDS FREE I'LL...
flurP
SlorP
GRRAH!!
IT'S HIT-TING ME!!
STOP!! I'LL KICK YOUR SCRAWNY BUTTS!!
AAAH!
PLEASE!!!
IT MUST BE GETTING DARK BY NOW...
YOU LOSE ALL SENSE OF TIME IN THIS PLACE.

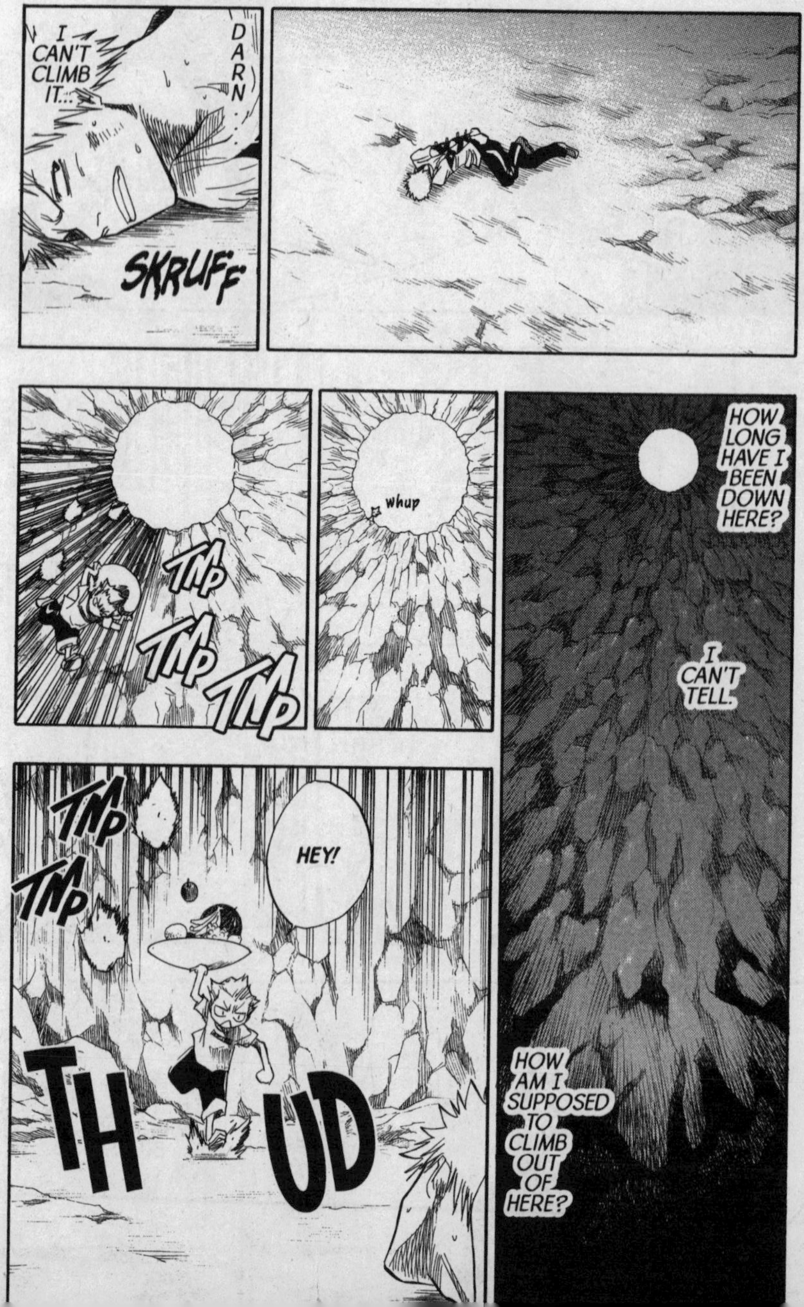
DARN...
I CAN'T CLIMB IT...
SKRUFF
HOW LONG HAVE I BEEN DOWN HERE?
I CAN'T TELL.
HOW AM I SUPPOSED TO CLIMB OUT OF HERE?
whup
TMP
TMP
TMP
TMP
TMP
HEY!
THUD

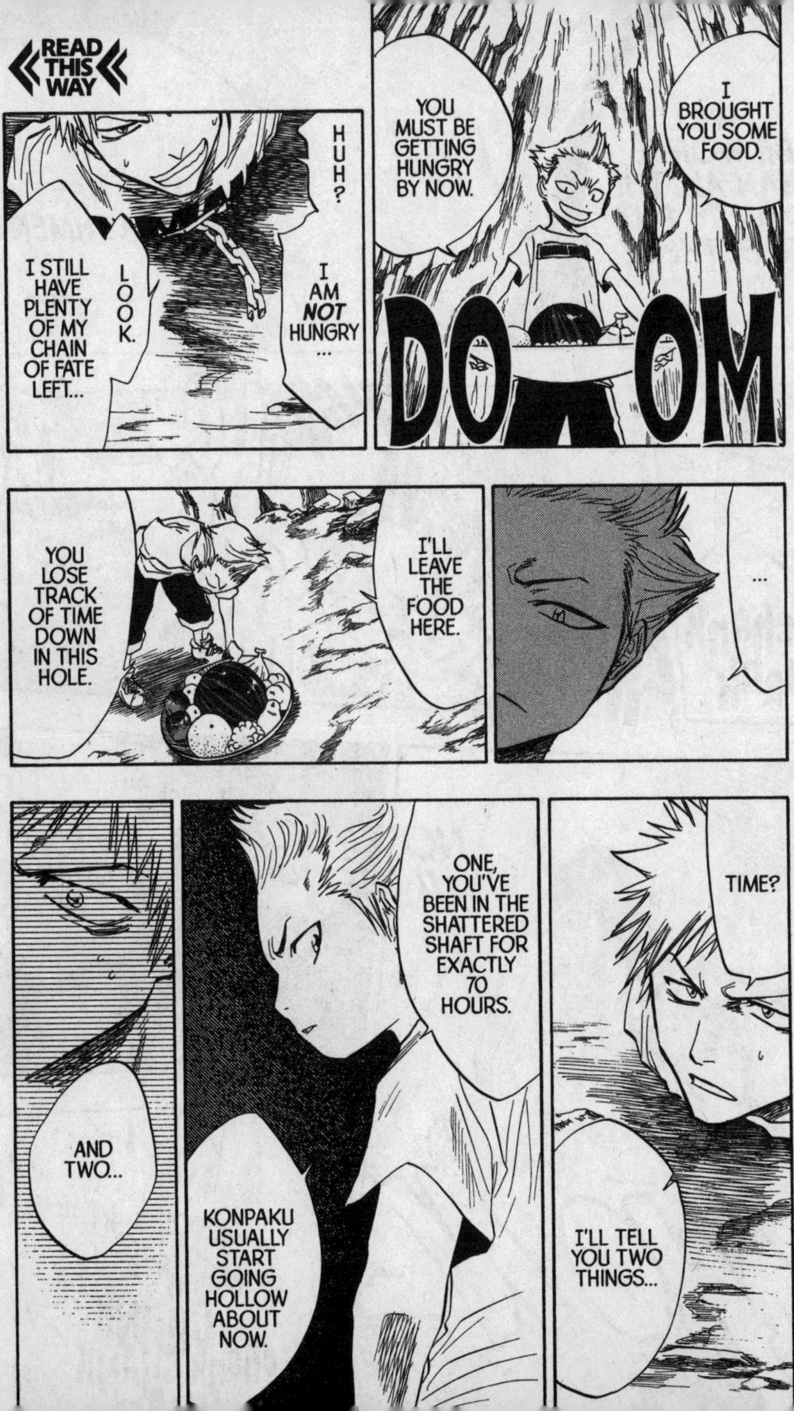
READ THIS WAY
I BROUGHT YOU SOME FOOD.
YOU MUST BE GETTING HUNGRY BY NOW.
DOOM
HUH?
I AM NOT HUNGRY ...
LOOK.
I STILL HAVE PLENTY OF MY CHAIN OF FATE LEFT...
...
I'LL LEAVE THE FOOD HERE.
YOU LOSE TRACK OF TIME DOWN IN THIS HOLE.
TIME?
I'LL TELL YOU TWO THINGS...
ONE, YOU'VE BEEN IN THE SHATTERED SHAFT FOR EXACTLY 70 HOURS.
KONPAKU USUALLY START GOING HOLLOW ABOUT NOW.
AND TWO...

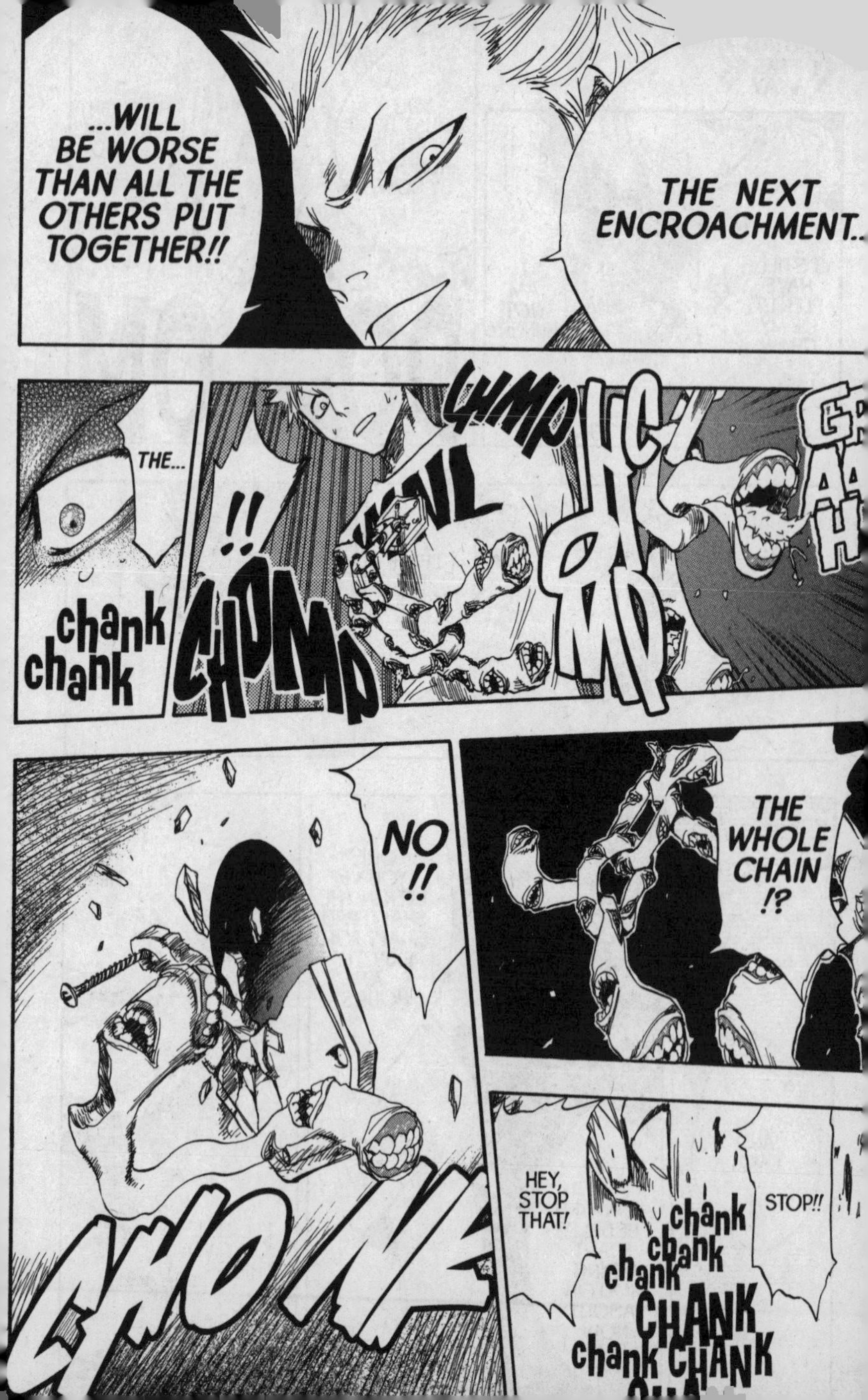
THE NEXT ENCROACHMENT...
...WILL BE WORSE THAN ALL THE OTHERS PUT TOGETHER!!
CHOMP
!!
THE...
chank chank
THE WHOLE CHAIN !?
NO !!
STOP!!
HEY, STOP THAT!
chank chank chank CHANK chank CHANK

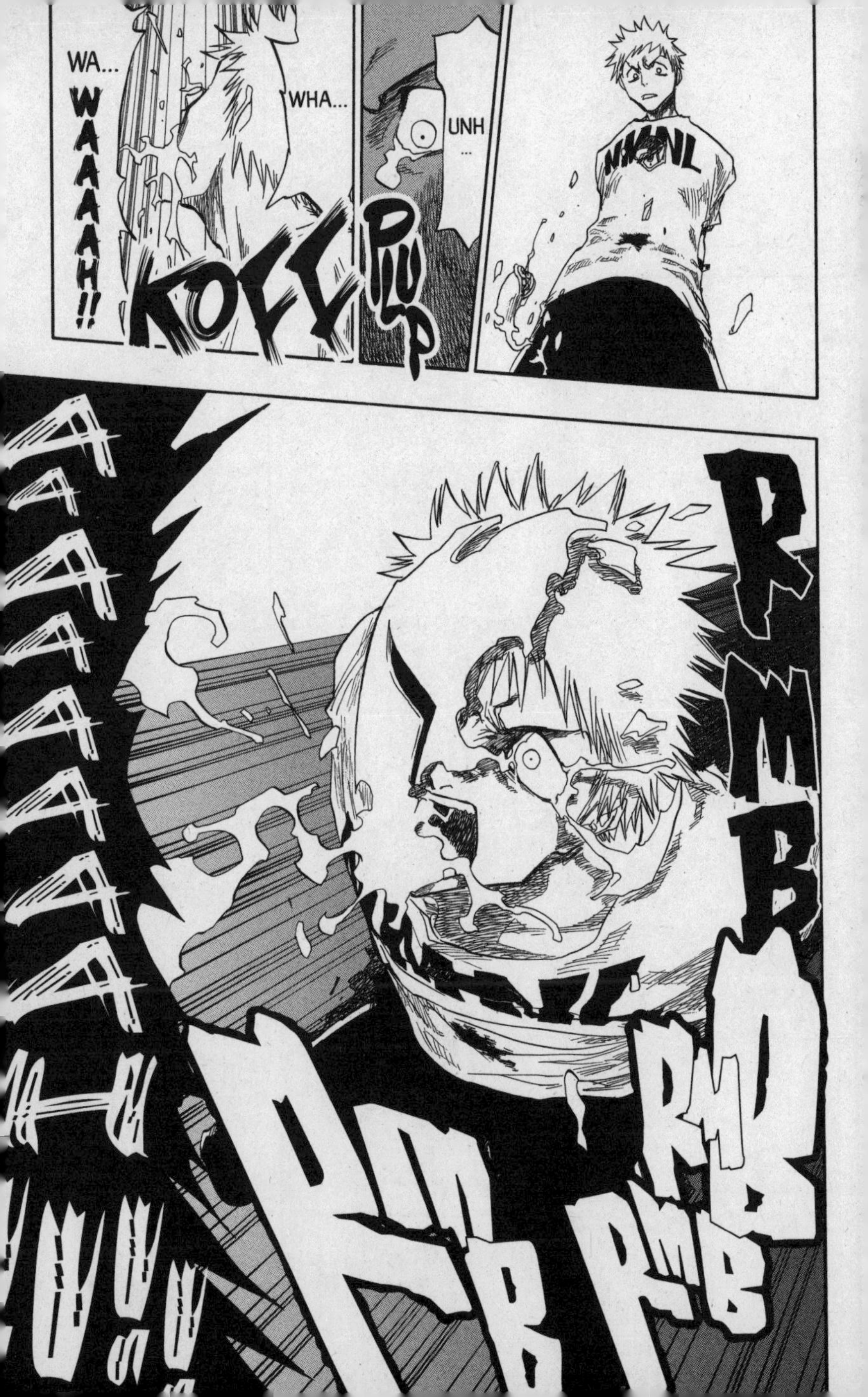
UNH ...
PULUP
WHA...
KOFF
WA... WAAAAAH!!

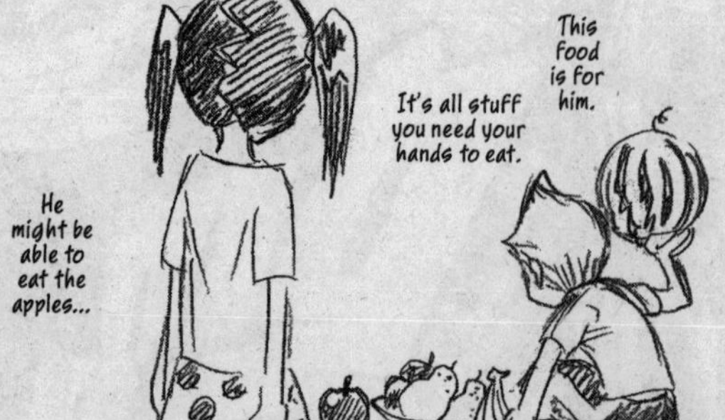
This food is for him.
It's all stuff you need your hands to eat.
He might be able to eat the apples...

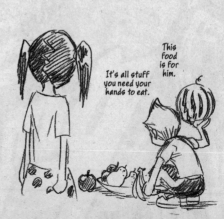

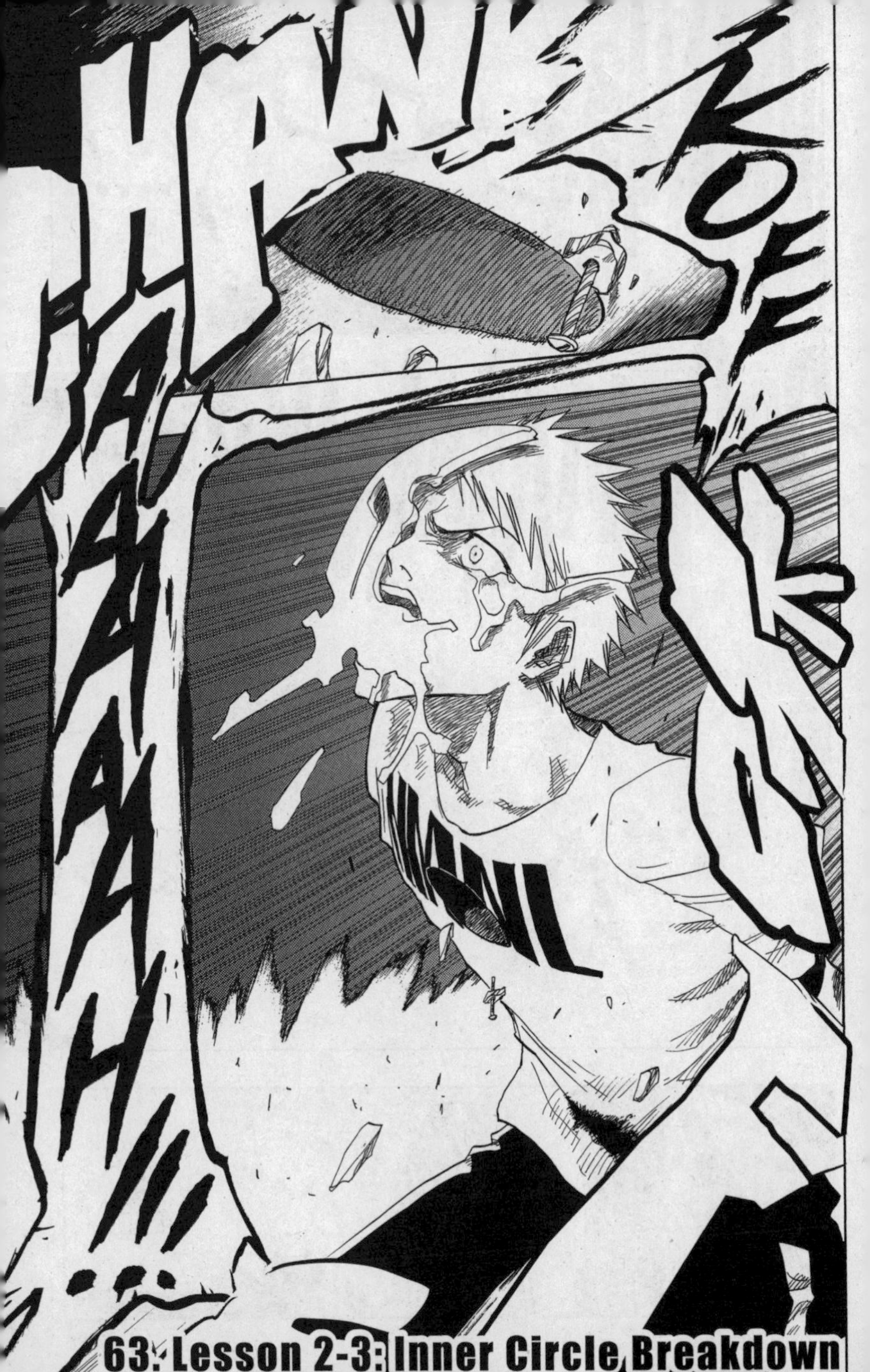

63. Lesson 2-3: Inner Circle Breakdown

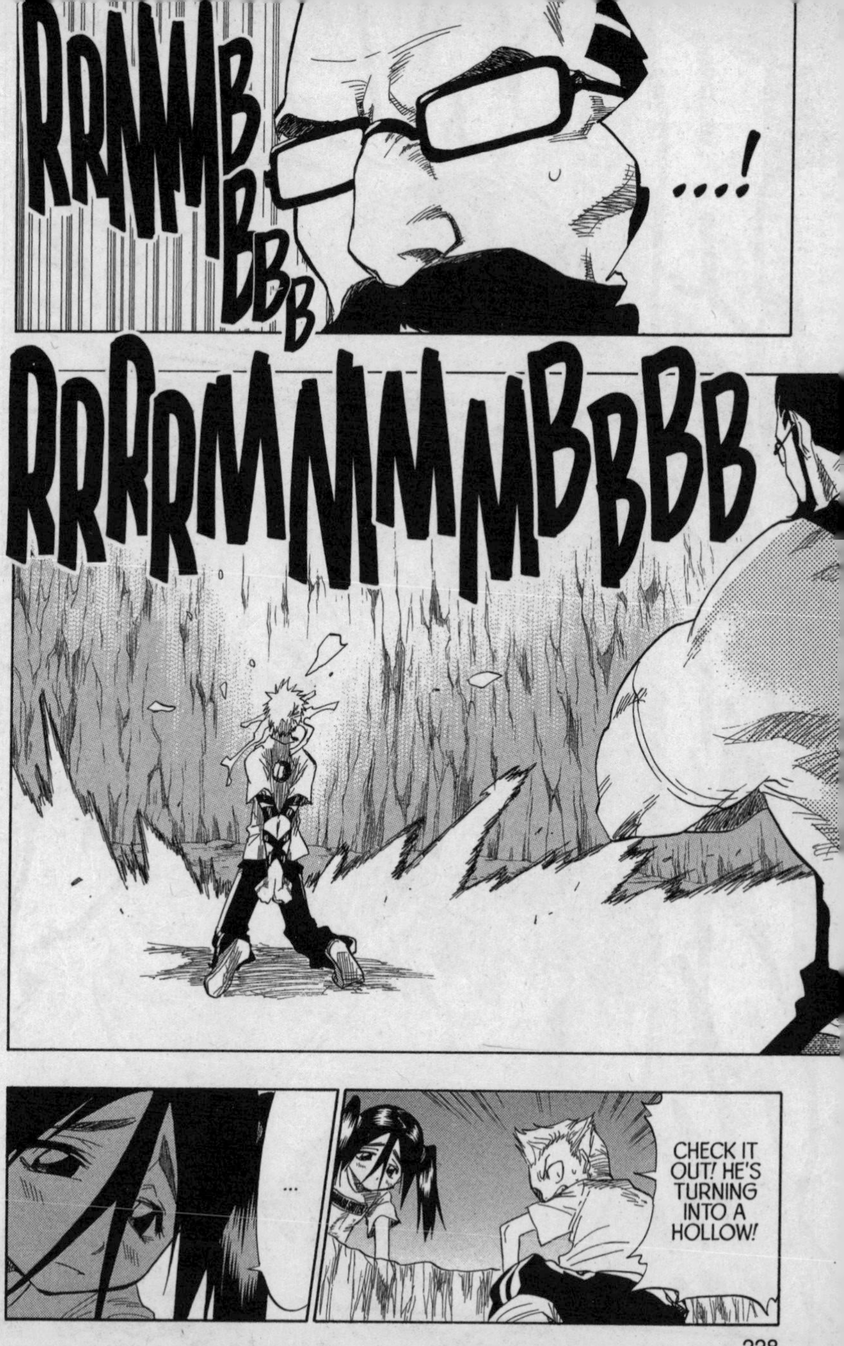

RRMMBBBB
...!
RRRMMMMBBBB
CHECK IT OUT! HE'S TURNING INTO A HOLLOW!
...

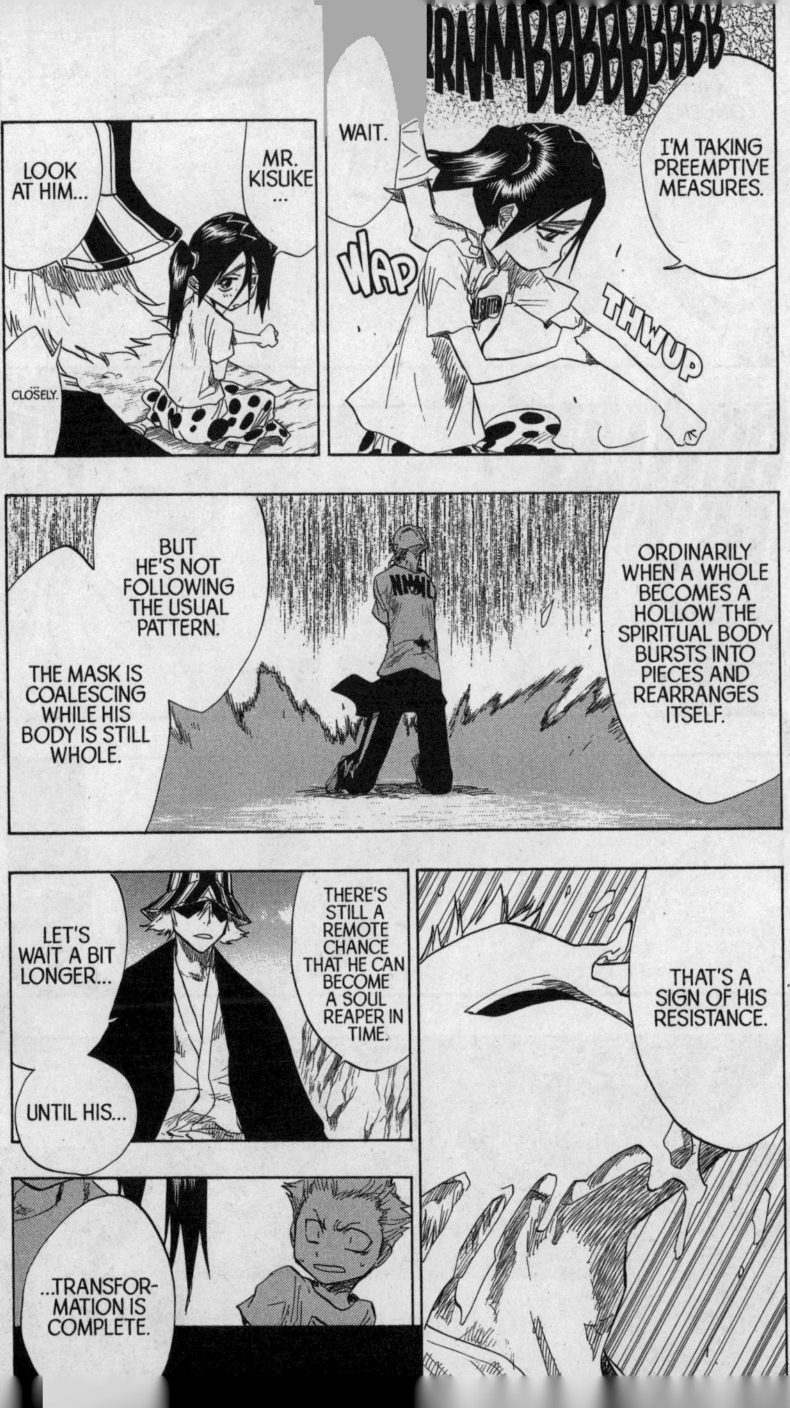

RNMBBBBBBBBB
I'M TAKING PREEMPTIVE MEASURES.
THWUP
WAP
WAIT.
MR. KISUKE ...
LOOK AT HIM...
...CLOSELY.
ORDINARILY WHEN A WHOLE BECOMES A HOLLOW THE SPIRITUAL BODY BURSTS INTO PIECES AND REARRANGES ITSELF.
BUT HE'S NOT FOLLOWING THE USUAL PATTERN.
THE MASK IS COALESCING WHILE HIS BODY IS STILL WHOLE.
THAT'S A SIGN OF HIS RESISTANCE.
THERE'S STILL A REMOTE CHANCE THAT HE CAN BECOME A SOUL REAPER IN TIME.
LET'S WAIT A BIT LONGER...
UNTIL HIS...
...TRANSFORMATION IS COMPLETE.

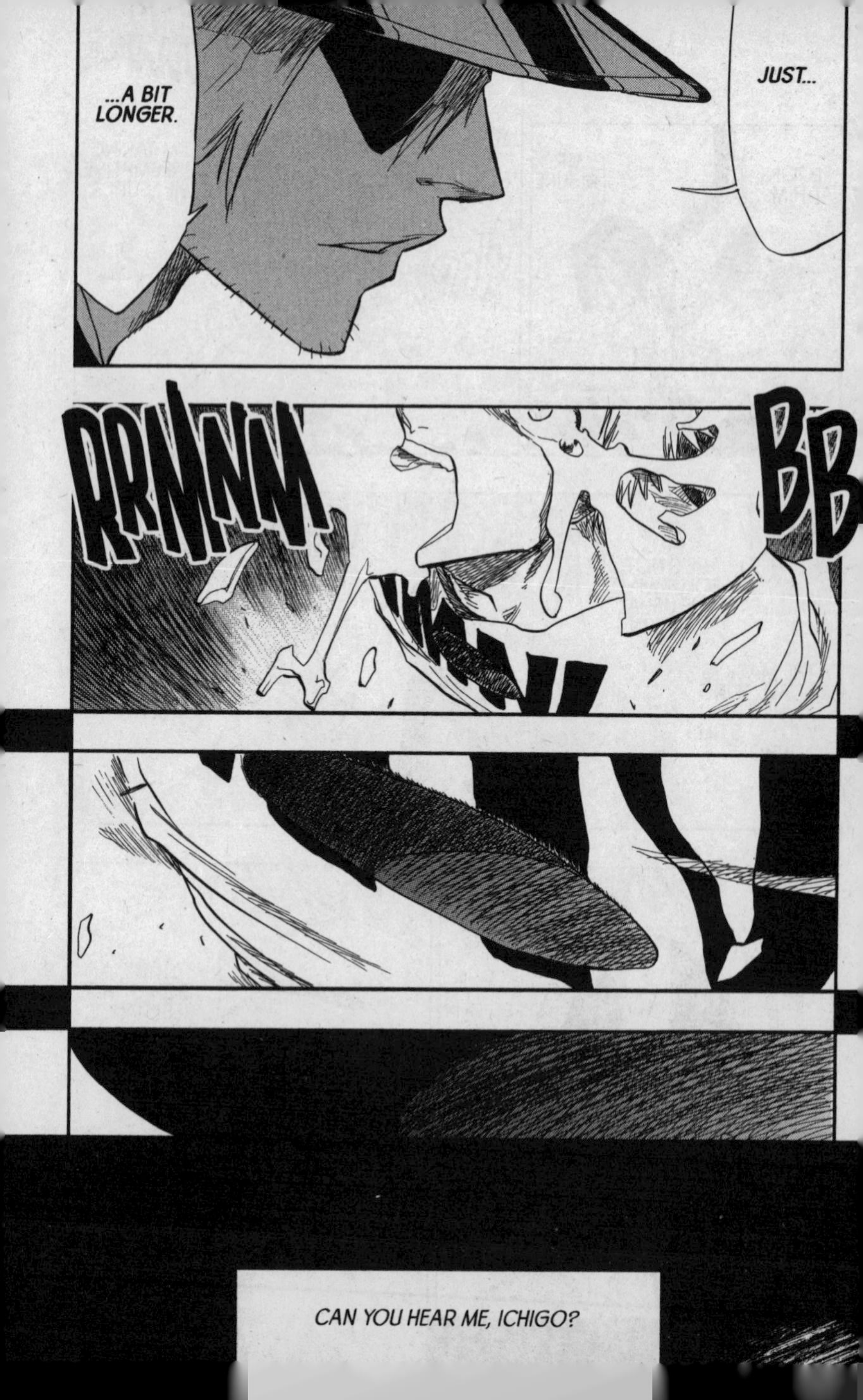
JUST...
...A BIT LONGER.
RRMNNM
BB
CAN YOU HEAR ME, ICHIGO?

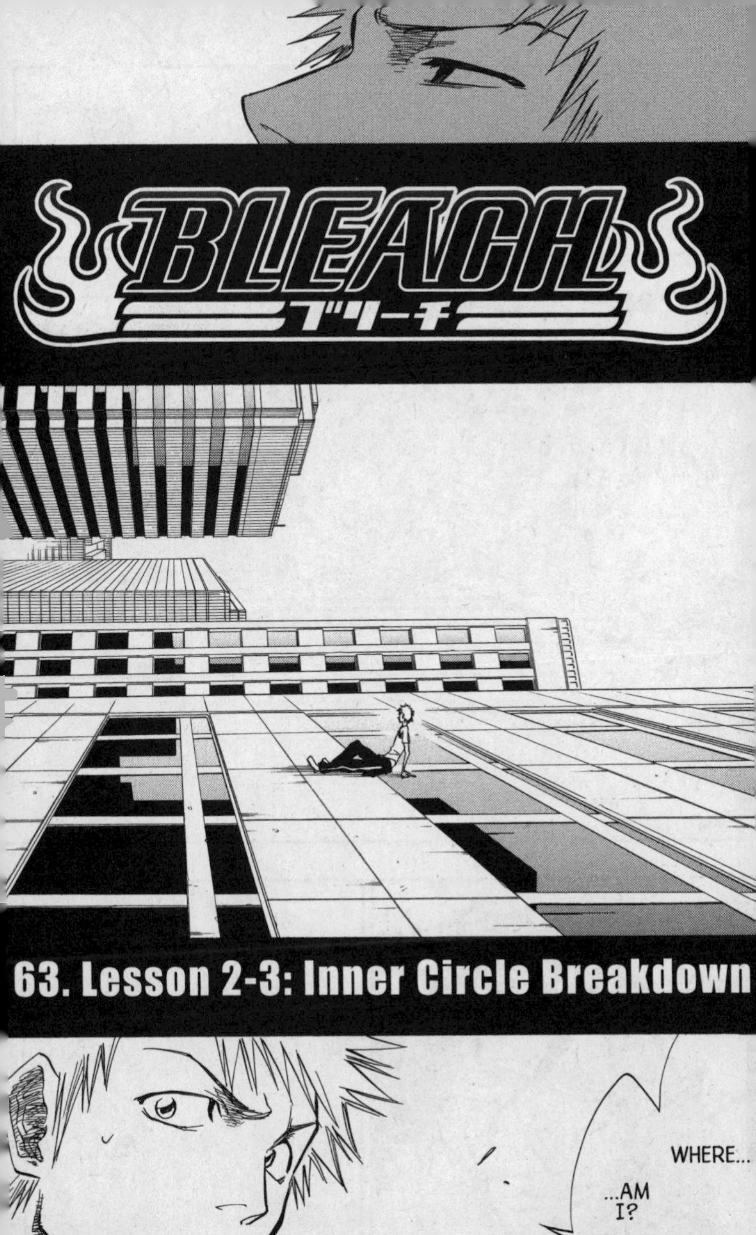
BLEACH
ブリーチ
63. Lesson 2-3: Inner Circle Breakdown
WHERE...
...AM I?

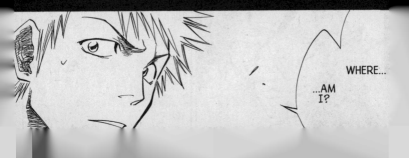

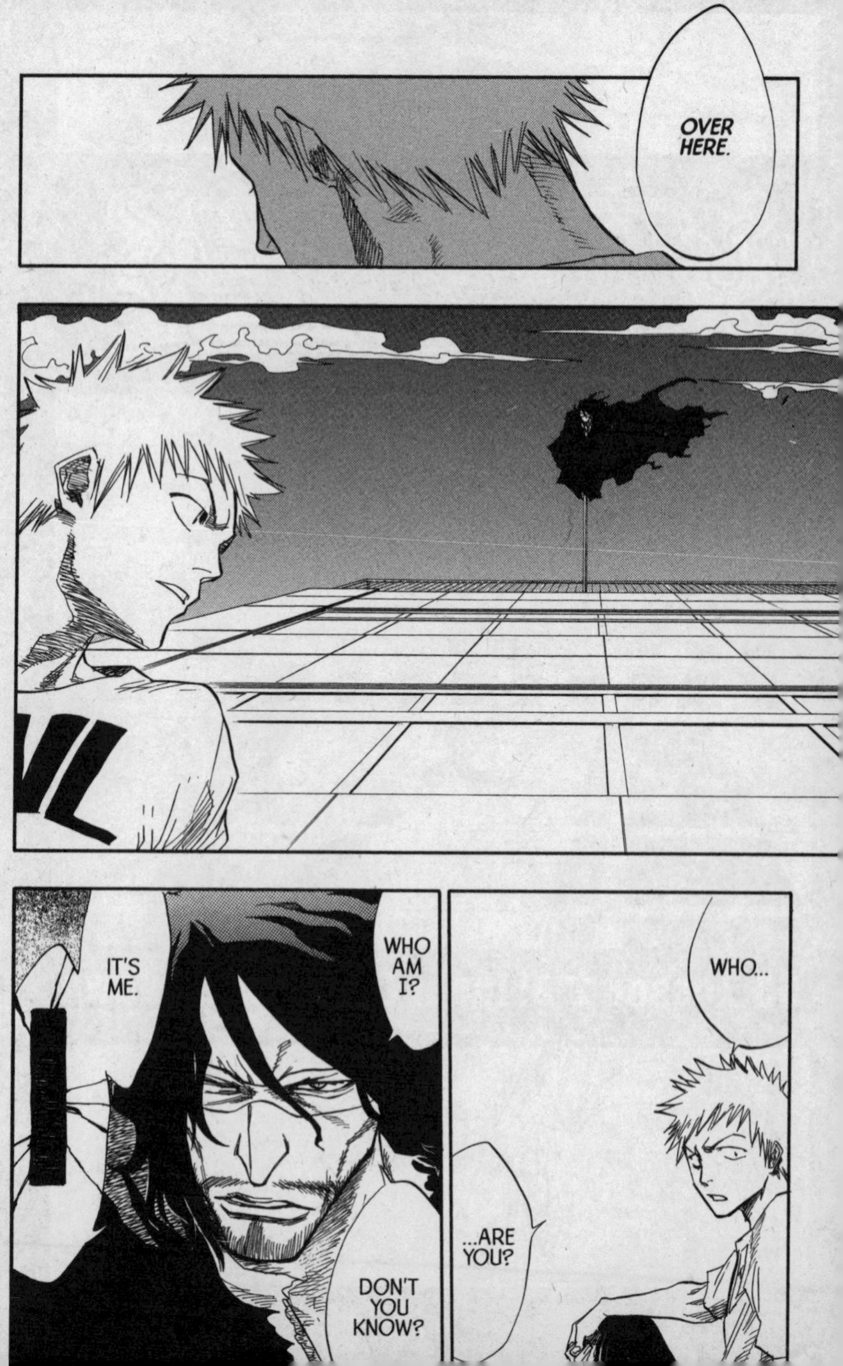
OVER HERE.
WHO...
...ARE YOU?
WHO AM I?
IT'S ME.
DON'T YOU KNOW?

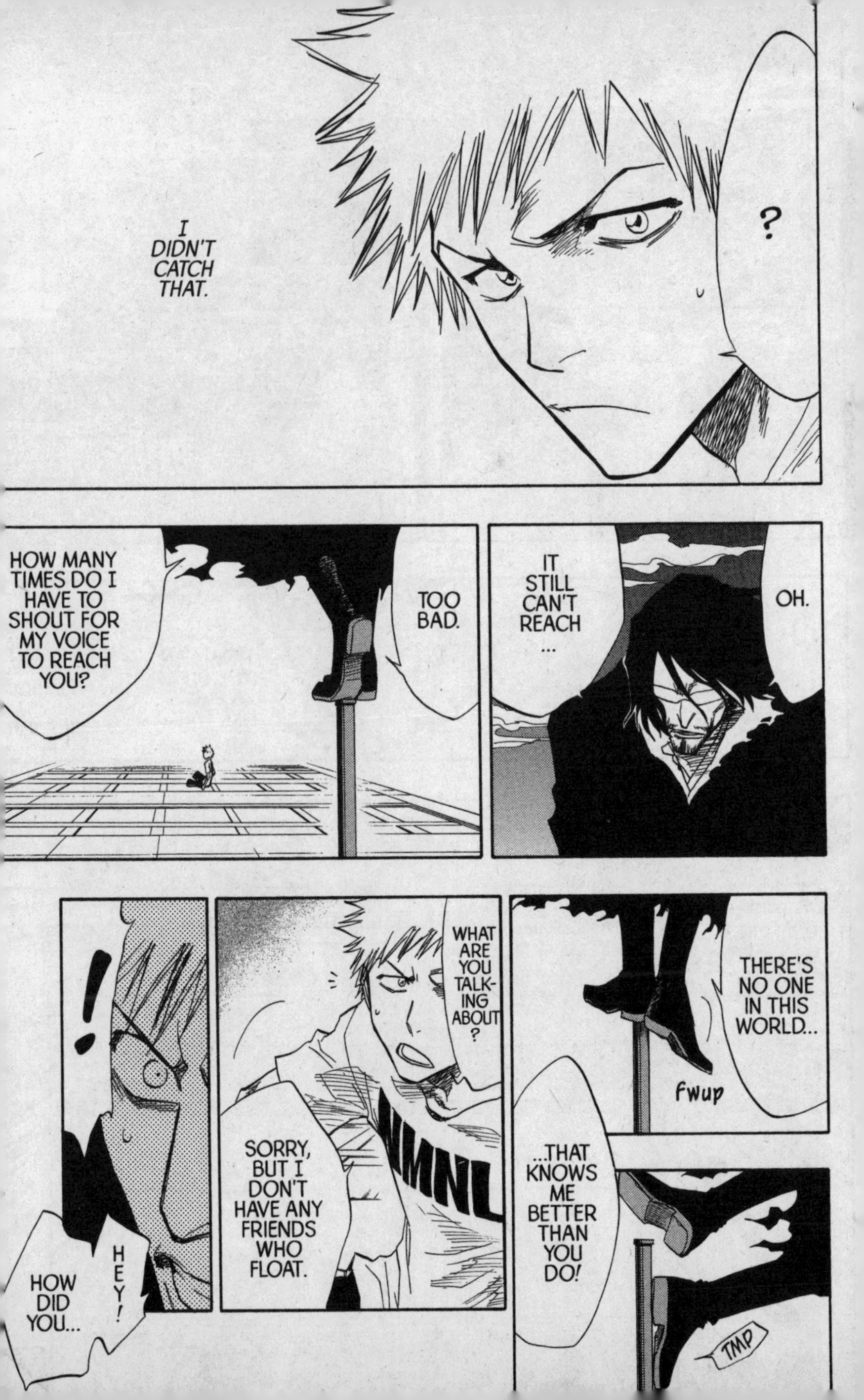
?
I DIDN'T CATCH THAT.
OH.
IT STILL CAN'T REACH ...
TOO BAD.
HOW MANY TIMES DO I HAVE TO SHOUT FOR MY VOICE TO REACH YOU?
THERE'S NO ONE IN THIS WORLD...
fwup
...THAT KNOWS ME BETTER THAN YOU DO!
TMP
WHAT ARE YOU TALKING ABOUT?
SORRY, BUT I DON'T HAVE ANY FRIENDS WHO FLOAT.
!
HEY!
HOW DID YOU...

HOW CAN YOU SIT IN A PLACE LIKE THAT?

HOW STRANG

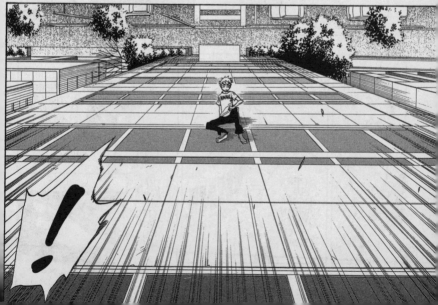

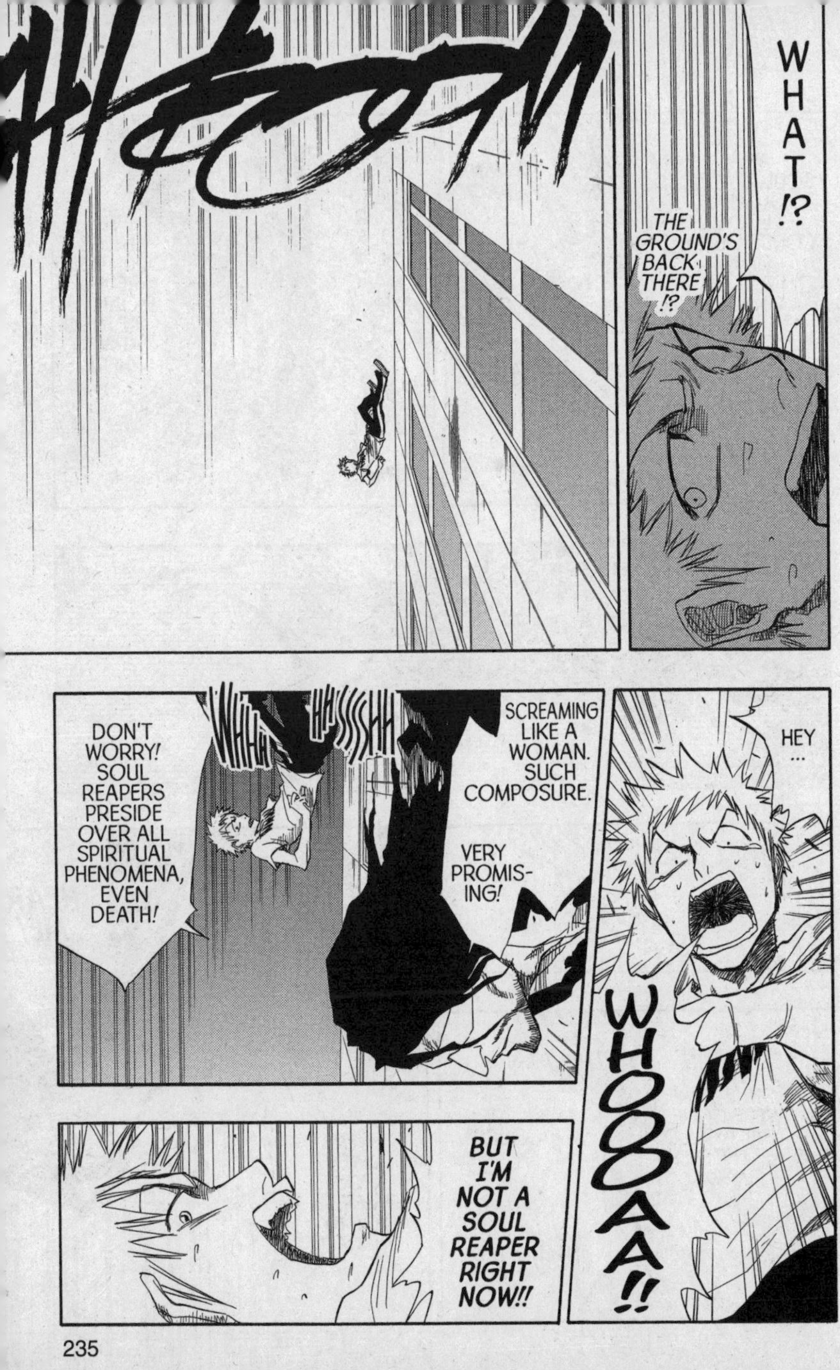
WHAT!?
THE GROUND'S BACK THERE!?
HEY ...
WHOOOAA!!
SCREAMING LIKE A WOMAN. SUCH COMPOSURE.
VERY PROMISING!
DON'T WORRY! SOUL REAPERS PRESIDE OVER ALL SPIRITUAL PHENOMENA, EVEN DEATH!
BUT I'M NOT A SOUL REAPER RIGHT NOW!!

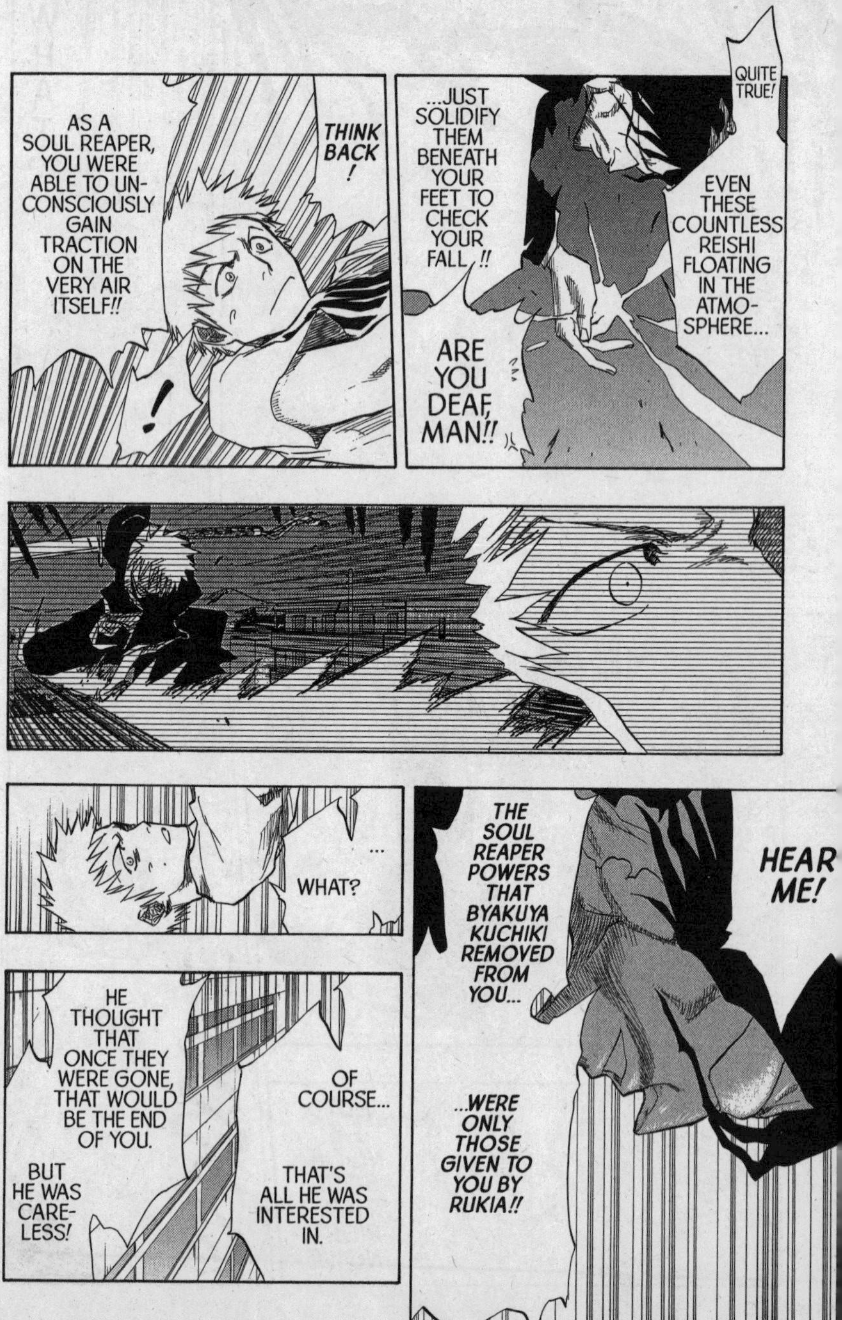
QUITE TRUE!
EVEN THESE COUNTLESS REISHI FLOATING IN THE ATMOSPHERE...
...JUST SOLIDIFY THEM BENEATH YOUR FEET TO CHECK YOUR FALL!!
ARE YOU DEAF, MAN!!
THINK BACK!
AS A SOUL REAPER, YOU WERE ABLE TO UN-CONSCIOUSLY GAIN TRACTION ON THE VERY AIR ITSELF!!
!
HEAR ME!
THE SOUL REAPER POWERS THAT BYAKUYA KUCHIKI REMOVED FROM YOU...
...WERE ONLY THOSE GIVEN TO YOU BY RUKIA!!
...
WHAT?
OF COURSE...
HE THOUGHT THAT ONCE THEY WERE GONE, THAT WOULD BE THE END OF YOU.
THAT'S ALL HE WAS INTERESTED IN.
BUT HE WAS CARE-LESS!

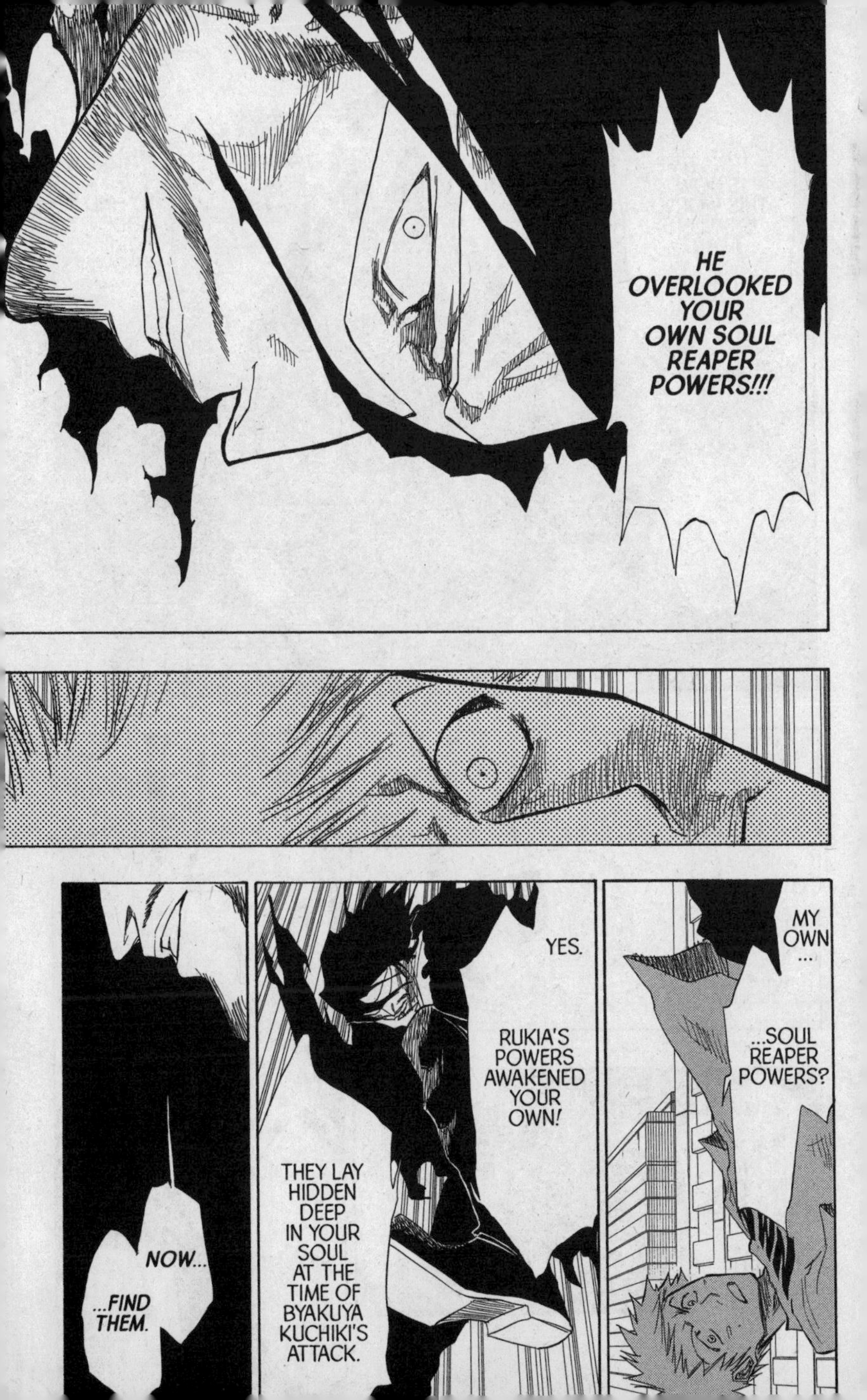
HE OVERLOOKED YOUR OWN SOUL REAPER POWERS!!!
MY OWN...
...SOUL REAPER POWERS?
YES.
RUKIA'S POWERS AWAKENED YOUR OWN!
THEY LAY HIDDEN DEEP IN YOUR SOUL AT THE TIME OF BYAKUYA KUCHIKI'S ATTACK.
NOW...
...FIND THEM.

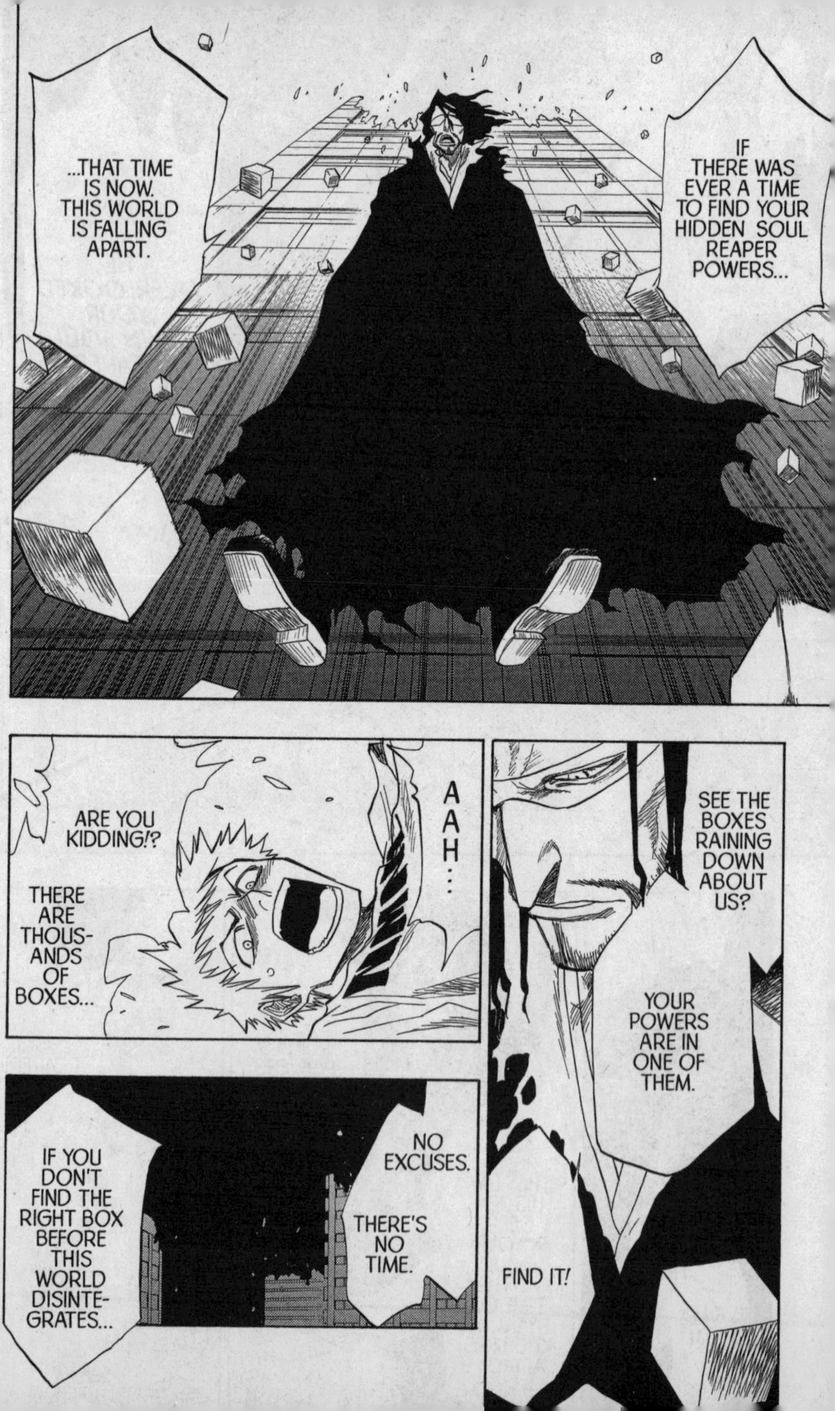
IF THERE WAS EVER A TIME TO FIND YOUR HIDDEN SOUL REAPER POWERS...
...THAT TIME IS NOW. THIS WORLD IS FALLING APART.
SEE THE BOXES RAINING DOWN ABOUT US?
AAH...
ARE YOU KIDDING!?
THERE ARE THOUSANDS OF BOXES...
YOUR POWERS ARE IN ONE OF THEM.
NO EXCUSES.
THERE'S NO TIME.
IF YOU DON'T FIND THE RIGHT BOX BEFORE THIS WORLD DISINTEGRATES...
FIND IT!

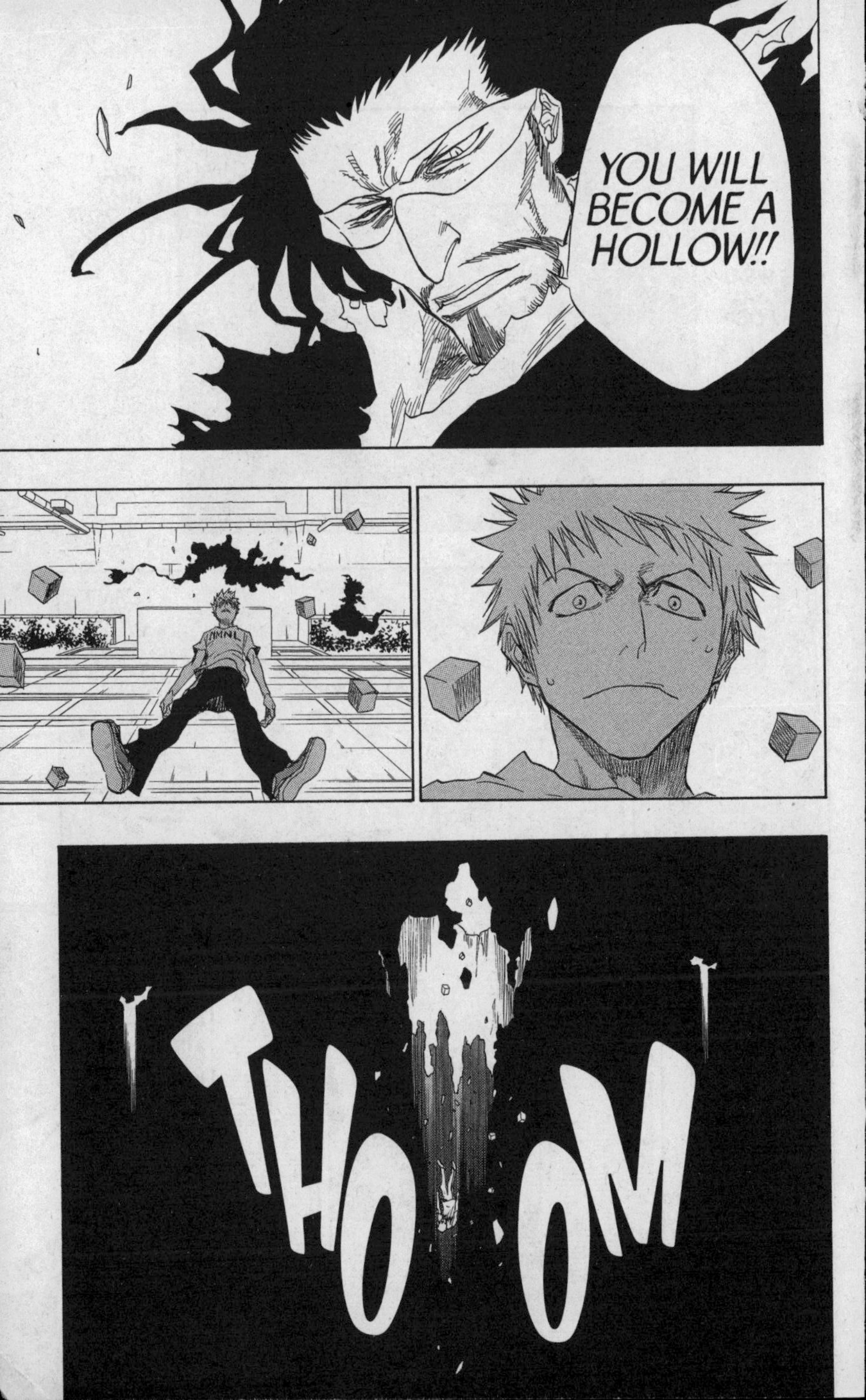
YOU WILL BECOME A HOLLOW!!
THO OM

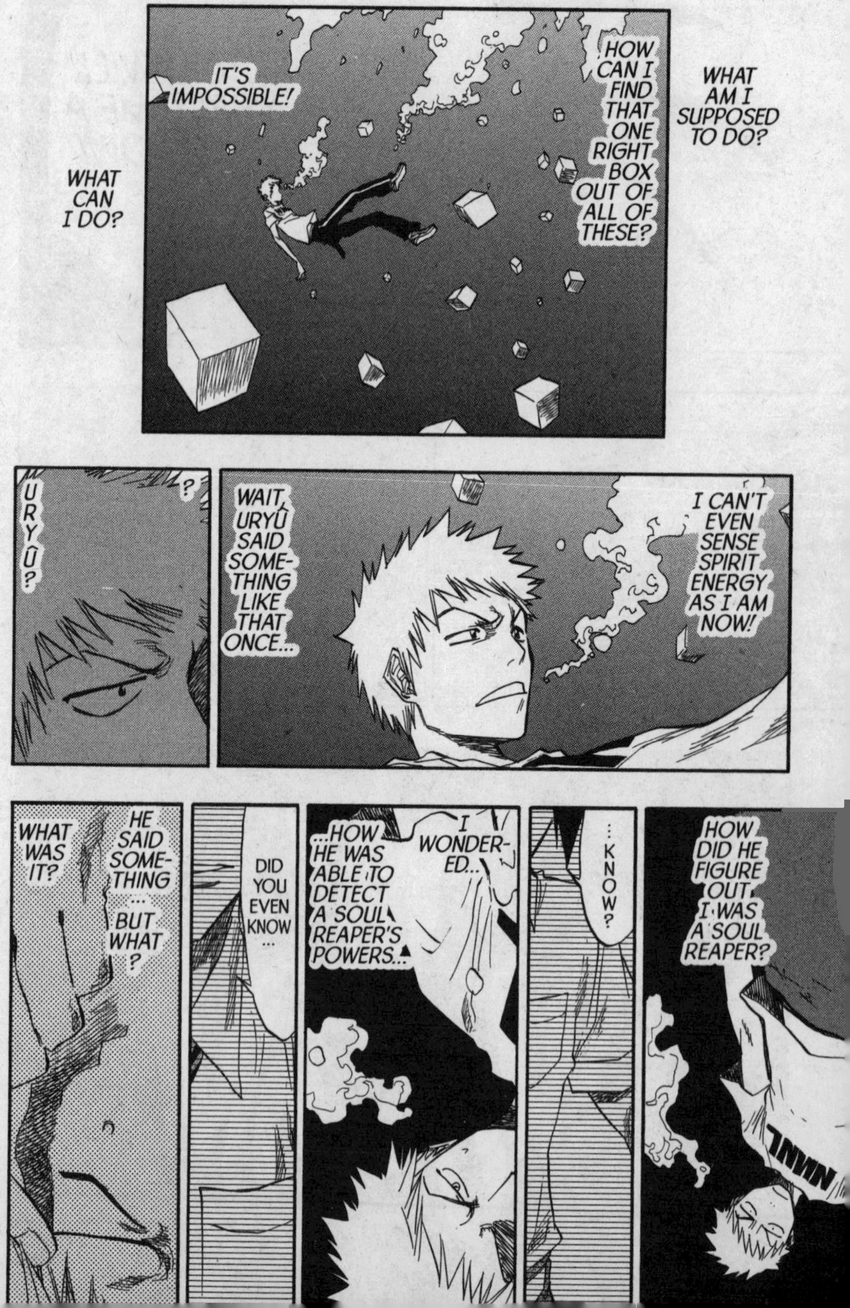
WHAT AM I SUPPOSED TO DO?
HOW CAN I FIND THAT ONE RIGHT BOX OUT OF ALL OF THESE?
IT'S IMPOSSIBLE!
WHAT CAN I DO?
I CAN'T EVEN SENSE SPIRIT ENERGY AS I AM NOW!
WAIT, URYŪ SAID SOMETHING LIKE THAT ONCE...
?
URYŪ?
HOW DID HE FIGURE OUT I WAS A SOUL REAPER?
...KNOW?
I WONDERED...
...HOW HE WAS ABLE TO DETECT A SOUL REAPER'S POWERS...
DID YOU EVEN KNOW...
HE SAID SOMETHING... BUT WHAT?
WHAT WAS IT?

READ THIS WAY

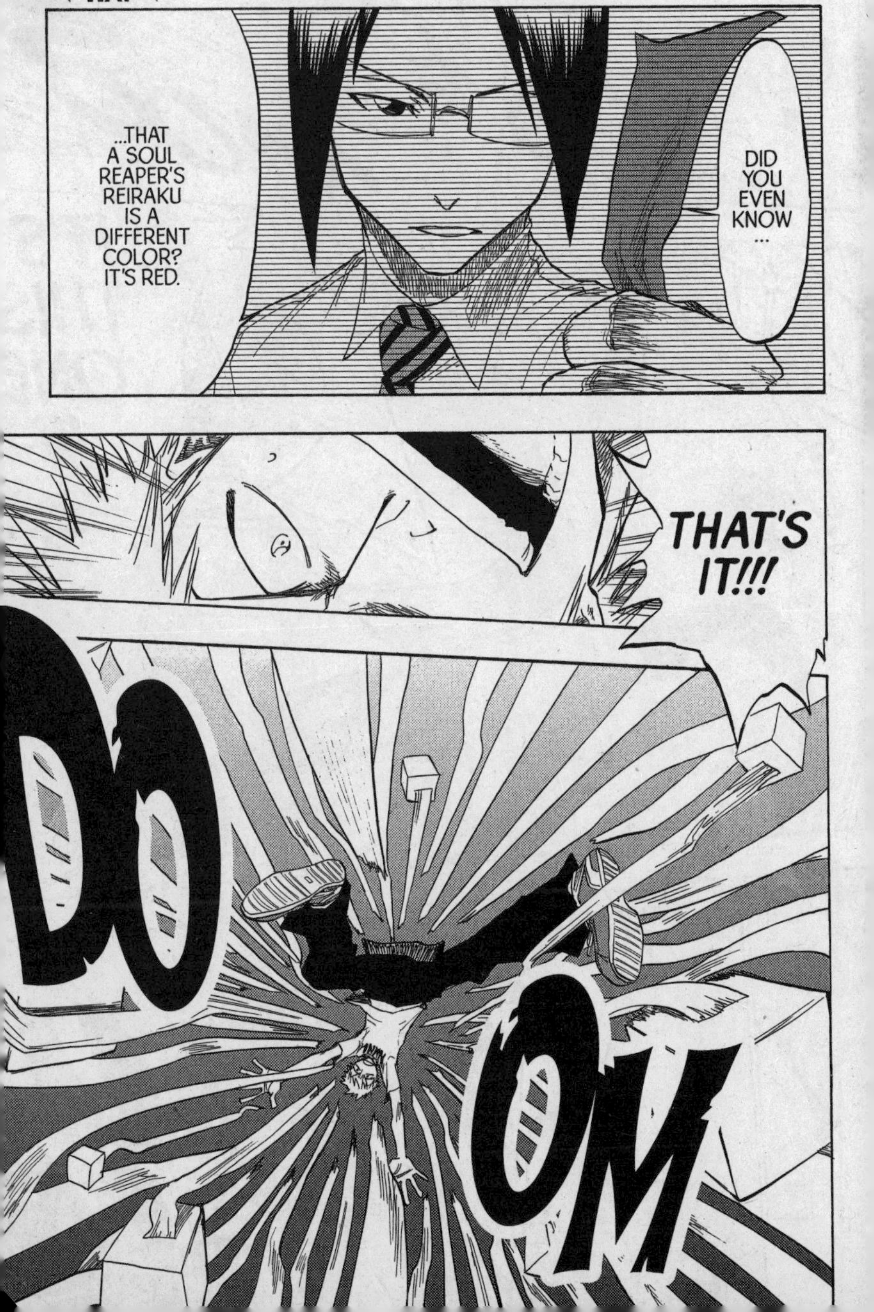
DID YOU EVEN KNOW ...
...THAT A SOUL REAPER'S REIRAKU IS A DIFFERENT COLOR? IT'S RED.
THAT'S IT!!!
DOOM

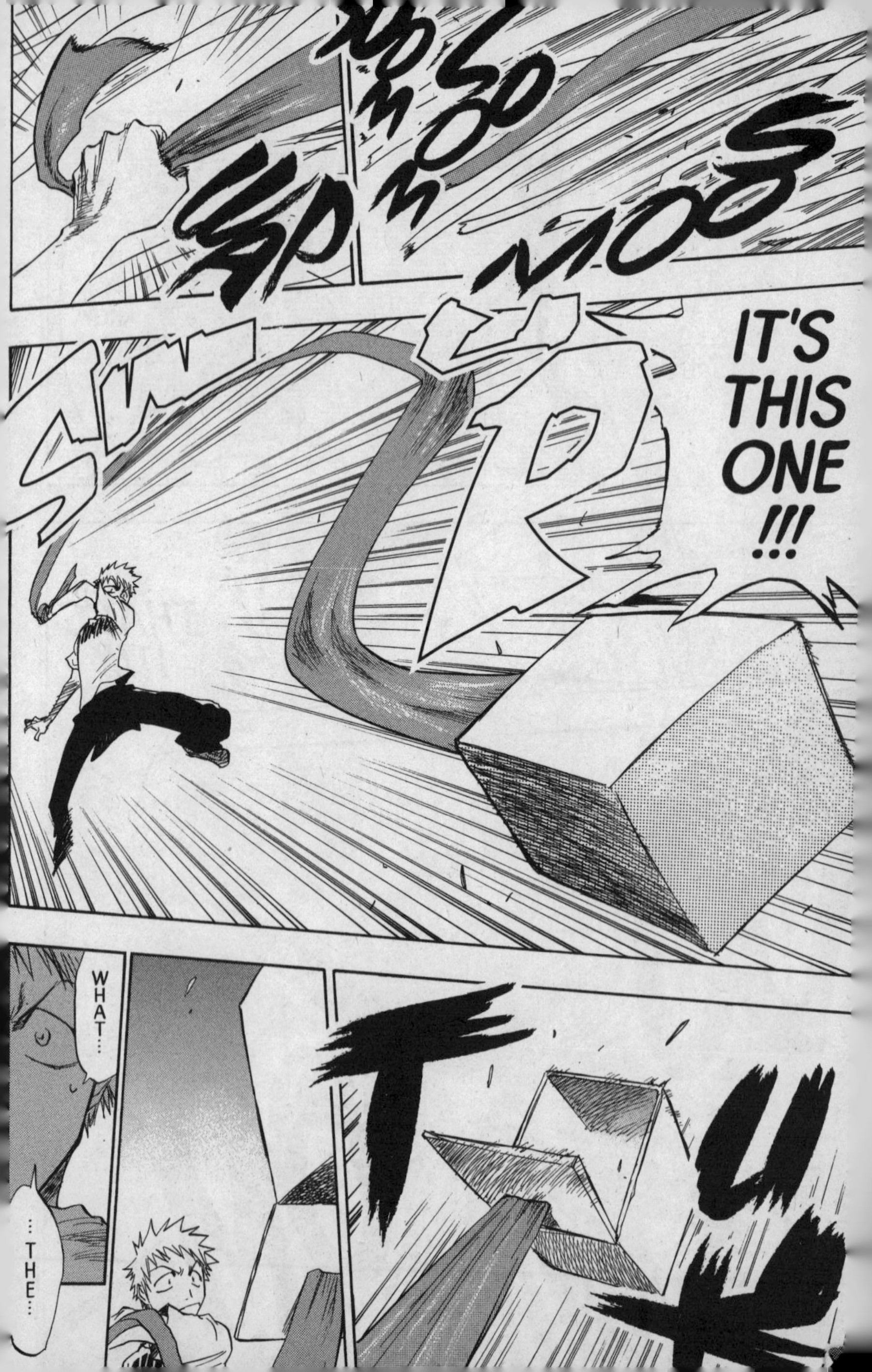
IT'S THIS ONE !!!
WHAT…
…THE…

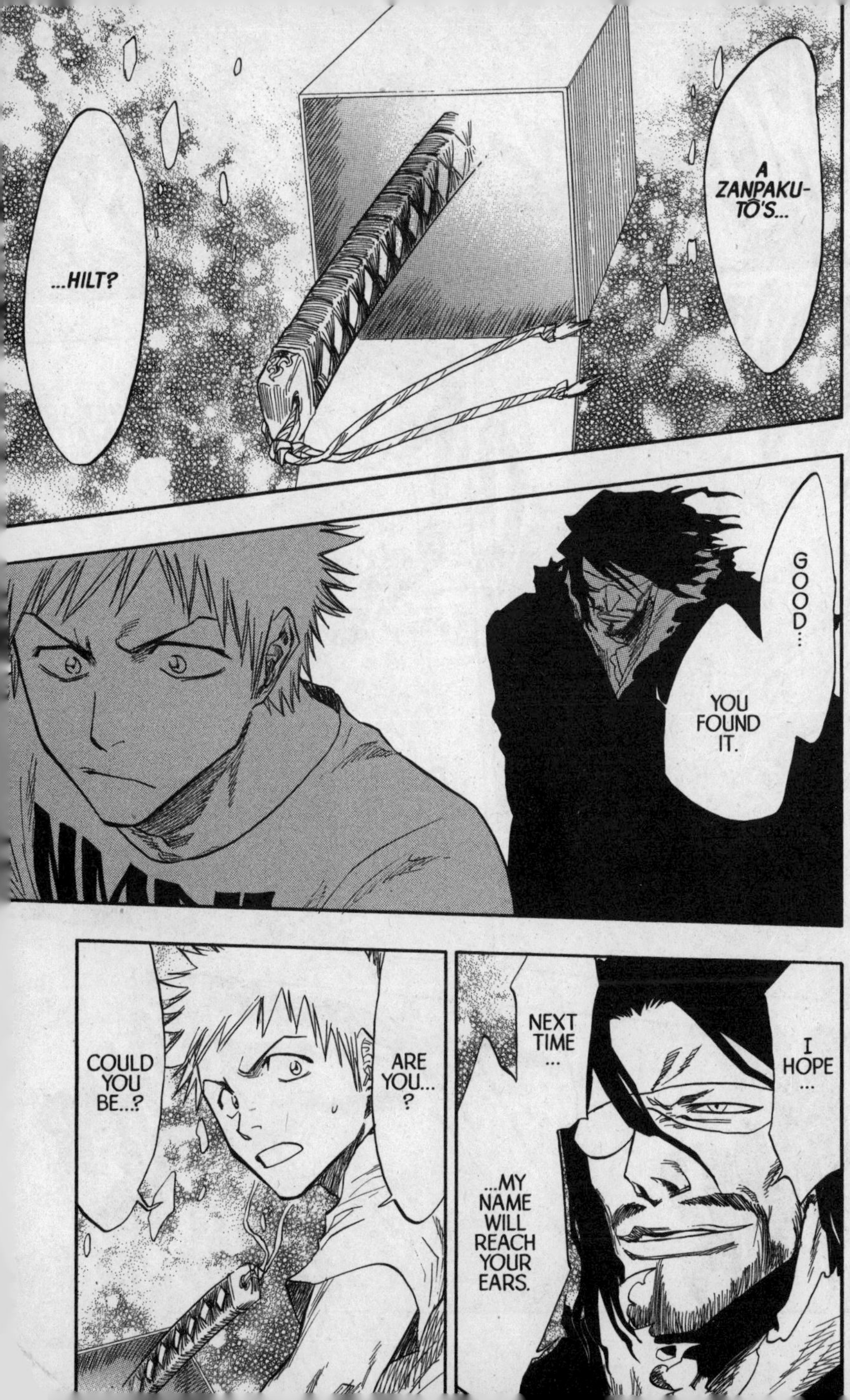
A ZANPAKU-TŌ'S...
...HILT?
GOOD...
YOU FOUND IT.
I HOPE...
NEXT TIME...
...MY NAME WILL REACH YOUR EARS.
ARE YOU...?
COULD YOU BE...?

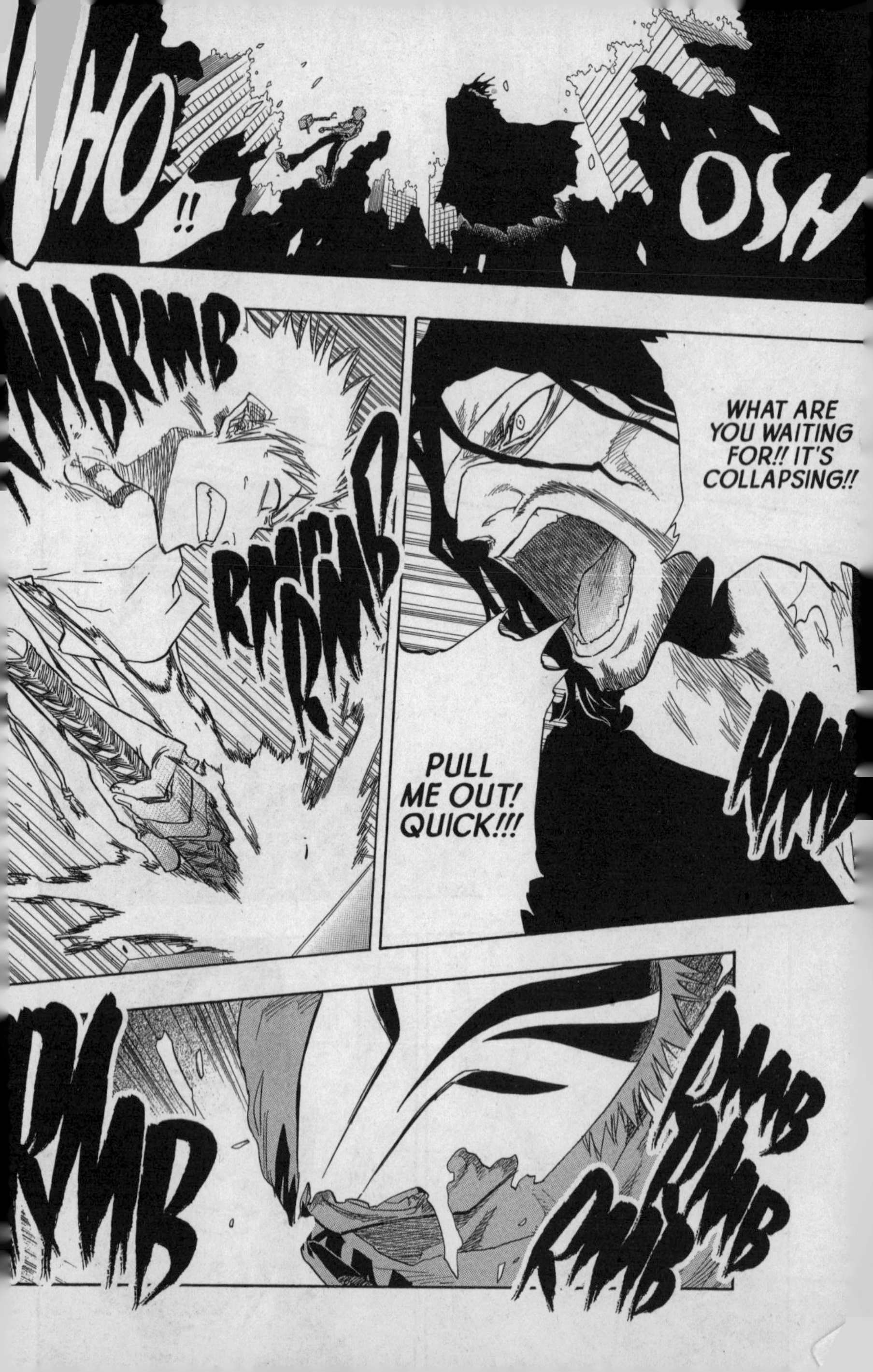

WHO
OSH
!!
WHAT ARE YOU WAITING FOR!! IT'S COLLAPSING!!
PULL ME OUT! QUICK!!!

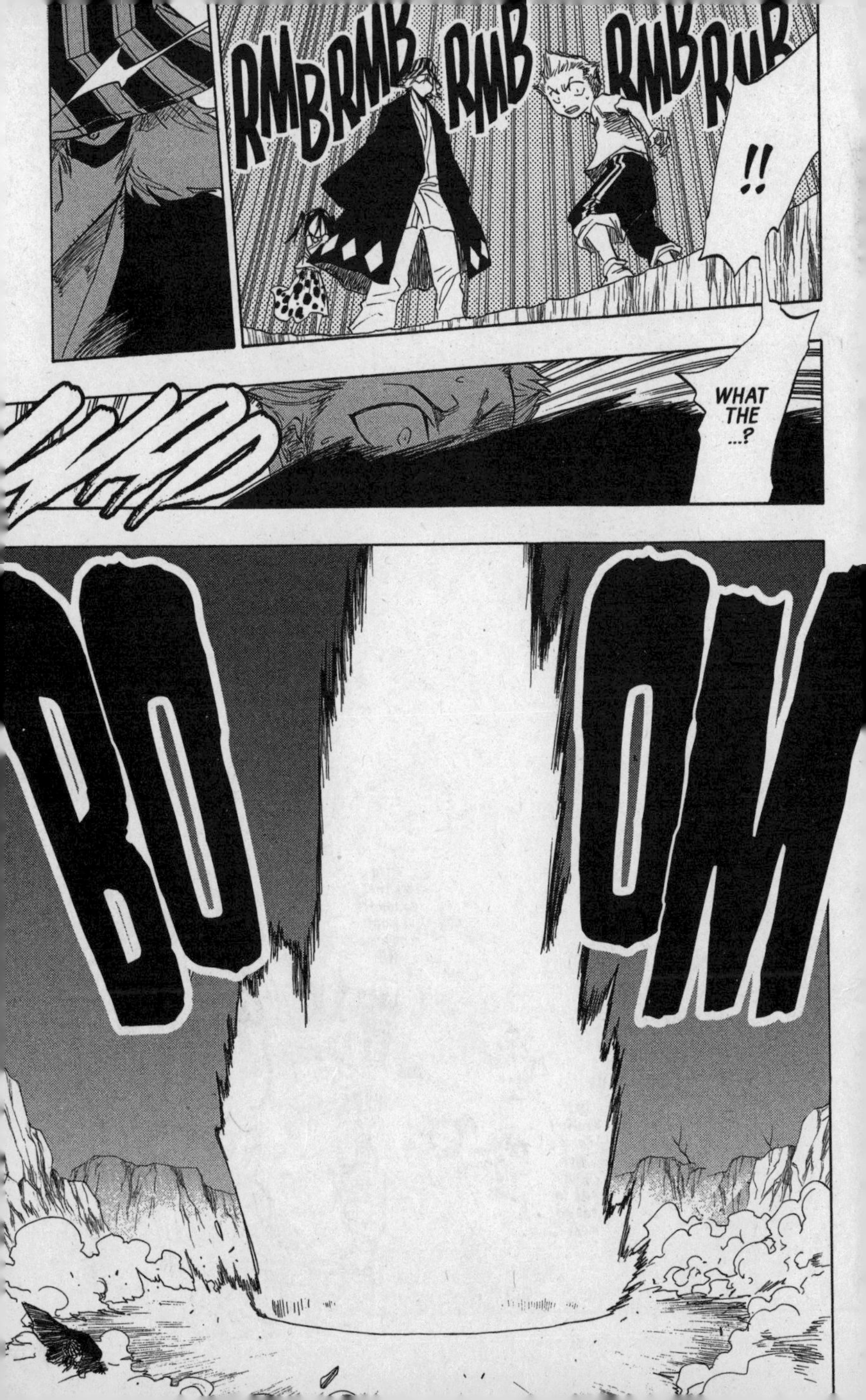
RMBRMB RMB RMBRUB
!!
WHAT THE ...?
BO
OM

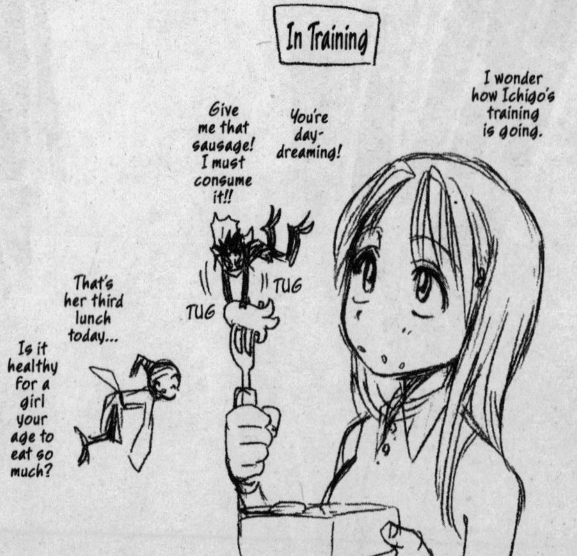
In Training
I wonder how Ichigo's training is going.
You're day-dreaming!
Give me that sausage! I must consume it!!
TUG
TUG
That's her third lunch today...
Is it healthy for a girl your age to eat so much?

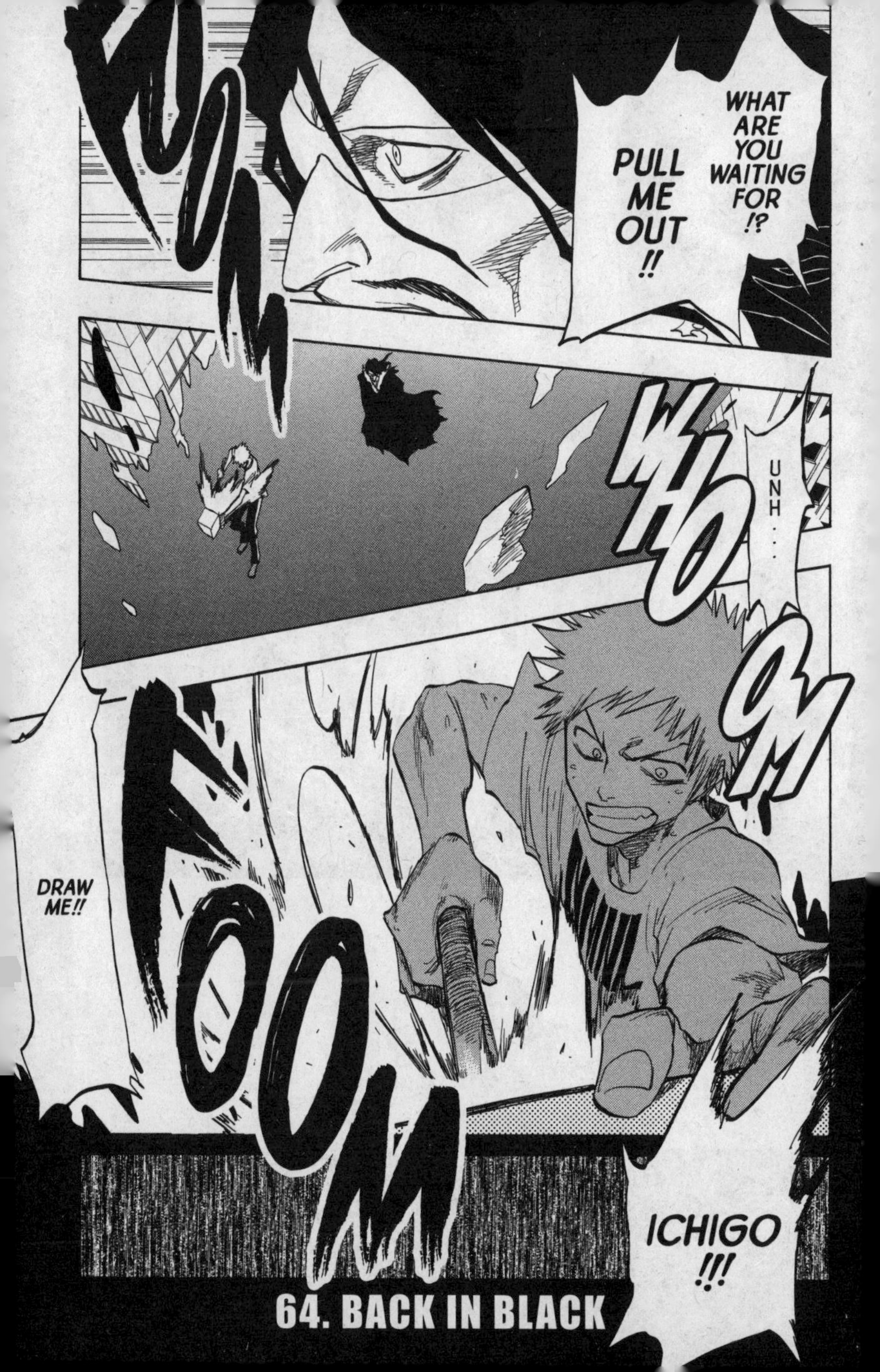
WHAT ARE YOU WAITING FOR !?
PULL ME OUT !!
UNH...
DRAW ME!!
ICHIGO !!!
64. BACK IN BLACK

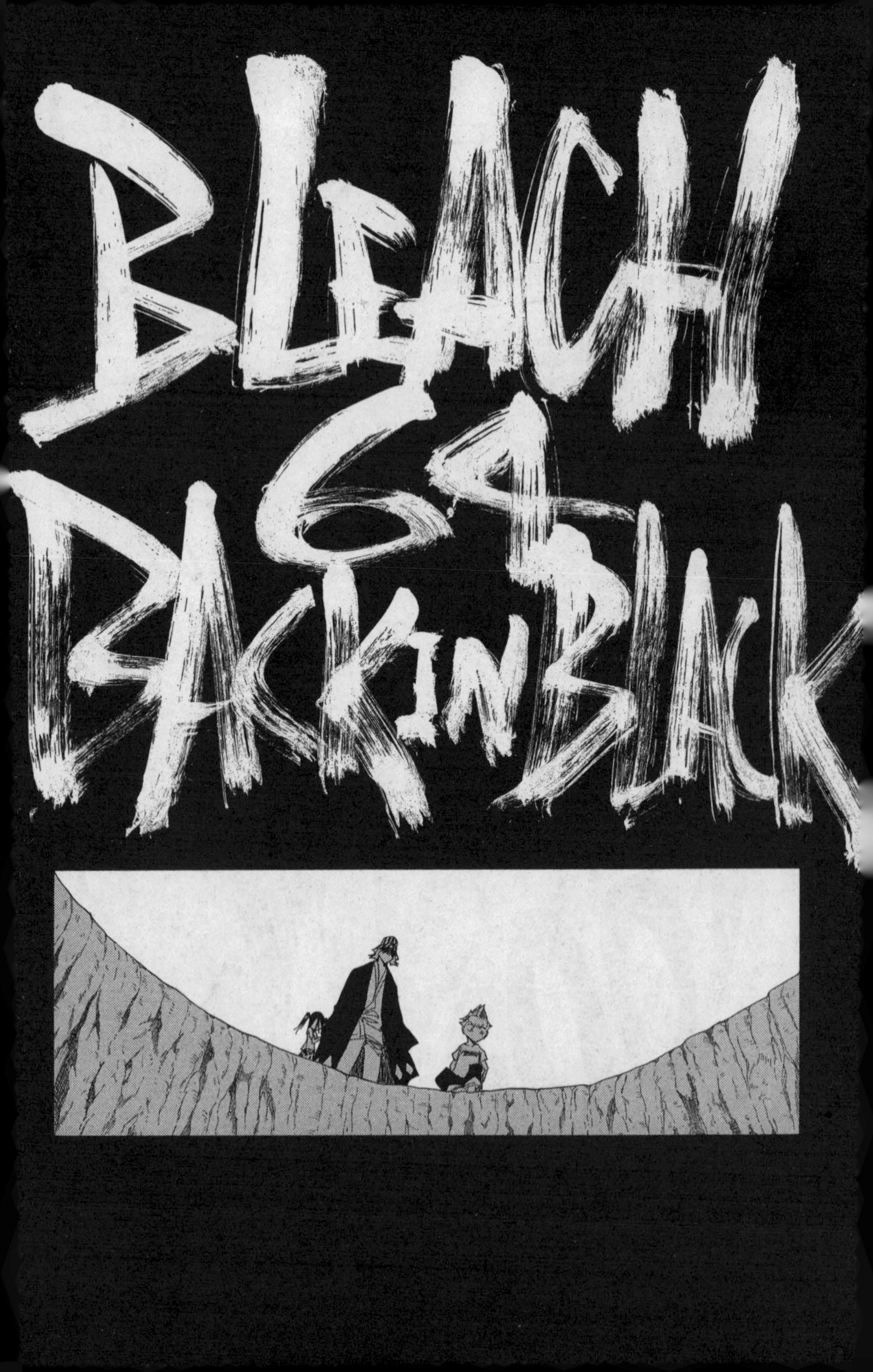
BLEACH
64
BACK IN BLACK

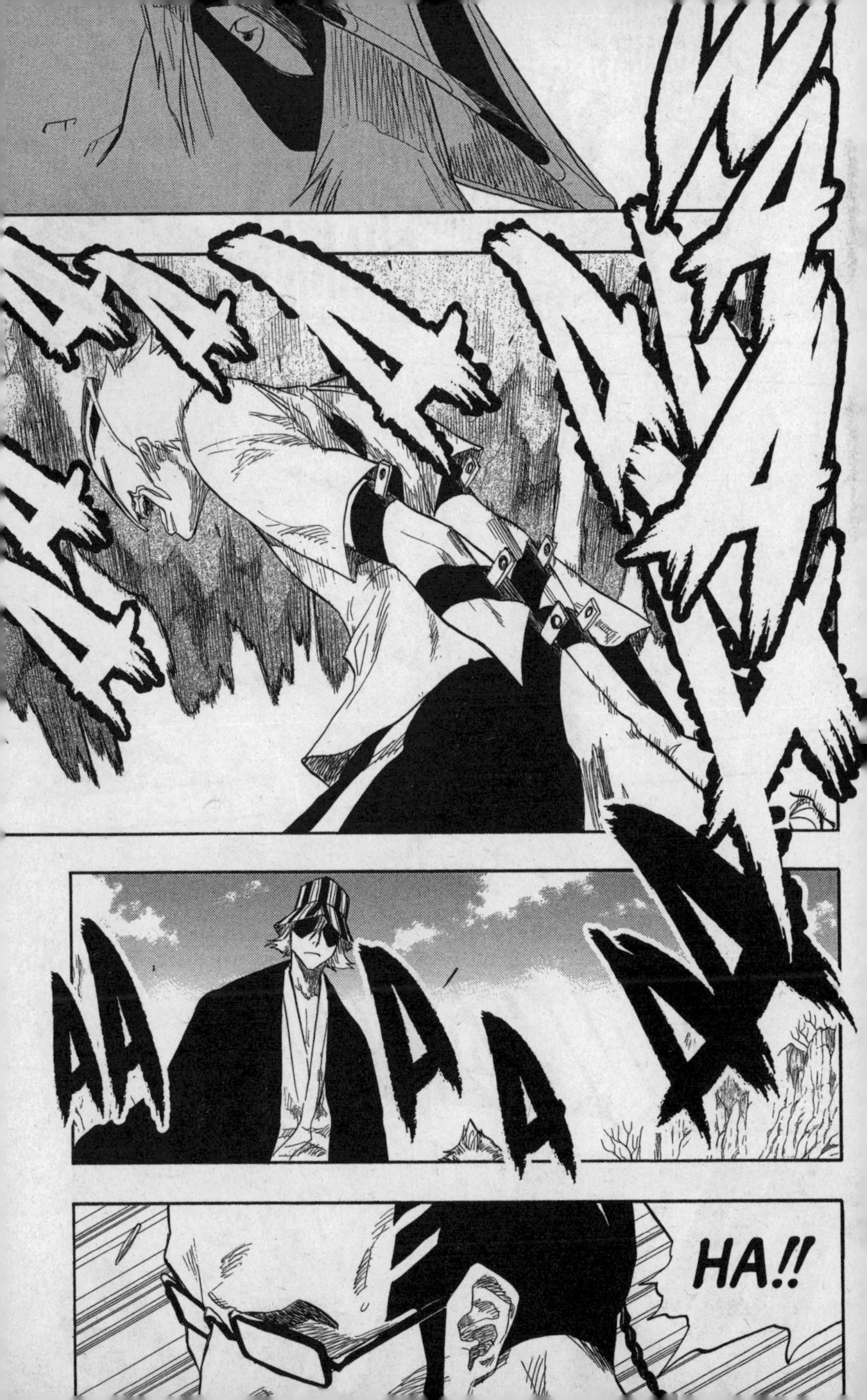
HA!!

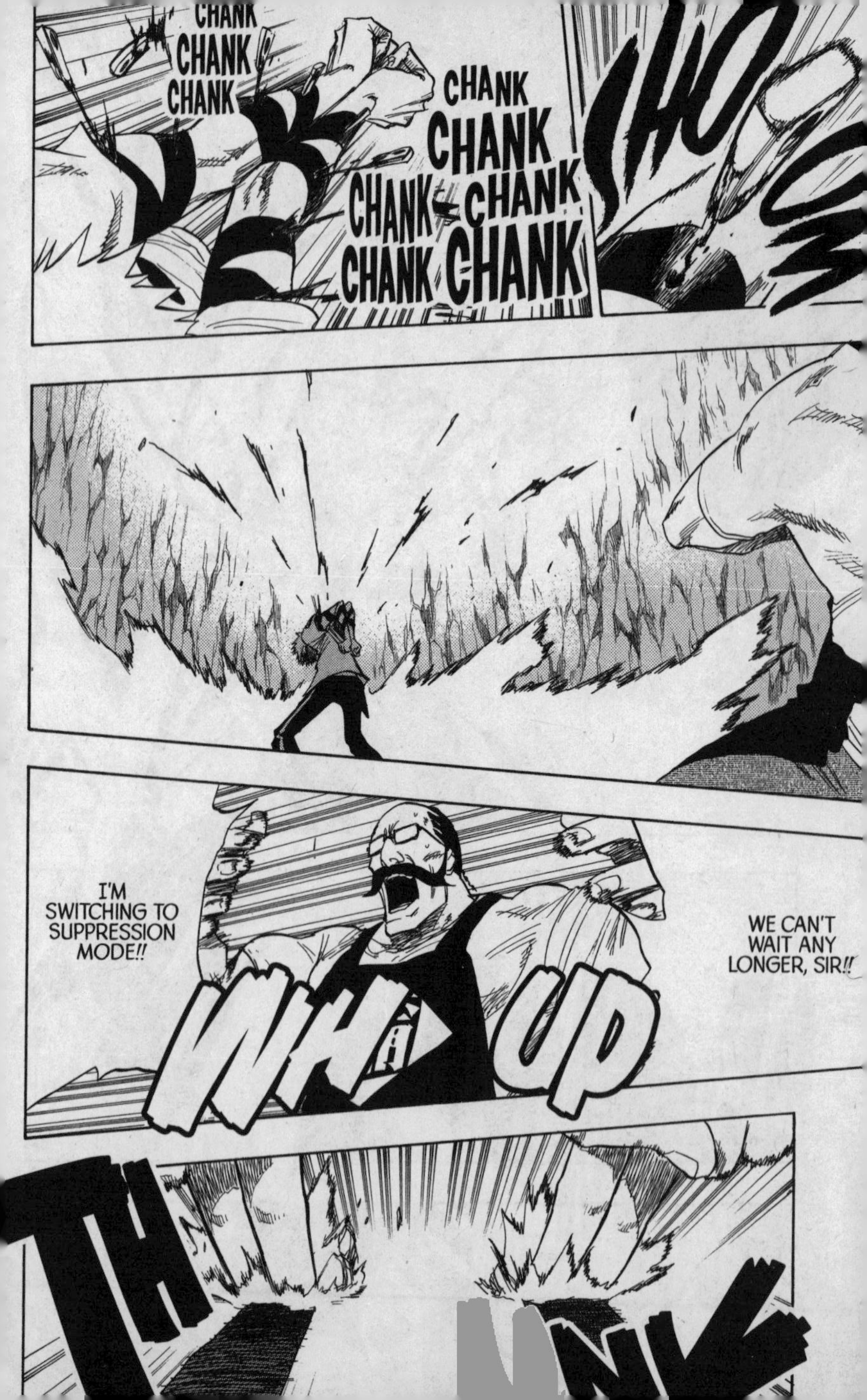
CHANK
CHANK
CHANK-CHANK
CHANK CHANK
CHANK
CHANK
CHANK
WE CAN'T WAIT ANY LONGER, SIR!!
I'M SWITCHING TO SUPPRESSION MODE!!

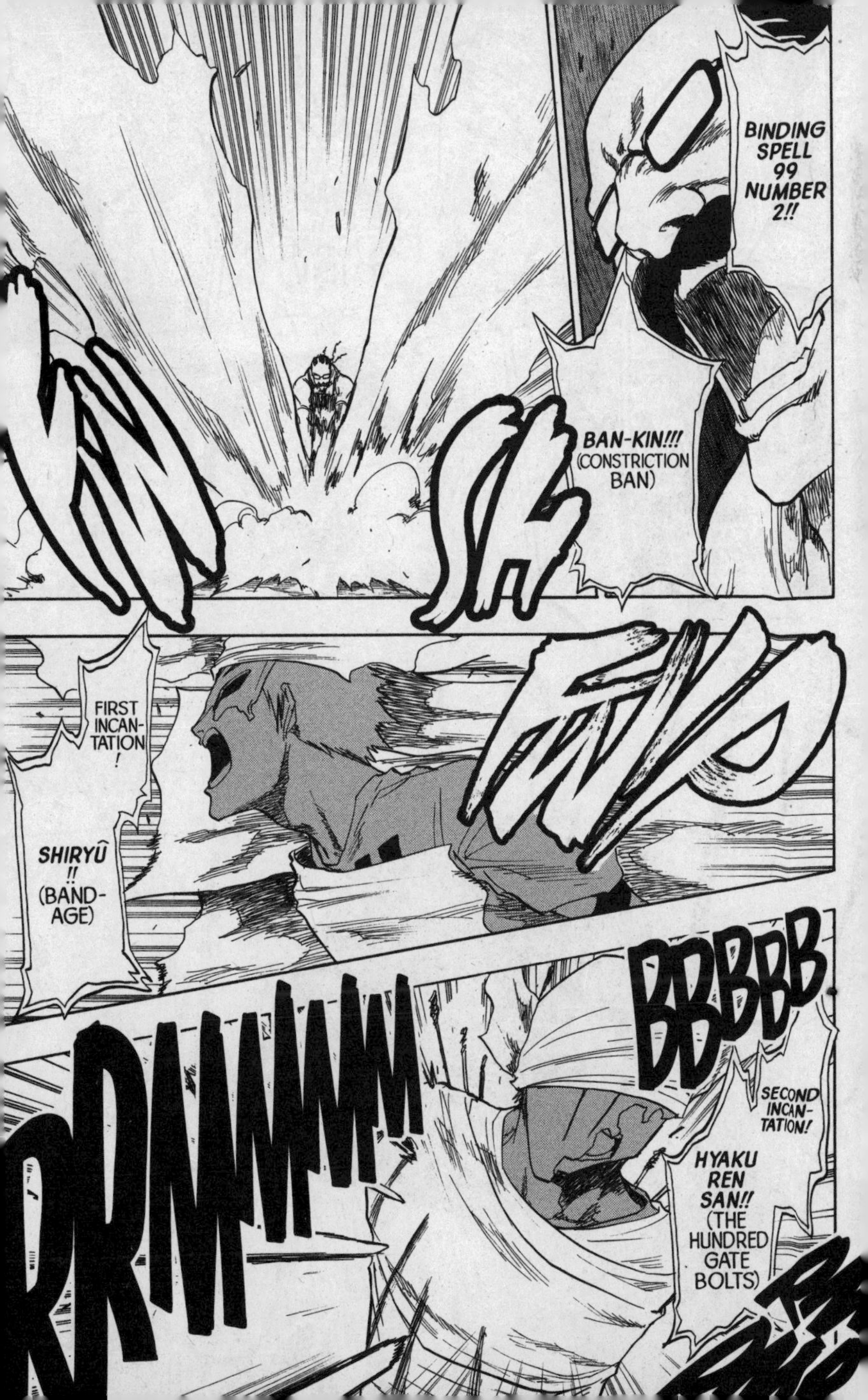
BINDING SPELL 99 NUMBER 2!!
BAN-KIN!!! (CONSTRICTION BAN)
FIRST INCANTATION!
SHIRYÛ!! (BANDAGE)
BBBBB
SECOND INCANTATION!
HYAKU REN SAN!! (THE HUNDRED GATE BOLTS)

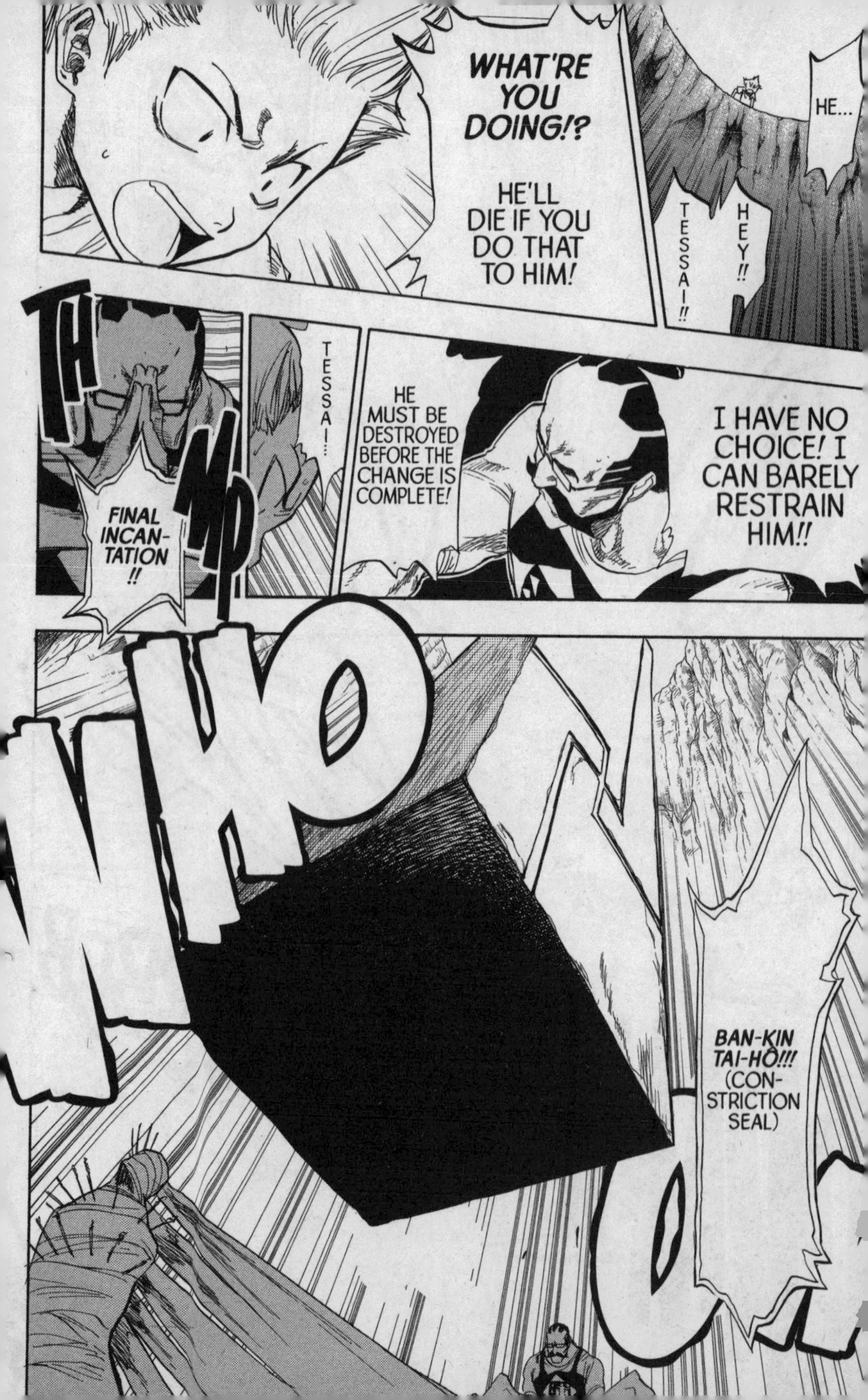
HE...
HEY!!
TESSAI!!
WHAT'RE YOU DOING!?
HE'LL DIE IF YOU DO THAT TO HIM!
I HAVE NO CHOICE! I CAN BARELY RESTRAIN HIM!!
HE MUST BE DESTROYED BEFORE THE CHANGE IS COMPLETE!
TESSAI...!
FINAL INCANTATION!!
BAN-KIN TAI-HŌ!!! (CONSTRICTION SEAL)

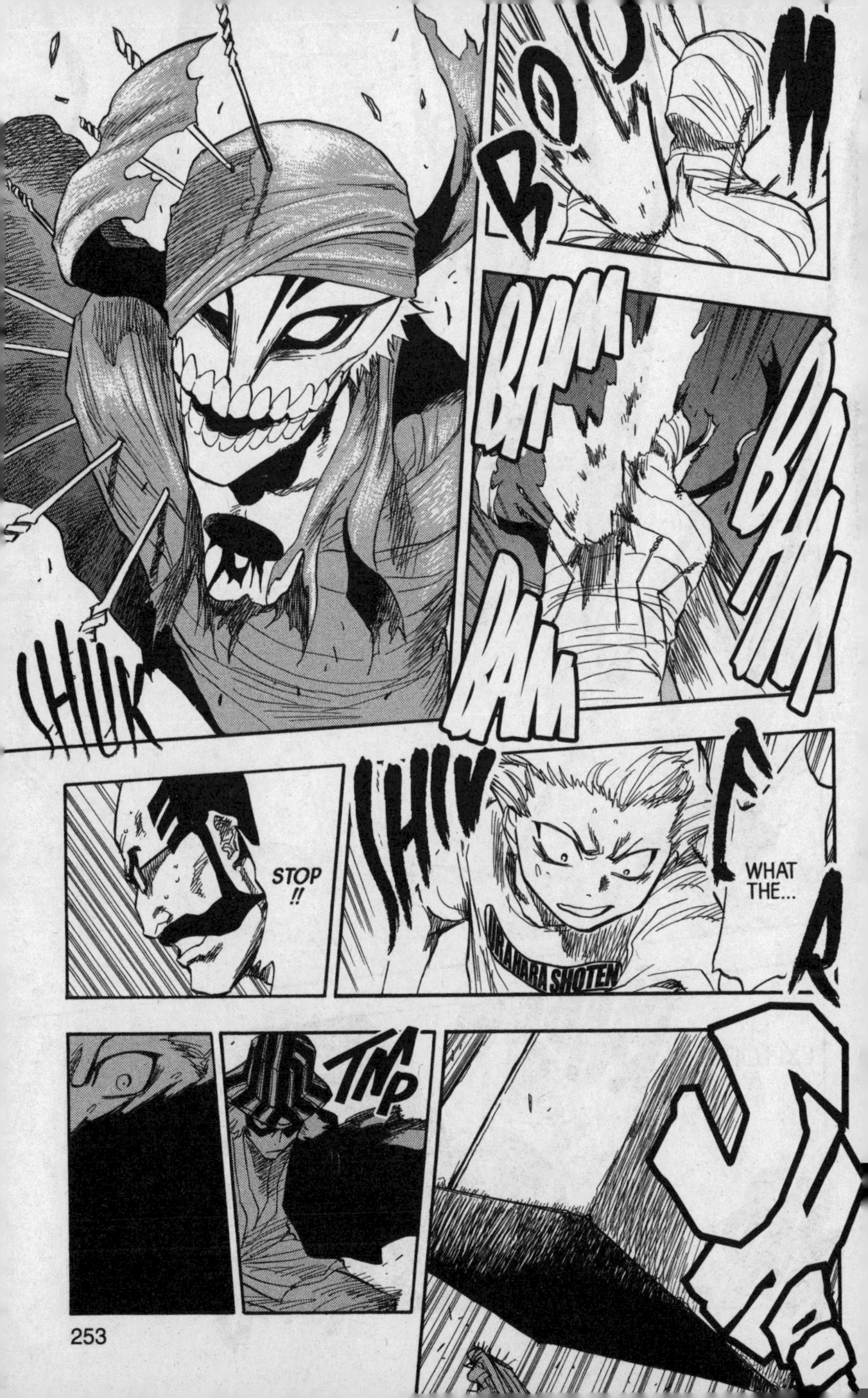
BOOM
BAM
BAM
BAM
CHUK
WHAT THE...
SHIV
URAHARA SHOTEN
STOP !!

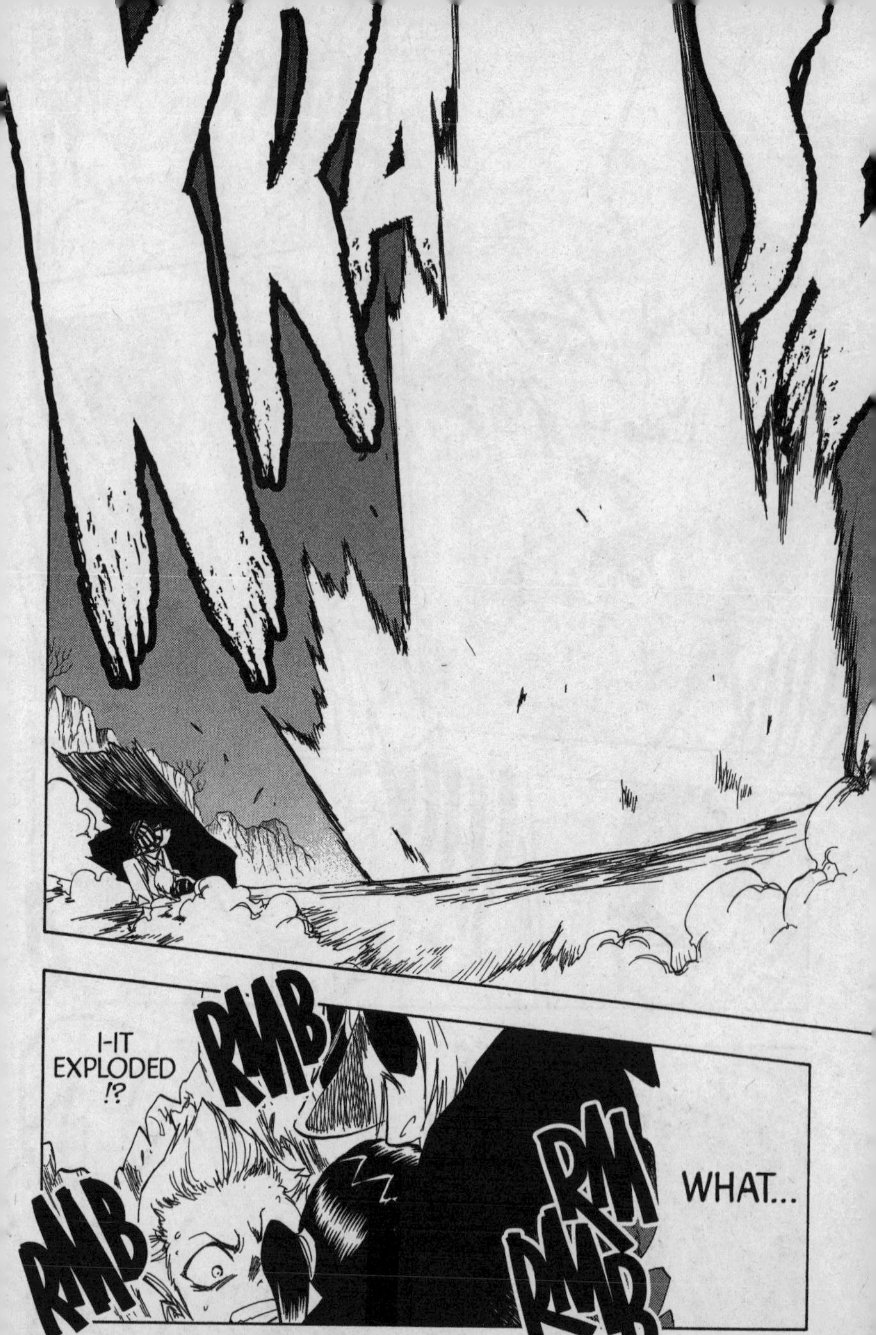
WHAT...
RMB
RMB
I-IT EXPLODED !?
RMB
RMB

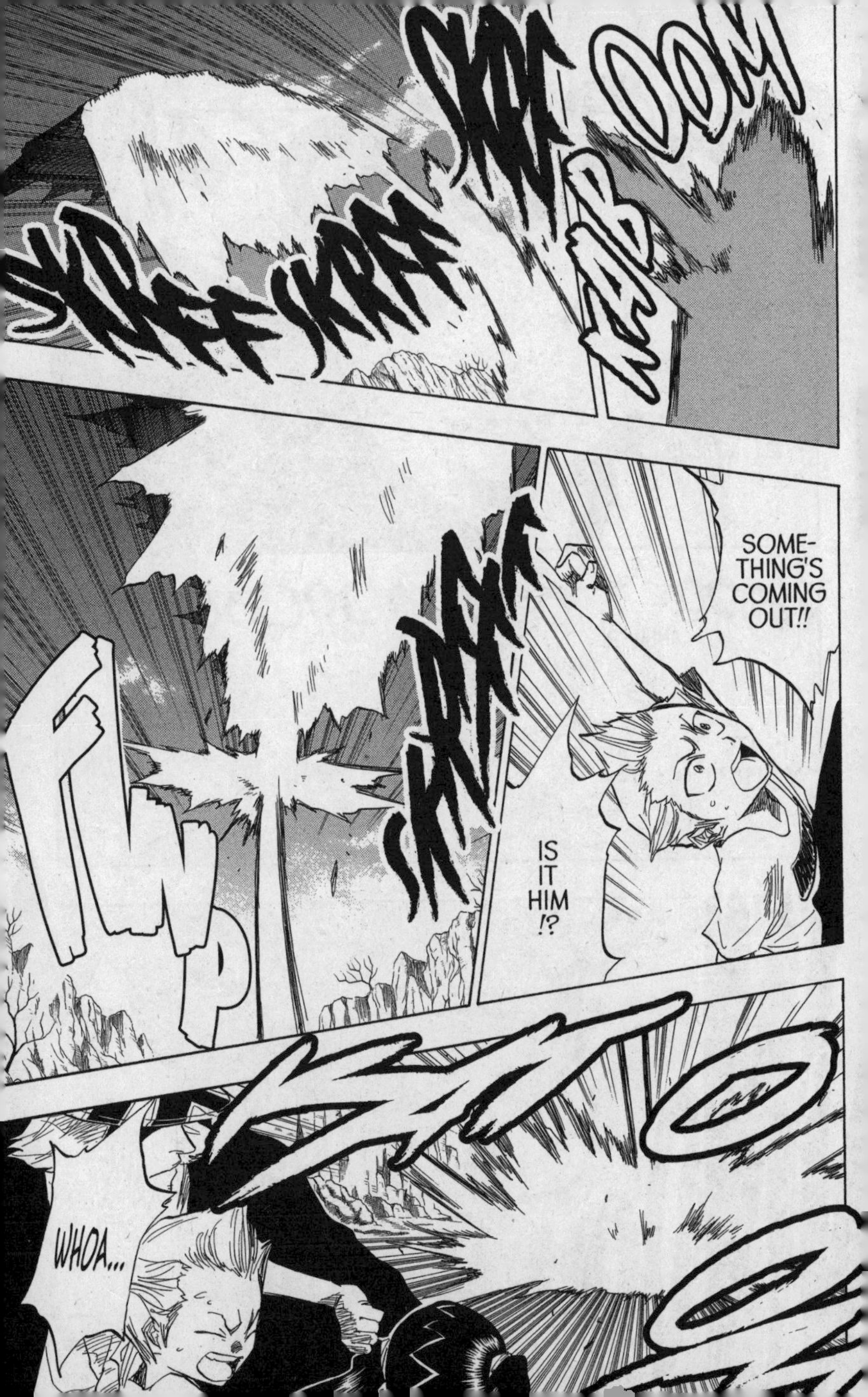
SOME-THING'S COMING OUT!!
IS IT HIM!?
WHOA...

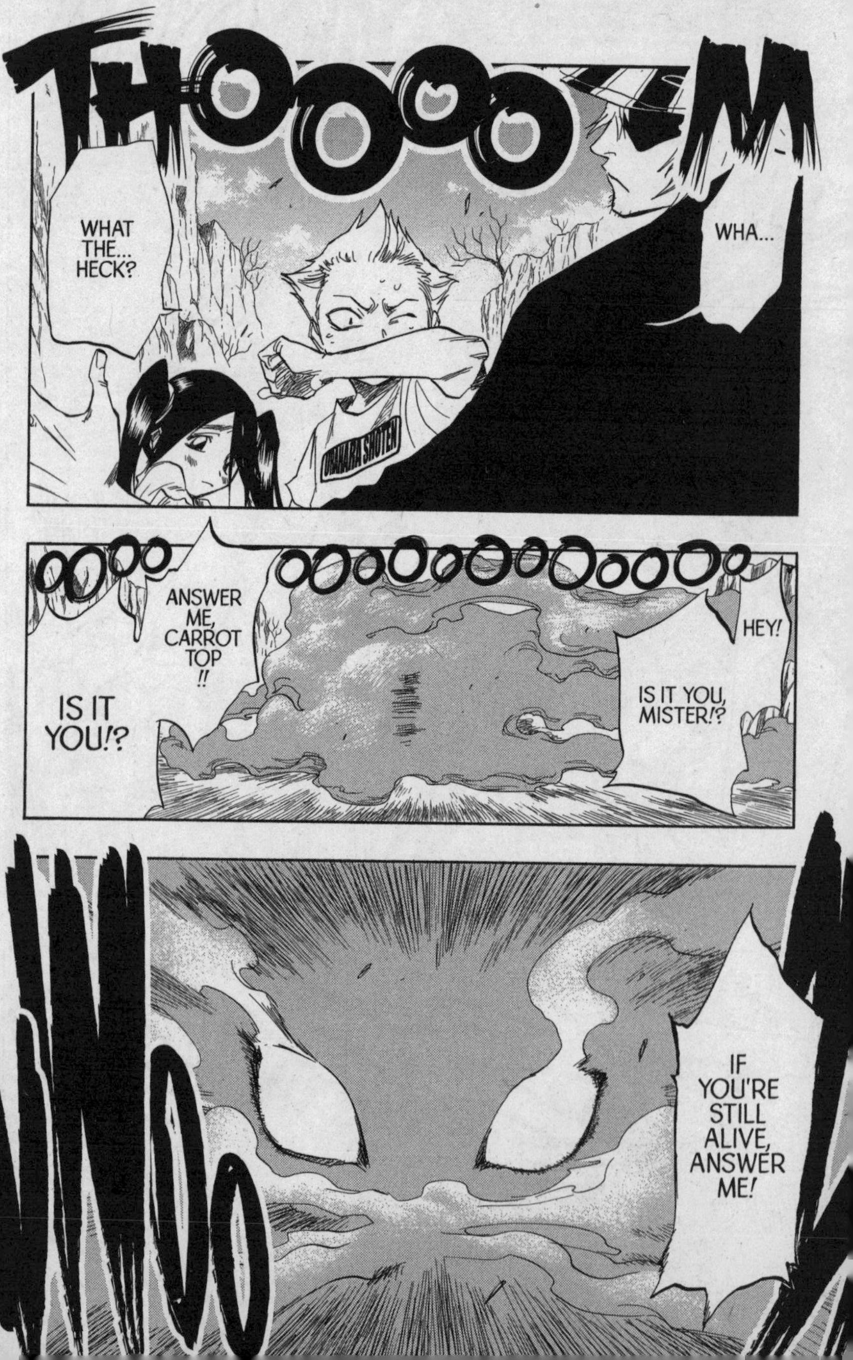
THOOOOOM
WHA...
WHAT THE... HECK?
URAHARA SHOTEN
HEY!
IS IT YOU, MISTER!?
ANSWER ME, CARROT TOP!!
IS IT YOU!?
IF YOU'RE STILL ALIVE, ANSWER ME!

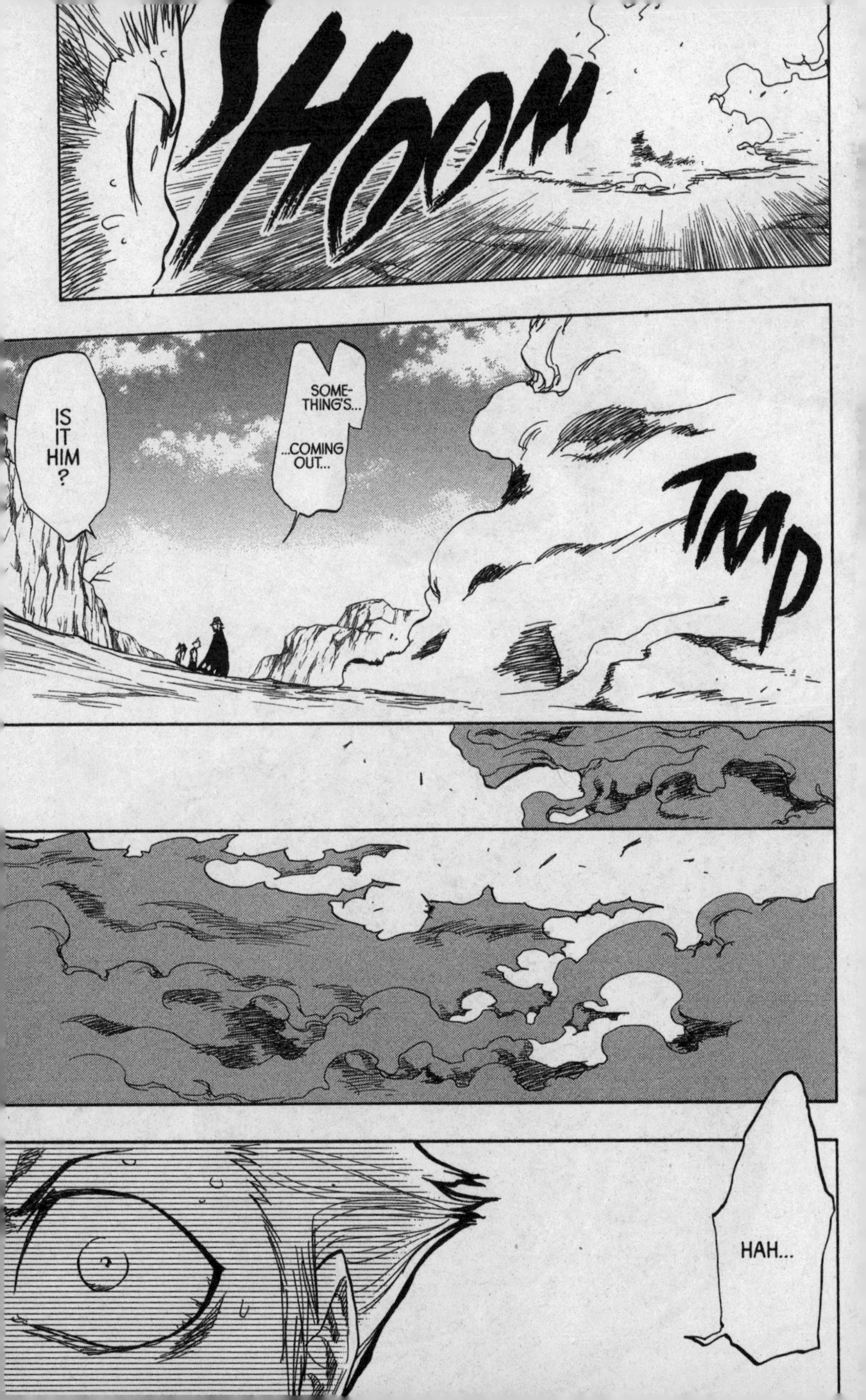
SHOOM
SOME-THING'S... ...COMING OUT...
IS IT HIM?
TMP
HAH...

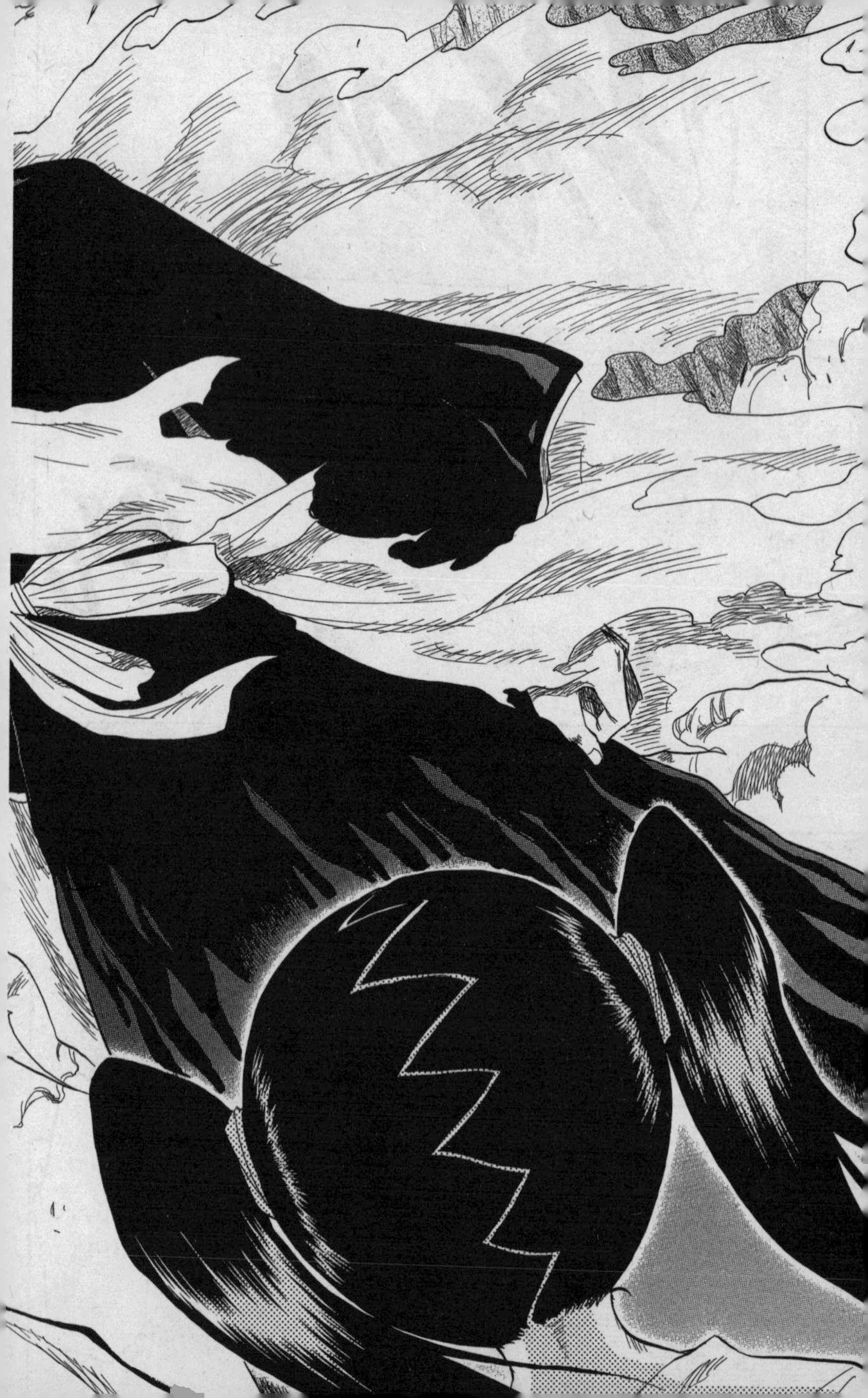

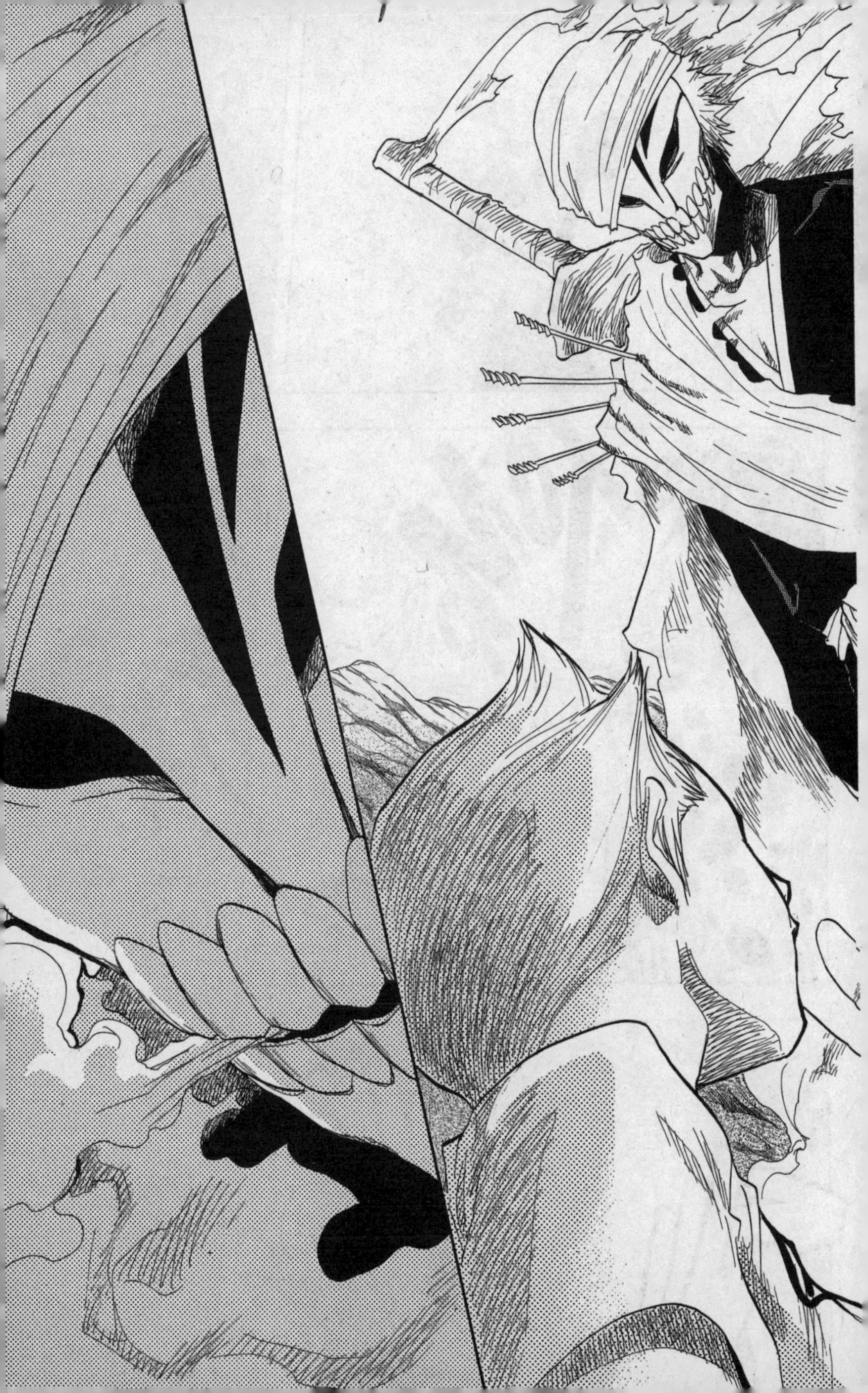

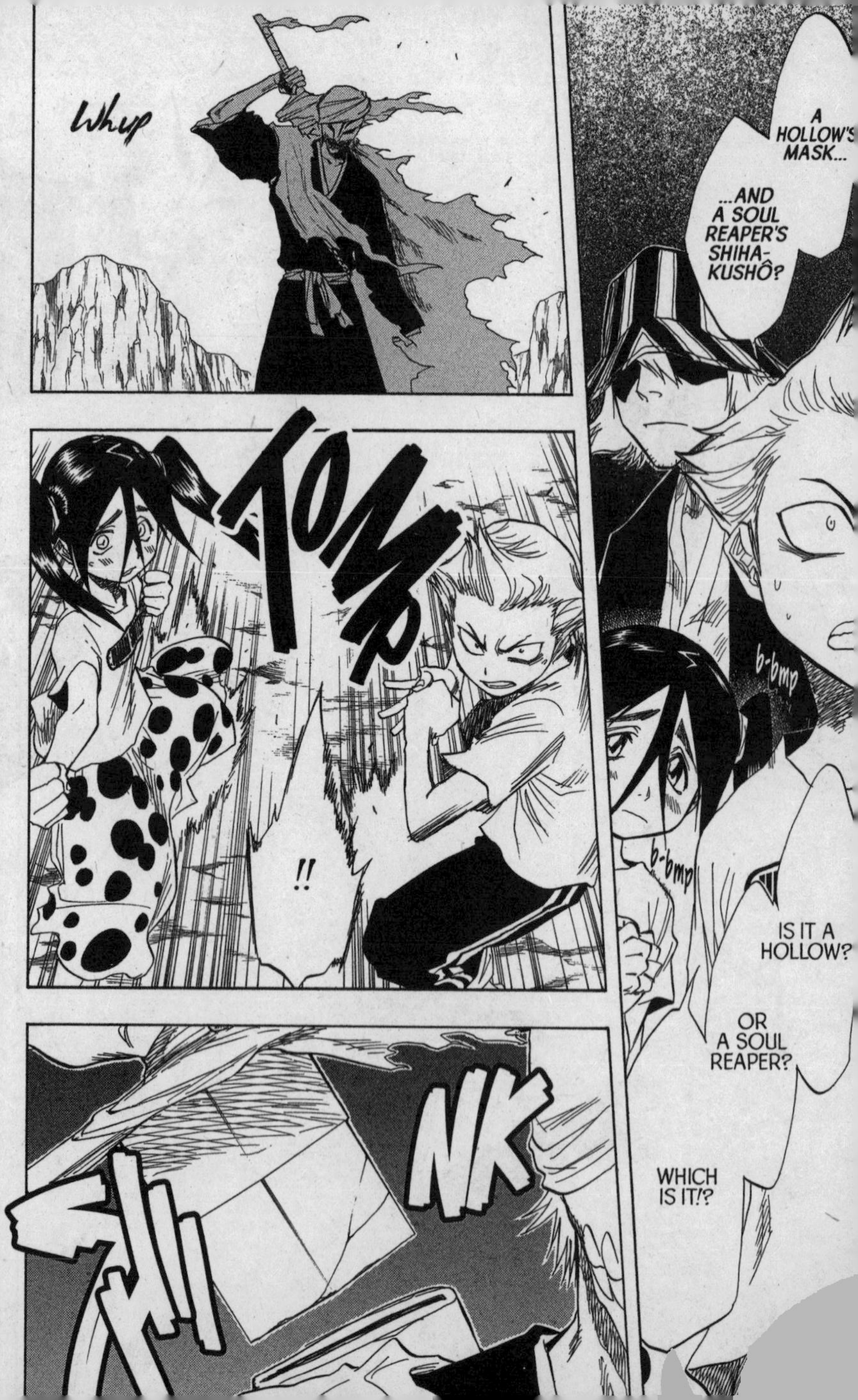
A HOLLOW'S MASK...
...AND A SOUL REAPER'S SHIHAKUSHÔ?
b-bmp
b-bmp
IS IT A HOLLOW?
OR A SOUL REAPER?
WHICH IS IT!?
Whup
TOMP
!!
NK

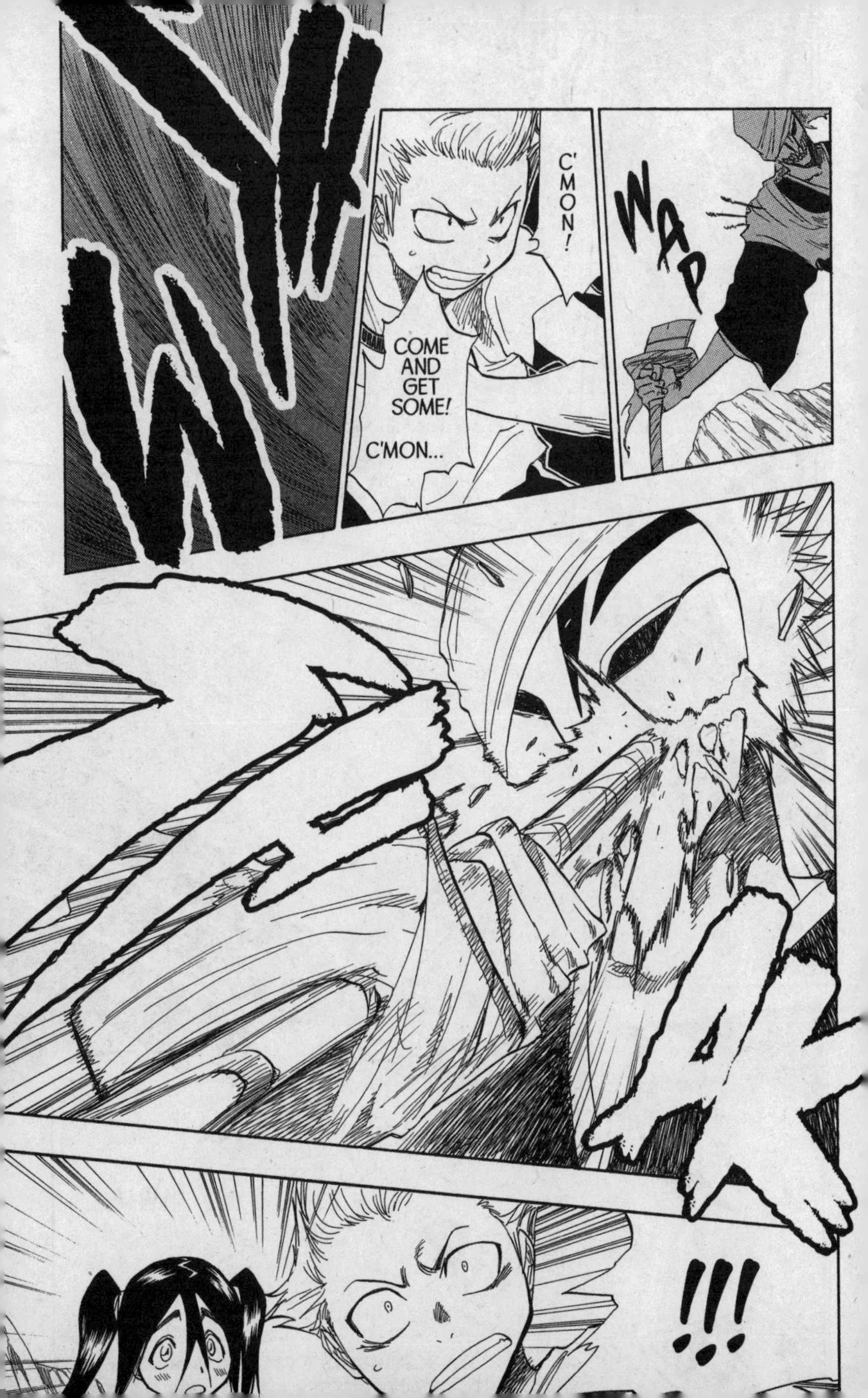
WAP
C'MON!
COME AND GET SOME!
C'MON...
!!!

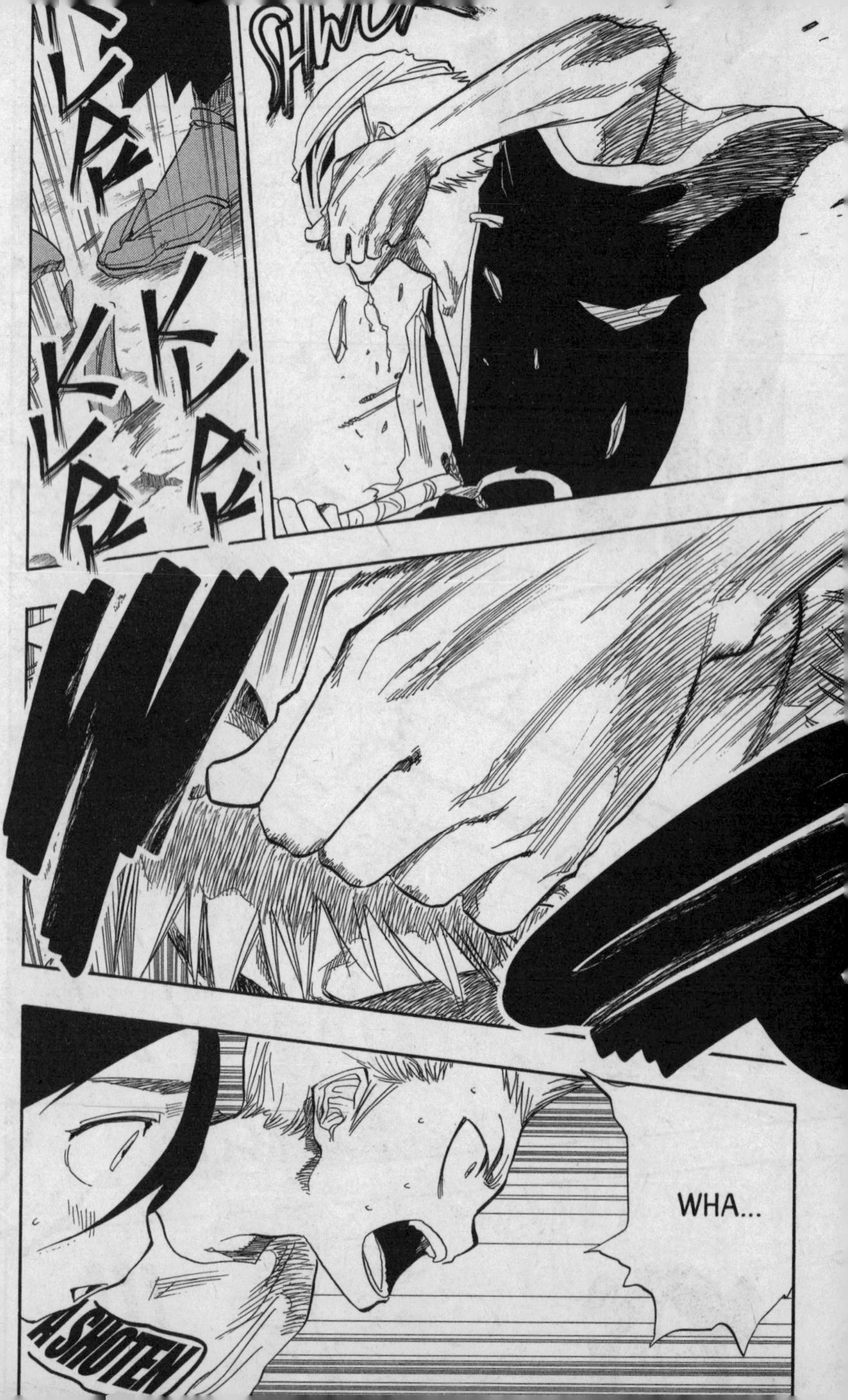
WHA...
A SHOTEN

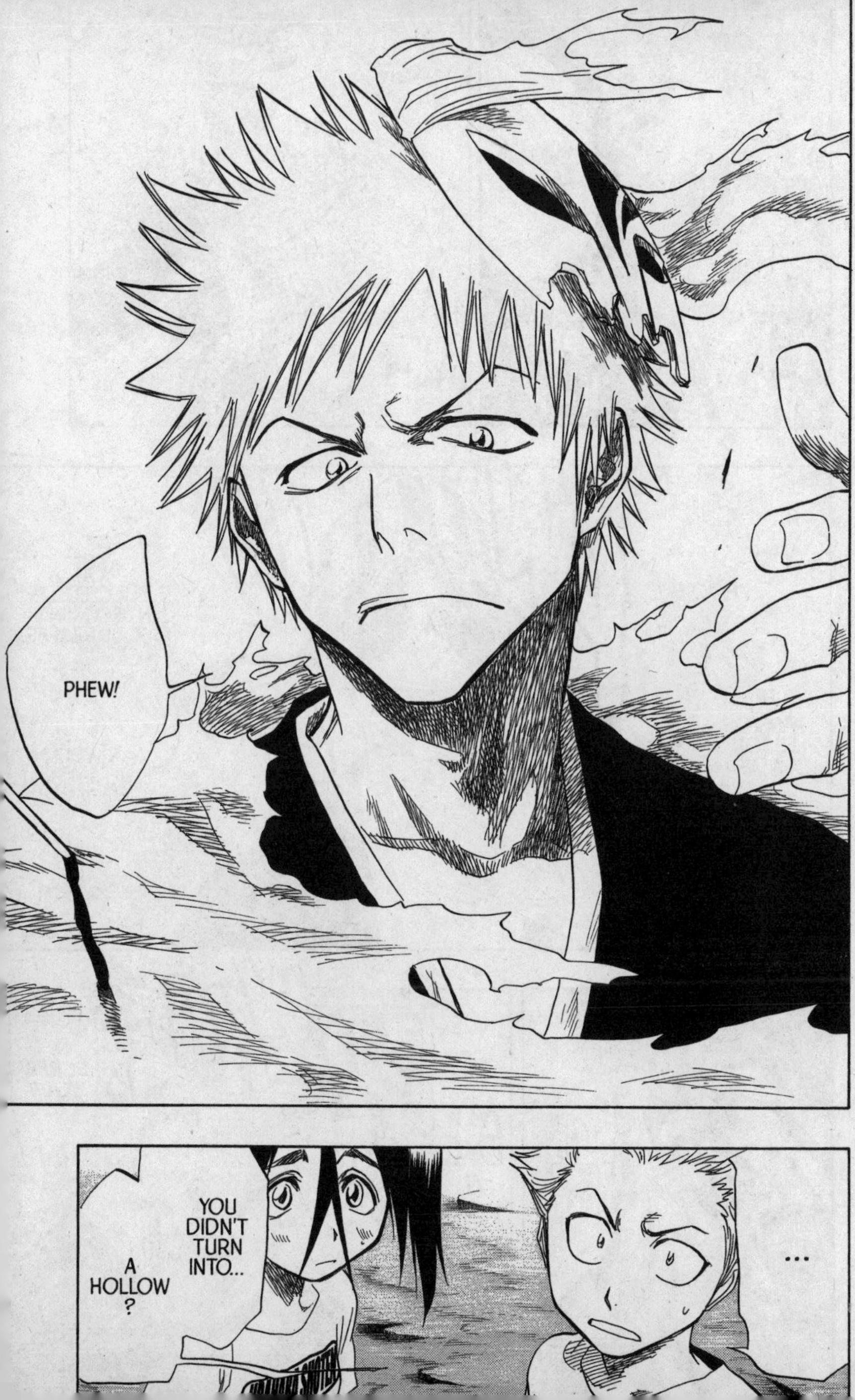
PHEW!
...
YOU DIDN'T TURN INTO...
A HOLLOW?

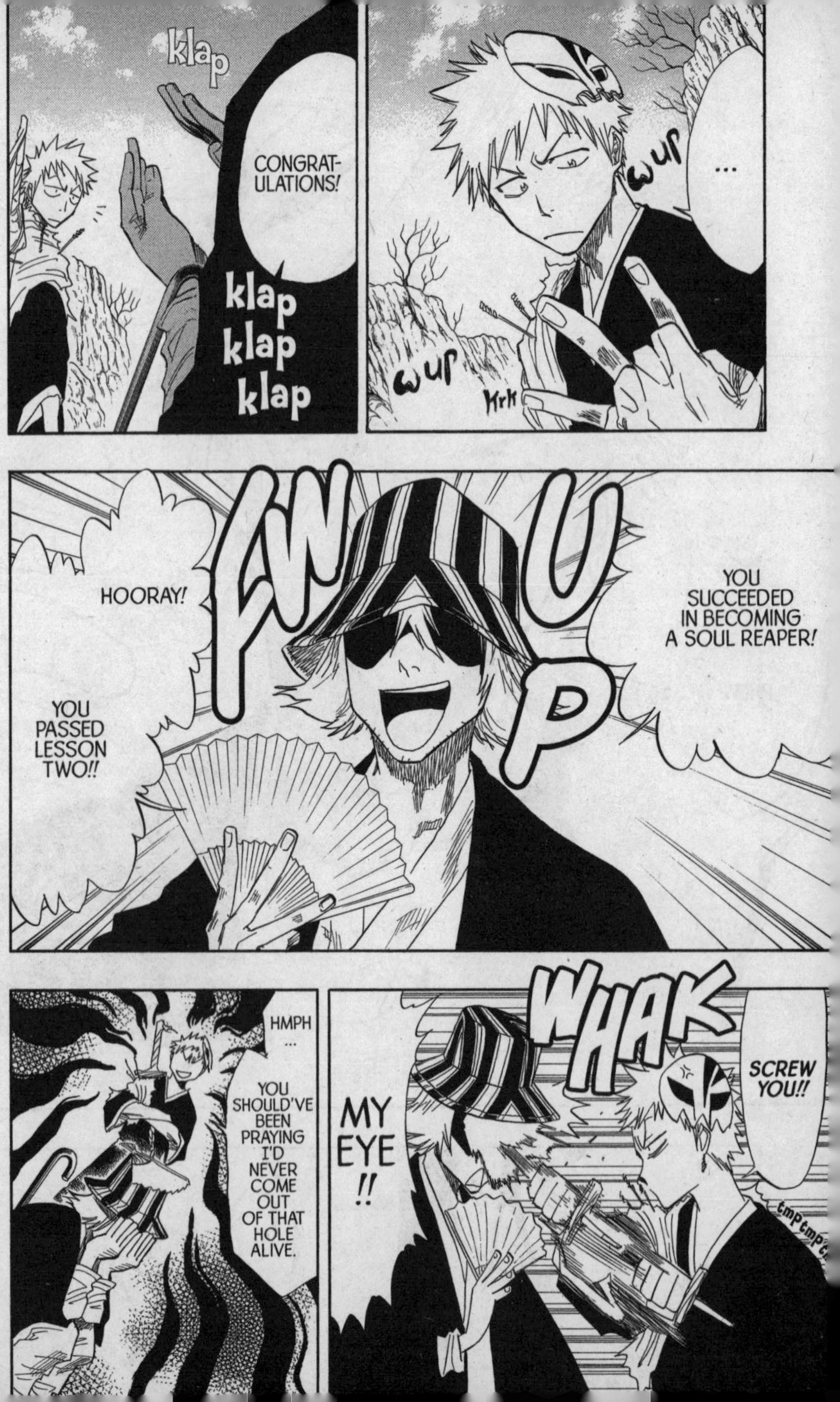
...
wup
Krk
wup
klap
CONGRAT-ULATIONS!
klap
klap
klap
YOU SUCCEEDED IN BECOMING A SOUL REAPER!
FWUP
HOORAY!
YOU PASSED LESSON TWO!!
SCREW YOU!!
WHAK
MY EYE!!
HMPH ...
YOU SHOULD'VE BEEN PRAYING I'D NEVER COME OUT OF THAT HOLE ALIVE.

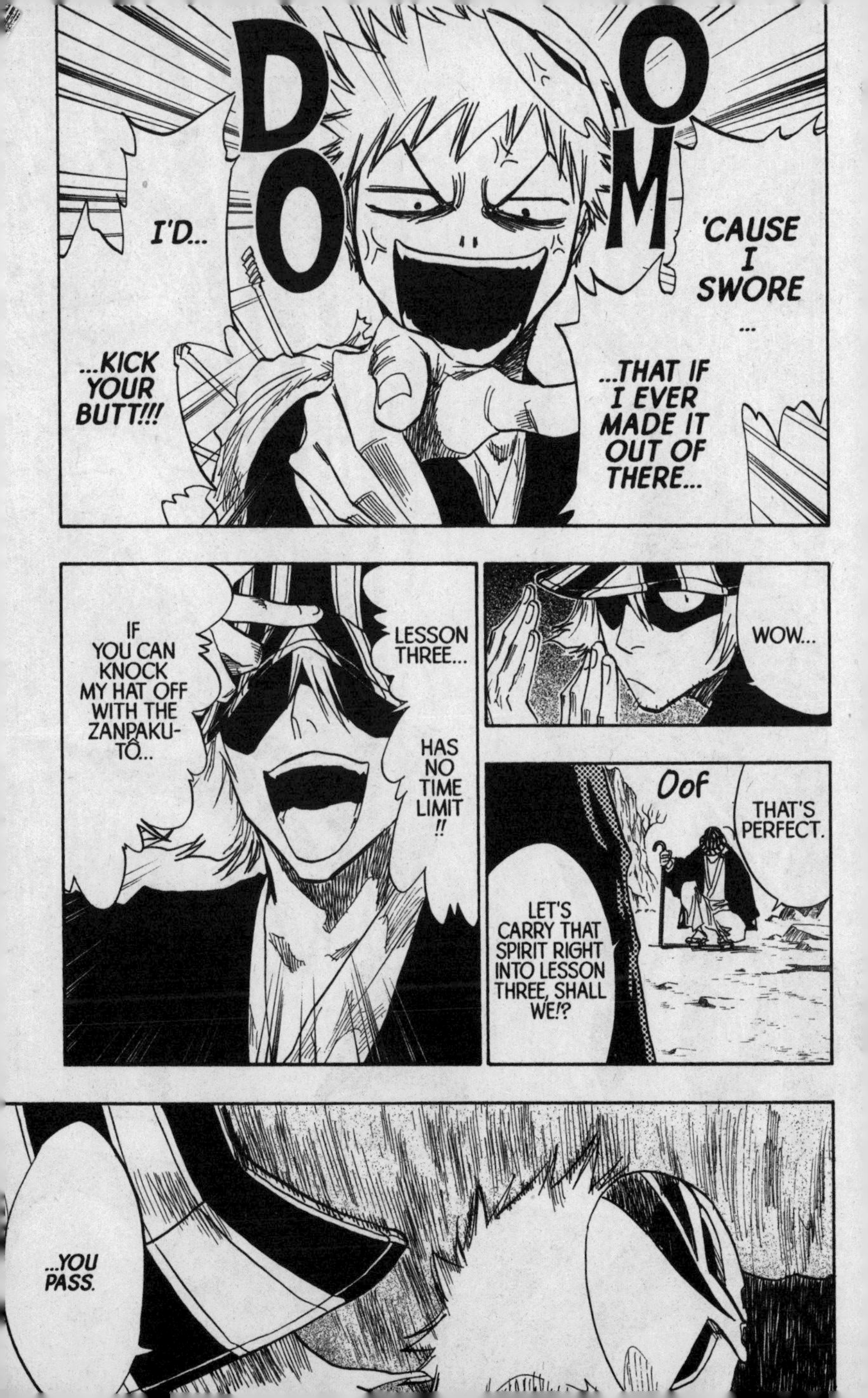
'CAUSE I SWORE ...
...THAT IF I EVER MADE IT OUT OF THERE...
I'D...
DOOM
...KICK YOUR BUTT!!!
WOW...
THAT'S PERFECT.
Oof
LET'S CARRY THAT SPIRIT RIGHT INTO LESSON THREE, SHALL WE!?
LESSON THREE...
HAS NO TIME LIMIT !!
IF YOU CAN KNOCK MY HAT OFF WITH THE ZANPAKU-TŌ...
...YOU PASS.

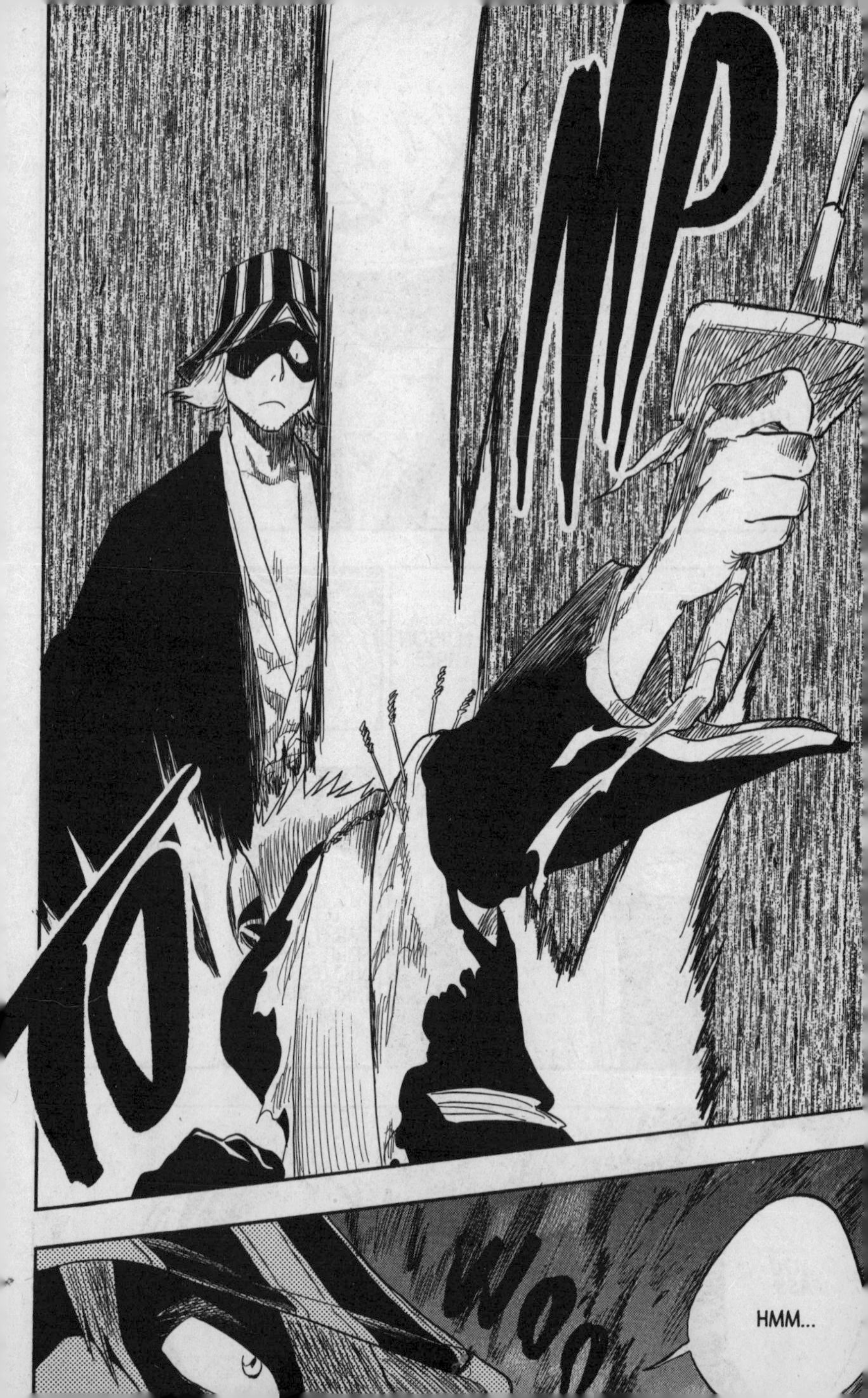
MP
HMM...

READ THIS WAY

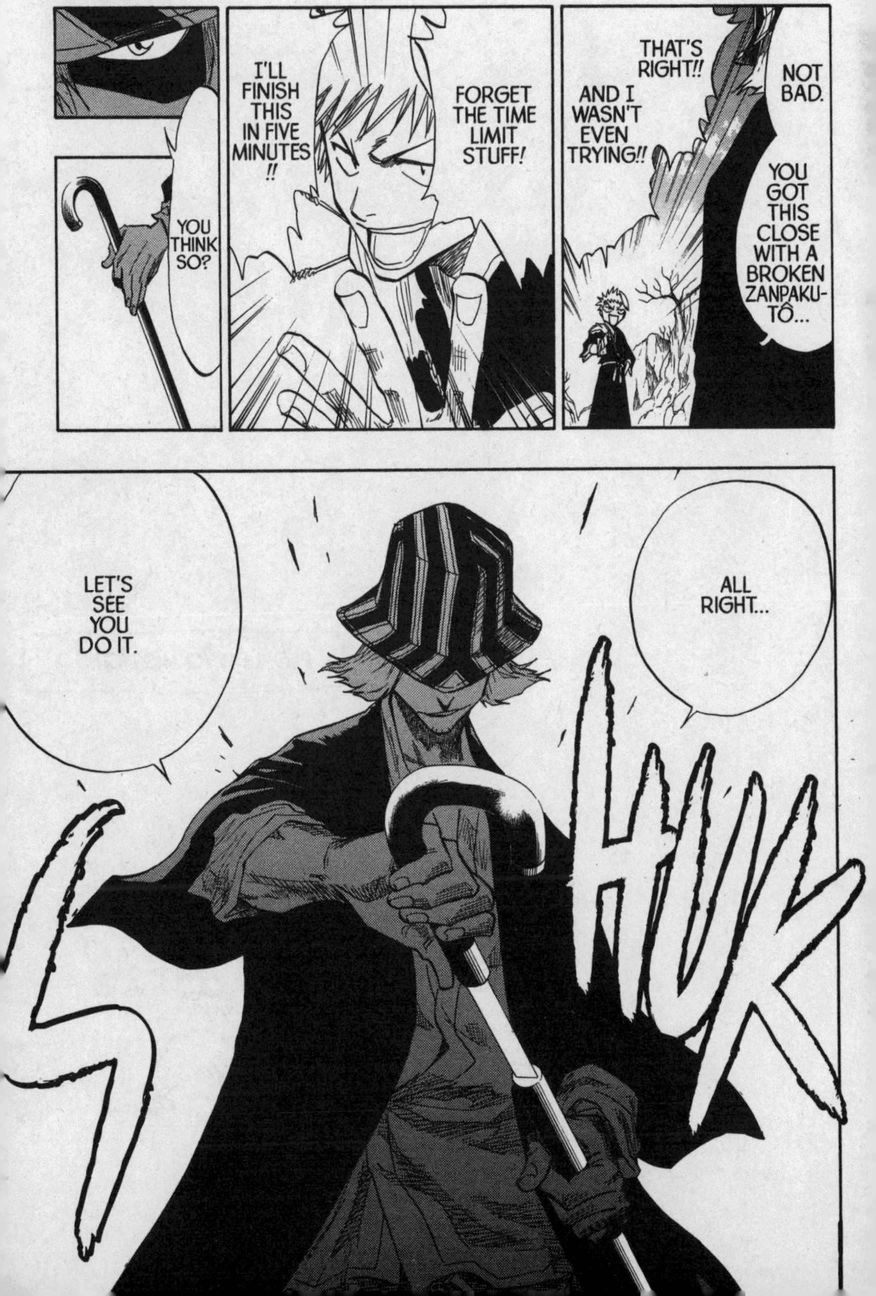
NOT BAD.
YOU GOT THIS CLOSE WITH A BROKEN ZANPAKU-TÔ...
THAT'S RIGHT!!
AND I WASN'T EVEN TRYING!!
FORGET THE TIME LIMIT STUFF!
I'LL FINISH THIS IN FIVE MINUTES!!
YOU THINK SO?
ALL RIGHT...
LET'S SEE YOU DO IT.
SHUK

PEOPLE WHO MISS ICHIGO

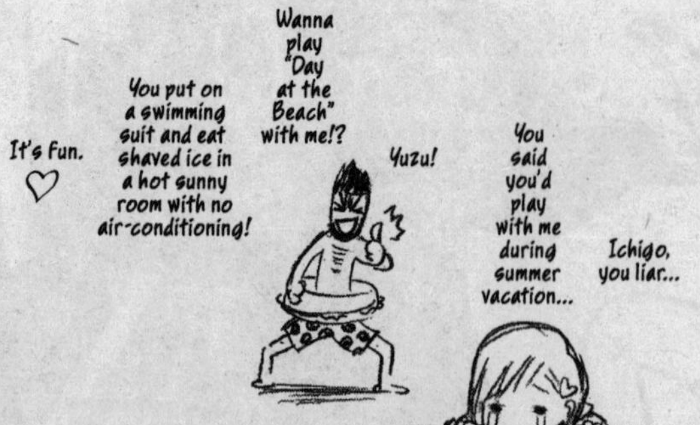
Ichigo, you liar...
You said you'd play with me during summer vacation...
Yuzu!
Wanna play "Day at the Beach" with me!?
You put on a swimming suit and eat shaved ice in a hot sunny room with no air-conditioning!
It's fun. ♡

65. Collisions

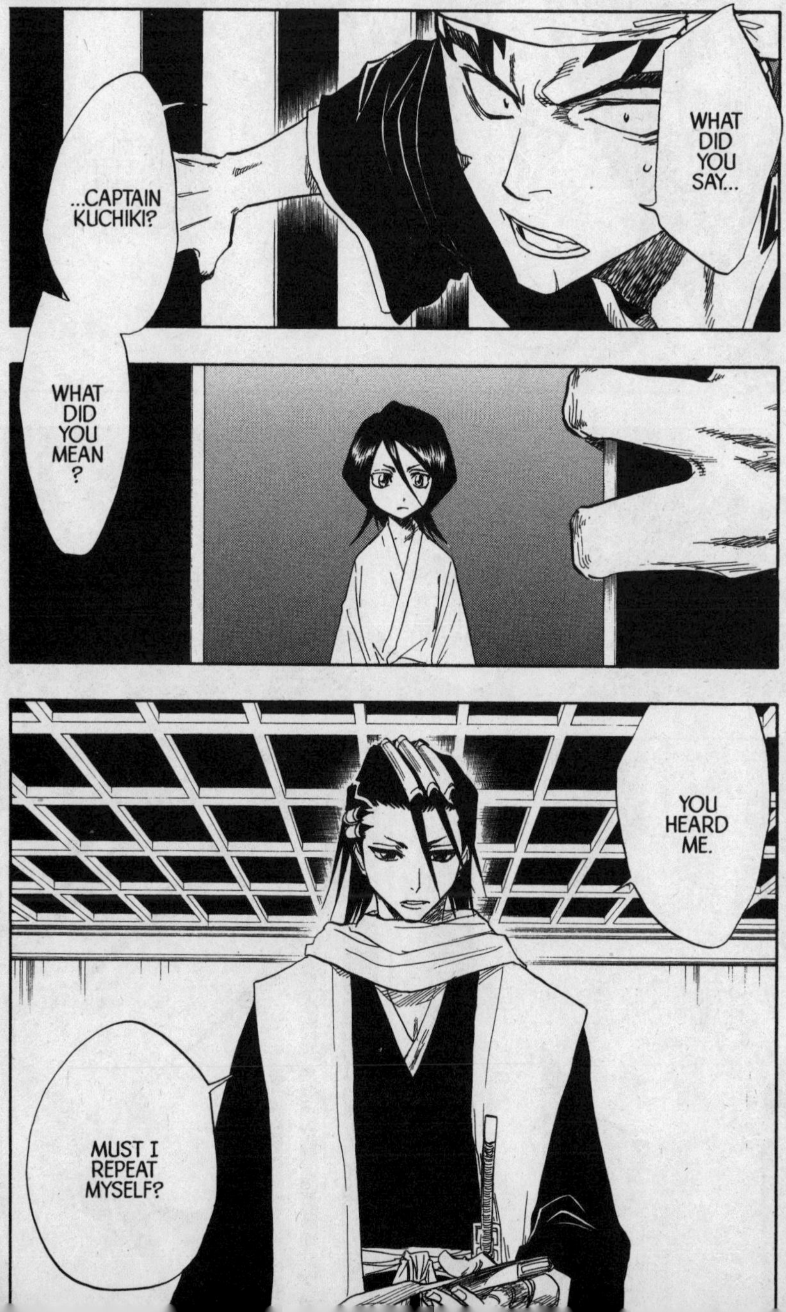
WHAT DID YOU SAY...
...CAPTAIN KUCHIKI?
WHAT DID YOU MEAN?
YOU HEARD ME.
MUST I REPEAT MYSELF?

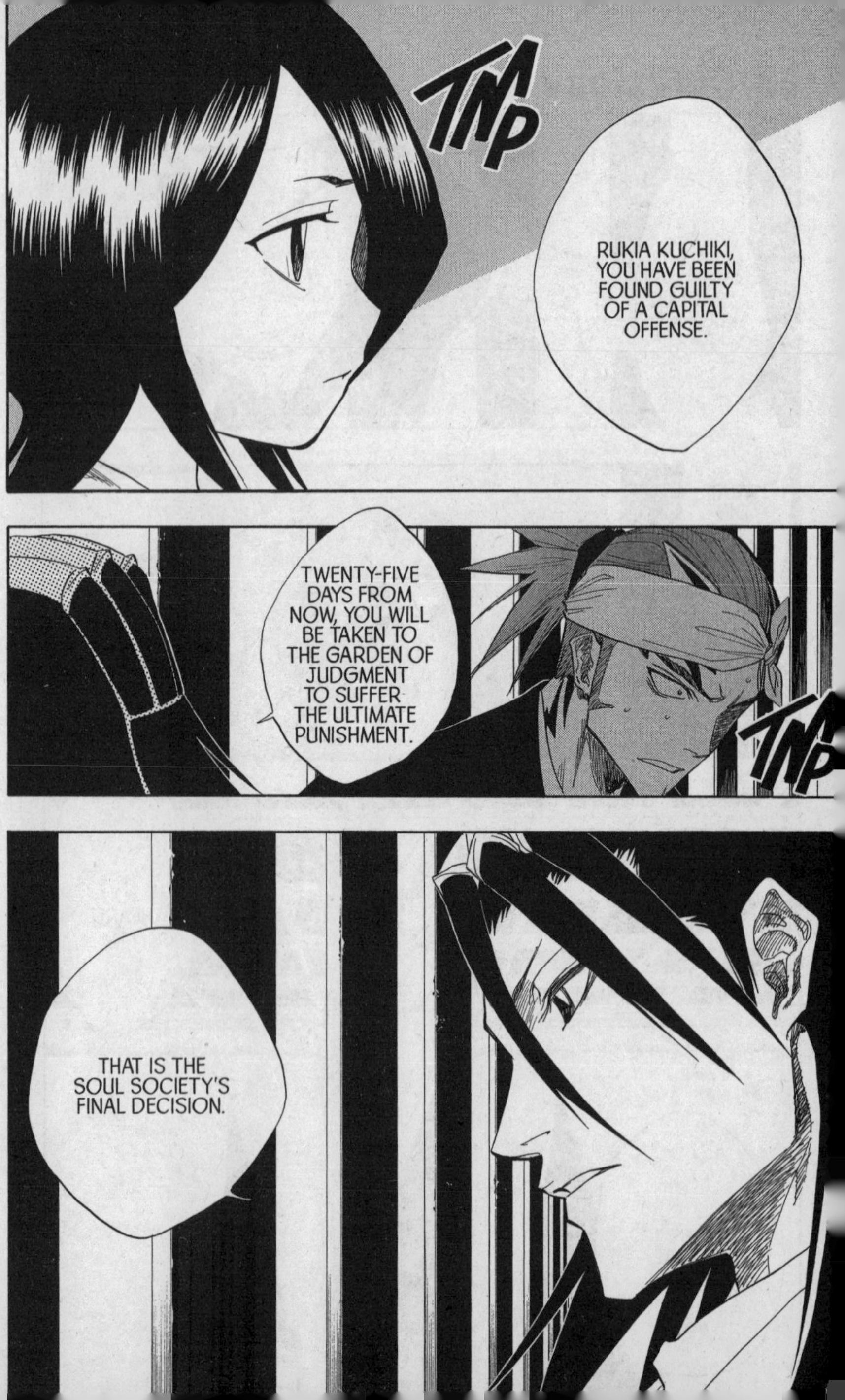
TMP
RUKIA KUCHIKI, YOU HAVE BEEN FOUND GUILTY OF A CAPITAL OFFENSE.
TWENTY-FIVE DAYS FROM NOW, YOU WILL BE TAKEN TO THE GARDEN OF JUDGMENT TO SUFFER THE ULTIMATE PUNISHMENT.
TMP
THAT IS THE SOUL SOCIETY'S FINAL DECISION.

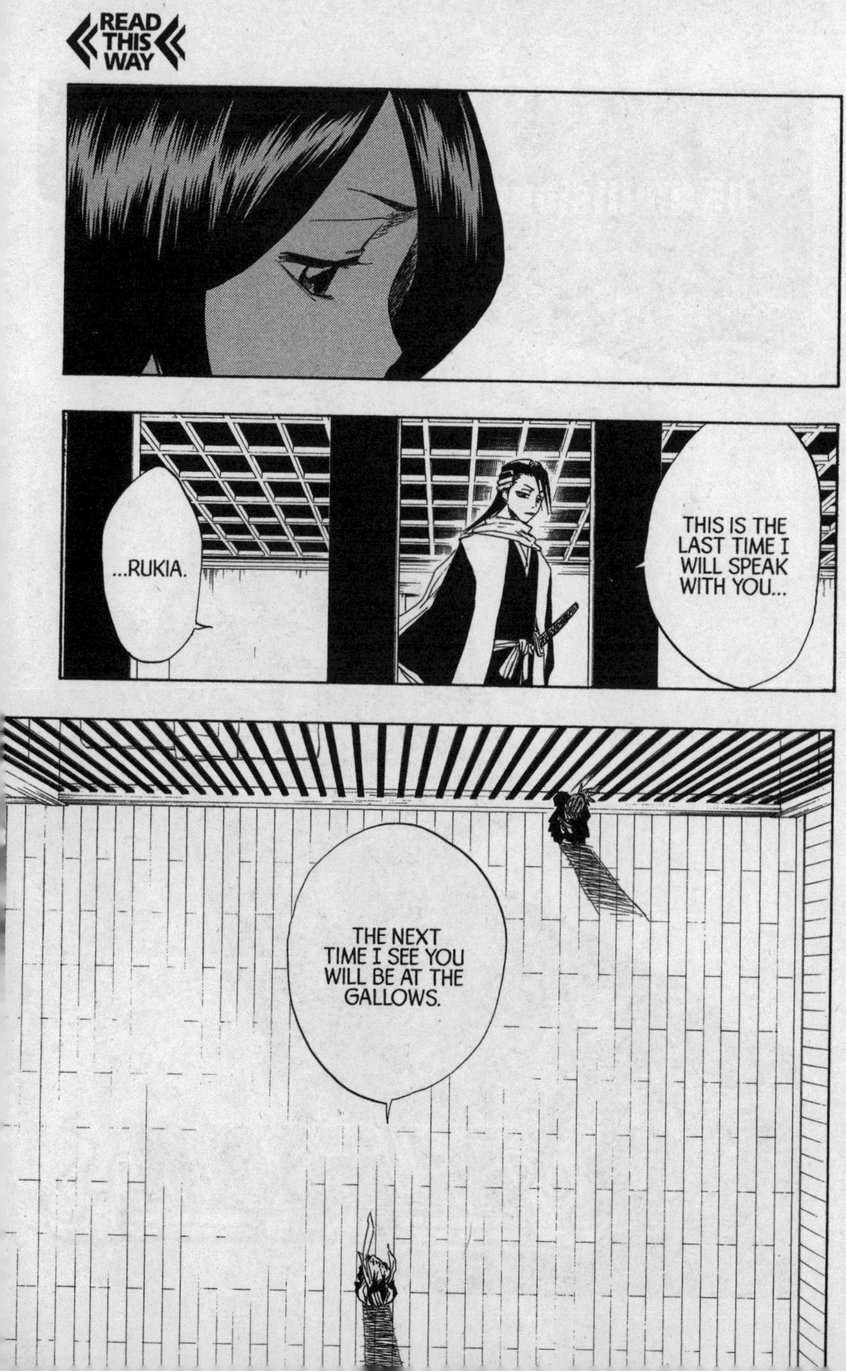
READ THIS WAY
THIS IS THE LAST TIME I WILL SPEAK WITH YOU...
...RUKIA.
THE NEXT TIME I SEE YOU WILL BE AT THE GALLOWS.

65. Collisions

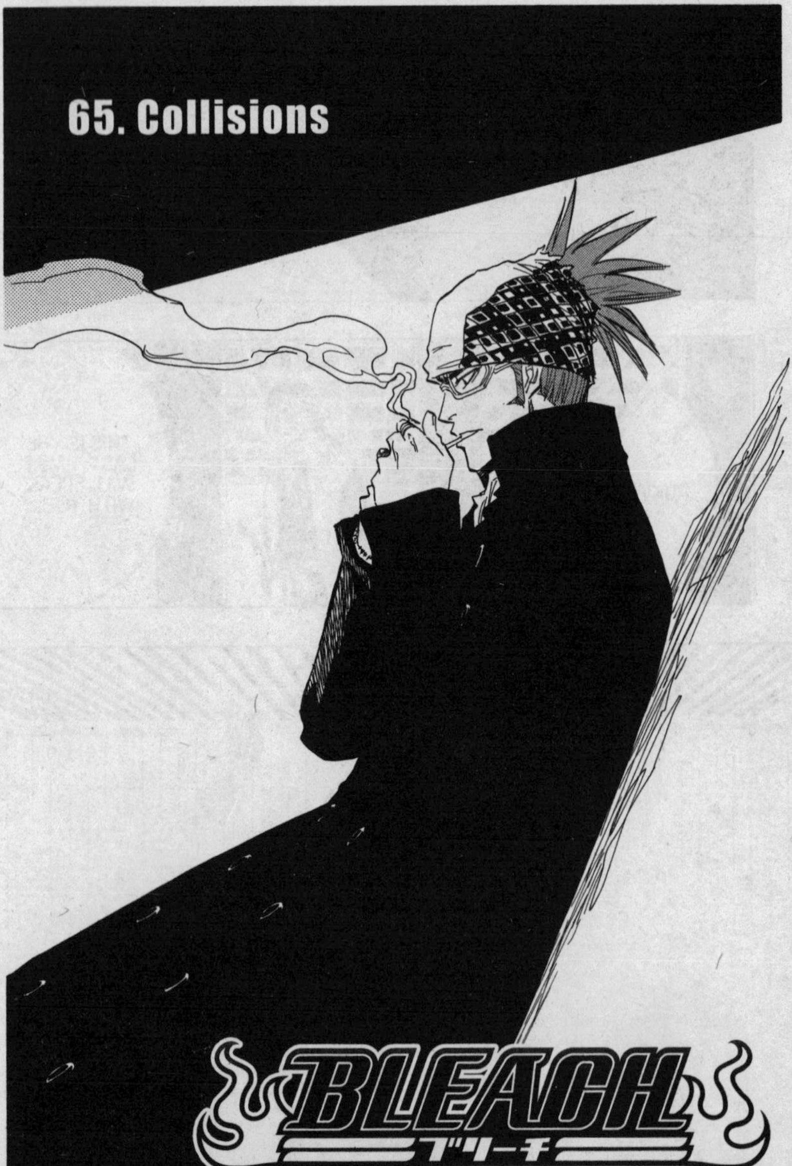
BLEACH
ブリーチ

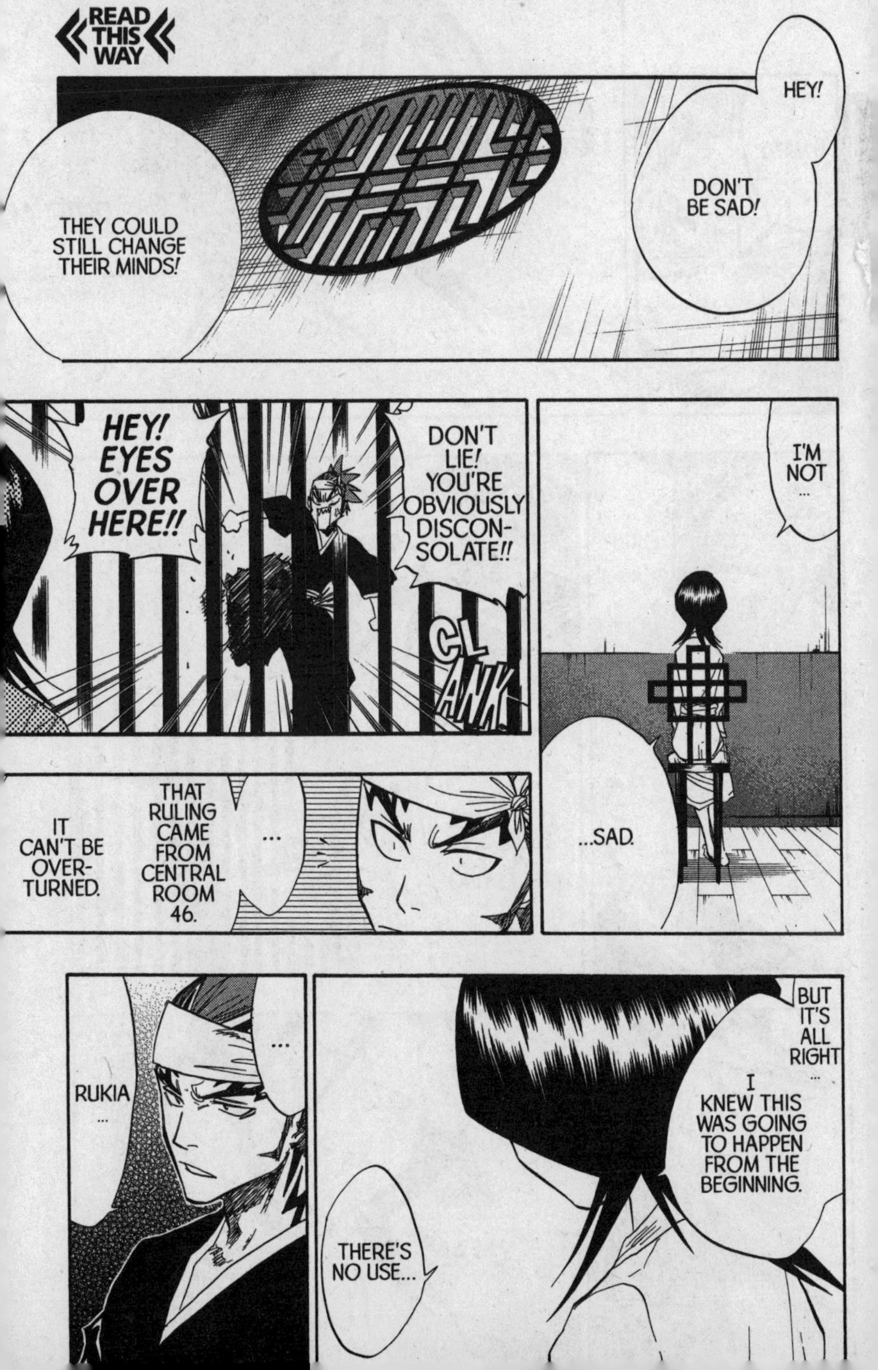
READ THIS WAY
HEY!
DON'T BE SAD!
THEY COULD STILL CHANGE THEIR MINDS!
I'M NOT ...
...SAD.
DON'T LIE! YOU'RE OBVIOUSLY DISCON-SOLATE!!
HEY! EYES OVER HERE!!
CLANK
...
THAT RULING CAME FROM CENTRAL ROOM 46.
IT CAN'T BE OVER-TURNED.
BUT IT'S ALL RIGHT ...
I KNEW THIS WAS GOING TO HAPPEN FROM THE BEGINNING.
THERE'S NO USE...
...
RUKIA ...

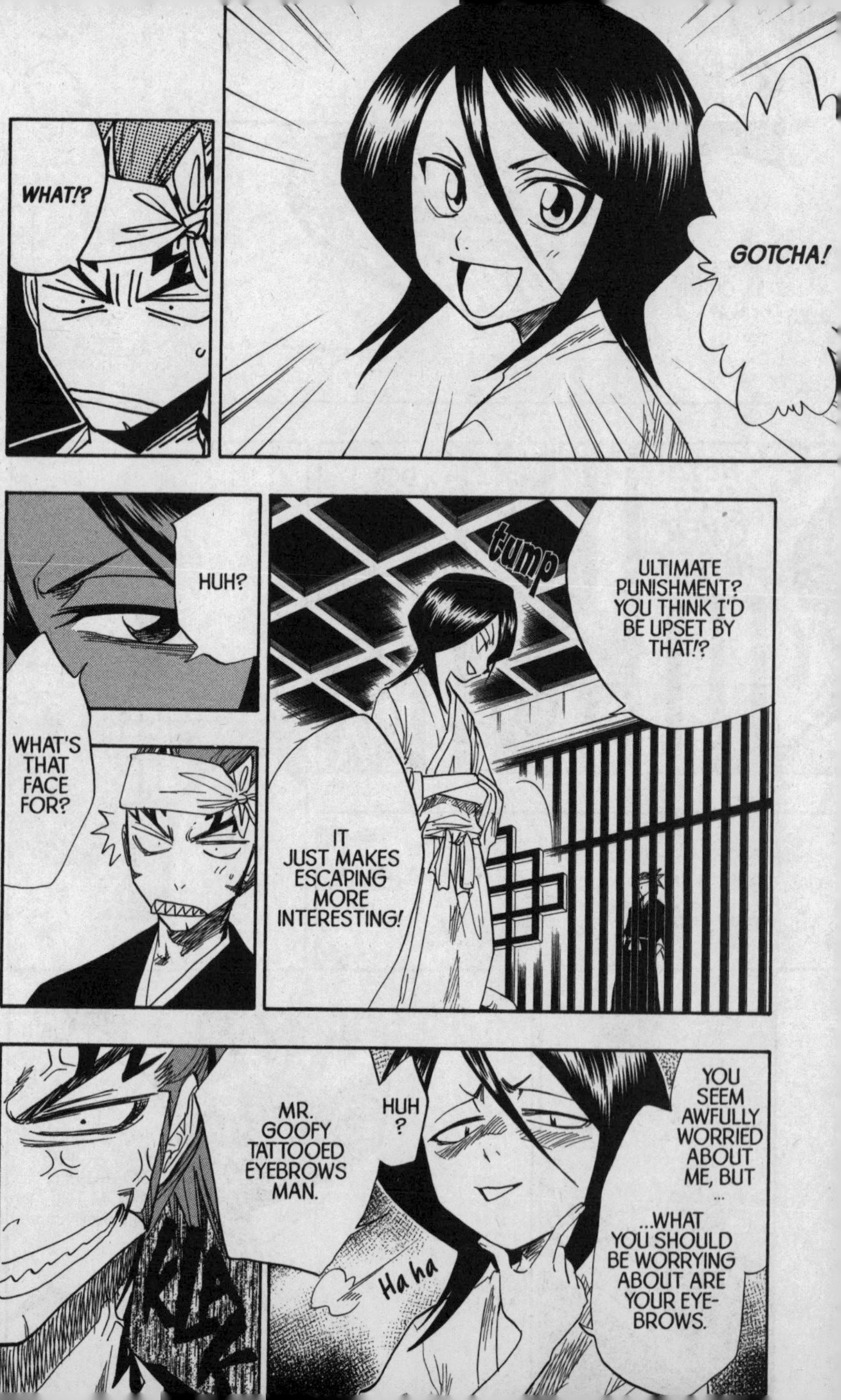
GOTCHA!
WHAT!?
tump
ULTIMATE PUNISHMENT? YOU THINK I'D BE UPSET BY THAT!?
IT JUST MAKES ESCAPING MORE INTERESTING!
HUH?
WHAT'S THAT FACE FOR?
YOU SEEM AWFULLY WORRIED ABOUT ME, BUT...
...WHAT YOU SHOULD BE WORRYING ABOUT ARE YOUR EYE-BROWS.
HUH?
MR. GOOFY TATTOOED EYEBROWS MAN.
Ha ha

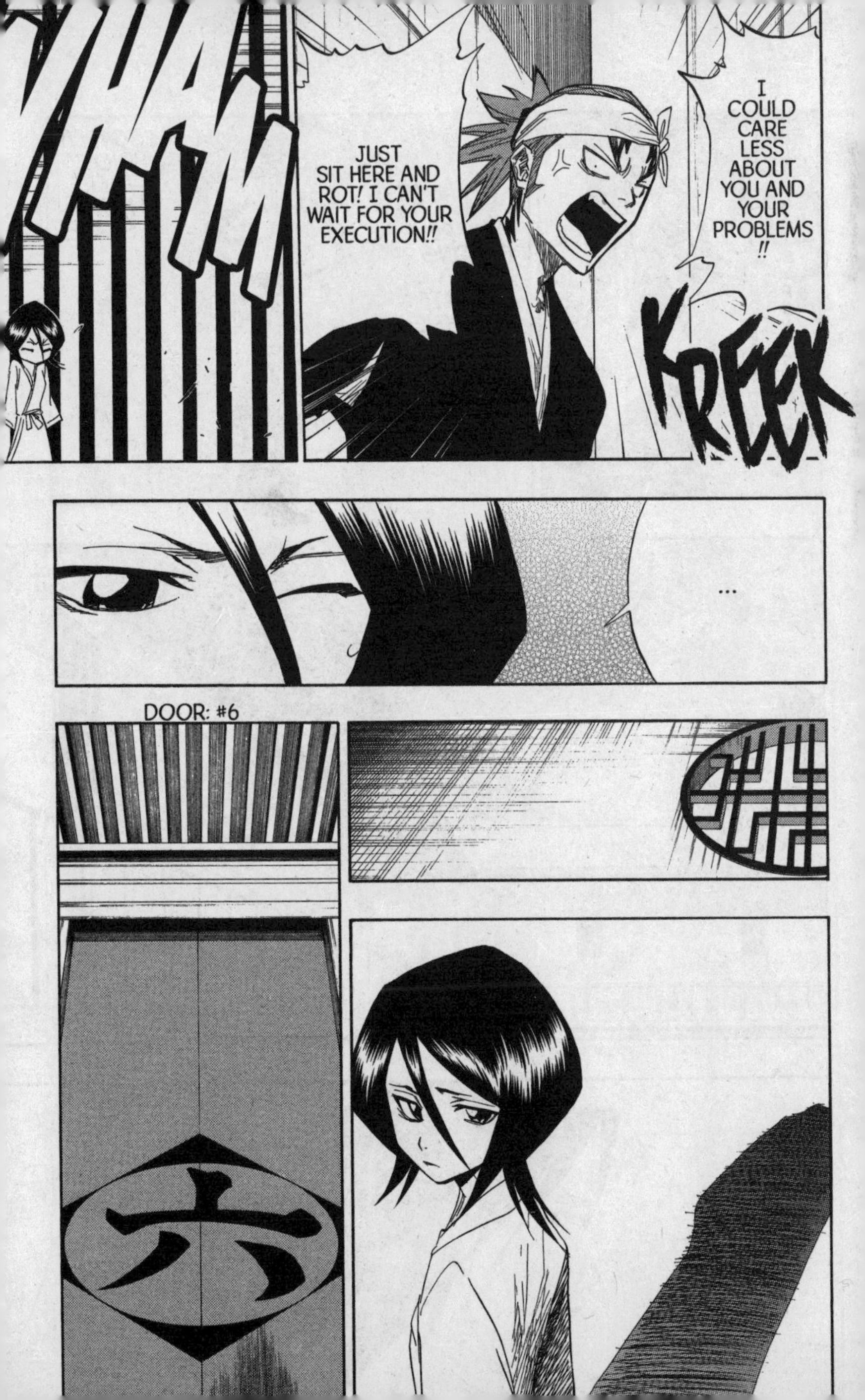
I COULD CARE LESS ABOUT YOU AND YOUR PROBLEMS!!
KREEK
JUST SIT HERE AND ROT! I CAN'T WAIT FOR YOUR EXECUTION!!
WHAM
...
DOOR: #6

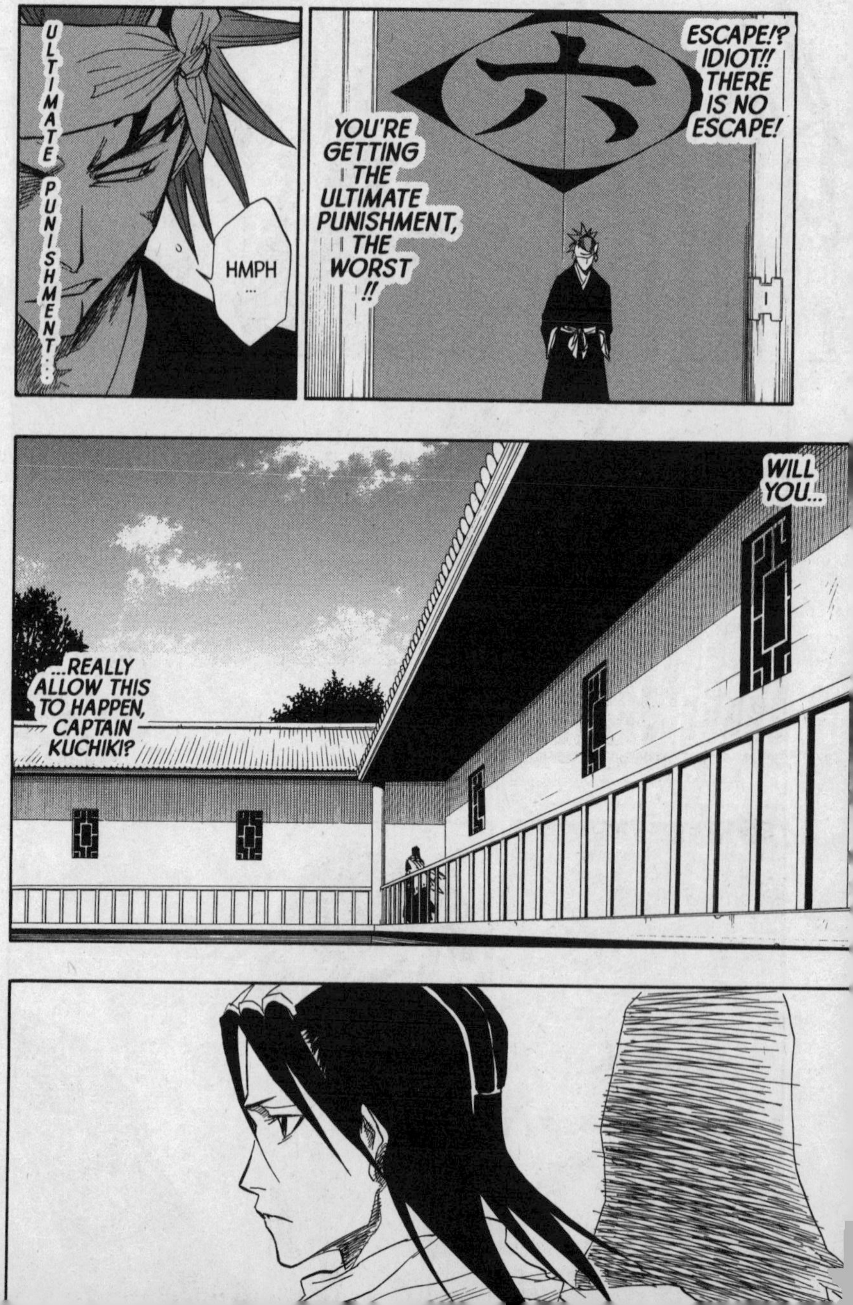
ESCAPE!? IDIOT!! THERE IS NO ESCAPE!
YOU'RE GETTING THE ULTIMATE PUNISHMENT, THE WORST!!
HMPH...
ULTIMATE PUNISHMENT...
WILL YOU...
...REALLY ALLOW THIS TO HAPPEN, CAPTAIN KUCHIKI!?

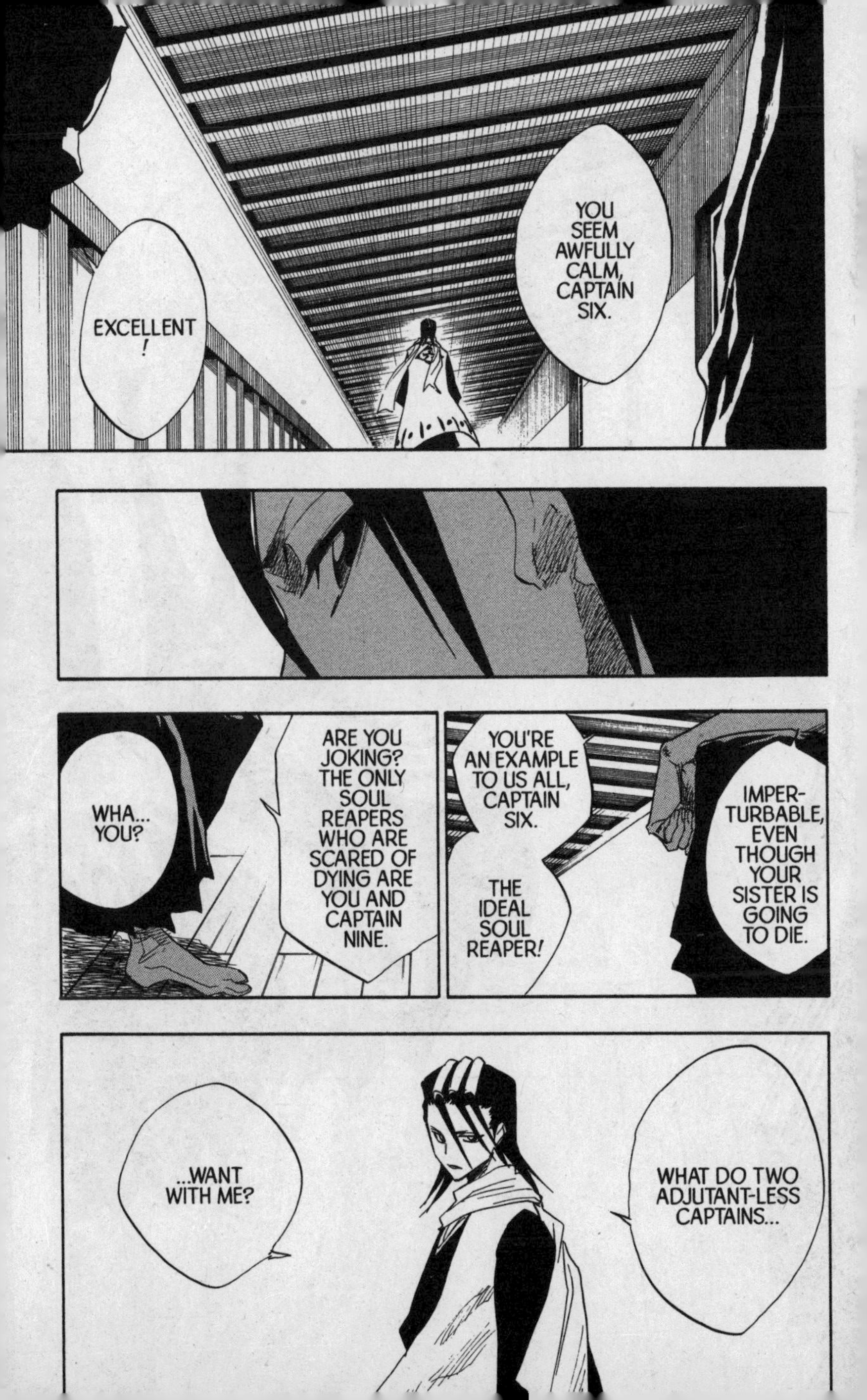
YOU SEEM AWFULLY CALM, CAPTAIN SIX.
EXCELLENT!
IMPER-TURBABLE, EVEN THOUGH YOUR SISTER IS GOING TO DIE.
YOU'RE AN EXAMPLE TO US ALL, CAPTAIN SIX.
THE IDEAL SOUL REAPER!
ARE YOU JOKING? THE ONLY SOUL REAPERS WHO ARE SCARED OF DYING ARE YOU AND CAPTAIN NINE.
WHA... YOU?
WHAT DO TWO ADJUTANT-LESS CAPTAINS...
...WANT WITH ME?

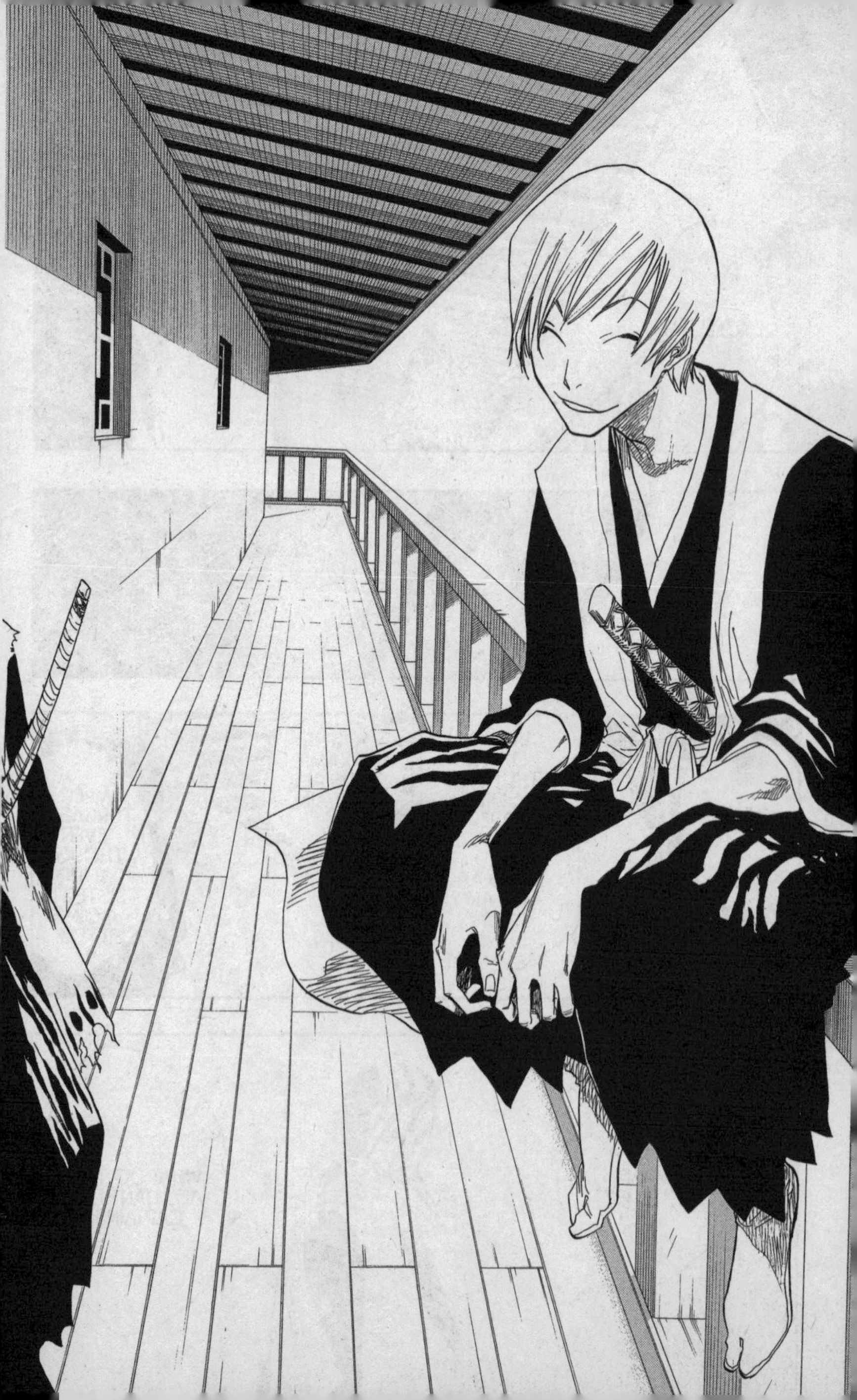

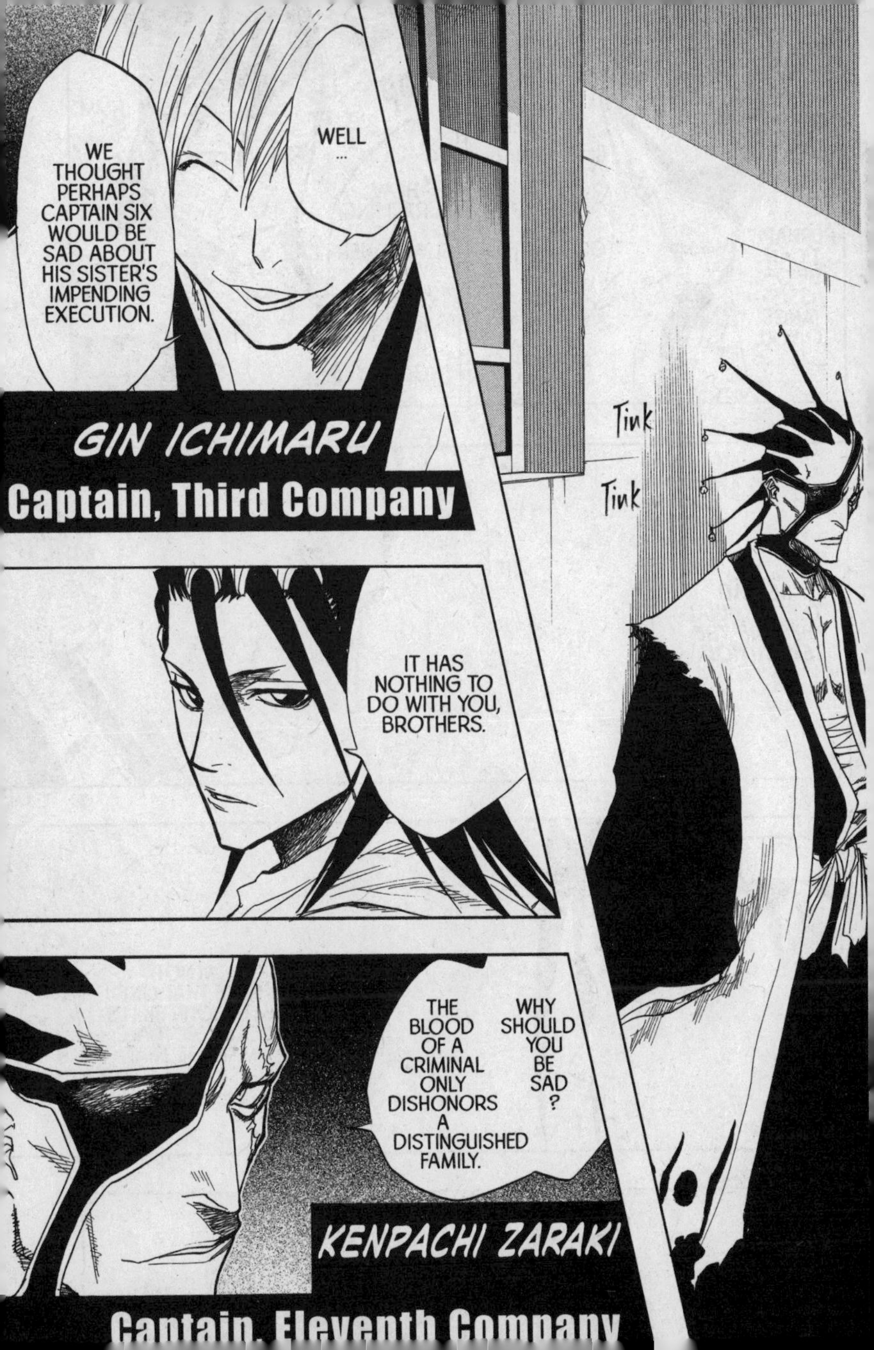
WE THOUGHT PERHAPS CAPTAIN SIX WOULD BE SAD ABOUT HIS SISTER'S IMPENDING EXECUTION.
WELL ...
GIN ICHIMARU
Captain, Third Company
Tink
Tink
IT HAS NOTHING TO DO WITH YOU, BROTHERS.
WHY SHOULD YOU BE SAD ?
THE BLOOD OF A CRIMINAL ONLY DISHONORS A DISTINGUISHED FAMILY.
KENPACHI ZARAKI
Captain, Eleventh Company

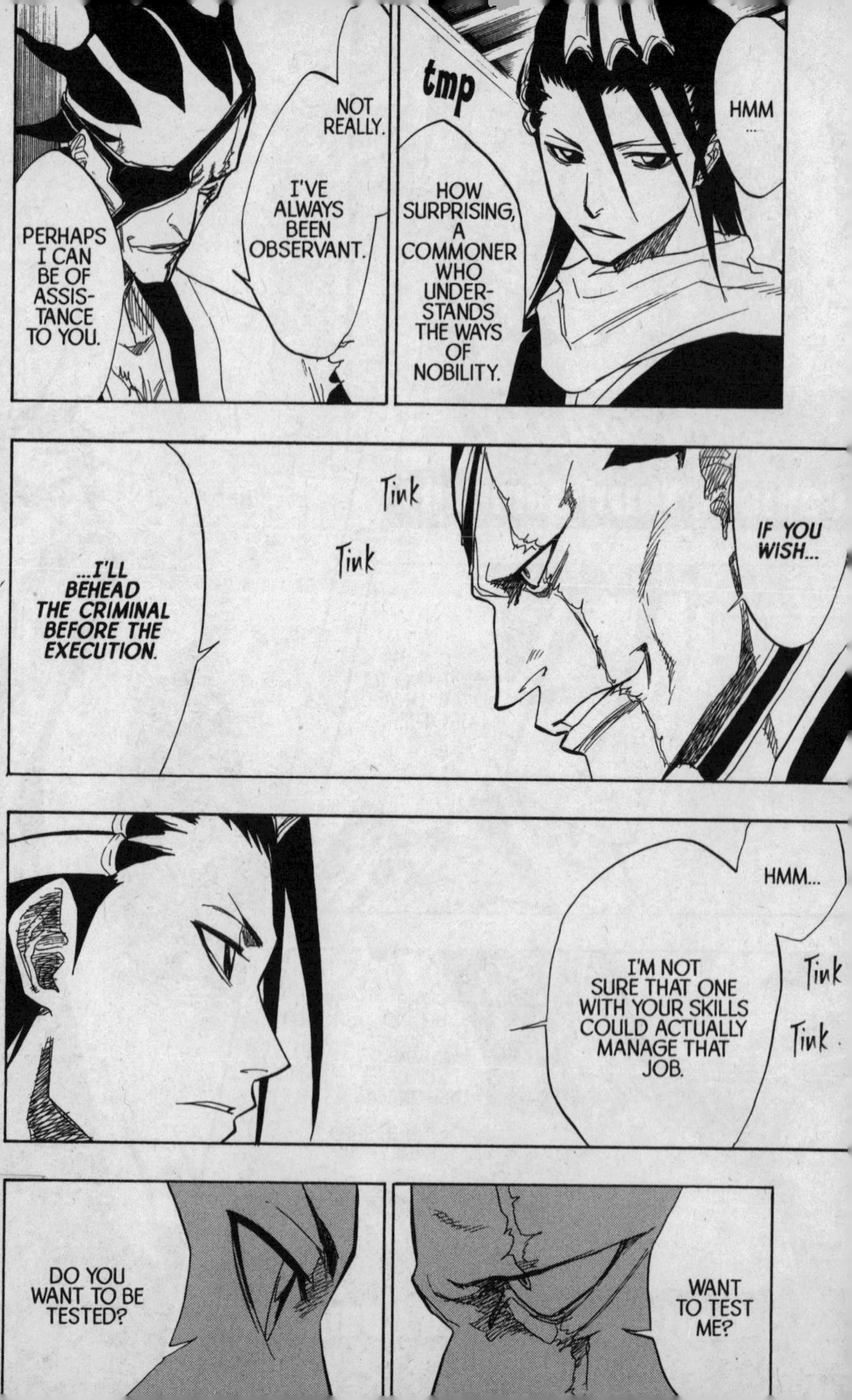
HMM ...
tmp
HOW SURPRISING, A COMMONER WHO UNDER-STANDS THE WAYS OF NOBILITY.
NOT REALLY.
I'VE ALWAYS BEEN OBSERVANT.
PERHAPS I CAN BE OF ASSIS-TANCE TO YOU.
IF YOU WISH...
Tink
Tink
...I'LL BEHEAD THE CRIMINAL BEFORE THE EXECUTION.
HMM...
I'M NOT SURE THAT ONE WITH YOUR SKILLS COULD ACTUALLY MANAGE THAT JOB.
Tink
Tink
WANT TO TEST ME?
DO YOU WANT TO BE TESTED?

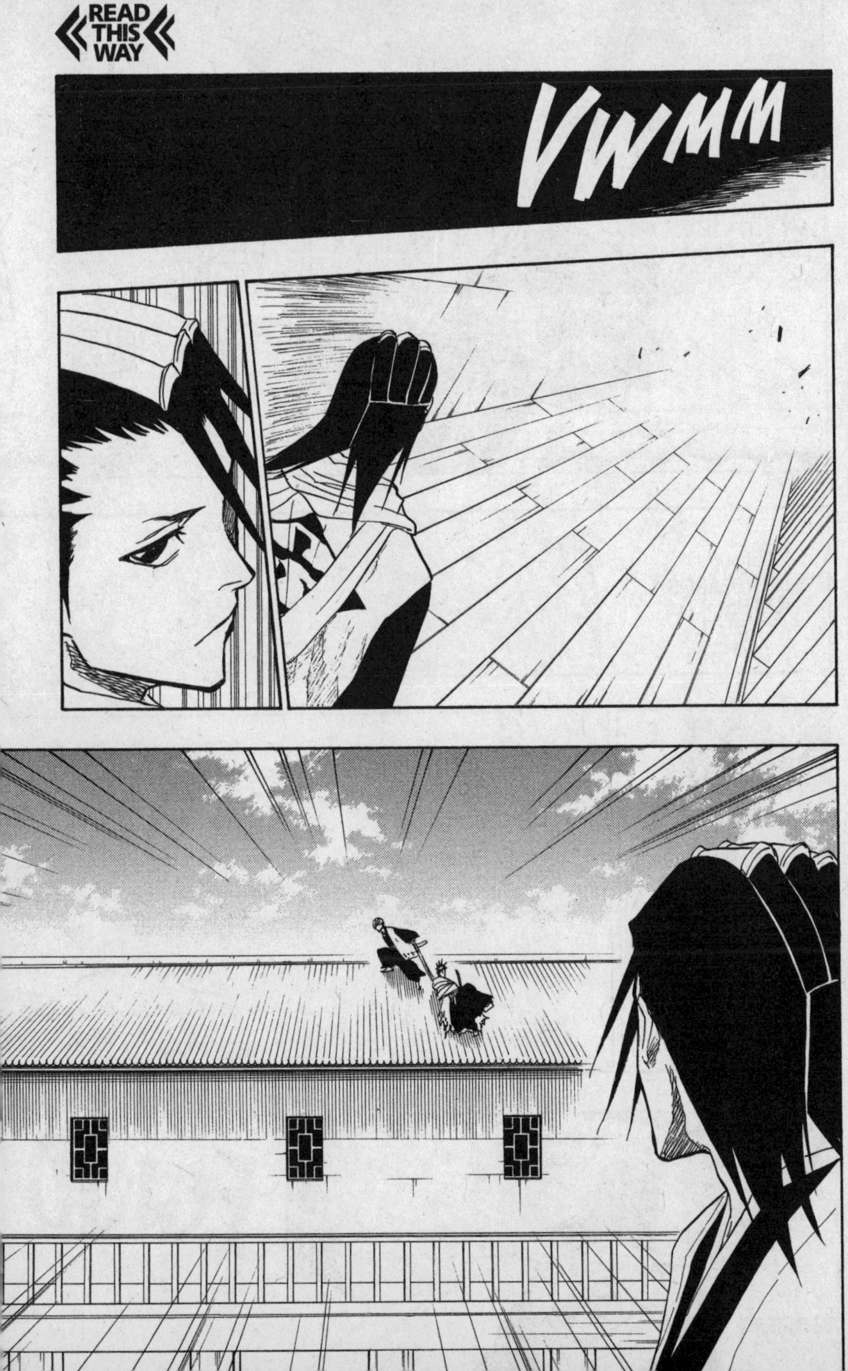
READ THIS WAY
VWMM

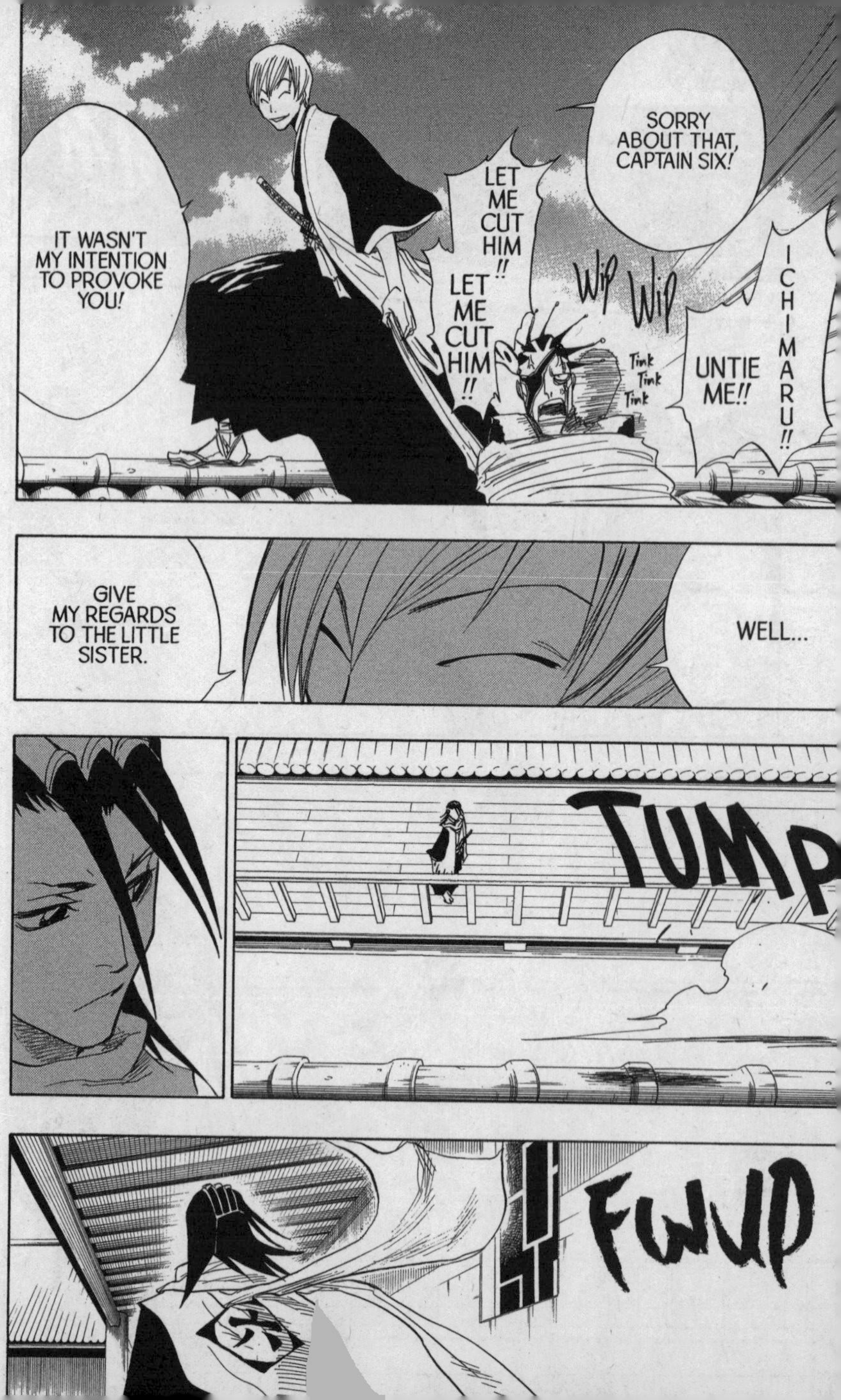
SORRY ABOUT THAT, CAPTAIN SIX!
ICHIMARU!! UNTIE ME!!
Wip Wip
Tink Tink Tink
LET ME CUT HIM!! LET ME CUT HIM!!
IT WASN'T MY INTENTION TO PROVOKE YOU!
WELL...
GIVE MY REGARDS TO THE LITTLE SISTER.
TUMP
FWUP

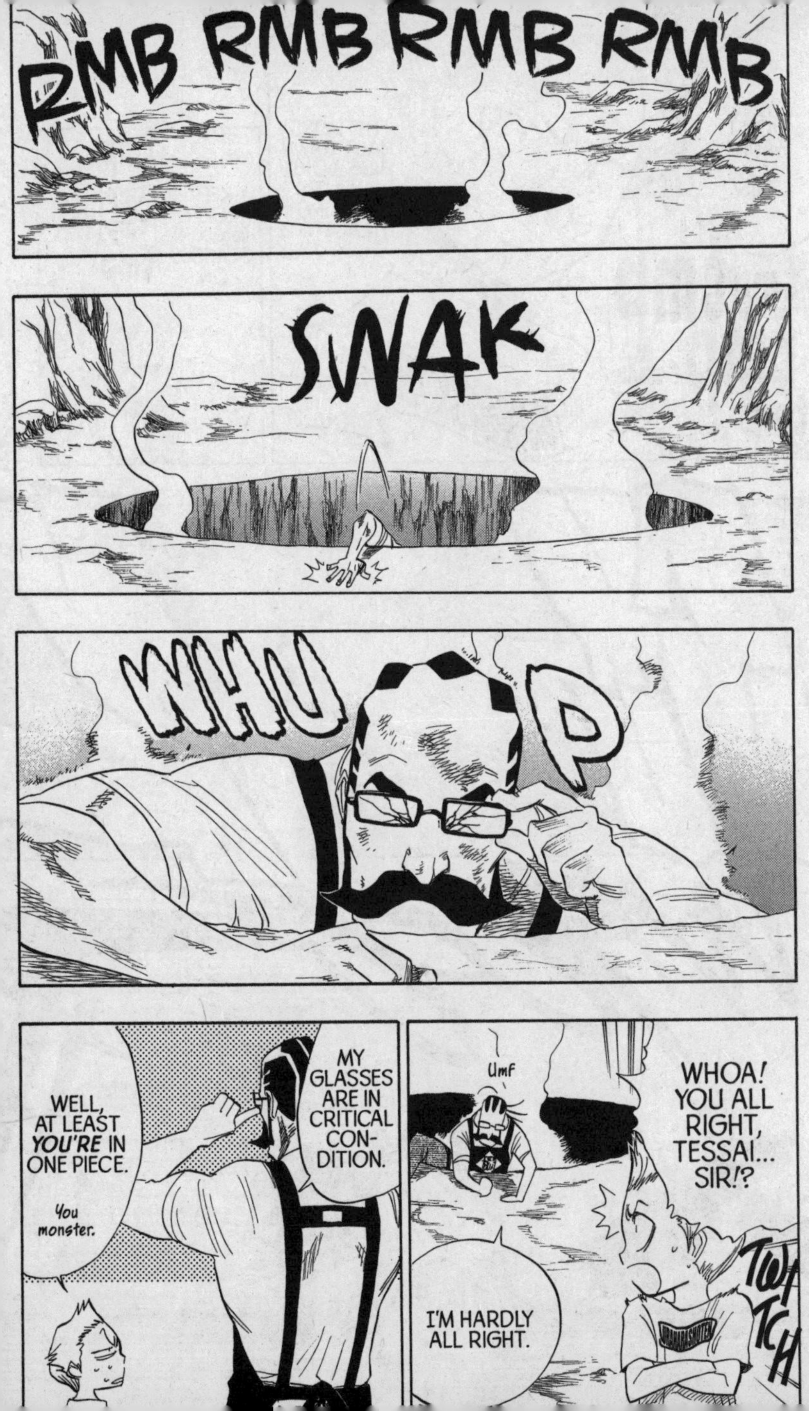
RMB RMB RMB RMB RMB
SWAK
WHUMP
WHOA! YOU ALL RIGHT, TESSAI... SIR!?
Umf
I'M HARDLY ALL RIGHT.
TWITCH
MY GLASSES ARE IN CRITICAL CON-DITION.
WELL, AT LEAST *YOU'RE* IN ONE PIECE.
You monster.

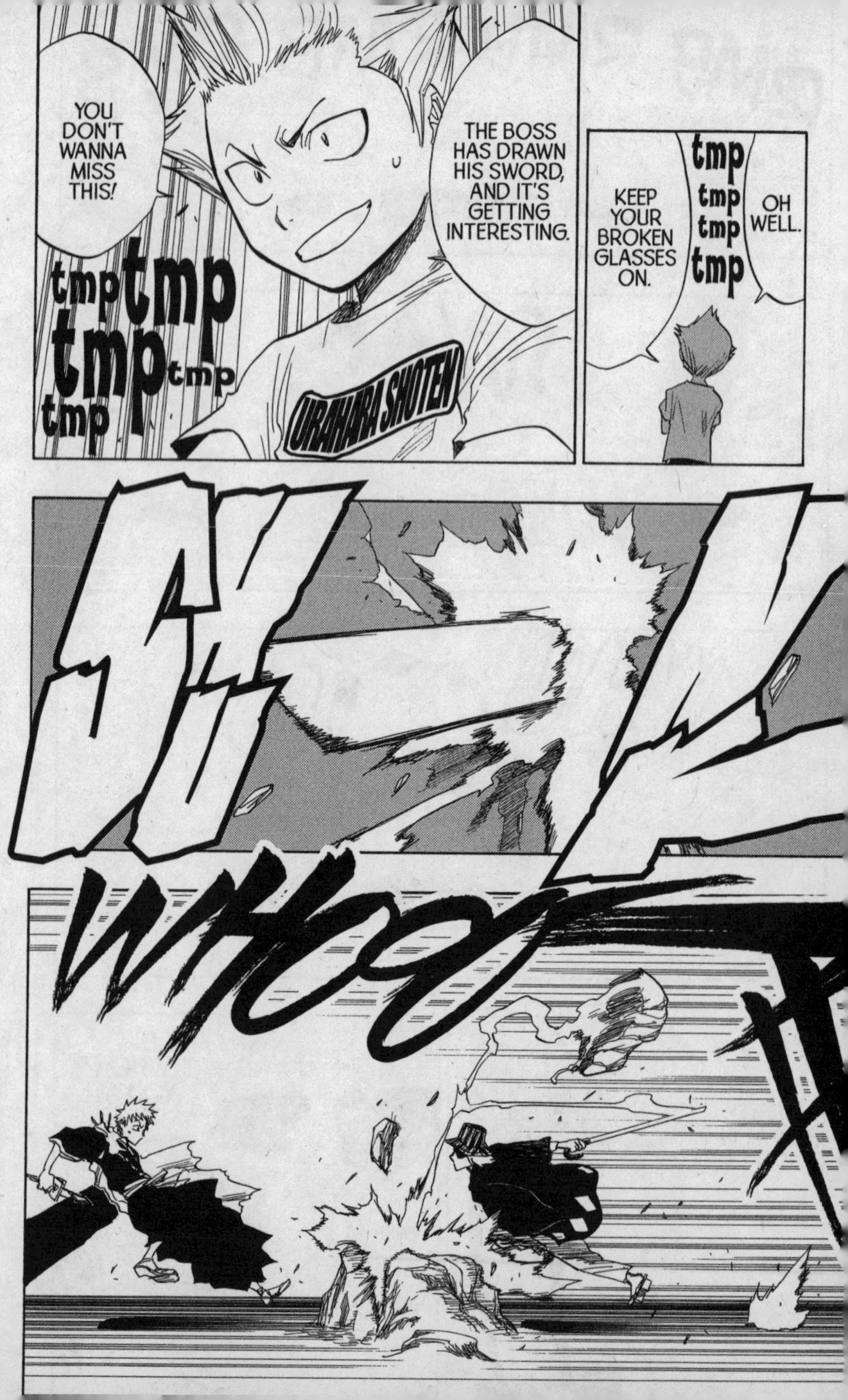
OH WELL.
tmp tmp tmp tmp
KEEP YOUR BROKEN GLASSES ON.
THE BOSS HAS DRAWN HIS SWORD, AND IT'S GETTING INTERESTING.
YOU DON'T WANNA MISS THIS!
tmp tmp tmp tmp tmp
URAHARA SHOTEN

READ THIS WAY

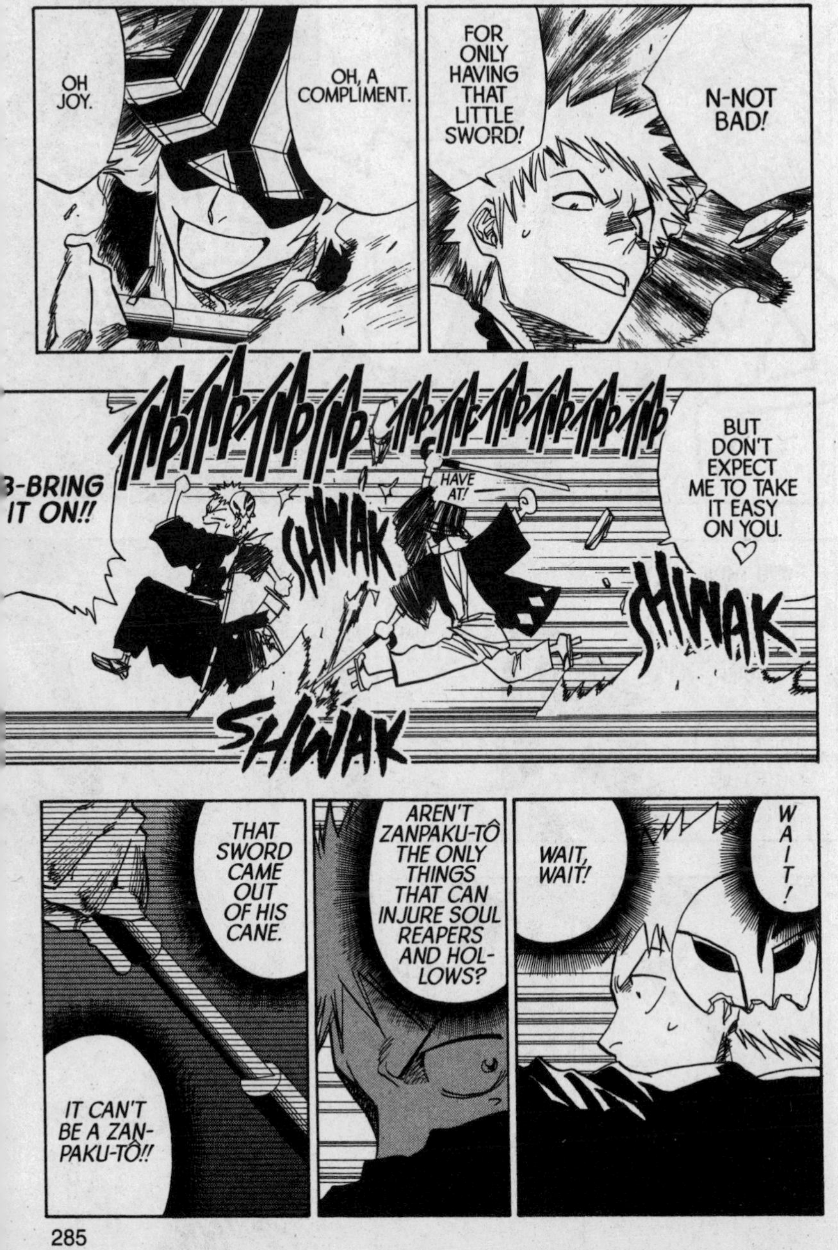

N-NOT BAD!
FOR ONLY HAVING THAT LITTLE SWORD!
OH, A COMPLIMENT.
OH JOY.
BUT DON'T EXPECT ME TO TAKE IT EASY ON YOU. ♡
TMP TMP TMP TMP TMP TMP TMP TMP TMP TMP
SHWAK
HAVE AT!
SHWAK
SHWAK
B-BRING IT ON!!
WAIT!
WAIT, WAIT!
AREN'T ZANPAKU-TÔ THE ONLY THINGS THAT CAN INJURE SOUL REAPERS AND HOLLOWS?
THAT SWORD CAME OUT OF HIS CANE.
IT CAN'T BE A ZANPAKU-TÔ!!

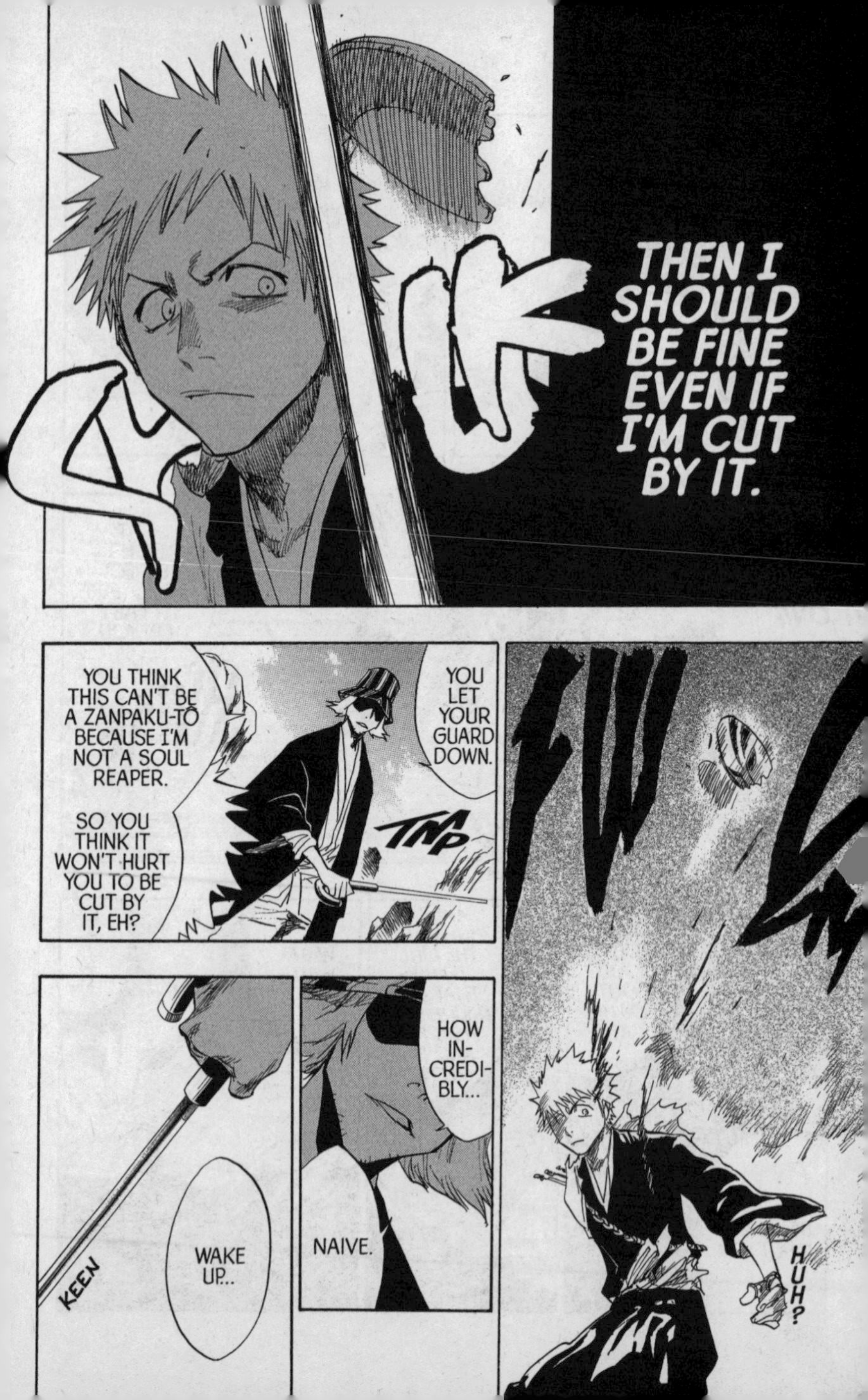
THEN I SHOULD BE FINE EVEN IF I'M CUT BY IT.
HUH?
YOU LET YOUR GUARD DOWN.
TMP
YOU THINK THIS CAN'T BE A ZANPAKU-TŌ BECAUSE I'M NOT A SOUL REAPER.
SO YOU THINK IT WON'T HURT YOU TO BE CUT BY IT, EH?
HOW IN-CREDI-BLY...
NAIVE.
WAKE UP...
KEEN

....!

krak
krak
krak

...BENIHIME,
THE RED
PRINCESS.

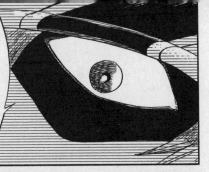

THIS
BLADE
IS VERY
MUCH A...

DOOM

...ZANPAKU-TÔ.

PEOPLE WHO MISS ICHIGO (2)

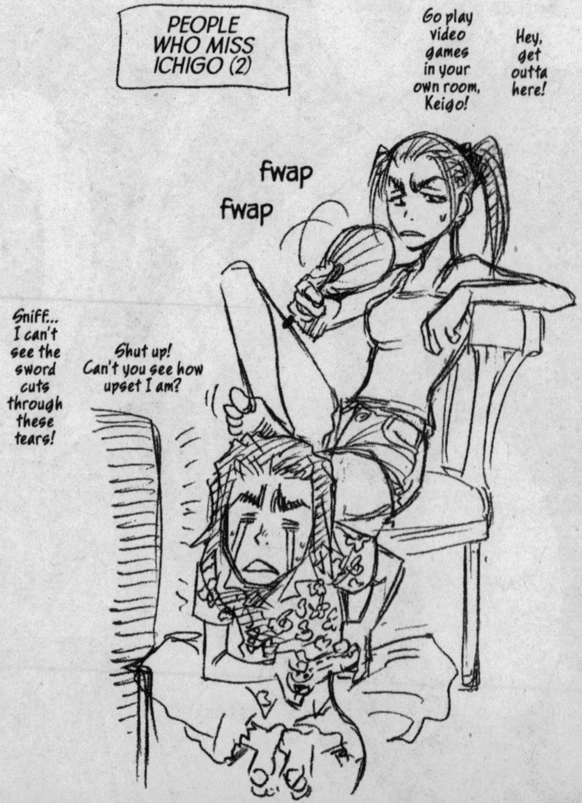
Hey, get outta here!
Go play video games in your own room, Keigo!
fwap
fwap
Shut up! Can't you see how upset I am?
Sniff... I can't see the sword cuts through these tears!

66. THE BLADE AND ME

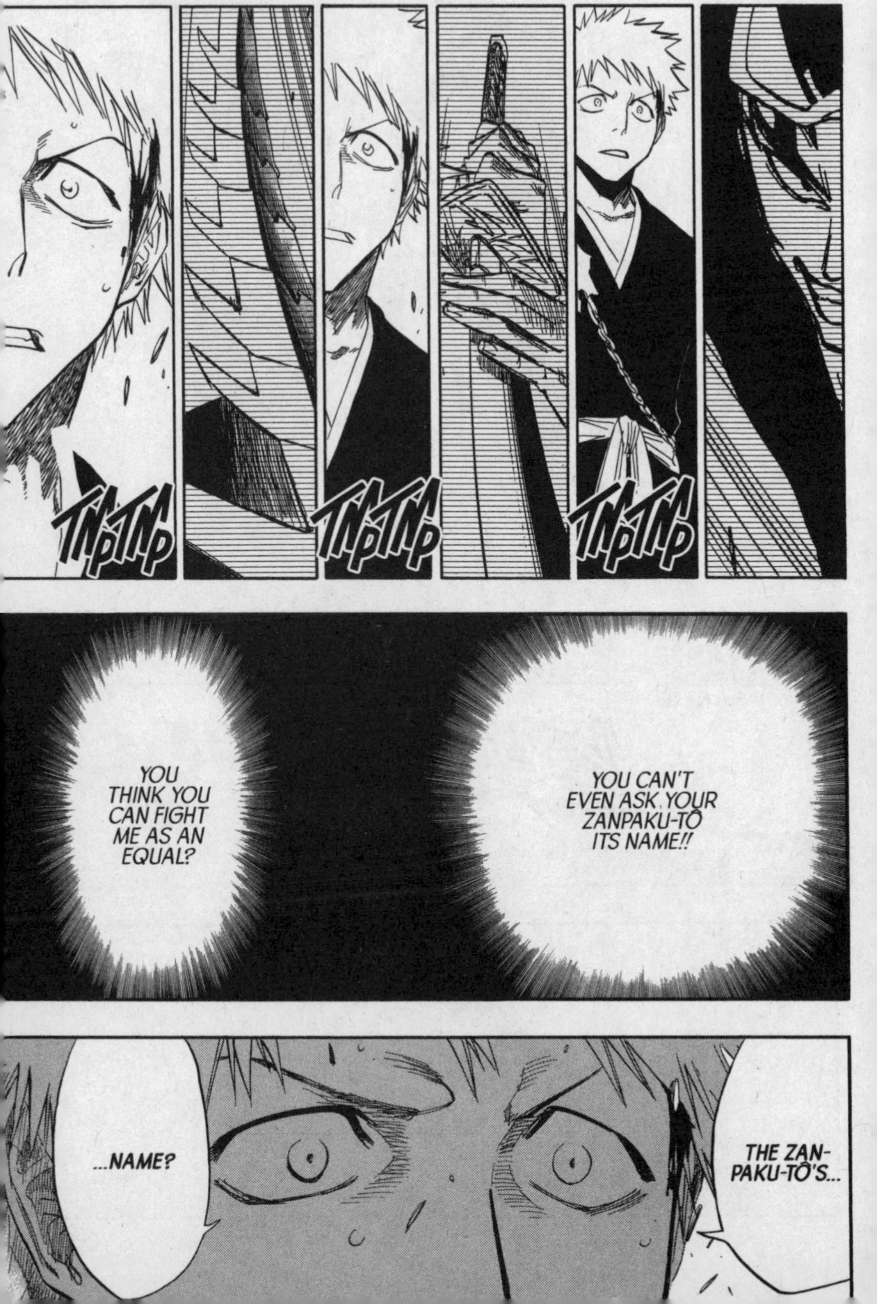
TMPTMP
TMPTMP
TMPTMP
YOU CAN'T EVEN ASK YOUR ZANPAKU-TÔ ITS NAME!!
YOU THINK YOU CAN FIGHT ME AS AN EQUAL?
THE ZAN-PAKU-TÔ'S...
...NAME?

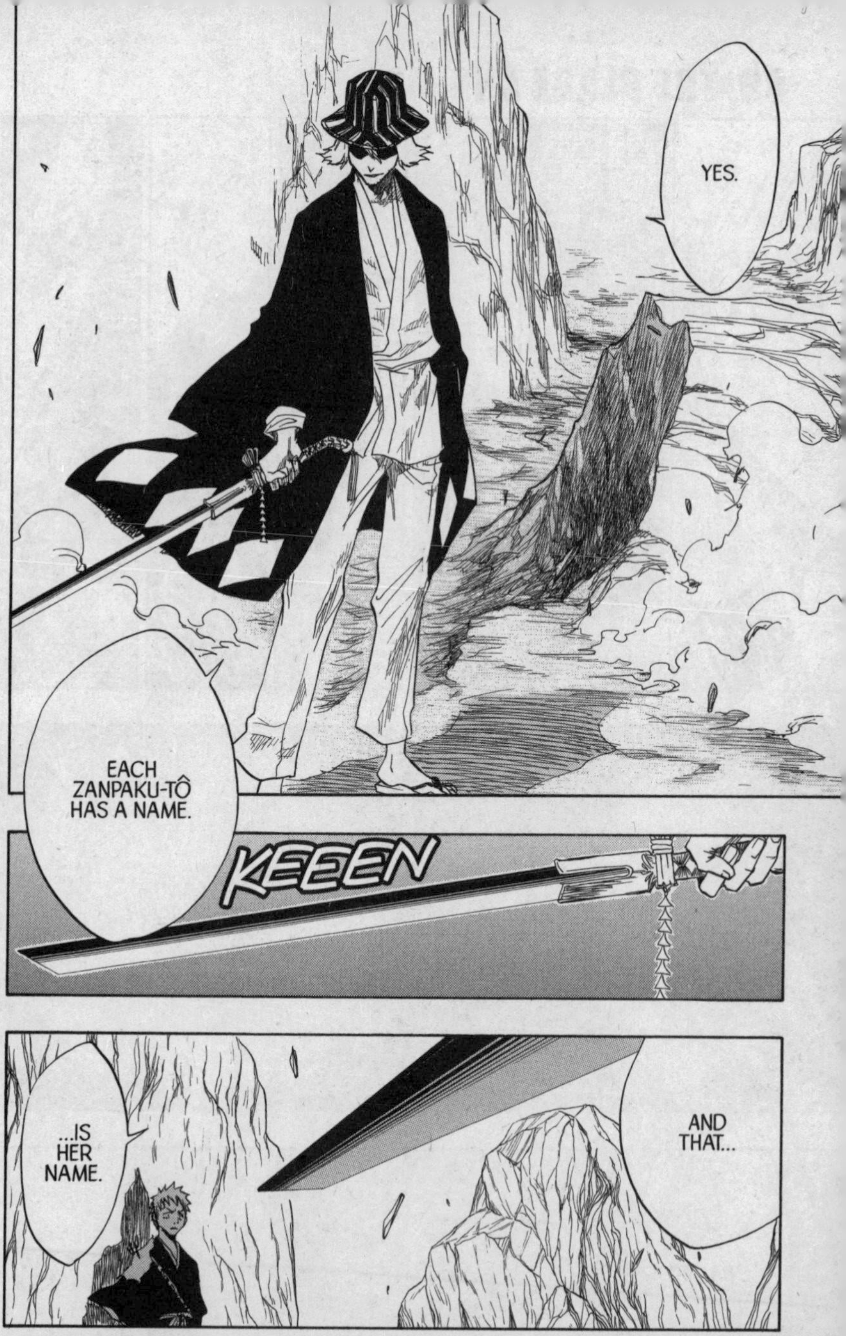
YES.
EACH ZANPAKU-TÔ HAS A NAME.
KEEEN
AND THAT...
...IS HER NAME.

READ THIS WAY

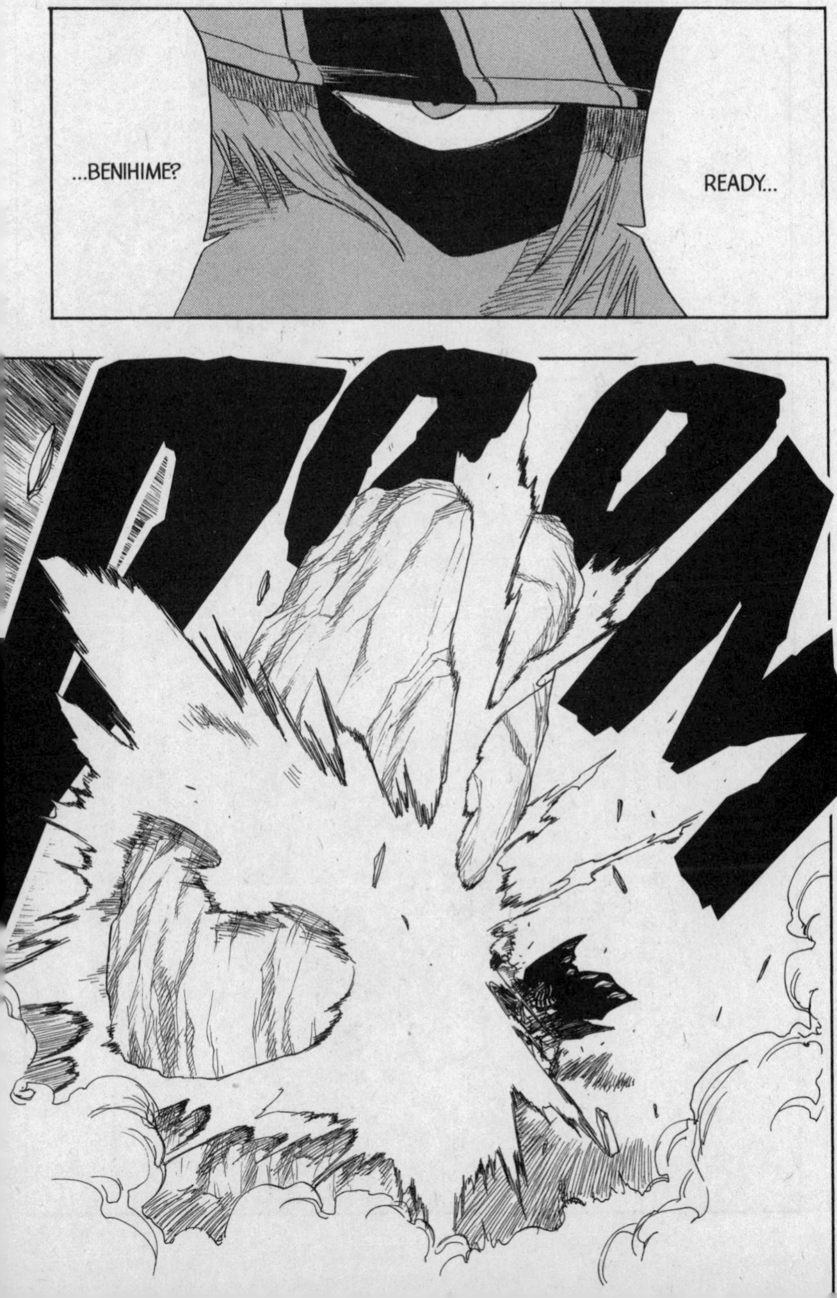
READY...
...BENIHIME?

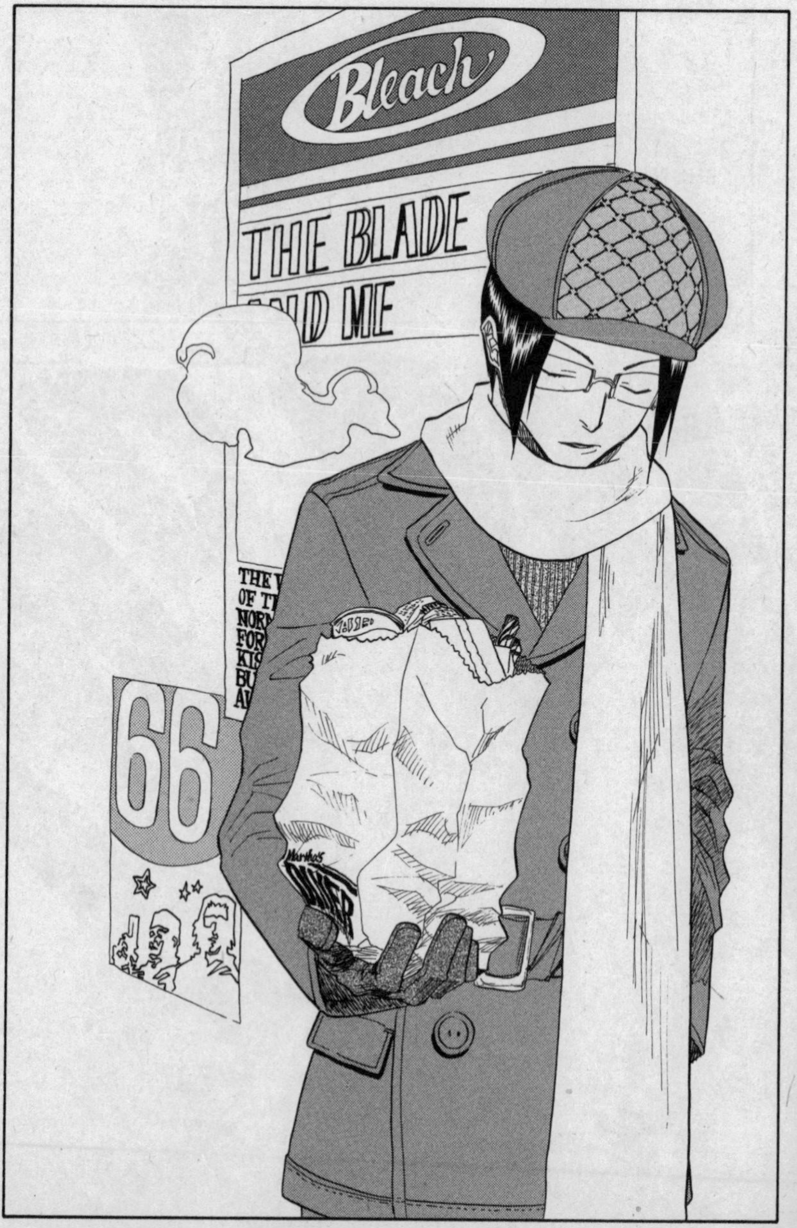
Bleach
THE BLADE
66

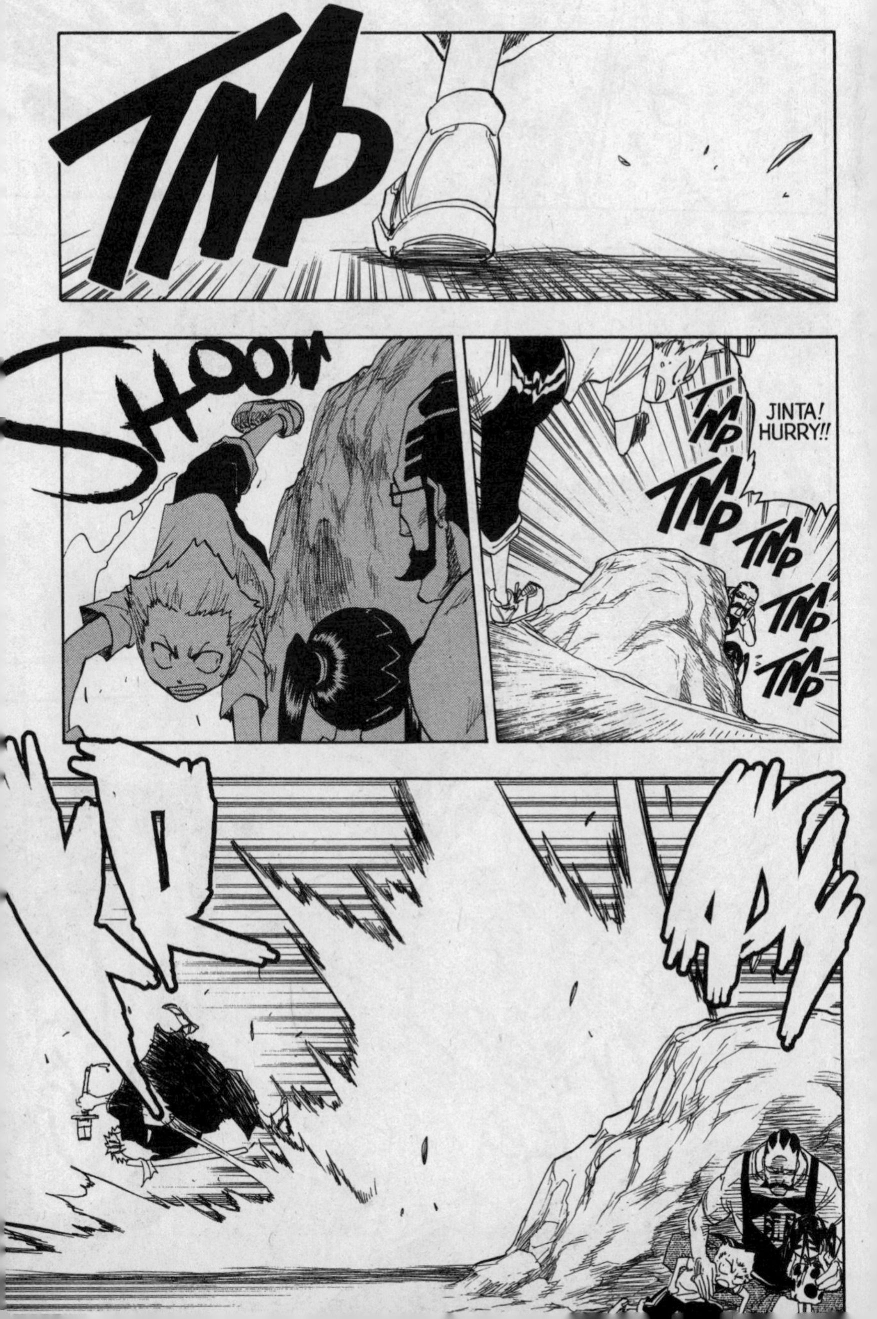
TMP
JINTA! HURRY!!
TMP
TMP
TMP
TMP
TMP
TMP
SHOOM

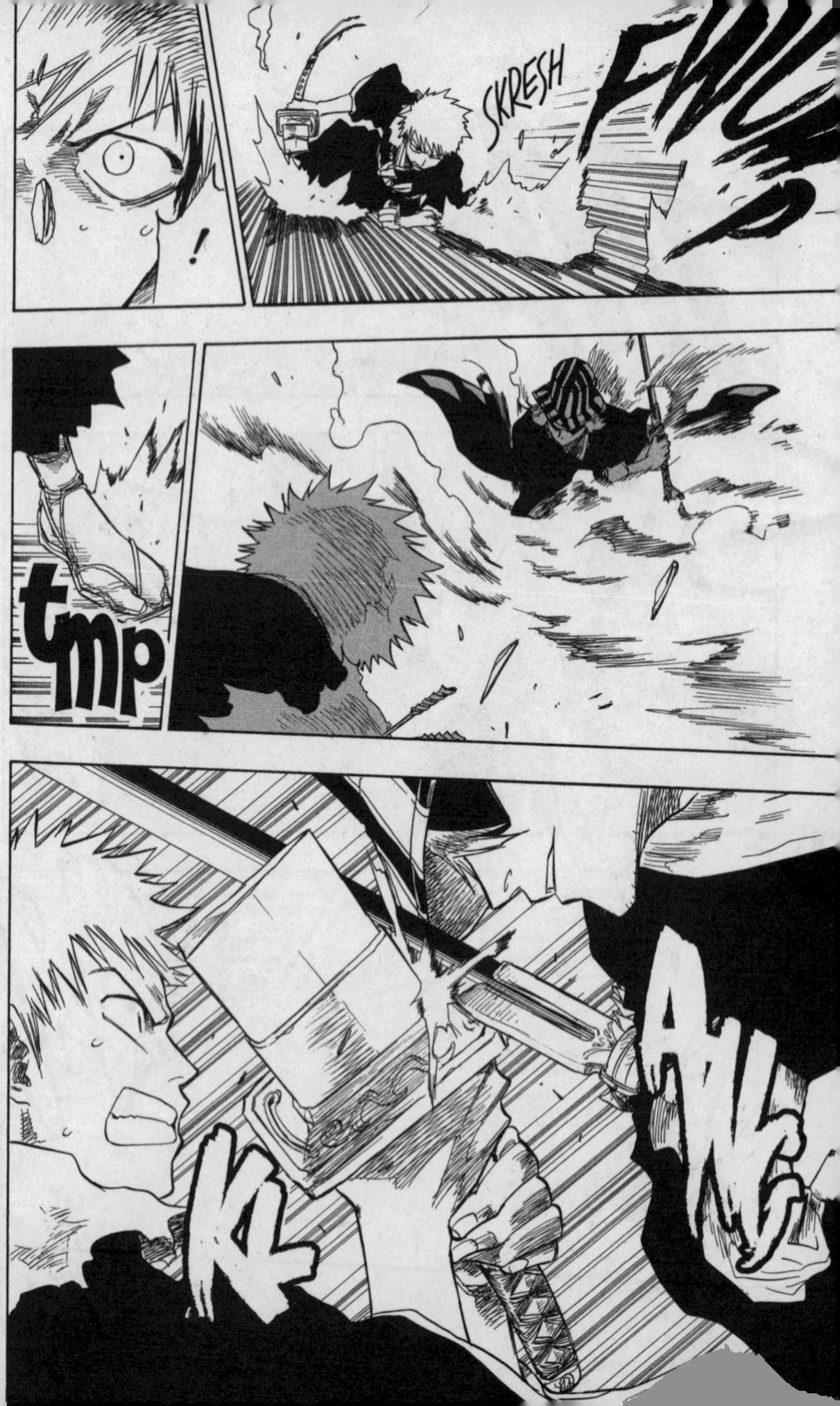
FWUMP
SKRESH
!
tmp
KLANG

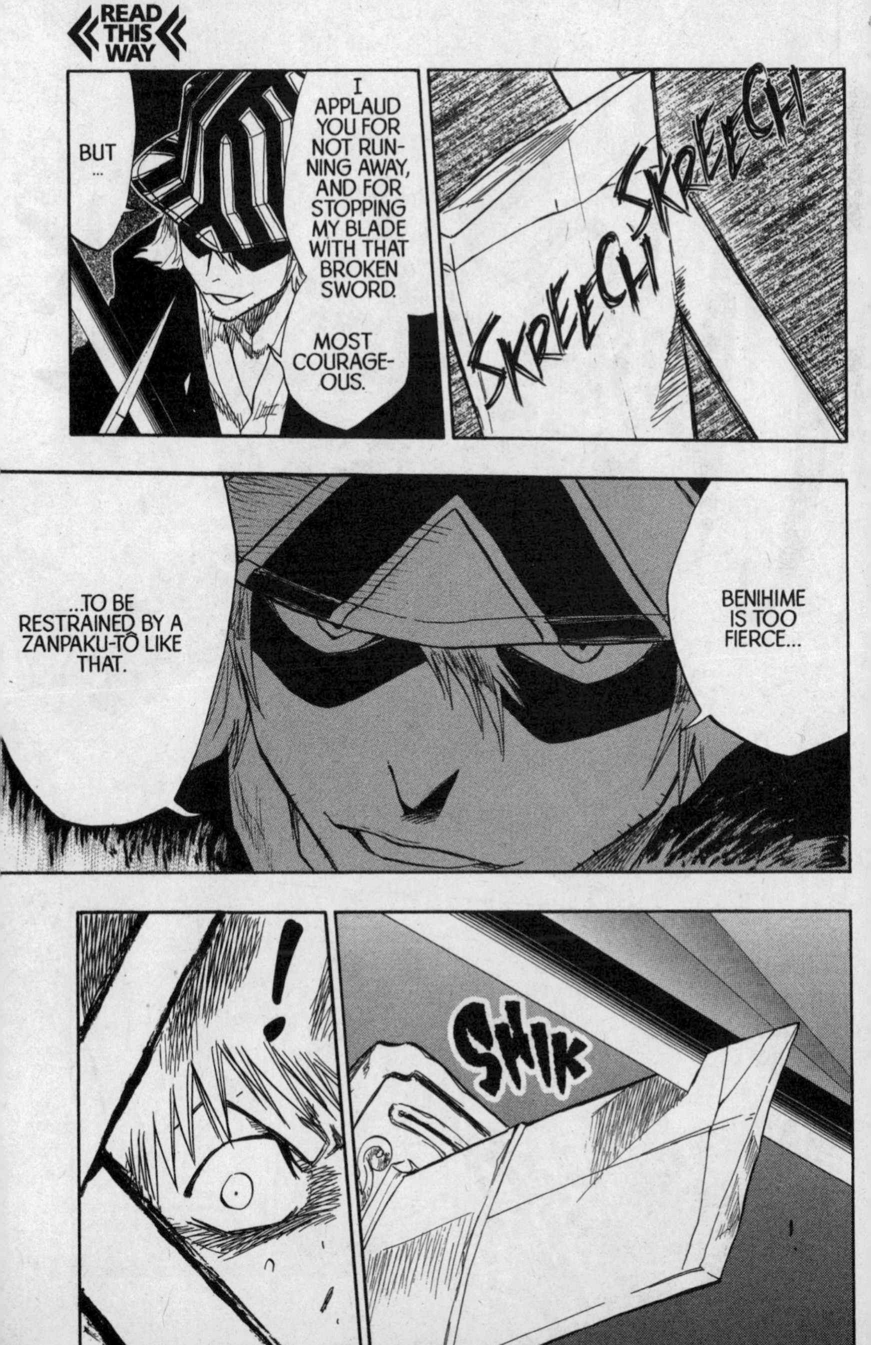
READ THIS WAY
SKREECH SKREECH
I APPLAUD YOU FOR NOT RUNNING AWAY, AND FOR STOPPING MY BLADE WITH THAT BROKEN SWORD.
MOST COURAGEOUS.
BUT ...
BENIHIME IS TOO FIERCE...
...TO BE RESTRAINED BY A ZANPAKU-TÔ LIKE THAT.
SHIK
!

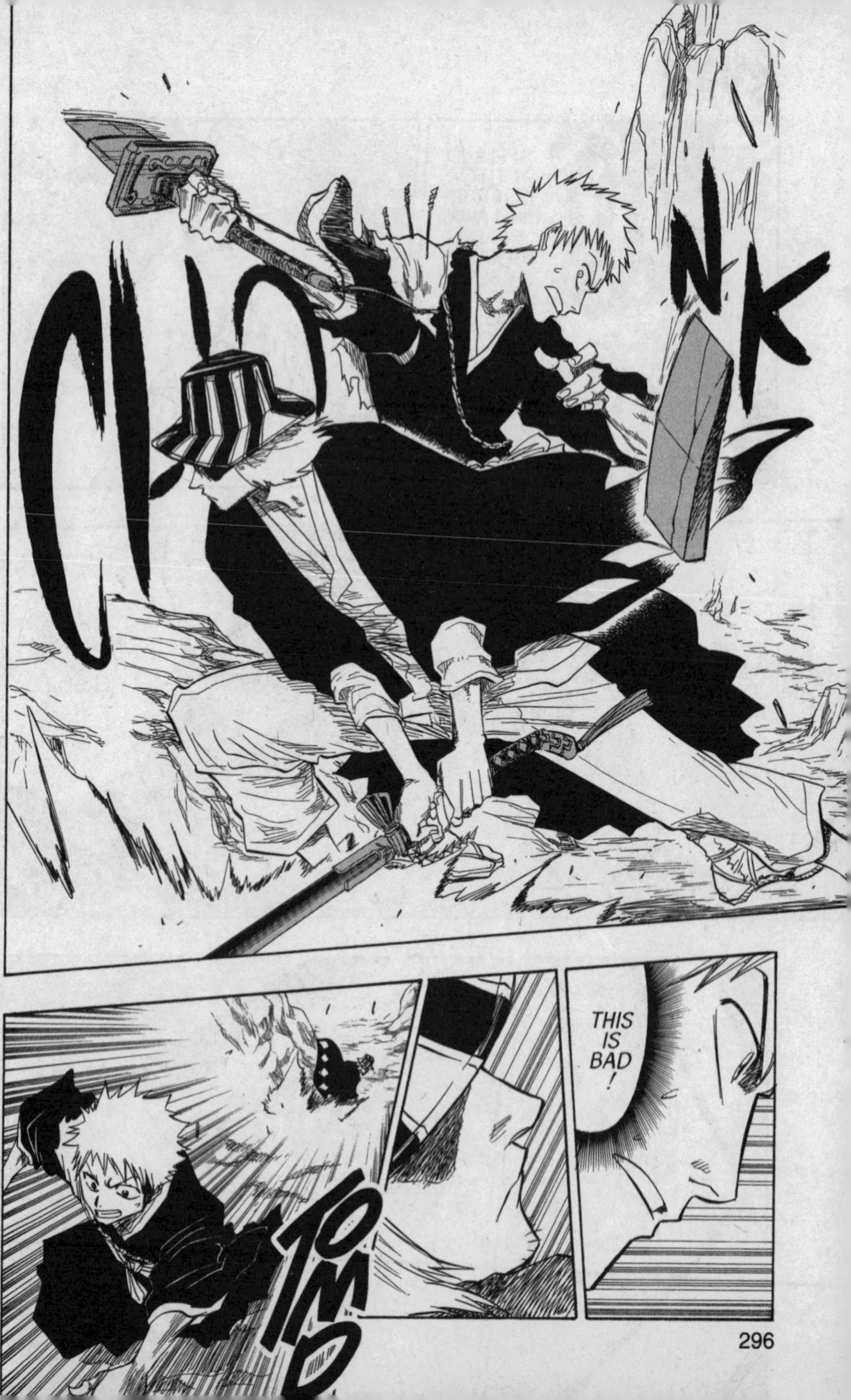
THIS IS BAD!

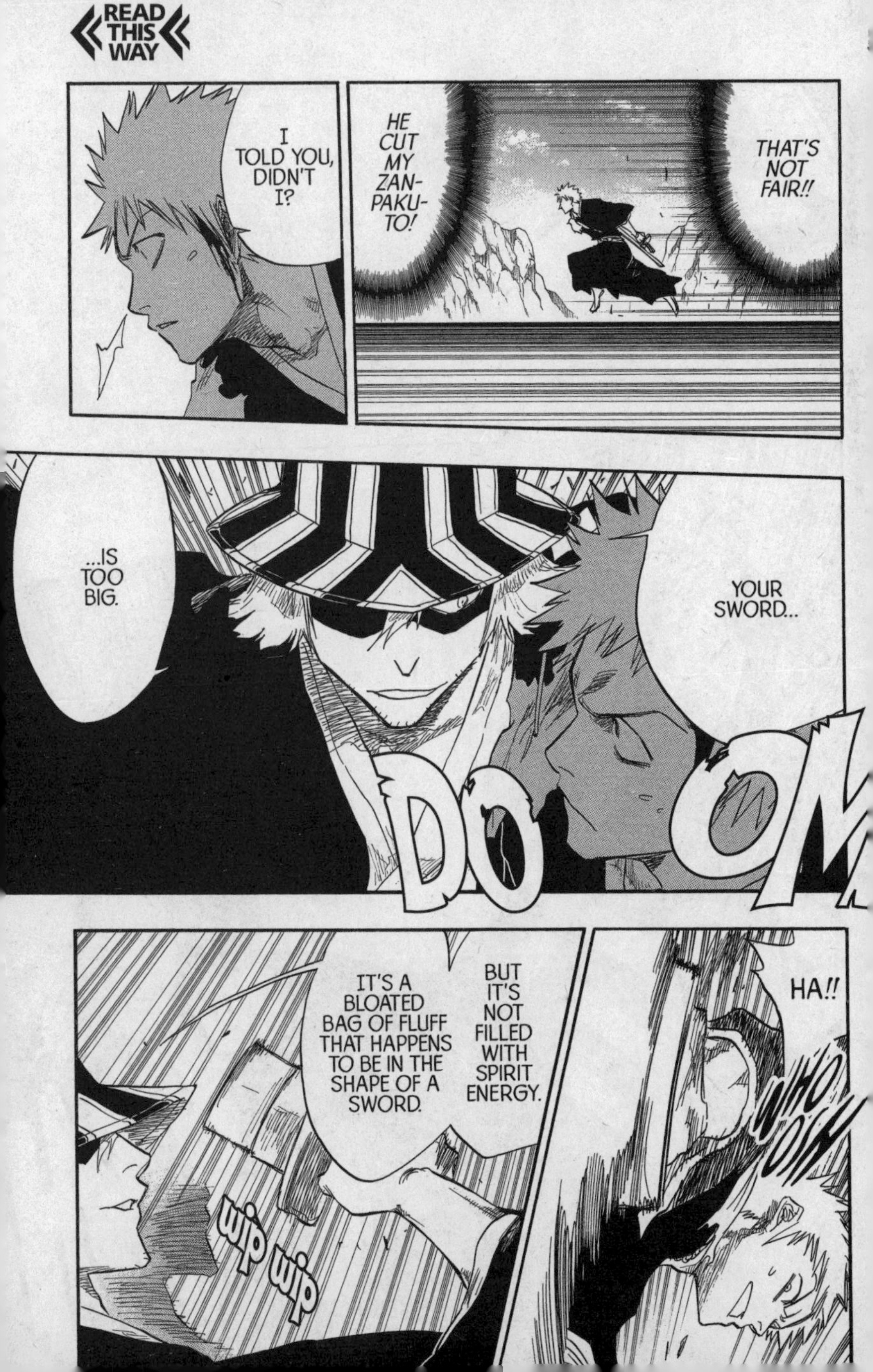
READ THIS WAY
THAT'S NOT FAIR!!
HE CUT MY ZAN-PAKU-TO!
I TOLD YOU, DIDN'T I?
YOUR SWORD...
...IS TOO BIG.
DOOM
HA!!
BUT IT'S NOT FILLED WITH SPIRIT ENERGY.
IT'S A BLOATED BAG OF FLUFF THAT HAPPENS TO BE IN THE SHAPE OF A SWORD.
wip wip

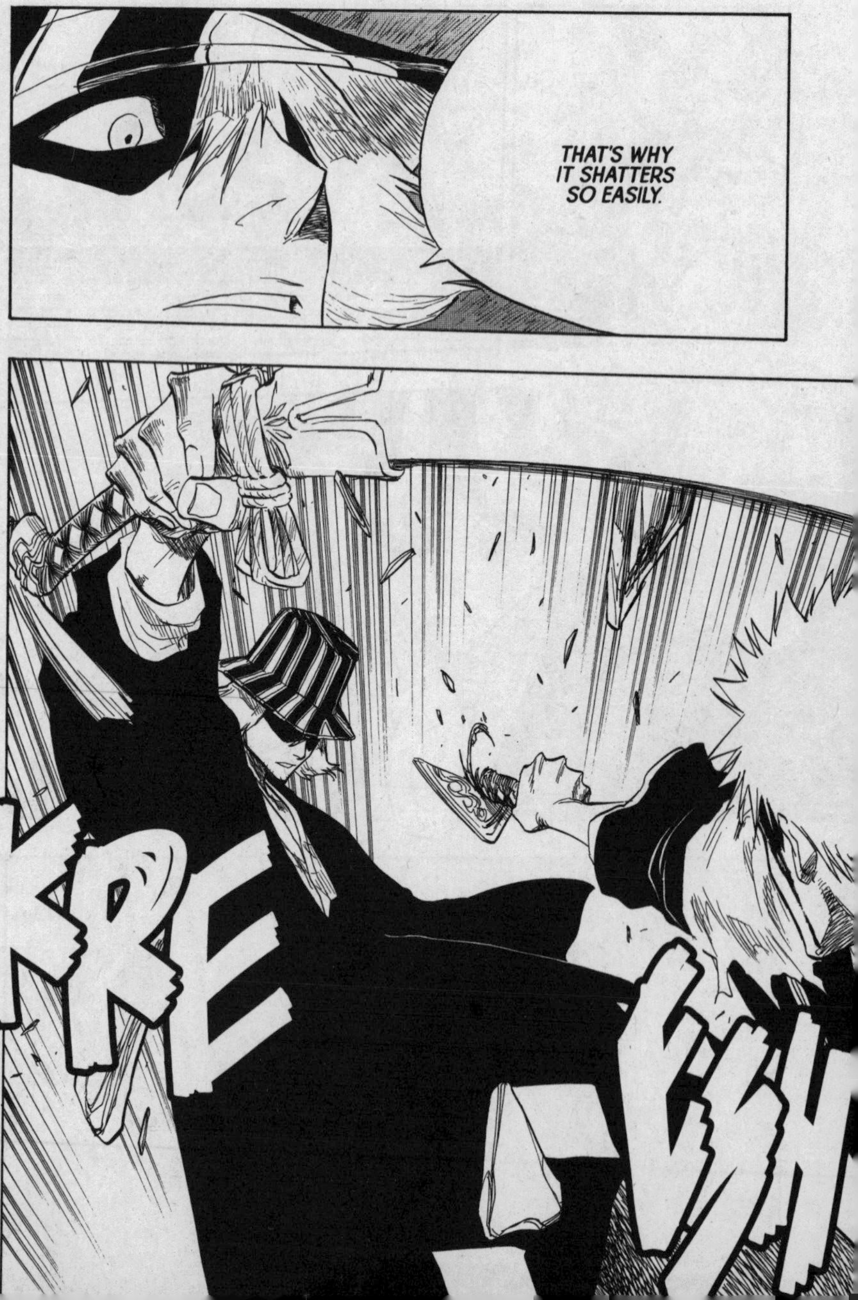
THAT'S WHY IT SHATTERS SO EASILY.

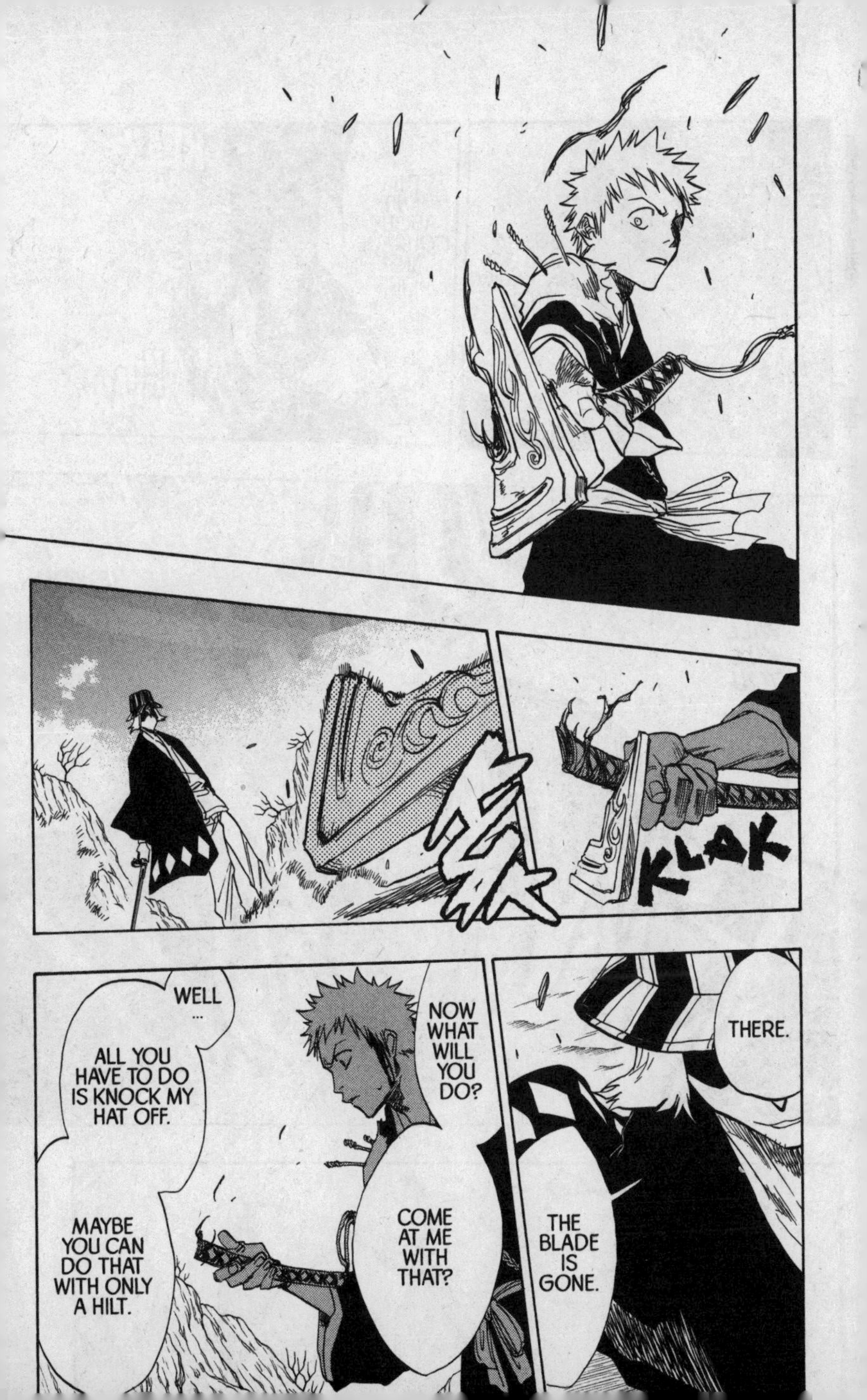
KLAK
THERE.
THE BLADE IS GONE.
NOW WHAT WILL YOU DO?
COME AT ME WITH THAT?
WELL ...
ALL YOU HAVE TO DO IS KNOCK MY HAT OFF.
MAYBE YOU CAN DO THAT WITH ONLY A HILT.

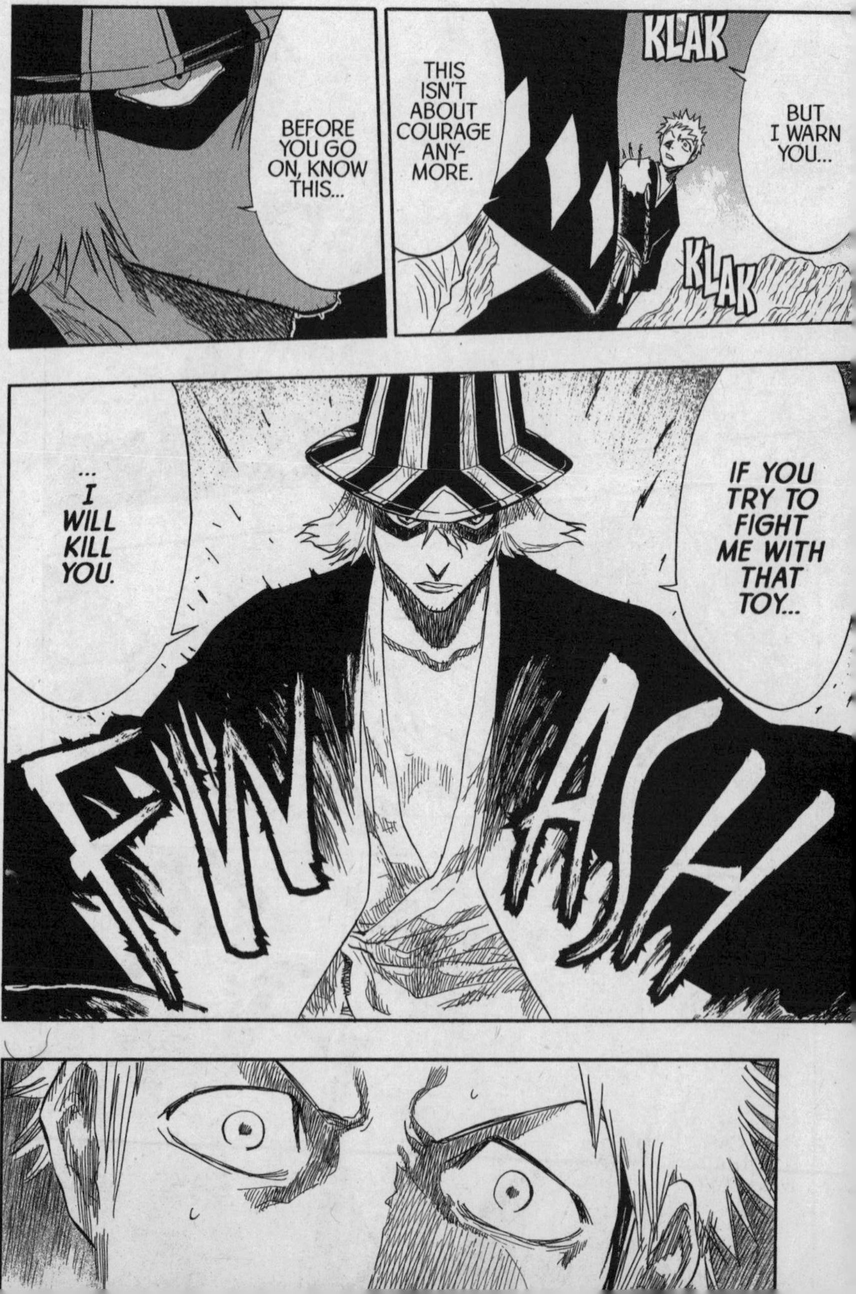
KLAK
BUT I WARN YOU...
KLAK
THIS ISN'T ABOUT COURAGE ANY-MORE.
BEFORE YOU GO ON, KNOW THIS...
IF YOU TRY TO FIGHT ME WITH THAT TOY...
FWASH
... I WILL KILL YOU.

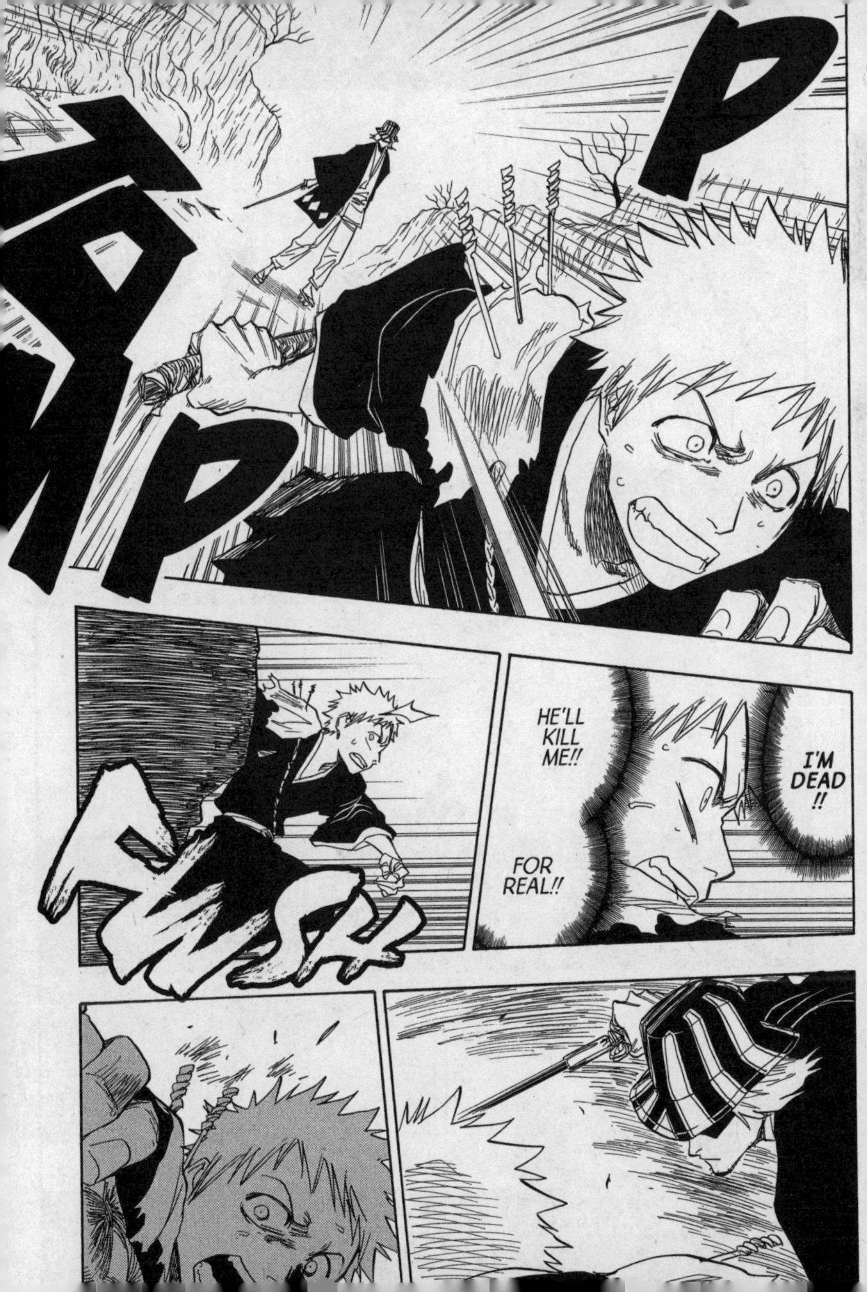
I'M DEAD !!
HE'LL KILL ME!!
FOR REAL!!

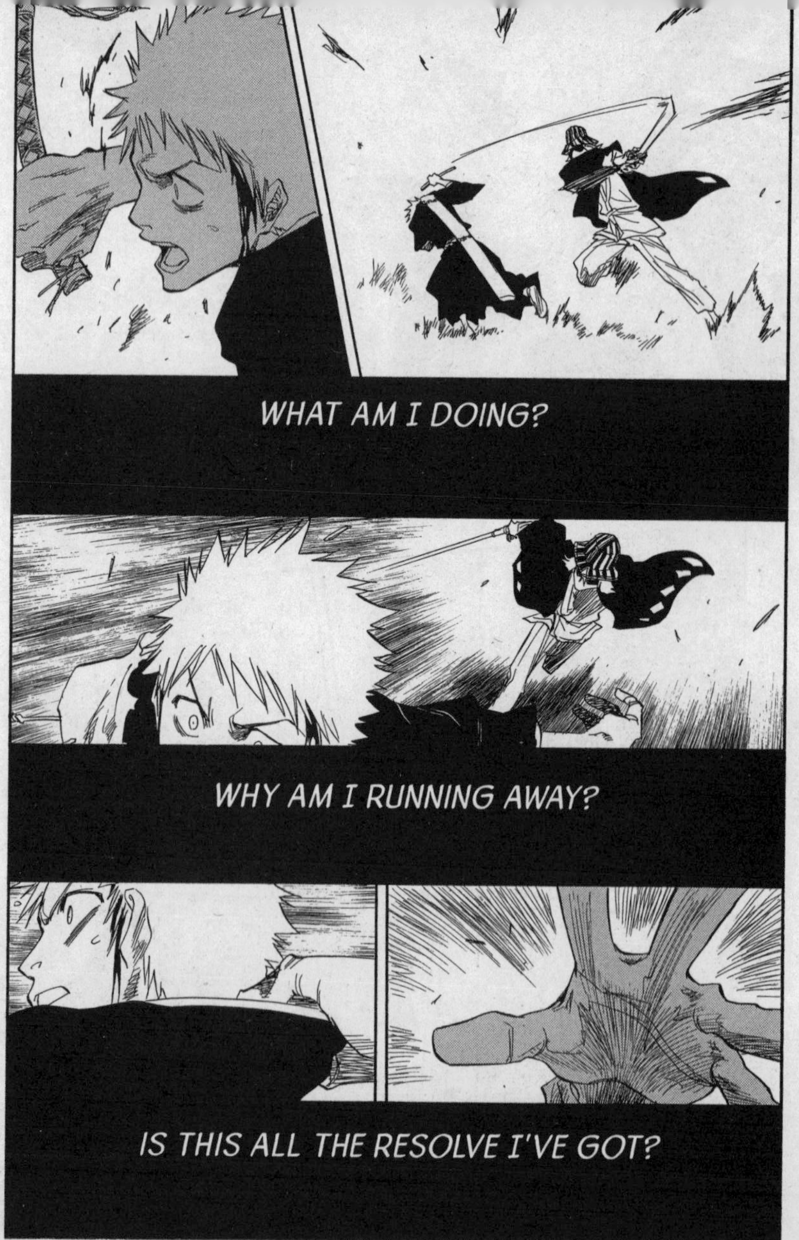
WHAT AM I DOING?
WHY AM I RUNNING AWAY?
IS THIS ALL THE RESOLVE I'VE GOT?

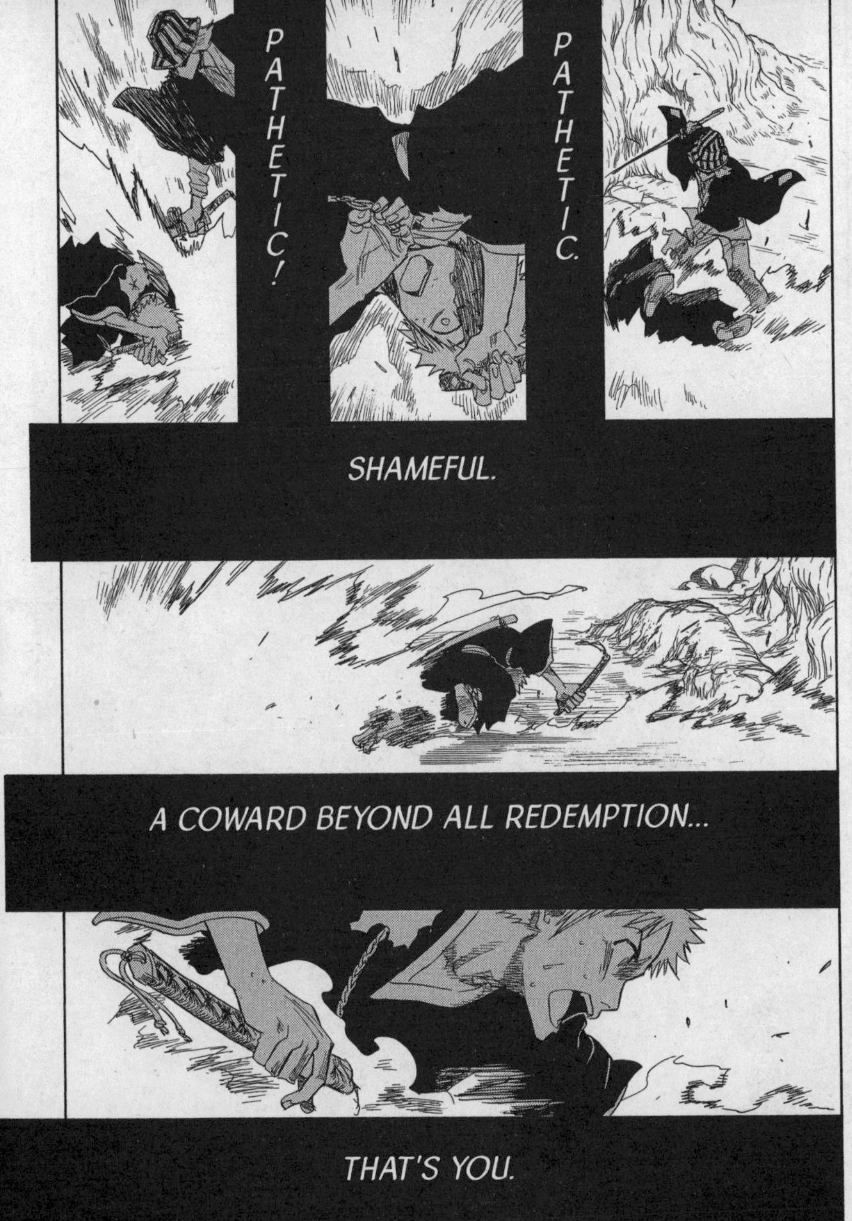
PATHETIC.
PATHETIC!
SHAMEFUL.
A COWARD BEYOND ALL REDEMPTION...
THAT'S YOU.

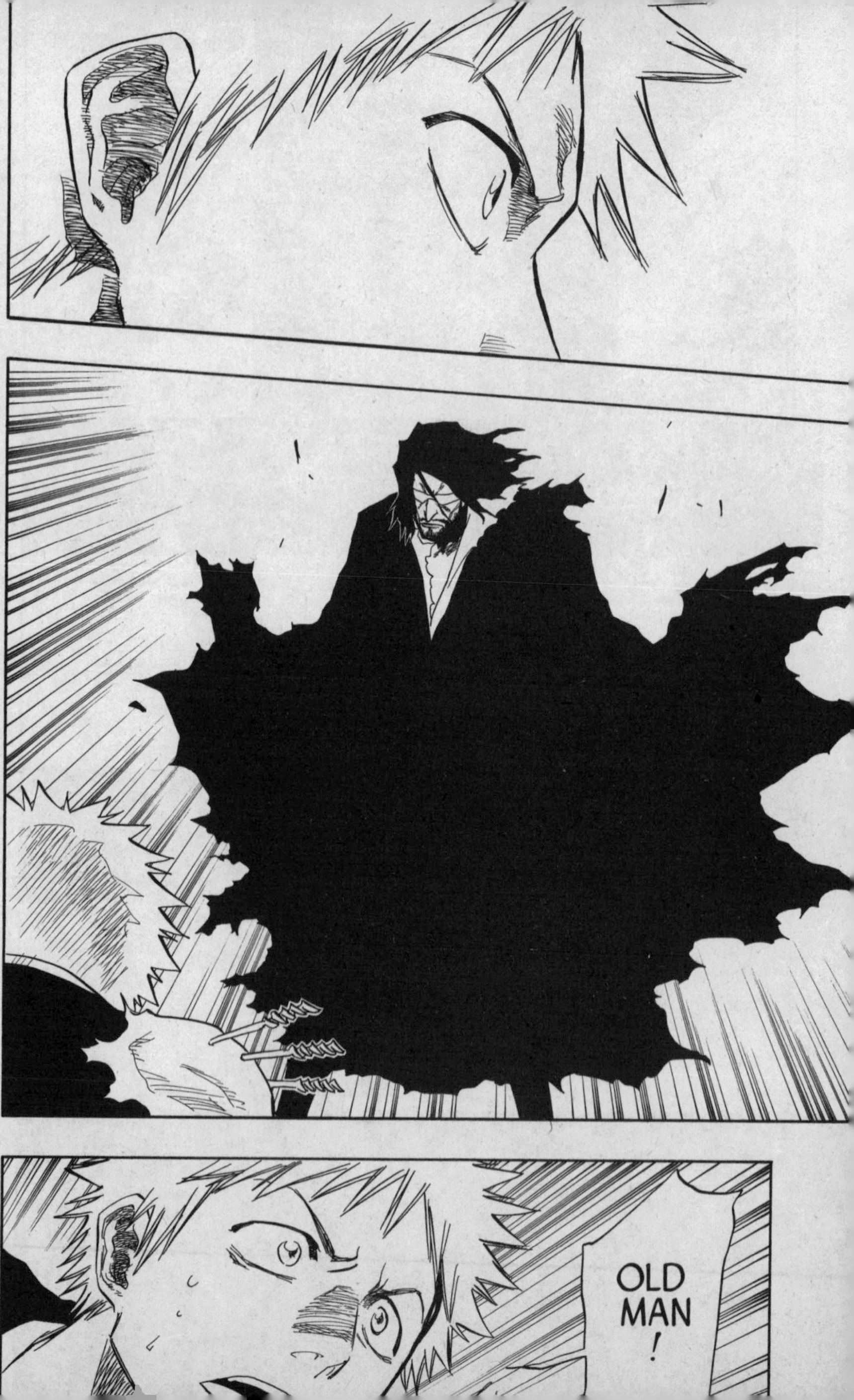
OLD MAN!

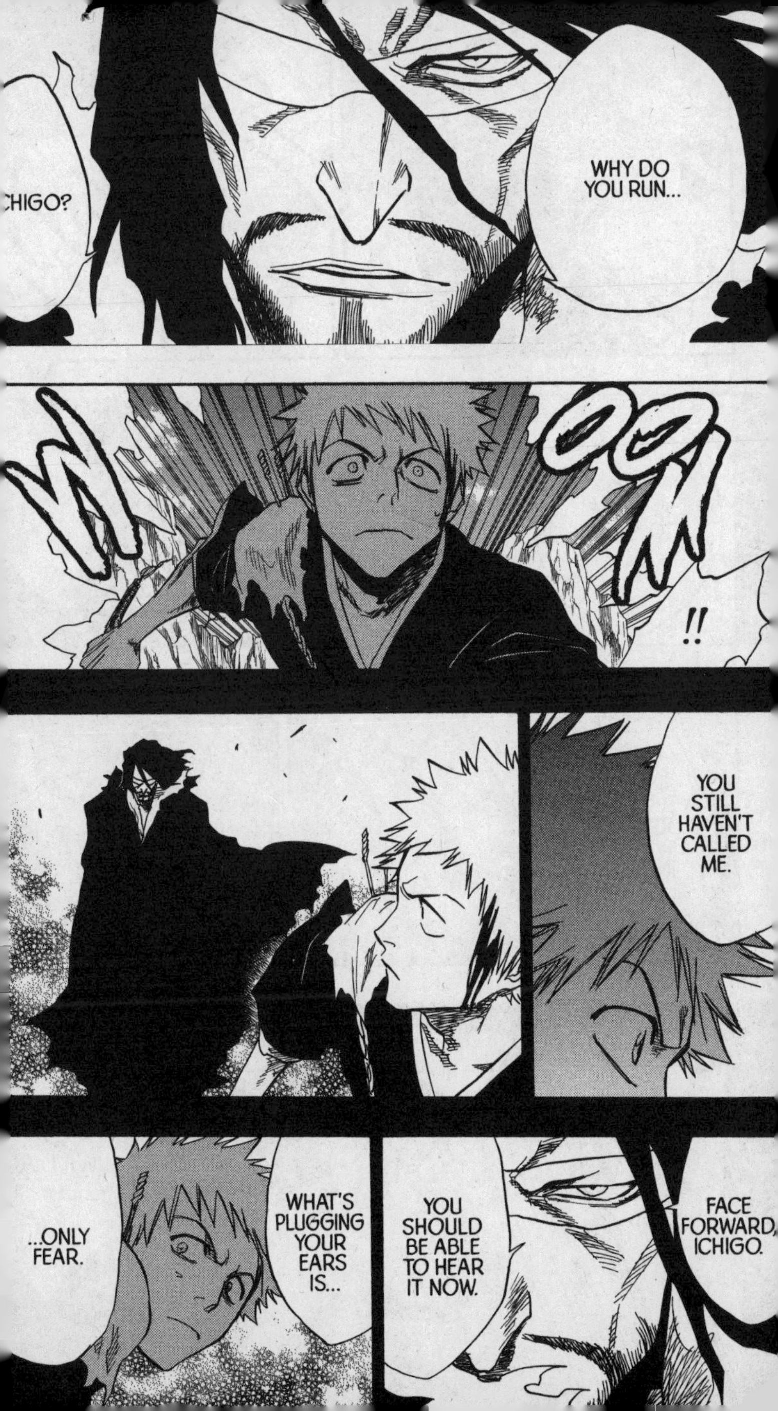
WHY DO YOU RUN...
CHIGO?
!!
YOU STILL HAVEN'T CALLED ME.
FACE FORWARD, ICHIGO.
YOU SHOULD BE ABLE TO HEAR IT NOW.
WHAT'S PLUGGING YOUR EARS IS...
...ONLY FEAR.

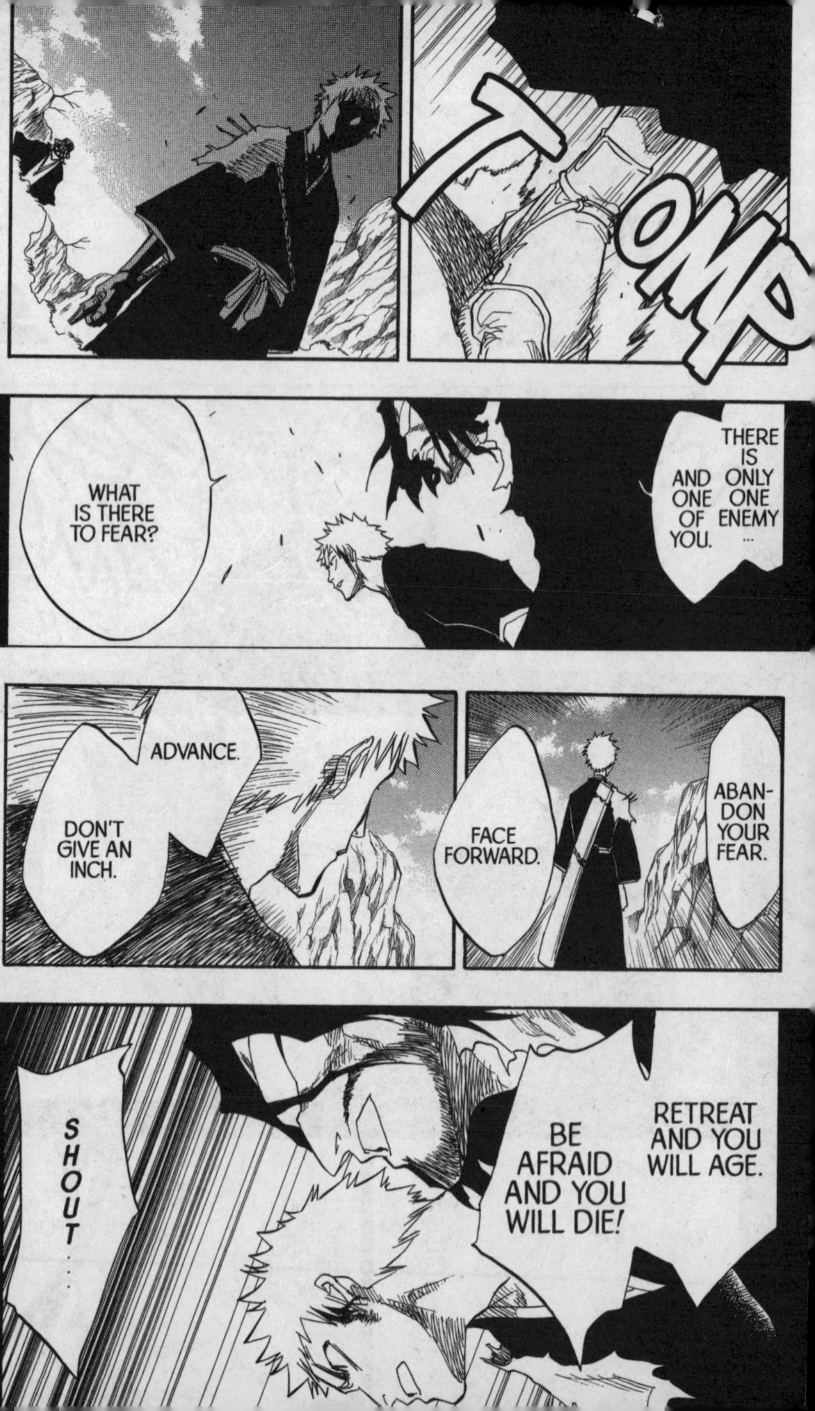
TOMP
THERE IS ONLY ONE ENEMY ...
AND ONE OF YOU.
WHAT IS THERE TO FEAR?
ABAN-DON YOUR FEAR.
FACE FORWARD.
ADVANCE.
DON'T GIVE AN INCH.
RETREAT AND YOU WILL AGE.
BE AFRAID AND YOU WILL DIE!
SHOUT...

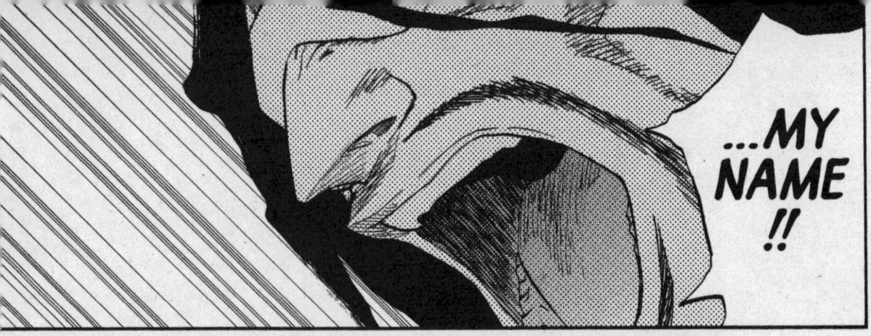
...MY NAME !!
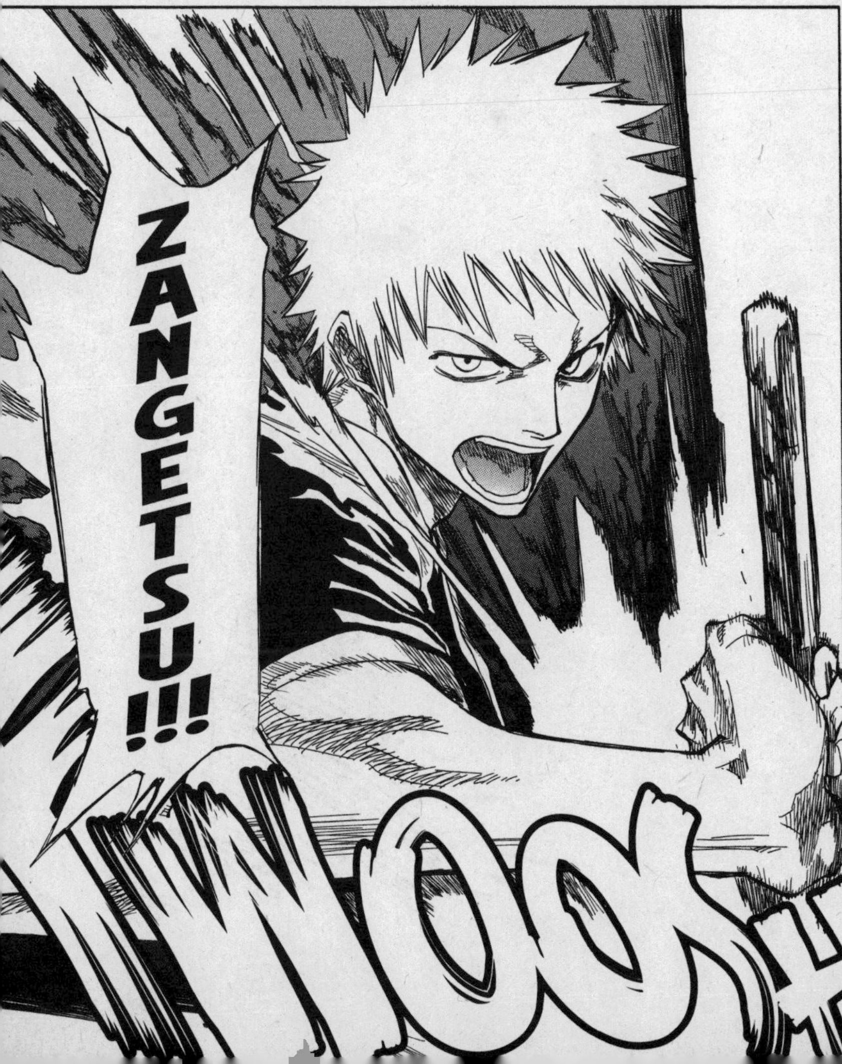
ZANGETSU!!!
WOOSH

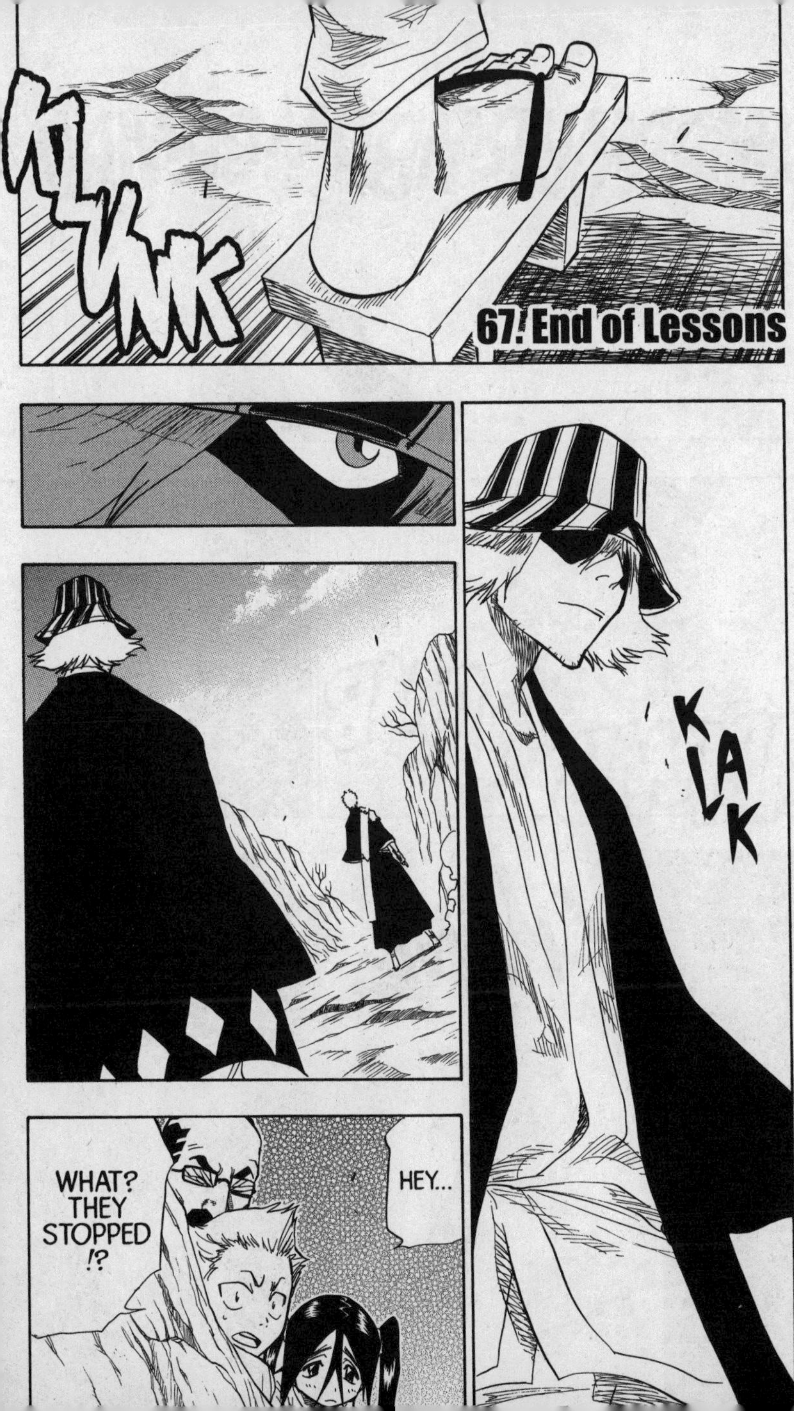
KLUNK
67. End of Lessons
KLAK
HEY...
WHAT? THEY STOPPED !?

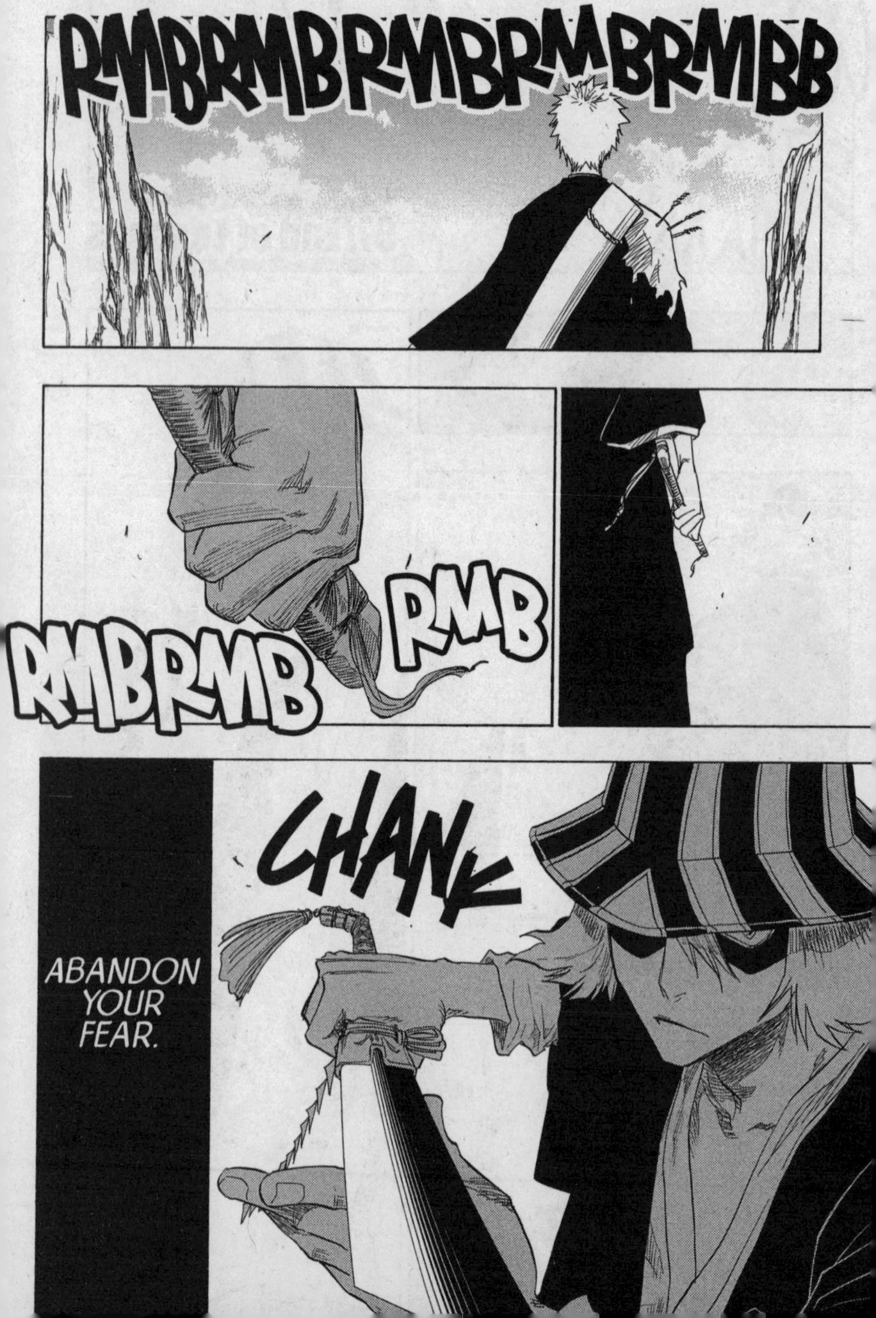
RMBRMBRMBRMBRMBB
RMB
RMBRMB
CHANK
ABANDON YOUR FEAR.

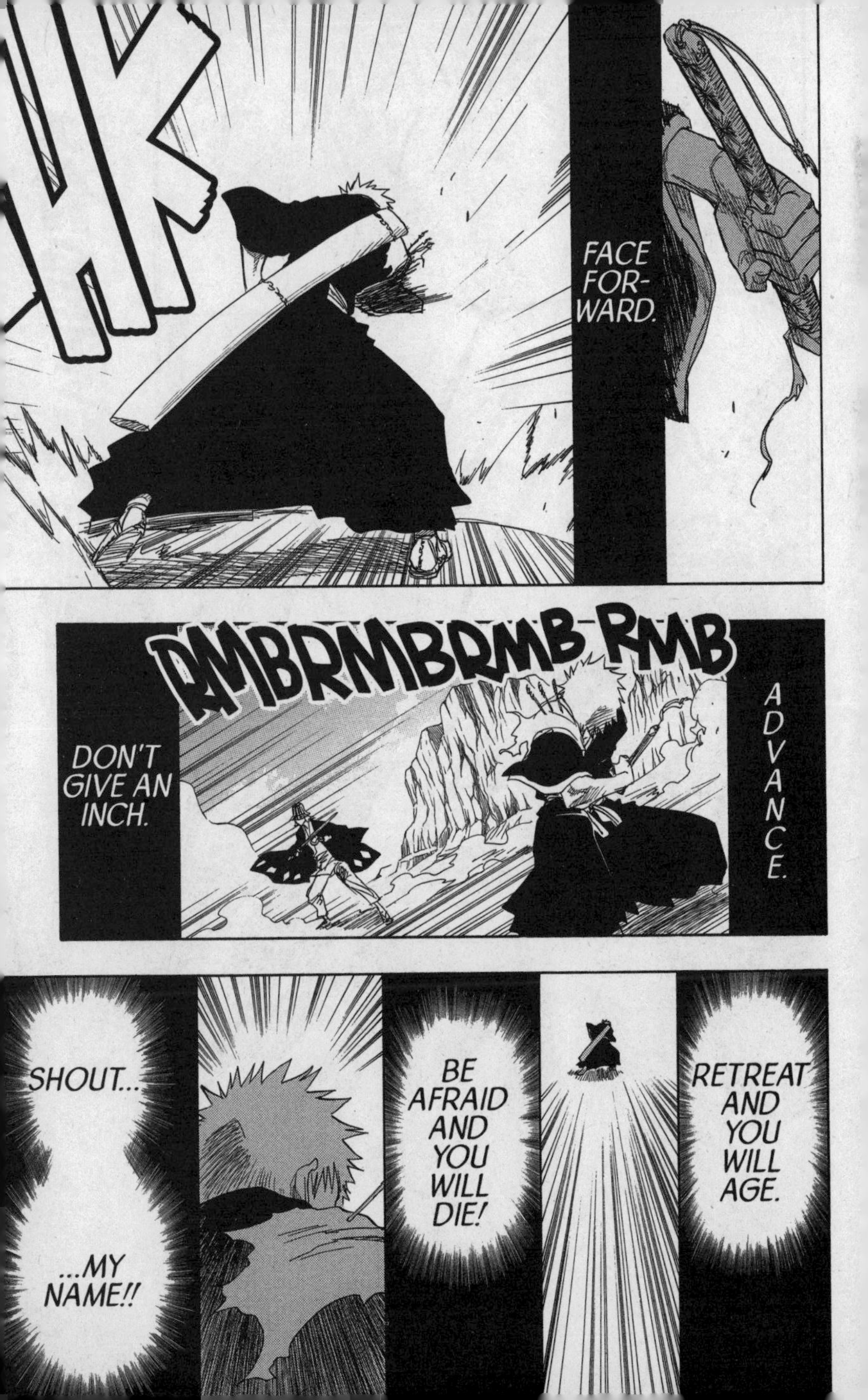
FACE FOR-WARD.
RMBRMBRMB RMB
ADVANCE.
DON'T GIVE AN INCH.
RETREAT AND YOU WILL AGE.
BE AFRAID AND YOU WILL DIE!
SHOUT...
...MY NAME!!

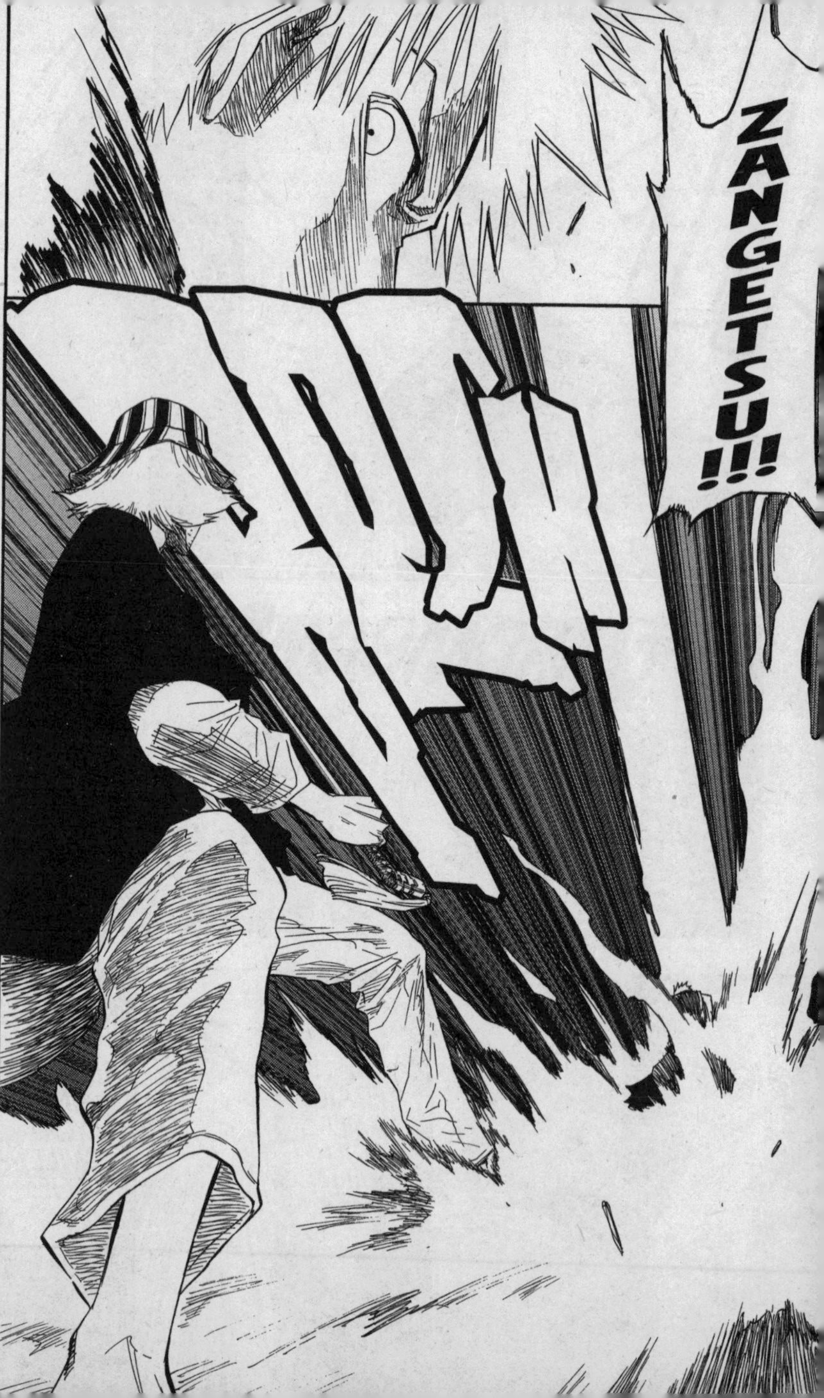
ZANGETSU!!!

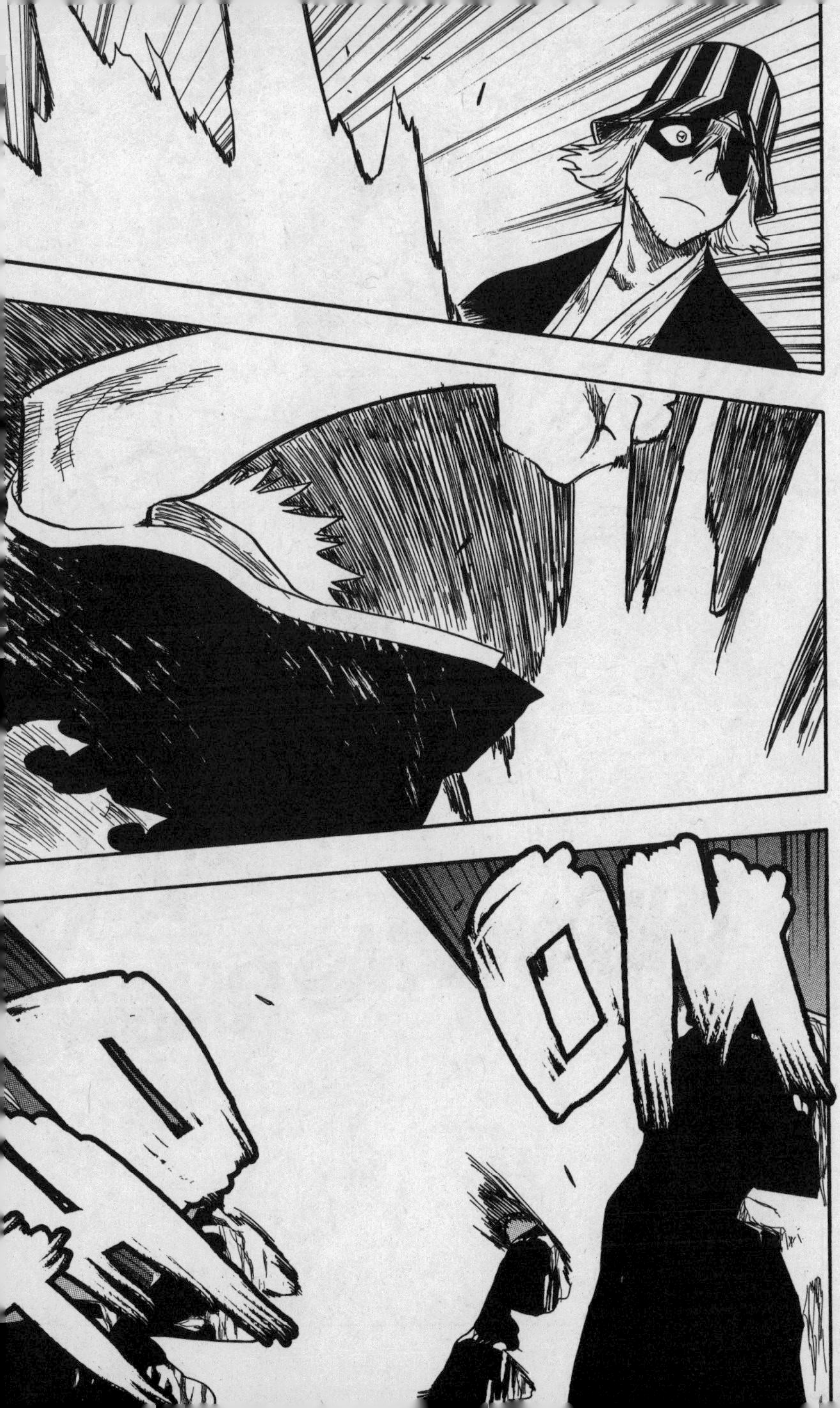

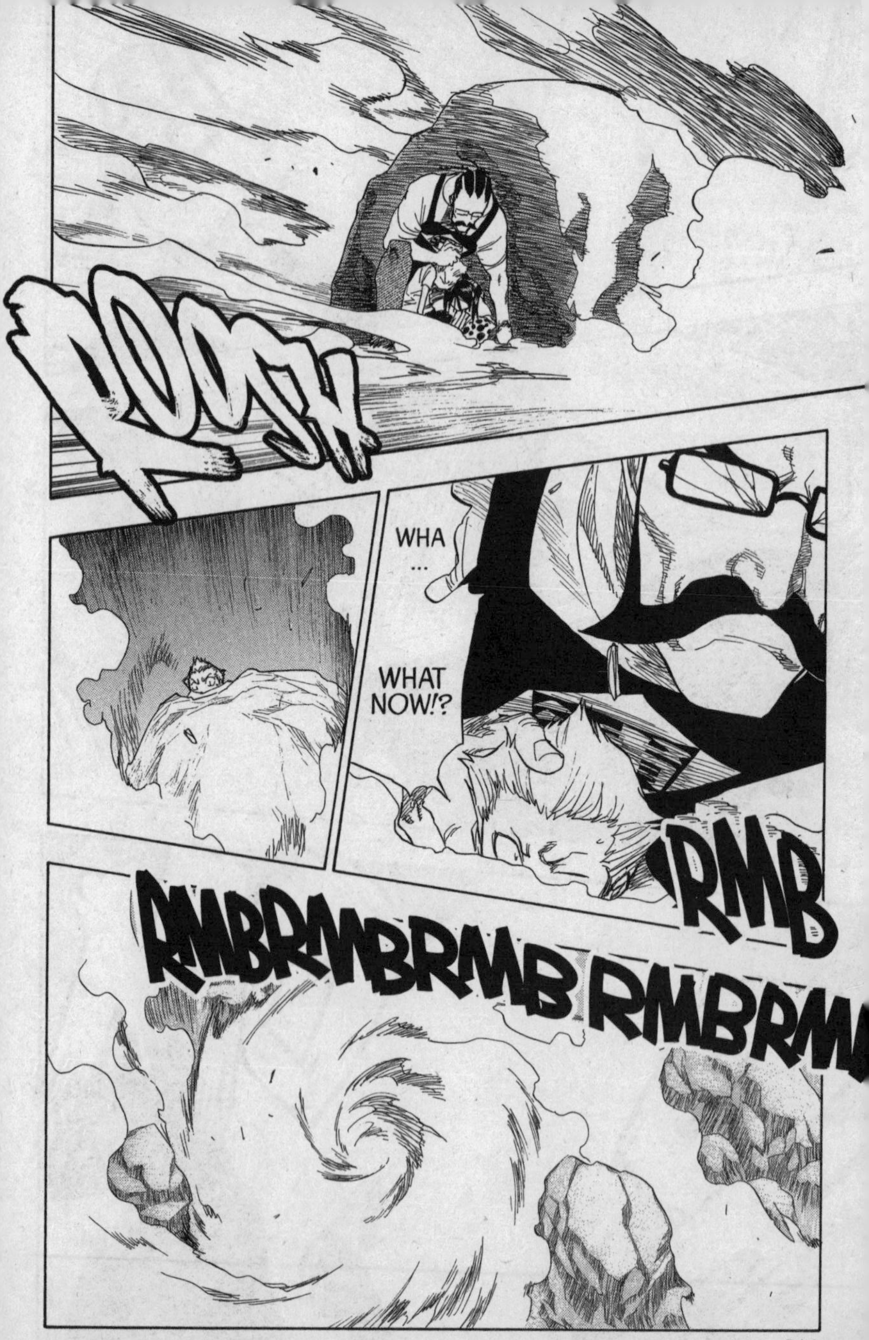
DOOSH
WHA ...
WHAT NOW!?
RMB
RMBRMBRMB RMBRM

RRMMBB

RRMMBB

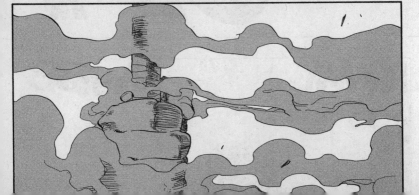

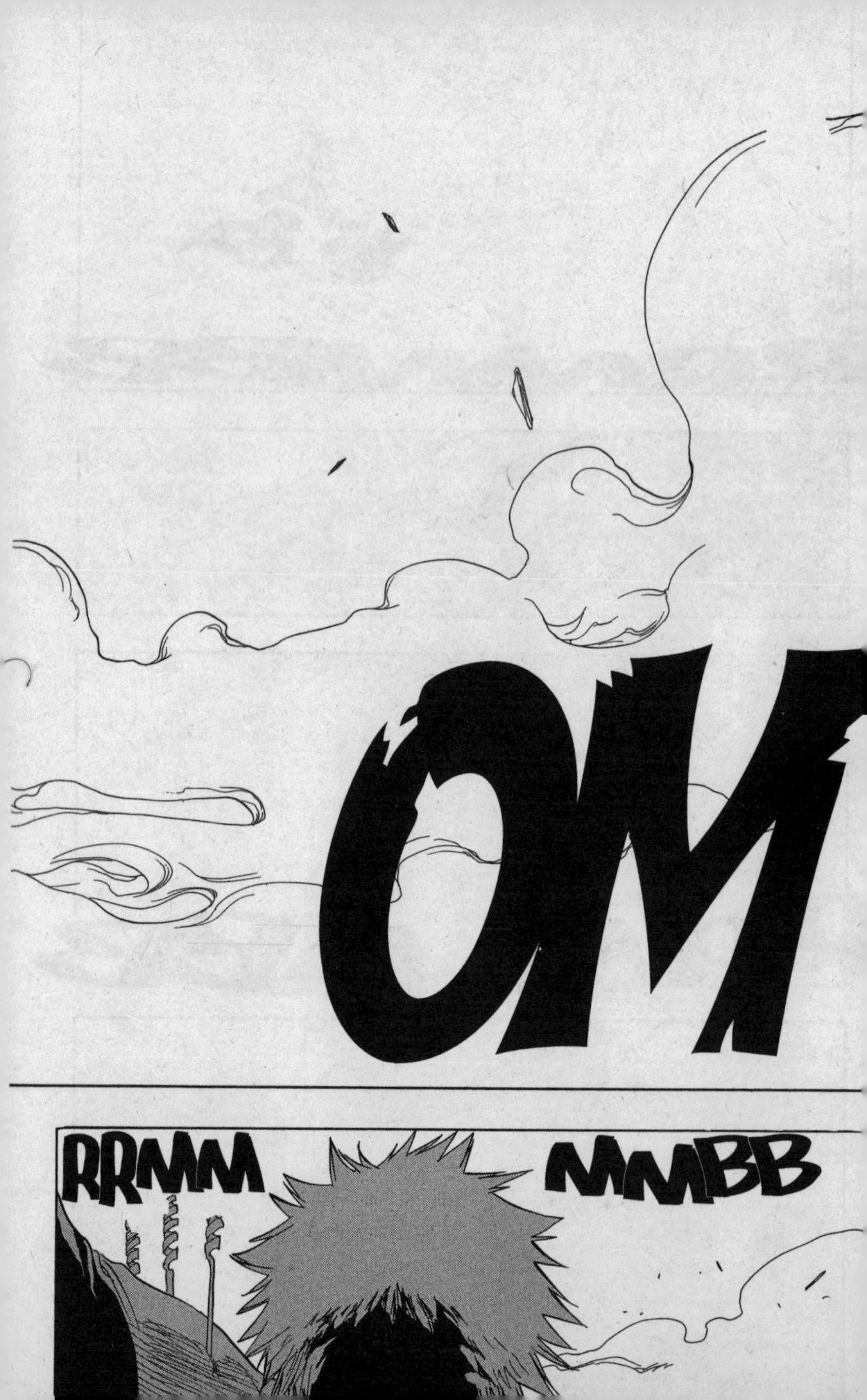
OM
RRMMM
MMBB

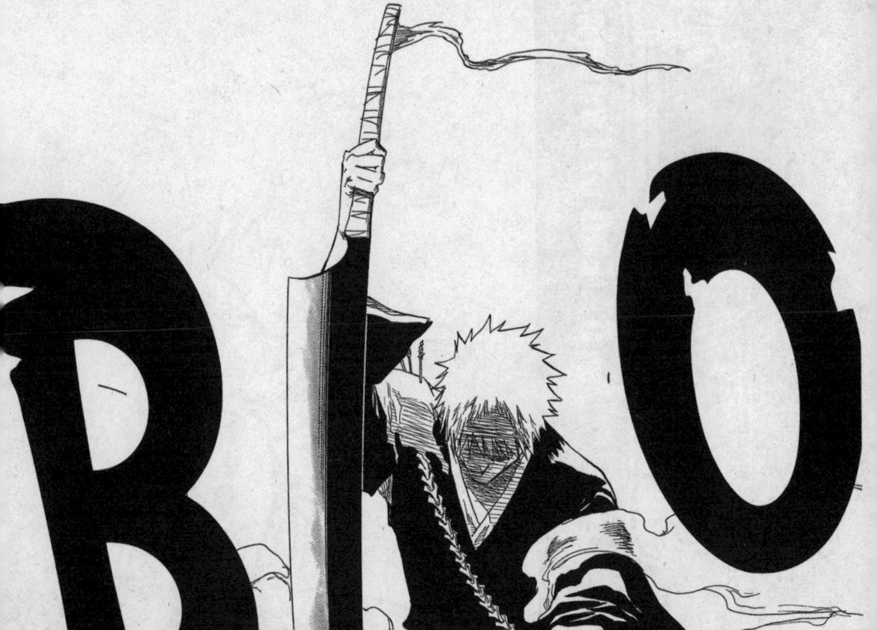
BO

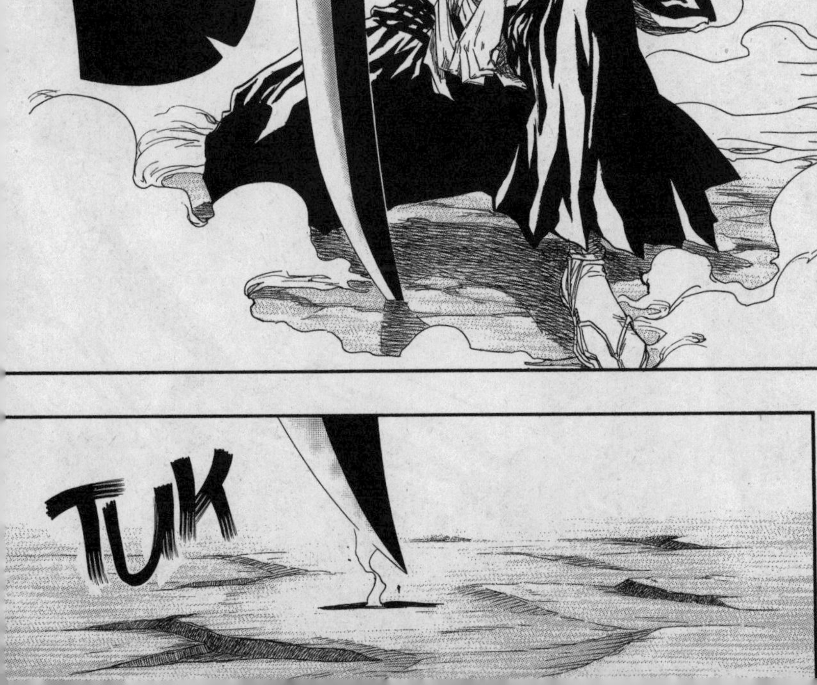
TUK

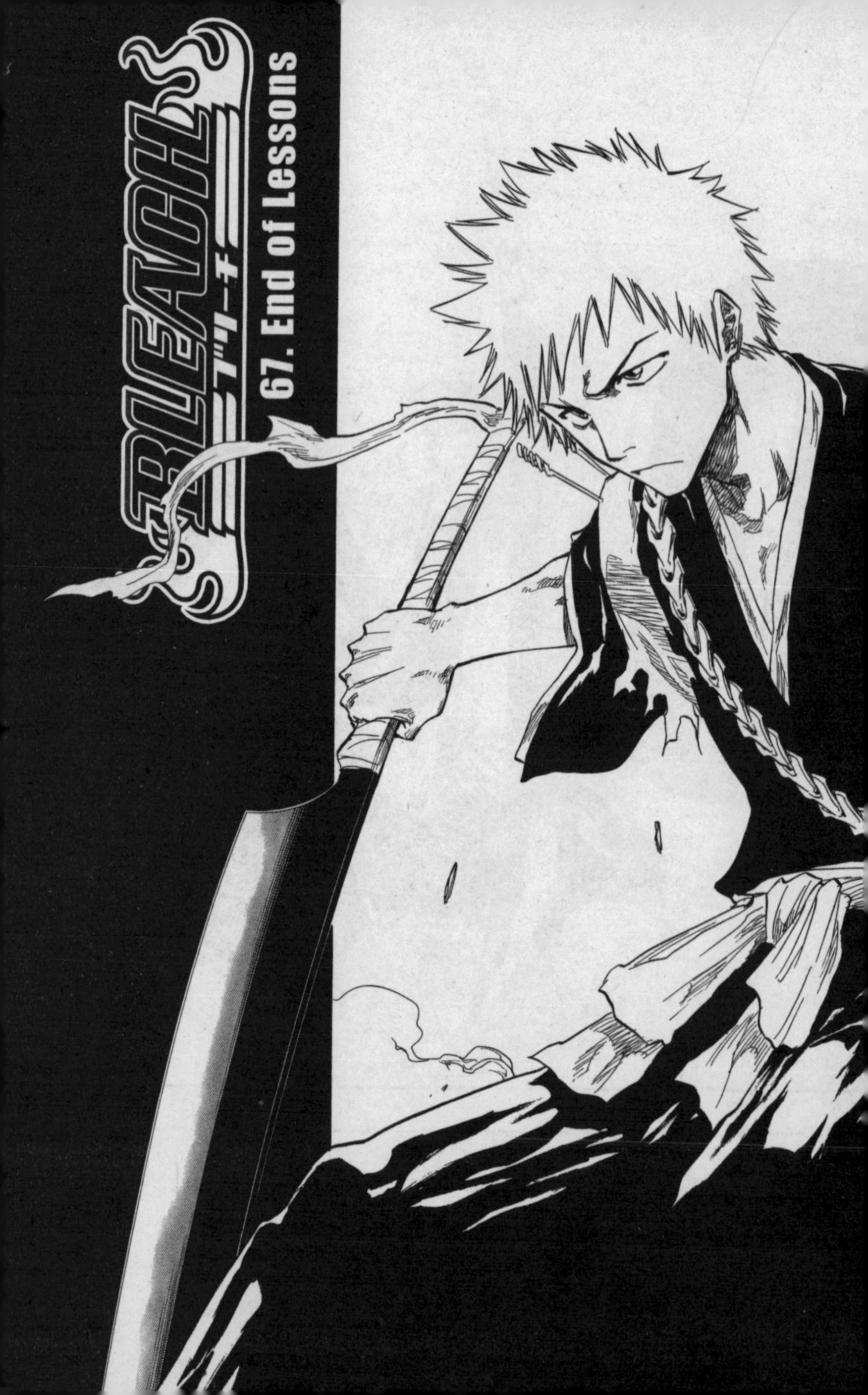
BLEACH
ブリーチ
67. End of Lessons

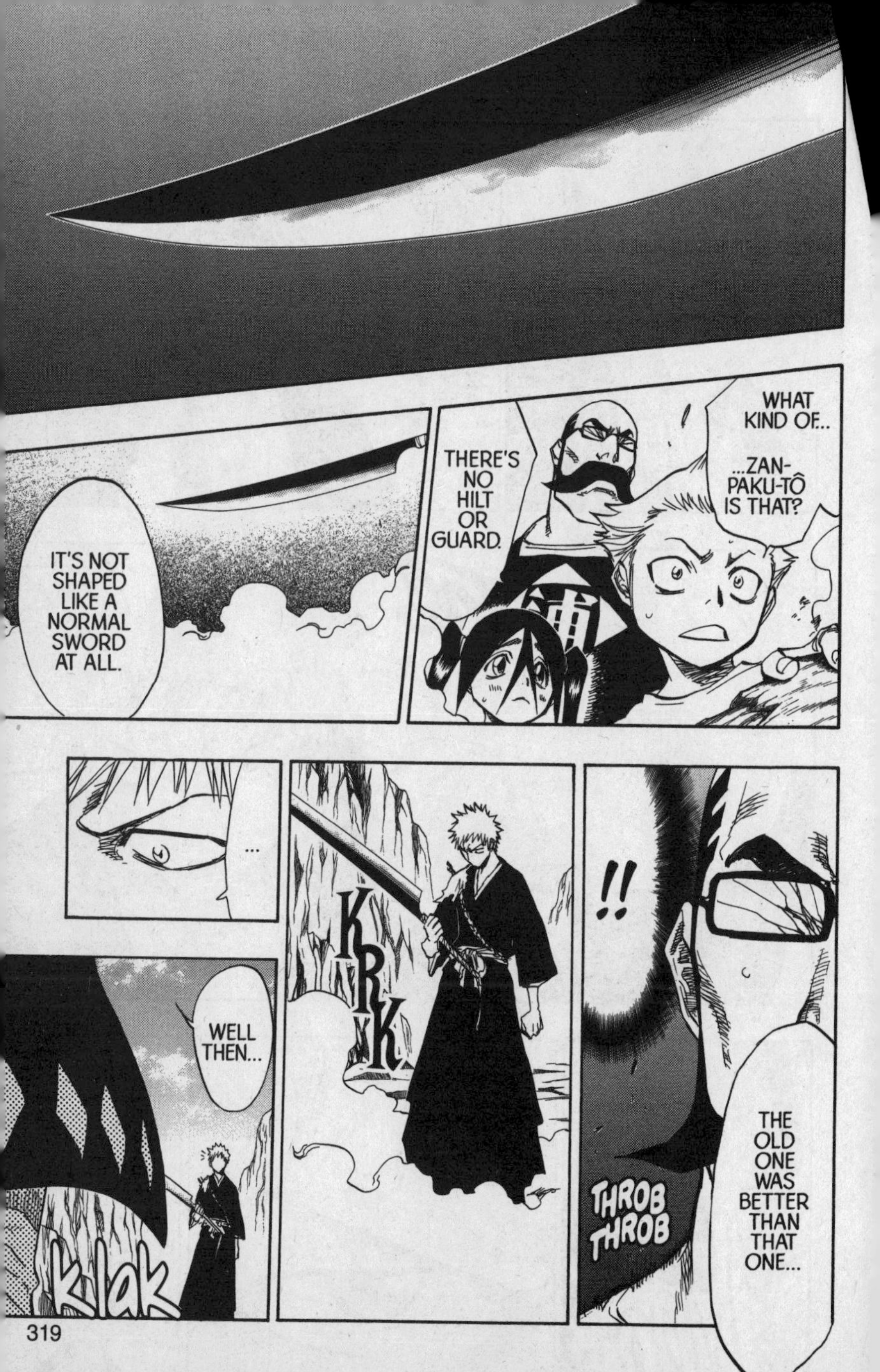
WHAT KIND OF...
...ZAN-PAKU-TÔ IS THAT?
THERE'S NO HILT OR GUARD.
IT'S NOT SHAPED LIKE A NORMAL SWORD AT ALL.
!!
...
KRK
THE OLD ONE WAS BETTER THAN THAT ONE...
THROB THROB
WELL THEN...
klak

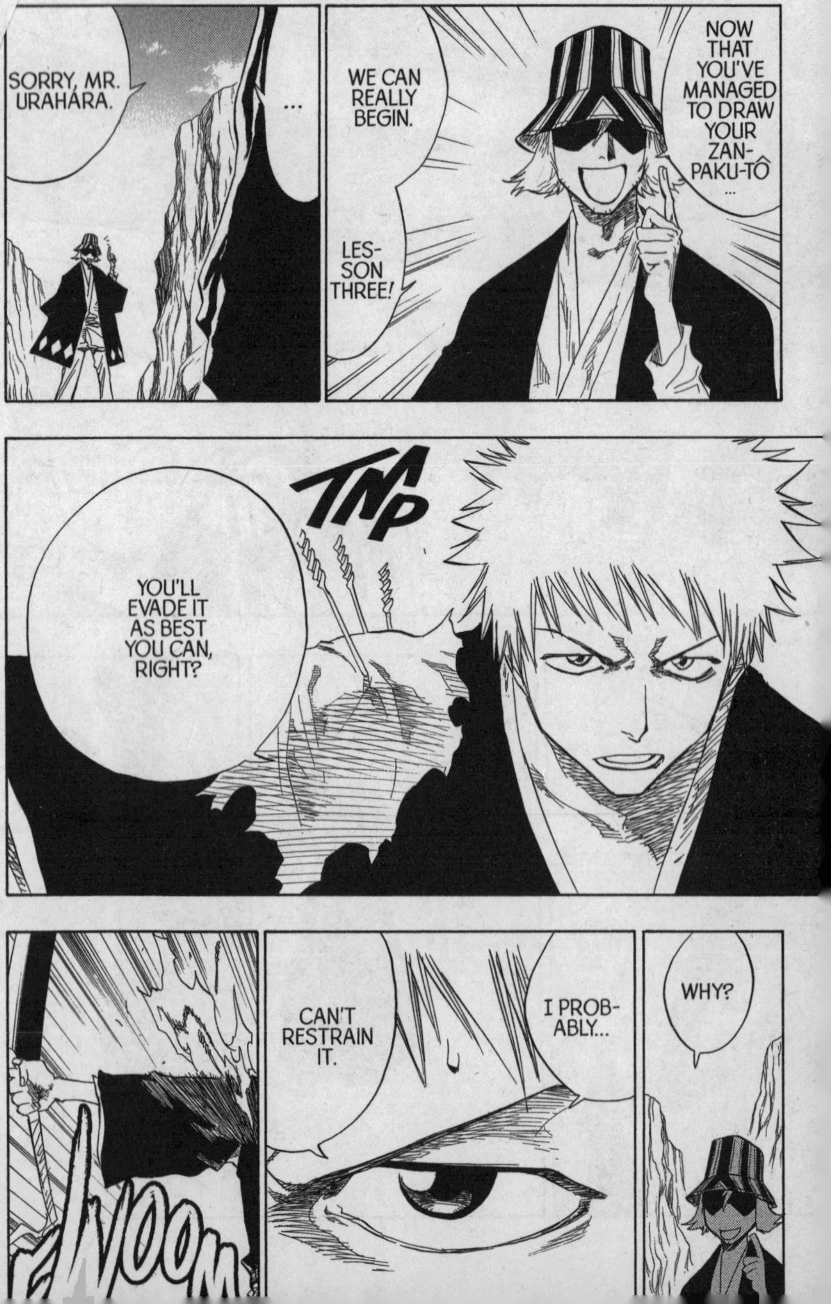
NOW THAT YOU'VE MANAGED TO DRAW YOUR ZAN-PAKU-TÔ...
WE CAN REALLY BEGIN.
LES-SON THREE!
...
SORRY, MR. URAHARA.
TMP
YOU'LL EVADE IT AS BEST YOU CAN, RIGHT?
WHY?
I PROB-ABLY...
CAN'T RESTRAIN IT.
VOOM

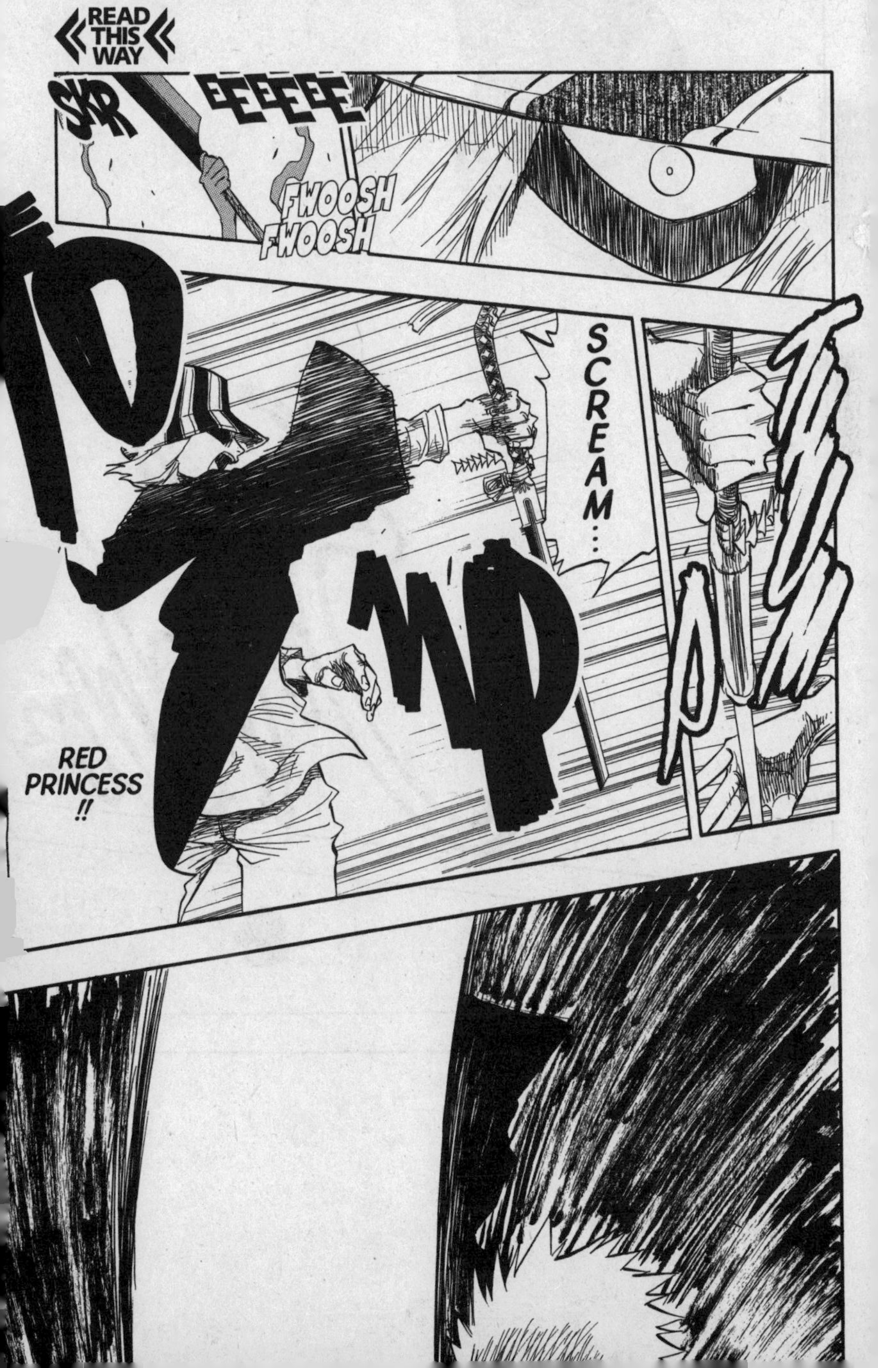
READ THIS WAY
SKREEEEEE
FWOOSH FWOOSH
SCREAM...
RED PRINCESS!!

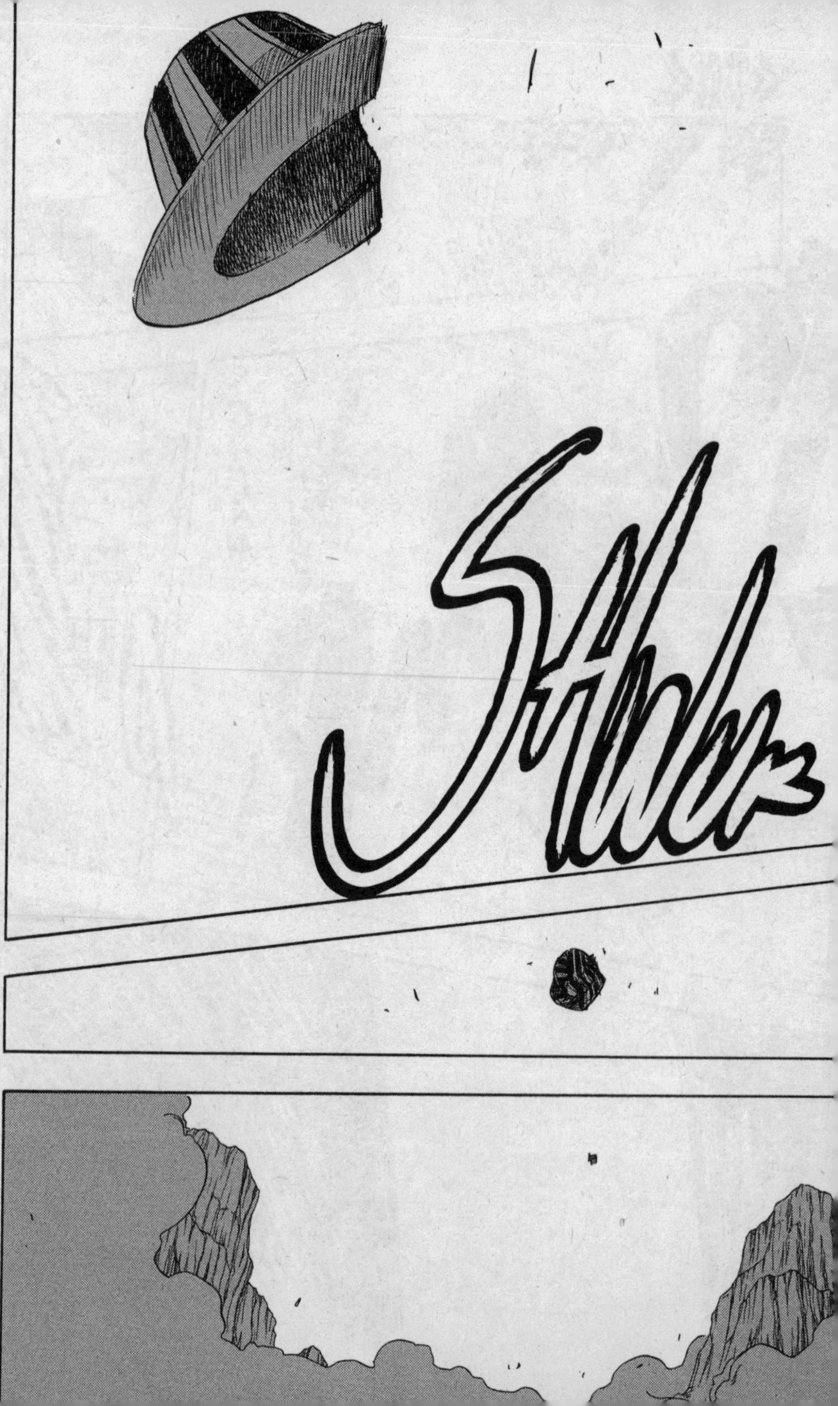

READ THIS WAY

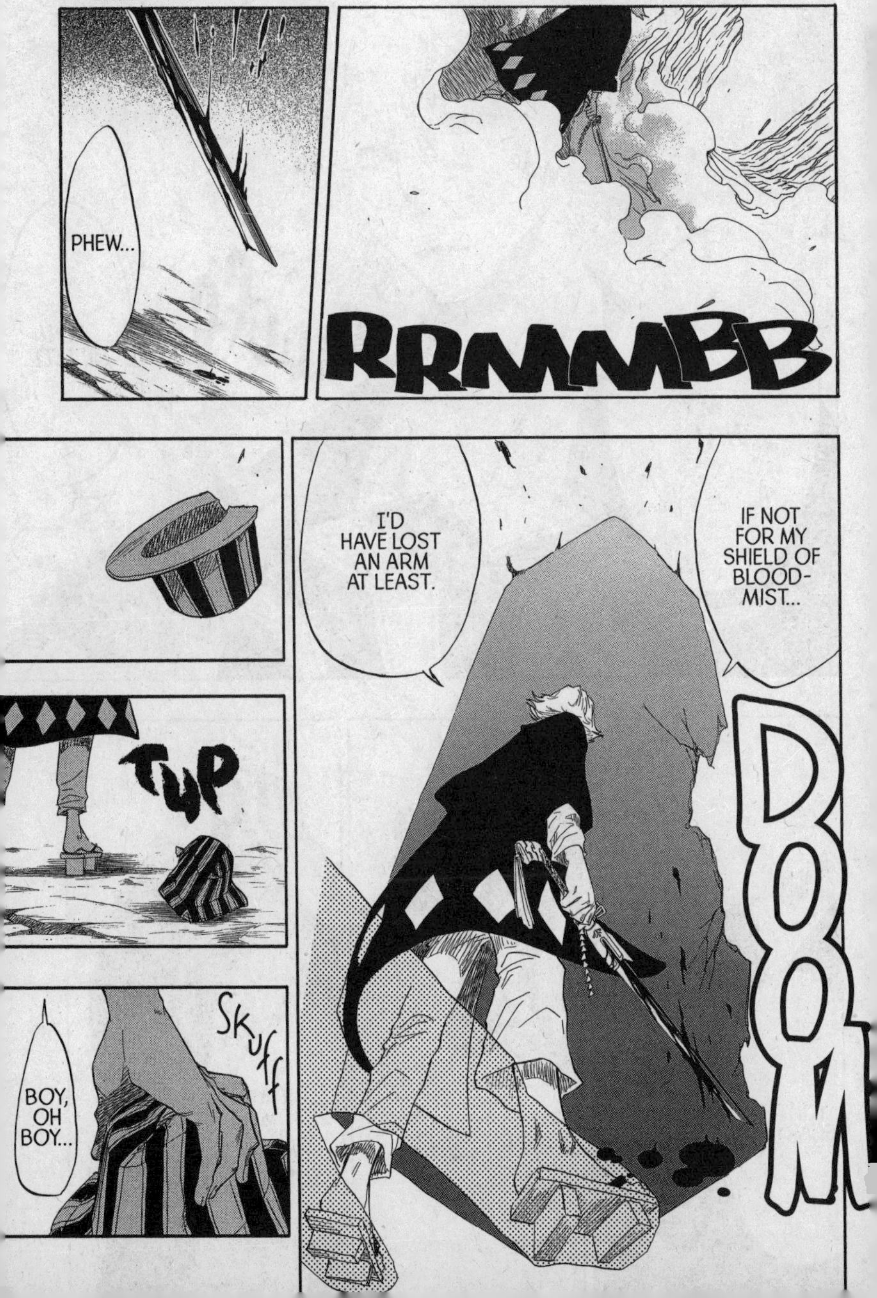

RRMMBB
PHEW...
IF NOT FOR MY SHIELD OF BLOOD-MIST...
I'D HAVE LOST AN ARM AT LEAST.
DOOM
TUP
SKUFF
BOY, OH BOY...

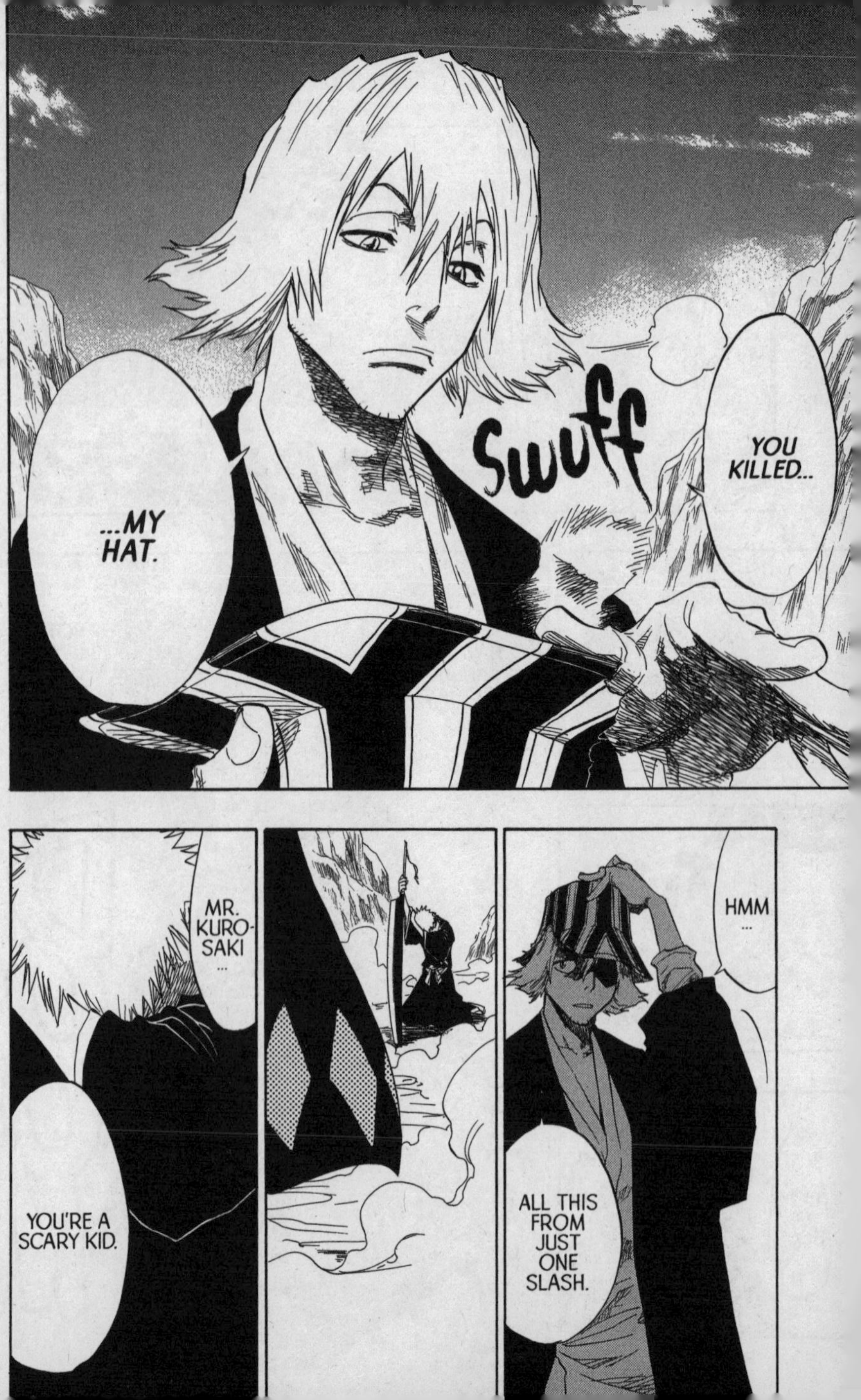
YOU KILLED...
Swuff
...MY HAT.
HMM ...
ALL THIS FROM JUST ONE SLASH.
MR. KURO-SAKI ...
YOU'RE A SCARY KID.

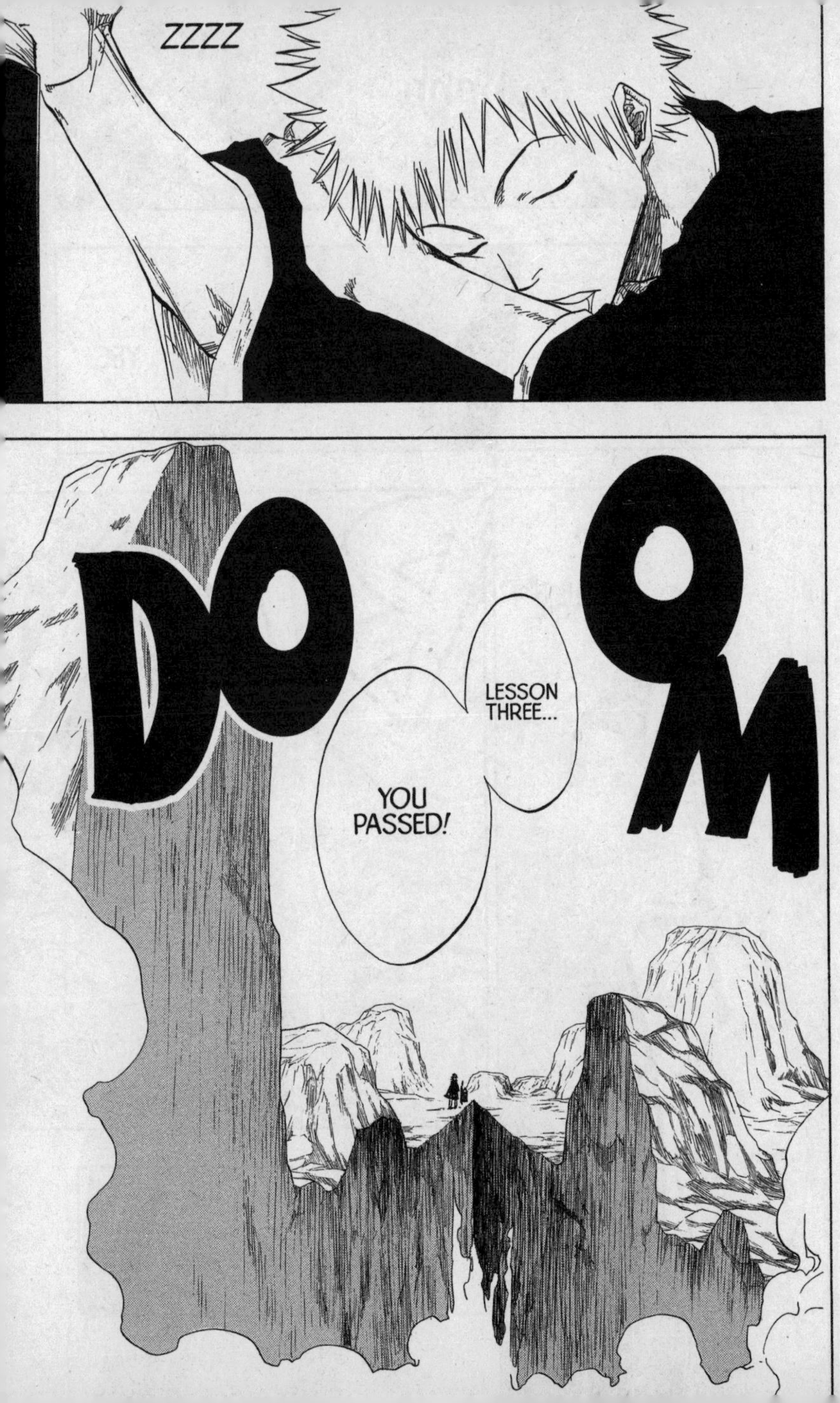
ZZZZ
DOOM
LESSON THREE...
YOU PASSED!

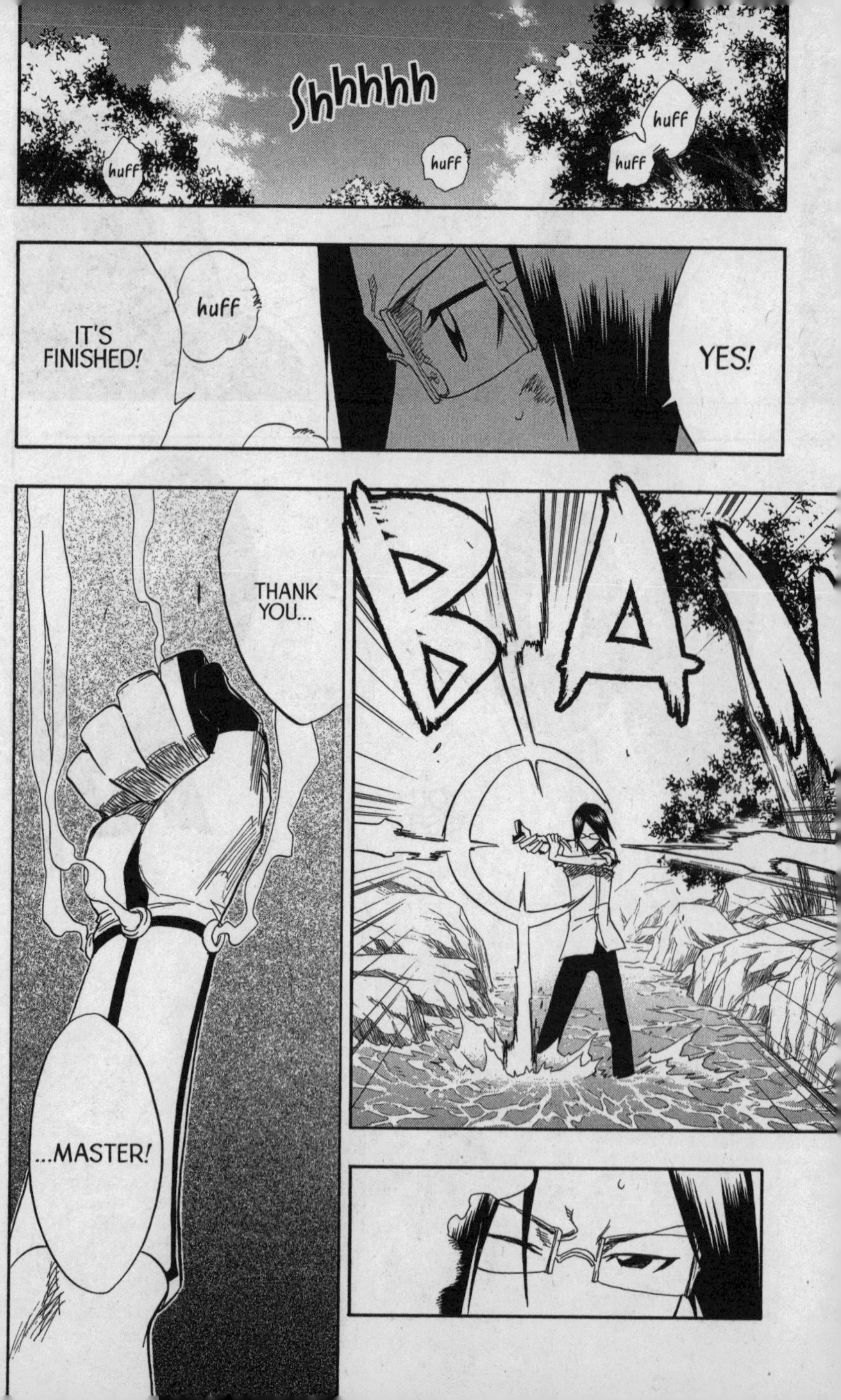
Shhhhh
huff
huff
huff
huff
YES!
huff
IT'S FINISHED!
BAN
THANK YOU...
...MASTER!

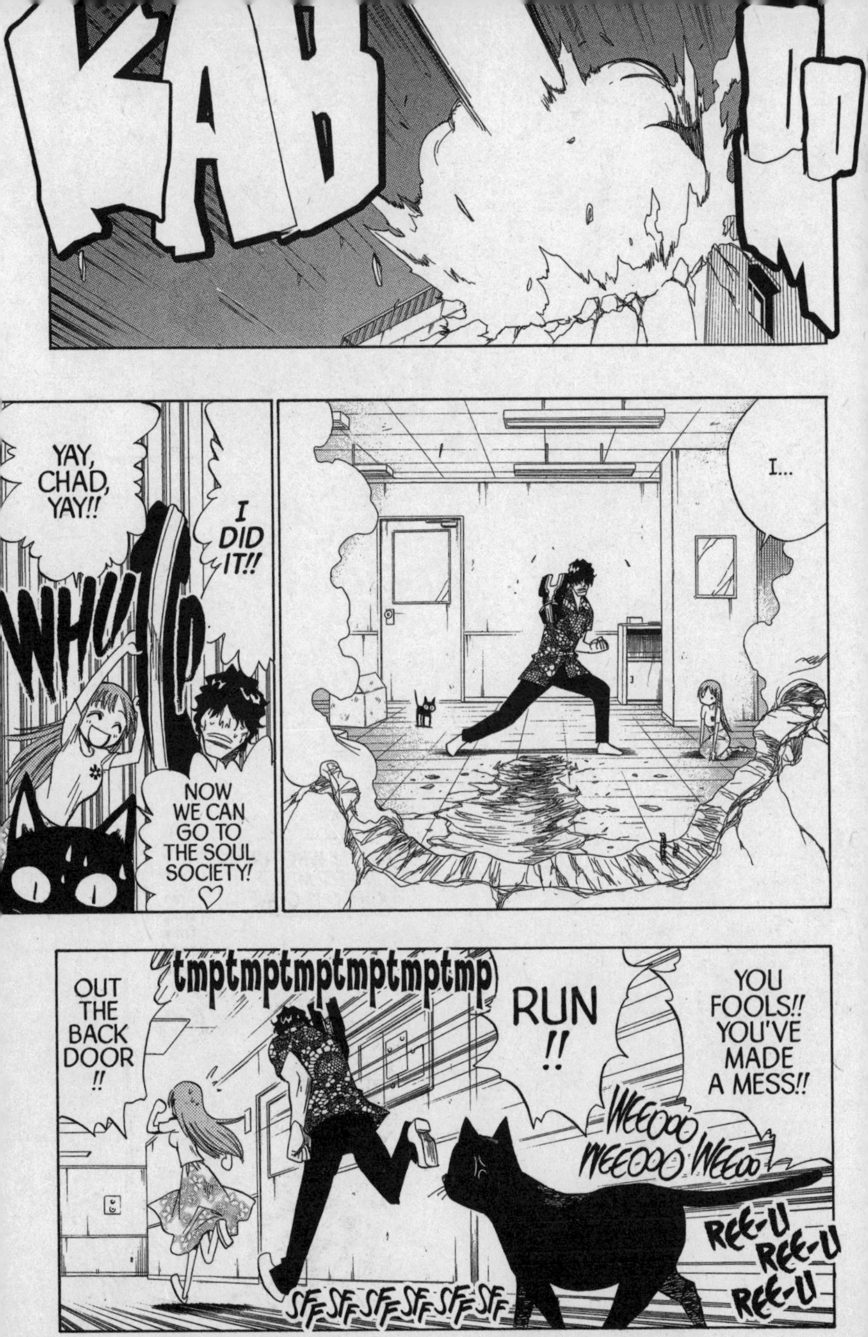
KABOOM
I...
YAY, CHAD, YAY!!
I DID IT!!
WHUMP
NOW WE CAN GO TO THE SOUL SOCIETY! ♡
YOU FOOLS!! YOU'VE MADE A MESS!!
RUN!!
OUT THE BACK DOOR!!
tmptmptmptmptmptmp
WEEOOO WEEOOO WEEOO
REE-U REE-U REE-U
SFF SFF SFF SFF SFF SFF

PEOPLE WHO ARE
IN DEEP MUD IF
ICHIGO IS GONE

I ran
away
from
home to
escape
from

But if I
have to
sleep
out
on the
street
much
longer,
I'll be
a dirty
rag!

68. The Last Summer Vacation

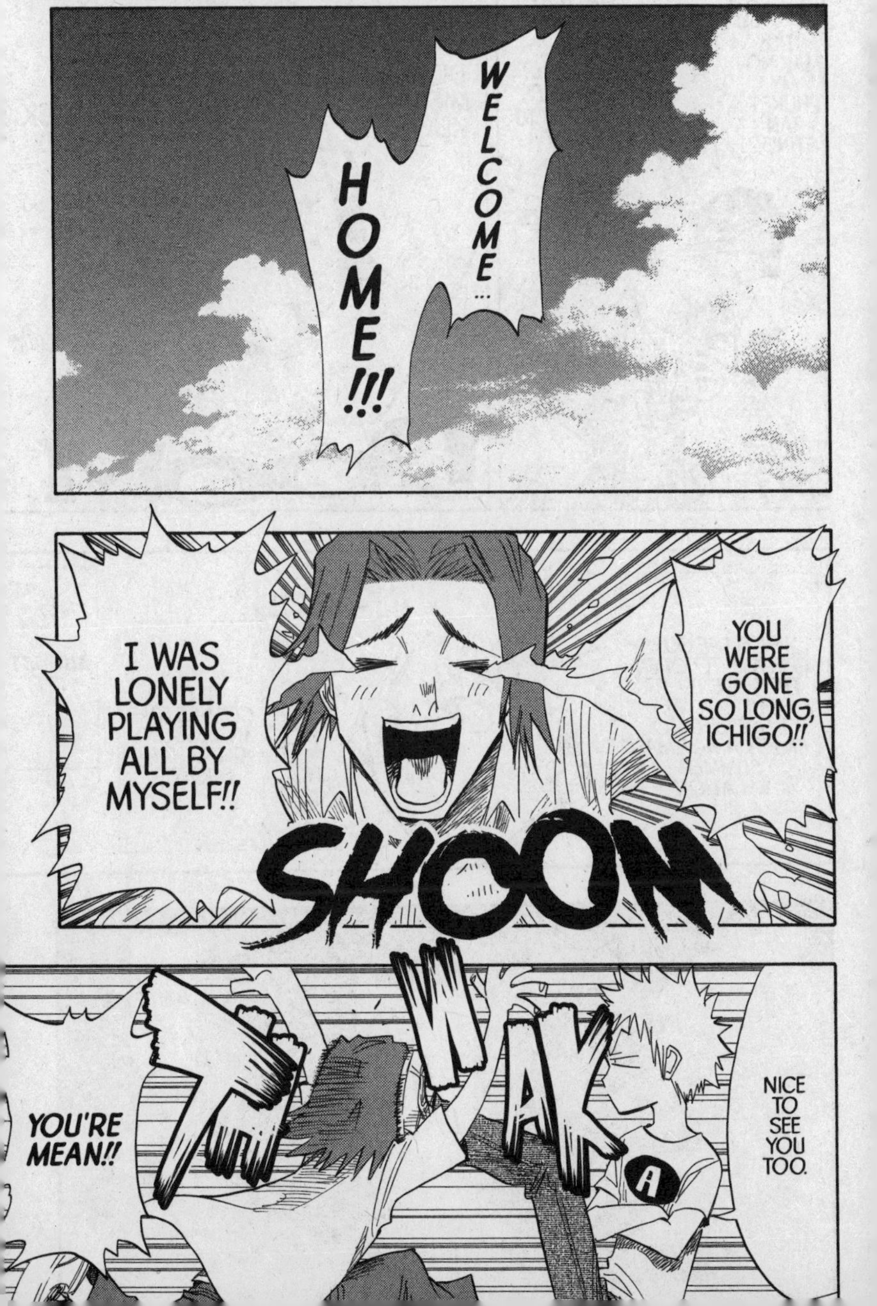
WELCOME HOME!!!
...
I WAS LONELY PLAYING ALL BY MYSELF!!
YOU WERE GONE SO LONG, ICHIGO!!
SHOOM
NICE TO SEE YOU TOO.
THWAK
YOU'RE MEAN!!

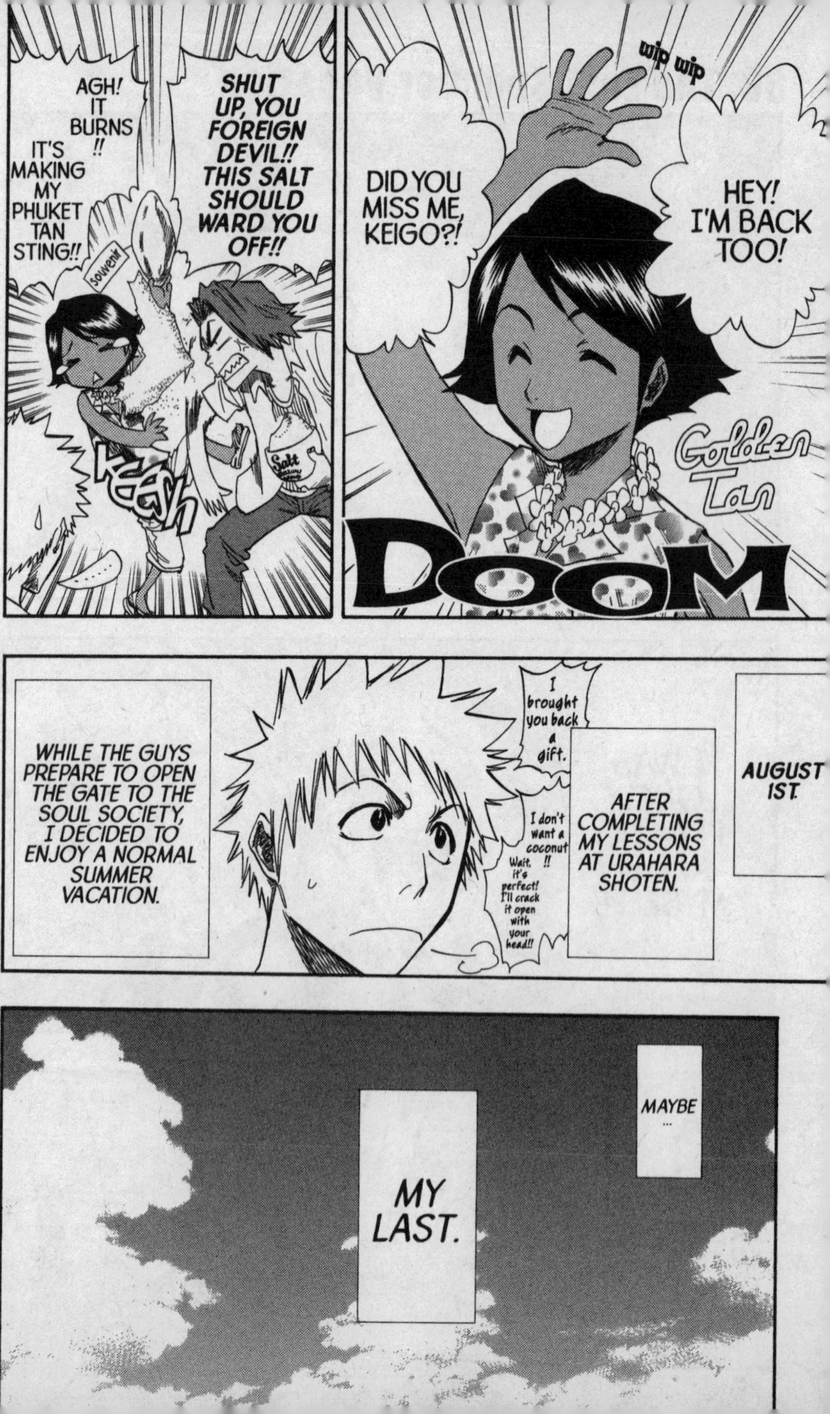
wip wip
HEY! I'M BACK TOO!
DID YOU MISS ME, KEIGO?!
Golden Tan
DOOM
SHUT UP, YOU FOREIGN DEVIL!! THIS SALT SHOULD WARD YOU OFF!!
AGH! IT BURNS!!
IT'S MAKING MY PHUKET TAN STING!!
souvenir
Salt
AUGUST 1ST.
AFTER COMPLETING MY LESSONS AT URAHARA SHOTEN.
I brought you back a gift.
I don't want a coconut!!
Wait, it's perfect! I'll crack it open with your head!!
WHILE THE GUYS PREPARE TO OPEN THE GATE TO THE SOUL SOCIETY, I DECIDED TO ENJOY A NORMAL SUMMER VACATION.
MAYBE...
MY LAST.

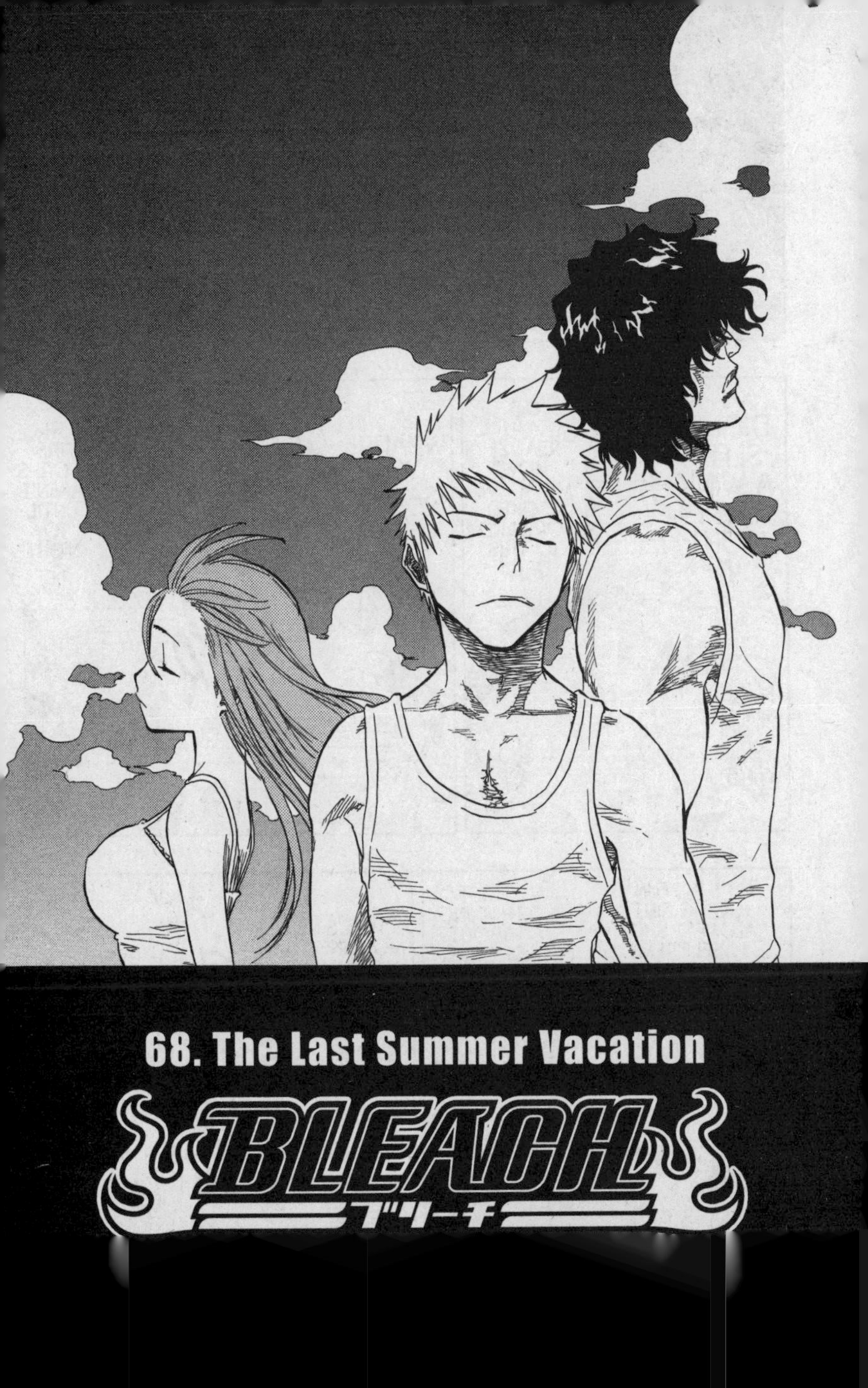

68. The Last Summer Vacation

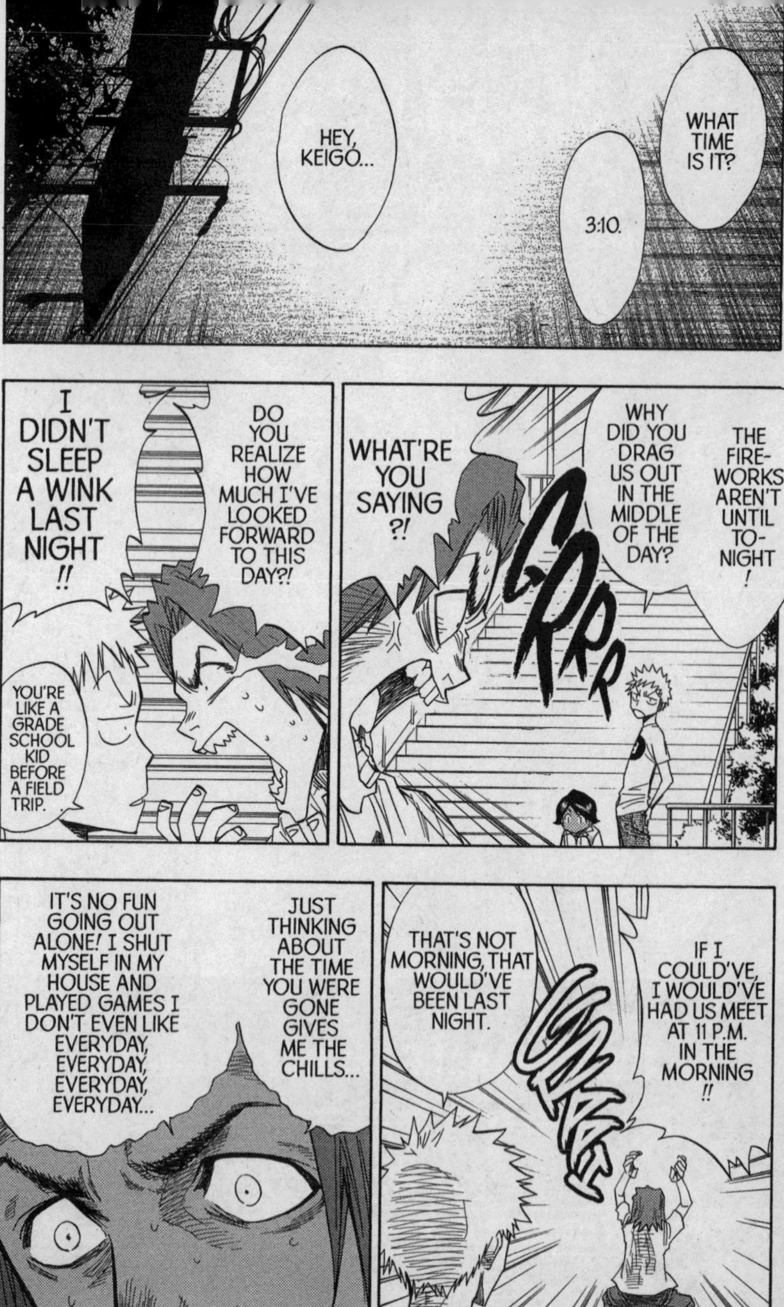
WHAT TIME IS IT?
3:10.
HEY, KEIGO...
THE FIRE-WORKS AREN'T UNTIL TO-NIGHT!
WHY DID YOU DRAG US OUT IN THE MIDDLE OF THE DAY?
GRRRR
WHAT'RE YOU SAYING?!
DO YOU REALIZE HOW MUCH I'VE LOOKED FORWARD TO THIS DAY?!
I DIDN'T SLEEP A WINK LAST NIGHT!!
YOU'RE LIKE A GRADE SCHOOL KID BEFORE A FIELD TRIP.
IF I COULD'VE, I WOULD'VE HAD US MEET AT 11 P.M. IN THE MORNING!!
THAT'S NOT MORNING, THAT WOULD'VE BEEN LAST NIGHT.
JUST THINKING ABOUT THE TIME YOU WERE GONE GIVES ME THE CHILLS...
IT'S NO FUN GOING OUT ALONE! I SHUT MYSELF IN MY HOUSE AND PLAYED GAMES I DON'T EVEN LIKE EVERYDAY, EVERYDAY, EVERYDAY, EVERYDAY...

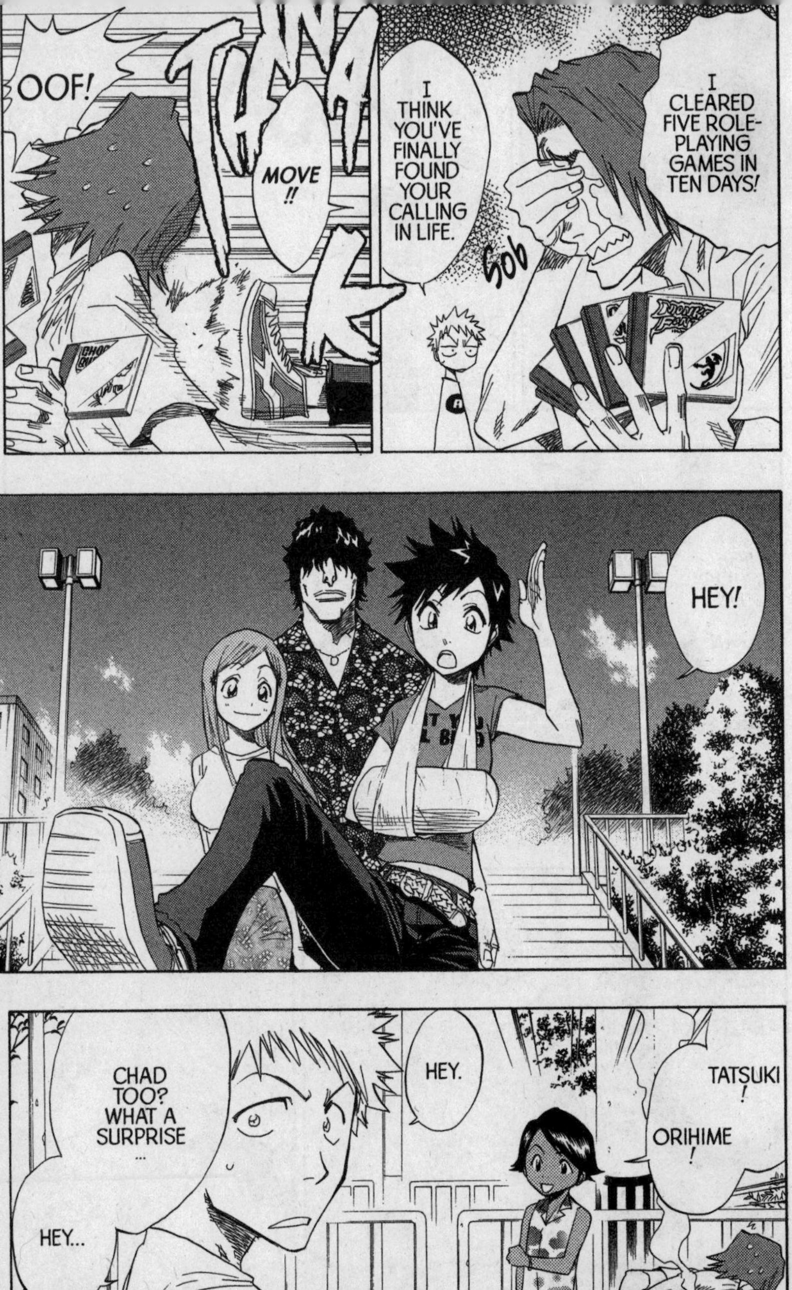
I CLEARED FIVE ROLE-PLAYING GAMES IN TEN DAYS!
Sob
I THINK YOU'VE FINALLY FOUND YOUR CALLING IN LIFE.
THWA
MOVE!!
OOF!
HEY!
TATSUKI! ORIHIME!
HEY.
CHAD TOO? WHAT A SURPRISE...
HEY...

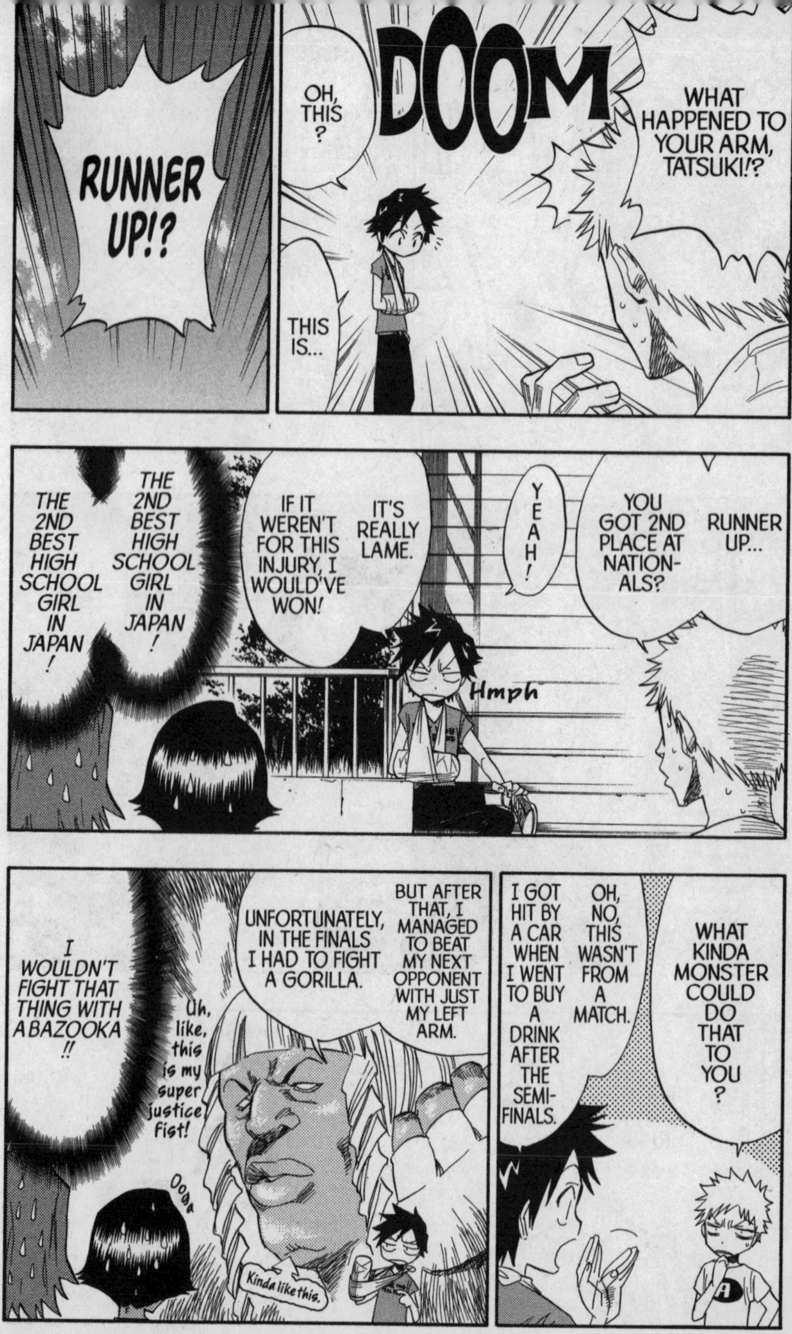
WHAT HAPPENED TO YOUR ARM, TATSUKI!?
DOOM
OH, THIS?
THIS IS...
RUNNER UP!?
RUNNER UP...
YOU GOT 2ND PLACE AT NATIONALS?
YEAH!
IT'S REALLY LAME.
IF IT WEREN'T FOR THIS INJURY, I WOULD'VE WON!
Hmph
THE 2ND BEST HIGH SCHOOL GIRL IN JAPAN!
THE 2ND BEST HIGH SCHOOL GIRL IN JAPAN!
WHAT KINDA MONSTER COULD DO THAT TO YOU?
OH, NO, THIS WASN'T FROM A MATCH.
I GOT HIT BY A CAR WHEN I WENT TO BUY A DRINK AFTER THE SEMI-FINALS.
BUT AFTER THAT, I MANAGED TO BEAT MY NEXT OPPONENT WITH JUST MY LEFT ARM.
UNFORTUNATELY, IN THE FINALS I HAD TO FIGHT A GORILLA.
Uh, like, this is my super justice fist!
Ooga
Kinda like this.
I WOULDN'T FIGHT THAT THING WITH A BAZOOKA!!

READ THIS WAY

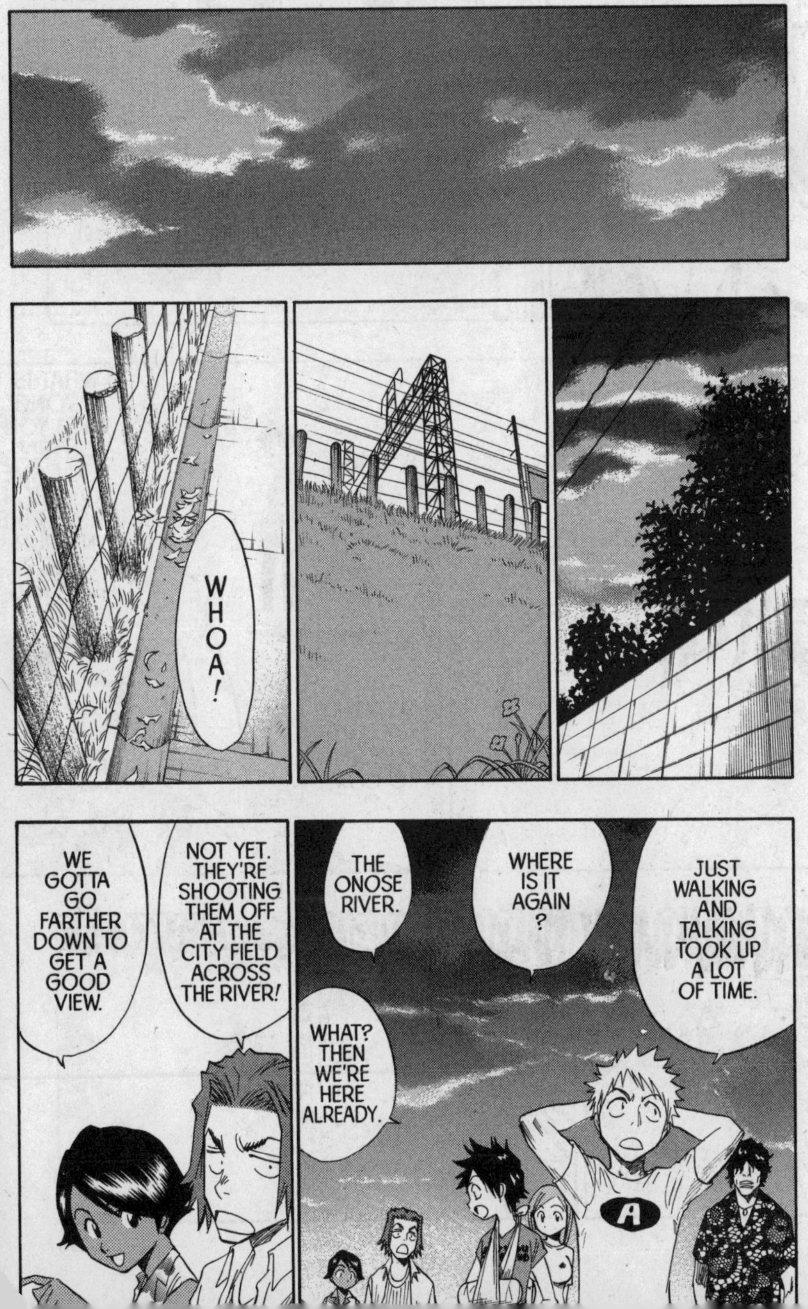
WHOA!
JUST WALKING AND TALKING TOOK UP A LOT OF TIME.
WHERE IS IT AGAIN?
THE ONOSE RIVER.
WHAT? THEN WE'RE HERE ALREADY.
NOT YET. THEY'RE SHOOTING THEM OFF AT THE CITY FIELD ACROSS THE RIVER!
WE GOTTA GO FARTHER DOWN TO GET A GOOD VIEW.

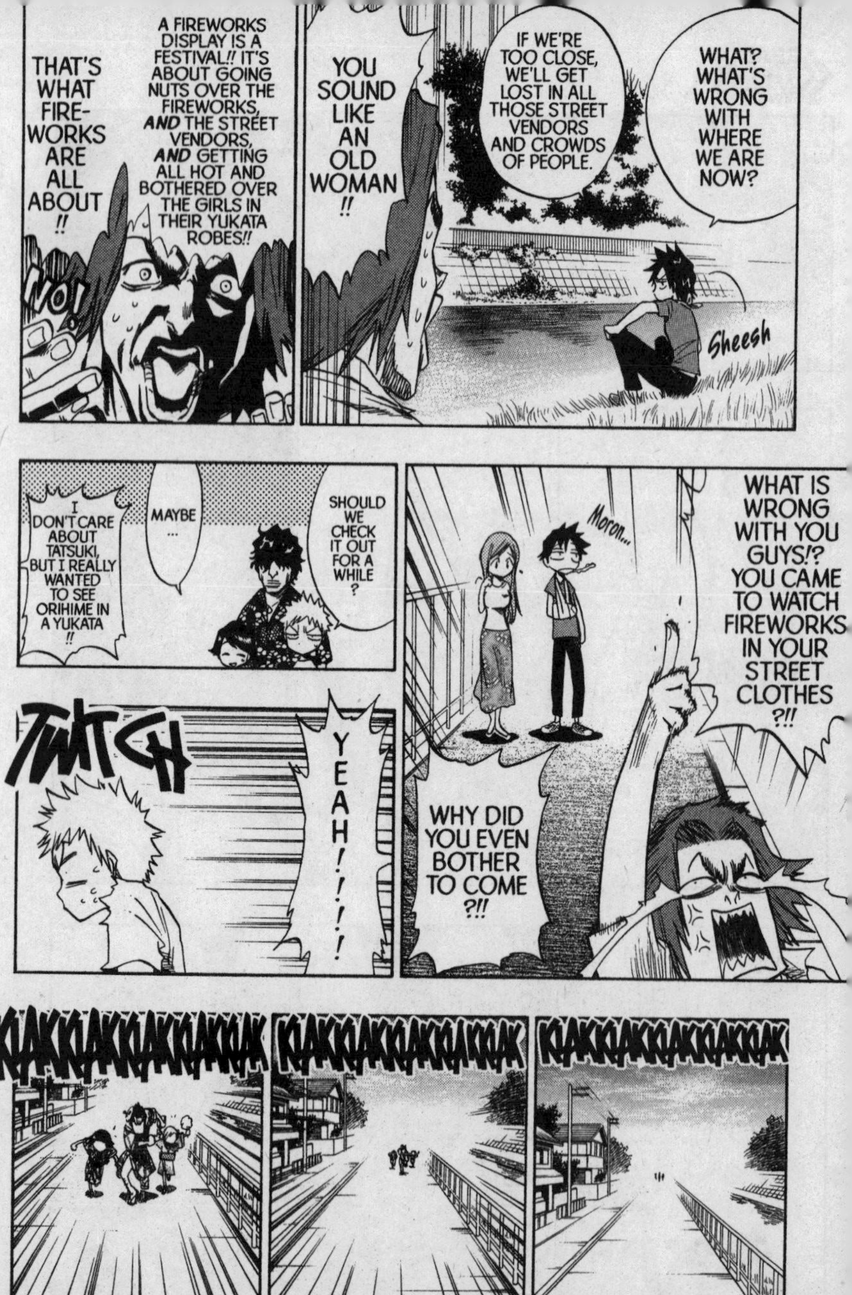

WHAT? WHAT'S WRONG WITH WHERE WE ARE NOW?
IF WE'RE TOO CLOSE, WE'LL GET LOST IN ALL THOSE STREET VENDORS AND CROWDS OF PEOPLE.
Sheesh
YOU SOUND LIKE AN OLD WOMAN!!
A FIREWORKS DISPLAY IS A FESTIVAL!! IT'S ABOUT GOING NUTS OVER THE FIREWORKS, AND THE STREET VENDORS, AND GETTING ALL HOT AND BOTHERED OVER THE GIRLS IN THEIR YUKATA ROBES!!
THAT'S WHAT FIRE-WORKS ARE ALL ABOUT!!
WHAT IS WRONG WITH YOU GUYS!? YOU CAME TO WATCH FIREWORKS IN YOUR STREET CLOTHES?!!
Moron...
WHY DID YOU EVEN BOTHER TO COME?!!
SHOULD WE CHECK IT OUT FOR A WHILE?
MAYBE...
I DON'T CARE ABOUT TATSUKI, BUT I REALLY WANTED TO SEE ORIHIME IN A YUKATA!!
YEAH!!!!!
TWITCH
KIAKKIAKKIAKKIAKKIAK
KIAKKIAKKIAKKIAKKIAK
KIAKKIAKKIAKKIAKKIAK

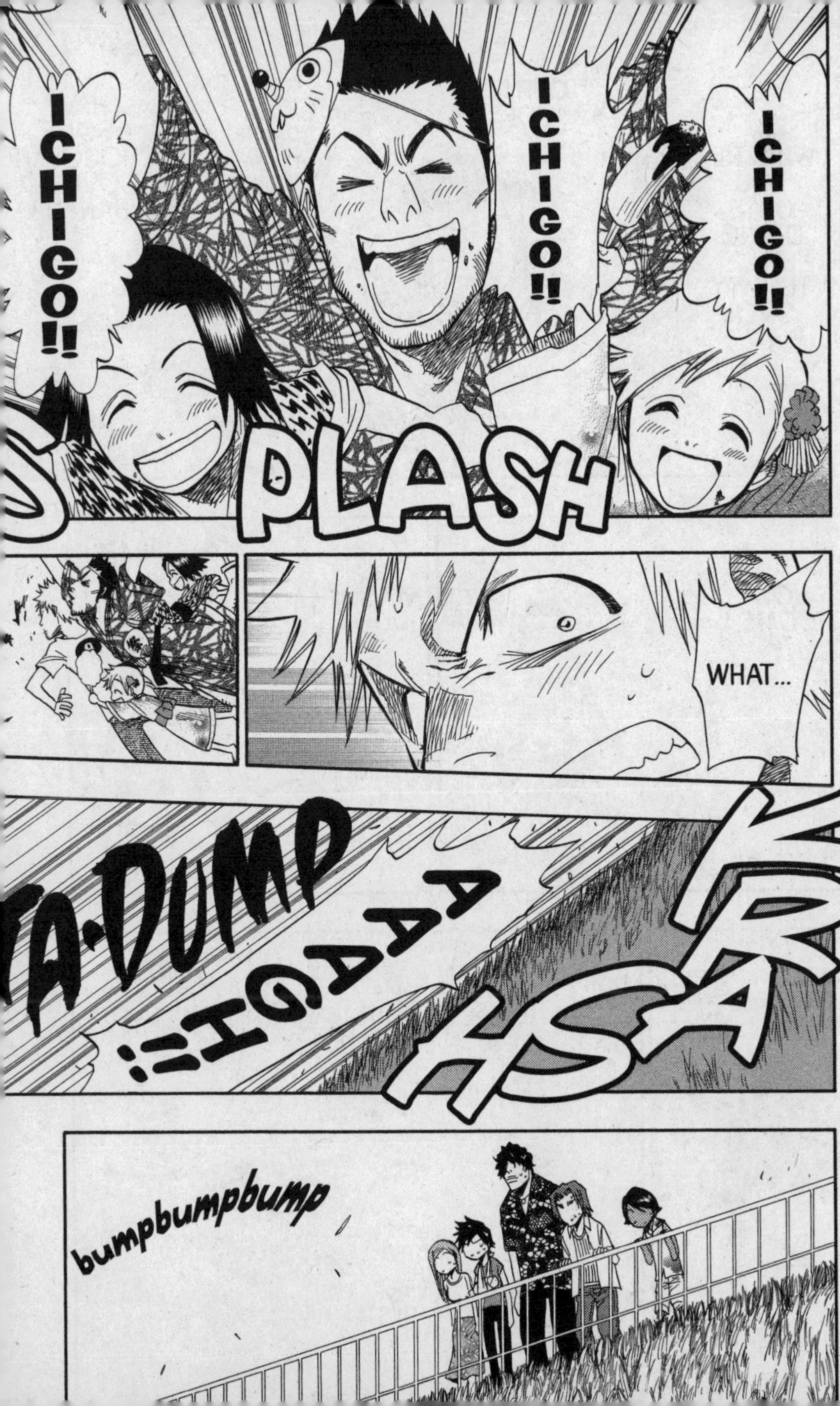

ICHIGO!!
ICHIGO!!
ICHIGO!!
SPLASH
WHAT...
KRASH
IGAAA!!
TA-DUMP
bumpbumpbump

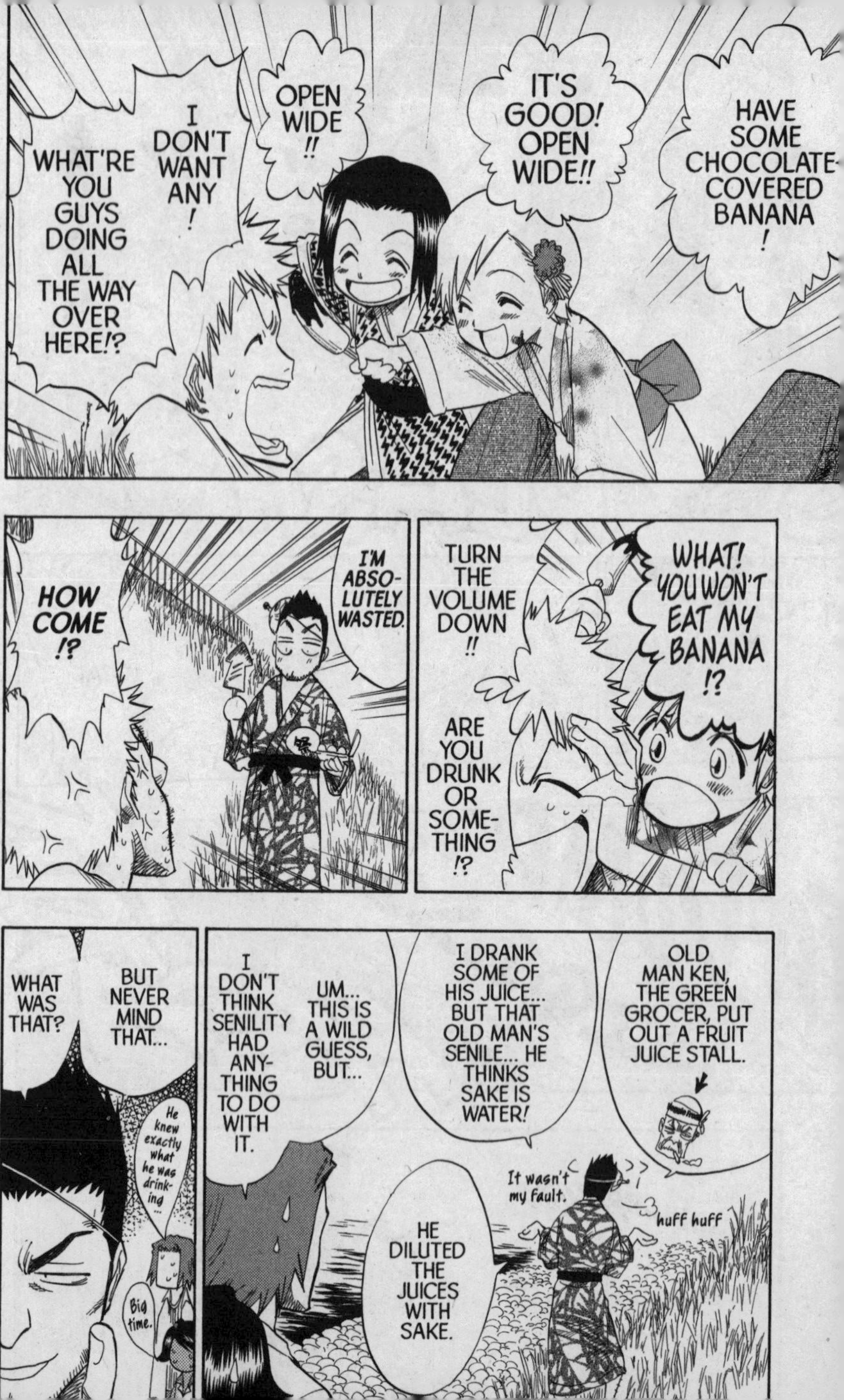
HAVE SOME CHOCOLATE-COVERED BANANA!
IT'S GOOD! OPEN WIDE!!
OPEN WIDE!!
I DON'T WANT ANY!
WHAT'RE YOU GUYS DOING ALL THE WAY OVER HERE!?
WHAT! YOU WON'T EAT MY BANANA!?
TURN THE VOLUME DOWN!!
ARE YOU DRUNK OR SOMETHING!?
I'M ABSOLUTELY WASTED.
HOW COME!?
OLD MAN KEN, THE GREEN GROCER, PUT OUT A FRUIT JUICE STALL.
I DRANK SOME OF HIS JUICE... BUT THAT OLD MAN'S SENILE... HE THINKS SAKE IS WATER!
It wasn't my fault.
huff huff
UM... THIS IS A WILD GUESS, BUT...
I DON'T THINK SENILITY HAD ANYTHING TO DO WITH IT.
HE DILUTED THE JUICES WITH SAKE.
BUT NEVER MIND THAT...
WHAT WAS THAT?
He knew exactly what he was drinking...
Big time.

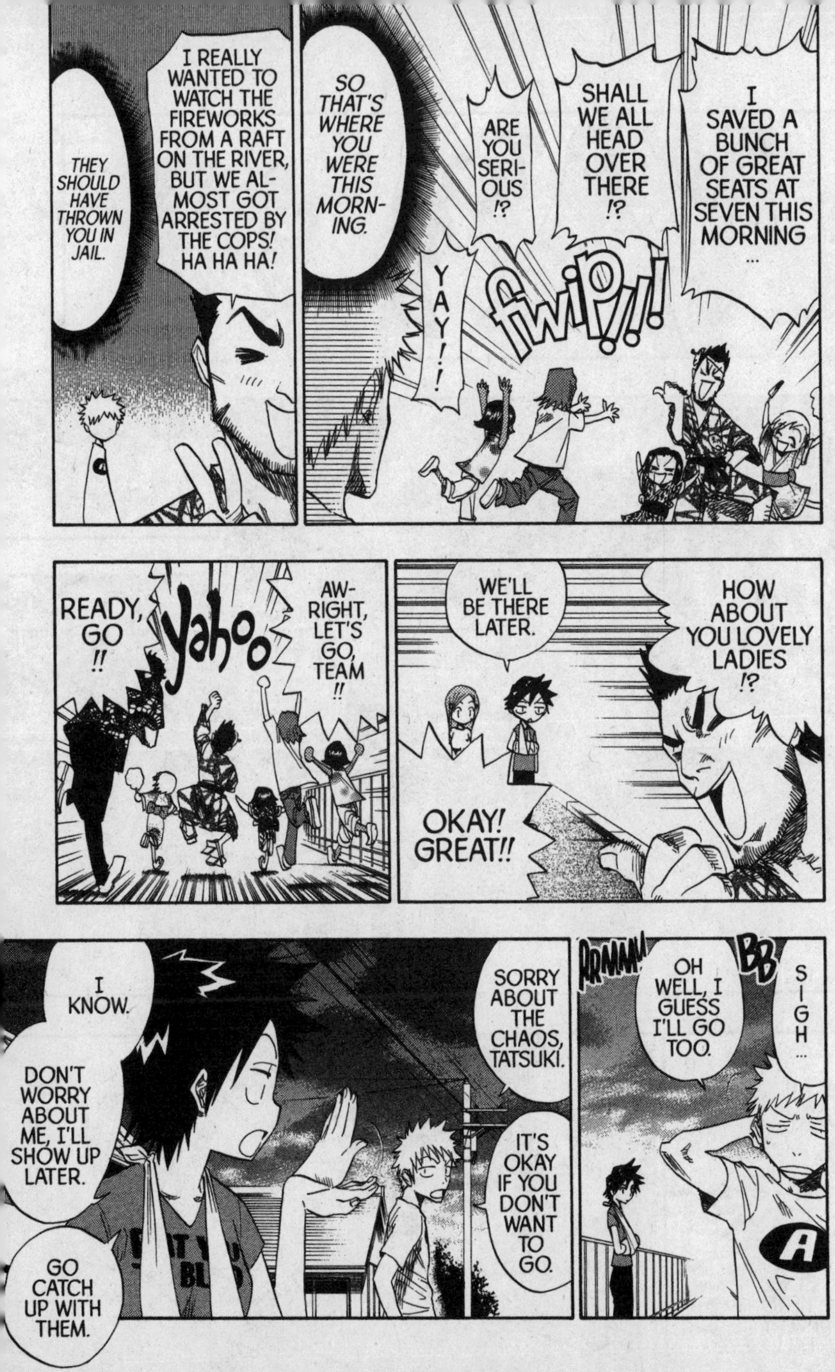
I SAVED A BUNCH OF GREAT SEATS AT SEVEN THIS MORNING...
SHALL WE ALL HEAD OVER THERE!?
ARE YOU SERIOUS!?
FWIP!!!
YAY!!
SO THAT'S WHERE YOU WERE THIS MORNING.
I REALLY WANTED TO WATCH THE FIREWORKS FROM A RAFT ON THE RIVER, BUT WE ALMOST GOT ARRESTED BY THE COPS! HA HA HA!
THEY SHOULD HAVE THROWN YOU IN JAIL.
HOW ABOUT YOU LOVELY LADIES!?
WE'LL BE THERE LATER.
OKAY! GREAT!!
AW-RIGHT, LET'S GO, TEAM!!
YAHOO
READY, GO!!
SIGH...
RRMMM
BB
OH WELL, I GUESS I'LL GO TOO.
SORRY ABOUT THE CHAOS, TATSUKI.
IT'S OKAY IF YOU DON'T WANT TO GO.
I KNOW.
DON'T WORRY ABOUT ME, I'LL SHOW UP LATER.
GO CATCH UP WITH THEM.

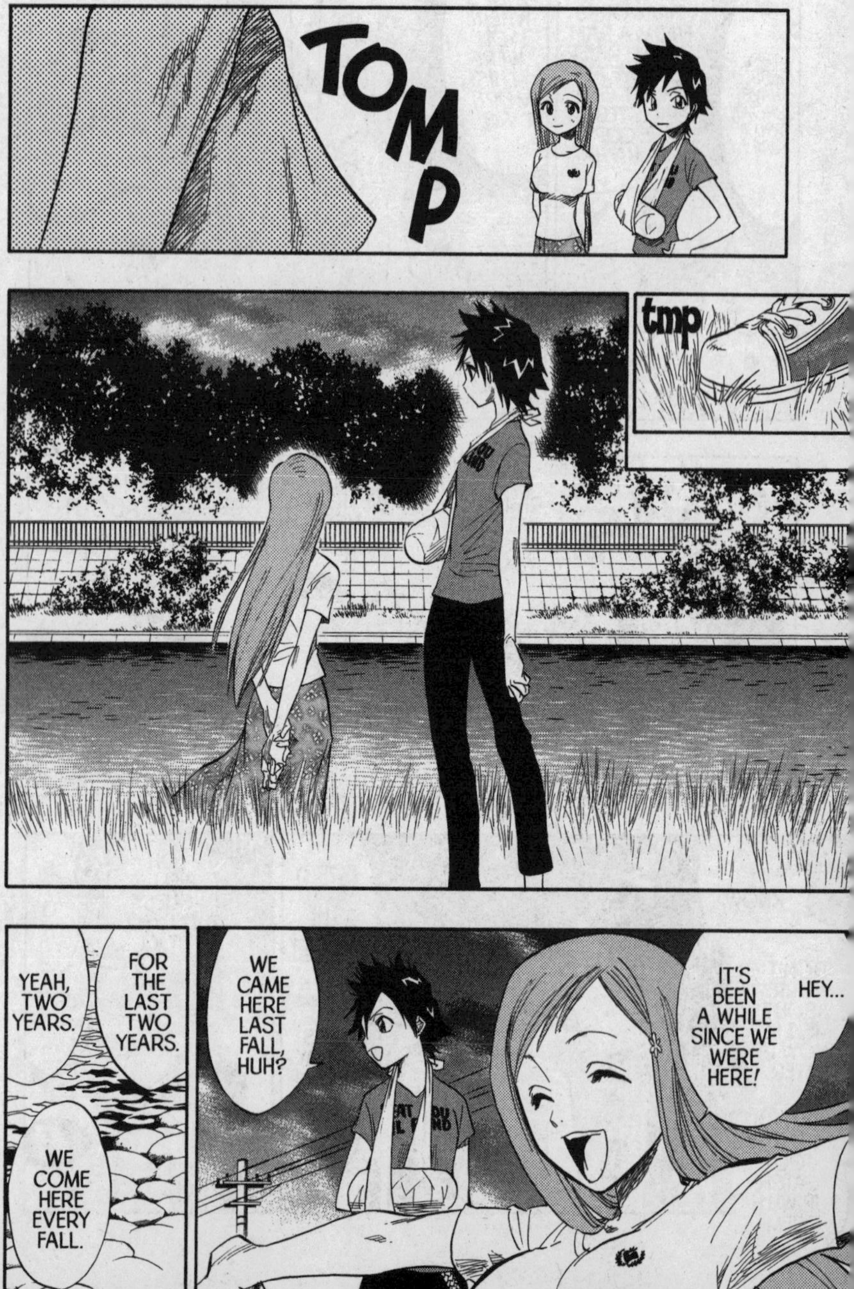
TOMP
tmp
HEY...
IT'S BEEN A WHILE SINCE WE WERE HERE!
WE CAME HERE LAST FALL, HUH?
FOR THE LAST TWO YEARS.
YEAH, TWO YEARS.
WE COME HERE EVERY FALL.

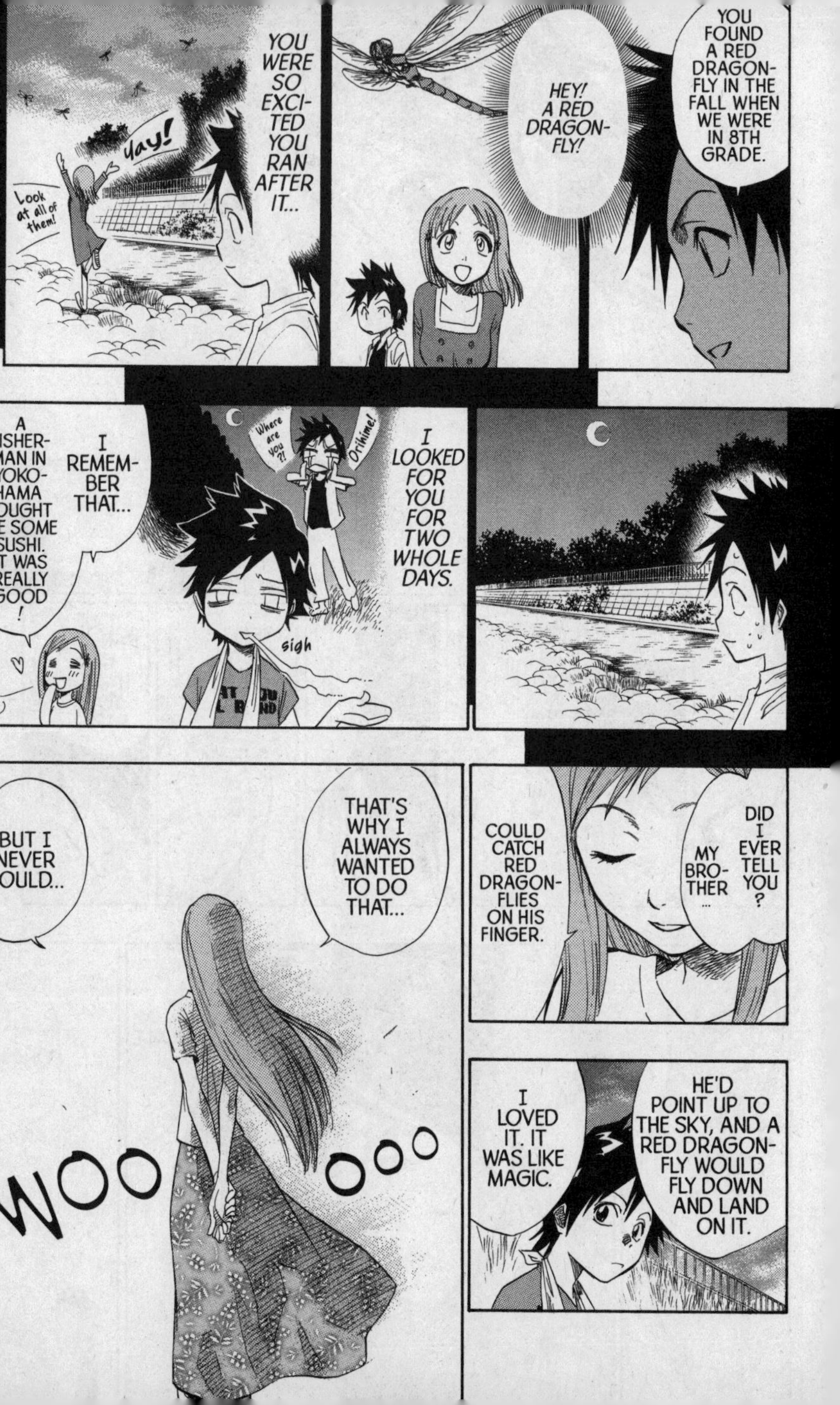
YOU FOUND A RED DRAGON-FLY IN THE FALL WHEN WE WERE IN 8TH GRADE.
HEY! A RED DRAGON-FLY!
YOU WERE SO EXCI-TED YOU RAN AFTER IT...
Yay!
Look at all of them!
I LOOKED FOR YOU FOR TWO WHOLE DAYS.
Orihime!
Where are you?!
sigh
I REMEM-BER THAT...
A FISHER-MAN IN YOKO-HAMA BOUGHT ME SOME SUSHI. IT WAS REALLY GOOD!
DID I EVER TELL YOU?
MY BRO-THER...
COULD CATCH RED DRAGON-FLIES ON HIS FINGER.
HE'D POINT UP TO THE SKY, AND A RED DRAGON-FLY WOULD FLY DOWN AND LAND ON IT.
I LOVED IT. IT WAS LIKE MAGIC.
THAT'S WHY I ALWAYS WANTED TO DO THAT...
BUT I NEVER COULD...
WOOOOO

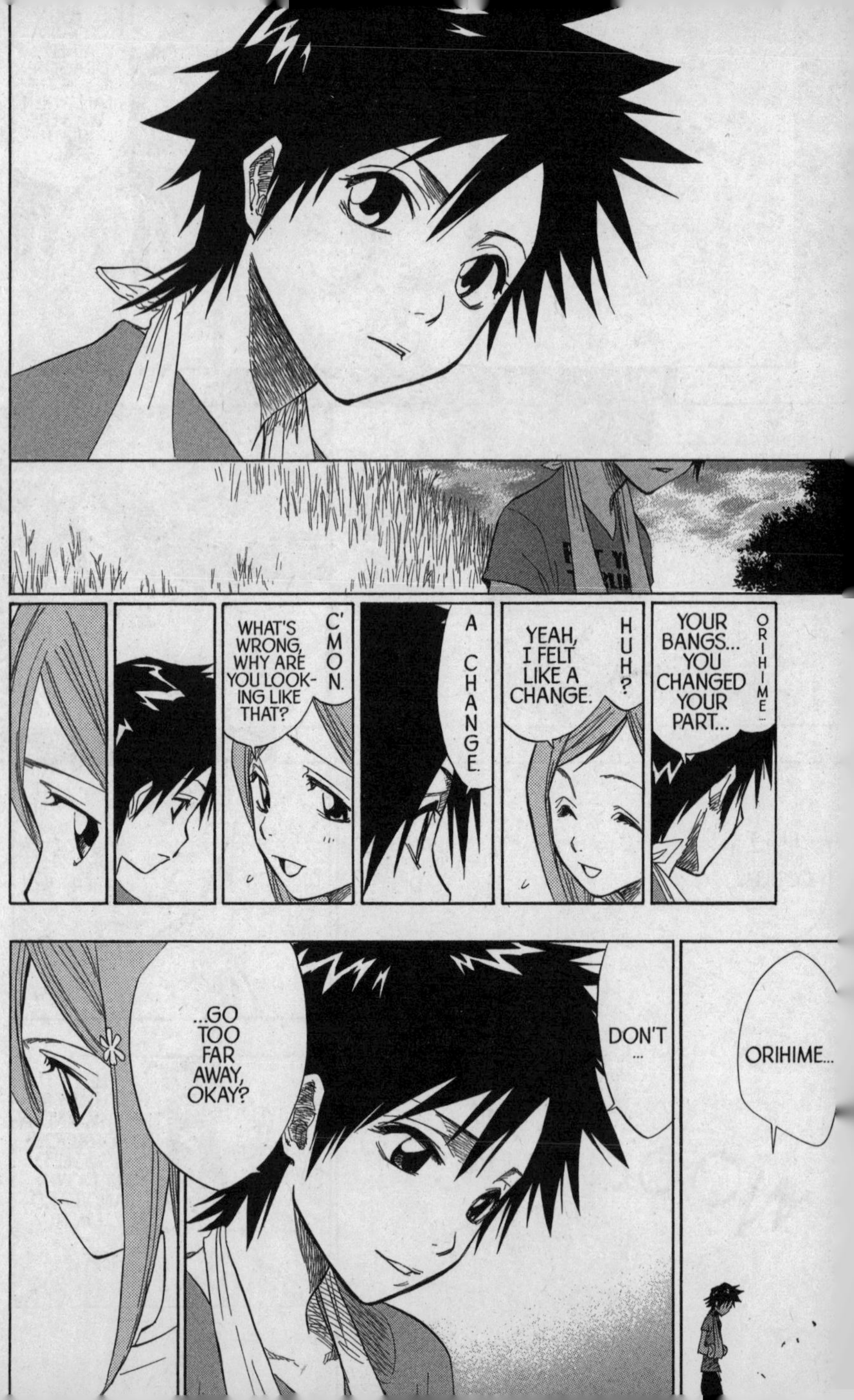
ORIHIME...
YOUR BANGS... YOU CHANGED YOUR PART...
HUH?
YEAH, I FELT LIKE A CHANGE.
A CHANGE.
C'MON.
WHAT'S WRONG, WHY ARE YOU LOOKING LIKE THAT?
ORIHIME...
DON'T...
...GO TOO FAR AWAY, OKAY?

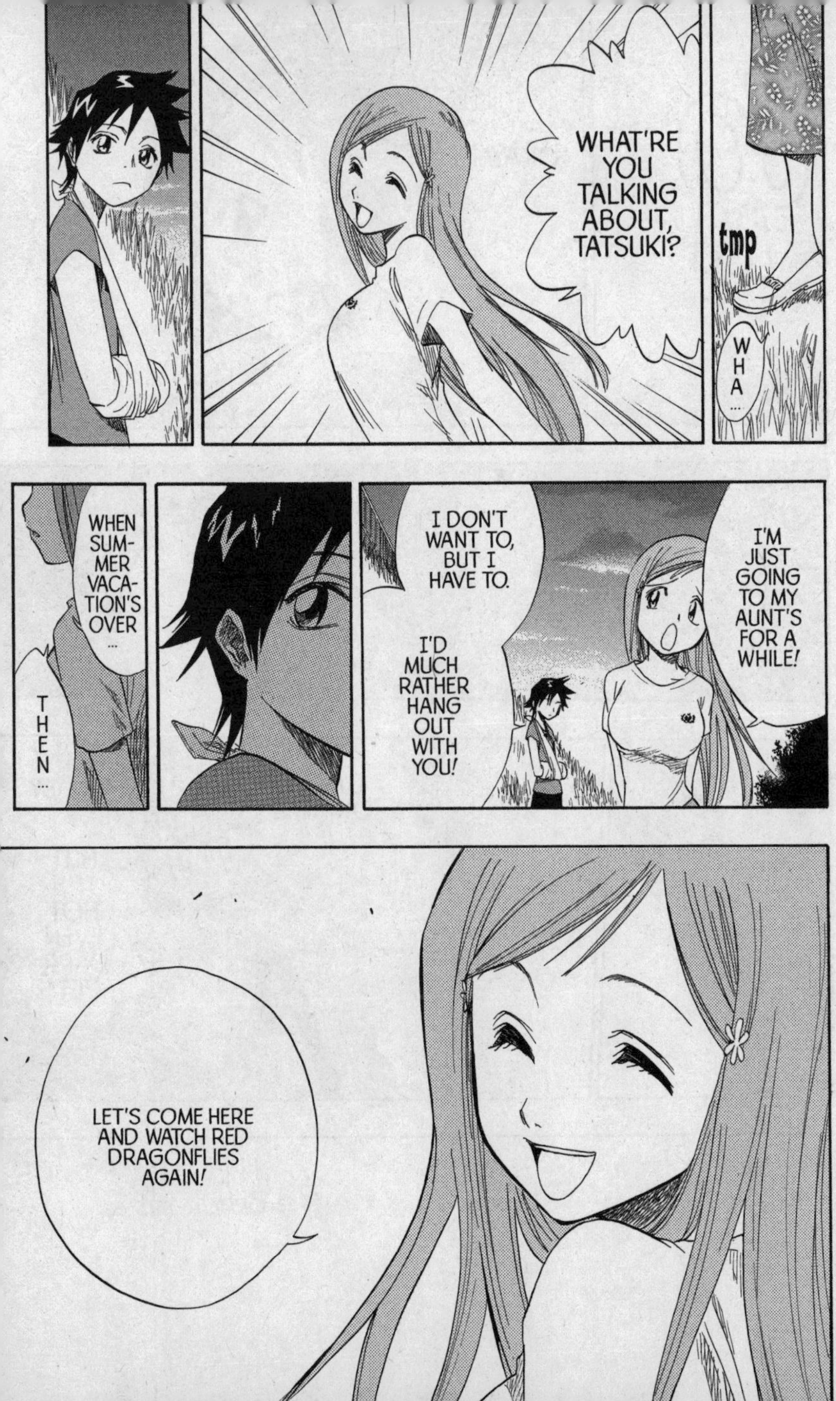
tmp
WHA...
WHAT'RE YOU TALKING ABOUT, TATSUKI?
I'M JUST GOING TO MY AUNT'S FOR A WHILE!
I DON'T WANT TO, BUT I HAVE TO.
I'D MUCH RATHER HANG OUT WITH YOU!
WHEN SUMMER VACATION'S OVER...
THEN...
LET'S COME HERE AND WATCH RED DRAGONFLIES AGAIN!

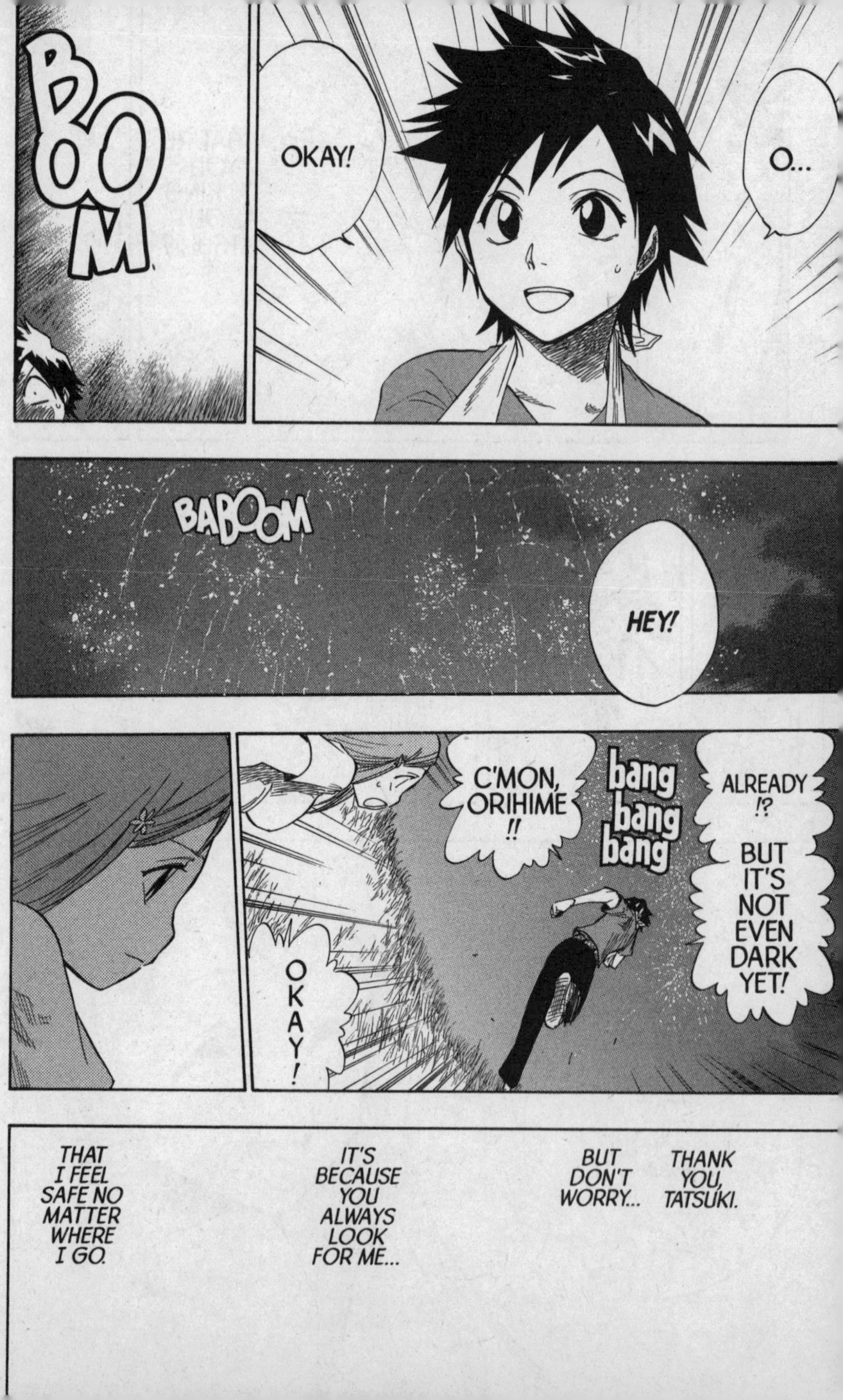
O...
OKAY!
BOOM
HEY!
BABOOM
ALREADY!? BUT IT'S NOT EVEN DARK YET!
bang bang bang
C'MON, ORIHIME!!
OKAY!
THANK YOU, TATSUKI.
BUT DON'T WORRY...
IT'S BECAUSE YOU ALWAYS LOOK FOR ME...
THAT I FEEL SAFE NO MATTER WHERE I GO.

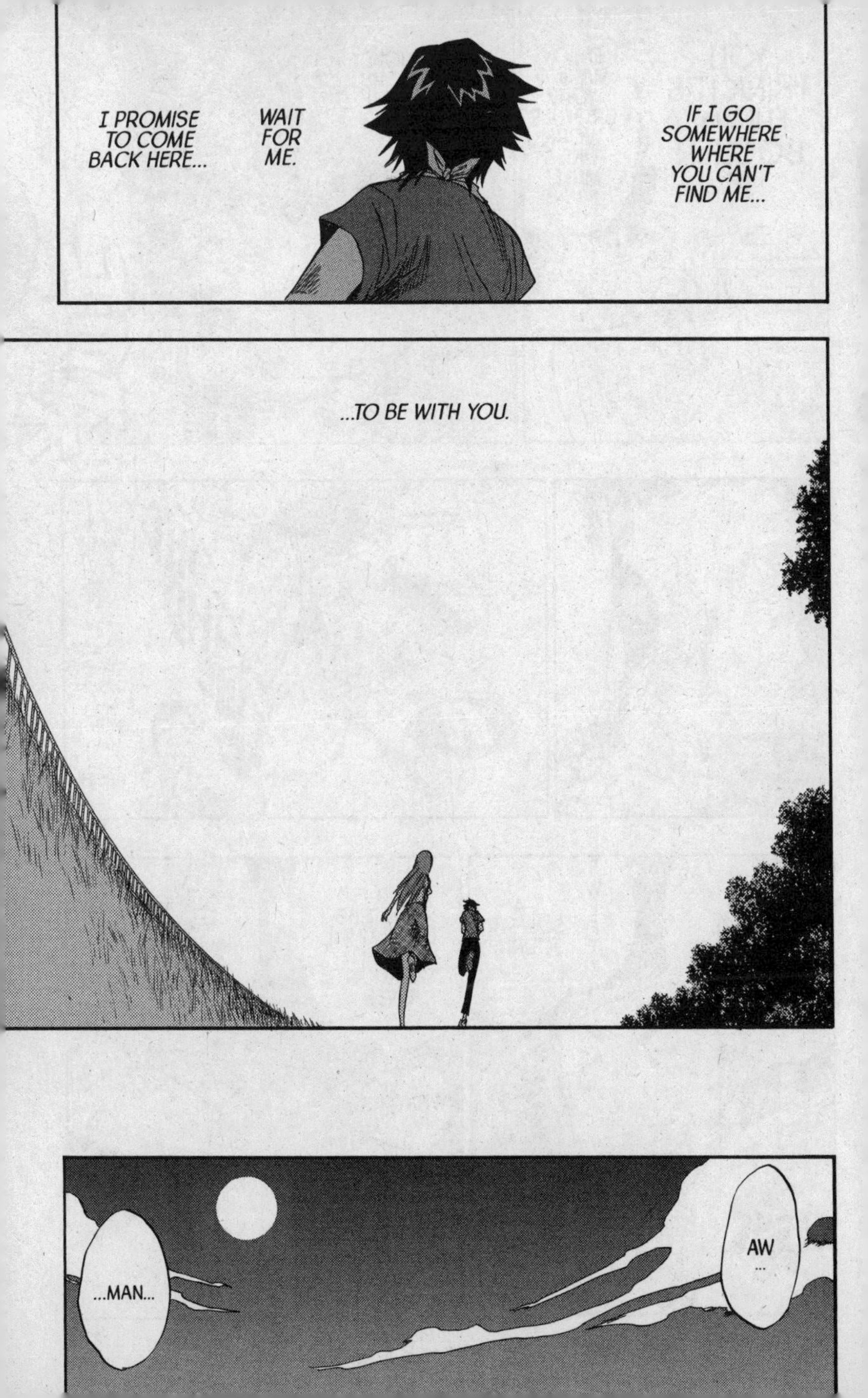
IF I GO SOMEWHERE WHERE YOU CAN'T FIND ME...
WAIT FOR ME.
I PROMISE TO COME BACK HERE...
...TO BE WITH YOU.
AW ...
...MAN...

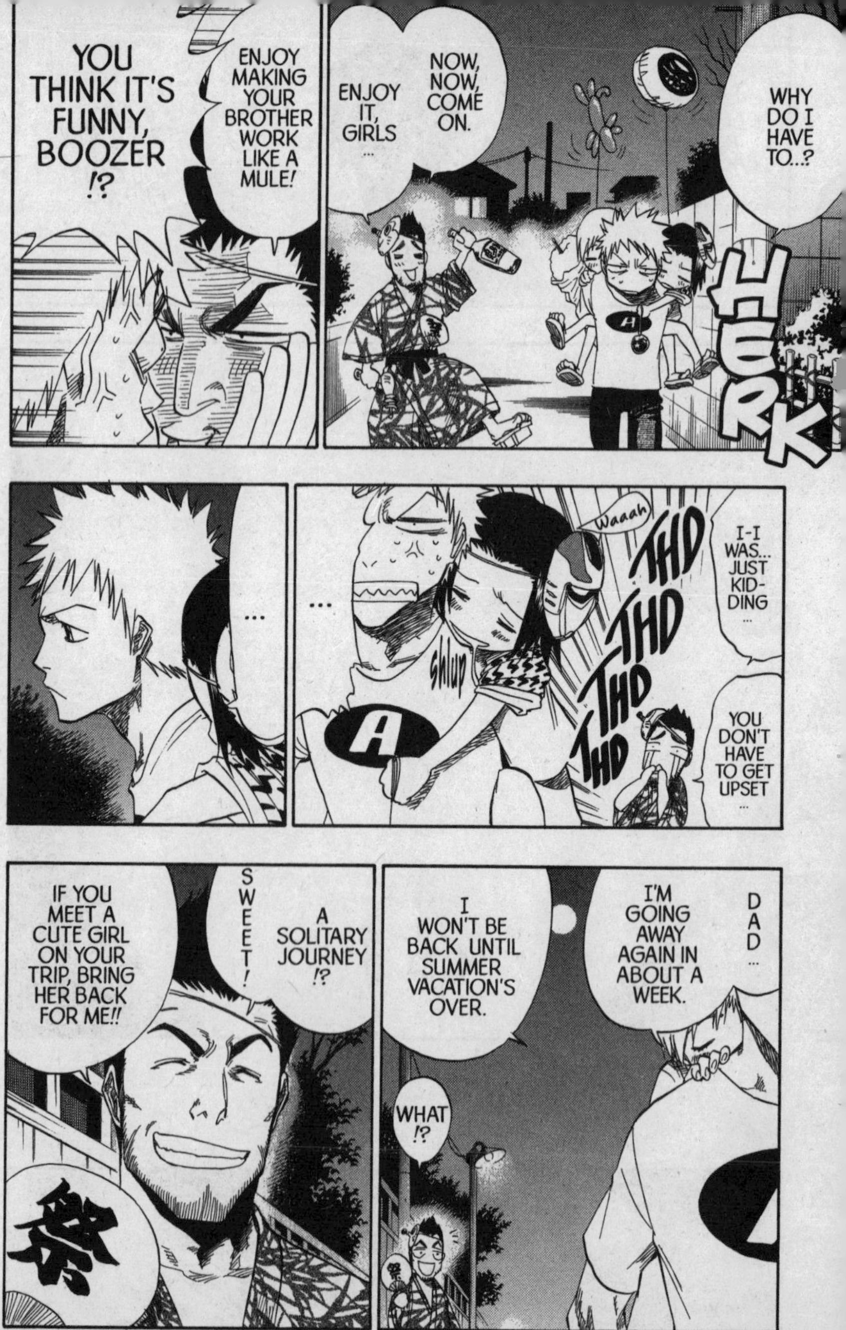

WHY DO I HAVE TO..?
HERK
NOW, NOW, COME ON.
ENJOY IT, GIRLS ...
ENJOY MAKING YOUR BROTHER WORK LIKE A MULE!
YOU THINK IT'S FUNNY, BOOZER !?
I-I WAS... JUST KIDDING ...
YOU DON'T HAVE TO GET UPSET ...
Waaah
THD THD THD THD THD
shlup
...
...
DAD ...
I'M GOING AWAY AGAIN IN ABOUT A WEEK.
I WON'T BE BACK UNTIL SUMMER VACATION'S OVER.
WHAT !?
A SOLITARY JOURNEY !?
SWEET!
IF YOU MEET A CUTE GIRL ON YOUR TRIP, BRING HER BACK FOR ME!!

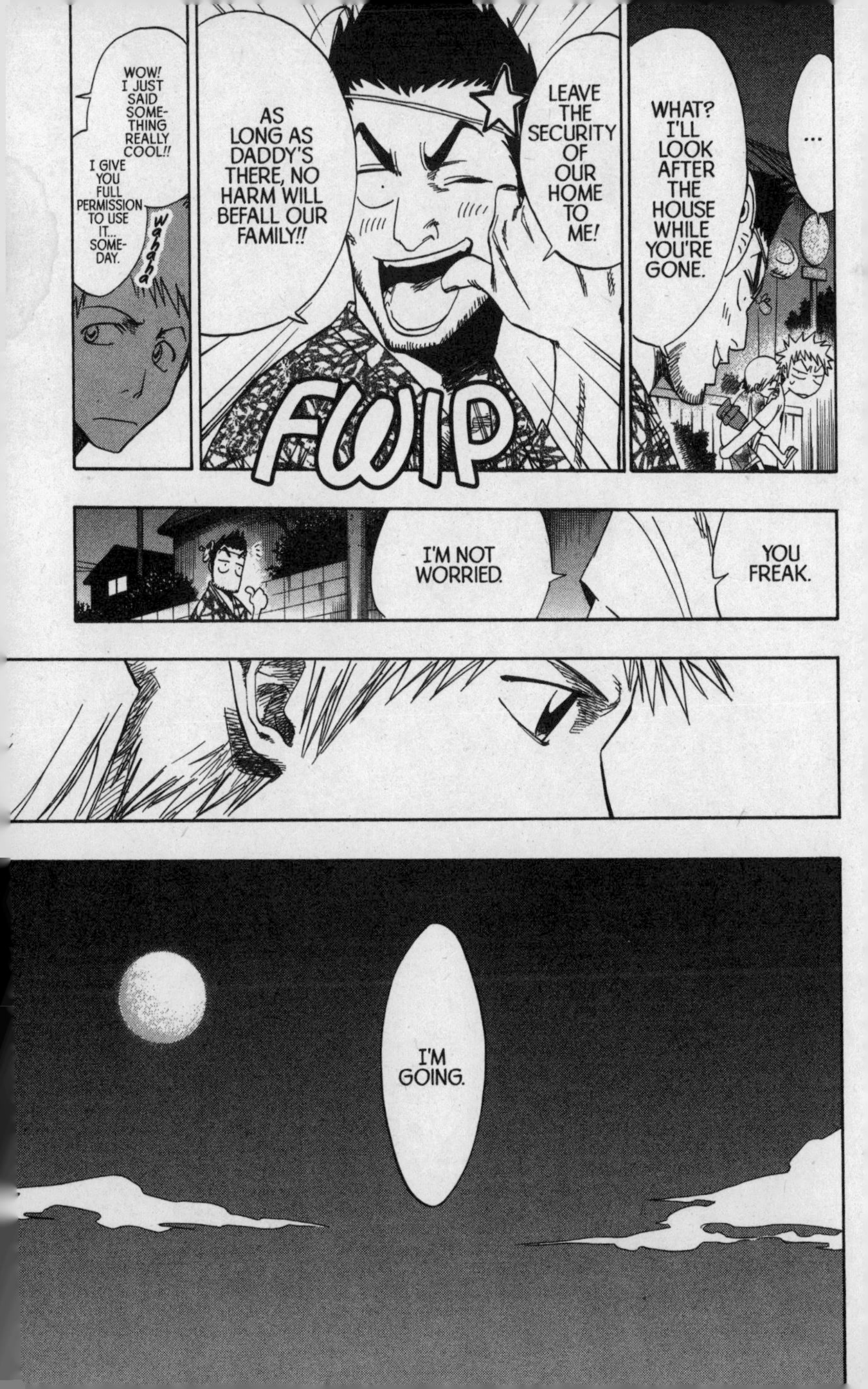

...
WHAT? I'LL LOOK AFTER THE HOUSE WHILE YOU'RE GONE.
LEAVE THE SECURITY OF OUR HOME TO ME!
AS LONG AS DADDY'S THERE, NO HARM WILL BEFALL OUR FAMILY!!
FWIP
WOW! I JUST SAID SOMETHING REALLY COOL!!
I GIVE YOU FULL PERMISSION TO USE IT... SOMEDAY.
Wahaha
YOU FREAK.
I'M NOT WORRIED.
I'M GOING.

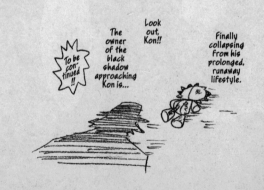

Finally collapsing from his prolonged, runaway lifestyle.
Look out, Kon!!
The owner of the black shadow approaching Kon is...
To be continued!!

69. 25:00 gathering

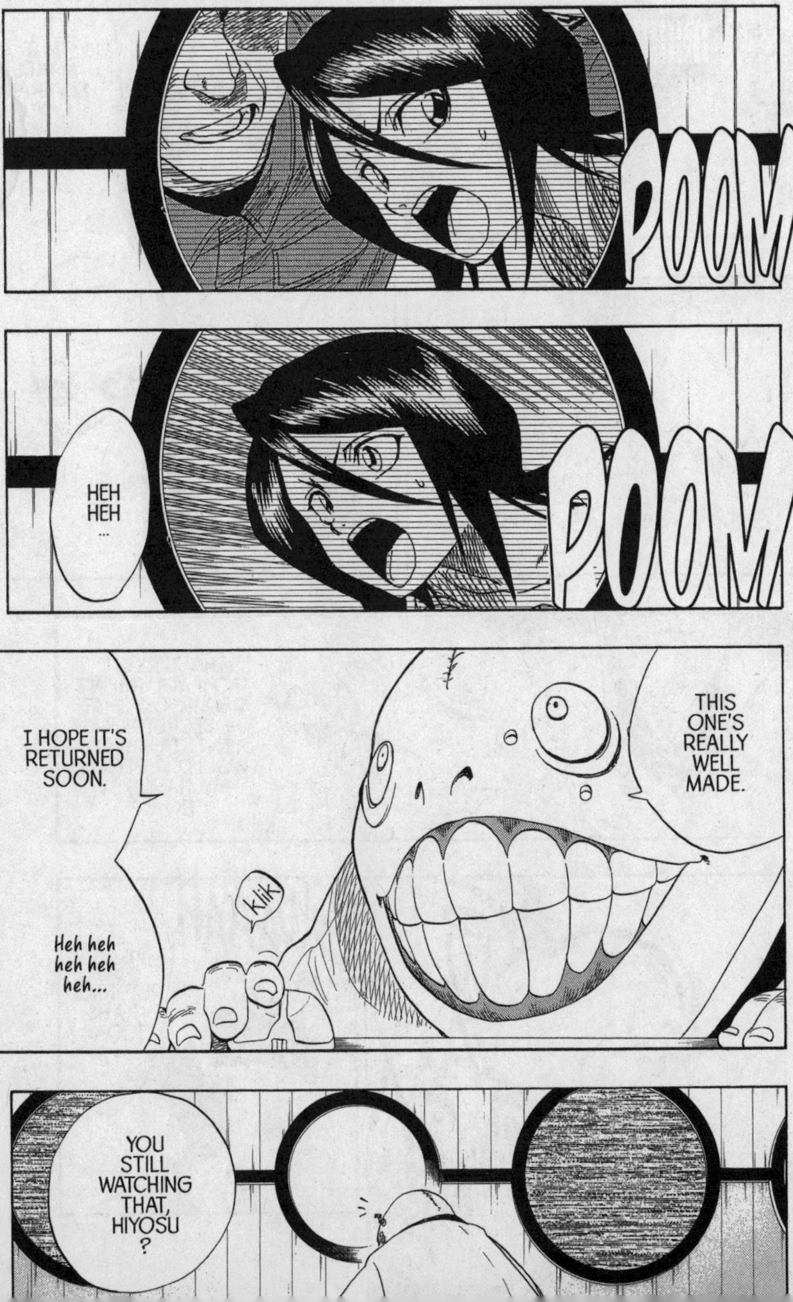
POOM
POOM
HEH HEH ...
THIS ONE'S REALLY WELL MADE.
klik
I HOPE IT'S RETURNED SOON.
Heh heh heh heh heh...
YOU STILL WATCHING THAT, HIYOSU ?

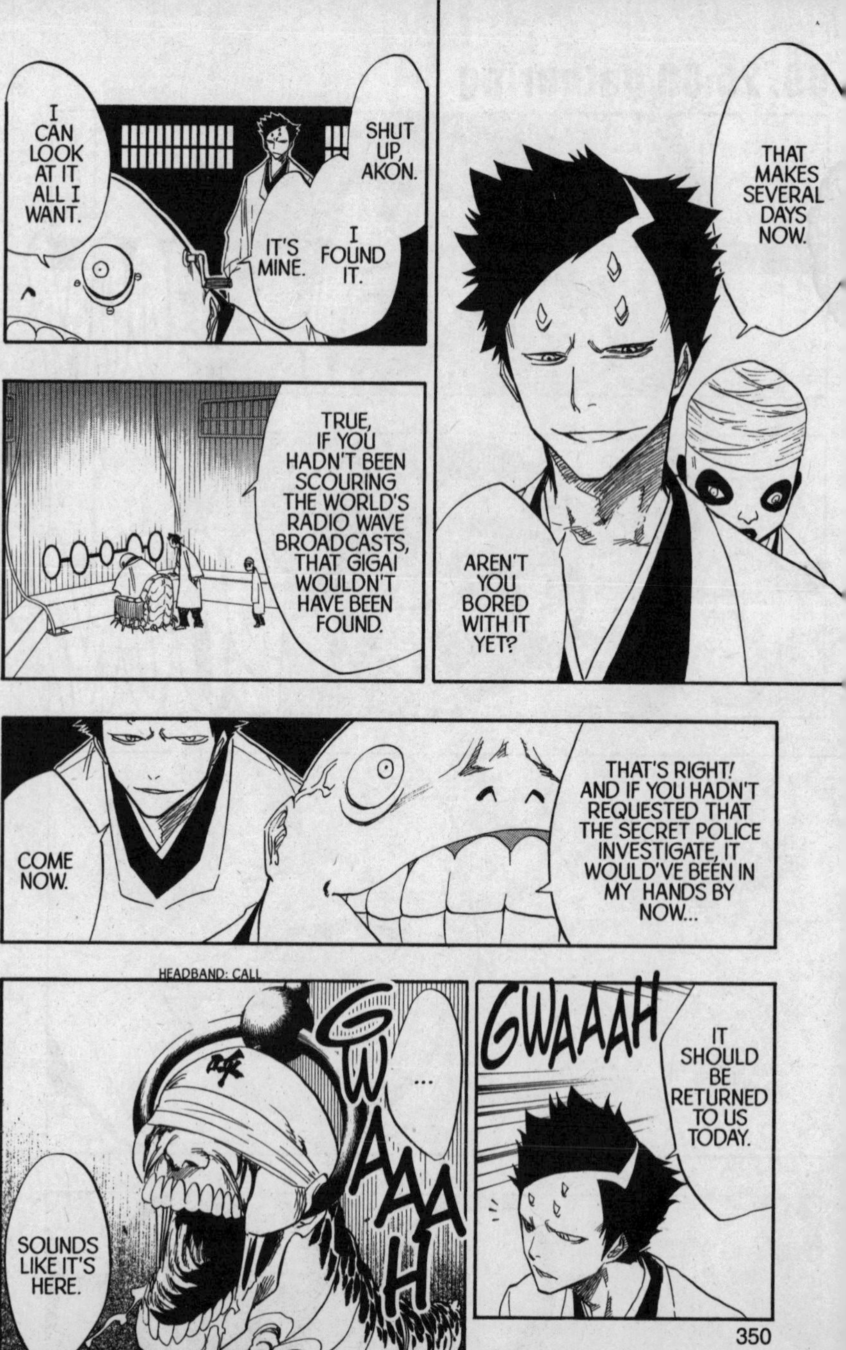

THAT MAKES SEVERAL DAYS NOW.
AREN'T YOU BORED WITH IT YET?
SHUT UP, AKON.
I FOUND IT.
IT'S MINE.
I CAN LOOK AT IT ALL I WANT.
TRUE, IF YOU HADN'T BEEN SCOURING THE WORLD'S RADIO WAVE BROADCASTS, THAT GIGAI WOULDN'T HAVE BEEN FOUND.
THAT'S RIGHT! AND IF YOU HADN'T REQUESTED THAT THE SECRET POLICE INVESTIGATE, IT WOULD'VE BEEN IN MY HANDS BY NOW...
COME NOW.
GWAAAH
IT SHOULD BE RETURNED TO US TODAY.
HEADBAND: CALL
GWAAAAH
...
SOUNDS LIKE IT'S HERE.

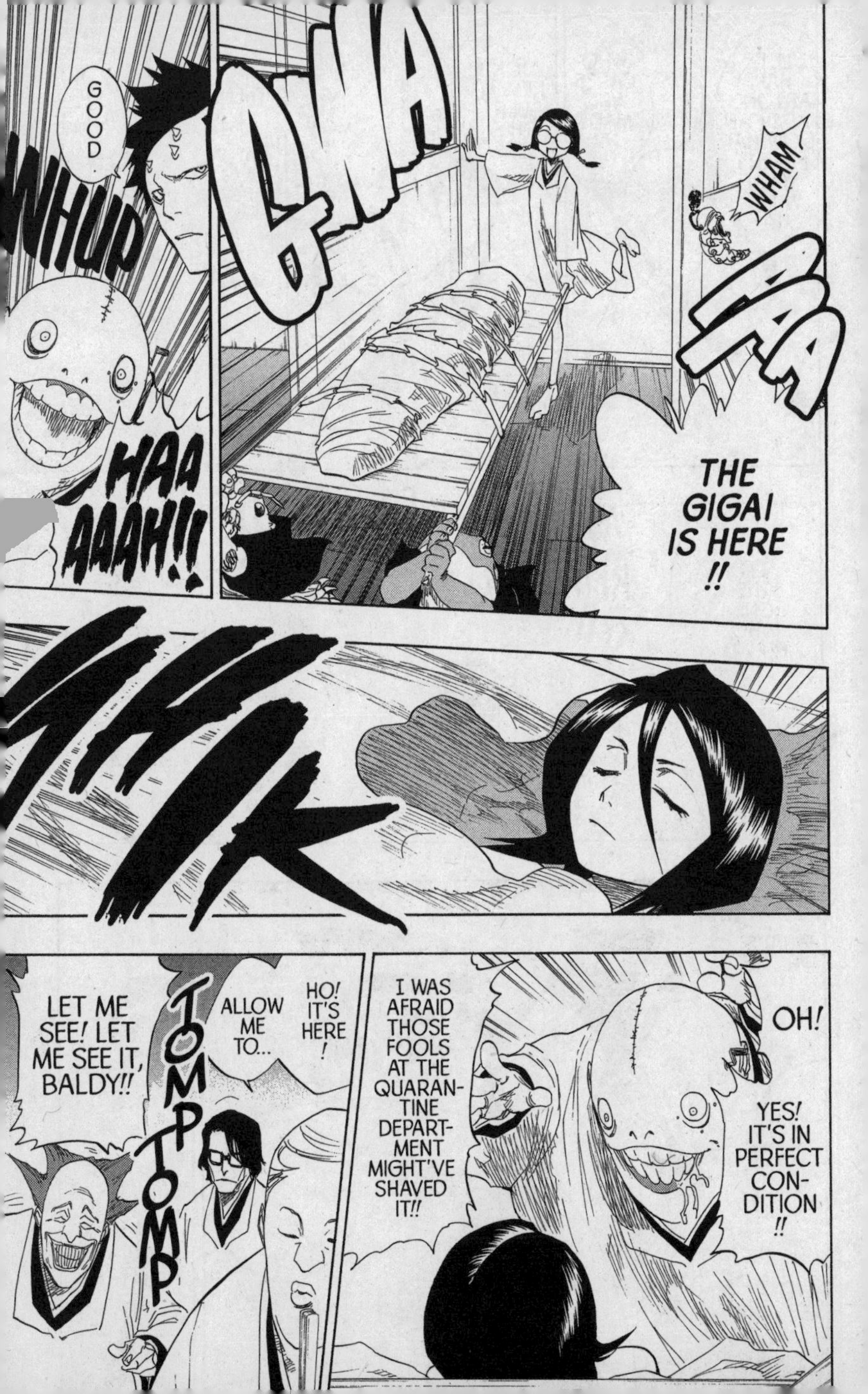
WHAM
THE GIGAI IS HERE!!
GWHA
GOOD
WHUP
HAAAAAH!!
OH!
YES! IT'S IN PERFECT CON-DITION!!
I WAS AFRAID THOSE FOOLS AT THE QUARAN-TINE DEPART-MENT MIGHT'VE SHAVED IT!!
HO! IT'S HERE!
ALLOW ME TO...
TOMP TOMP TOMP
LET ME SEE! LET ME SEE IT, BALDY!!

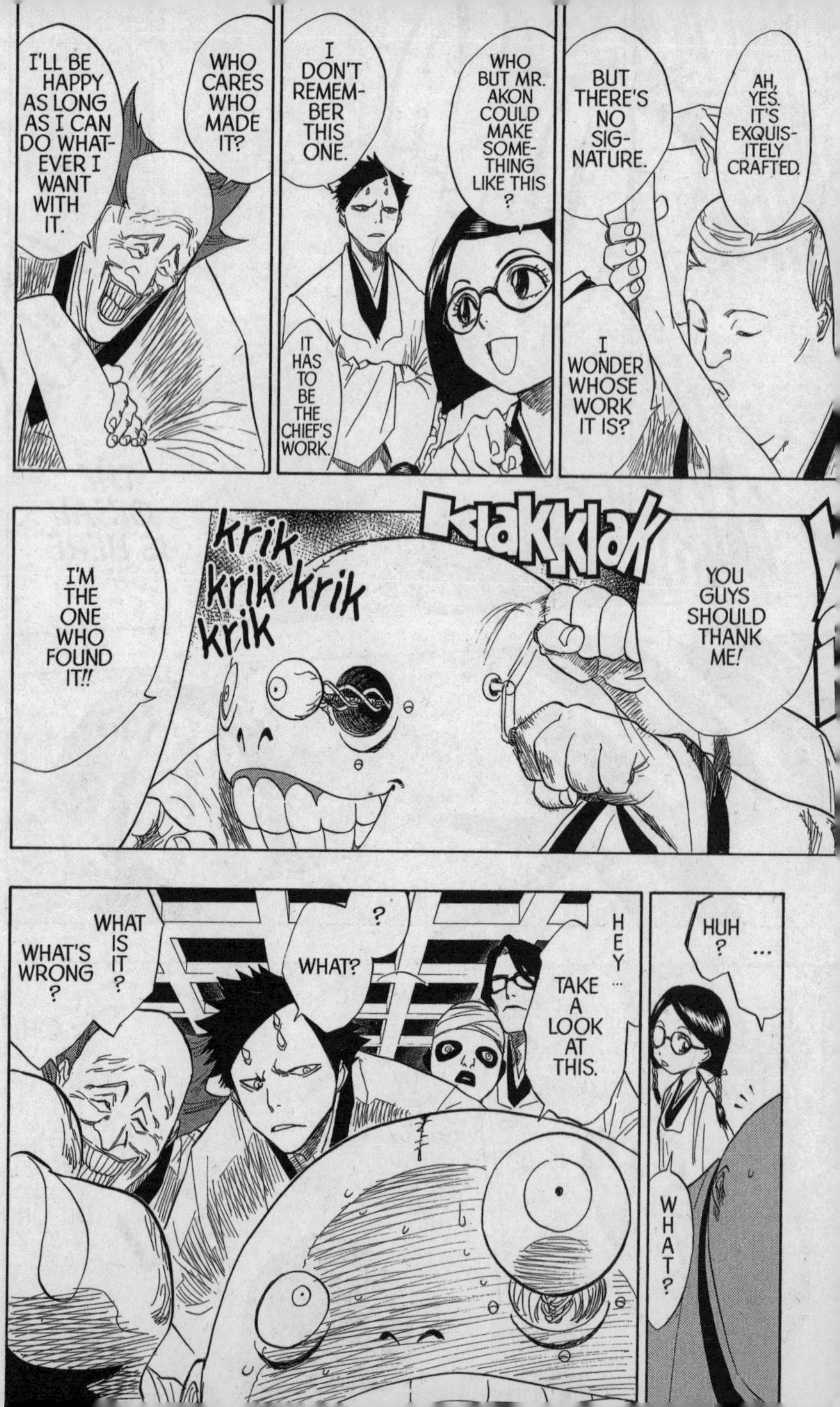
AH, YES. IT'S EXQUISITELY CRAFTED.
BUT THERE'S NO SIGNATURE.
I WONDER WHOSE WORK IT IS?
WHO BUT MR. AKON COULD MAKE SOMETHING LIKE THIS?
I DON'T REMEMBER THIS ONE.
IT HAS TO BE THE CHIEF'S WORK.
WHO CARES WHO MADE IT?
I'LL BE HAPPY AS LONG AS I CAN DO WHATEVER I WANT WITH IT.
KLAKKLAK
YOU GUYS SHOULD THANK ME!
krik krik krik krik
I'M THE ONE WHO FOUND IT!!
HUH? ...
WHAT?
HEY... TAKE A LOOK AT THIS.
?
WHAT?
WHAT IS IT?
WHAT'S WRONG?

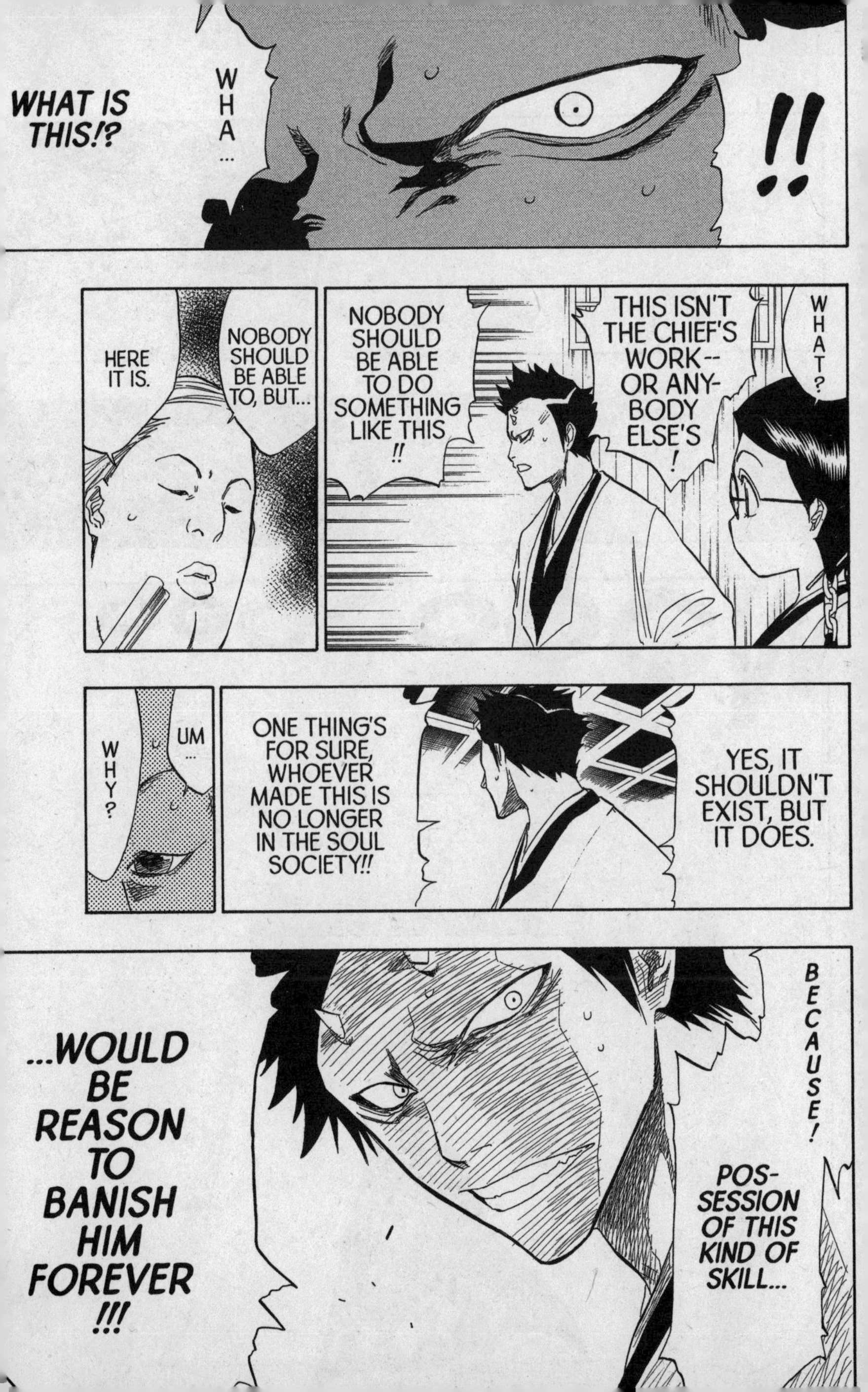
!!
WHA...
WHAT IS THIS!?
WHAT?
THIS ISN'T THE CHIEF'S WORK-- OR ANYBODY ELSE'S!
NOBODY SHOULD BE ABLE TO DO SOMETHING LIKE THIS!!
NOBODY SHOULD BE ABLE TO, BUT...
HERE IT IS.
YES, IT SHOULDN'T EXIST, BUT IT DOES.
ONE THING'S FOR SURE, WHOEVER MADE THIS IS NO LONGER IN THE SOUL SOCIETY!!
UM...
WHY?
BECAUSE!
POSSESSION OF THIS KIND OF SKILL...
...WOULD BE REASON TO BANISH HIM FOREVER!!!

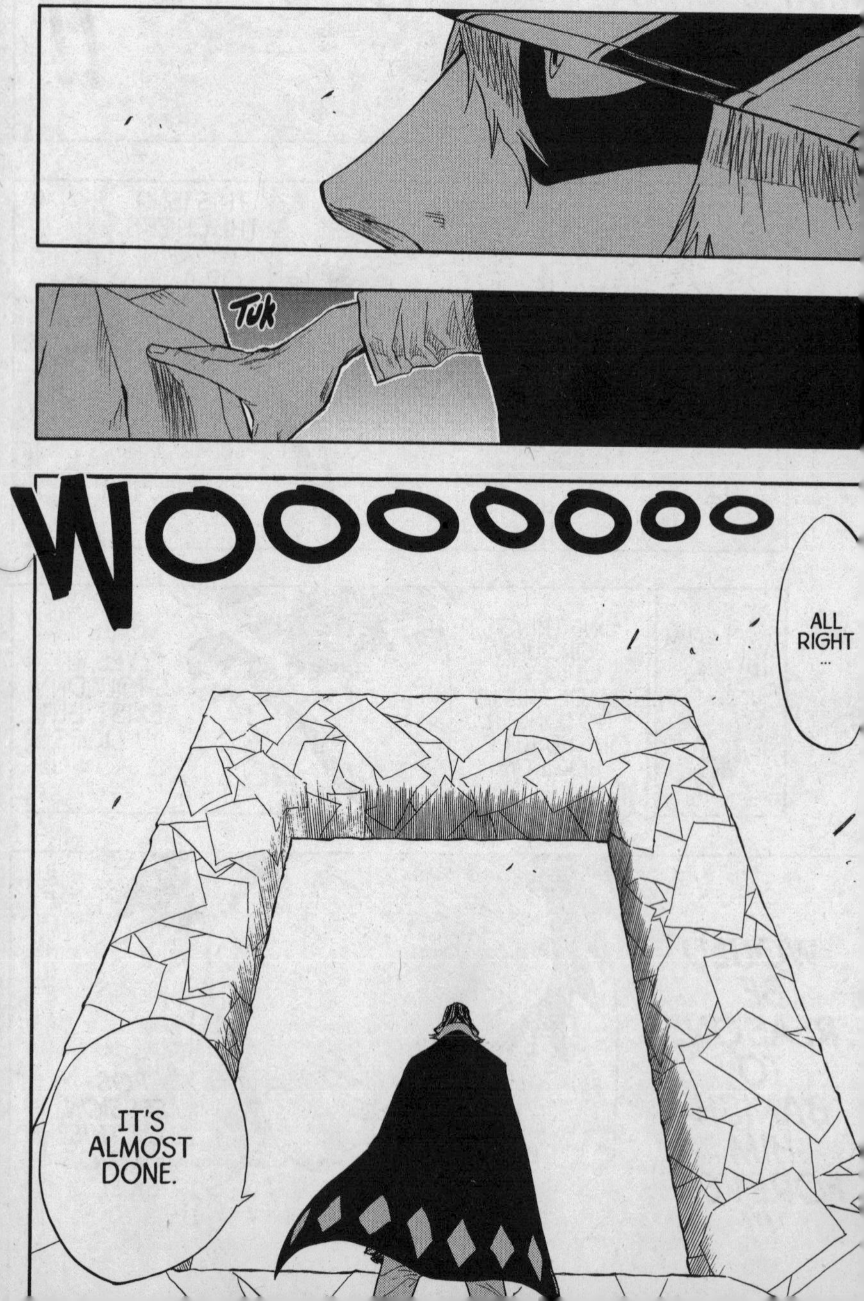
TUK
WOOOOOOO
ALL RIGHT ...
IT'S ALMOST DONE.

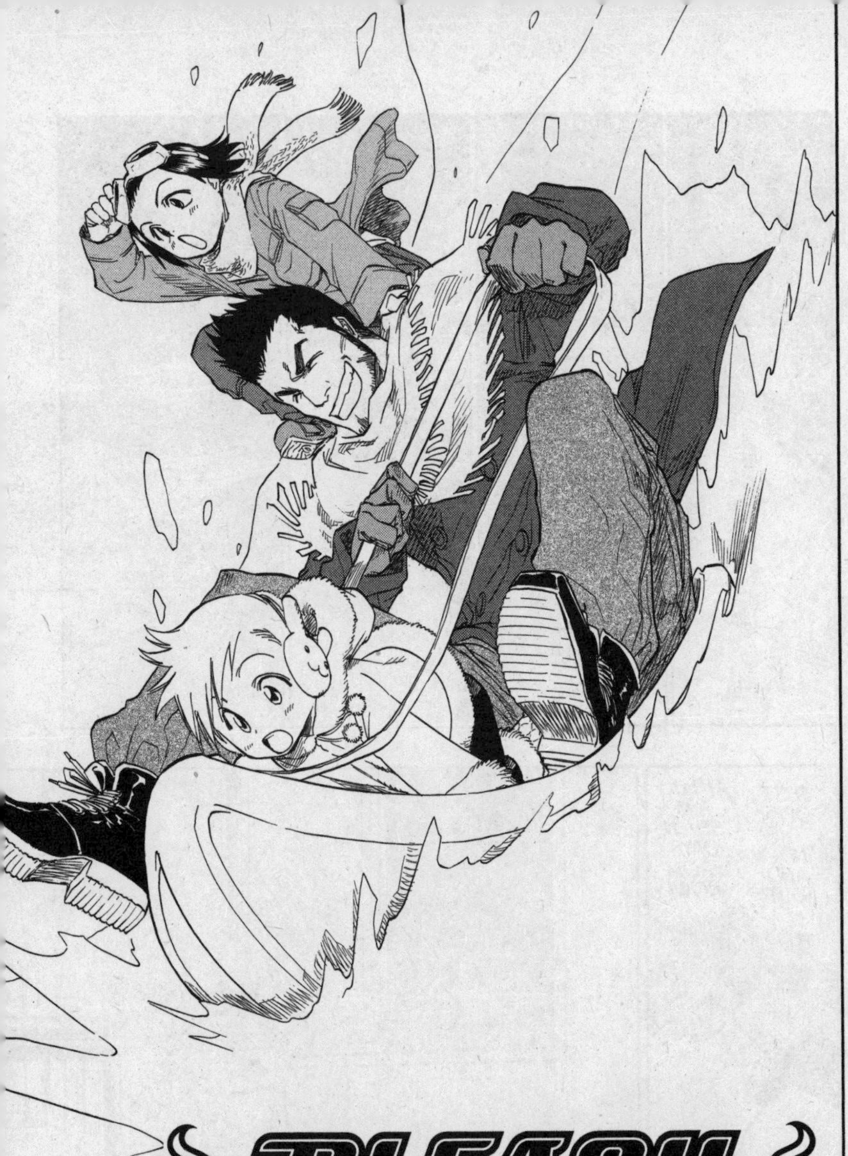

BLEACH

ブリーチ

69. 25:00 gathering

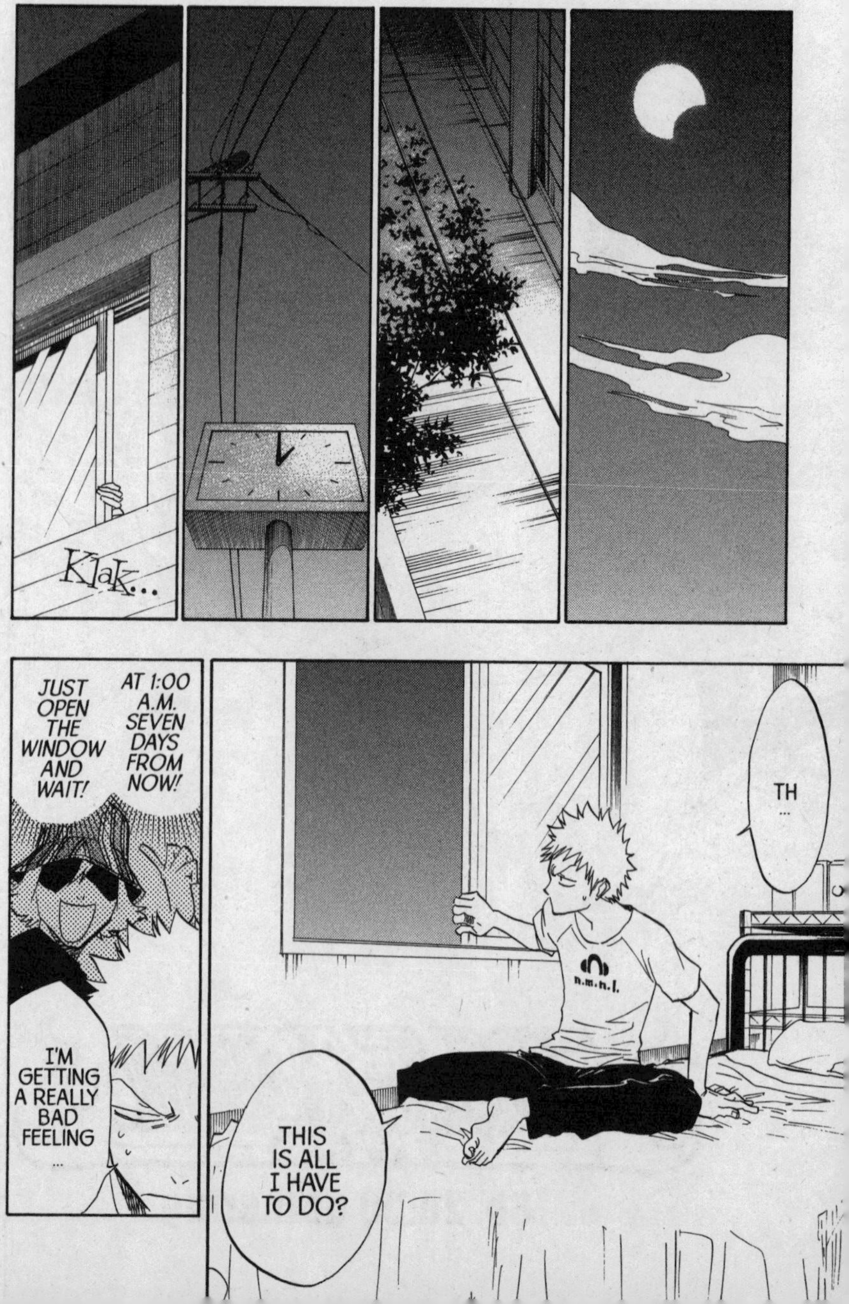
Klak...
JUST OPEN THE WINDOW AND WAIT!
AT 1:00 A.M. SEVEN DAYS FROM NOW!
I'M GETTING A REALLY BAD FEELING ...
TH ...
THIS IS ALL I HAVE TO DO?

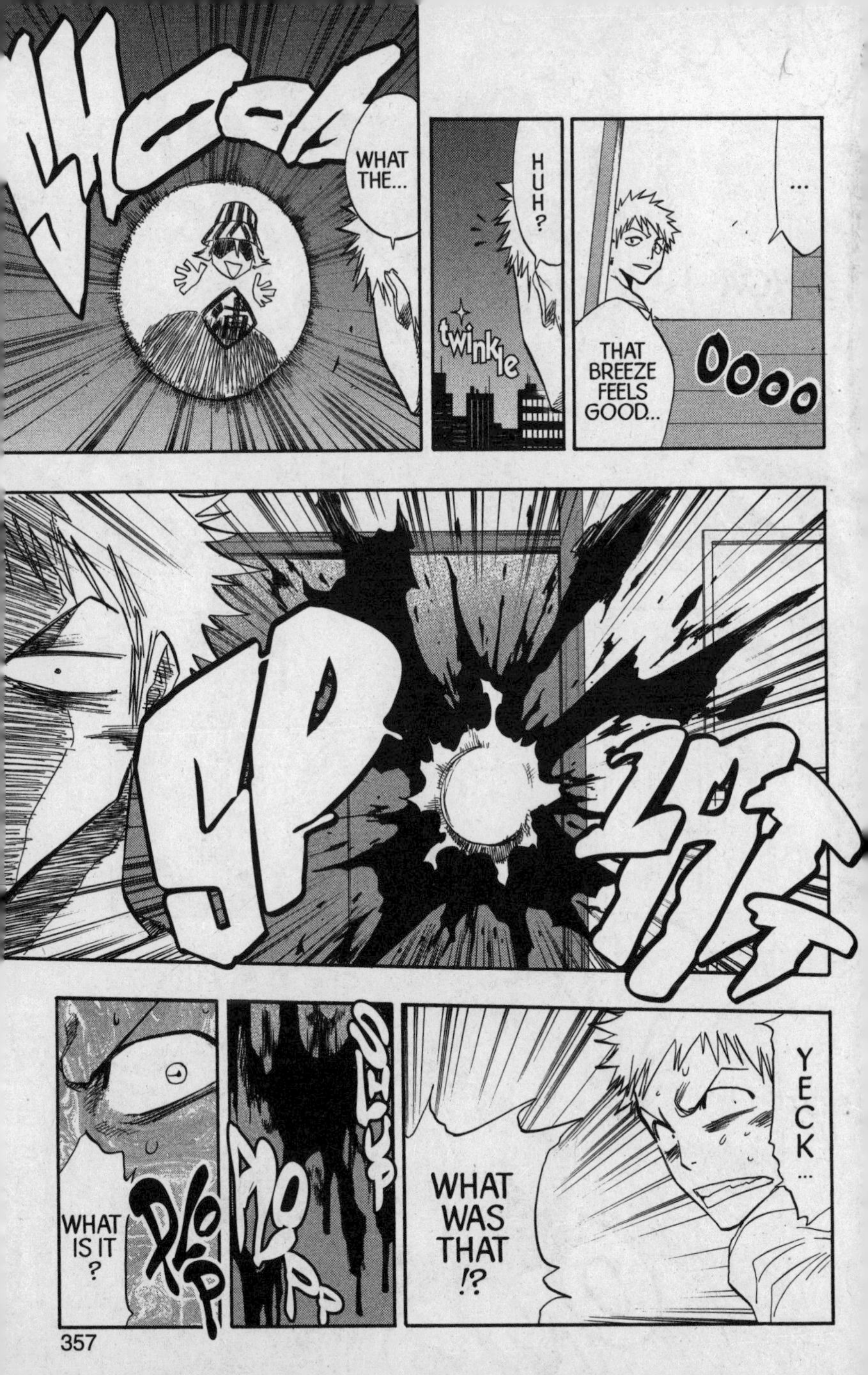
...
THAT BREEZE FEELS GOOD...
OOOO
HUH?
twinkle
WHAT THE...
SPLAT
YECK...
WHAT WAS THAT!?
WHAT IS IT?
PLOP

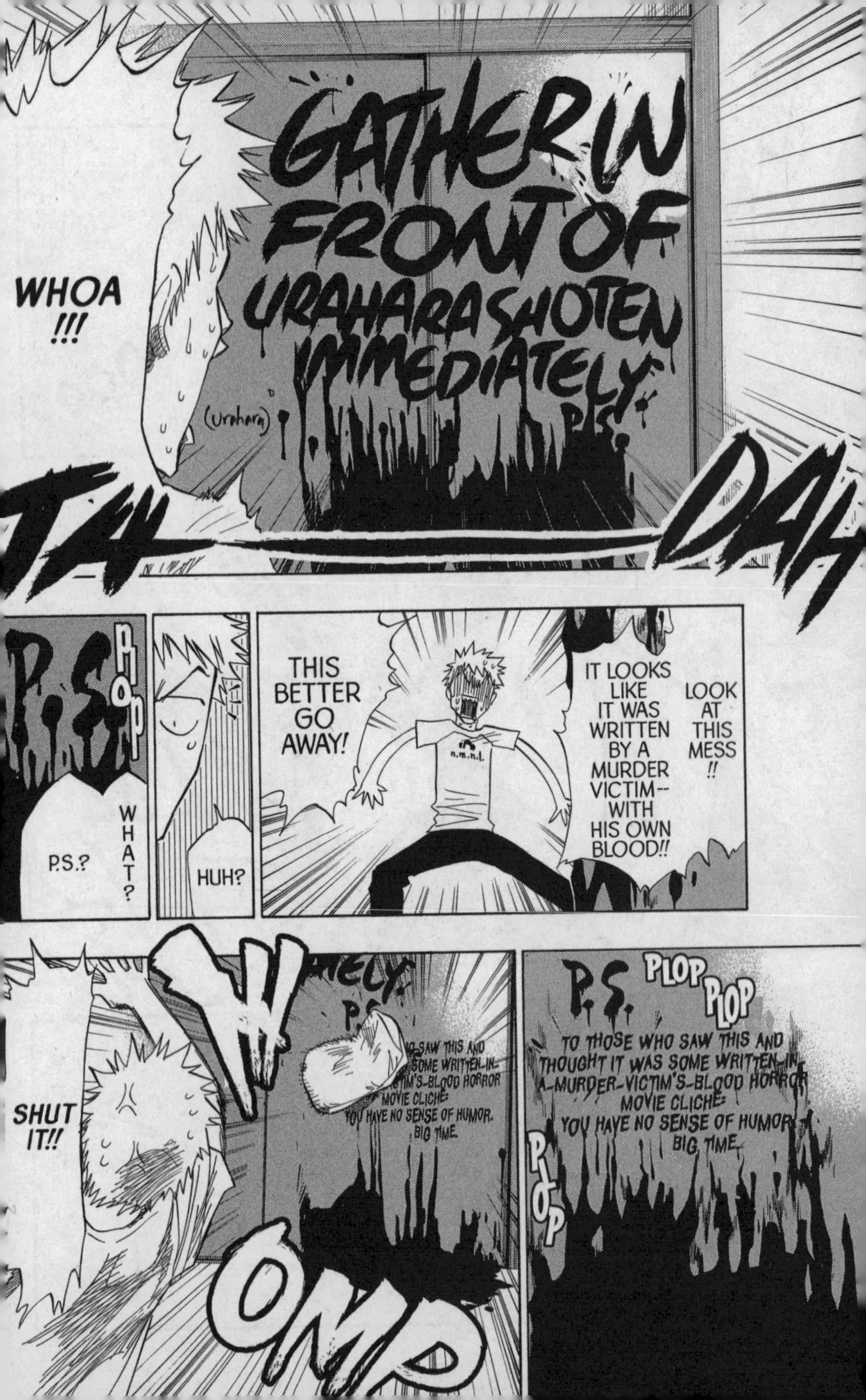
GATHER IN FRONT OF URAHARA SHOTEN IMMEDIATELY.
(urahara)
P.S.
WHOA!!!
TA-DAH
LOOK AT THIS MESS!!
IT LOOKS LIKE IT WAS WRITTEN BY A MURDER VICTIM--WITH HIS OWN BLOOD!!
THIS BETTER GO AWAY!
HUH?
P.S.
plop
WHAT?
P.S.?
P.S.
PLOP PLOP
TO THOSE WHO SAW THIS AND THOUGHT IT WAS SOME WRITTEN-IN-A-MURDER-VICTIM'S-BLOOD HORROR MOVIE CLICHE:
YOU HAVE NO SENSE OF HUMOR.
BIG TIME.
PLOP
SHUT IT!!

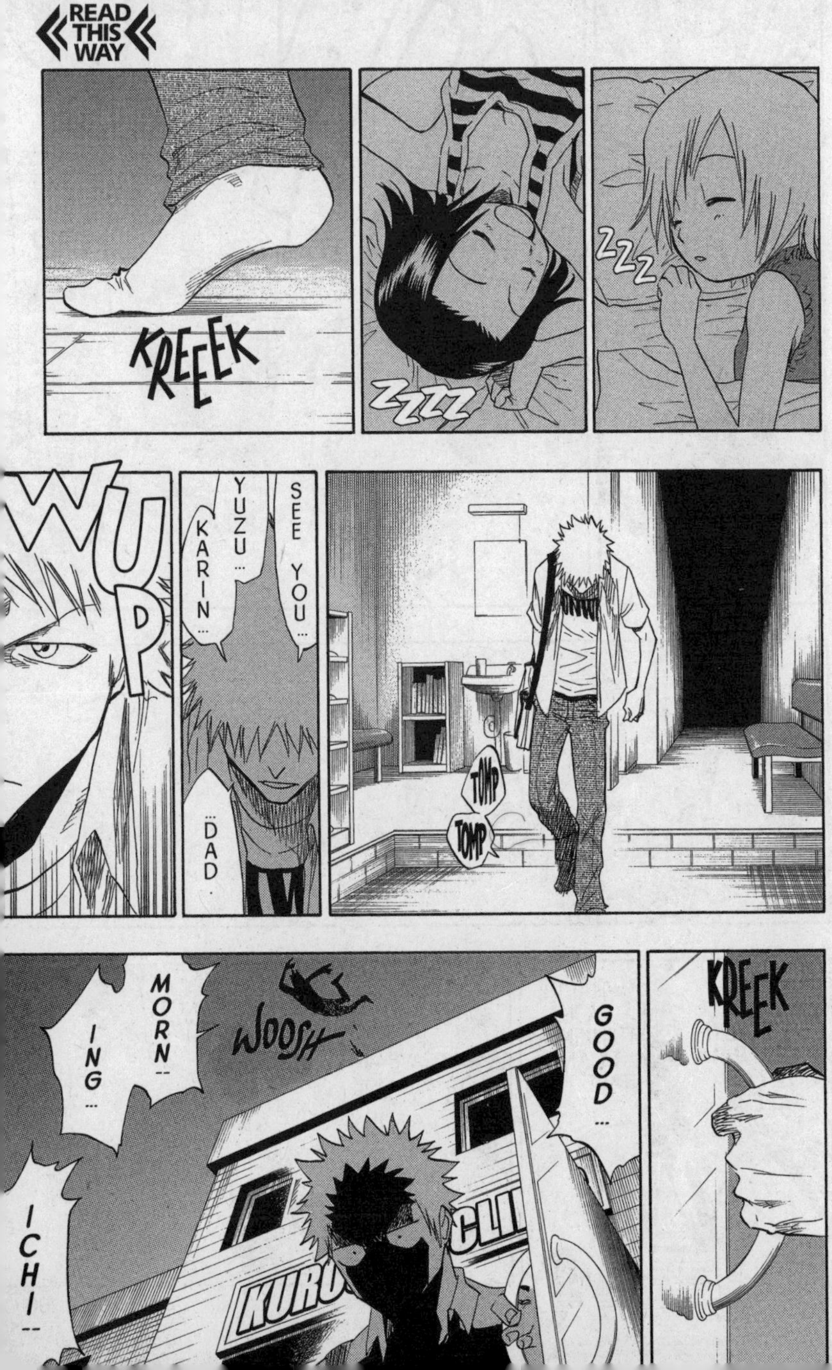
READ THIS WAY
ZZZ
ZZZZ
KREEEK
TOMP
TOMP
SEE YOU...
YUZU...
KARIN...
...DAD.
WUP
KREEK
GOOD...
MORN--
ING...
WOOSH
ICHI--
KURO
CLI

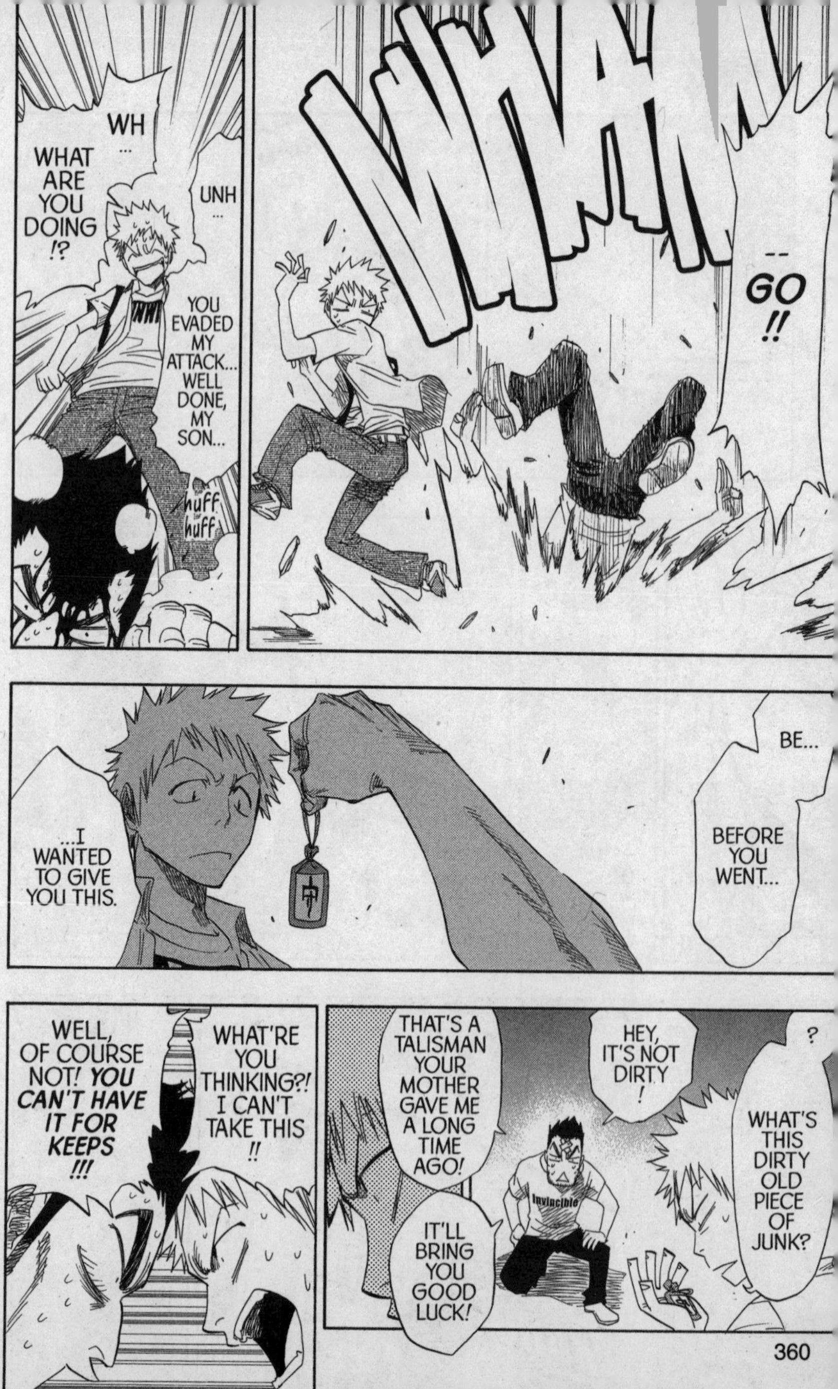
--GO!!
WHAM
UNH...
WH... WHAT ARE YOU DOING!?
YOU EVADED MY ATTACK... WELL DONE, MY SON...
huff huff
BE...
BEFORE YOU WENT...
...I WANTED TO GIVE YOU THIS.
?
WHAT'S THIS DIRTY OLD PIECE OF JUNK?
HEY, IT'S NOT DIRTY!
THAT'S A TALISMAN YOUR MOTHER GAVE ME A LONG TIME AGO!
IT'LL BRING YOU GOOD LUCK!
Invincible
WHAT'RE YOU THINKING?! I CAN'T TAKE THIS!!
WELL, OF COURSE NOT! ***YOU CAN'T HAVE IT FOR KEEPS!!!***

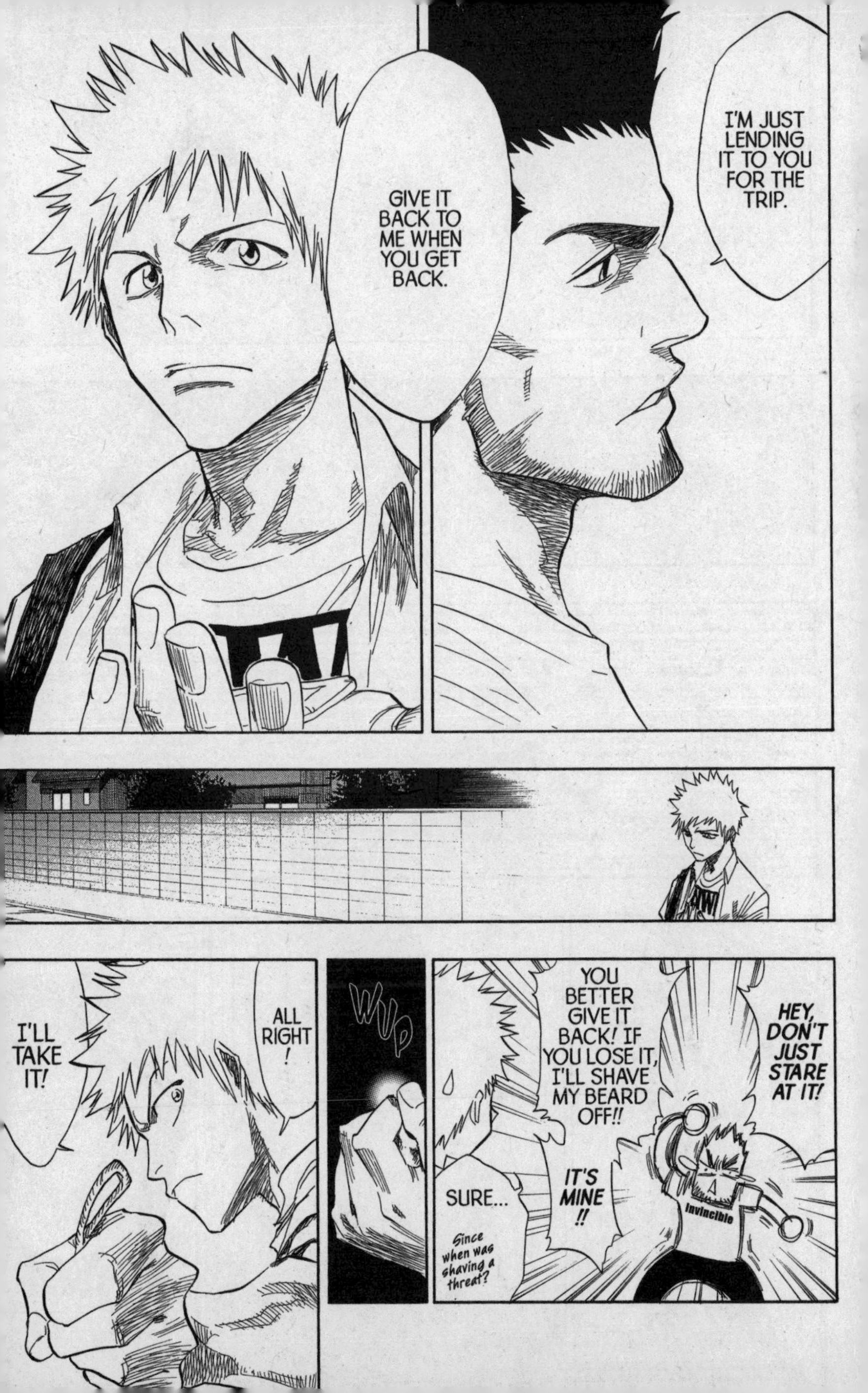

I'M JUST LENDING IT TO YOU FOR THE TRIP.
GIVE IT BACK TO ME WHEN YOU GET BACK.
HEY, DON'T JUST STARE AT IT!
YOU BETTER GIVE IT BACK! IF YOU LOSE IT, I'LL SHAVE MY BEARD OFF!!
IT'S MINE!!
Invincible
SURE...
Since when was shaving a threat?
WUP
ALL RIGHT!
I'LL TAKE IT!

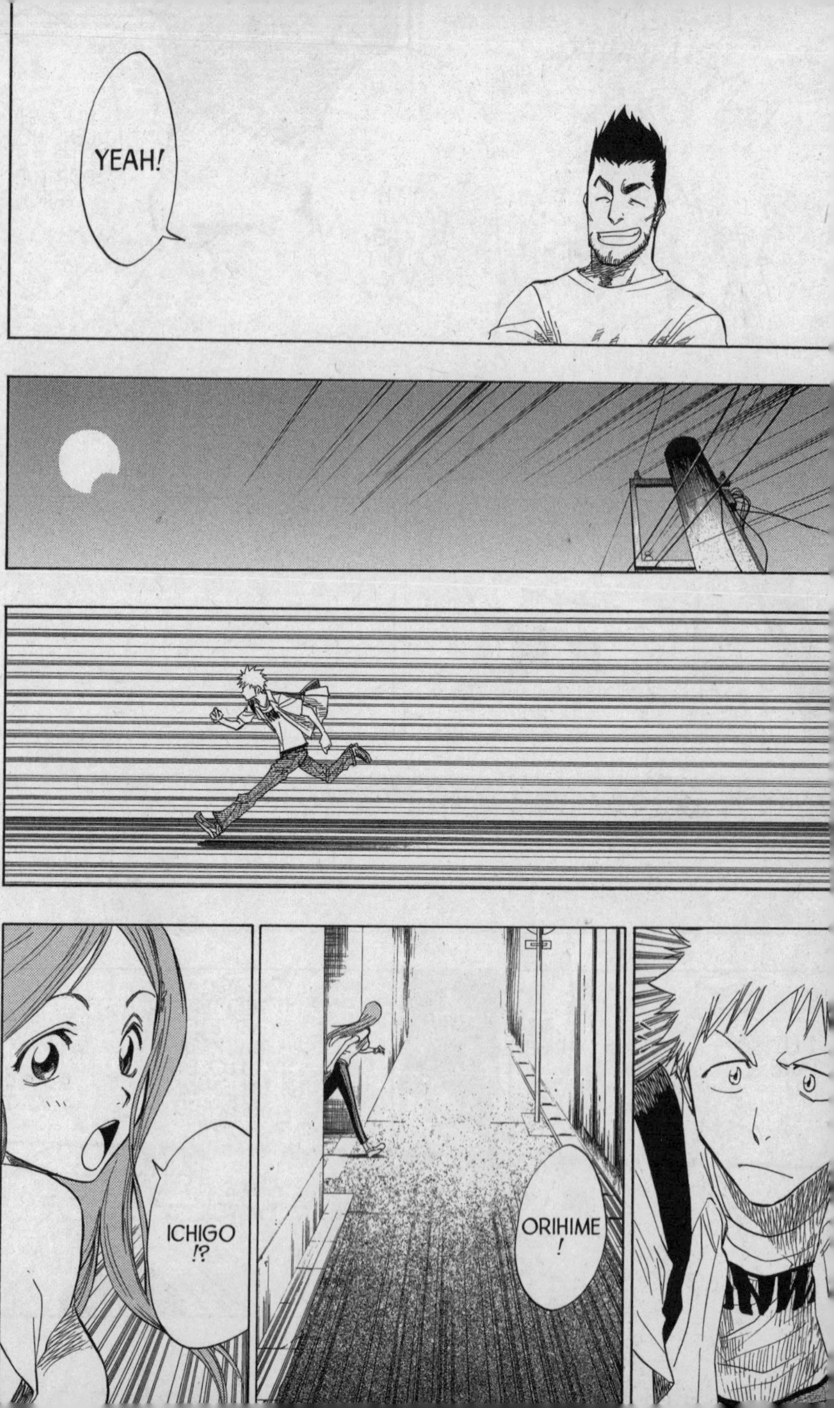
YEAH!
ORIHIME!
ICHIGO!?

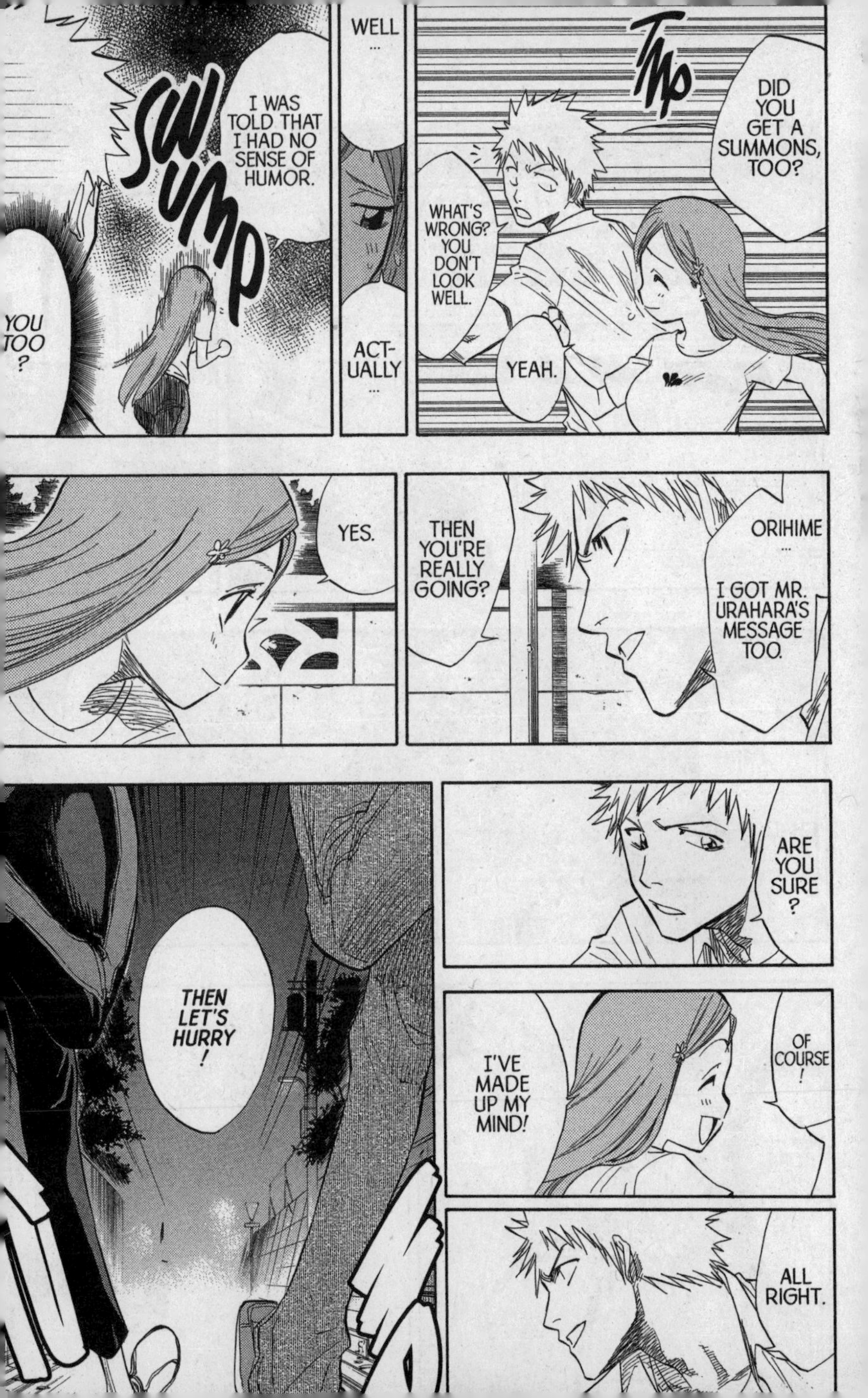
TMP
DID YOU GET A SUMMONS, TOO?
WHAT'S WRONG? YOU DON'T LOOK WELL.
YEAH.
WELL ...
ACT-UALLY ...
SWUMP
I WAS TOLD THAT I HAD NO SENSE OF HUMOR.
YOU TOO ?
ORIHIME ...
I GOT MR. URAHARA'S MESSAGE TOO.
THEN YOU'RE REALLY GOING?
YES.
ARE YOU SURE ?
OF COURSE !
I'VE MADE UP MY MIND!
ALL RIGHT.
THEN LET'S HURRY !

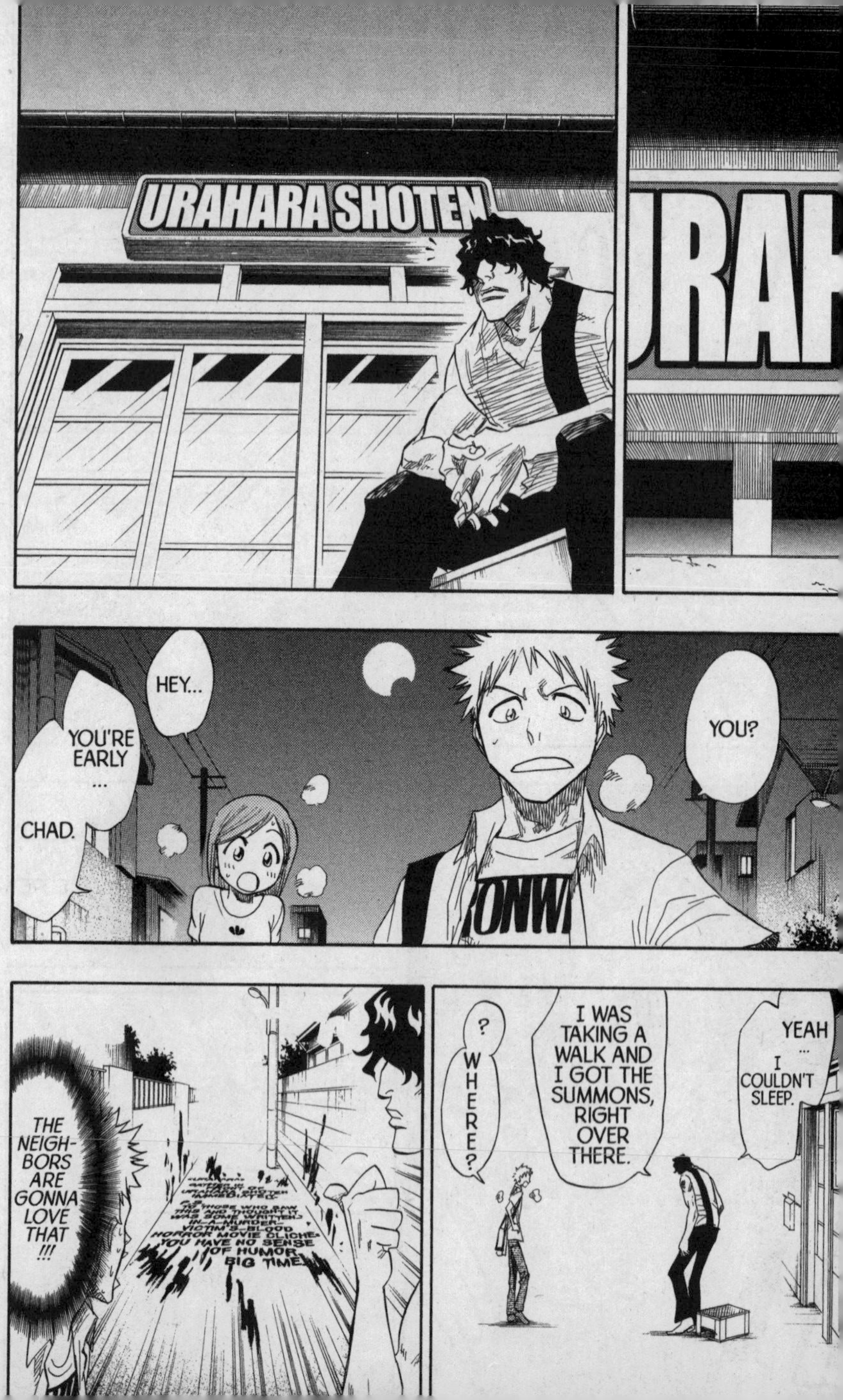
URAHARA SHOTEN
YOU?
HEY...
YOU'RE EARLY ...
CHAD.
YEAH ... I COULDN'T SLEEP.
I WAS TAKING A WALK AND I GOT THE SUMMONS, RIGHT OVER THERE.
? WHERE?
P.S. TO THOSE WHO SAW THIS AND THOUGHT IT WAS SOME WRITTEN-IN-A-MURDER-VICTIM'S-BLOOD HORROR MOVIE CLICHE. YOU HAVE NO SENSE OF HUMOR. BIG TIME.
THE NEIGH-BORS ARE GONNA LOVE THAT!!!

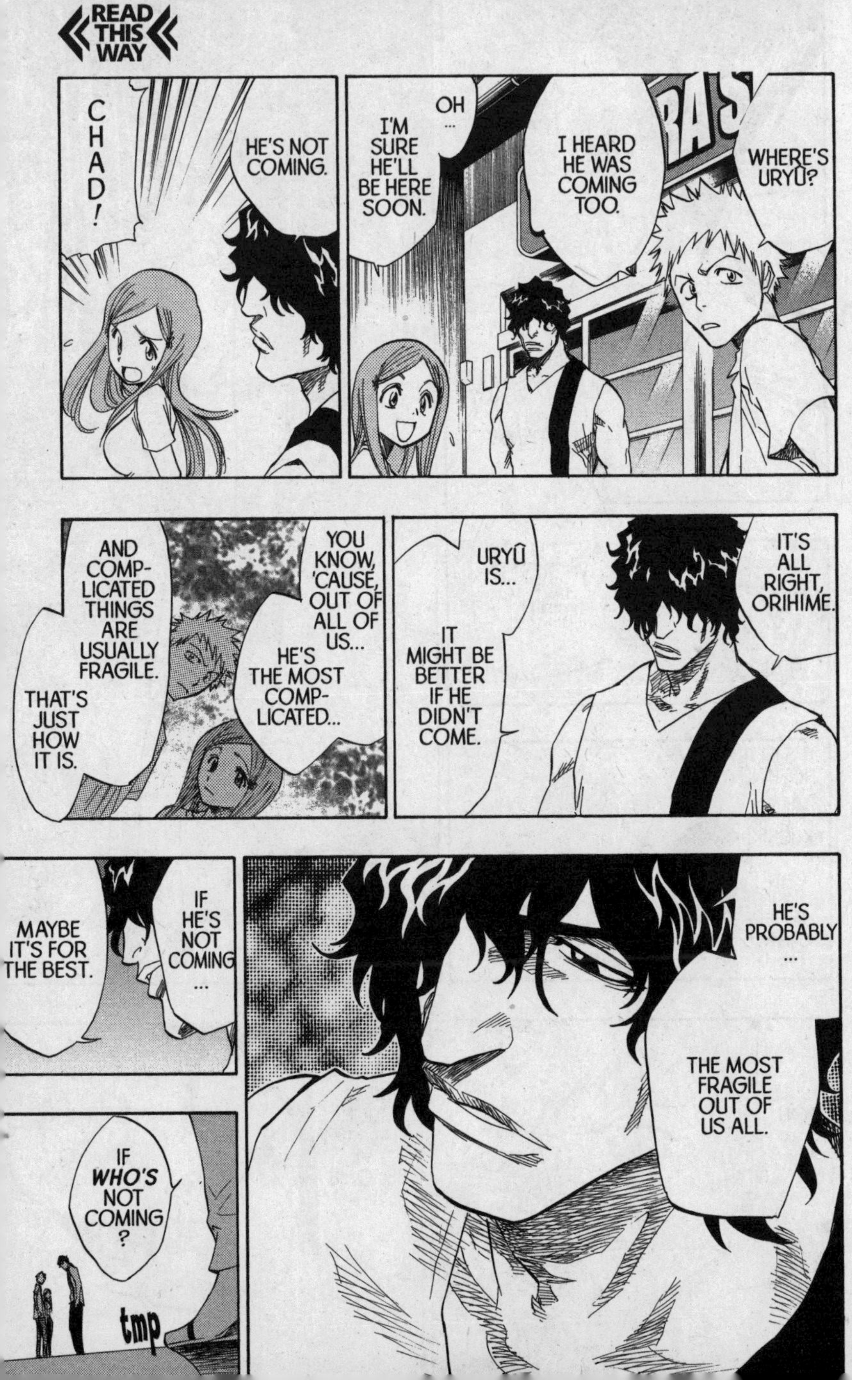
READ THIS WAY
WHERE'S URYŪ?
I HEARD HE WAS COMING TOO.
OH...
I'M SURE HE'LL BE HERE SOON.
HE'S NOT COMING.
CHAD!
IT'S ALL RIGHT, ORIHIME.
URYŪ IS...
IT MIGHT BE BETTER IF HE DIDN'T COME.
YOU KNOW, 'CAUSE, OUT OF ALL OF US...
HE'S THE MOST COMPLICATED...
AND COMPLICATED THINGS ARE USUALLY FRAGILE.
THAT'S JUST HOW IT IS.
HE'S PROBABLY...
THE MOST FRAGILE OUT OF US ALL.
IF HE'S NOT COMING...
MAYBE IT'S FOR THE BEST.
IF *WHO'S* NOT COMING?
tmp

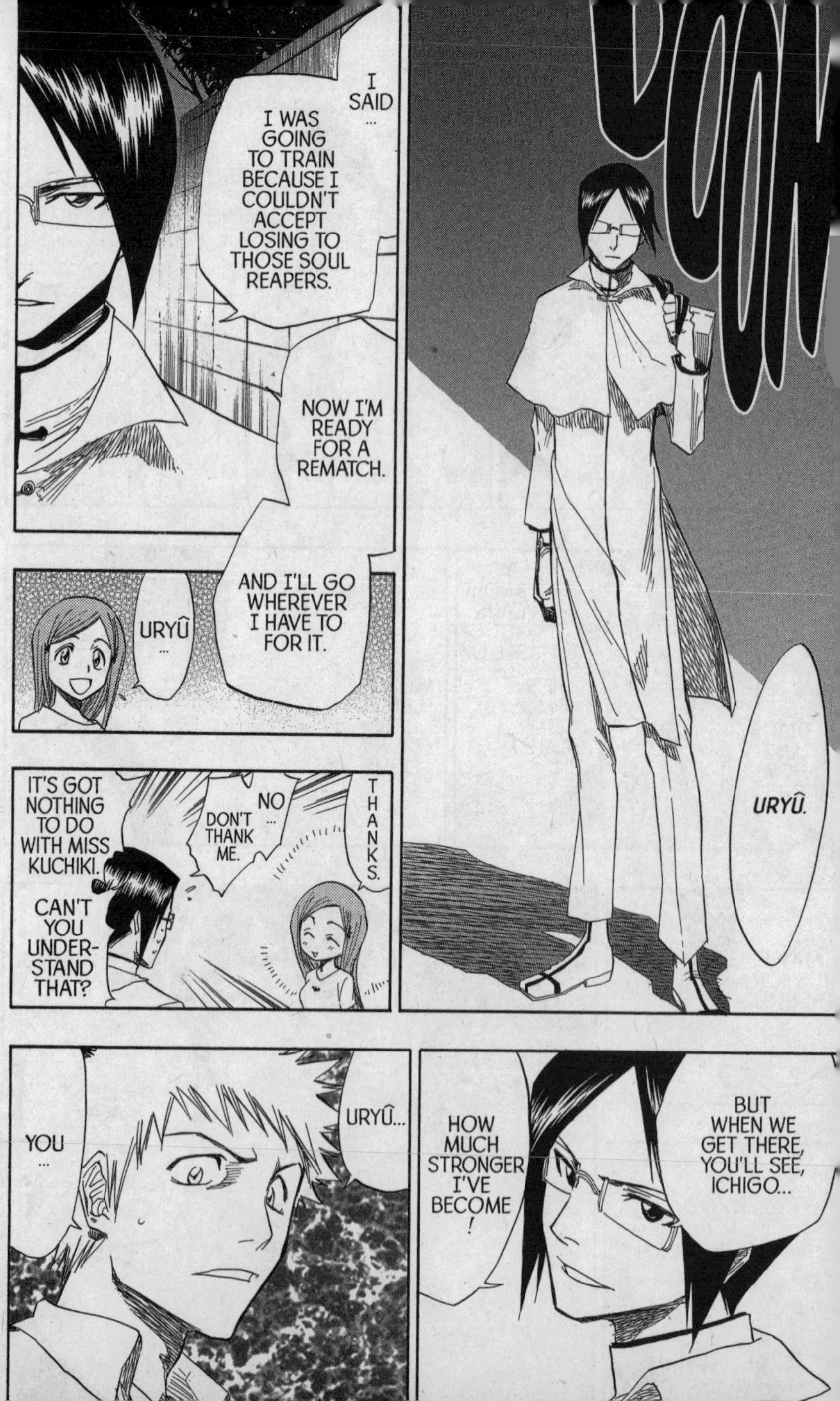

URYÛ.
I SAID ...
I WAS GOING TO TRAIN BECAUSE I COULDN'T ACCEPT LOSING TO THOSE SOUL REAPERS.
NOW I'M READY FOR A REMATCH.
AND I'LL GO WHEREVER I HAVE TO FOR IT.
URYÛ ...
THANKS.
NO ...
DON'T THANK ME.
IT'S GOT NOTHING TO DO WITH MISS KUCHIKI.
CAN'T YOU UNDER-STAND THAT?
BUT WHEN WE GET THERE, YOU'LL SEE, ICHIGO...
HOW MUCH STRONGER I'VE BECOME !
URYÛ...
YOU ...

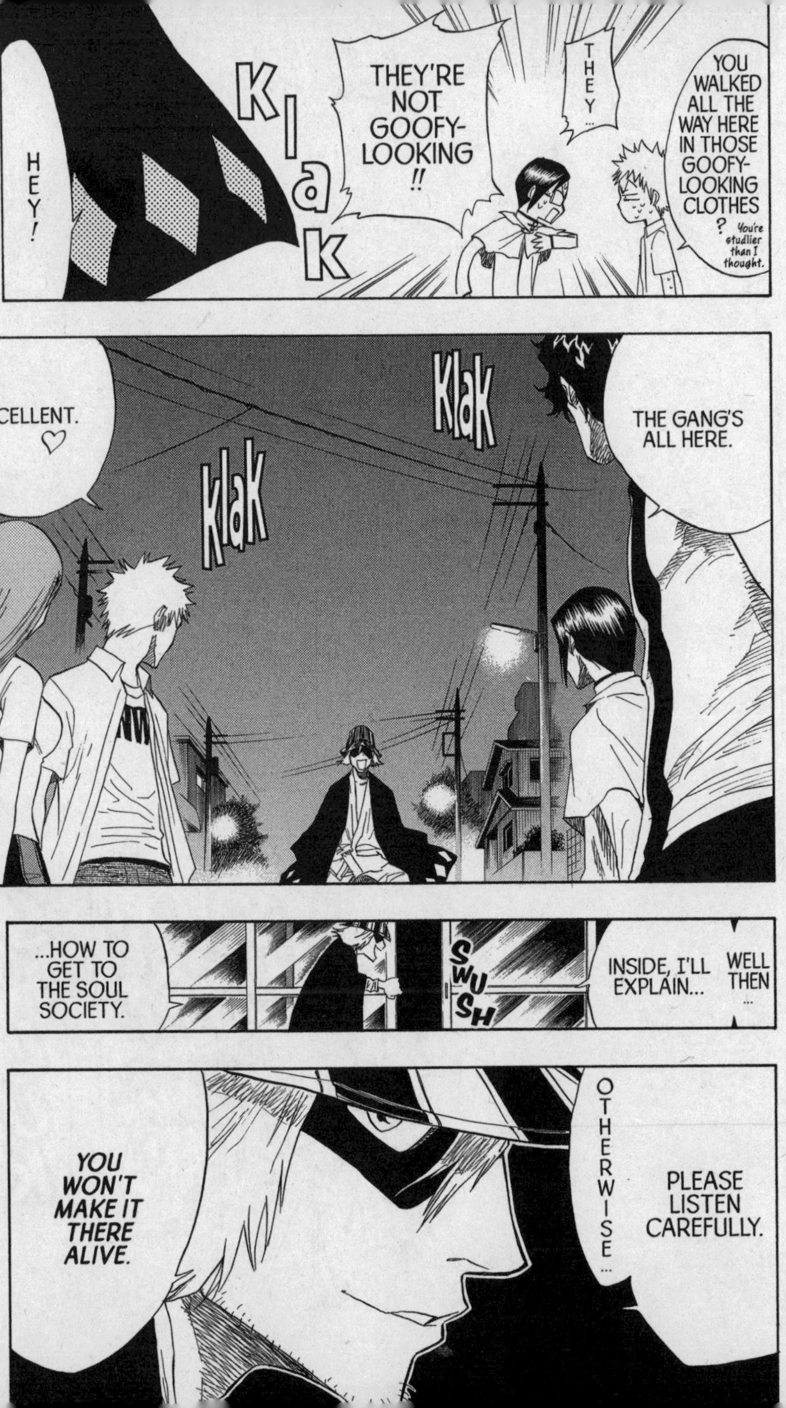
YOU WALKED ALL THE WAY HERE IN THOSE GOOFY-LOOKING CLOTHES?
You're studlier than I thought.
THEY...
THEY'RE NOT GOOFY-LOOKING!!
Klak
HEY!
THE GANG'S ALL HERE.
Klak
Klak
EXCELLENT. ♡
WELL THEN...
INSIDE, I'LL EXPLAIN...
SWUSH
...HOW TO GET TO THE SOUL SOCIETY.
PLEASE LISTEN CAREFULLY.
OTHERWISE...
YOU WON'T MAKE IT THERE ALIVE.

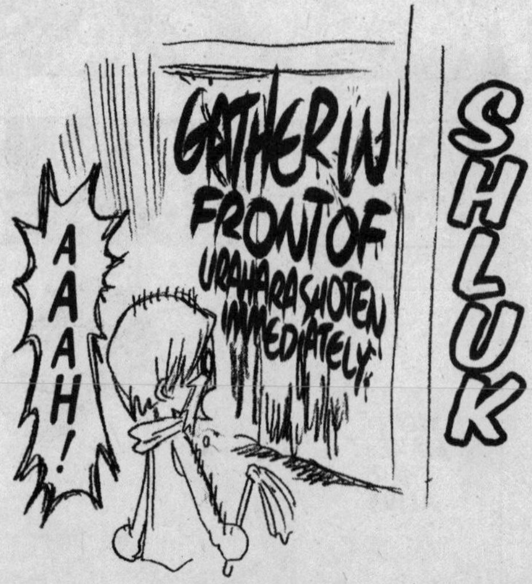
SHLUK
GATHER IN FRONT OF URAHARA SHOTEN IMMEDIATELY.
AAAAH!

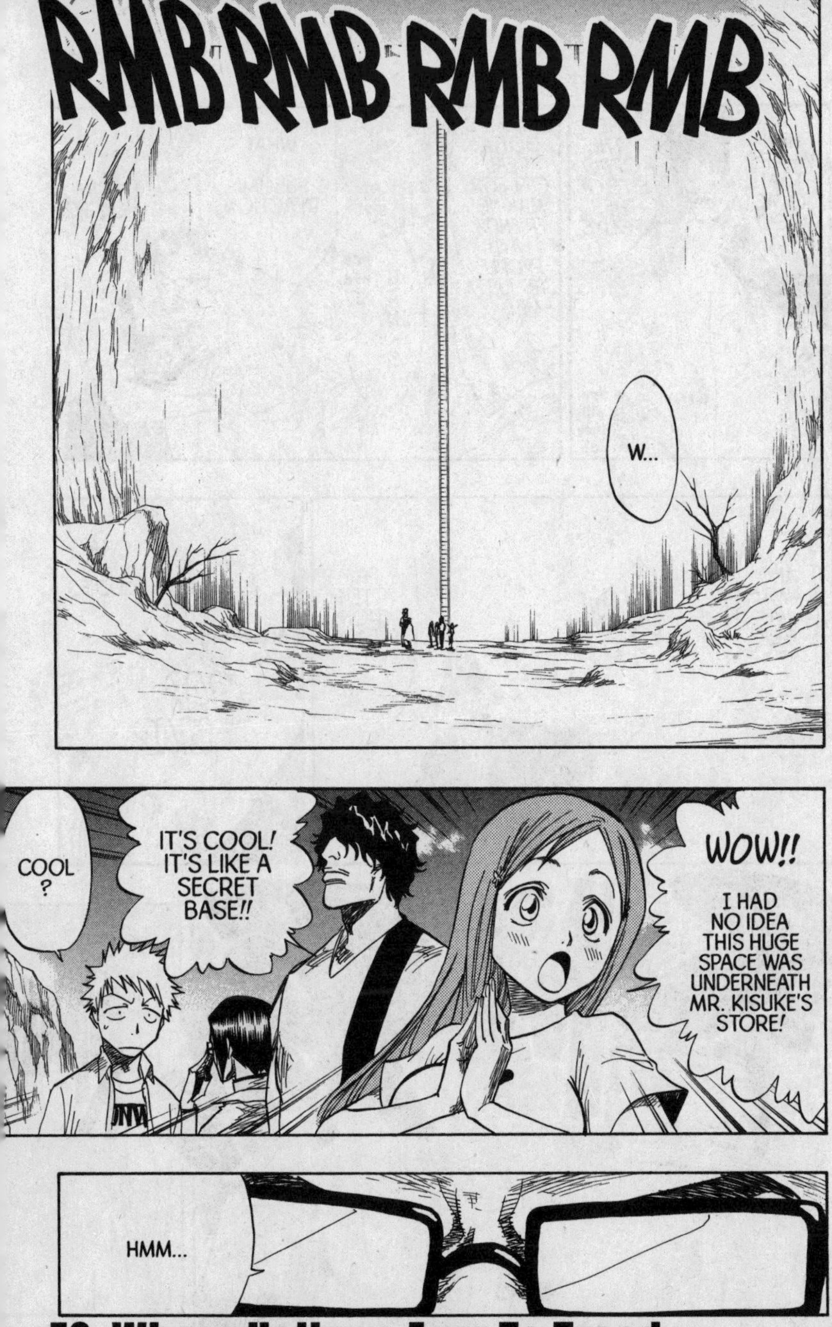
RMB RMB RMB RMB
W...
WOW!!
I HAD NO IDEA THIS HUGE SPACE WAS UNDERNEATH MR. KISUKE'S STORE!
IT'S COOL! IT'S LIKE A SECRET BASE!!
COOL?
HMM...

70. Where Hollows Fear To Tread

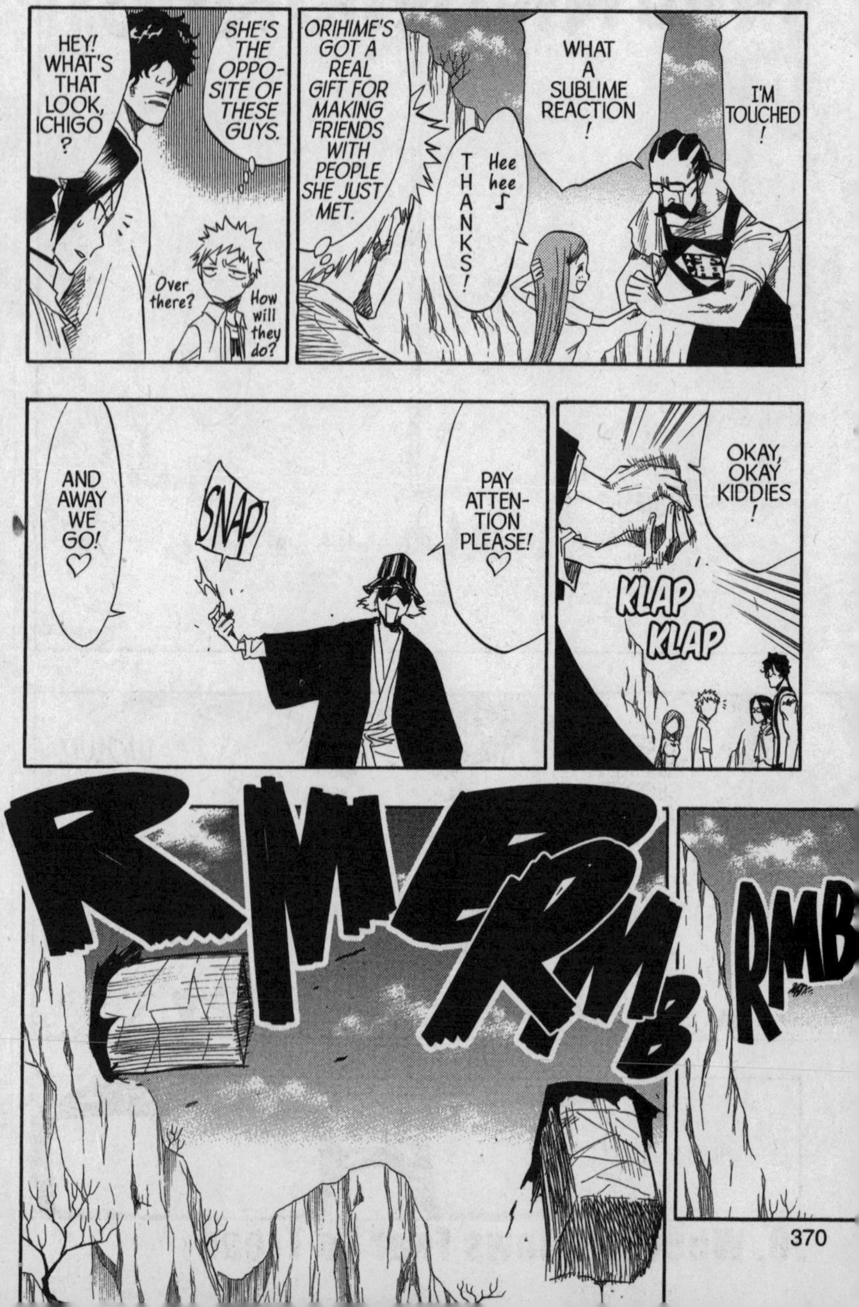
ORIHIME'S GOT A REAL GIFT FOR MAKING FRIENDS WITH PEOPLE SHE JUST MET.
I'M TOUCHED!
WHAT A SUBLIME REACTION!
THANKS!
Hee hee ♪
SHE'S THE OPPOSITE OF THESE GUYS.
HEY! WHAT'S THAT LOOK, ICHIGO?
Over there?
How will they do?
OKAY, OKAY KIDDIES!
KLAP KLAP
PAY ATTENTION PLEASE! ♡
SNAP
AND AWAY WE GO! ♡
RMB
RMBRMB

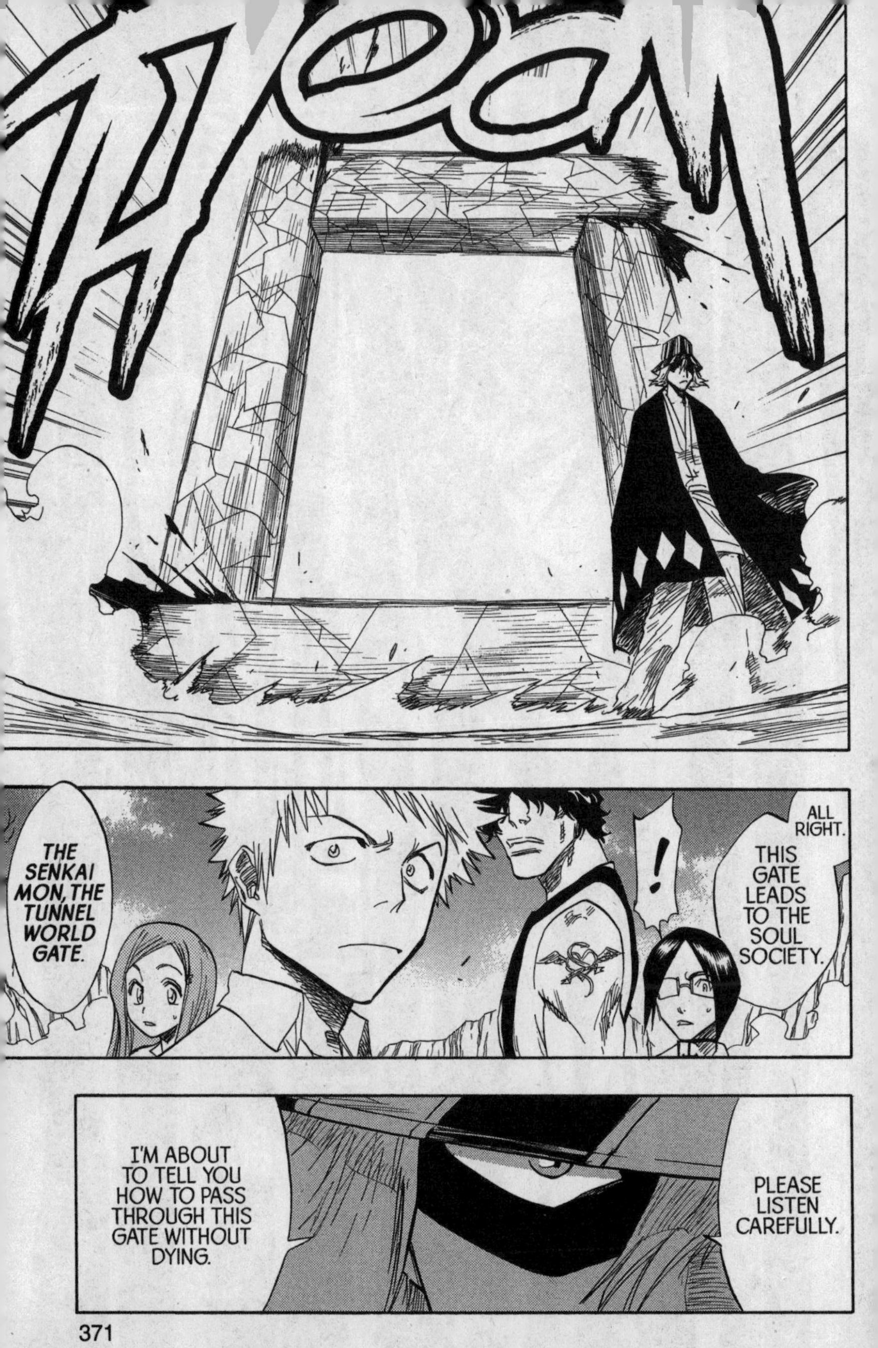
VOOM
ALL RIGHT.
THIS GATE LEADS TO THE SOUL SOCIETY.
!
THE SENKAI MON, THE TUNNEL WORLD GATE.
PLEASE LISTEN CAREFULLY.
I'M ABOUT TO TELL YOU HOW TO PASS THROUGH THIS GATE WITHOUT DYING.

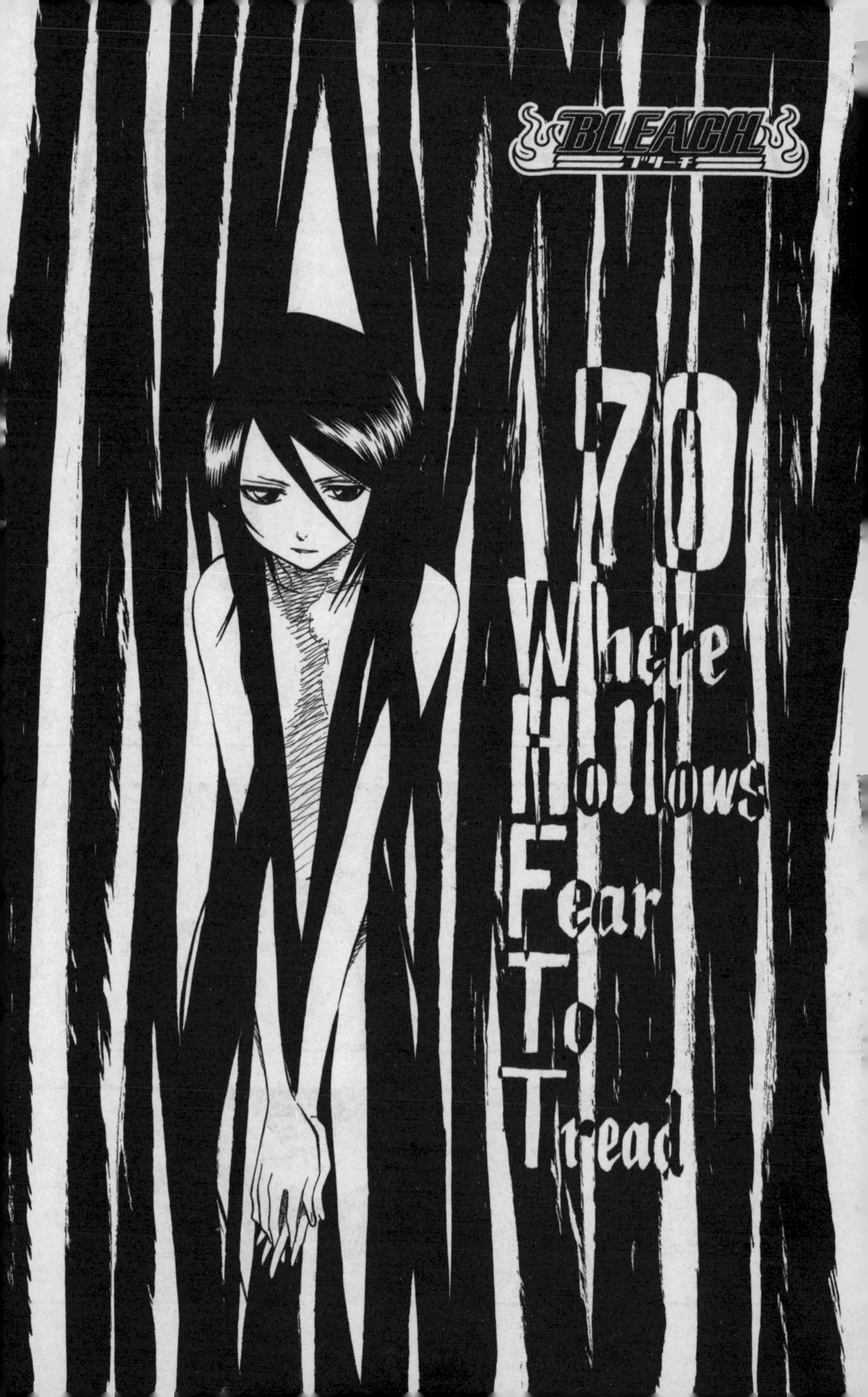
BLEACH
ブリーチ
70
Where Hollows Fear To Tread

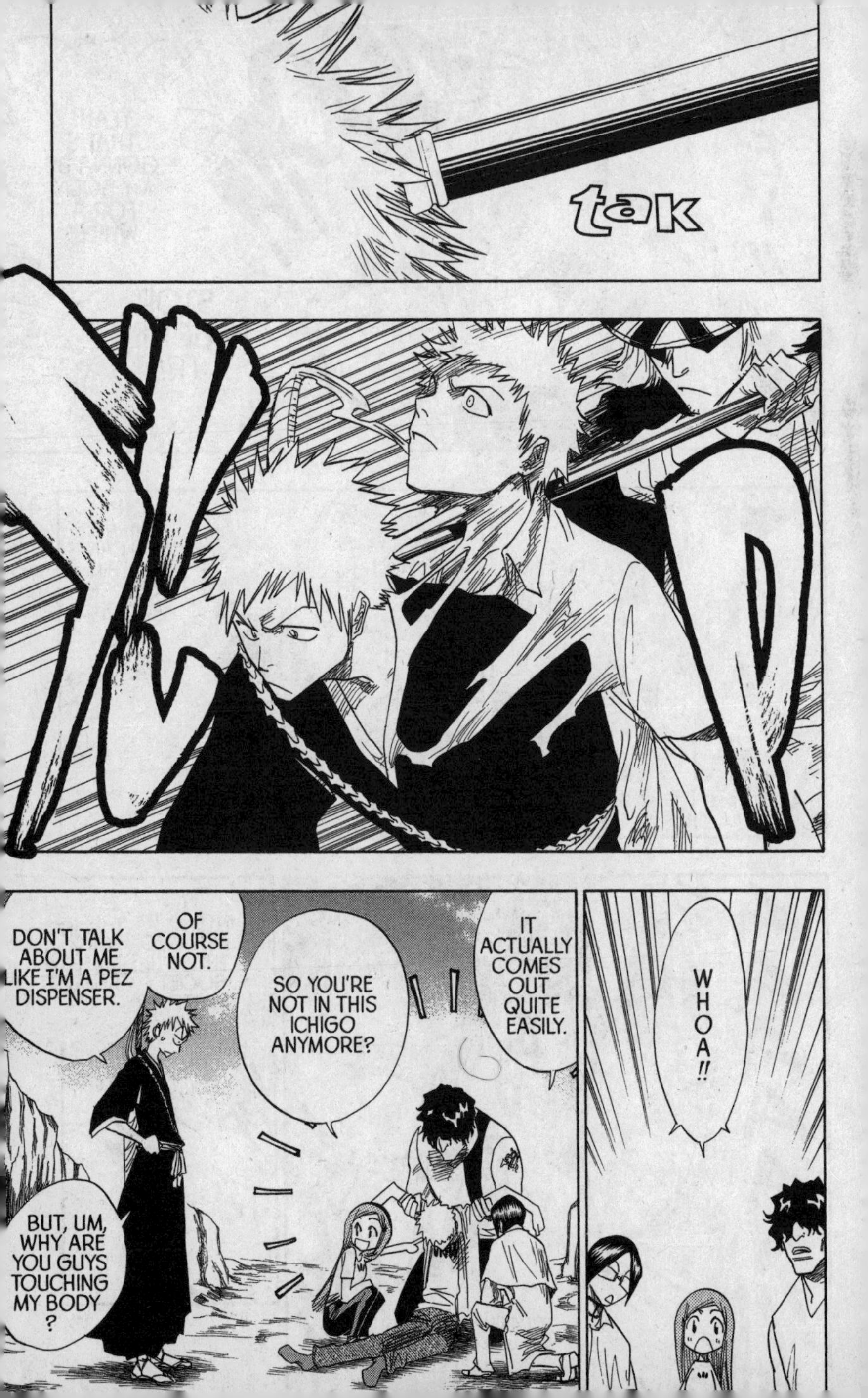
tak
WHOA!!
IT ACTUALLY COMES OUT QUITE EASILY.
SO YOU'RE NOT IN THIS ICHIGO ANYMORE?
OF COURSE NOT.
DON'T TALK ABOUT ME LIKE I'M A PEZ DISPENSER.
BUT, UM, WHY ARE YOU GUYS TOUCHING MY BODY?

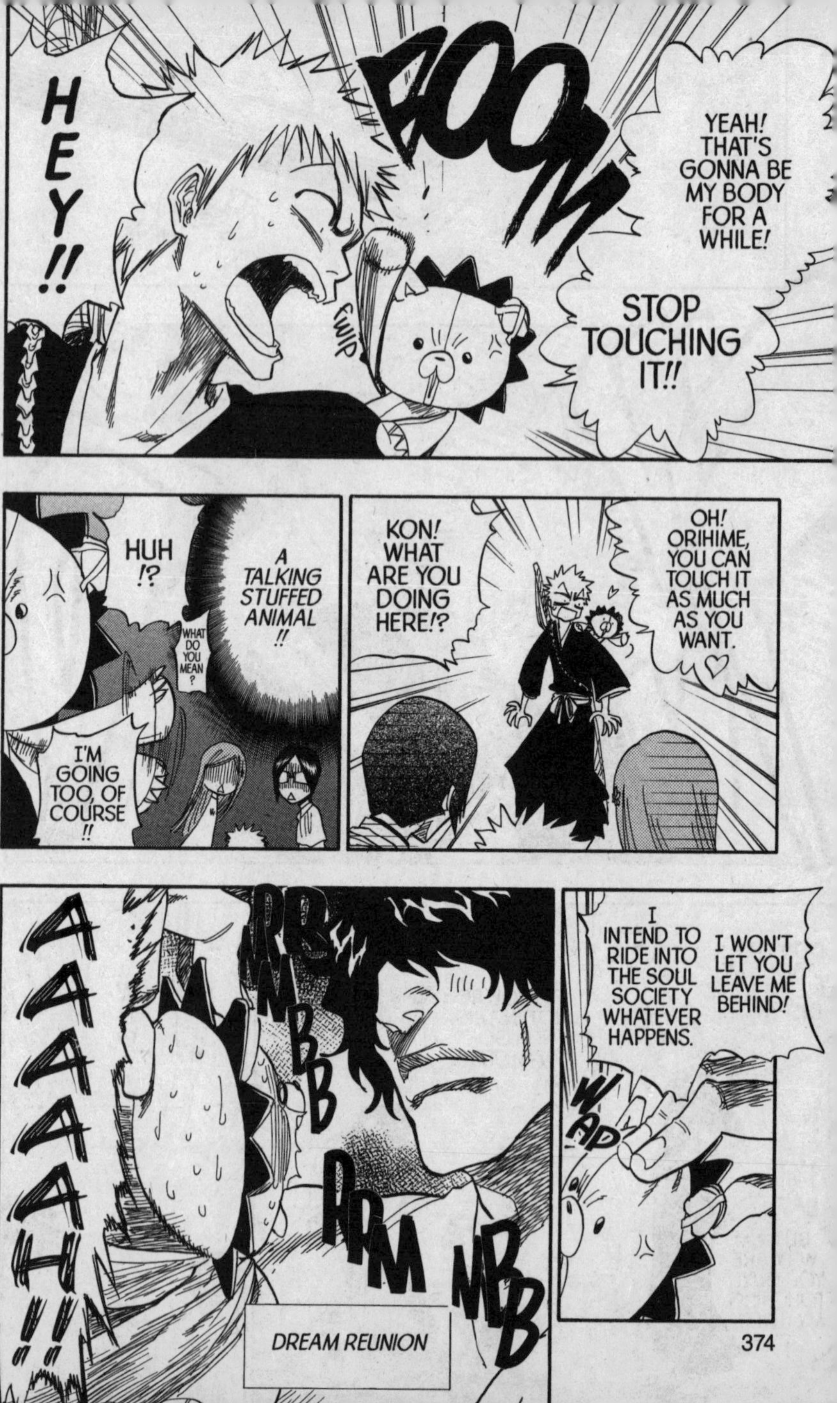
YEAH! THAT'S GONNA BE MY BODY FOR A WHILE!
STOP TOUCHING IT!!
ZOOM
FWIP
HEY!!
OH! ORIHIME, YOU CAN TOUCH IT AS MUCH AS YOU WANT.
KON! WHAT ARE YOU DOING HERE!?
A TALKING STUFFED ANIMAL!!
HUH!?
WHAT DO YOU MEAN?
I'M GOING TOO, OF COURSE!!
I WON'T LET YOU LEAVE ME BEHIND!
I INTEND TO RIDE INTO THE SOUL SOCIETY WHATEVER HAPPENS.
WAD
RRRMNBB
RRRMNBB
AAAAAAH!!

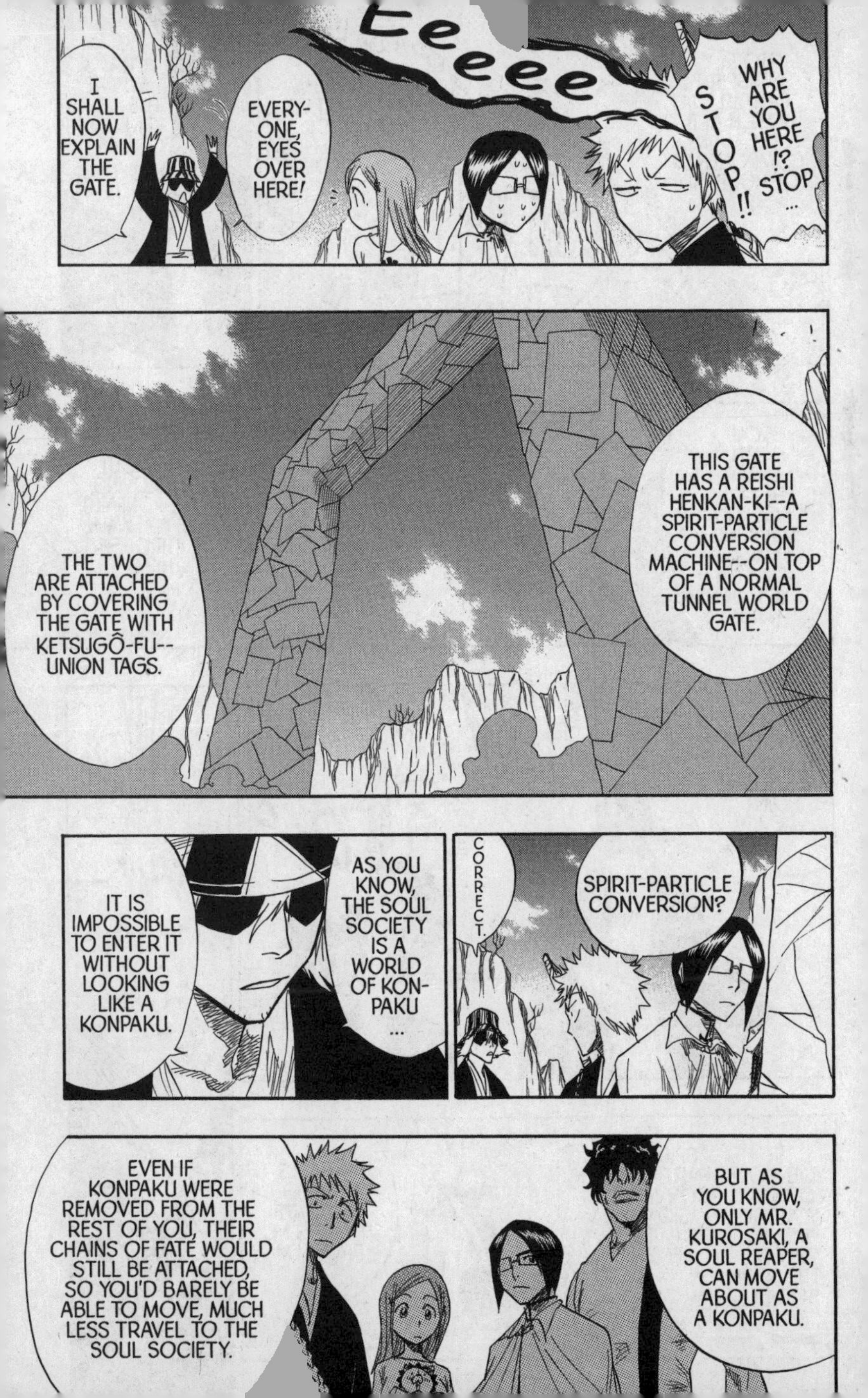
eeeee
WHY ARE YOU HERE!? STOP...
STOP!!
EVERYONE, EYES OVER HERE!
I SHALL NOW EXPLAIN THE GATE.
THIS GATE HAS A REISHI HENKAN-KI--A SPIRIT-PARTICLE CONVERSION MACHINE--ON TOP OF A NORMAL TUNNEL WORLD GATE.
THE TWO ARE ATTACHED BY COVERING THE GATE WITH KETSUGŌ-FU--UNION TAGS.
SPIRIT-PARTICLE CONVERSION?
CORRECT.
AS YOU KNOW, THE SOUL SOCIETY IS A WORLD OF KONPAKU...
IT IS IMPOSSIBLE TO ENTER IT WITHOUT LOOKING LIKE A KONPAKU.
BUT AS YOU KNOW, ONLY MR. KUROSAKI, A SOUL REAPER, CAN MOVE ABOUT AS A KONPAKU.
EVEN IF KONPAKU WERE REMOVED FROM THE REST OF YOU, THEIR CHAINS OF FATE WOULD STILL BE ATTACHED, SO YOU'D BARELY BE ABLE TO MOVE, MUCH LESS TRAVEL TO THE SOUL SOCIETY.

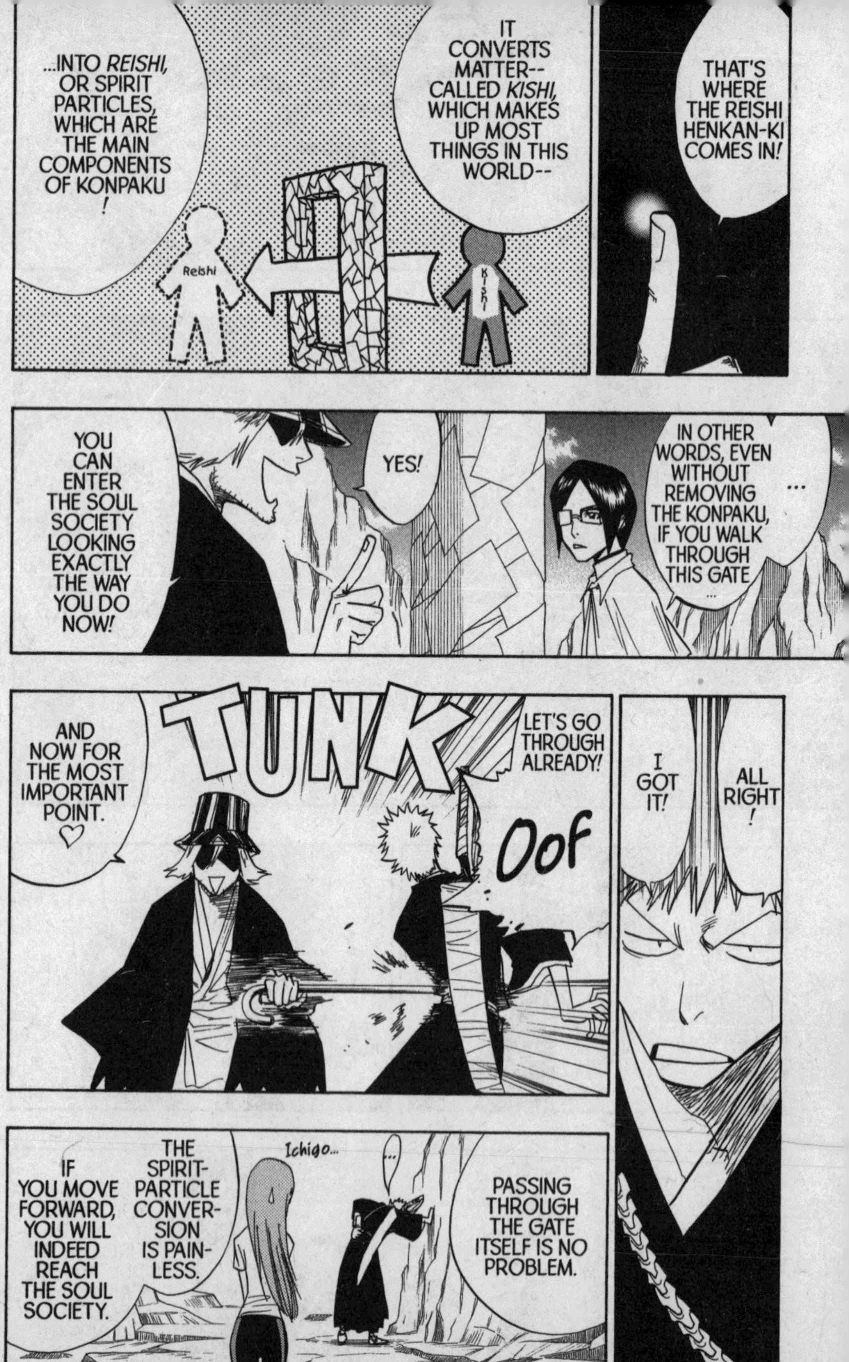
THAT'S WHERE THE REISHI HENKAN-KI COMES IN!
IT CONVERTS MATTER-- CALLED *KISHI*, WHICH MAKES UP MOST THINGS IN THIS WORLD--
...INTO *REISHI*, OR SPIRIT PARTICLES, WHICH ARE THE MAIN COMPONENTS OF KONPAKU!
Kishi
Reishi
IN OTHER WORDS, EVEN WITHOUT REMOVING THE KONPAKU, IF YOU WALK THROUGH THIS GATE...
...
YES!
YOU CAN ENTER THE SOUL SOCIETY LOOKING EXACTLY THE WAY YOU DO NOW!
ALL RIGHT!
I GOT IT!
LET'S GO THROUGH ALREADY!
TUNK
Oof
AND NOW FOR THE MOST IMPORTANT POINT. ♡
PASSING THROUGH THE GATE ITSELF IS NO PROBLEM.
...
Ichigo...
THE SPIRIT-PARTICLE CONVERSION IS PAINLESS.
IF YOU MOVE FORWARD, YOU WILL INDEED REACH THE SOUL SOCIETY.

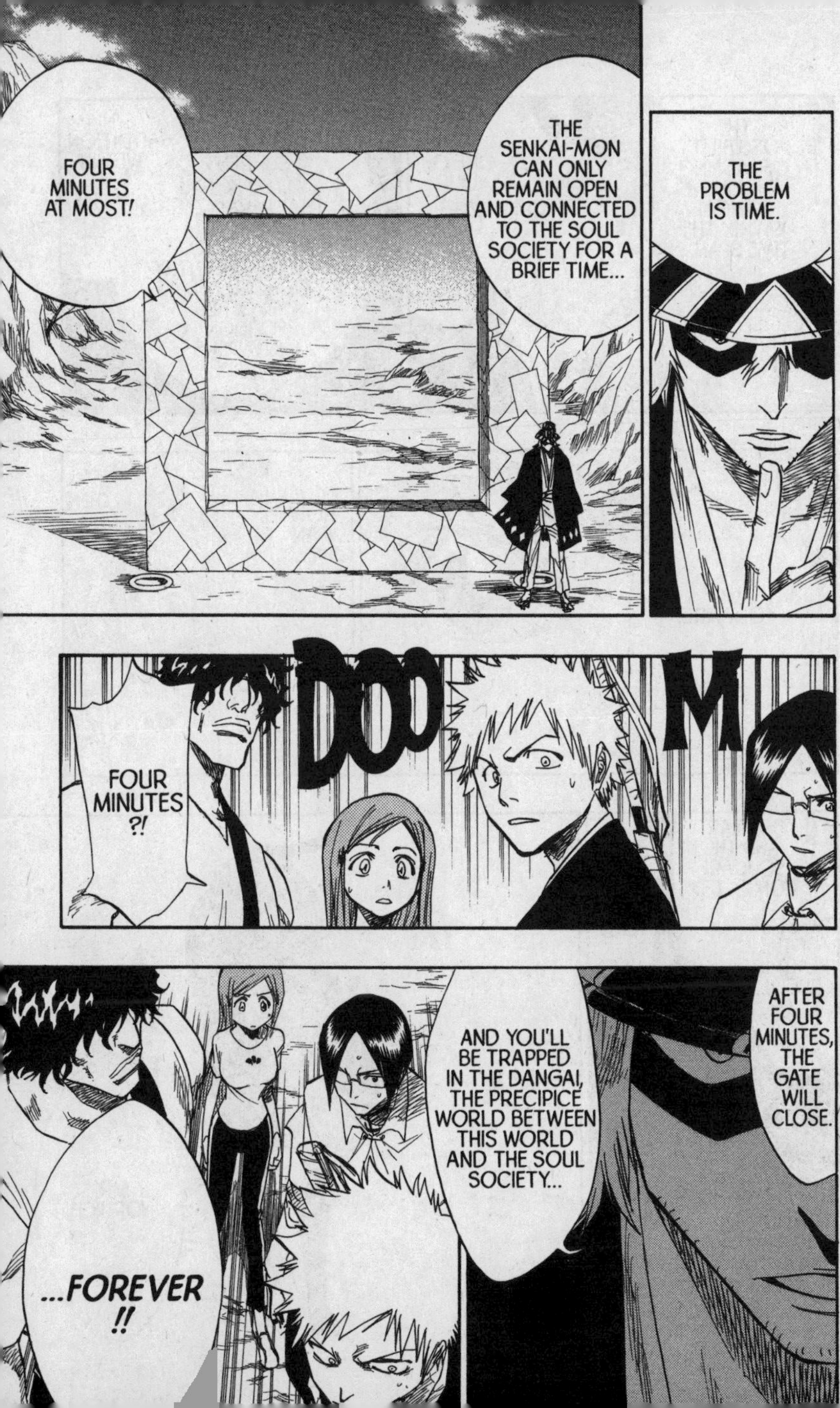
THE PROBLEM IS TIME.
THE SENKAI-MON CAN ONLY REMAIN OPEN AND CONNECTED TO THE SOUL SOCIETY FOR A BRIEF TIME...
FOUR MINUTES AT MOST!
DOOM
FOUR MINUTES ?!
AFTER FOUR MINUTES, THE GATE WILL CLOSE.
AND YOU'LL BE TRAPPED IN THE DANGAI, THE PRECIPICE WORLD BETWEEN THIS WORLD AND THE SOUL SOCIETY...
...FOREVER !!

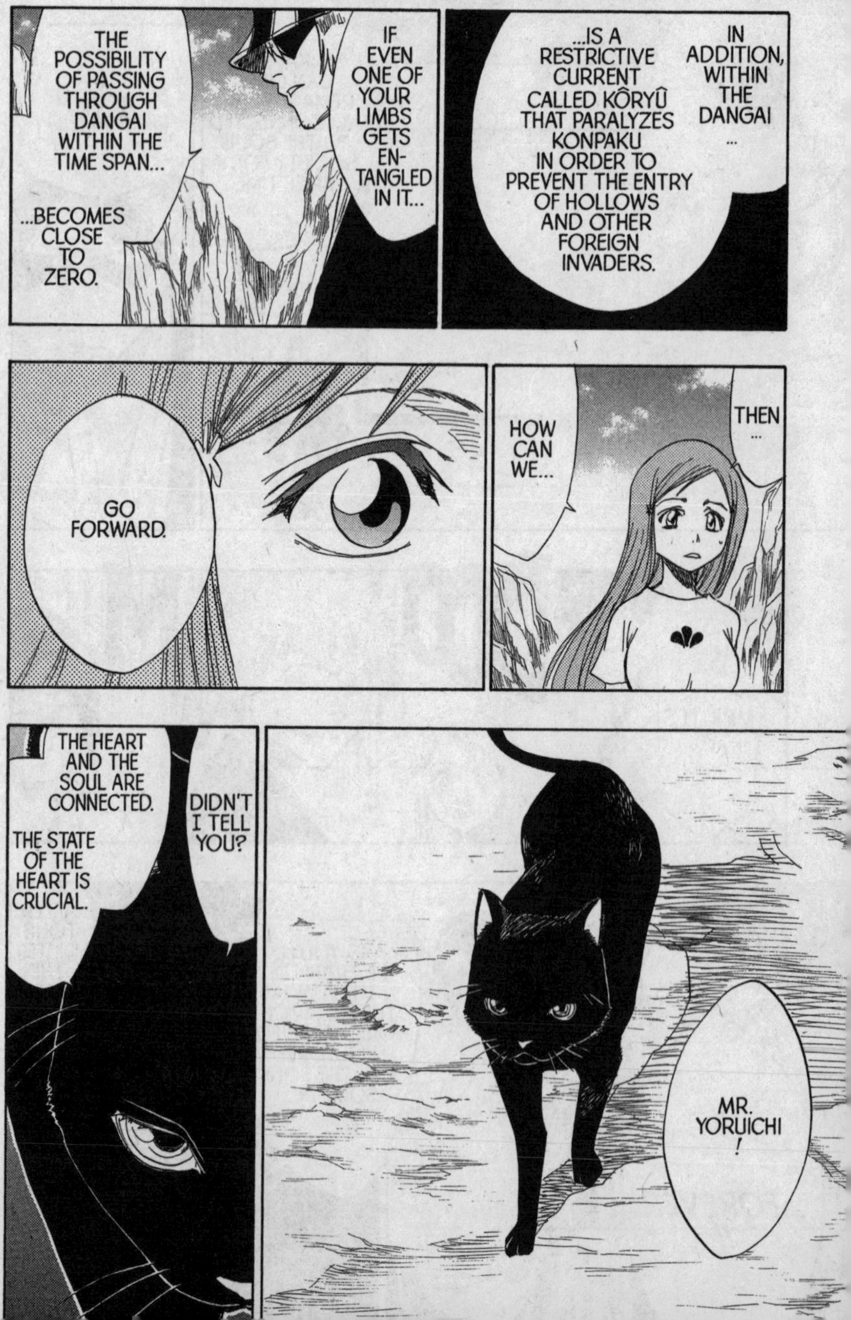
IN ADDITION, WITHIN THE DANGAI...
...IS A RESTRICTIVE CURRENT CALLED KÔRYÛ THAT PARALYZES KONPAKU IN ORDER TO PREVENT THE ENTRY OF HOLLOWS AND OTHER FOREIGN INVADERS.
IF EVEN ONE OF YOUR LIMBS GETS EN-TANGLED IN IT...
THE POSSIBILITY OF PASSING THROUGH DANGAI WITHIN THE TIME SPAN...
...BECOMES CLOSE TO ZERO.
THEN...
HOW CAN WE...
GO FORWARD.
MR. YORUICHI!
DIDN'T I TELL YOU?
THE HEART AND THE SOUL ARE CONNECTED.
THE STATE OF THE HEART IS CRUCIAL.

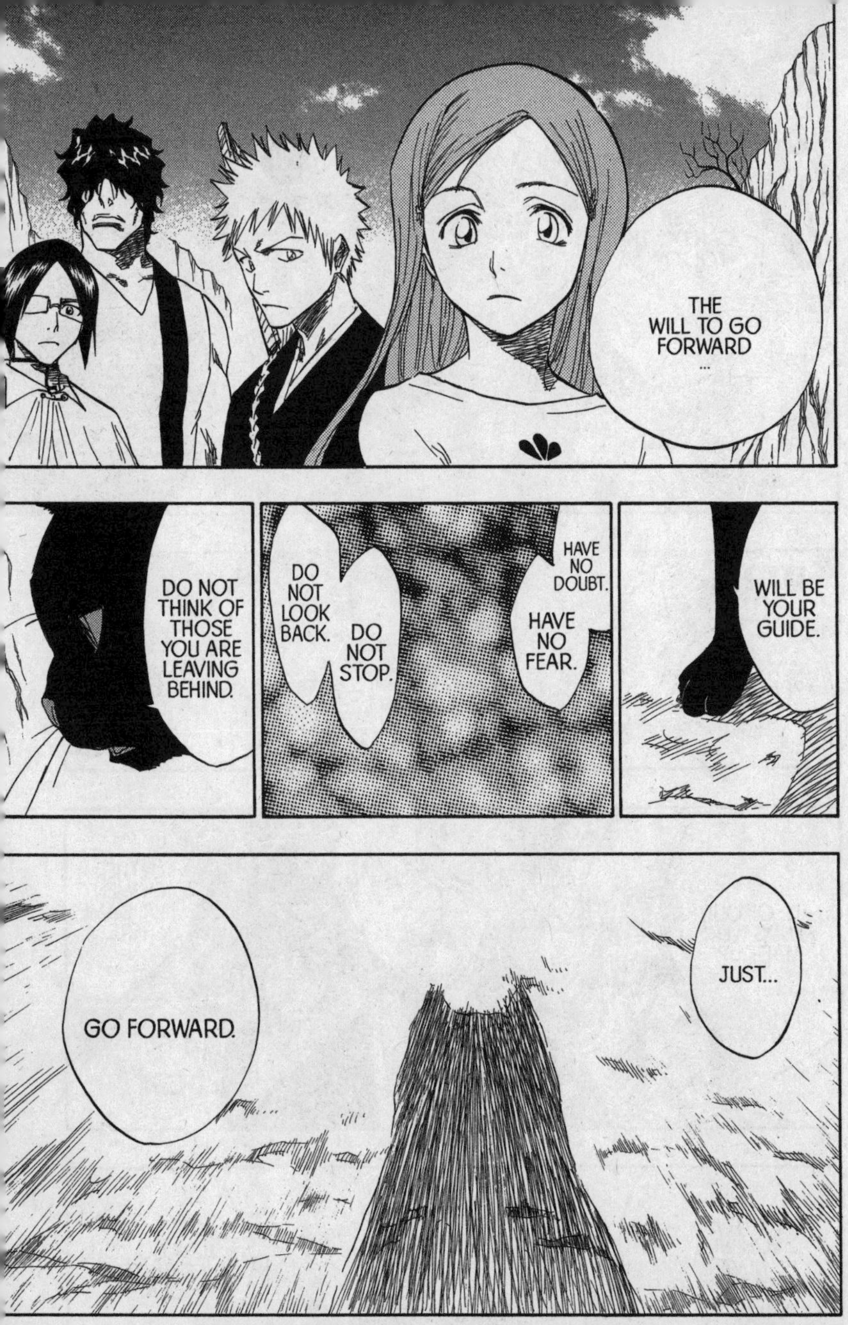
THE WILL TO GO FORWARD ...
WILL BE YOUR GUIDE.
HAVE NO DOUBT.
HAVE NO FEAR.
DO NOT STOP.
DO NOT LOOK BACK.
DO NOT THINK OF THOSE YOU ARE LEAVING BEHIND.
JUST...
GO FORWARD.

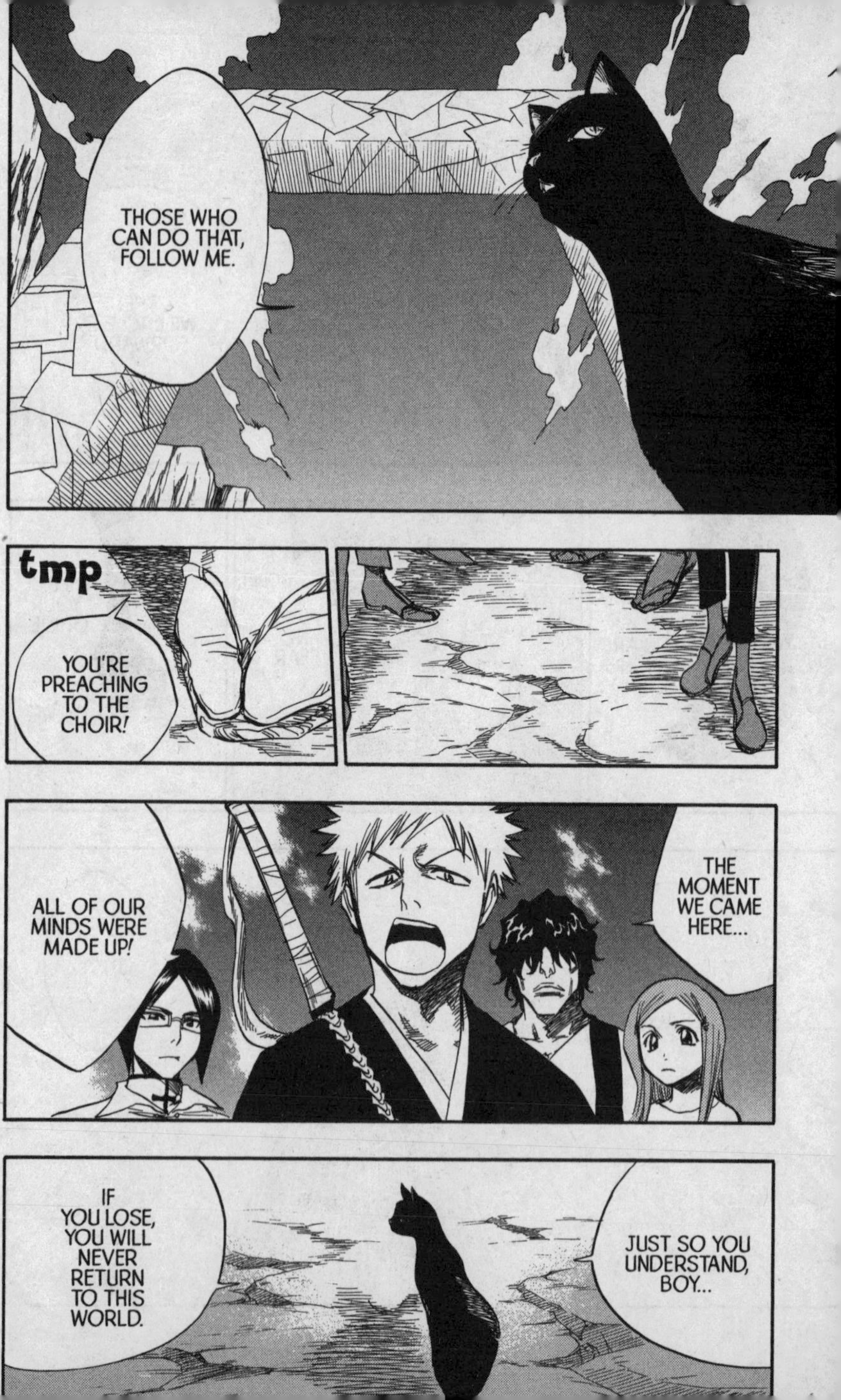
THOSE WHO CAN DO THAT, FOLLOW ME.
tmp
YOU'RE PREACHING TO THE CHOIR!
THE MOMENT WE CAME HERE...
ALL OF OUR MINDS WERE MADE UP!
JUST SO YOU UNDERSTAND, BOY...
IF YOU LOSE, YOU WILL NEVER RETURN TO THIS WORLD.

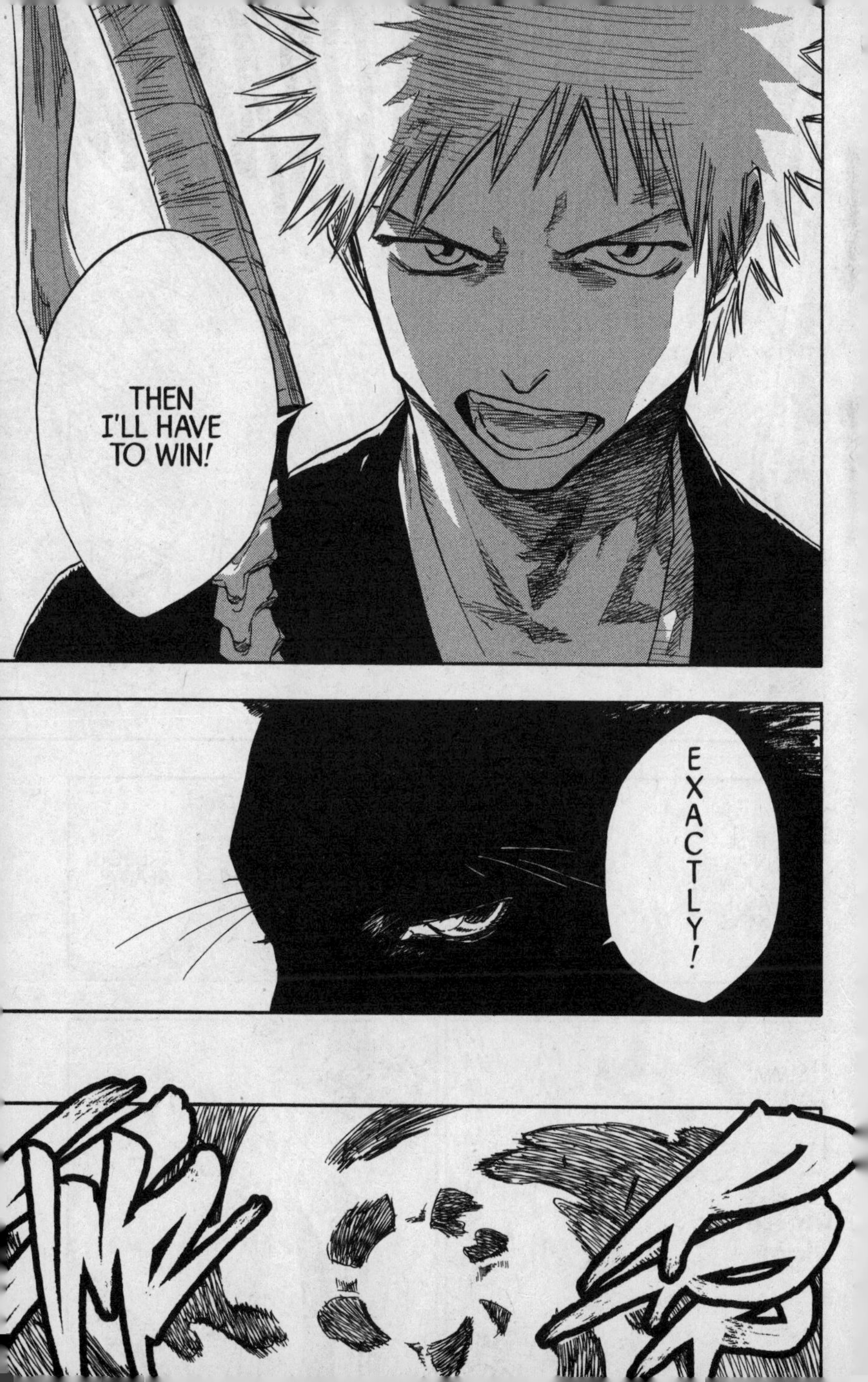
THEN I'LL HAVE TO WIN!
EXACTLY!

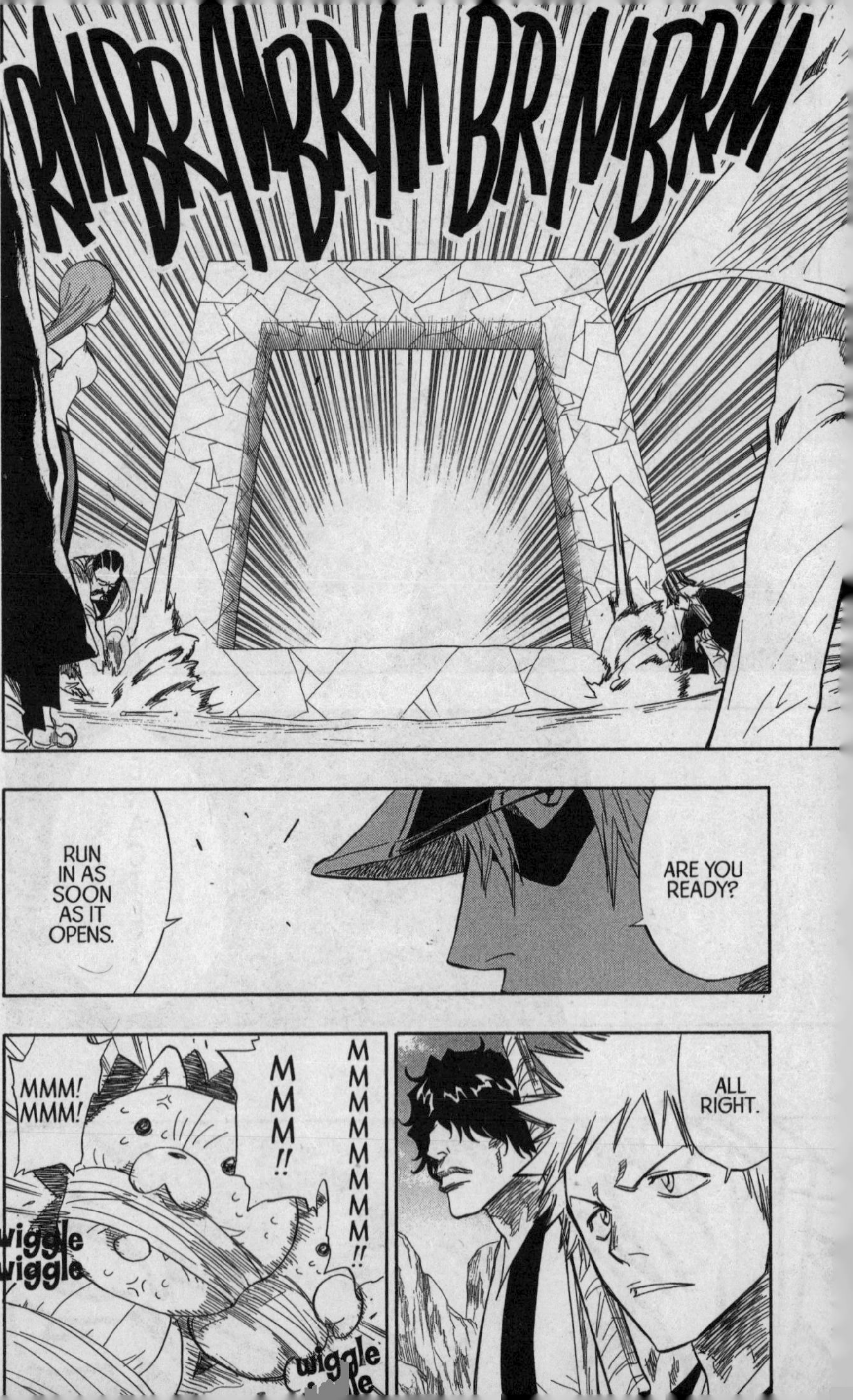
BRMBRMBRM BRMBRM
ARE YOU READY?
RUN IN AS SOON AS IT OPENS.
ALL RIGHT.
MMMMMMMMM!!
MMM!!
MMM! MMM!
wiggle wiggle
wiggle

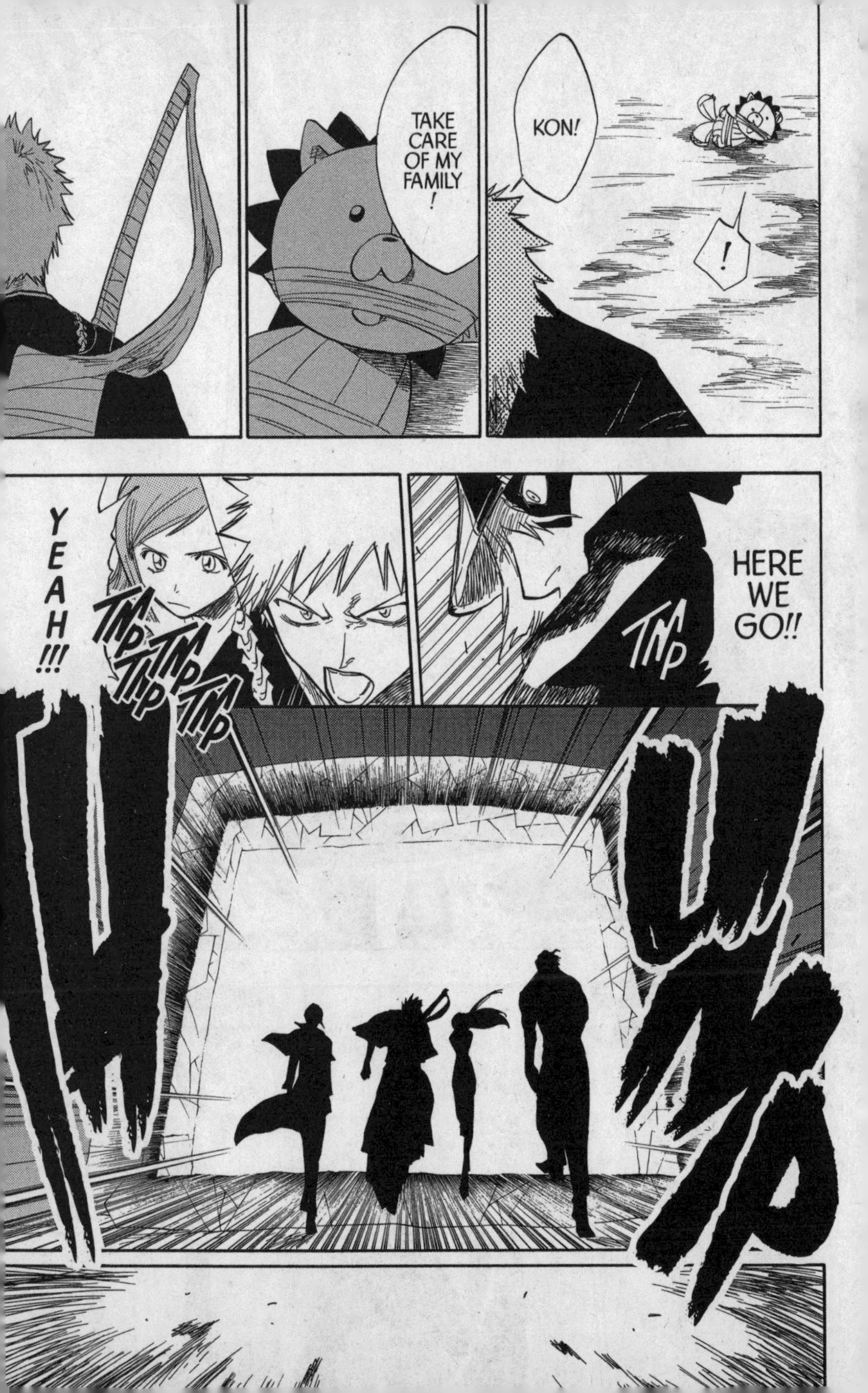
!
KON!
TAKE CARE OF MY FAMILY!
HERE WE GO!!
TMP
YEAH!!!
TMP TMP TMP TMP

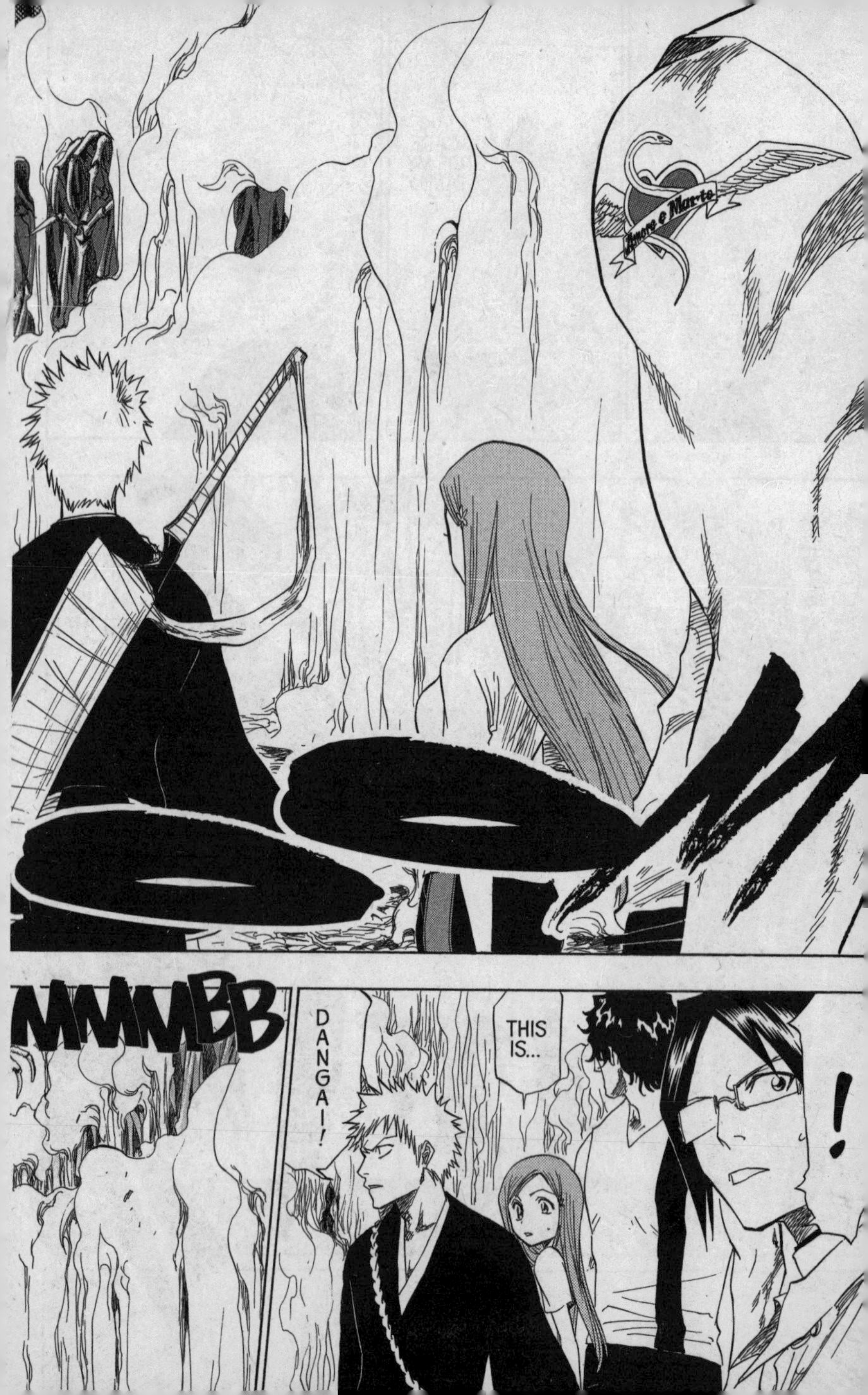
MMMMBB
!
THIS IS...
DANGAI!

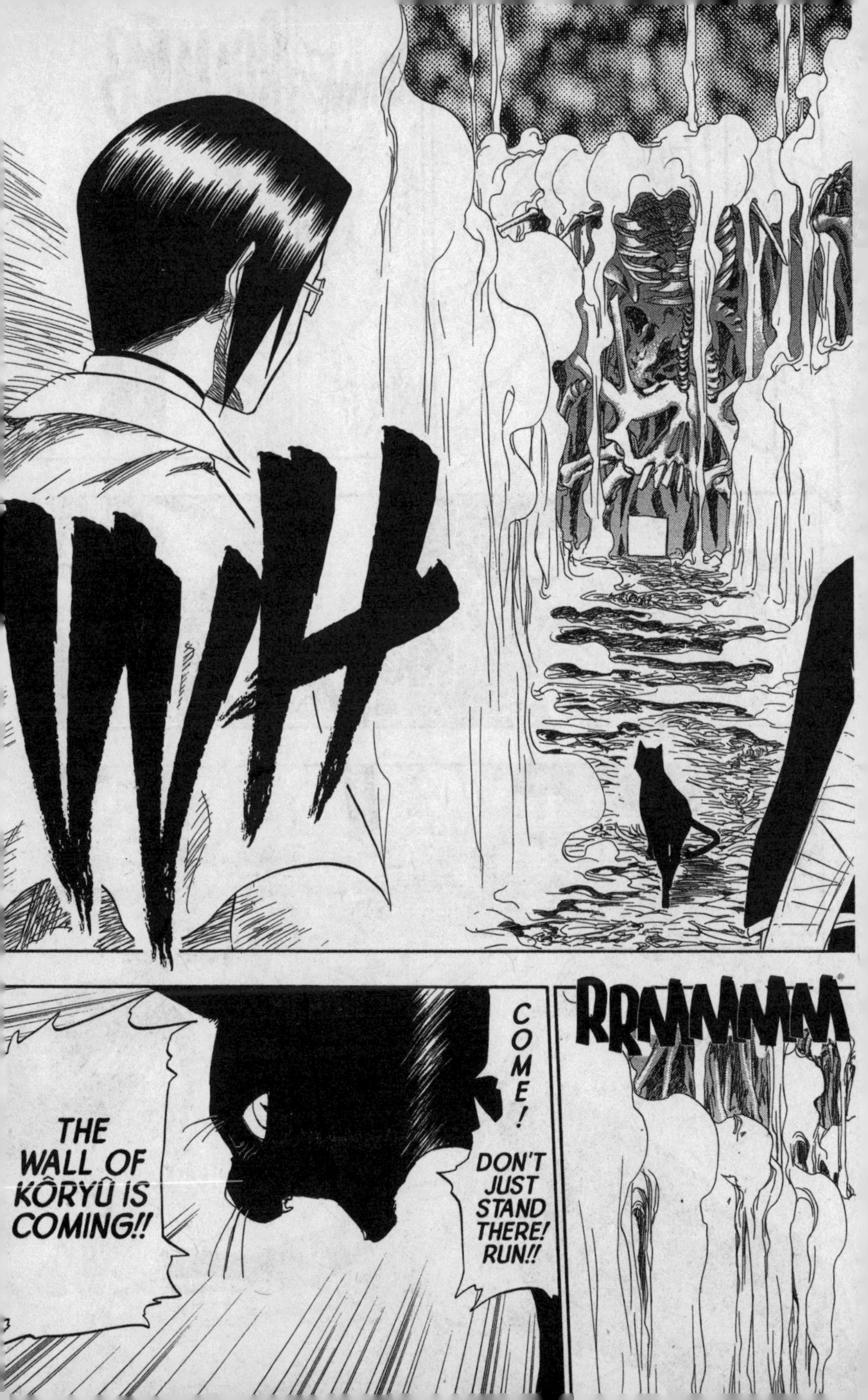
RRMMMM
COME!
DON'T JUST STAND THERE! RUN!!
THE WALL OF KÔRYÛ IS COMING!!

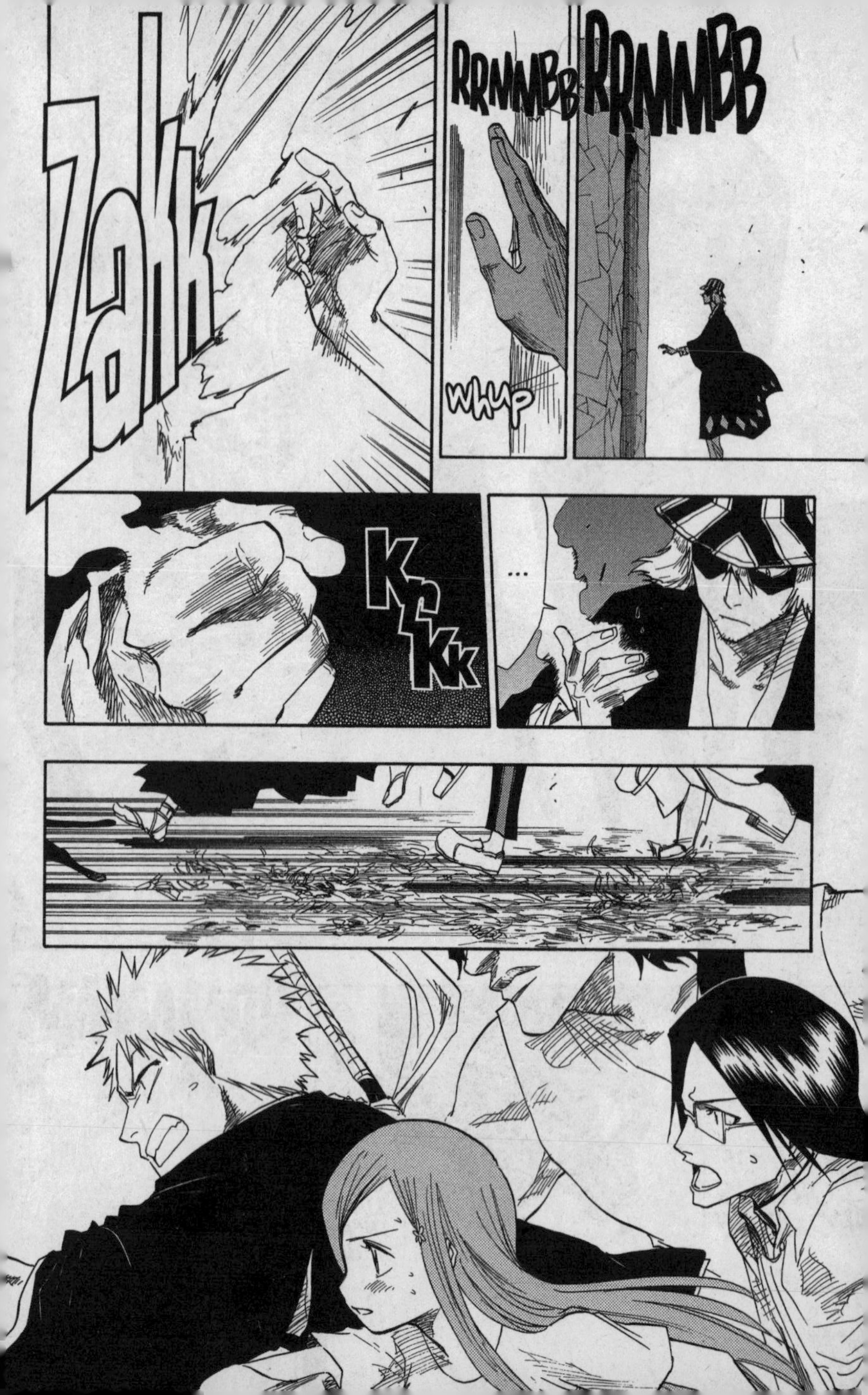
RRMMBB
RRNMBB
whup
Zakk
...
KnKk

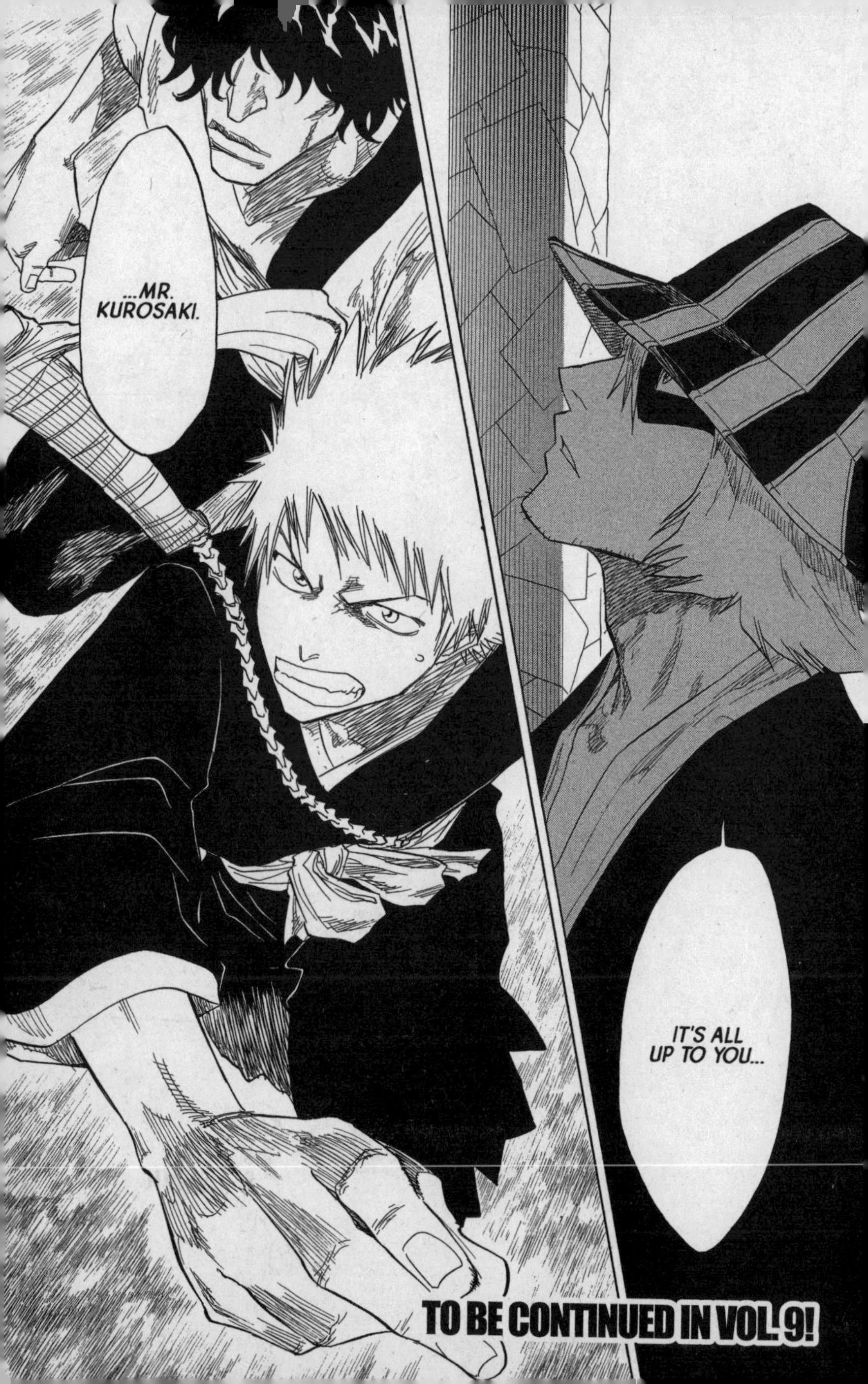

...MR. KUROSAKI.
IT'S ALL UP TO YOU...
TO BE CONTINUED IN VOL. 9!

Just when I thought he was here to stay!!

waah

Ichigo took off again!!

waah

Bleach Extra!! Radio-Kon3

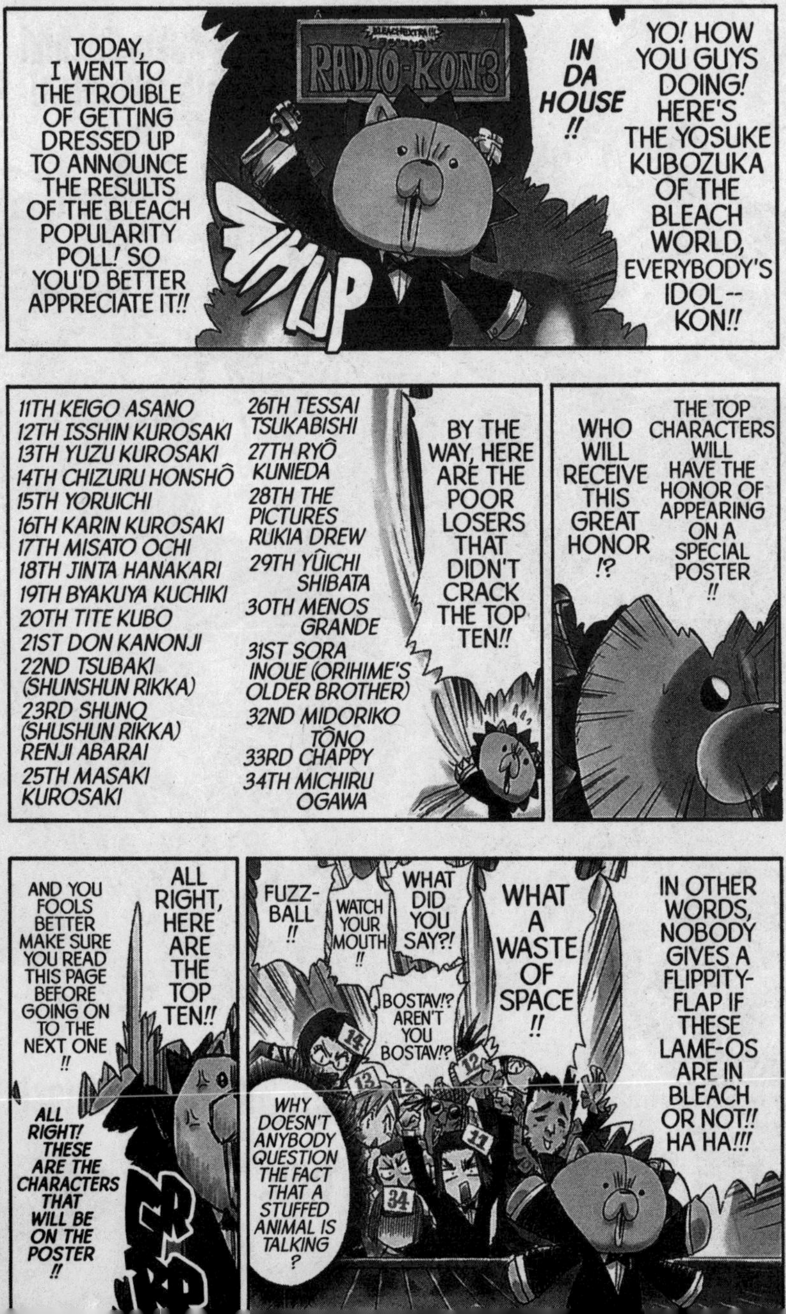

RADIO-KON3
YO! HOW YOU GUYS DOING! HERE'S THE YOSUKE KUBOZUKA OF THE BLEACH WORLD, EVERYBODY'S IDOL-- KON!!
IN DA HOUSE !!
TODAY, I WENT TO THE TROUBLE OF GETTING DRESSED UP TO ANNOUNCE THE RESULTS OF THE BLEACH POPULARITY POLL! SO YOU'D BETTER APPRECIATE IT!!
THE TOP CHARACTERS WILL HAVE THE HONOR OF APPEARING ON A SPECIAL POSTER !!
WHO WILL RECEIVE THIS GREAT HONOR !?
BY THE WAY, HERE ARE THE POOR LOSERS THAT DIDN'T CRACK THE TOP TEN!!
11TH KEIGO ASANO
12TH ISSHIN KUROSAKI
13TH YUZU KUROSAKI
14TH CHIZURU HONSHÔ
15TH YORUICHI
16TH KARIN KUROSAKI
17TH MISATO OCHI
18TH JINTA HANAKARI
19TH BYAKUYA KUCHIKI
20TH TITE KUBO
21ST DON KANONJI
22ND TSUBAKI (SHUNSHUN RIKKA)
23RD SHUNO (SHUSHUN RIKKA)
RENJI ABARAI
25TH MASAKI KUROSAKI
26TH TESSAI TSUKABISHI
27TH RYÔ KUNIEDA
28TH THE PICTURES RUKIA DREW
29TH YÛICHI SHIBATA
30TH MENOS GRANDE
31ST SORA INOUE (ORIHIME'S OLDER BROTHER)
32ND MIDORIKO TÔNO
33RD CHAPPY
34TH MICHIRU OGAWA
IN OTHER WORDS, NOBODY GIVES A FLIPPITY-FLAP IF THESE LAME-OS ARE IN BLEACH OR NOT!! HA HA!!!
WHAT A WASTE OF SPACE !!
WHAT DID YOU SAY?!
WATCH YOUR MOUTH !!
FUZZ-BALL !!
BOSTAV!? AREN'T YOU BOSTAV!?
WHY DOESN'T ANYBODY QUESTION THE FACT THAT A STUFFED ANIMAL IS TALKING ?
ALL RIGHT, HERE ARE THE TOP TEN!!
AND YOU FOOLS BETTER MAKE SURE YOU READ THIS PAGE BEFORE GOING ON TO THE NEXT ONE !!
ALL RIGHT! THESE ARE THE CHARACTERS THAT WILL BE ON THE POSTER !!

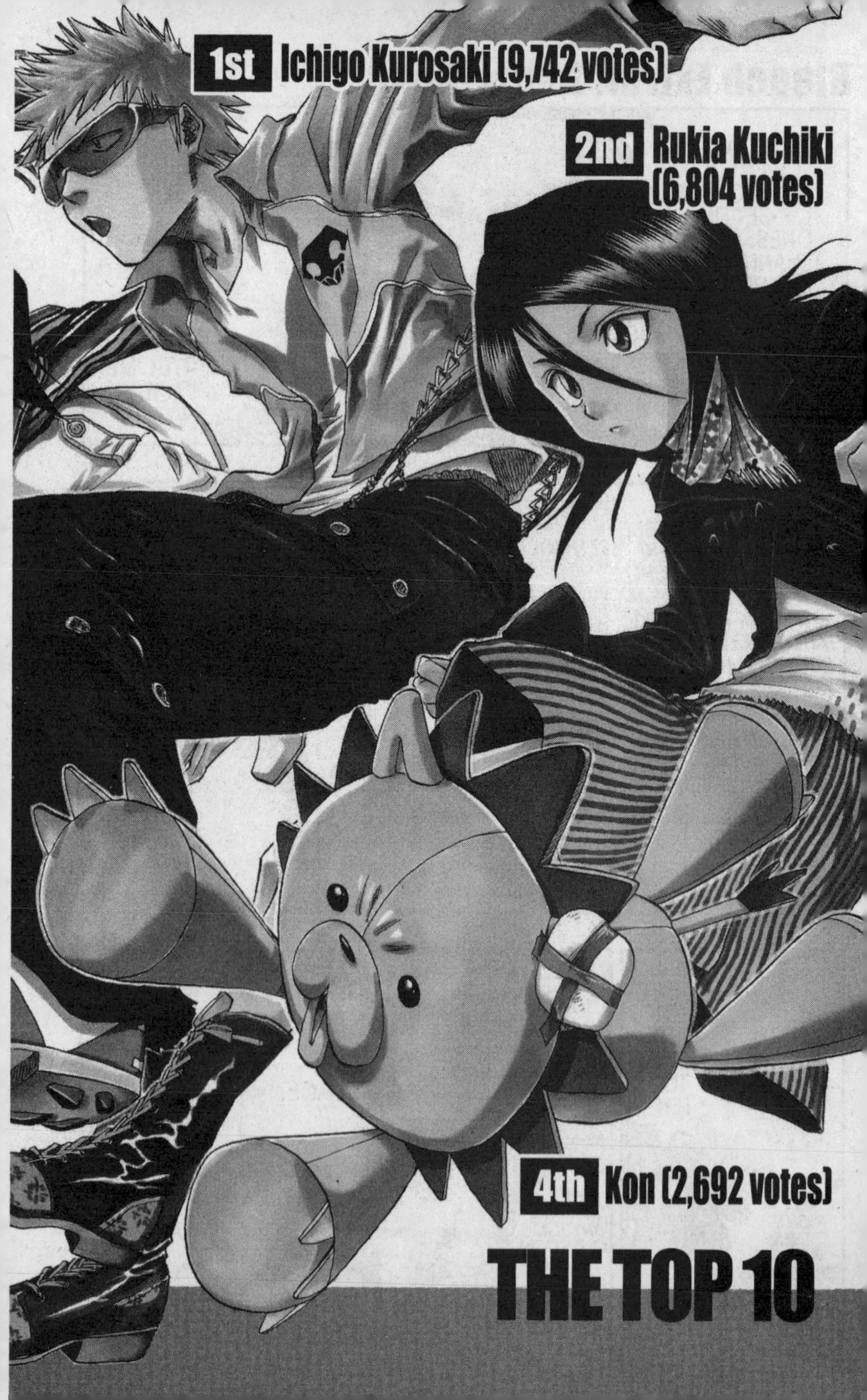
1st Ichigo Kurosaki (9,742 votes)
2nd Rukia Kuchiki (6,804 votes)
4th Kon (2,692 votes)
THE TOP 10

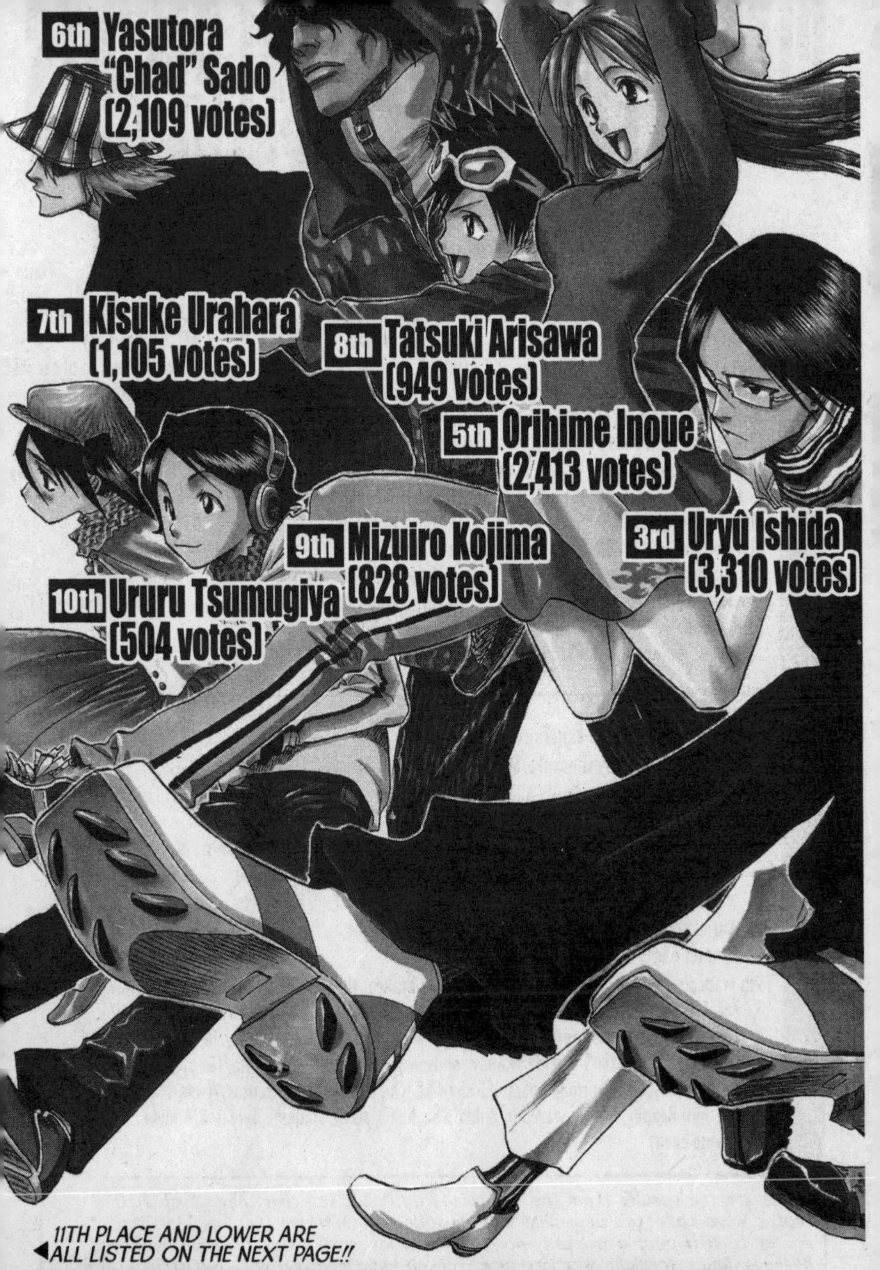
6th Yasutora "Chad" Sado (2,109 votes)
7th Kisuke Urahara (1,105 votes)
8th Tatsuki Arisawa (949 votes)
5th Orihime Inoue (2,413 votes)
3rd Uryû Ishida (3,310 votes)
9th Mizuiro Kojima (828 votes)
10th Ururu Tsumugiya (504 votes)

◀11TH PLACE AND LOWER ARE ALL LISTED ON THE NEXT PAGE!!

BLEACH POPULARITY POLL RESULTS

These results are based on a poll conducted in the pages of WEEKLY SHONEN JUMP, Japan. Who's your favorite BLEACH character? Send your answers to: SHONEN JUMP c/o VIZ, LLC P.O. Box 77010, San Francisco, CA 94107 ATTN: BLEACH Popularity Contest

BLEACH POPULARITY POLL RESULTS

THE COMPLETE LIST

Popularity Vote Complete Results

The number of votes are in ()

11th Keigo Asano (496)
12th Isshin Kurosaki (488)
13th Yuzu Kurosaki (482)
14th Chizuru Honshō (475)
15th Yoruichi (471)
16th Karin Kurosaki (462)
17th Misato Ochi (459)
18th Jinta Hanakari (457)
19th Byakuya Kuchiki (446)
20th Tite Kubo (395)
21st Don Kanonji (390)
22nd Tsubaki (Shunshun Rikka) (382)
23rd Shunō (Shushun Rikka) (374)

11 thru 50

Renji Abarai (374)
25th Masaki Kurosaki (351)
26th Tessai Tsukabishi (333)
27th Ryō Kunieda (292)
28th The pictures Rukia drew (281)
29th Yūichi Shibata (268)
30th Menos Grande (236)
31st Sora Inoue (203)
32nd Midori Tōno (166)
33rd Soul Candy Chappy (132)
34th Michiru Ogawa (107)
35th Shunshun Rikka (104)
36th Lilly (Shunshun Rikka) (85)
37th Ayame (Shunshun Rikka) (69)
38th The ghost girl in episode 1 (41)

39th Mahana (28)
40th Uryū's teacher (25)
41st Shigeo (22)
42nd The weirdo of the R&D Department (15)
43rd Grand Fisher (12)
44th Soul Candy Yuki (11)
45th Soul Candy Alfred (9)
Ôshima (9)
47th Acidwire (8)
48th Hollow (7)
Old man from vegetable store (7)
Cookie (7)

---

51 thru 79

51st Harutoki/Soul Candy Kaneshiro (6 votes each)
53rd Enraku/Soul Candy Ginosuke/Soul Candy Pupples/Principal/Micchan (5 votes each)
58th Soul Candy Schteiner/Soul Candy Gringo/Soul Candy Diana/Bostav/Teacher Kagine/Hinagiku (4 votes each)
64th Hitomi Victoria Odagiri/Soul Candy Blues/Soul Candy Claudia/Baigon/Spirit of the bad bear/
The Hollow Shrieker put out/Fishbone D/Yama-chan/Melon/Hashigami (3 votes each)
74th Shrieker/The grandpa and son during blackout/Toshi-Rin/Marianne/Magic Girl Megalon (2 votes each)
79th Francois/Just Kon's doll/Snake Whistle/The parakeet that's not Yuichi/Caterpillar Hollow/
The doll that Uryū fixed/The person who raced Orihime and Ichigo in Orihime's fantasy/
The clerk girl at CD store/Desk used for throwing/Akutabi Ganma/Nancy/Hexapods/
Dad's Great Whistle/Schneider/Randy Johnson/Ino/Kaneda/Kuroage-Ha/The spirit of the office
worker Konsōed in episode one/The Inoki-like Ichigo in Orihime's fantasy/Iwao/Mikami/
The Soul Reaper that appeared in Rukia's flashback scene/Madame Akiyama/Abuelo
(1 vote each)

---

*These are the results from the 1st Popularity Poll taken from August of 2002
(votes were collected beginning with episode 51). Offering the Top Ten Character
Poster to 100 people worked--we received a lot more votes than we expected.
Byakuya, Renji, Yoruichi--who are new--ranked high; one guy voted 200 times for
Miss Ochi; there was one vote for a character from my previous work (Akutabi
Gamma); and there were a lot of maniacs. Looking at all the results, I think it came
out pretty interestingly. It was fun. I hope we can do it again in the summer...*

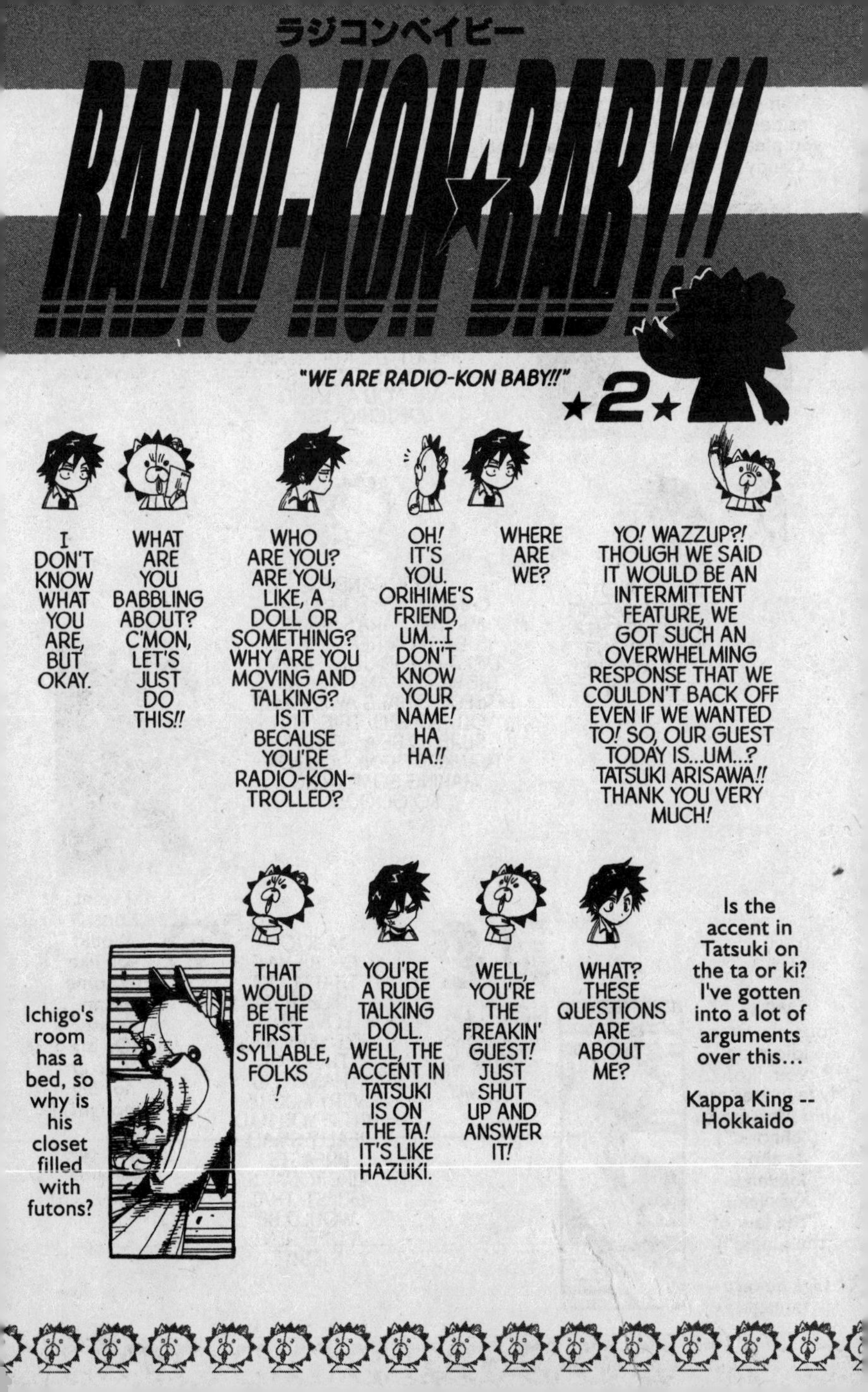
ラジコンベイビー
RADIO-KON★BABY!!
"WE ARE RADIO-KON BABY!!"
★2★
YO! WAZZUP?! THOUGH WE SAID IT WOULD BE AN INTERMITTENT FEATURE, WE GOT SUCH AN OVERWHELMING RESPONSE THAT WE COULDN'T BACK OFF EVEN IF WE WANTED TO! SO, OUR GUEST TODAY IS...UM...? TATSUKI ARISAWA!! THANK YOU VERY MUCH!
WHERE ARE WE?
OH! IT'S YOU. ORIHIME'S FRIEND, UM...I DON'T KNOW YOUR NAME! HA HA!!
WHO ARE YOU? ARE YOU, LIKE, A DOLL OR SOMETHING? WHY ARE YOU MOVING AND TALKING? IS IT BECAUSE YOU'RE RADIO-KON-TROLLED?
WHAT ARE YOU BABBLING ABOUT? C'MON, LET'S JUST DO THIS!!
I DON'T KNOW WHAT YOU ARE, BUT OKAY.
Is the accent in Tatsuki on the ta or ki? I've gotten into a lot of arguments over this...
Kappa King -- Hokkaido
WHAT? THESE QUESTIONS ARE ABOUT ME?
WELL, YOU'RE THE FREAKIN' GUEST! JUST SHUT UP AND ANSWER IT!
YOU'RE A RUDE TALKING DOLL. WELL, THE ACCENT IN TATSUKI IS ON THE TA! IT'S LIKE HAZUKI.
THAT WOULD BE THE FIRST SYLLABLE, FOLKS!
Ichigo's room has a bed, so why is his closet filled with futons?

The other day, I used my handicraft skills to full effect and made a Kon (see photo). But without the insides, it's not a genuine Kon. Will you please tell me how to make Soul Candy or where I can buy some?
-- Rose, Nagasaki

Tatsuki, you're good friends with Ichigo, so you must know this one, right?

Asuka Koizumi--Kanagawa

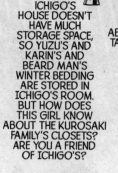

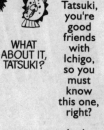

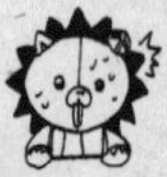

WHAT ABOUT IT, TATSUKI?

ICHIGO'S HOUSE DOESN'T HAVE MUCH STORAGE SPACE, SO YUZU'S AND KARIN'S AND BEARD MAN'S WINTER BEDDING ARE STORED IN ICHIGO'S ROOM. BUT HOW DOES THIS GIRL KNOW ABOUT THE KUROSAKI FAMILY'S CLOSETS? ARE YOU A FRIEND OF ICHIGO'S?

SOUL CANDY CAN ONLY BE FOUND AT MR. URAHARA'S SHOP. IS THIS FOR REAL!? YOU DID A GOOD JOB!!! EVEN THE WEIGHT AND SIZE ARE PERFECT!! THAT'S AWESOME!! YOU CAN SELL THIS!! IT'S SURE TO BE A BIG HIT!! THANKS!! THANK YOU FOR MAKING SOMETHING SO GOOD!!!

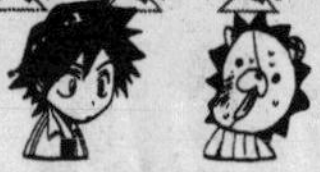

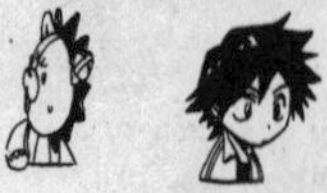

YOU'RE RIGHT, THIS IS AMAZING. YOU'D BE CUTE IF YOU DIDN'T MOVE AROUND LIKE THAT.

...

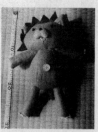

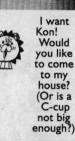

I want Kon! Would you like to come to my house? (Or is a C-cup not big enough?)

Yumiko--Saitama

YAHOO!!! C!? HA HA!! THAT'LL DO NICELY!! I LOVE ANY SIZE SERVINGS THOUGH! THANK YOU VERY MUCH!! BUT IF YOU HAD REALLY SMALL BREASTS, LIKE TODAY'S GUEST, THAT WOULD BE A DIFFERENT STORY!!

I'M ALSO A C, BY THE WAY...

NO !!!?

What four-character idiom do you like? (My favorites are *Shiri Metsuretsu* ("chaotic") and *Jakuniku Kyôshoku* ("the law of the jungle").

♡ Oga Sukaru--Yamagata

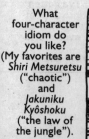

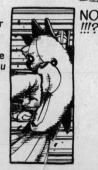

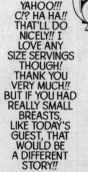

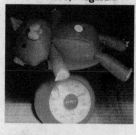

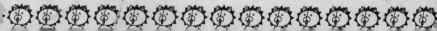

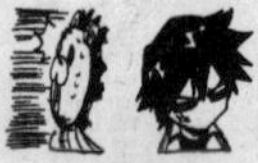

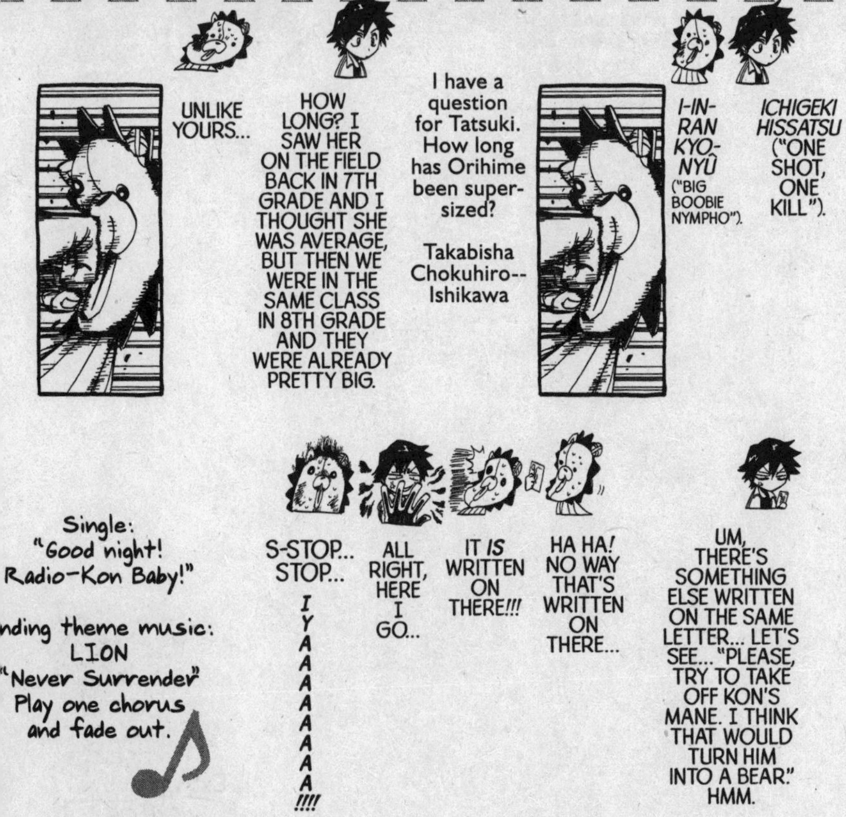
ICHIGEKI HISSATSU ("ONE SHOT, ONE KILL").
I-IN-RAN KYO-NYÛ ("BIG BOOBIE NYMPHO").
I have a question for Tatsuki. How long has Orihime been super-sized?
Takabisha Chokuhiro--Ishikawa
HOW LONG? I SAW HER ON THE FIELD BACK IN 7TH GRADE AND I THOUGHT SHE WAS AVERAGE, BUT THEN WE WERE IN THE SAME CLASS IN 8TH GRADE AND THEY WERE ALREADY PRETTY BIG.
UNLIKE YOURS...
UM, THERE'S SOMETHING ELSE WRITTEN ON THE SAME LETTER... LET'S SEE... "PLEASE, TRY TO TAKE OFF KON'S MANE. I THINK THAT WOULD TURN HIM INTO A BEAR." HMM.
HA HA! NO WAY THAT'S WRITTEN ON THERE...
IT *IS* WRITTEN ON THERE!!!
ALL RIGHT, HERE I GO...
S-STOP... STOP...
IYAAAAAAAAAA!!!!
Single: "Good night! Radio-Kon Baby!"
nding theme music: LION "Never Surrender" Play one chorus and fade out.

Now accepting letters!!

Any kind of question is fine!! Questions are chosen at random, but the acceptance rate for postcards is probably higher than for letters!! The third guest will be Uryû Ishida!! Include your question, name, address, age, and telephone number and send it all to the address below!

SHONEN JUMP c/o VIZ, LLC
P.O. Box 77010, San Francisco, CA 94107
ATTN: "Bleach" Radio-Kon Baby!!

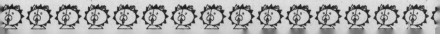

Extra

URYÛ ON AUGUST 1st

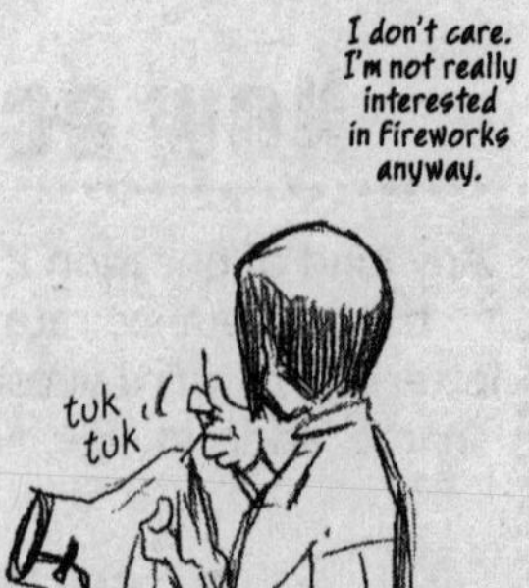
I don't care. I'm not really interested in fireworks anyway.
tuk tuk

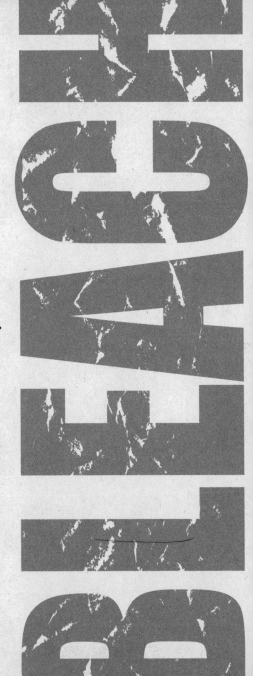

I have a stereo at home. I bought it in junior high with money I earned delivering newspapers—I know it's a cliché. I've used it for over ten years.

Recently, it hasn't been working well. I thought about replacing it, but even if I bought the latest, coolest unit, I'd probably still miss this one. So I can't bring myself to buy a new one. In other words, I'm a wimp.

-Tite Kubo

BLEACH

BLEACH
ブリーチ

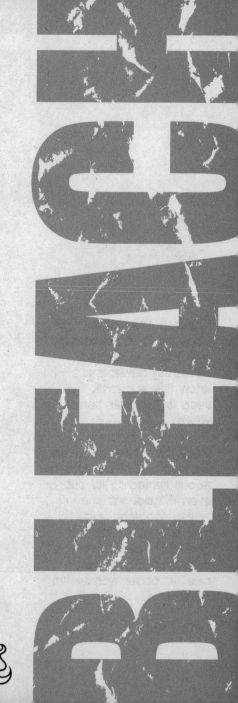

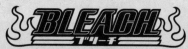

Oh, all of us dream
That we are flying the skies
With our eyes open

BLEACH9 FOURTEEN DAYS FOR CONSPIRACY

STARS AND

Yoruichi

Orihime Inoue

Ichigo Kurosaki

★ plot

One fateful night, Ichigo Kurosaki encounters Soul Reaper Rukia Kuchiki and ends up helping her do her job—which is cleansing lost souls called Hollows and guiding them to the Soul Society. Eventually, Ichigo grows powerful and defeats the behemoth Menos Grande. Now Rukia has been condemned to death in the Soul Society. To save her, Ichigo, Orihime, Chad, and Uryû have endured rigorous training. With their feline guide, Yoruichi, they finally enter the Soul Society. But do they have what it takes to save Rukia—or themselves?!!

BLEACH ALL

Jidanbô

Yasutora "Chad" Sado

Uryû Ishida

STORIES

BLEACH 9

FOURTEEN DAYS FOR CONSPIRACY

Contents

71. INTRUDERZ

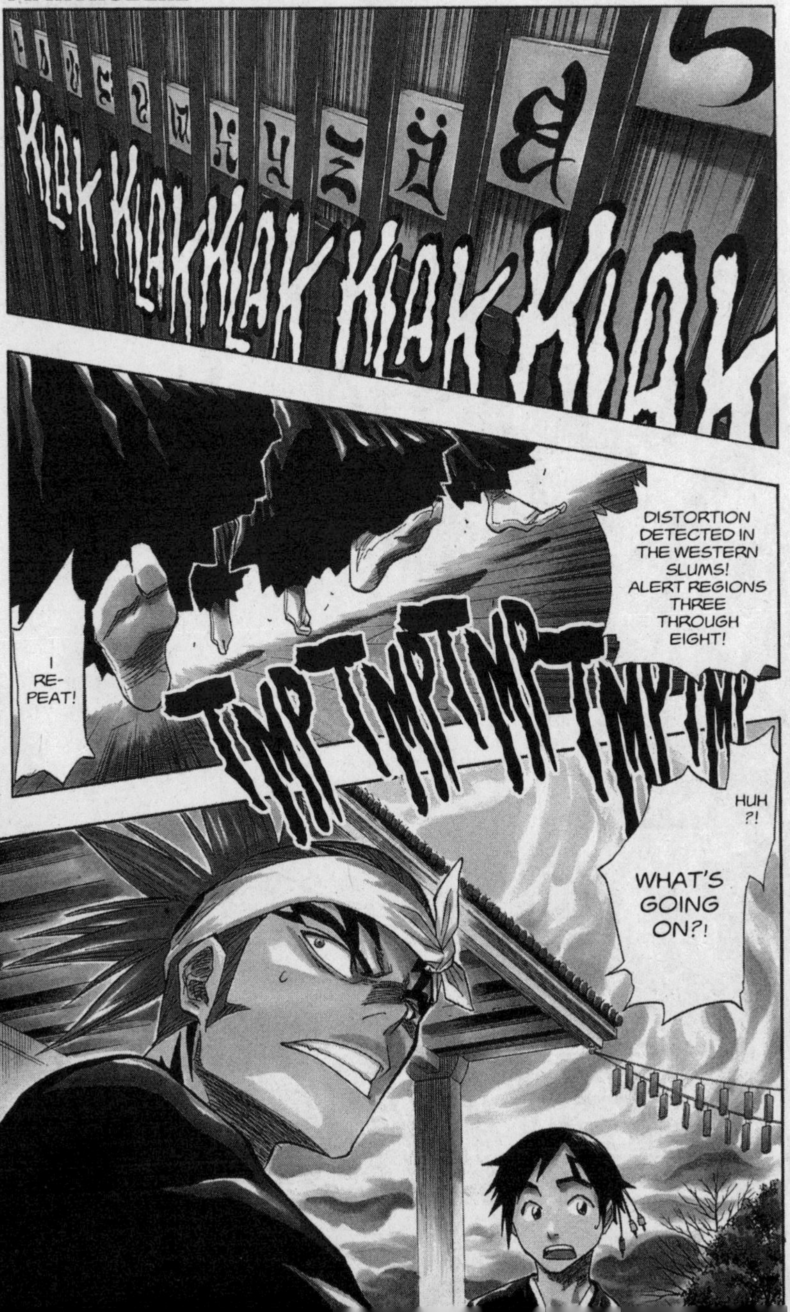
KLAK KLAK KLAK KLAK KLAK
DISTORTION DETECTED IN THE WESTERN SLUMS! ALERT REGIONS THREE THROUGH EIGHT!
I RE-PEAT!
TMP TMP TMP TMP TMP
HUH ?!
WHAT'S GOING ON?!

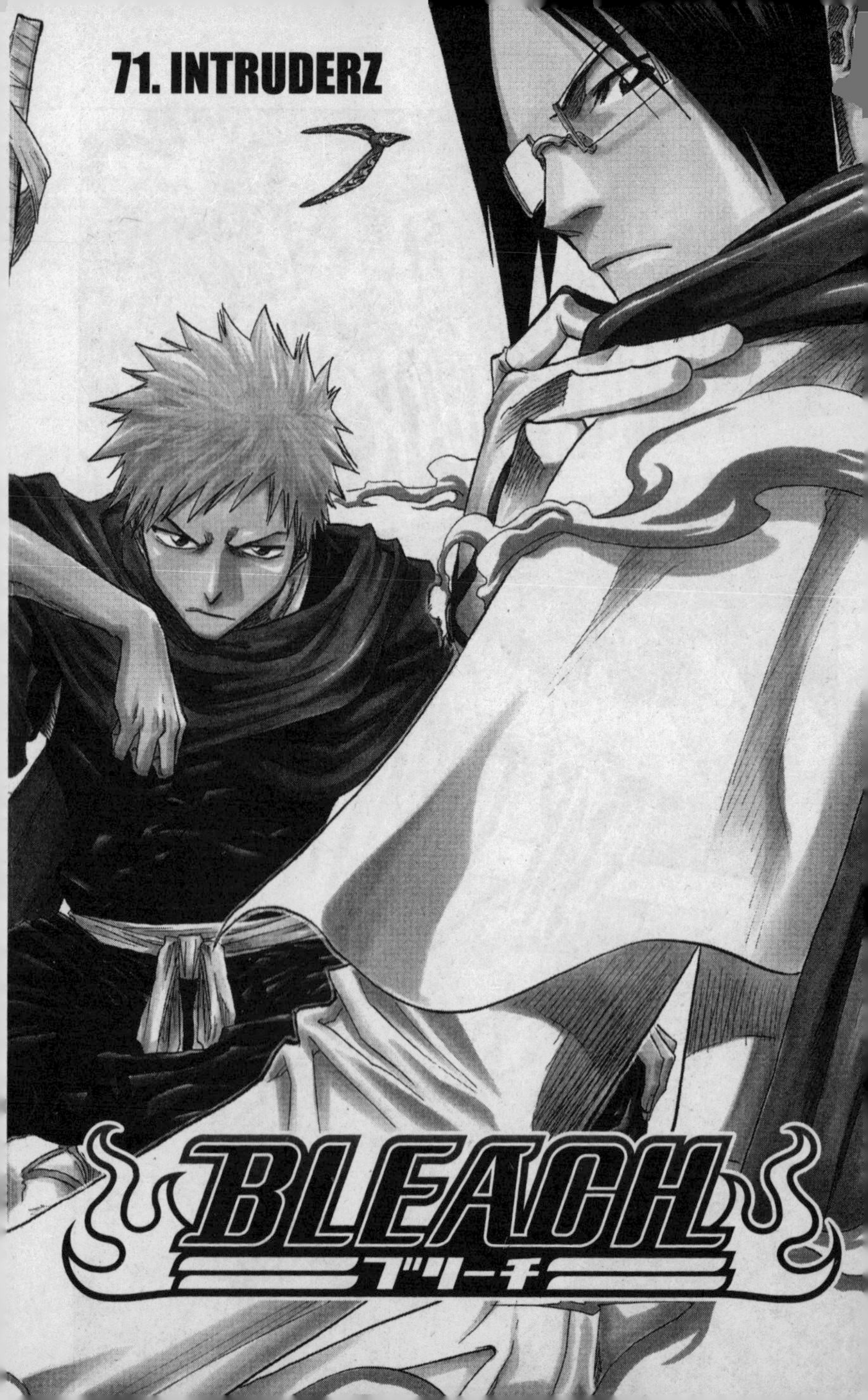
71. INTRUDERZ
BLEACH
ブリーチ

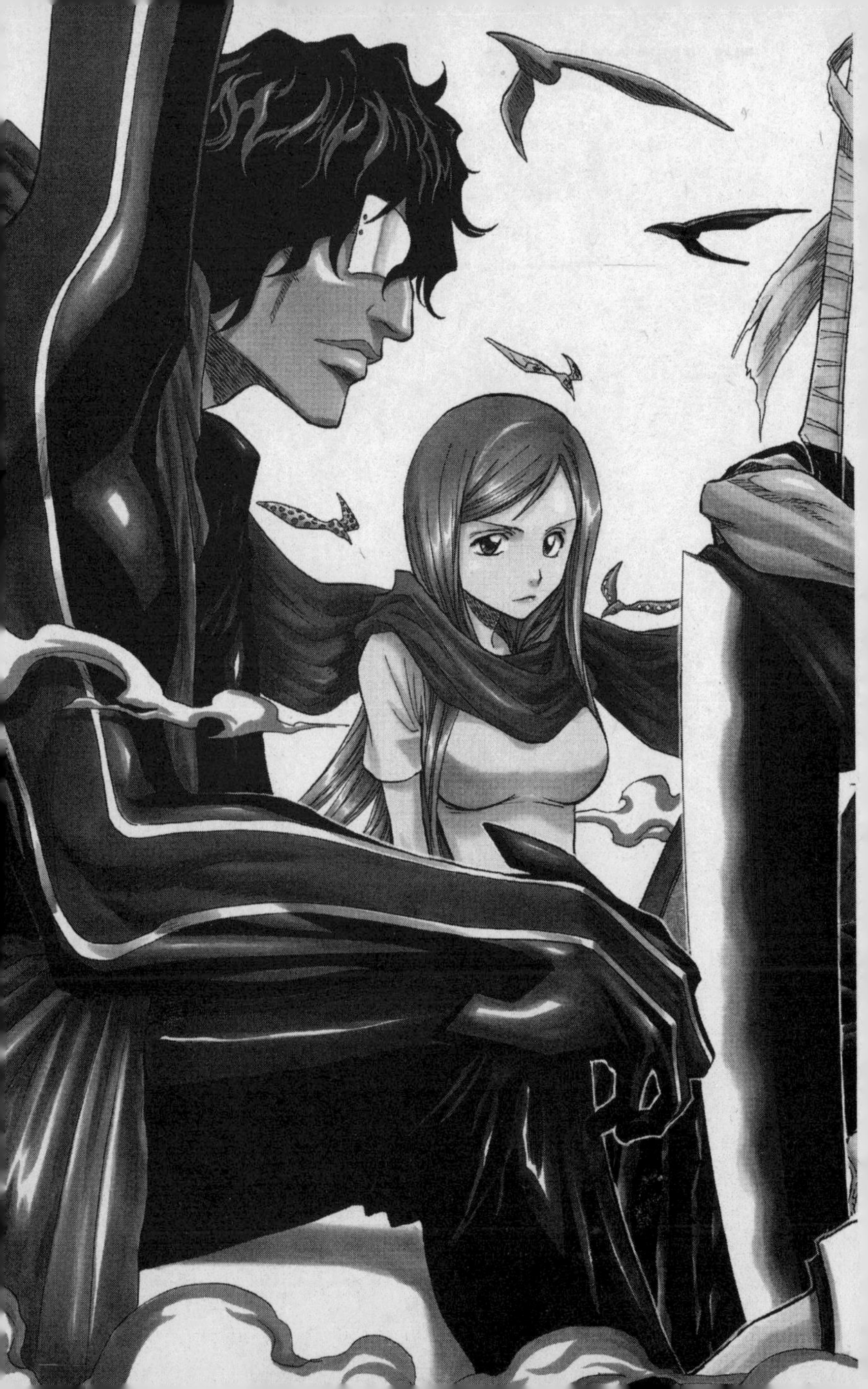

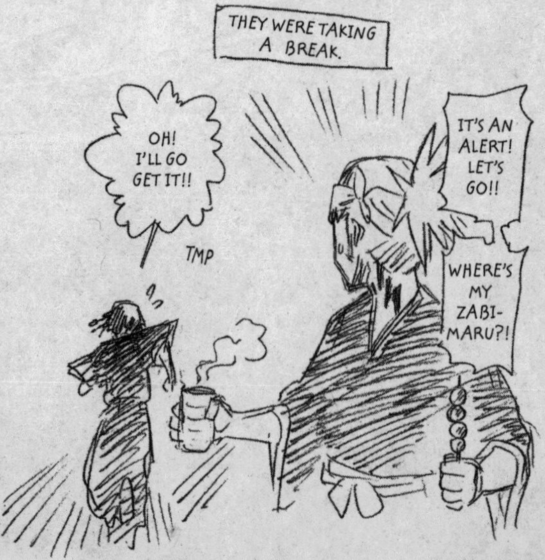
THEY WERE TAKING A BREAK.
IT'S AN ALERT! LET'S GO!!
WHERE'S MY ZABI-MARU?!
OH! I'LL GO GET IT!!
TMP

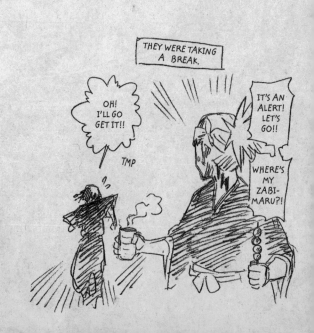

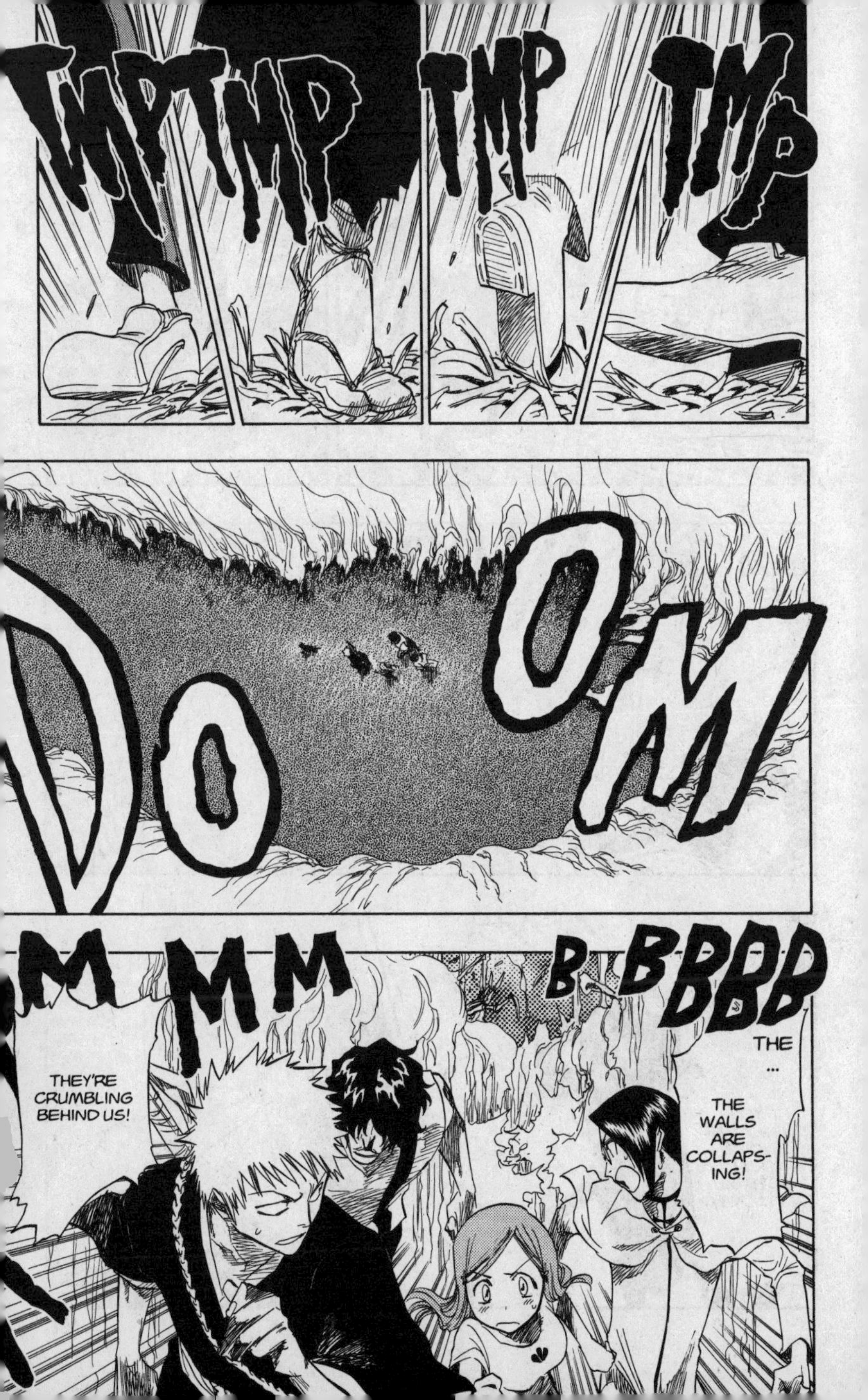
TMP TMP
TMP
TMP
TMP
DOOM
MMM
BBBBB
THE ...
THE WALLS ARE COLLAPS-ING!
THEY'RE CRUMBLING BEHIND US!

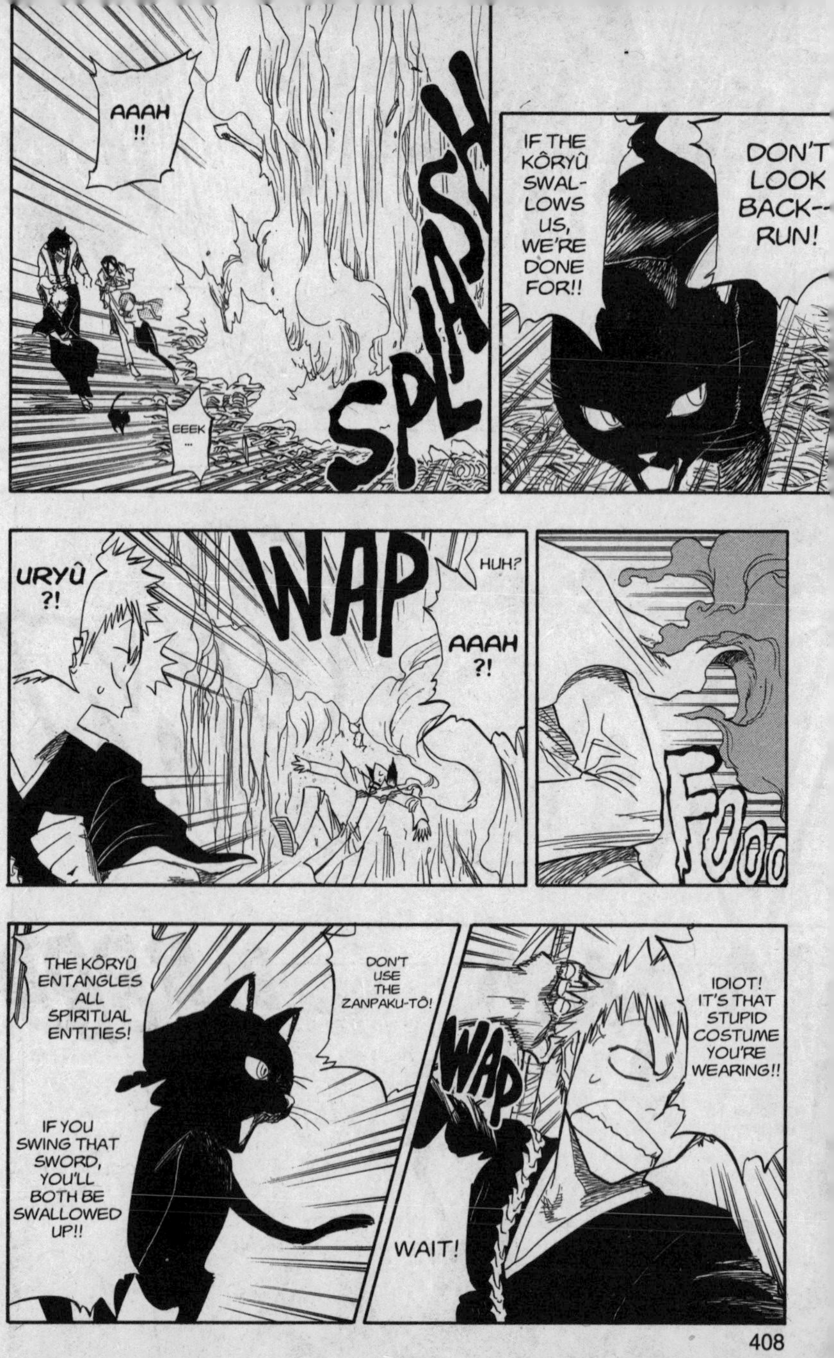
DON'T LOOK BACK--RUN!
IF THE KÔRYÛ SWAL-LOWS US, WE'RE DONE FOR!!
SPLASH
AAAH !!
EEEK ...
FOOO
HUH?
AAAH ?!
WAP
URYÛ ?!
IDIOT! IT'S THAT STUPID COSTUME YOU'RE WEARING!!
WAP
WAIT!
DON'T USE THE ZANPAKU-TÔ!
THE KÔRYÛ ENTANGLES ALL SPIRITUAL ENTITIES!
IF YOU SWING THAT SWORD, YOU'LL BOTH BE SWALLOWED UP!!

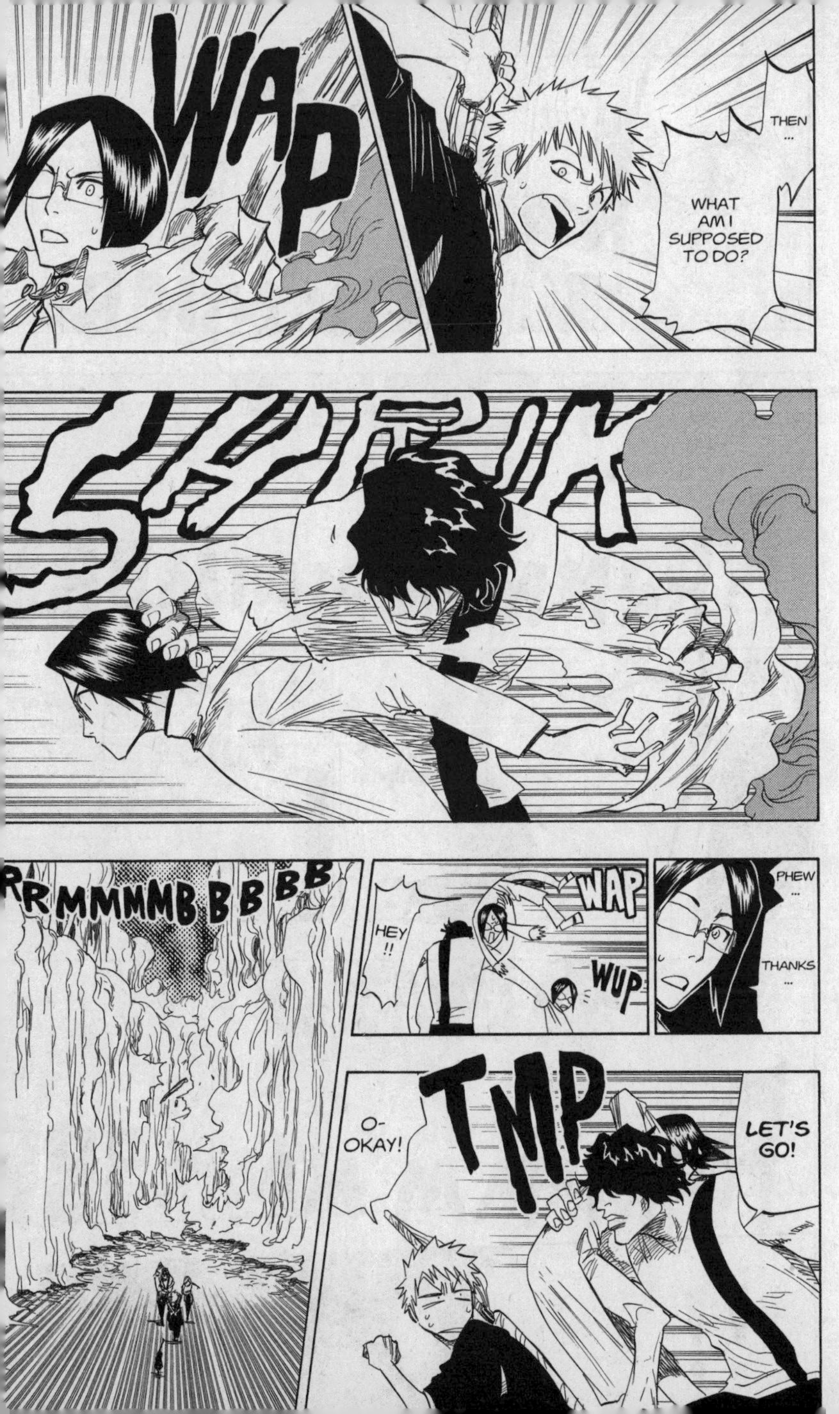
THEN ...
WHAT AM I SUPPOSED TO DO?
WAP
PHEW ...
THANKS ...
HEY !!
WAP
WUP
RRMMMMB B B BB
LET'S GO!
TMP
O-OKAY!

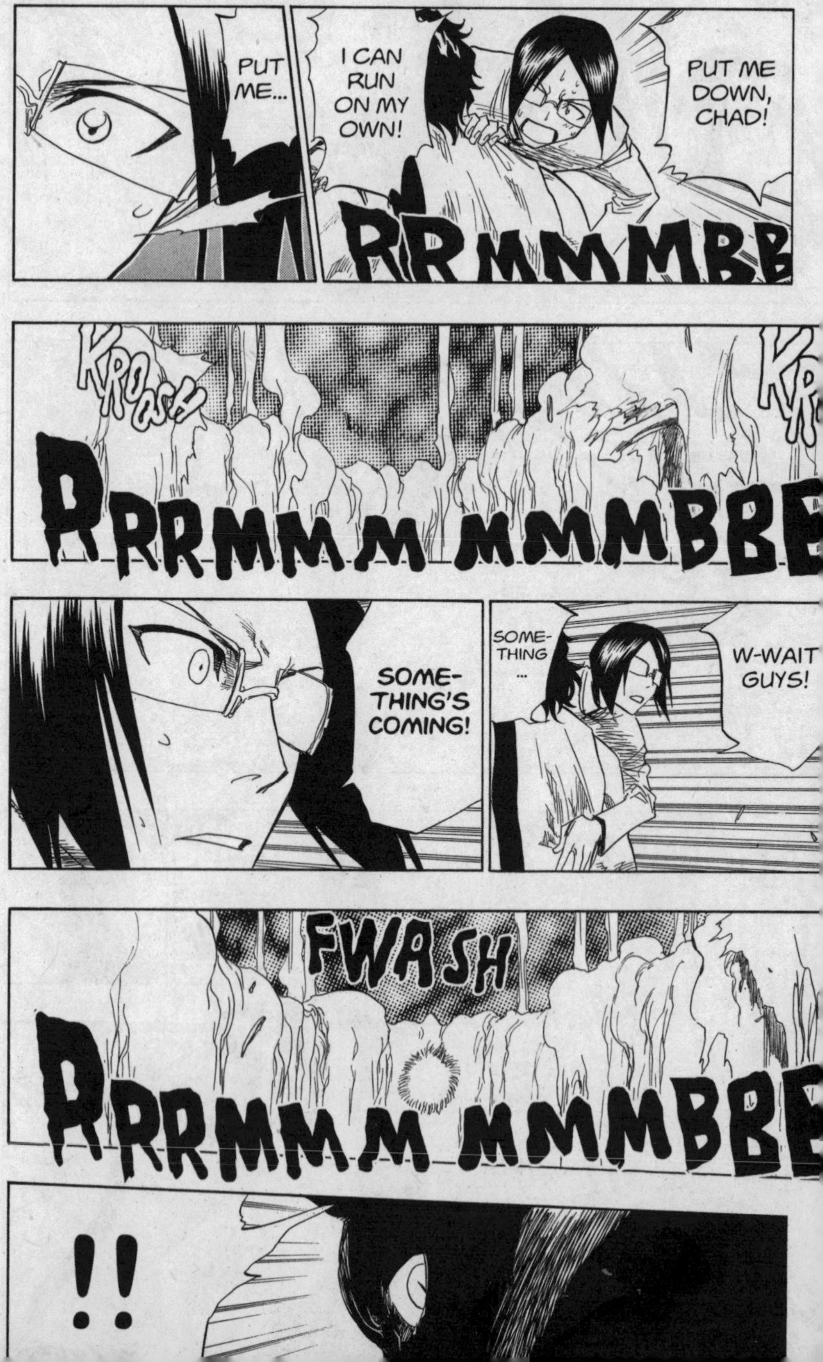
PUT ME DOWN, CHAD!
I CAN RUN ON MY OWN!
PUT ME...
RRMMMBB
KROSH
RRRMMM MMMBBE
W-WAIT GUYS!
SOME-THING ...
SOME-THING'S COMING!
FWASH
RRRMMM MMMBBE
!!

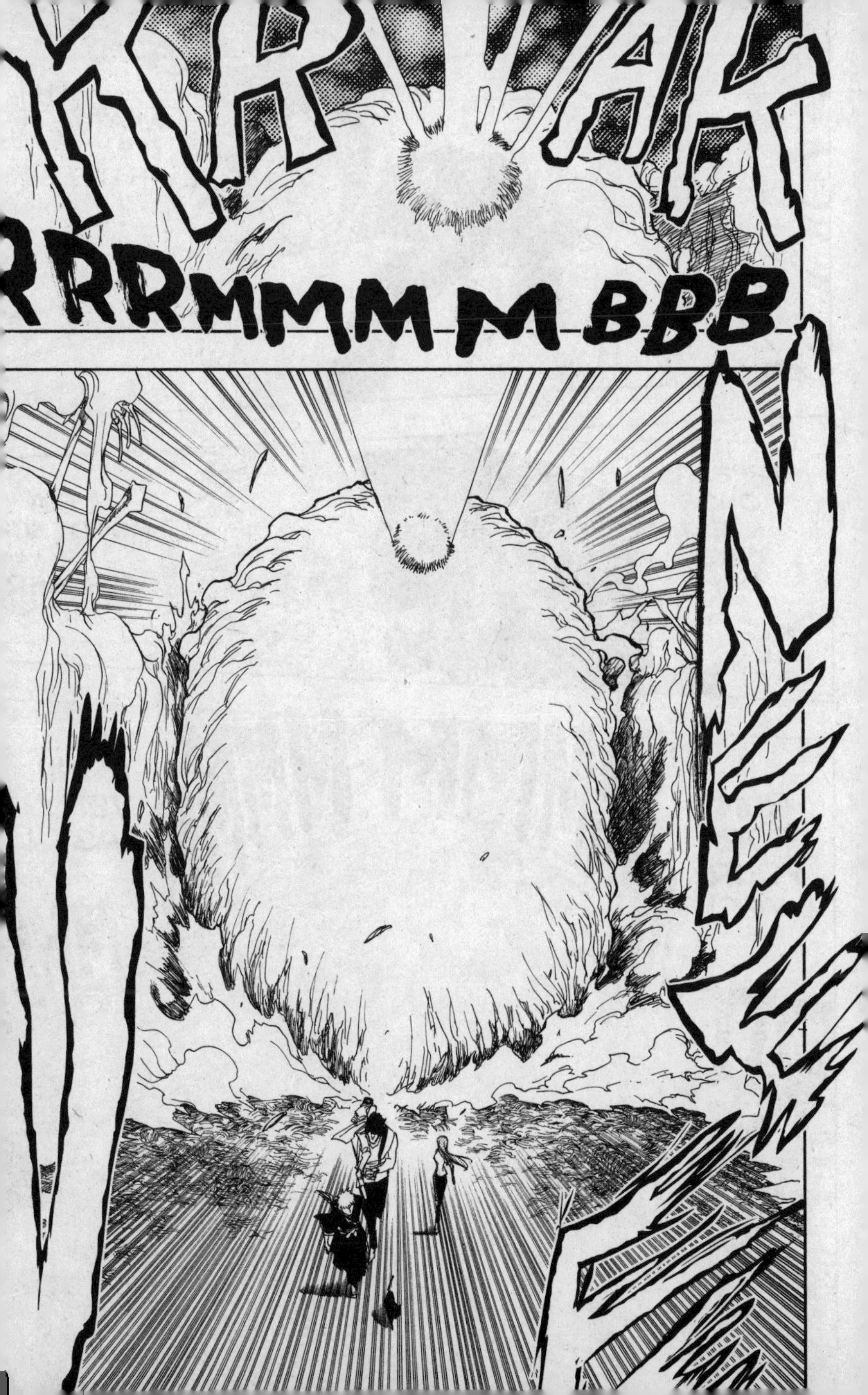
RRRMMMMBBB

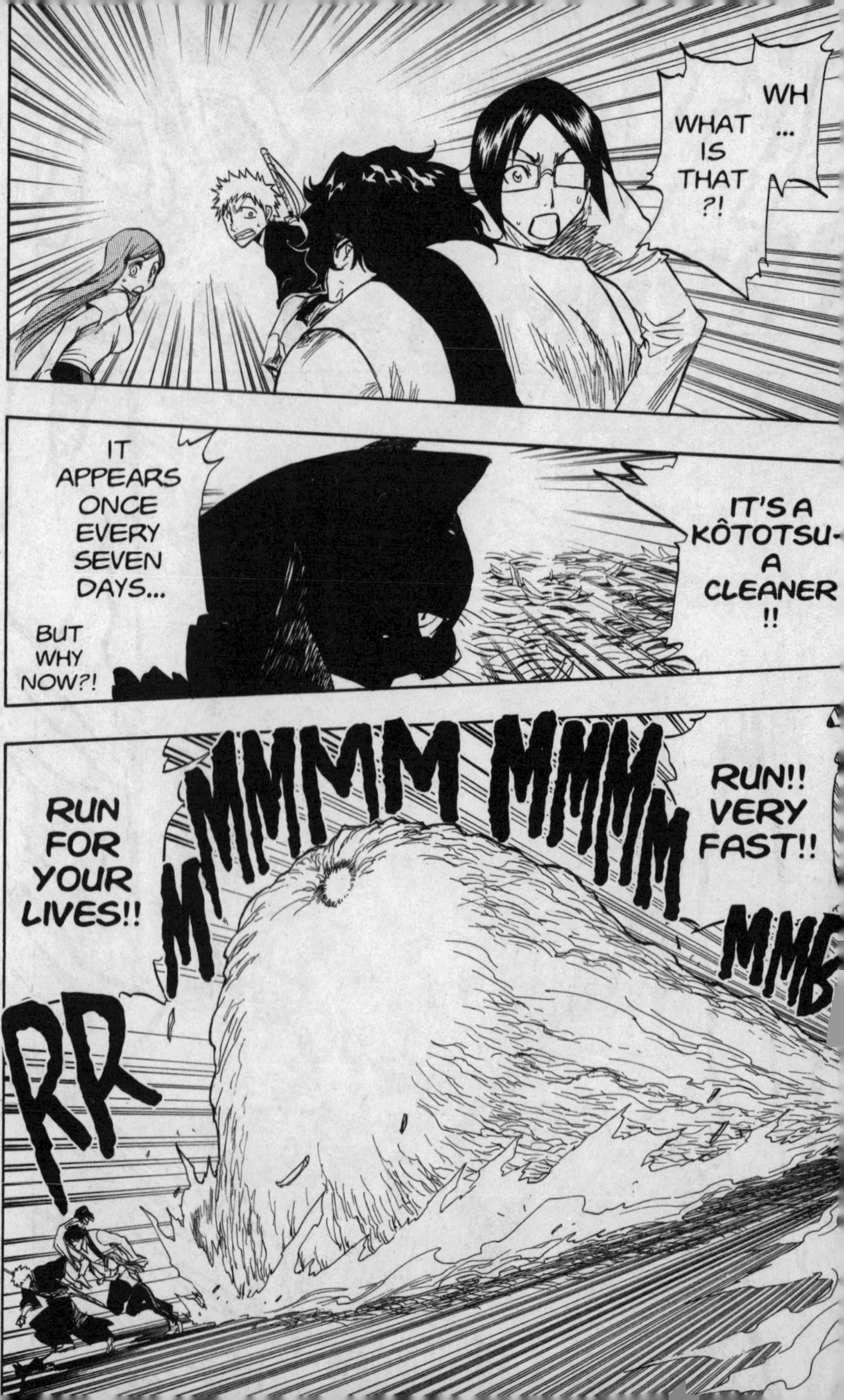
WH ...
WHAT IS THAT ?!
IT'S A KÔTOTSU- A CLEANER !!
IT APPEARS ONCE EVERY SEVEN DAYS...
BUT WHY NOW?!
RUN!! VERY FAST!!
MMMMM MMMMM MMB
RUN FOR YOUR LIVES!!
RR

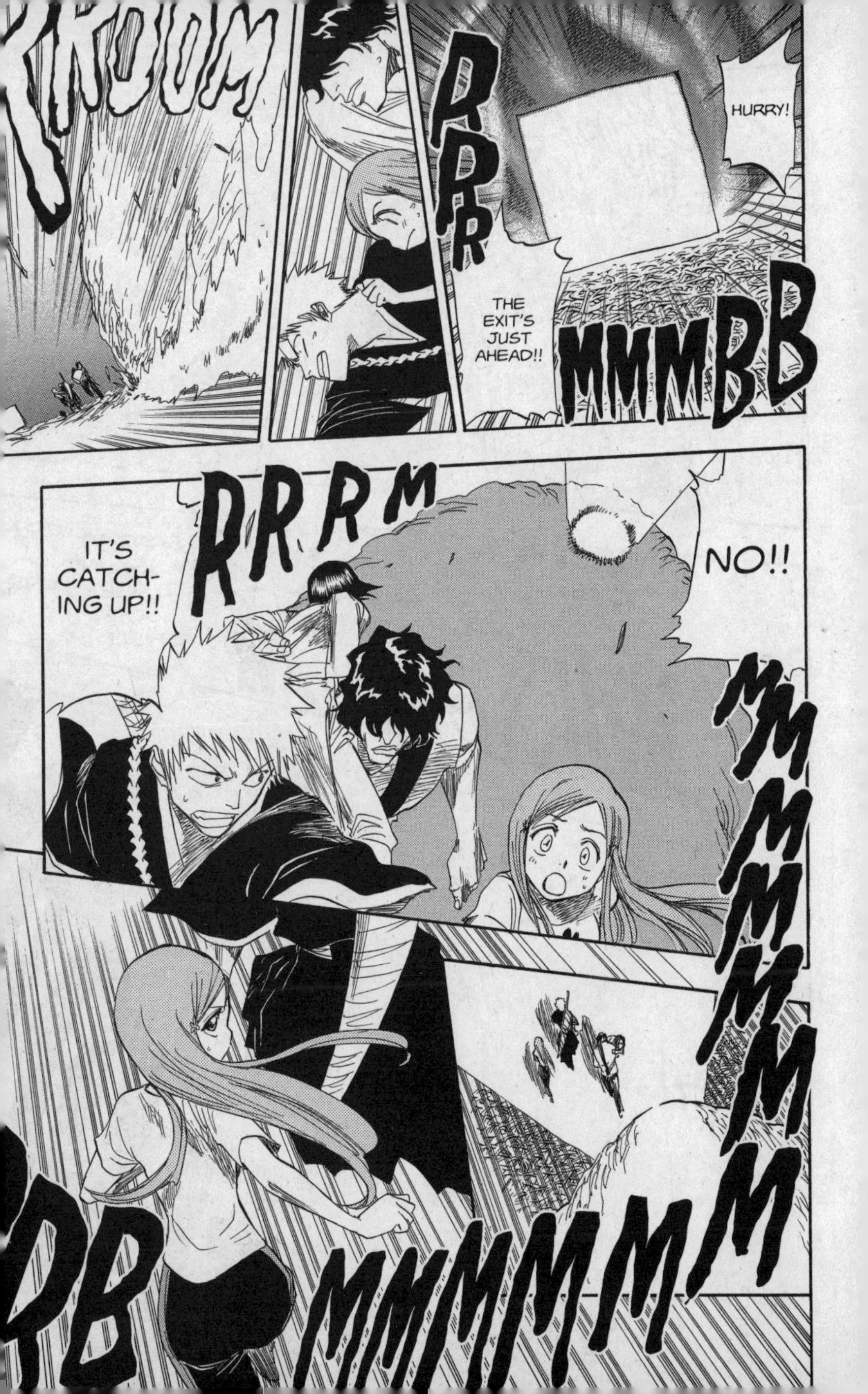
HURRY!
RRR
KROOM
THE EXIT'S JUST AHEAD!!
MMMBB
NO!!
RRRM
IT'S CATCH-ING UP!!
MMMMMMMMM
RB MMMMMMM

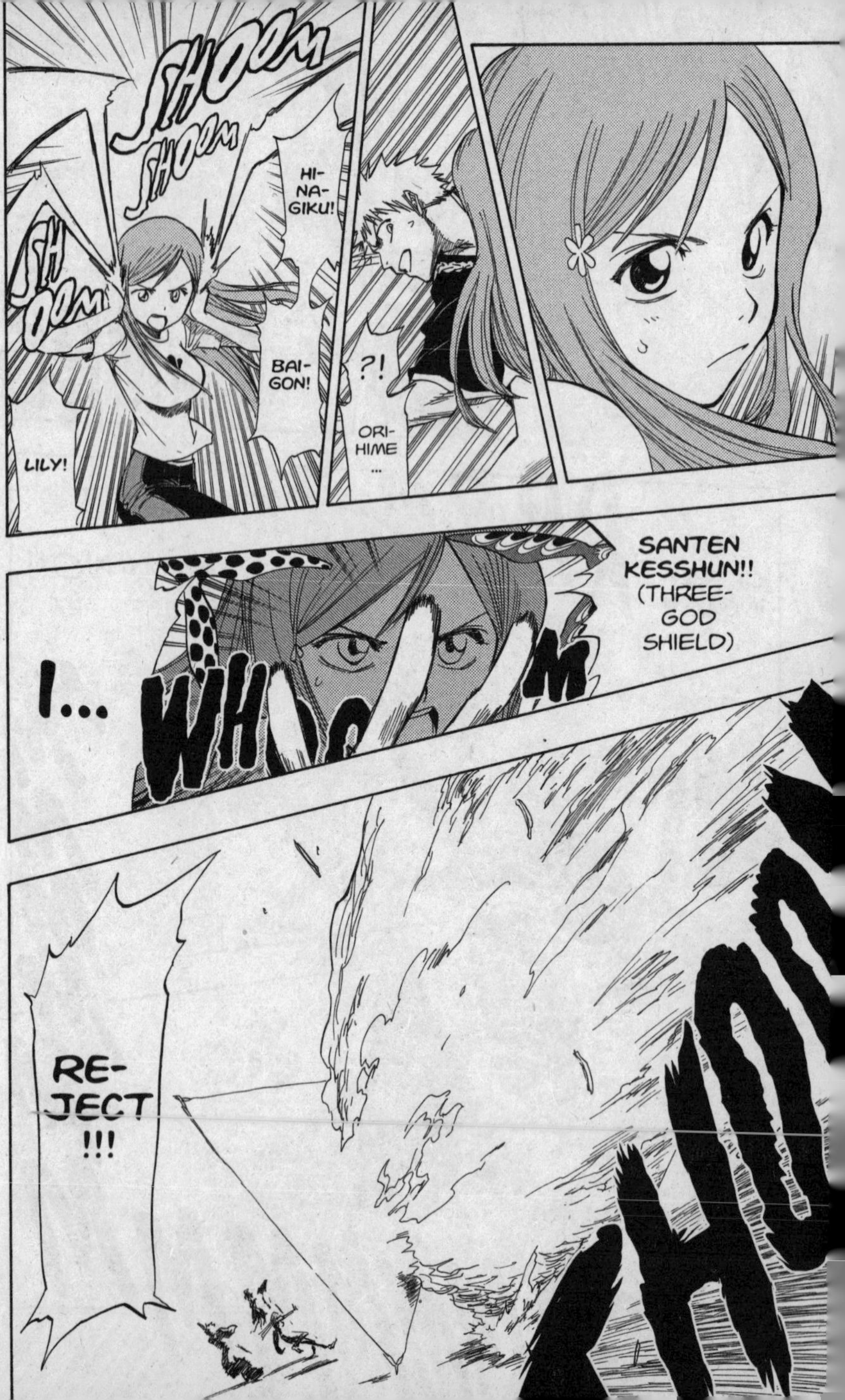
?!
ORI-HIME ...
SHOOM
SHOOM
HI-NA-GIKU!
BAI-GON!
SHOOM
LILY!
SANTEN KESSHUN!! (THREE-GOD SHIELD)
I...
RE-JECT !!!

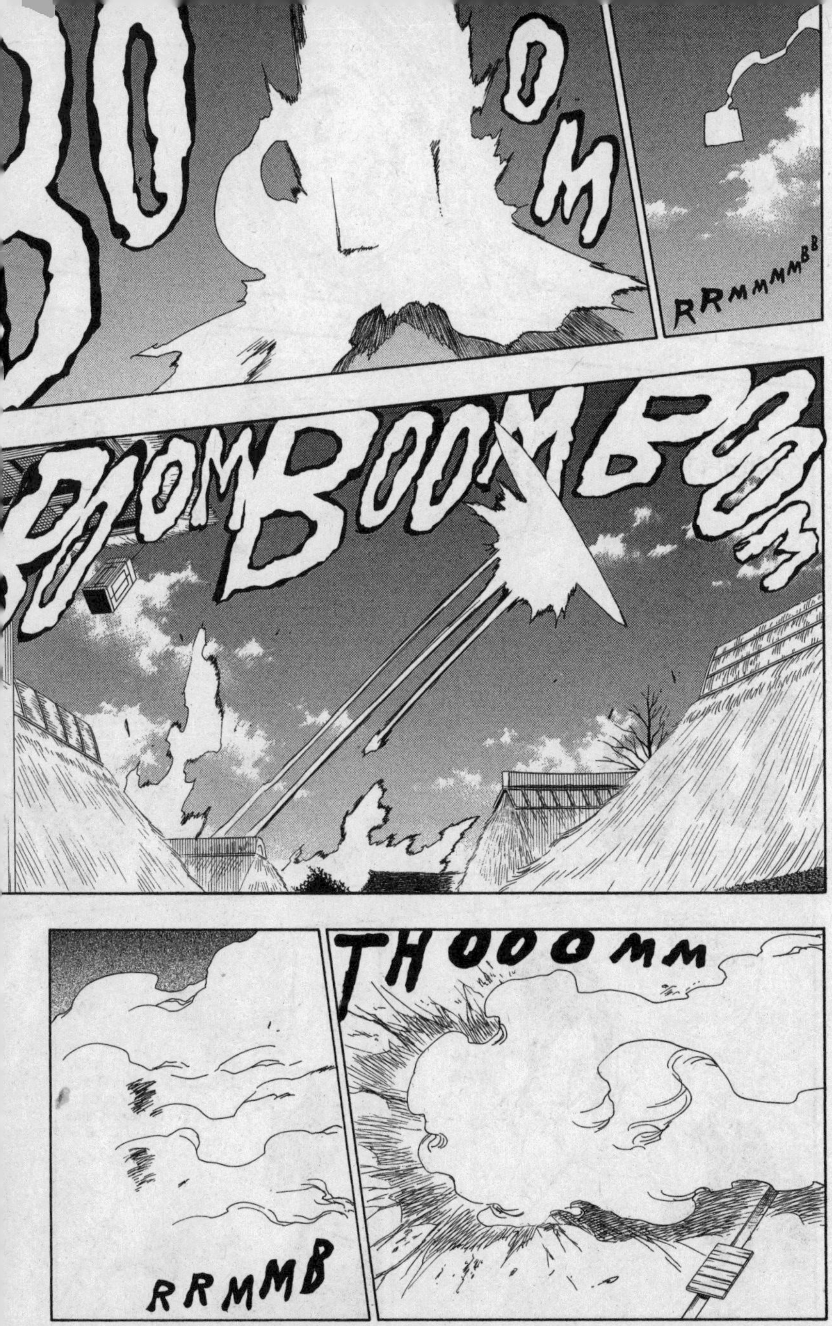
RRMMMMBB
BOOM
BOOM BOOM BOOM
THOOOMM
RRMMB

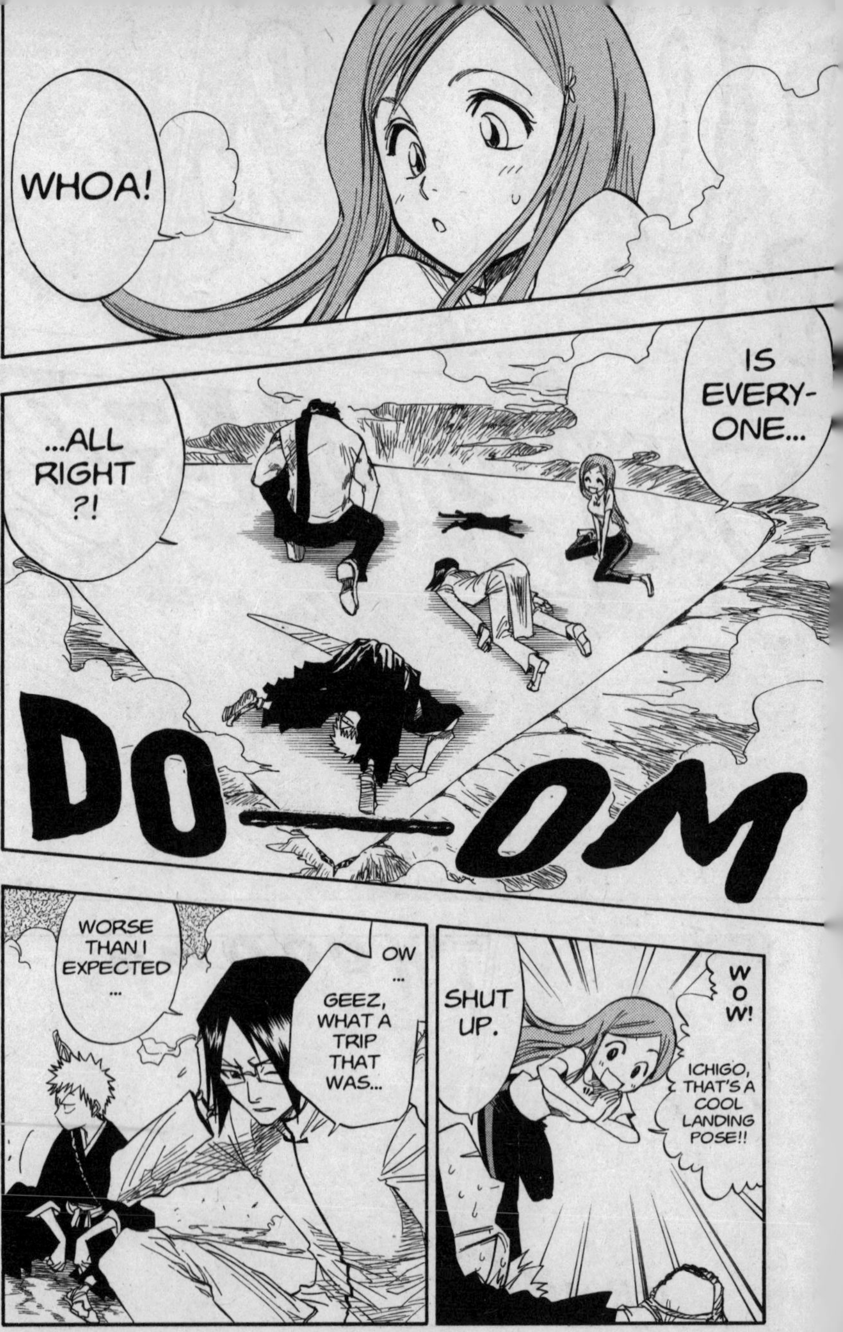
WHOA!
IS EVERY-ONE...
...ALL RIGHT?!
DO—OM
WOW!
ICHIGO, THAT'S A COOL LANDING POSE!!
SHUT UP.
OW ... GEEZ, WHAT A TRIP THAT WAS...
WORSE THAN I EXPECTED ...

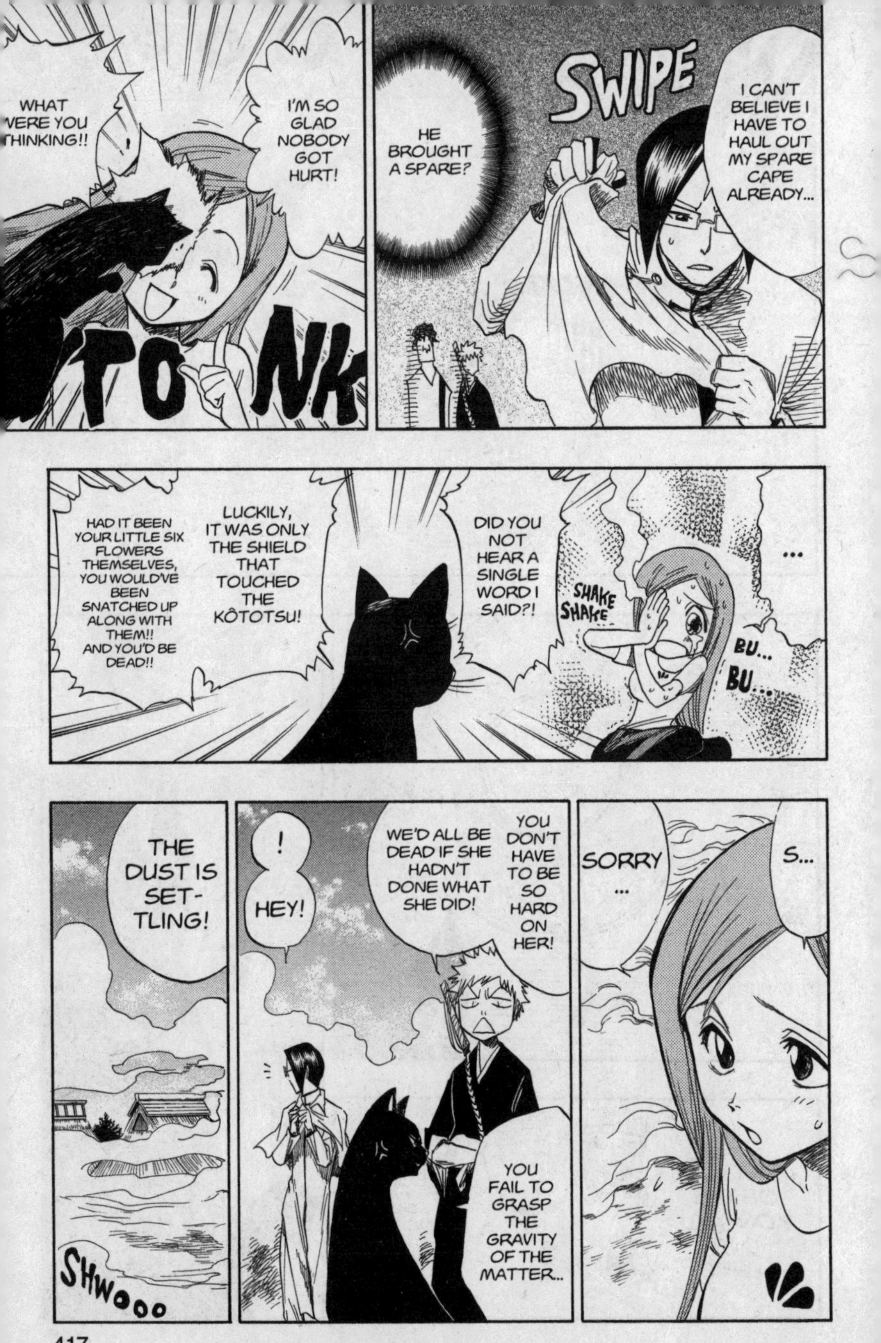
SWIPE
I CAN'T BELIEVE I HAVE TO HAUL OUT MY SPARE CAPE ALREADY...
HE BROUGHT A SPARE?
I'M SO GLAD NOBODY GOT HURT!
TONK
WHAT WERE YOU THINKING!!
...
BU... BU...
SHAKE SHAKE
DID YOU NOT HEAR A SINGLE WORD I SAID?!
LUCKILY, IT WAS ONLY THE SHIELD THAT TOUCHED THE KÔTOTSU!
HAD IT BEEN YOUR LITTLE SIX FLOWERS THEMSELVES, YOU WOULD'VE BEEN SNATCHED UP ALONG WITH THEM!! AND YOU'D BE DEAD!!
S...
SORRY...
YOU DON'T HAVE TO BE SO HARD ON HER!
WE'D ALL BE DEAD IF SHE HADN'T DONE WHAT SHE DID!
YOU FAIL TO GRASP THE GRAVITY OF THE MATTER...
!
HEY!
THE DUST IS SET-TLING!
SHWOOO

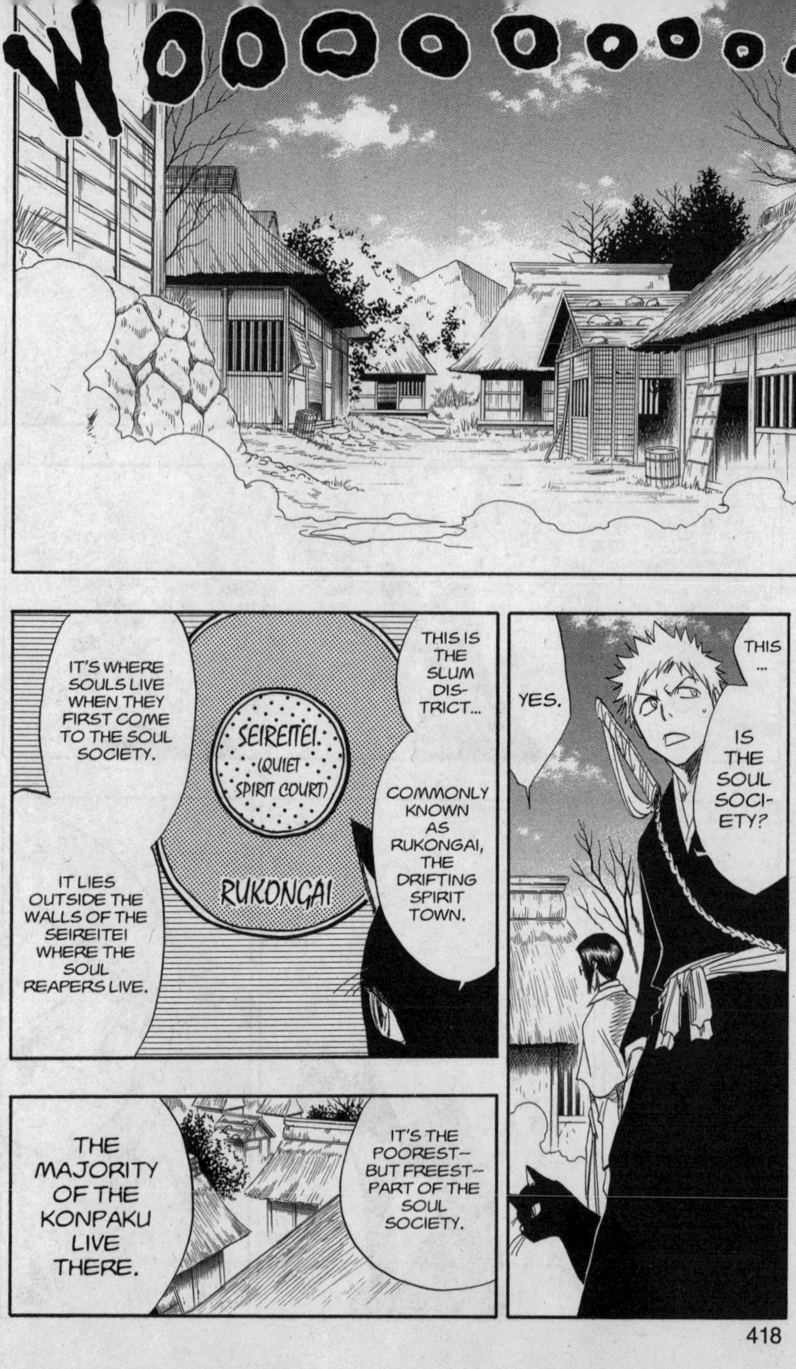
WOOOOOOOOO
THIS ... IS THE SOUL SOCIETY?
YES.
THIS IS THE SLUM DISTRICT...
COMMONLY KNOWN AS RUKONGAI, THE DRIFTING SPIRIT TOWN.
IT'S WHERE SOULS LIVE WHEN THEY FIRST COME TO THE SOUL SOCIETY.
SEIREITEI (QUIET SPIRIT COURT)
RUKONGAI
IT LIES OUTSIDE THE WALLS OF THE SEIREITEI WHERE THE SOUL REAPERS LIVE.
IT'S THE POOREST--BUT FREEST--PART OF THE SOUL SOCIETY.
THE MAJORITY OF THE KONPAKU LIVE THERE.

READ THIS WAY

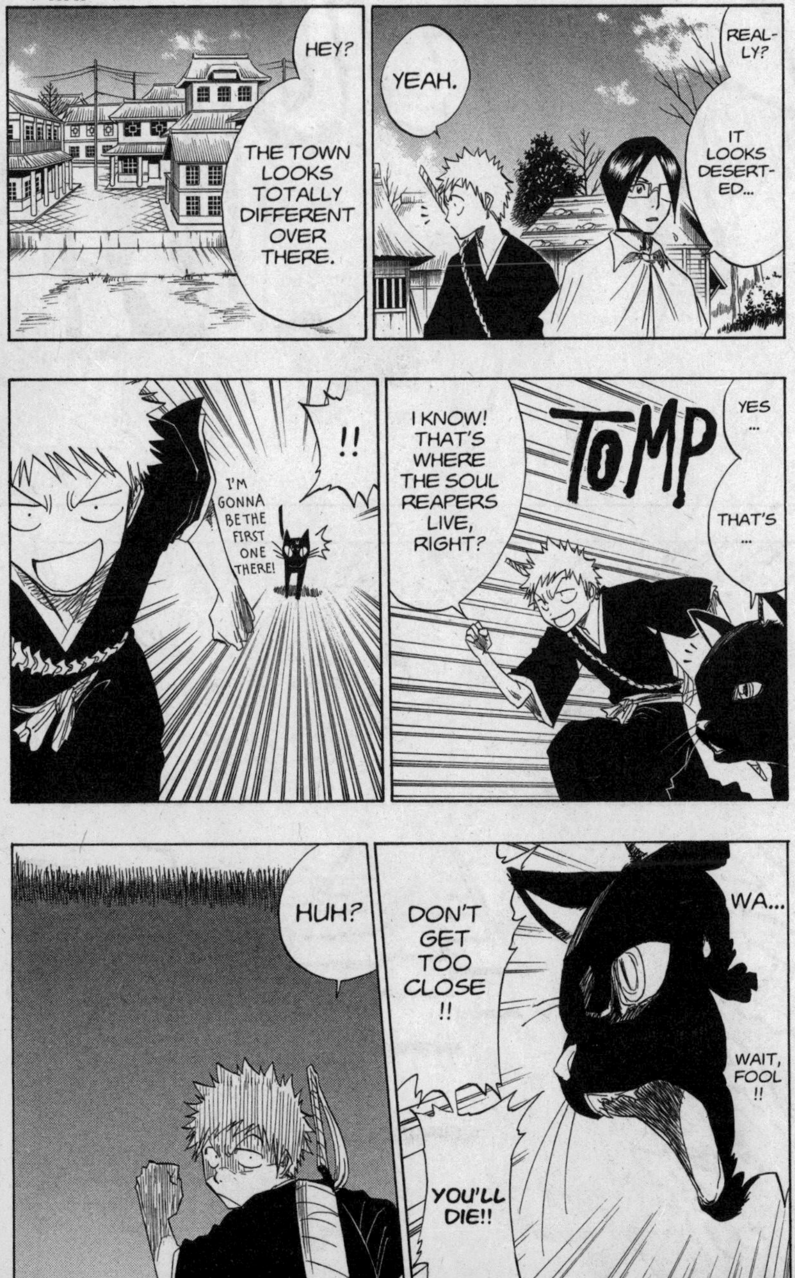
REAL-LY?
YEAH.
IT LOOKS DESERT-ED...
HEY?
THE TOWN LOOKS TOTALLY DIFFERENT OVER THERE.
YES...
THAT'S...
TOMP
I KNOW! THAT'S WHERE THE SOUL REAPERS LIVE, RIGHT?
!!
I'M GONNA BE THE FIRST ONE THERE!
WA...
DON'T GET TOO CLOSE!!
WAIT, FOOL!!
YOU'LL DIE!!
HUH?

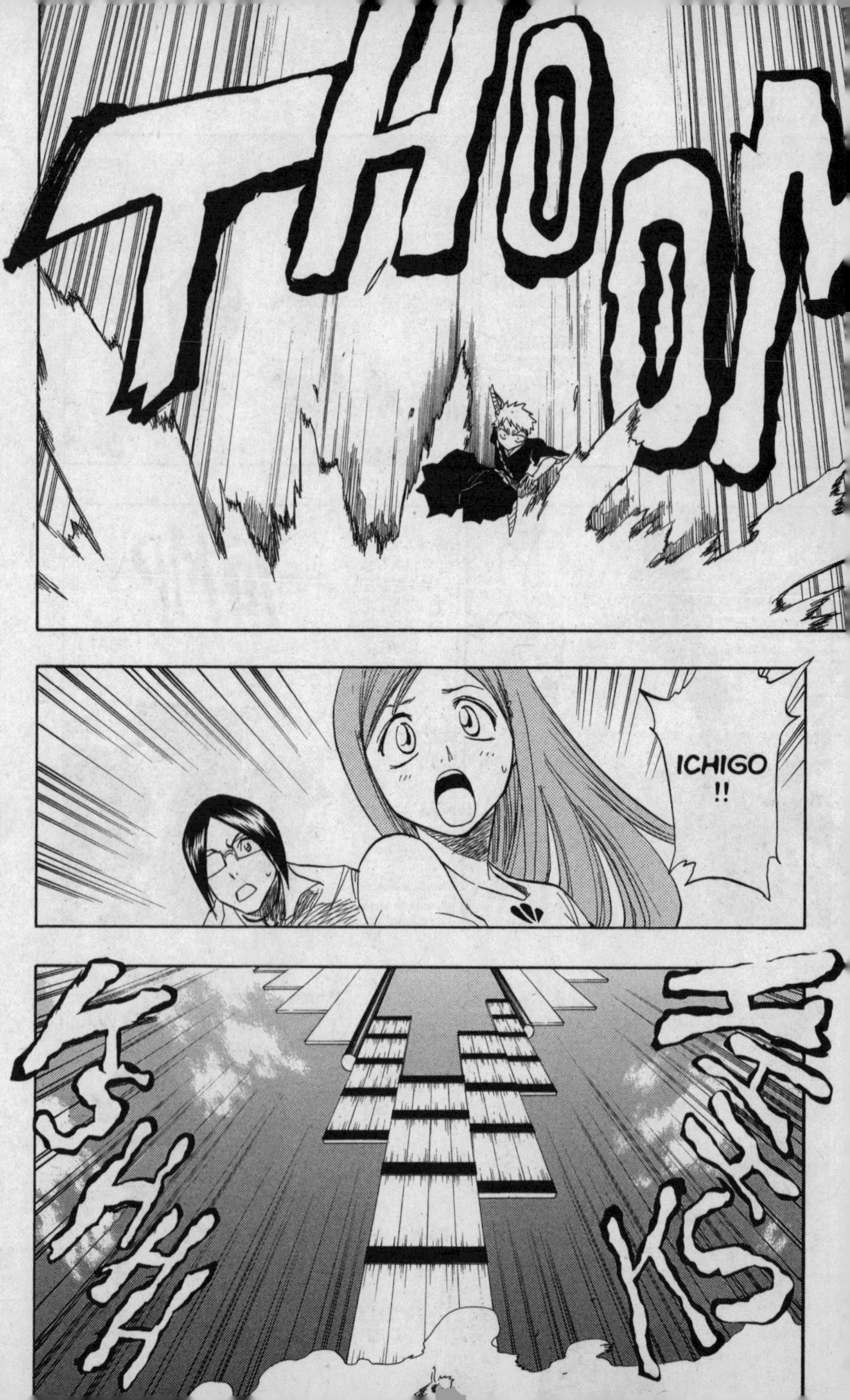
THOOM
ICHIGO !!
KSHHH

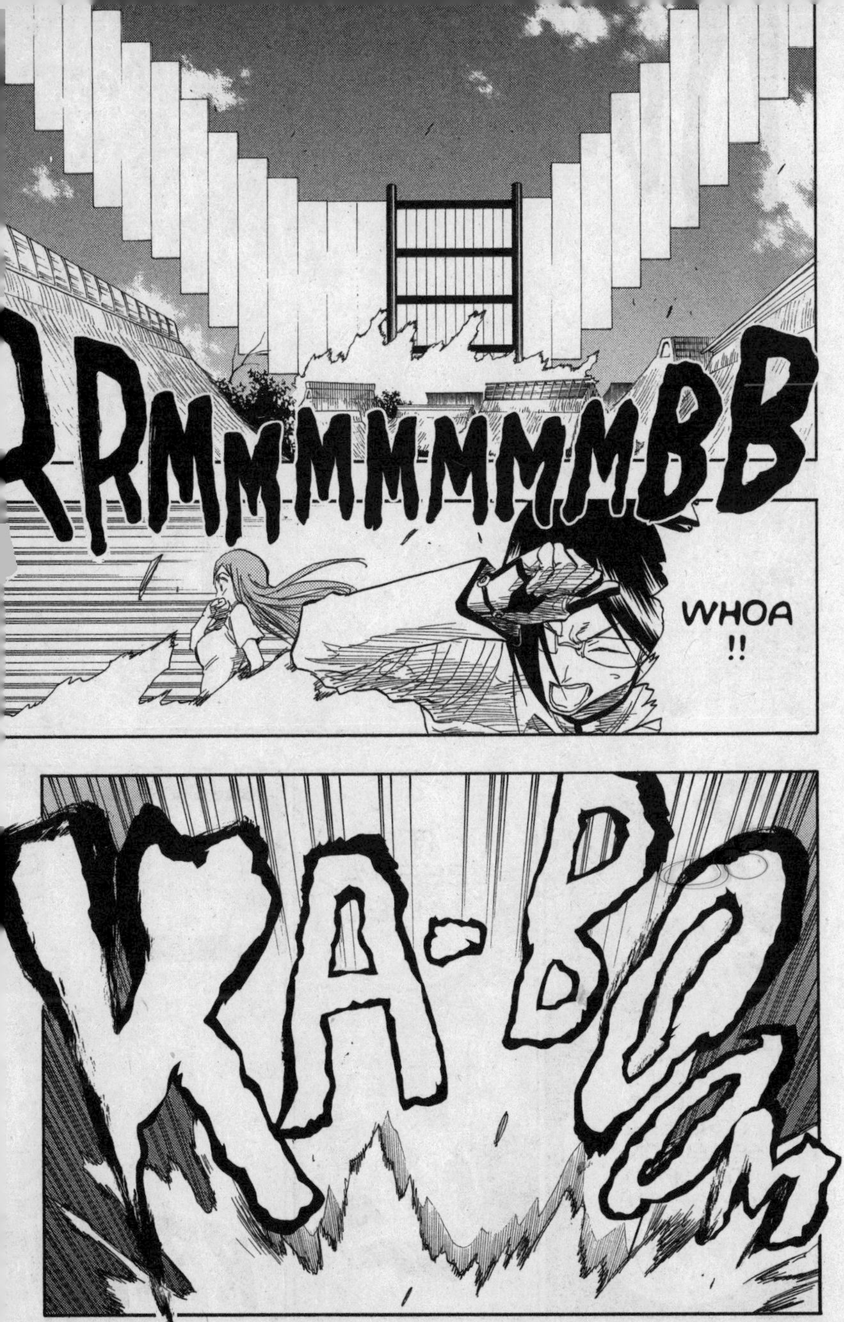
RRMMMMMMMBB
WHOA !!
KA-BOOM

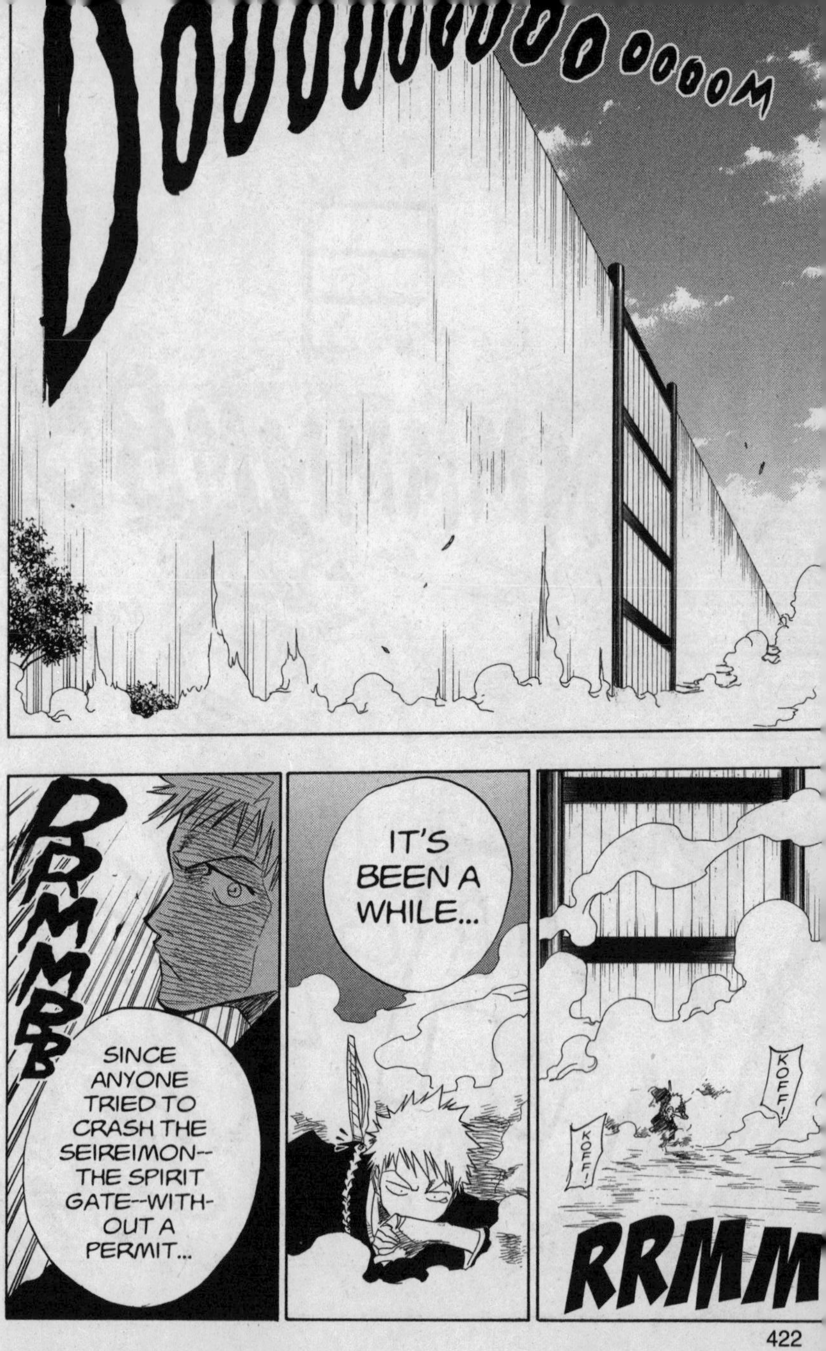
DOOOOOOOOOOOOOM
RRMM
KOFF!
KOFF!
IT'S BEEN A WHILE...
SINCE ANYONE TRIED TO CRASH THE SEIREIMON--THE SPIRIT GATE--WITHOUT A PERMIT...
BRRMMBB

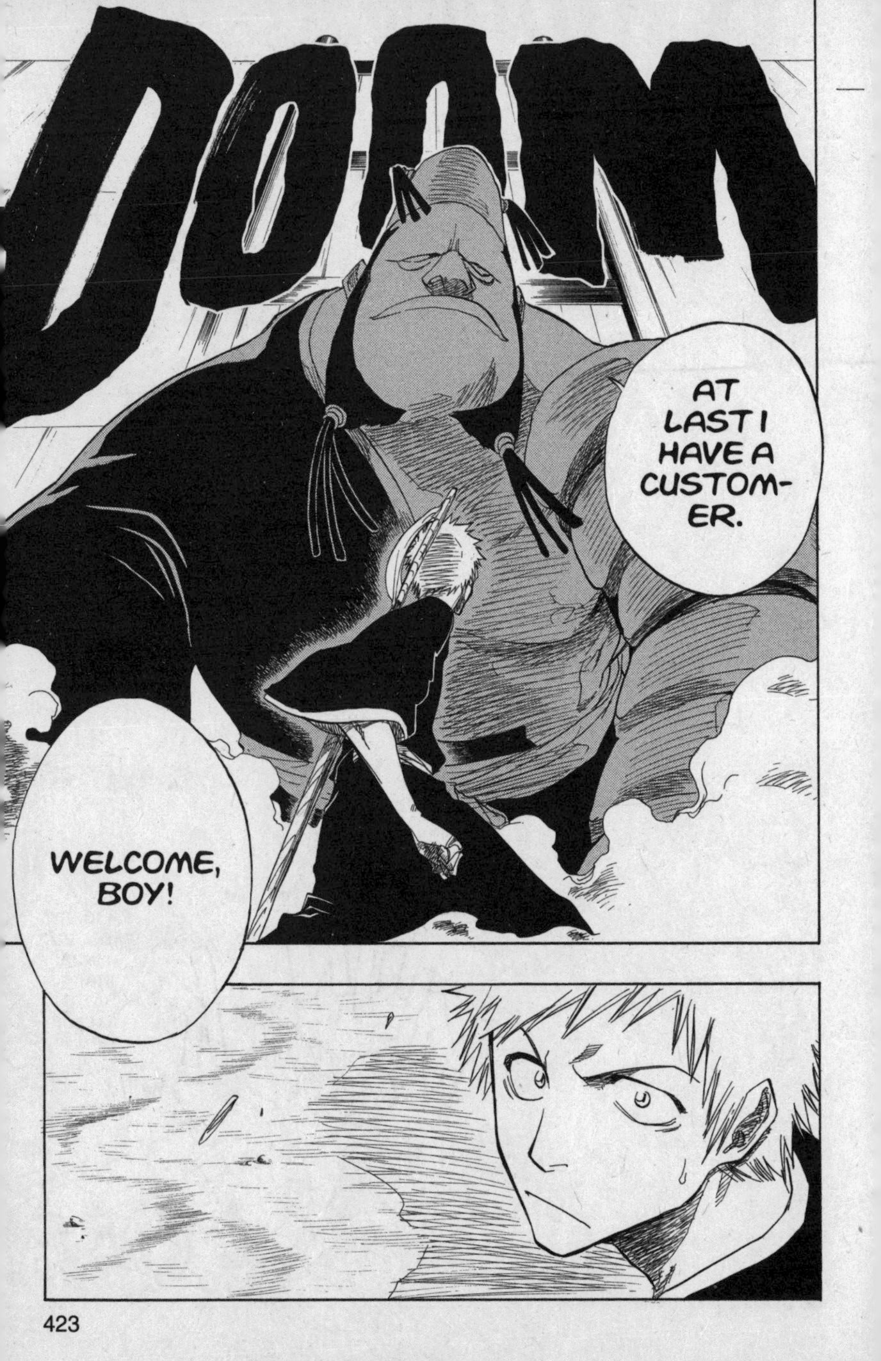
DOOM
AT LAST I HAVE A CUSTOMER.
WELCOME, BOY!

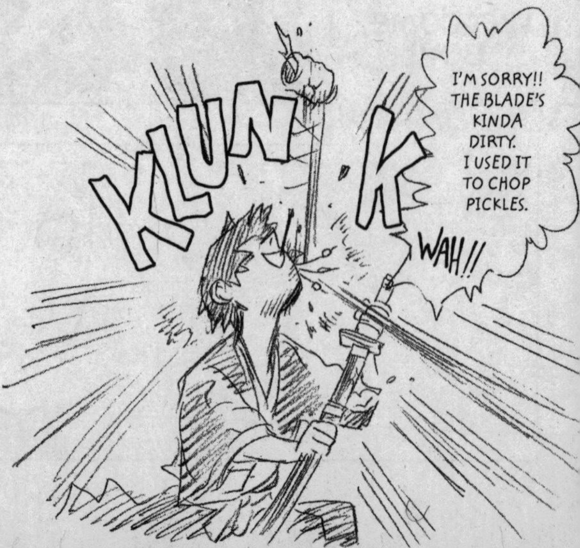
KLUNK
WAH!!
I'M SORRY!! THE BLADE'S KINDA DIRTY. I USED IT TO CHOP PICKLES.

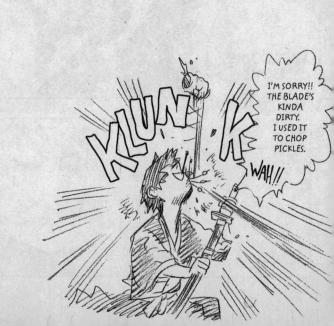

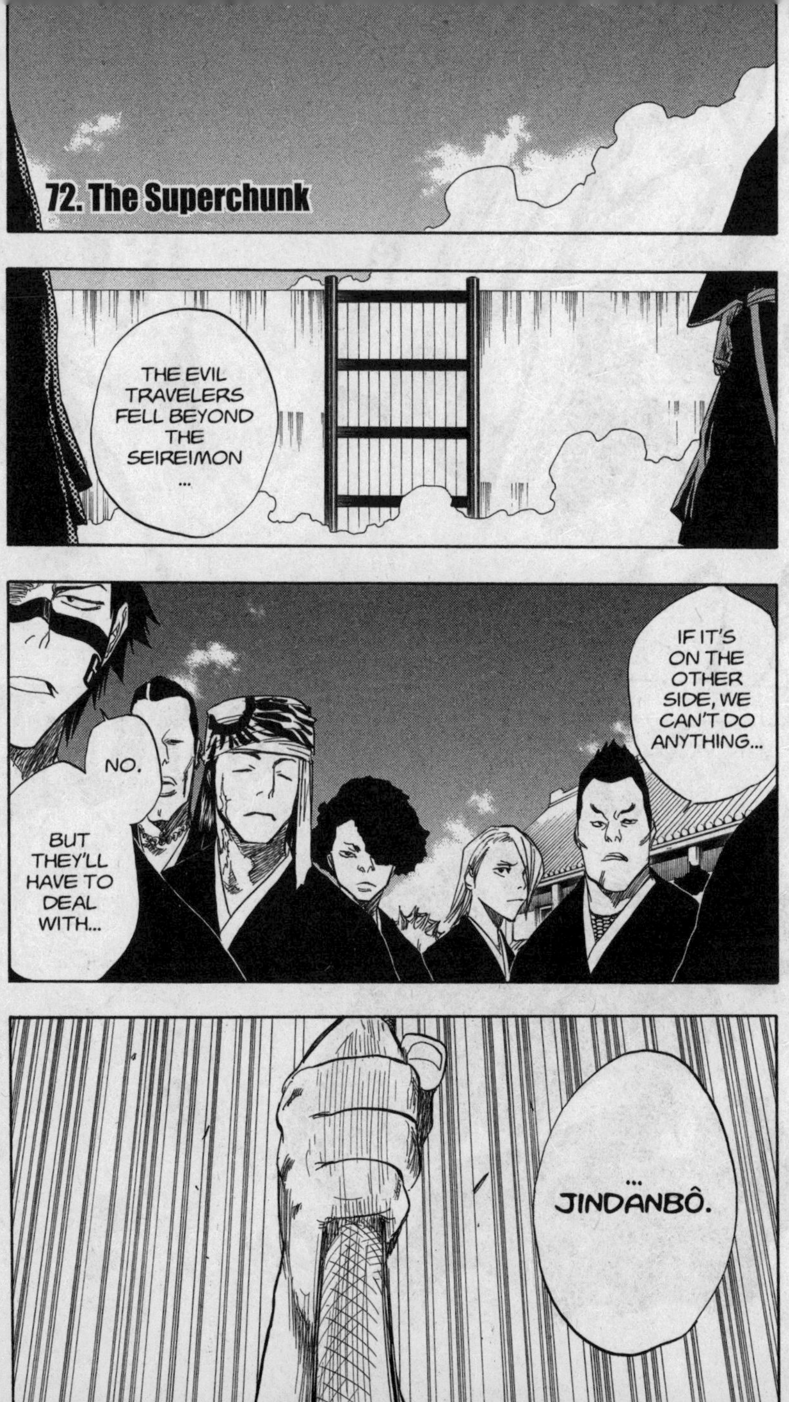
72. The Superchunk
THE EVIL TRAVELERS FELL BEYOND THE SEIREIMON ...
IF IT'S ON THE OTHER SIDE, WE CAN'T DO ANYTHING...
NO.
BUT THEY'LL HAVE TO DEAL WITH...
... JINDANBÔ.

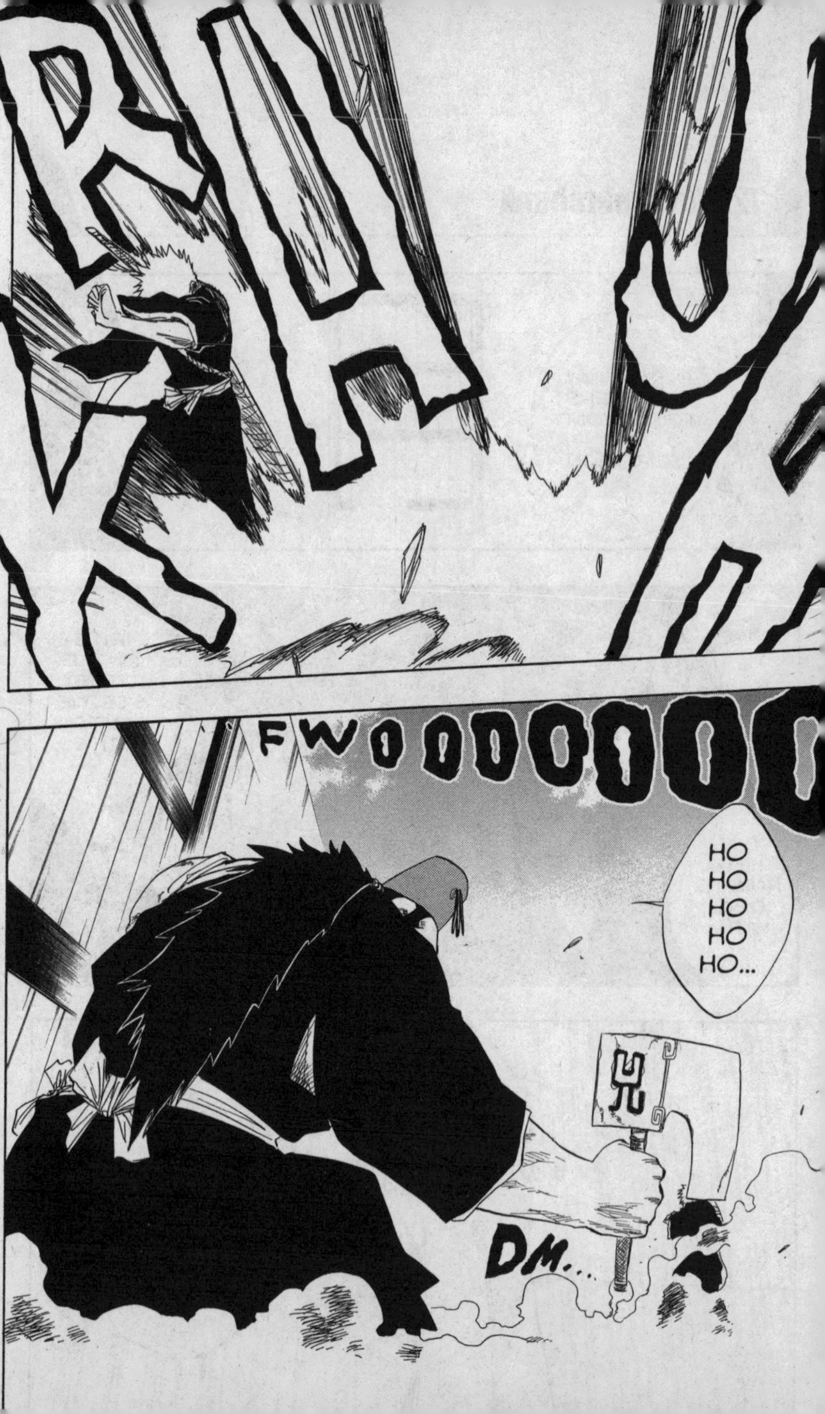
RAH
FWOOOOOOOOO
HO HO HO HO HO...
DM...

AX: JI--FIRST CHARACTER OF JINDANBÔ'S NAME

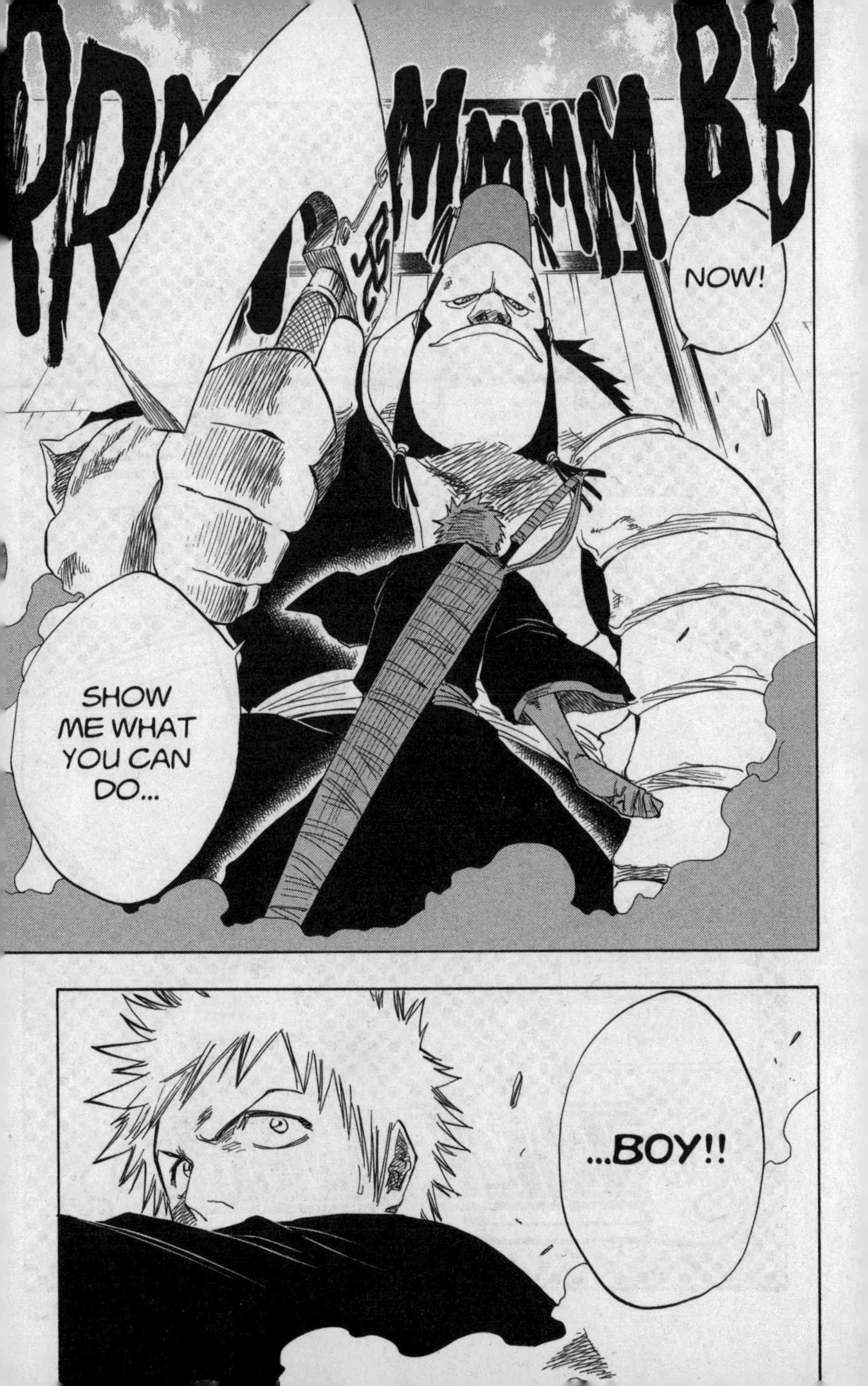
NOW!
SHOW ME WHAT YOU CAN DO...
...BOY!!

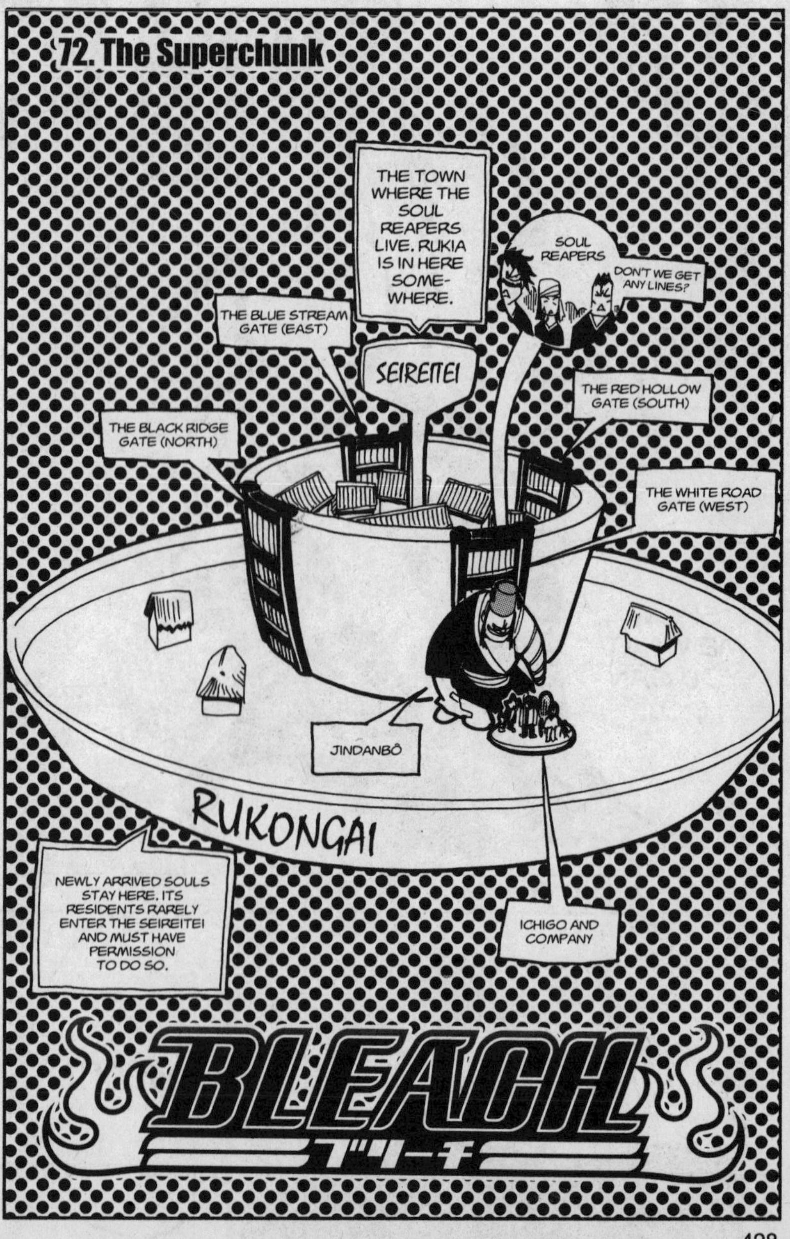
72. The Superchunk
THE TOWN WHERE THE SOUL REAPERS LIVE. RUKIA IS IN HERE SOMEWHERE.
SOUL REAPERS
DON'T WE GET ANY LINES?
THE BLUE STREAM GATE (EAST)
SEIREITEI
THE RED HOLLOW GATE (SOUTH)
THE BLACK RIDGE GATE (NORTH)
THE WHITE ROAD GATE (WEST)
JINDANBÔ
RUKONGAI
NEWLY ARRIVED SOULS STAY HERE. ITS RESIDENTS RARELY ENTER THE SEIREITEI AND MUST HAVE PERMISSION TO DO SO.
ICHIGO AND COMPANY
BLEACH
ブリーチ

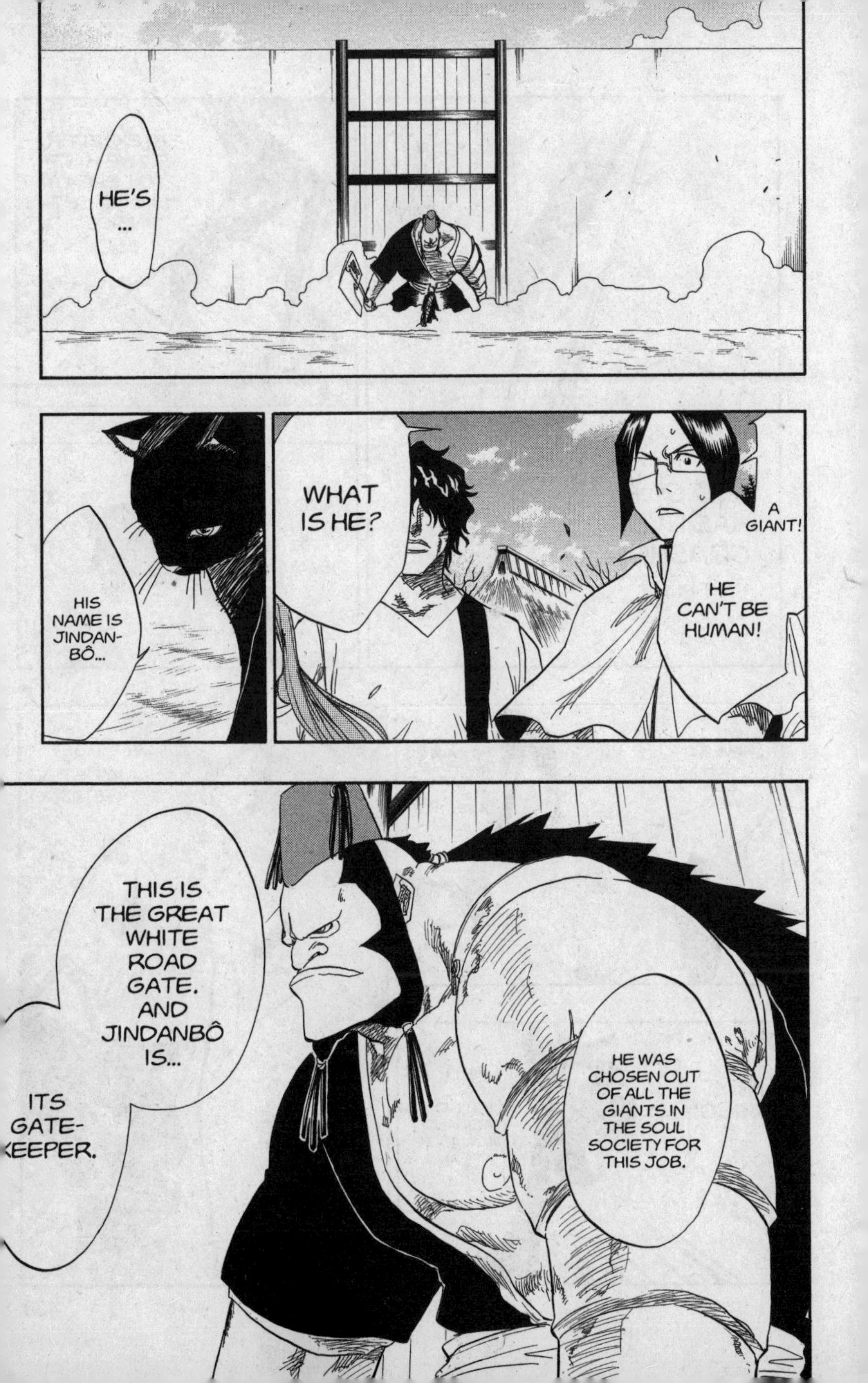
HE'S ...
A GIANT!
HE CAN'T BE HUMAN!
WHAT IS HE?
HIS NAME IS JINDANBÔ...
THIS IS THE GREAT WHITE ROAD GATE. AND JINDANBÔ IS...
HE WAS CHOSEN OUT OF ALL THE GIANTS IN THE SOUL SOCIETY FOR THIS JOB.
ITS GATE-
EEPER.

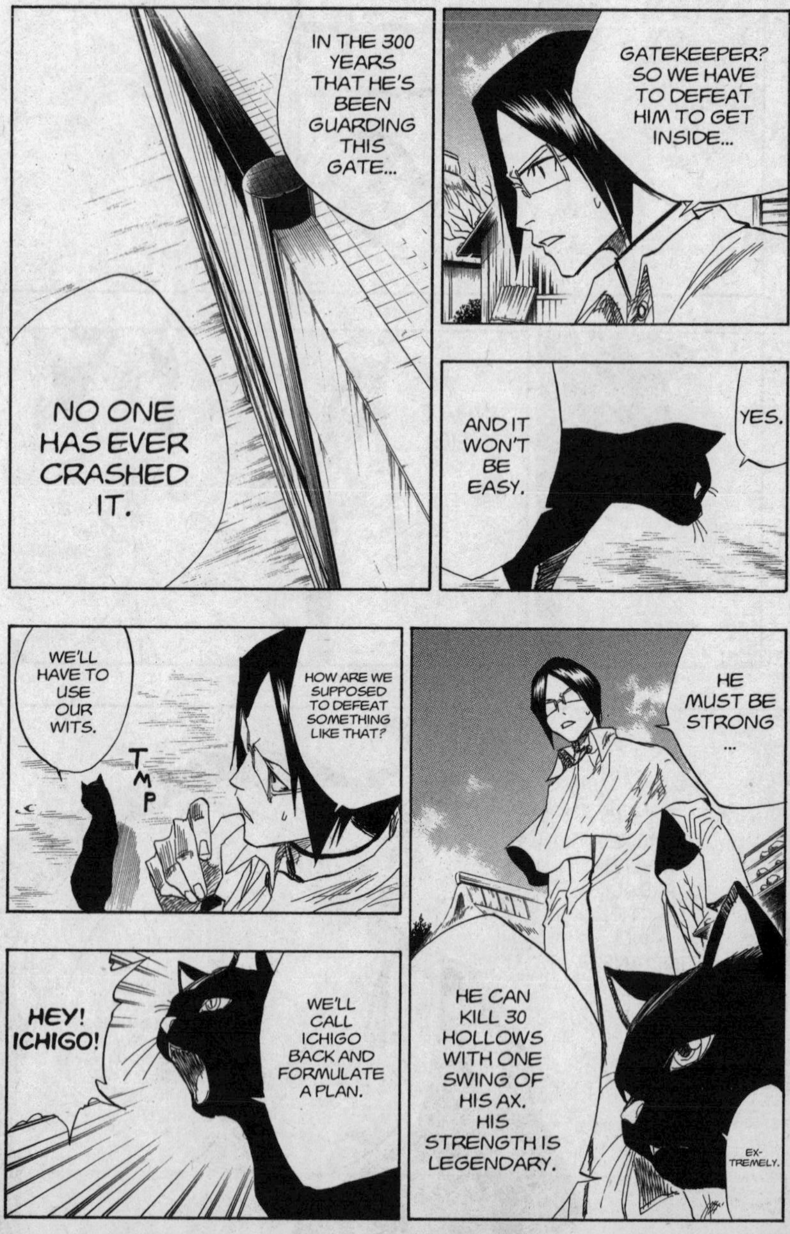
GATEKEEPER? SO WE HAVE TO DEFEAT HIM TO GET INSIDE...
YES.
AND IT WON'T BE EASY.
IN THE 300 YEARS THAT HE'S BEEN GUARDING THIS GATE...
NO ONE HAS EVER CRASHED IT.
HE MUST BE STRONG ...
EX-TREMELY.
HE CAN KILL 30 HOLLOWS WITH ONE SWING OF HIS AX. HIS STRENGTH IS LEGENDARY.
HOW ARE WE SUPPOSED TO DEFEAT SOMETHING LIKE THAT?
TMP
WE'LL HAVE TO USE OUR WITS.
WE'LL CALL ICHIGO BACK AND FORMULATE A PLAN.
HEY! ICHIGO!

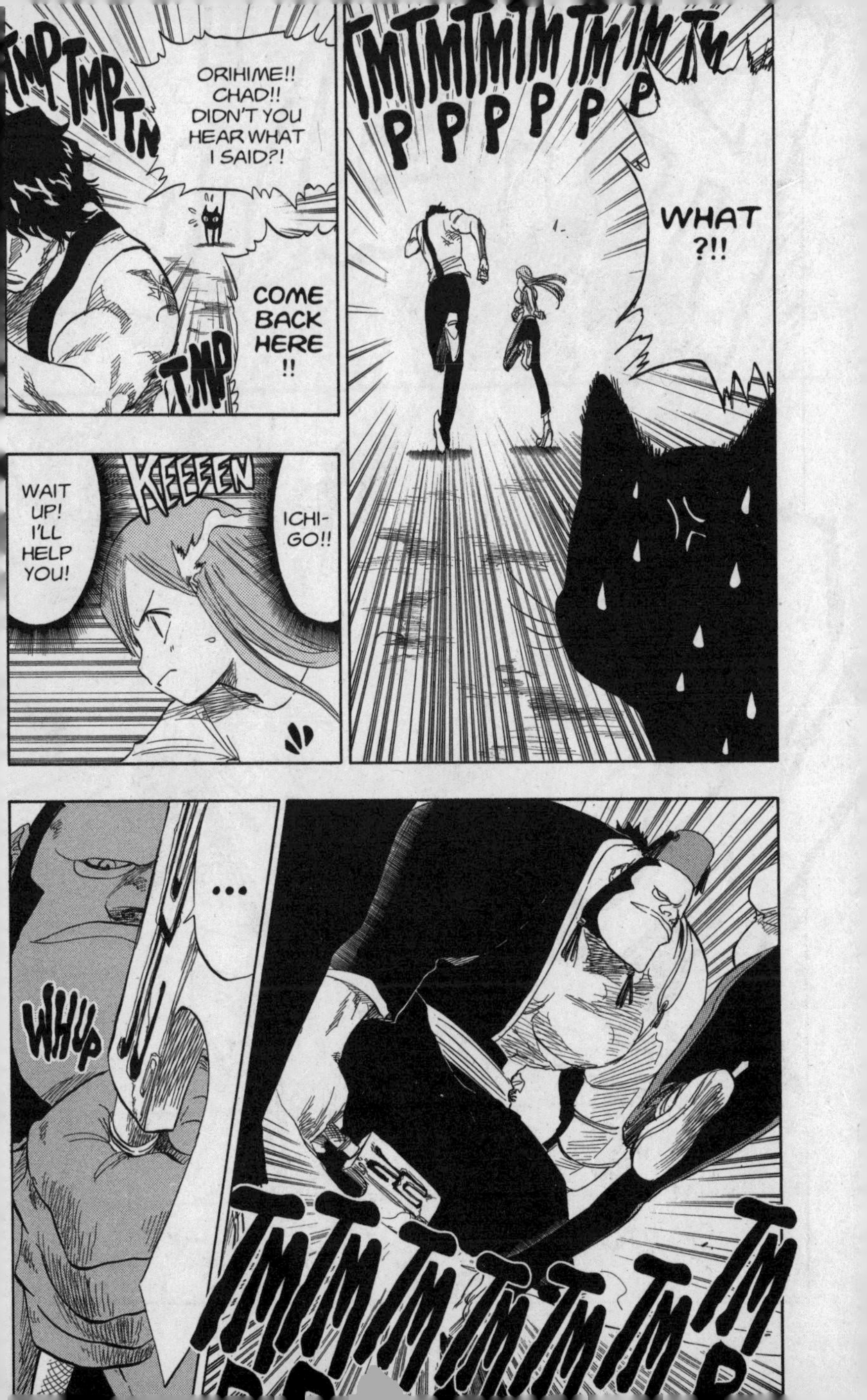

TMTMTMTMTMTMTMTN PPPPPP
WHAT ?!!
TMPTMPTN
ORIHIME!! CHAD!! DIDN'T YOU HEAR WHAT I SAID?!
COME BACK HERE !!
TMP
ICHI-GO!!
KEEEEN
WAIT UP! I'LL HELP YOU!
TMTMTMTMTMTMTMTMTM
...
WHUP

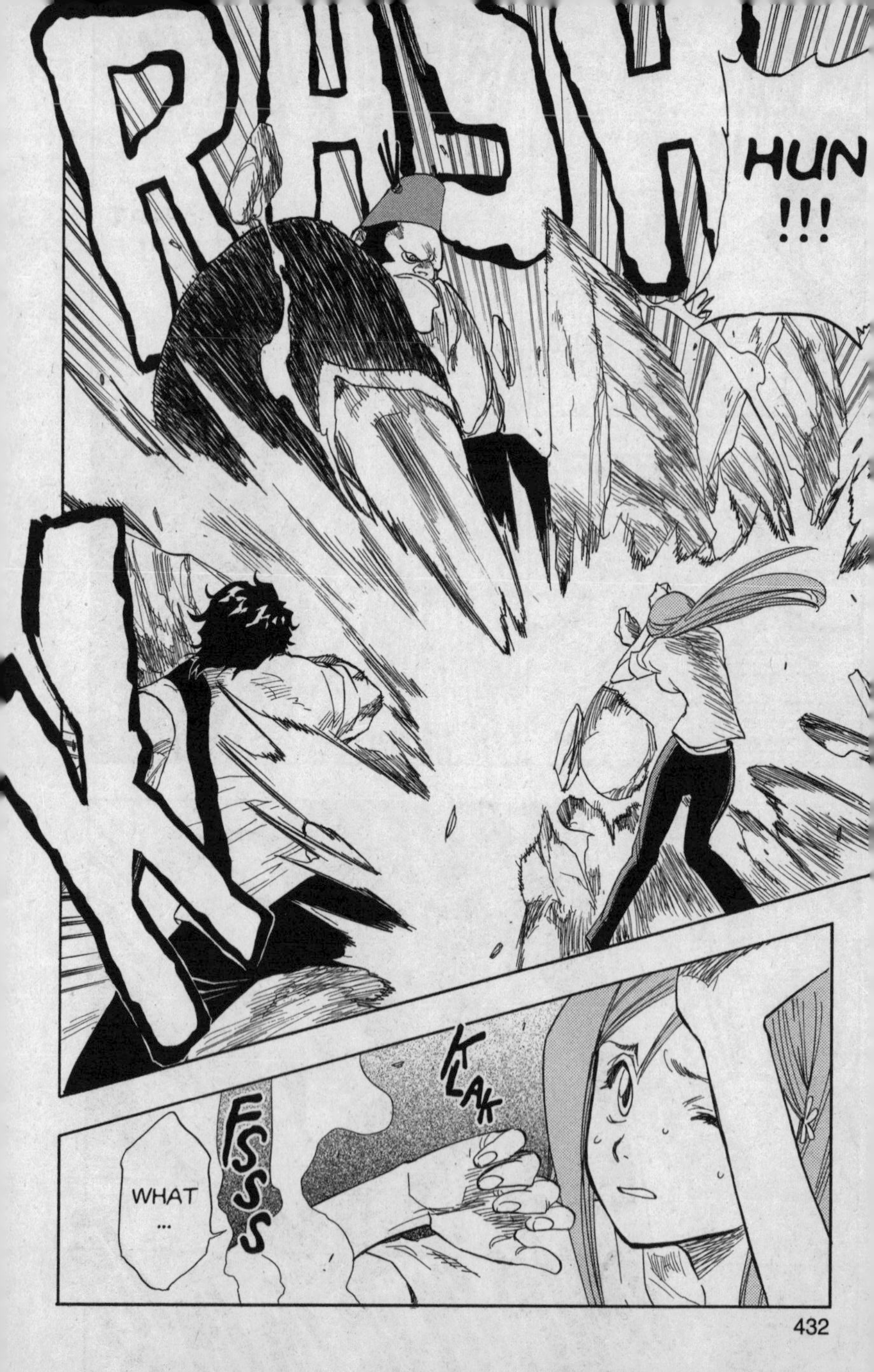
HUN !!!
KLAK
FSSS
WHAT ...

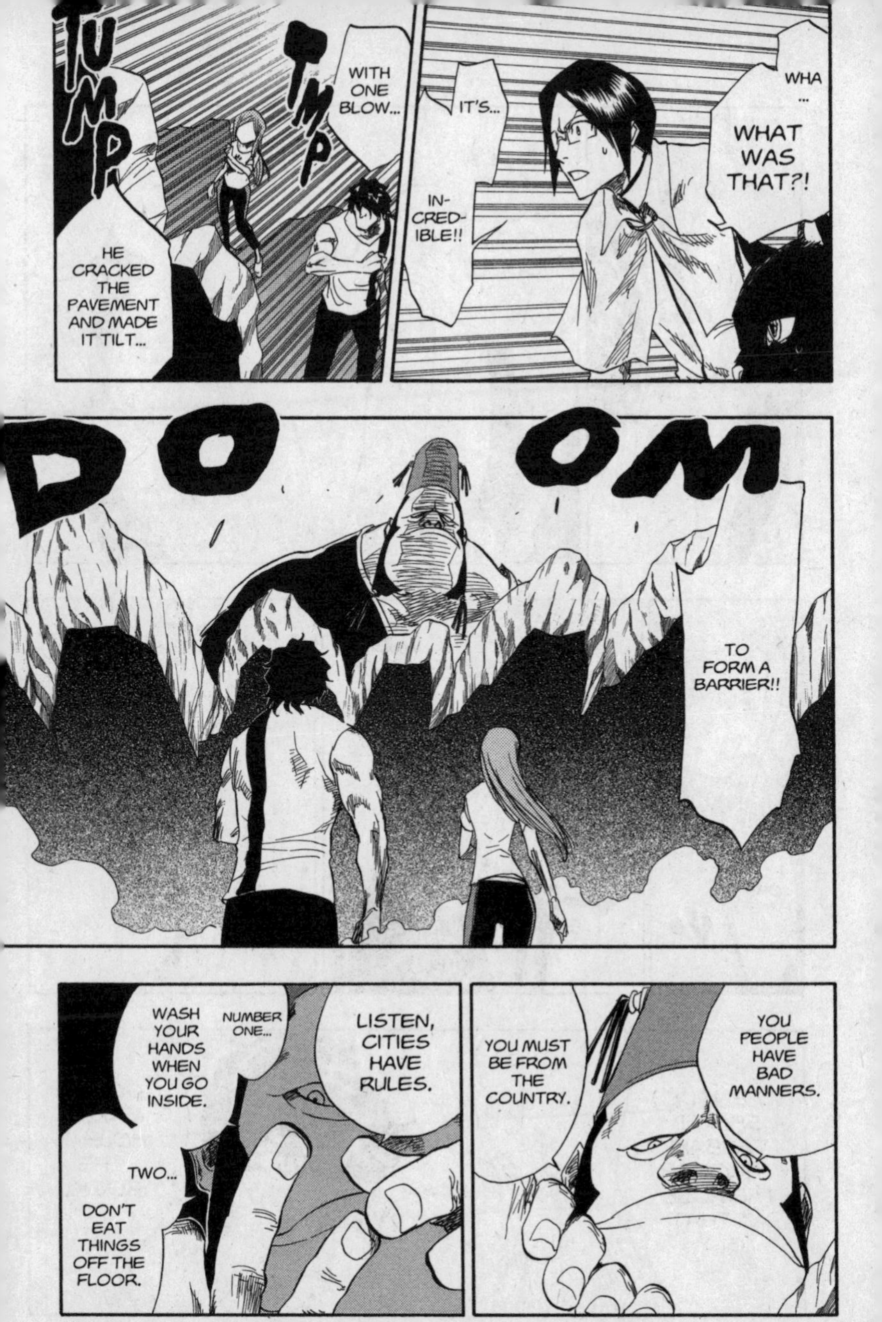
WHA... WHAT WAS THAT?!
IT'S...
INCREDIBLE!!
TMP
WITH ONE BLOW...
TUMP
HE CRACKED THE PAVEMENT AND MADE IT TILT...
DOOM
TO FORM A BARRIER!!
YOU PEOPLE HAVE BAD MANNERS.
YOU MUST BE FROM THE COUNTRY.
LISTEN, CITIES HAVE RULES.
NUMBER ONE...
WASH YOUR HANDS WHEN YOU GO INSIDE.
TWO...
DON'T EAT THINGS OFF THE FLOOR.

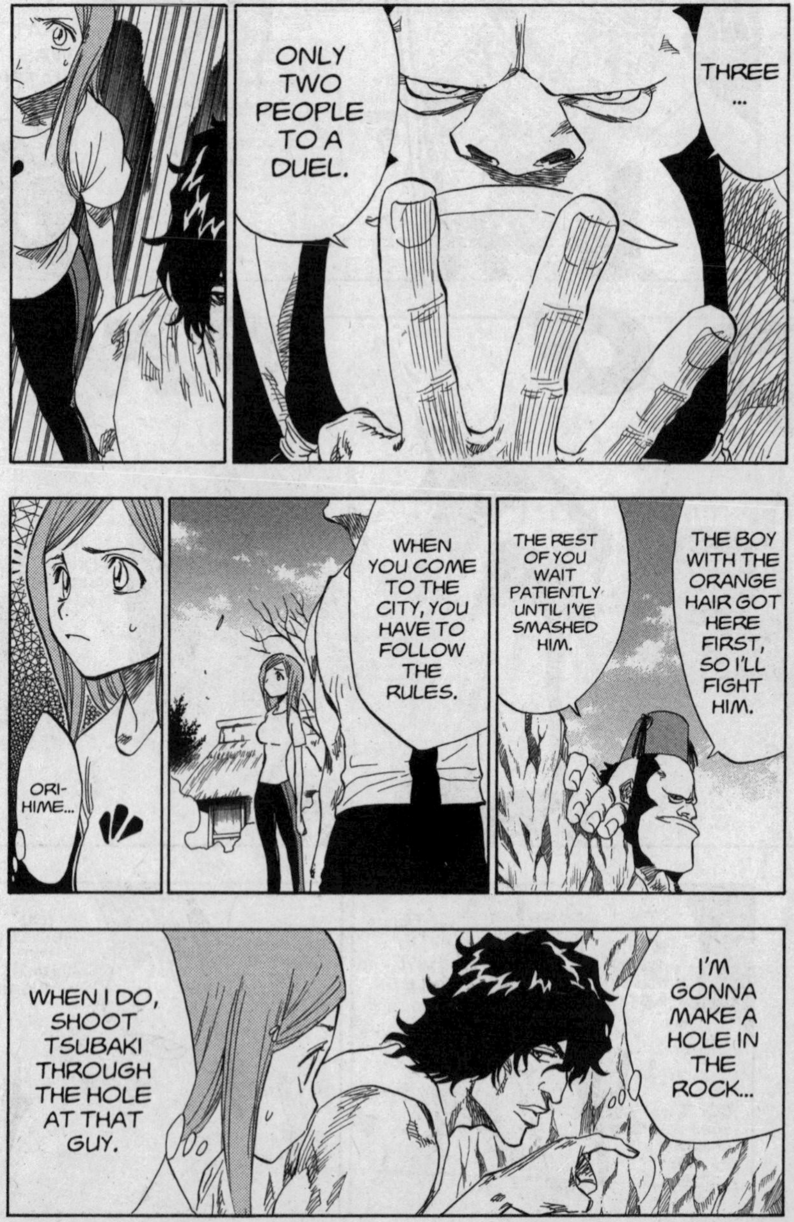
THREE...
ONLY TWO PEOPLE TO A DUEL.
THE BOY WITH THE ORANGE HAIR GOT HERE FIRST, SO I'LL FIGHT HIM.
THE REST OF YOU WAIT PATIENTLY UNTIL I'VE SMASHED HIM.
WHEN YOU COME TO THE CITY, YOU HAVE TO FOLLOW THE RULES.
ORI-HIME...
I'M GONNA MAKE A HOLE IN THE ROCK...
WHEN I DO, SHOOT TSUBAKI THROUGH THE HOLE AT THAT GUY.

READ THIS WAY

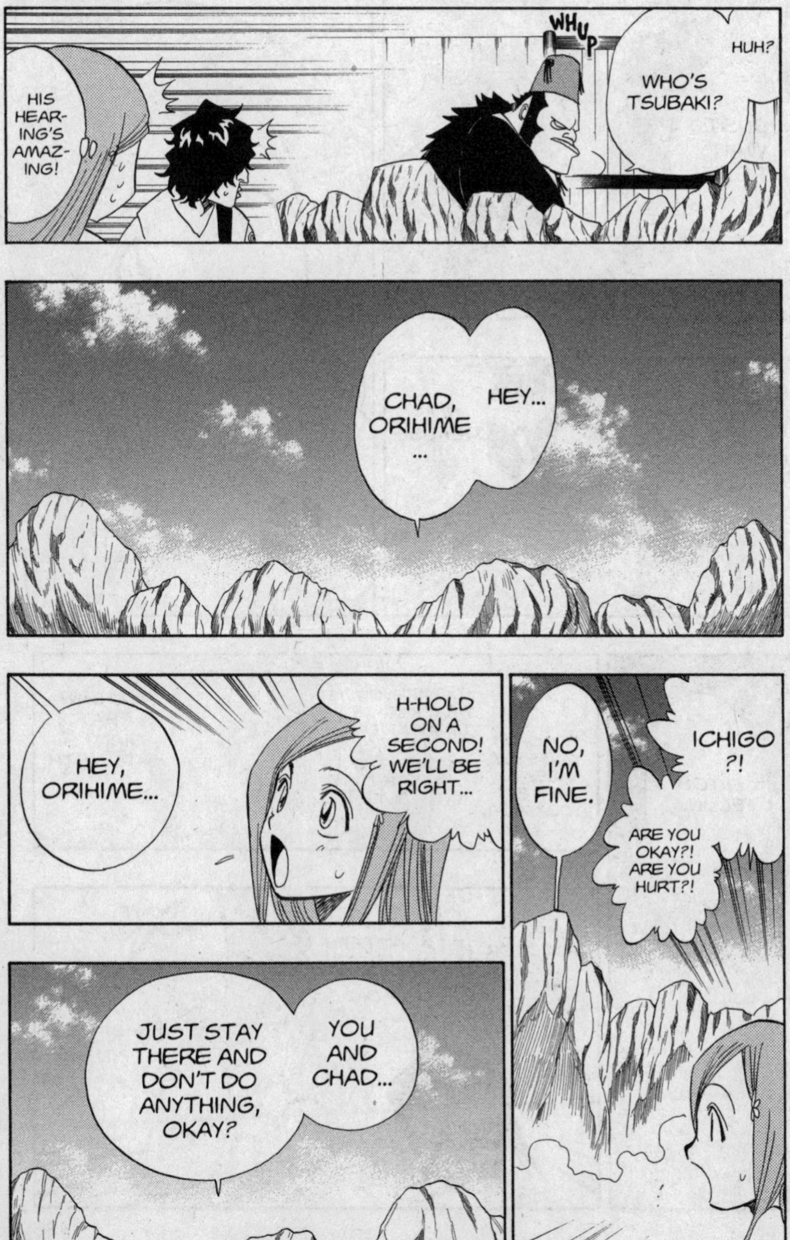
HUH? WHO'S TSUBAKI?
WHUP
HIS HEARING'S AMAZING!
HEY... CHAD, ORIHIME...
ICHIGO?!
ARE YOU OKAY?! ARE YOU HURT?!
NO, I'M FINE.
H-HOLD ON A SECOND! WE'LL BE RIGHT...
HEY, ORIHIME...
YOU AND CHAD...
JUST STAY THERE AND DON'T DO ANYTHING, OKAY?

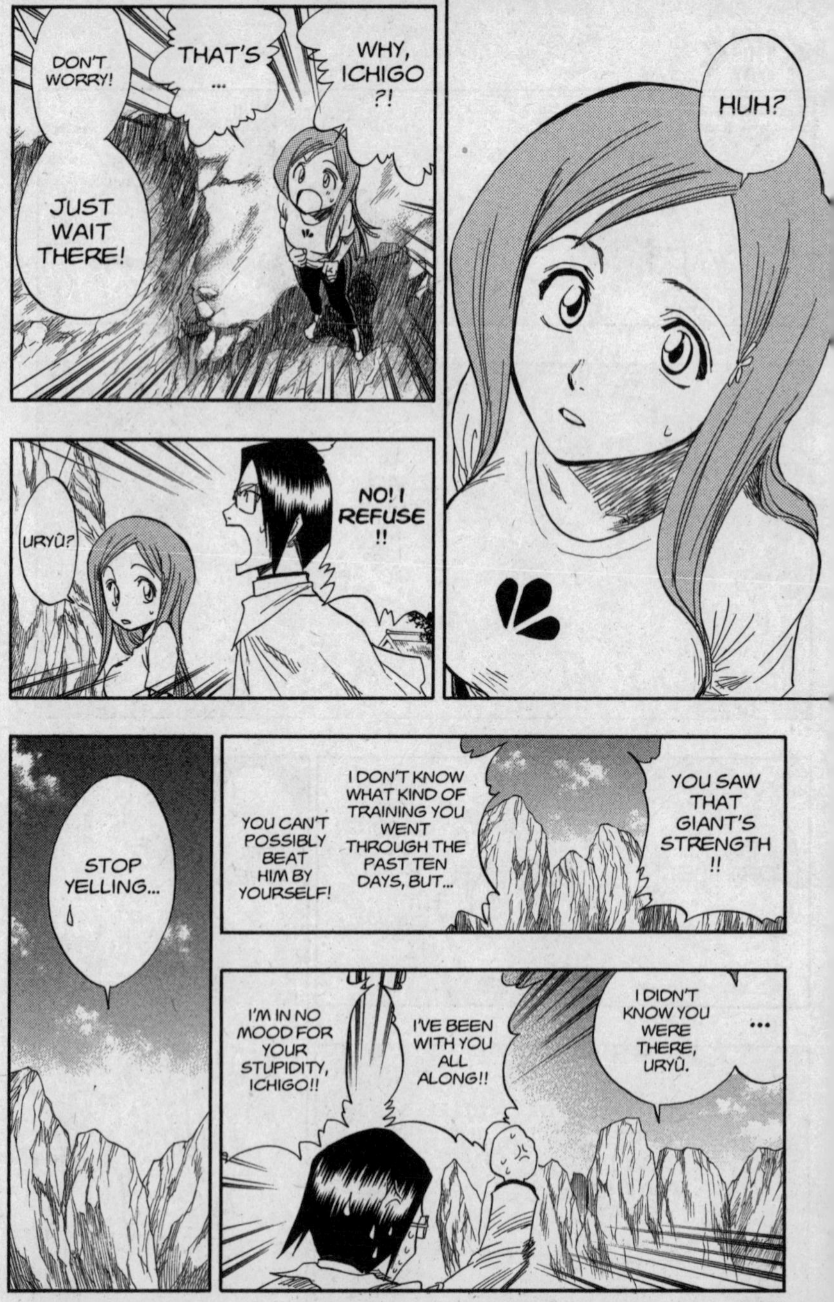
HUH?
WHY, ICHIGO ?!
THAT'S ...
DON'T WORRY!
JUST WAIT THERE!
NO! I REFUSE !!
URYÛ?
YOU SAW THAT GIANT'S STRENGTH !!
I DON'T KNOW WHAT KIND OF TRAINING YOU WENT THROUGH THE PAST TEN DAYS, BUT...
YOU CAN'T POSSIBLY BEAT HIM BY YOURSELF!
...
I DIDN'T KNOW YOU WERE THERE, URYÛ.
I'VE BEEN WITH YOU ALL ALONG!!
I'M IN NO MOOD FOR YOUR STUPIDITY, ICHIGO!!
STOP YELLING...

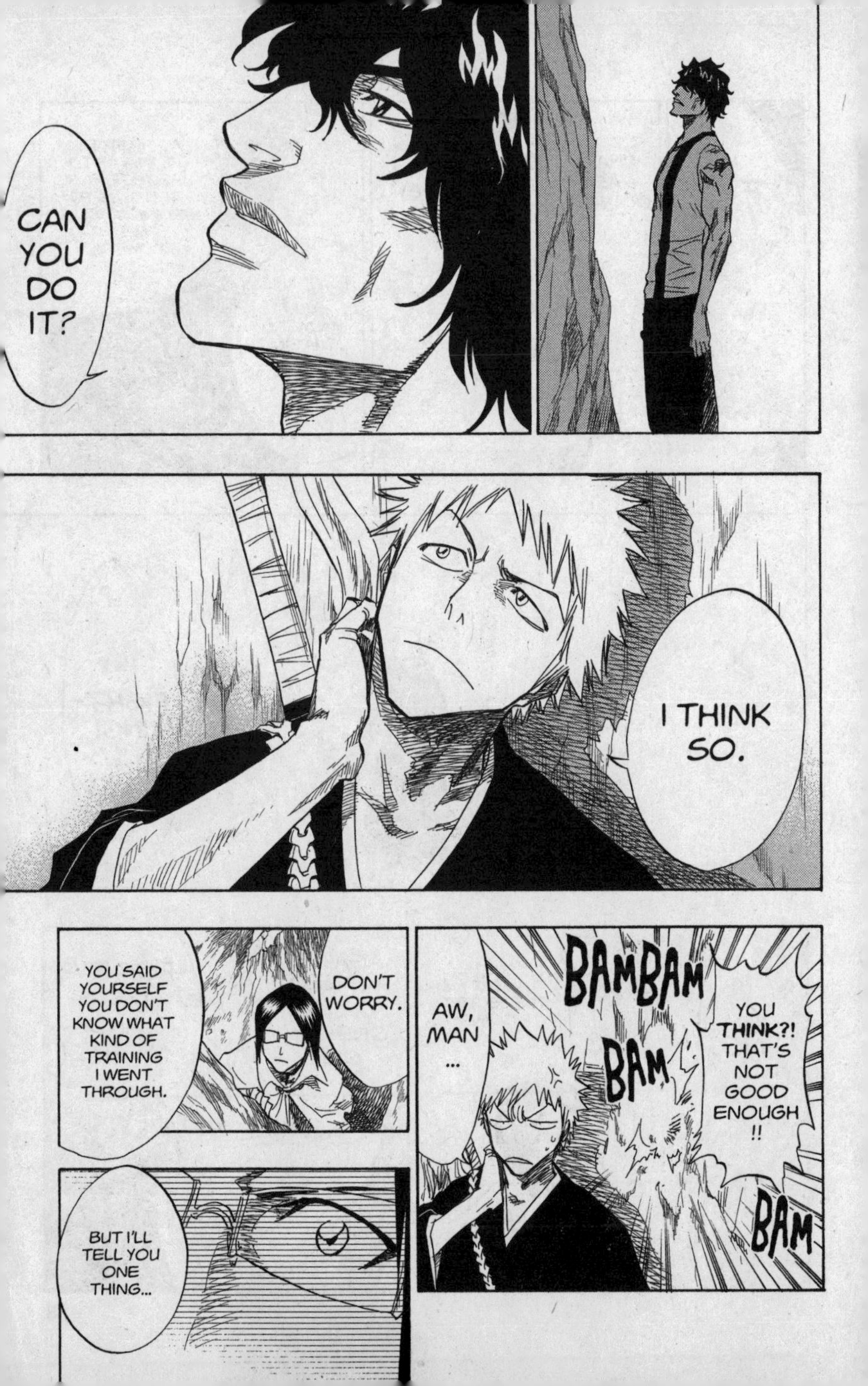
CAN YOU DO IT?
I THINK SO.
YOU THINK?! THAT'S NOT GOOD ENOUGH!!
BAMBAM
BAM
BAM
AW, MAN ...
DON'T WORRY.
YOU SAID YOURSELF YOU DON'T KNOW WHAT KIND OF TRAINING I WENT THROUGH.
BUT I'LL TELL YOU ONE THING...

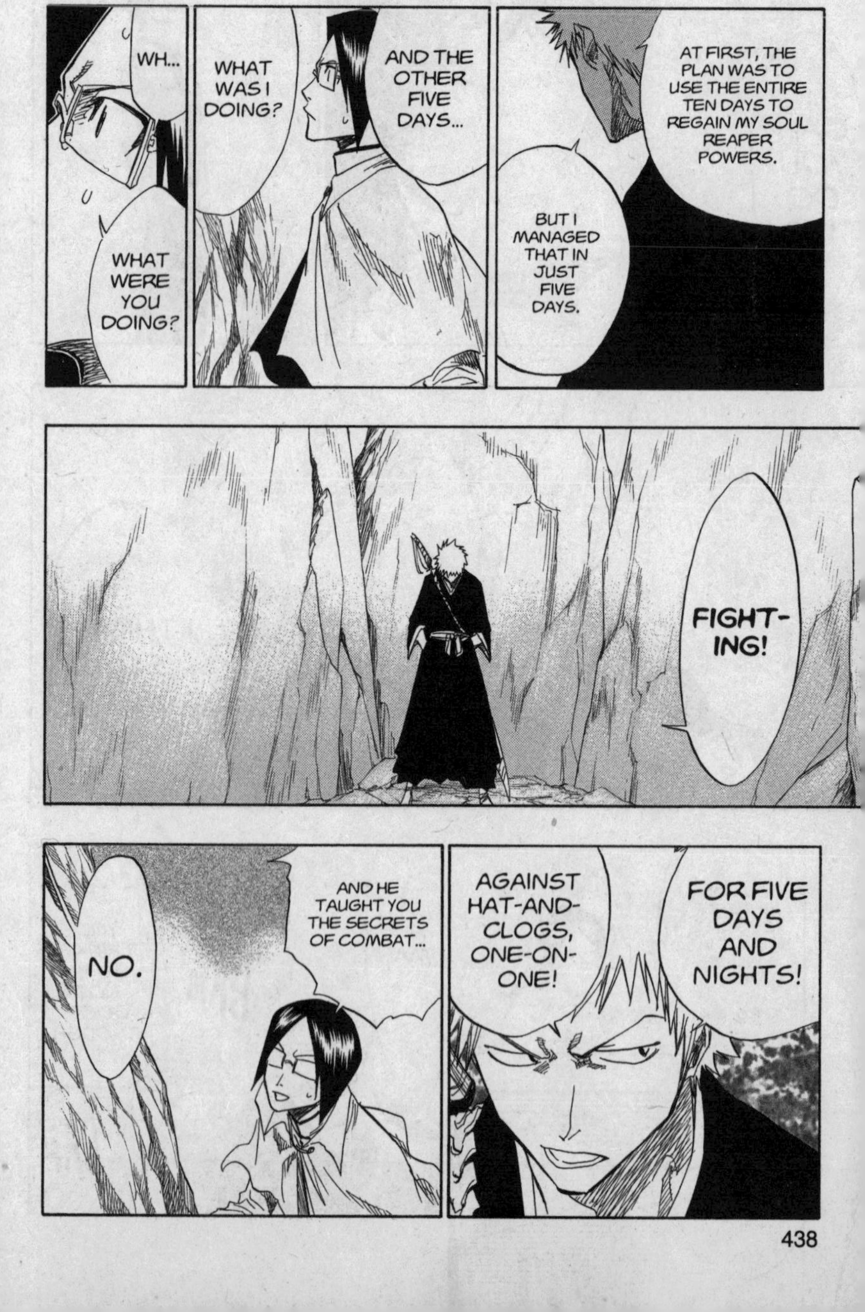
AT FIRST, THE PLAN WAS TO USE THE ENTIRE TEN DAYS TO REGAIN MY SOUL REAPER POWERS.
BUT I MANAGED THAT IN JUST FIVE DAYS.
AND THE OTHER FIVE DAYS...
WHAT WAS I DOING?
WH...
WHAT WERE YOU DOING?
FIGHT-ING!
FOR FIVE DAYS AND NIGHTS!
AGAINST HAT-AND-CLOGS, ONE-ON-ONE!
AND HE TAUGHT YOU THE SECRETS OF COMBAT...
NO.

READ THIS WAY

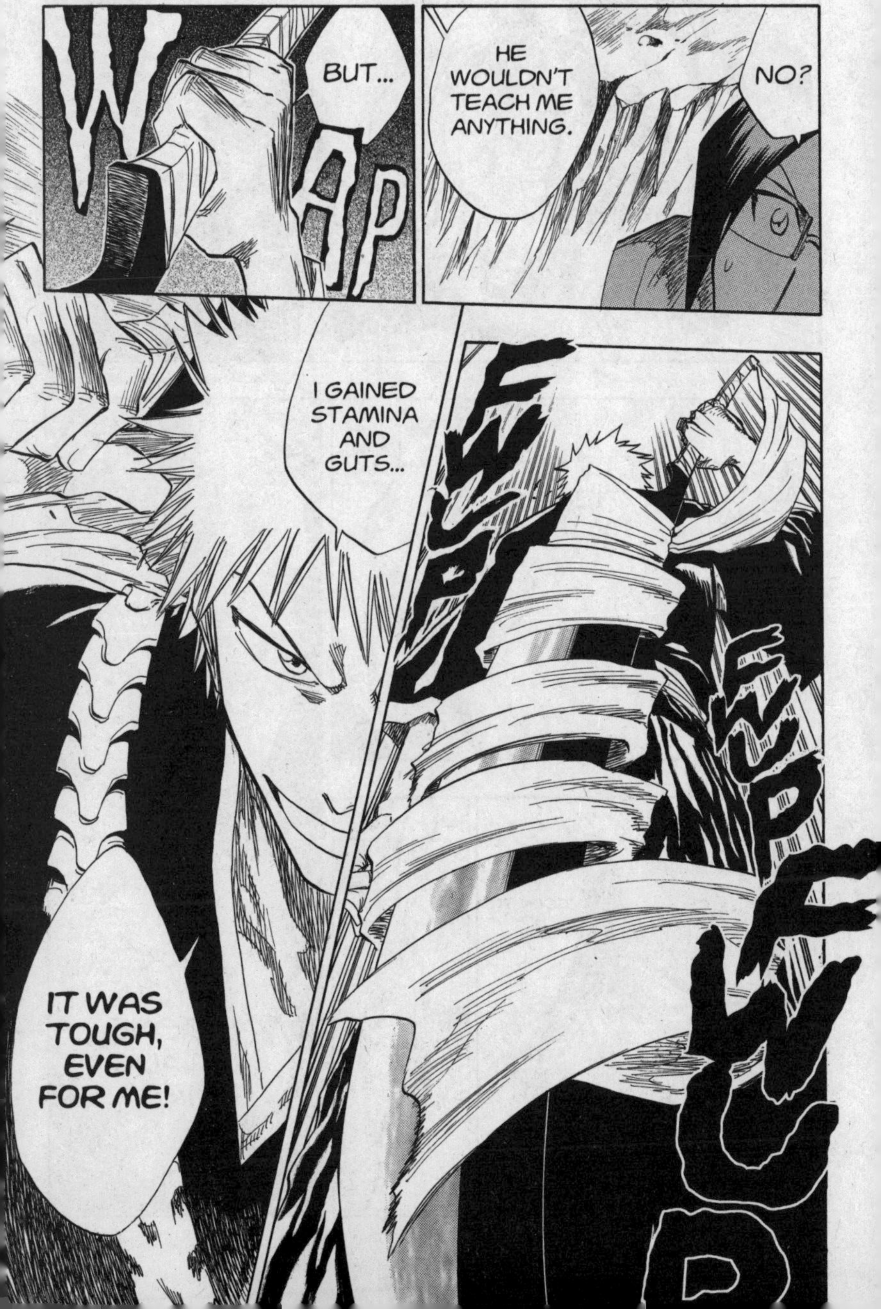
NO?
HE WOULDN'T TEACH ME ANYTHING.
BUT...
WAP
I GAINED STAMINA AND GUTS...
IT WAS TOUGH, EVEN FOR ME!

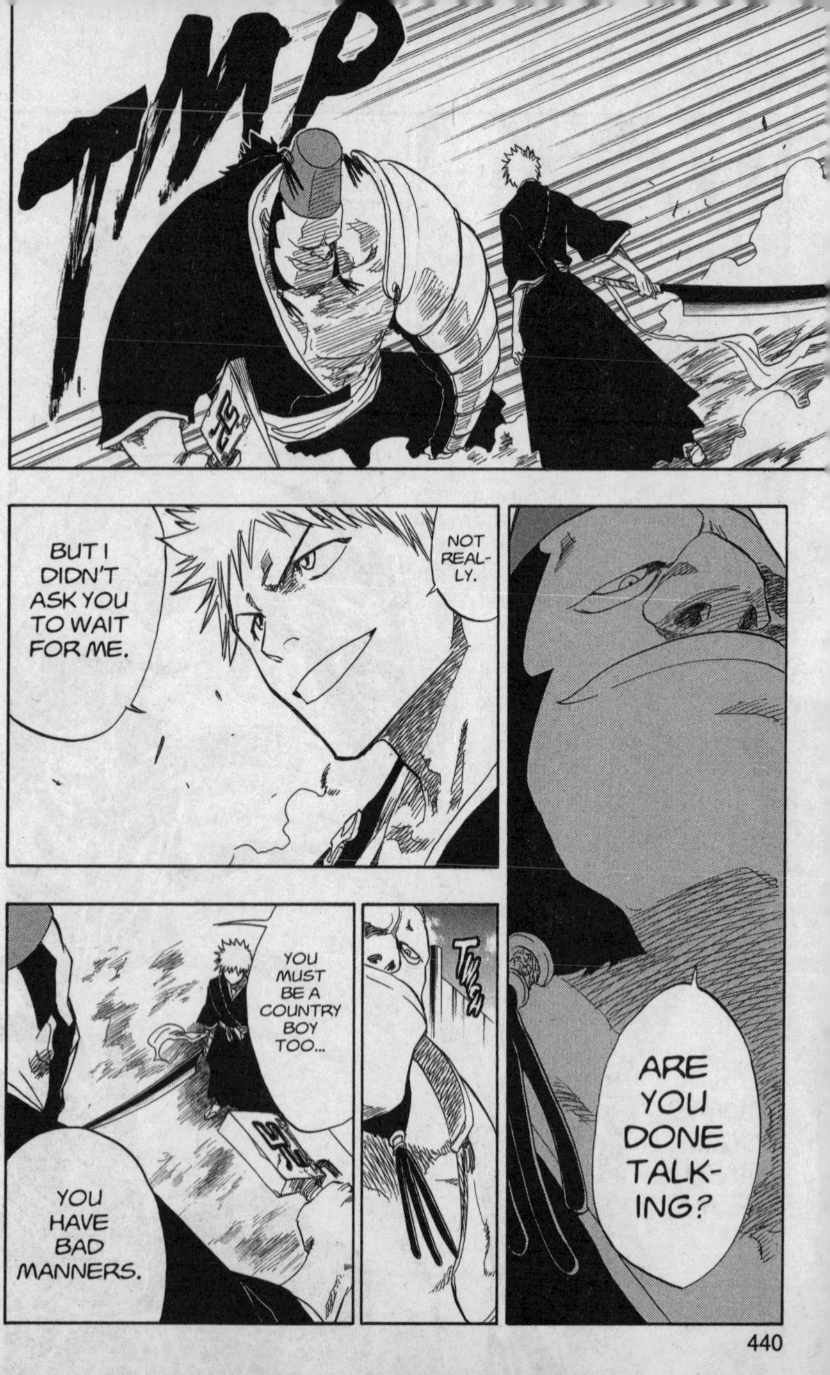
TMP
ARE YOU DONE TALKING?
NOT REALLY.
BUT I DIDN'T ASK YOU TO WAIT FOR ME.
TWSH
YOU MUST BE A COUNTRY BOY TOO...
YOU HAVE BAD MANNERS.

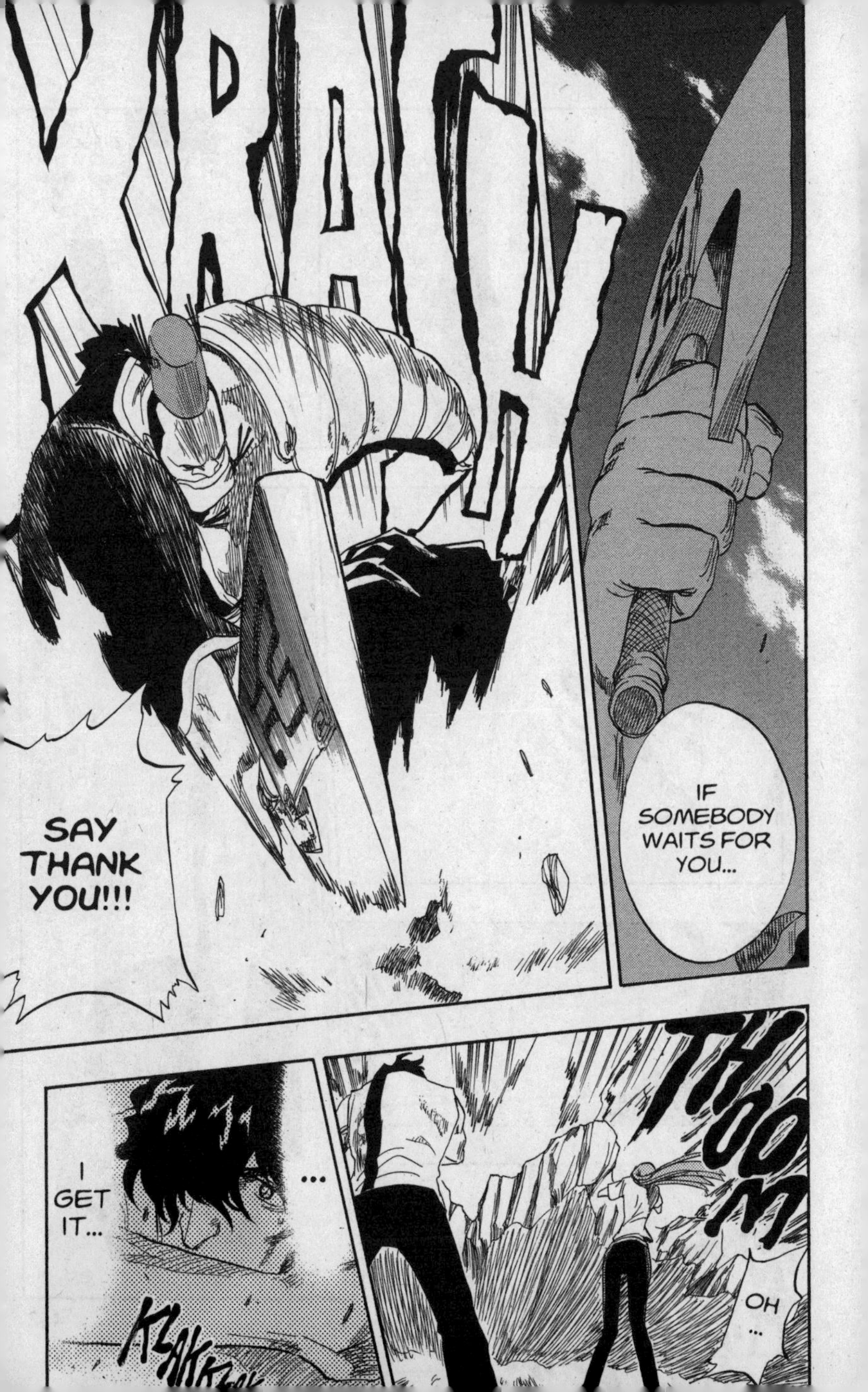
IF SOMEBODY WAITS FOR YOU...
SAY THANK YOU!!!
THOOM
OH ...
...
I GET IT...

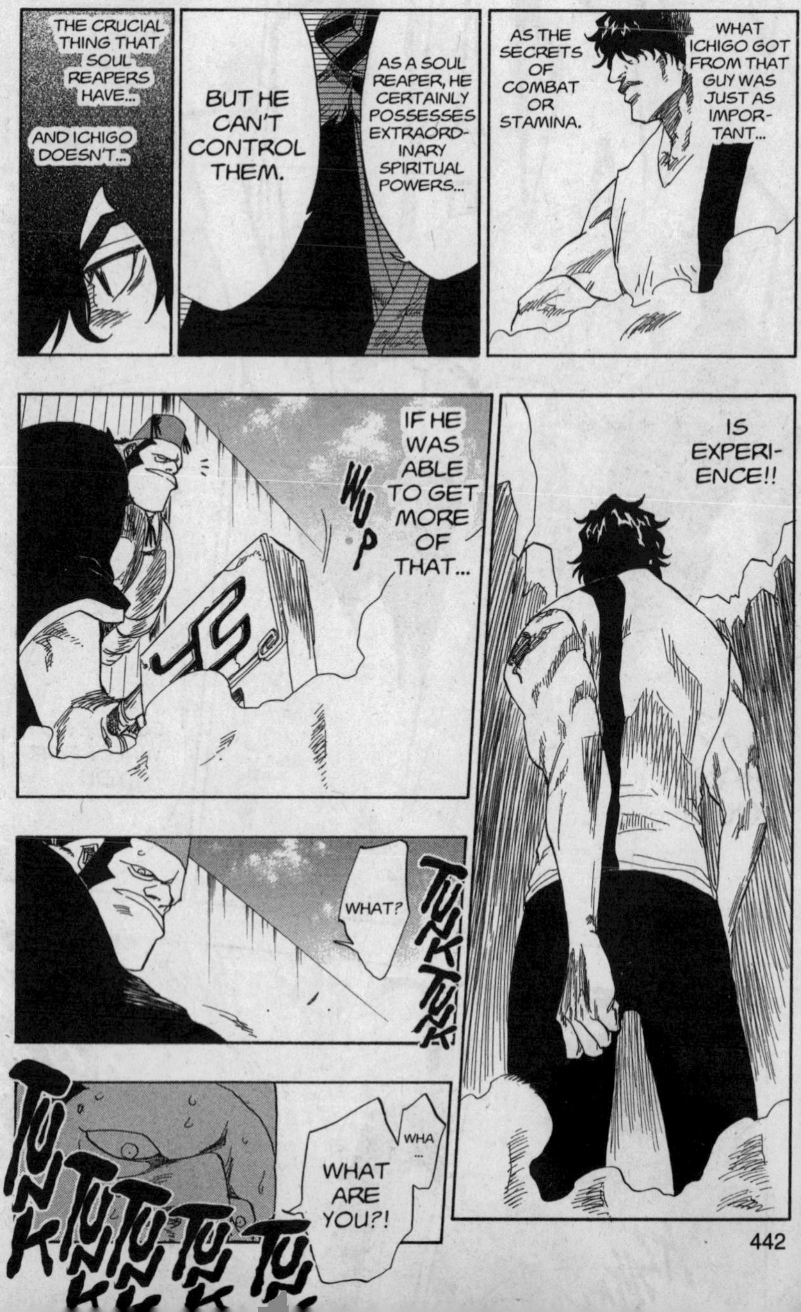
WHAT ICHIGO GOT FROM THAT GUY WAS JUST AS IMPORTANT...
AS THE SECRETS OF COMBAT OR STAMINA.
AS A SOUL REAPER, HE CERTAINLY POSSESSES EXTRAORDINARY SPIRITUAL POWERS...
BUT HE CAN'T CONTROL THEM.
THE CRUCIAL THING THAT SOUL REAPERS HAVE...
AND ICHIGO DOESN'T...
IS EXPERIENCE!!
IF HE WAS ABLE TO GET MORE OF THAT...
WUP
WHAT?
TUNK TUNK
WHA...
WHAT ARE YOU?!
TUNK TUNK TUNK TUNK TUNK

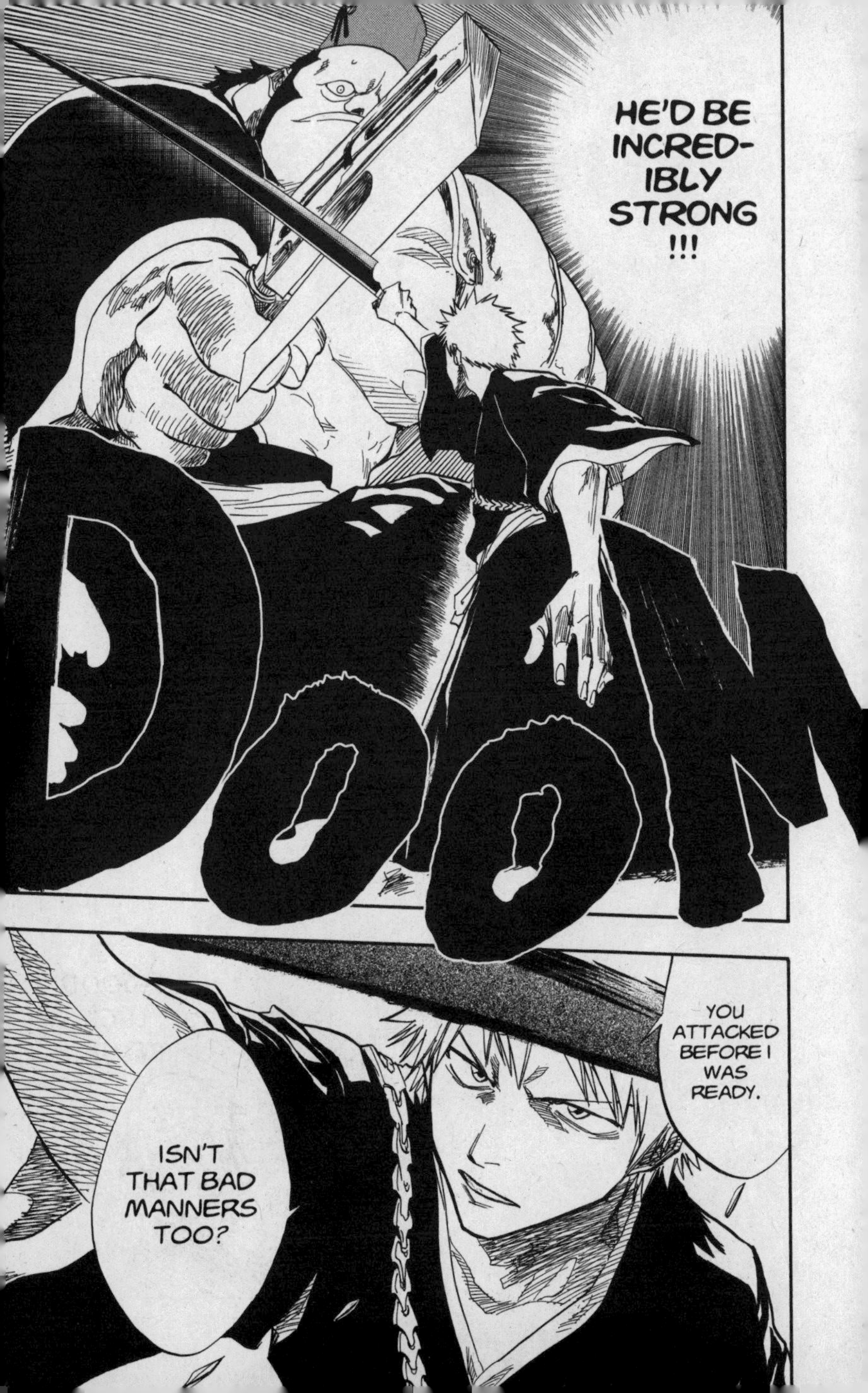
HE'D BE INCRED-IBLY STRONG !!!
DOOM
YOU ATTACKED BEFORE I WAS READY.
ISN'T THAT BAD MANNERS TOO?

G-GOOD
LUCK,
RENJI...

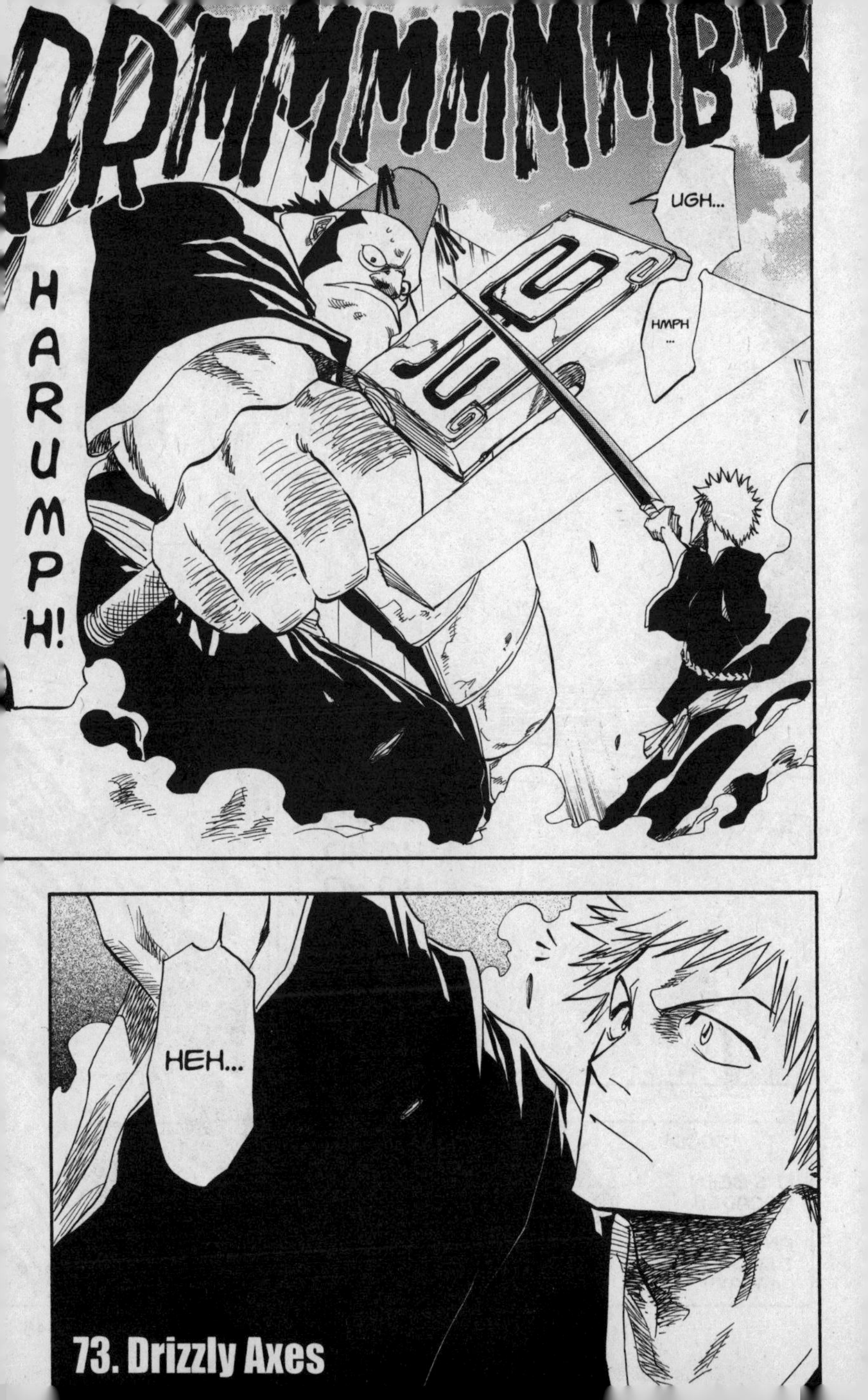
DRMMMMMMBB
UGH...
HMPH...
HARUMPH!
HEH...

73. Drizzly Axes

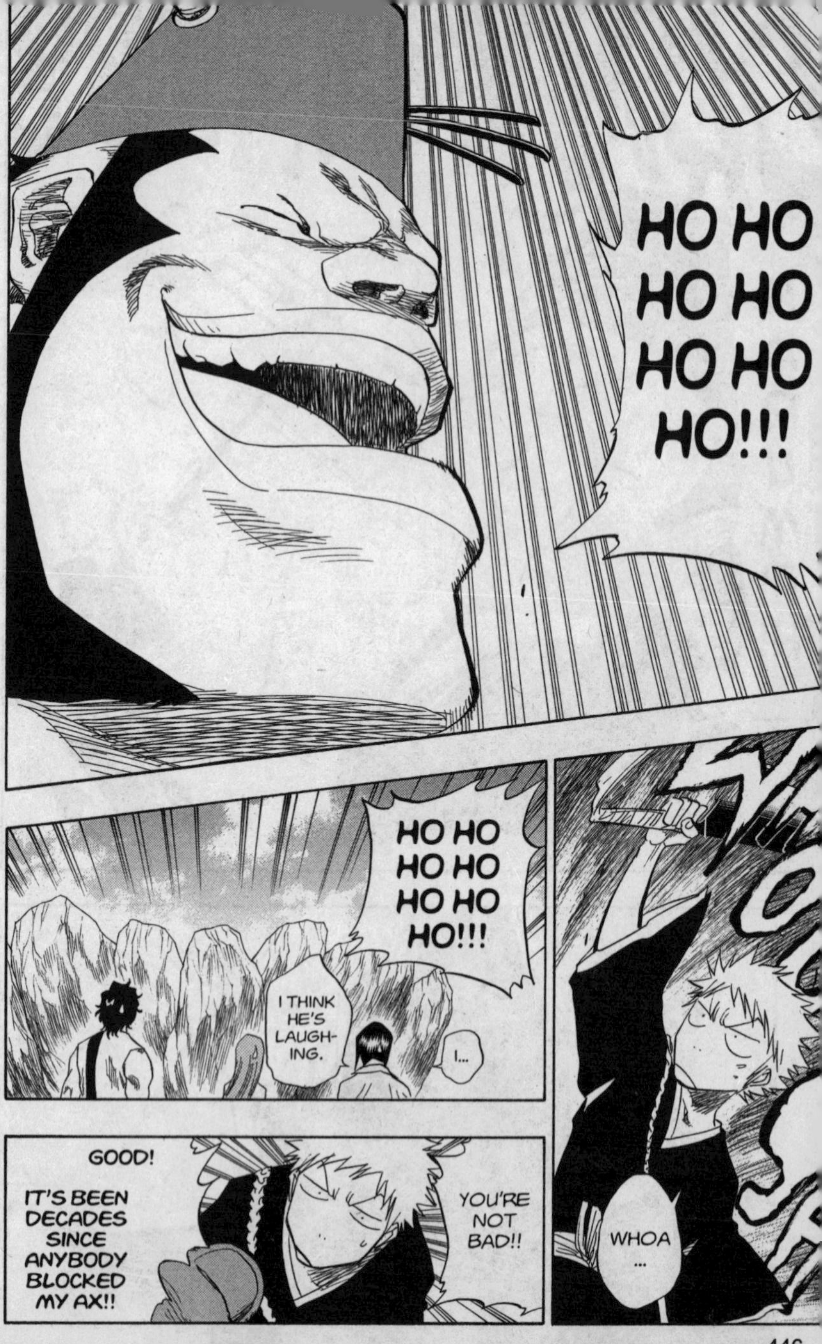
HO HO HO HO HO HO HO!!!
WHOA ...
HO HO HO HO HO HO HO!!!
I...
I THINK HE'S LAUGHING.
YOU'RE NOT BAD!!
GOOD!
IT'S BEEN DECADES SINCE ANYBODY BLOCKED MY AX!!

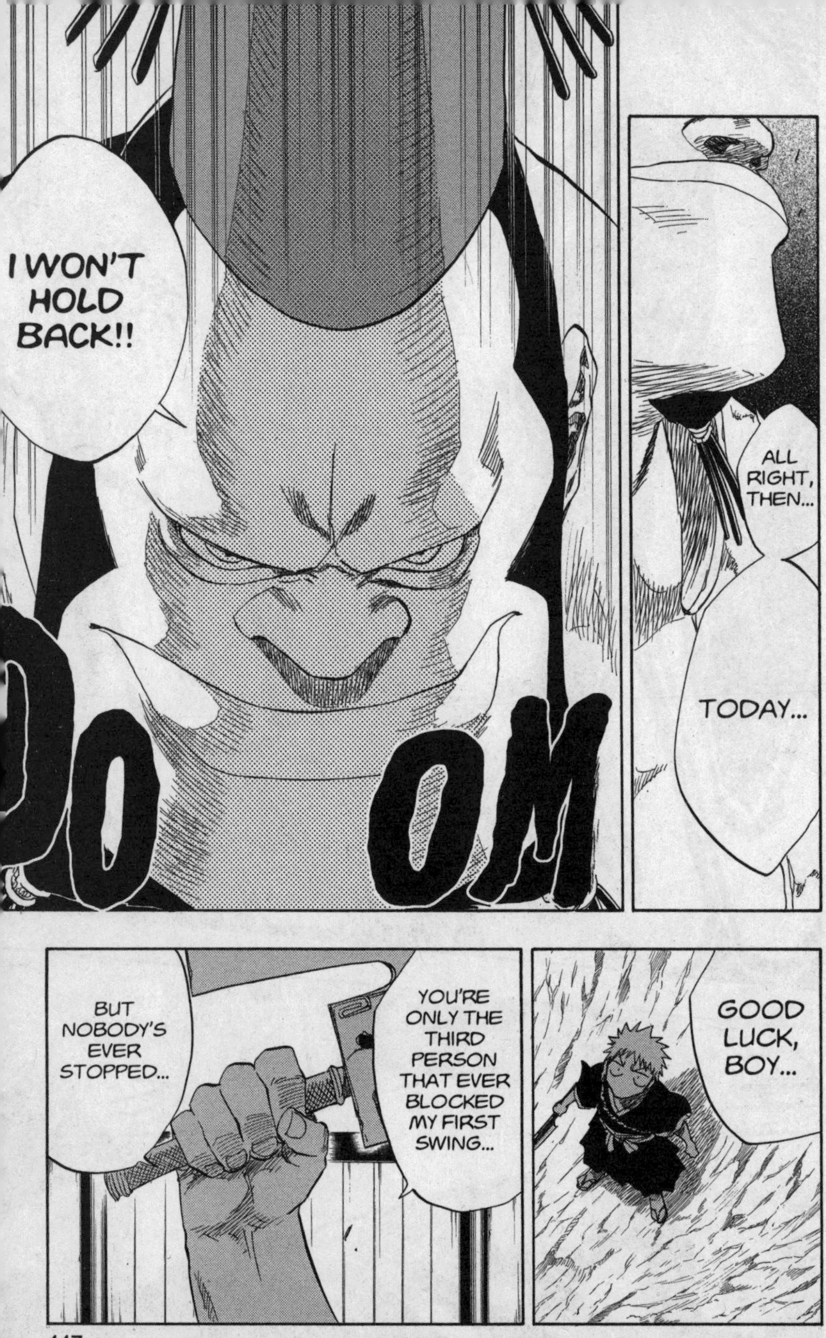
ALL RIGHT, THEN...
TODAY...
I WON'T HOLD BACK!!
GOOD LUCK, BOY...
YOU'RE ONLY THE THIRD PERSON THAT EVER BLOCKED MY FIRST SWING...
BUT NOBODY'S EVER STOPPED...

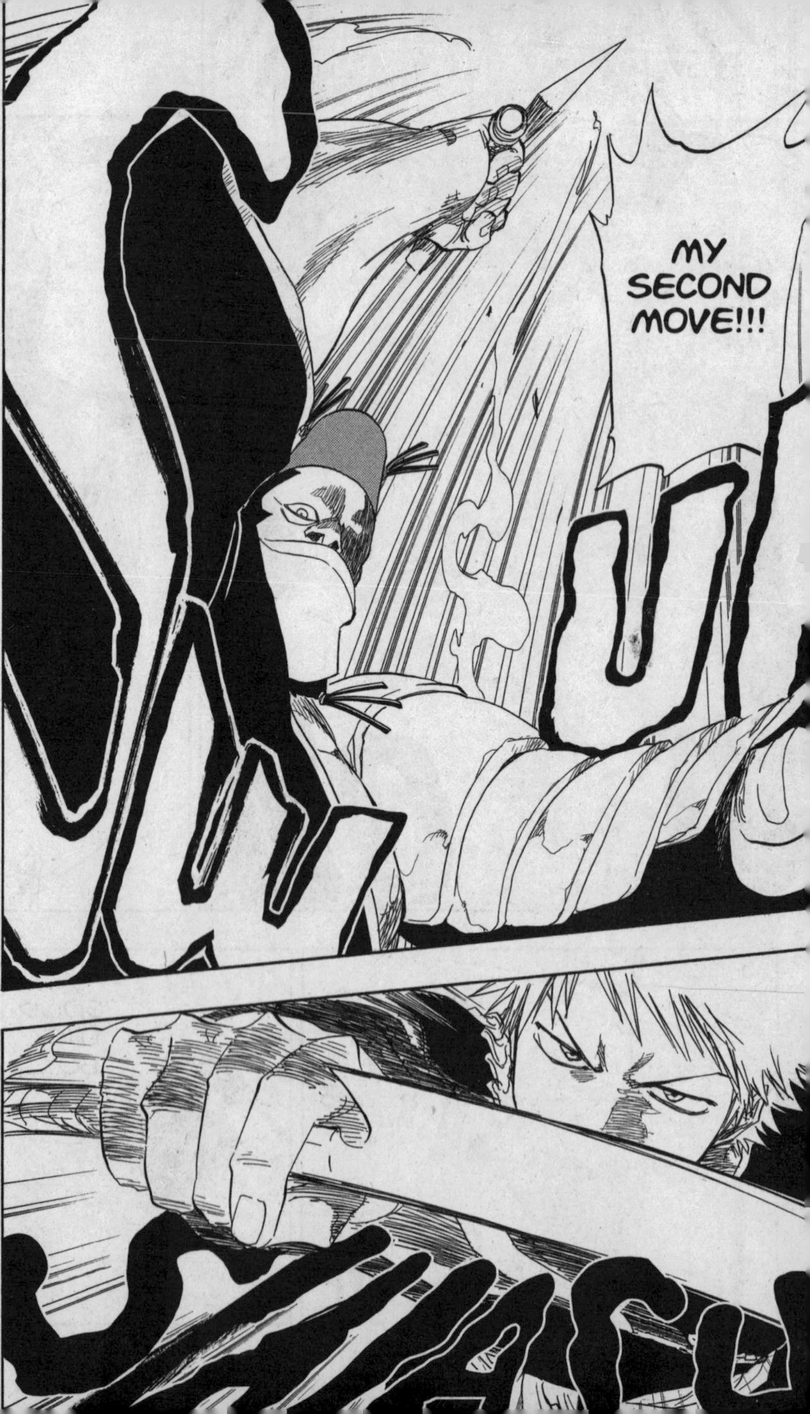
MY SECOND MOVE!!!

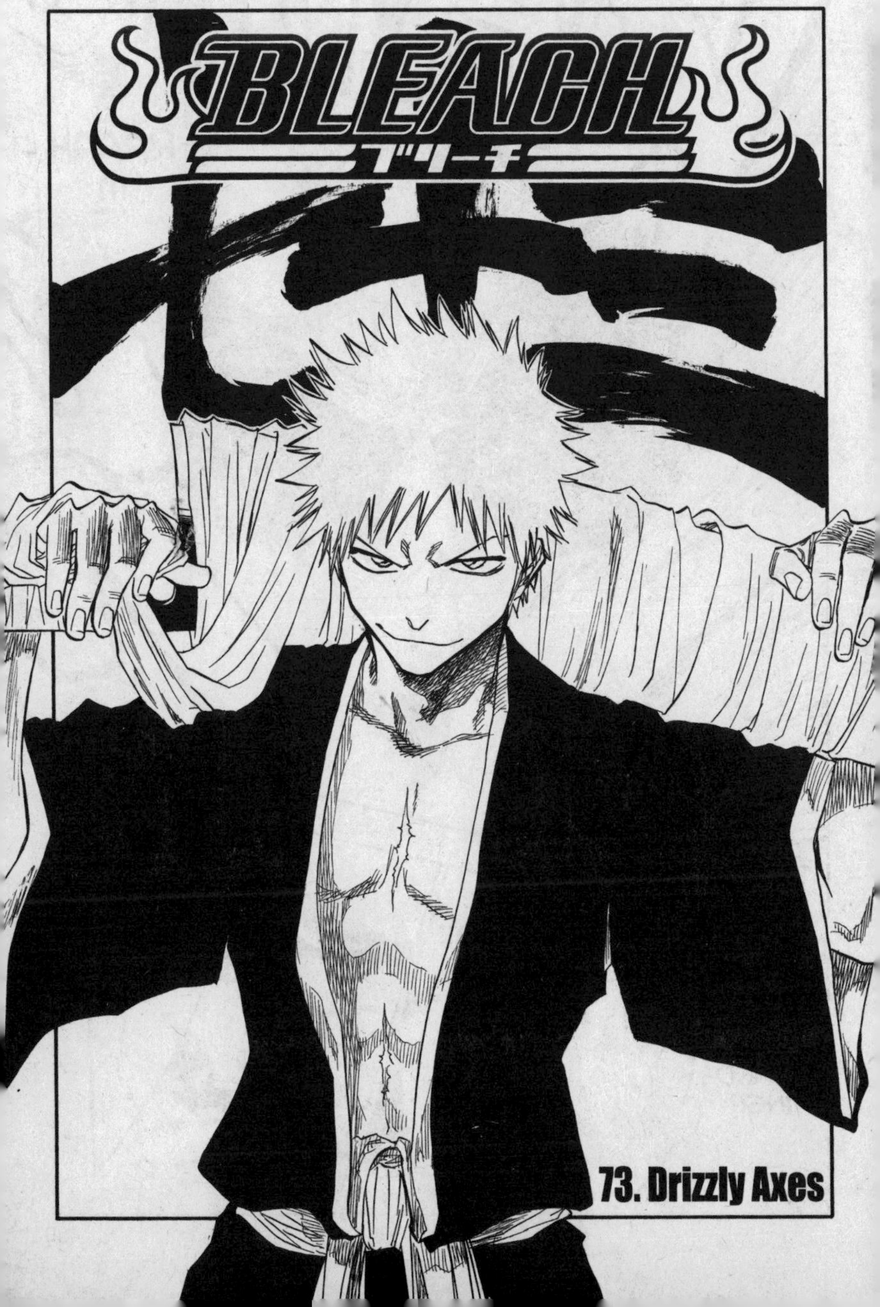
BLEACH
ブリーチ
73. Drizzly Axes

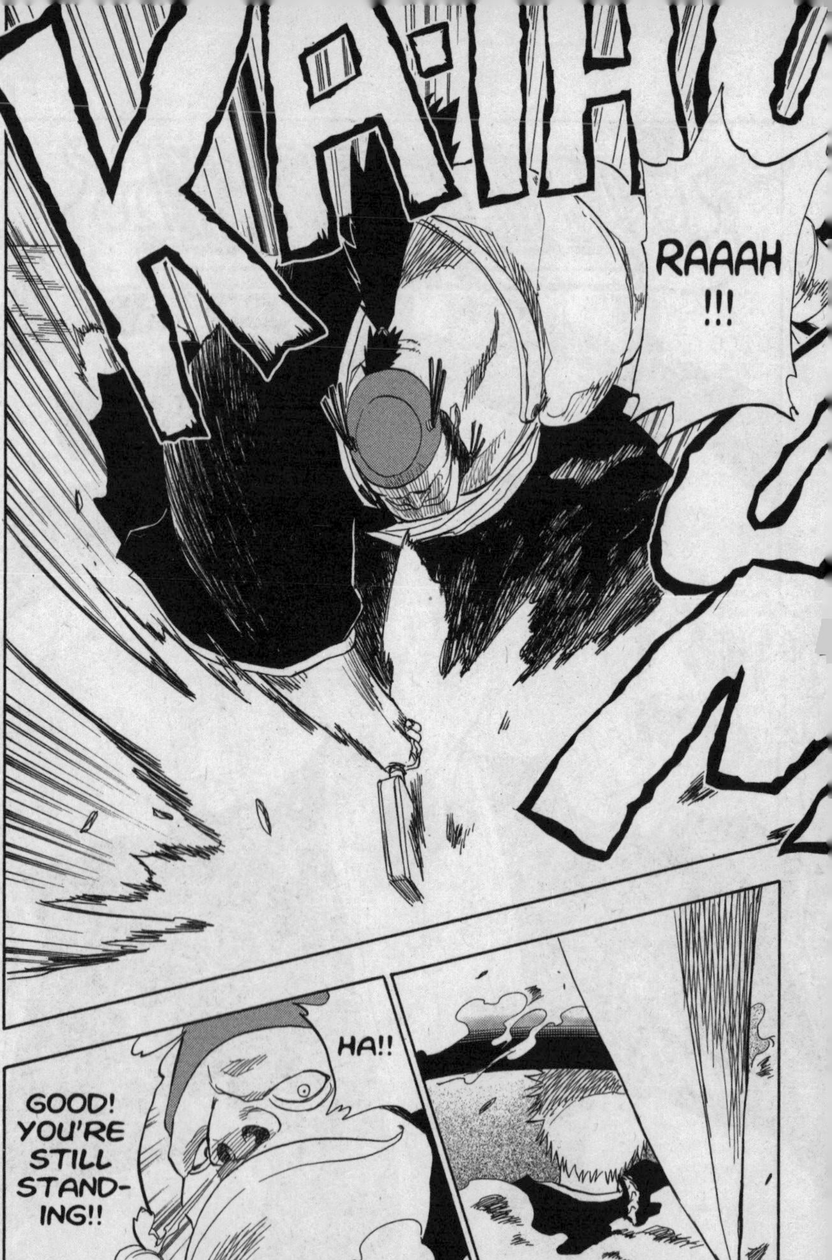
RAAAH !!!
HA!!
GOOD! YOU'RE STILL STAND-ING!!

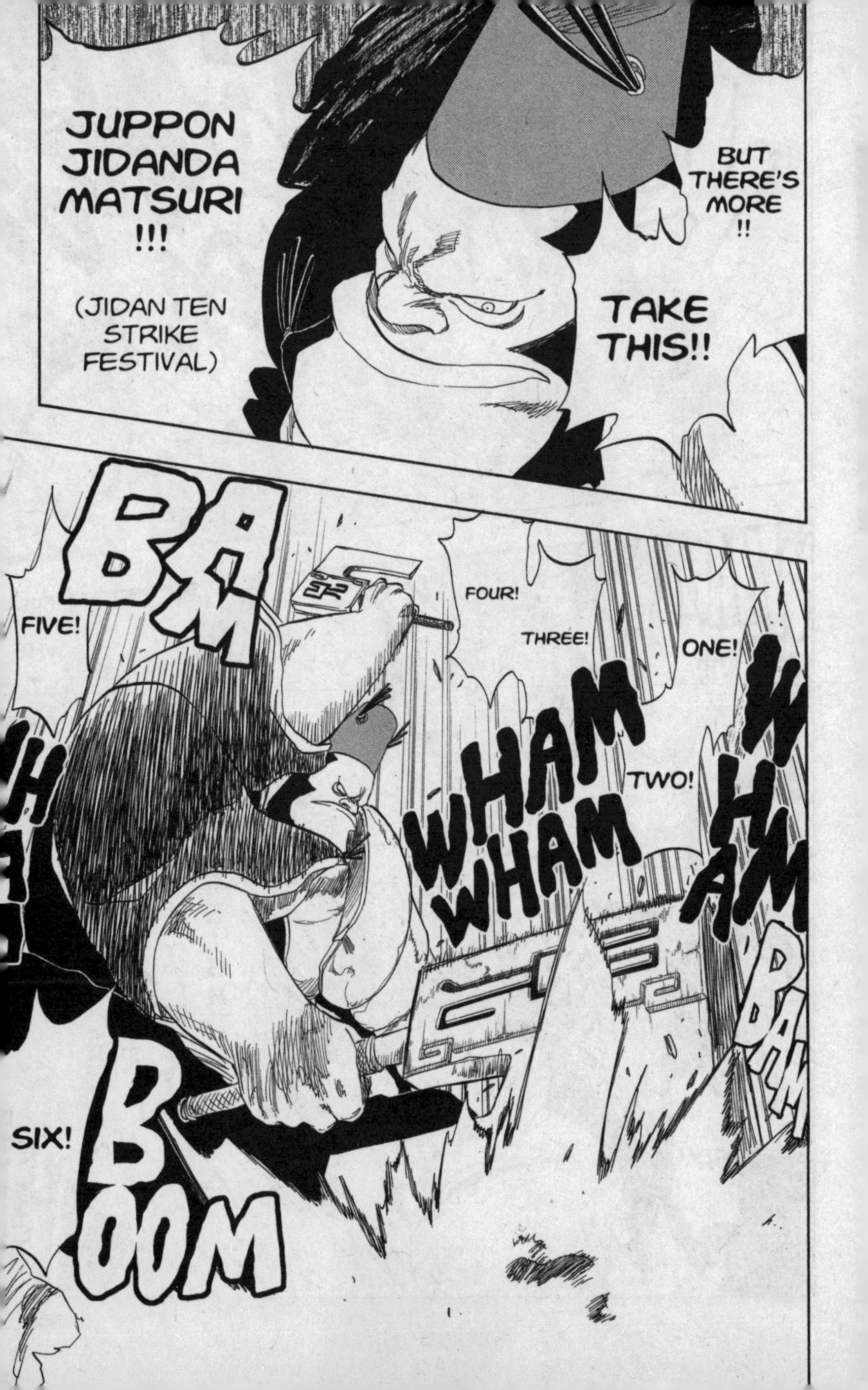
BUT THERE'S MORE !!
TAKE THIS!!
JUPPON JIDANDA MATSURI !!!
(JIDAN TEN STRIKE FESTIVAL)
ONE!
TWO!
WHAM
WHAM
THREE!
FOUR!
BAM
FIVE!
SIX!
BOOM

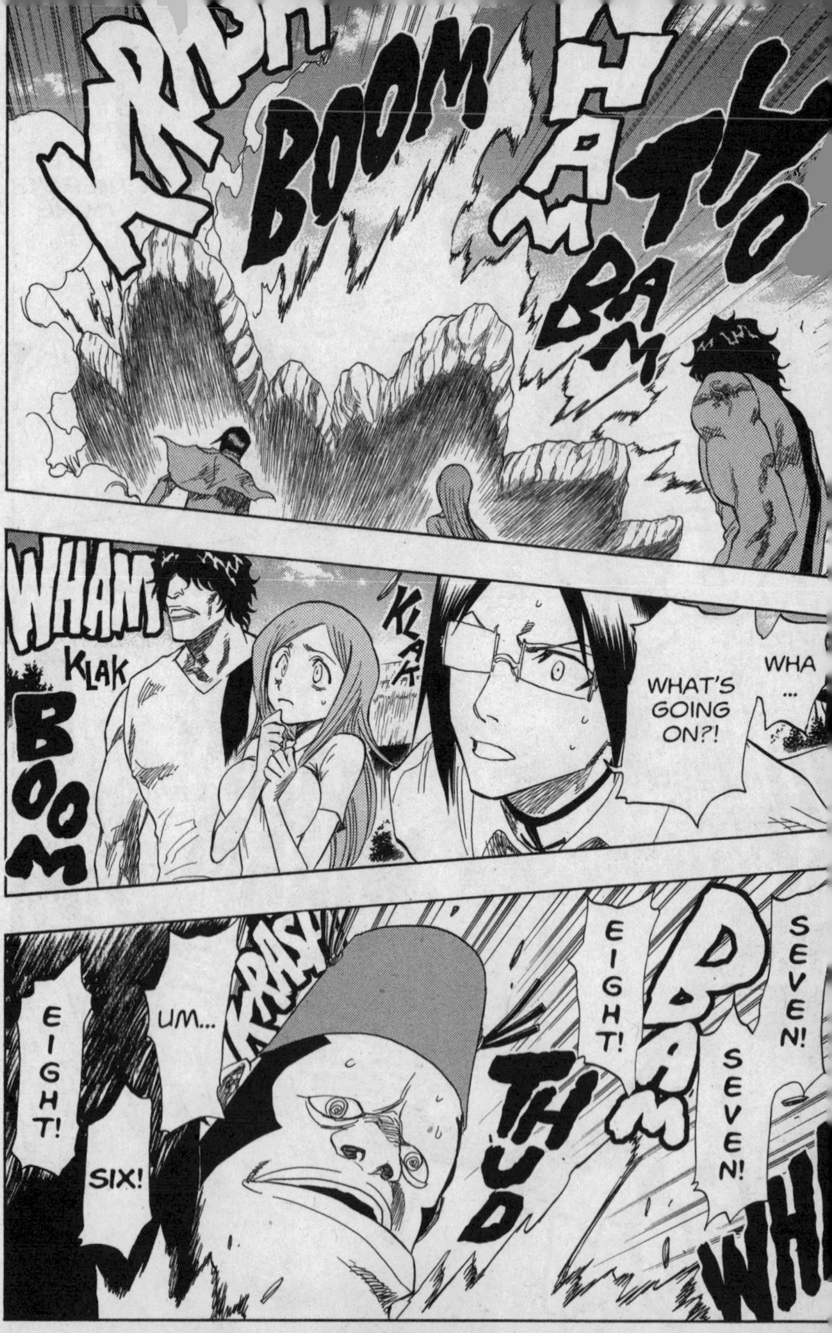
BOOM
BAM
WHA
...
WHAT'S GOING ON?!
KLAK
KLAK
WHAM
BOOM
SEVEN!
SEVEN!
EIGHT!
BAM
THUD
UM...
EIGHT!
SIX!

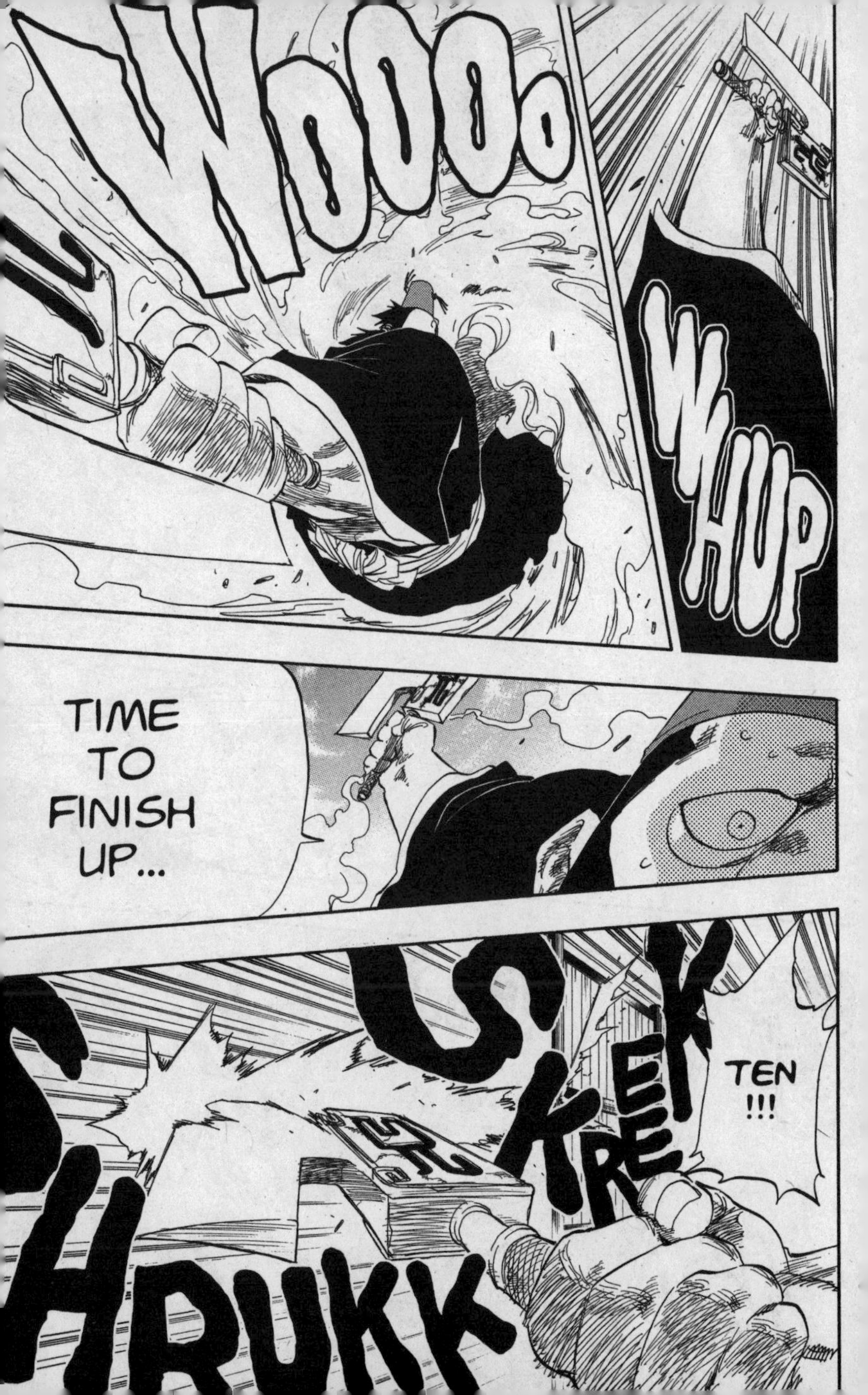
WHUP
WHOOOO
TIME TO FINISH UP...
TEN !!!
HRUKK

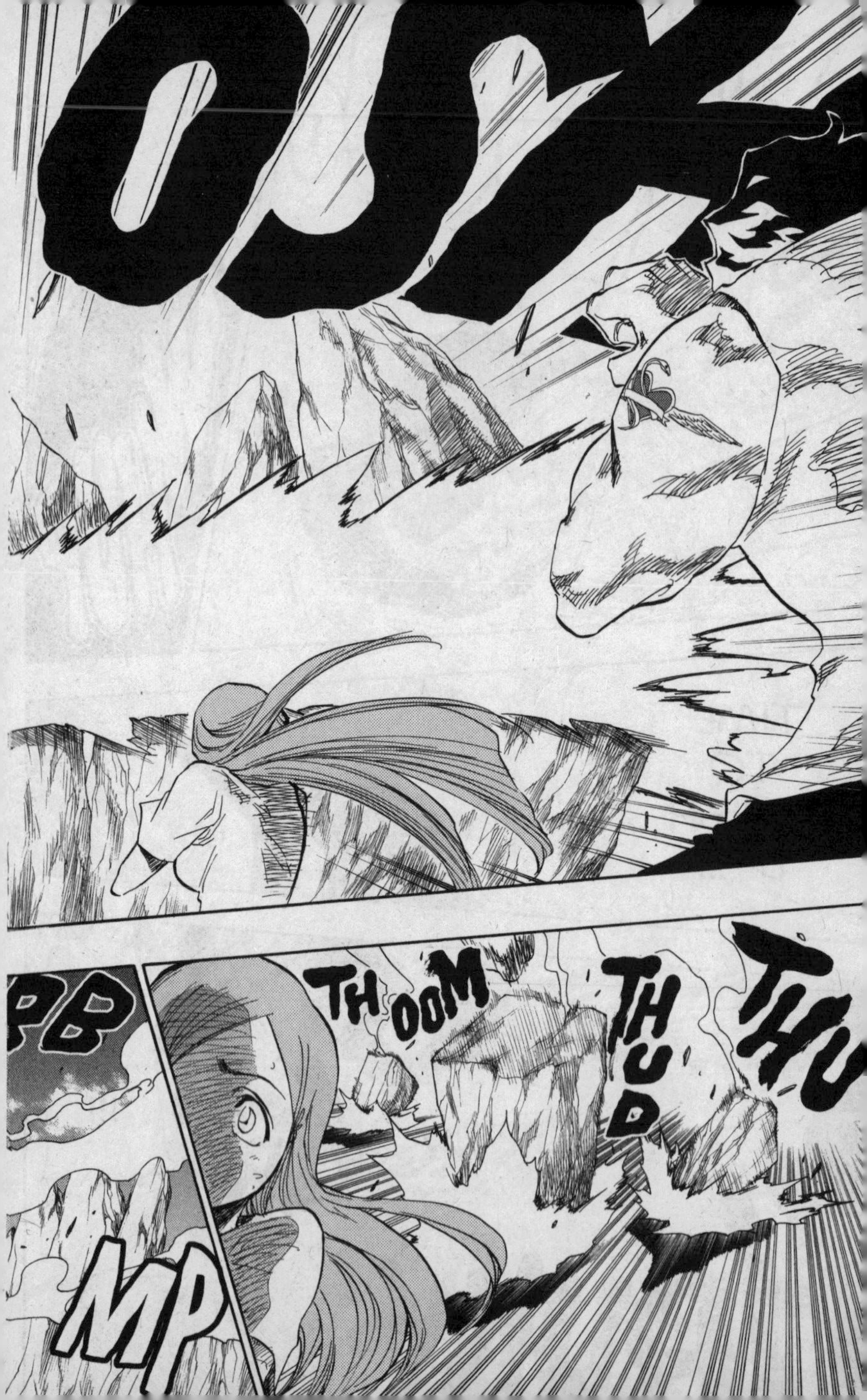
THU
THUD
THOOM
MP

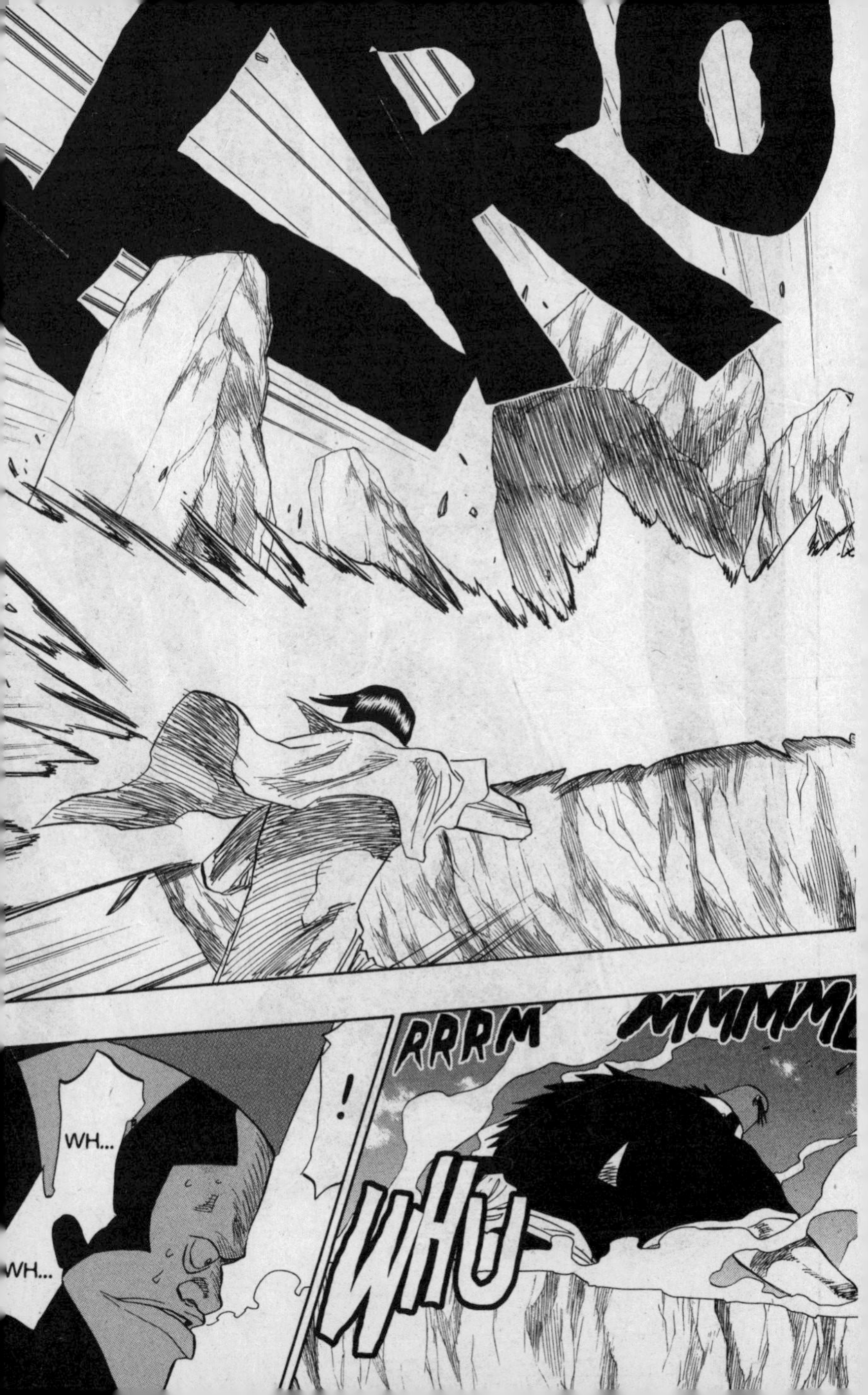
RO
RRRM
MMMMM
WHU
!
WH...
WH...

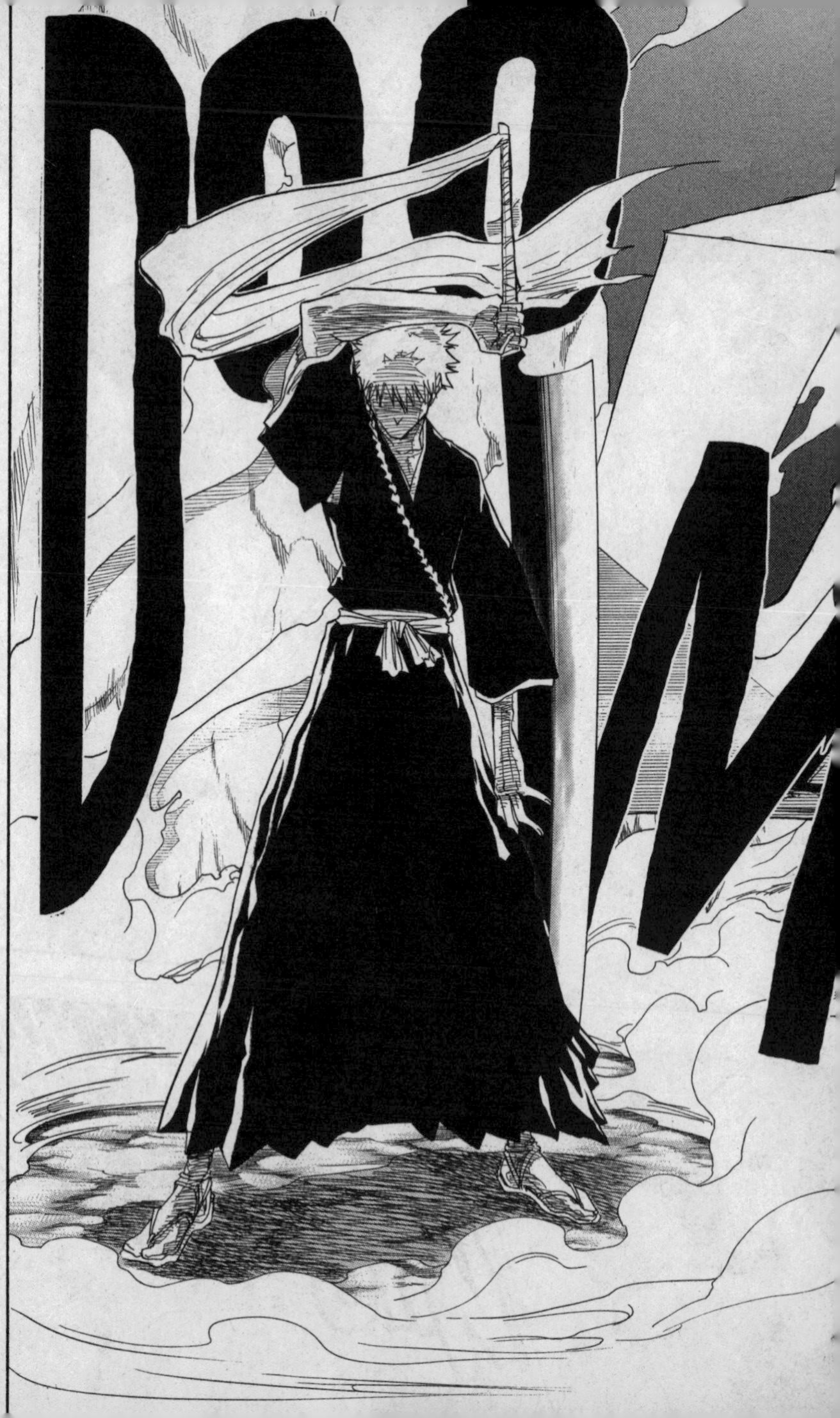
DOOM

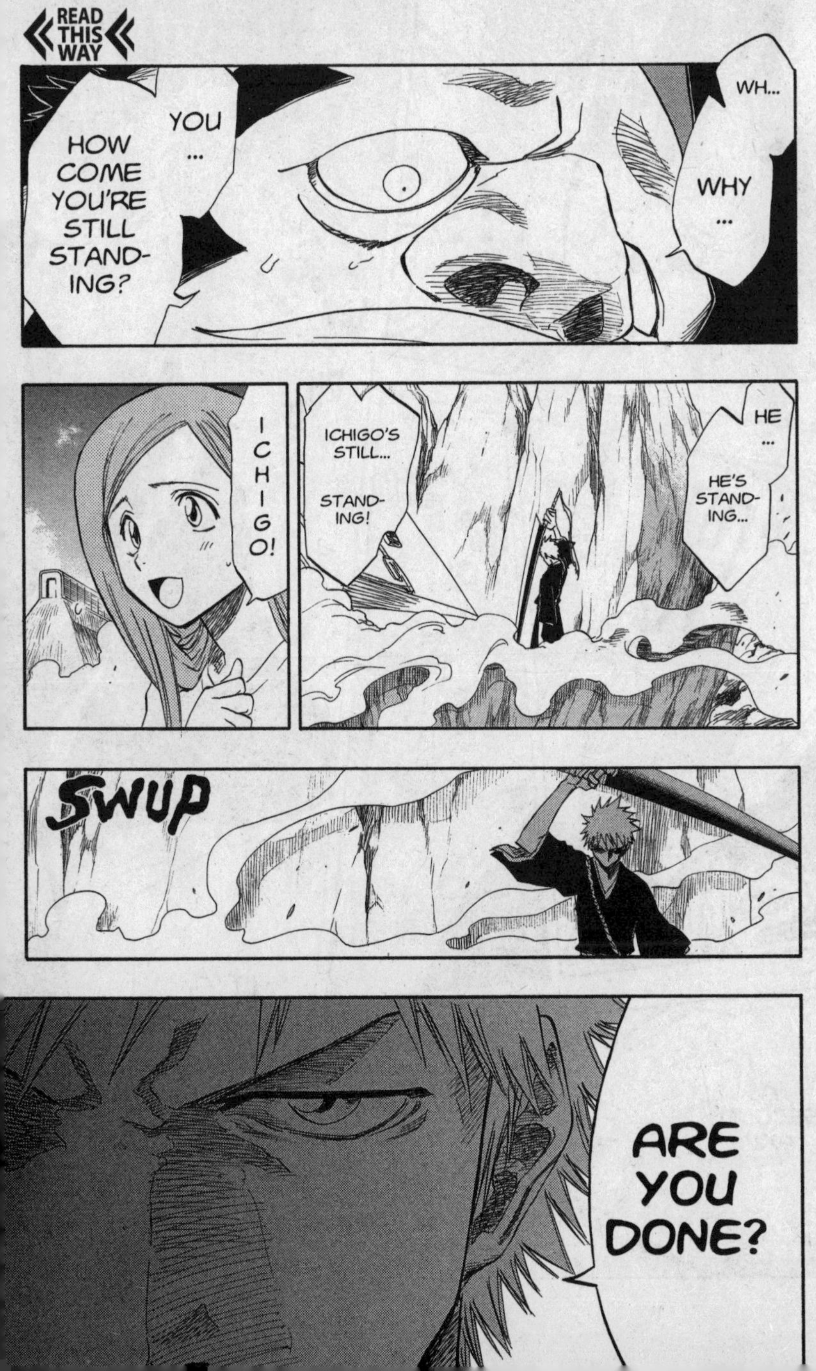
READ THIS WAY
WH... WHY...
YOU... HOW COME YOU'RE STILL STANDING?
HE... HE'S STANDING...
ICHIGO'S STILL... STANDING!
ICHIGO!
SWUP
ARE YOU DONE?

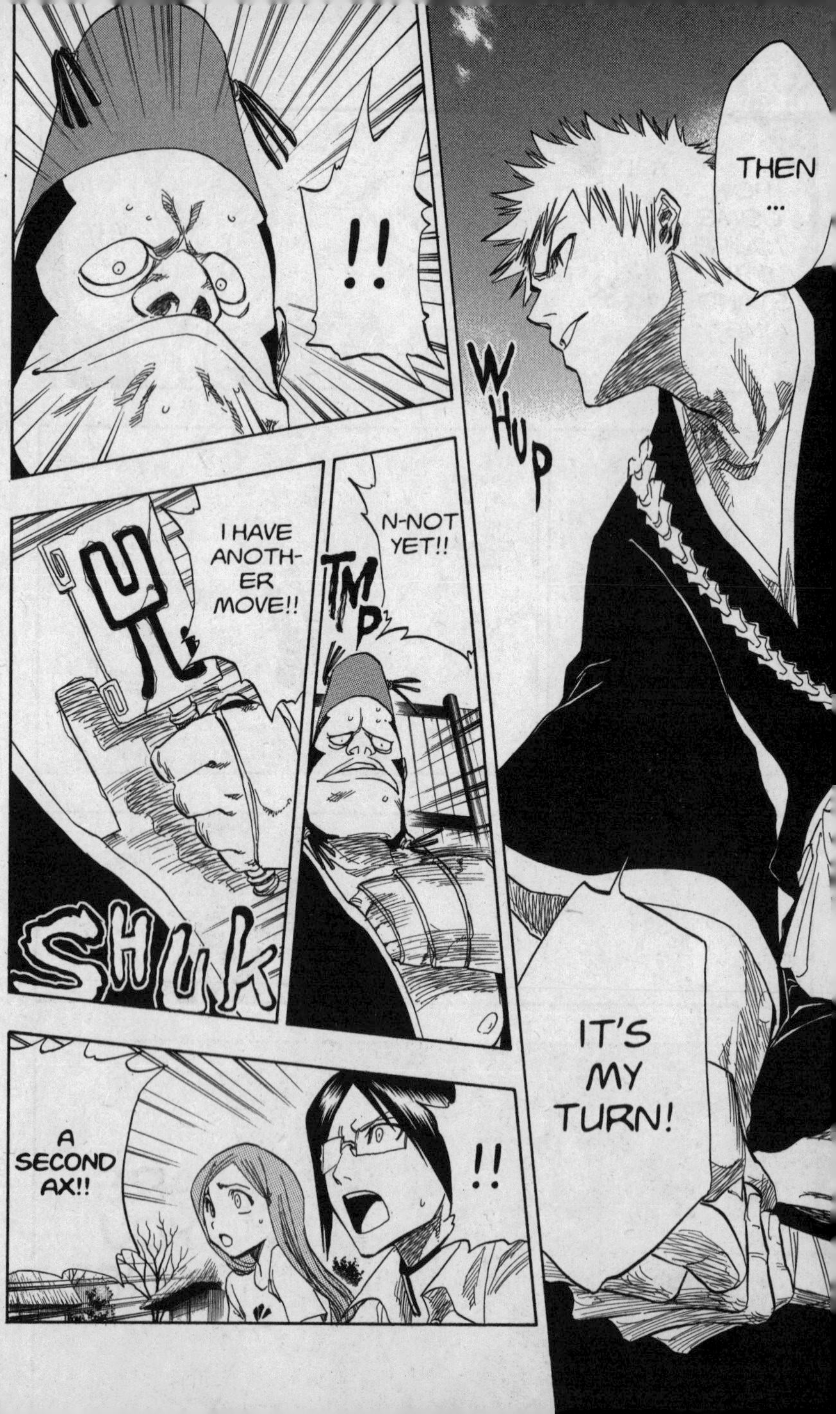

THEN ...
!!
WHUP
N-NOT YET!!
TMP
I HAVE ANOTHER-ER MOVE!!
SHUK
IT'S MY TURN!
!!
A SECOND AX!!

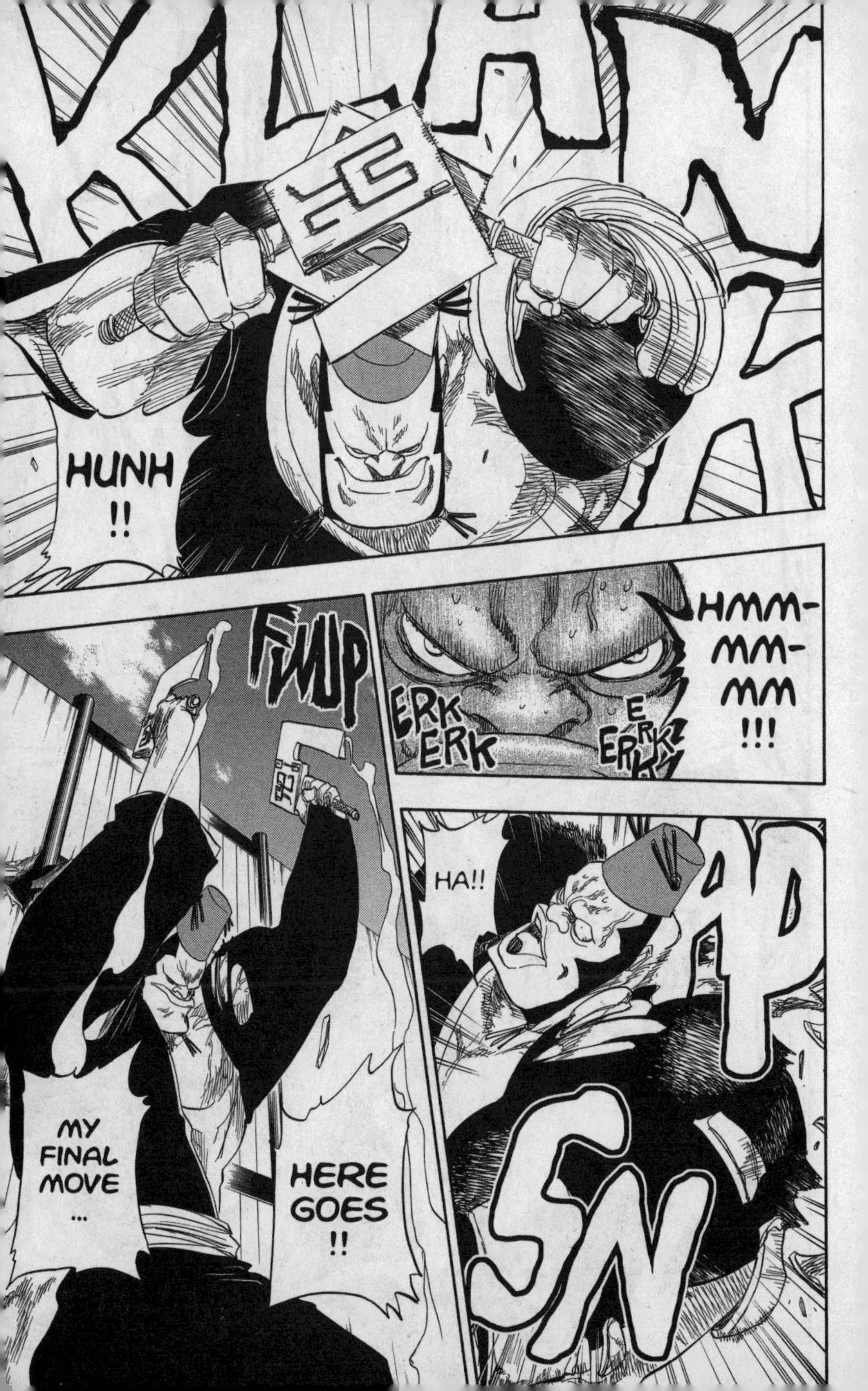
HUNH !!
HMM-MM-MM !!!
ERK ERK
ERK ERK
FWUP
HA!!
HERE GOES !!
MY FINAL MOVE ...

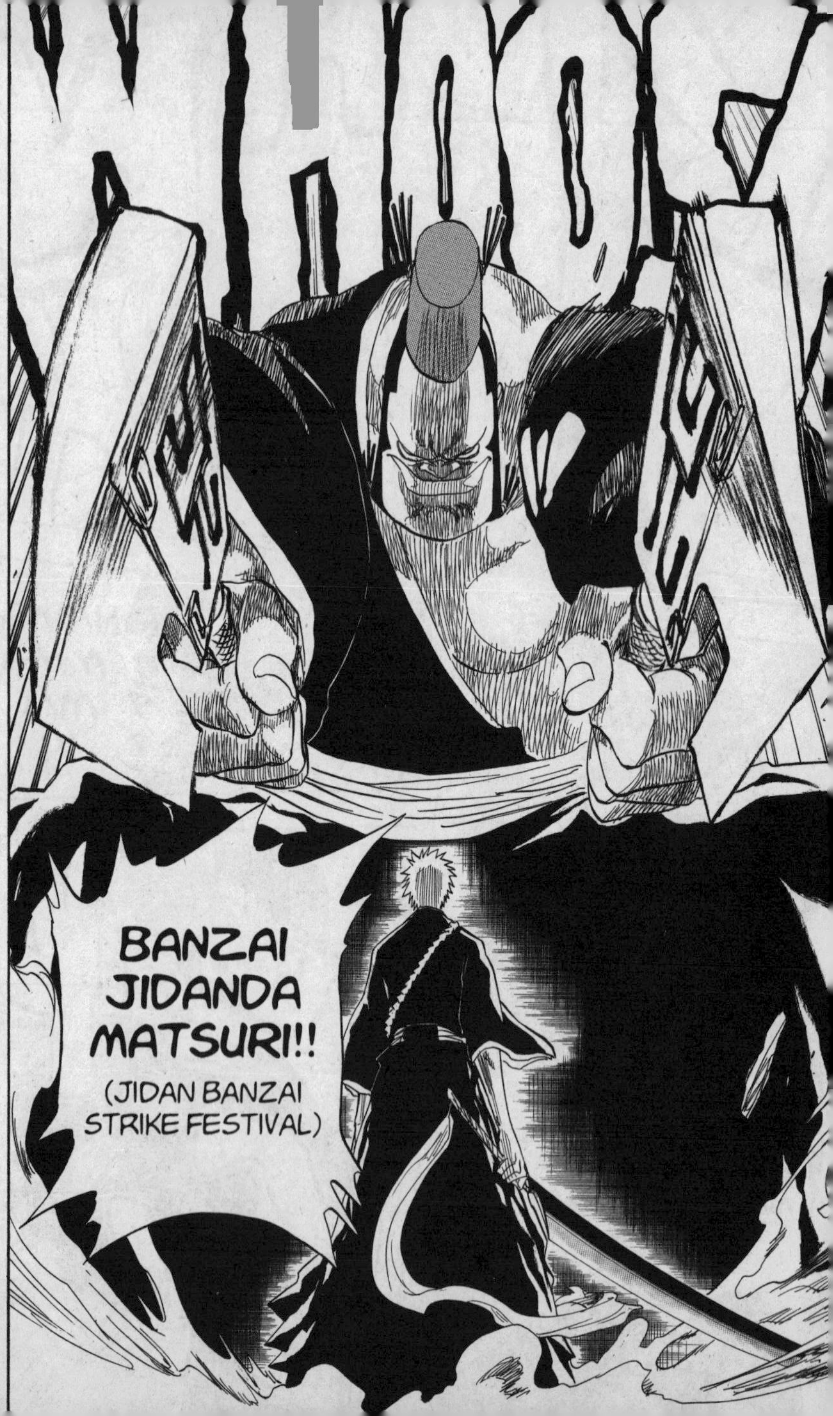
BANZAI JIDANDA MATSURI!!
(JIDAN BANZAI STRIKE FESTIVAL)

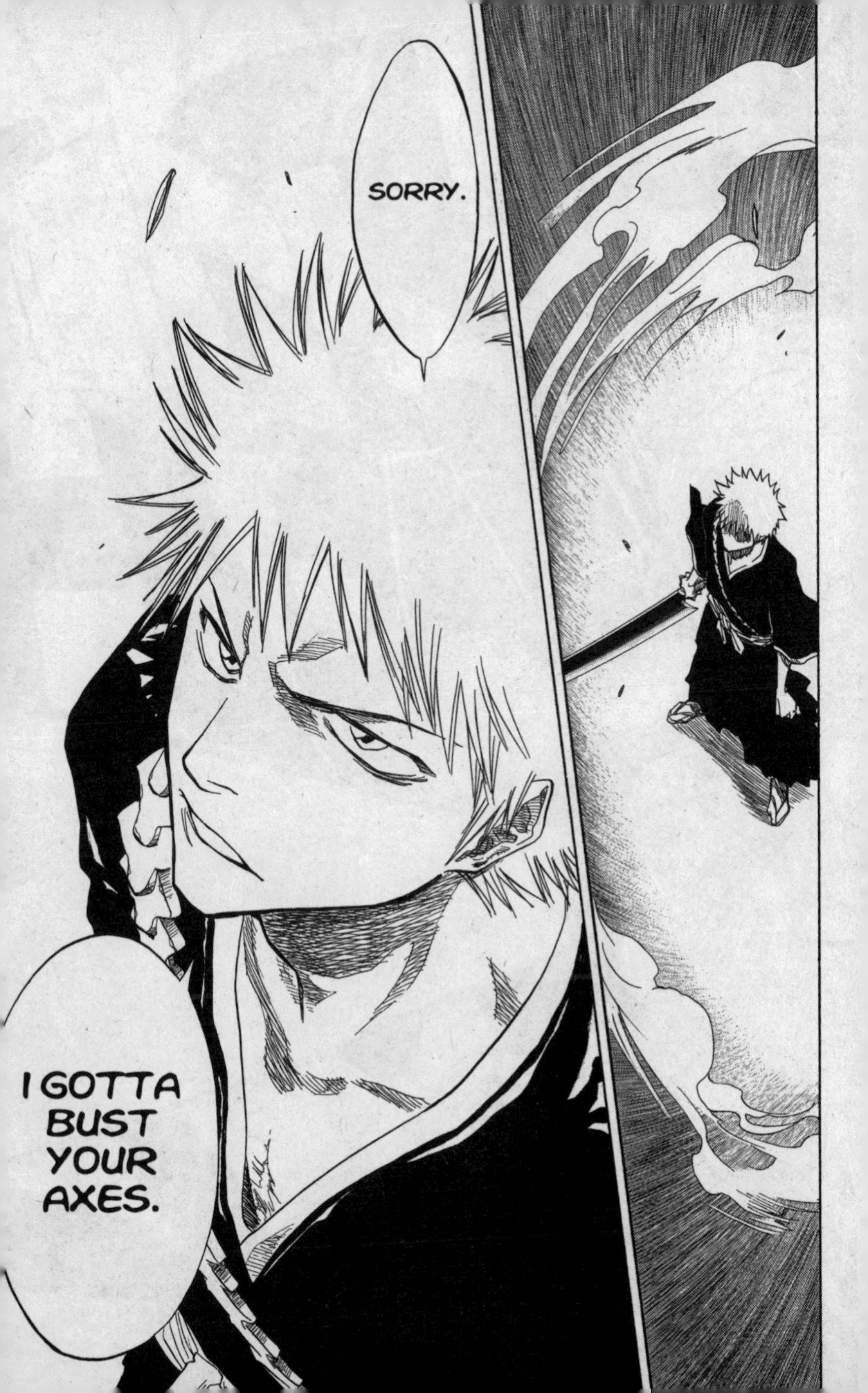
SORRY.
I GOTTA BUST YOUR AXES.

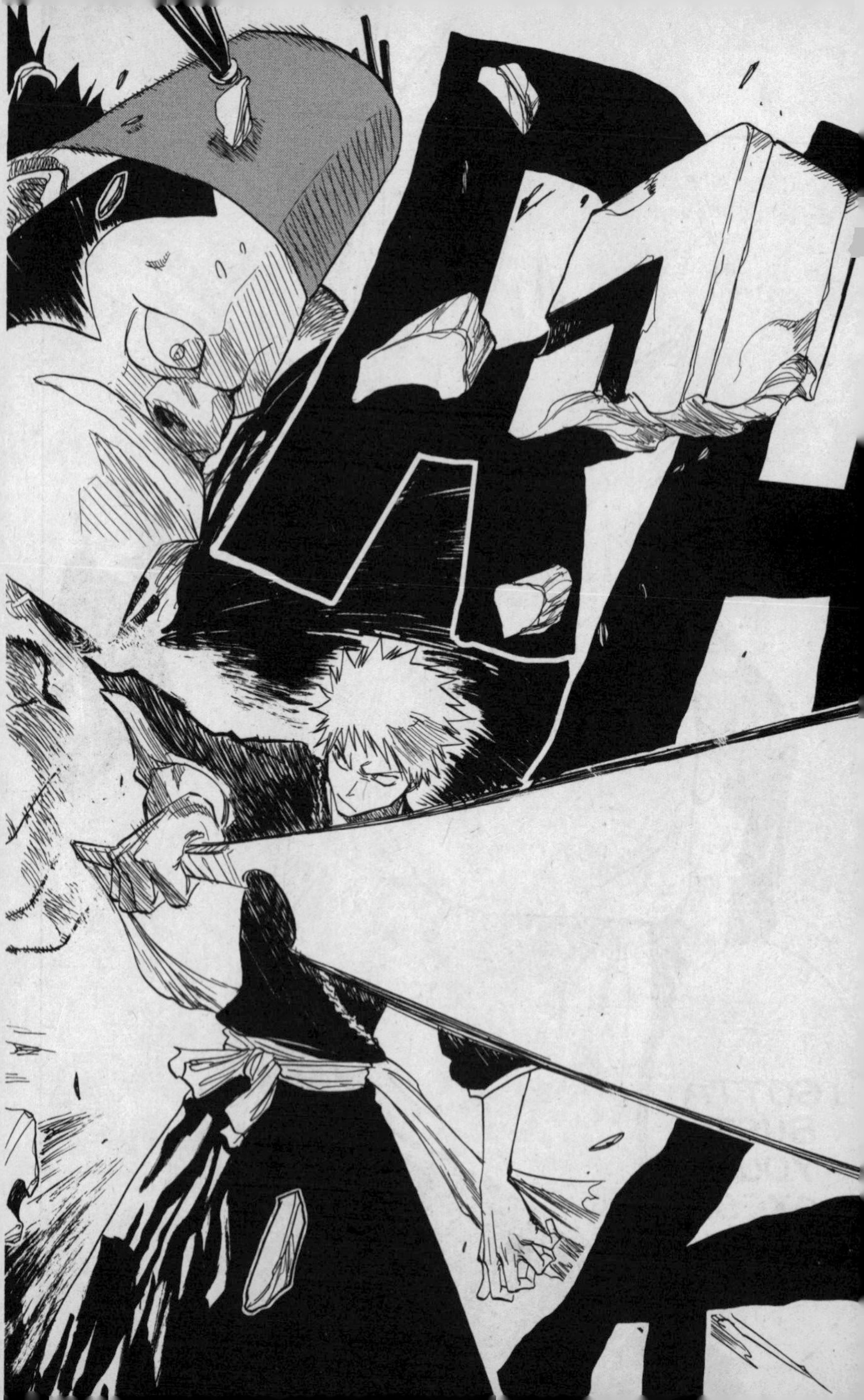

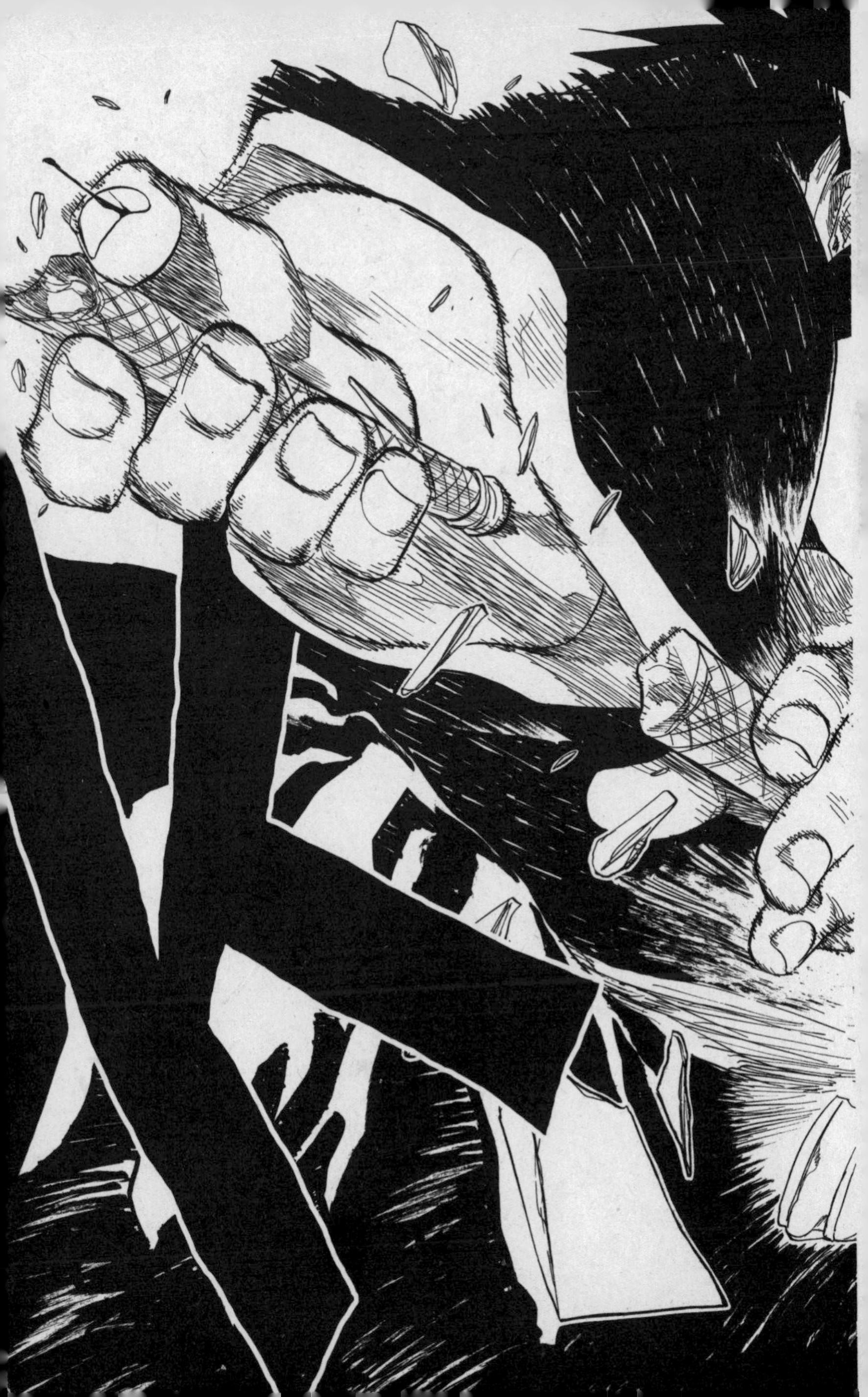

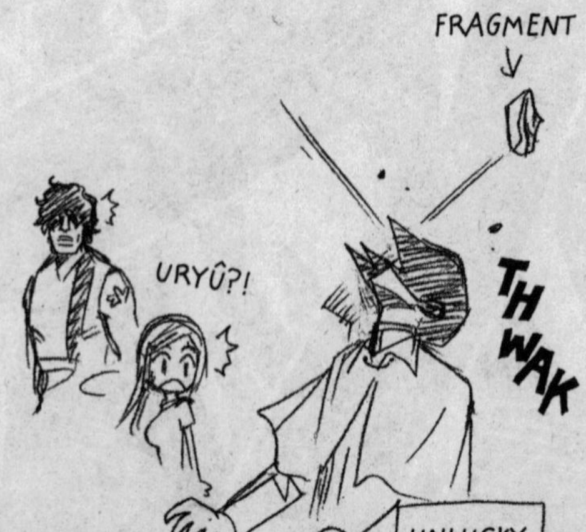
FRAGMENT
URYÛ?!
THWAK
UNLUCKY

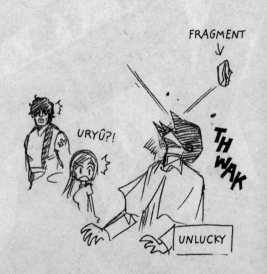

74. Armlost, Armlost

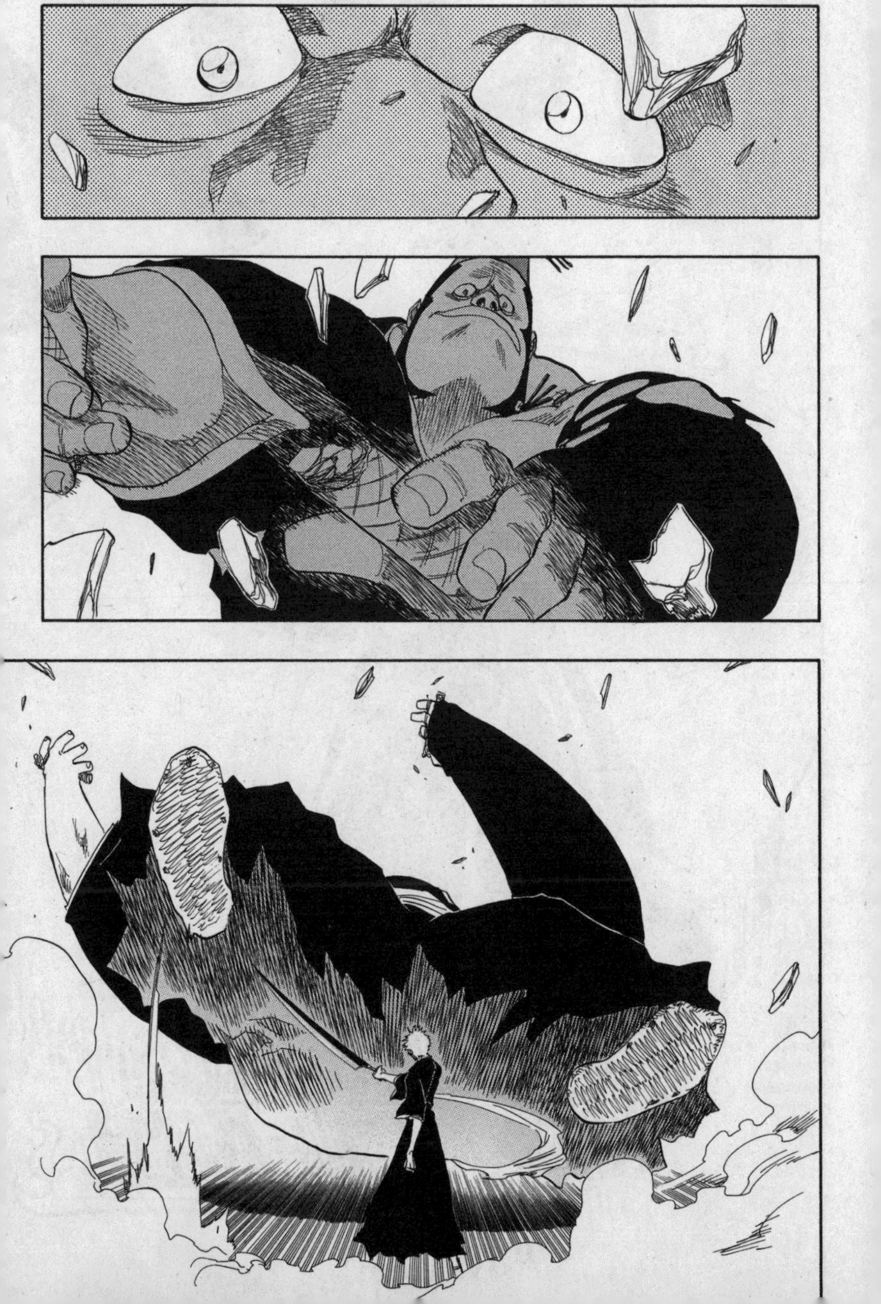

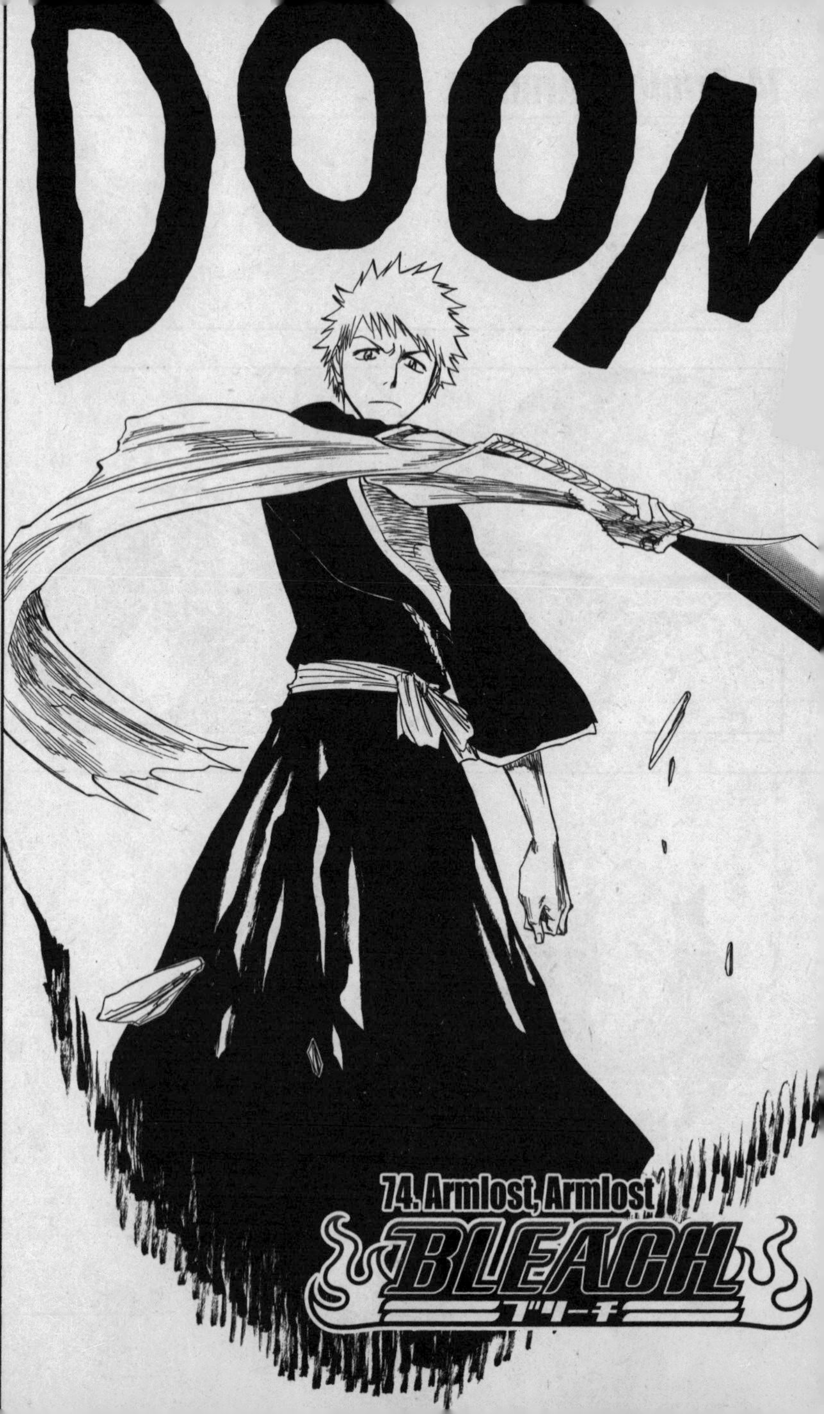
DOON
74. Armlost, Armlost
BLEACH
ブリーチ

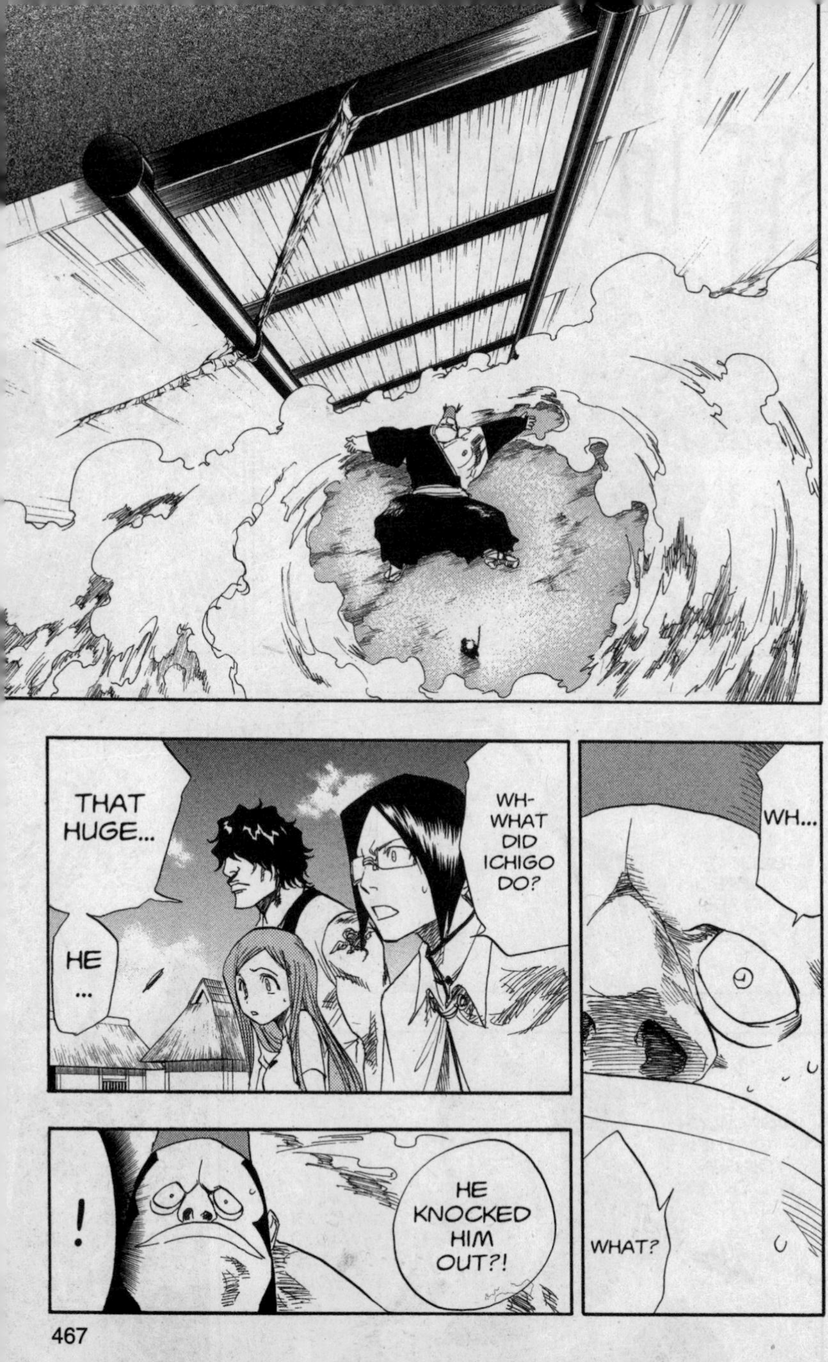
WH...
WHAT?
WH- WHAT DID ICHIGO DO?
THAT HUGE...
HE ...
HE KNOCKED HIM OUT?!
!

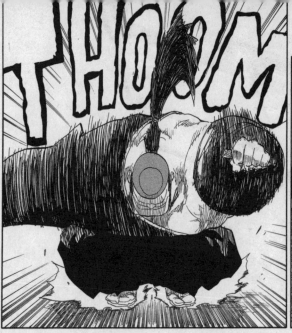

THOOM

THUD

TH-THAT COULD'VE BEEN BAD!

I CAN'T BELIEVE I SLIPPED AND FELL ON MY BUTT!

WHOA!!

HA HA!

YOU DON'T KNOW MUCH IF YOU THINK YOU CAN KNOCK ME OUT!!

HUH?!

WHAT'S THAT LOOK?! OH, YOU THOUGHT I WAS OUT, DIDN'T YOU?!

AX...

THAT'S WHY I HATE HICKS! THEY'RE IGNORANT!

JUST WAIT. ONE MORE WHACK WITH MY...

KRK

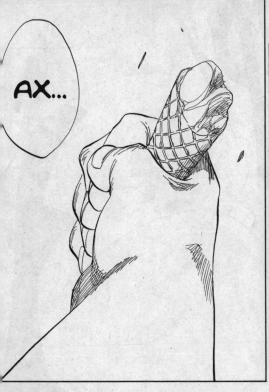

MY...

BOTH MY AXES?!

MY AXES ARE...

MY AX?!

...

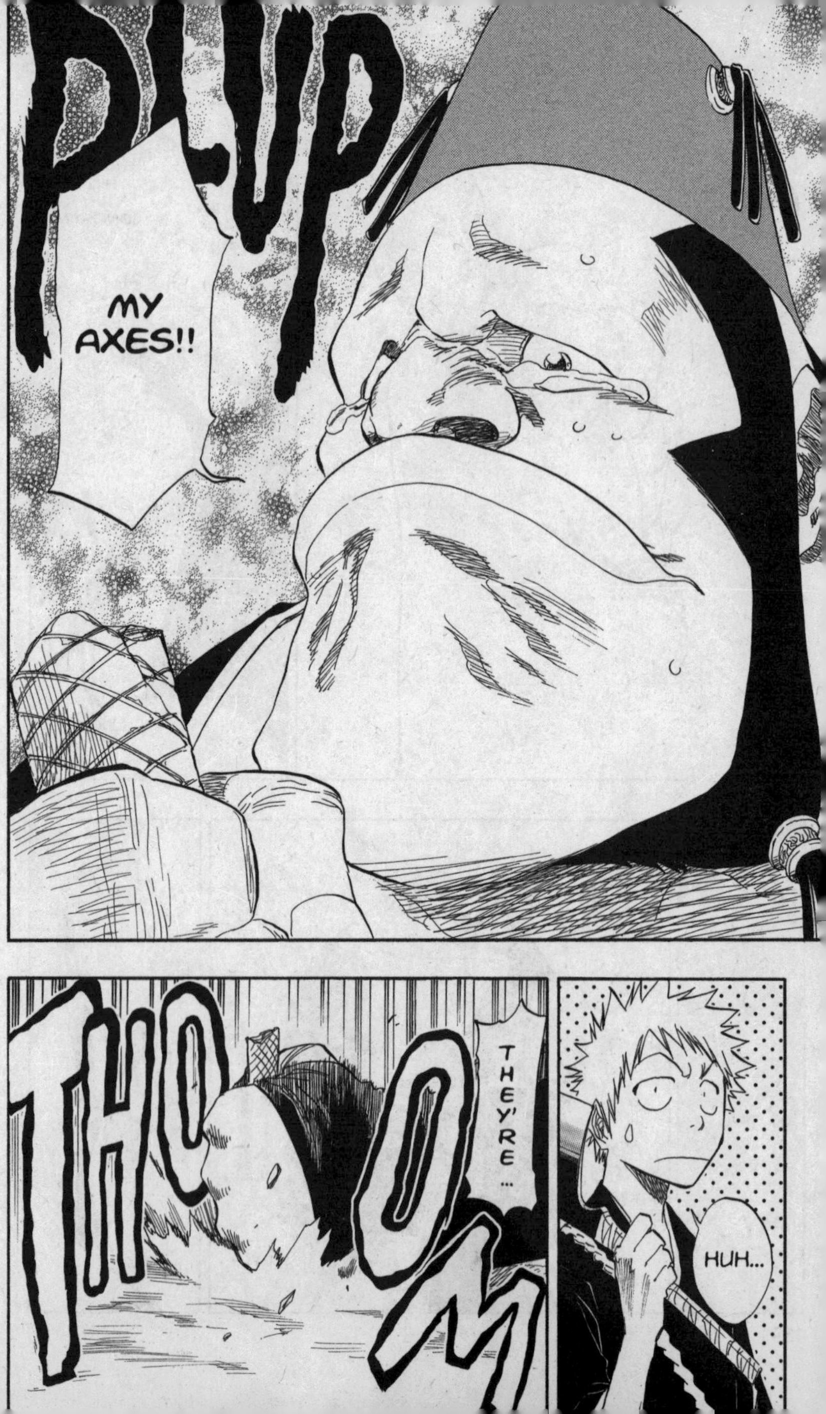
P-UP
MY AXES!!
HUH...
THEY'RE ...
THOOM

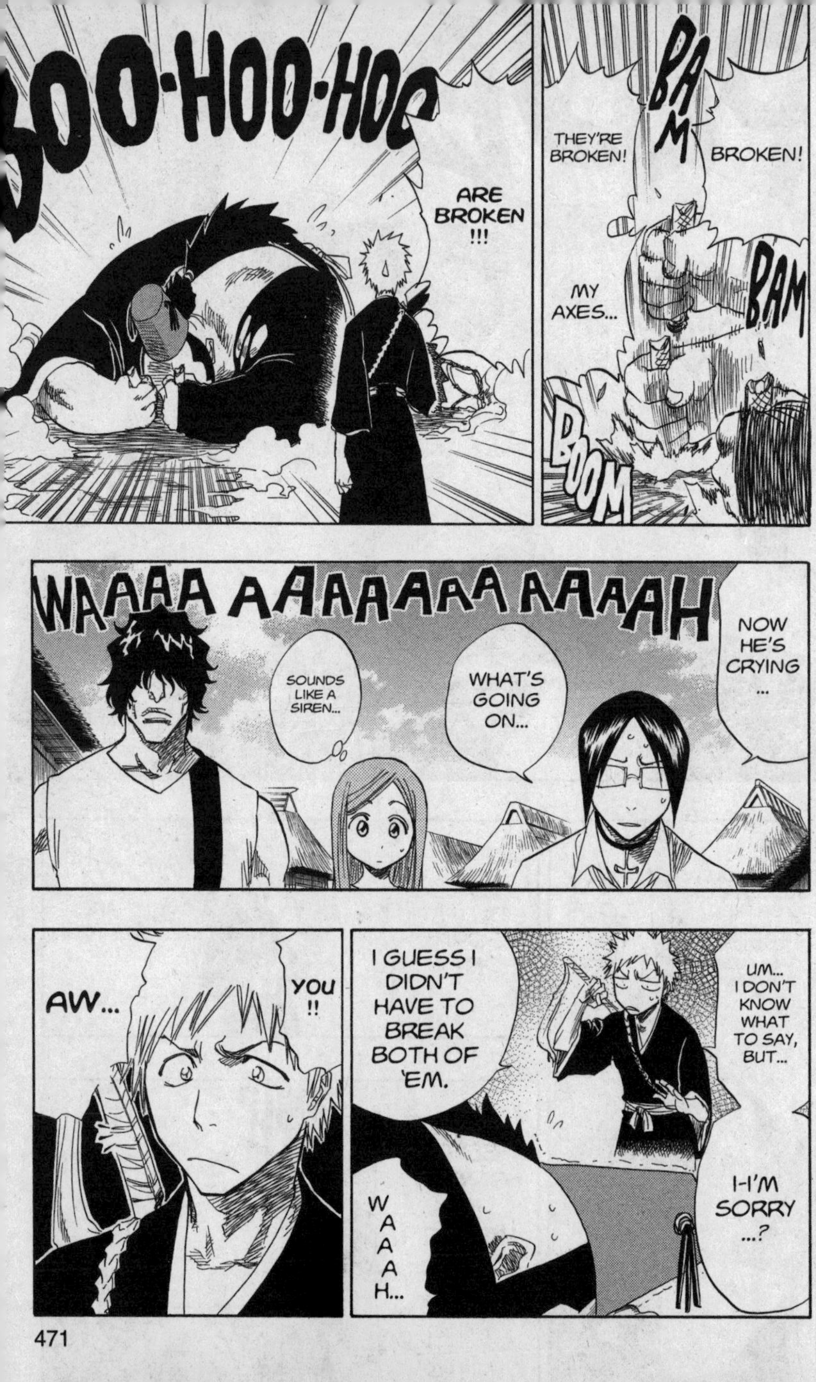
BAM
THEY'RE BROKEN!
BROKEN!
BAM
MY AXES...
BOOM
ARE BROKEN!!!
SOO-HOO-HOO
WAAAA AAAAAAAA AAAAH
NOW HE'S CRYING...
WHAT'S GOING ON...
SOUNDS LIKE A SIREN...
UM... I DON'T KNOW WHAT TO SAY, BUT...
I-I'M SORRY...?
I GUESS I DIDN'T HAVE TO BREAK BOTH OF 'EM.
WAAAAH...
YOU!!
AW...

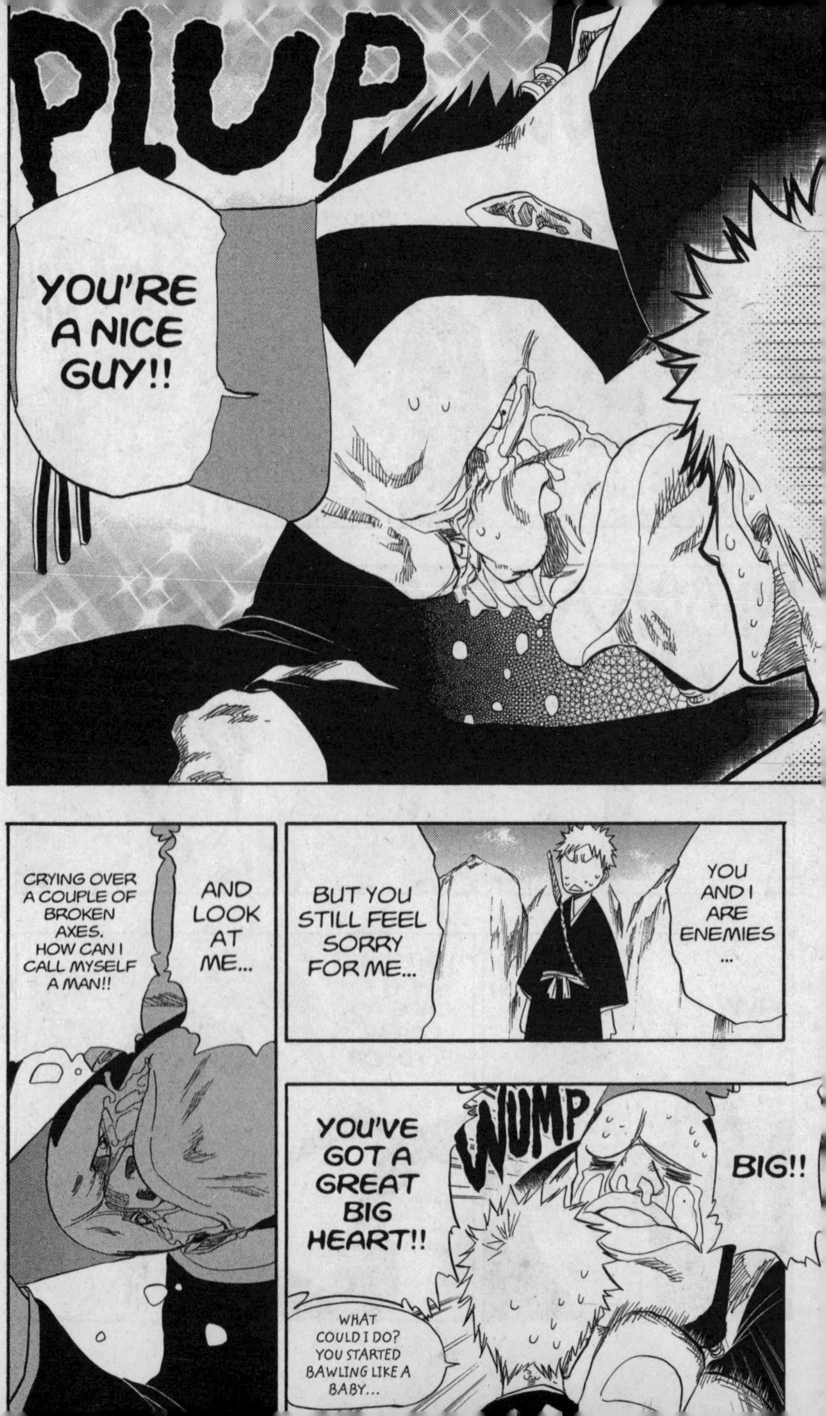
PLUP
YOU'RE A NICE GUY!!
YOU AND I ARE ENEMIES...
BUT YOU STILL FEEL SORRY FOR ME...
AND LOOK AT ME...
CRYING OVER A COUPLE OF BROKEN AXES. HOW CAN I CALL MYSELF A MAN!!
BIG!!
WUMP
YOU'VE GOT A GREAT BIG HEART!!
WHAT COULD I DO? YOU STARTED BAWLING LIKE A BABY...

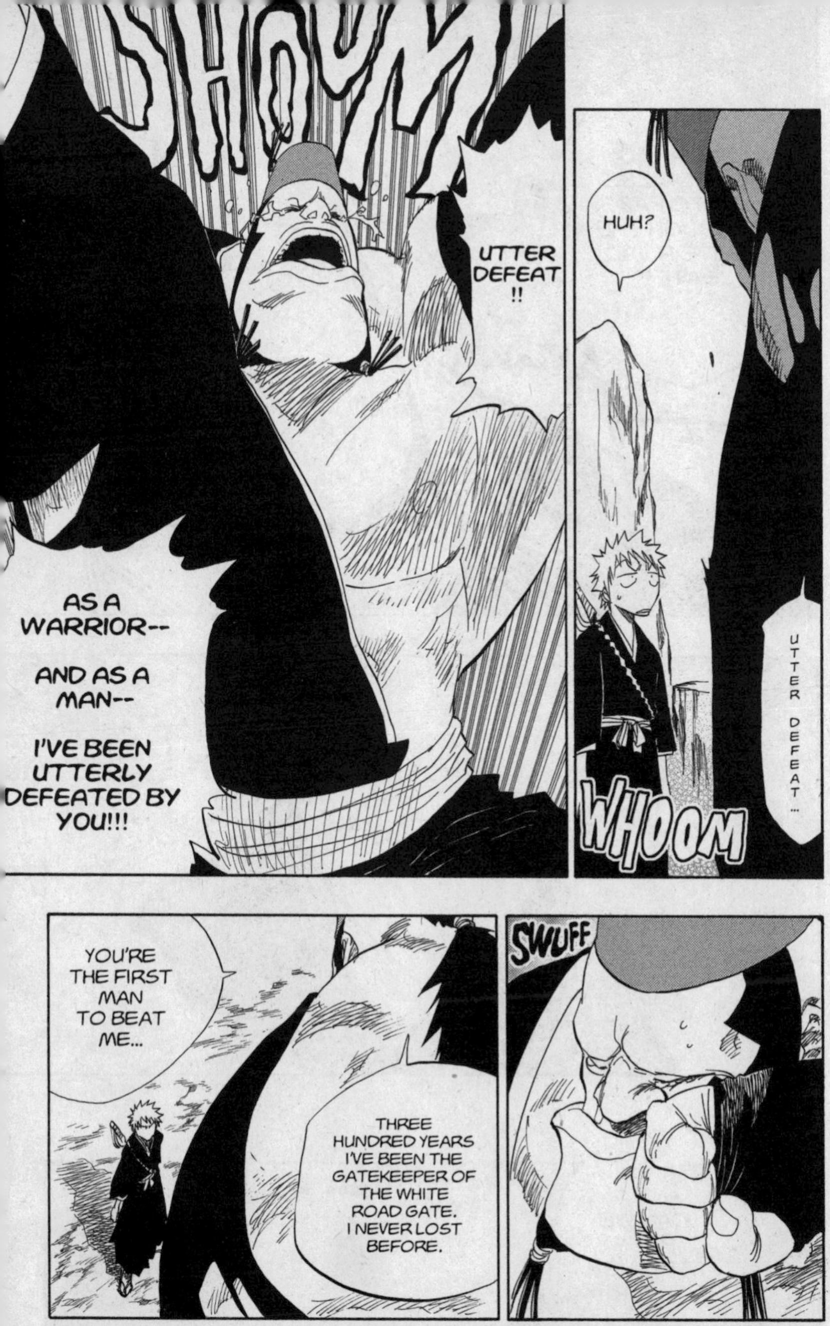
HUH?
UTTER DEFEAT...
WHOOM
SHOOM
UTTER DEFEAT!!
AS A WARRIOR--
AND AS A MAN--
I'VE BEEN UTTERLY DEFEATED BY YOU!!!
SWUFF
YOU'RE THE FIRST MAN TO BEAT ME...
THREE HUNDRED YEARS I'VE BEEN THE GATEKEEPER OF THE WHITE ROAD GATE. I NEVER LOST BEFORE.

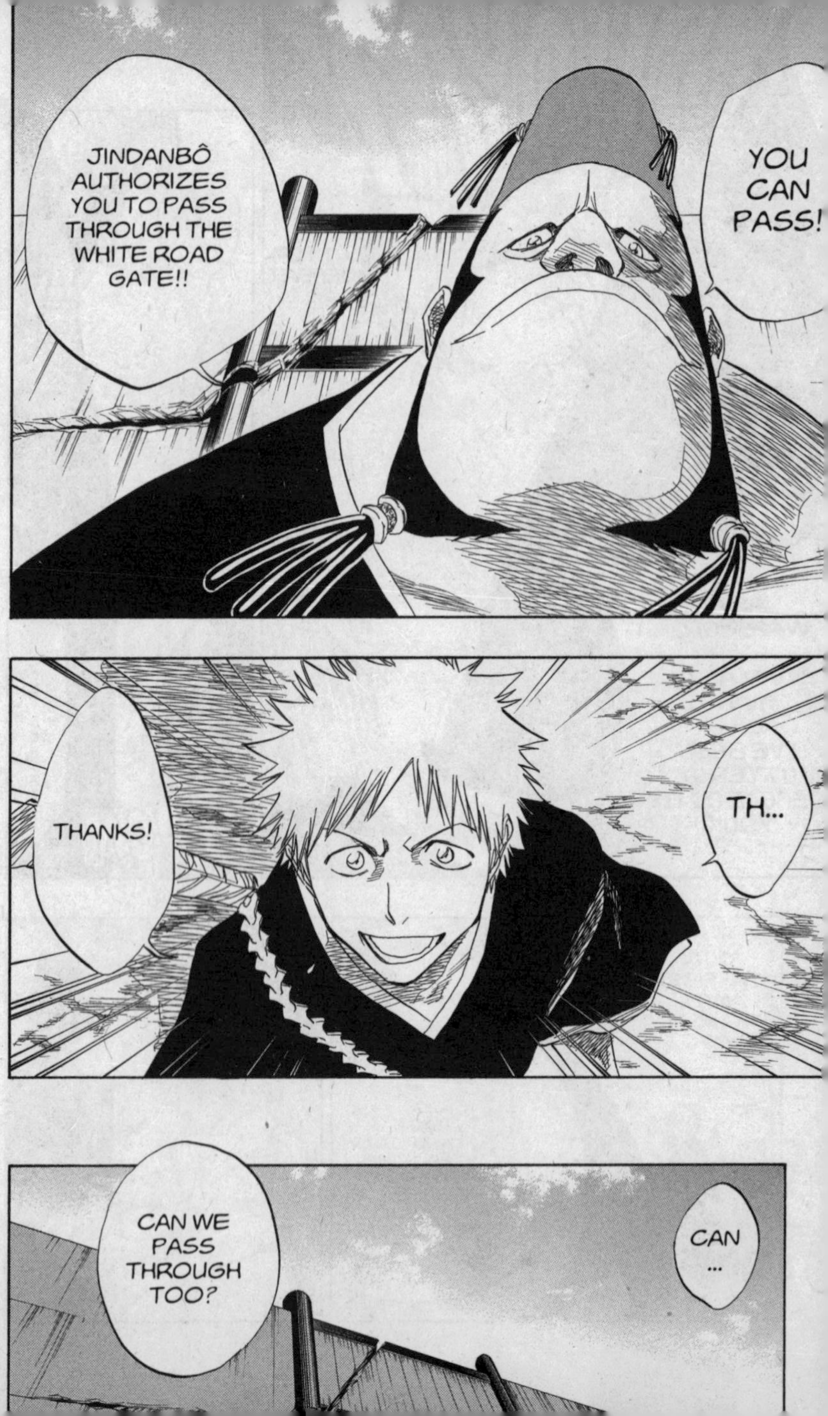
YOU CAN PASS!
JINDANBÔ AUTHORIZES YOU TO PASS THROUGH THE WHITE ROAD GATE!!
TH...
THANKS!
CAN ...
CAN WE PASS THROUGH TOO?

READ THIS WAY

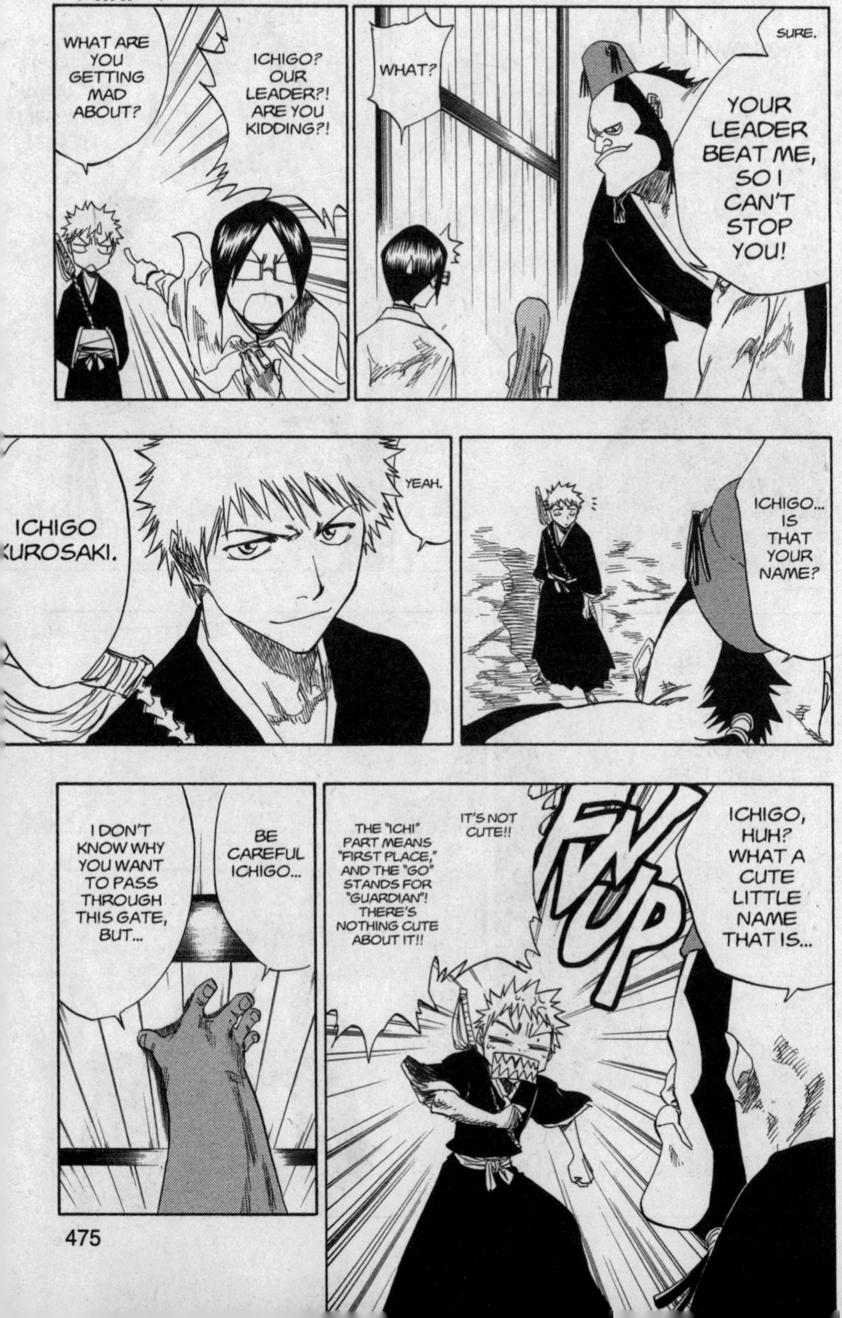
SURE.
YOUR LEADER BEAT ME, SO I CAN'T STOP YOU!
WHAT?
ICHIGO? OUR LEADER?! ARE YOU KIDDING?!
WHAT ARE YOU GETTING MAD ABOUT?
ICHIGO... IS THAT YOUR NAME?
YEAH.
ICHIGO KUROSAKI.
ICHIGO, HUH? WHAT A CUTE LITTLE NAME THAT IS...
FWUP
IT'S NOT CUTE!!
THE "ICHI" PART MEANS "FIRST PLACE," AND THE "GO" STANDS FOR "GUARDIAN"! THERE'S NOTHING CUTE ABOUT IT!!
BE CAREFUL ICHIGO...
I DON'T KNOW WHY YOU WANT TO PASS THROUGH THIS GATE, BUT...

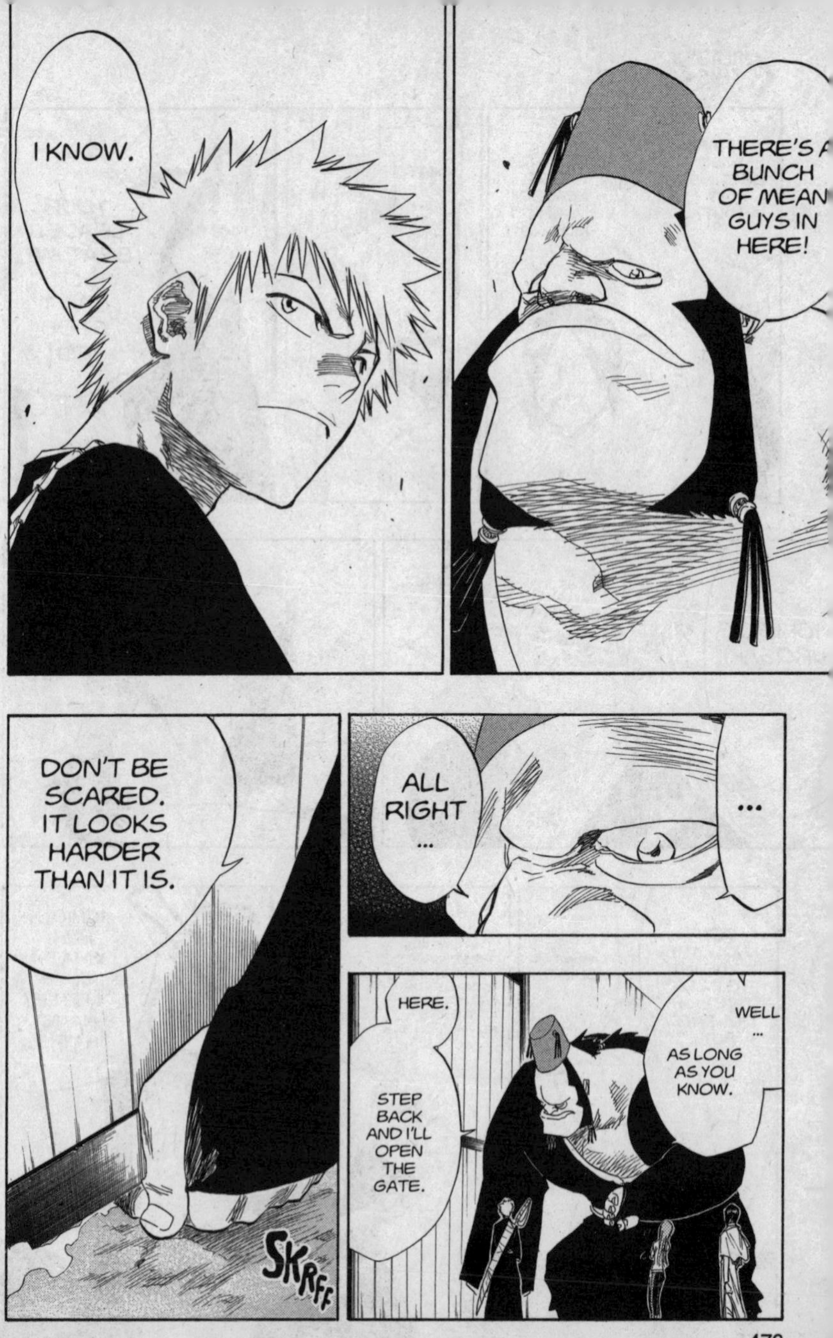
THERE'S A BUNCH OF MEAN GUYS IN HERE!
I KNOW.
...
ALL RIGHT ...
DON'T BE SCARED. IT LOOKS HARDER THAN IT IS.
SKRFF
WELL ... AS LONG AS YOU KNOW.
HERE.
STEP BACK AND I'LL OPEN THE GATE.

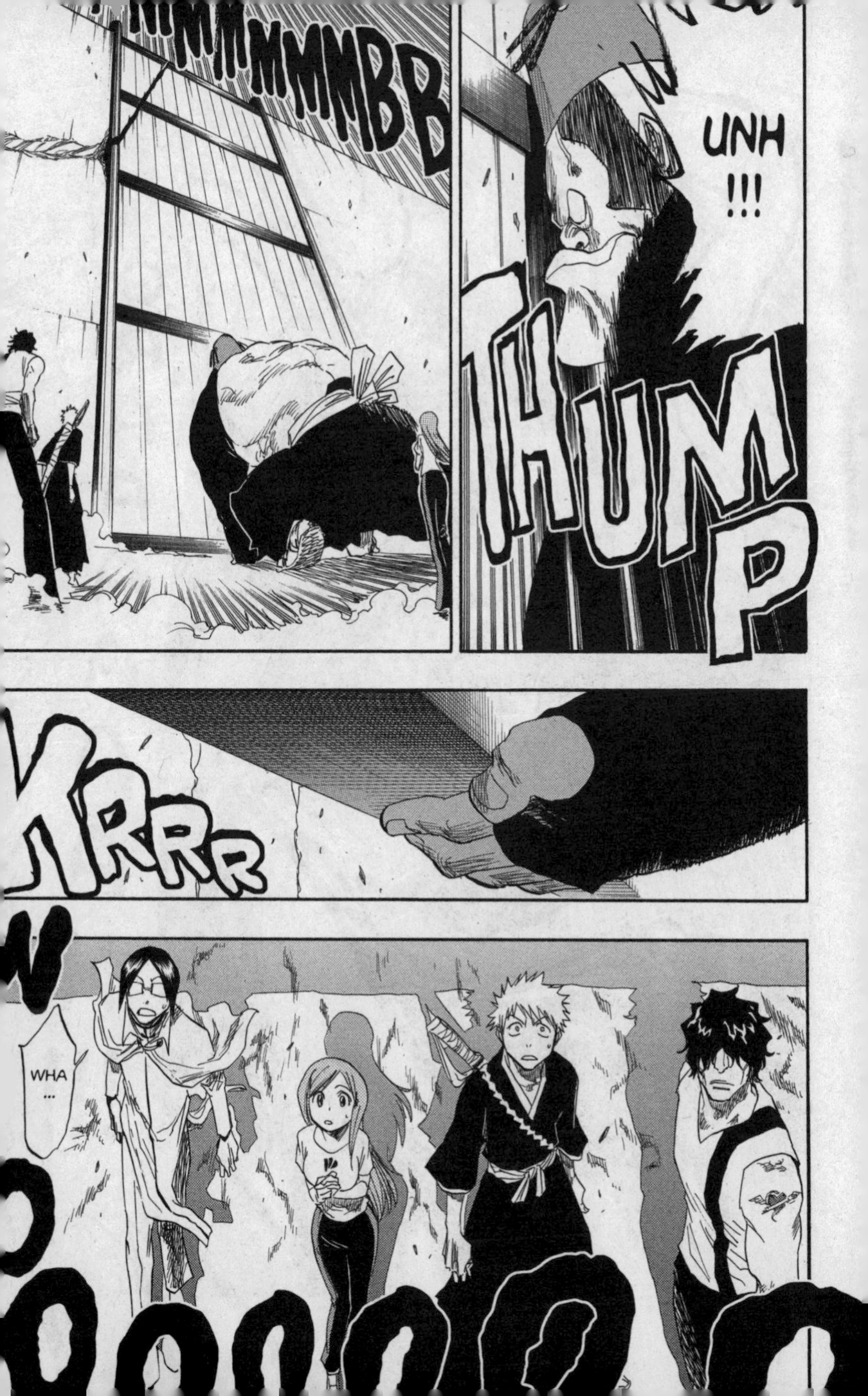

UNH
!!!
THUMP
MMMMMBB
VRRR
WHA
...

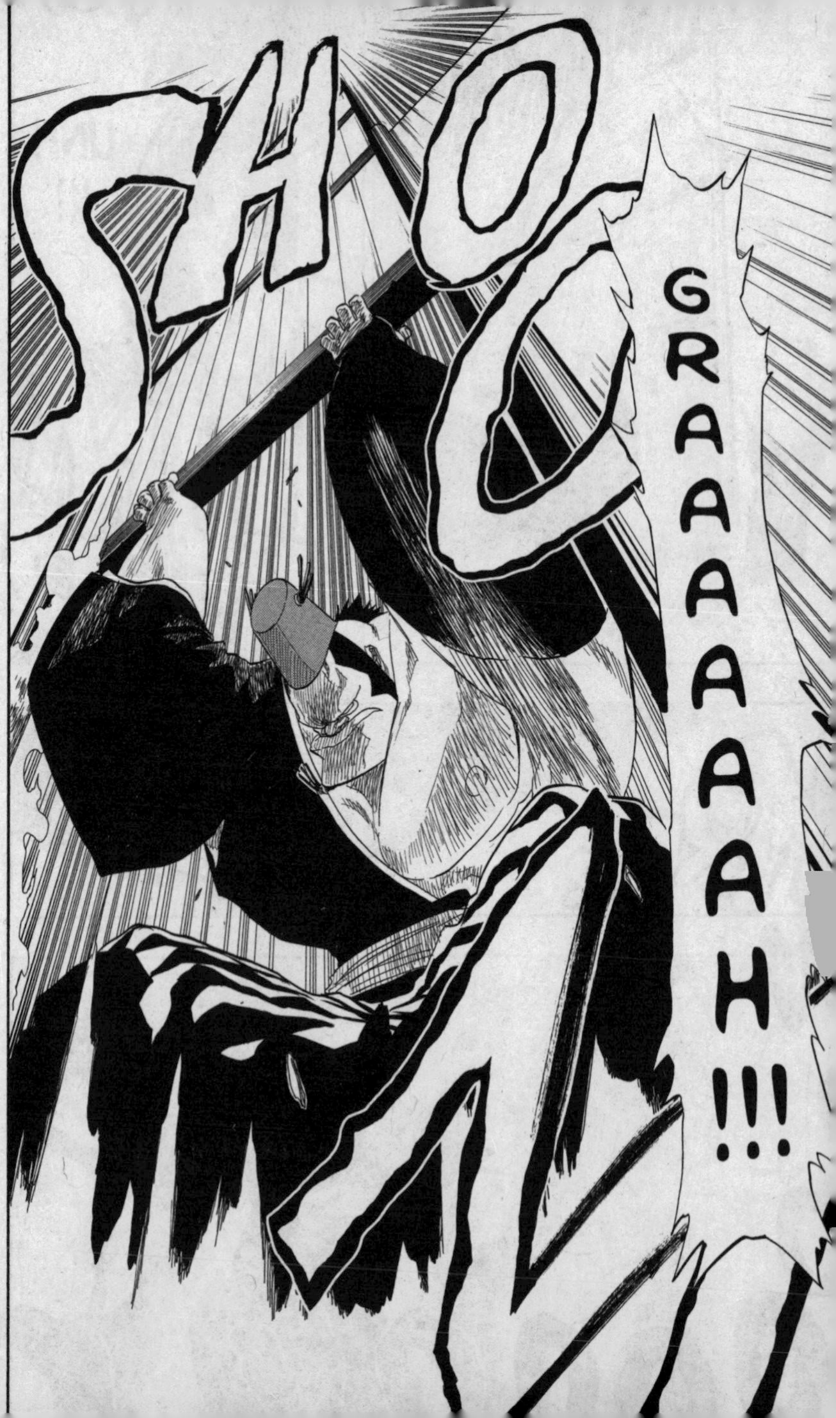
GRAAAAAAH!!!

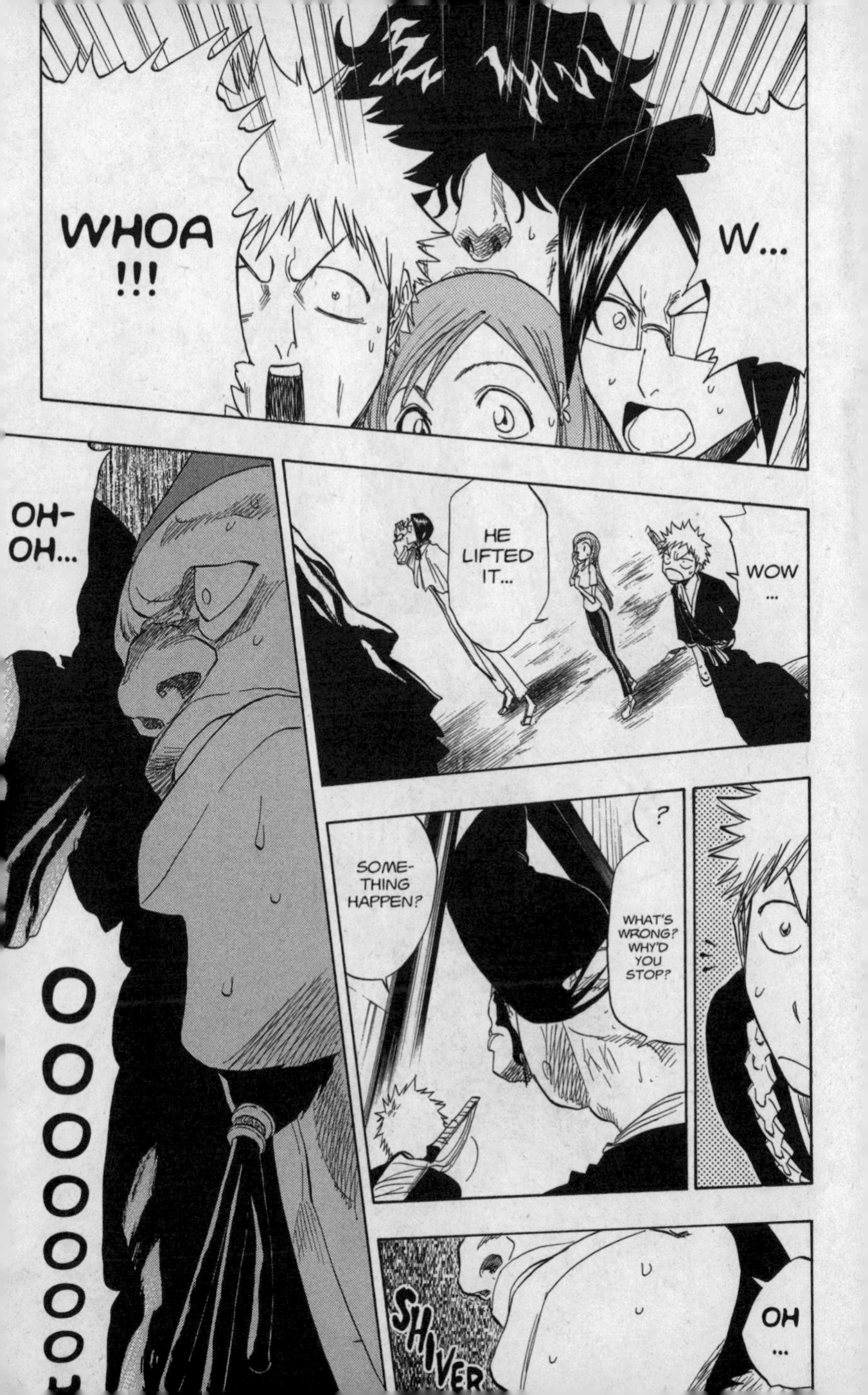
W...
WHOA !!!
WOW ...
HE LIFTED IT...
OH-OH...
?
WHAT'S WRONG? WHY'D YOU STOP?
SOME-THING HAPPEN?
OOOOOOOOOH
OH ...
SHIVER

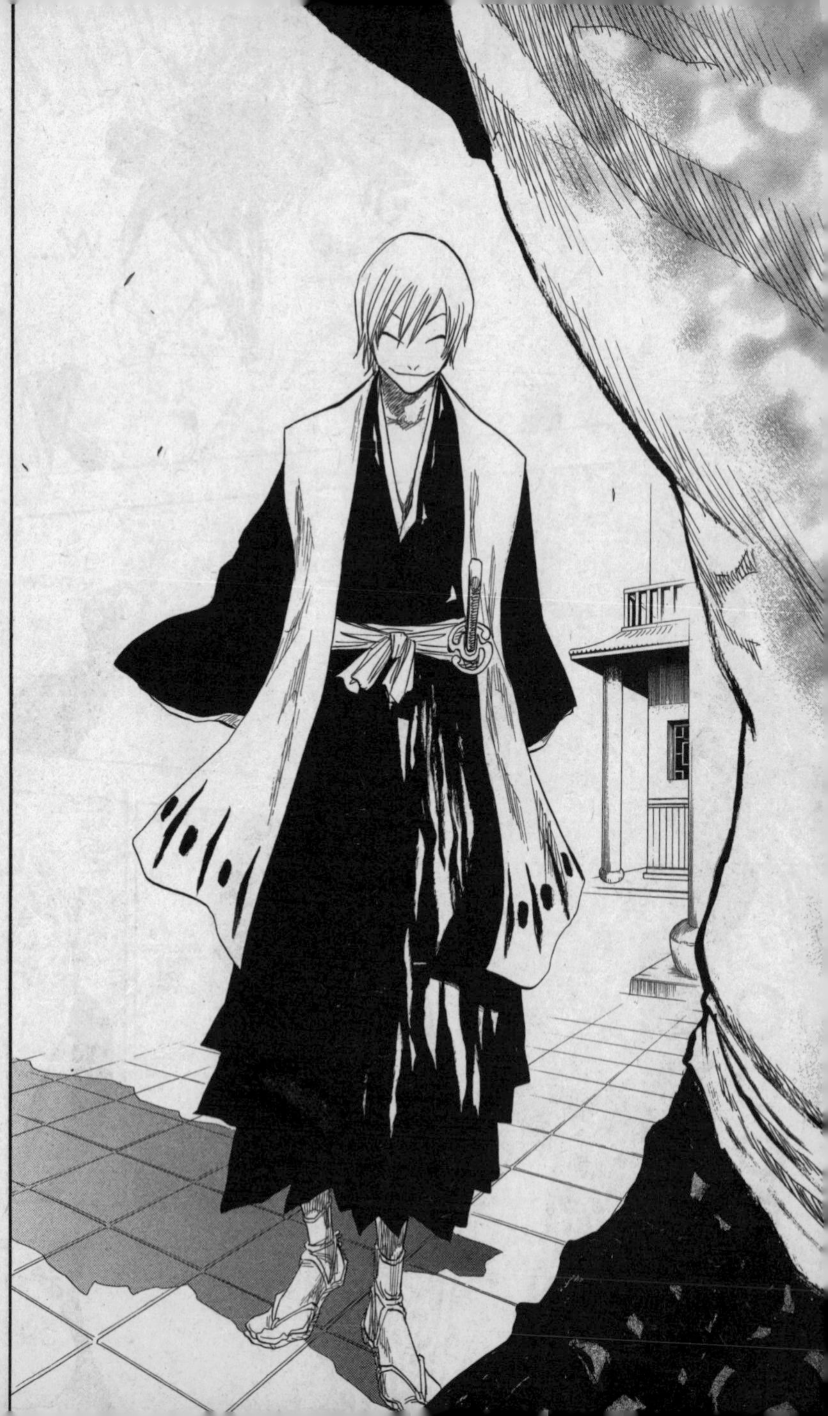

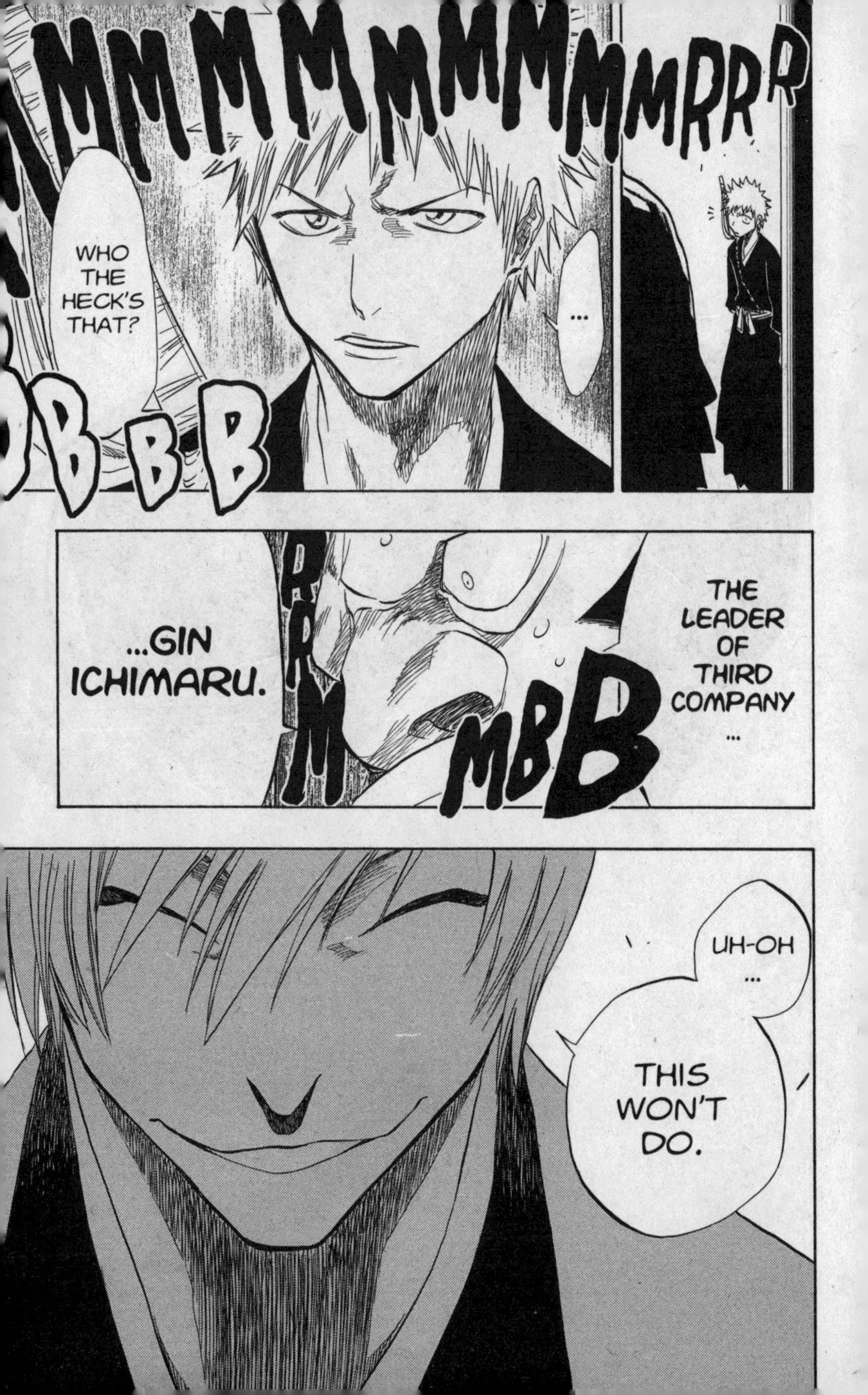

MMMMMMMMMRRR
...
WHO THE HECK'S THAT?
BBB
THE LEADER OF THIRD COMPANY ...
...GIN ICHIMARU.
RRRMMBB
UH-OH ...
THIS WON'T DO.

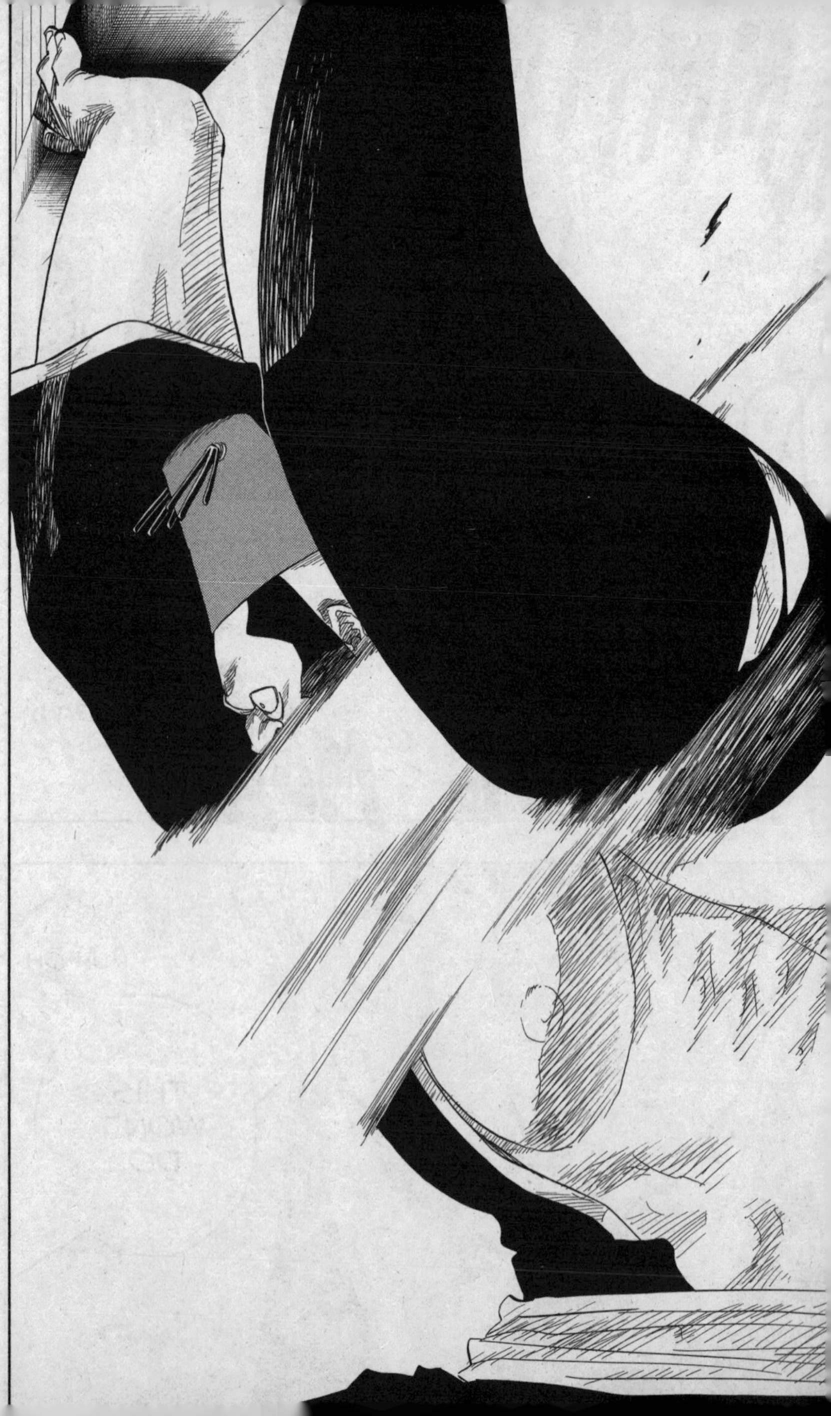

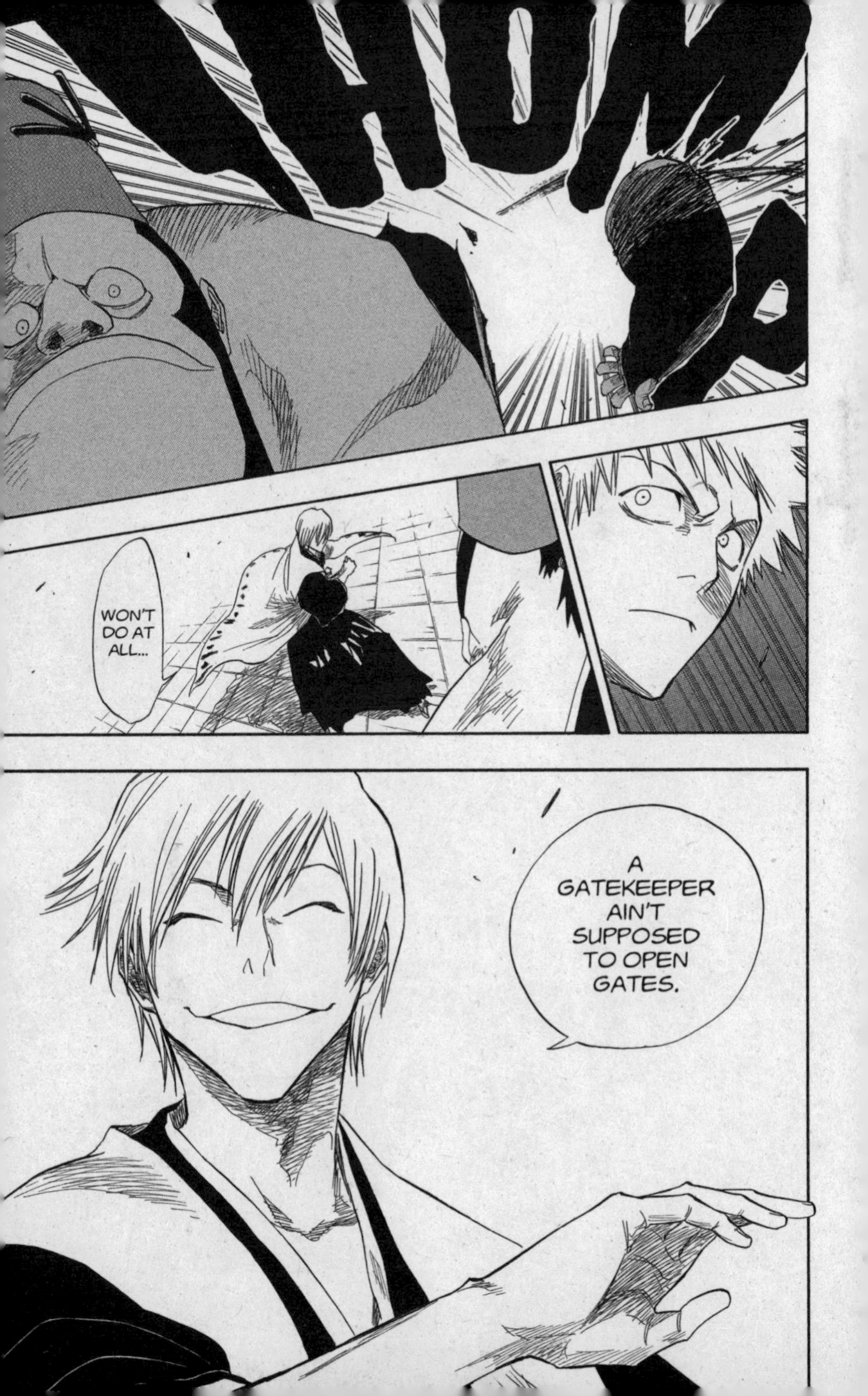
WON'T DO AT ALL...
A GATEKEEPER AIN'T SUPPOSED TO OPEN GATES.

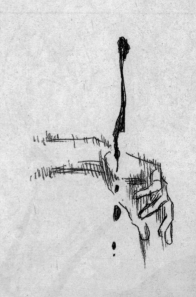

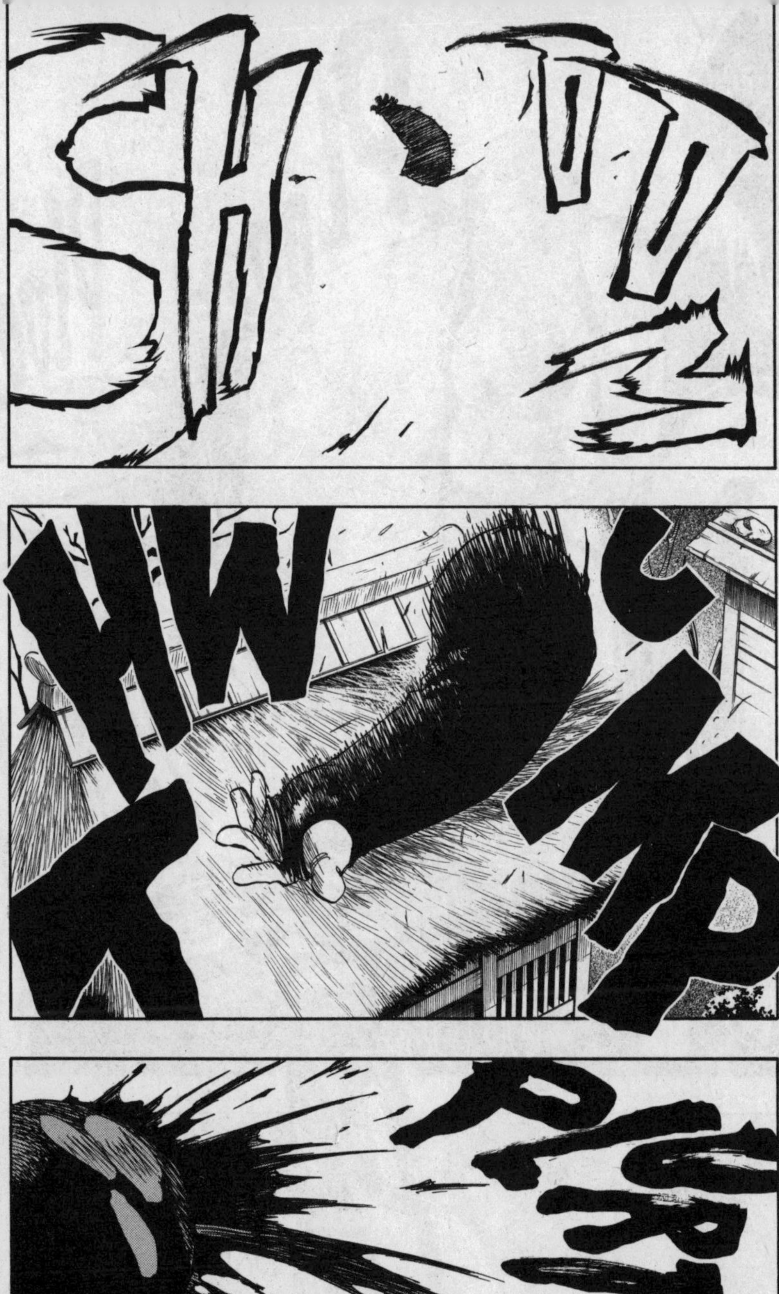

75. Crimson Rain

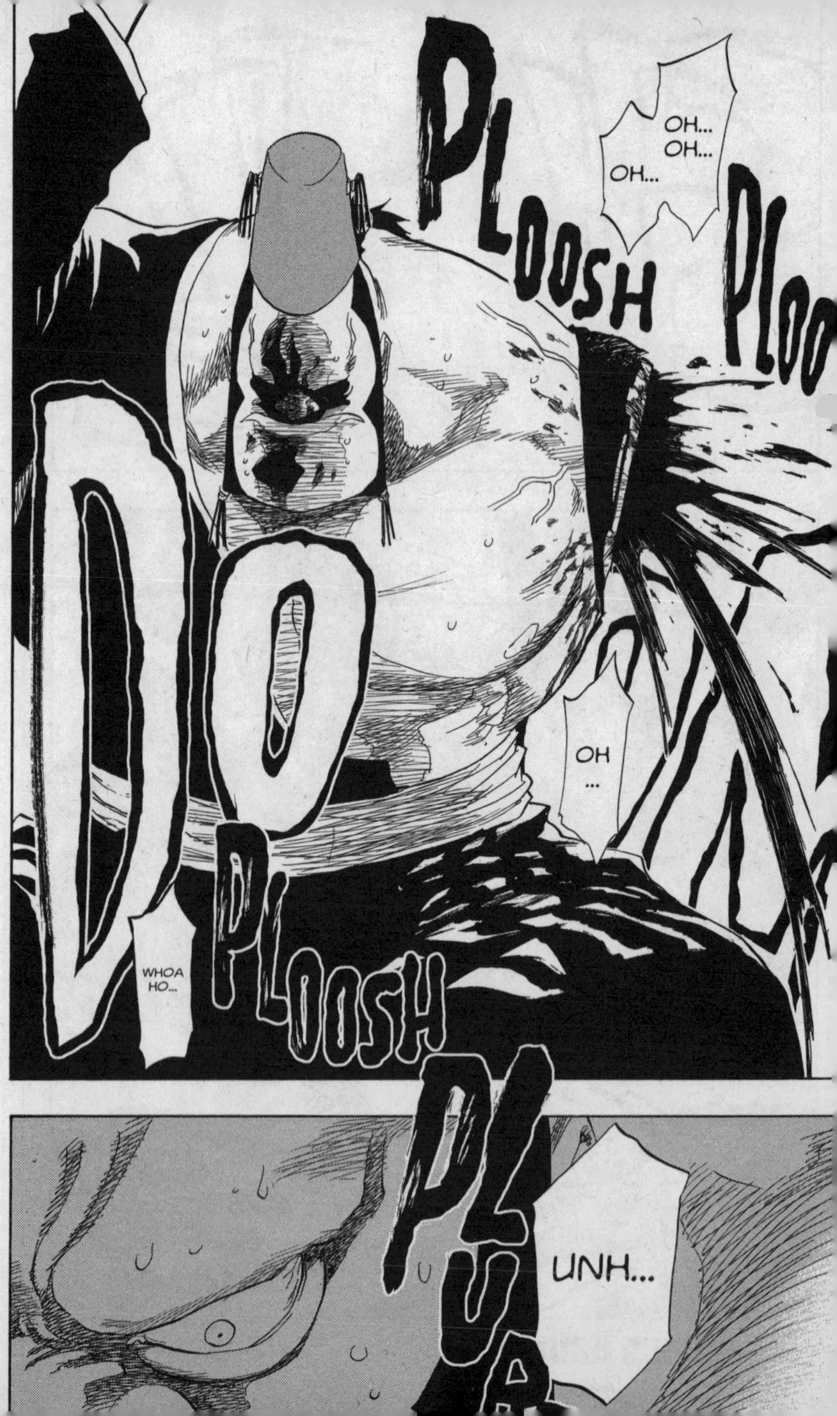

OH... OH... OH...
PLOOSH
PLOO
OH ...
DO
WHOA HO...
PLOOSH
UNH...
PL

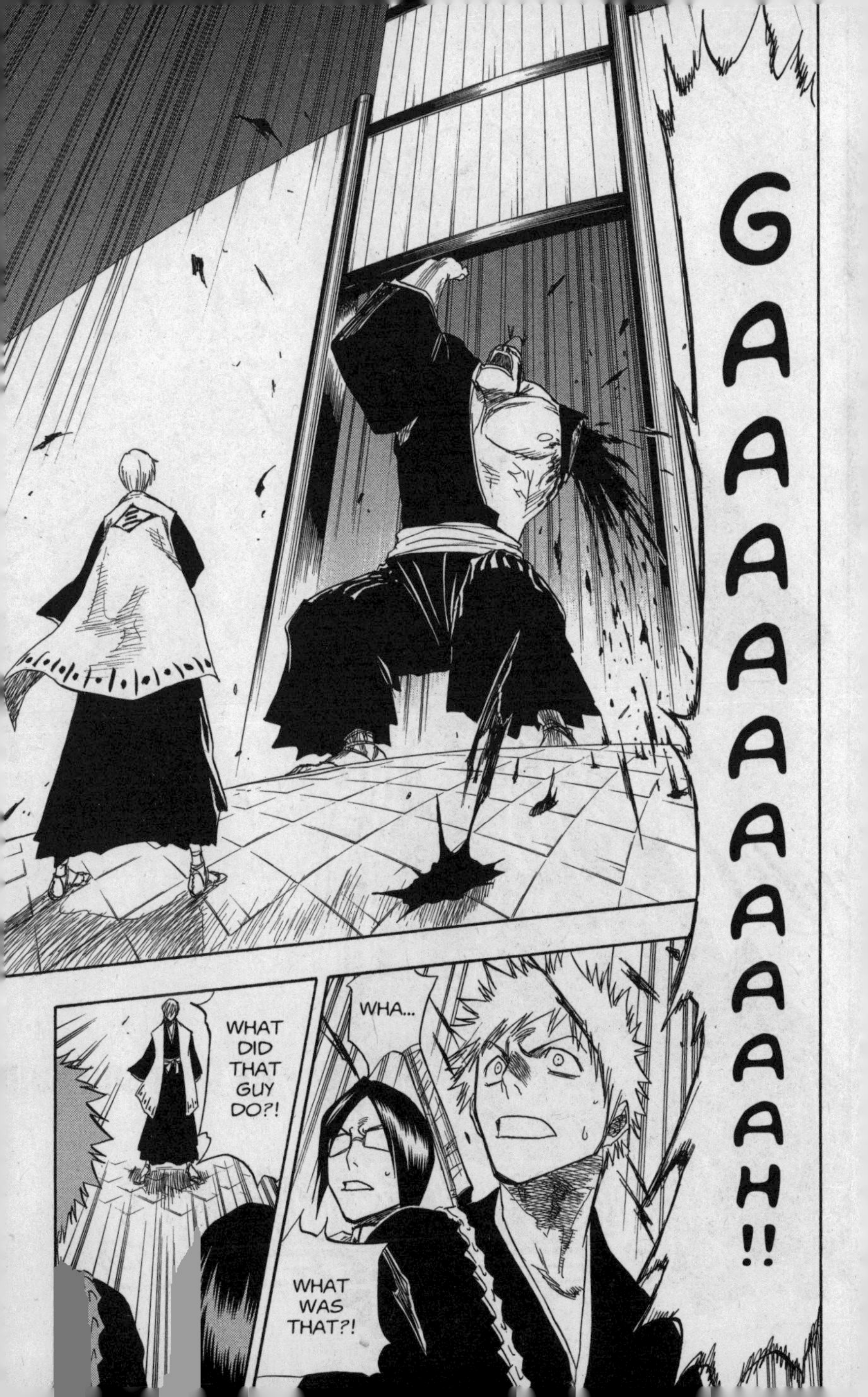
GAAAAAAAAAAAH!!
WHA...
WHAT DID THAT GUY DO?!
WHAT WAS THAT?!

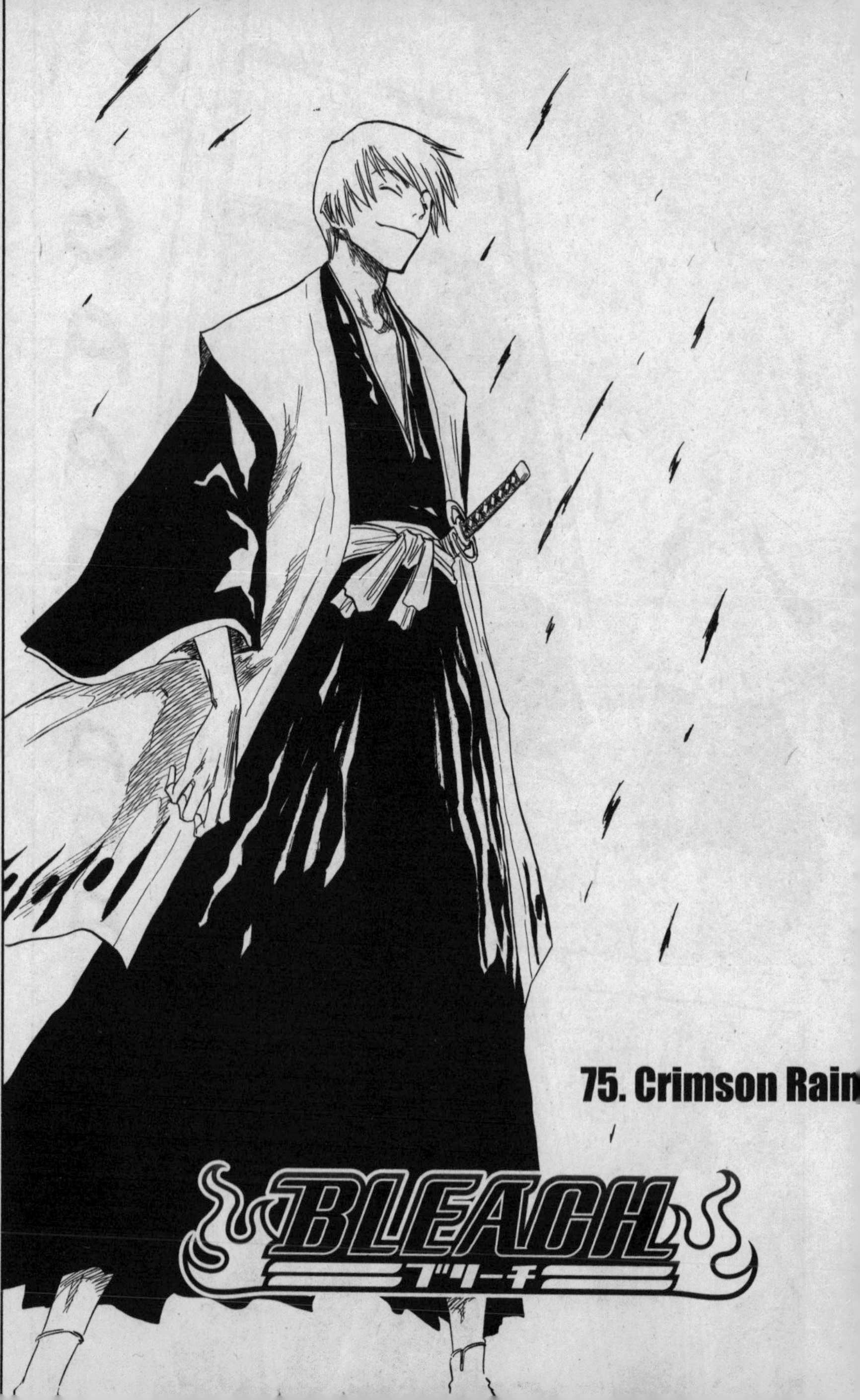
75. Crimson Rain
BLEACH
ブリーチ

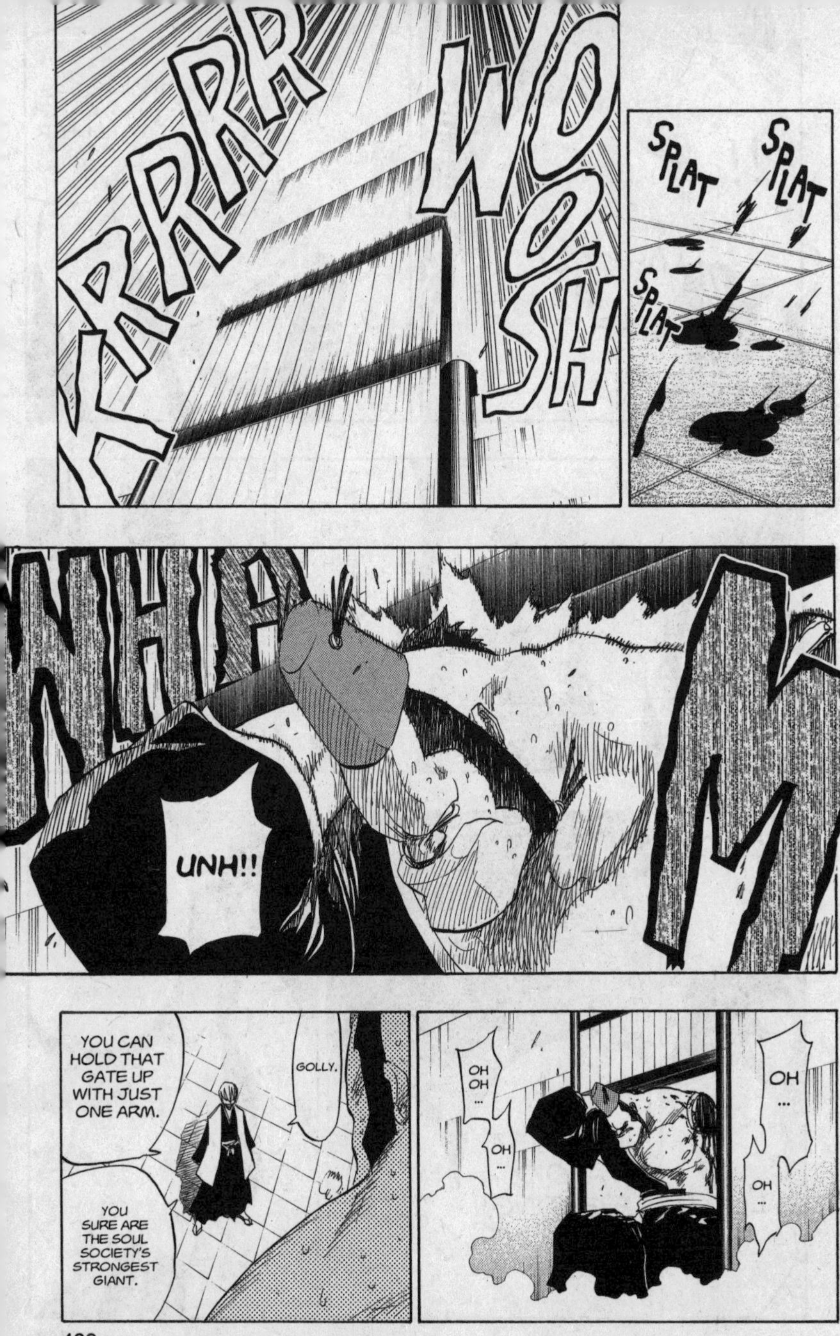
SPLAT
SPLAT
SPLAT
KRRRR
WOOSH
WHAM
UNH!!
OH ...
OH ...
OH OH ...
OH ...
GOLLY.
YOU CAN HOLD THAT GATE UP WITH JUST ONE ARM.
YOU SURE ARE THE SOUL SOCIETY'S STRONGEST GIANT.

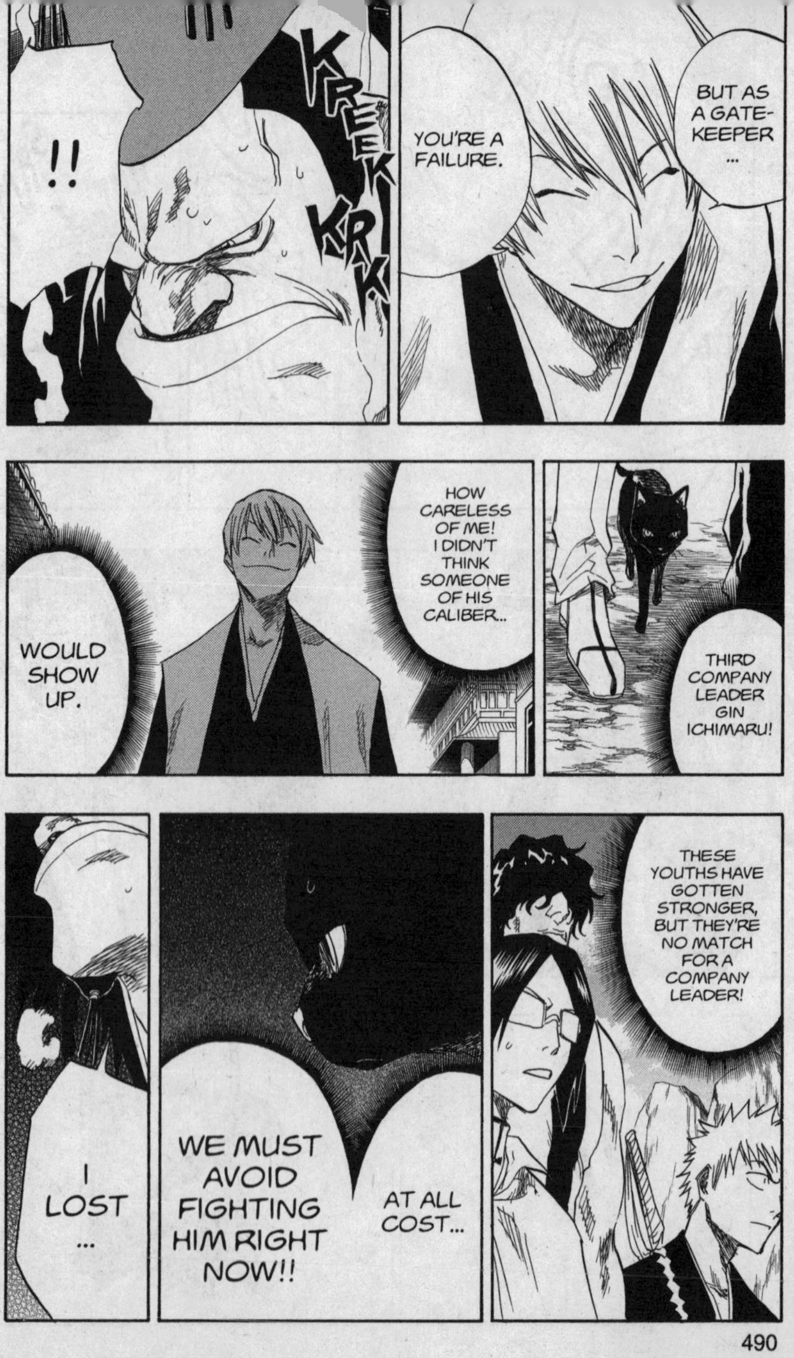
BUT AS A GATE-KEEPER ...
YOU'RE A FAILURE.
KREEK
KRK
!!
THIRD COMPANY LEADER GIN ICHIMARU!
HOW CARELESS OF ME! I DIDN'T THINK SOMEONE OF HIS CALIBER...
WOULD SHOW UP.
THESE YOUTHS HAVE GOTTEN STRONGER, BUT THEY'RE NO MATCH FOR A COMPANY LEADER!
AT ALL COST...
WE MUST AVOID FIGHTING HIM RIGHT NOW!!
I LOST ...

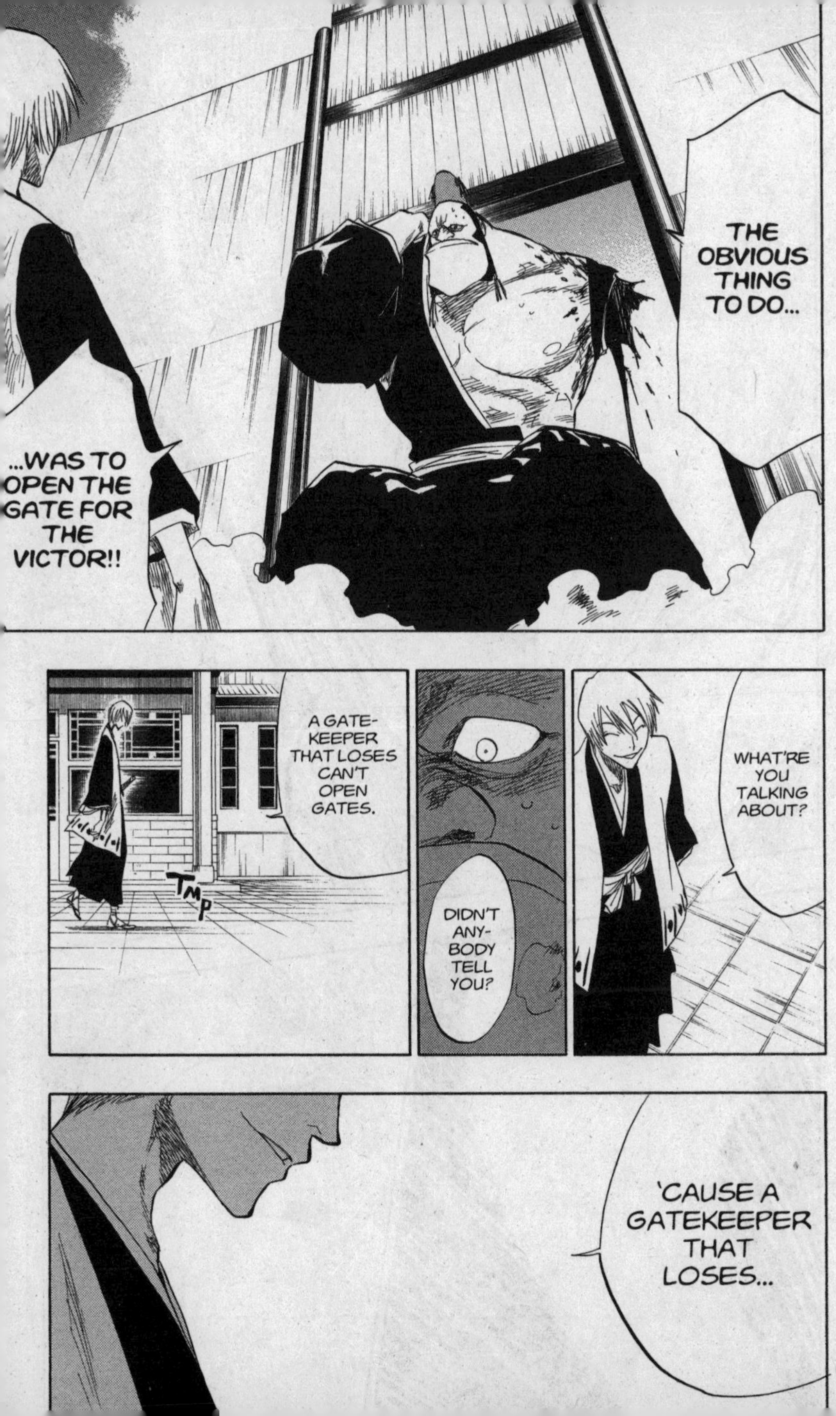
THE OBVIOUS THING TO DO...
...WAS TO OPEN THE GATE FOR THE VICTOR!!
WHAT'RE YOU TALKING ABOUT?
DIDN'T ANY-BODY TELL YOU?
A GATE-KEEPER THAT LOSES CAN'T OPEN GATES.
TMP
'CAUSE A GATEKEEPER THAT LOSES...

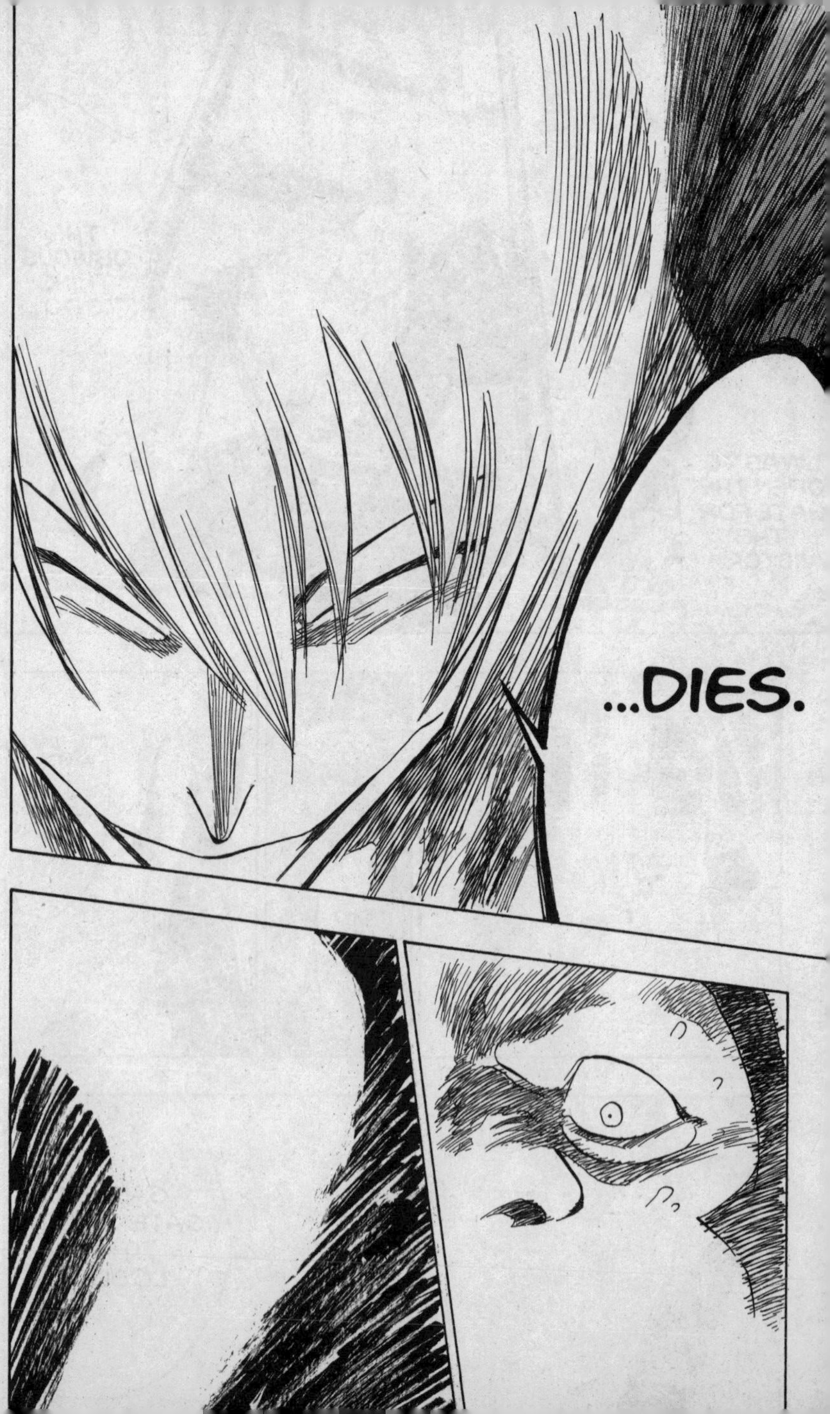
...DIES.

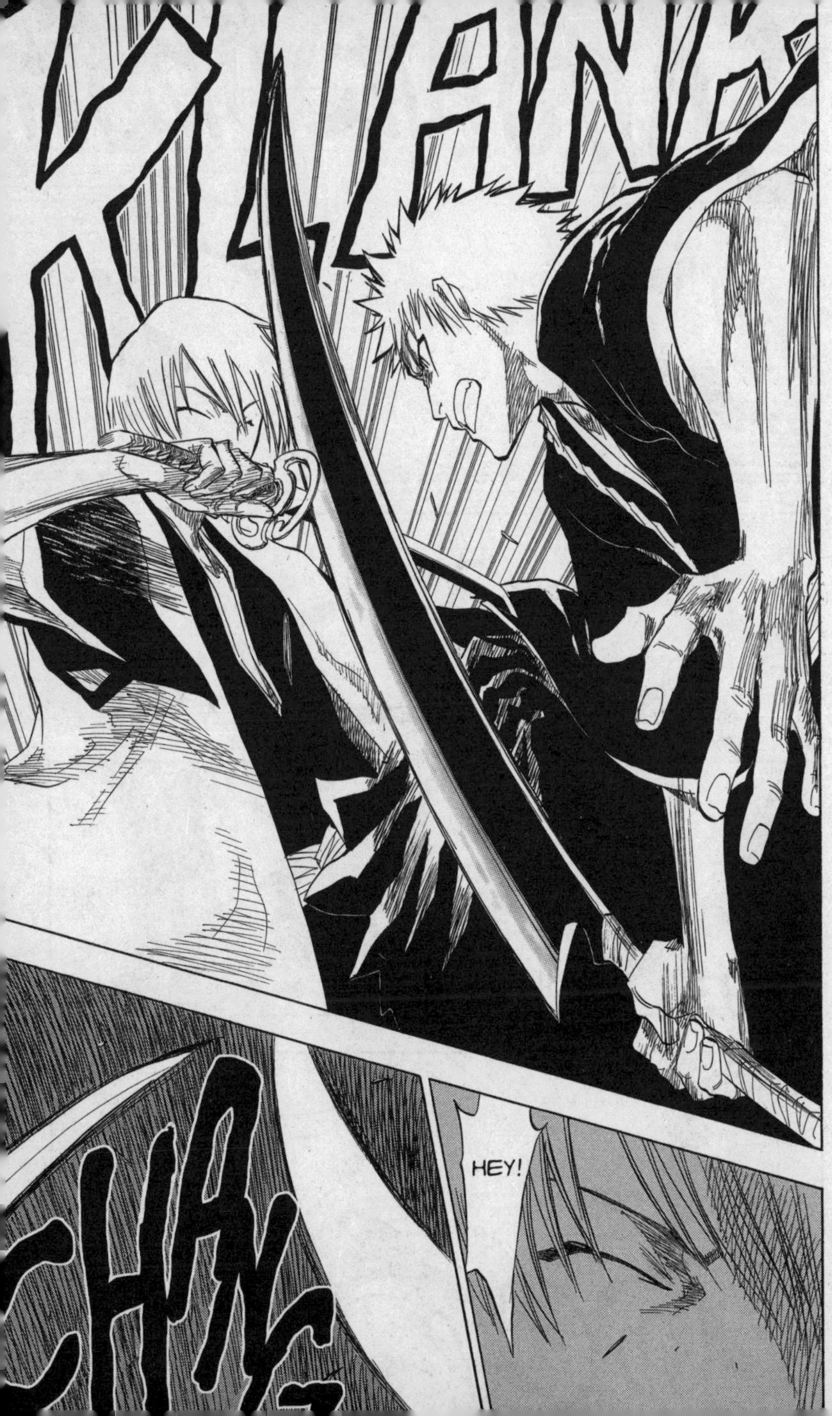
HEY!

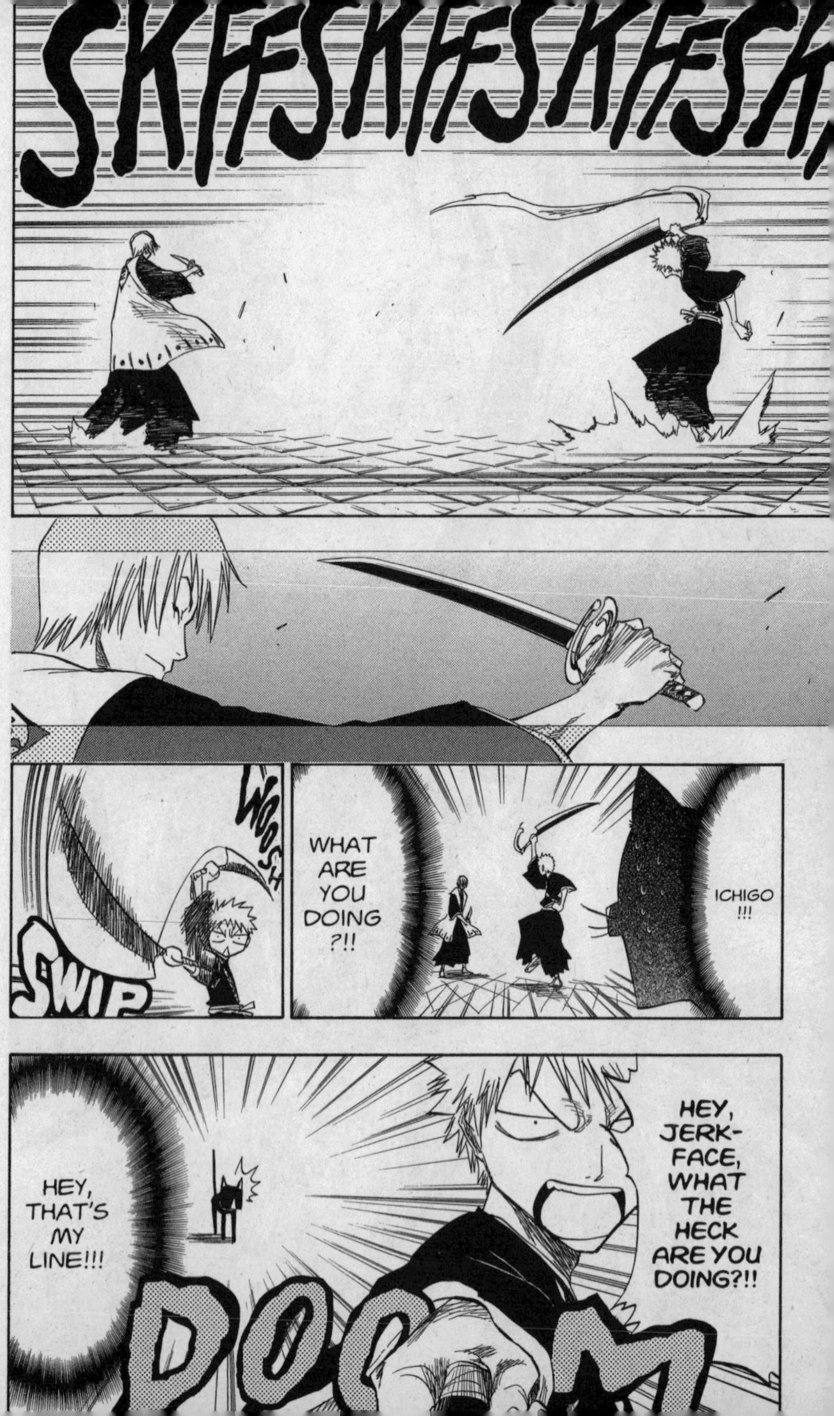
SKFSKFSKFSK
ICHIGO!!!
WHAT ARE YOU DOING?!!
WOOSH
SWIP
HEY, JERK-FACE, WHAT THE HECK ARE YOU DOING?!!
HEY, THAT'S MY LINE!!!
DOOM

READ THIS WAY

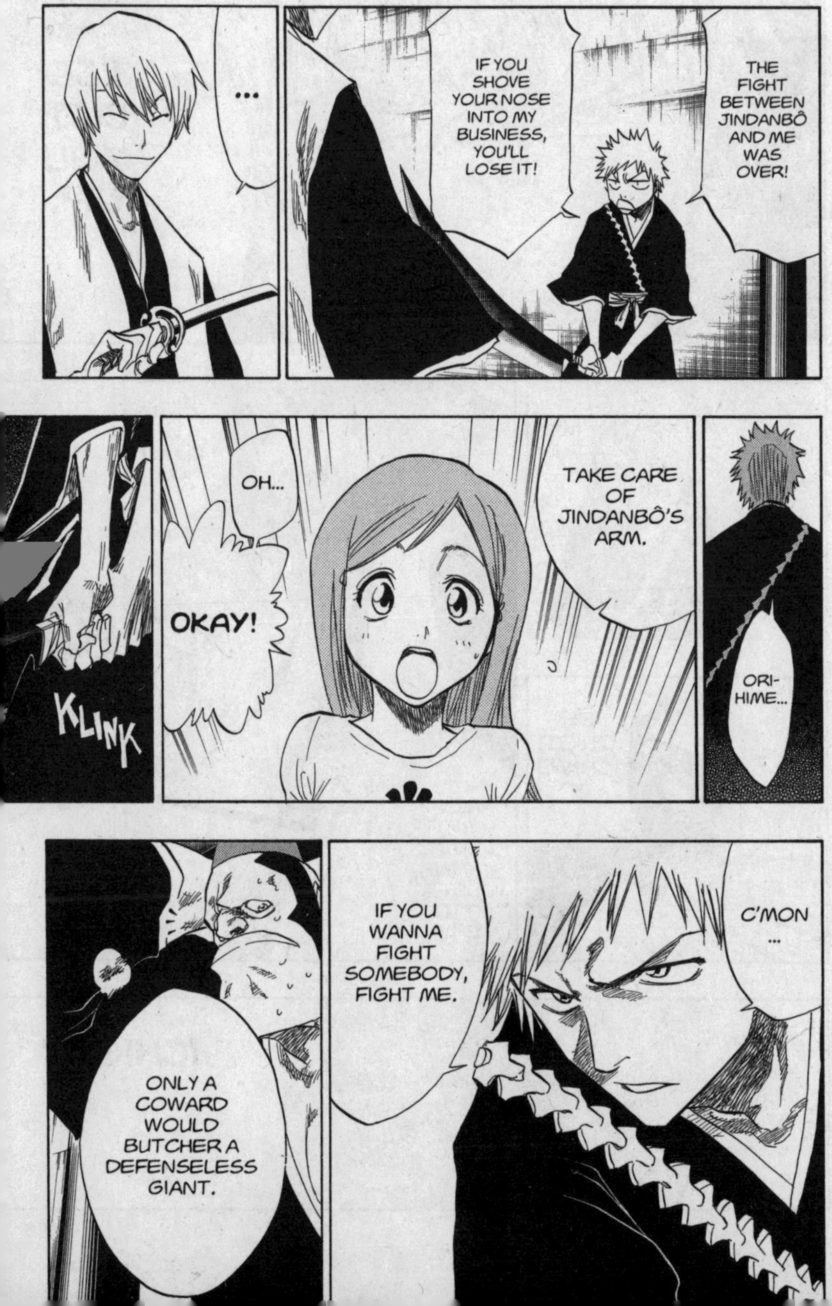

THE FIGHT BETWEEN JINDANBÔ AND ME WAS OVER!
IF YOU SHOVE YOUR NOSE INTO MY BUSINESS, YOU'LL LOSE IT!
...
ORI-HIME...
TAKE CARE OF JINDANBÔ'S ARM.
OH...
OKAY!
KLINK
C'MON ...
IF YOU WANNA FIGHT SOMEBODY, FIGHT ME.
ONLY A COWARD WOULD BUTCHER A DEFENSELESS GIANT.

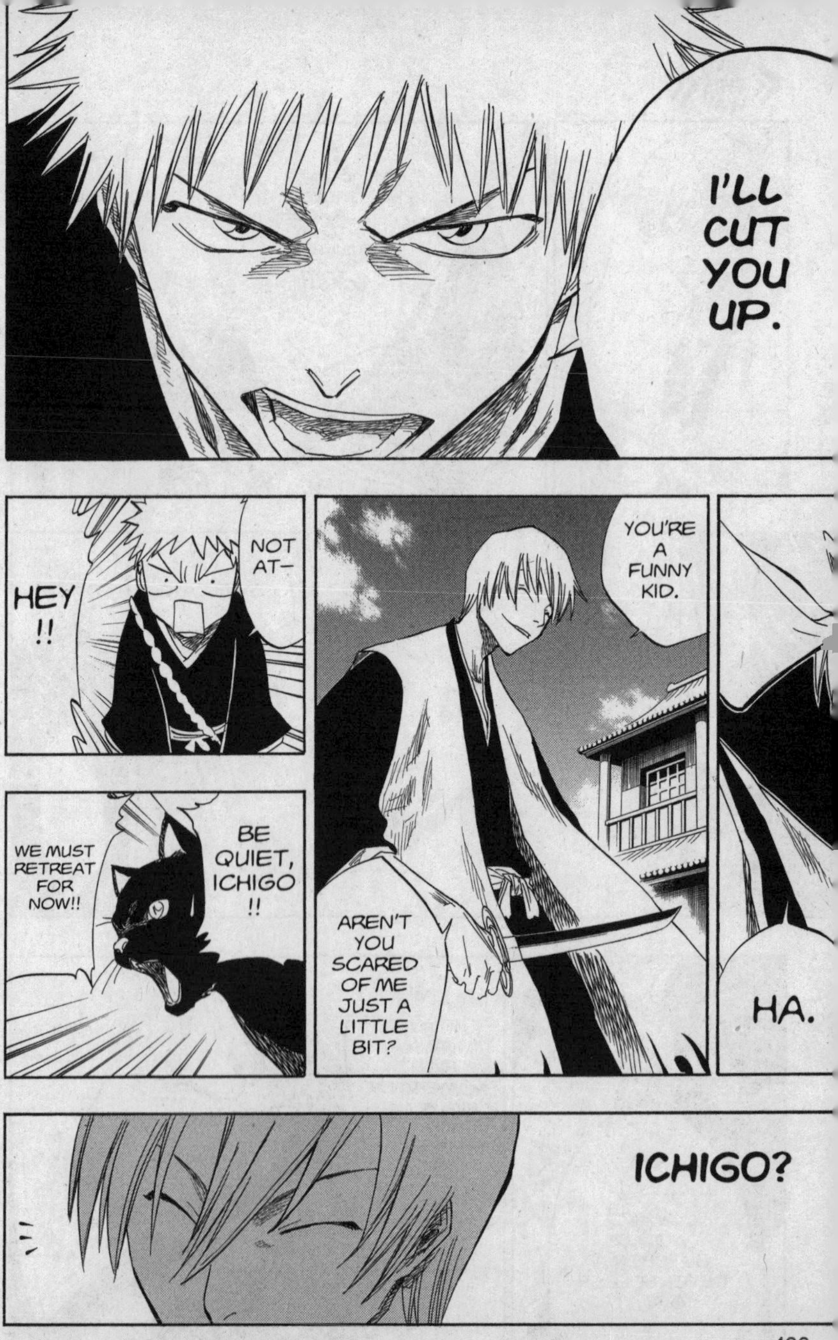
I'LL CUT YOU UP.
HA.
YOU'RE A FUNNY KID.
AREN'T YOU SCARED OF ME JUST A LITTLE BIT?
NOT AT—
HEY!!
BE QUIET, ICHIGO!!
WE MUST RETREAT FOR NOW!!
ICHIGO?

READ THIS WAY

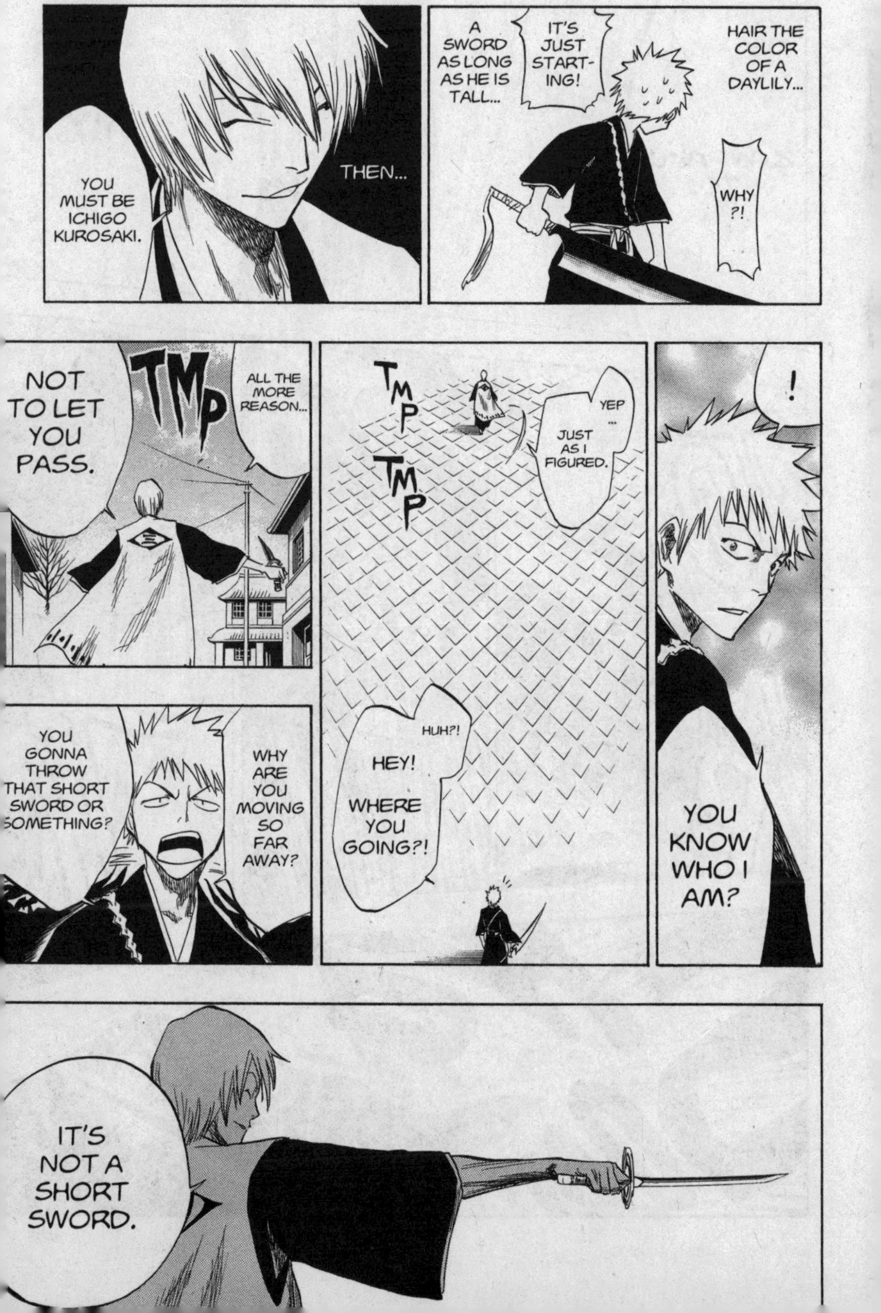
HAIR THE COLOR OF A DAYLILY...
A SWORD AS LONG AS HE IS TALL...
IT'S JUST START-ING!
WHY?!
THEN...
YOU MUST BE ICHIGO KUROSAKI.
!
YOU KNOW WHO I AM?
YEP... JUST AS I FIGURED.
TMP TMP
ALL THE MORE REASON...
NOT TO LET YOU PASS.
TMP
HUH?!
HEY! WHERE YOU GOING?!
WHY ARE YOU MOVING SO FAR AWAY?
YOU GONNA THROW THAT SHORT SWORD OR SOMETHING?
IT'S NOT A SHORT SWORD.

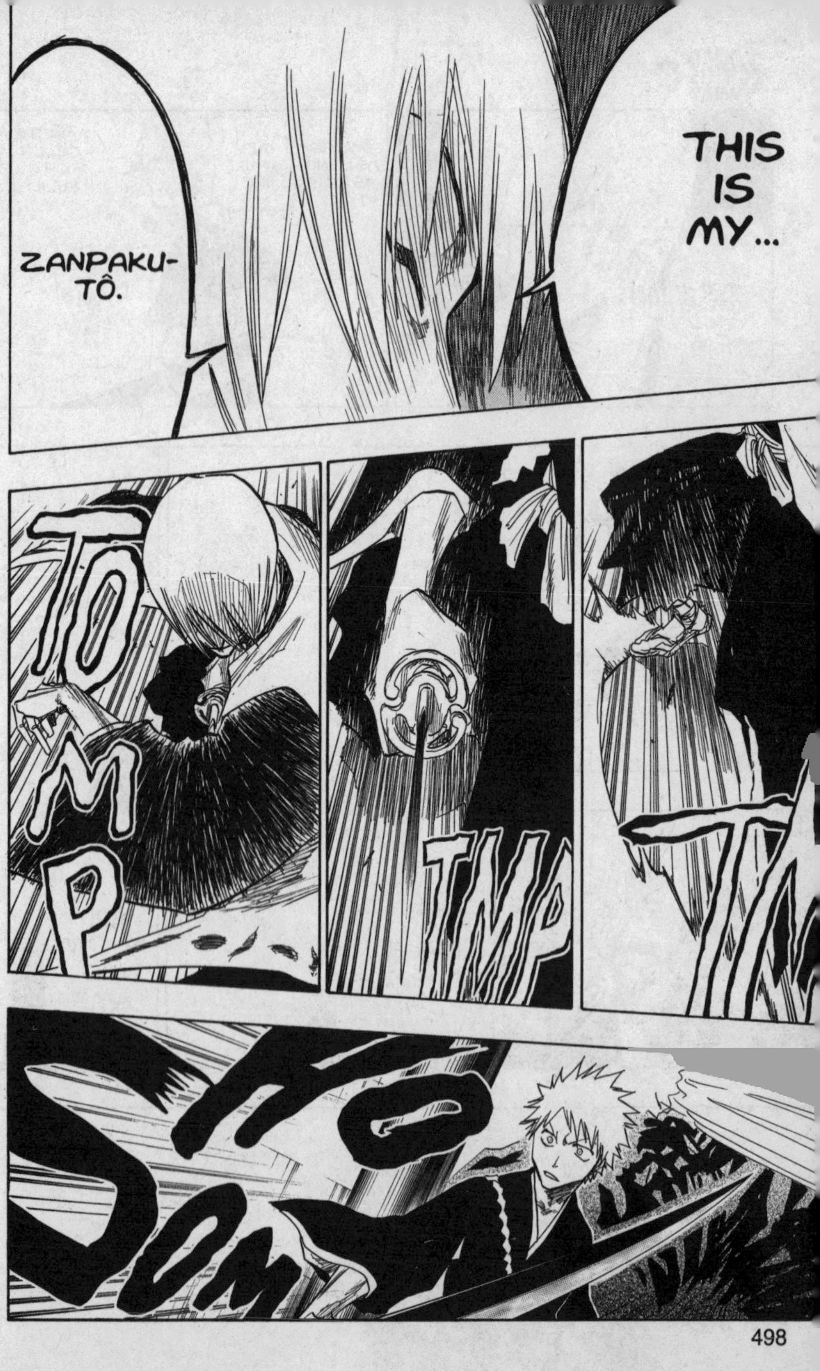
THIS IS MY...
ZANPAKU-TÔ.
TMP
TOMP

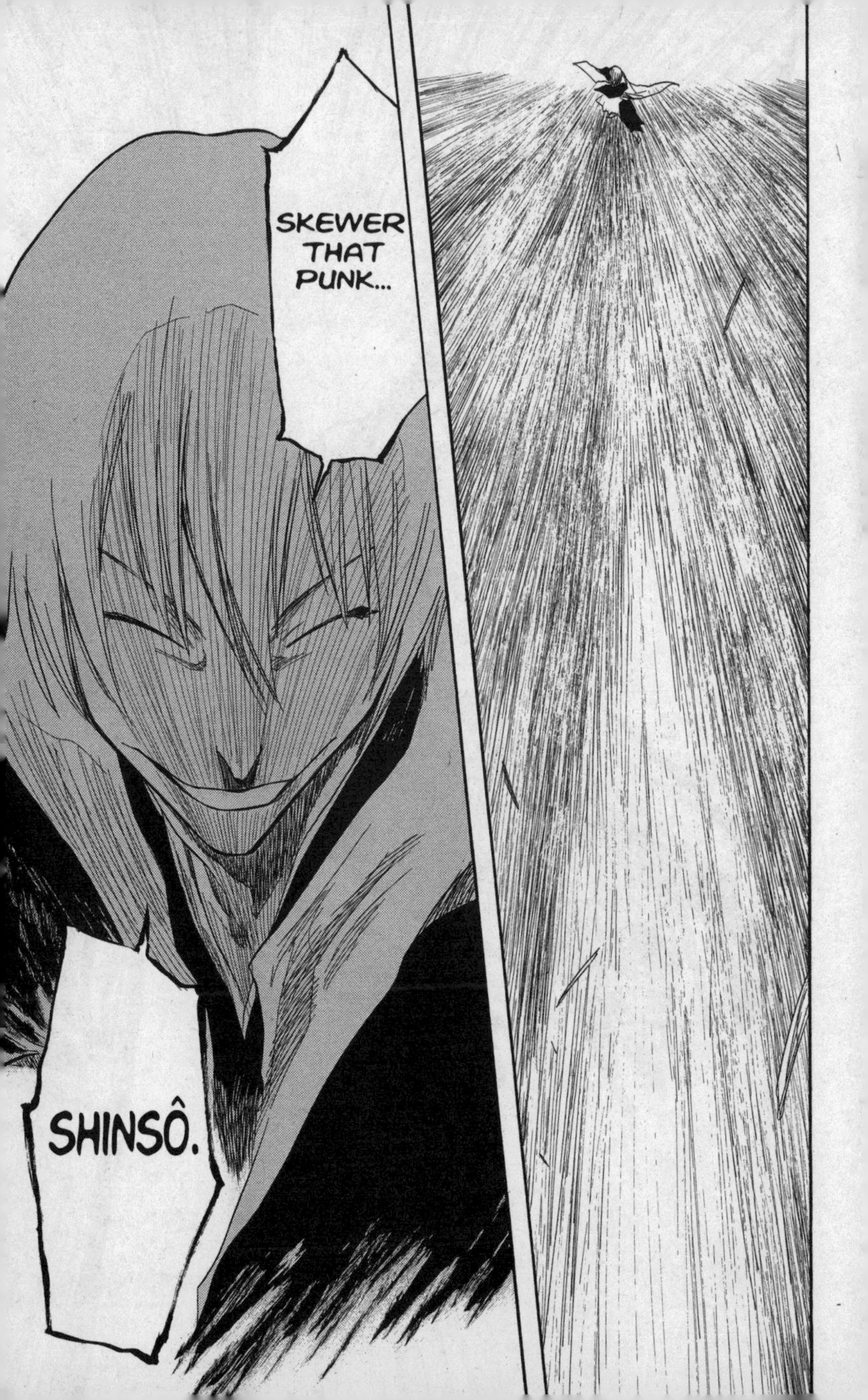
SKEWER THAT PUNK...
SHINSÔ.

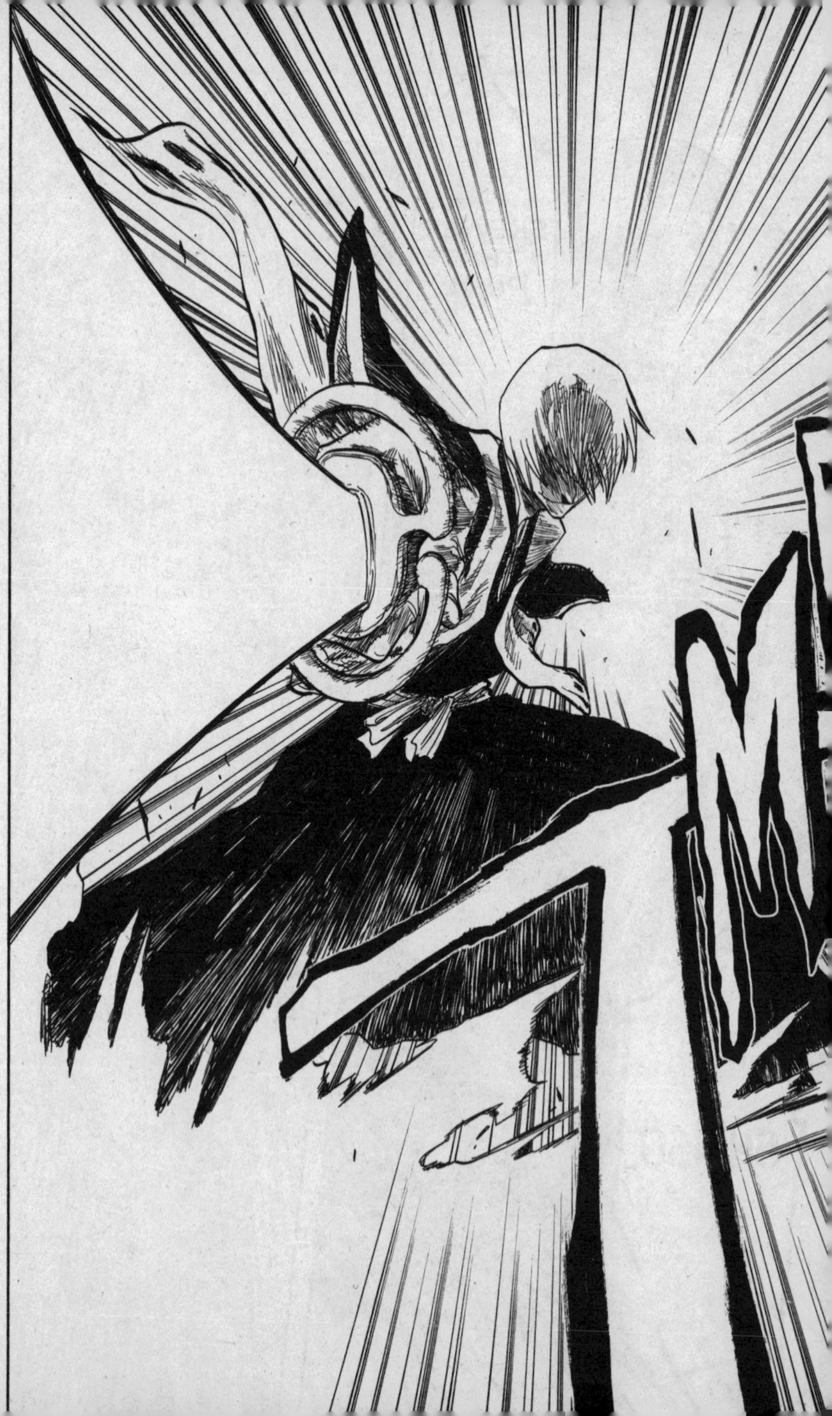

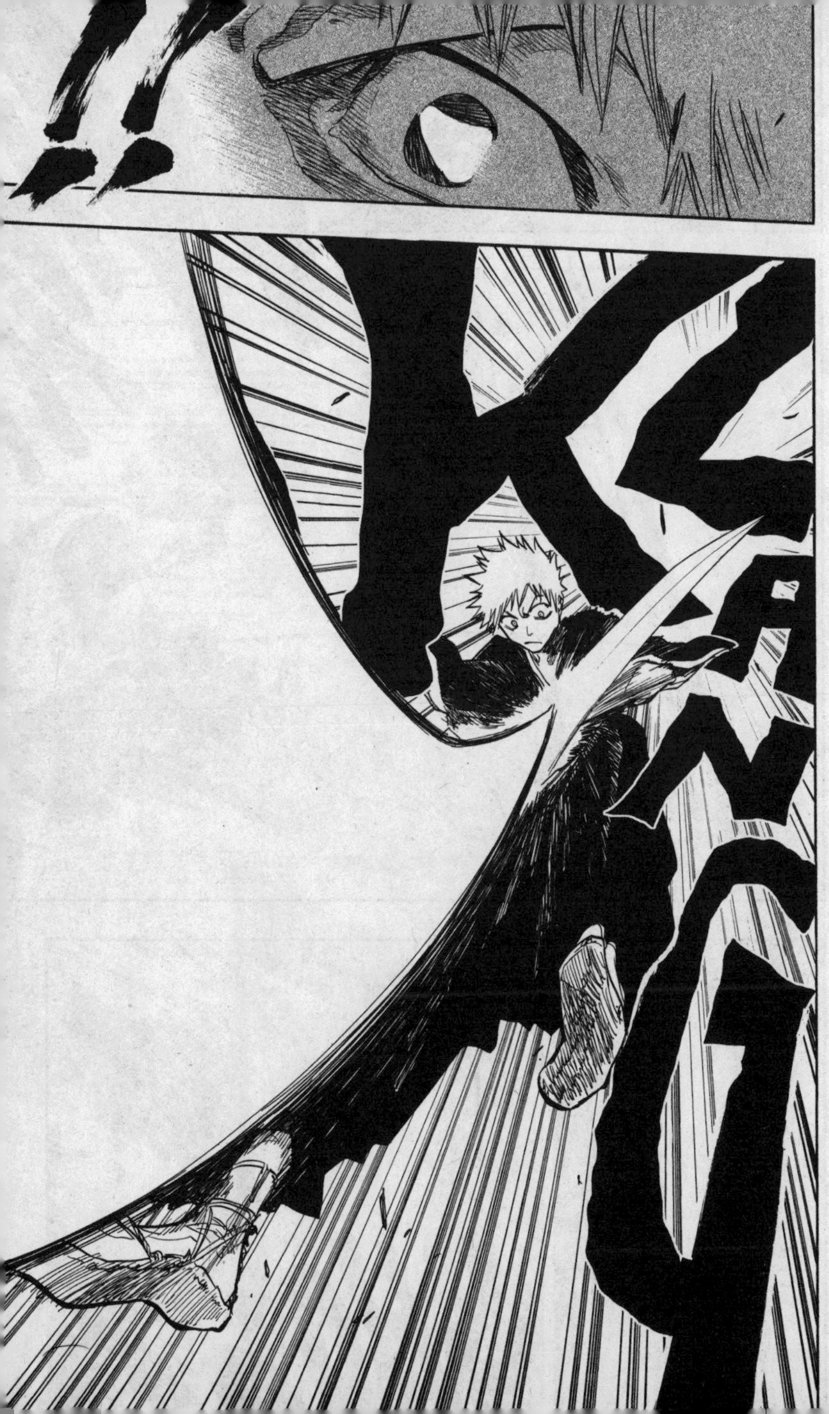
!!

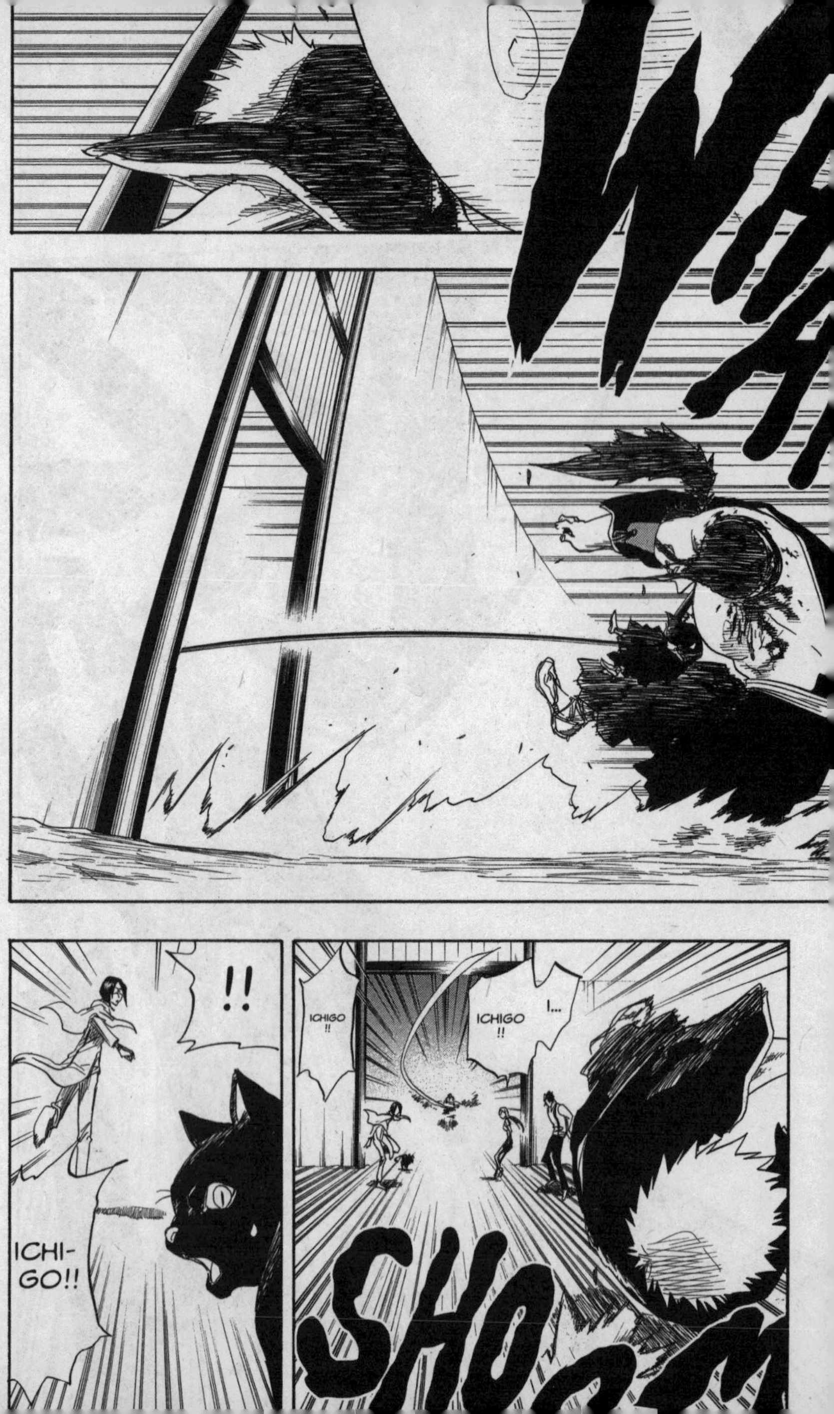
I...
ICHIGO !!
ICHIGO !!
!!
ICHI-GO!!

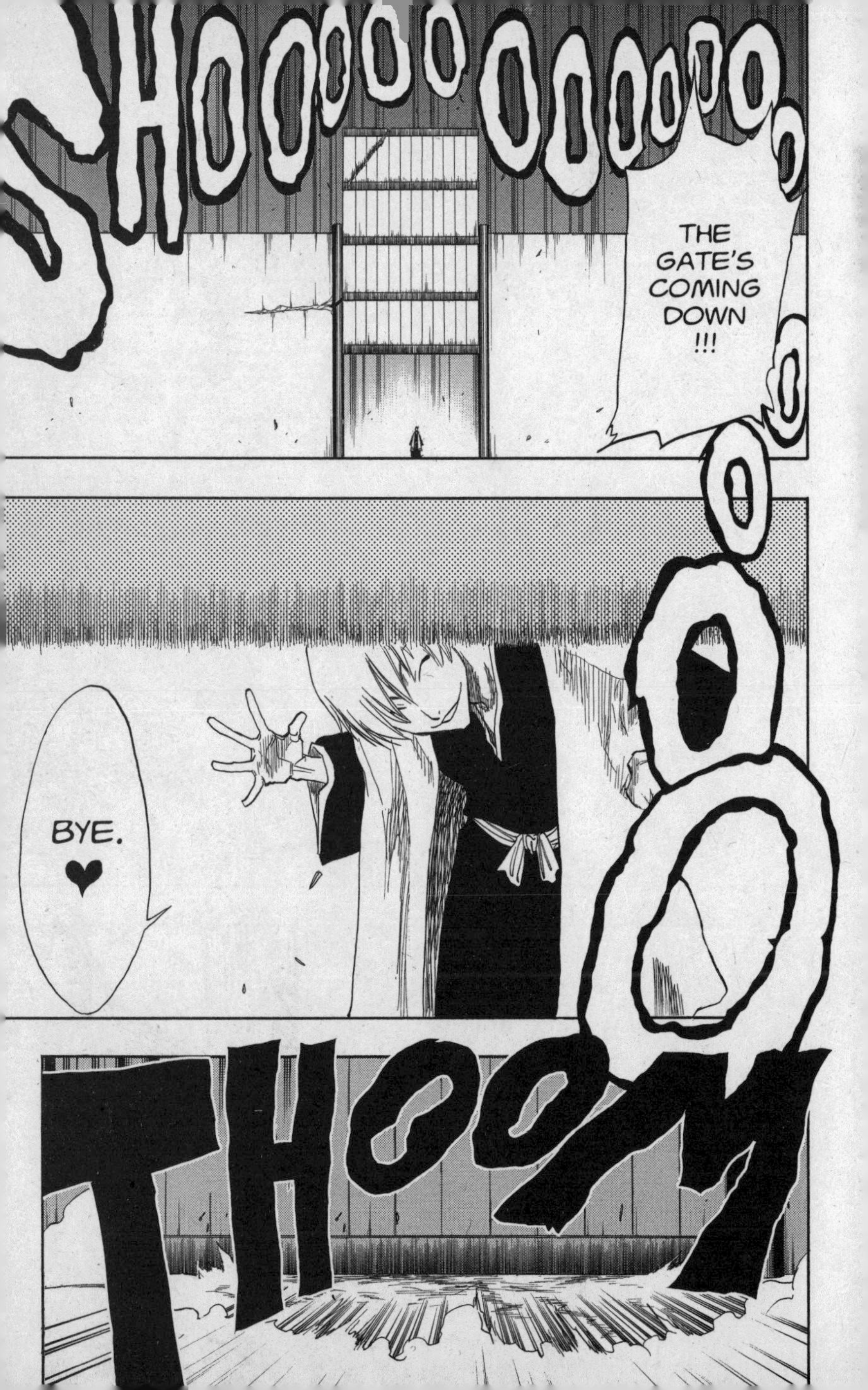
SHOOOOOOOOOOOO
THE GATE'S COMING DOWN!!!
BYE. ♥
THOOOM

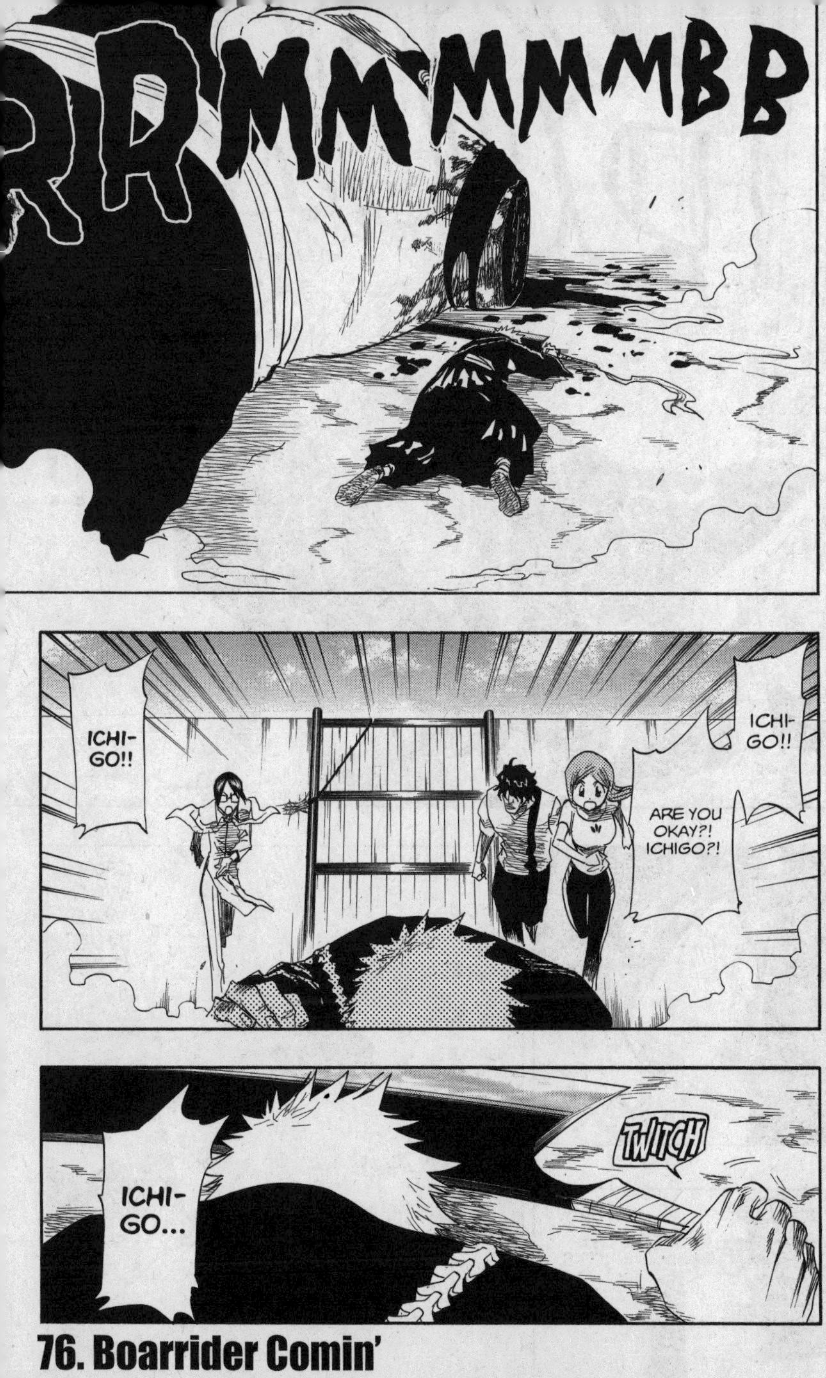
RRMMMMMMBB
ICHI-GO!!
ARE YOU OKAY?! ICHIGO?!
ICHI-GO!!
TWITCH
ICHI-GO...

76. Boarrider Comin'

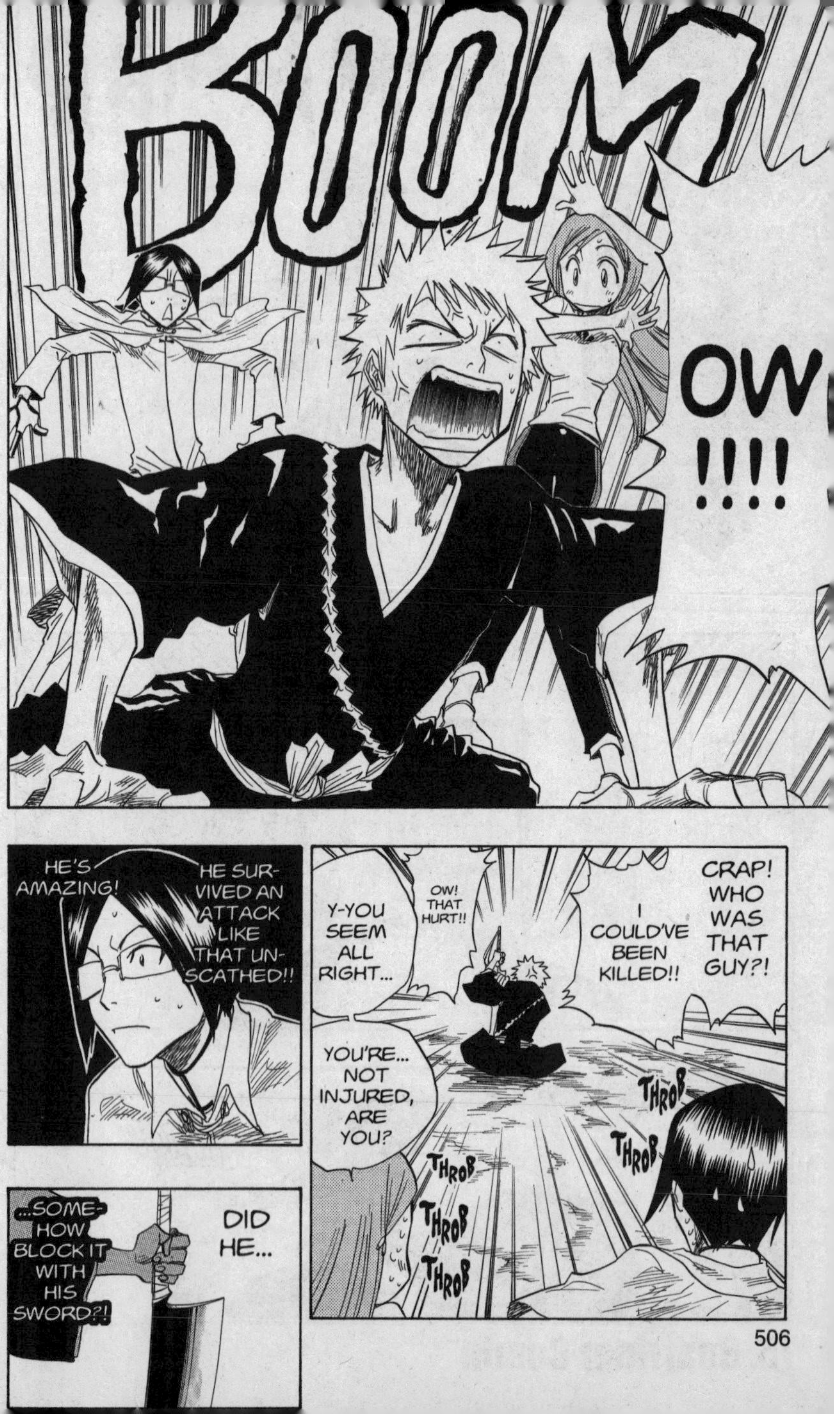
BOOM
OW !!!!
CRAP! WHO WAS THAT GUY?!
I COULD'VE BEEN KILLED!!
OW! THAT HURT!!
Y-YOU SEEM ALL RIGHT...
YOU'RE... NOT INJURED, ARE YOU?
THROB THROB THROB THROB THROB
HE SURVIVED AN ATTACK LIKE THAT UNSCATHED!!
HE'S AMAZING!
DID HE...
...SOMEHOW BLOCK IT WITH HIS SWORD?!

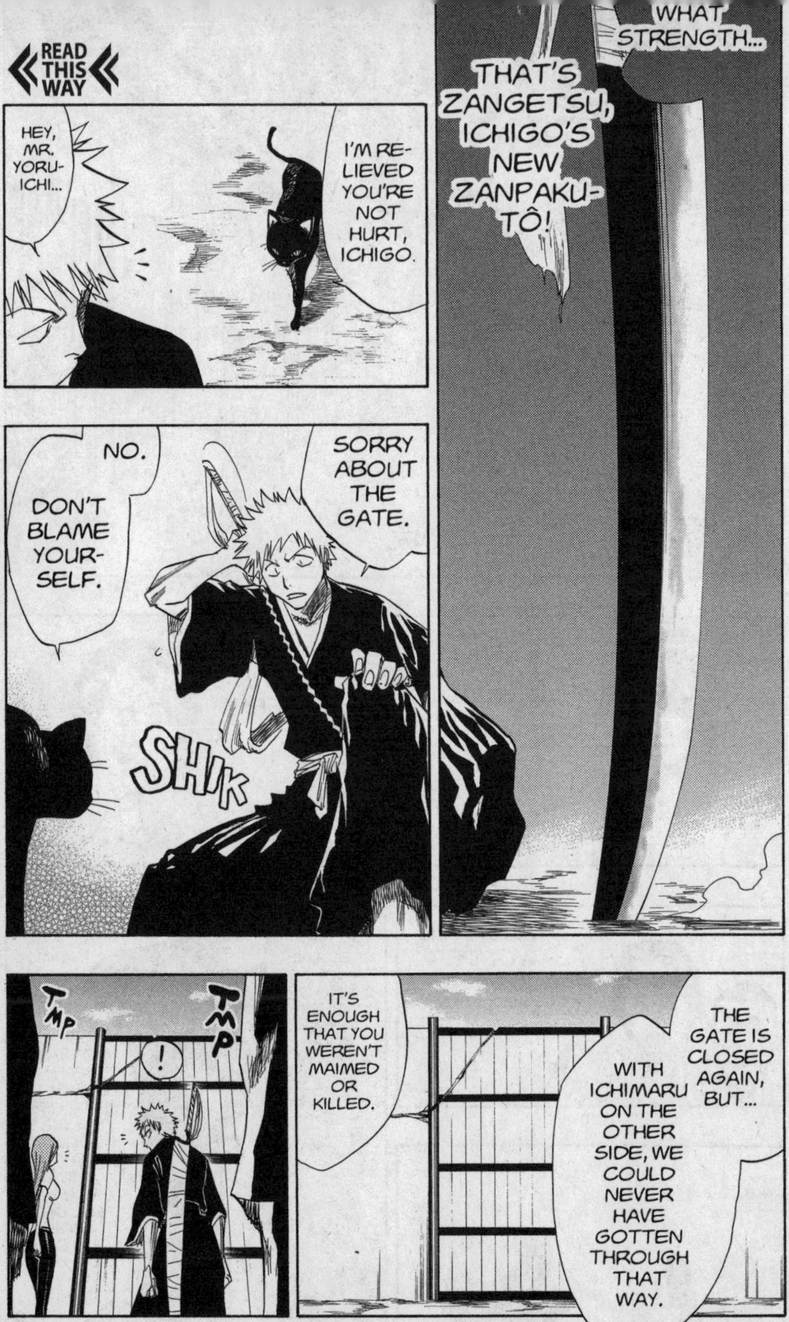
READ THIS WAY
WHAT STRENGTH...
THAT'S ZANGETSU, ICHIGO'S NEW ZANPAKU-TÔ!
I'M RE-LIEVED YOU'RE NOT HURT, ICHIGO.
HEY, MR. YORU-ICHI...
SORRY ABOUT THE GATE.
NO.
DON'T BLAME YOUR-SELF.
SHIK
THE GATE IS CLOSED AGAIN, BUT...
WITH ICHIMARU ON THE OTHER SIDE, WE COULD NEVER HAVE GOTTEN THROUGH THAT WAY.
IT'S ENOUGH THAT YOU WEREN'T MAIMED OR KILLED.
TMP
TMP
!

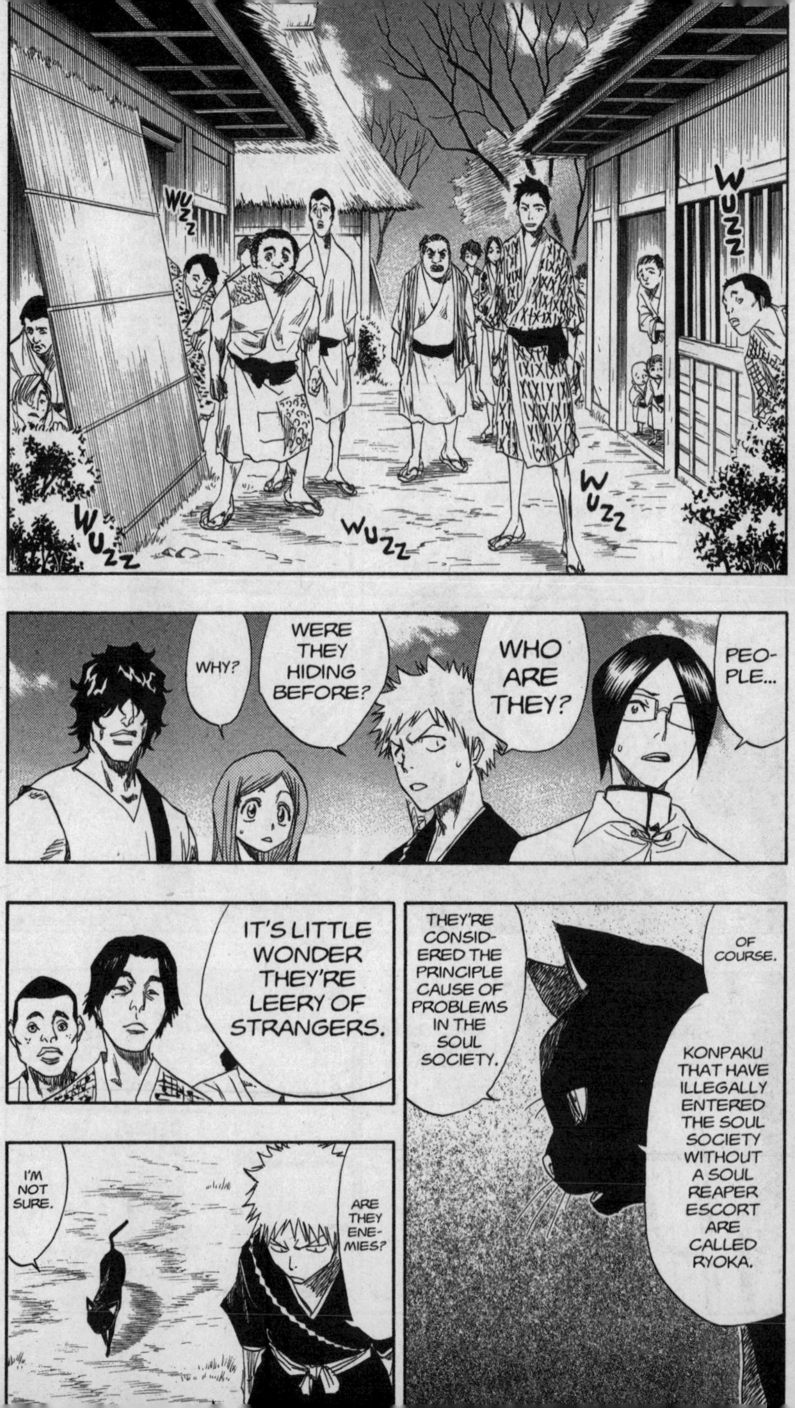
WUZZ
WUZZ
WUZZ
WUZZ
WUZZ
PEO-PLE...
WHO ARE THEY?
WERE THEY HIDING BEFORE?
WHY?
OF COURSE.
KONPAKU THAT HAVE ILLEGALLY ENTERED THE SOUL SOCIETY WITHOUT A SOUL REAPER ESCORT ARE CALLED RYOKA.
THEY'RE CONSIDERED THE PRINCIPLE CAUSE OF PROBLEMS IN THE SOUL SOCIETY.
IT'S LITTLE WONDER THEY'RE LEERY OF STRANGERS.
ARE THEY ENEMIES?
I'M NOT SURE.

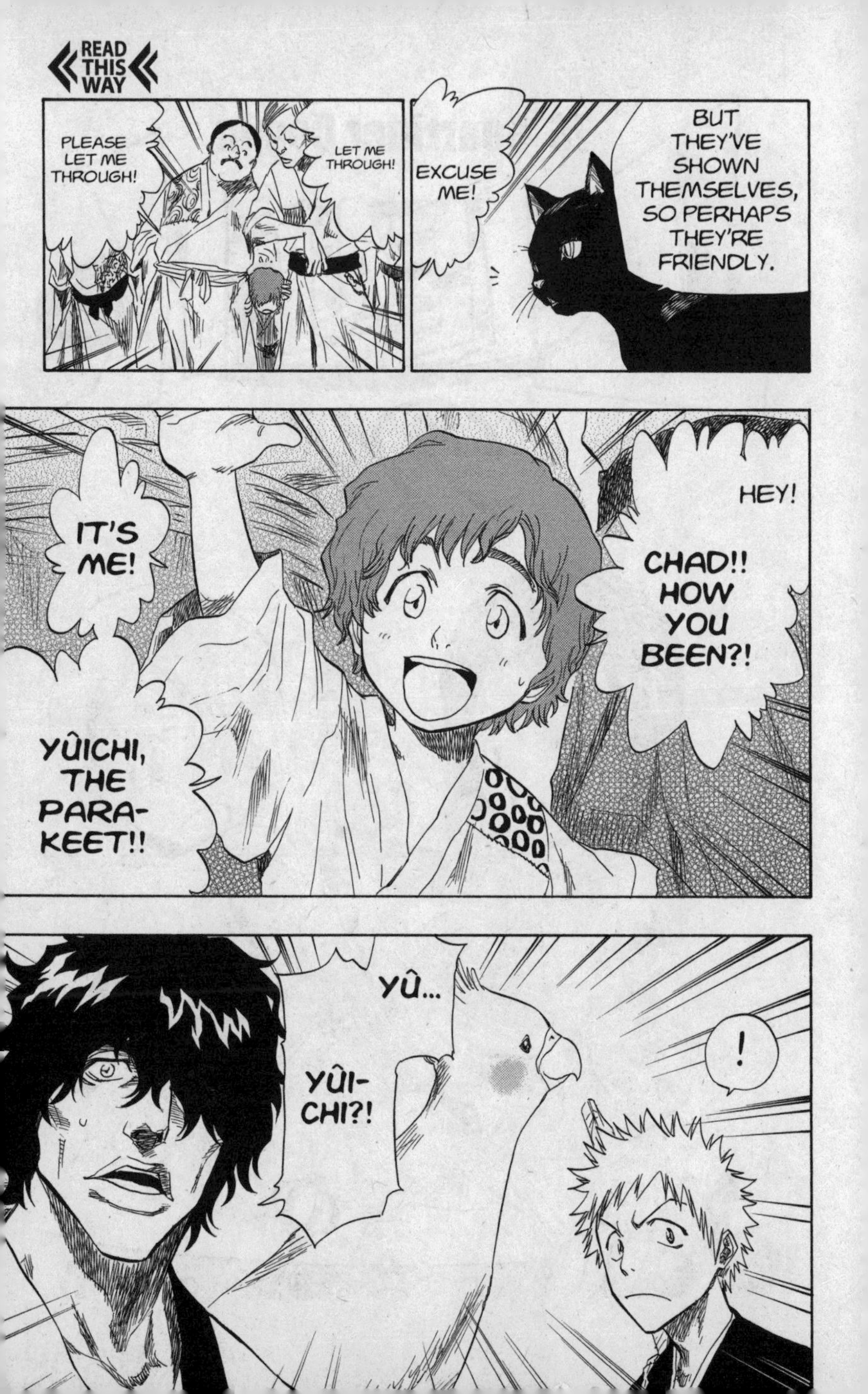
READ THIS WAY
BUT THEY'VE SHOWN THEMSELVES, SO PERHAPS THEY'RE FRIENDLY.
EXCUSE ME!
LET ME THROUGH!
PLEASE LET ME THROUGH!
HEY!
CHAD!! HOW YOU BEEN?!
IT'S ME!
YÛICHI, THE PARA-KEET!!
!
YÛ...
YÛI-CHI?!

76. Boarrider Comin'

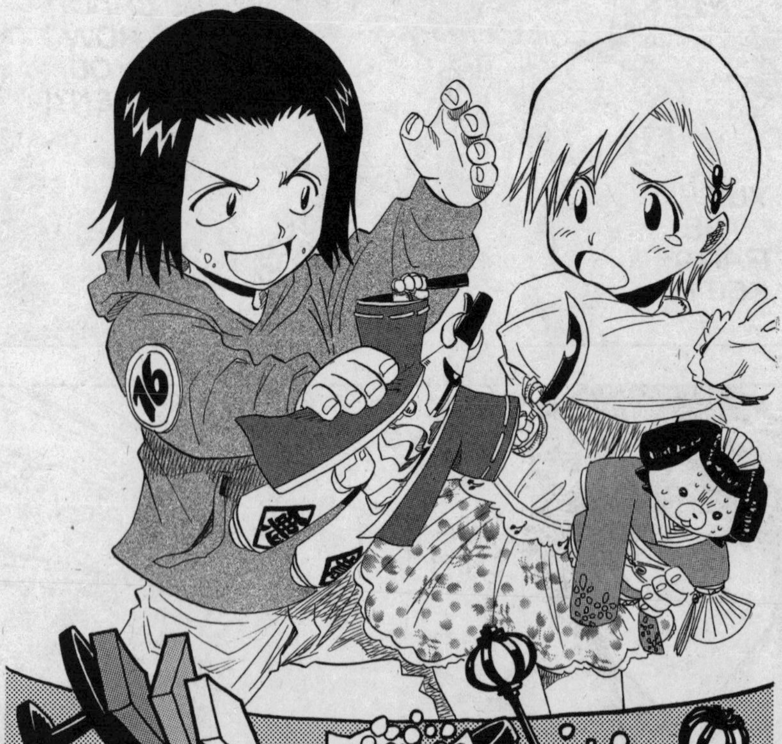

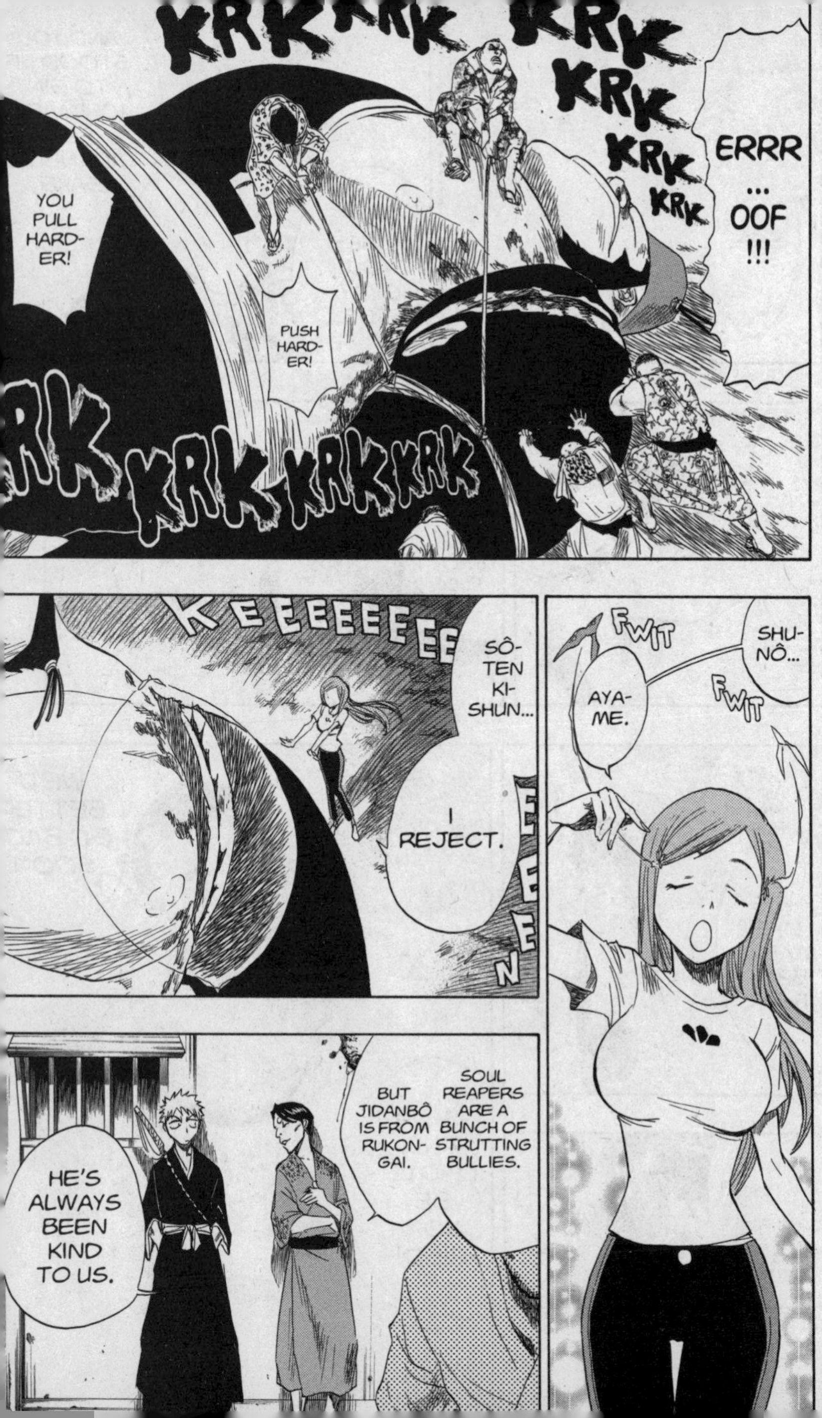

KRKKRK KRK
KRK
KRK
KRK
ERRR ... OOF !!!
YOU PULL HARDER!
PUSH HARDER!
KRK KRK KRKKRK
SHUNÔ...
AYAME.
FWIT
FWIT
SÔTEN KISHUN...
I REJECT.
KEEEEEEEEEEEEN
SOUL REAPERS ARE A BUNCH OF STRUTTING BULLIES.
BUT JIDANBÔ IS FROM RUKONGAI.
HE'S ALWAYS BEEN KIND TO US.

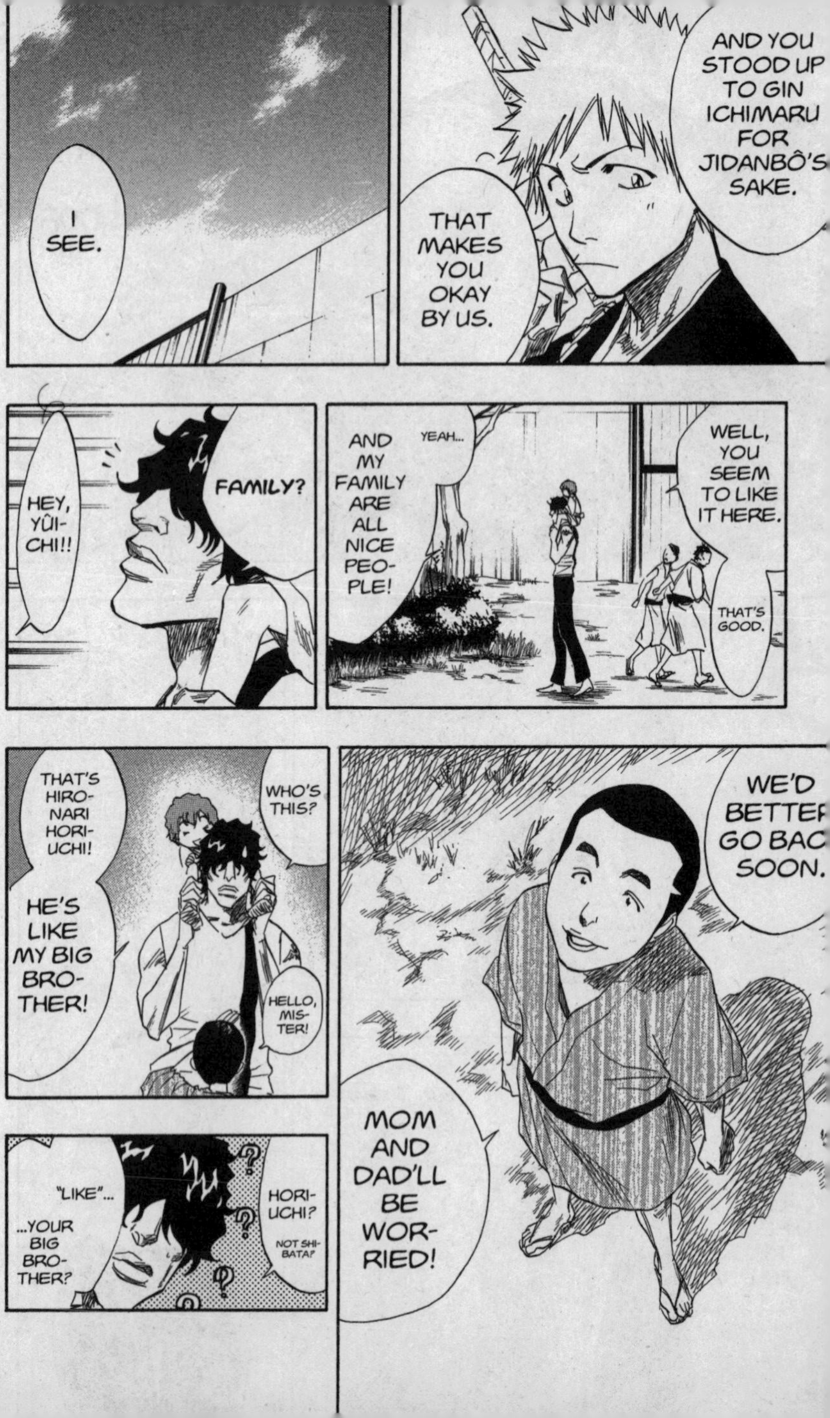
AND YOU STOOD UP TO GIN ICHIMARU FOR JIDANBÔ'S SAKE.
THAT MAKES YOU OKAY BY US.
I SEE.
WELL, YOU SEEM TO LIKE IT HERE.
THAT'S GOOD.
YEAH...
AND MY FAMILY ARE ALL NICE PEOPLE!
FAMILY?
HEY, YÛICHI!!
WE'D BETTE GO BAC SOON.
MOM AND DAD'LL BE WORRIED!
WHO'S THIS?
THAT'S HIRONARI HORIUCHI!
HE'S LIKE MY BIG BROTHER!
HELLO, MISTER!
HORIUCHI?
NOT SHIBATA?
"LIKE"...
...YOUR BIG BROTHER?

READ THIS WAY

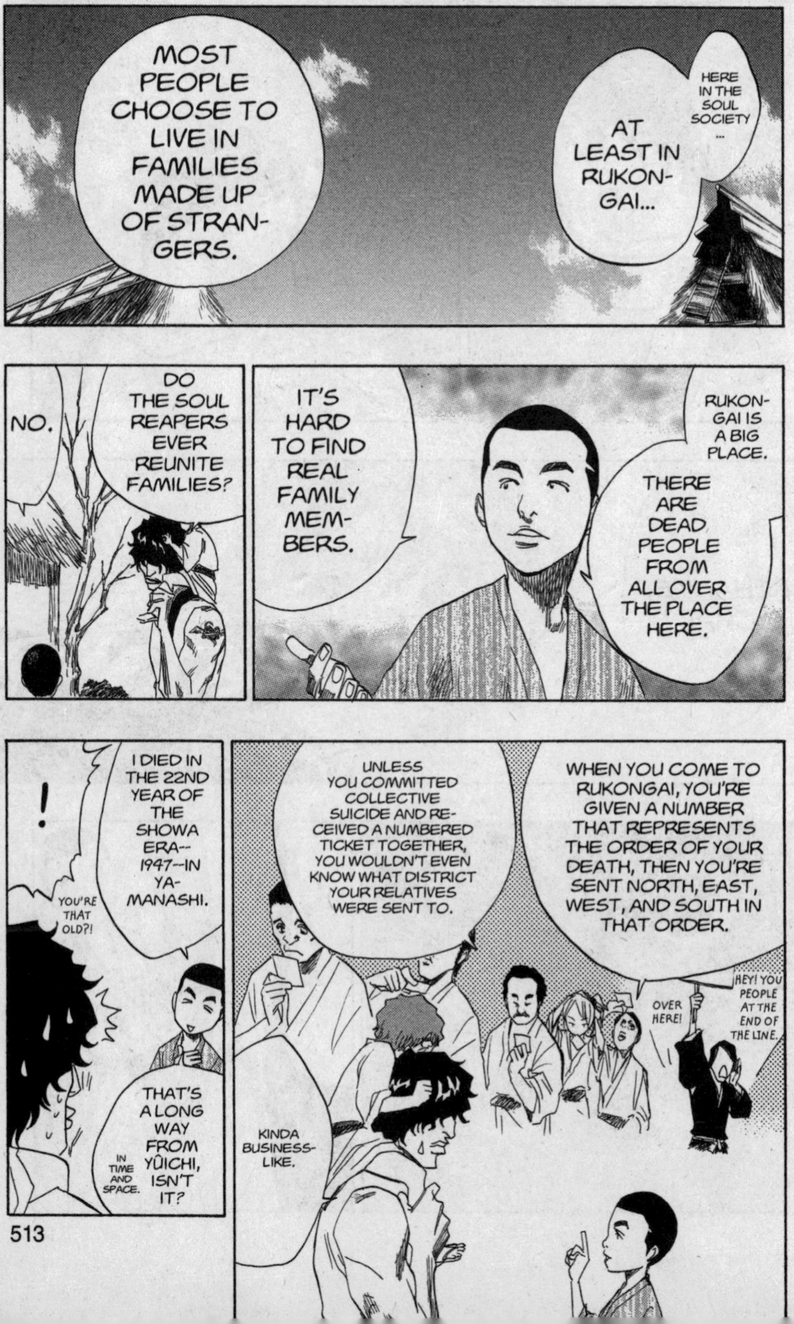
HERE IN THE SOUL SOCIETY...
AT LEAST IN RUKON-GAI...
MOST PEOPLE CHOOSE TO LIVE IN FAMILIES MADE UP OF STRAN-GERS.
RUKON-GAI IS A BIG PLACE.
THERE ARE DEAD PEOPLE FROM ALL OVER THE PLACE HERE.
IT'S HARD TO FIND REAL FAMILY MEM-BERS.
DO THE SOUL REAPERS EVER REUNITE FAMILIES?
NO.
WHEN YOU COME TO RUKONGAI, YOU'RE GIVEN A NUMBER THAT REPRESENTS THE ORDER OF YOUR DEATH, THEN YOU'RE SENT NORTH, EAST, WEST, AND SOUTH IN THAT ORDER.
UNLESS YOU COMMITTED COLLECTIVE SUICIDE AND RE-CEIVED A NUMBERED TICKET TOGETHER, YOU WOULDN'T EVEN KNOW WHAT DISTRICT YOUR RELATIVES WERE SENT TO.
HEY! YOU PEOPLE AT THE END OF THE LINE.
OVER HERE!
KINDA BUSINESS-LIKE.
I DIED IN THE 22ND YEAR OF THE SHOWA ERA--1947--IN YA-MANASHI.
!
YOU'RE THAT OLD?!
THAT'S A LONG WAY FROM YÛICHI, ISN'T IT?
IN TIME AND SPACE.

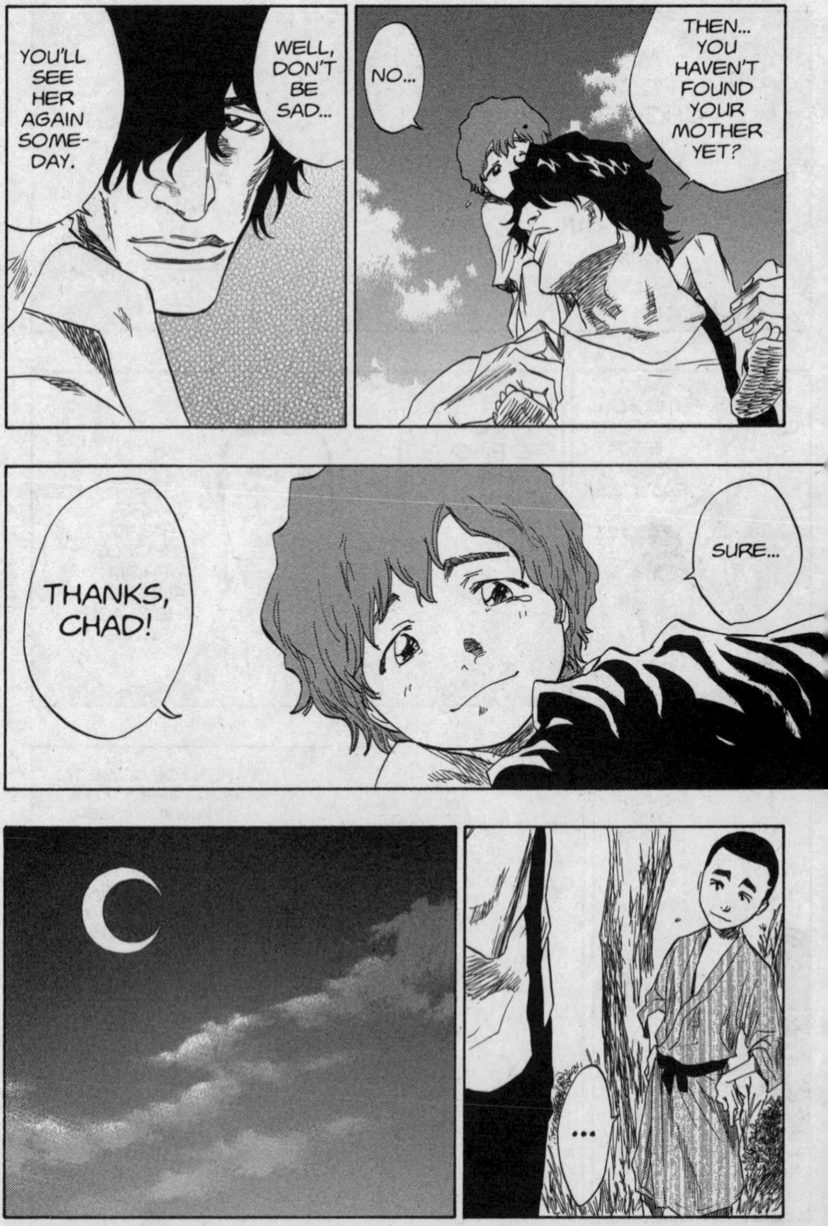
THEN... YOU HAVEN'T FOUND YOUR MOTHER YET?
NO...
WELL, DON'T BE SAD...
YOU'LL SEE HER AGAIN SOME-DAY.
SURE...
THANKS, CHAD!
...

READ THIS WAY

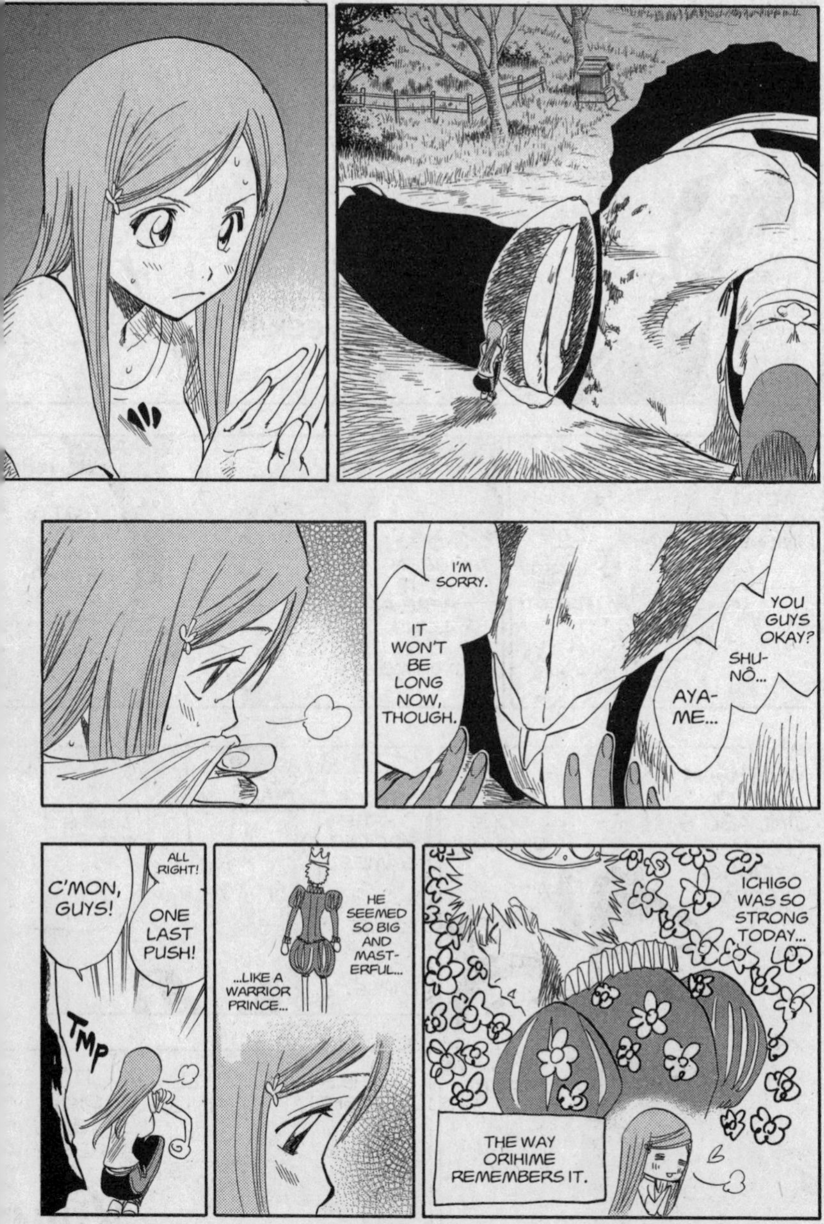
YOU GUYS OKAY?
SHU-NÔ...
AYA-ME...
I'M SORRY.
IT WON'T BE LONG NOW, THOUGH.
ICHIGO WAS SO STRONG TODAY...
THE WAY ORIHIME REMEMBERS IT.
HE SEEMED SO BIG AND MASTERFUL...
...LIKE A WARRIOR PRINCE...
ALL RIGHT!
ONE LAST PUSH!
C'MON, GUYS!
TMP

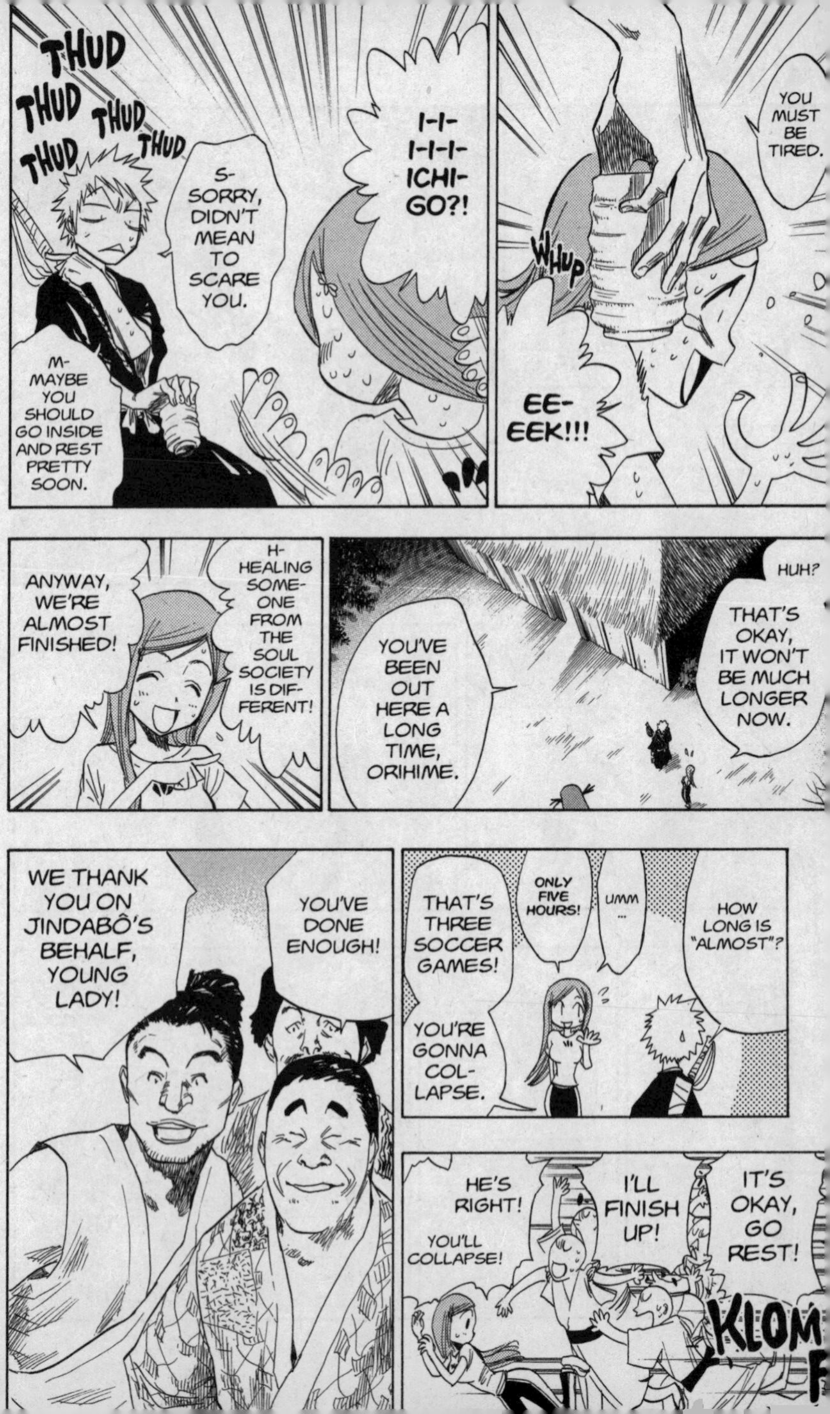
YOU MUST BE TIRED.
WHUP
EE-EEK!!!
I-I-I-I-I-ICHI-GO?!
THUD THUD THUD THUD THUD
S-SORRY, DIDN'T MEAN TO SCARE YOU.
M-MAYBE YOU SHOULD GO INSIDE AND REST PRETTY SOON.
YOU'VE BEEN OUT HERE A LONG TIME, ORIHIME.
HUH?
THAT'S OKAY, IT WON'T BE MUCH LONGER NOW.
H-HEALING SOMEONE FROM THE SOUL SOCIETY IS DIFFERENT!
ANYWAY, WE'RE ALMOST FINISHED!
HOW LONG IS "ALMOST"?
UMM...
ONLY FIVE HOURS!
THAT'S THREE SOCCER GAMES!
YOU'RE GONNA COLLAPSE.
IT'S OKAY, GO REST!
I'LL FINISH UP!
HE'S RIGHT!
YOU'LL COLLAPSE!
KLOM
YOU'VE DONE ENOUGH!
WE THANK YOU ON JINDABÔ'S BEHALF, YOUNG LADY!

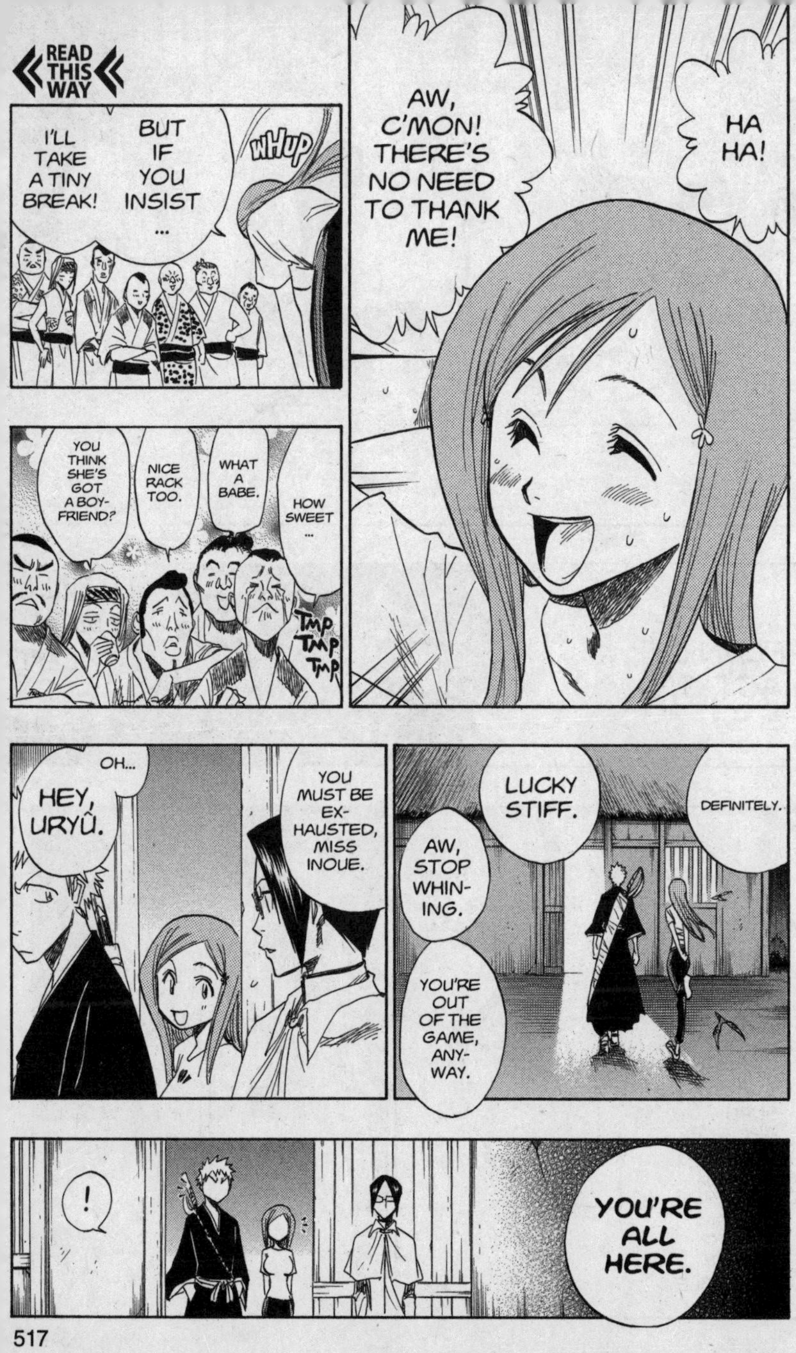
READ THIS WAY
HA HA!
AW, C'MON! THERE'S NO NEED TO THANK ME!
wHUp
BUT IF YOU INSIST ...
I'LL TAKE A TINY BREAK!
HOW SWEET ...
WHAT A BABE.
NICE RACK TOO.
YOU THINK SHE'S GOT A BOY-FRIEND?
TMP TMP TMP
DEFINITELY.
LUCKY STIFF.
AW, STOP WHINING.
YOU'RE OUT OF THE GAME, ANYWAY.
YOU MUST BE EXHAUSTED, MISS INOUE.
OH...
HEY, URYÛ.
YOU'RE ALL HERE.
!

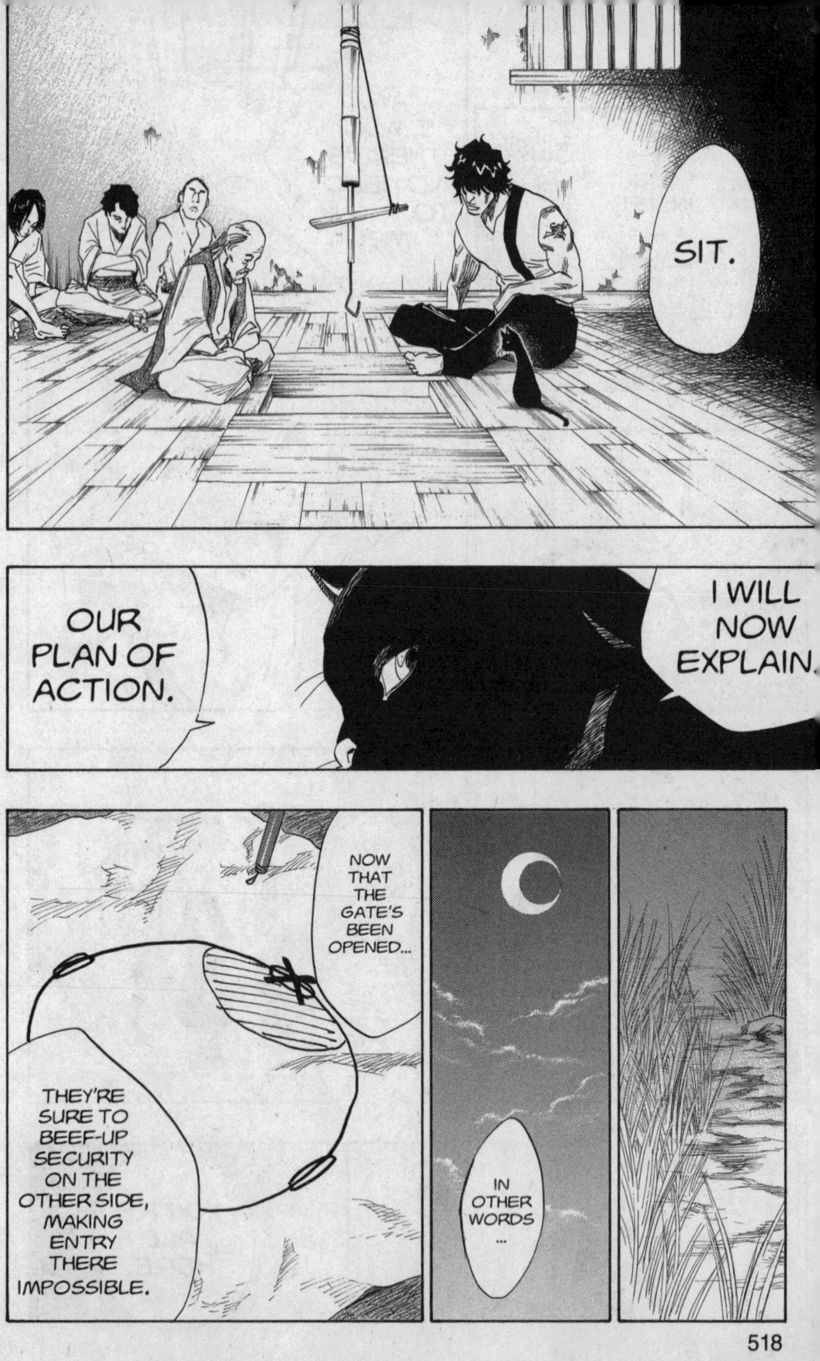
SIT.
I WILL NOW EXPLAIN.
OUR PLAN OF ACTION.
IN OTHER WORDS...
NOW THAT THE GATE'S BEEN OPENED...
THEY'RE SURE TO BEEF-UP SECURITY ON THE OTHER SIDE, MAKING ENTRY THERE IMPOSSIBLE.

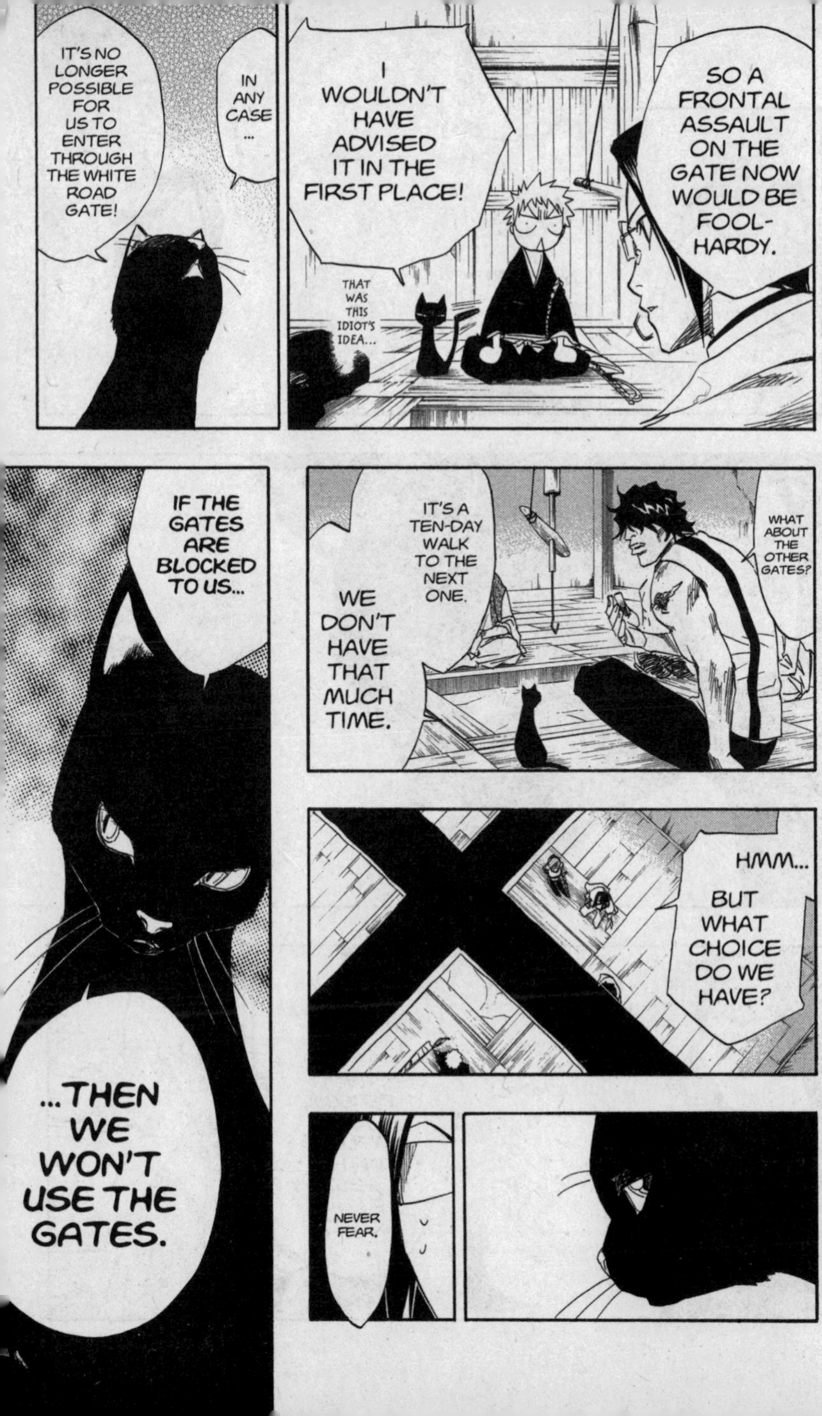

SO A FRONTAL ASSAULT ON THE GATE NOW WOULD BE FOOL-HARDY.
I WOULDN'T HAVE ADVISED IT IN THE FIRST PLACE!
THAT WAS THIS IDIOT'S IDEA...
IN ANY CASE...
IT'S NO LONGER POSSIBLE FOR US TO ENTER THROUGH THE WHITE ROAD GATE!
WHAT ABOUT THE OTHER GATES?
IT'S A TEN-DAY WALK TO THE NEXT ONE.
WE DON'T HAVE THAT MUCH TIME.
HMM...
BUT WHAT CHOICE DO WE HAVE?
NEVER FEAR.
IF THE GATES ARE BLOCKED TO US...
...THEN WE WON'T USE THE GATES.

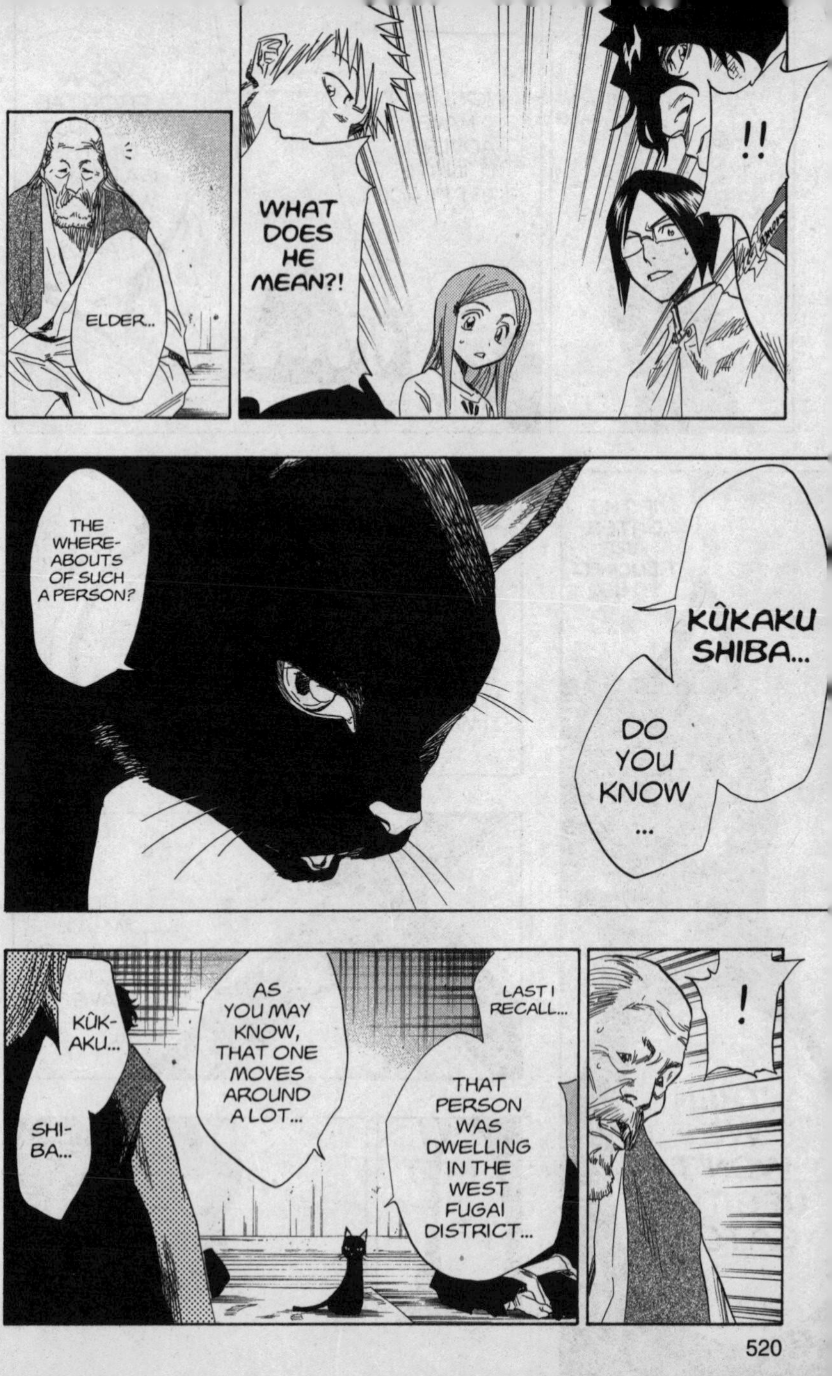
!!
WHAT DOES HE MEAN?!
ELDER...
KÛKAKU SHIBA...
DO YOU KNOW ...
THE WHERE-ABOUTS OF SUCH A PERSON?
!
LAST I RECALL...
THAT PERSON WAS DWELLING IN THE WEST FUGAI DISTRICT...
AS YOU MAY KNOW, THAT ONE MOVES AROUND A LOT...
KÛK-AKU...
SHI-BA...

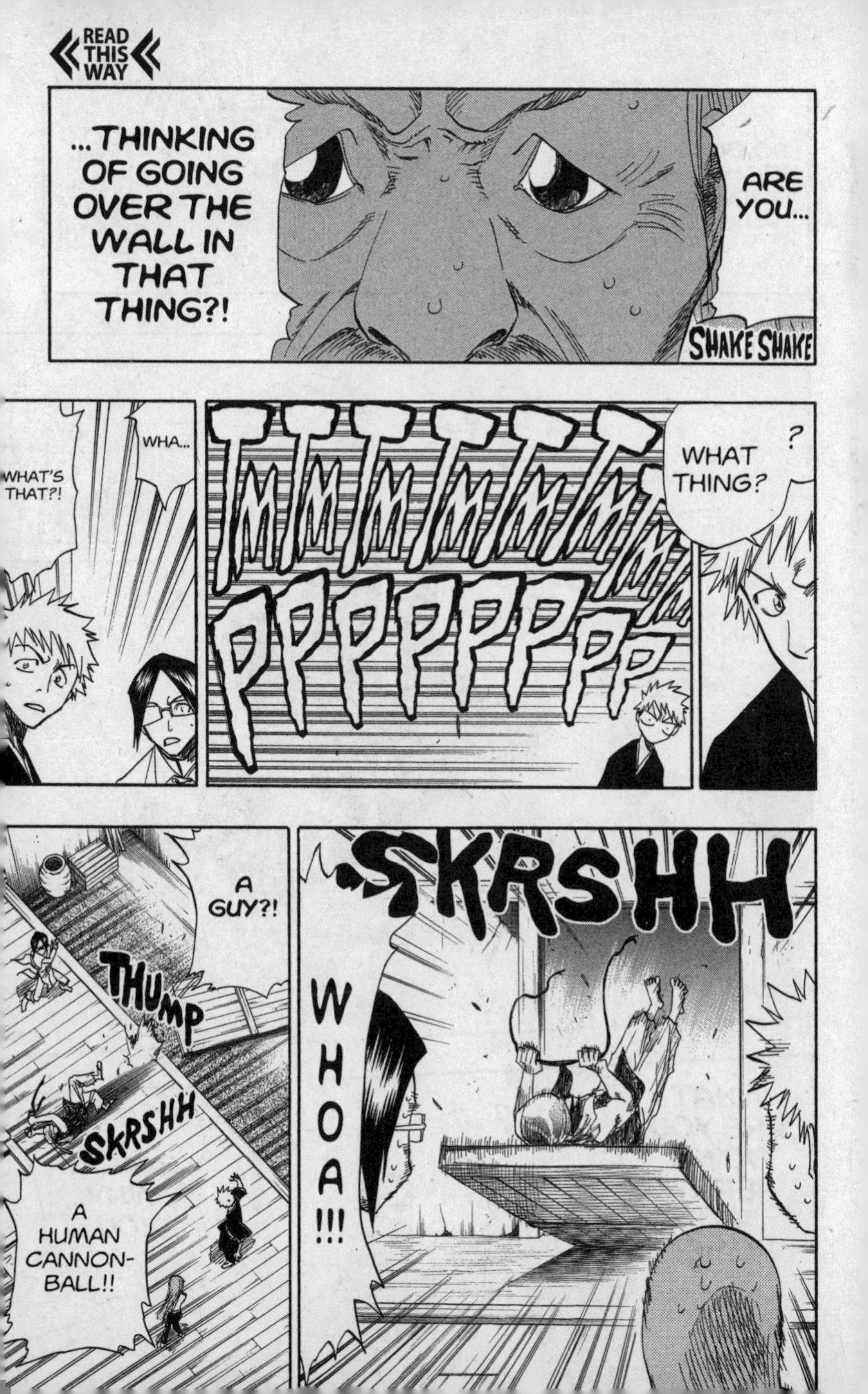
READ THIS WAY
ARE YOU...
...THINKING OF GOING OVER THE WALL IN THAT THING?!
SHAKE SHAKE
?
WHAT THING?
TMMMMMMM
PPPPPPPP
WHA...
WHAT'S THAT?!
SKRSHH
WHOA!!!
A GUY?!
THUMP
SKRSHH
A HUMAN CANNON-BALL!!

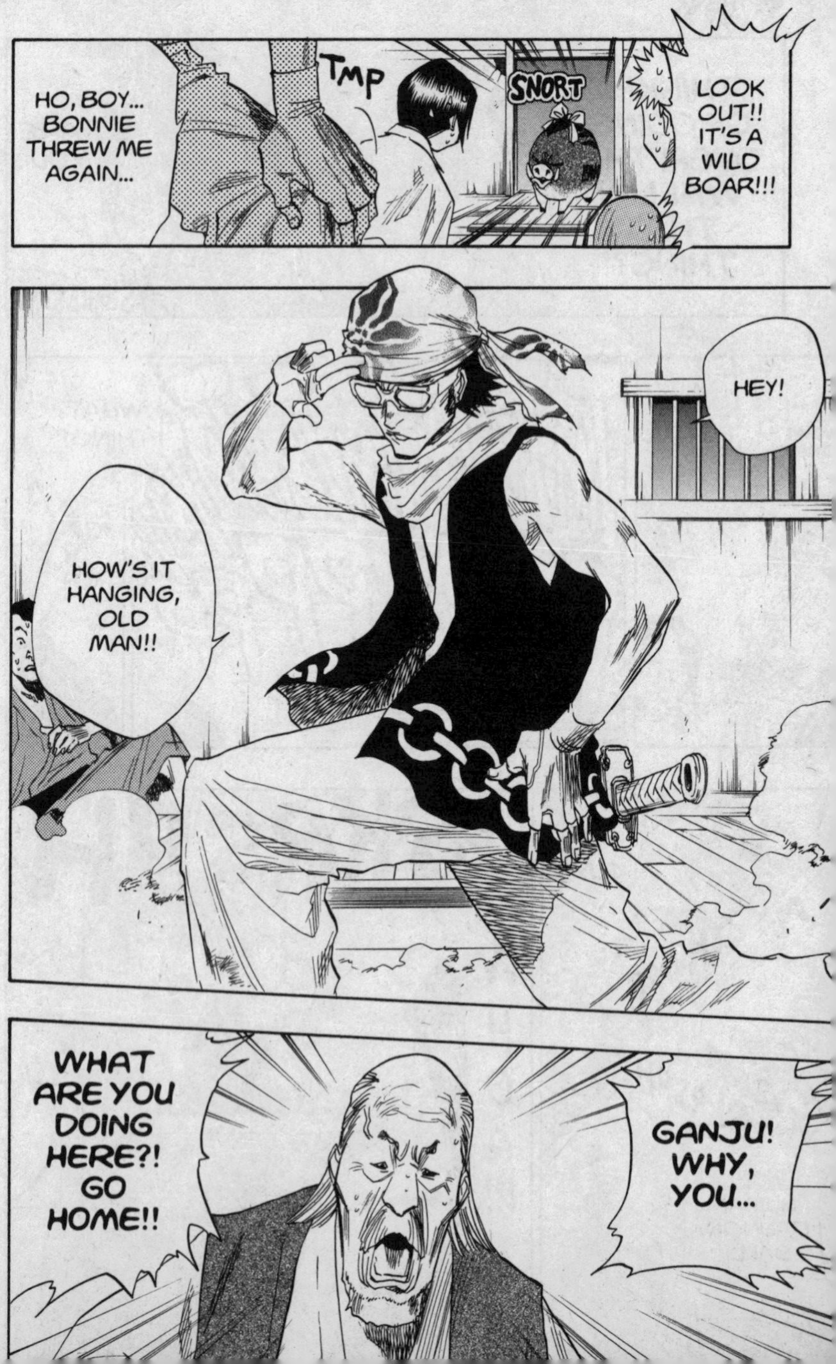
LOOK OUT!! IT'S A WILD BOAR!!!
SNORT
TMP
HO, BOY... BONNIE THREW ME AGAIN...
HEY!
HOW'S IT HANGING, OLD MAN!!
GANJU! WHY, YOU...
WHAT ARE YOU DOING HERE?! GO HOME!!

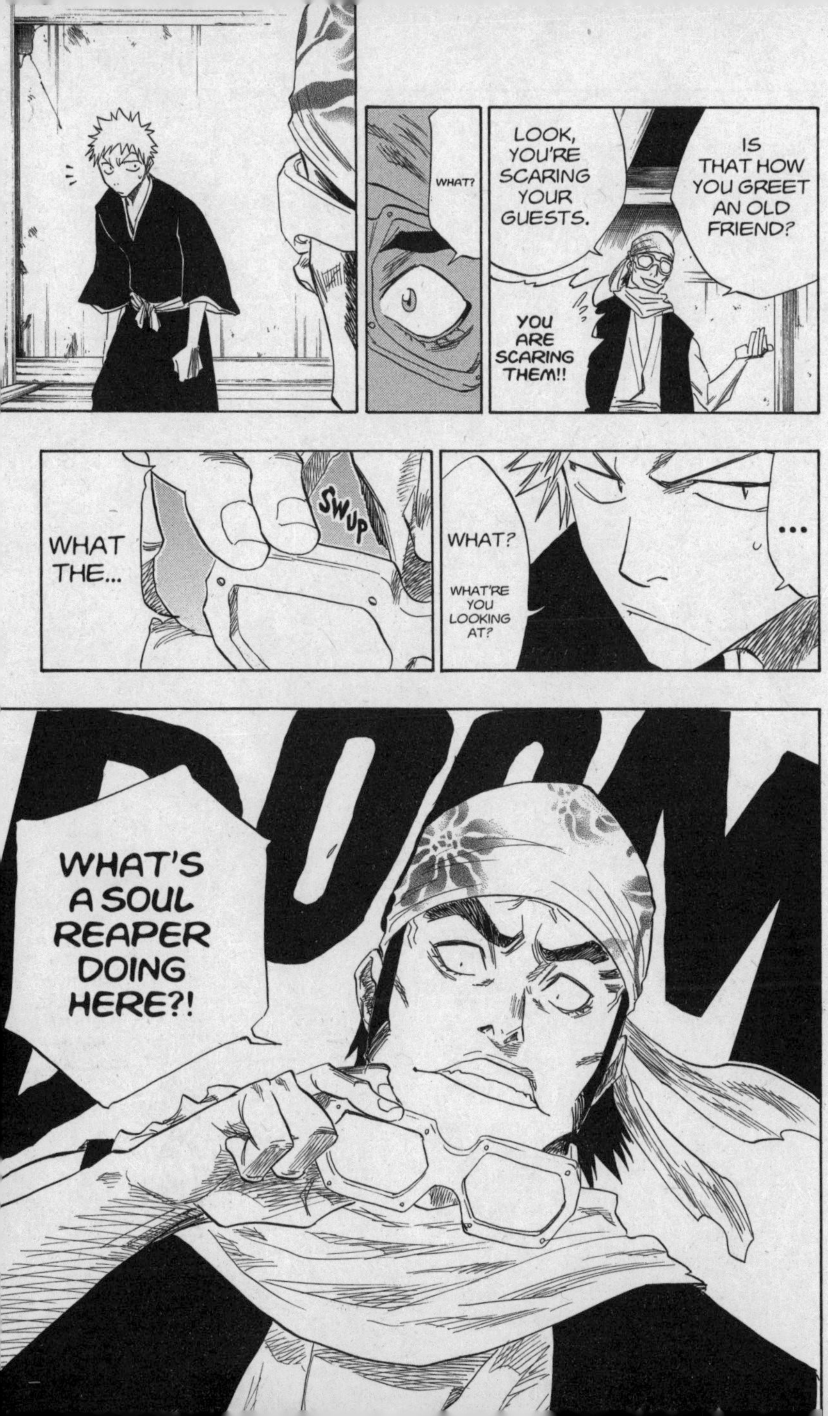
IS THAT HOW YOU GREET AN OLD FRIEND?
LOOK, YOU'RE SCARING YOUR GUESTS.
YOU ARE SCARING THEM!!
WHAT?
...
WHAT?
WHAT'RE YOU LOOKING AT?
SWUP
WHAT THE...
WHAT'S A SOUL REAPER DOING HERE?!

WILL YOU
COME PLAY
WITH ME
AGAIN
SOMEDAY...

CHAD?

77. My Name Is Ganju

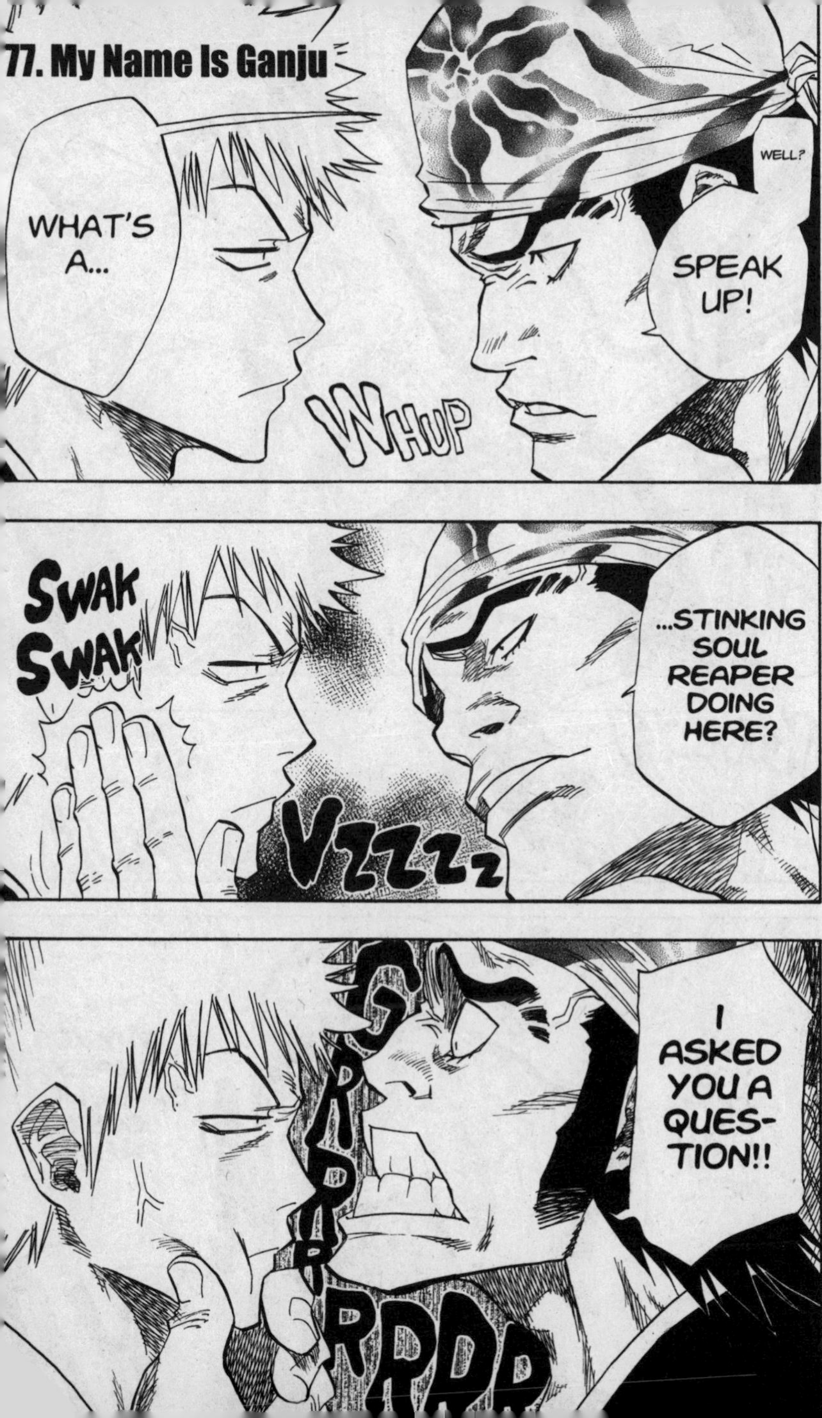
WELL?
SPEAK UP!
WHAT'S A...
WHUP
SWAK SWAK
...STINKING SOUL REAPER DOING HERE?
VZZZz
I ASKED YOU A QUES-TION!!

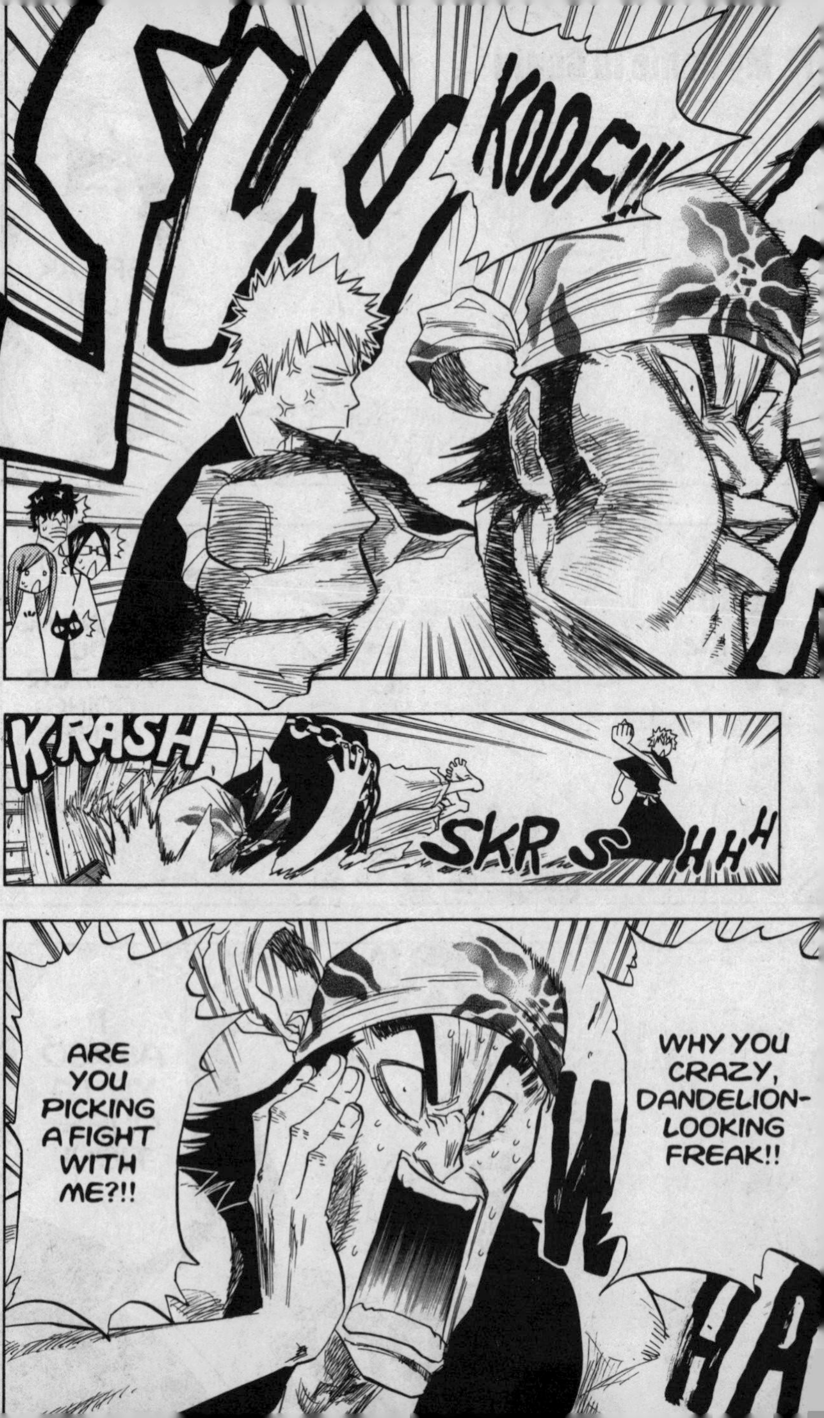
KOOF!!!
KRASH
SKRS HHH
WHY YOU CRAZY, DANDELION-LOOKING FREAK!!
ARE YOU PICKING A FIGHT WITH ME?!!

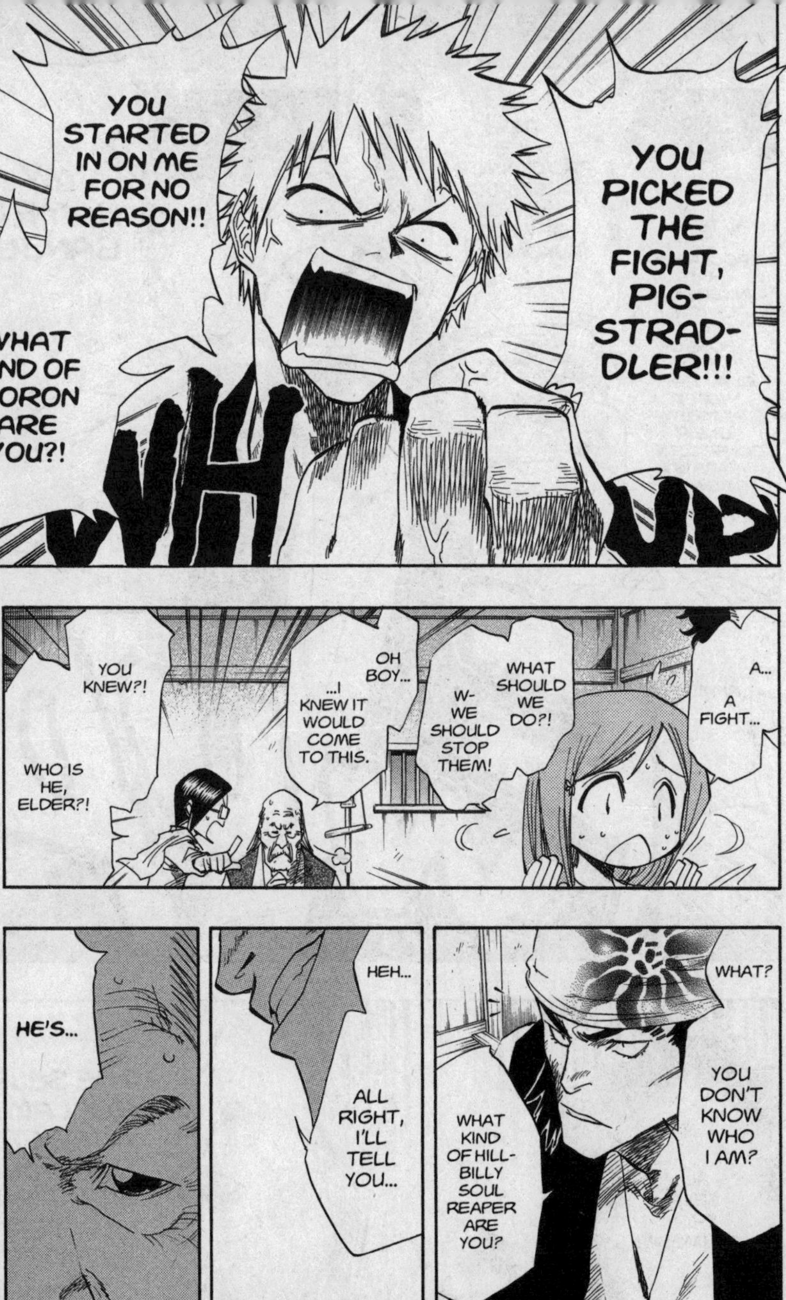
YOU PICKED THE FIGHT, PIG-STRADDLER!!!
YOU STARTED IN ON ME FOR NO REASON!!
WHAT KIND OF MORON ARE YOU?!
A... A FIGHT...
WHAT SHOULD WE DO?!
W-WE SHOULD STOP THEM!
OH BOY...
...I KNEW IT WOULD COME TO THIS.
YOU KNEW?!
WHO IS HE, ELDER?!
WHAT?
YOU DON'T KNOW WHO I AM?
WHAT KIND OF HILL-BILLY SOUL REAPER ARE YOU?
HEH...
ALL RIGHT, I'LL TELL YOU...
HE'S...

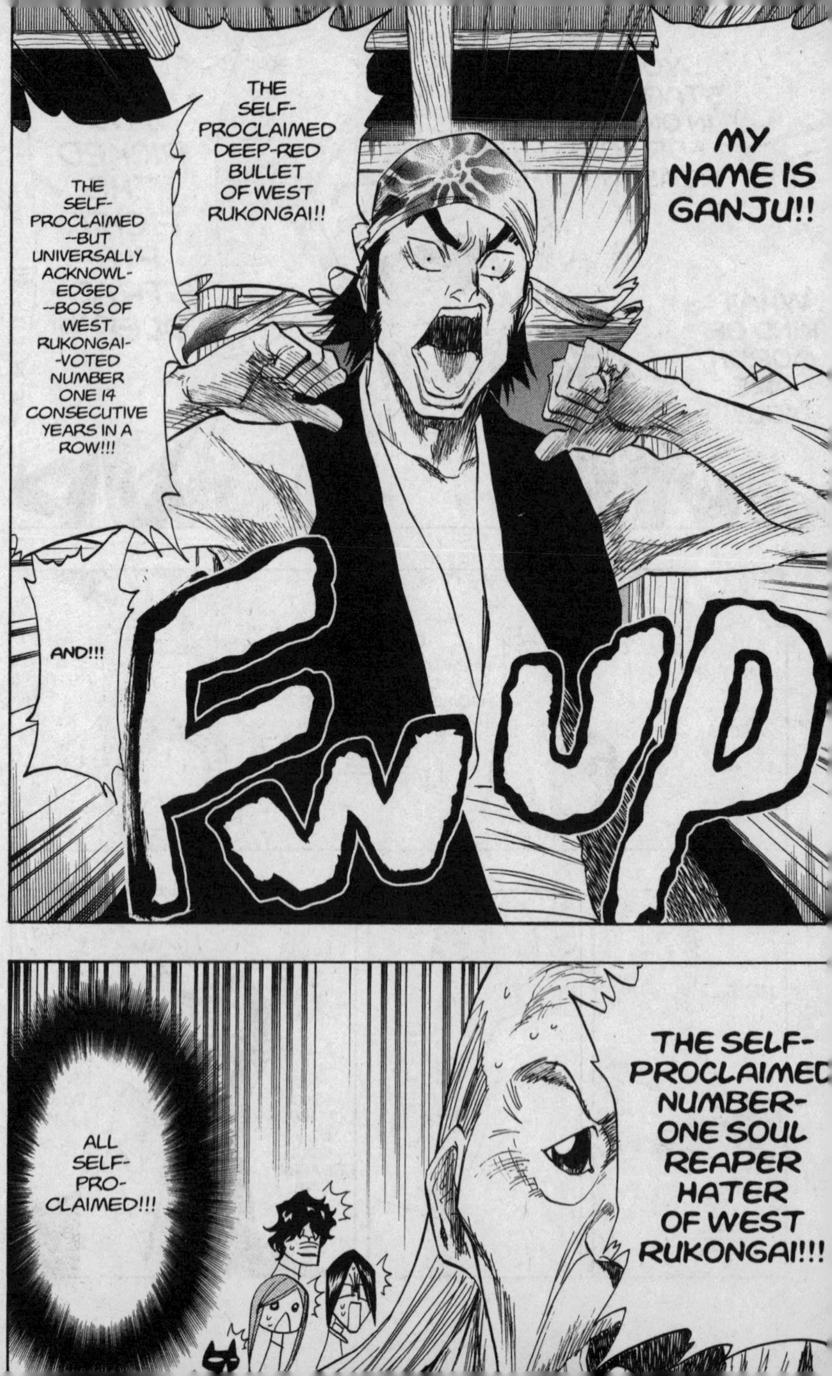
MY NAME IS GANJU!!
THE SELF-PROCLAIMED DEEP-RED BULLET OF WEST RUKONGAI!!
THE SELF-PROCLAIMED --BUT UNIVERSALLY ACKNOWL-EDGED --BOSS OF WEST RUKONGAI--VOTED NUMBER ONE 14 CONSECUTIVE YEARS IN A ROW!!!
AND!!!
FWUD
THE SELF-PROCLAIMED NUMBER-ONE SOUL REAPER HATER OF WEST RUKONGAI!!!
ALL SELF-PRO-CLAIMED!!!

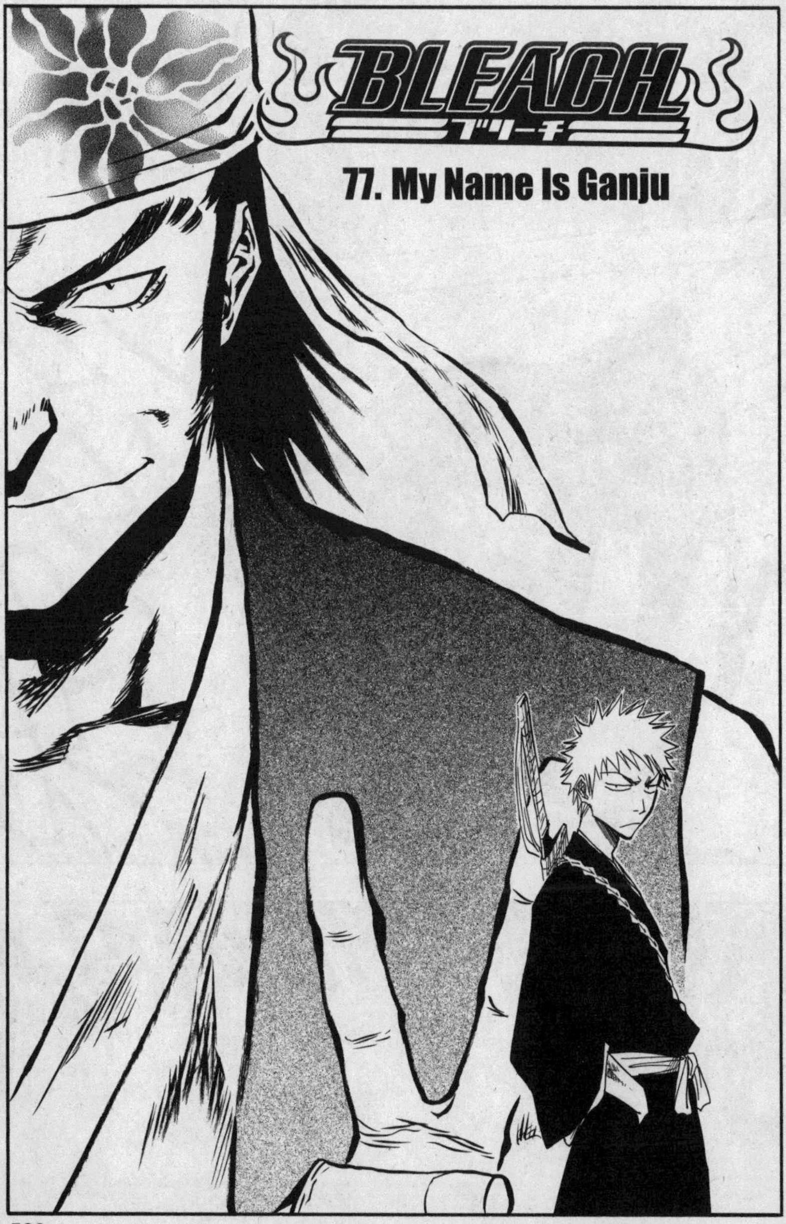
BLEACH
ブリーチ
77. My Name Is Ganju

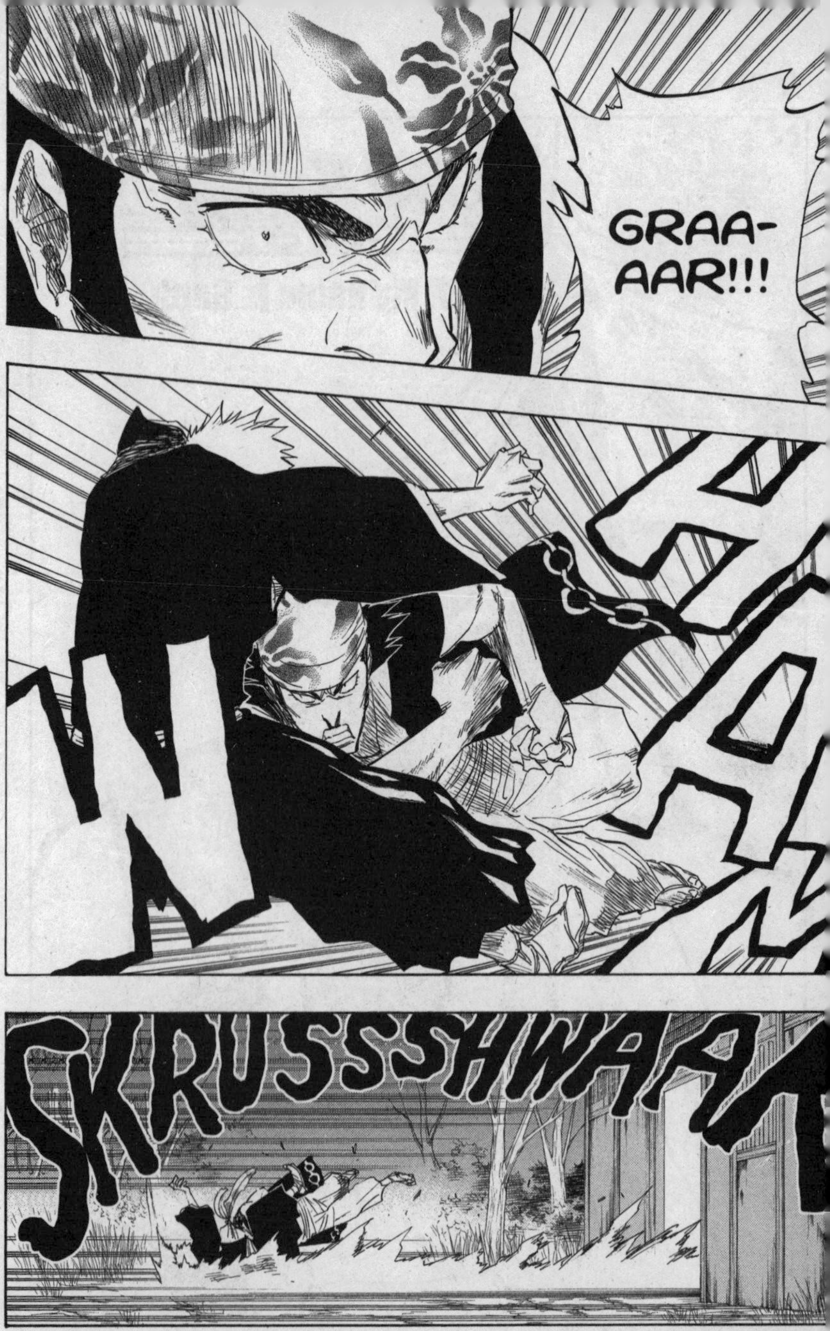
GRAA-
AAR!!!
SKRUSSSHWAAK

READ THIS WAY

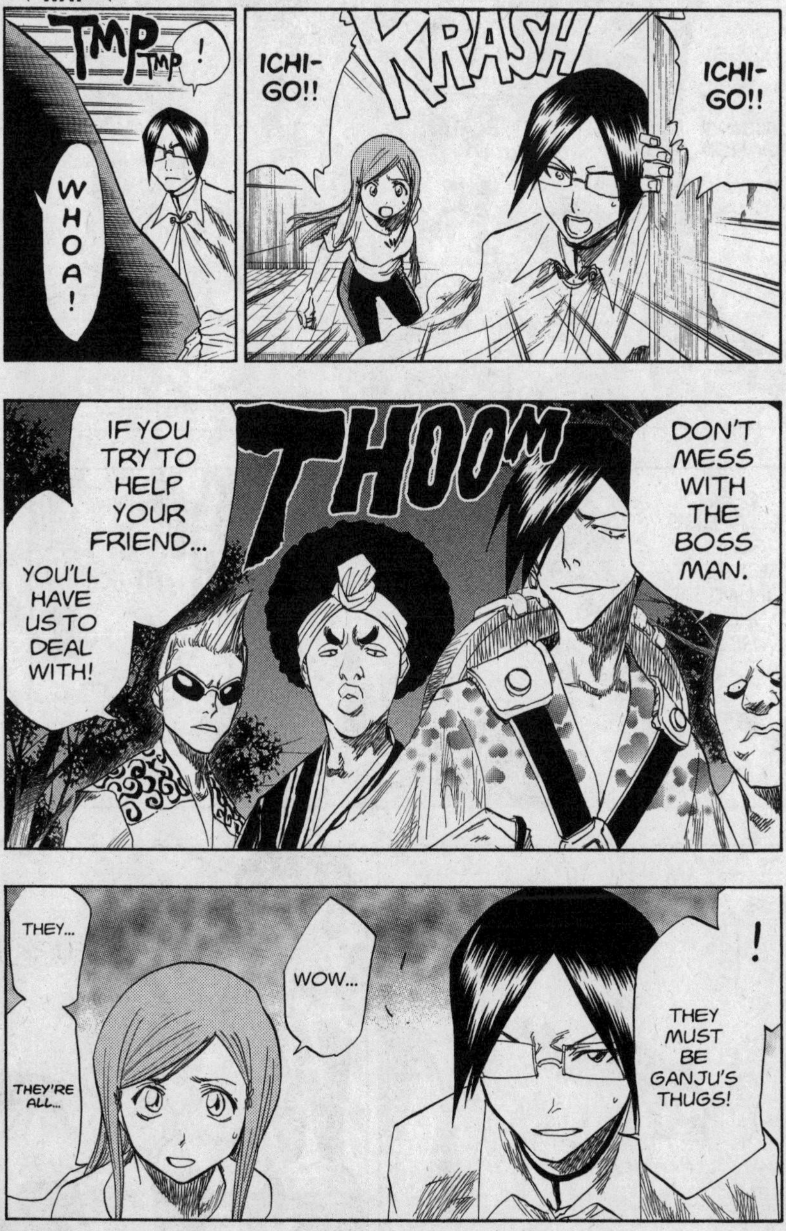
KRASH
ICHI-GO!!
ICHI-GO!!
TMP TMP
!
WHOA!
DON'T MESS WITH THE BOSS MAN.
THOOM
IF YOU TRY TO HELP YOUR FRIEND...
YOU'LL HAVE US TO DEAL WITH!
!
THEY MUST BE GANJU'S THUGS!
WOW...
THEY...
THEY'RE ALL...

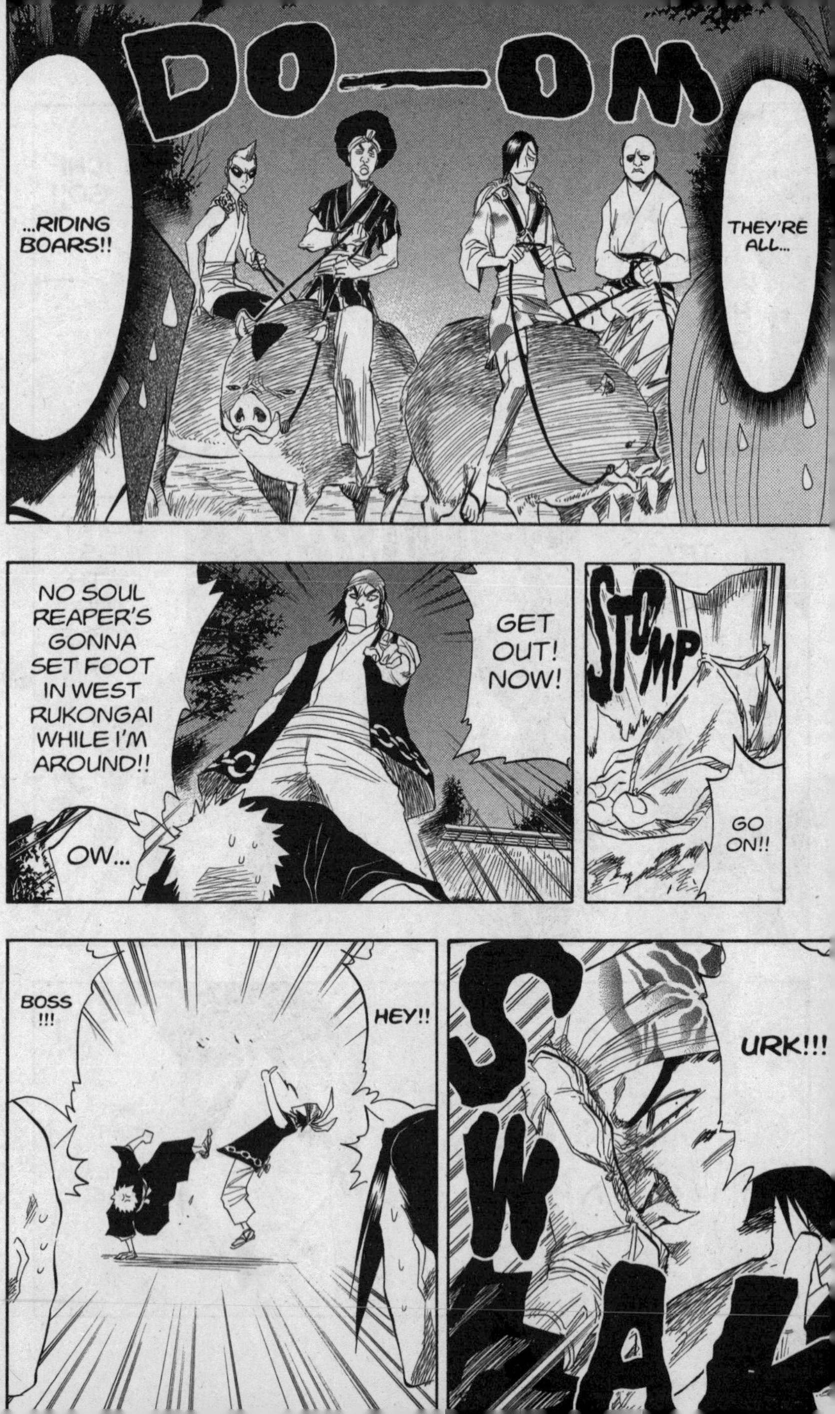
DO—OM
THEY'RE ALL...
...RIDING BOARS!!
STOMP
GO ON!!
GET OUT! NOW!
NO SOUL REAPER'S GONNA SET FOOT IN WEST RUKONGAI WHILE I'M AROUND!!
OW...
URK!!!
HEY!!
BOSS !!!

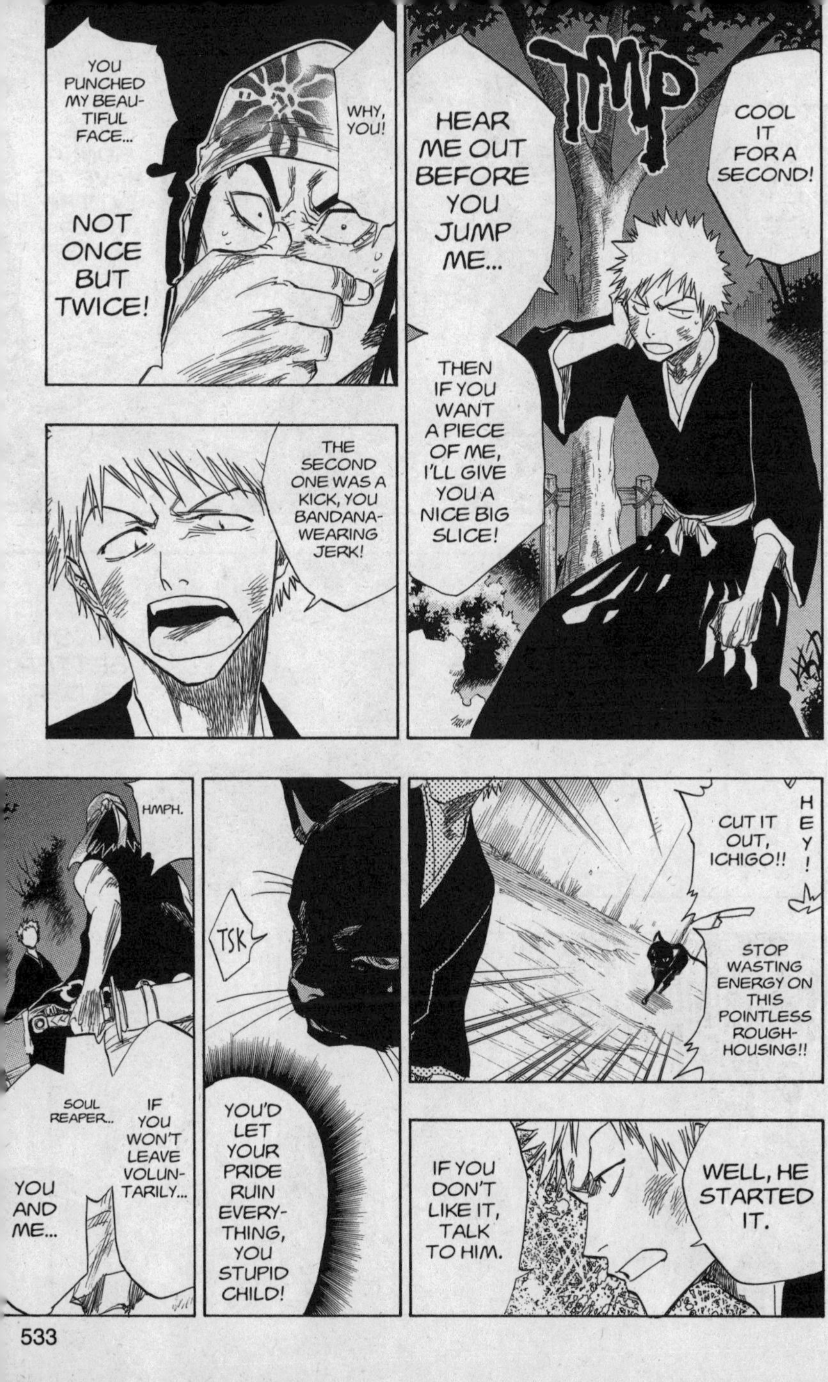

TMP
COOL IT FOR A SECOND!
HEAR ME OUT BEFORE YOU JUMP ME...
THEN IF YOU WANT A PIECE OF ME, I'LL GIVE YOU A NICE BIG SLICE!
WHY, YOU!
YOU PUNCHED MY BEAU-TIFUL FACE...
NOT ONCE BUT TWICE!
THE SECOND ONE WAS A KICK, YOU BANDANA-WEARING JERK!
HEY!
CUT IT OUT, ICHIGO!!
STOP WASTING ENERGY ON THIS POINTLESS ROUGH-HOUSING!!
WELL, HE STARTED IT.
IF YOU DON'T LIKE IT, TALK TO HIM.
TSK
YOU'D LET YOUR PRIDE RUIN EVERY-THING, YOU STUPID CHILD!
HMPH.
SOUL REAPER...
IF YOU WON'T LEAVE VOLUN-TARILY...
YOU AND ME...

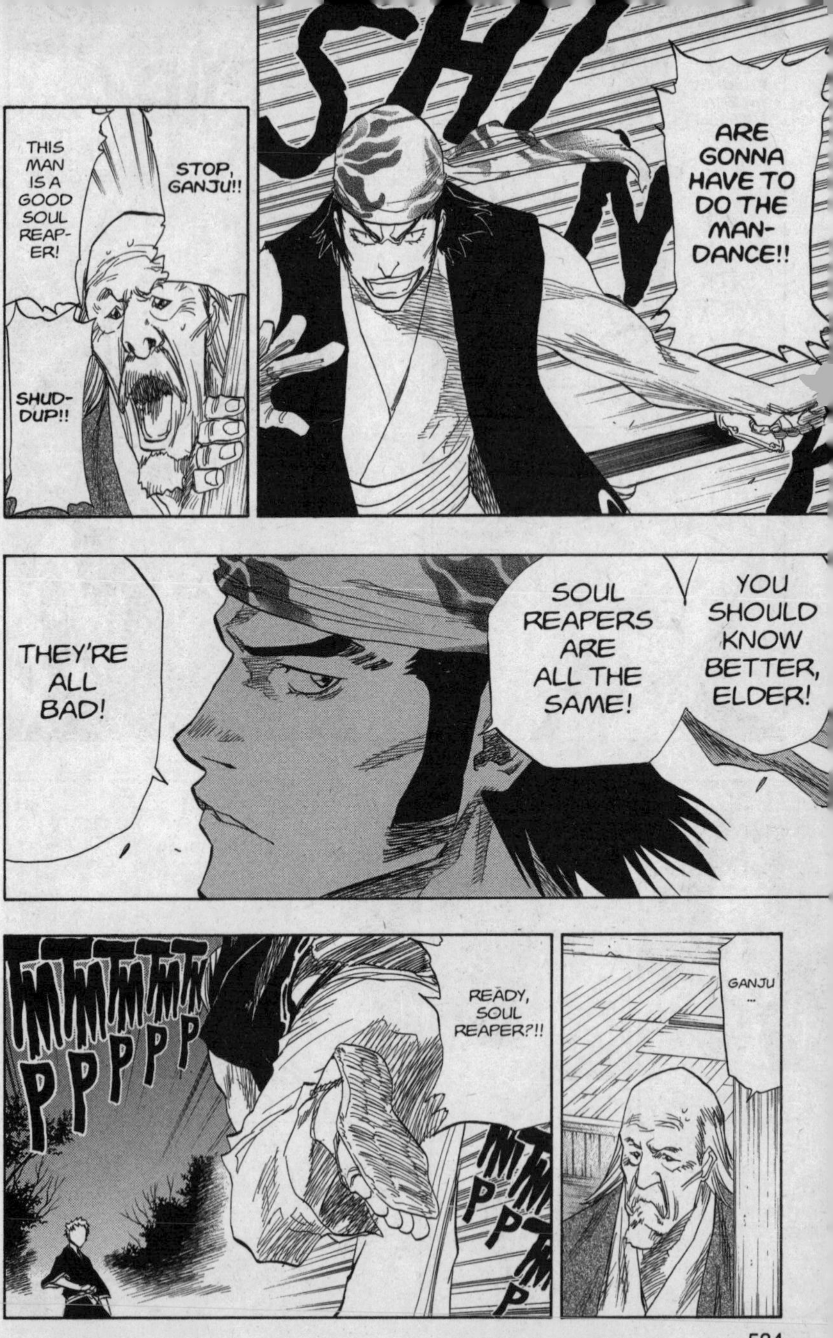
ARE GONNA HAVE TO DO THE MAN-DANCE!!
STOP, GANJU!!
THIS MAN IS A GOOD SOUL REAPER!
SHUD-DUP!!
YOU SHOULD KNOW BETTER, ELDER!
SOUL REAPERS ARE ALL THE SAME!
THEY'RE ALL BAD!
GANJU ...
READY, SOUL REAPER?!!

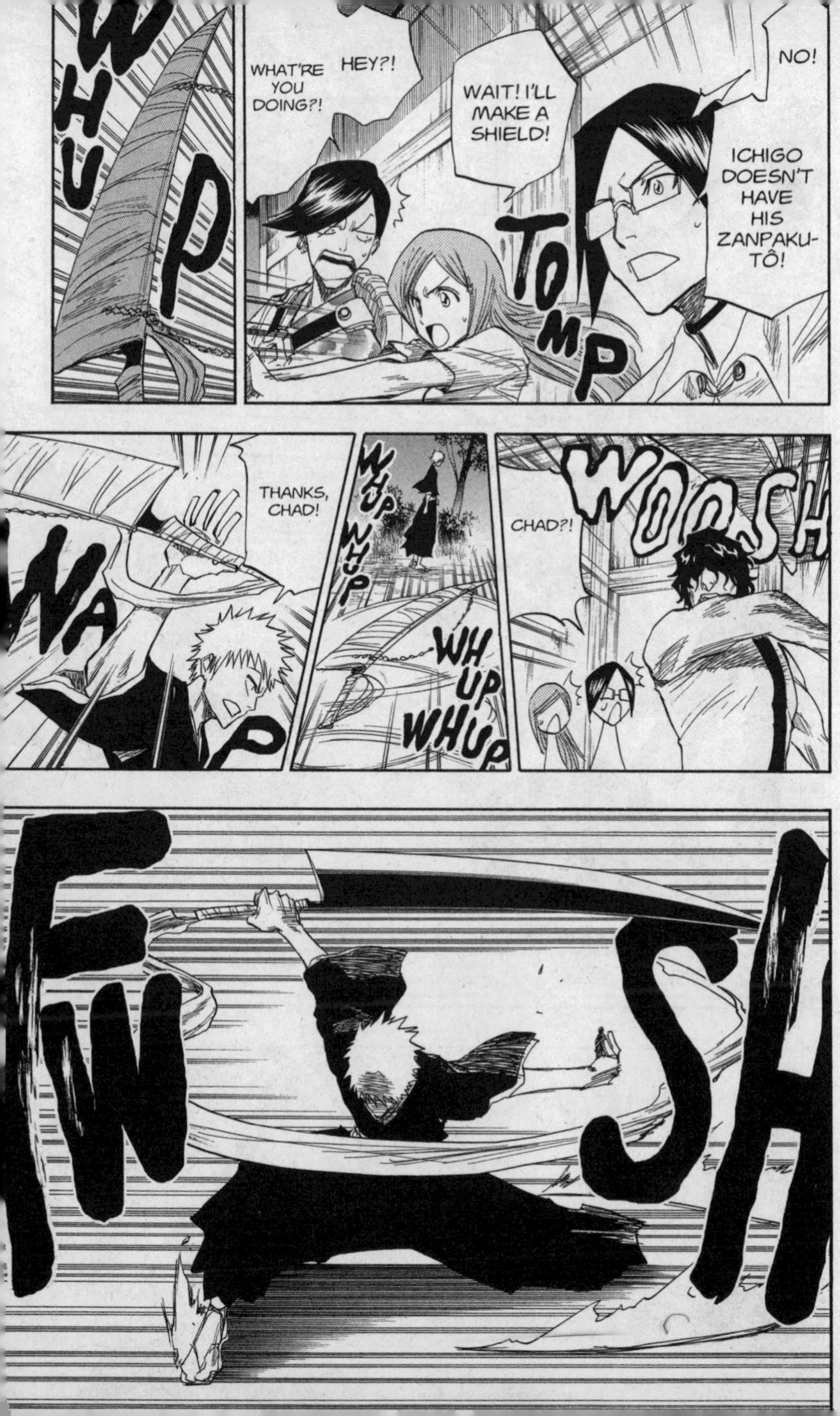

NO!
ICHIGO DOESN'T HAVE HIS ZANPAKU-TÔ!
WAIT! I'LL MAKE A SHIELD!
TOMP
HEY?!
WHAT'RE YOU DOING?!
WHUP
WOOSH
CHAD?!
WHUP WHUP
WHUP WHUP
THANKS, CHAD!
FWSH

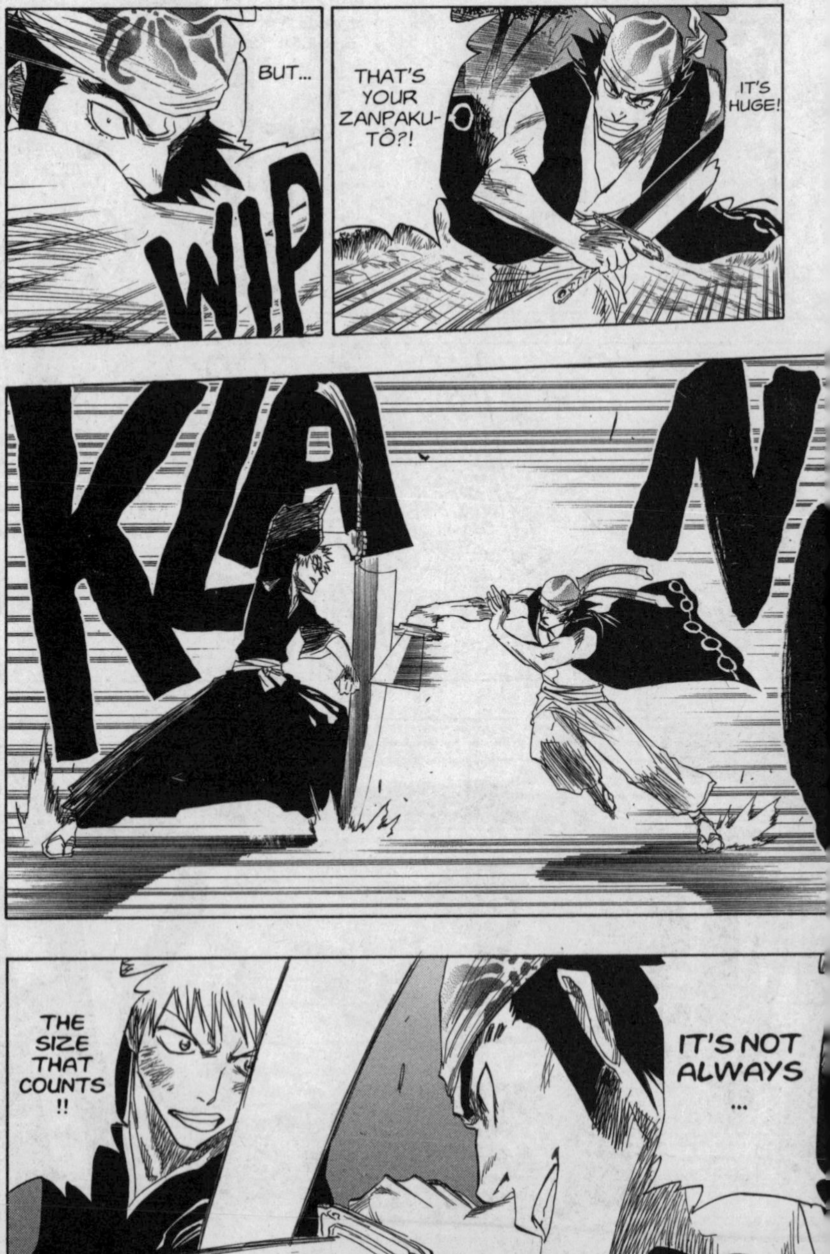

IT'S HUGE!
THAT'S YOUR ZANPAKU-TÔ?!
BUT...
WIP
KLA
N
IT'S NOT ALWAYS ...
THE SIZE THAT COUNTS !!

READ THIS WAY

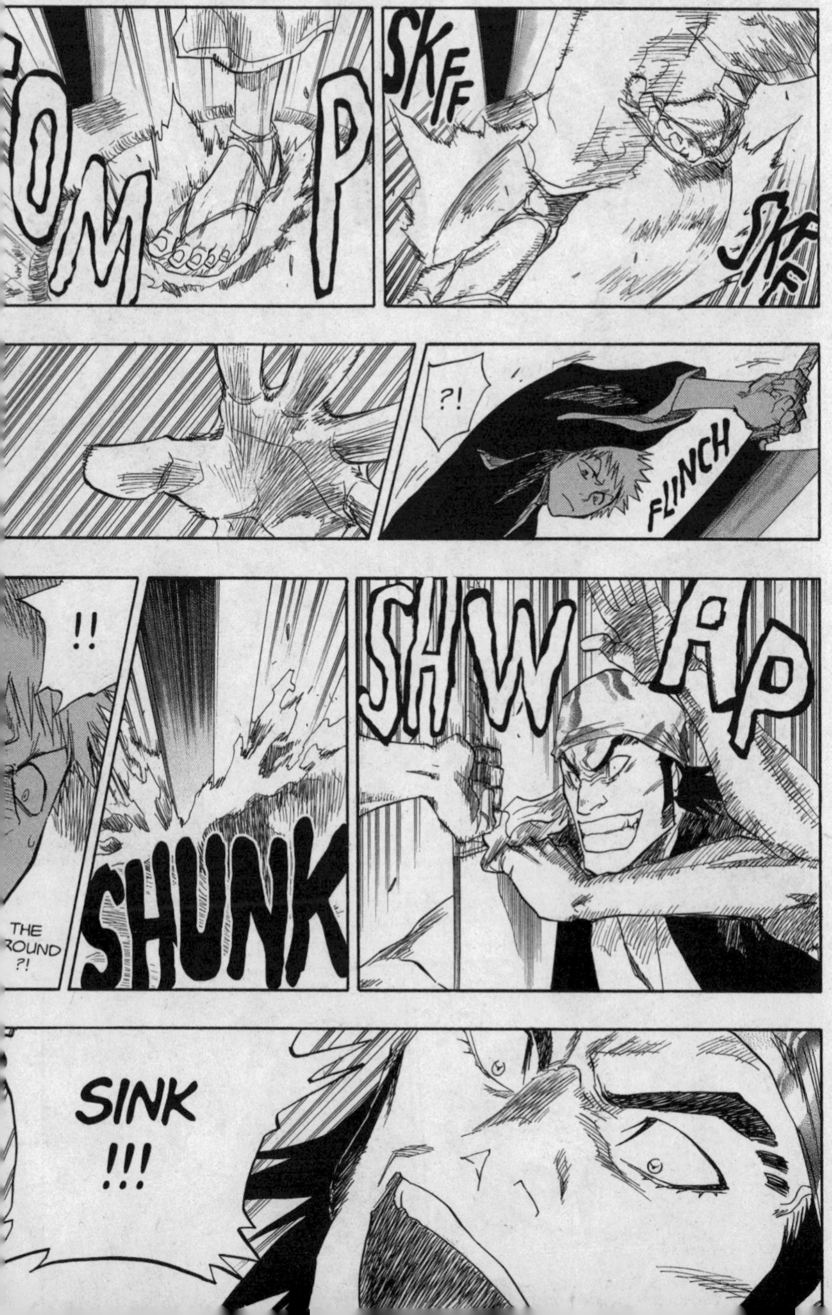
SKFF
SKFF
OMP
?!
FLINCH
SHWAP
SHUNK
!!
THE
ROUND
?!
SINK
!!!

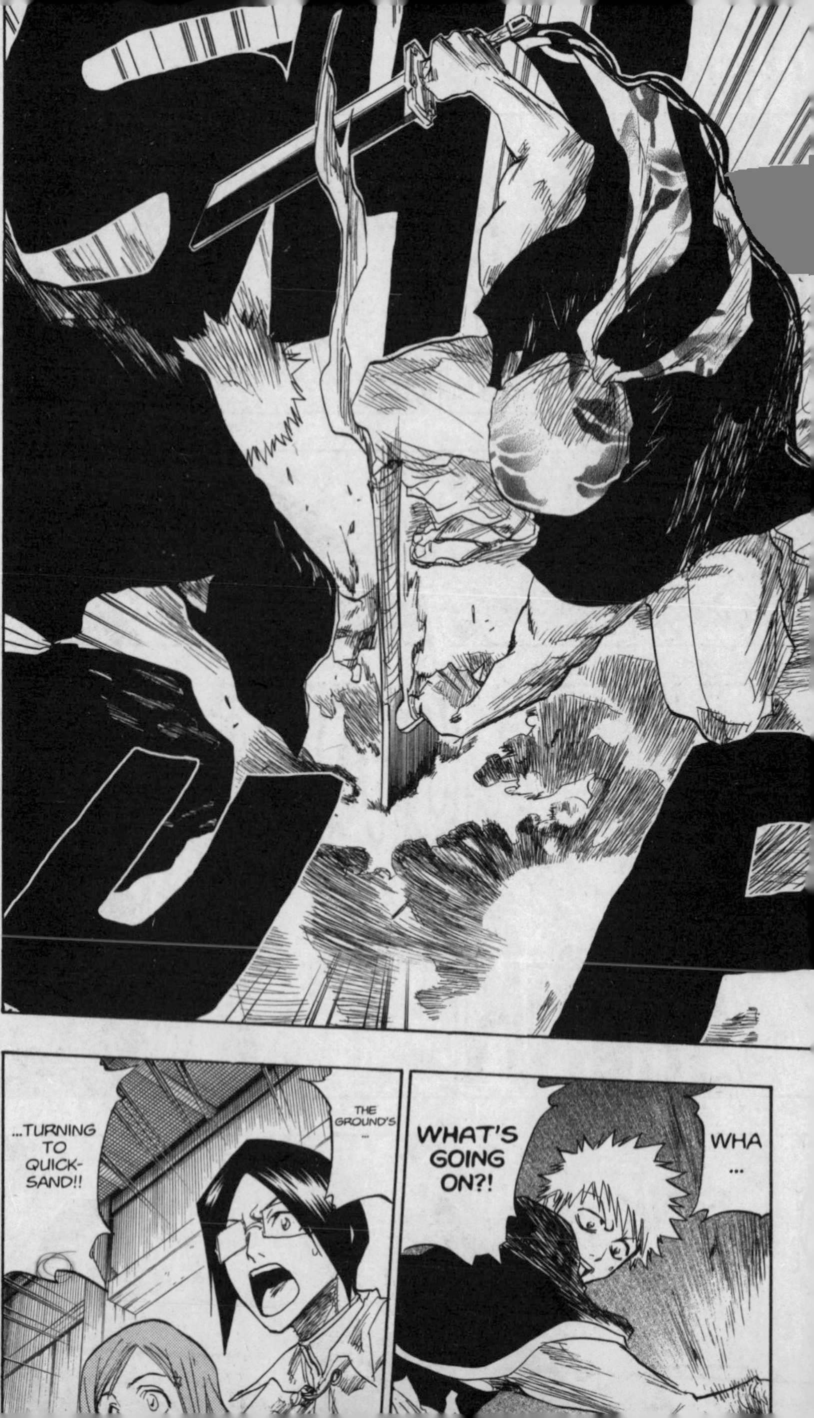
WHA ...
WHAT'S GOING ON?!
THE GROUND'S ...
...TURNING TO QUICK-SAND!!

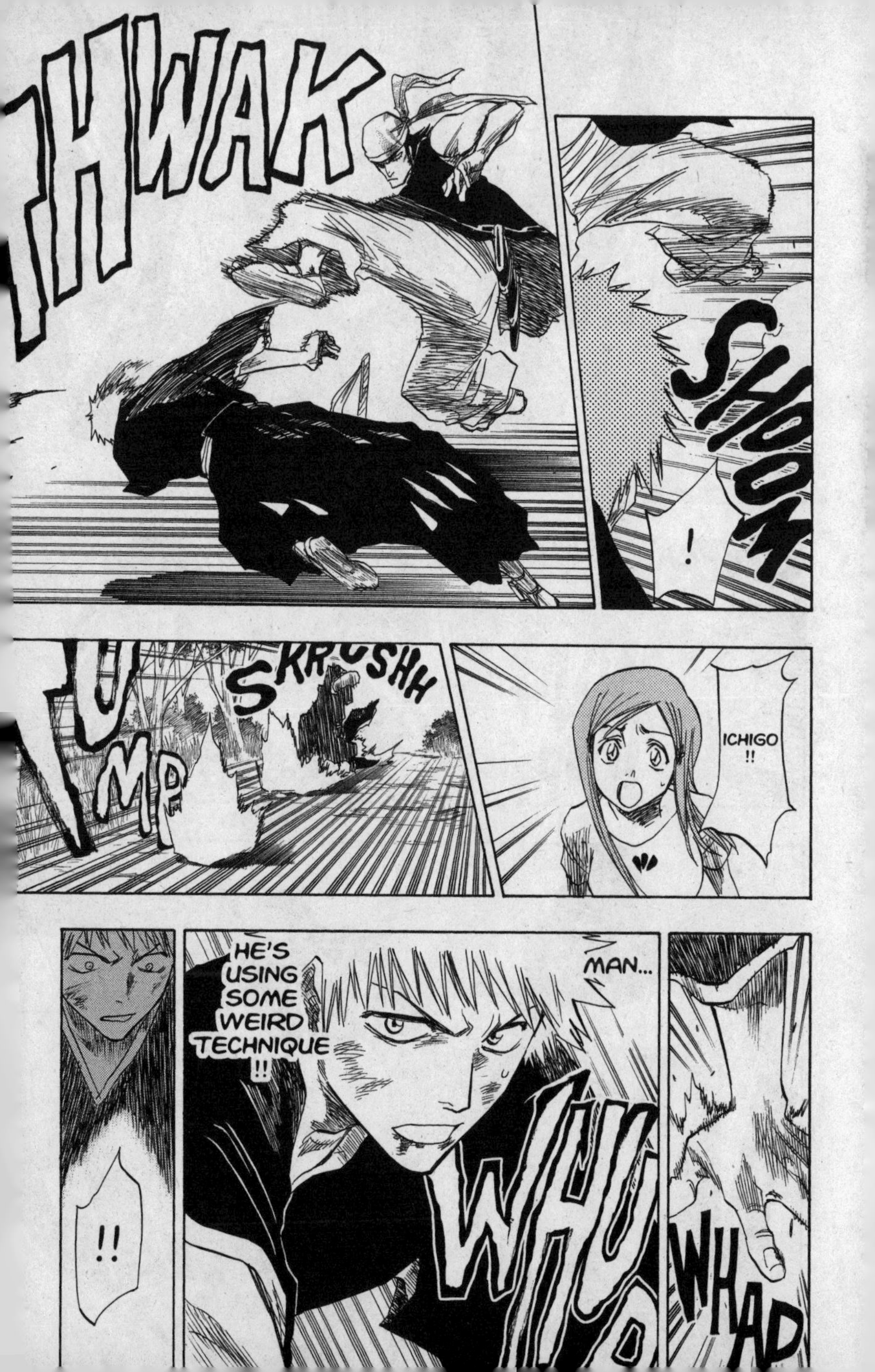

SHOOM
!
THWAK
ICHIGO !!
SKRCSHH
THUMP
WHAD
MAN...
HE'S USING SOME WEIRD TECHNIQUE !!
WHU
!!

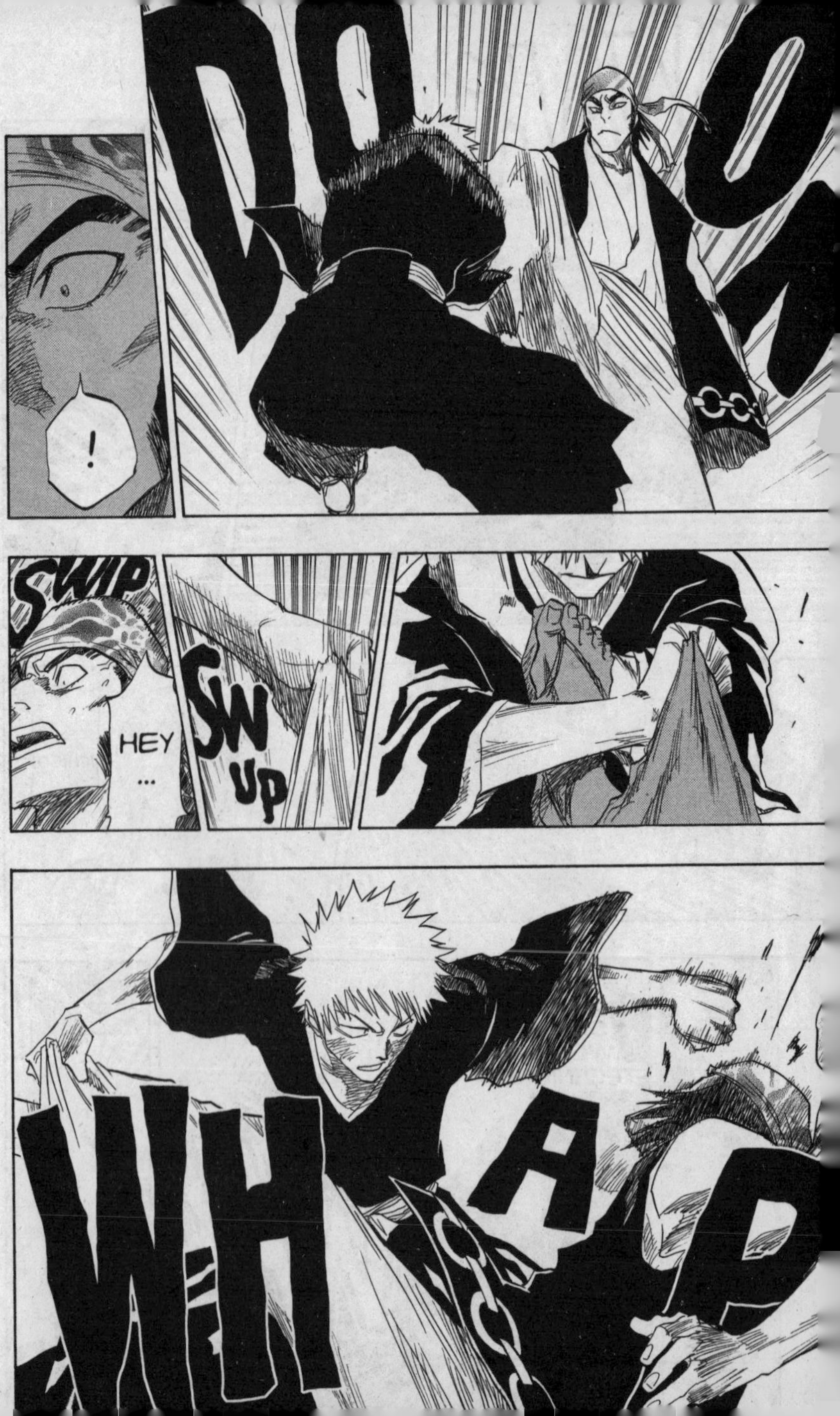

DOO
!
SWIP
SWUP
HEY ...
WHAP

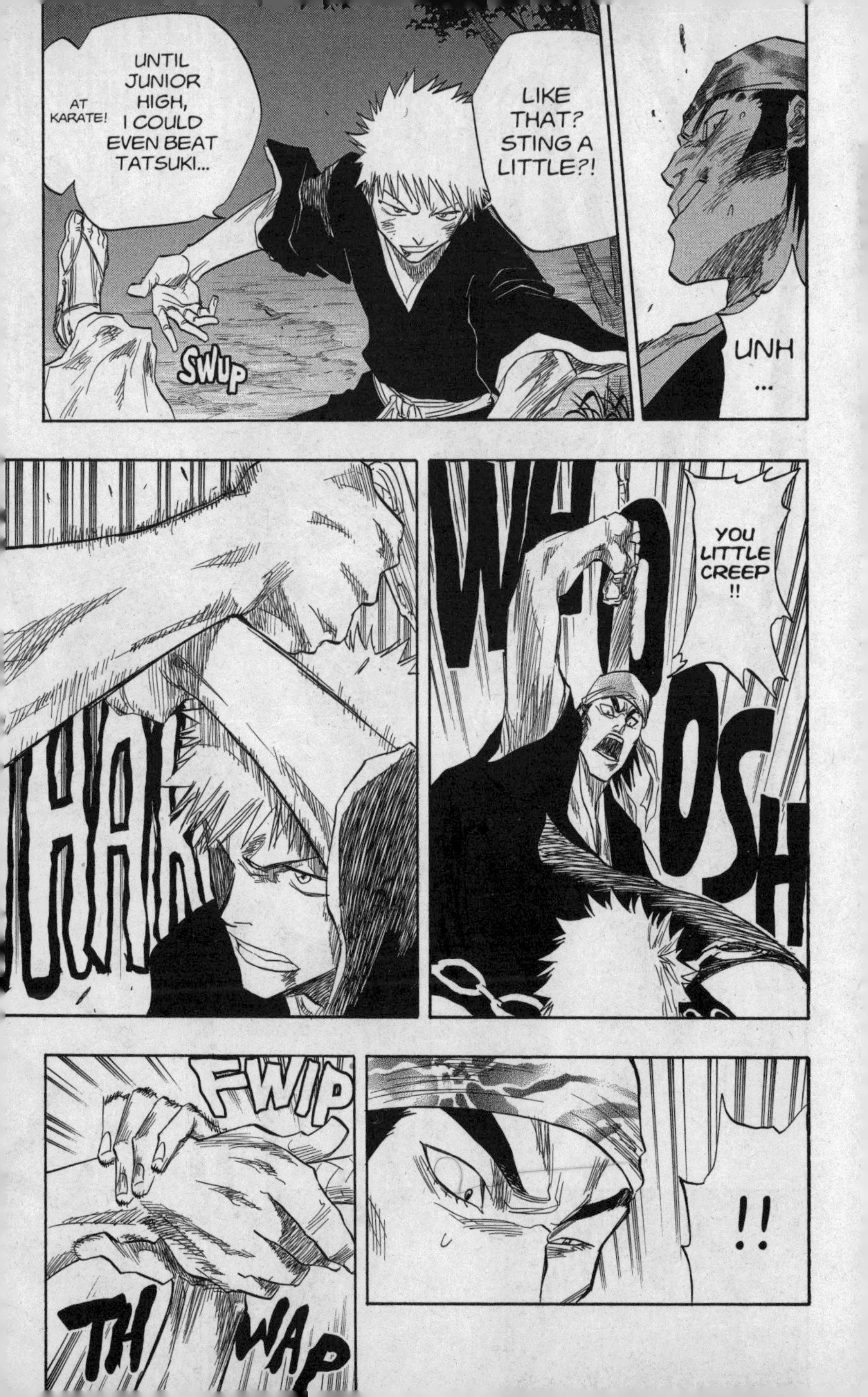
UNH
...
LIKE THAT? STING A LITTLE?!
UNTIL JUNIOR HIGH, I COULD EVEN BEAT TATSUKI...
AT KARATE!
SWUP
YOU LITTLE CREEP !!
WHOOSH
THAK
!!
FWIP
THWAP

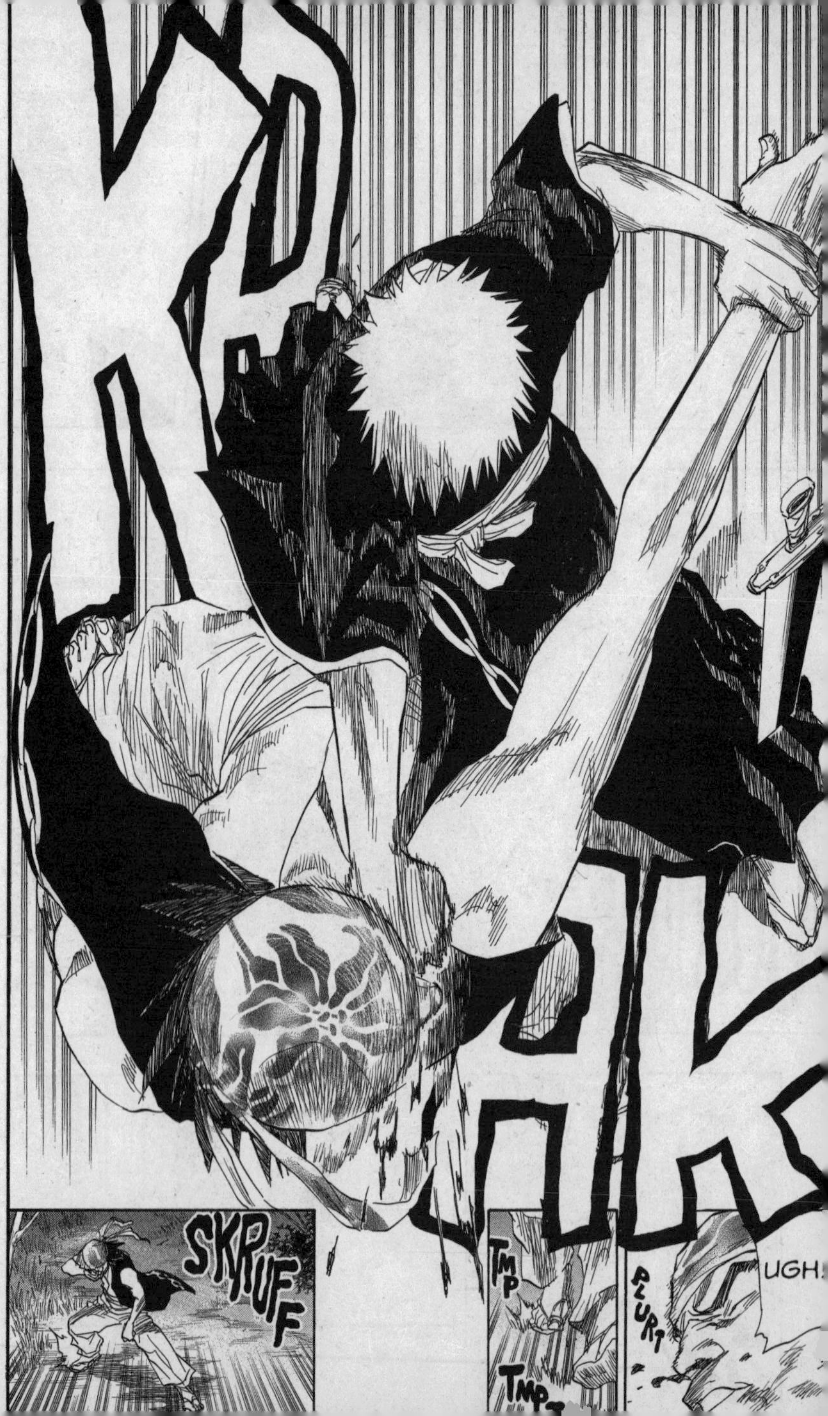
SKRUFF
TMP
TMP..
PLURT
UGH

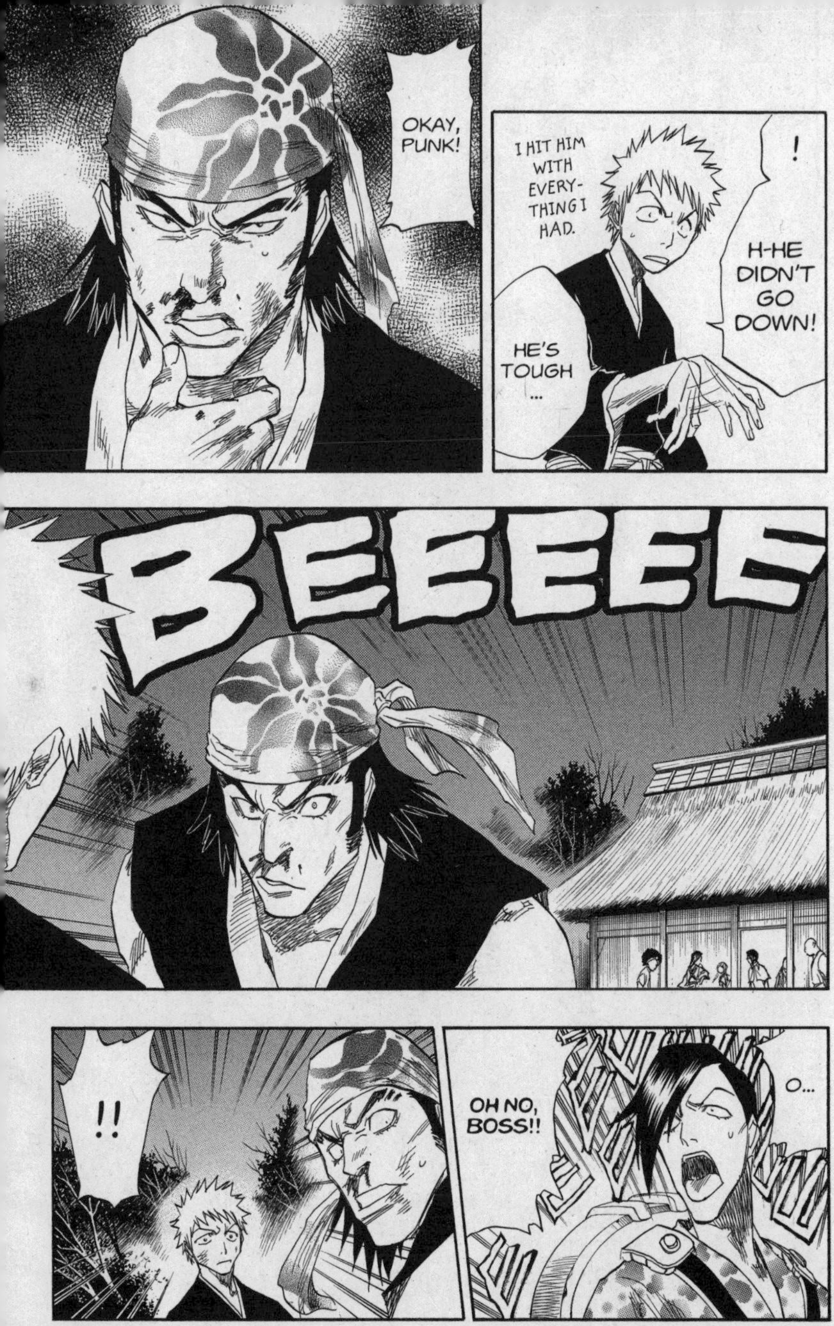
!
H-HE DIDN'T GO DOWN!
I HIT HIM WITH EVERY-THING I HAD.
HE'S TOUGH ...
OKAY, PUNK!
BEEEEE
O...
OH NO, BOSS!!
!!

GANJU'S GANG

TOP

REAL NAME:
KENJI
YAMASHITA
WORST
STREET
FIGHTER.
WORST
ARGUER,
TOO.

FEVER

REAL NAME:
MITSURU
ISHINO
HAS
ABSOLUTELY
NO
RHYTHM.

HAWK

REAL NAME:
TAICHI
MIYAMOTO
HENCHMAN
NUMBER
ONE.
GOOD AT
COOKING.

DUMBBELL

REAL NAME:
SADATOMO
SAIONJI
A GENIUS AT
CARING FOR
ANIMALS.

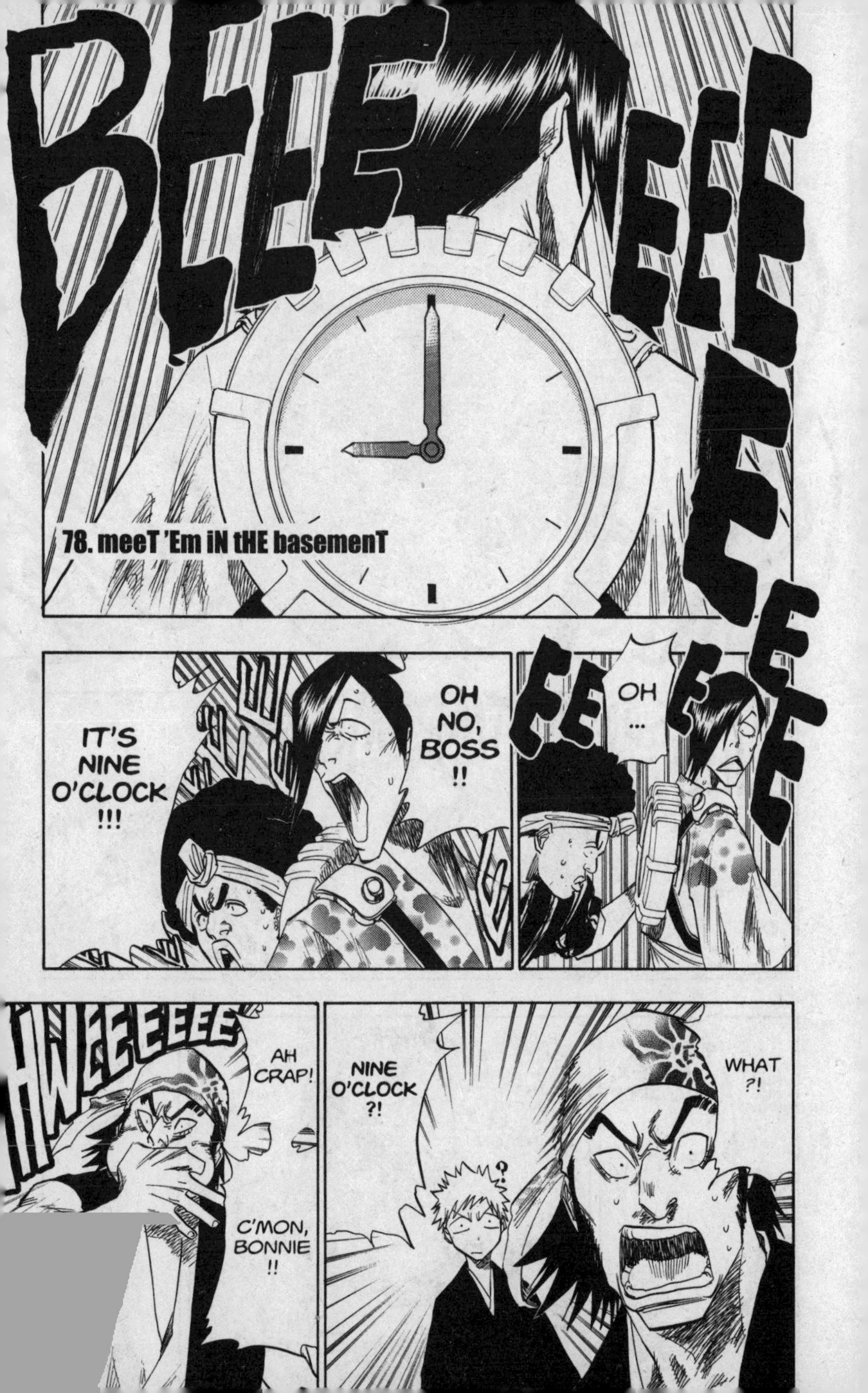
BEEEEEEEEEEEEE
78. meeT 'Em iN tHE basemenT
OH ...
OH NO, BOSS !!
IT'S NINE O'CLOCK !!!
WHAT ?!
NINE O'CLOCK ?!
AH CRAP!
C'MON, BONNIE !!
HWEEEEEE

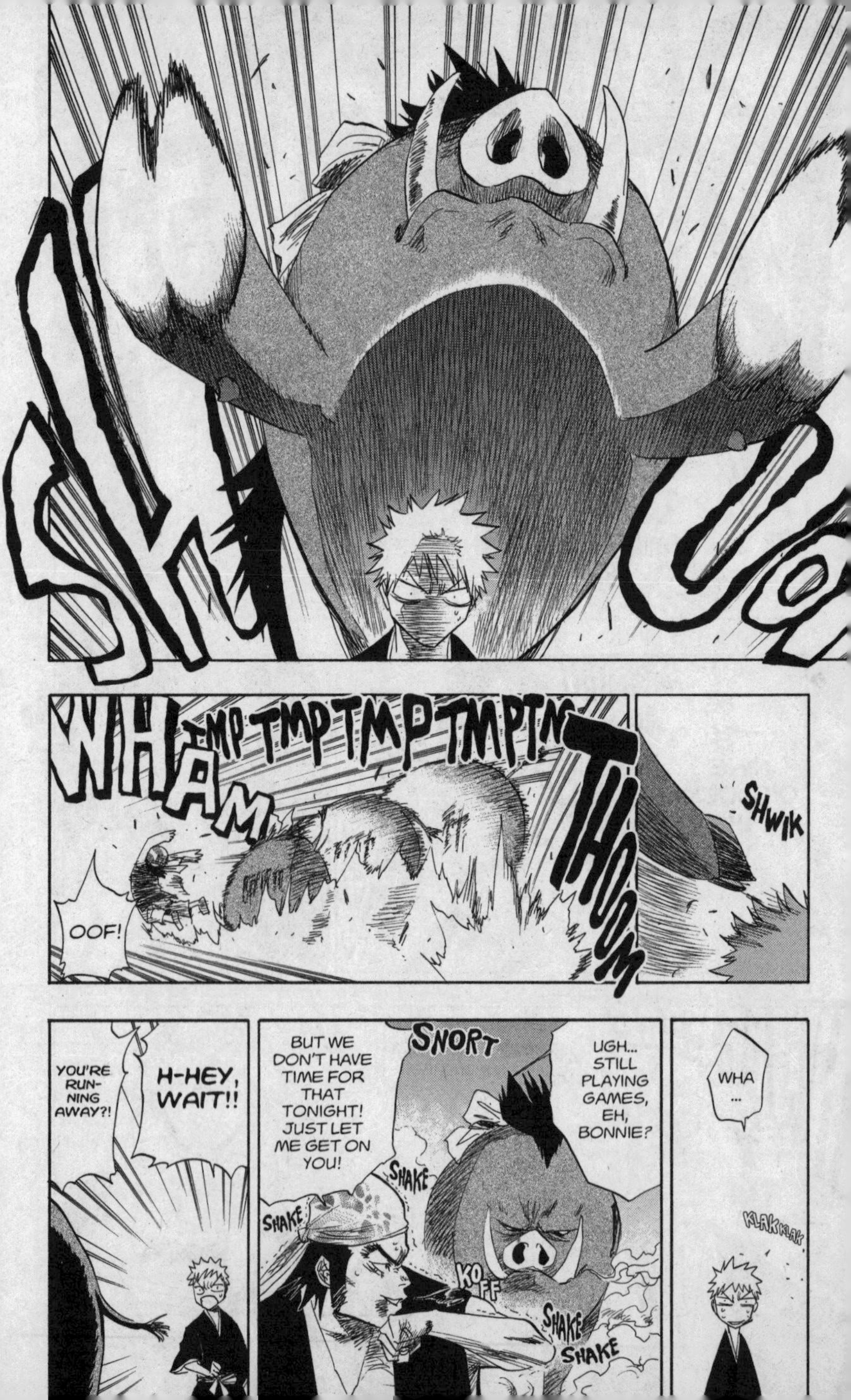
SHWIK
THOOOM
TMP TMP TMP TMP TMP TMP TM
WHAM
OOF!
WHA ...
KLAK KLAK
UGH... STILL PLAYING GAMES, EH, BONNIE?
SNORT
BUT WE DON'T HAVE TIME FOR THAT TONIGHT! JUST LET ME GET ON YOU!
SHAKE
SHAKE
KOFF
SHAKE
SHAKE
H-HEY, WAIT!!
YOU'RE RUN-NING AWAY?!

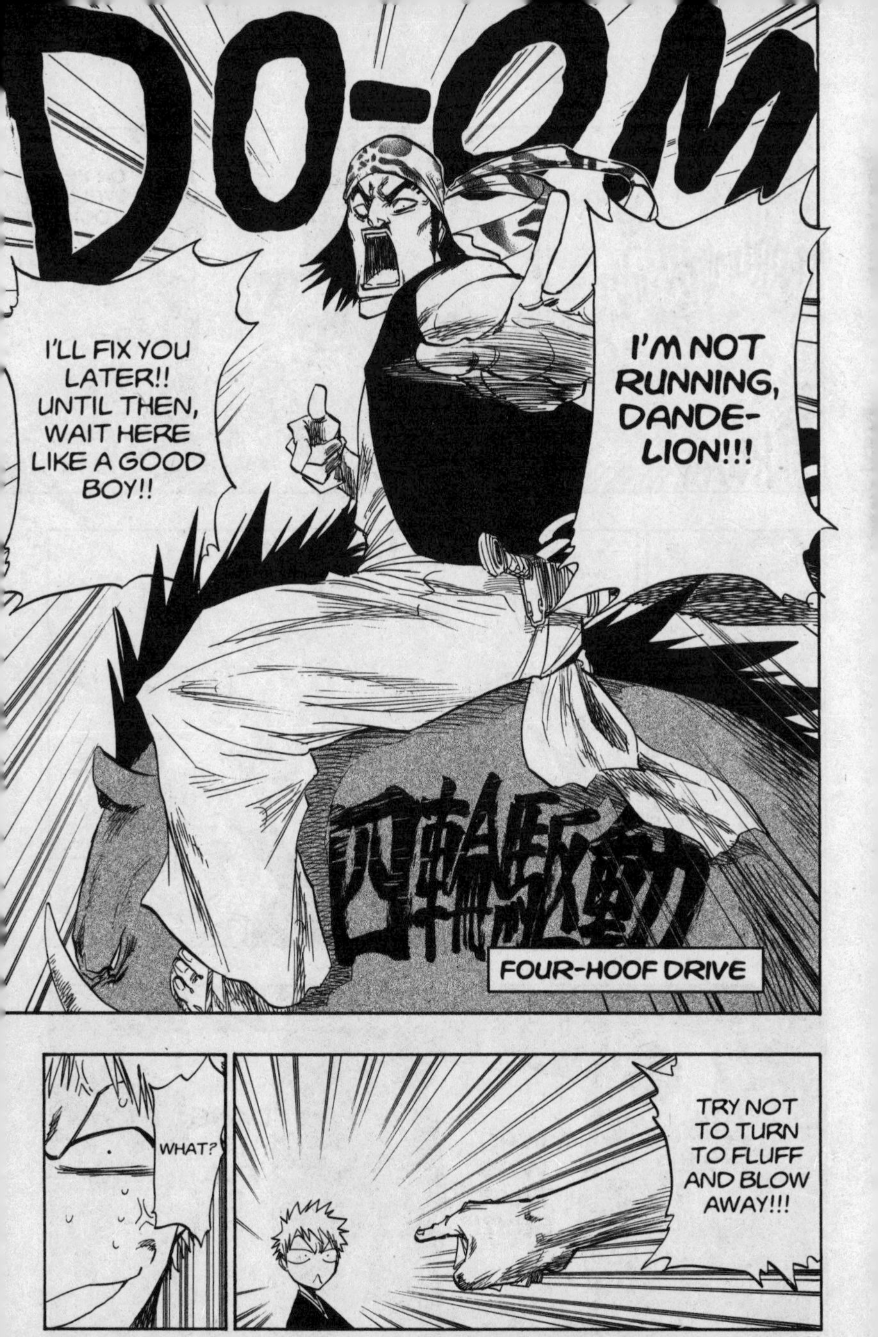
DO-OM
I'M NOT RUNNING, DANDE- LION!!!
I'LL FIX YOU LATER!! UNTIL THEN, WAIT HERE LIKE A GOOD BOY!!
FOUR-HOOF DRIVE
TRY NOT TO TURN TO FLUFF AND BLOW AWAY!!!
WHAT?

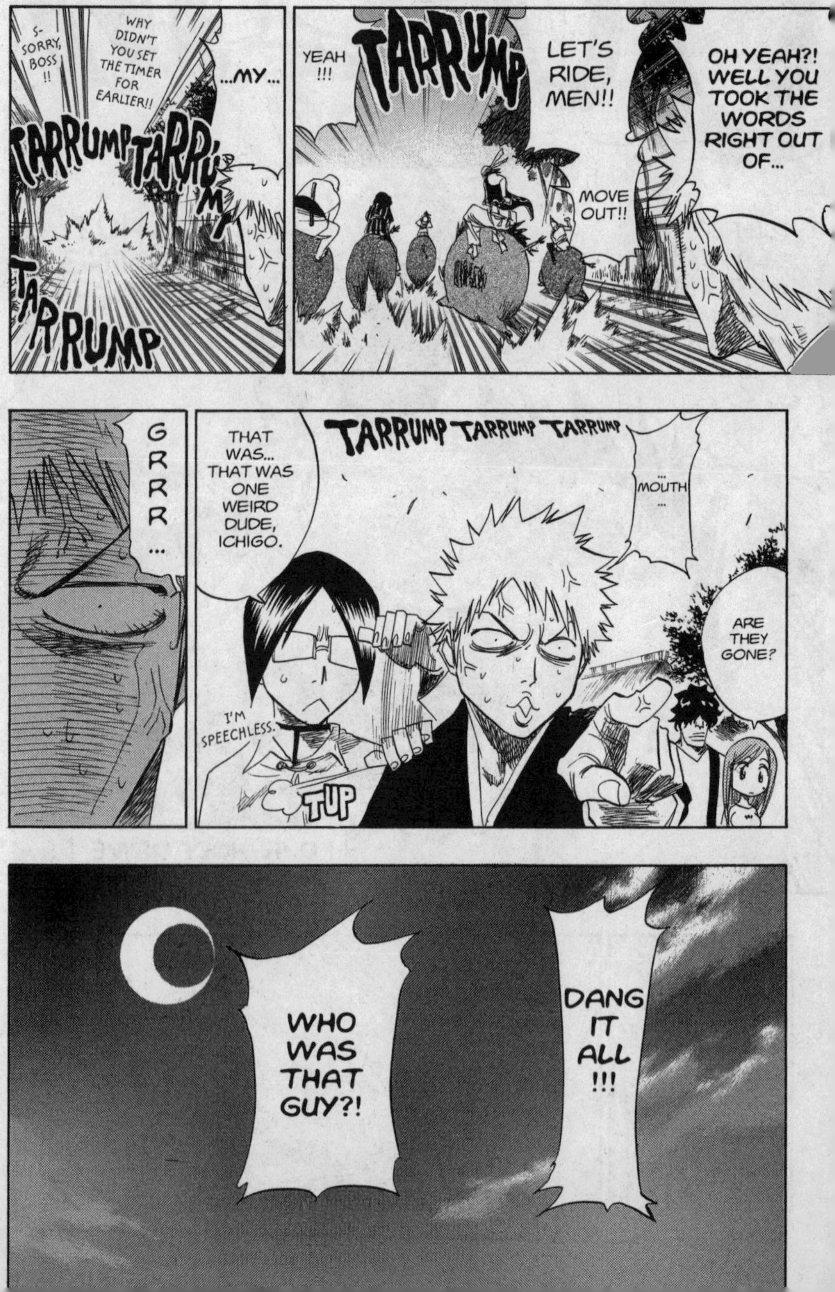
OH YEAH?! WELL YOU TOOK THE WORDS RIGHT OUT OF...
LET'S RIDE, MEN!!
MOVE OUT!!
TARRUMP
YEAH!!!
...MY...
WHY DIDN'T YOU SET THE TIMER FOR EARLIER!!
S-SORRY, BOSS!!
TARRUMP TARRUMP
TARRUMP
...MOUTH...
ARE THEY GONE?
TARRUMP TARRUMP TARRUMP
THAT WAS... THAT WAS ONE WEIRD DUDE, ICHIGO.
I'M SPEECHLESS.
TUP
GRRR...
DANG IT ALL!!!
WHO WAS THAT GUY?!

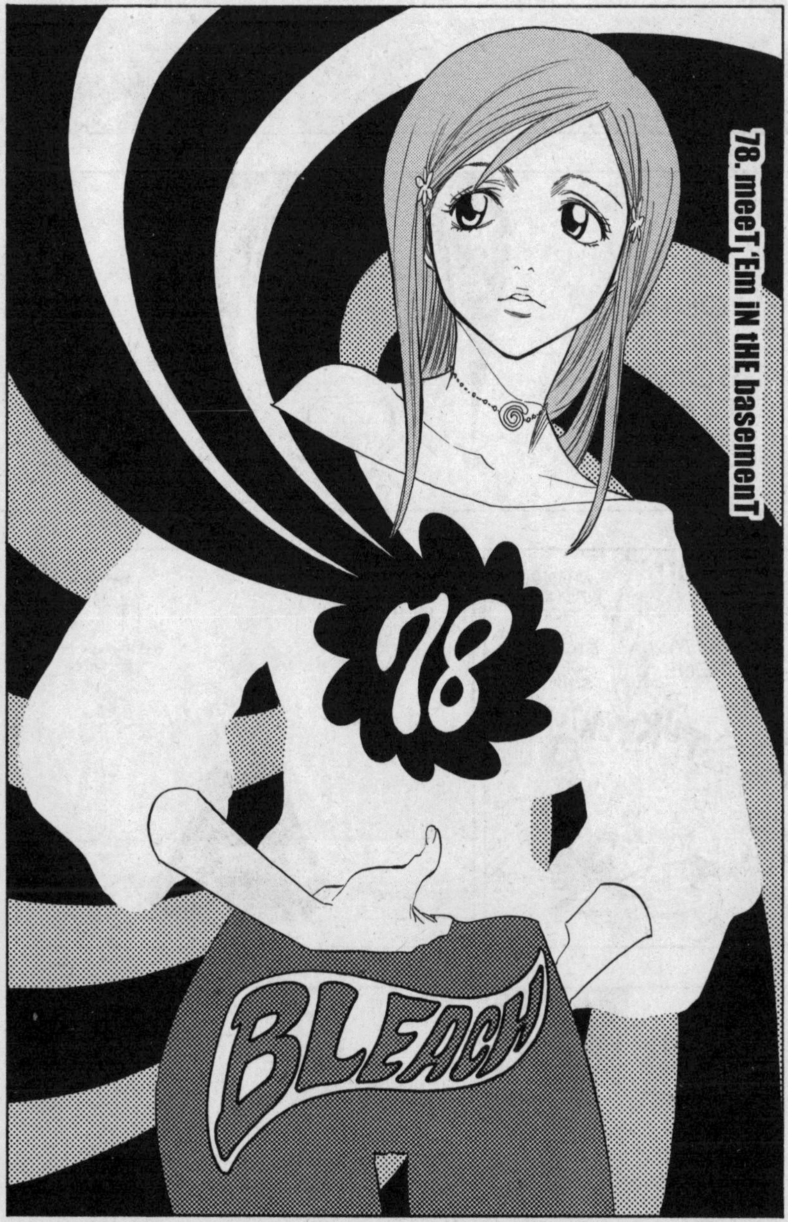
78. meeT 'Em iN tHE basemenT
78
BLEACH

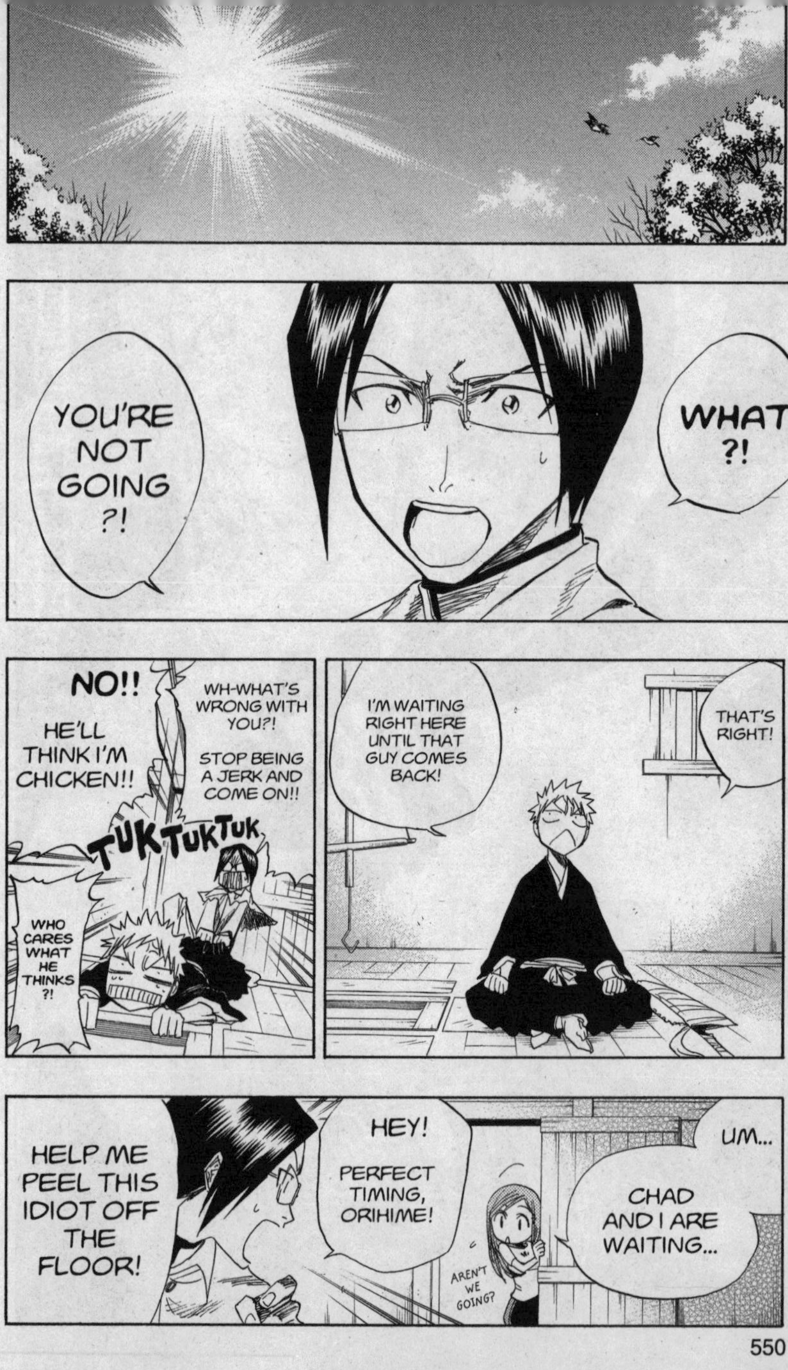
WHAT?!
YOU'RE NOT GOING?!
THAT'S RIGHT!
I'M WAITING RIGHT HERE UNTIL THAT GUY COMES BACK!
WH-WHAT'S WRONG WITH YOU?!
STOP BEING A JERK AND COME ON!!
NO!!
HE'LL THINK I'M CHICKEN!!
TUK TUK TUK
WHO CARES WHAT HE THINKS?!
UM...
CHAD AND I ARE WAITING...
AREN'T WE GOING?
HEY!
PERFECT TIMING, ORIHIME!
HELP ME PEEL THIS IDIOT OFF THE FLOOR!

READ THIS WAY

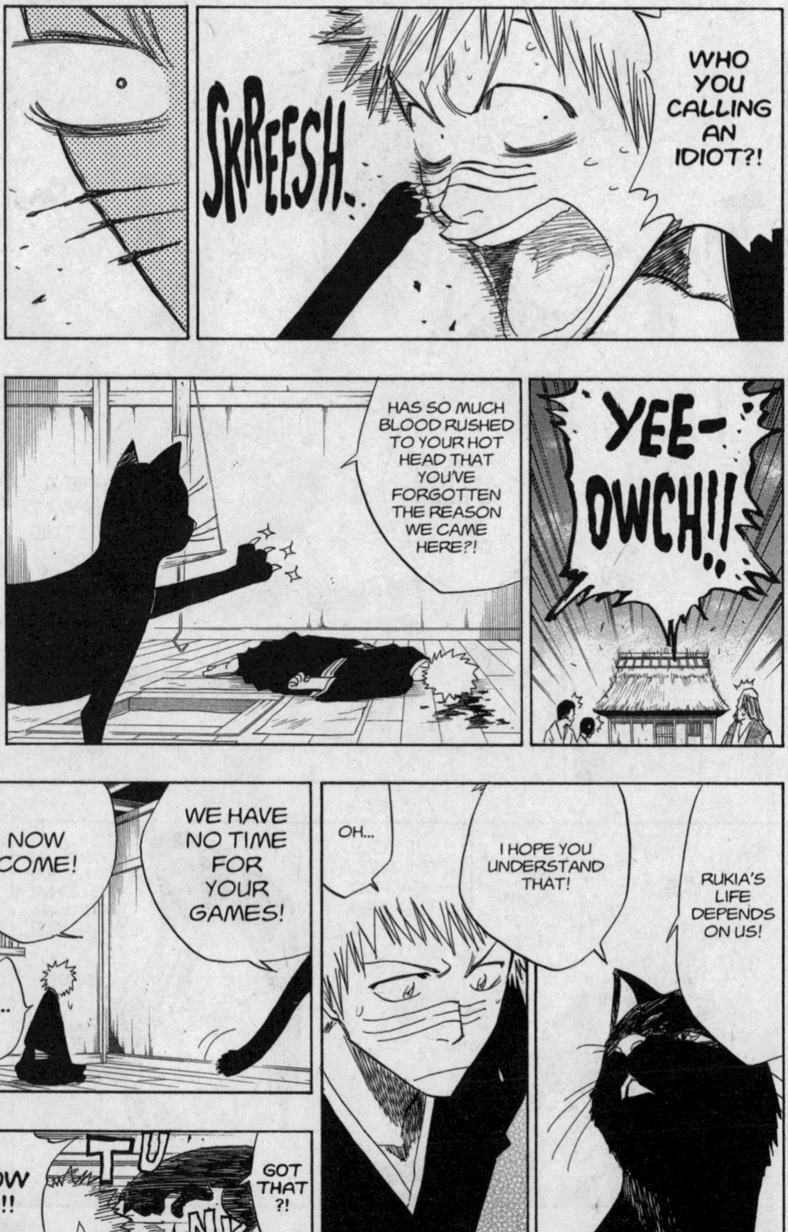
WHO YOU CALLING AN IDIOT?!
SKREESH
YEE-OWCH!!
HAS SO MUCH BLOOD RUSHED TO YOUR HOT HEAD THAT YOU'VE FORGOTTEN THE REASON WE CAME HERE?!
RUKIA'S LIFE DEPENDS ON US!
I HOPE YOU UNDERSTAND THAT!
OH...
WE HAVE NO TIME FOR YOUR GAMES!
NOW COME!
...
GOT THAT?!
TUNK
OW!!

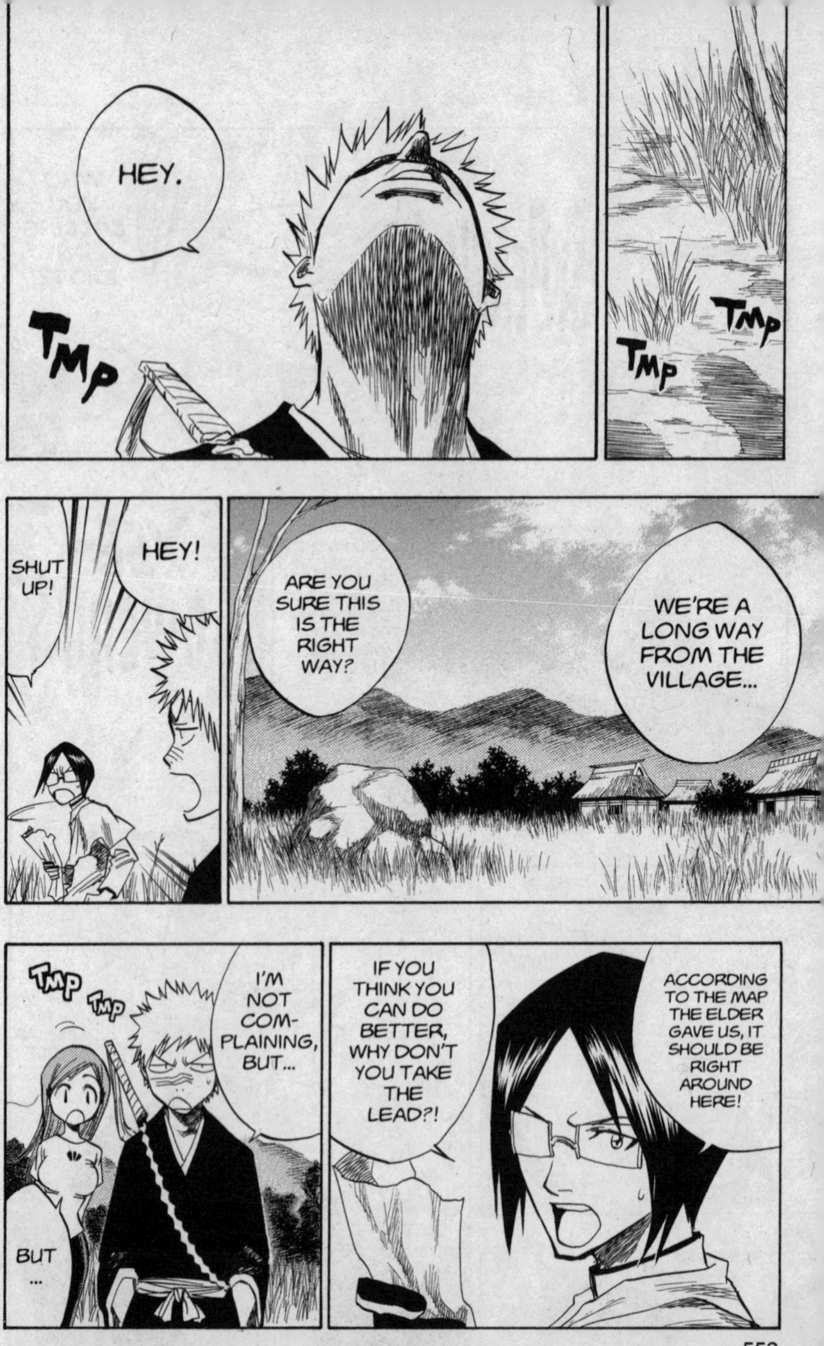
TMP
TMP
HEY.
TMP
WE'RE A LONG WAY FROM THE VILLAGE...
ARE YOU SURE THIS IS THE RIGHT WAY?
HEY!
SHUT UP!
ACCORDING TO THE MAP THE ELDER GAVE US, IT SHOULD BE RIGHT AROUND HERE!
IF YOU THINK YOU CAN DO BETTER, WHY DON'T YOU TAKE THE LEAD?!
I'M NOT COM-PLAINING, BUT...
TMP
TMP
BUT ...

READ THIS WAY

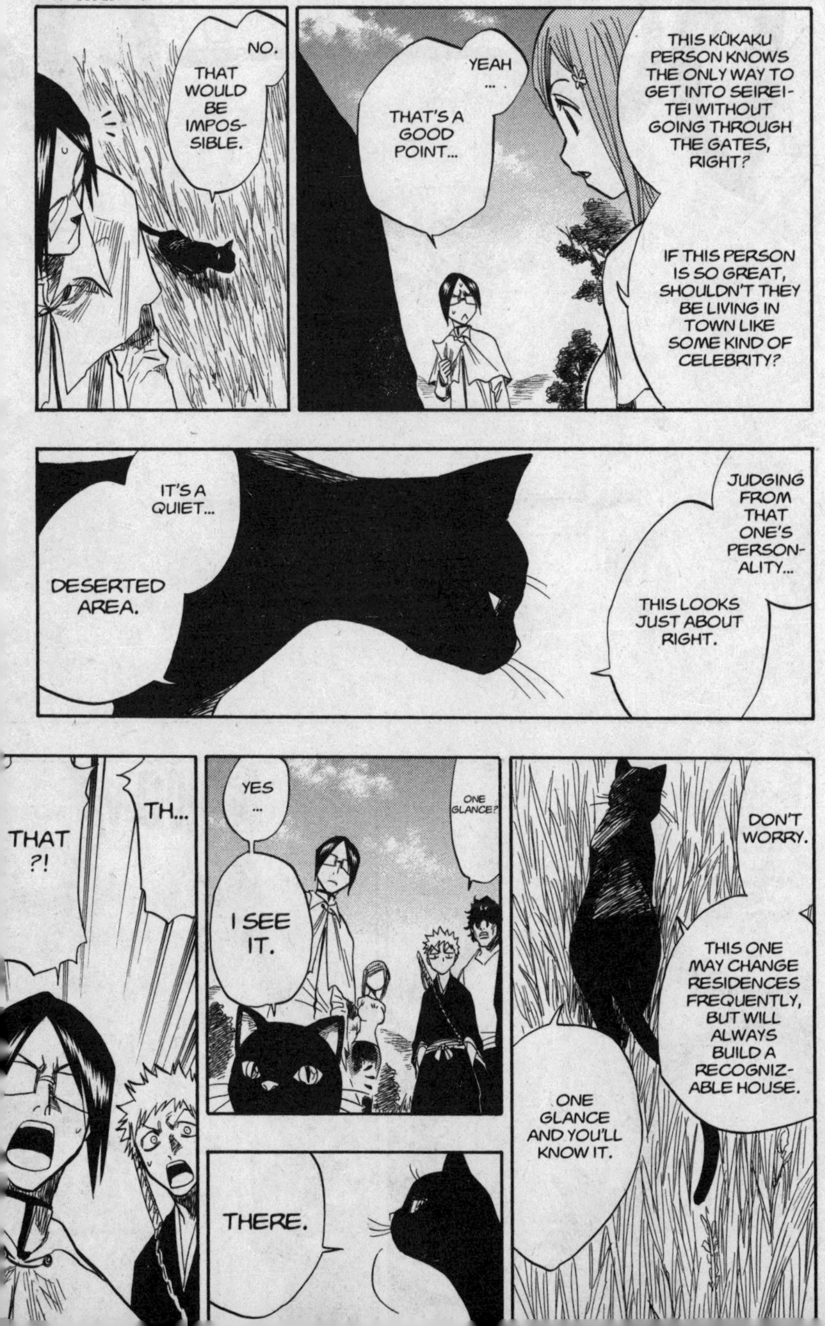

THIS KÛKAKU PERSON KNOWS THE ONLY WAY TO GET INTO SEIREI-TEI WITHOUT GOING THROUGH THE GATES, RIGHT?
IF THIS PERSON IS SO GREAT, SHOULDN'T THEY BE LIVING IN TOWN LIKE SOME KIND OF CELEBRITY?
YEAH... THAT'S A GOOD POINT...
NO. THAT WOULD BE IMPOSSIBLE.
JUDGING FROM THAT ONE'S PERSONALITY... THIS LOOKS JUST ABOUT RIGHT.
IT'S A QUIET... DESERTED AREA.
DON'T WORRY.
THIS ONE MAY CHANGE RESIDENCES FREQUENTLY, BUT WILL ALWAYS BUILD A RECOGNIZABLE HOUSE.
ONE GLANCE AND YOU'LL KNOW IT.
ONE GLANCE?
YES... I SEE IT.
THERE.
TH...
THAT?!

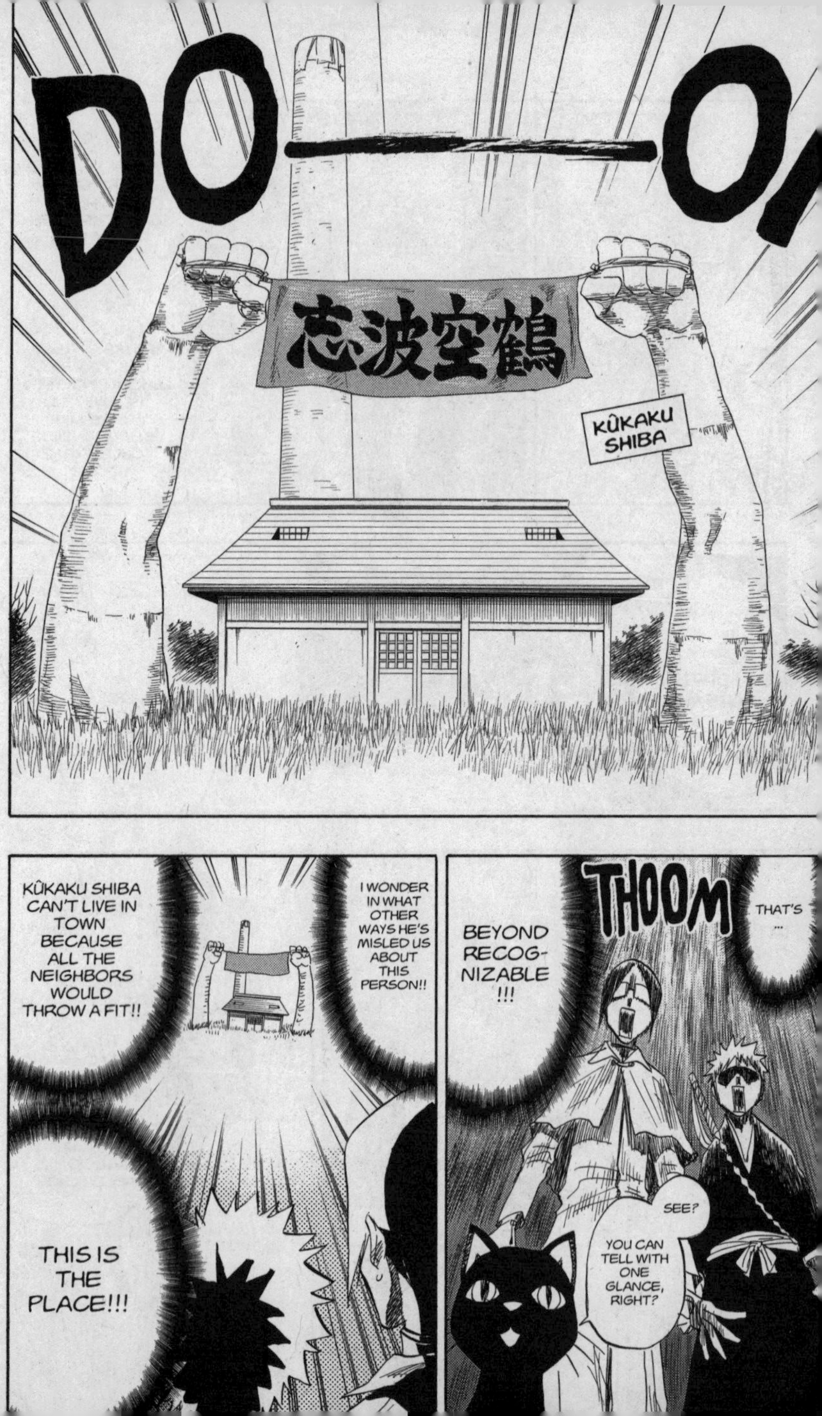
DO—O
志波空鶴
KÛKAKU SHIBA
THOOM
THAT'S ...
BEYOND RECOG-NIZABLE!!!
SEE?
YOU CAN TELL WITH ONE GLANCE, RIGHT?
I WONDER IN WHAT OTHER WAYS HE'S MISLED US ABOUT THIS PERSON!!
KÛKAKU SHIBA CAN'T LIVE IN TOWN BECAUSE ALL THE NEIGHBORS WOULD THROW A FIT!!
THIS IS THE PLACE!!!

READ THIS WAY

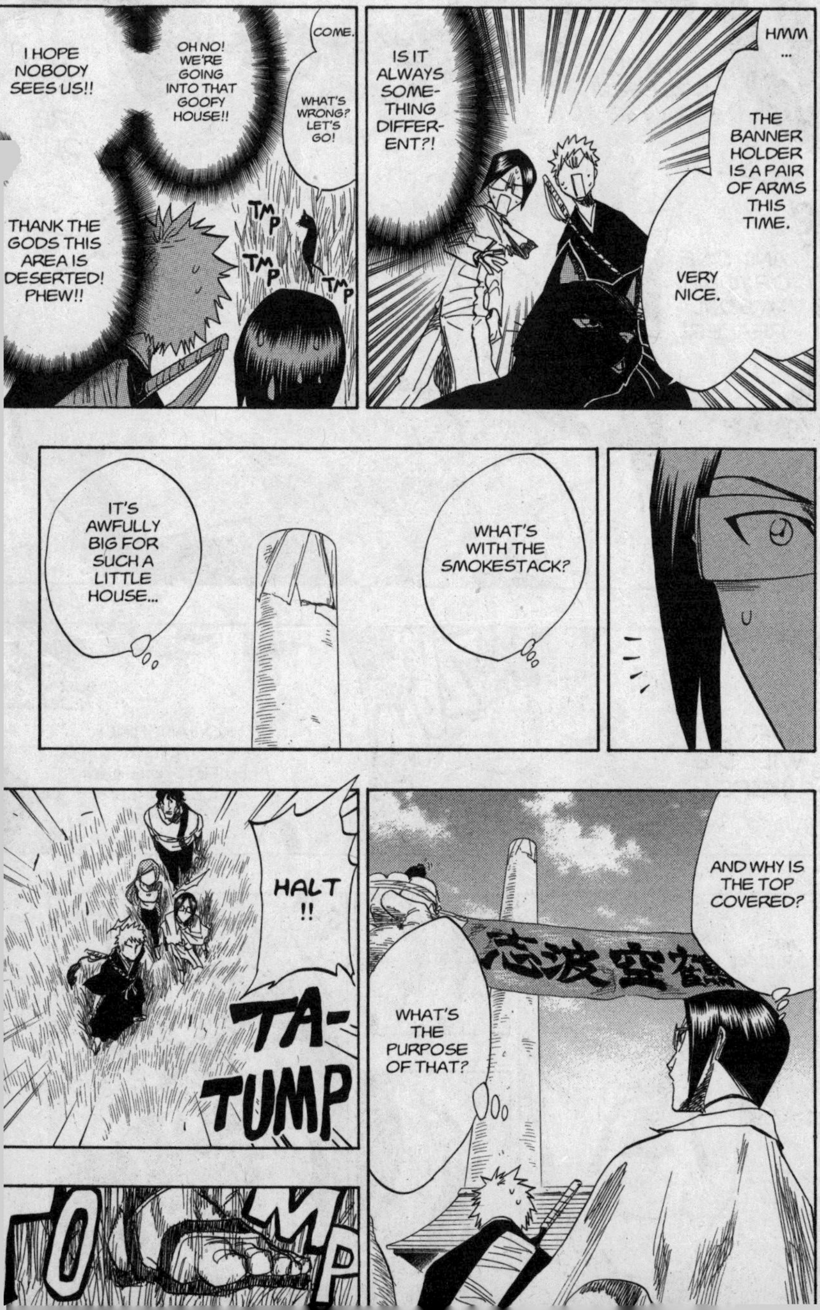

HMM ...
THE BANNER HOLDER IS A PAIR OF ARMS THIS TIME.
VERY NICE.
IS IT ALWAYS SOME-THING DIFFER-ENT?!
COME.
WHAT'S WRONG? LET'S GO!
OH NO! WE'RE GOING INTO THAT GOOFY HOUSE!!
I HOPE NOBODY SEES US!!
THANK THE GODS THIS AREA IS DESERTED! PHEW!!
TMP
TMP
TMP
WHAT'S WITH THE SMOKESTACK?
IT'S AWFULLY BIG FOR SUCH A LITTLE HOUSE...
AND WHY IS THE TOP COVERED?
WHAT'S THE PURPOSE OF THAT?
HALT !!
TA-TUMP

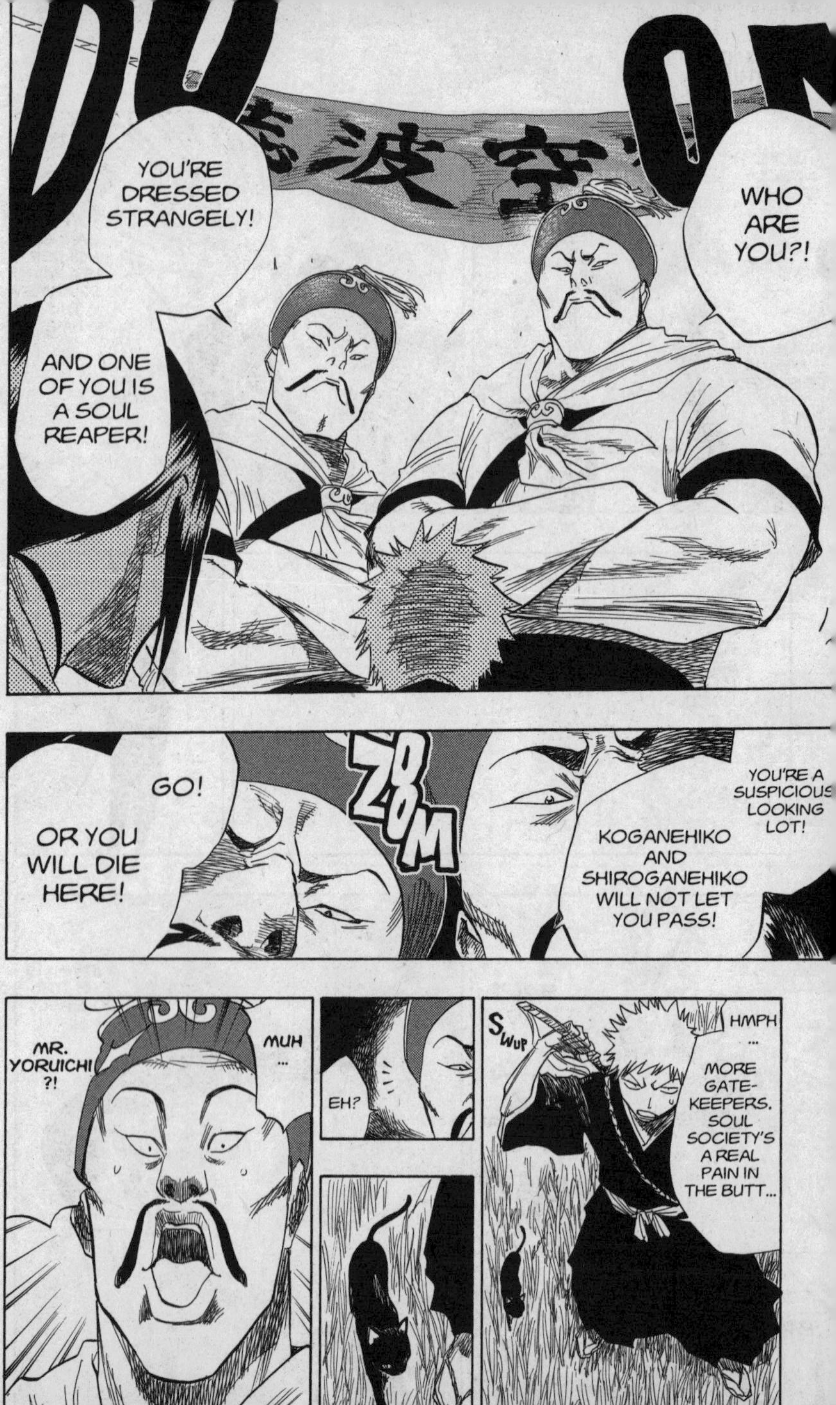
WHO ARE YOU?!
YOU'RE DRESSED STRANGELY!
AND ONE OF YOU IS A SOUL REAPER!
YOU'RE A SUSPICIOUS LOOKING LOT!
KOGANEHIKO AND SHIROGANEHIKO WILL NOT LET YOU PASS!
ZOOM
GO!
OR YOU WILL DIE HERE!
HMPH ...
SWUP
MORE GATE-KEEPERS. SOUL SOCIETY'S A REAL PAIN IN THE BUTT...
EH?
MUH ...
MR. YORUICHI ?!

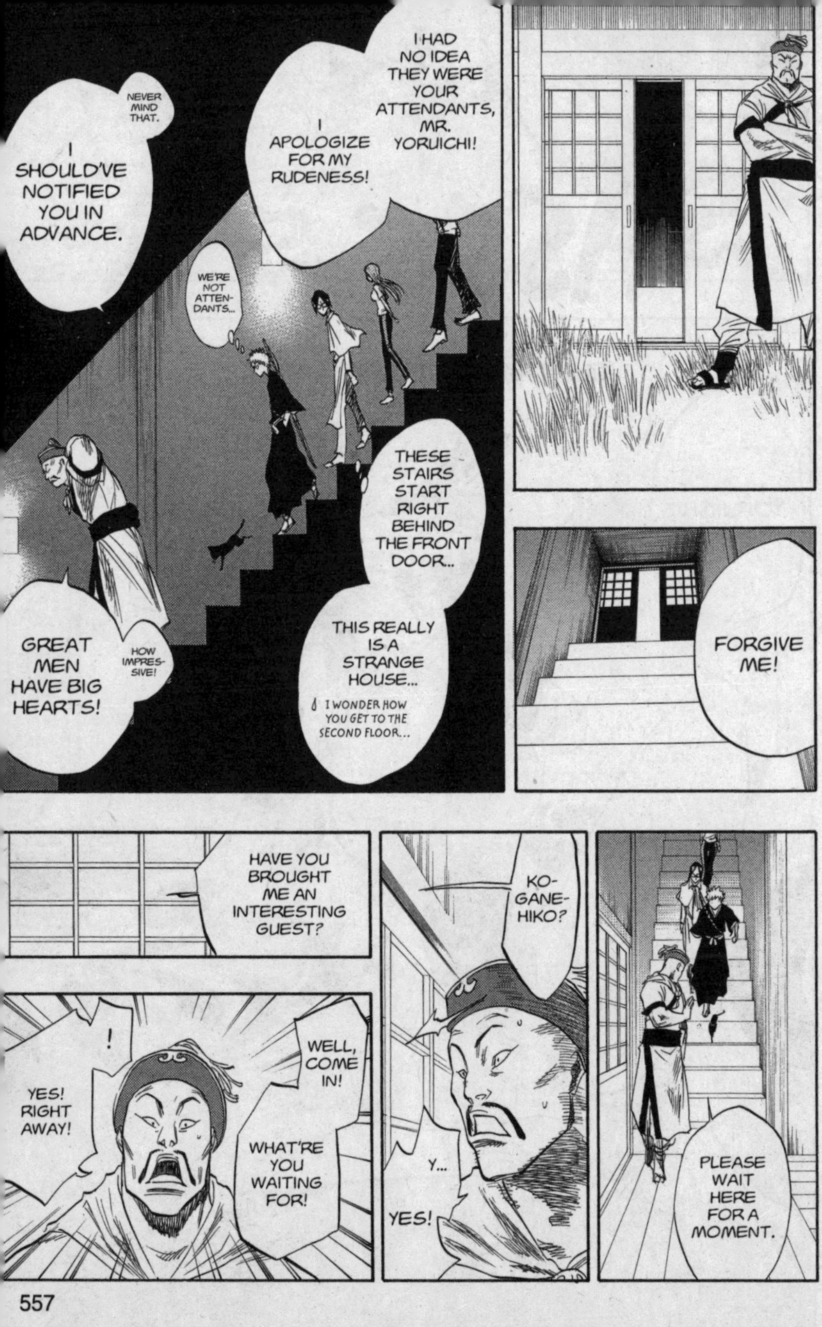
FORGIVE ME!
I HAD NO IDEA THEY WERE YOUR ATTENDANTS, MR. YORUICHI!
I APOLOGIZE FOR MY RUDENESS!
NEVER MIND THAT.
I SHOULD'VE NOTIFIED YOU IN ADVANCE.
WE'RE NOT ATTENDANTS...
THESE STAIRS START RIGHT BEHIND THE FRONT DOOR...
THIS REALLY IS A STRANGE HOUSE...
I WONDER HOW YOU GET TO THE SECOND FLOOR...
GREAT MEN HAVE BIG HEARTS!
HOW IMPRESSIVE!
PLEASE WAIT HERE FOR A MOMENT.
KO-GANE-HIKO?
Y...
YES!
HAVE YOU BROUGHT ME AN INTERESTING GUEST?
!
YES! RIGHT AWAY!
WELL, COME IN!
WHAT'RE YOU WAITING FOR!

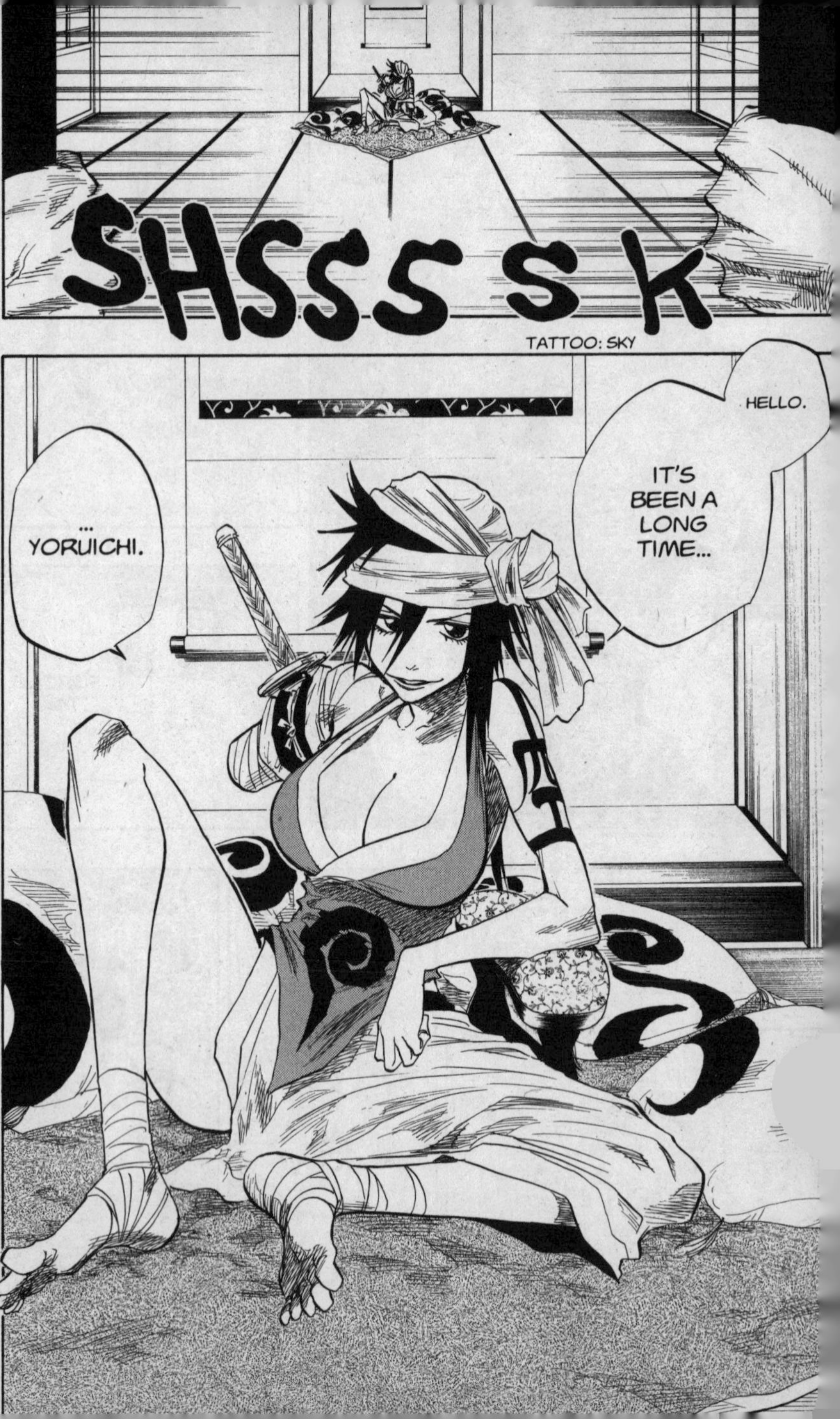
SHSSS S K
TATTOO: SKY
HELLO.
IT'S BEEN A LONG TIME...
... YORUICHI.

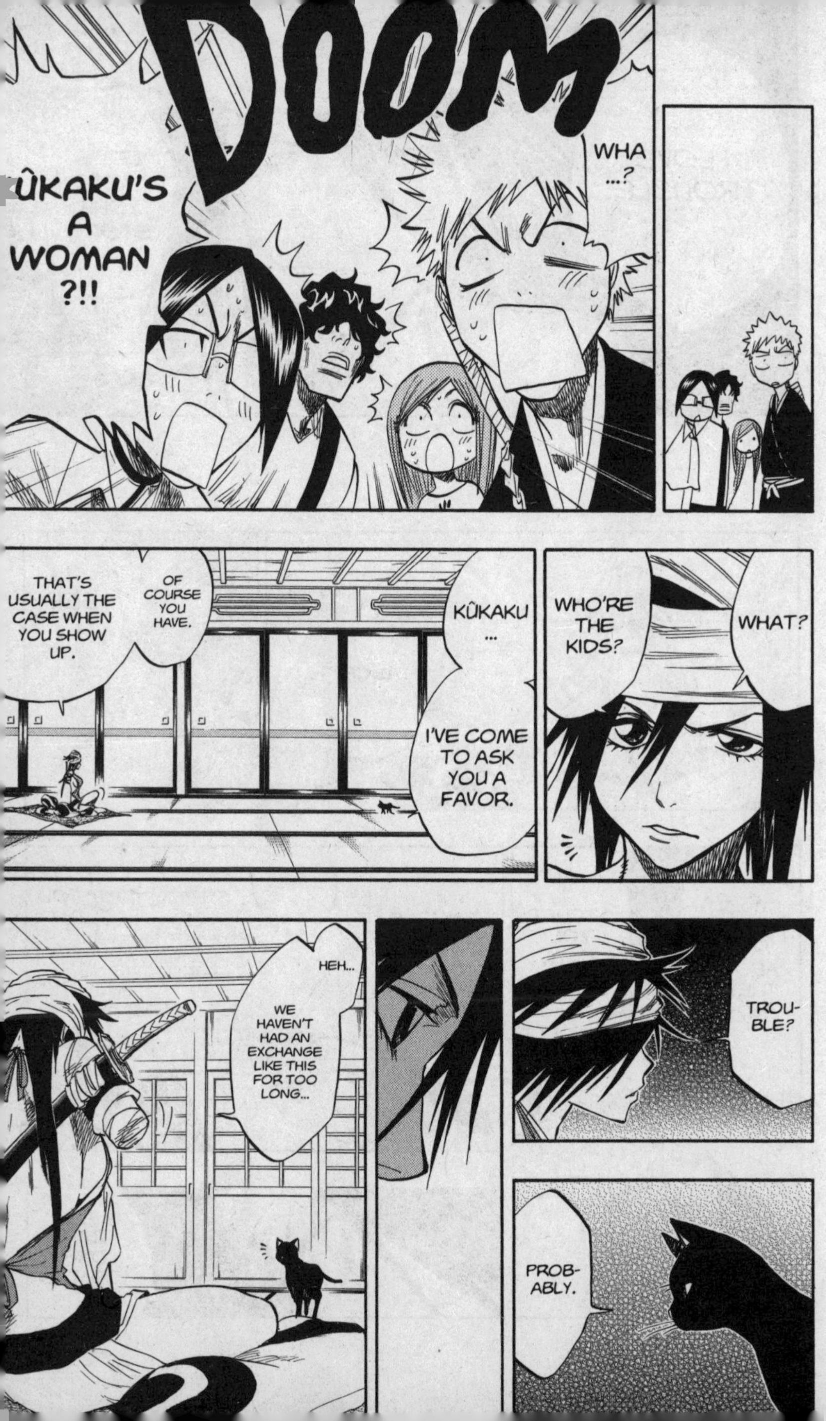

WHA ...?
DOOM
ÛKAKU'S A WOMAN?!!
WHAT?
WHO'RE THE KIDS?
KÛKAKU ...
I'VE COME TO ASK YOU A FAVOR.
OF COURSE YOU HAVE.
THAT'S USUALLY THE CASE WHEN YOU SHOW UP.
TROU-BLE?
PROB-ABLY.
HEH...
WE HAVEN'T HAD AN EXCHANGE LIKE THIS FOR TOO LONG...

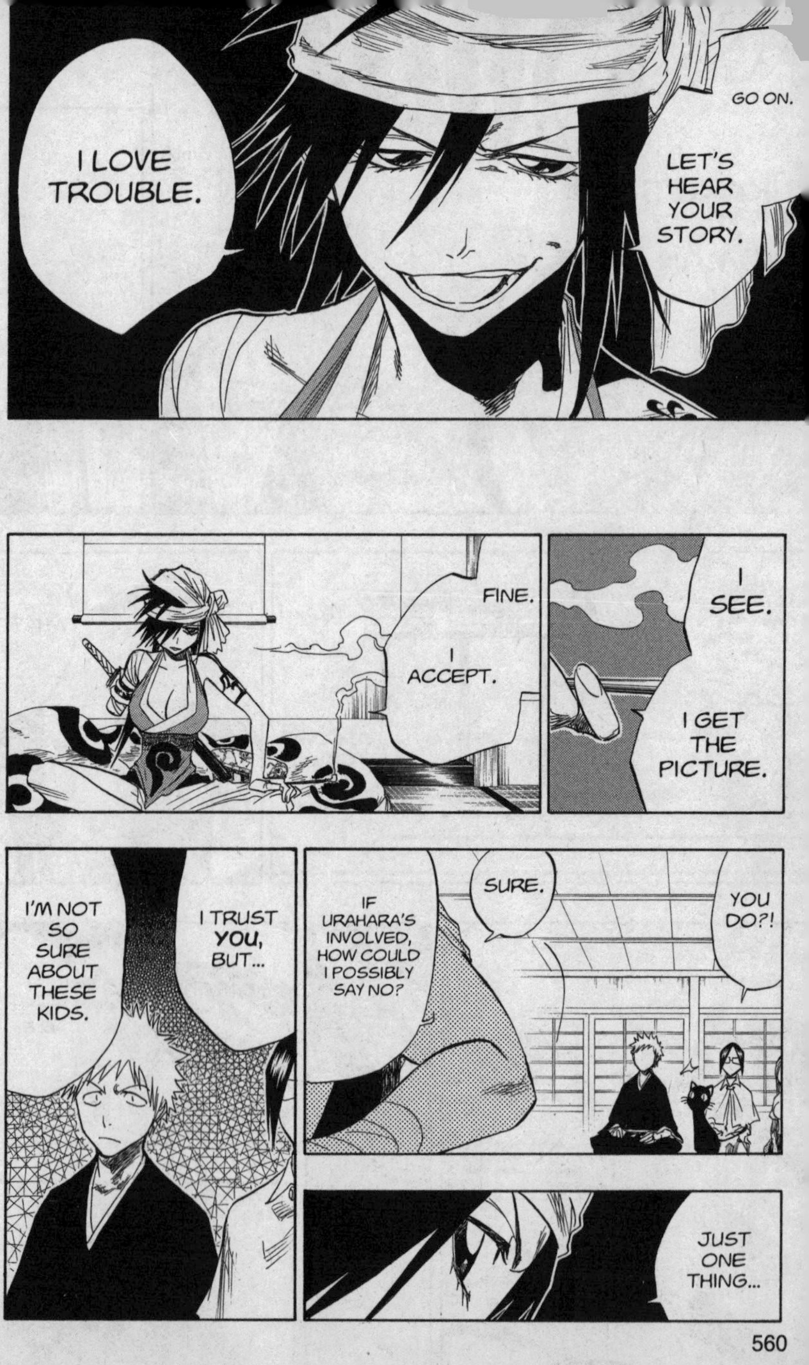
GO ON.
LET'S HEAR YOUR STORY.
I LOVE TROUBLE.
I SEE.
I GET THE PICTURE.
FINE.
I ACCEPT.
YOU DO?!
SURE.
IF URAHARA'S INVOLVED, HOW COULD I POSSIBLY SAY NO?
I TRUST **YOU,** BUT...
I'M NOT SO SURE ABOUT THESE KIDS.
JUST ONE THING...

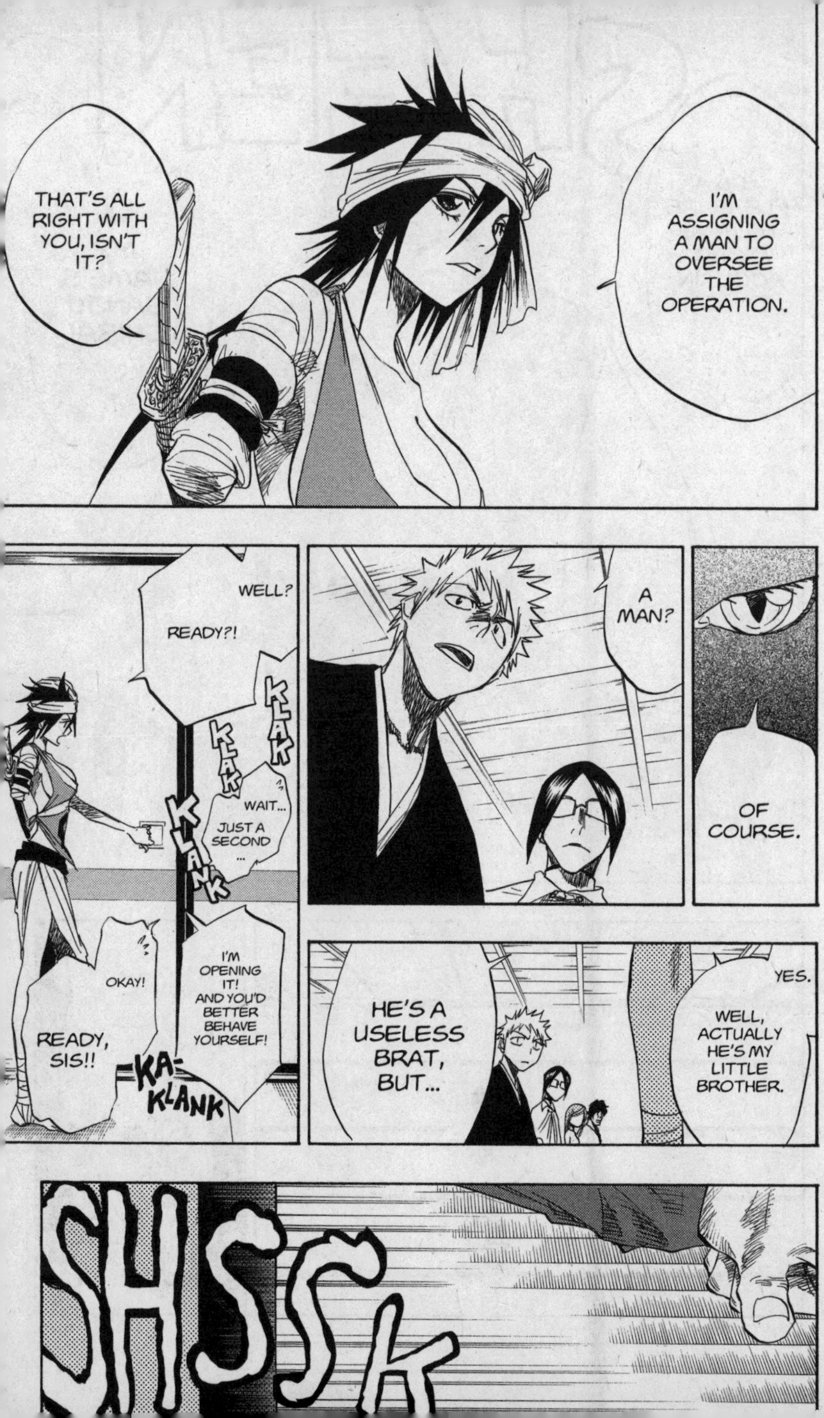
I'M ASSIGNING A MAN TO OVERSEE THE OPERATION.
THAT'S ALL RIGHT WITH YOU, ISN'T IT?
OF COURSE.
A MAN?
YES.
WELL, ACTUALLY HE'S MY LITTLE BROTHER.
HE'S A USELESS BRAT, BUT...
WELL?
READY?!
KLAK
KLAK
WAIT... JUST A SECOND...
KLANK
I'M OPENING IT! AND YOU'D BETTER BEHAVE YOURSELF!
OKAY!
READY, SIS!!
KA-KLANK
SHSSK

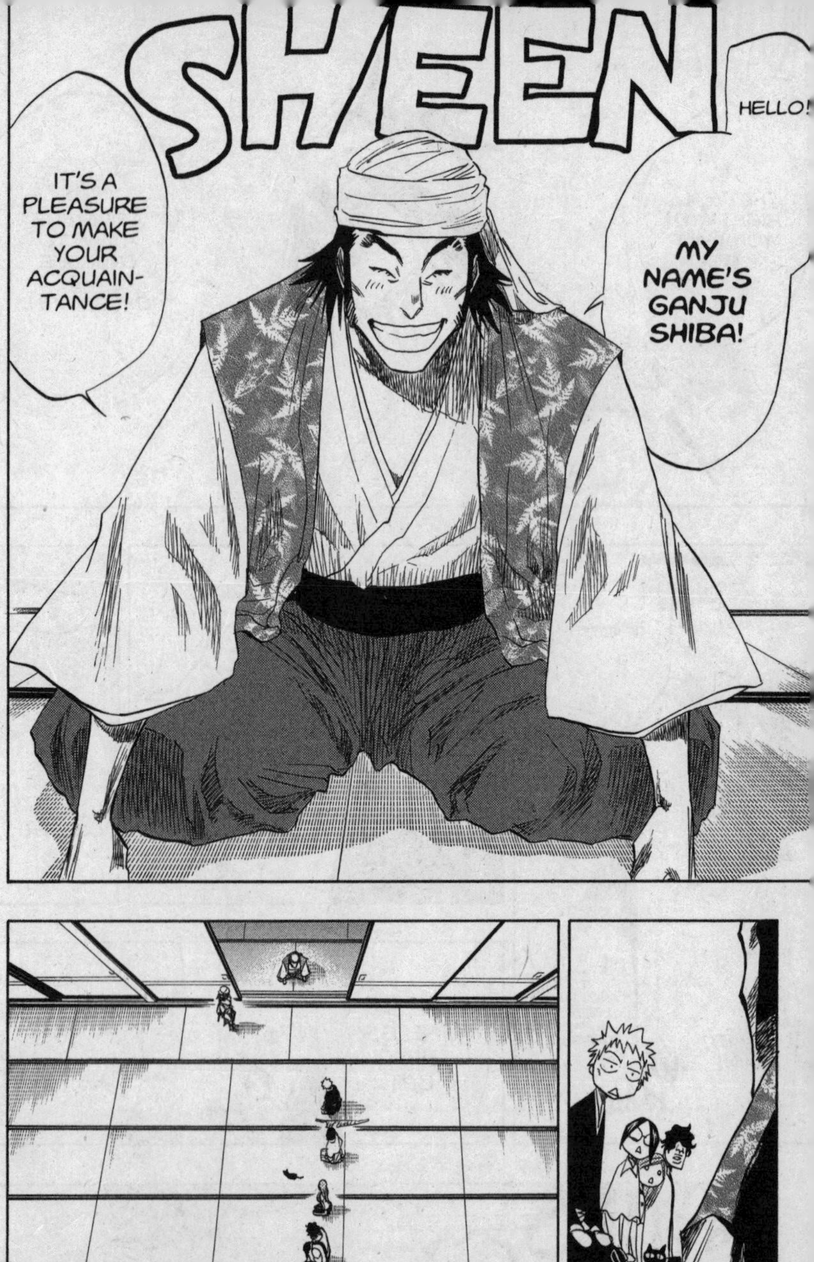
SHEEN
HELLO!
MY NAME'S GANJU SHIBA!
IT'S A PLEASURE TO MAKE YOUR ACQUAIN-TANCE!

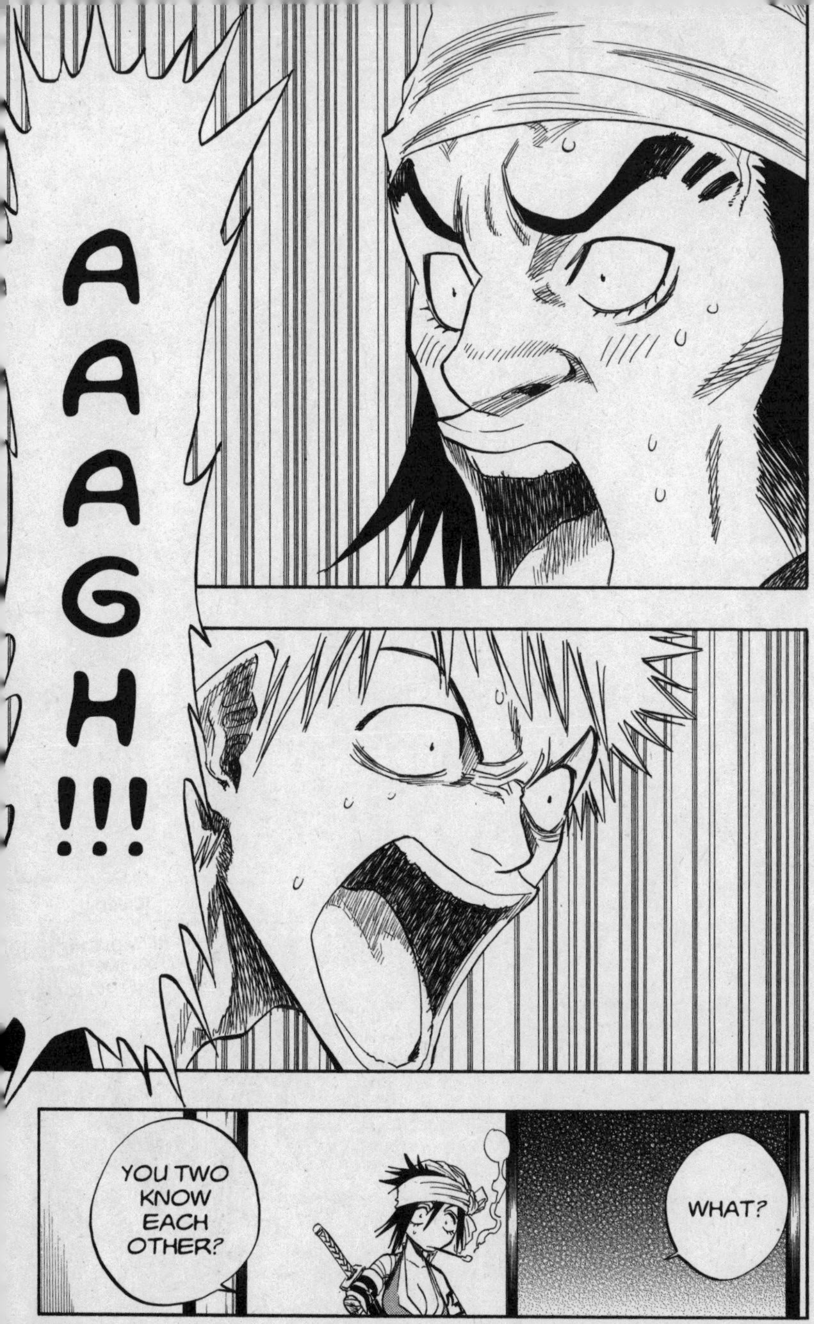
AAAGH!!!
WHAT?
YOU TWO KNOW EACH OTHER?

ICHIGO...

YOU'VE BEEN OVERREACTING TO EVERYTHING SINCE YOU GOT TO THE SOUL SOCIETY.

ARE YOU JUST TIRED OR ARE YOU WORRIED ABOUT US?

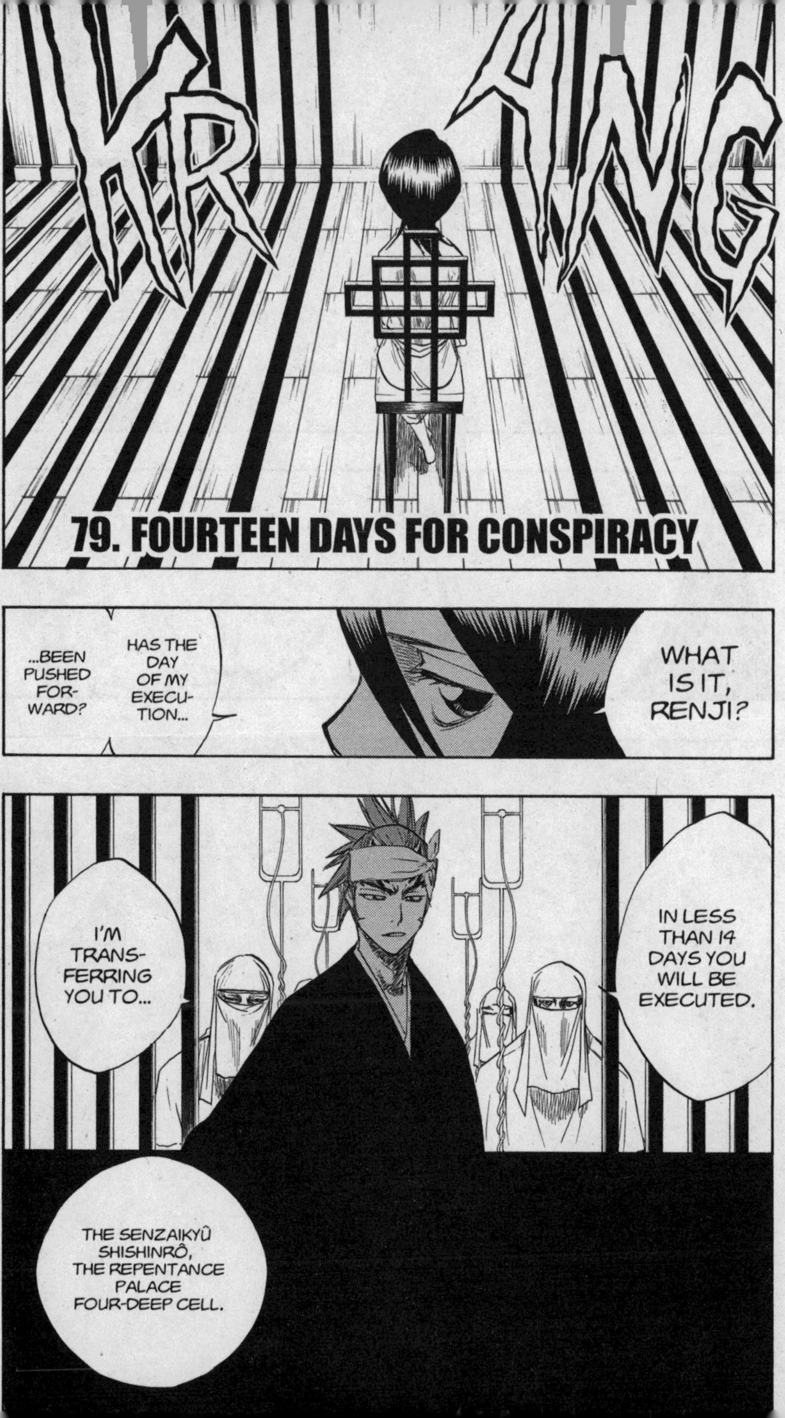
KR ANG
79. FOURTEEN DAYS FOR CONSPIRACY
WHAT IS IT, RENJI?
HAS THE DAY OF MY EXECUTION...
...BEEN PUSHED FORWARD?
IN LESS THAN 14 DAYS YOU WILL BE EXECUTED.
I'M TRANSFERRING YOU TO...
THE SENZAIKYÛ SHISHINRÔ, THE REPENTANCE PALACE FOUR-DEEP CELL.

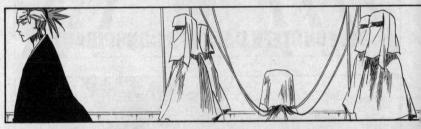

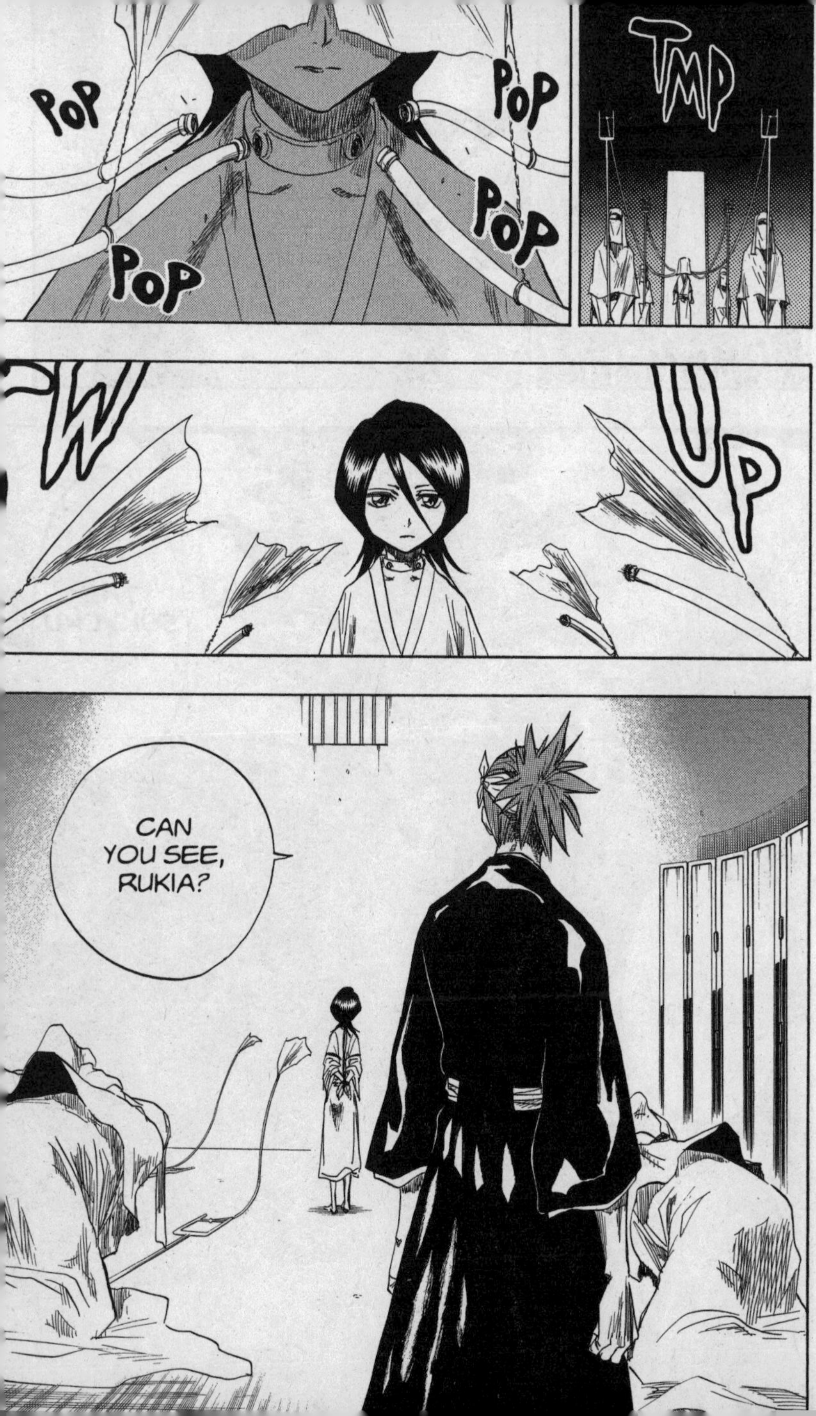
TMP
POP
POP
POP
POP
WHUP
CAN YOU SEE, RUKIA?

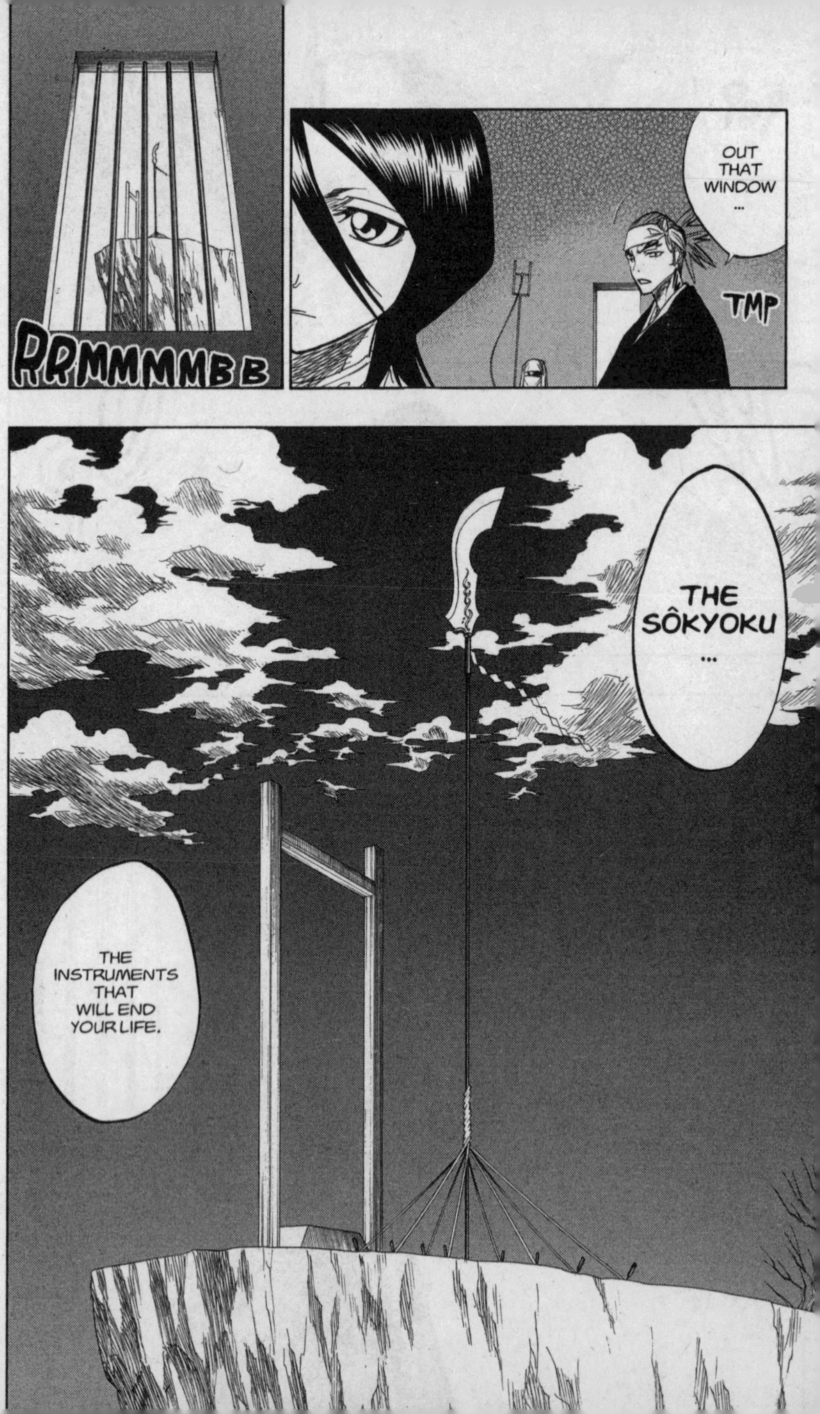
OUT THAT WINDOW ...
TMP
RRMMMMBB
THE SÔKYOKU ...
THE INSTRUMENTS THAT WILL END YOUR LIFE.

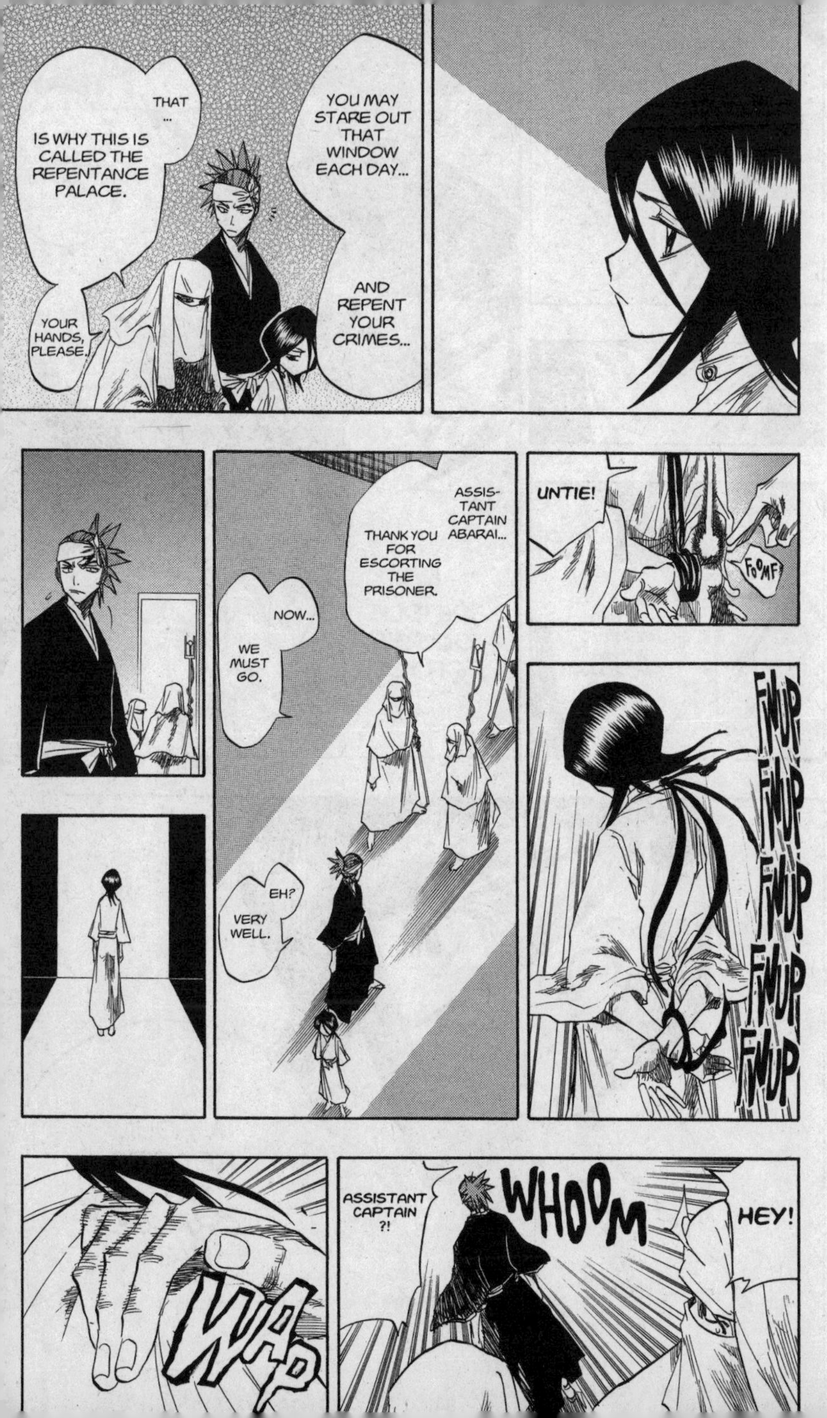
YOU MAY STARE OUT THAT WINDOW EACH DAY...
AND REPENT YOUR CRIMES...
THAT ...
IS WHY THIS IS CALLED THE REPENTANCE PALACE.
YOUR HANDS, PLEASE.
UNTIE!
FOOMF
FWUP FWUP FWUP FWUP FWUP FWUP
ASSISTANT CAPTAIN ABARAI...
THANK YOU FOR ESCORTING THE PRISONER.
NOW...
WE MUST GO.
EH?
VERY WELL.
HEY!
WHOOM
ASSISTANT CAPTAIN ?!
WAP

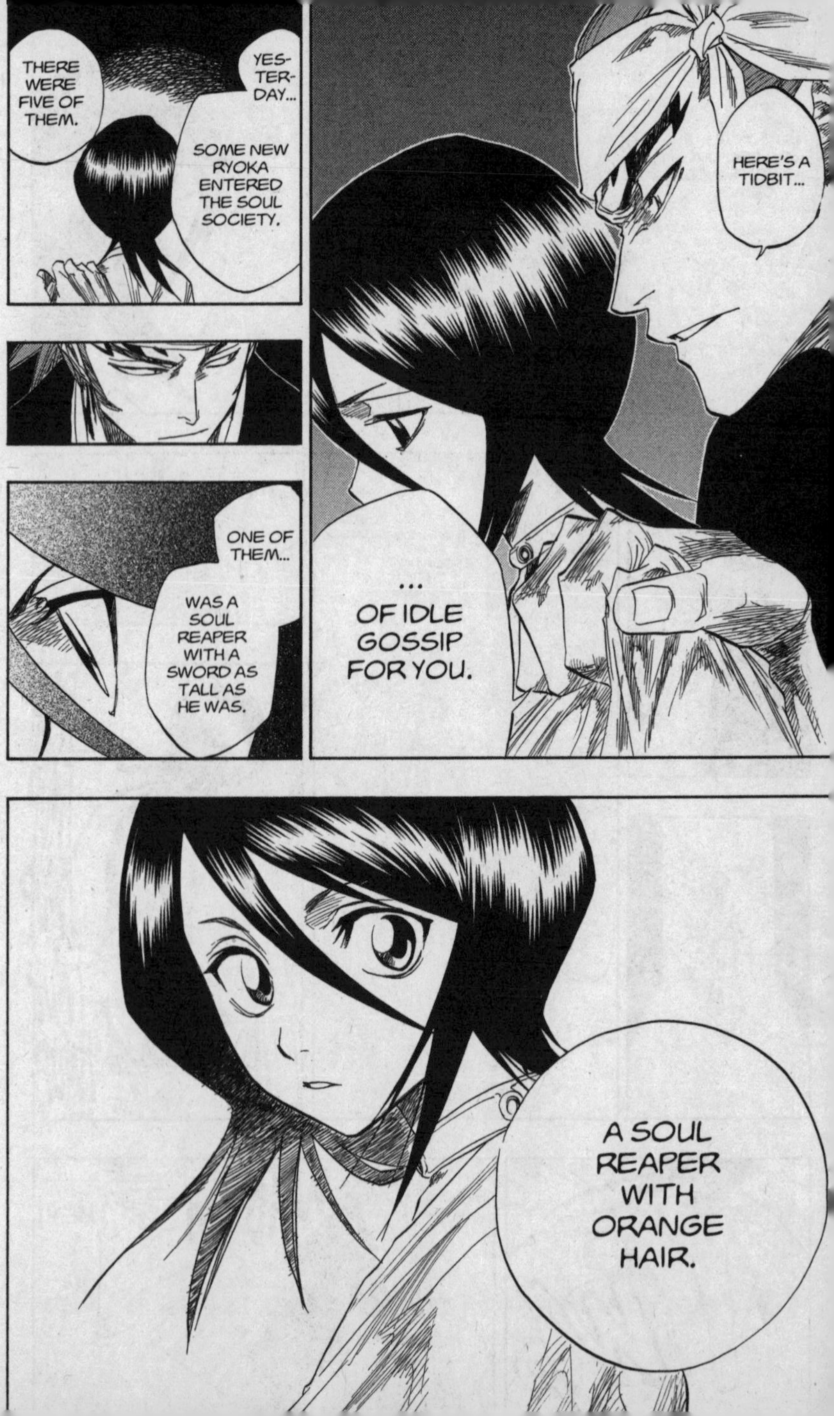
HERE'S A TIDBIT...
...OF IDLE GOSSIP FOR YOU.
YESTERDAY...
SOME NEW RYOKA ENTERED THE SOUL SOCIETY.
THERE WERE FIVE OF THEM.
ONE OF THEM...
WAS A SOUL REAPER WITH A SWORD AS TALL AS HE WAS.
A SOUL REAPER WITH ORANGE HAIR.

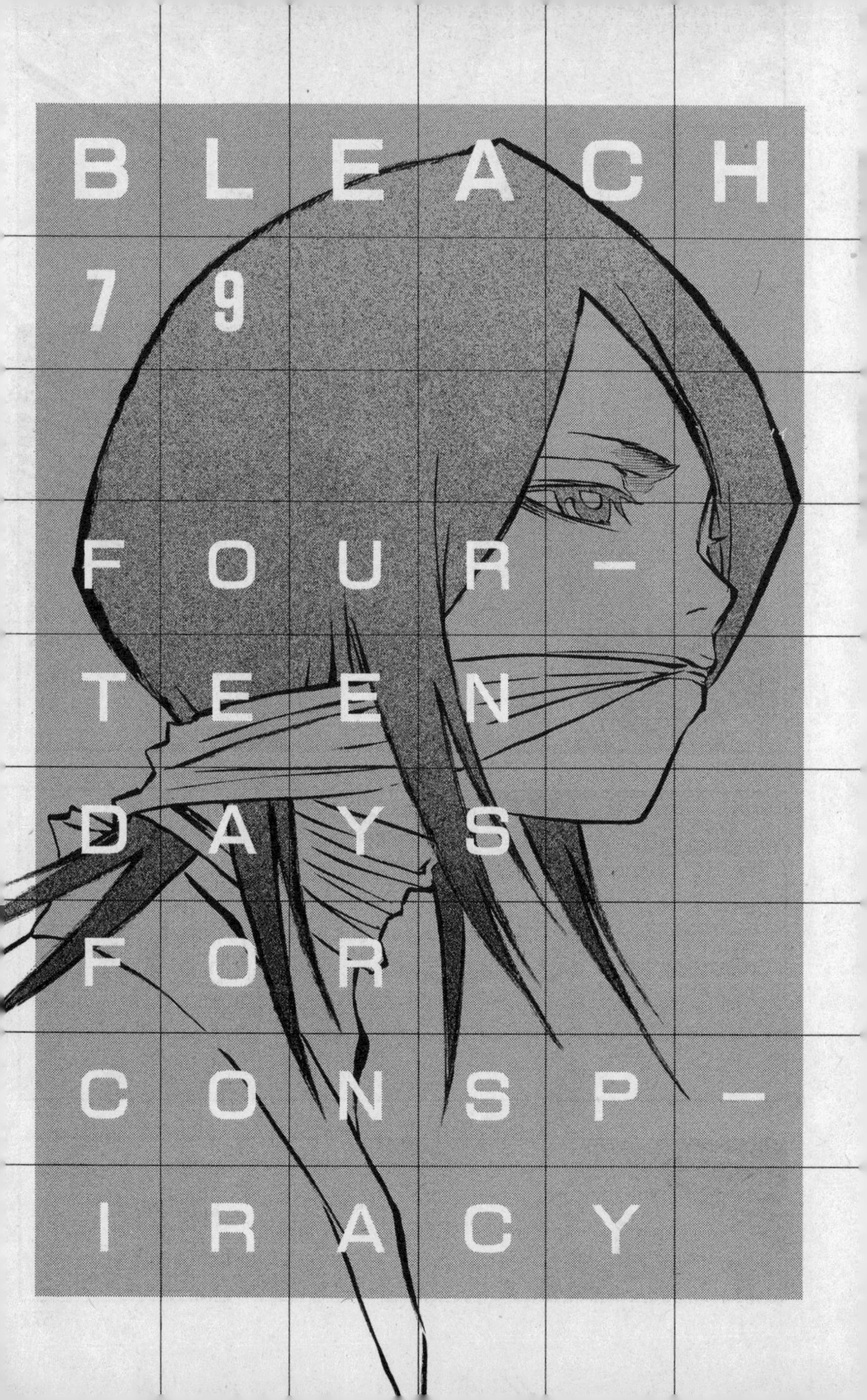
BLEACH
79
FOUR-
TEEN
DAYS
FOR
CONSP-
IRACY

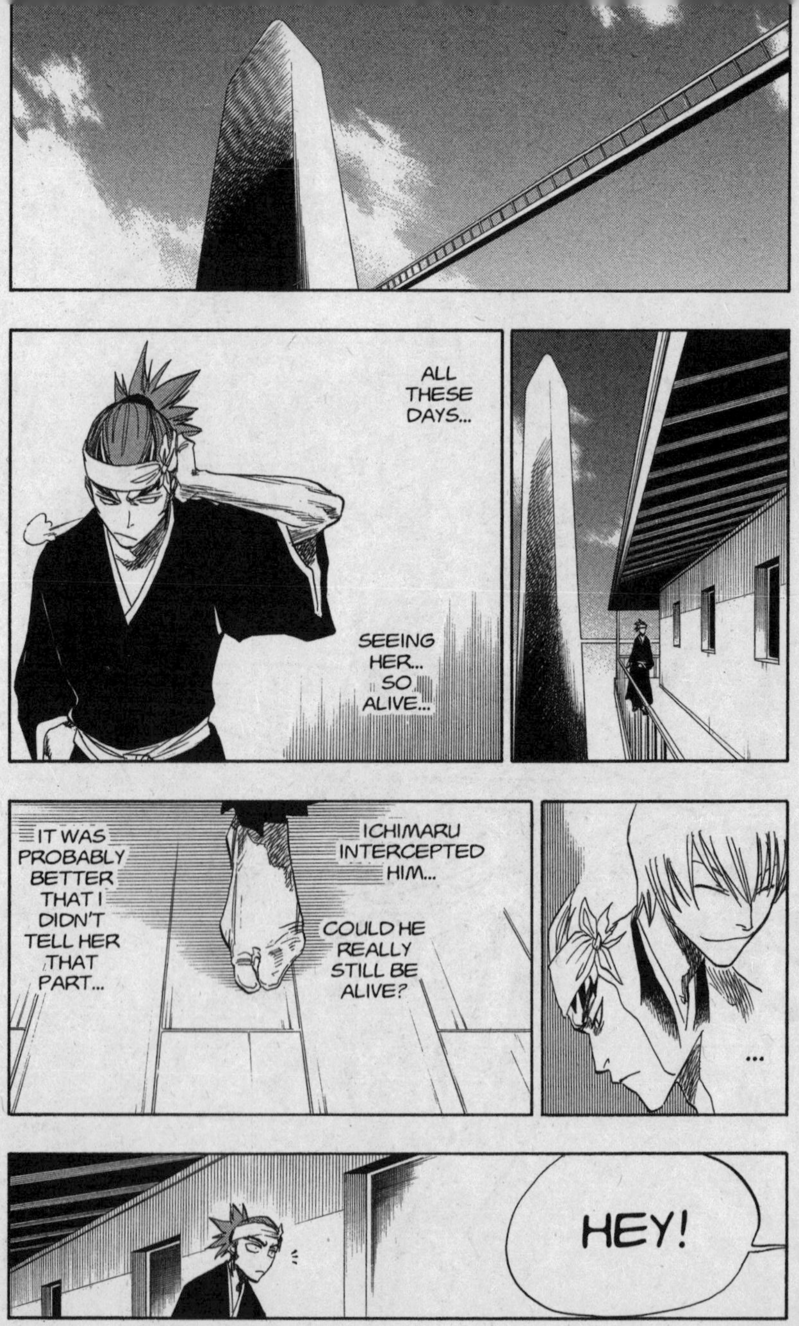
ALL THESE DAYS...
SEEING HER... SO ALIVE...
...
ICHIMARU INTERCEPTED HIM...
COULD HE REALLY STILL BE ALIVE?
IT WAS PROBABLY BETTER THAT I DIDN'T TELL HER THAT PART...
HEY!

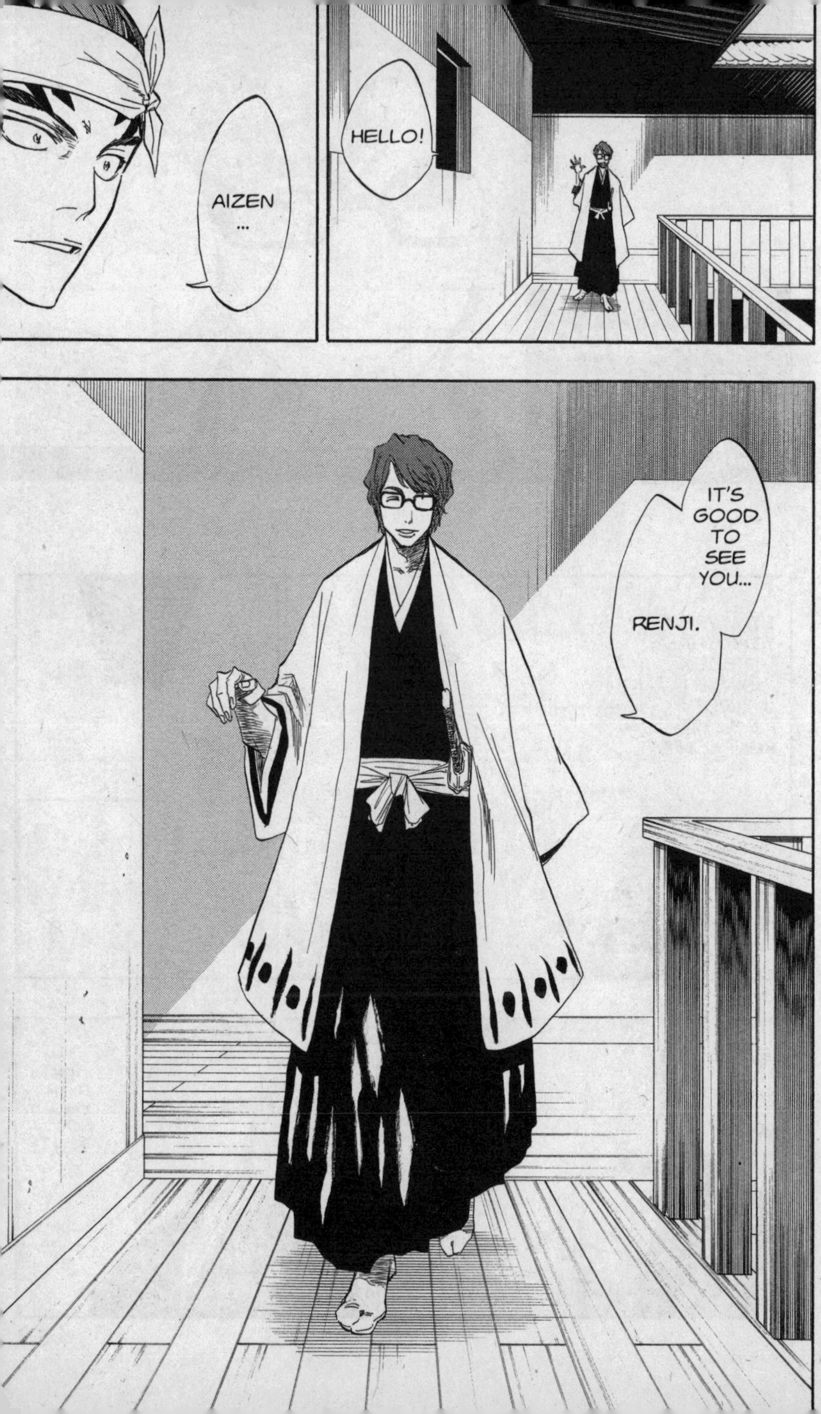
HELLO!
AIZEN ...
IT'S GOOD TO SEE YOU...
RENJI.

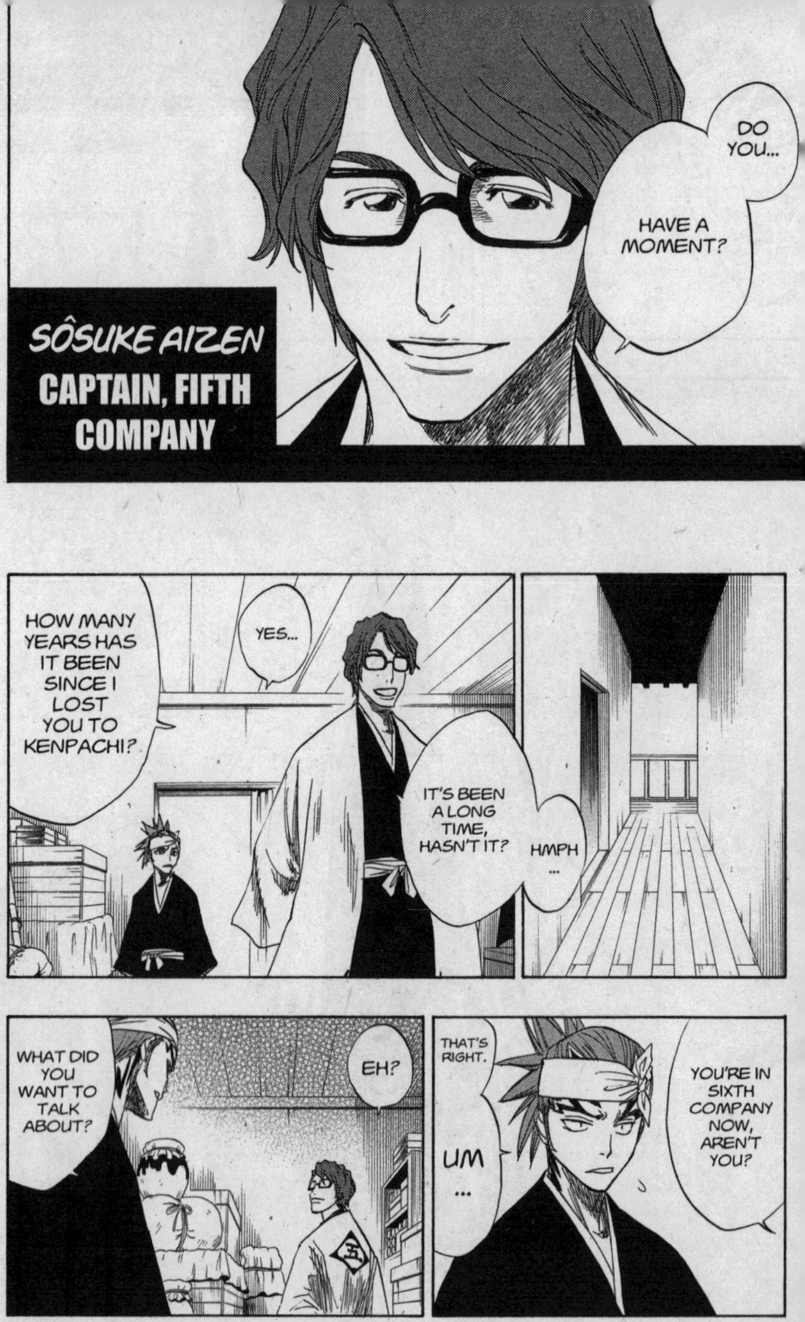
DO YOU...
HAVE A MOMENT?
SÔSUKE AIZEN
CAPTAIN, FIFTH COMPANY
HMPH ...
IT'S BEEN A LONG TIME, HASN'T IT?
YES...
HOW MANY YEARS HAS IT BEEN SINCE I LOST YOU TO KENPACHI?
YOU'RE IN SIXTH COMPANY NOW, AREN'T YOU?
THAT'S RIGHT.
UM ...
EH?
WHAT DID YOU WANT TO TALK ABOUT?

READ THIS WAY

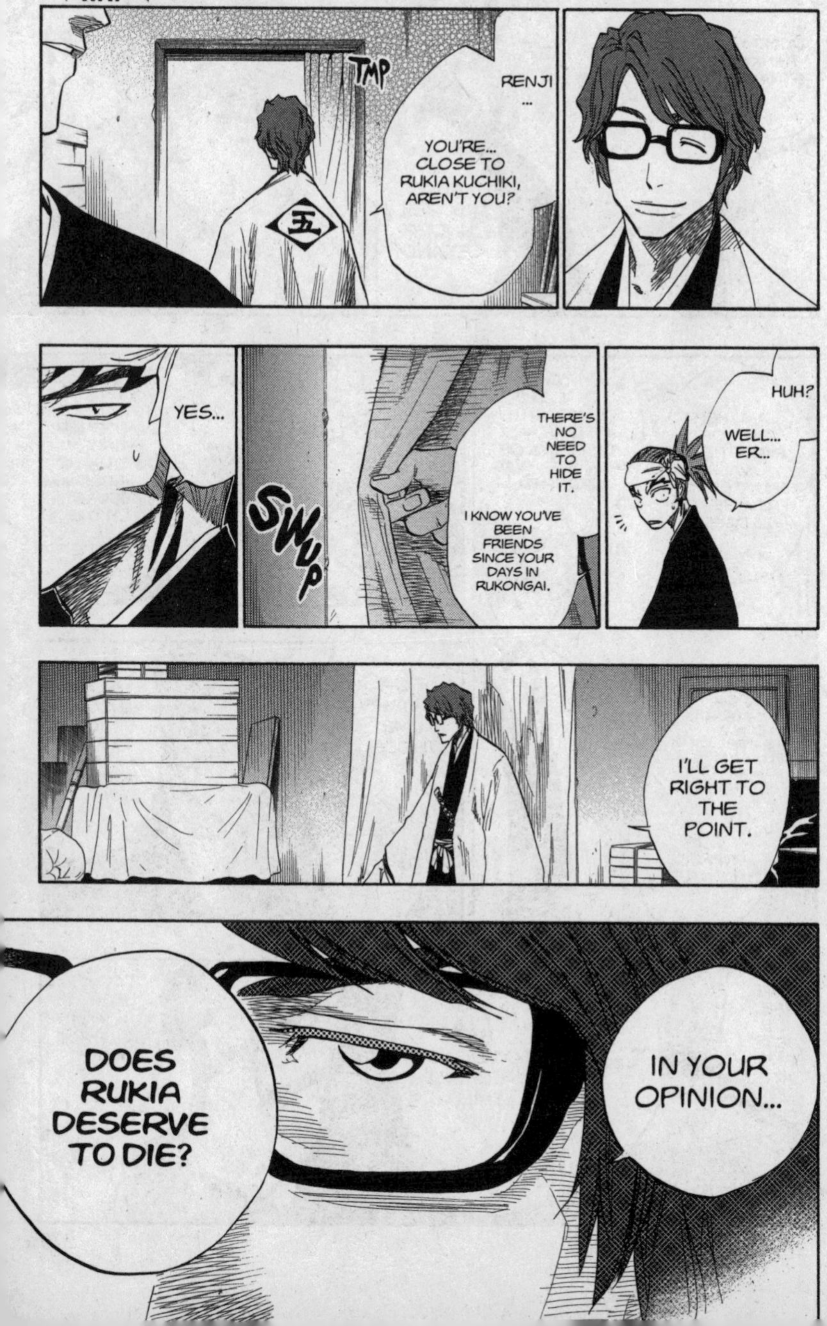
TMP
RENJI ...
YOU'RE... CLOSE TO RUKIA KUCHIKI, AREN'T YOU?
HUH?
WELL... ER...
THERE'S NO NEED TO HIDE IT.
I KNOW YOU'VE BEEN FRIENDS SINCE YOUR DAYS IN RUKONGAI.
SWUP
YES...
I'LL GET RIGHT TO THE POINT.
IN YOUR OPINION...
DOES RUKIA DESERVE TO DIE?

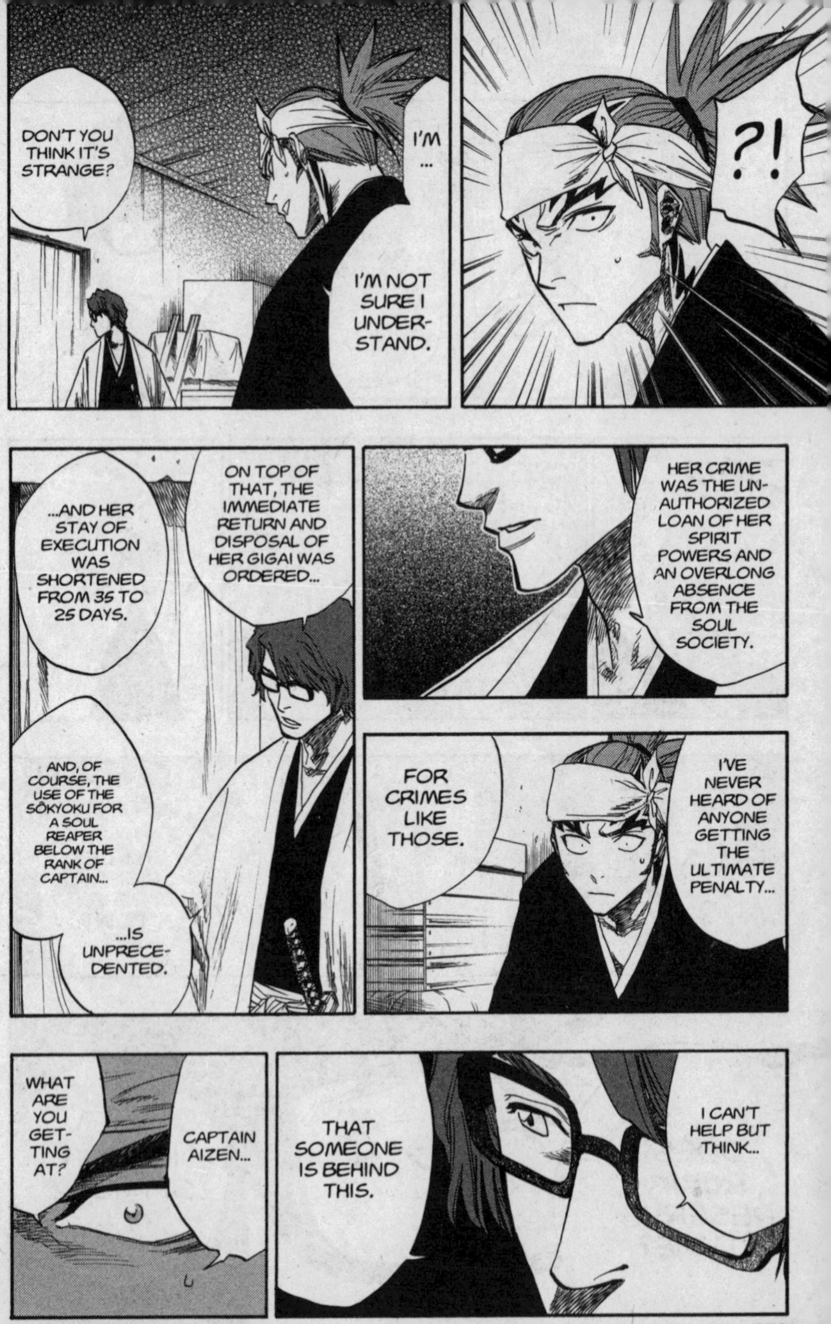
?!
I'M ...
I'M NOT SURE I UNDER-STAND.
DON'T YOU THINK IT'S STRANGE?
HER CRIME WAS THE UN-AUTHORIZED LOAN OF HER SPIRIT POWERS AND AN OVERLONG ABSENCE FROM THE SOUL SOCIETY.
I'VE NEVER HEARD OF ANYONE GETTING THE ULTIMATE PENALTY...
FOR CRIMES LIKE THOSE.
ON TOP OF THAT, THE IMMEDIATE RETURN AND DISPOSAL OF HER GIGAI WAS ORDERED...
...AND HER STAY OF EXECUTION WAS SHORTENED FROM 35 TO 25 DAYS.
AND, OF COURSE, THE USE OF THE SÔKYOKU FOR A SOUL REAPER BELOW THE RANK OF CAPTAIN...
...IS UNPRECE-DENTED.
I CAN'T HELP BUT THINK...
THAT SOMEONE IS BEHIND THIS.
CAPTAIN AIZEN...
WHAT ARE YOU GETTING AT?

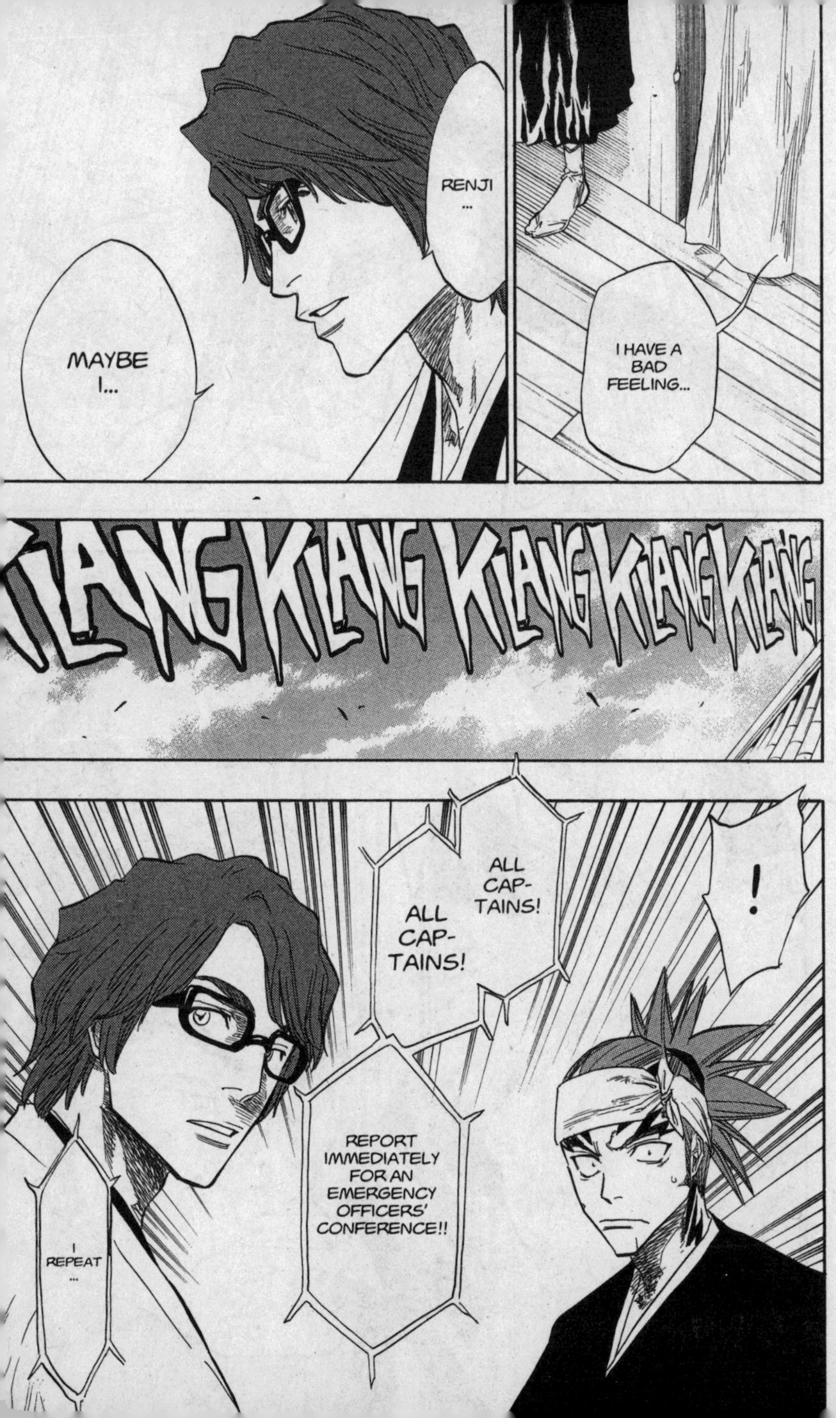
I HAVE A BAD FEELING...
RENJI ...
MAYBE I...
LANG KLANG KLANG KLANG KLANG
!
ALL CAP-TAINS!
ALL CAP-TAINS!
REPORT IMMEDIATELY FOR AN EMERGENCY OFFICERS' CONFERENCE!!
I REPEAT ...

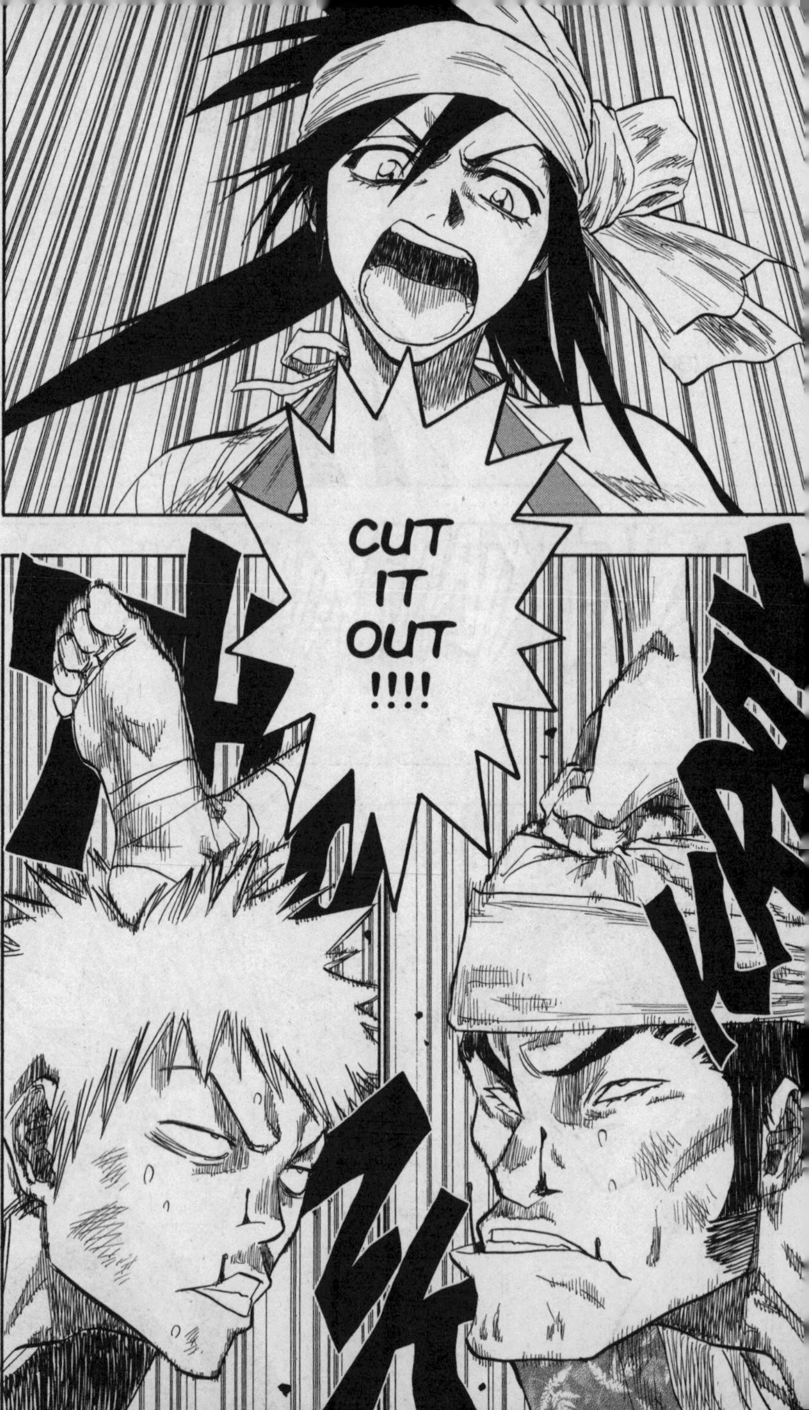
CUT IT OUT !!!!

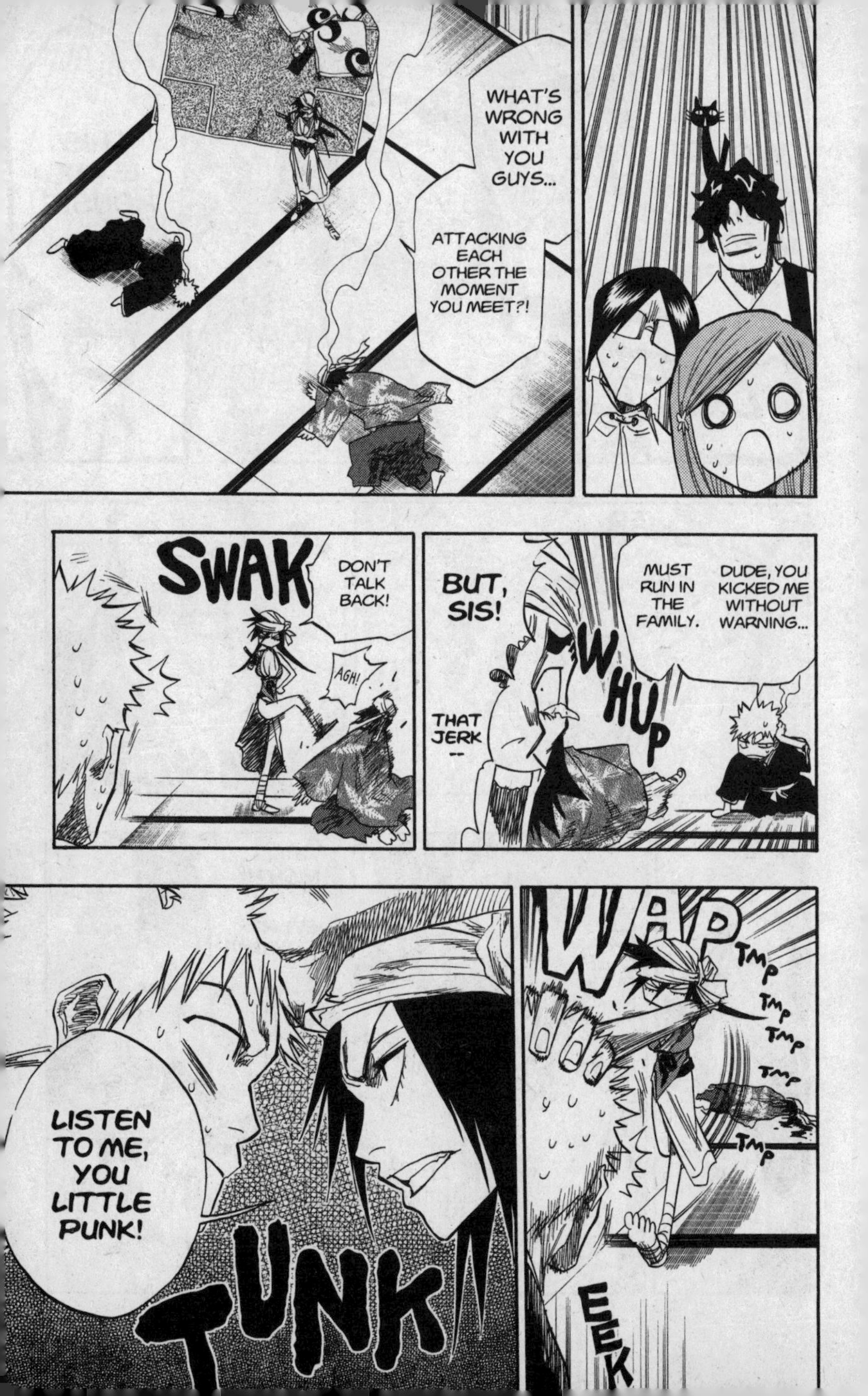
WHAT'S WRONG WITH YOU GUYS...
ATTACKING EACH OTHER THE MOMENT YOU MEET?!
DUDE, YOU KICKED ME WITHOUT WARNING...
MUST RUN IN THE FAMILY.
WHUP
BUT, SIS!
THAT JERK --
DON'T TALK BACK!
SWAK
AGH!
WAP
TMP TMP TMP TMP TMP
EEK
LISTEN TO ME, YOU LITTLE PUNK!
TUNK

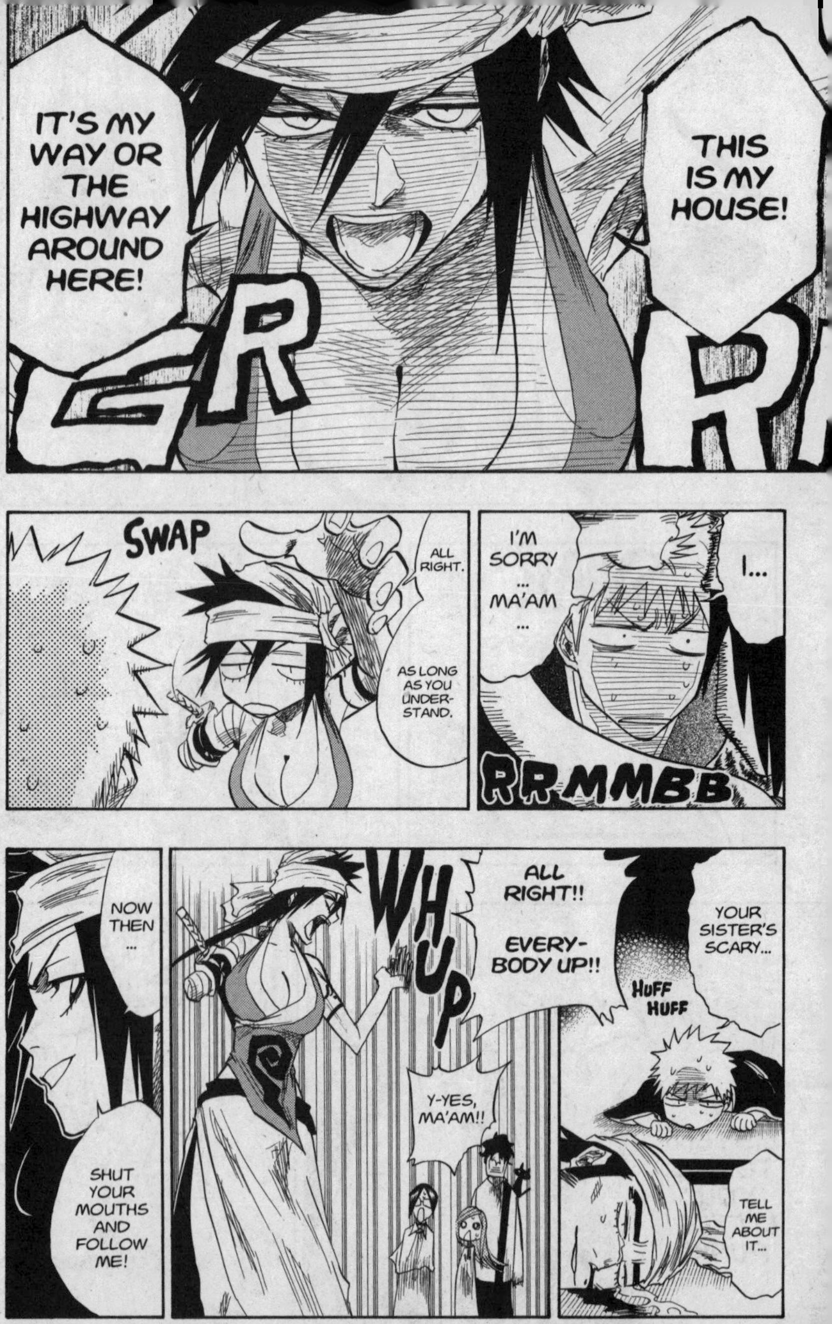
THIS IS MY HOUSE!
IT'S MY WAY OR THE HIGHWAY AROUND HERE!
GRR
I...
I'M SORRY ... MA'AM ...
RRMMBB
ALL RIGHT.
AS LONG AS YOU UNDER-STAND.
SWAP
YOUR SISTER'S SCARY...
HUFF HUFF
TELL ME ABOUT IT...
ALL RIGHT!!
EVERY-BODY UP!!
WHUP
Y-YES, MA'AM!!
NOW THEN ...
SHUT YOUR MOUTHS AND FOLLOW ME!

READ THIS WAY

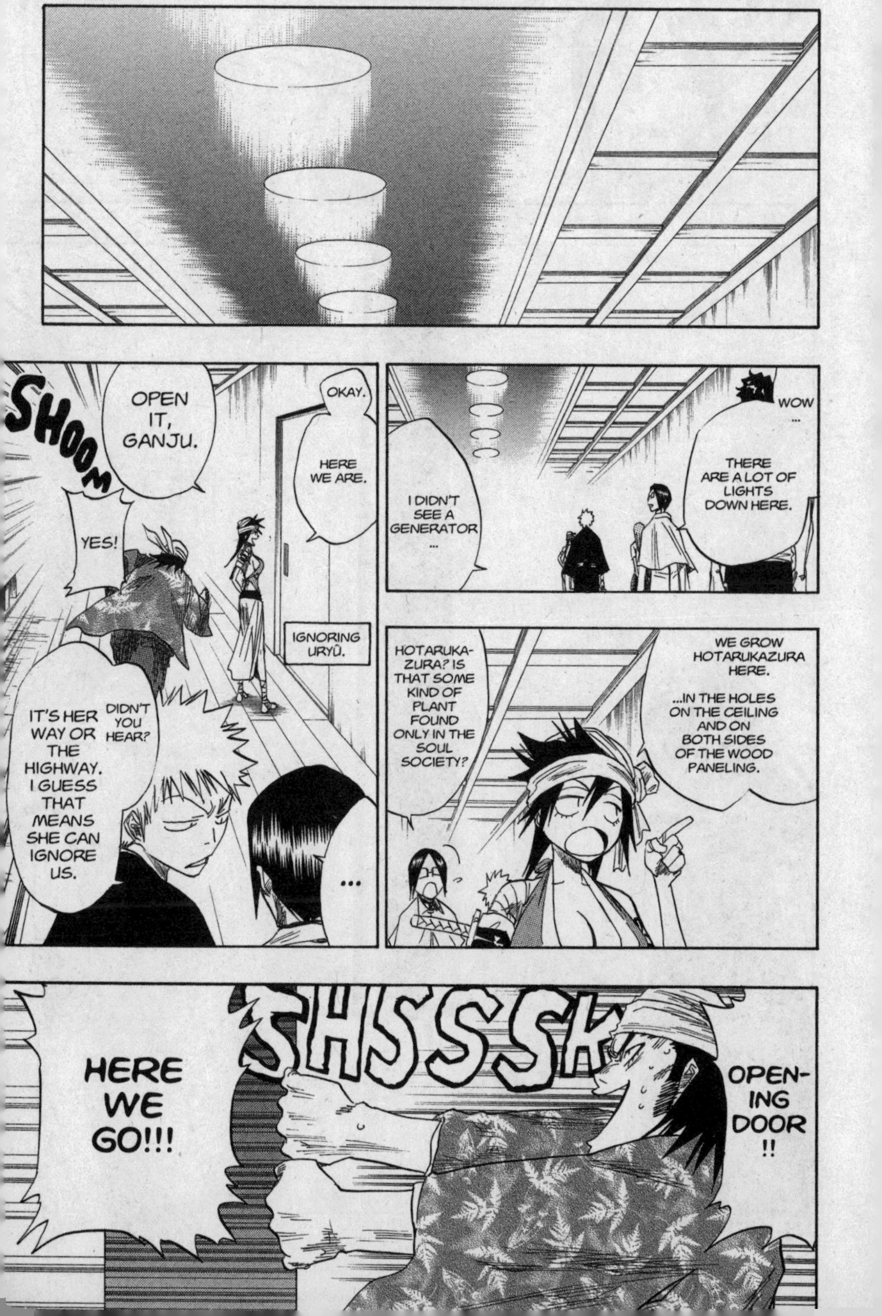
WOW...
THERE ARE A LOT OF LIGHTS DOWN HERE.
I DIDN'T SEE A GENERATOR...
OKAY.
HERE WE ARE.
OPEN IT, GANJU.
SHOOM
YES!
WE GROW HOTARUKAZURA HERE.
...IN THE HOLES ON THE CEILING AND ON BOTH SIDES OF THE WOOD PANELING.
HOTARUKAZURA? IS THAT SOME KIND OF PLANT FOUND ONLY IN THE SOUL SOCIETY?
IGNORING URYÛ.
DIDN'T YOU HEAR?
IT'S HER WAY OR THE HIGHWAY. I GUESS THAT MEANS SHE CAN IGNORE US.
...
OPEN-ING DOOR !!
SHSSSK
HERE WE GO!!!

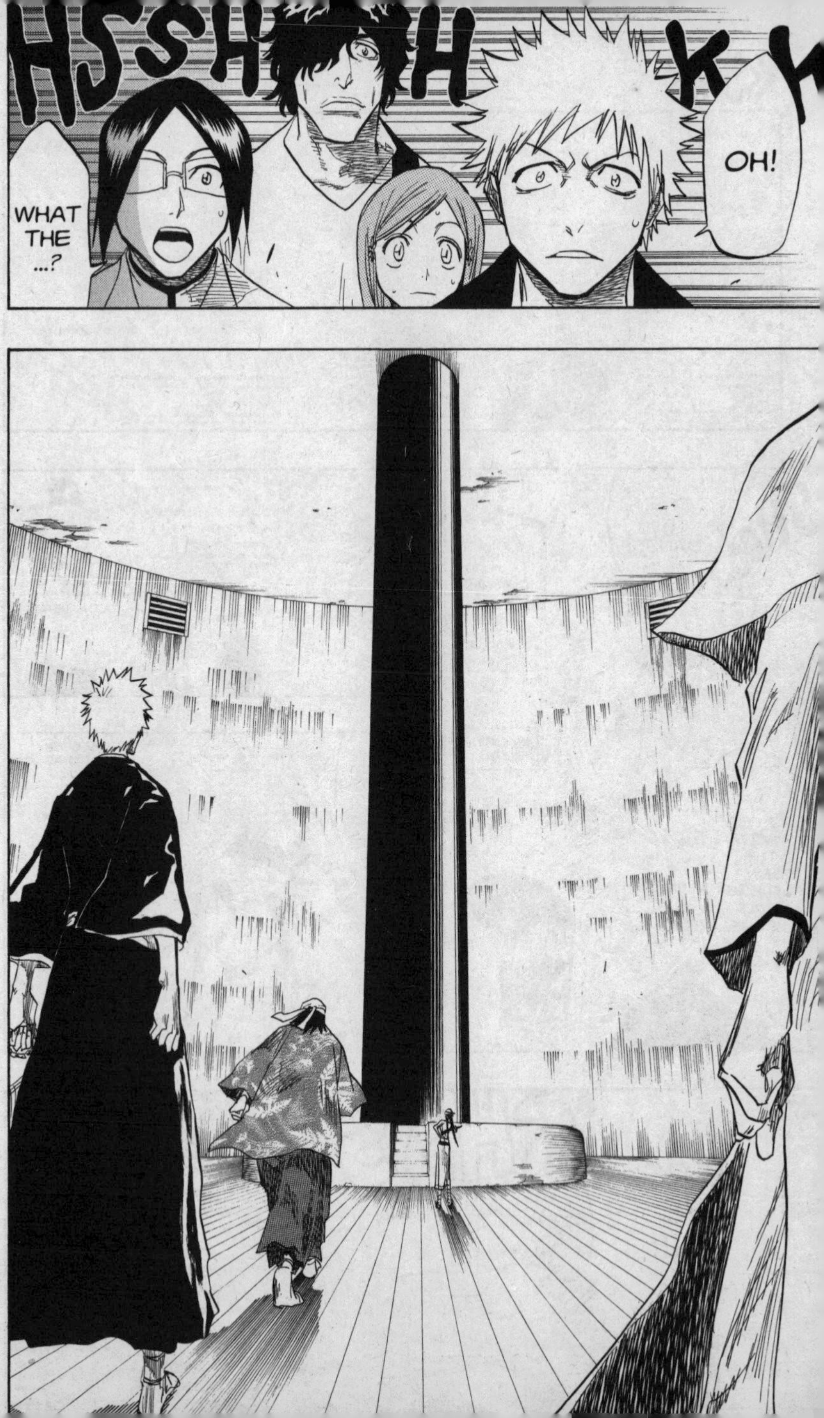
HSSHHH
KK
OH!
WHAT THE ...?

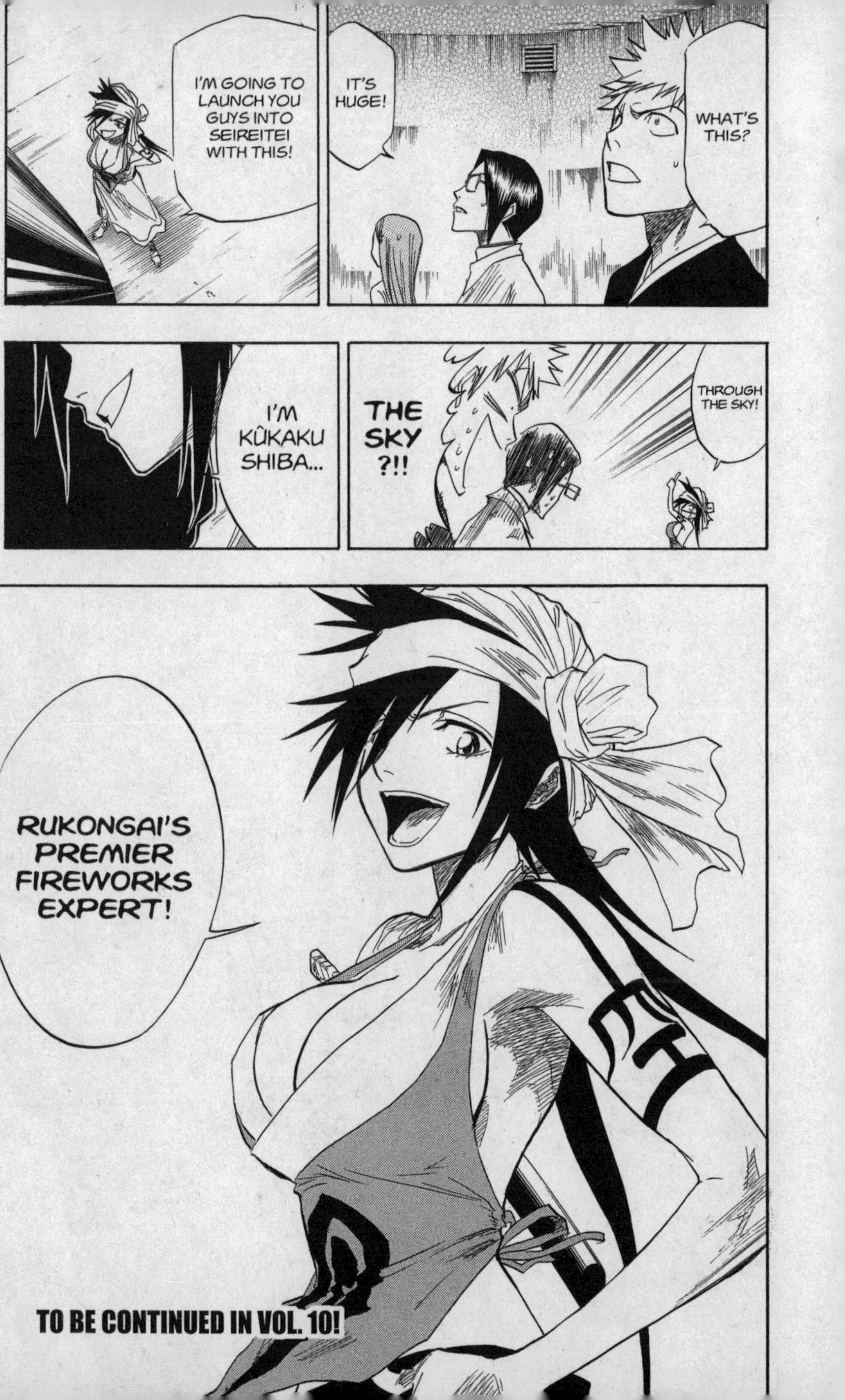
WHAT'S THIS?
IT'S HUGE!
I'M GOING TO LAUNCH YOU GUYS INTO SEIREITEI WITH THIS!
THROUGH THE SKY!
THE SKY ?!!
I'M KÛKAKU SHIBA...
RUKONGAI'S PREMIER FIREWORKS EXPERT!
TO BE CONTINUED IN VOL. 10!

KÛKAKU'S HOUSES--SCULPTURAL ARCHITECTURE (A FEW EXAMPLES)
KÛKAKU SHIBA
TITLE: HANDSTAND
TITLE: FIRST LOVE
KÛKAKU SHIBA
KÛKAKU SHIBA
TITLE: THE CHAMPION
THE LATEST VERSION DOESN'T SEEM SO BAD, NOW...
...

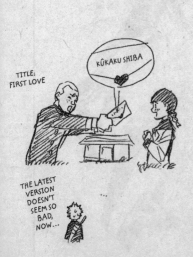

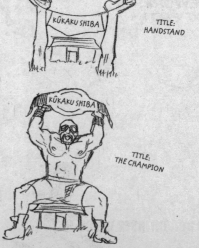

Here is some important **BLEACH** data!!

Thirteen Court Guard Companies	CAPTAIN BYAKUYA KUCHIKI--SIXTH COMPANY	クチキ・ビャクヤ

180 CM

63 KG

D.O.B. JANUARY 31

•28TH HEAD OF DISTINGUISHED ARISTOCRATIC KUCHIKI FAMILY

•WEARS THE KENSEIKAN (PULL STAR SILENCE), AN ORNAMENT ALLOWED ONLY TO NOBLES-- A SERIES OF SEMI-TUBES THAT CLAMP TO THE HAIR

•WEARS GINPAKU KAZANO-HANA USUGINU (SILVERY-WHITE WINDFLOWER SILK GAUZE), A SCARF WORN BY GENERATIONAL HEAD OF FAMILY, WOVEN BY A MASTER WEAVER, THE THIRD INHERITOR TO KUROEMON TSUJISHIRO. ONE OF THESE COSTS AS MUCH AS TEN HOUSES.

•LIKES BALLOON FLOWERS, MOONLIGHT WALKS, SPICY FOOD

THEME SONG
Giovanni Mirabassi
"Je Chante Pour
Passer Le Temps"
RECORDED IN
"AVANTI!"

Thirteen Court Guard Companies	ASSISTANT CAPTAIN RENJI ABARAI--SIXTH COMPANY	アバライ・レンジ

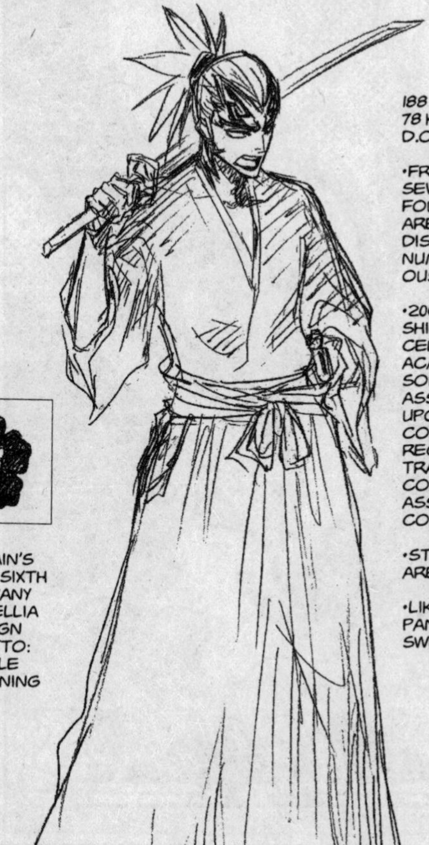

188 CM
78 KG
D.O.B. AUGUST 31

•FROM INUZURI, RUKONGAI'S SEVENTY-EIGHTH DISTRICT. THE FOUR QUARTERS OF RUKONGAI ARE EACH DIVIDED INTO 80 DISTRICTS. THE HIGHER THE NUMBER, THE MORE DANGEROUS THE DISTRICT.

•2066TH TERM GRADUATE OF SHINÔREIJUTSUIN, THE CENTRAL SPIRITUAL ARTS ACADEMY, ALSO KNOWN AS SOUL REAPER ACADEMY. ASSIGNED TO FIFTH COMPANY UPON GRADUATING, HIS COMBAT ABILITY WAS SOON RECOGNIZED AND HE WAS TRANSFERRED TO ELEVENTH COMPANY. PROMOTED TO ASSISTANT CAPTAIN OF SIXTH COMPANY ONE MONTH AGO.

•STRANGE EYEBROWS ARE TATTOOS

•LIKES TAIYAKI (FISH-SHAPED PANCAKES FILLED WITH SWEAT BEAN JAM)

THEME SONG
HAZU FEATURING
Ill-Bosstino
"NORAINU"
("STRAY DOG")
RECORDED IN
"The NEWBORN"

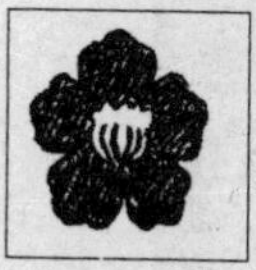

CAPTAIN'S BADGE, SIXTH COMPANY
CAMELLIA DESIGN
MOTTO: NOBLE REASONING

Next Volume Preview

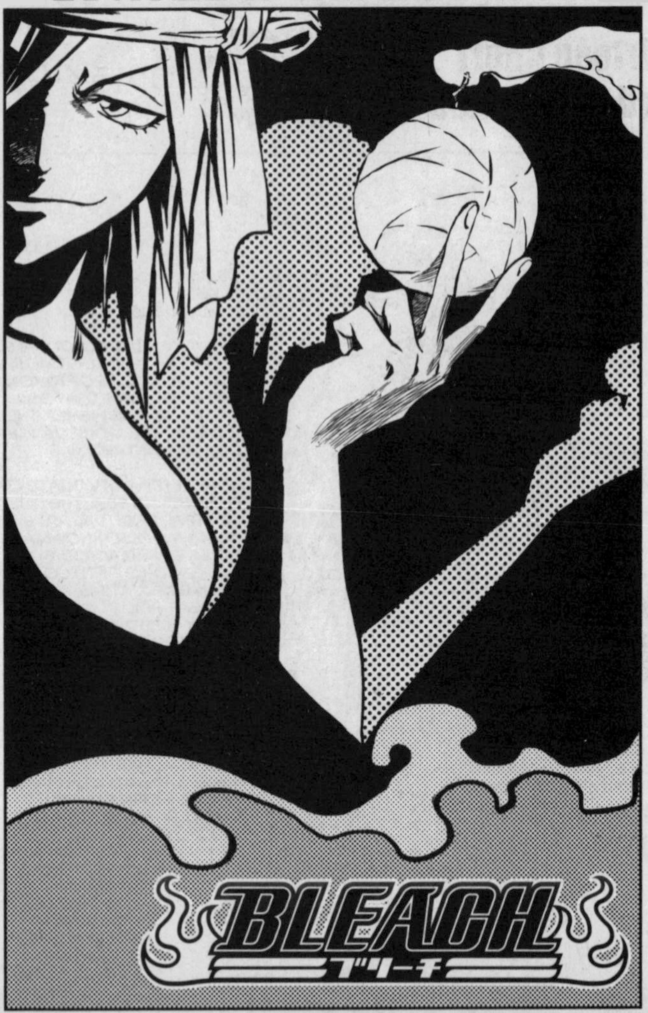
BLEACH
ブリーチ

With explosives-expert Kûkaku's assistance, Ichigo's crew is one step closer to finally infiltrating the Soul Society and busting Rukia out of the big house. To successfully break though the Soul Society's powerful barrier, Ichigo will (once again) be forced to control his seemingly endless reservoir of spiritual energy…without blowing everything up. Back at Soul Society HQ, the top captains of the Soul Reapers are assembled so they can figure out how to deal with their unwanted guests.

Available now!

A BRUSH WITH THE AFTERLIFE

All Colour But The Black

THE ART OF BLEACH

By Tite Kubo, creator of *ZOMBIEPOWDER*.

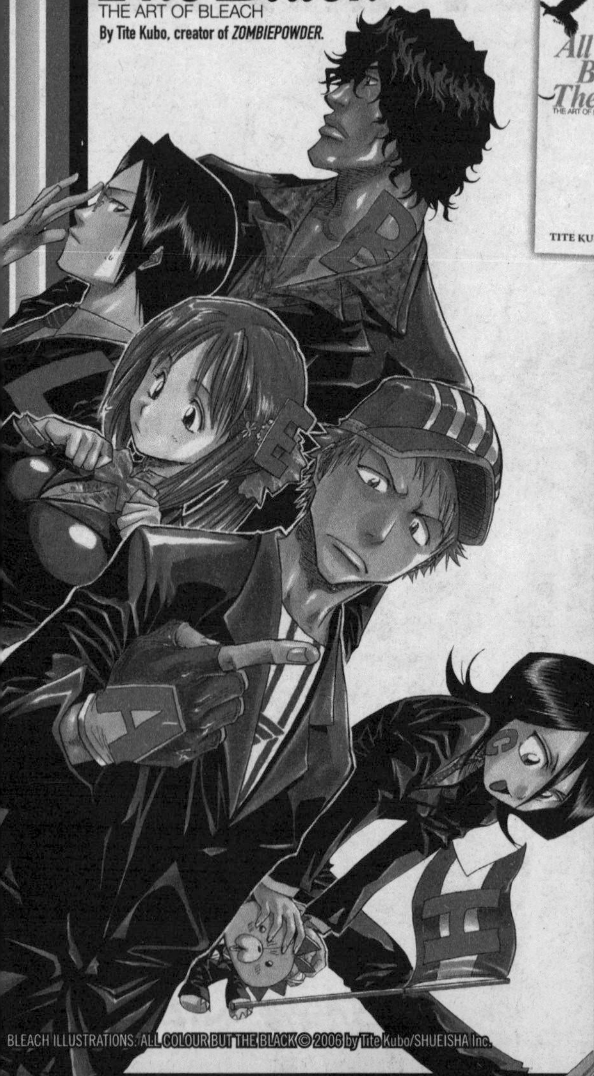

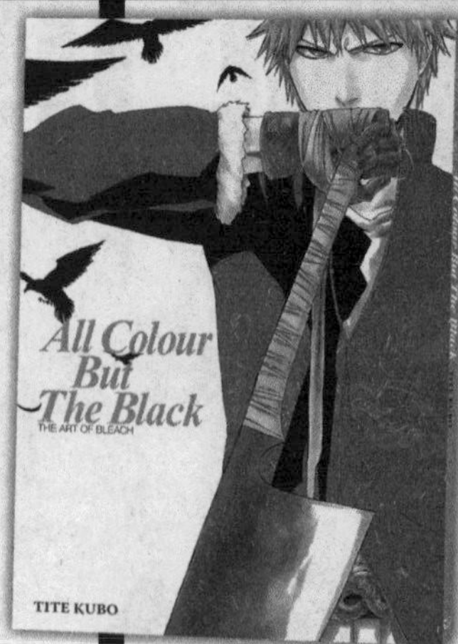
All Colour
But
The Black
THE ART OF BLEACH
TITE KUBO

EXPLORE THE WORLD OF *BLEACH* THROUGH THIS HIGH-QUALITY ART BOOK SHOWCASING ARTWORK FROM TITE KUBO'S POPULAR MANGA SERIES, WHICH INCLUDES:

- Vibrant illustrations, including art from volumes 1-19
- An annotated art guide
- Extra character information

PLUS, AN EXCLUSIVE POSTER!

COMPLETE YOUR *BLEACH* COLLECTION WITH *THE ART OF BLEACH: ALL COLOUR BUT THE BLACK*— GET YOURS TODAY!

On sale at www.shonenjump.com
Also available at your local bookstore and comic store.

SHONEN JUMP www.shonenjump.com
VIZ media www.viz.com